Building the Steel String
ACOUSTIC GUITAR

Building the Steel String
ACOUSTIC GUITAR

R.M. MOTTOLA

Credits & Copyrights

This book is original work based on the author's observations and experience. Quantitative data and other specifications are taken from publicly available sources or from the author's observations or from credited sources.

Except as noted all photos and drawings are by the author.

All brand names and model names are properties of their respective rights holders.

Disclaimer of Liability: Although every effort was made to ensure that the information in this book was accurate at the time of publication, the author does not assume and does hereby disclaim any liability for any damage, loss, or disruption caused by errors or omissions. Information in this book is provided as-is, without any express or implied warranty. This book provides a detailed description of some guitar construction projects. It is not an instruction manual. It is made available for informational purposes only.

© 2021 by R.M. Mottola All rights reserved. No part of this book covered by copyrights hereon may be reproduced or copied without written permission except as allowed by fair use with included attribution.

Please address all correspondence to the author using the URL below. Please note that due to time constraints I cannot answer lutherie questions.

https://www.LiutaioMottola.com/contact.htm

ISBN-13: 978-1-7341256-1-0   (B&W softcover)

First edition, October 2021

Contents

	Acknowledgments	vii
	About the Author	ix
Chapter 1:	Introduction	1
Chapter 2:	Roughing Out the Neck	15
Chapter 3:	The Fretboard	35
Chapter 4:	The Neck Joint and Headstock	55
Chapter 5:	The Headplate and Decoration	67
Chapter 6:	Further Refinement of the Neck	87
Chapter 7:	Carving the Neck	97
Chapter 8:	The Body Mold	113
Chapter 9:	Bending the Sides of the Guitar	129
Chapter 10:	The Garland	149
Chapter 11:	The Back Plate	169
Chapter 12:	The Top Plate and Its Rosette	193
Chapter 13:	Bracing the Top Plate	217
Chapter 14:	Assembling the Body	243
Chapter 15:	Body Decoration	261
Chapter 16:	Installing the Frets	301
Chapter 17:	Fitting and Attaching the Neck	315
Chapter 18:	Preparing for Finishing	341
Chapter 19:	Applying the Finish	349
Chapter 20:	The Bridge	383
Chapter 21:	Fret Dressing	413
Chapter 22:	The Final Details	427
Chapter 23:	Stringing Up and Setting Up	449

Chapter 24:	Coda	463
Appendix A:	Online Annex	465
Appendix B:	Simple Router Jig for Planing Thin Plates	466
Appendix C:	Guitar Body Vise	469
Appendix D:	Guitar Neck Rest	471
Appendix E:	Finish Scrapers	472
	Glossary of Lutherie Terms	474
	Wood Species Mentioned in This Book	481
	Luthiers Mentioned in This Book	483
	Index	484

Acknowledgments

Although it is conventional to put the acknowledgments section of a book at the end, the fact is that without the people and assets listed here, this book in its present state would not exist. For this reason I am listing and saying my thanks for all the assistance right up front. I am pleased and proud to point out that the people that have offered assistance in the creation of this book hail from all over the world.

People

It continues to be my great good fortune to be surrounded by lutherie subject matter experts, and my greater fortune that so many of them enthusiastically answered my requests for assistance with this book. Collegiality and personal friendship have their limits, and asking someone to critically examine a technical manuscript of almost 500 pages is a big ask. In the book world it's sort of like asking someone to help you move house, including your workshop full of stationary power tools and your extensive collections of antique safes and grand pianos. The people listed following this paragraph provided substantial help in one or more of the following: reviewing drafts, providing needed corrections and augmentation, copy editing, and proofreading. My sincere thanks to them all for their considerable efforts.

James Buckland is a music professor at Presbyterian College in Clinton, South Carolina, a guitarist, and a long time luthier, specializing in early Romantic period music and instruments. He has an encyclopedic knowledge of historical and modern musical instruments. He is a frequent author of articles in *American Lutherie*. In addition to providing considerable input on the draft of this book, his Guild of American Luthiers Convention lecture and subsequent *American Lutherie* article "19th Century Guitar Making Techniques" was key to my initial understanding of an important concept in lutherie, that expert work is readily accomplished with the use of very simple and easy to build jigs and fixtures. That concept is a key part of the construction techniques described in this book.

John Calkin is a luthier and lutherie author from Greenville, Virginia. He has repaired and built guitars in his own shop for a long time, and was on the staff of the Huss & Dalton Guitar Company for many years. He is a frequent contributor to a number of online lutherie discussion groups. In addition to guitars he builds ukuleles and cigar box guitars, and is a proponent of what he calls Outlaw Lutherie, which is fundamentally a process by which stringed musical instrument construction can be made available to all, regardless of woodworking ability. John is one of my fellow *American Lutherie* contributing editors, and was particularly influential when I first started building guitars. He has a great and uncanny ability to quickly analyze complex instrument designs and construction processes and extract their essential elements.

Richard Curtis is a long time Boston area guitarist. He has worked as a professional musician, a woodworker, a writer, and a software engineer. In addition to his invaluable copy editing and proofreading skills, his musical and woodworking background make him a perfect match for the target audience of this book. He has provided excellent comments and corrections to initial drafts.

Sjaak Elmendorp from the Netherlands began his lutherie career before retiring from his primary career as a commercial scientist specializing in polymer physics. He has built a wide range of plucked stringed instruments, from historical reproductions to modern steel string guitars. Sjaak has written a number of lutherie articles for *American Lutherie*. Although possessing a strong theoretical background, he is eminently pragmatic. His comments and suggestions on early drafts of this book have been invaluable.

Mark French is a professor of mechanical engineering technology at Purdue University and the author of the books *Engineering the Guitar*, *Technology of the Guitar*, and *Acoustic Guitar Design*. He teaches guitar construction as the basis for a practical understanding of engineering technology, and is a frequent author of articles in *American Lutherie* and *Savart Journal*. He does regular consultation work with a number of large guitar manufacturers. Mark has an infectious interest in guitar lutherie at all levels. His inputs to this book have been most valuable.

Christine King was a member of the production staff of the venerable New England birding publication *Bird Observer*. It is my suspicion that she has the entire *Chicago Manual of Style* committed to memory. Probably more than one edition. She provided comprehensive copy editing and proofreading of this book. Although not a luthier, she has extensive lutherie knowledge, accumulated over many years of patient listening while her luthier husband (me) talked her ear off.

Leonardo Lospennato is an accomplished luthier in Berlin, specializing in electric guitars and basses. He is the author of the highly regarded books *Electric Guitar and Bass Design* and *Electric Guitar Making & Marketing* and was the editor of the magazine *Sustain*, the journal of the Fellowship of European Luthiers. He teaches electric guitar and bass construction to an international clientele. Leonardo is another luthier with an infectious enthusiasm for the craft. His adeptness at teaching this subject made him an ideal reviewer for early drafts of this book.

Graham McDonald is a long time luthier from Australia specializing in mandolin and ukulele family instruments. He is a frequent *American Lutherie* contributor and is a prolific author of lutherie books. He contributes regularly to a number of online lutherie discussion groups. His catalog includes *The Bouzouki Book*, *The Mandolin Project: A Workshop Guide to Building Mandolins*, *The Mandolin: A History*, and *The Ukulele: An Illustrated Workshop Manual*. I have been a long time admirer of Graham's work since attending one of his Guild of American Luthiers convention presentations a number of years back. His willingness to review early drafts of this book is a great honor to me.

Austin Mottola is a guitarist and molecular biologist currently doing post doc work in Tel Aviv. He was an ideal reviewer of drafts of this book due to his interest in guitars and guitar construction. That he is a scientist not easily intimidated by large documents was a big plus. That he is my nephew is also a big plus.

Anamaría Paredes specializes in restoration, repair, and construction of guitars and Colombian Andean instruments. Based in Bogotá, Colombia, she worked for many years in the shop of her well-known father Alberto Paredes until his semi-retirement from lutherie. She has written articles for *American Lutherie*. I was honored to coauthor one of those. Her attention to detail in lutherie work is also apparent in her work reviewing early drafts of this book.

Frederick (Federico) Sheppard is a luthier now specializing in Spanish guitars, including historical reproductions. He is the foremost expert on the life and music of composer and classical guitarist Agustín Barrios, and is coauthor of the book *The Diary of Agustín Barrios Mangoré*. Frederick is a frequent *American Lutherie* author. He is another of those rare people with encyclopedic lutherie knowledge. He lives and works in Green Bay, Wisconsin, and in Spain. When in Spain, Frederick is lutherie artist in residence at Carrion de los Condes.

This book is greatly enhanced with additional contributions from the following people. **Darcy Kuronen** is emeritus curator of the musical instrument collection of the Museum of Fine Arts Boston and author of the book *Dangerous Curves: The Art of the Guitar*. He provided valuable guidance on the section in the introduction on the history of the guitar. Seattle area photographer and webmaster **Steve McElrath** provided expert photo editing consulting and photo editing script development. Artistic design consulting was provided by my brother, New York City artist, sculptor and art fabricator **Milo Mottola**. **Tim Olsen** is the founder of the Guild of American Luthiers and the editor of *American Lutherie*. He provided commentary on the first few chapters of the book, and specified a number of general improvements.

Photos not taken by the author were generously provided by **Mike Doolin**, **Sjaak Elmendorp**, and **Anamaría Paredes**.

The result of all this assistance from so many talented people is a book that is far better in every way than it was in its initial draft form. Any remaining shortcomings are my own.

Although not contributing directly to this book, there are a number of people who have been supportive and influential throughout my lutherie career. These folks made it possible for me to get to the place to be able to write this book. I owe my start in lutherie to the late Jim Mouradian. The knowledge shared by members of the lutherie group New England Luthiers, and by those of the Guild of American Luthiers has been essential to my own development as a luthier. I am grateful to everyone that has taken the time over the years to answer my questions and critique my work.

Software and Other Assets

Free software and other assets were used in the creation of this book. Thanks to everyone for making your work products freely available.

Bulk plain text editing was performed using the Notepad++ text editor. Bulk photo processing was done using the ImageMagick image editing software suite. FotoSketcher by David Thoiron was used for artistic processing of the cover photo. QR codes were generated using Zint Barcode Studio by Robin Stuart. Some photos appearing in the book were taken using the Open Camera app for Android devices.

The book is set using the Tex Gyre Termes font. Music notation is set in the Bravura Text font by Steinberg. Cover and chapter titles are set in Amarante by Karolina Lach. The chapter title graphics are inspired by graphics in the LyxBook Deco layout.

The basic layout design and color palette for the cover were borrowed from an old magazine cover of the August 1904 issue of McClure's magazine.

About the Author

A former engineer, R.M. Mottola has been building electric and acoustic guitars and bass guitars since 1994. He maintains the popular Liutaio Mottola Lutherie Information website (https://LiutaioMottola.com). He is a contributing editor and the technology editor for *American Lutherie*, the journal of the Guild of American Luthiers, and has written over sixty articles on guitar construction and related topics. He organizes the Science and Technology Seminars at Guild of American Luthiers conventions. He is the author of the definitive reference book *Mottola's Cyclopedic Dictionary of Lutherie Terms*. R.M. is the editor of the *Savart Journal*, the open access online research journal of science and technology of stringed musical instruments, and has written a number of research articles on topics of geometry, acoustics, and psychoacoustics of stringed musical instruments. He has provided editorial input to many popular books on lutherie and stringed musical instruments. R.M. is a member of the regional lutherie group New England Luthiers and lives in the Boston area.

1 Introduction

This book provides a detailed account of the construction of the steel string acoustic guitar. Information of this type is available from many sources – there are books, videos, hands-on classes, as well as all sorts of instructional material on the Internet. What is different about this book is that the construction details here have been purposely designed for the guitar-building novice. The information provided here is optimized for the person with some woodworking experience and general-purpose woodworking tools who wants to build a guitar, but without a steep learning curve; without a large outlay for special-purpose guitar-building tools; and with little time dedicated to the construction of special jigs and fixtures.

I built my first guitar in 1995. The effort was for the most part self-directed, but I was fortunate to be able to get expert advice and considerable encouragement from an expert – Boston-area luthier and repairman Jim Mouradian (1951–2017).

By the way, a *luthier* is a person that builds stringed musical instruments, and *lutherie* is the process of building such instruments. I will preferentially use these terms throughout this book. Before embarking on my lutherie career I was an engineer. This background would turn out to influence a lot of the ways I did things as a guitar builder, but one thing that was quite significant has to do with taking notes. I am an inveterate note-taker. Although at the time of the construction of my first instrument the last thing on my mind was writing a book about guitar construction, my construction notes from all of my instruments would turn out to be very useful for this effort. This is particularly the case where the notes contained information on those construction steps I found to be most challenging as a novice instrument builder.

After finishing my first instrument I was hooked on lutherie and immediately began a second. To the end of better understanding the construction process, I read what books were available at the time about guitar construction. From these I realized a very significant fact about lutherie – there are different ways of accomplishing the same task. A guitar is a complex construction and there are a lot of steps to building one. The construction techniques detailed in each book varied from each other. I was fascinated by this and would continue to explore the consequences of this throughout my lutherie career.

As is the case with every luthier I know, the more instruments I built the more time I spent accumulating tools and building jigs and fixtures. The tools included general-purpose woodworking tools as well as a wide variety of specialty lutherie tools. The jigs and fixtures were mostly shop built. These and the specialty tools help to make a number of the operations involved in building a guitar quicker and also make it easier to attain a high level of precision.

While all of this guitar building and shop outfitting was going on I was increasing my awareness of and contact with other luthiers. This was primarily the result of joining the Guild of American Luthiers and reading the organization's journal *American Lutherie*. One result of all this contact with other luthiers was to open up my understanding that there were even more ways to perform the various construction processes than I had realized from reading the available books on the subject. Along these lines the GAL also introduced to me the idea that there is no one right way to do things. I would consider this idea throughout my early lutherie career. In fact I would actively test it, modifying my building techniques to try a different approach to one or more of the building steps with every instrument. And my fascination with the variety of lutherie techniques grew as I also started to consider historical construction techniques. Demonstrations of such techniques by many subject matter experts, including Clinton, South Carolina, guitarist, luthier, and professor James Buckland, and explanations of others by British historian and author James Westbrook, introduced me to the ways that historical luthiers worked.

The guitar listening sessions at the GAL conventions clearly impressed upon me that there was no right way to do things. These conventions, usually held every three years, feature listening sessions for classical guitars, steel string acoustic guitars, and ukuleles. Each listening session works like this: There is one room and one player who plays one piece of music on all of the instruments submitted for the session. There are usually dozens of instruments in each session. Instrument makers are not identified until after their guitars are played. The upshot of all this is that the only thing that substantially varies during the session is the guitar being played. This makes it possible to critically evaluate the sonic differences in a large number of guitars, in an environment that closely resembles one in which guitars are typically played. And since the room, player, and musical program are the same for all guitars, session listeners can have some confidence that any differences they hear among instruments are attributable to the instruments themselves. Not knowing who made each instrument before it is played eliminates any prejudice a listener may have for or against the builder. When I attend these sessions I keep my eyes closed or avert my gaze as each instrument is presented to the player and then played. In this way I also eliminate any bias I may have that is based on the size or shape or materials of the guitar. I keep track of the guitars I like the best, and I will spend a substantial amount of time during each convention polling people that attend the listening sessions about their personal favorites as well. And I always make a point of interviewing the builders of the instruments I liked the best, asking them about their building techniques.

From these listening sessions and from many years of evaluating the sonic properties of guitars under less-formal conditions and under conditions imposed by strict scientific experimental methods, I can confidently make a few related assertions. The first assertion is that it is rare to find a truly bad sounding guitar. This should be extremely liberating and confidence-building for the novice guitar maker. Given reasonable and conventional guitar design and guitar-building techniques, the likelihood that a novice can build a good sounding first instrument is practically guaranteed. But wait, it gets even better. The second assertion is that in my experience there is not all that much difference between the majority of good sounding guitars and the very best sounding guitars. Given similar body size and strings, sonic differences between the good and the great are quite subtle. So not only is it very likely that a novice guitar builder's first instrument will sound good, it is also very likely that it will sound very close to that of the best-sounding instruments available. Many highly experienced luthiers I know still have the first instruments they built and are generally still quite pleased with the way those instruments sound.

The third assertion I'll make comes from the information I've collected about the design and construction of the best sounding instruments I've heard. The assertion is that there doesn't seem to be *any* correlation between how good an instrument sounds and the specific techniques used to build it. None whatsoever. Some of the best-sounding guitars I've heard were built by builders that simply built to the dimensions specified in a plan. Others were built in a manner that involved some sort of individualized "tuning" of the major parts of the instrument or of the completed instrument. For some builders, these tuning operations can be described as ad hoc or intuitive. For others they are quite technical and may involve audio measurement equipment. But again, when I interview the builders of the guitars I have heard which possess above-average sonic qualities and ask about construction techniques, those techniques are all over the map.

This fact is of primary importance for a book aimed at documenting a guitar building sequence appropriate for the novice builder. Since there are many ways to perform each of the many steps required to build a guitar, and since all of these ways seem to be able to yield guitars of superior sonic quality, we can make use of *any* of these ways and not have to worry about sacrificing sound quality. And since it is not necessary to sacrifice sound quality, construction techniques can be selected for other qualities, like ease of implementation for example. This explains why there are such a wide variety of building techniques among luthiers. Individual builders make use of those construction techniques that are familiar to them, that make use of their skills and knowledge, and that make use of the tools available to them. Individual luthiers are each under unique constraints of time and economics, and these also influence which building techniques are employed.

In my own building projects I of course made use of my own set of construction techniques based on all of these factors. But as mentioned, the subject of the variety of techniques always interested me and I studied this in some depth. The subject was so intriguing to me that, starting in 2017 I embarked upon what amounts to a research project to select a series of guitar construction steps intended to produce optimal results for the novice guitar builder. This selection was informed by my shop notes of my own novice experiences and those of the many novice builders I have come in contact with via my lutherie information website LiutaioMottola.com, my work as a contributing editor for *American Lutherie*, and the beginner guitar builders I have advised or taught directly.

Author's website

Following the initial selection of techniques I spent the next few years building instruments using only those techniques, just to test the validity of the approach and to make any necessary refinements. The construction techniques described in this book are the results of that research project. This process of guitar building is certainly not the only way for a novice to do things but it is based on a careful selection of construction techniques with the success of a novice builder's guitar construction project as its primary goal.

I'll finish up this introduction by briefly describing the qualities that were used to select the techniques specified in this book. This list also incorporates what can be considered prerequisites for making practical use of the techniques described.

Likelihood of Success – This is really the most important criterion used to select from the many different ways of performing each lutherie operation. If a technique can successfully be used by a lutherie novice, then it could be considered for inclusion in the process. All of the other qualities listed below relate to this one.

Woodworking Skills – The construction of a guitar is an advanced woodworking project. Woodworking experience should be considered a requirement before attempting to tackle such a project. The likelihood of success is highest of course for someone already possessing advanced woodworking skills. But if construction techniques are specified which do not themselves require advanced woodworking skills, successful guitar construction can be accomplished without those skills. The construction techniques detailed in this book have been selected to require a minimum of woodworking skills. In particular no advanced joinery is required. Those construction steps that are unique to guitar construction are also broken down into sequences of simpler and more manageable steps.

General Woodworking Tools – A wide variety of woodworking tools are available and different tools can often be applied to a given woodworking task. On the surface it would seem that the tools in each woodworker's arsenal would vary greatly and that this more than anything would determine just how each lutherie construction step was done. My experience though indicates that the majority of folks intending to begin a lutherie project have a good collection of basic woodworking tools. This observation was confirmed with polling conducted on my website for a period of years. Most of the techniques described in this book that use power tools make use of bandsaw, drill press, and hand held routers. Operations demonstrated using hand tools make use of chisels, block plane and other small planes, flat bottom spoke shave, card scraper and Japanese backsaw. A more complete discussion of tools appears later in this chapter. Here, the most important point is that the tools used in the descriptions of construction techniques in this book are those that the majority of guitar builder novices already own and are familiar with. The techniques were selected specifically to avoid the use of fancy, esoteric, and expensive woodworking tools. About the only general purpose woodworking tool useful in this work that is not ubiquitous in every shop is a thickness sander. But this is an expensive tool, so alternative methods for working thin and wide boards to thickness are explained.

Specialized Lutherie Tools – Most experienced luthiers have invested a lot of money in specialized tools that aid in the construction of a guitar. That cost can be a serious barrier to entry into the lutherie field, and for this reason, the construction process described in this book makes use of as few of them as is possible. There are some times when such tools are used, and these are always cases where there really isn't an alternative that provides the needed accuracy and ease, or where the likelihood of success of an operation is substantially higher when the specialized tool is used. I also make exceptions for those specialized lutherie tools that are relatively inexpensive.

Shop-built Jigs and Fixtures – Luthiers use shop-built jigs and fixtures to make certain construction tasks quicker and more precise. Most experienced luthiers make use of several of these. But the problem with such jigs for the novice is that they take time to build. This time is amortized over the construction of many instruments for the experienced builder. For the novice, a reliance on a large number of shop-built jigs significantly increases the time it takes to build a first instrument. The construction process described here makes use of as few shop-built jigs as possible, in an attempt to reduce the project completion time and maintain interest and enthusiasm for the novice guitar maker. And with the exception of one fixture, all shop-built jigs and fixtures used in the Project are simple, cheap, disposable, and very quick to build. These simple jigs provide precision to construction steps without requiring a lot of time and money to build them.

Safety – I can't tell you how many times I have seen a shop-built jig or fixture and blanched at how dangerous the thing was. Woodworkers are exposed to enough dangers just using the hand and power tools that we typically use to do our work. I have no desire to add to that danger by constructing jigs and fixtures that are simple but also dangerous. This particularly applies to shop-built fixtures that require electrical wiring or that heat up. I've got enough to worry about without adding the dangers of electrocution and fire to the list. I categorically rejected any jigs or fixtures that I considered to represent too much of a safety hazard from consideration for use in guitar construction.

Manufactured Components – The use of manufactured components and subassemblies can shorten the time it takes to complete a guitar building project. Use of such components can also reduce the need for specialty tools. For the most part the construction process does not make use of many manufactured components with the exception of the fret wire, the tuning machines, and the neck reinforcing trussrod. This latter component may be shop-built but it is rare for modern luthiers to do so, and so no instructions are provided for building a trussrod in the shop. Inexpensive and well-designed trussrods are readily available. In a few cases the availability of other manufactured components or of operations performed outside of the shop are mentioned as alternatives.

Simplicity – In cases where there are a lot of ways to perform a task, the way which is simplest and fastest was generally preferred as long as it was consistent with likely favorable outcome. Construction of a guitar is a time consuming process. Keeping the overall project time down helps to maintain enthusiasm for the project and makes the work more enjoyable.

Appropriate for a Self-Directed Project – There are a number of construction techniques that really only work well when introduced in a formal guitar building class or personalized instruction. Although I have not made a detailed study of this, it appears that there are some techniques the introduction of which just work better when they are individualized for each student. Books such as this one can sometimes suggest a few alternative ways of doing things, but the print medium just doesn't support substantial individualization. So techniques that appear here have been selected to work well when presented in a book to be used in a self-directed project. My lutherie information website has been up and running for many years, and not a day goes by that I don't receive questions from novice luthiers, each working in isolation. After answering thousands of such questions, the construction techniques that work well for novices working independently have become apparent.

Assembly Time – Decreasing the amount of time it takes a novice to build a guitar is worthwhile, if for no other reason than to help maintain interest and enthusiasm for the project. So in cases where there are several ways to accomplish something, the quickest way will usually be taken unless doing so conflicts with other more important criteria. Note that there is often a conflict between speed of assembly and likelihood of success. In the construction methods described here, the latter always takes precedence.

Organization of the Book

This book is organized into chapters that each represent one major construction effort. These are ordered in a sensible sequence. As a general rule each chapter begins with an overview discussion of the construction that will be detailed in the chapter. It will contain background material of interest, which is sometimes historical or theoretical or technical in nature. Note that this overview section does *not* get into the nitty gritty details of construction. That is left for a subsequent section specifically about construction. The construction description part of the chapter is organized as a series of construction operations, each with a sequence of numbered construction steps. Construction operations are indicated by a heading that begins with a check box and looks like this:

☐ **Construction Operation**

There may or not be some descriptive text following the heading, but a series of numbered construction steps will always follow.

A book of this sort generally begins with an introduction detailing all terminology and general structural descriptions. In this book this is mostly relegated to the individual chapters. Doing so eliminates what many consider to be an overwhelming amount of detail before construction even begins. In this book most technical information is presented in the chapter in which it is referenced.

The terminology used to describe the work is discussed early in each chapter. The first instance of each lutherie term that is not likely to be commonly understood appears in *italics*, and these terms are defined in a glossary appearing at the end of the book. Lutherie is a specialized class of woodworking, and a guitar construction project is an exercise in advanced woodworking. As such, it is assumed that in addition to possessing general woodworking skills, a person beginning a guitar construction project will be familiar with essential woodworking terminology. This by way of saying that essential woodworking terms are neither called out at first use nor are they defined in the glossary. Terminology encountered in the text which is unfamiliar should be looked up using a general Internet search.

Special lutherie tools and materials needed for construction are discussed early in each chapter as well. Although in books such as this it is conventional to fully list all tools and materials needed before beginning a construction operation, in this book tools and materials needed for construction appear only when special tools and materials are used. Again, lutherie is an advanced class of woodworking, so this book assumes a well-equipped woodworking shop, at least as far as general woodworking tools go. Later in this chapter is a discussion of the general tools and supplies needed before a guitar construction project is begun.

The layout and construction work described in each chapter is broken down into a number of logical construction operations, and these in turn are divided into a number of simple construction steps. This logical layout makes the descriptions easy to follow. Some chapters contain sidebar discussions related to the design or construction at hand. These provide additional information for those interested in it, without breaking the general construction description flow.

Included at the end of the book are appendices containing instructions for the construction of some jigs and fixtures which may be of use to novice builders working in a shop that is minimally equipped. Sometimes the text of a chapter will reference external sources of information such as other books, journal articles, or web pages. Information needed to access these external sources appears as end notes to the chapter.

Notational Conventions

Formatting and notational conventions used in this book are listed here so that you may know what they mean before you encounter them.

Dimensions

Although the book is intended primarily for readers in the USA it is also intended to be useful to all readers. Linear dimensions are generally presented in both inches and millimeters. Readers should be aware that the values in millimeters are simply direct mechanical conversions from inches, usually to one decimal place. These will often look funny to those using the metric system, but please just round these values to whole millimeters where that is appropriate.

Fractions of inches are presented either as vulgar fractions or as decimal fractions, depending on the conventions generally used for the item that is being described. For example dimensions used to describe most woodworking objects use vulgar fractions, e.g. 2¼″ (57.2MM). Vulgar fractions as small as 1/64 are used. Decimal inch fractions are used in cases where more precision is required (for example, when denoting fret placement on the fretboard) or where doing so is conventional. An example of the later is expressing the diameter of strings, e.g. 0.013″ (0.33MM).

URLs

URLs are written in a sans serif font and are often accompanied by a QR code for easy access.

Sidebars

Sidebars are denoted by a light gray background color, and contain discussions relevant to the topic at hand without unduly interrupting the flow of the text.

Italics

It has already been mentioned that italics are used to denote a lutherie term the first time it is used. Italics are also used for emphasis and to denote non-English words. Lutherie is quite interesting in that so much of its terminology makes use of non-English words. In order to prevent the text from being overrun with italics, in this book I do not italicize any lutherie terms with non-English origins, but instead limit this particular use of italics to Latin binomials, used to identify wood species. So, first use of unfamiliar lutherie terms, emphatic words, and Latin binomials are all italicized. It is always apparent from context which of these are indicated by the use of italics.

Wood Species

Wood species are specified by common name followed by Latin binomial, for example Honduras mahogany (*Swietenia macrophylla*). All wood species referenced in the text are listed in an appendix by Latin binomial. The appendix includes the common name(s) of each wood and lists a number of the important mechanical properties useful in selecting wood for a lutherie project. People sometimes balk at the use of the Latin names for wood species, but their use is really the only way to specify wood species in an unambiguous way.

Numbering of Photos, Figures, and Tables

Photos, figures, and tables are each numbered sequentially in each chapter. So, all photos in a chapter will be numbered sequentially by appearance, starting with 1. The same goes for figures (drawings), which are distinct from photos and are numbered in their own sequence. Same with tables.

Attention Icons

Some pieces of information are important enough that they are called out with special attention icons. The list of icons used follows.

Important Points – Paragraphs which contain important points begin with a pointing finger icon, like this example paragraph:

This is a really important point, as you can tell by the fact it begins with the important point pointing finger icon.

Screw-ups – Mistakes are inevitable when undertaking any project, but some are common enough that they are worth noting. Paragraphs that include information on common mistakes are preceded by an icon of an up-pointing wood screw, like this example paragraph:

In addition to serving as a warning for a possible mistake, the text in paragraphs like this will often describe how the mistake can be remedied.

Thinking Ahead – Sometimes during a construction operation, an action must be taken in preparation for a construction operations that will occur later in the book, maybe even in a different chapter.

Descriptions of the action and explanations of why it is performed now, and what future operation it will affect, are called out with the thought bubble icon.

Practice – Some operations really should be practiced a few times before attempting them on an instrument under construction.

These actions are called out with this icon of a young woman practicing the guitar.

Left-Handed Construction – For the most part the acoustic steel string guitar is symmetrical and as such is suitable for both right-handed and left-handed use. But there are some important steps which must be performed differently if a left-handed instrument is being built.

These actions are called out with this icon of a left hand. There are surprisingly few such instances.

Save For Later – It is often the case that a jig or simple tool is made for use in a construction operation. It is generally the case that the jig or tool can be discarded when the construction operation has been performed. The cases when the jig or tool should be retained for construction operations that appear much later in the book are called out with the familiar icon for saving things from computer software.

This jig or tool should be saved for later use in a similar construction operation.

Online Annex

There is always some amount of useful information that is subject to change frequently. Inclusion of such information in a printed book means that the book quickly becomes out of date. In this book, all such information is put in an online annex that is referenced by the printed book. In this way the changeable information can be kept up to date. Information maintained online includes the plans and templates for the example guitars built in the book; a list of suppliers of lutherie materials, tools and services; and errata that were found in the text of the book following its publication. It is a wise idea to refer to the errata section *before* getting into the book, and to note corrections on their appropriate pages. The URLs of external website resources are also included in the online annex. URLs and QR codes for the sections of the online annex can be found in Appendix A.

About the Photos and Diagrams

The book contains many photos and diagrams. For the most part the photos are edited for clarity and conventional composition, but there are a few photos that have been enhanced in some way to make the important details stand out. This often makes for a peculiar looking photograph, but form follows function in these cases. The most common such enhancements are substantial changes to contrast, and the overwriting of pencil lines to make them stand out better.

Diagrams are used in cases where an extreme focus on certain details is required. Diagrams of three dimensional objects are usually presented in *orthographic projection*. Diagrams are also used to show what in a real instrument are subtle geometrical features. These are often cartoon drawings, in which the feature of note is exaggerated to make it more visible and obvious.

Very Brief History of the Acoustic Guitar

In my observation, a section on the history of the guitar seems to be a requirement for any comprehensive work describing the instrument's construction. Also in my observation, these are rarely read. So my goal here is to discharge my obligation in a very brief history that focuses on those aspects of the history which were most influential in the construction of the modern steel string acoustic guitar. It's short. There are many great books on the subject of guitar history, and any one of them offers a far more comprehensive picture than what is in this brief introduction. I am particularly fond of two such books.[1, 2] Both are currently out of print but readily available used.

Early history of most stringed musical instruments is largely speculative. The fundamental problem is that these instruments are quite delicate and easily damaged, so few examples of really early instruments survive to the current day. But we are pretty sure of this: plucked stringed instruments with the familiar waisted body shape of guitars did exist in Europe by the mid-1500s. These were *gut string* instruments, usually with four *courses* of two strings each. Tuning was accomplished by violin style pegs. The frets were made of gut and tied to the neck, in the same manner as for lutes.

These instruments would change over time to have five courses of gut strings. Probably the most obvious additional evolution was in the adaptation of solid frets, usually made of ivory or metal. For the most part, development of the instrument until the late 1700s was not particularly energetic. But a change in the popularity of the instrument and a change in repertoire for it induced a number of significant changes during the Classical and Romantic periods. Stringing evolved to the modern six single strings during this period, likely related to the availability of mass-produced thin wire, which made it practical to make wire-wound bass strings. The number of frets increased, placing additional frets on the top, above the soundhole. Bridges that used pins to anchor the strings made their appearance.

The Industrial Revolution would make mechanical tuning machines available as a replacement for wooden tuning pegs. These began to be in use in the early 1800s, and by the end of that century would be the most common mechanism for tuning. The body gradually changed shape during the Romantic period, becoming wider (though still narrow by modern standards), with a more pronounced waist.

The 1800s brought considerable experimentation with the bracing structure of the top plate as well, with various configurations being tried. One style that was adapted by C.F. Martin positioned the main braces of the top in a crossed configuration shaped like the letter "X." This bracing configuration would survive as the most common one used in modern steel string acoustic guitars.

Romantic period guitars were primarily gut string instruments but there was considerable experimentation among builders and players with steel strings during this period. Guitar factories in the USA in the late 19th and early 20th centuries built instruments specifically for the use of steel strings. This is an important point in the evolution of the modern steel string guitar. Instruments built for gut strings could not always withstand the considerably increased string tension imposed by steel strings. Installation of steel strings on guitars not specifically built for them regularly resulted in dramatically shortened instrument life.

Although a number of guitar manufacturers were producing guitars intended for use with steel strings, it wasn't until the early part of the 20th century that the C.F. Martin company produced guitars specifically intended for steel strings. At this point, the structural prototype of the contemporary steel string acoustic guitar was complete. Tuning machines, a pin bridge, metal frets, a fretboard that extends over the body, a body with a pronounced waist, an "X" braced top, and six steel strings pretty much define the modern instrument.

Steel string guitar development from then until now consisted mostly in continued increases of the size of the body. Although body size increases were generally advertised as intended to increase the loudness of the guitar, this was always more a marketing pitch than an acoustic reality. Smaller body instruments are quite loud. What increased body size actually did acoustically was to increased the guitar's bass response. It is interesting that acoustic guitar body size increased during the course of the 20th century to the quite large size generally called Jumbo, but that general preferences in the latter part of the 20th century and early part of the 21st century tended to shift back to sizes that were somewhat smaller than the largest available. Musical instrument taste and fashion is ever changing, but as of this writing the most popular size acoustic steel string guitar is what is generally referred to as the "OM" size, taking the size designation of a popular C.F. Martin model.

Evolution and innovation never stops. Modern luthiers continue to experiment with the instrument, with bracing, materials, and manufacturing being areas of considerable interest.

The Basic Structure of the Guitar

The finer details of the structure of the guitar are presented in the individual construction chapters where they are relevant. Here, those details of the basic structure of the guitar that serve as background for the rest of the book are presented. The overall structure of the instrument is pretty obvious from even casual observation, but there are important details of the structure that are either hidden within, or are subtle enough that they may not be obvious.

The guitar has two major subassemblies, the neck and the body. The neck consists of the headstock, the neck shaft and heel, and the fretboard. Inside the neck shaft and under the fretboard is a *trussrod*, which provides additional stiffness and, in modern guitars, a mechanism for relatively fine adjustment of the curvature of the fretboard. The body of the guitar consists of the sides, the top, and back, each with their associated bracing, and blocks at neck end and tail end. All of this structure is visible from outside the guitar and through the soundhole. The latter view may require the use of strategically placed mirrors.

For the majority of steel string guitars, the neck and body are built independently and then attached together in one of the final assembly operations. The joint used to connect neck and body varies. Traditional instruments make use of some type of

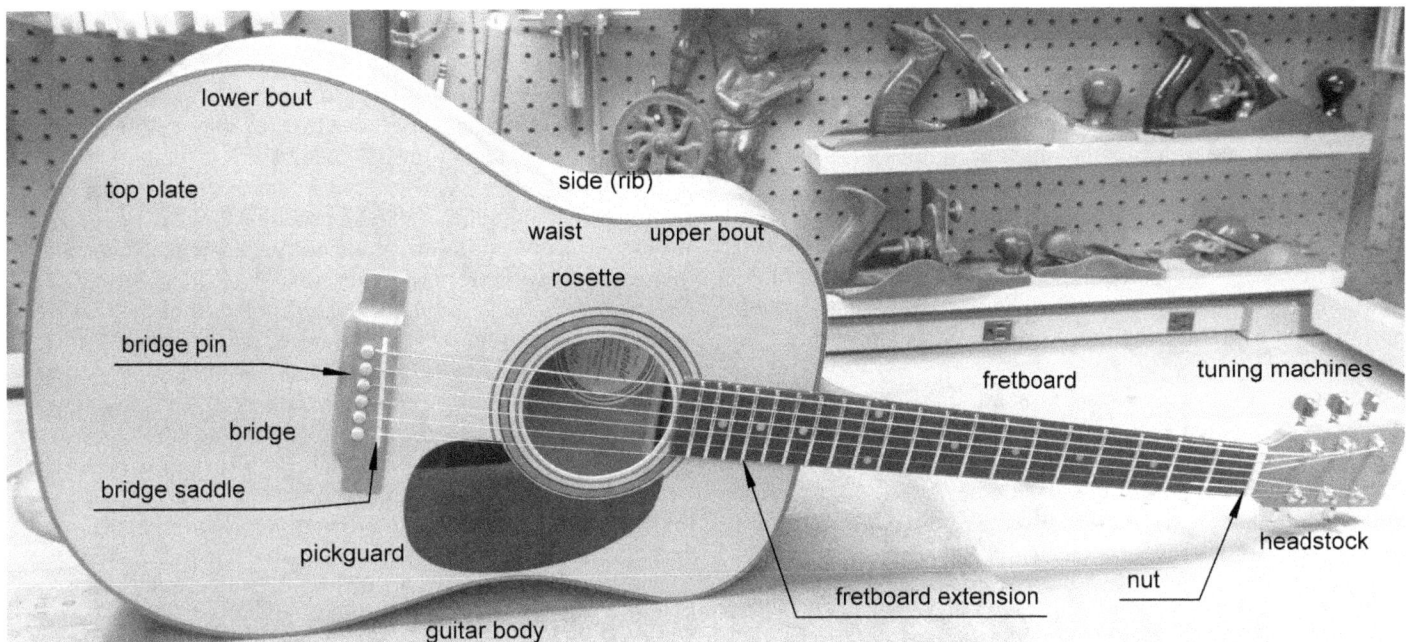

mortise and tenon joint, usually a dovetail, glued together. Such joints are usually completely invisible in the completed instrument. Some modern (and some historical) guitars make use of metal hardware to effect the neck joint. It is usually the case when hardware is used that at least some of that hardware is visible in the completed instrument. The example instruments described in this book make use of a simple hardware neck joint.

One of the subtle details of the gross structure of the guitar that is easy to overlook is the pitch of the neck relative to the body. It is usually the case in modern steel string guitars that the neck is pitched back a subtle 1° or a bit more. This is done to accommodate *plate arching* and to ensure an appropriate height for the bridge.

Plate arching is another subtle feature of the gross structure of the acoustic steel string guitar. Both the top and back plates are generally arched to some degree. Arching of the top plate is usually much more subtle than that of the back. Arching is nominally performed to help the instrument maintain critical geometry in the presence of seasonal changes in humidity and also in the presence of the deforming tension of the strings. There are a number of ways in which plate arching is implemented[3] and the overall geometric considerations can be quite complex.[4] But there are basically two classes of plate arching implementation: *spherical doming* and *ad hoc arching*. The latter is used in this book because it requires no special-purpose fixtures.

Again, this information is presented here for the purpose of general background for the rest of the book. Specific details of the structure are presented where they are directly applicable.

Designation of the Sides of the Guitar

This book follows the common practice of designating the left side and right side of the guitar as if the instrument is oriented neck end up and its top plate is being viewed. If a guitar is played right-handed, the player will look down onto the left side of the instrument, and the right side will be pointing towards the floor.

Tools

General Woodworking Tools

As mentioned, polling indicates that the vast majority of folks interested in building a first guitar have well equipped woodworking shops. For the most part, construction examples

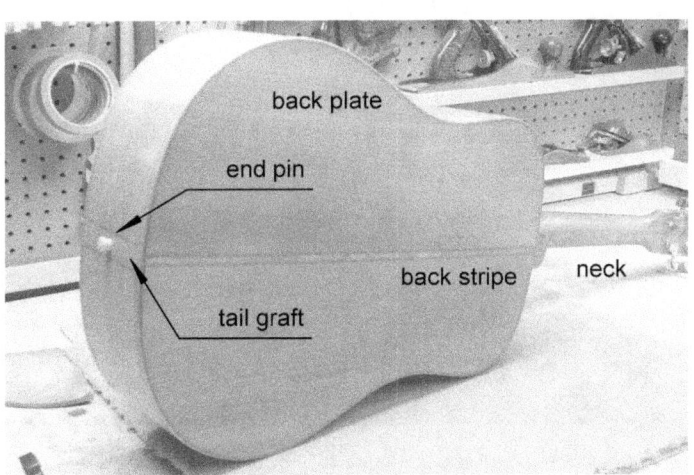

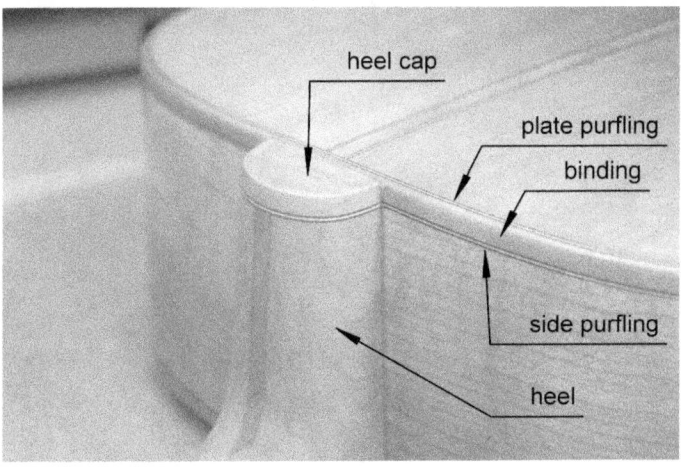

throughout the book will use a variety of common general woodworking tools, with preference for those which best illustrate the construction step being described. It is also the case that some key construction operations are described using a variety of tools that luthiers commonly use for these tasks.

Power Tools

Power tools regularly used in the examples include drill press, band saw, trim router, larger plunge router, and handheld power drill. A stationary spindle sander is often used in the examples, but drill press mounted sanding drums are readily substituted.

Of course, it is possible to perform all of the operations demonstrated using these power tools with various hand tools instead. But complete use of hand tools is not common these days, and as such is generally not the best way to demonstrate construction tasks to a large and diverse readership. This is not to dismiss woodworkers that prefer working extensively with hand tools. Those that prefer to work this way generally have highly developed skills and would have no problem, say, planing a thin plate to thickness using only hand planes. But this is out of the scope of experience for most woodworkers these days, and a guitar building project is probably not the best time to begin learning to acquire such skills. All that said, the book does provide a description of jointing the halves of the top and back plates of the guitar using the hand plane, as one of the options for this operation.

Hand Tools

But that is not to say that most of the construction operations described in the book involve power tools. A number of common woodworking hand tools are used in some of the examples. These tools were selected based on their general familiarity to modern woodworkers and their common use among practicing luthiers. These are tools that can be found in most any woodworking shop, including the shops of woodworkers that work primarily with power tools.

Hand tools were used in the examples for all of the carving operations because these specific operations are largely unfamiliar to many woodworkers and their use supports slow and sure work. Carving tools include a flat sole spokeshave, coarse and medium flat/rounded rasps, sanding boards, and a card scraper and its associated burnisher. Rasps can range from the very inexpensive cheese grater style (the stainless steel ones work very well), to the more expensive conventional cabinetmakers' rasps, to the still more expensive hand stitched rasps.

Sanding boards are flat boards to which Pressure Sensitive Adhesive (PSA) sandpaper has been attached. Because they are such inexpensive shop-built tools that can easily and cheaply be built to spec, sanding boards are used often in the construction examples. A possibly underappreciated property of sanding boards is that they are practically guaranteed to sand a perfectly flat surface, as long as the area being sanded is always in contact with the board while sanding. This property is heavily relied upon in lutherie construction.

***Photo 1-5**– Short and long luthiers' cam clamps are shown in this gluing operation on the top plate of the guitar.*

Card scrapers are extremely useful hand scrapers that are often used in the examples, but it should be pointed out that almost any operation where a card scraper is used can be done with sandpaper just as well.

About Clamps

The old saying among woodworkers that one can never have enough clamps is certainly true for lutherie. In addition to the general arsenal of clamps found in any woodworking shop, lutherie shops usually contain a number of specialty clamps as well. There are special clamps needed to attach the bridge to the guitar top. These are discussed in the chapter on the construction of that component.

Luthiers are fond of using wooden cam clamps for most clamping operations, so much so that these are usually referred to as luthiers' cam clamps. These are ideal for guitar construction for a number of reasons. Although wooden cam clamps cannot apply as much clamping pressure as some other types, the pressure they can apply is more than adequate for lutherie assembly tasks. In fact, there are a number of assembly tasks that require a light touch with the clamps, and cam clamps are ideal for those. The pads of wooden cam clamps are padded with cork, so the clamps can be applied directly to delicate wood surfaces. Wooden cam clamps are also quite light in weight, and this helps to decrease distortion of delicate assemblies when clamping them together.

While on the subject of clamping pressure, I should point out the purpose of clamps is to apply enough pressure to achieve adequate distribution of the glue in the joint, *not* to force an ill-fitting joint into contact. This is a general rule for woodworking, but it is even more important when making something as delicate as a guitar. If a C-clamp is required to close a joint, that joint has not been fitted well enough.

One of the major advantages offered by the luthiers' cam clamp is a clamping depth which is typically greater than that of other styles of clamps. The typical "short" jaw wooden cam clamp has a depth of 4¼″ (108mm) and the longer clamp offers a depth of 7½″ (190.5mm). Many of the construction descriptions in this book depend on these depths, and so clamps of this style are a requirement for following the construction descriptions. A total of ten of the 4¼″ (108mm) deep clamps and four of the 7½″ (190.5mm) are required for some of the construction described here.

Due to the geometry of the clamping mechanism of luthiers' cam clamps, they tend to pull the work that is in contact with the cam jaw toward the bar of the clamp when the clamp is tightened. This can alternately be viewed as a bug or a feature of this style of clamp. It is often the case that assembly descriptions will specify clamp placement in order to work around this tendency of the clamps to pull. It is just as often the case that clamp placement is specified to take advantage of this tendency.

Another type of clamp which is used in quantity in guitar construction is the 1″ (25.4mm) spring clamp. These are used in one particular operation, gluing the linings to the insides of the guitar sides. A minimum of 12 of these are required. 36 or more would be even better.

Measuring Tools

Rulers of various lengths of the type found in any woodworking shop are used frequently in the examples. Flexible rulers are used for the measurement of curved parts. Certain specialty rulers are used in some construction options and are described in the text where those tools are needed. General purpose digital calipers are readily available and can be quite inexpensive these days, and so they are used in a lot of the construction examples.

One measuring tool that is not always found among the collection in a typical wood shop is a set of automotive style feeler gauges. These are ideal for many of the precision measuring and marking operations of guitar construction and as such these are often found in the examples. They are also inexpensive and readily available.

Specialty Lutherie Tools

These will not be individually called out here, but are described in the context of the construction operations that use them. I mentioned earlier that the described construction process makes limited use of specialty tools, but that there are some operations for which their use greatly improves the likelihood of success for the novice luthier. All such tools are readily available from lutherie suppliers.

About Planing/Sanding Thin Parts to Thickness

Lutherie is by definition advanced woodworking, so basic woodworking operations are not given much in the way of detailed explanation in these pages. But there is one operation which is prudent to discuss, and that is the thickness planing (or sanding) of thin parts in general and of large thin parts in particular. There are several large panels that go into the guitar which must be reliably planed quite thin, about 3⁄32″ (2.4mm), and accurately. Although in my polling I found that most novice luthiers have access to a planer, these machines unfortunately cannot be used to plane pieces that thin. The most commonly used power tool to do this is the stationary thickness sander, but this is an expensive tool that is not found in every woodworking shop. Fortunately there are some inexpensive options to the use of this tool.

One readily available option is to simply have the wood supplier sand the pieces to thickness. Almost all lutherie wood suppliers offer this option for a reasonable extra charge. Woodworkers that are very proficient with hand planes can use those tools for this purpose. Another option is a drill press mounted device generally called a Safe-T-Planer. These are inexpensive, at least compared to the cost of a thickness sander, and can be reliably used on the larger panels if some sort of backing board and drill press extension table are used.

A reliable and quite safe option is a shop built planing jig for use with a router and a large diameter bottom cleaning router bit. Such jigs can be complex, but a description for a *very* simple jig of this type is provided in Appendix B.

Materials

In keeping with the general organization of this book, descriptions of the materials used in guitar construction are generally located in the chapters where each material is first used. So here only general background information is presented.

Lutherie Wood

There is a common lutherie myth that certain woods have particular musical qualities and that these are the woods which must be used for lutherie applications. Although where particular wood species are concerned this is truly a myth, when it comes to the condition of the wood and some of its mechanical features, there is indeed a difference between wood that is suitable for use in a guitar and that which would be more suitable for other woodworking projects. A guitar is a very light structure that must be able to vibrate freely but also support considerable string tension. And it must do this while maintaining some very tight dimensional tolerances over long periods of time. To these ends, the materials it is made of must be stiff, strong, and dimensionally stable. Some of the materials must also be light in weight.

What is most required for stability are:

• wood species that are reasonably dimensionally stable with changes in humidity;

• wood that has been thoroughly dried to a moisture content that reduces further shrinkage;

• straightness of grain (so any dimensional changes that do happen are uniformly expressed);

• and wood that is *quartersawn* (so differential dimensional changes can be managed by the orientation of the wood in the instrument).

It is certainly possible for knowledgeable luthiers to select wood from general wood suppliers that suits the purpose, but by far the easiest way for a lutherie novice to obtain wood with such qualities is to purchase it from a specialty lutherie wood supplier, and to be sure the wood meets these requirements.

Glue

A guitar is primarily held together by glued joints, so glue is an extremely important component of the finished instrument. There are a number of glues that are used in lutherie. The most common ones are listed here. In the described construction process a limited number of glues are used. Each has its own advantages and disadvantages. As such, the use of each type of glue is limited to certain applications. The glues used in the construction process are indicated with an asterisk in the following list.

Hot Hide Glue

This is the traditional woodworking glue, and it has been used in lutherie for hundreds of years. It is made of boiled animal protein. It comes dry and must be mixed and kept within a fairly critical range of temperature and viscosity for use. It is the preferred glue for many luthiers. Hot hide glue (often abbreviated HHG) cures by drying out and cooling. It has unique

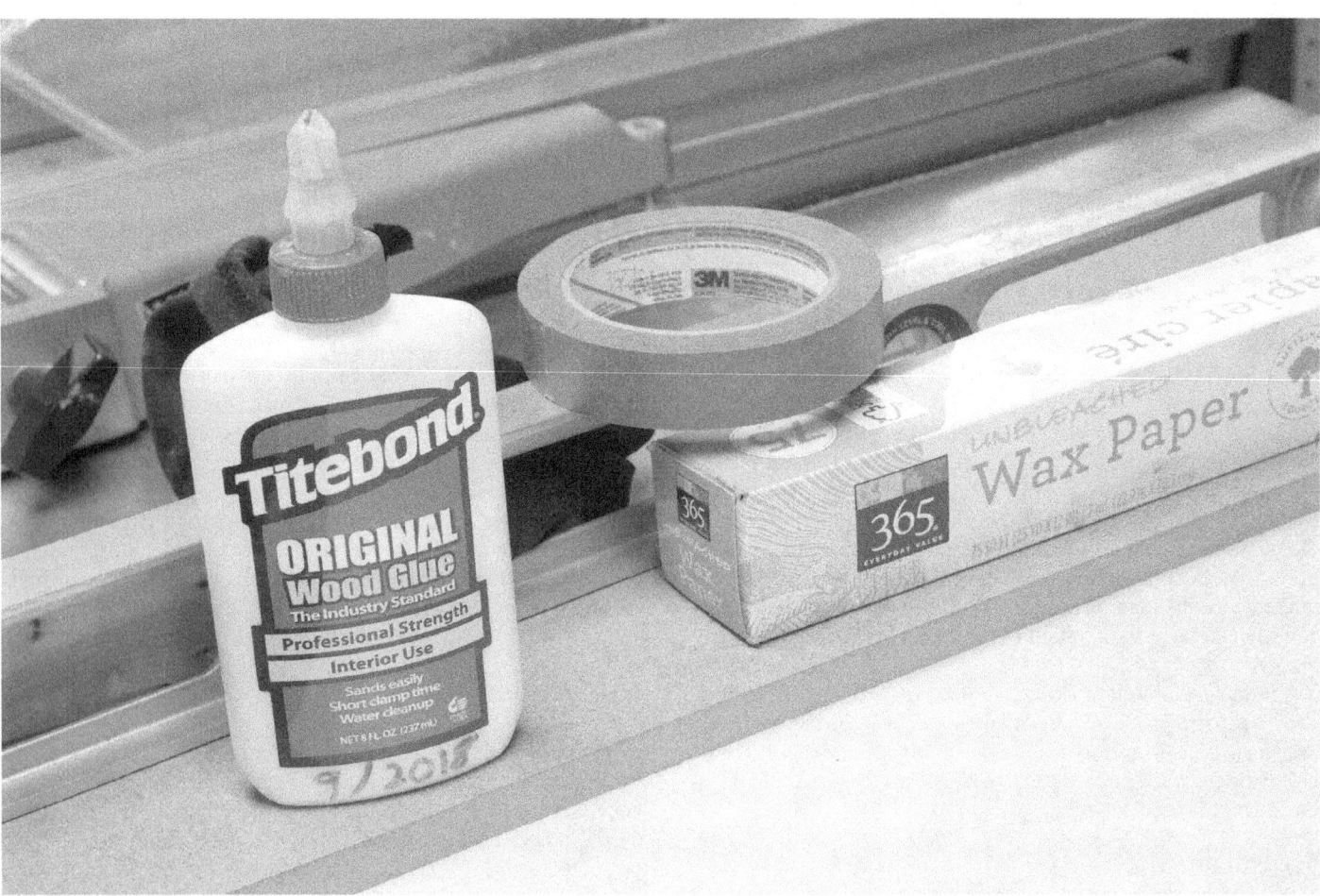

***Photo 1-6**– Woodworking glue, masking tape, and wax paper are essential supplies.*

application requirements because parts glued with it must be positioned quickly before the glue cools. When the glue does cool it grabs, stabilizing the joint. These unique qualities are different enough from other glues that the gluing process is often quite different if this glue is used than it would be if another glue was used.

Hot hide glue is not used in the described construction process in this book. Guitar lutherie requires a number of complex gluing and clamping configurations that can be daunting to lutherie novices, even under ideal conditions. These applications are made all the more daunting by the requirement for speed. Given the criteria used to select construction methods for the construction process, particularly those for likelihood of success, existing woodworking skills, simplicity, and presentation in book format, hot hide glue could not reasonably be considered for use here.

Liquid Hide Glue

Issues presented by hot hide glue have been fully understood since it was first used. It is not clear when, but at some time in the past woodworkers found that the addition of urea to hot hide glue would prevent it from solidifying at room temperature, so the glue could be used as an easy to apply liquid. Liquid hide glue was used industrially since at least the early part of the 20th century. Commercial liquid hide glues are readily available. Its use in lutherie is quite rare. The glue works well, but it has a very short shelf life (measured in months). When old or under conditions of even slightly cold temperatures, it often does not cure. Most luthiers I know that have tried this glue have eventually had a gluing operation where the glue failed to cure, which caused them to abandon its use. Because there are more reliable alternatives, liquid hide glue is not used in the construction process described in the book.

Fish Glue

Most commonly used in bookbinding applications, fish glue is similar to hide glue but is made of fish protein. It is liquid at room temperature and so is quite easy to use. Some luthiers that would use hot hide glue but want something more convenient use fish glue for instrument assembly. Because other options are readily available, fish glue is not used in the described construction process

Woodworking Glue*

This general category of glue is more properly named aliphatic resin glue. It is generally yellow in color, so it is often called yellow glue. But that yellow color is not inherent to the glue itself, so there are glues of this class that are white in color or that have been dyed to match the color of dark woods. Woodworking glue is readily available, has a long shelf life, and is easy to apply and use. It is used in the described construction process for all these reasons. Woodworking glue cures by drying.

As a general rule I don't like to name specific products in the book, but in this case the ubiquity of one brand (Titebond) and the fact that they offer multiple variations which need to be differentiated requires me to do so. Although other glues in the Titebond line offer better moisture resistance, for lutherie applications the original Titebond glue (sometimes referred to as Titebond I) is generally preferred. The glue line is generally more invisible with this product. Moisture resistance is rarely an issue for glue used to assemble guitars. Stringed instruments are not subject to the weather, and in the case where a cured glue joint must be opened it is very useful to use heat and moisture to do that.

Of particular use for lutherie novices are woodworking glues which offer longer setting time. This gives the luthier more time to set up the more complicated gluing and clamping operations. There is a glue in the Titebond line called Titebond Extend which offers longer setting time. Its use is highly recommended.

Epoxy*

The main advantage offered by epoxy for certain lutherie applications is that is cures chemically, not by drying. As such, it does not shrink when it cures. It also does not wet the wood, which would subject the wood to some expansion while gluing, and later to slow shrinking. For the majority of lutherie applications this is not an issue, but there is one special case where the expansion of the wood during gluing and its slow shrinkage afterward can cause some problems. That case is the lamination of pieces, where the area of the glued surface is large and oriented with the grain of the wood. This case mostly occurs when pieces are laminated together for the neck of the guitar.

A traditional putty for filling gaps and holes is made of glue and sanding dust. When made with epoxy, this putty is quick and easy to use because it does not shrink as it cures, and so a single application is almost always sufficient. Both of these applications for epoxy are used in the described construction process.

Cyanoacrylate Glue*

The major feature of this class of glues is its quick bonding. There are a number of lutherie gluing applications where small pieces can be glued quickly using only hand pressure for clamping. This greatly speeds the time it takes to complete these steps.

Cyanoacrylate glue comes in various viscosities. In the described construction process, both medium viscosity and thin viscosity are used. Thin viscosity cyanoacrylate glue has the extremely useful quality of being able to wick into the finest gaps, and it is used extensively in lutherie to take advantage of that quality.

It should be noted that for lutherie applications cyanoacrylate glues are usually best applied using disposable plastic droppers called micro transfer pipettes. These are available from lutherie suppliers and also from laboratory suppliers.

It should also be noted that for safety, cyanoacrylate glue, particularly the thin viscosity glue, should never be used unless cyanoacrylate glue solvent is on hand. The solvent is acetone.

Polyurethane Glue

This is an interesting glue, but it is not used in lutherie. The glue cures chemically in the presence of water. But the quality that makes it most unsuitable for lutherie applications is that the glue expands while it cures, which makes it impossible to make a glue joint that doesn't have a visible glue line.

Miscellaneous Materials

Wood Products

The construction operations described here make heavy use of two manufactured wood products for various jigs, fixtures, and cauls. These are medium density fiberboard (MDF) and melamine coated particleboard. These sheet goods are inexpensive and readily available. They are also quite flat and dimensionally stable, *as long as they don't get wet*. The melamine board makes very nice sanding boards. In addition to being very flat, PSA sandpaper sticks well to the melamine veneer surface and is easy to remove when the times comes to replace it.

Cork or Rubber Sheets

These materials are used whenever a hard padded surface is needed. Small amounts are used in various cauls and clamping fixtures. Plain cork sheet material is available in rolls from home centers. It is quite inexpensive. Sheet rubber and cork/rubber composite sheets are available from industrial suppliers. These latter materials hold up better and are more expensive than plain cork.

Double Stick Tape

A very thin polyester tape with adhesive on both surfaces is used extensively in the construction process. This tape is often used to tape down router templates for template routing applications. It is available from suppliers of router bits and from lutherie suppliers. Although fairly expensive as far as consumable products go, it is a great time saver for temporary attachment of various things. In the described construction process it is even used to put some jigs and fixtures together.

Wax paper

Small pieces of this readily available material are regularly used in applications where a glue proof barrier is needed.

Sandpaper

The conventional range of sandpaper used in general woodworking is used in lutherie as well. The woodworking construction descriptions in this book will indicate use of Coated Abrasives Manufacturers' Institute (CAMI) grits in the range of 60 through 320. This is the most common sandpaper grit specification for sandpaper sold in the USA. CAMI grits are indicated by plain numbers, with no additional preceding letters. Note that, in this grit range, the grit specifications of the Federation of European Producers Association (FEPA) are all close enough to the CAMI grits so that they are considered to be interchangeable. FEPA sandpaper grits are preceded by the letter "P."

Finer grits are specified in the construction descriptions for use on finishing materials. Grits in the CAMI range of 400 through 1000 are indicated. Note that for these finer grits, the

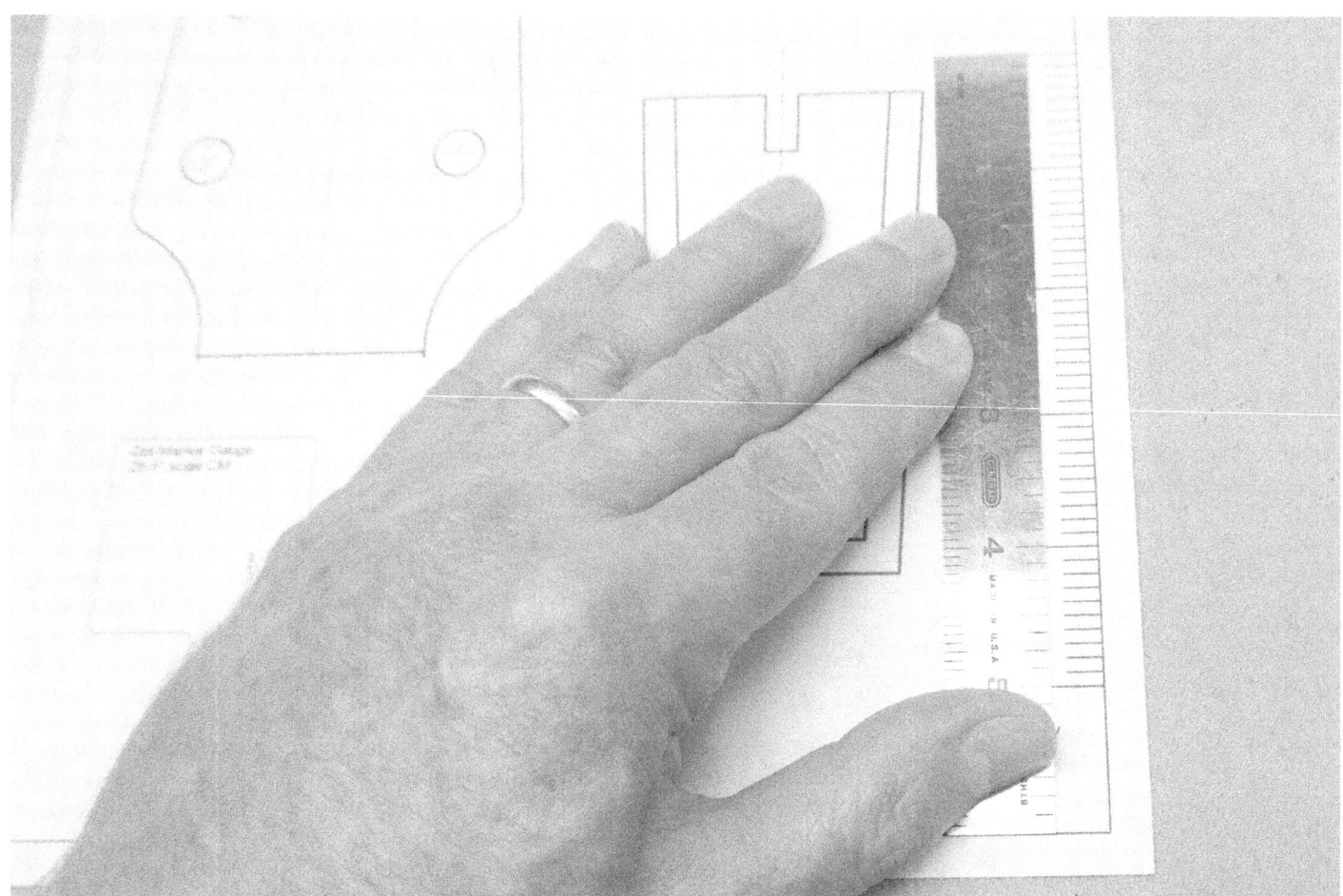

Photo 1-6– *Verifying the printed scale on a template page to be sure the templates are the correct size.*

"P" grits are *not* interchangeable. More information on this is available in the chapter on finishing.

Pressure Sensitive Adhesive (PSA) backed sandpaper is used extensively for sanding boards. Although a wide variety of grits are useful, all construction operations described can make use of only three grits, 60, 80, and 180.

General Construction Topics

As has been mentioned, the construction of a guitar is an advanced woodworking project. The more advanced woodworking skills possessed by the lutherie novice, the higher the likelihood of a successful instrument. This is particularly the case when some of that woodworking experience has been in the construction of small and detailed objects that require a high degree of dimensional accuracy during construction, and that must retain a high degree of dimensional accuracy afterwards. A guitar is a small and finely fitted bit of woodworking. It is also an extremely light structure that has to hold up to considerable string tension and maintain a high degree of dimensional accuracy over time and changing environmental conditions. Those conditions include varying temperature and humidity. Although the former is generally not much of an issue except in the extremes, the latter is an important issue that must be addressed at construction time.

Accuracy of Dimensions

In my observation, many novice luthiers have experience building things out of wood that require a high degree of dimensional accuracy. It is also the case that experienced woodworkers that don't can readily adapt to the requirements imposed by guitar construction. The dimensions given for many components in this book typically require accuracy of greater than 1/64" (0.4mm). Lutherie novices whose previous woodworking experience is with assemblies which require less accuracy are advised to keep this in mind. The construction descriptions provide details of how needed accuracy can be achieved in places where it is required.

Humidity Control

Wood expands and contracts with changes in its internal moisture content. For a lot of objects constructed out of wood, this is not an issue or at least not much of an issue. But for guitars it is an absolutely critical issue. The lightweight structure of a guitar must remain playable within a wide range of relative humidity. This requires wood species choices and grain orientation of certain parts of the instrument to be made with the expansion and contraction of the wood in mind. The lightweight structure requires the use of some very thin and broad pieces of wood, and changes in humidity can result in cracking of these pieces if changes in dimension are extreme.

For this reason it is almost always necessary to maintain the humidity of the place in which the wood materials and the construction subassemblies are stored to within a fairly narrow range. Here in New England, relative humidity ranges throughout the year from around 30% or less in the winter to around 80% or more in the summer. This is typical for a lot of the temperate climates around the world. A guitar built at 80% relative humidity is highly likely to crack if it is subject to prolonged periods at 30%, which would be the case during pretty much any winter.

Note that there are places in the world where this is not an issue. Colombian luthier Anamaría Paredes builds instruments under the relatively high and relatively stable humidity conditions of Bogotá, but for the most part these instruments will live their lives in that same environment, so the likelihood of serious cracking is pretty low.

The solution for those of us that work in temperate climates with large seasonal swings in relative humidity is to build under controlled humidity conditions, keeping the relative humidity in the range of 40% to 55%. This is in the middle of the expected humidity swing in most temperate climates. An instrument built under these conditions will still swell with increased humidity and shrink with decreased humidity, but it will not do so severely.

Maintaining ideal relative humidity in the construction environment often presents a problem. The first thing that is necessary is to have some way of actually measuring relative humidity in the shop. Fortunately, inexpensive digital humidity gauges are readily available. Another (usually) fortunate thing is that the internal moisture content of wood changes fairly slowly, so spikes in atmospheric humidity are not much of a concern. We care about the long term humidity trends.

Low relative humidity in the shop is dealt with by installing a humidifier. High relative humidity is dealt with by installing a dehumidifier, but in a lot of cases simply air conditioning the shop will remove enough moisture to keep it within specs. In my shop I have to humidify for three months in the winter, and dehumidify for three months in the summer.

Note that some luthiers don't bother to control the humidity in the entire shop, choosing instead to control humidity just in a small room or closet where the wood to be used and the guitar in its current state of construction is stored when it is not actively being worked on. This approach works out very well and is far less costly than trying to control the humidity of the entire shop.

One last word on this subject. A luthier never really knows the humidity conditions under which purchased wood was stored, so it is always a sound idea to purchase wood that will be used in a lutherie project well in advance of actual construction and to store that wood under humidity control for a while before beginning the project. For thin wood bought from a reputable lutherie wood dealer, that is used for the top, back, and sides of the guitar, a month is usually a sufficient amount of time for the wood to acclimate.

Plans and Templates

The construction descriptions in this book detail the construction of two example instruments, an OM style guitar and a Dreadnought style guitar. PDF files containing full size plans for these example instruments can be downloaded from the online annex of this book, found in Appendix A. The construction descriptions here make heavy use of templates, the files of which can also be downloaded. Most of the templates are simply copies of parts of the drawings in the plans. Other templates are available for various gauges that aid in fitting parts of the guitar. Still others are used to make special-purpose sanding boards that are used when fitting the neck to the guitar body.

For each example instrument there is one plan. There is also one template book, one neck-fitting sanding board template set, and a template used to slot the nut, for a total of three template files to be downloaded in addition to the file for the plan.

After the plan and templates are downloaded they must be printed out. The instrument plans are color engineering drawings (blueprints) which must be printed out on Arch E (36˝ (914MM) × 48˝ (1219MM)) or larger size paper. For European users, the plans can be printed onto B0 size paper. Most people don't have a printer that can handle paper of this size. Various businesses provide printing services that can handle this. Most online office supply stores offer this service, and there are specialty blueprint printing companies as well. A web search for "blueprint printing" will provide a number of printing resources. Printing prices are reasonable. It is a good idea to have two copies of the plan printed, so one can be cut up for use in construction of the body mold.

The templates are all sized for standard ANSI Letter size (8.5˝ (215.9MM) × 11˝ (279.4MM)) stock, and can be printed on most computer printers. For European users, the templates can be printed onto A4 size paper. The template book and the neck fitting sanding board template set are most usefully printed onto card stock. This makes templates cut out from the books easy to trace. The nut slotting template is unique in that it is printed onto computer label stock. Details of this are included before use of that template is discussed.

A very important step is verifying proper printing size of the plan and each template page. Plans and templates *must* be printed out *actual size*, not fitted to the page, and not explicitly enlarged or reduced. There are rulers marked in inches printed down one side and across the bottom of all plans and templates. These are used to verify that the pages have been printed actual size. An accurate ruler with fine graduations is used to measure these printed rulers (**photo 1-6**). If they measure accurately then the page has been accurately printed to size.

Note that most commercial large format printers used to print out the plans will likely print correctly sized plans. Home computer printers are more prone to size inaccuracies, particularly along the vertical axis. As mentioned, the templates are commonly printed out on home computer printers. If the vertical printed ruler does not measure accurately, the template(s) should be discarded and another printer should be found for printing the templates.

---

1. Kuronen, Darcy (2000). *Dangerous Curves: The Art of the Guitar*. MFA Publications. ISBN13: 978-0878464852.

2. Evans, Tom; Evans, Mary Anne (1977). *Guitars: From the Renaissance to Rock*. Paddington Press. ISBN13 : 978-0709209874

3. Mottola, R.M. (2005). Rib Depth of Guitars with Spherically Domed Plates. *American Lutherie #84*, p. 22.

4. Mottola, R.M. (2012). Fretboard/Top Plate Geometry of the Flattop Guitar. *American Lutherie #111*, p. 32.

2 Roughing Out the Neck

The guitar consists of two major subassemblies, the neck and the body. Either one can be approached first in a guitar building project, but in this book the neck is built first. This order of construction follows that of luthiers such as Sylvan Wells of Bay State Guitars, who considers the neck to be the essence of the instrument.

This chapter contains information on the initial steps in the construction of the guitar neck. These include shaping the wood blank that will be the basis of the neck, cutting the side profile of the neck out of the blank, installing a reinforcing dowel in the heel, and routing the channel for the trussrod. But before the specifics of construction are presented, a general introduction to this topic is made.

The first step in the construction of the neck subassembly is the selection of neck blank materials. There are three options here, a *rectangular cross-section neck blank* (which for brevity I'll refer to hereafter as simply a rectangular blank), a variation on that, where the blank is made of vertically laminated pieces, or an *assembled neck blank*. The first is a solid piece of wood of rectangular cross-section that is large enough in all dimensions so that the basic shape of the neck can be cut from it. The second option, which is a common variation of the first approach, is to laminate such a solid blank from thinner boards. **Figure 2-1** shows the side profile of a neck superimposed over the outline of a rectangular blank. The third option is to assemble the neck blank from pieces that are closer in dimension to the neck profile. See **figure 2-2**. All of these options are

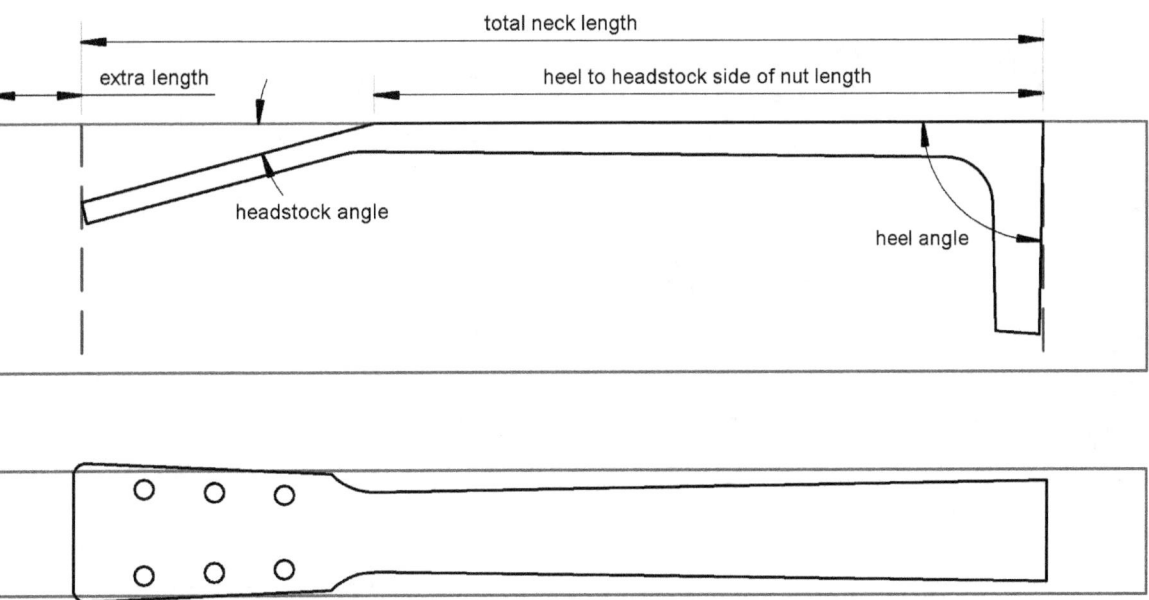

***Figure 2-1**– Schematic of a rectangular cross-section neck blank, with outlines of the neck drawn over its side and top surfaces. Note the blank must be longer than the neck; it must be deeper than the length of the heel, which is the same as the depth of the guitar body at the neck joint; and the blank must be a little wider than the width of the neck shaft at the heel end. Note also that the total width of the headstock is often wider than the neck blank. Wood will be added at a later construction step to support the full width of the headstock.*

Figure 2-2– Side view schematic of an assembled neck blank, with the side profile of the neck drawn over the side surface. The blank is assembled out of a solid heel block and a board. One end of the board is cut off at a shallow angle, then the off cut is flipped over and glued back on to form the headstock part. Here too the blank must be longer than the finished neck will be.

common, and the choice of which to use is often made based primarily on availability and cost of materials. So all are detailed here. Lutherie wood suppliers generally offer neck materials for both solid rectangular blanks and assembled blanks.

Wood Selection

It is important that wood used for the neck of the guitar (and all other parts of the guitar for that matter) be fully dry. The industry standard for dry wood is approximately 12% moisture content. Wood moisture meters are readily available, but if one is not available in the shop, a practical alternative is to simply purchase wood from a reputable lutherie wood supplier. It is prudent whenever possible to procure wood well in advance of starting the lutherie project, and then storing it in the shop. A few weeks or months will allow the moisture content of the wood to stabilize relative to the relative humidity of the shop.

Selecting a wood species for the neck is optimally accomplished by first specifying what we require the neck to do, and then choosing wood that meets those requirements. The guitar neck must be strong enough and stiff enough to support the tension of the guitar strings. It must be dimensionally stable, even with changes in humidity. Because the guitar neck is fashioned by carving, the wood used must be easy to shape by carving. The wood must be readily available and reasonably priced.

For the most part, we really don't have to worry too much about strength and stiffness when selecting a wood species. The completed guitar neck will have a substantial steel trussrod embedded inside, and this will provide enough strength and stiffness no matter the wood species used. As a practical matter, the lutherie novice will not necessarily have to be concerned with the other requirements either, if the wood for the neck is purchased from a reputable lutherie wood supplier. Such suppliers will only offer neck blanks from wood species that are known to be suitable for guitar necks.

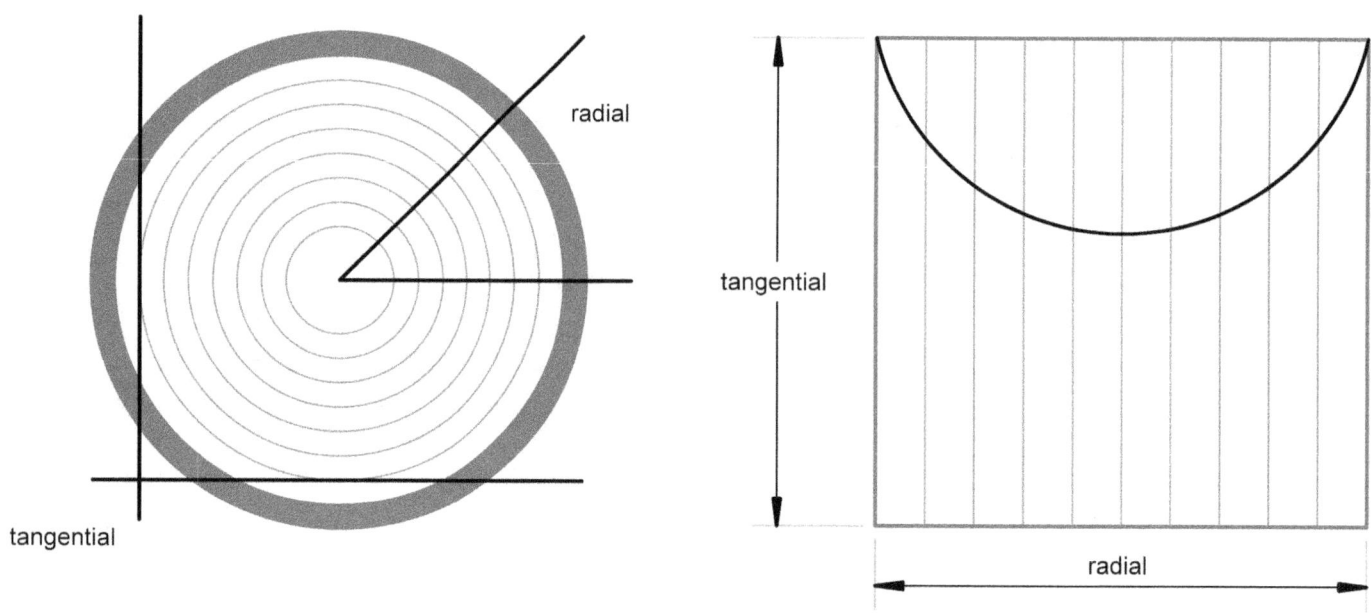

Figure 2-3– Schematic views of end grain of a log and of a quartersawn neck blank. As wood dries out it shrinks more tangential to the growth rings than it does radially to the growth rings. The ratio of shrinkage is different for each wood species. Honduras mahogany has low shrinkage and a low shrinkage ratio, making it very stable no matter how it is cut. When other species are used for neck blanks, the blanks should be quartersawn. This will result in most of the change in dimension with change in humidity in the thickness of the wood. For a guitar neck, small changes in thickness are not much of an issue.

Photo 2-1 – *End grain of a solid Honduras mahogany (*Swietenia macrophylla*) neck blank. Note that bastard grain orientation is fine due to the stability of this species.*

The traditional material for the neck of a steel string guitar is Honduras mahogany (*Swietenia macrophylla*), and its use is highly recommended. As mentioned, the neck of an acoustic guitar must be light in weight and stiff, and it also must be dimensionally stable. A guitar is a structure that must be light in weight and also maintain close dimensional tolerances. Even small dimensional changes with changes in humidity can wreak havoc on a guitar. Honduras mahogany is ideal for guitar necks because it is light in weight, easy to carve, and it is dimensionally stable with humidity changes. This species is unique in that its shrinkage specs are roughly the same *tangential* to the growth rings of the wood and *radial* to the growth rings as well. See **figure 2-3**. Note that no wood species shrinks much along the length of the board. The consequences of low shrinkage in general and similar shrinkage both across and with the growth rings mean that a Honduras mahogany neck will be stable no matter what the grain orientation is for the board(s) from which it is cut (**photo 2-1**).

This is a good place to point out that *Swietenia macrophylla* is endangered and thus protected. As such, it is expensive, and availability is limited. As a result, wood dealers sell a variety of so-called mahoganies, some of which are not even of the same genus (*Swietenia*) as that of the genuine material. Fortunately, such woods can make excellent guitar necks if the blanks are properly cut. A popular species for necks at the time of this writing is sapele (*Entandrophragma cylindricum*). Likewise, almost any medium weight hardwood can be used to make a guitar neck if properly cut. As used here, the term "properly cut" means that there is no twist along the length, that there is little *runout*, and that the board is either perfectly *quartered* or close to it. Most wood species will shrink and expand with changes in humidity, mostly along the growth rings. Ideally, a guitar neck doesn't change much in dimension at all with changes in humidity, and this is essentially the case if it is made of Honduras mahogany. The next best thing is if it only changes in thickness with changes in humidity, because thickness changes here don't have any serious consequences for the geometry of the instrument.

Based on all this, the decision of selection of wood species and the construction option for the neck blank goes as follows. Honduras mahogany can be used no matter its grain orientation (*quartersawn*, *flat sawn*, *bastard grain*) for either a rectangular or assembled blank. Other hardwood species can be used for either type of blank if the board(s) is perfectly quartered or only a few degrees off quarter. A special case is a rectangular blank that is made by laminating a number of boards together. It is possible to construct a laminated rectangular blank from flat sawn or bastard grain boards so that distorting changes in dimensions relative to changes in humidity in each of the laminations mostly cancel each other out. More information on this is provided in the following section.

The above discussion focuses on dimensional stability. But as mentioned, there are other qualities to consider when selecting wood to use for the construction of a guitar neck. One of the most important, particularly in the context of the construction process described in this book, is how easy it is to carve, since the shaft and heel parts of the neck will be carved to shape. As mentioned, Honduras mahogany is ideal in this regard. Basswood (*Tilia americana*) is a light colored wood that is also easy to carve. Most medium density hardwoods with fine, straight grain carve fairly well. Some that work well are the soft maples such as eastern soft maple (*Acer rubrum*) or European sycamore (*Acer pseudoplatanus*), American cherry (*Prunus serotina*), and black walnut (*Juglans nigra*). Some that should probably be avoided, particularly by wood-carver novices include oak (*Quercus* spp.) and similar woods that don't carve well because the grain is so stringy, and tulip poplar (*Liriodendron tulipifera*), which tends to fuzz up when carved and sanded. Novices should probably avoid figured woods of any species, which all present carving difficulties.

As well as not being difficult to carve, wood used to construct a guitar neck should be clear of defects. When a rectangular blank is used, any defects in the wood should fall outside of the pattern of the neck.

Rectangular Neck Blank Option

This overview section provides general information on this type of neck blank, but it also contains important concepts and terminology for both types.

The major advantage to starting construction with a rectangular cross-section neck blank is that no time and effort is needed to assemble the blank. But there are some disadvantages to this approach. Rectangular neck blanks are generally more expensive, less available, and are certainly more wasteful of wood. But on that latter point, I do find that I can always put the cut-offs to good use for fashioning blocks and other parts. Perhaps the most important potential disadvantage to using a rectangular blank is that the headstock may be more prone to breaking if the completed instrument takes a fall. This is because the headstock is completely composed of short-grain wood, and this is prone to cracking when stressed (**figure 2-4**). Still, many production instruments have been made using rectangular neck blanks, and they hold up well enough. The necks of the classic 20th century guitars from Gibson and Martin were all

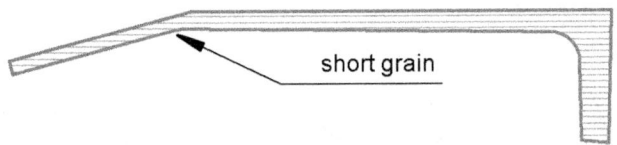

Figure 2-4 – *Necks cut from a solid block of rectangular cross-section may be more prone to cracking of the headstock due to short grain there.*

constructed in this manner. Many accomplished luthiers continue to use this traditional construction.

Finished Dimensions of a Rectangular Neck Blank

As indicated in the caption of **figure 2-1** the finished dimensions of a rectangular cross-section neck blank must be longer than the neck; deeper than the length of the heel, which is the same as the depth of the guitar body at the neck joint; and a little wider than the width of the neck shaft at the heel end. The first two of these measurements can be taken from the side view of the neck subassembly on the guitar plan. I recommend the finished blank be at least 1″ (25.4MM) longer than the neck on both the headstock and the heel ends, for a total extra length of at least 2″ (50.8MM). More extra length is better. This extra length is necessary because the critical distance of the body end of heel to the location of the nut cannot be precisely determined until after the top surface of the headstock is planed. The example instruments in this book have total neck lengths of 20⅝″ (524MM), so rectangular cross-section neck blanks for these instruments should be at least 22⅝″ (575MM) long.

The finished blank must also be a bit deeper than the length of the heel, which is the same as the depth of the guitar body at the neck joint. The example instruments have different heel lengths. For the OM style Tripletta, the heel is 3⅞″ (98.4MM) long. The heel of the dreadnought style Paura is 4 9/16″ (115.9MM) long.

The finished blank should be a little wider than the width of the neck shaft at the body end of the heel. The necks of the example instruments are 2 5/32″ (54.8MM) wide here. I recommend adding at least 7/32″ (5.6MM) to each side to get the width of the finished neck blank. So for either instrument, a finished neck blank width of 2⅝″ (66.7MM) will work fine. Note that the calculated finished width of the blank may not be wide enough to completely cover the width of the headstock (see **figure 2-1**). This is not a problem, as the headstock width will be built up with the addition of wood "ears" during a subsequent construction step.

On the other hand, if a blank wide enough to include the entire width of the headstock is available, it certainly can be used. But note that there is a practical limit to the width of the blank of 2⅞″ (73MM) if the blank is to be worked using a conventional table saw with 10″ (254MM) diameter blade, and 3″ (76.2MM) tall sanding drums mounted on the drill press.

For convenience, finished dimensions for a rectangular neck blank for the example instruments appear in **table 2-1**. Remember, the dimensions above and in the table are finished dimensions, so procured blanks that are not "surfaced four sides" (S4S) must be large enough to allow for surfacing. Details on surfacing appear in a bit, but first the option for laminating up a blank is discussed.

Laminated Rectangular Neck Blank Variation

As mentioned, laminating the blank from thinner boards allows the use of more readily available flat sawn or bastard grain (rift sawn) wood, but can still yield a stable neck. Such material may not be available from lutherie wood suppliers, but is available from general suppliers of hardwood lumber. Although a neck blank can be laminated from any number of pieces, the theory of how this works is most readily described using a two-piece laminated blank as an example. To compose a two-piece laminated blank, a single long flat sawn board is cut in half crosswise and the two halves are "flip-matched" for lamination. When this is done, the end grain of the resulting blank shows

Length	≥22⅝″	(575MM)
Depth (Tripletta OM)	≥3⅞″	(98.4MM)
Depth (Paura Dreadnought)	≥4 9/16″	(115.9MM)
Width	2⅝″	(66.7MM)

***Table 2-1**– Finished dimensions for a rectangular cross-section neck blank suitable for the guitars in the recommended plans that accompany this book.*

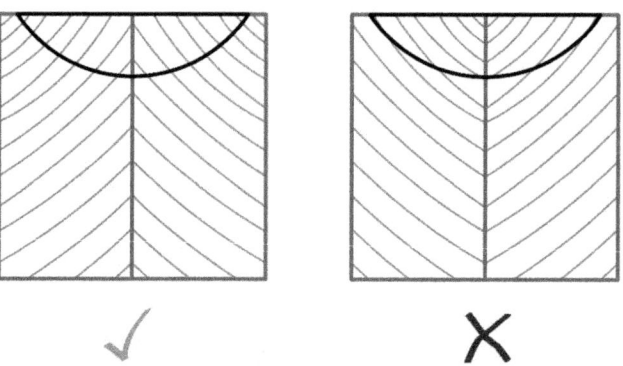

***Figure 2-5** – To improve appearance, bastard grain (rift sawn) laminations are oriented so the grain lines run as perpendicular to the outline of the neck shaft as possible.*

***Photo 2-2** – Cutting and flip matching a board yields a two-piece laminated neck blank. The end grain of the two halves are approximately mirror images.*

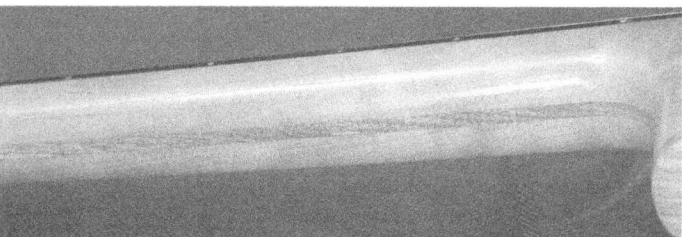

***Photo 2-3** – A narrow center lamination of a different wood species in the neck blank results in a neck with a stripe down the middle.*

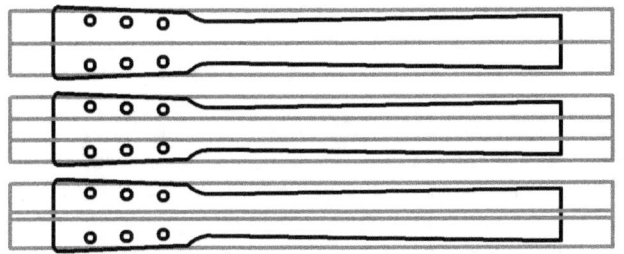

Figure 2-6 – Typical two-piece and three piece lamination patterns for laminated rectangular cross-section neck blanks. Note that no matter what pattern is used, joints between laminations should never cross the outline of the side of the neck shaft. Another way to put this is that the entire side of the shaft must be situated within a single lamination.

approximately a mirror image on either side of the lamination seam. See **photo 2-2**. In theory, any distortion resulting from changes in humidity in one of the laminated pieces is compensated by equal and opposite distortion in the other piece. In practice this construction has been used extensively for hard maple (*Acer saccharum*) electric bass necks and even though this wood is not particularly stable, the resulting laminated necks are very much so.

The end grain of laminated blanks should be as symmetrical about the vertical centerline as possible. Likewise the width and species of the laminations. If bastard grain wood is used, the finished neck shaft will look better if the grain can be oriented so that it runs as perpendicular to the outline of the cross section of the finished neck as possible. See **figure 2-5**. Although all sorts of patterns are possible, the most commonly used are the two-piece flip-matched lamination described above, a three-piece lamination made of equal-width pieces made with a flat sawn center piece and two flip-matched side pieces, and a three-piece lamination made with a narrow flat sawn center piece and two wider flip-matched side pieces. Note that the latter style is often made with the center piece of a contrasting color wood, resulting in a center stripe in the finished neck, as shown in **photo 2-3**. The common lamination patterns are shown schematically in **figure 2-6**.

The total width of the stacked laminations must add up to at least 2⅝″ (66.7mm), the same minimum thickness as for a solid blank, as indicated in **table 2-1**. So for a two-piece laminated blank the stock should first be planed to 1⁵⁄₁₆″ (33.3mm) before being cut in half. For a three-piece blank where all the laminations are the same thickness, the stock should be planed to ⅞″ (22.2mm). The thickness of the laminations of a three-piece blank with a thin center stripe will depend on the thickness of the stripe. For a typical ¼″ (6.4mm) center stripe, the side laminations should be 1³⁄₁₆″ (30.2mm).

Assembled Neck Blank Option

The major advantage of the assembled neck blank is that the wood for it is generally less expensive than for the rectangular cross-section blank, and also more readily available. The main disadvantage is that some additional assembly is required, but this is neither a difficult nor time-consuming task.

A minor disadvantage is that there may be no spare material available to use for the headstock ears, which will be needed to widen the headstock in a subsequent assembly operation. When considering this option, it is wise to figure out where to get the material for the two ears, which each will be approximately ½″ (12.7mm) square and 6″ (152.4mm) long.

The material to fashion this style of blank is generally available from lutherie suppliers as two separate pieces, a board that will be fashioned into the headstock and neck shaft, and a block that will be used for the heel (**photo 2-4**). Although it is generally not used in the construction of steel string guitars, another option for the heel is to laminate up a heel block from several pieces cut from the board used for the neck shaft and headstock. This is called a *stacked heel*. Since its use is atypical for steel string guitars, construction of the stacked heel is not detailed in this book.

When ordering these materials sight unseen, I always ask the supplier to match the pieces for color and appearance of the grain.

Refer to **figure 2-2** for a schematic drawing of the assembled neck blank and its relationship to the finished neck.

Finished Dimensions of an Assembled Neck Blank

These are essentially the same as for the rectangular blank. But since the blank will be assembled from two pieces of wood, the dimensions of those pieces must be individually considered. The board that will be used for the headstock and neck shaft must be just a bit wider than the widest part of the shaft in the finished instrument. When that board is planed smooth, its thickness must be thicker than the thickest part of the shaft of the finished instrument. This board must be longer than the total length of the finished neck. Here I recommend an extra length of at least 3″ (76.2mm) longer than the finished neck. In addition to providing for adjustment to the eventual location of the nut, this extra length is needed to compensate for the angle of the headstock and also for the trimming necessary to cut off and fit the headstock piece.

The finished width of the heel block should be the same as that of the board used for the headstock and shaft. It must be thick enough (deep enough) so that when it is glued onto the shaft piece the combined depth will be greater than that of the

Photo 2-4 – The two pieces of wood used for an assembled neck blank. The top board is used to fashion the headstock and neck shaft, and the block is used for the heel.

Length of shaft part	≥23⅝″	(600.1mm)
Thickness of shaft part	≥⅞″	(22.2mm)
Width of shaft part and heel block	≥2⅝″	(66.7mm)
Length of heel block	≥4″	(101.6mm)
Depth of heel block (Tripletta OM)	≥3″	(76.2mm)
Depth of heel block (Paura Dreadnought)	≥3¹¹⁄₁₆″	(93.7mm)

Table 2-2 – Finished dimensions for the two pieces needed for an assembled neck blank for the example guitars.

heel of the finished instrument. And it should be at least 4″ (101.6mm) long. It must be long enough to include the thickest part of the heel plus the transition curve from heel to shaft, plus at least another 1½″ (38.1mm). Finished dimensions for the two pieces needed for an assembled neck blank for the example guitars are provided in **table 2-2**.

The Surfaces of the Neck Blank

For purposes of description of construction in this chapter, it is useful to unambiguously name the four broad surfaces of the neck blank. Looking at the side view in **figure 2-1,** and looking at **figure 2-2**, the top surface of the blank will be referred to as the *fretboard surface*. This is the surface onto which the fretboard will eventually be glued. The bottom surface in those figures is straightforwardly referred to as the *bottom surface*. Imagine that the blank in the figures is sitting on its side on the bench, with the headstock oriented to the left, and you are looking down on it. The surface in contact with the bench is referred to as the *reference surface*. This is the surface that will usually be in contact with the table of various stationary power tools, such as table saws and bandsaws, drill press, and spindle and disc sanders. The surface opposite the reference surface (the side view surface you are looking at in **figures 2-1** and **2-2**) is referred to as the *layout surface*. In general, this is the surface that will be marked up with the profile of the neck for cutting operations.

Note that in the figures and photos the neck will usually be shown with the headstock oriented to the left, which is the same orientation that a right-handed player would generally view the neck while playing. Although this consistency of orientation is useful in identifying the surfaces, it is also very useful to write the names of the surfaces right on the blank in pencil, and to refresh these labels whenever they are obliterated by woodworking operations.

Layout and Construction

One thing to keep in mind during the construction process for both types of blanks at all steps: the reference surface and the fretboard surface must be kept square. Failure to do so can result in a neck that is too small in one or more dimensions, and such an error is often not recoverable.

Initial Construction of the Rectangular Neck Blank Option

This section contains construction details for a rectangular cross-section neck blank. Construction of the assembled neck blank is discussed in the following section.

Description of constructing a laminated blank appears first. In the case of a solid blank this is skipped over, to the construction section on surfacing the blank.

☐ **Laminating the Blank**

The blank is laminated by gluing the laminations together. For all gluing operations, it is a really good idea to perform a dry run of the assembly process to be sure all needed tools and materials are on hand, and to be sure the assembly can be performed before the glue sets up.

I recommend using 30 minute epoxy to laminate the neck blank, and in any gluing operation where broad surfaces are glued together and where it is not necessary for the glue joint to be reversible for repair work at some time in the future. The major advantage of epoxy is that it does not wet the wood, and therefore does not cause it to expand in size at the glue joint. This expansion has little consequence for thinner pieces of wood, but can be consequential when broad surfaces are glued together. Instruments with laminated necks and thin finishes tend to develop tiny ridges at the glue lines when regular wood glue is used. It takes months or years for these ridges to develop, and they are caused by eventual shrinking of the wood next to the glue line. These can be felt by the player. Such ridges don't develop when epoxy is used for neck blank lamination.

1. The wood to use for the laminations should be cut generously wider and longer than the finished depth and length

Photo 2-5 – *Applying epoxy to the first lamination with a notched spreader. The bench top is protected with newspaper. The clamps and cauls that will be used to clamp up the blank are seen in the background.*

Photo 2-6 – *The laminated blank is clamped. Cauls are used to protect the blank from damage from the C-clamps.*

dimensions for the blank in **table 2-1** because the laminations will move around a bit during lamination and will have to be squared up after the glue dries. If this is not possible, the blank can be clamped together dry with the pieces well-aligned, and then drilled for screws or dowels that will keep the laminations in alignment during gluing. Of course, if this is done these holes should be made outside of the pattern of the neck. The stock is then planed to the thicknesses needed for the chosen lamination pattern, and the laminations generously cut to length.

2. The laminations are fitted together dry, checked for accuracy of end grain orientation, then the stack of laminations is placed on its side on the bench, the bench top having been first covered with newspaper to protect it from glue squeeze-out.

3. Enough 30 minute epoxy glue to cover one side of each lamination is mixed up. One at a time, each lamination is flipped off the stack onto the newspaper-covered bench. Glue is applied with a fine notched plastic spreader to ensure an even coating, so the entire surface is covered with glue (**photo 2-5**). The next laminate is flipped over onto the first, glue is applied. The entire process is repeated until all laminations are now re-stacked.

4. The stack is picked up and placed on the bench so the grain of the laminations is now vertical, and clamps are applied, with cauls if needed, and tightened just gently. Clamping near the edges of the blank is most important because this is where the wood that will end up in the finished neck is. The laminations usually slip out of position a bit, so the entire stack is pushed back into shape before the clamps are tightened fully. Once the clamps are tight, the stack can be oriented any way while the glue cures (**photo 2-6**). The glue is allowed to fully cure (about 24 hours) before the clamps are removed.

☐ **Surfacing the Blank**

1. The blank is surfaced to the finished dimensions specified in **table 2-1**, using whatever tools are familiar and available. The surfaced blank should be rectangular, with accurate 90° angles between adjacent surfaces. This operation can be quickly performed using a well set up jointer (**photo 2-7**). If a hand plane,

Photo 2-7 – The rough blank is easily surfaced and squared up using a well set up jointer.

| Neck heel end to headstock side of nut | 14¹¹⁄₃₂″ (364.3mm) |
| Headstock angle | 15° |

***Table 2-3**– Dimensions related to the location and angle of the headstock for the example guitars. To calculate the distance from the heel end of the neck blank to the headstock side of the nut, add distance in the first row of the table to the amount of extra length allocated to the heel end of the neck blank.*

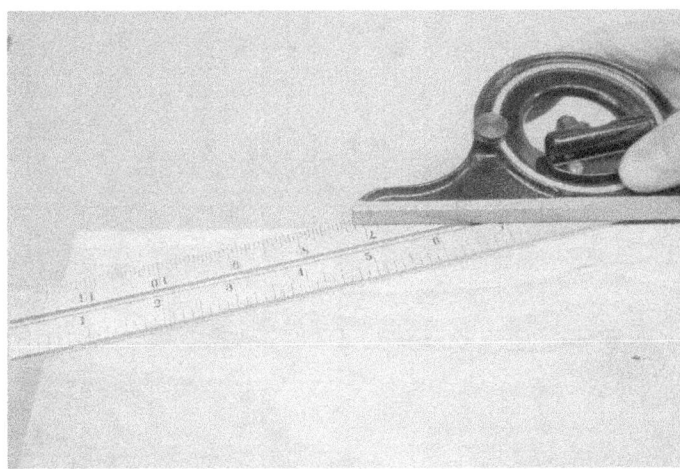

***Photo 2-8** – A protractor is used to draw the line representing the top surface of the headstock. The line extends from the headstock side of the nut to the end of the blank.*

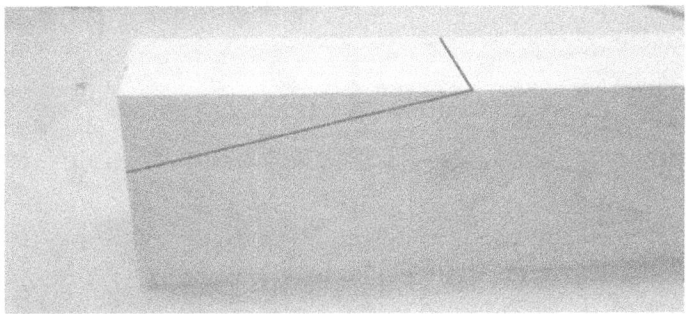

***Photo 2-9** – The line is drawn on the layout surface of the blank and also on the reference surface (not seen in this photo).*

straightedge, and square are used, it is really only necessary to flatten and square up two adjacent surfaces. These surfaces are the top of the blank (that is, the fretboard surface) and the reference surface. Although no special care is needed to flatten the layout surface, it should be cleaned up well enough so that lines can be accurately drawn on it using pencil and straightedge. There is really no need to clean up the bottom surface at all. In cases where tools are available to do this quickly and easily it is generally useful to straighten and square these surfaces though. The ends of the blank should be trimmed square to the top and side surfaces. To avoid mistakes, after the blank is surfaced it is useful to write the name of each surface on the respective surfaces of the blank in pencil. As subsequent operations obliterate these labels they should be refreshed.

☐ **Cutting the Headstock Top Surface**

The next step is laying out, cutting, and flattening the top surface of the headstock. The angle of the headstock of steel string guitars varies from about 12° to 15° and the angle is not critical

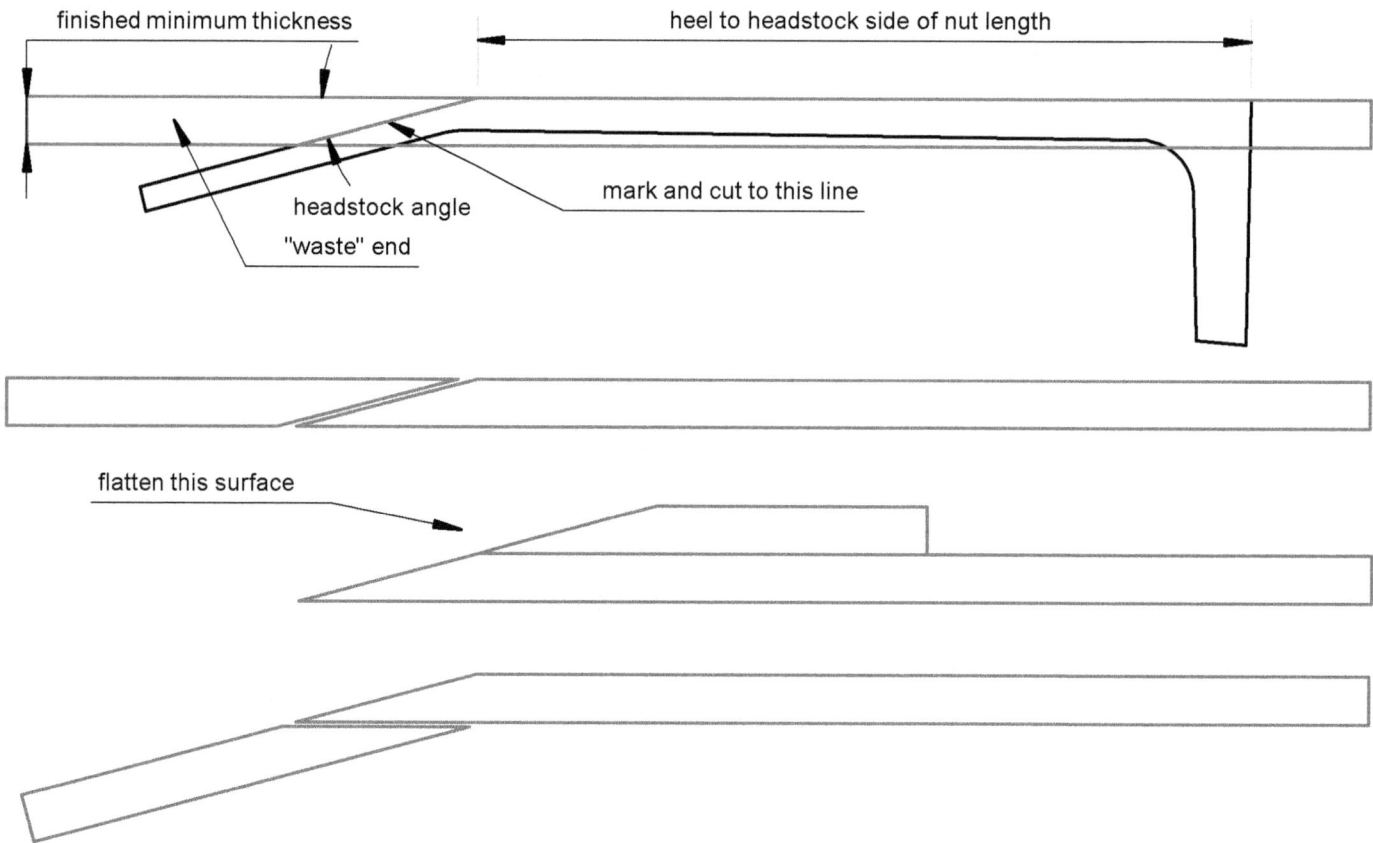

Figure 2-7 – *Schematic of construction of the neck shaft and headstock part of the assembled neck blank. The headstock portion is cut off the board and the cut surfaces are aligned then planed smooth and flat. The headstock portion is then flipped over and glued to the underside of the shaft portion.*

within this range. The example instruments both use a 15° headstock angle.

1. A pencil mark is made on the fretboard surface representing the location of the headstock side of the nut. This is measured from the heel end of the neck blank as the distance in the finished instrument from heel end to headstock side of nut, plus

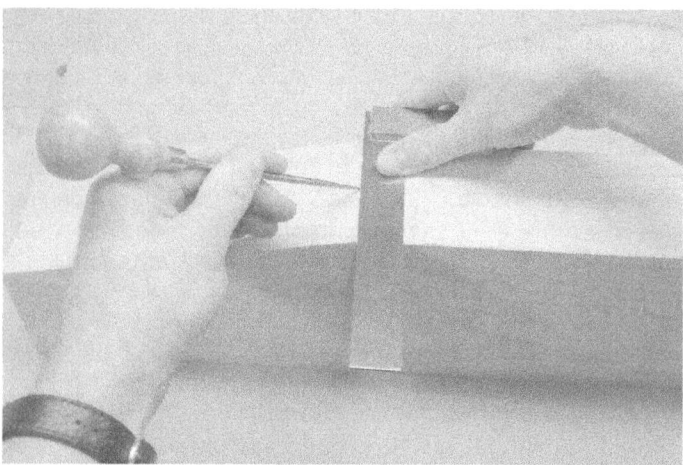

Photo 2-10 – *After the headstock top surface is cut and refined the edge between it and the fretboard surface is marked with a scratch awl. This will serve as a reference for all subsequent layout operations.*

however much extra length was added to the blank at the heel end. See **table 2-3**. For the example instruments the heel to fretboard side of nut distance is 14¹¹⁄₃₂″ (364.3mm). If 1″ (25.4mm) of extra length was added to the heel end of the blank, the total distance is 15¹¹⁄₃₂″ (389.7mm). This distance is measured down the fretboard surface from the heel end of the blank, and a mark is made there in pencil. A square is used with the head against the reference surface, to fully mark this location across the entire width of the fretboard surface in pencil. The ends of this line are extended just a bit onto the reference and layout surfaces of the blank.

2. A protractor is used to draw the line representing the top surface of the headstock onto the layout surface. This line extends from the nut line all the way to the headstock end of the blank (**photos 2-8, 2-9**). The protractor is also used to draw this line onto the reference surface, then these lines are connected across the headstock end surface of the blank.

3. The blank is cut to this line using bandsaw or hand saw, then the sawn surface is cleaned up and flattened using a plane, large diameter drill press-mounted sanding drum or spindle sander, or a small sanding board. Following initial flattening, the surface is further refined and flattened with the small sanding board. Care is taken when flattening this surface to be sure that the edge formed between this surface and the fretboard surface remains perpendicular to the length of the blank. Ideally this

edge will fall exactly on the penciled nut line, but often it will end up a bit in front or behind. As long as the offset from this edge to the penciled nut line is smaller than the extra length allocated to the blank at the ends, all will be fine. There is really no need to hew exactly to the lines penciled on the layout and reference surfaces either. It is important only that the surface be flat and the edge between it and the fretboard surface is perpendicular to the reference surface.

4. This edge will now represent the location of the headstock side of the nut. All subsequent layout will reference this edge. It is best to mark this edge accurately and permanently, using a square and a scratch awl (**photo 2-10**). If the scribed line is difficult to see it can be highlighted with pencil.

5. Construction continues at the section entitled "Continuing Construction of the Neck Blank."

Initial Construction of the Assembled Neck Blank Option

☐ Surfacing the Pieces of the Blank

1. The board that will be used to make the neck shaft and headstock is cut to length as specified in **table 2-2**. Both of the broad surfaces of this board are gluing surfaces so they must be planed or sanded smooth and flat and parallel, using planer, thickness sander, or hand plane. This board is thicknessed as specified in **table 2-2**. One side of the board will be designated and marked in pencil as the reference surface, and this must be planed smooth as well, and made square to the broad surfaces. The remaining side is designated as the layout surface. It is useful to plane this smooth and square too. In any case, the board is planed or ripped to width as described.

2. The heel block will be trimmed to the same width as the neck shaft board. One side of the block is marked as the reference surface. The top surface of the block will be glued to the bottom surface of the shaft board, so that surface must be planed smooth, flat, and square to the reference surface.

☐ Constructing the Shaft and Headstock Parts

The operations involved in this step are shown schematically in **figure 2-7**.

1. The neck shaft/headstock board is cut at an angle into two pieces. The location of the cut is first measured and the line of the cut is drawn on the layout surface of the board. The location of the cut is where the headstock side of the nut will be in the finished guitar. To locate this, a measurement is taken from the body end of the heel to the headstock side of the nut on the guitar plan. This value is provided for the example guitars in **table 2-3**. To this is added half the extra length that was included in the length of the neck shaft/headstock board. This total distance is measured from the heel end of the board and marked in pencil on the fretboard surface. A square is used to draw a line across the width of the board on the fretboard surface at this location.

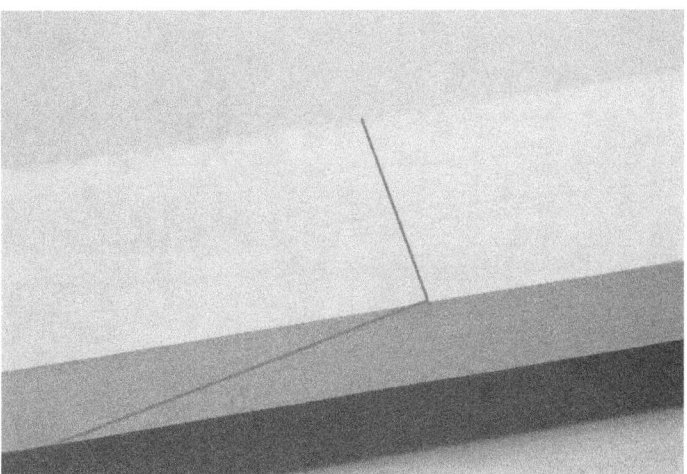

Photo 2-11 – The location of the cut is drawn on the top and layout side of the board.

Photo 2-12 – When using the bandsaw, the cut can more safely be made if the board is first clamped to a thick rectangular piece of scrap.

Photo 2-13 – The two pieces after the board is cut. The headstock part is on top and the neck shaft part is underneath.

Photo 2-14 – The parts are clamped together so the cut surfaces can be planed and flattened as a single surface.

Photo 2-15 – *A coarse grit sanding board can be used to flatten the surface. Then a finer grit sanding board can be used to smooth the surface and refine the edges square to the stock.*

Photo 2-17 – *A disc sander works well for this application.*

Photo 2-16 – *A hand plane can be used to flatten the surfaces. Note that there is a backer board of the same width as the pieces. This supports the thin sharp edge at the end.*

Photo 2-18 – *The pieces, oriented the way they will be glued together.*

Photo 2-19 – *The neck shaft piece is clamped down to an assembly board made of (in this photo, fake wood grained) melamine covered particle board. The fretboard surface (facing away in the photo) must be square to the surface of the assembly board.*

2. Next a protractor is used to draw the line of the cut on the layout side of the board, as in **photo 2-8**. The angle of the line is the same as the headstock angle. This value is also provided for the example guitars in **table 2-3**. The result of the above two steps are shown in **photo 2-11**.

3. The board is cut on this line, keeping the saw blade on the headstock side (short side) of the line. Various saws can be used to make the cut.

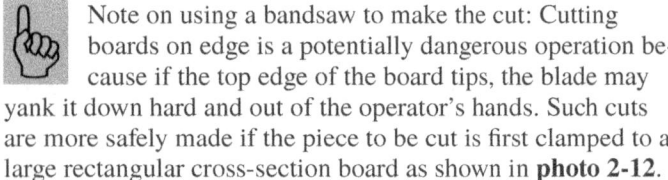 Note on using a bandsaw to make the cut: Cutting boards on edge is a potentially dangerous operation because if the top edge of the board tips, the blade may yank it down hard and out of the operator's hands. Such cuts are more safely made if the piece to be cut is first clamped to a large rectangular cross-section board as shown in **photo 2-12**.

The cut surfaces will have to be cleaned up no matter what saw is used. Resulting parts are shown in **photo 2-13**.

4. Now the pieces are oriented with the headstock piece on top of the neck shaft piece, so the cut surfaces are aligned, as shown in **figure 2-6** and **photos 2-13** and **2-14**. The pieces are clamped together (**photo 2-14**) and then the cut surfaces are flattened and smoothed. Some options for doing this include using a coarse grit sanding board followed by a finer grit sanding board (**photo 2-15**); using a finely set hand plane (**photo 2-16**); or using a disc sander (**photo 2-17**). Whatever tools are used to perform this operation, it is important that the planed surface is flat, and that both the sharp edge of the end of the neck shaft piece and the edge between the cut surface and the top surface of the headstock piece remain square to the sides. A square is used to check, and adjustments are made as necessary. The fine grit sanding board is useful in making these

adjustments. A small amount of added pressure on one side or the other while sanding can move the angle of these edges one way or the other.

5. After the surfacing is done, the pieces are unclamped and oriented as shown in **photo 2-18** to check to see if they will form a smooth, flat, and continuous headstock top surface. If not, additional flattening and squaring using the technique described above will be necessary. Note that close-fitting is extremely important for this and all glued joints. The pieces must fit perfectly when examined dry and simply held together in the hands. It should never be assumed that clamping pressure can be used to compensate for ill-fitting joints.

☐ Assembling the Shaft and Headstock Parts

In order to maintain registration of the two pieces while gluing, the pieces are glued together while clamped to a flat glue-proof assembly board, and two glue-proof clamping cauls are used as well. Any flat material with a coat of paste wax to prevent glue from sticking can be used for these purposes. Melamine covered particle board is ideal. It is inexpensive and glue doesn't stick to the melamine surfaces, so no waxing is required.

As with all gluing operations, it is wise to do a dry run to be sure of clamp placement and alignment before actually committing to glue.

Photo 2-22 – *The headstock piece is clamped down to the assembly board and cauls are clamped to both sides of the joint. The cauls in the photo are made of waxed pieces of scrap wood. Cauls made of melamine covered particle board work well in this application.*

Photo 2-23 – *Another view of the clamping arrangement showing the joint and the cauls.*

1. An assembly board of ¾″ (19.1mm) thick melamine covered particle board is cut approximately 8″ (203.2mm) wide by 24″ (609.6mm) long. From the same material, two clamping cauls 2⅝″ (66.7mm) wide by 4″ (101.6mm) long are cut.

2. Two clamps are used to clamp the neck shaft piece on its side to the assembly board as shown in **photo 2-19**, being sure there is enough room for the headstock piece. Note the placement of the clamps, one on one side of the assembly board and the other on the other side. Luthier's cam clamps tend to pull the work toward their bars when tightened. Although this tendency can cause problems, it can also be used for alignment purposes. The board must be clamped down so that the fretboard surface is perpendicular to the surface of the assembly board. This is checked with a square. If the board is out of square, the clamps can be tightened and loosened (and more clamps added if needed) to pull the board into alignment.

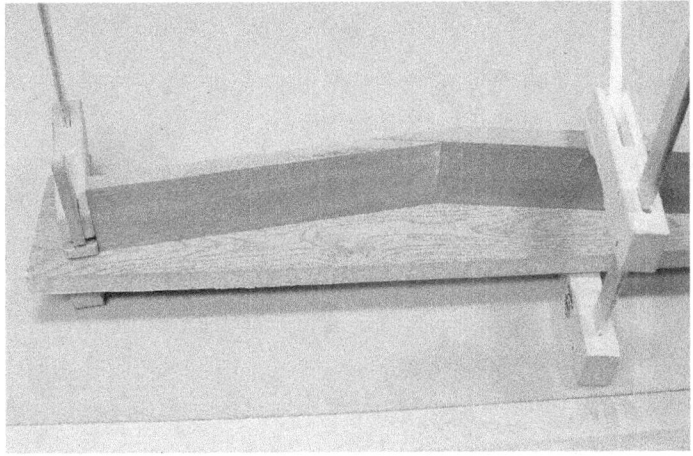

Photo 2-20 – *A single clamp (shown here on the left) is positioned as a stop for the headstock piece to prevent it from slipping out of position while gluing.*

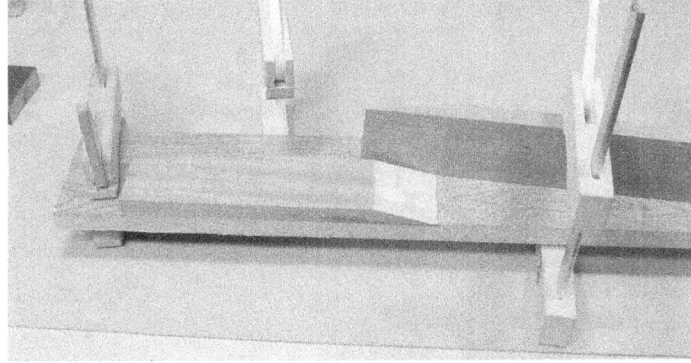

Photo 2-21 – *Glue is applied to the gluing surface of the headstock piece.*

3. The headstock piece is positioned on the assembly board and a clamp is clamped down to the assembly board only, just behind and in contact with the end of the headstock piece. This clamp serves as a stop, to prevent the headstock piece from sliding during gluing (**Photo 2-20**).

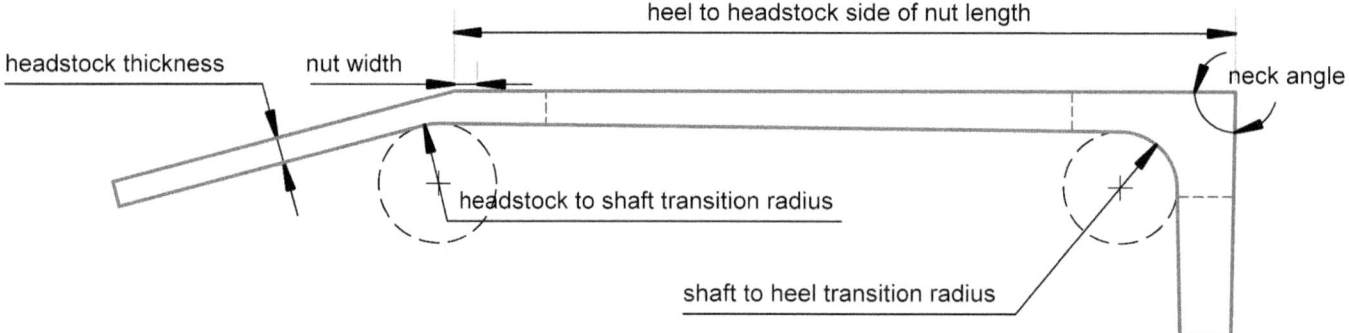

Figure 2-8 – *Critical dimensions used to lay out the side profile of the neck. The dashed lines represent locations where thickness measurements of the neck shaft and the heel are taken. See **table 2-4** for the values of these dimensions for the example instruments.*

4. Glue is applied to completely cover the gluing surface of the headstock piece as shown in **photo 2-21**. The "Goldilocks principle" is used when applying glue: Too much glue will make it difficult to assemble the pieces, because the glue acts as a lubricant and the pieces to be joined will readily slip around on it. Too little glue will make for a weak glue joint.

5. One caul is positioned against the underside of the headstock with one end butted up to the sharp right end of the headstock piece. The other caul is placed on the opposite side of the headstock piece, covering the joint. Two clamps are used to lightly clamp the joint together. If an adequate amount of glue was applied, there will be some squeeze-out when the clamps are applied.

6. Two more clamps are positioned to clamp the headstock piece down to the assembly board, one from each side, and lightly clamped (**photos 2-22, 2-23**). Alignment of all the pieces is checked, then the clamps clamping the joint and those clamping the headstock piece down to the assembly board are alternately tightened a bit at a time, checking alignment with each tightening.

7. The glue is allowed to cure at least two hours before the clamps are removed and the assembly is removed from the assembly board.

8. The reference side and the layout side are flattened as necessary by rubbing them on a large sanding board. If alignment was well maintained during gluing, not much work will be needed here. The sides must remain square to the fretboard surface. This is checked with a square.

9. The top surface of the headstock is flattened on a sanding board (**photo 2-24**). While this is done, the edge between the headstock top surface and the fretboard surface must remain square to the reference surface. If it is out of square a bit, biasing pressure on one side or the other while sanding with the sanding board will bring the edge back to square.

10. This edge will now represent the location of the headstock side of the nut. All subsequent layout will reference this edge. This edge in now accurately and permanently marked using a square and a scratch awl. See **photo 2-10**.

☐ **Adding the Heel Part**

The heel block is glued to the neck shaft and headstock assembly using the assembly board to maintain registration. For this operation, working over just one end of the assembly board will make it easier to place the clamps.

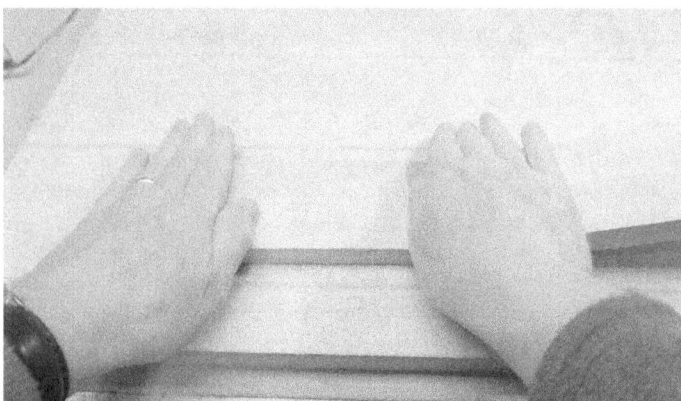

Photo 2-24 – *The top surface of the headstock is sanded flat and smooth on the sanding board. The edge between this surface and the fretboard surface must be made square to the reference side of the neck shaft piece.*

Photo 2-25 – *The clamping arrangement for gluing the heel block to the neck shaft and headstock assembly.*

Neck heel end to headstock side of nut	14 11/32"	(364.3mm)
Nut width	1/4"	(6.4mm)
Headstock thickness	15/32"	(11.9mm)
Neck angle	89°	
Shaft thickness, 1" (25.4mm) from nut	≥5/8"	(15.9mm)
Shaft thickness, 2 1/4" (57.2mm) from heel	≥3/4"	(19.1mm)
Heel thickness, 2" (50.8mm) from fretboard	≥1 1/32"	(26.2mm)
Heel thickness, 2 3/4" (69.9mm) from fretboard (Tripletta OM)	≥15/16"	(23.8mm)
Heel thickness, 2 3/4" (69.9mm) from fretboard (Paura Dreadnought)	≥31/32"	(24.6mm)
Headstock to shaft transition radius	1 3/32"	(27.8mm)
Shaft to heel transition radius	1 1/32"	(26.2mm)
Heel length (Tripletta OM)	3 7/8"	(98.4mm)
Heel Length (Paura Dreadnought)	4 9/16"	(115.9mm)

Table 2-4 – *Values of critical dimensions used to lay out the side profile of the neck of the example guitars.*

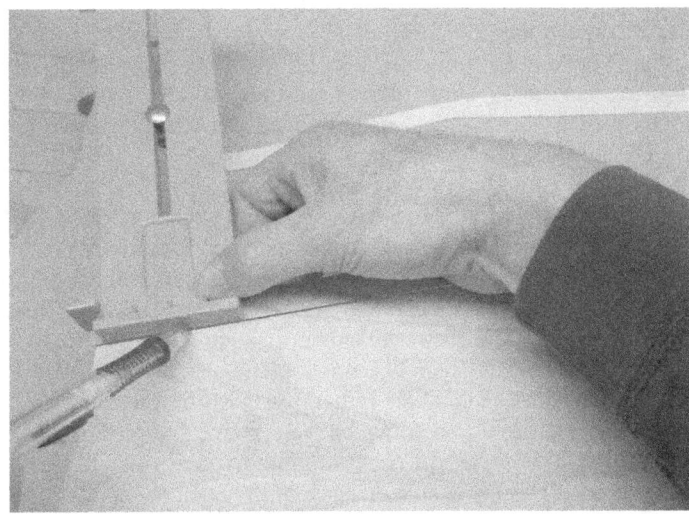

Photo 2-26 – *Using a marking gauge to mark the bottom edge of the headstock. The fence of the marking gauge is against the top surface of the headstock.*

1. The location of the heel end of the neck is marked on the layout side in pencil. The distance from the headstock side of the nut to the end of the neck is given in **table 2-3**.

2. The mark made in the previous step is used to locate the heel block. The body end of the heel block *must end up a little past this mark*.

3. Glue is applied to the gluing surface of the heel block. The heel is lightly clamped to the shaft with two clamps, one from each end. A glue-proof caul is placed on top of the joint, and two clamps are used to lightly clamp the pieces down to the assembly board. See **photo 2-25** for the clamping arrangement. The position of the heel block relative to the mark for the heel end of the neck is checked, and the block is repositioned as necessary. All clamps are sequentially tightened, checking for alignment and contact of the pieces with the assembly board.

4. The glue is allowed to cure at least two hours before unclamping and removing the neck from the assembly board.

5. The reference and layout sides are flattened on the sanding board, being sure the fretboard surface remains square to these sides.

Continuing Construction of the Neck Blank

Instructions for continuing construction are the same for both types of neck blanks. The fretboard surface of the blank is marked with some critical reference lines. The side profile of the entire neck is transferred to the blank, then the profile is cut out and the surfaces smoothed. The side profile of the neck shaft and heel can be transferred to the layout side of the neck blank in one of two ways: The entire profile can be cut out from the side view on the instrument plan and then used as a template, or the profile can be transferred from measurements taken from the instrument plan. Critical measurements used in these construction steps are shown in **figure 2-8** and specified in **table 2-4**.

☐ Scribing Heel and Nut Locations

In a previous step, the location of the headstock side of the nut was scribed onto the fretboard surface of the neck blank. Now, two other locations will be scribed onto that surface relative to that scribed line.

1. The value for the neck heel end to the headstock side of the nut is taken from **table 2-4**. This distance is then measured from the scribed line on the fretboard surface representing the headstock side of the nut. A mark is made on the fretboard surface at this distance. Then a square and scratch awl are used to scribe a line across the fretboard surface at the mark.

2. The value for the nut width is taken from **table 2-4**. This distance is then measured from the scribed line on the fretboard surface representing the headstock side of the nut. A mark is made on the fretboard surface at this distance. Then a square and scratch awl are used to scribe a line across the fretboard surface at the mark.

☐ Laying Out Headstock Thickness and Heel End

1. The thickness of the headstock is marked on the layout side of the neck blank using a marking gauge set to the value for the thickness of the headstock from **table 2-4**. See **photo 2-26**. The top of the headstock is used as the reference surface to guide the marking gauge. The end of the headstock is not marked at this time. The line representing the bottom of the headstock should extend right to the end of the blank.

The thickness of the headstock is somewhat critical. Tuning machines will be mounted here in the finished instrument, and the range of total headstock thickness that they can accommodate is limited, usually centered around 9/16" (14.3mm). It is rare for tuning machine manufacturers and lutherie suppliers to provide this specification. For this reason, it is a good idea to have the tuning machines that will be used on the guitar on hand before construction begins, so the range of headstock thickness that can be accommodated can be measured. Note that the final thickness of the headstock will be greater than the thickness of the headstock part of the neck blank, because a headplate will be added at a later construction step.

2. The body end of the heel is marked on the layout surface using a protractor set to the neck angle specified in **table 2-4**. Note that this neck angle is measured between the fretboard surface and what will be the body end of the heel surface. This line is located at the neck heel end location previously scribed on the fretboard surface. The line should extend all the way from fretboard surface to the bottom surface of the blank. A matching line should be drawn on the reference surface of the neck blank as well, and the ends of these two lines should be connected across the bottom surface of the blank using a square. Note that although just a small difference from 90°, the neck angle is *critical* and should be accurately measured and drawn.

□ **Laying Out Neck Shaft and Heel Profile**

The profile of the neck shaft gets thicker toward the heel, and the profile of the heel gets thinner toward its end. Although some customization of the thickness is possible, these should not be made any thinner than indicated by the plan and the values in **table 2-4**. Inside the neck shaft of the finished instrument there will be a metal trussrod, and inside the heel will be installed threaded inserts that attach the neck to the guitar body. Minimum thicknesses are required to provide ample room for these components.

The profiles of shaft and heel can be transferred to the blank either by using the side view of the neck on the plan as a template, or by using the measurements provided in **table 2-4**.

Option 1: Using the Plan as a Template

1. The side view of the neck shaft and heel is carefully cut from the plan, using scissors or a hobby knife. If the knife is used, a straightedge can also be used to guide the cut for the straight parts of the outline.

2. The cut out piece is used as a template. It is positioned onto the layout side of the neck blank, aligned with the fretboard surface edge and also with the nut and heel end locations, and taped in place with a few small pieces of tape.

3. The profile of the shaft and heel are carefully drawn in pencil, following the edge of the template. The template is removed. Results are shown in **photos 2-27** and **2-28**.

4. A straightedge and pencil are used to extend the lines of the heel down to the bottom edge of the blank.

5. If the headstock angle changed a bit during operations to flatten the headstock top surface, the arc that transitions between the bottom of the headstock and the shaft may no longer be accurate. This arc can be redrawn using a circle template or a compass, or it may simply be drawn freehand.

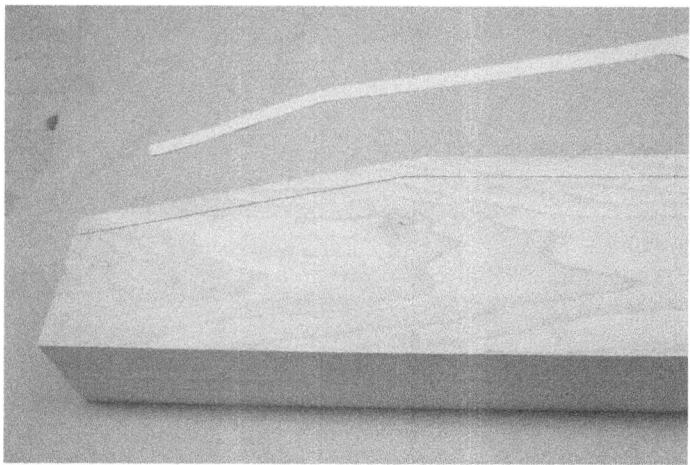

Photo 2-27 – Headstock end of neck blank with profile drawn on it.

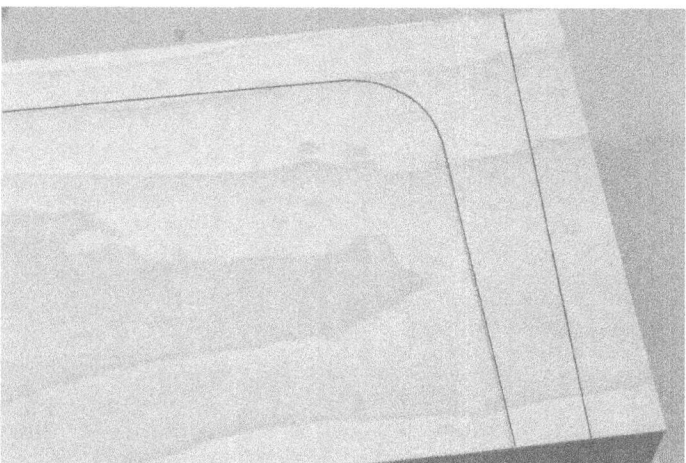

Photo 2-28 – Heel end of neck blank with profile drawn on it.

Option 2: Drawing the Profile from Measurements

1. **Table 2-4** contains two thickness measurements for the neck shaft, one located at a distance from the nut mark and the other located at a distance from the heel end mark. It also contains two heel thickness measurements at distances from the fretboard surface. Each of these is measured and marked on the layout surface of the blank, as indicated by the dashed lines in **figure 2-8**.

2. A straightedge is used to connect the bottoms of the two marks representing the bottom of the neck shaft. This line is extended well into the headstock and the heel.

3. The straightedge is used to connect the left ends of the two marked thickness lines for the heel, too.

4. The intersection between neck shaft and heel profile lines is rounded over (filleted) as indicated in **figure 2-8**. The radius of the roundover is given in **table 2-4**. This can be drawn using an appropriately sized circle template (but note that circle templates are usually marked in circle diameters), or by using a compass.

Photo 2-29 – After cutting out the waste from the inside, the neck looks like this.

5. The intersection of the bottom of the headstock and bottom of the neck shaft is also rounded over in similar fashion, using the radius value in **table 2-4**.

□ **Cutting Out and Smoothing the Neck Profile**

1. The waste on the underside of the headstock and neck shaft and on the inside of the heel are removed first, staying well away from the lines due to the thickness of the blank. It is wise to try to remove the waste in one piece if possible.

 The waste piece should be saved for use in making pieces that will be used to extend the width of the headstock. That operation is covered in a subsequent chapter.

Photo 2-30 – The cut surface can be smoothed using the spindle sander (pictured) or a sanding drum mounted on the drill press. The neck is backed up with a large square block to keep the sanded surface square to the table.

Photo 2-31 – A simple shop-built accessory table screwed to the drill press table allows the bottom edge of the drill press mounted sanding drum to be below the surface of the table. This means the drum can sand right down to the bottom edge of the work.

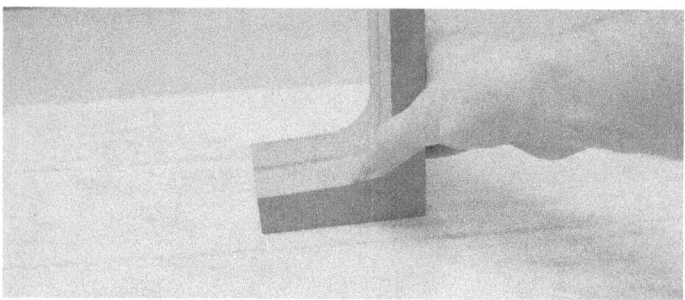

Photo 2-32 – If the heel end is trimmed with the bandsaw or other saw that does not provide perfect precision, the cut surface is cleaned up flat and square on the sanding board.

with various hand held saws. In this case it is prudent to first drill through the blank at the two transition curves, using a 2″ (50.8mm) diameter Forstner bit. Some luthiers like to use a hole saw for this.

2. The resulting cut surface can be smoothed using a spindle sander or a drill press-mounted sanding drum (**photo 2-30**). A large diameter drum is used first to remove material quickly, followed by a 2″ (50.8mm) diameter drum to work the transition curves. No matter what style of blank was used, the neck is now thin in profile and should be backed up with a large square cross-section block to keep the sanded surfaces square to the sides of the neck.

Note that when using a drill press-mounted drum sander, it is useful to construct and use a simple table that allows the bottom edge of the sanding drum to be slightly below the top surface of the table (**photo 2-31**). This allows sanding right down to the bottom of the surface to be sanded.

3. The back of the headstock is sanded flat using a hard sanding block. During this process the thickness of the headstock should be regularly checked to be sure the top and back surfaces remain parallel.

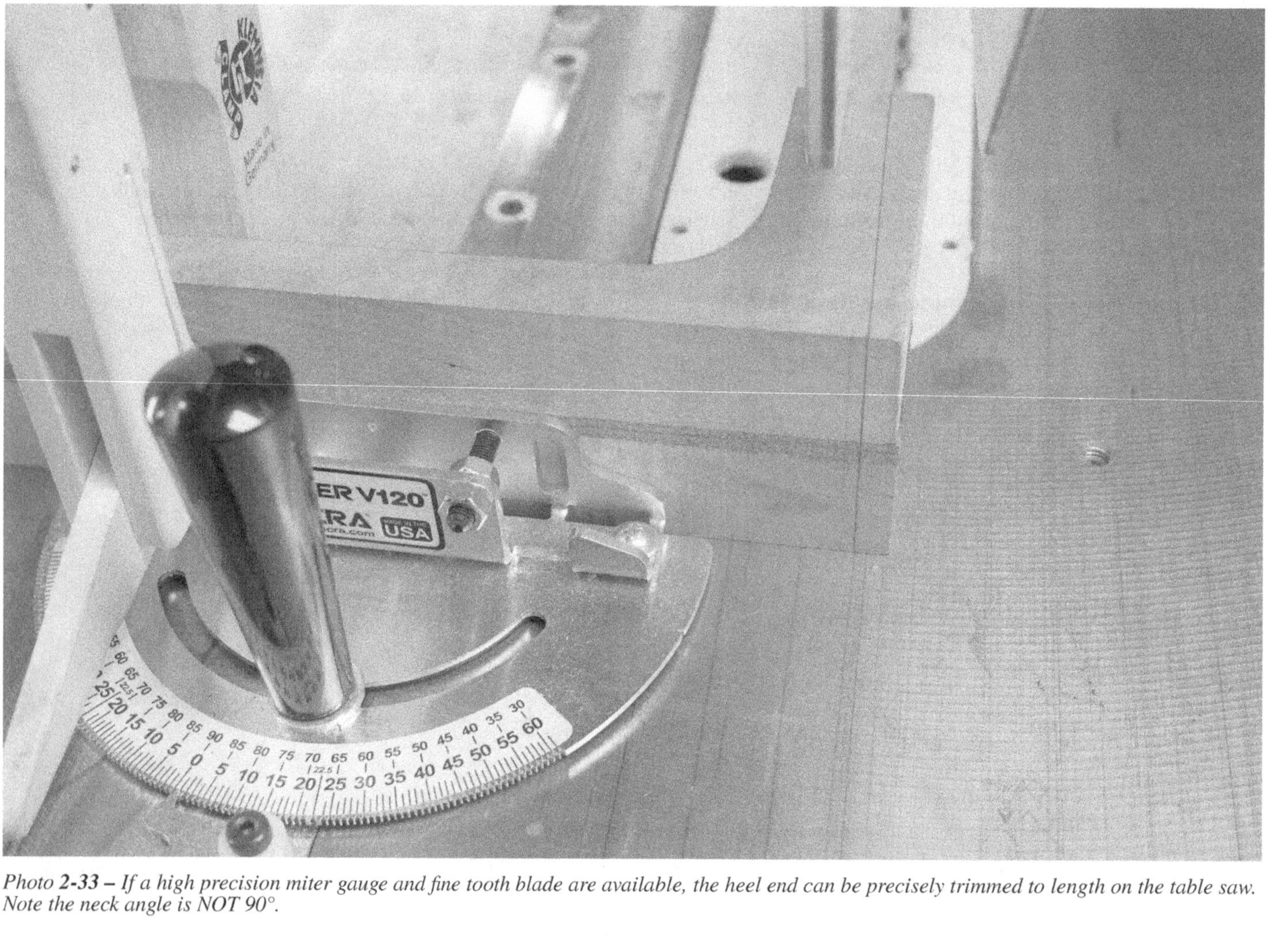

The bandsaw is the ideal tool for this purpose. It should first be set up with the blade square to the table and checked with thick scrap wood to be sure it leaves cut surfaces that are perpendicular to the table when cutting thick wood. If an assembled neck blank is used, the blank should be clamped to a large rectangular cross-section block of wood first, to avoid the dangerous possibility of the blank tipping and the saw yanking the blank down into the table. See **photo 2-12**. Backing up the blank with such a block also helps to ensure that the cuts will be square to the reference surface of the blank. After the cut is made, the neck will look like **photo 2-29**. Note that the cut can be made

Photo 2-33 – If a high precision miter gauge and fine tooth blade are available, the heel end can be precisely trimmed to length on the table saw. Note the neck angle is NOT 90°.

4. The body end of the heel is trimmed to the marked line. This can be done with the bandsaw and then the surface refined on the sanding board (**photo 2-32**). During sanding it is important to regularly check that the neck angle is retained and that the body end surface remains square to the sides of the neck. If a high precision miter gauge is available, trimming the heel to length can be done on the table saw fitted with a very fine blade (**photo 2-33**). It is possible to make this cut with a conventional miter gauge by repeatedly making trial cuts on scrap, measuring the resulting angle with a protractor and adjusting the miter gauge angle, until the proper angle is achieved on a trial cut.

5. The heel is trimmed to length. Heel length measurements for the example instruments appear in **table 2-4**.

6. A marking gauge is used to scribe a longitudinal centerline on all top, bottom, and end surfaces of the neck. The marking gauge should reference the reference side of the neck. Care should be taken to not scribe too deeply on the bottom surfaces of headstock and shaft and the inside surface of the heel, as these are now close to finished dimensions. Note that if the neck has been laminated from two pieces, the glue line between the pieces serves as a longitudinal centerline. A flexible plastic ruler can be used to mark the centerline inside the transition curves, or these areas can remain unmarked.

The roughed out neck will now look like that pictured in **photo 2-34**.

Photo 2-34 – *The roughed out neck.*

Photo 2-35 – *Drilling the hole for the dowel in the heel.*

About Trussrods

Modern steel string guitars invariably have adjustable metal trussrods embedded in their necks. The trussrod adds mass and stiffness to the neck. The added stiffness helps to maintain rigidity under string tension. Adjustment of the trussrod provides control over neck relief (bowing of the neck) and as a consequence of action (string height above the frets).

Trussrods began to appear regularly in the necks of guitars primarily during the 20th century. The first examples were usually simple metal stiffening bars. A later advancement was to make the rod adjustable in one direction. Such rods are generally referred to as *single-acting trussrods* or *compression trussrods*. Tightening the adjustment nut or screw of such rods decreases front bow of the fretboard. Some simple implementations of single-acting trussrods need to be fitted into the neck using a carefully cut spline with a long curved surface. There are also single-acting rods that can be fitted into a simple routed channel.

A more modern advancement is the double-acting trussrod. These can be tightened in two directions and as such can decrease back bow or front bow of the fretboard. Double-acting rods are typically configured as one rod or bar fixed over another adjustable rod, with the two rods held together by threaded blocks at each end.

The example instruments make use of double-acting trussrods. These are readily available from general lutherie suppliers and from custom trussrod manufacturers. See the online annex on sources of tools and supplies in Appendix A for more details. Trussrods come in various lengths for various types of instruments. For steel string acoustic guitars like the example guitars, with necks that meet the body at the 14th fret, a trussrod of 14¼″ (362mm) overall length and approximately 13¼″ (336.6mm) measured from end block to end block is required. Note that lutherie suppliers will use one or the other of these measurements to denote the length of their trussrods and this is a source of confusion when comparing rods from different suppliers. Note also that the width and height of the neck channel required for the trussrod may differ depending on the supplier.

The example instruments mount the trussrod so access to the adjustment nut is inside the instrument. The alternative is to provide access to the adjustment nut at the headstock. Both are commonly used in modern guitars. Inside-the-instrument access is used in the example instruments primarily because it requires less woodworking to do so. It also results in a neck that is stronger at the headstock, because wood does not have to be removed to form the pocket to provide access to the adjustment nut.

Trussrods are available with various types of adjusting nuts. For use with acoustic guitars it is best to use rods that are adjusted using an Allen key. This is particularly the case when the adjuster will be positioned inside the guitar. Note that some trussrods that are generally dimensioned using inch units will use a metric Allen key for adjustment. It is essential to have on hand the proper size key for the trussrod.

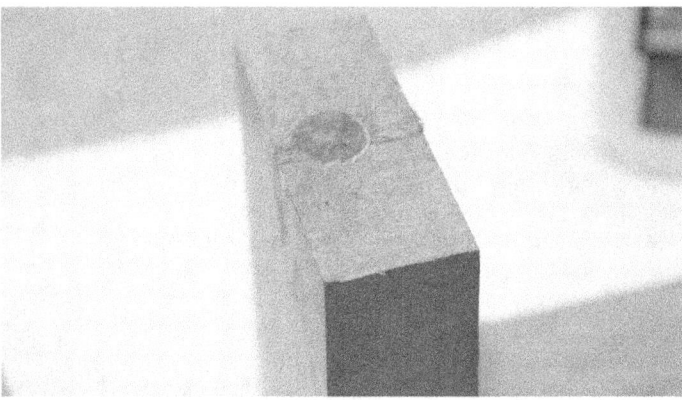

Photo 2-36 – *Dowel glued into the heel and cut flush with heel bottom.*

☐ **Installing the Heel Reinforcing Dowel**

The example instruments make use of a bolt-on neck joint. The body is attached to the neck with two bolts which screw into threaded inserts embedded in the neck heel. I'll provide more information about this joint and the threaded inserts in later chapters, but here I want to point out that there are no threaded inserts available that are specifically designed to be threaded into the end grain of hardwood. It turns out that there are a number of types of inserts that work well in this application for *some* types of wood. In order to make it so that a wider variety of inserts can be used in a wider variety of wood species, it is worthwhile to provide at least some cross grain wood for the inserts to screw into. This is accomplished easily by gluing a hardwood dowel into the heel, a construction detail used by a number of luthiers including California luthier and educator Harry Fleishman.

1. The center point for a hole to be drilled for the dowel is marked on the bottom surface of the heel. The mark is made on the centerline, ⅜″ (9.5mm) in from the body contact surface, and pricked with an awl.

2. A ½″ (12.7mm) diameter brad point drill bit is chucked in the drill press. The neck is positioned fretboard surface down on a flat piece of hardwood scrap to prevent the exit of the bit from blowing out the grain. It is positioned for drilling at the marked center point, and clamped down.

3. The hole is drilled through the heel (**photo 2-35**). If quill travel of the drill press or drill bit length is too short to drill all the way through, the hole is drilled as deep as possible. The neck is removed from the drill press. If the hole could not be drilled all the way through, the bit is chucked in the hand drill and drilling of the through hole is continued with the neck clamped onto the hardwood scrap.

4. A length of ½″ (12.7mm) diameter hardwood dowel is cut to the length of the heel. Its edges are chamfered. The dowel is test-fitted in the drilled hole. Although it should not fall through, the fit should not be tight either, because when glue is applied it will swell the wood. The surface of the dowel is sanded for a smooth fit. It is desirable to cut some grooves in the dowel to allow excess glue someplace to go. This can be done using a triangular file.

5. Glue is applied to the entire surface of the dowel, and the dowel is fitted into the hole. If it is possible for the fretboard end of the dowel to be positioned so it is not quite flush with the fretboard surface of the neck, and if excess glue is removed from the fretboard surface of the neck now, that will simplify later cleanup of this surface. The glue is allowed to cure at least two hours.

6. The fretboard surface is cleaned of any dried glue by stroking it a few times across the surface of a sanding board. Any scribed reference lines that have been affected by doing this are refreshed. Excess dowel length can be cut from the heel end using a flush cutting plug cutter saw or similar saw (**photo 2-36**).

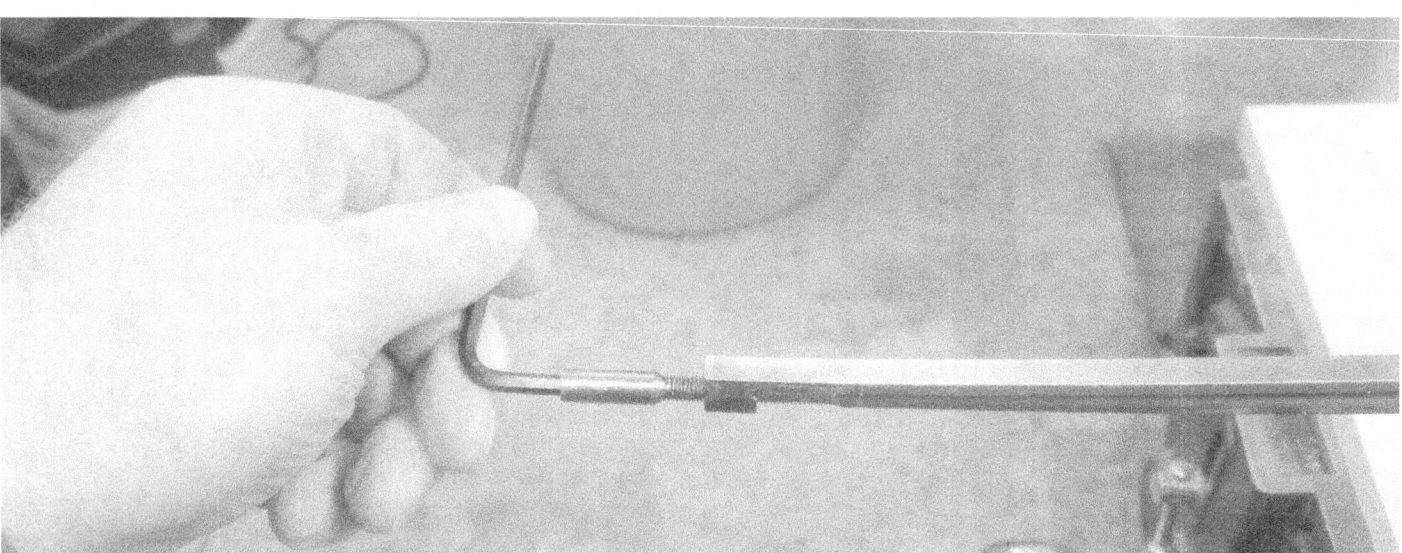

Photo 2-37 – *Checking operation of the trussrod.*

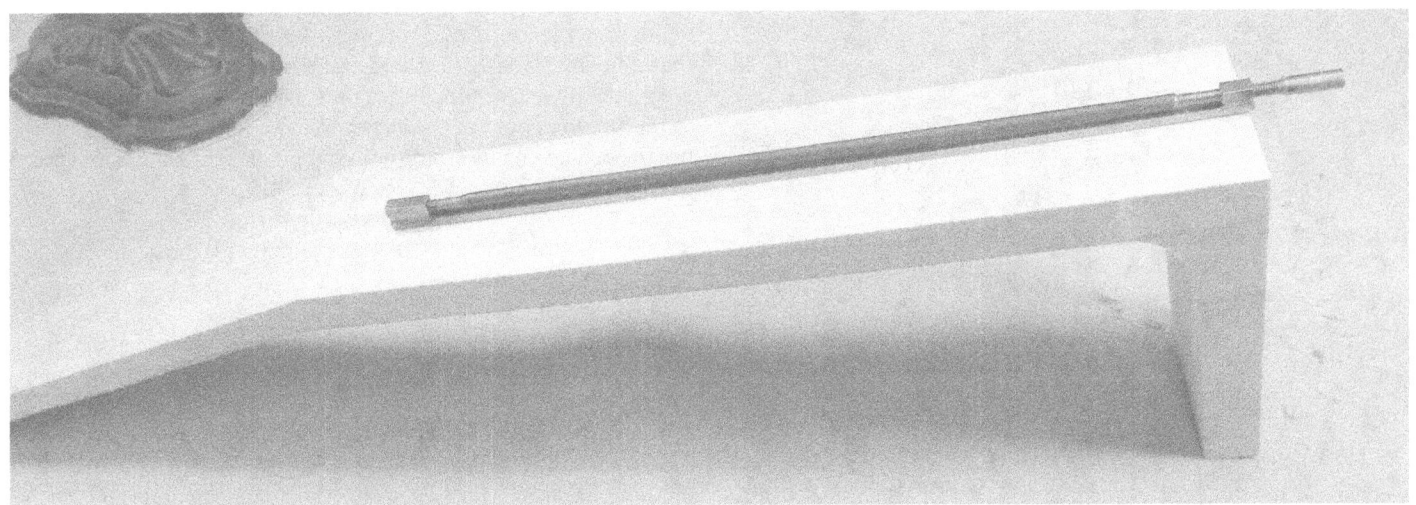

Photo 2-38 – *The trussrod is positioned on the neck so the end of the end block on the adjuster end is aligned with the heel end of the neck.*

☐ Routing the Trussrod Slot

The example guitars use *double acting trussrods* of 14¼″ (362MM) overall length, with adjusters that are turned using an Allen wrench, and that drop into a routed channel. See the sidebar for more general information about trussrods. The width and depth of the channel for the trussrod will depend on the trussrod. Each manufacturer will provide this information for the trussrods they sell, but it is always a good idea to have the trussrod in hand before routing the channel. The construction details that follow assume that this is the case. Also needed for the job is a straight or spiral router bit with diameter of the width of the channel to be routed.

The construction method detailed here makes use of a handheld router but this task could certainly be accomplished using a router table if one is available. Some luthiers make this cut using the table saw.

Materials
    Neck assembly
    Trussrod (see text)
Tools
    Router with edge guide
    Router bit with diameter of width of trussrod
    Allen key to adjust trussrod

1. Operation of the trussrod is checked. The trussrod end block near the adjuster is clamped in the vise and the Allen key is used to adjust the rod in both directions, checking for smooth operation and checking to be sure it bends. The rod is examined for any breaks or other defects. See **photo 2-37**. If the rod checks out OK it is adjusted to its neutral position for subsequent steps. Neutral position can be felt while turning the adjuster: The rod does not "fight" turning so much when at the neutral position.

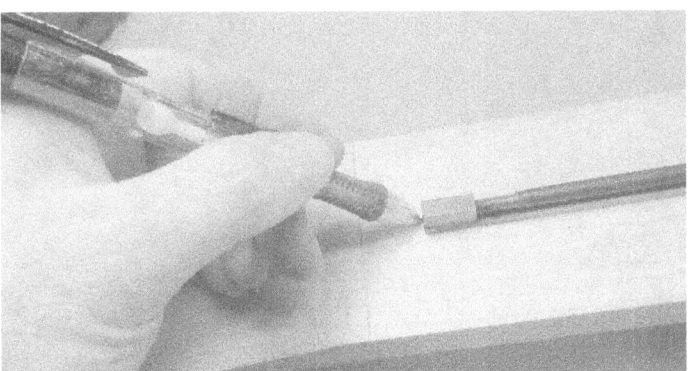

Photo 2-39 – *The location of the other end of the trussrod is marked on the centerline of the fretboard surface.*

2. The trussrod is placed on top of the fretboard surface along the centerline of the neck so the end of the end block near the adjuster lines up with the heel end of the neck. The adjuster will extend 1″ (25.4MM) past the heel end of the neck (**photo 2-38**). A pencil is used to mark the location of the other end of the trussrod onto the fretboard surface at the centerline (**photo 2-39**).

Photo 2-40 – *The neck is clamped in the bench vise for routing. Note the wedges of wood under the shaft of the neck to help support the weight of a heavy router. The clamp on the headstock will be used in a subsequent step as a stop to prevent the router from routing the channel too long.*

3. The neck is securely mounted for routing with the edge guide against the reference surface. The neck can be clamped by the heel at one end of the bench vise, and then wedges of wood between the underside of the shaft and the top of the vise at the other end are used to support that part of the shaft (**photo 2-40**). An alternative is to put wedges between the headstock

Photo 2-41 – *The router positioned in the middle of its channel routing movement from left to right. The right end of the edge guide will contact the clamp on the headstock at the end of the movement. The clamp acts as a stop to prevent the router from routing the channel too long.*

Photo 2-42 – *The trussrod is installed in the channel with the adjuster nut down. The top surface of the trussrod must end up flush with the fretboard surface of the neck. If it is too high it will interfere with the fretboard. If it is too low it may rattle around in the slot.*

depth intervals of ⅛″ (3.2mm) until the channel is nearly to the required depth for the trussrod. Additional shallow final cuts are made after this. Much care must be taken with the final cuts to be sure the depth of the channel is not too shallow and not too deep. The channel is thoroughly cleaned of debris and the trussrod is fitted and checked for depth.

 The trussrod goes in the channel with the adjuster side *down* (**photo 2-42**).

7. The trussrod is removed from the channel and set aside. It will be installed during a later assembly operation.

8. Using the centerline on the heel end surface as a reference, the centerline is continued a short way (at least ¼″ (6.4mm)) onto the floor of the trussrod slot. This will be important for later work on the heel. Feeler gauges are often useful in making this mark.

and the front of the bench, then clamp the headstock to the bench front. However the neck is mounted, it must be secure and it must provide unimpeded access to the reference surface for the router edge guide.

4. The router is set up with bit and edge guide and adjusted to cut the channel right down the centerline marked on the fretboard surface. It is important that the bit be centered. If a plunge router is used, it is possible to check centering by plunging to just lightly touch the surface and then checking the resulting mark for centering.

5. The router is slid to the right until the edge of the bit just aligns with the end-of-trussrod mark made in step 2. A clamp is placed to serve as a stop to prevent the router from moving beyond this point (**photo 2-41**). After the clamp is placed, the router is moved and a check is made to be sure the stop is accurately placed.

6. The depth of cut is set to ⅛″ (3.2mm) for the initial cut. The initial cut should be very short, just enough to again check for proper centering of the bit on the centerline. If that checks out, the full length of the channel is cut. Additional cuts are made at

3 The Fretboard

Although the fretboard is a relatively simple component of the guitar, it must be constructed with precision, because its dimensions are critical to the construction of the guitar as a whole. The criticality of some of its dimensions, like the location of the slots that will hold the frets, is probably obvious. If the frets are not located accurately, the guitar will not play in tune. But possibly less obvious is the need to build the fretboard so that it is symmetrical about its centerline, and the need to build it to precise width at both ends. Doing so will keep string spacing and bridge width of the finished guitar within specs. Even the thickness of the fretboard is critical, because its thickness will have an effect on the height of the bridge and saddle.

The finished fretboard is trapezoidal in shape when viewed from the front, the sides diverging from the nut end to the soundhole end (**figure 3-1**). The sides are straight, and so to describe the overall taper we could either specify the width at the nut end and the angle the sides form with the nut end, or we could specify the width at the nut and the width at some other point along the length. For layout and construction purposes the latter is the conventional way it is done. Generally, the taper is described by specifying the width at the nut end and also the width at the point where the neck joins the body, which for modern steel string guitars including the example instruments is also where the 14th fret is located.

For steel string guitars, the top surface of the fretboard, which will be referred to as the *playing surface*, is generally *cambered*, that is, it is curved from side to side (**figure 3-2**). The term *radiused* is also commonly used. The amount of cambering is specified by the *camber radius*, or simply the radius. Actually imparting the camber to the playing surface is not described in the construction section of this chapter, but will be described in a later chapter. But the camber radius will be touched upon in this chapter because it affects the depth of the fret slots.

As can be seen in **figure 3-2**, the end profile of the frets is sort of a rounded over "T" shape. The lower part of that shape is called the *fret tang*, and this fits into a sawn fret slot on the fretboard. Actually installing the frets is not described in this chapter either, but laying out and sawing the fret slots *is* described here, as well as alternatives to doing this in the shop. And, although not critical to the construction of the example instruments, for the curious this chapter does contain information on how and why the frets are located where they are on the fretboard.

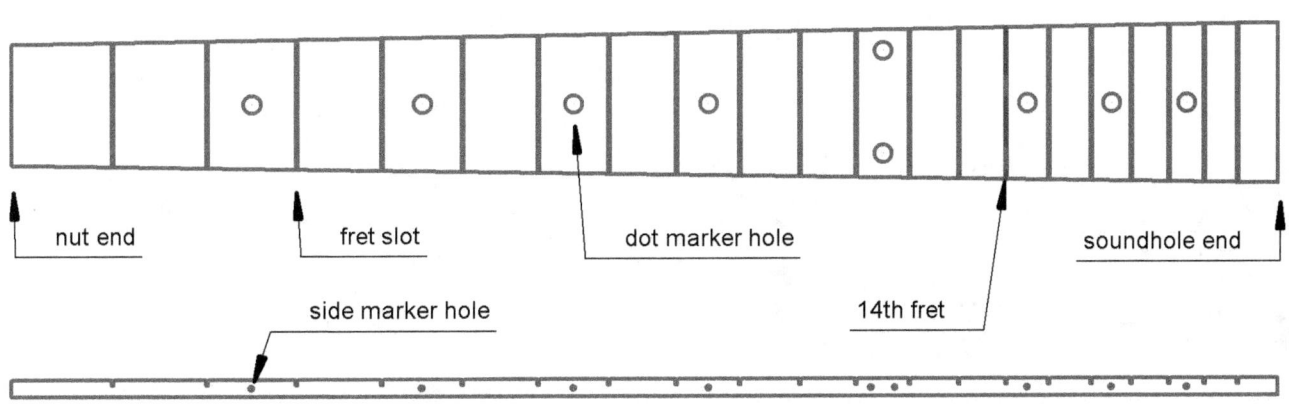

Figure 3-1 – *Schematic of front and side views of the fretboard.*

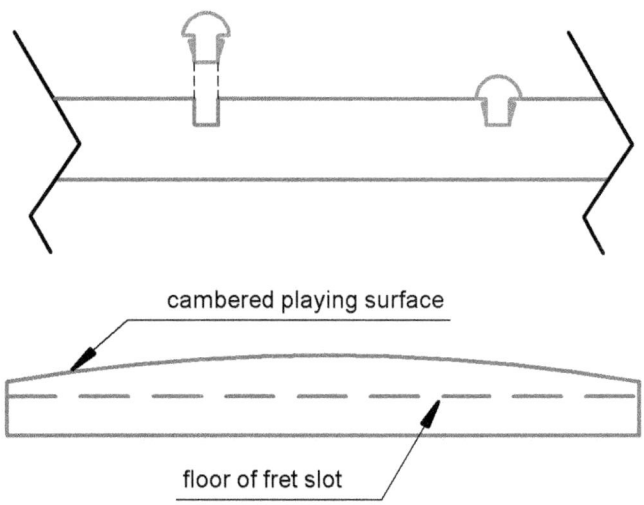

Figure 3-2 – Schematic close-up of the side of the fretboard, showing installation of frets in the fret slots (top), and of the end of the fretboard, showing playing surface camber and the floor of the fret slots.

In addition to the frets, the fretboard also has position markers. The simplest form of these are round dots made of some contrasting material, and these are fitted in drilled holes (**photo 3-1**). The location and drilling of those holes is also described in detail in the construction section of this chapter.

Wood Selection

I mentioned in the introductory material in the previous chapter on roughing out the neck that quartersawn wood is highly desired for that part of the guitar, because it results in a more stable neck. The same goes for wood used for the guitar fretboard. It turns out that this is even more important here, because fretboards are generally made of the denser hardwoods, and denser hardwoods tend to have even greater shrinkage than the wood species generally used for the neck. Stability of the neck with changes in humidity is extremely important. Using a quartersawn fretboard will help achieve that stability.

It is desirable to select a material for use as a fretboard based on the task that it must perform. The material should be hard and resistant to abrasion from strings and players' fingers. It should hold frets well in sawn slots. And it should be dimensionally stable with changes of humidity. Actually on that last point what is really required is that it be *as* dimensionally stable as the material used for the instrument neck, because it will be glued to that neck, and if the two materials exhibit different rates of dimensional change with changes in humidity it will cause the neck to bend with changes in humidity.

If we look at historical choices for fretboard material, it is apparent that stability of the neck with changes in humidity was not always much of a consideration. What *was* an important historical consideration is how the fretboard looks. The preference was for dark woods. It was generally the case that inexpensive instruments used fretboards of inexpensive and light colored hardwoods such as soft maple (*Acer rubrum* or similar), painted black to resemble ebony (*Diospyros* spp.). More expensive instruments would generally have fretboards made of a more expensive wood such as one of the rosewoods. East Indian rosewood (*Dalbergia latifolia*) or Brazilian rosewood (*Dalbergia nigra*) were commonly used. The most expensive instruments usually had fretboards made of some sort of ebony (*Diospyros* spp.).

Painted maple is currently out of favor for even inexpensive instruments these days due to its long association with cheap guitars. Although maple is a perfectly good wood for use as a fretboard, the black paint treatment of yore does not generally hold up well under hard playing, and the worn-through look of a painted fretboard is generally not considered a good look.

Modern instruments at all price points continue to use East Indian rosewood as a fretboard material. It looks good, holds up well, and is highly compatible with mahogany (*Swietenia macrophylla*) and similar woods used for guitar necks, as far as stability with changes in humidity go. As of this writing, it is becoming endangered and it is getting more expensive. Still, if it is available this is an excellent choice for the fretboard.

Ebony is highly problematic for fretboard use. It is endangered and expensive. Its major historical visual appeal was that it is truly black in color, but true black ebony fretboard blanks are essentially impossible to find anymore. Ebony is also a poor choice when it comes to stability with change in humidity. It expands and contracts a lot. If an ebony fretboard is quartersawn, this expansion and contraction will generally not twist or bend the neck in any major way, but low humidity does result in width shrinkage which causes the fret ends to stick out, and in extreme cases may result in cracking of the fretboard. I generally will not use ebony except when appropriate in historical reproduction instruments.

All of the negatives associated with ebony have spurred much investigation into alternatives. One of the best of these is phenolic impregnated wood, generally referred to as *impreg* in the wood industry, although the term is rarely used by lutherie wood suppliers. This material is made by impregnating light colored (and often domestic) hardwood with phenolic resin and black pigment. The resulting material has all of the desirable characteristics of ebony but it is also fairly inexpensive and quite stable with changes in humidity. A related material is compressed and impregnated wood, wood panels made up of thin pieces impregnated with phenolic resin and compressed together. The industry name for this material is *compreg*, but again lutherie suppliers rarely if ever use the term. Fretboards made of these materials are available from a number of lutherie suppliers, sold under various brand names.

The general issues with endangerment of traditional tropical hardwoods for fretboards has induced luthier suppliers to offer more species than were commonly used in the past. I won't list any of these here, as availability and popularity tends to change rapidly.

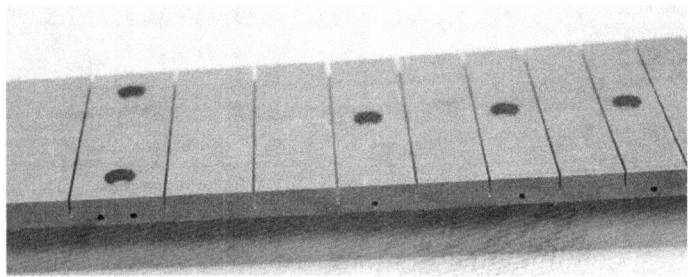

Photo 3-1 – Close-up of fretboard after fret slots are cut, fretboard is trimmed to final shape and dimensions, and holes for dot markers and side markers are drilled. The playing surface is not cambered at this point in construction.

Photo 3-2 – Classical guitars made by the author. The instrument in front is made completely from domestic wood species and features a black locust fretboard.

One last point. For the guitar builder that gravitates toward domestic species and is willing to buck tradition, there are some nice domestic species here in the USA which make excellent fretboards, but are light in color. A well-quartered piece of black locust (*Robinia pseudoacacia*) or hickory (*Carya* spp.) will work fine in this application (**photo 3-2**). Note though that these species are generally not available from typical lutherie wood suppliers.

Construction Options

Lutherie suppliers will generally carry rectangular guitar fretboard blanks in various wood species. These are sized to be suitable for most guitars, including the example guitars. **Table 3-1** lists the minimum dimensions for rectangular fretboard blanks needed to construct the fretboards of the example instruments. These days, the guitar builder has other options besides working from a plain rectangular blank. Some lutherie suppliers offer rectangular blanks that have been pre-slotted for the frets. Making use of a pre-slotted blank can eliminate the work involved with laying out and sawing the fret slots.

 A rectangular pre-slotted blank for use in the construction of the example guitars must be slotted for a scale length of 25.5″ (647.7mm) and contain *at least* 20 frets. The number of fret slots is important. Note that the scale length must be *exactly* 25.5″ (647.7mm).

 Some suppliers also offer fretboard blanks that have been pre-cambered (pre-radiused), eliminating that step in the construction process. These should be avoided because they are not compatible with the construction details outlined in this book. Although it may appear that purchasing a pre cambered fretboard will save some work, in fact many of the otherwise simple jigs presented here would have to be modified to accommodate it.

Rectangular fretboard blank thickness	≥¼″	(6.4mm)
Rectangular fretboard blank width	≥2⅜″	(60.3mm)
Rectangular fretboard blank length	≥18½″	(470mm)
Slotted fretboard scale length	25.5″	(647.7mm)
Slotted fretboard number of fret slots	≥20	

Table 3-1– Dimensions for fretboard blanks for the construction of the example guitars.

 Some suppliers offer unslotted fretboards that are tapered, that is, not rectangular. These should be avoided because they are not compatible with the construction details here for fret slotting.

Although most of the off-the-shelf fretboard options available from lutherie suppliers are not compatible with the construction process described in this book, there is a construction option that can be used to eliminate the step of slotting the fretboard. The fretboard can be slotted by a lutherie CNC fabrication shop, or by a lutherie supplier that has CNC equipment. Although CNC fret slotting is more expensive than other ways to do that, a CNC shop can also cut custom design position inlays and the pockets for them.

The construction descriptions in this and a subsequent chapter include all the steps needed to fashion the fretboard starting from a simple blank. A few different options are included for laying out the frets, and a few different options are included for trimming the sides of the fretboard as well.

 While fretboard purchasing options are being considered, it would be a good idea to purchase an additional piece of wood of the same species as the fretboard and at least the dimensions of the *fretboard extension* – that part of the fretboard that overhangs the guitar top in the finished instrument. Although it may not be necessary, this extra piece of wood may be needed to fashion a shim under the fretboard extension. One option to obtain such wood is to purchase an extra long fretboard blank, one intended for use in an electric bass. This will provide plenty of additional material. Another option is to purchase an extra headplate of the same species as that of the fretboard.

About Scale Length and Fret Spacing

Although none of the information in this section is necessary to build a guitar from plans, I offer it for those curious about the relationship between scale length and fret spacing.

Scale Length

The scale length of a stringed instrument is the nominal vibrating length of the open string, realized as the nominal distance between the nut and the bridge saddle. Historically, guitar scale lengths vary a lot. Three of the five surviving baroque guitars built by Stradivari have scale lengths of 29$\frac{7}{32}$″ (742mm), a length that is considered to be all but unplayable. Contrast this to the scale lengths typical of 19th century English guitars, which had scale lengths around 24¾″ (628.7mm). Modern acoustic steel string guitars feature a variety of scale lengths, but most differ only slightly, and hover around 25.4″ (645.2mm), which is the standard used by guitars made by C.F. Martin. Note that the example guitars in this book use a scale length of 25.5″ (647.7mm).

The question of why there are so many similar scale lengths is an interesting one. If one were to attempt to engineer an optimal scale length, the major factors to be considered would be playability and good tone. A scale length that is too long, like that of the Stradivari guitars mentioned above, makes fingering difficult for all players except those with exceptionally long fingers. A too short scale length could also cause fingering problems, particularly for players with big hands. Although this is an oversimplification, it is generally the case that the tone of vibrating strings is improved with longer scale lengths. Too short a scale length makes for noticeable inharmonicity, particularly on the lower strings and the higher frets.

It is likely that the small range of scale lengths used in modern guitars evolved as a reasonable compromise between playability and pleasing tone. It is not known definitively why there are so many different scale lengths that vary from each other by just a tiny amount, but this probably had to do with errors introduced when attempting to copy the scale length of an instrument from simple measurements. In any case, these differences are so small from a playing perspective, that all these minor variations in scale length are functionally equivalent.

But this does *not* mean that a guitar builder can simply chose any scale length. This is a critical dimension that is the basis for other dimensions of the finished instrument. In fact, when guitars are designed, the scale length is usually the first thing that is specified, and most other dimensions are based on that. Consequently it is important that the scale length to use be taken from the plan that is used.

One final point about scale length: It was mentioned above that the scale length of a stringed instrument is the nominal distance between the nut and the bridge saddle. For fretless instruments such as those of the violin family the scale length (also called *mensure*) is *exactly* this distance. But for fretted instruments, the bridge saddle is usually moved a bit farther away from the nut in an effort to improve intonation of the fretted notes. This additional compensatory length is called *compensation*. It will be discussed in more detail in the chapter on the bridge. But here it is important to note that simply measuring the distance between nut and bridge saddle of an existing guitar will not yield an accurate indication of scale length, due to this additional compensation.

Fret Spacing

It is clear from looking at a fretted instrument that the placement of the frets follows a pattern. No matter the scale length of the instrument, the distance between frets gets increasingly smaller the farther away from the nut. The spacing is designed to provide optimal intonation, and it mimics the relationship between the frequencies of the notes. Before looking at that in more detail, it is useful to consider that this designed spacing is relatively modern, and that other methods were used in the past.

Early fretted instruments such as lutes had frets that were made of pieces of gut that were looped around the shaft of the neck and tied in place. Since tied frets could be slid up and down the neck, it is likely that fret placement was initially done simply by trial and error. A fret would be tied in position, the note struck, the intonation of the note assessed, and the fret moved to correct intonation accordingly. It wouldn't take too many iterations to home in on the correct location for the fret. Each of the frets would be placed in the same manner. Because the frets looped right around the shaft of the neck, it was easy to move them inadvertently during playing, and so every player of such an instrument would have been adept at relocating the frets.

Since the initial setting up of the frets was a time-consuming process, it is likely that someone would have taken measurements of the fret locations of a well-set-up instrument, for use in setting up the next instrument of that same scale length. It is

Fret#	Note	Freq. (Hz)	Freq. ÷ Prev. Note Freq.
0	A2	110	—
1	A♯2 | B♭2	116.541	1.059...
2	B2	123.471	1.059...
3	C3	130.813	1.059...
4	C♯3 | D♭3	138.591	1.059...
5	D3	146.832	1.059...
6	D♯3 | E♭3	155.563	1.059...
7	E3	164.814	1.059...
8	F3	174.614	1.059...
9	F♯3 | G♭3	184.997	1.059...
10	G3	195.998	1.059...
11	G♯3 | A♭3	207.652	1.059...
12	A3	220	1.059...

Table 3-2 – *Table of frequencies of the notes of the first twelve frets on the A string of the guitar. The fourth column contains the approximate value of the frequency of the note, divided by the frequency of the previous note. These resulting values are all the same. This number is called the twelfth root of two, and it defines the relationship between the frequencies of notes in equal temperament.*

also likely that from these measurements, someone would have noticed that the distance from the nut to the first fret was approximately 1/18th the distance of the nut to the bridge. And it is further likely that it would have been noticed that the distance between the first and second frets was approximately 1/18th the distance from the first fret to the bridge. The same relationship occurs for every fret on up the neck. The name for this proportional relationship is called the *rule of 18*.

Note the consistent use of the phrase "it is likely" in the above paragraph. We know about the rule of 18 but we really don't know anything about its origin. Thus the speculation. Its occult roots notwithstanding, luthiers have made use of the rule of 18 for locating fret positions right up into the latter half of 20th century. In fact many modern luthiers still use it. This is particularly true of luthiers like James Buckland, a music professor in Clinton South Carolina, and a builder of reproductions of early Romantic period guitars. Builders of reproductions of historical instruments generally want them to be built *exactly* as the original instruments were.

As mentioned above, the more modern method used to calculate fret locations is based on the frequencies of the equal temperament notes. Most of us that are musicians don't know the frequencies of all the notes off the tops of our heads, but we generally know that the frequency of the A above middle C is 440Hz. If we need to know other note frequencies they can easily be looked up in references like the table on my website at

https://www.liutaiomottola.com/formulae/freqtab.htm.

We know that the frequency of oscillation is higher for higher pitched notes and lower for lower pitched notes. We also know that the frequency of a note an octave above a base note is twice that of the base note, and the frequency of a note an octave below a base note is half that of the base note. **Table 3-2** shows the frequencies of the first twelve notes on the guitar A string, each on a row of the table. The last column of each row contains the value obtained when the frequency of the note is divided by the frequency of the previous note. You can see in the table that for each note that value is the same, 1.059, to three decimal places.

Table Of note freqs.

Fret#	ΔLoc. (″)	Prev. ΔLoc. ÷ ΔLoc.
0	—	—
1	1.431	—
2	1.351	1.059...
3	1.275	1.059...
4	1.204	1.059...
5	1.136	1.059...
6	1.072	1.059...
7	1.012	1.059...
8	0.955	1.059...
9	0.902	1.059...
10	0.851	1.059...
11	0.803	1.059...
12	0.758	1.059...

Table 3-3 – Table of inter-fret distances for the first twelve frets of a guitar with a scale length of 25.5″. The second column, labeled ΔLoc., contains the distance between the fret and the previous fret, the inter-fret distance. The third column contains the result of the previous inter-fret distance divided by the current one. In all cases this is 1.059..., the twelfth root of two.

This value is known as the *twelfth root of two*, and it describes the relative frequency of each equal temperament note.

From that we know that the twelfth root of two is the proportion that governs the frequencies of notes. In fact, this same value also governs the placement of frets on a modern fretted instrument. Take a look at **table 3-3**. This table shows the inter-fret distances for the first 12 frets of a guitar with a scale length of 25.5″ (647.7mm). We know just from observation that the inter-fret distances get smaller the farther away from the nut. The table provides actual inter-fret values. The third column of the table shows the result of dividing the inter-fret distance from the previous row by that of the current row. That result in all cases is 1.059, the twelfth root of two.

This comparison between frequencies of notes and inter-fret distances shows that fret spacing is directly related to the frequency spacing of notes, but it does not directly show how the locations of the frets are calculated. There are a number of ways to do this. One simple way is to calculate a divisor that can be used in exactly the same way that the number 18 is used when applying the rule of 18. That divisor can be calculated by dividing the scale length of any instrument by the distance from nut to first fret. Using a scale length of 25.5″ and dividing that by the distance from nut to first fret for this scale length, the result is 17.817, expressed to three decimal places. Again, this fret spacing constant is used exactly as described when making use of the rule of 18.

These days there is really no need to do the math to calculate fret spacing. There are many calculators available to do this, such as the one found on my website at

https://www.liutaiomottola.com/formulae/fret.htm.

Fret spacing calculator

That webpage includes much additional information for those that want to explore this subject more deeply. Another great resource that explains the math in more detail is the article "Google Calculator and the Guitar's Magic Number"[1] by William Leirer.

I want to repeat again that lutherie novices should not attempt to alter the scale length from that found in the guitar plan that is being worked from. Small changes in scale length will be imperceptible to the player, but will require changes to bridge placement, top bracing, soundhole placement, and possibly other things as well.

About Fretboard Width

The width of the fretboard should have a profound effect on the feel of the guitar, and with guitar players coming in all shapes and sizes, it would be logical to assume that guitars would come with fretboards of various widths too. They do of course, but within the class of steel string acoustic guitars these differences are quite small and probably are not all that significant. This may seem like something which a builder might want to customize, but I would urge caution to the first-time guitar maker, and suggest sticking to the plan being worked from. Neck width will have an effect on string spacing, which affects bridge dimensions like bridge pin spacing. Even something as seemingly trivial as making the nut end of the fretboard a bit narrower could result in enough widening of the bridge pin hole spacing to require changes to the internal bracing of the guitar top. Best to stick to the plan, and reserve customization for a subsequent instrument. Note that the width of the necks for the example instruments assumes a conventional fretboard width. Also note that most lutherie wood suppliers size fretboard blanks very closely to the ultimate conventional size of the fretboard.

About Playing Surface Camber/Radius

Although the construction information in this chapter does not cover cambering the fretboard playing surface, the topic needs to be touched upon here, because it could impact the depth of the fret slots, and fret slotting *is* covered in this chapter. Basically the issue is, the smaller the radius of camber, the deeper the fret slots must be. This can be visualized by taking a look again at **figure 3-2**. The slots for the frets are cut at a depth relative to the top surface of the uncambered fretboard. Cambering the fretboard makes the slots shallower at their ends than in the middle. The fret slots must be deep enough at the ends to accommodate the full depth of the tangs of the frets. This is standardized for all fretwire to 0.07″ (1.8mm). If the radius of camber is smaller, the depth of the slots at the ends will be shallower, so in order to accommodate a small radius camber, the fret slots would have to be cut deeper.

Fretboard camber is another area where a lot of variation is theoretically possible, but for steel string acoustic guitars there really isn't that much variation. The most common radius is 12″ (304.8mm).

An interesting thing about fretboard radius is that it varies greatly with different styles of guitar. Classical guitars and many historical instruments have fretboards that are completely flat. Some modern electric guitars feature fretboards with just a small amount of camber, typically with radii around 16″ (406.4mm). As mentioned most steel string acoustic guitars make use of a 12″ (304.8mm) radius. Some early electric guitars use radii of 9″ (228.6mm) or less.

Conventional wisdom has it that small radius fretboards make chording more comfortable, but there are no ergonomic studies which actually support this. Plus, classical guitarists don't seem to have problems playing chords on perfectly flat

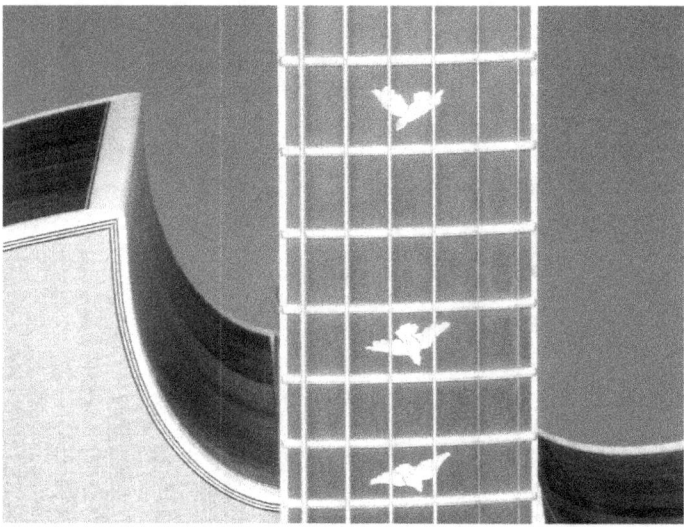

Photo 3-3 – *Beautiful inlaid dove position markers on a guitar by Mike Doolin. The inlays were designed and cut by Nancy Conescu.*

fretboards. Players generally feel that flatter fretboards are preferable for instruments that are played using deep string bends, because they don't "note out" and buzz as much when such bends are performed. This observation is supported by some research on the geometric relationship between strings and fret tops during deep string bends.[2]

For construction of a steel string acoustic guitar I recommend a camber radius of between 12″ (304.8mm) and 16″ (406.4mm). Radii smaller than that may require changes to the construction of the bridge. The acoustic guitar bridge generally has a flat top surface with a slot in it, in which the saddle is mounted and protrudes. Smaller radius fretboard camber requires a smaller radius camber to the top of the saddle, and this may require a shorter bridge and more saddle exposure. For lutherie novices, best not to go there. Stick to the range specified above.

About Position Markers

Here there are a lot of options even for the novice guitar builder. Steel string guitars typically have position markers in the playing surface of the fretboard, and also on the side of the fretboard facing the player. The modern convention is to place these at frets 3, 5, 7, 9, 12, 15, 17, and 19 for an instrument with 20 frets. Markers can be simple dots or fancy inlays as in **photo 3-3**. Some players prefer the clean look of no position markers at all. Another option is to put an inlaid marker only at fret 12.

There are a lot of options for materials for the markers. Simple dots can be made from precut discs of plastic or shell, which are readily available from lutherie suppliers. Discs can also be cut from plastic rods. Any material that is hard enough to stand up to the abrasion that a guitar fretboard will be subject to can be used.

The construction steps later in this chapter deal with simple dot markers only. Builders that want fancier inlays and have the skill to do the inlay work can certainly go that route. Another common option is to have a fretboard and inlays made by a custom lutherie CNC shop.

Layout and Construction

The following sequences of construction steps assume starting with a fretboard blank of adequate size. Not all of these steps will apply in the case where the starting point is a pre-slotted fretboard, of course. Note also that the locations of the frets are critical to good intonation of the finished guitar, so great care is taken to accurately lay out and saw the fret slots.

Planing to Thickness

Blanks from lutherie suppliers may already be planed to thickness. For the example instruments, final planed thickness of the blank should be ¼″ (6.4mm). Once planed the blank must be perfectly flat with no twist or bow at this thickness.

☐ **Planing and Marking the Fretboard Blank**

1. The general dimensions of the blank required are specified in **table 3-1**. The broad surfaces of the blank are first planed flat and coplanar to each other, with the thickness of the blank ending up at ¼″ (6.4mm). A hand plane and bench hook can be used, as can a thickness sander or a planer. If a plane or planer is used it is important to avoid planing into the grain, to avoid taking large chunks out of the surface. Depending on the species of the wood of the blank, the amount of runout, and the amount of figure, it may be prudent to avoid use of the planer altogether. The woods generally used for fretboards are unfortunately prone to splitting, unless scrupulous care is taken not to work into the grain when using edge tools. It is possible that a moderate amount of tear-out on the surface of the fretboard that will be the gluing surface will be acceptable. If the surfaces are abrasively planed, they should be surfaced to at least 80 grit.

2. One broad surface is designated the gluing surface, and is so marked in pencil. One end is designated the nut end, and this is marked in pencil too. This designation is usually done based on a purely visual assessment of the fretboard, but also may be done to put defects in one of the broad surfaces where they will not be seen, and also to put defects near one end of the blank where they will be cut off when the fretboard is trimmed to length. If the board has noticeable runout, the nut end should be selected as the end that it is possible to plane toward.

3. One side of the blank is ripped or planed straight and perpendicular to the broad surfaces. This will be the reference surface, and should be marked accordingly in pencil. Because I prefer to always work whenever possible with the neck oriented with the nut end to my left, when the fretboard is sitting on the bench playing surface up and nut end to the left, the reference surface should be the side farthest away from the front of the bench. Ripping or planing the other side parallel to the reference surface is advised, as long as the minimum width can be retained.

4. A marking gauge is used to *lightly* scribe a centerline down the center of the entire length of the playing surface, using the reference surface as a guide. It is useful to also scribe a centerline on the gluing surface as well.

5. The nut end of the blank is trimmed square to the reference surface. This can be done using table saw and miter gauge, disc sander and miter gauge, or accurate miter box and back saw.

Fret Slotting

As mentioned, options for slotting the fretboard include purchasing a pre-slotted board (if one with at least 20 fret slots can be had), having the board custom slotted by a lutherie CNC shop, or doing the slotting in the shop. Lutherie suppliers often offer tool systems for fret slotting. These generally include CNC-cut fret-slotting templates that can be used with either a table saw jig and special blade, or with a special-purpose miter box. Such systems do a great job but are expensive, so their use is not considered for the construction process described in this book. However, the individual templates are fairly inexpensive, so a method for marking fret locations using such a template is provided.

In the instructions that follow, the fret slots are cut using a special purpose backsaw that is available from lutherie suppliers. This saw cuts a kerf that is 0.022″ (0.56mm) or 0.023″ (0.58mm) wide, which accommodates the tang of standard commercial fret wire. This kerf width is critical. These saws are fairly inexpensive.

☐ **Marking Fret Locations**

Accurate fret location is critical to good intonation of the finished instrument. The marking operations must be done with considerable precision. Positions are marked using a knife. The resulting marks are thin and short and can be difficult to see on dark colored wood. It helps to see the resulting marks if they are filled with powdered chalk or any other fine white powder such as baking soda after they are made.

Option 1: Using a Ruler

This is a tedious, time-consuming and error-prone method. Results should be carefully double-checked to be sure they are accurate. The method makes use of a 24″ long engraved steel ruler that is graduated in $1/100$ths of an inch. Note the absence of metric units equivalences here because I am unaware of the existence of metric rulers with equivalent gradation. Although many luthiers achieve excellent results using rulers with coarser gradations, I can't recommend that approach for lutherie novices. Note that the specified ruler is not inexpensive, and this should be considered when deciding which layout method to use if such a ruler will have to be purchased.

Materials
  The fretboard blank
  Melamine board
  Flat solid wood or MDF as thick as the ruler is wide
  Double sided polyester tape
Tools
  24″ long engraved steel ruler, graduated in $1/100^{th}$ of an inch
  Hobby knife or marking knife
  Magnifying headgear
  Lamp
  Scissors
  Clamps

Photo 3-4 – A fence and stop block are clamped down to the base board. Two clamps are used as "feet" to support the front of the base board.

Photo 3-5 – The fretboard is attached to the base board using double sided tape. It is positioned against the fence and against the stop block. The ruler is attached to the fence using double sided tape, too. It is resting on top of the fretboard, and is positioned against the stop block so its zero position is the same as the nut end of the fretboard.

1. A base board is cut from melamine board approximately 24″ (609.6mm) long by 12″ (304.8mm) wide.

2. A fence is cut from stock that is approximately as thick as the ruler is wide. The fence should be as long as the base board. The fence should be planed square.

Fret#	From Nut	Fret#	From Nut
1	1.43″	11	11.99″
2	2.78″	12	12.75″
3	4.06″	13	13.47″
4	5.26″	14	14.14″
5	6.40″	15	14.78″
6	7.47″	16	15.38″
7	8.48″	17	15.95″
8	9.43″	18	16.48″
9	10.34″	19	16.99″
10	11.19″	20	17.47″

Table 3-4 – Table of fret locations for the example instruments, which have a scale length of 25.5″ and 20 frets. Fret locations are given as distances from the nut. Values are presented to two decimal places so that a ruler graduated in hundredths of an inch can be used to lay out fret locations on the fretboard.

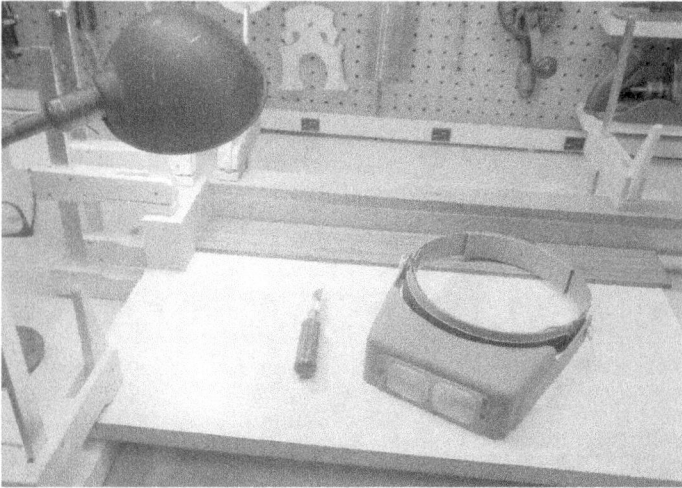

Photo 3-6 – Ready to begin marking the fret locations on the fretboard. A headband magnifier and a strong light are necessary to count the fine engraved lines of the ruler. The marking is done using a hobby knife or marking knife.

Photo 3-7 – The position of the lamp is moved as marking proceeds up the fretboard so it is always shining on the ruler near where the current mark will be made.

Photo 3-8 – When the appropriate mark on the ruler is identified, the point of the knife is inserted into the engraved groove and gently slid down until it is touching the surface of the fretboard. It is then pressed into the fretboard to mark the fret location.

3. A stop block is cut from the same or similar squared up material as used for the fence. The stop block is cut approximately 3″ (76.2mm) long. Its ends must be trimmed square to the long surfaces.

4. Clamps are used to mount the fence and stop block to the base board as shown in **photo 3-4**. The stop block end is mounted square to the front surface of the fence. After it is clamped in place this is checked with a square and adjusted again if necessary. Note that a couple of clamps are used simply as "feet" to support the front of the base board.

5. A few pieces of the double-sided tape, each approximately ½″ (12.7mm) square, are cut and used to attach the fretboard to the base board. The tape is attached to the gluing surface of the fretboard and the protective paper is removed. The fretboard is positioned on the base board with the reference surface against the fence and the nut end against the stop block. Then it is pressed down to the base board to secure it in place.

6. A few pieces of the double-sided tape are used to attach the ruler to the fence. The ruler is positioned so it is sitting on the fretboard and so its end is against the stop block. This aligns its zero position with the nut end of the fretboard. Then it is pressed in place against the fence to secure the tape (**photo 3-5**). Note that the positioning described assumes the zero position of the ruler is at its left end. If the zero position of the ruler is located in from its end, the stop block must be unclamped and the zero mark on the ruler lined up with the nut end of the fretboard. Once in place, the stop block can be repositioned and clamped.

7. The location of the first fret is marked on the fretboard. A headband magnifier and strong light are necessary to perform this operation with accuracy (**photo 3-6**). The lamp is moved into position to shine on the approximate location of the first fret (**photo 3-7**). The location of the first fret is taken from **table 3-4** for the example guitars, which use a scale length of 25.5″ (647.7mm). The engraved mark for this location is identified on the ruler. The tip on the blade of the hobby knife is inserted into the engraved mark on the ruler, and gently drawn down until the blade is touching the top surface of the fretboard (**photo 3-8**). Pressure is applied to the knife so it makes a definitive mark on the surface of the fretboard.

8. The locations of the 2nd through the 20th frets are similarly marked. The example instruments have 20 frets.

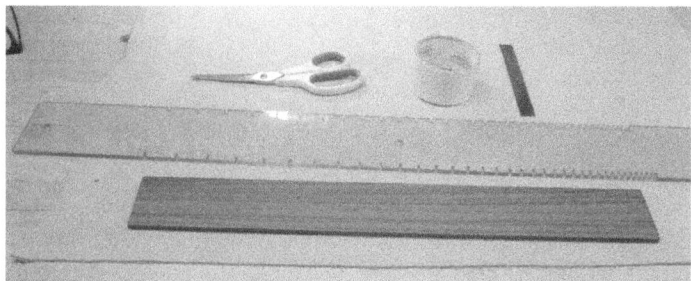

Photo 3-9 – A plastic template (center) for a commercial fret slotting system can be used to mark the fret locations on the fretboard.

9. The marked locations of the frets are checked carefully at least once. It is useful to begin each check by placing the tip of the knife blade in the mark, then sliding the tip up into the engraved mark on the ruler, and then counting back the number of marks to the next labeled mark on the ruler.

10. The ruler and any tape are removed from the fence. The fretboard is removed from the base board.

Option 2: Using a Commercial Template

Lutherie suppliers offer fret slot cutting systems that make use of CNC-cut plastic templates. An example is shown in **photo 3-9**. Although these templates are designed specifically for each supplier's proprietary fret slotting tools, they can be readily used to mark fret locations by hand. These templates have slots cut into their edges at the positions of the frets. The slots are intended to engage a locating pin, but can be used to guide a marking knife. Fret slotting templates are fairly inexpensive, and they generally cost about the same amount as a finely graduated precision ruler. These templates generally have location slots for two different scale lengths, one on each side of the template. A template for a scale length of 25.5˝ is required for construction of the example guitars. Note that using the template as described here requires it to be taped to the playing surface of the fretboard blank, so that surface must be flat. Note also that the first slot on the template is for the location of the nut, *not* the location of the first fret.

Materials
    The fretboard blank
    Double sided polyester tape
Tools
    Plastic fretting template, 25.5˝ scale length (see text)
    Small steel ruler
    Hobby knife or marking knife
    Scissors

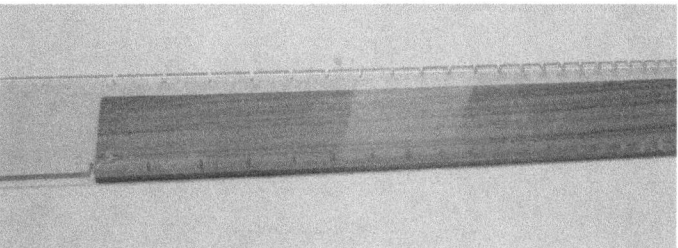

Photo 3-12 – The template attached to the fretboard top using double-sided tape, after it has been aligned with the nut end of the fretboard.

Photo 3-10 – A small ruler or other flat thin piece of metal is used to align the right wall of the nut location slot of the template with the nut end of the fretboard.

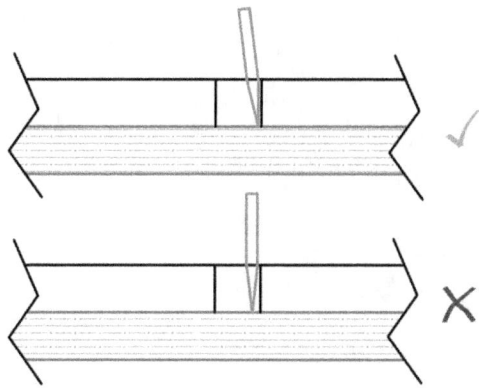

Figure 3-3 – If a hobby knife or other knife with a blade with a double bevel is used to make the mark, the bevel, not the side of the blade, must be held flat against the right wall of the template slot.

Photo 3-11 – Another view of the process of aligning the right wall of the nut slot of the template with the nut end of the fretboard.

Photo 3-13 – Marking the location of a fret onto the playing surface of the fretboard.

Photo 3-14 –*The thickness of the fence block is adjusted, so when the back of the fret-slotting saw is resting on the top of the block, the distance from the bottom of the block to the bottom of the saw teeth is the required depth of the fret slots.*

Photo 3-15 – *A close-up view of measuring the exposure of the saw below the bottom of the fence block.*

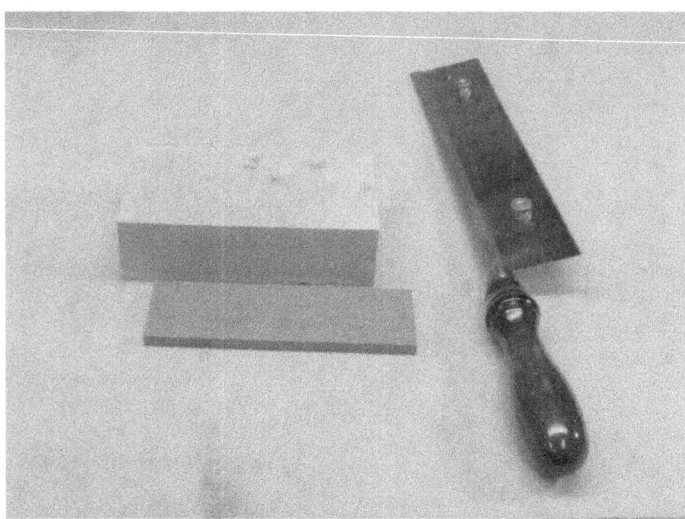

Photo 3-16 – *A scrap of wood is fashioned into a fence for the fence block. When the fence block is sitting on top of the fretboard, the fence will ride against the side of the fretboard. This keeps the saw cut perpendicular to the fretboard side.*

1. The fret slotting template will be attached to the playing surface of the fretboard using double-sided tape, with its edge aligned with one side of the fretboard and the right wall of the template's nut-location slot aligned with the nut end of the fretboard. First, small pieces of double-sided tape are cut and applied to the playing surface of the fretboard, and the backing paper is removed.

2. The template is lightly positioned on top of the fretboard, with its edge aligned with that of the fretboard. A small ruler is inserted into the nut-location slot of the template and used to align the right wall of the nut-location slot with the nut end of the fretboard (**photos 3-10** and **3-11**).

3. After the template is aligned on the fretboard, pressure is applied to stick the template in place so it will not move while marking (**photo 3-12**).

4. A hobby or marking knife is used to transfer the location of the right wall of the template slot for the first fret to the fretboard surface. If a marking knife is used, the flat of the blade is pressed to the right wall of the template slot. If a hobby knife is used, the *bevel* of the blade is pressed flat against the right wall of the template slot. Once positioned, the knife is pressed down to mark the top of the fretboard.

 Note that the mark must be made *exactly* at the location of the right wall of the template slot; so if a hobby knife is used the *bevel* of the blade must be in contact with this wall, *not* the side of the blade. See **figure 3-3**.

5. The locations of frets 2 through 20 are marked in similar fashion. Note that the template will have location slots for more than 20 frets (**photo 3-13**). Marks should only be made for 20 frets.

6. The template and tape are removed from the fretboard.

☐ Sawing the Fret Slots

The fret slots are sawn using a special purpose fret slotting saw, available from lutherie suppliers. This looks like a typical small back saw, but it cuts a kerf that is exactly as wide as is required to accommodate the tangs of the frets. There is some variation in these saws depending on supplier. Some are European style back saws and some are Japanese style back saws that cut on the pull stroke. Both styles work fine. Some of these saws come equipped with an adjustable depth stop. These generally cost more but are highly recommended.

Although sawing the slots is essentially a simple operation there are two critical aspects which should be kept in mind. The slots must be cut perpendicular to the surface of the fretboard and perpendicular to the reference edge. And they must be cut to a consistent depth that will be deep enough to accommodate fret installation. Further, the slots must be cut neatly, without marring the surface of the fretboard. To meet these requirements, the slots are cut using a simple shop-built fence block with a depth stop. During sawing, the fretboard is clamped securely to the bench or a workboard, and the fence block is clamped securely to the fretboard. This allows both hands to be free for precision sawing.

Fret slot depth	5/32″	(4mm)
Fretboard length	17¹⁵⁄₁₆″	(455.6mm)
Fretboard width at nut	1²³⁄₃₂″	(43.7mm)
Half width at nut	55/64″	(21.8mm)
Fretboard width at 14th fret	2⁵⁄₃₂″	(54.8mm)
Half width at 14th fret	1⁵⁄₆₄″	(27.4mm)
Fretboard width at soundhole end	2⁹⁄₃₂″	(57.9mm)
Half width at soundhole end	1⁹⁄₆₄″	(29mm)

Table 3-5– Critical dimensions for the fretboard of the example instruments.

Materials
   The fretboard blank
   Scrap wood for fashioning the fence block (see text)
   Wood screws (see text)
Tools
   Fret slotting saw
   Small ruler
   Clamps

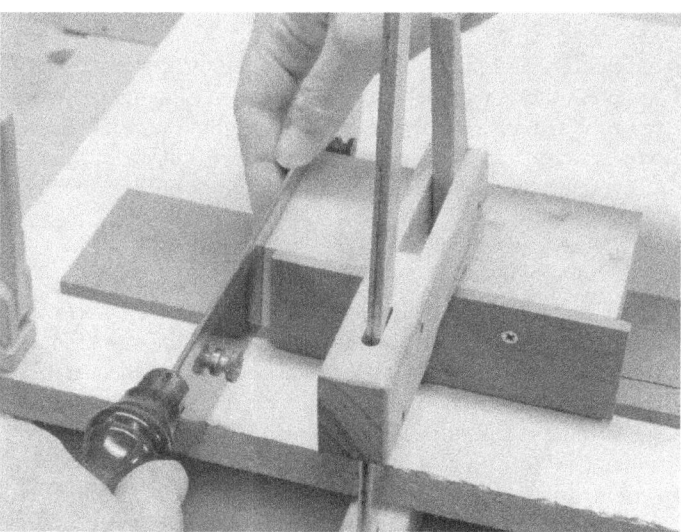

Photo 3-17 – The completed fence block in use to make a trial cut on a stand-in for the fretboard, made of MDF. The fence piece is attached to the front of the fence block with wood screws, and it extends below the bottom edge, so it can bear against the side of the fretboard. The fence block is clamped in place on the fretboard with its end aligned with one of the fret location marks previously made on the fretboard top. The saw blade is pressed firmly against the end of the fence block while the cut is made. The depth of the cut stops when the back of the saw contacts the top of the fence block.

1. A simple fence block is cut from a scrap of thick wood. All surfaces of the block must be square to the others. The dimensions of this block will depend mostly on the dimensions of the fretting saw. This being the case, the fretting saw must be on hand before the fence block can be fashioned. The finished block should be approximately 6″ (152.4mm) long. Its width should be the same as that of the fretboard. The thickness of the block should be such that, when it is placed against the side of the blade of the fret-slotting saw with its top surface against the underside of the saw back, the distance between the bottom of the block and the bottom of the saw teeth will equal the target fret slot depth, 5/32″ (4mm), as shown in **table 3-5**. This relationship is shown in **photos 3-14** and **3-15**. Note that even though the fence block is a quickly fashioned and disposable tool, this particular dimension is critical, and should be measured and cut with precision.

2. A general strategy for fashioning this block is to select a piece of scrap that is more than thick enough and to plane it down to the target thickness. If a piece of scrap thick enough is not readily available, a blank can be laminated up out of thinner stock. A planer or thickness sander can be used to quickly and accurately plane to thickness, but these tools impose a minimum length on the piece that they can safely handle. So, if such tools are used, the stock is planed to thickness first and then cut to length.

3. A fence for the fence block is fashioned from thin scrap. This fence is used to keep the end of the fence block perpendicular with the reference surface of the fretboard. It should be shorter in length than the length of the fence block and roughly as wide as the fence block is thick. It is mounted on the side of the fence block so its bottom edge hangs 3/16″ (4.8mm) below the bottom of the fence block, and is attached with wood screws. See **photos 3-16** and **3-17**. The ends of this fence must not protrude beyond the ends of the fence block.

4. If the fret slotting saw has a depth stop, it is set to the same depth of cut, as indicated in **table 3-5**. A check is made to be

Photo 3-18 –The fingers of the hand not holding the saw are used to keep the blade constantly in full contact with the end of the fence block while sawing.

sure the depth stop hardware does not interfere with the fence block. If it does, the depth stop hardware should be removed from the saw.

5. One or more test cuts are made on a piece of scrap. It is useful to have a stand-in for the fretboard, fashioned from scrap wood, that can be used to make some test cuts. The purpose of the test cuts is to be sure things can be set up for comfortable cutting, and to be sure accurate cuts can be made. The stand-in fretboard with the fence block on top can be clamped directly to the bench, or a base board such as that used in the fret location marking operation can be used. I prefer to use the base board, because it puts the saw at a more comfortable height for sawing.

Note the position of my hands in **photos 3-17** and **3-18**. One hand holds the handle of the saw, while the fingers of the other hand press the saw blade gently but positively flat against the end of the fence block. It is useful to determine which orientation works best. In the photos, I am sawing with my left hand and pressing the saw blade with my right. The other way may be more comfortable.

Sawing should proceed with ever-so-gentle sawing pressure. It is critical that the saw blade does not jump out of the kerf during sawing, so the finger pressure holding the blade to the fence block is critical. Once the back of the saw reaches the top of the fence block, there will be a distinct reduction in the force needed to push (or pull) the saw, which will be felt in the sawing hand. At this point it is important to be sure the saw back is in contact with the top of the fence block along its entire width. This will indicate that the kerf is of even depth. It is *not* a good idea to continue sawing at this point. Doing so will wear the top surface of the fence block, and this will make subsequent cuts a bit deeper.

After the test cut(s) is made, the depth of cut is checked for accuracy. If it is not accurate, the height of the fence block and, if applicable, the height of the saw depth stop must be adjusted accordingly, and the test cut(s) made again.

Photo 3-19 – *A long ruler is used to mark the length of the fretboard.*

Photo 3-20 – *The fretboard can be trimmed to length using the table saw with a fine blade, zero clearance insert, and the miter gauge.*

6. The first fret slot is cut. The fence block is fitted and clamped down so that its cutting end is aligned with the mark for the first fret from the nut end of the fretboard. The fence block should be oriented so that its cutting end is on the opposite side of the mark from the nut end of the fretboard. This orientation will end up making the centerline of the resulting kerf closer to the nut by half the thickness of the kerf. Although it may seem that this will adversely affect intonation, in fact it will have a positive effect on intonation, at least mathematically, but in any case it will not have an adverse effect on audible intonation. The slot is cut in the same manner as per the test cut made in the previous step.

7. The rest of the fret slots for frets 2 through 20 are cut in the same manner as the first one. The fence block is retained for use in cutting the fretboard to length.

Trimming the Fretboard to Shape

These operations are straight forward, but it should again be noted that fretboard wood is hard, dense, and stiff, and is prone to splitting. When using edge tools for final trimming it is imperative that cuts are *not* made into the grain. Doing so can result in a split in the fretboard which is not repairable. Three options are presented here for trimming the sides to final dimensions. The descriptions of each of these specify the orientation of the cuts to avoid splitting of the grain.

□ **Trimming Fretboard to Length, Rough Trimming Sides**

1. The length of the fretboard for the example guitars is presented in **table 3-5**. A long ruler is used to measure from the nut end of the fretboard, down the centerline, and a mark is made at the indicated length (**photo 3-19**). A square is used to continue this mark across the fretboard from side to side. Note that if a pre-slotted fretboard is used the fretboard is trimmed to length at the slot for fret 21.

2. The fretboard is cut to length at this mark. Any appropriate tool can be used to make the cut. A table saw with a fine blade (80 or 100 tooth), zero clearance insert, and miter guide can be used (**photo 3-20**). The fence block and fret-slotting saw setup used to saw the fret slots can be used, and after the cut is made to fret slot depth, the fence block can be removed and the cut continued right through the fretboard. After the cut is made the surface of the cut should be sanded smooth.

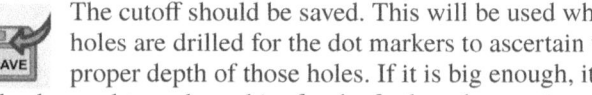 The cutoff should be saved. This will be used when the holes are drilled for the dot markers to ascertain the proper depth of those holes. If it is big enough, it may also be used to make a shim for the fretboard extension.

3. The scribed centerline is now extended down both the nut end and the soundhole end of the fretboard. If a centerline has not already been scribed down the center of the gluing surface, that should be done now. These marks will be needed in subsequent operations.

4. The locations of the fretboard sides are marked on the playing surface at the nut end, 14th fret, and at the soundhole end (**table 3-5**). These marks should be made using a precision

ruler, as offsets from the centerline. So, for each of the locations, half the half width of the fretboard at this location is taken from the table, and marks are made at that distance from the centerline, on both sides of the centerline.

5. A straightedge and pencil are used to connect the three marks for one side of the fretboard, then the other. If the three marks don't align, then one or more of them are not in the right place, and the marks should be measured and made again. After lines representing both sides of the fretboard have been drawn, all six of the half widths should be measured again to be sure they are correct before cutting. Note that accurate half widths guarantee that the fretboard is the correct width and also guarantee that it is symmetrical on both sides of the centerline.

6. Excess material is rough trimmed off the sides using the bandsaw or a similar tool.

☐ Finish Trimming of the Fretboard Sides

Three options are provided. The first makes use of a hand plane and bench hook. The second method uses a sanding board and a simple fence. The third method uses a router and two flush cutting bits.

 No matter what method is used to final trim the sides of the fretboard, it is vital that the width of the fretboard at the nut end, 14th fret, and soundhole end are accurate, and that the half widths on both sides of the centerline at these locations are also accurate. Making sure these measurements are accurate will ensure that the fretboard is accurately sized and also symmetrical about the centerline. Small and seemingly minor deviations here can end up having major consequences that will necessitate changes in string spacing and bridge construction in later construction steps.

Option 1: Using the Hand Plane and Bench Hook

1. The fretboard is placed so its nut end is against the stop of a bench hook of appropriate length, with the side to be trimmed hanging over the side of the bench hook a bit. A finely set hand plane is used on its side to trim the fretboard side down to near the mark (**photo 3-21**). The other side is done in like fashion, again with the nut end of the fretboard against the stop.

Note that many fretboard blanks do not have perfectly straight grain and may have runout near the sides. It may be necessary in some cases to plane from the other direction.

2. The width of the fretboard at nut and soundhole ends are checked, straightness of the sides is checked, and trimming of the sides is continued, with care taken to trim equally on both sides, until the target widths are achieved.

Option 2: Using the Sanding Board and Simple Fence

1. The sides of the fretboard are scrubbed on a large sanding board with 80 grit sandpaper, to trim the sides close to the marks. The fretboard should be held as perpendicular to the surface of the sanding board as possible.

2. A long board of rectangular cross section and approximately 1½″ (38MM) thick is clamped to the sanding board for use as a fence.

3. The width of the fretboard at nut and soundhole ends are checked, and sanding of the sides is continued with the gluing

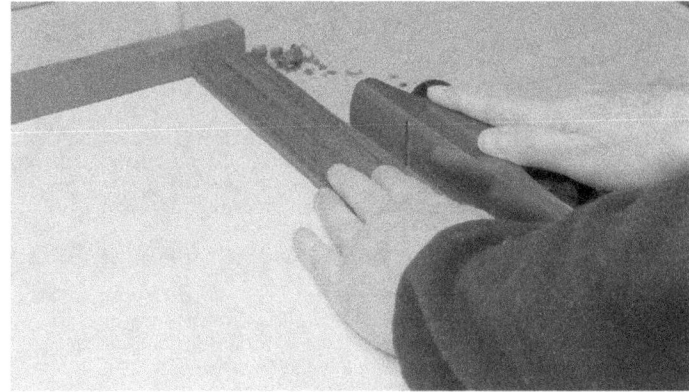

Photo 3-21 – *The sides of the fretboard are trimmed to final dimensions using a hand plane and bench hook.*

Photo 3-22 – *To keep the sides square to the broad surfaces of the fretboard, they are sanded on the sanding board using a simple fence. The front surface of the fence must be straight and perpendicular to the top surface of the sanding board.*

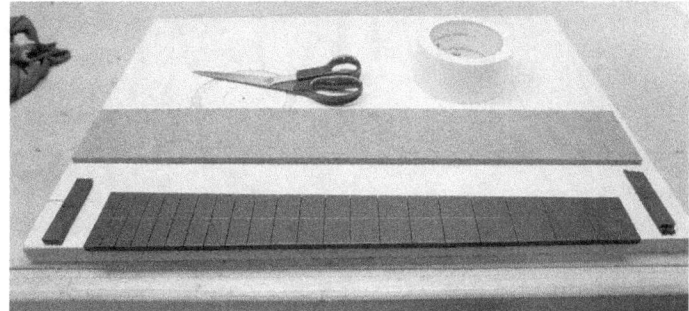

Photo 3-23 – *The components needed to do the final trimming of the fretboard sides using router and pattern bits. The rectangular template (center) is made of MDF and has straight ripped sides. The fretboard is in the front center. Two small spacer pieces are at the ends of the fretboard. Here they are cutoffs from the fretboard but they can be of any material of the same thickness as the fretboard.*

Photo 3-24 – Squares of double stick-tape are stuck to the back surface (gluing surface) of the fretboard. Smaller pieces of the tape are stuck down near the front corners of the base board. These are used to secure the two spacer pieces.

Photo 3-25 – The fretboard is mounted with the side to be trimmed overhanging the front edge of the base board. The spacer pieces are stuck down to the baseboard near the ends. Squares of double-stick tape are stuck to the playing surface of the fretboard.

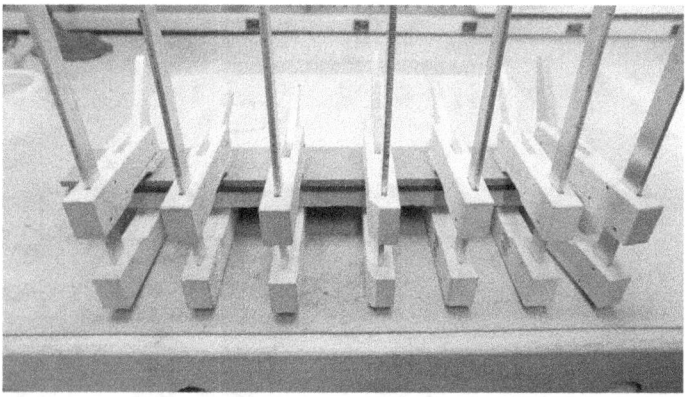

Photo 3-26 – The straight edge of the template has been aligned with the pencil line on the fretboard indicating the location of the side. It is important that the template is stuck securely to the fretboard, and that the fretboard is stuck securely to the base board for routing. A line of clamps is used to exert pressure so the double-stick tape holds well. Then the clamps are removed.

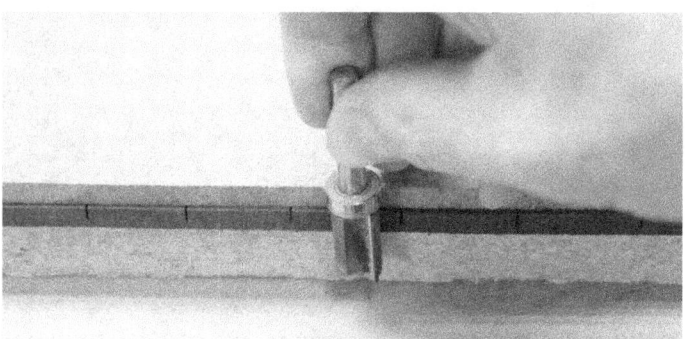

Photo 3-27 – A trimming bit with a top mounted bearing is used to trim the side to the line. The bearing follows the straight edge of the template.

surface of the fretboard held in contact with the fence. Care is taken to sand equally on both sides, until the target widths are achieved (**photo 3-22**).

Option 3: Using the Router and Flush-Cutting Bits

This method makes use of a simple pattern (the straight edge of a thin board) and flush-cutting bits (also called pattern bits) in a router, to trim the sides of the fretboard to final dimensions. Two things must be avoided when performing these cuts: an unsafe climb cut, and cutting into the grain. Due to the properties of most woods used for fretboards, attempting to rout into the grain (i.e. to rout from the nut end toward the soundhole end of the fretboard) is practically guaranteed to split the fretboard. For this reason, and also because the lines marking the locations of the sides of the fretboard are on the playing surface, both a top bearing and a bottom bearing flush-cutting bit are required.

Materials
    The fretboard blank
    Melamine board for use as a base board (see text)
    ¼″ (6.4MM) thick MDF or tempered hardboard (see text)
    Double-sided tape
Tools
    Router
    Top bearing flush-cutting router bit, at least ½″ (12.8MM)
        diameter, ¾″ (19.1MM) cutting length
    Bottom bearing flush-cutting router bit, at least ½″ (12.8MM)
        diameter, at least ½″ (38MM) cutting length
    Scissors
    Metal or plastic putty knife

1. A piece of melamine board is cut or repurposed for use as a base board. This should be approximately 24″ (609.6MM) long and at least 12″ (304.8MM) wide.

2. A piece of ¼″ (6.4MM) thick MDF or tempered hardboard 24″ (609.6MM) long and approximately 3″ (76.2MM) wide is cut to

Photo 3-28 – Routing proceeds from left to right. Notice the spacer between the right end of the template and the base board. It prevents the weight of the router from levering the template down after the router has been moved past the end of the fretboard.

use as a pattern. One long edge of this piece should be ripped straight.

3. Two small spacer pieces are cut from any ¼″ (6.4mm) thick stock. Each piece should be approximately 3″ (76.2mm) long by 1″ (25.4mm) wide. Base board, pattern, fretboard, and spacer pieces are shown in **photo 3-23**.

4. Steps 4 through 11 are followed to trim the right side of the fretboard. Squares of double-stick tape are cut and stuck to the gluing (back) surface of the fretboard. Two smaller strips of the tape are cut and stuck down to the base board as shown in **photo 3-24**. The backing paper is removed from all the tape pieces and the fretboard is flipped over so the playing surface is up. The fretboard is stuck down to the base board, oriented with the soundhole end (wide end) to the left, the nut end (narrow end) to the right, and with the pencil line indicating the location of the near side overhanging the front end of the base board just a bit. In a later step, the router will be used to rout the waste off down to the line, and the router bit should not contact the front edge of the base board when this is done.

5. The two spacer pieces are stuck down to the tape near each end of the fretboard.

6. Additional squares of the tape are cut and stuck down to the playing surface of the fretboard, as shown in **photo 3-25**.

7. Now the backing paper is removed from the tape, and the template is placed on top of the fretboard with its straight edge carefully aligned with the pencil line showing the location of the side. After the edge is well aligned with the marked line, the template is pressed firmly in place.

8. To be sure the template is well stuck down to the fretboard and will not move during routing, a few clamps are applied along the length of the fretboard to set the tape (**photo 3-26**), then the clamps are removed. This sets the adhesive of the tape.

9. The router bit with the top bearing is selected. During routing, the bearing will run along the straight edge of the template (**photo 3-27**) and the bit will trim the side to the marked line. The bit is mounted in the router collet, and the depth of cut is adjusted so the bearing will ride on the template edge and the fretboard side will be completely trimmed.

10. Routing starts with the router bit against the template and to the left of the left end of the fretboard (**photo 3-28**), and proceeds left to right until the bit has moved past the right end of the fretboard. Note the purpose of the spacer pieces, which is to support the template from bending at the ends under the weight of the router.

11. The template is carefully removed from the fretboard and the fretboard is carefully removed from the base board. Note that a metal or plastic putty knife may be needed to unstick things. Due to the fret slots, it is very easy to crack the fretboard if it is bent. All the tape is removed from the template, fretboard, and base board. The spacer pieces are left in place, stuck to the base board.

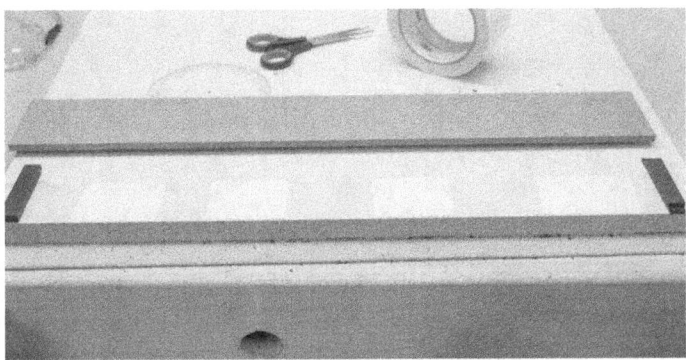

Photo 3-29 – The template straight edge has been stuck down to the playing surface of the fretboard, aligned with the left side location line, which is facing away from us in this photo. Squares of double-stick tape are applied to the baseboard as shown.

Photo 3-30 – The spacer pieces are removed, then the template and fretboard assembly is flipped over, template side down, so the side of the fretboard to be trimmed overhangs the front edge of the base board.

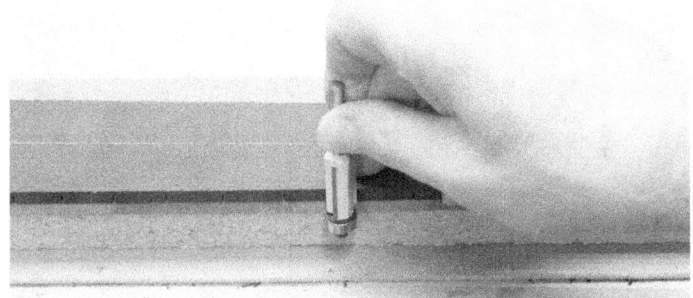

Photo 3-31 – A bottom bearing bit is used for this cut. The bearing rides on the straight edge of the template.

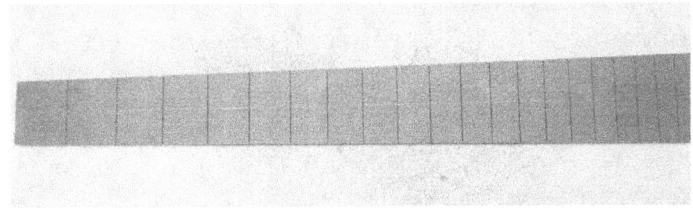

Photo 3-32 – Fretboard with sides trimmed to final dimensions.

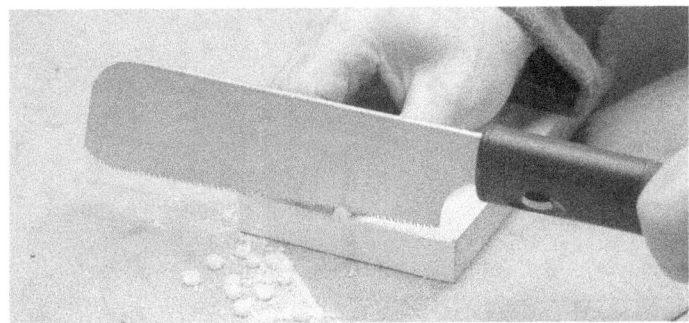

Photo 3-33 – Slicing plastic dots for use as dot markers from a plastic rod.

12. The left side of the fretboard is now trimmed. The fretboard is oriented with the playing surface up and the soundhole end to the left. Squares of tape are cut and stuck down along the playing surface of the fretboard. The backing paper is removed.

13. The template is placed gently on top of the fretboard, aligning the straight edge of the template with the line marking the left side of the fretboard, which is facing away from the front edge of the base board. The template is pressed down firmly so the tape sticks.

14. Squares of tape are cut and stuck down to the base board near the front edge, in the location where the fretboard will be for routing (**photo 3-29**). The backing paper is removed. The small spacer pieces are also removed from the baseboard and discarded. They are not needed here and may be in the way, because the template will be on the bottom.

15. The template and fretboard assembly is flipped over, template surface down, and gently oriented so the marked line to be cut extends a bit over the front edge of the base board. The wider soundhole end of the fretboard must be to the left. The gluing surface of the fretboard is now up (**photo 3-30**).

16. As in step 8, a line of clamps are applied to put pressure on the tape and make everything stick together well. The clamps are then removed.

17. The top-bearing bit is removed from the router and the bottom-bearing bit (**photo 3-31**) is inserted, and the router depth is adjusted for the cut. The bearing will run against the template and the cutter will trim the side of the fretboard.

18. As in step 10, routing proceeds from left to right.

19. The fretboard is removed from the template, the template from the base board, as well as all the tape sticking to various surfaces. Following this and other fretboard side trimming options, the fretboard will look as shown in **photo 3-32**.

Locating and Drilling Holes for Dot Markers

Pre-cut shell and plastic dots are available from lutherie suppliers for use as dot markers. The instructions that follow are for marking the locations of the dots and drilling the holes for them. Inserting the dots is left until after the fretboard has been cambered, an operation detailed in another chapter. But the marker dots that will be used must be on hand now, so holes of correct diameter and depth can be drilled.

Some suppliers may offer a number of different sizes, but typical dots for the playing surface are ¼″ (6.4MM) in diameter and typical dots for the side of the fretboard are ³⁄₃₂″ (2.4MM) in diameter. Dots made of shell material like abalone and mother of pearl (MOP) are typically at least 0.05″ (1.3MM) thick. I don't recommend dots that are any thinner than that. Plastic dots are often thicker. Another source of plastic dots is to buy plastic rod and cut dots off the rod in the shop (**photo 3-33**). Plastic rods are available from lutherie suppliers for side marker dots, but these dots are *not* cut prior to installation.

☐ **Marking Centers for the Dot Markers**

The example instruments have 20 fret fretboards. The following instructions are for locating and marking the centers for dot markers on the fretboard playing surface and the side surface, at the conventional locations. These are at frets 3, 5, 7, 9, 12, 15, 17, and 19. With the exception of fret 12 which has two dots, all the other locations will have a single dot. Two options are presented for performing this operation. The fist uses a precision ruler to measure locations for the dot centers. The second method uses a special gauge which comes with the template books for the example instruments.

Option 1: Using a Ruler

1. The first fret on the fretboard to have a marker is fret 3. The distance between that fret and the one previous to it is measured along the centerline of the fretboard, using a precision ruler. Half of this distance is calculated and located on the ruler, and a pencil mark is made across the centerline at that location.

2. Step 1 is repeated for frets 5, 7, and 9, each of which will also have a single dot.

3. Fret 12 will have two dot markers. These are generally approximately centered between the low E and A strings, and between the high E and B strings, respectively. For the example instruments the centers of the dots are each located ¾″ (19.1MM) from the centerline. The ruler is used to measure this distance from the centerline and a line parallel to the centerline is drawn. Then the ruler is used to measure the distance between frets 11 and 12 along this line. Half that distance is taken and an intersecting mark is made at the center point of the dot. This is repeated for the other dot of the pair.

4. Step 1 is repeated for frets 15, 17, and 19, each of which will also have a single dot, located on the centerline.

5. Steps 1 and 2 are repeated on the left side of the fretboard if the instrument will be right-handed. When marking the side there is no centerline, so marks should all be lines that extend the full thickness of the fretboard.

 If the instrument will be left-handed then the side dot marks are made on the right side of the fretboard.

6. Fret 12 also gets a double dot marker on the fretboard side. A similar location line is penciled between frets 11 and 12. Then the ruler is used to mark a parallel line ⅛″ (3.2MM) on both sides of the original mark. The original mark is now erased to avoid confusion when it comes time to drill the holes.

7. Step 4 is repeated on the fretboard side to mark locations for the single dots for frets 15, 17, and 19.

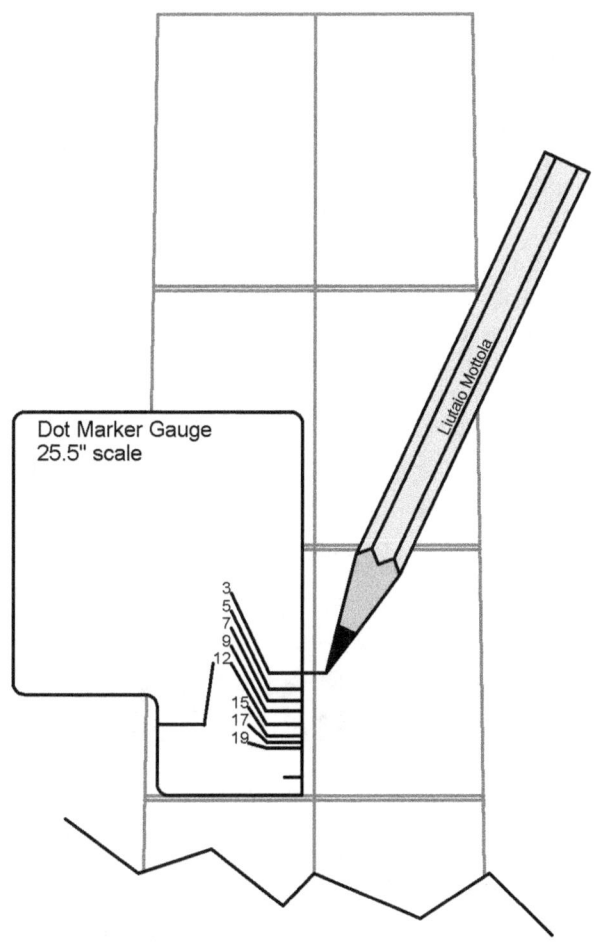

Figure 3-4 – Using the dot marker location gauge to mark the location of the dot marker for the third fret.

8. All of the marks are now visually checked to be sure they are accurately placed. If anything looks amiss, measuring and marking are re-done where necessary to correct the problem.

Option 2: Using the Dot Marker Location Gauge

A file containing a book of templates is available for each of the example instruments. If not already done, the pages of the template book are printed out on card stock. Included with the templates is a simple gauge that is used to lay out the centers for the dot markers. This is cut out using knife or scissors.

1. With the fretboard in a vertical orientation and nut end up, the base of the gauge is aligned with the slot for fret 3, and the right edge of the gauge is aligned with the fretboard centerline. A pencil mark is made next to the line on the gauge labeled 3, as shown in **figure 3-4**.

2. The locations of the centers for the dot markers for frets 5, 7, 9, 15, 17, and 19 are marked in the same manner.

3. For fret 12, the gauge is positioned in the same manner, but a pencil mark is made next to the line on the left indented edge of the gauge labeled 12, as shown in **photo 3-34**. A small pencil

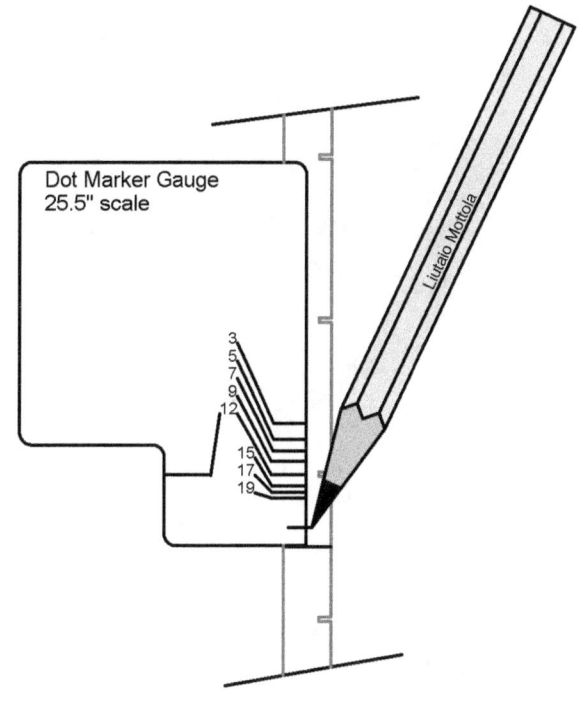

Figure 3-5 – Using the dot marker location gauge to mark the location of one of the double dots at the twelfth fret on the side of the fretboard.

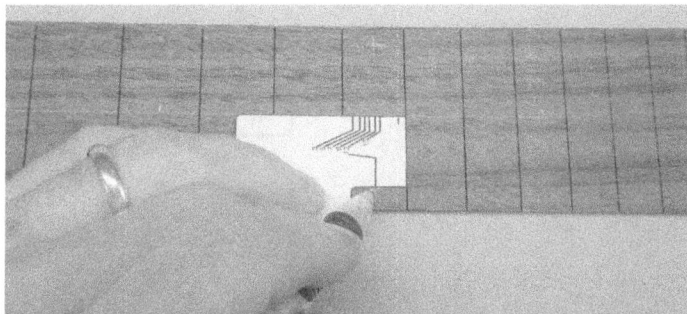

Photo 3-34 – The gauge is used to mark the location of the center of one of the double dots on the twelfth fret.

Photo 3-35 – The thickness of the dot is transferred to the side of the fretboard cutoff, to be used as a depth gauge for setting the drilling depth.

Photo 3-36 – The quill stop of the drill press is adjusted to drill a hole in the fretboard cutoff that is approximately as deep as the dot is thick. The fit of the dot in the hole is checked, and the quill stop is re-adjusted if the hole is too shallow or too deep.

2. The drill press is set up with a brad point bit of the diameter of the dots. A flat backing board and a hold down clamp are used. The table height should be adjusted so the point of the bit is just a fraction above the top surface of the fretboard cutoff. The quill stop of the drill press is set to stop drilling when the flat bottom part of the bit is at the depth of the pencil line marked on the side of the cutoff. That represents the depth of hole required to match the thickness of the dot.

3. A test hole is drilled in the cutoff (**photo 3-36**) and a dot is inserted to check the hole depth. If the depth is not correct the quill stop is re-adjusted. This process is repeated until the dot fits flush with the surface of the fretboard cutoff. I generally make a note of how tightly the dots fit the holes. This

Photo 3-37 – The dot centers that have been marked in pencil are pricked with an awl. The pricked centers will precisely locate the point of the brad point bit which will be used to drill the holes.

mark is also made tracing the left indented edge of the gauge. The two pencil marks form a sort of half cross.

4. Keeping the base of the gauge aligned with the slot for fret 12, the gauge is slid over until the left indented edge of the gauge is aligned with the fretboard centerline. Then a half cross mark is made next to the line on the *right* edge of the gauge labeled 12.

5. The locations of the side single side dots are marked in similar fashion. It helps to hold the fretboard in the vise while marking the side dots. A small mark is made for each single side dot. These marks are then extended across the thickness of the fretboard, using the pencil and a small square.

6. Fret 12 gets a double dot side marker. The gauge is used to mark as for a single dot. Then the base of the gauge is moved so it is aligned with that mark, and a mark is made next to the very small unlabeled line near the base, on the right edge of the gauge (**figure 3-5**). The gauge is now moved so that small unlabeled line is aligned with the original mark, and a mark is made next to the corner between the base and the right edge of the gauge. So now there are three marks here. The original center mark is erased to avoid confusion when drilling the holes.

Photo 3-38 – The single dot holes are drilled at the pricked centers using a brad point bit.

☐ **Drilling Holes for the Playing Surface Dot Markers**

Drilling the holes for the dot markers is done using the drill press and an appropriately sized brad point bit. This is pretty straightforward, but due to the thin size of the dots, care must be taken to drill holes that are *exactly* the correct depth for them.

1. A simple gauge is made to use when setting the drill press quill stop for drilling these holes. The saved cutoff from the fretboard is placed on the bench and one of the dots is placed on the bench beside it, touching the side of the cutoff. The top surface of the dot is traced onto the side of the cutoff in pencil (**photo 3-35**). The cutoff is flipped over to be used as a gauge.

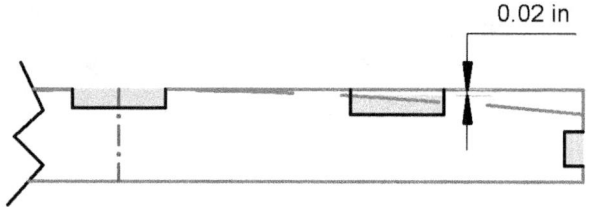

Figure 3-6 – The holes for the double dots must be drilled a bit deeper than the holes for the single dots. The former are located near the sides of the fretboard. When the fretboard playing surface is cambered these holes will get shallower.

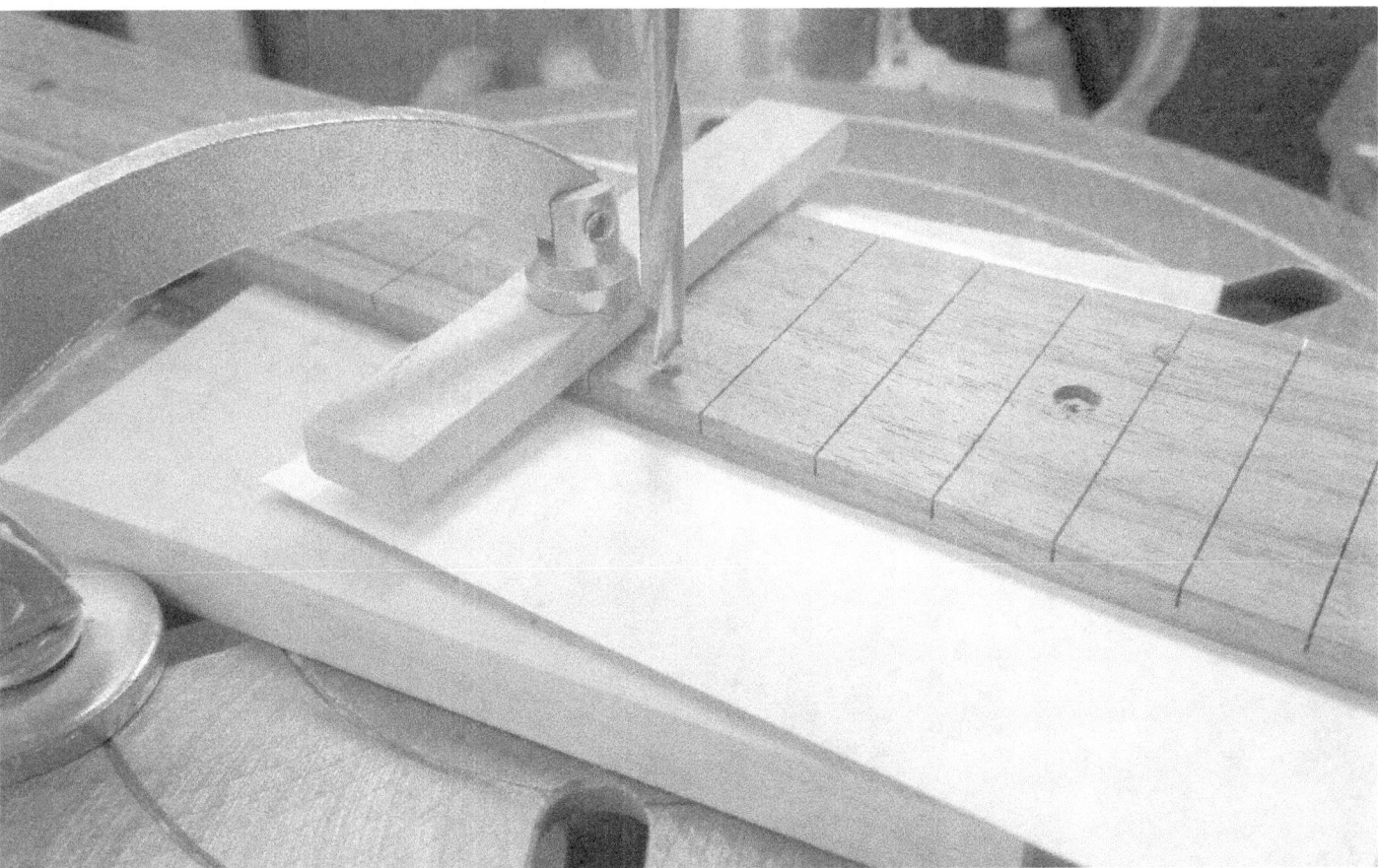

Photo 3-39 – *Two sheets of card stock are placed under the fretboard to raise it up, so the holes for the double dots will end up a bit deeper.*

information will be of use later, when the dots are glued in. To remove dots in the cutoff when making these drilling depth adjustments, the awl is used to firmly pierce the surface of the wood right next to the edge of the dot. It can then be used to lever the dot out of the bore.

4. An awl is used to prick the center marks for all of the playing surface dots (**photo 3-37**). Note that even small off-center location variations are often visible, so care should be taken to locate the point of the awl in the centerline groove before pricking each center.

5. The cutoff is removed and the fretboard is positioned on the drill press table. Holes for all the playing surface single dots (but *not* the double dots) are drilled, using the drill press as set up, and centering the point of the drill bit in each pricked center mark (**photo 3-38**). To center the bit, a pricked center is positioned directly under the point of the bit. The fretboard is lifted with the fingers until the pricked center engages the bit point. The fretboard is held in this position with one hand, while the press lever is pressed, which will press the fretboard to the table. The lever is held to keep the fretboard in position, while the hold down clamp is thrown to clamp the fretboard in place for drilling. Drilling feed should be quite slow to avoid chipping out the edges of the holes. All debris should be removed from the table before each drilling because this will affect the depth of the hole if the fretboard is placed on top of debris.

6. The double dot holes must be drilled 0.02″ (0.5MM) deeper than the single dot holes. If this is not done, those holes will end up being too shallow after the playing surface of the fretboard is cambered. See **figure 3-6**. The most straightforward way to do this is to place a sheet of 0.5MM veneer or card stock between the fretboard and the drill press table while drilling these two holes (**photo 3-39**). Note that a standard business card or the readily available 110LB (298GSM) card stock for computer printers is 0.01″ (0.25MM) thick, so two thicknesses of either can be used in this application. Note also that standard 20LB (75GSM) printer paper is typically 0.005″ (0.13MM) thick, so four thicknesses of this can be used as a spacer.

7. The dots are not glued in place at this time. The fretboard has yet to be cambered, and this operation will be done using coarse sandpaper, which can put deep scratches in shell and plastic dots which will be difficult to sand out. The dots will be installed after the fretboard has been cambered and sanded to fit grit.

☐ **Drilling Holes for the Fretboard Side Dot Markers**

Side dots cannot be accurately lined up using pricked centers. There is no centerline marked on the side of the fretboard and all of the marks locating the centers of the side dots are drawn right across the thickness of the fretboard. The holes for the side dots will be drilled at a fixed offset from the gluing surface of the fretboard. The reference is the gluing surface, because the thickness of the side of the fretboard will be less after

Photo 3-40 – A stack of feeler gauges adding up to 0.040″ (1mm) is used to set the distance between the front surface of the fence and the surface of the drill bit.

Photo 3-41 – The fretboard is clamped to the fence with its side aligned with the top of the fence, and one of the center marks for a side dot positioned directly below the point of the bit. Then the hole is drilled.

the fretboard is cambered (see again **figure 3-6**), and in fact it will vary in thickness from the nut end to the soundhole end.

1. A board to use as a fence on the drill press table is cut or selected. The board should be flat and rectangular, and be a bit wider than the fretboard is at the soundhole end. If should be thick enough so it can be clamped down to the table without the clamps extending over the front surface. The fence is clamped to the drill press table and checked for squareness with the table.

2. A standard twist bit of the diameter of the side dots or side dot rod is chucked into the drill press.

3. The quill stop is adjusted so the tip of the bit stops approximately 3/32″ (2.4mm) below the top of the fence.

4. An 0.040″ (1mm) feeler gauge (or a stack of feeler gauges that add up to that thickness) is placed against the front of the fence near the top, and the fence or table is moved until the side of the bit is in contact with the surface of the feeler gauge (**photo 3-40**). The table and fence are secured in this position, re-checked using the feeler gauge, and repositioned if necessary.

5. For each hole, the fretboard is positioned with its gluing (back) surface in contact with the fence; and the side to be drilled aligned with the top of the fence; and one of the dot location marks directly below the point of the drill bit. The fretboard is clamped in this position to the fence, using two clamps or large spring clamps. Positioning of the fretboard is checked again, then the hole is drilled (**photo 3-41**).

6. The side marker dots are also not installed at this time.

---

1. Leirer, William. (2008) Google Calculator and the Guitar's Magic Number. *American Lutherie #86*, p.62.

2. Mottola, R.M. (2014) Guitar Fretboard Camber and Action in the Context of String Bending. *Savart Journal* vol.1, #4.

4 The Neck Joint and Headstock

A number of different joints have been used to attach the necks to the bodies of stringed musical instruments. These range from simple joints to some that are quite mechanically complex. The necks of the violins built by the Cremonese master builders were simply glued and nailed in place. Lutes also used this simple means of neck attachment. Later instruments made use of glued joints that were some form of the mortise and tenon joints familiar in all types of woodworking. Modern steel string acoustic guitars evolved directly from 19th century European gut string guitars. A variety of neck joints were in use at that time and place. One that was common is a variant of the simple mortise and tenon called the dovetail joint, in which a dovetail-shaped tenon fits into a similarly shaped mortise (**figure 4-1**, **photo 4-1**). Until recent years, this was the most commonly used neck joint for steel string guitars built in the USA.

Although an excellent joint, the dovetail joint was not chosen for use in the construction process described here. It is a difficult joint to render by hand, and although there are many modern woodworkers who are quite comfortable in making these joints by hand, most are not. These days, templates and router bits are available to help make these joints quickly, but the process of aligning these templates for use, and the process of fitting joints that were not originally built in perfect alignment, is somewhat tedious and difficult to describe.

There are a number of excellent modern neck joints, too. Just about every luthier and guitar factory uses a neck joint of their own design, optimized for their own style of construction. Although I'd like to mention and discuss all of them here, time and space do not permit doing so. But I will give a little shout-out for two. The modern joint used by Taylor Guitars is a model of efficient simplicity: It makes use of laser-cut shims for neck angle adjustment. The fully-adjustable neck joint designed by Portland Oregon luthier Mike Doolin provides for full adjustment of the neck, even while the guitar is strung up.[1]

The neck joint used in the example guitars is called a bolt-on butt joint. The neck is attached to the body with two bolts. These bolts are inserted into holes in the neck block inside the guitar body, and they thread into inserts in the heel of the neck. The heel simply butts against the neck end of the body. See **figure 4-2**, **photos 4-2 – 4-4**. In the example instruments, this part of the body is flat, as is the body contact surface of the heel. This makes the necessary process of adjusting the position and

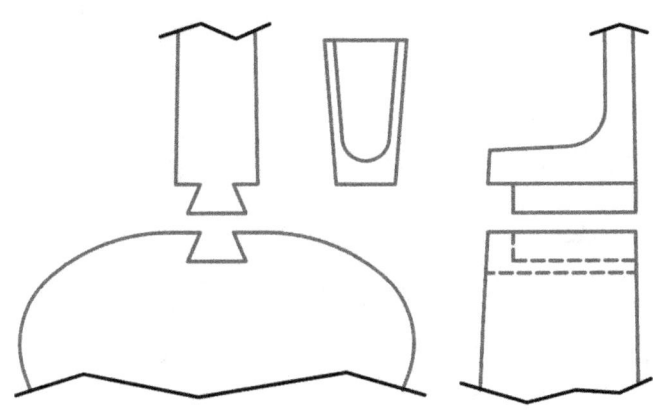

Figure 4-1– Schematic top view, end view, and side view cross-section of a typical dovetail neck joint.

Photo 4-1– The neck is removed from an antique guitar, revealing the parts of the dovetail neck joint. When the joint is fitted, the tenon is pressed into the mortise from the top.

attitude of the neck relative to the body quite simple and straightforward to demonstrate and describe. This joint works well for one-of-a-kind guitars, and it works particularly well for novice luthiers, because they are able to quickly and reliably build it and fit it.

Photo 4-2 – *A body with the back off, showing the holes that are drilled through the body and the internal neck block for the bolts that will attach neck and body.*

Photo 4-3 – *This photo, taken during a much later sanding operation, shows the inside surface of the heel of the neck, with the cheeks that will contact the body.*

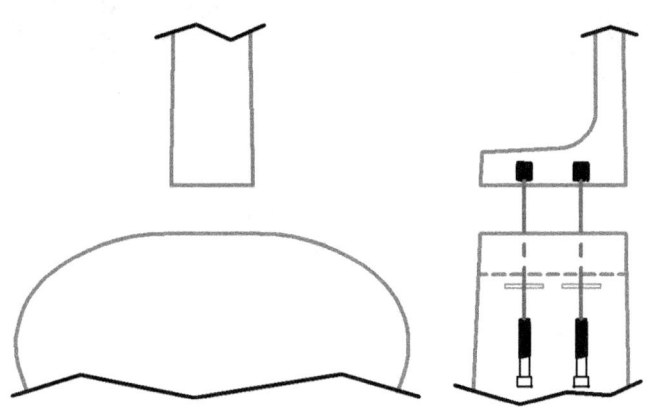

Figure 4-2 – *Schematic top view and side view cross-section of the bolt-on butt neck joint used in the example guitars.*

There was a time not too many years ago when people worried that the use of a bolt-on neck joint would have adverse effects on the sound of the guitar. Fortunately, experience has demonstrated that this is not the case, and bolt-on necks are used by most modern factories and also by many hand builders of steel string and classical guitars. The neck joint used in the example guitars is most similar to the joint used by the Canadian guitar manufacturer Godin in their Seagull line of acoustic steel string guitars. It sounds good, it is simple to build, and it is simple to fit and adjust.

Layout and Construction

There are two construction operations detailed in this chapter. The first is the installation of threaded inserts in the guitar body contact surface of the neck heel. The second is extending the width of the headstock. Both of these operations use templates taken from the first page of the template book for the example guitar under construction. The templates should be accurately cut out using scissors or a knife and straightedge.

Installing the Threaded Inserts

Two threaded inserts are installed in the guitar body contact surface of the heel. Before this is done however, a shallow pocket is excavated from this surface, which will reduce the area that will contact the guitar body to two narrow cheeks on both sides of the heel. The cheeks can be seen in **photo 4-3,** and the effect they have on the heel contact with the guitar body can be seen in **photo 4-4**. The reason this is done is to make it easier to trim down this part of the heel when making adjustments, when the neck is eventually fitted to the body. This is also a service to the future luthier that will reset the neck when the guitar eventually needs that work done.

Installation of the threaded inserts is a straightforward process, but care must be taken that the holes they fit into are drilled perpendicular to the heel surface and are of accurate depth. The heel is not very thick and will later be carved, and so it is important that the holes drilled into it are not made too deep. Installation of the inserts is done using a simple

Photo 4-4 – *This is how the joint looks when bolted together. Again, the back is off this instrument, but in a finished instrument the bolts are inserted through the soundhole and into the holes drilled through the neck block.*

disposable jig which keeps the bit of a hand drill perpendicular for drilling, and also keeps the insert perpendicular to the hole while it is being inserted. This simple jig makes it possible to install the inserts without use of the drill press, which would require a large and somewhat complicated fixture to allow drilling into the end of the long neck.

About Threaded Inserts

There are a variety of styles of threaded inserts available for woodworking applications. It is highly unfortunate that there don't appear to be industry standard names for these various styles. To further add to the confusion, inserts intended for wood rarely include descriptions that indicate *exactly* what kind of wood and what grain orientation they will work in. So, much of the information on the appropriateness of different styles of inserts must be gleaned by trial and error. Fortunately this has been done, and the novice builder can (and should) rely on threaded inserts sold by lutherie suppliers specifically for the purpose of bolt-on necks.

The three basic styles of threaded inserts are shown in **photo 4-5**. The flanged and tapered style of insert is often found in hardware stores and home centers. It is intended for use in particleboard and it is *not* suitable for the task at hand. The two other styles pictured are both suitable for the construction operations to be described. One is a flangeless "knife edge" insert, which works well in most medium density hardwoods. This style of insert is available from lutherie suppliers specifically for this purpose. The other recommended style of insert is a flangeless self-tapping machine insert often referred to as a Tap-Loc insert. It is intended for soft metals, but works well in the application at hand. A small study indicated that this style of insert provided moderately better holding strength than other styles when installed in the end grain of mahogany (*Swietenia macrophylla*).[2] This style works particularly well in the end grain of very dense hardwoods. I prefer these inserts for lutherie beginners because they require less effort to install.

No matter which style of insert is selected, the insert itself should be close to, but no longer than, ½″ (12.7mm) long, and have an internal ¼″-20 thread. Note that I am not including a metric equivalent for the threads here, although I am sure suitable equivalents are available. Whatever inserts are used, it is important to obtain and heed the manufacturer's suggestion for the drill size to use for the holes.

☐ Pocketing the End of the Heel

Construction details provided here use a small router and small bottom-cleaning pattern bit, which do the work quickly and cleanly. This operation can also be done using knife and chisel to excavate the pocket, followed by cleaning up the surface of the pocket with sandpaper on a small sanding block.

Materials
    Neck assembly
    Heel end template
    Masking tape
    ¼″ (6.4mm) thick MDF to use as templates
    Double-sided tape
Tools
    Small router or laminate trimmer
    Short bottom-cleaning router pattern bit with top bearing

---

1. Scribed centerlines should already be in place on the body contact surface of the heel, the bottom of the heel, and a short way down the floor of the trussrod slot. If any of these are missing, they are marked at this time. The floor of the trussrod

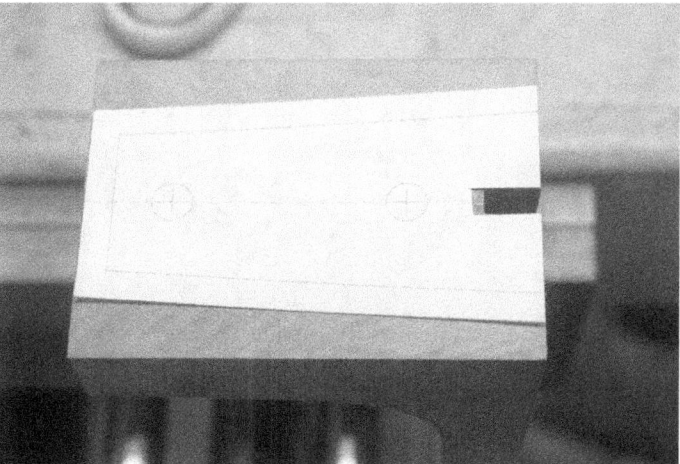

Photo 4-6 *– The template is fitted to the heel, aligned with the fretboard edge and the centerline. Note that the trussrod slot in the template has been cut a little deep to expose the centerline of the heel at that end.*

Photo 4-5 *– Three common styles of threaded inserts. The leftmost style is intended for use in particleboard and should not be used. The center style is a flangeless insert often described as having "knife edge" external threads. It works well when threaded into the end grain of most medium density hardwoods, and is available from lutherie suppliers. The rightmost style is a self-tapping machine insert intended for soft metal, often called a Tap-Loc insert. It works well in the end grain of very hard woods. Note that in this photo that the insertion end of each insert is pointing down.*

Photo 4-7 *– The heel end is shown with the outline of the guitar heel (outside lines) and the walls of the heel surface pocket (inside lines) marked in pencil.*

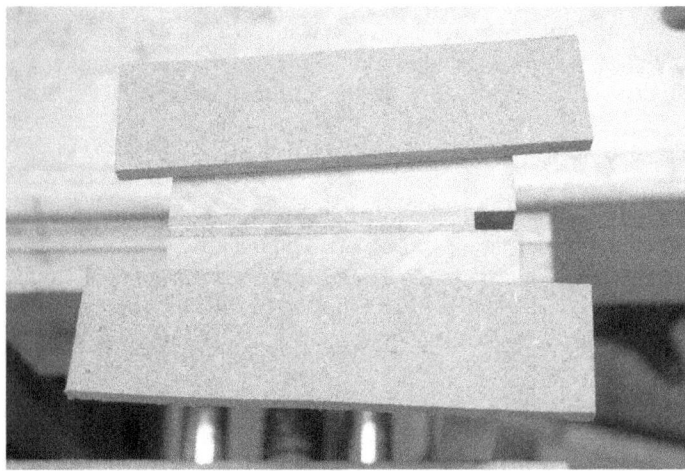

Photo 4-8 – The templates are fixed to the lines representing the walls of the pocket using double-sided tape, and pressed firmly into place.

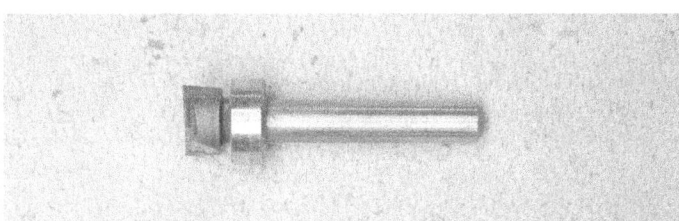

Photo 4-9 – A shallow bottom-cleaning pattern bit with a top bearing is used to cut the pocket.

Photo 4-10 – The pocket is excavated using the small router.

Photo 4-11 – The finished heel pocket.

slot is most easily marked by pressing a stack of automotive-style feeler gauges against one wall of the slot, and then scribing onto the floor, tracing the surface of the inner feeler gauge.

2. The card stock heel template for the guitar is cut out with knife and straightedge or with scissors. The trussrod slot in the template is also cut out, using the knife. Note this should be cut out a bit deeper than indicated on the template. This makes it easier to see the centerline when the template is positioned over the heel.

3. The neck assembly is clamped in the vise vertically so the heel end is facing up and is level.

4. The top edge of the template is aligned with the fretboard surface edge of the heel, and the template centerline is aligned with the centerline on the trussrod slot floor and with the centerline scribed on the heel surface (**photo 4-6**). Once aligned, the template is lightly taped in place with masking tape.

5. The sides of the heel are traced in pencil from the template onto the heel end. The template is removed, but saved for a later operation. The heel is currently longer than it will be in the finished instrument. If the lines just drawn do not extend all the way to the bottom of the heel, a straightedge and pencil are used to extend them to the bottom edge. Two lines are now drawn parallel to the lines representing the sides of the heel, each inside and offset ¼″ (6.4MM). These mark the walls of the heel pocket (**photo 4-7**).

6. A strip of ¼″ (6.4MM) thick MDF approximately 16″ (406.4MM) long is ripped straight and 2″ (50.8MM) wide, and then cut in half. These pieces will be used as templates to guide the bearing of the pattern router bit. Each one is aligned with one of the lines marking a wall of the pocket (**photo 4-8**). Double-sided tape is used to stick these templates down to the heel. As has been done in past operations, a clamp is used to apply pressure to be sure the tape adhesive sticks well, and then the clamp is removed.

7. A shallow bottom-cleaning pattern bit (**photo 4-9**) is fit into a small trim router, and the depth is set to cut ⅛″ (3.2MM) below the surface of the heel. The cut is checked to be sure the bearing of the bit will ride against the walls of the templates.

8. The pocket is excavated (**photo 4-10**), avoiding pressing too hard against the sides of the templates. Then the templates and any remaining tape are removed (**photo 4-11**).

9. The centerline is now redrawn down the floor of this pocket.

☐ Assembling the Threaded Insert Fitting Jig

This simple disposable jig is made of pieces of melamine board stuck together with double-sided tape. It provides drilled holes which serve as bushings to keep the pilot holes drilled into the heel perpendicular to it. It also provides a hole to help keep the inserts straight while they are being inserted. See **figure 4-3** and **photo 4-12**.

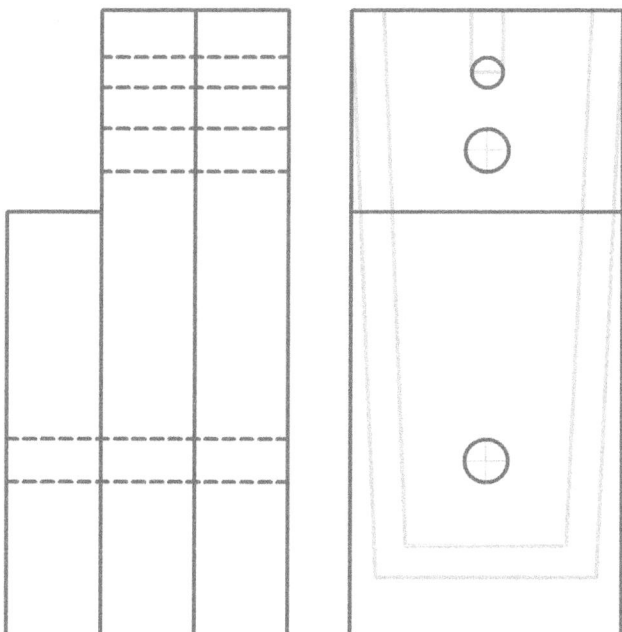

Figure 4-3 – Schematic side view and front view of the shop-built jig used to fit the threaded inserts. The jig is made from three pieces of melamine-covered particle board, taped together with double-sided tape. The jig is sized to be the same height and width as the untrimmed heel of the neck, which is probably longer than its finished length at this point in construction. Note in the front view that the heel template is superimposed over the surface of the jig, and that the jig is longer than the template. Two holes are drilled through the jig, which will serve as bushings to guide the drilling of the pilot holes for the threaded inserts. A third hole (topmost hole) is also drilled through. This one is used as a bushing to guide the insertion tool for the inserts.

Photo 4-12 – The completed threaded-insert fitting jig. The thinner end with the two holes is the fretboard end of the jig.

Photo 4-13 – The three parts of the jig. The part resting on the other two is shorter in length. Centerlines are drawn on all surfaces of all pieces.

Materials
  Neck assembly
  Heel end template
  ¾" (19.1mm) thick melamine board
  Double–sided tape
  80-grit PSA sandpaper
  ¼"-20 x 4" bolt
Tools
  Brad point drill bit for threaded insert (see text)
  ¼" brad point drill bit
  awl

---

1. A strip of ¾" (19.1mm) thick melamine board is cut the same width as the heel and approximately 16" (406.4mm) long. When this is cut using the table saw, the simplest way to get the width to be the same as the heel is to trap the heel between fence and saw blade, then lock the fence and remove the neck assembly. Two pieces are cut from this length, each as long as the heel. A shorter piece is also cut. The card stock heel template is placed on the heel end as in **photo 4-6**. The distance from the bottom of the heel up the centerline to a point ½" (12.7mm) beneath the center of the *upper* insert on the template is measured. This is the length the third piece of melamine board is cut to.

2. Longitudinal centerlines are marked on all surfaces on all three pieces, including on both ends (**photo 4-13**).

3. Double-sided tape is applied to cover one broad surface of one of the long pieces. The two long pieces are stuck together so their mating surfaces are perfectly aligned, yielding essentially one thicker rectangular block (**figure 4-4.1**). This assembly is most easily done by clamping a large rectangular block of wood to the table saw table, butt against the table saw fence. The two pieces of melamine board are assembled working in the corner between fence and wood block (**photo 4-14**). Once stuck together, the pieces are clamped in the vise to apply pressure to the adhesive of the double-sided tape (**photo 4-15**). This sets the adhesive.

4. The card stock heel template is placed on one of the broad melamine covered surfaces of the block, with its top edge aligned with the edge of the block and its centerline aligned with that of the block as well. The template is taped in place with a couple of small pieces of masking tape. Using an awl, the centers of the threaded inserts are pricked right through the template into the melamine (**photo 4-16**). The tape and card stock template are removed.

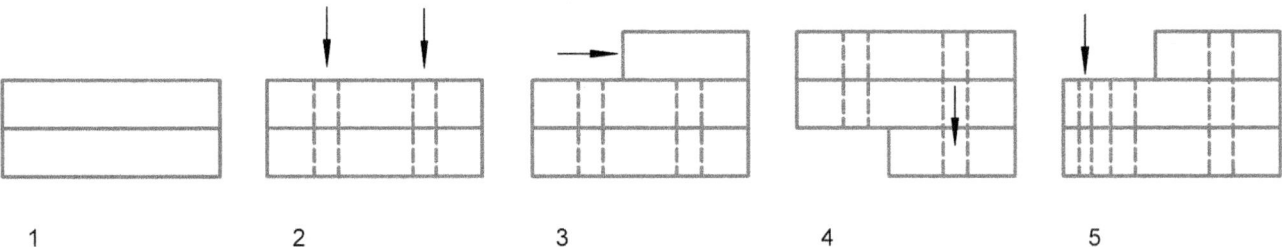

Figure 4-4 – *Assembly of the threaded insert fitting jig. 1. The two long pieces are laminated together. 2. The holes which will serve as guides for drilling the pilot holes in the neck heel are drilled through the jig. 3. The shorter piece is laminated to the rest of the jig. 4. The jig is flipped over, and the lower guide hole is continued through the added shorter piece. 5. The jig is flipped over, and the hole which will serve to guide the threaded insert insertion tool is drilled through the jig.*

5. 80-grit PSA sandpaper is stuck to the opposite surface of the block and trimmed (**photo 4-17**). The sandpaper helps to hold the jig in place on the heel during use.

6. The drill press is fitted with a brad point bit of the appropriate diameter for a pilot hole for the threaded inserts that will be used. The block is placed sandpaper side down on a backing board on the drill press table. Through holes are drilled through the block at the pricked centers (**figure 4-4.2**).

The exact drill bit size specified by the manufacturer of the threaded inserts *must* be used. Depending on the insert, the drill bit may be sized in $\frac{1}{32}$″ or $\frac{1}{64}$″.

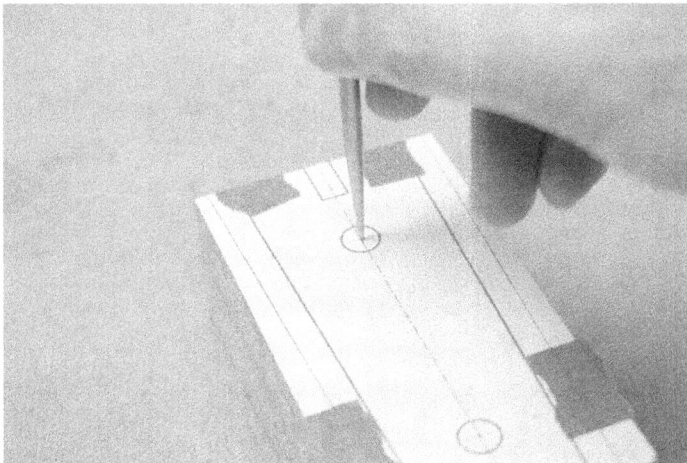

Photo 4-16 – *The template is aligned with the top edge of the block and the block centerline, and taped in place. The template will probably not be as long as the block, because the template is as long as the finished heel of the guitar, and the block is the length of the heel in its current state. Hole centers for the inserts are pricked right through the template using an awl.*

Photo 4-14 – *A rectangular block of wood is clamped down to the table saw extension table, flush against the fence. The block and the fence provide an inside corner which is used to align the two pieces of the jig.*

Photo 4-15 – *The assembly is clamped in the vise to set the adhesive of the double-sided tape that hold the pieces together.*

Photo 4-17 – *PSA sandpaper is attached to the opposite surface of the block. This helps prevent the jig from sliding around in use.*

Although a set of brad point drill bits is a requirement for lutherie work, not every shop will have a set of such finely denominated bits. In that case, and if the drill press quill has adequate travel, the following method can be used to drill the holes.

The twist bit needed to drill the pilot hole for the inserts is selected. A brad point bit that is approximately the same overall *length* as the twist bit is also selected. It doesn't matter what the diameter of the brad point bit is, because it will be used only to center the work. The brad point bit is chucked into the drill press, the block is positioned on the drill press table with a backing board, and the height of the drill press table is adjusted so the distance between the point of the bit and the top surface of the block to be drilled is enough so that the bit can be removed from the chuck without moving table or block. The table is locked. The block is centered to drill one of the holes by raising it up by hand until the point of the bit engages the pricked center mark, holding the block in place against the bit point while lowering the drill press quill to pin the block to the backing board, and holding it pinned in place while clamping it in place with the drill press table clamp. The work is now centered for drilling the hole. Without moving the table or the work, the brad point bit is removed from the chuck and replaced with the twist bit that will be used to drill the hole. The hole is drilled through the block. The process is repeated for the other hole.

7. Double-sided tape is used to attach the final, shorter, piece to the front of the block (the surface that is not covered with sandpaper), aligned with the bottom and side edges (**figure 4-4.3**). This will cover up the lower drilled hole. The assembly is clamped in the vise to set the adhesive of the tape. PSA sandpaper is applied to the surface of this piece and then trimmed.

8. The jig is flipped over, then using the lower pilot hole as an alignment guide, the drill press is used to drill the lower hole through this short piece (**figure 4-4.4, photo 4-18**).

9. The jig is placed on the bench with the long part down and the shorter part up. The awl is used to prick a center roughly halfway between the top edge and the top of the upper pilot hole along the centerline on the remaining surface without PSA. This can be eyeballed. The drill press is used to drill a ¼" hole through the block at this center (**figure 4-4.5**). The jig is now complete, as seen in **photo 4-12**.

10. An insertion tool is made by cutting the head off a ¼"-20 × 4" long bolt with a hacksaw, then filing or grinding the rough edges of the bolt shaft smooth. A handle is made from wood scrap so the insertion tool can be pressed down in use. A blind ¼" hole is drilled in the center of one surface of this handle block. The hole will be used to engage the end of the insertion tool. See **photo 4-19**.

☐ **Drilling Pilot Holes for the Threaded Inserts**

The two larger diameter holes in the threaded-insert fitting jig will be used as bushings to guide a drill bit to drill blind pilot holes in the heel, for installation of the threaded inserts. Because the jig is made of such flimsy material, these bushing

Photo 4-18 – Using the hole drilled through two thicknesses of MDF as a guide, the lower hole is continued through the smaller part of the jig.

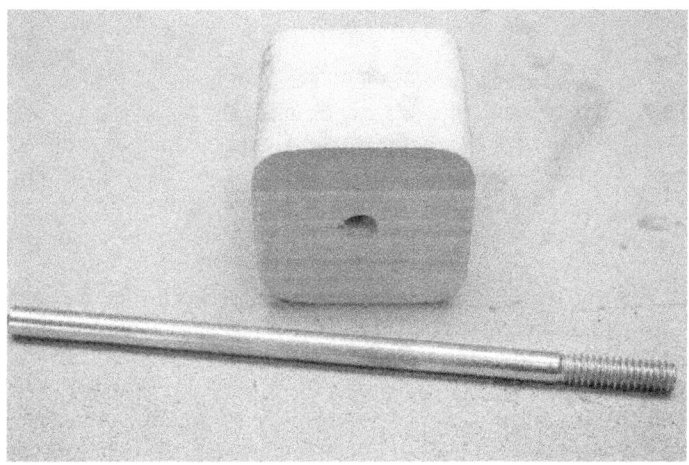

Photo 4-19 – The insertion tool for the threaded inserts (foreground) is made by sawing the head off a bolt. A wood handle is also fashioned that can be used to apply pressure to the end of the insertion tool during use.

Photo 4-20 – The jig is positioned as shown and its edges are aligned with those of the heel, then it is clamped in place. A twist drill bit of the appropriate diameter for the threaded inserts to be used is dropped into the bushing hole in the jig for the upper insert. A stack of feeler gauges that add up to the depth of the point of the drill bit are placed as shown, and then one of the threaded inserts is placed on top of that. The drill bit is marked for depth with masking tape, so the bottom edge of the tape is in line with the top surface of the insert. If a drill bit stop collar is available for the bit, it can be used in place of the tape depth marker.

holes will wear quickly, but when used with care they will be suitable for a single use. Note that the smaller diameter hole in the jig is *not* used in this operation.

Materials
    Neck assembly
    Masking tape
    Threaded inserts
Tools
    Clamps
    Threaded insert fitting jig
    Handheld drill
    Twist bit sized for threaded insert pilot hole (see text)
    Drill bit stop collar for above, if available
    Automotive feeler gauges

---

1. The neck assembly is clamped in the vise with the body contact surface of the heel up and level.

2. The threaded insert fitting jig is positioned on the heel and clamped down with one or more clamps. The jig is oriented as shown in **photo 4-20** and **figure 4-5.1**, with the thinner end in line with the fretboard surface edge of the neck. The clamp(s) should be positioned to provide drilling access to the bigger hole closest to the fretboard edge.

3. The pilot hole for the upper threaded insert is drilled first. The depth of the hole needed is determined and marked on the drill bit, as follows. The appropriate size twist bit for the pilot hole for the threaded inserts to be used is dropped into the drilled hole in the jig, so its point will be resting on the surface of the pocket on the heel. If one is available, a stop collar for that drill bit is placed onto the bit. A stack of automotive feeler gauges adding up to 0.126″ (6.4mm) is placed next to the drill bit, and one of the threaded inserts in placed on top of the gauges. The stop collar, if one is available, is adjusted so its bottom surface is in line with the top surface of the threaded insert, and then tightened in place. If no stop collar is available, the drill bit is marked with masking tape at the level of the top surface of the threaded insert. It helps when placing the stop collar or the tape to kneel down, so the top of the insert is at eye level. This is a critical measurement. These details are also shown in **photo 4-20**. Insert and feeler gauges are removed, and the bit is removed from the hole.

4. The bit is fitted into a hand held drill. The bit is again inserted in the hole in the jig until it bottoms out. When holding the drill, an attempt should be made to keep the bit as vertical as possible. The bored hole in the jig will guide the bit, but it should be kept in mind that the jig is made of soft material. Then the hole is drilled until the stop collar touches the top of the jig or until the bottom of the marking tape reaches the level of the top surface of the jig (**figure 4-5.2**).

 Note that a conventional twist drill bit tends to pull itself into the hole. This effect is even more pronounced when drilling down vertically. The hole must *not* be drilled too deep. When using a tape depth marker instead of a stop collar, it is critical that the bit *not* be allowed to drill below the level indicated by the tape, which can slip upward if it contacts the top surface of the jig.

5. The stop collar or tape is removed from the bit, and the bit is removed from the drill. Using the other guide hole in the jig, steps 3 and 4 are repeated to drill the pilot hole for the lower threaded insert (**figure 4-5.3**). If the clamp(s) are currently obscuring this hole, it should be repositioned to provide drilling access. Note that this hole in the jig goes through three thicknesses of melamine board, so the drilling depth setup described in step 3 *must* be repeated for this hole.

6. The jig is unclamped from the heel, the neck assembly is unclamped from the vise, and the pilot holes are thoroughly cleaned of all debris.

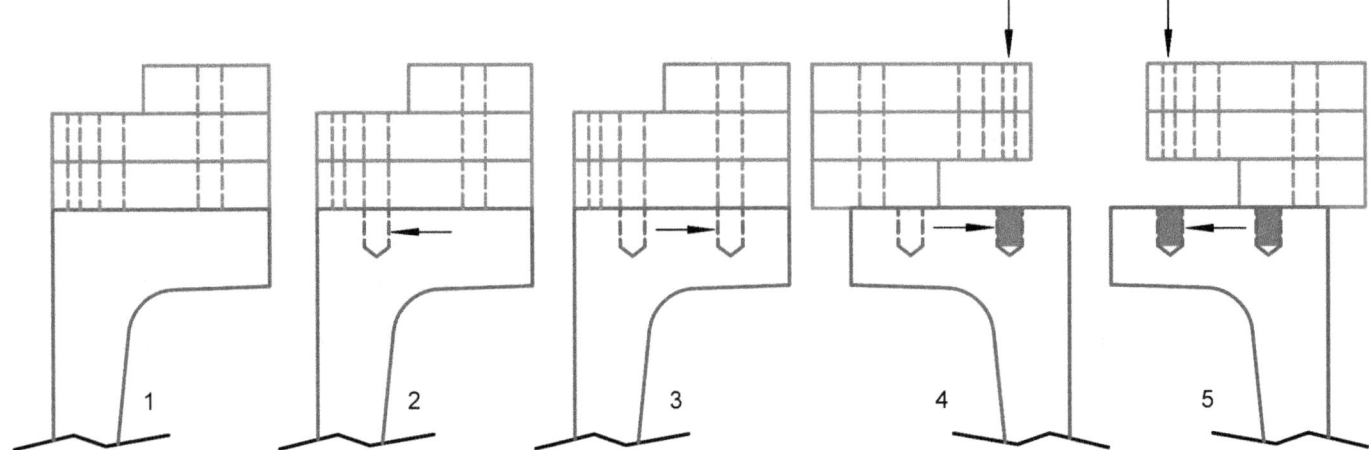

Figure 4-5 – *Using the threaded insert fitting jig. 1. The jig is clamped onto the heel, with the narrow end in line with the fretboard surface of the neck. 2. The pilot hole for the upper threaded insert is drilled in the heel. 3. Without moving the jig, the pilot hole for the lower threaded insert is drilled in the heel. 4. When the threaded inserts are installed, the neck is held in the vise with the heel pointing to the left, and the jig is flipped over. The guide hole in the jig for the insertion tool is positioned over the upper pilot hole when the jig is used to insert the upper threaded insert. 5. The guide hole in the jig for the insertion tool is positioned over the lower pilot hole when the jig is used to insert the lower threaded insert.*

☐ Inserting the Threaded Inserts in the Heel

The jig is flipped over, and used with the insertion tool to insert the threaded inserts into the pilot holes. The jig and tool keep the insert perpendicular to the heel while it is being screwed into place. The stepped underside of the jig provides space for the insert. One hand is used to apply insertion pressure, and the other hand turns a wrench which screws the insert into its bore. The amount of insertion pressure needed depends on the type of insert used. Self-tapping machine inserts require little insertion pressure. The knife edge style of insert requires quite a lot of insertion pressure.

If insufficient insertion pressure is applied to the knife edge style insert, turning the insert will not result in it being screwed into its bore. Instead, the external threads will behave like a drill bit, gouging out wood and enlarging the bore hole, and making it impossible for the insert to be securely inserted. Care must be taken to prevent this from happening.

It is prudent to practice and make one or more test insertions into the end grain of scrap wood of the same species that the neck is made from, to get a feel for the amount of insertion pressure required for proper insertion. The saved cutoff when the neck was trimmed to length is ideal for this.

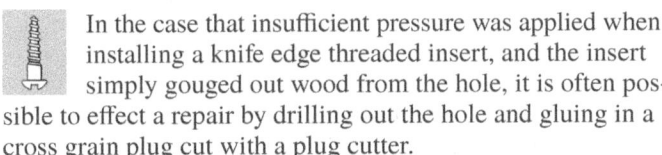

In the case that insufficient pressure was applied when installing a knife edge threaded insert, and the insert simply gouged out wood from the hole, it is often possible to effect a repair by drilling out the hole and gluing in a cross grain plug cut with a plug cutter.

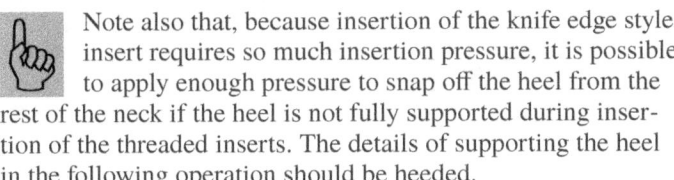

Note also that, because insertion of the knife edge style insert requires so much insertion pressure, it is possible to apply enough pressure to snap off the heel from the rest of the neck if the heel is not fully supported during insertion of the threaded inserts. The details of supporting the heel in the following operation should be heeded.

Materials
    Neck assembly
    Threaded inserts
    ¼"-20 nut and ¼" flat washer
    Thin cyanoacrylate glue
Tools
    Clamps
    Threaded insert fitting jig
    Threaded insert insertion tool
    Small square
    Open end wrench to turn nut
    Pliers

---

1. The insert nearest the fretboard end of the heel will be inserted first. The neck assembly is clamped in the vise with the heel end up and level. It is important that the vise is actually holding the sides of the entire heel, to prevent the heel from being snapped off during insertion of the threaded insert. In

Photo 4-21 – The neck assembly is clamped in the vise so the vise is fully clamping the sides of the heel. In this photo, the neck shaft is inside the right side of the vise jaws, and the bottom of the heel points to the left. The jig is flipped over for use in inserting the threaded inserts. In this photo, the insert nearest the fretboard is being inserted. The insertion tool is being pressed down with the wood handle on top during insertion. This pressure causes the insert to screw into the wood, rather than gouge wood out of the hole.

Photo 4-22 – The nut, washer, and threaded insert are threaded onto the insertion tool.

Photo 4-23 – A small square is used to check to be sure the shaft of the insertion tool is perpendicular to the top surface of the jig.

photo 4-21, the heel is *fully* clamped in the vise, and is pointing to the left.

2. A nut and washer are threaded onto the insertion tool. Enough thread is left showing so it will go about halfway into the insert. An insert is threaded on and tightened against the

Photo 4-24 – The nut is turned with an open end wrench. Pressure on the top of the insertion tool, plus turning the nut, screws the insert into the wood of the heel. Pressure on the top of the insertion tool must be maintained while the nut is turned. Care is taken to avoid trying to thread the insert deeper into the hole than there is room for it. As soon as the insert bottoms out in the hole, turning stops.

Photo 4-25 – The clamping configuration to use when inserting the threaded insert located near the bottom of the heel. There must be clearance for the clamp that holds the jig to the heel, but the heel must also be supported to prevent it from being snapped off if a lot of downward pressure is needed to insert the threaded insert. The heel is supported by a large block of scrap wood spanning the tops of the vise jaws, and wedges of wood as shown.

washer and nut by hand (**photo 4-22**). The insert is positioned vertically into the fretboard end pilot hole, then the ¼" hole in the jig is slipped over the shaft of the insertion tool, and the jig is positioned aligned with the sides of the heel. The shaft of the insertion tool should be vertical. This is checked with small square if necessary (**photo 4-23**). The jig is lightly clamped down with a single clamp as shown in **photo 4-21**, repositioned for verticality of the insertion tool if necessary, and then the clamp is tightened.

3. The handle is placed on top of the insertion tool shaft. Pressure is applied to the handle with one hand, while the other is used to turn the nut using the open end wrench (**photo 4-24**), driving and screwing the insert into the heel. Turning and pressing is continued until the washer *just* touches the floor of the heel. It is critical that the insert *not* be over tightened, as this will simply strip out wood and weaken the joint.

4. The clamp is removed and the jig is lifted off the shaft of the insertion tool. The shaft of the insertion tool is held firmly with pliers and the wrench is used to back off the nut. Then the insertion tool is threaded out of the threaded insert.

5. The neck assembly is removed from the vise.

6. The threaded insert near the bottom of the heel is inserted next. Providing support under the heel to prevent it from being snapped off with insertion pressure, while also providing access to the clamp that holds the jig in place, requires a different hold in the vise. Here, the heel is raised up above the top of the vise a few inches, so the vise is only clamped to the neck shaft. A thick block of scrap wood is bridged across the jaws of the vise and under the bottom of the heel. Wedges are placed between the block and the heel bottom, to support the heel and prevent downward insertion pressure from breaking the heel off. But space must be provided to position the clamp that will hold the jig in place on the heel, too. **Photo 4-25** shows this arrangement.

7. Steps 2 through 5 are repeated to install this threaded insert. The jig and insertion tool are removed. The installed inserts are pictured in **Photo 4-26**.

8. Thin cyanoacrylate glue is wicked between the threaded inserts and the wood surrounding them. This helps bind any wood that may have been loosened during the insertion operations. The glue is allowed to cure for a few hours before any attempt is made to screw bolts into the inserts, to prevent the possibility of the bolts getting glued into the inserts.

9. A ¼"-20 bolt is test threaded into each of the inserts to be sure there is no cyanoacrylate glue on the threads that will prevent a bolt from fully seating. If glue did get on the threads, it can be removed by running a tap in and out of each insert.

Photo 4-26 – Both threaded inserts inserted. The top surfaces of the threaded inserts end up approximately flush with the floor of the pocket in the heel. It is sometimes the case that the tops of the inserts end up a bit above the level of the floor.

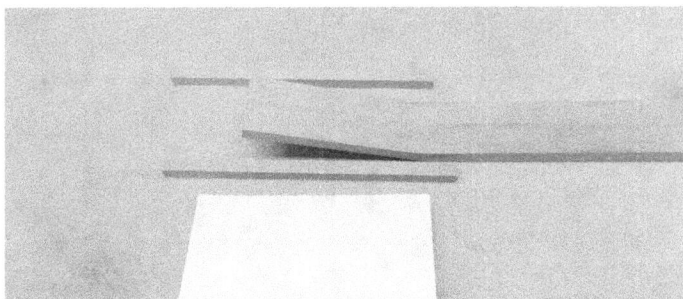

Photo 4-27 – The headstock end of the neck assembly and the two headstock ears. In the foreground is a melamine assembly board that will be used to keep all pieces aligned during gluing.

Attaching Headstock Ears

It is often the case that the neck blank is fashioned to be wide enough to cover the neck shaft and heel, but not quite wide enough to cover the width of the headstock, which is almost always wider than the rest of the neck assembly. The conventional way to deal with this is to extend the width of the headstock part only, with the addition of two headstock ears. These are simply small pieces of wood that are glued to the sides of the headstock. They can usually be fashioned out of the cutoffs from earlier trimming operations on the neck, but in any case should be fashioned from wood of the same species as the rest of the neck.

As is the case with all gluing and clamping operations, it is wise to do a dry run, to be sure all the right clamps are on hand and all can be placed before the glue begins to cure.

☐ Fashioning and Attaching the Headstock Ears

1. Two ears are fashioned out of the same wood species as used for the rest of the neck. Each of these should be wide enough so that the total width of the headstock part of the neck assembly will be enough to cover the finished width of the headstock. The headstock template from the template book can be used to check. For the example instruments, the ears should be approximately ½″ (12.7mm) wide. The ears should be fashioned to be exactly the same thickness as the headstock, if possible. If this is not possible, their thickness *must* err on the thick side. It is convenient if the ears are made as long as the headstock is. In case that is not possible, they must be made long enough (and, eventually glued in place where needed) to cover the widest part of the headstock. And they have to be at least long enough to be able to be clamped with two clamps. **Photo 4-27** shows the headstock and the two ears ready for gluing.

2. Because the plane of the top surface of the headstock must be retained, the ears will be glued to the headstock with the headstock top surface and ears all clamped down to a flat glue-proof piece of melamine board. The first step is to use one long and one standard length clamp to clamp the headstock face down on the melamine board. It helps to use a third clamp to prop up the neck shaft (**photo 4-28**).

3. Glue is applied to the gluing surfaces of the ears, and the ears are pressed in place on the sides of the headstock. Two clamps are used to clamp the ears to the headstock. These are placed and lightly clamped. One, or if there is room, two clamps are used to press each ear to the melamine assembly

Photo 4-28 – One long clamp and one standard length clamp are used to clamp the top of the headstock flat against the assembly board. On the right, a third clamp is used to prop up the neck shaft, to keep the headstock flat to the bench top.

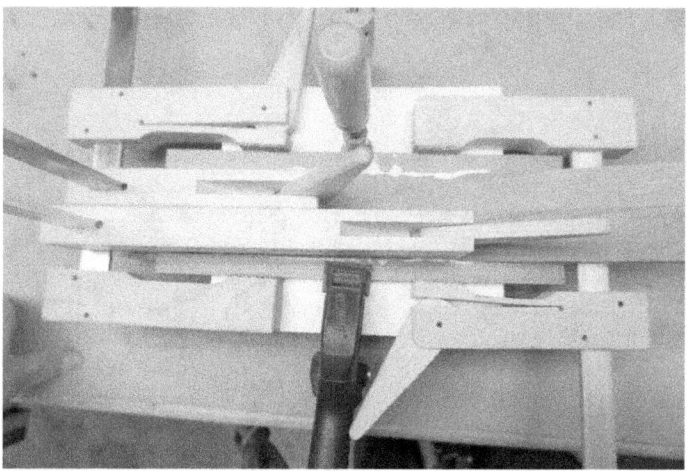

Photo 4-29 – Looking down on the clamping configuration for the headstock ears. Two clamps are used to clamp the ears to the sides of the headstock (left, right). One clamp is used to clamp each of the ears down to the assembly board. In the photo the far ear is clamped down with a bar clamp and the near ear is clamped down with a spring clamp.

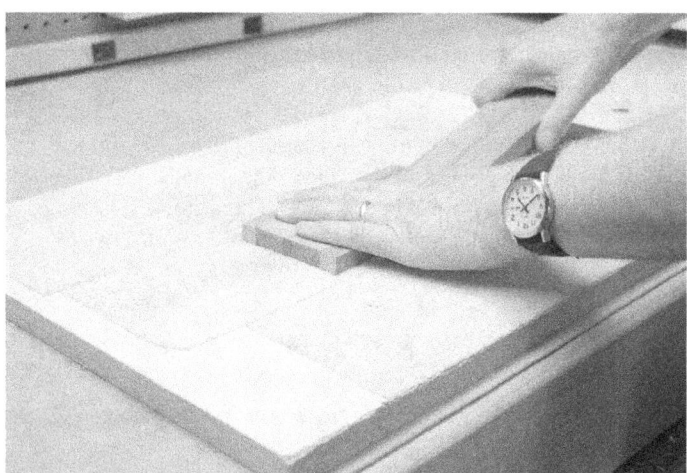

Photo 4-30 – Glue squeeze-out is cleaned from the headstock top surface using the sanding board.

Photo 4-31 – Re-scribing the location of the headstock side of the nut, following sanding of the top surface of the headstock.

Photo 4-32 – Glue squeeze-out is cleaned from the headstock back surface using sandpaper on a flat block.

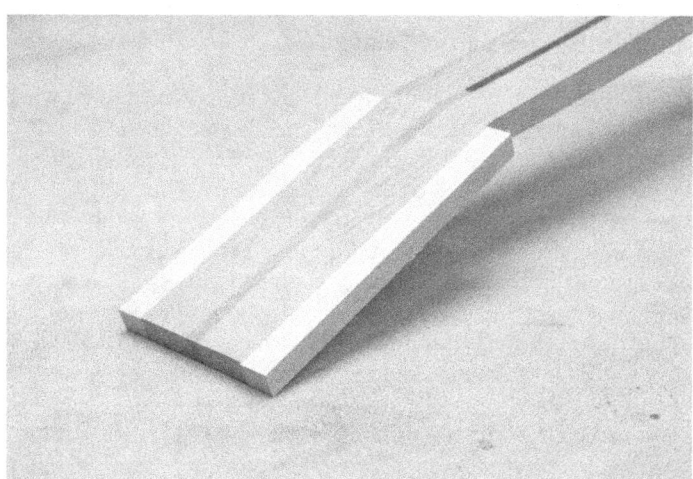

Photo 4-33 – Headstock with ears attached.

board (**photo 4-29**). These are also initially lightly clamped. Once all clamps are in position, they are successively tightened. The contact between ears and assembly board is checked again to be sure it is tight along the full length of both ears. Glue is allowed to cure for at least 2 hours before clamps are removed.

4. Glue squeeze-out is removed and the top surface of the headstock is flattened, using the sanding board (**photo 4-30**). Care should be taken to avoid obliterating the scribed line denoting the headstock side of the nut. If this line is damaged, it is refreshed using an awl and square (**photo 4-31**).

5. The back side of the headstock is flattened using sandpaper on a hard block (**photo 4-32**). The headstock with ears installed is pictured in **photo 4-33**.

---

1. Doolin, Mike; Fleishman, Harry. (2006) Modern Approaches to Adjustable Neck Joints. *American Lutherie #86*, p. 24.

2. Mottola, R.M. (2010) Testing Threaded Inserts. *American Lutherie #101* p. 54.

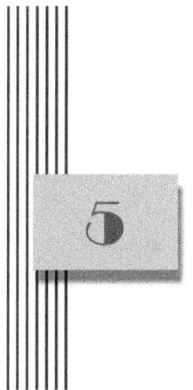

5. The Headplate and Decoration

The *headplate* is a thin piece of wood that covers the front of the headstock. Although this feature does not appear on all guitars, it does appear on most high end instruments. It is both functional and decorative. The two construction options presented earlier for roughing out the neck are strengthened by the addition of the headplate. When the neck is sawn from a solid block, there is short grain all along the headstock which is relatively easy to crack if the guitar suffers a blow in that area. The headplate helps to strengthen this short grain. And if neck construction involves scarf jointing the headstock on as a separate piece, the headplate glued over the scarf joint adds strength to this joint as well.

From a decorative perspective the headplate can provide a nice visual detail to the guitar if a particularly attractive piece of wood is used for this purpose. If the headstock will feature a decorative inlay, the headplate provides the "canvas" for that inlay. Often one or more sheets of *headplate veneer* are added between headstock and headplate, and these will show as decorative stripes on the sides of the headstock of the finished guitar.

The general construction of the headplate and headplate veneers are shown in **figure 5-1**. Note that the nut end of the headplate is mitered so it is perpendicular to the fretboard surface of the neck. This and the nut end of the fretboard form a channel into which the nut is mounted. **Photos 5-1** and **5-2** show the headplate of one of the guitars built during the development of the construction process described in this book. The headplate of this guitar features a simple understated inlay of a stylized letter "M", which I use to inlay most of my instruments.

I will point out that there are all sorts of decoration possible, but here I am only discussing additions to the headstock that identify the builder in some way. These are usually limited to the builder's name, or a logo or logotype monogram. Electric guitar luthier, author and educator Leonardo Lospennato mentions in his book *Electric Guitar and Bass Making and Marketing* that the headstock logo of most instruments is simply some form of the builder's name. This is certainly true for acoustic guitars as well. Some such guitars made in small shops often use a stylized form of the builder's monogram on the headstock, and occasionally you'll also see a simple pictorial logo.

The history and practice of headstock decoration is interesting. Baroque period guitars generally did not feature headstock identification, although the shape and style of the headstock would often identify the builder. This is still the case today with classical and flamenco guitars. Guitars from the 19th century also rarely included builder-identifying headstock markings.

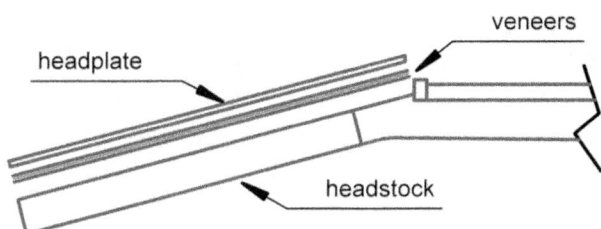

Figure 5-1 – *Schematic side view of headstock showing application of the headplate and the headplate veneers.*

Photo 5-1 – *The headplate of the Paura dreadnought style example guitar. The headplate is made of a decorative piece of black cherry (Prunus serotina) and includes a simple wood inlay of a stylized letter "M."*

Photo 5-2 – Side view of a headplate showing a single black headplate veneer.

There are some examples of instruments that included identifying marks stamped on the headstock, but if this was done it was invariably done on the back of the headstock.

Headstock front identification decoration really began in earnest in the early 20th century. Higher priced instruments with such markings were generally done using shell inlay, and lower priced instruments made do with silk screened *waterslip decals*. Shell inlay is done by cutting thin sheets of shell, such as mother of pearl or abalone, and then sawing shaped pieces out of these sheets with a fine saw. Pockets are excavated in the wood of the headplate, into which these shapes are fitted and glued. The inevitable small gaps between the inlay and the walls of the pocket are filled with pigmented filler to match the wood. Because shell inlay was done completely by hand, it was a time consuming process even when the inlay shapes were simple and small.

In contrast, the manufacture of waterslip decals was done in quantity. Sheets of heavy paper were sprayed with a thin coating of hide glue and allowed to dry. These were then silk screened with clear lacquer in the outline of the decal. If the decal was small then many identical outlines would be screened onto each sheet at the same time. The decal image was built up with the addition of successive colors of paint, also silk screened on and allowed to dry. To apply a decal it was simply cut from the sheet, dipped in warm water to soften the glue, then slipped off the paper backing onto the finished headplate.

These two forms of decoration continued to dominate through the century. Later advances in printing provided a lot more options for mass manufactured guitars. At the time of printing of this book, many low priced guitars feature identifying decoration that is printed directly to the headstock using UV cured pigments deposited by a printer designed to print directly to a surface. Inlay of shell material and other materials is also still common for guitars that sell at a higher price. Whereas in the past this type of inlay was done by hand, it is now done by CNC machines, which cut the inlay and the pocket into which it fits.

There are a wide variety of options for the implementation of headstock decoration. But the following discussion is limited to only those options that are readily available to the novice builder of guitars. Not discussed here are decoration options that can really only be cost effective in a production environment. Available options fall into two general categories: those that can be performed in the shop, and those that can be readily

and inexpensively contracted out. Note that each of the options presented has advantages and disadvantages, and also presents limitations to what decoration is possible. In some cases even the wood that can be used for the headplate is limited by the decoration option. For these reasons it is probably prudent to be familiar with all of these options, and then select one accordingly. In the following sections these options are discussed in a general way. Specific construction details appear in later sections of this chapter.

No Decoration Option

As mentioned, this was the choice for many years of acoustic guitar history. Advantages of this option are that any wood species can be used for the headplate, and this is by far the simplest, least inexpensive, and least time-consuming approach.

Clear Stickers Printed in the Shop Option

Anyone with a computer and inkjet printer can print a design onto the modern equivalent of waterslip decals, clear label stock, which can then be cut out and applied onto the headstock of the finished instrument. More finish is then applied on top of the label to protect it. The features of the design can be quite detailed, thin, and can have sharp points. There are some limitations inherent to this option though. Probably the most important one is that before a logo decal can be made, the artwork must be drawn using computer drawing software. For folks that are familiar with such software this is not a barrier. Fortunately for everyone else some drawing software is quite easy to learn, so this shouldn't be a barrier to anyone.

An important limitation to the use of clear stickers for headplate decoration is that the headplate must be made of wood which is light in color, such as one of the maples. Computer printer ink depends on a white or very light background if it is to be at all visible. See **photo 5-3**. In addition to being restricted to light wood backgrounds, the artwork must generally be drawn using darker colors.

Decals were traditionally used for less expensive instruments and so are always appropriate for reproductions of less expensive instruments, or instruments that attempt to attain that particular aesthetic. Contemporary guitar luthier Todd Cambio from Madison, Wisconsin, builds a line of instruments that hearken back aesthetically to the budget instruments produced by American factories in the early 20th century. Use of decals

Photo 5-3 – The headstock of a solid body electric guitar built by the author, decorated with a computer printed image on clear label stock. The headplate must be made of a light colored wood and the image color must be fairly dark for this to work. If the label stock is truly clear, its edges disappear when finish is applied over the label.

on the headstock and for other decoration help to attain this vibe.

White Stickers Printed in the Shop Option

Printing onto opaque white plastic label stock provides an advantage and a disadvantage compared to the use of clear label stock. The advantage is that the printed image is backed up by white, so any colors can be used, not just dark colors. The disadvantage is that any part of the finished design that is not covered by ink will show as white. One of the ramifications of this is that the insides of letters that enclose space, like "B", "O", and "Q" for example, will show white unless some other color is explicitly applied there. See **figure 5-2**. The other issue is that when cutting out the design from the label stock, the outline must be accurately cut, to eliminate any white from the outer edges of the design. The latter is all but impossible except for designs that have very simple outlines. For practical purposes what this means is that this option requires the design to have a simple and easy-to-cut outline.

Contracted Vinyl Decals or Stickers Option

A brief overview of the traditional method of manufacturing decals was previously presented. These days, decals and stickers are made commercially using special printers that print onto sheets of paper-backed vinyl and also cut out the outline of the image. These printers are expensive and so are not often found in a typical small woodworking shop or in most people's homes. But short-run vinyl printing services are readily available that can inexpensively print decals or stickers from the customer's artwork. This option provides all the same advantages as printing onto white plastic label stock in the shop, with the added advantage that the process can also accurately cut out the outline of the design. This makes it possible to make a design with a more complex outline than could be cut out by the luthier with a knife. There are limitations to how finely this cutting works, so it is a good idea to send artwork to the shop and ask how accurately the outline will be cut.

CNC Inlay Option

CNC machines are ubiquitous in guitar factories of every size and are becoming more common in the shops of individual builders. Most commercial small CNC routers are suitable for cutting inlays from shell, wood, and plastic sheet material, and can also rout the pocket into the headplate as well. This option is available even to shops without the equipment. These days

About Shell Inlay Materials

There are many varieties of shell material available for use in inlay work. The most commonly used in lutherie are mother of pearl (MOP) and abalone. Lutherie suppliers and specialist shell inlay material suppliers offer shell slices for inlay work. For the inlay work described here, the slices should be about 0.05″ (1.3MM) thick. These come as rectangular pieces that are a bit over 1″ (25.4MM) square, although bigger pieces are often available from some suppliers.

The size of the slices available imposes restrictions on the size of the design of course. For bigger designs, the options are to build the design up of smaller strokes, each of which can be cut out separately, or to put together a blank made of smaller pieces of shell edged together. It is often difficult to match the pieces for color, pattern, and chatoyancy unless a large assortment of pieces is available. It is especially difficult to match MOP. Fortunately, specialty shell inlay material suppliers can usually supply matched pieces on request.

A far easier solution for larger designs is to use laminated shell sheets which are available in quite large sizes. These are made of flaked abalone and polyester resin, and are available from most luthier suppliers.

Shell can be CNC cut using conventional carbide end mills. It is hand cut using standard jeweler's saw blades. Much care must be taken when hand sawing shell because it is brittle and delicate and so is easily cracked. Cracked pieces of MOP are generally discarded. There is really no way to repair the crack. But cracked pieces of abalone can usually be glued back together with cyanoacrylate glue. Because abalone has a fine multicolored pattern and because when it breaks it usually breaks on one of the lines between colors, repairs in abalone are almost always completely invisible. Laminated abalone sheets are quite tough and resistant to cracking during sawing. Cracks that do happen can also be repaired with cyanoacrylate glue

Figure 5-2 – Example showing issues with printing onto white label stock. In the left figure the letter was printed onto white plastic and then the outline was tediously trimmed. But the interior area shows the white color of the label stock. In the right figure the design includes the same letter on a simple circular field. The color of the field shows in the interior of the letter, and because the field is such a simple shape it is easy to cut the entire design out of the label stock.

Photo 5-4 – Inlay and pocket cut with a CNC router. The inlay is made of two pieces of MOP butted together. The pocket is cut by the machine to fit the inlay exactly. Neither inlay nor pocket have any sharp corner points, the radii of the corners being limited by that of the bit used to cut the inlay out. Note also that in addition to routing the pocket for the inlay, the machine also routed the outline of the headstock and the centers for drilling the holes for the tuning machines.

Photo 5-5 – *Features of a design cut by a CNC machine can be quite narrow, but cannot be any narrower than the diameter of the bit used to do the cutting. Here an outline version of my monogram logo is cut from abalone shell. The outline and the pocket are less than 0.031″ (0.8mm) wide.*

there are a number of services that provide custom CNC work to small shops at reasonable cost. In general when contracting for this service, the luthier provides the artwork (generally just the outline(s) of the inlay) and selects a headplate and shell material, and the shop will cut the inlay piece(s) and pocket(s) and send them. **Photo 5-4** shows a CNC cut headplate pocket from one of my instruments and the inlay that will go into it.

Shell inlay is traditionally found on high end guitars, and as such it is particularly appealing for handcrafted instruments. This process was traditionally done mostly by hand and so it was expensive and imprecise. The use of CNC machines makes the process far simpler and far less laborious. In general, any kind of wood can be used for the headplate. There are limitations to doing this using CNC routers. The biggest limitation is imposed by the diameter of the cutting bit used to cut the inlay and the pocket. No feature of the inlay can be narrower than the diameter of the cutting bit. And no point of the design can be sharper than the radius of the cutting bit either. Although most CNC routers can manage a 0.031″ (0.8MM) diameter bit without breaking it, some precision machines can use bits of even smaller diameter (**Photo 5-5**).

Hand Cut Inlay Option

This is the way shell inlay was traditionally done before machine cutting technology became available. There are still luthiers that do inlay this way, and the results are often spectacular. Instruments by some luthiers like Grit Laskin from Canada and the mother and daughter team of Kathy and Jimmi Wingert in Rancho Palos Verdes, California, are well known for the beauty of their inlay work. The design is cut out of the shell slices by hand, using a jeweler's saw with a fine blade, and then smoothed and refined using files. A shell piece is then traced onto the headplate, and the pocket is excavated using knives, tiny chisels, and a small router with small diameter bits. Alternatively, the design and a through pocket can be cut at the same time, marquetry style, using a jeweler's saw.

The major advantage of this option is that it requires few specialized and expensive tools. But there are many disadvantages. Although experts at hand cut inlay can inlay into almost anything, the lutherie novice with no prior experience in this technique should probably use only solid black headplate material such as black ebony or black phenolic impregnated wood. When the inevitable gaps between the inlay and the hand cut pocket are subsequently filled with black filler they become nearly invisible, resulting in a much neater looking job than if any other headplate color is used.

There are also limits to the size and shape of the features that can be cut by hand, particularly by a novice. Long, skinny pieces, and pieces with long runs of parallel lines are particularly difficult to cut by hand. Designs suitable for implementation in hand cut inlay will take these limitations into account.

Layout and Construction

No matter which decoration option is used, the first construction step is to prepare the headplate and then ascertain the area available for decoration. After this is accomplished one of the decoration options is taken. Each option has its own requirements for drawing, and these are enumerated here. Drawing is assumed to make use of some sort of computer drawing software. Many programs are available, and the following text does not assume any particular one.

Each option also has its own construction details of course. Note that for the options that involve printed stickers, these are printed but they are not applied at this time. Application will

Photo 5-6 – *Guitar with individual tuning machines.*

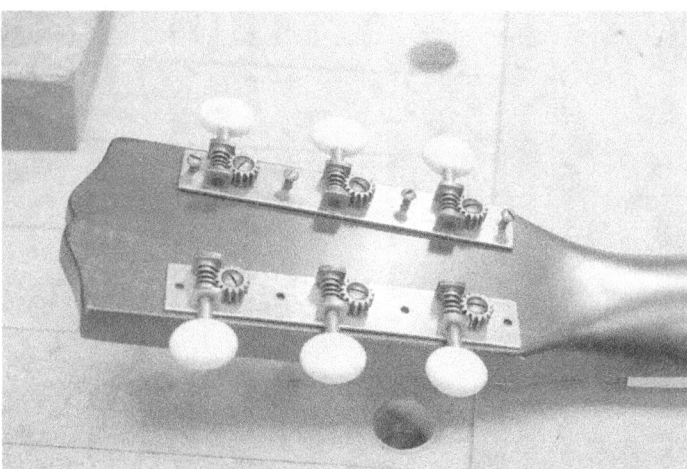

Photo 5-7 – *Guitar with three-on-a-plate tuning machines being installed*

happen much later in the construction process, as a step during the finishing of the instrument. Although it is possible to put off drawing and printing the stickers as well, it is advisable to do that now, just to be sure the label will fit.

Likewise for the inlay options. These are done now, and before the headplate is attached to the neck assembly, to be sure that they can be accomplished as planned. If an option is attempted at this time but the results are not satisfactory, the attempt can be made again, or a different option can be tried. The most that will be wasted (other than the builder's time and effort) by an unsatisfactory attempt at headplate decoration is a relatively inexpensive headplate.

Headplate Preparation and Layout

Selecting a headplate material is based on what decoration option is chosen. When the decoration will be printed onto a clear sticker, the headplate must be of some light colored wood such as one of the maples (*Acer* spp). If the decoration will be a hand cut inlay, the headplate should be black in color. This would suggest the use of ebony (*Diospyros* spp.) but unfortunately truly black ebony is rarely available. A better choice is to use a black phenolic impregnated wood headplate, which is truly black in color. If the decoration will be printed onto an opaque white sticker, or if it will be a CNC cut inlay, or if the headplate will remain undecorated, then any species and color of wood can be used for the headplate.

Headplate blanks are available from lutherie wood suppliers. It is a wise idea to buy headplates already planed to a thickness of 3/32″ (2.4MM) because it is a chore to do that work in the shop due to the thinness and small size of the piece. Suppliers also have precut veneers for use between headplate and the rest of the headstock. These veneers are typically 0.02″ (0.5MM) thick. It is typical to use anywhere from zero to three such veneers. How many to use depends on the decorative effect desired. It is typical to place light colored veneers against dark colored wood, and dark colored veneers against light colored wood. So for example, a dark colored headplate over a dark colored headstock would look good with a single light colored veneer, or a sandwich of light/dark/light veneers between them. A light colored headplate and a light colored headstock would look good with a single dark colored veneer or a dark/light/dark sandwich. A light headplate and dark headstock (or the other way around) would look good with an appropriately oriented dark/light veneer combination, or with no veneer at all.

When considering the stripe pattern that the veneers will give to the finished instrument, it is a good idea to think ahead to the *purfling* pattern that will be used to decorate around the guitar's *binding*. These will be implemented using thin precut strips of veneer. Most lutherie suppliers have veneer lines that match some but maybe not all of the headplate veneers they offer.

Typical guitar tuning machines will accommodate total finished headstock thickness (headstock, plus any veneers, plus headplate) of 1/2″ (12.7MM) to 5/8″ (15.9MM). Headplates are typically planed to be 3/32″ (2.4MM) thick. It is a good idea to have the headplate, the veneers, and the tuning machines on hand to be sure that everything will fit *before* the headstock is fully assembled. Having the machines on hand will also help in doing the layout work specified below.

Lutherie suppliers offer a wide variety of guitar tuning machines. Note that the tuning machine spacing on the templates for the two example instruments is suitable for most individual tuning machines (**photo 5-6**), but is *not* suitable for any three-on-a-plate machines (**photo 5-7**) that I know of. The spacing can be modified of course, but my recommendation to the luthier novice is to use individual machines, because the drilling of the holes for individual machines in the headstock is far more forgiving than it is for plated machines.

☐ **Preparing the Headplate**

Materials
    Headplate
    Headplate veneers
    Neck assembly
    Tuning machines
Tools
    Protractor

1. If it is not already, the headplate is planed to a thickness of 3/32″ (2.4MM). Note that this can be done using a hand plane and bench hook. The thicknessing router jig mentioned in Appendix B can also be used.

2. The minimum and maximum total headstock thickness that can be accommodated by the tuning machines is determined by examining (and maybe partially assembling) the machines.

3. The total thickness of headstock, veneers, and headplate are measured to be sure it falls within the range that can be accommodated by the machines. If necessary, the headplate can be thinned to 1/16″ (1.6MM). If the headstock must be further thinned

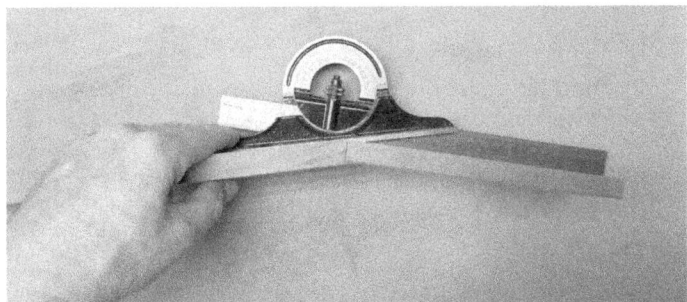

Photo 5-8 – *Measuring headstock angle with a protractor.*

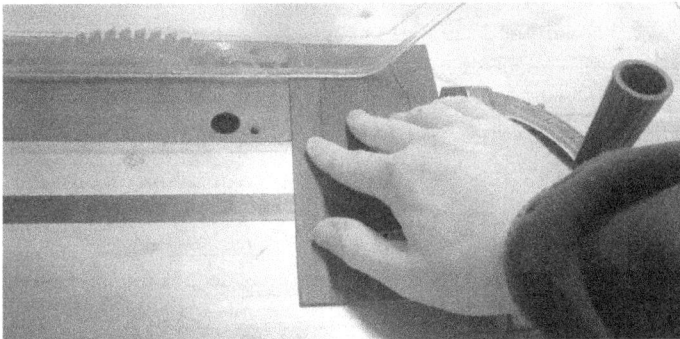

Photo 5-9 – *Sawing the bevel on one end of the headplate, using the table saw with a tilted fined-toothed blade.*

Photo 5-10 – *Trimming the end of the headplate to the angle of the headstock on the disc sander with table tilted.*

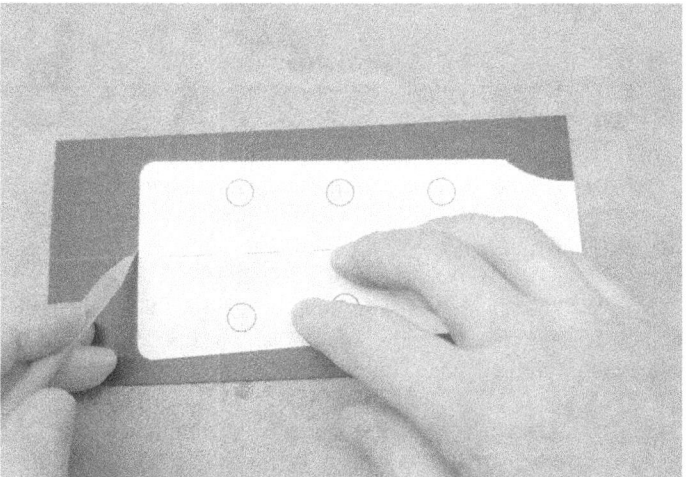

Photo 5-11 – *Tracing the outline of the headstock from the template onto the headplate.*

so the beveled end surface is perpendicular to the fretboard surface of the neck assembly.

□ **Headplate Layout**

In this operation, the bounds of the decoration area are determined for use in drawing the design. Then the headplate is marked for the eventual cutting of the outline of the headplate and the drilling of the holes for the tuning machines. Note that the following layout steps limit the decoration area to that part of the headplate that is above the topmost tuning machines. There is no reason why the decoration area cannot be extended down between the tuning machines as well of course.

Materials
  Headplate
  Headstock template
  Tuning machines
  Masking tape

1. The template page for the example instrument being built containing the headstock template is printed onto card stock and the template is cut out with scissors or knife. Note that the headstock templates for the two example instruments may be substituted for one another if desired.

2. The tuning machines are positioned on top of the template, with the centers of their tuning posts aligned with the post centers on the template. This is done to check to be sure the machines will fit at the locations indicated by the centers on the template.

3. The tuning machines are removed from the template, and the top surface hardware for the two topmost machines are centered over the center marks on the template. The top surface hardware consists of either a press-in or screw-in bushing, and possibly a decorative washer.

4. A horizontal line is drawn across the template approximately ¼″ (6.4mm) above the top surface hardware. This line represents the bottom boundary of the area of the headplate that can be decorated.

5. A line offset from the edges of the upper part of the template approximately ¼″ (6.4mm) is also drawn. This line represents the top and side boundaries of the area of the headplate that can

to meet thickness requirements, material should be taken off the back of the headstock instead.

4. One of the sides of the headplate is ripped or planed straight, to serve as a reference surface.

5. A protractor is used to measure the angle between headstock top surface and fretboard surface of the neck assembly (**photo 5-8**).

6. One end of the headplate is beveled to the angle measured. This operation can be done on the table saw with a fine blade, tilted to the measured angle (**photo 5-9**) or on a disc or belt sander with a tilting table (**photo 5-10**).

7. If the headplate will be used to inlay shell, the top surface of the headplate is sanded up to 150 grit. This is necessary because, once the shell is in place, the headplate cannot be sanded with any coarser grit. Doing so often puts deep scratches in the shell that are difficult or impossible to sand out. Note that the top surface of the headplate is the surface that will be on top when the headplate is temporarily positioned on the headstock

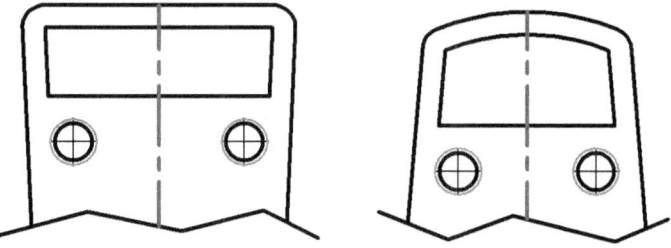

Figure 5-3 – *The area in which the headplate decoration can be placed is drawn on the headstock template. The measurements of this box will be used to limit the size of the decoration when it is drawn.*

Figure 5-4 – The design in this example is just a letter "B." It is drawn inside the black boundary box to be sure it will fit on the headplate. The design is then surrounded by a gray color closed curve, which indicates where the design should be cut when it is cut out from the printed label.

be decorated (**figure 5-3**). The measurements of the bounded area will be used in subsequent drawing operations.

6. A longitudinal centerline is drawn on the top surface of the headplate in pencil. If the headplate is dark in color, a light colored pencil is used. The centerline is continued down the nut end (beveled end) of the headplate.

7. The template is aligned with the nut end of the headplate and its centerline. It may be taped in place if necessary. The outline of the template is traced onto the surface of the headplate (**photo 5-11**).

Clear Plastic Sticker Made in the Shop Option

The decoration is drawn using computer drawing software, then inkjet printed onto clear plastic label stock. A number of label sheets are identified as "clear" but the plastic is actually translucent. Most "clear" address labels are really translucent. These are *not* ideal, because in the finished instrument the edges of the decoration will be visible. The label manufacturer Avery uses the term "Glossy Clear Film" to describe their truly clear labels. In addition to being made of truly clear plastic, the labels must be big enough to accommodate a typically sized headplate design.

Because the design will be printed onto labels, it is necessary that the drawing software used be able to accommodate labels as well. Most label manufacturers make simple drawing software available for use with their label products. This software is usually adequate for generating simple designs for headplate decoration.

☐ **Drawing the Design**

1. The drawing software is set up to use the selected labels.

2. A box representing the area that can be decorated is drawn, using the dimensions from the box that has been drawn on the headstock template in a previous operation.

3. The decoration is drawn so it fits in the box. The decoration must use only dark colors.

4. It is a good idea to draw a line enclosing the entire design. This will be used as a guide when cutting the design out of the printed label (**figure 5-4**).

5. The label is printed on an inkjet printer. Some software allows printing a single label rather than a whole sheet of labels.

6. Scissors or a knife are used to cut the design out of the label.

7. It is wise to preview the design by removing the backing and sticking it onto a piece of wood of the same species as the headplate. If adjustments need to be made to the design, the preview is removed and the above steps are repeated.

8. Once the design is acceptable, a few more labels are printed out. These are put aside until needed during finishing of the instrument.

White Plastic Sticker Made in the Shop Option

The process here is identical to the previous option, but instead of printing on clear label stock the design is printed onto white plastic label stock. The label manufacturer Avery uses the term "Durable White Film" to describe this material. Note the issues described earlier in this chapter with the use of white material. The design should put some color behind any enclosed spaces in lettering. The design should include an easy-to-cut-out field behind any lettering, as shown in **figure 5-2**. No step-by-step description is provided here, because the process is identical to that for shop-made clear plastic stickers.

Contracted White Vinyl Sticker Option

As mentioned, the printers that are used to make commercial labels can trim the outline even if it is fairly complex, so the design may not need to have a simple geometric background field, as is the case for shop-printed white film labels. **Figure 5-5** shows a simple single letter design that can be cut by a professional vinyl printer. Artwork is generated as for the previous two options, but the software should not be set up to print onto a specific label size. Commercial printers can generally print multiple copies of a design per sheet. Some commercial

Figure 5-5 – Even though the outline of the letter is fairly complex, all of the white label film can be trimmed off by a commercial vinyl printer.

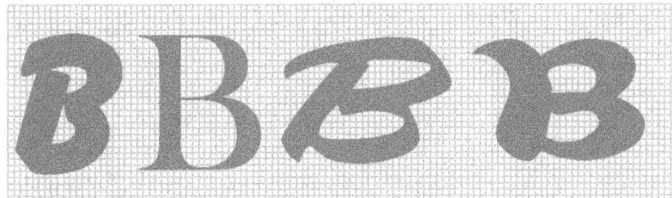

Figure 5-6 – Candidate fonts are previewed over a grid with line spacing that is the same as the diameter of the smallest bit that will be used to cut the inlay and its pocket. Some, like the second from the left are rejected outright because it is apparent there are too many features that are narrower than the grid spacing. The rest of the letters contain sharp points which cannot be rendered, but these can be modified to be less sharp.

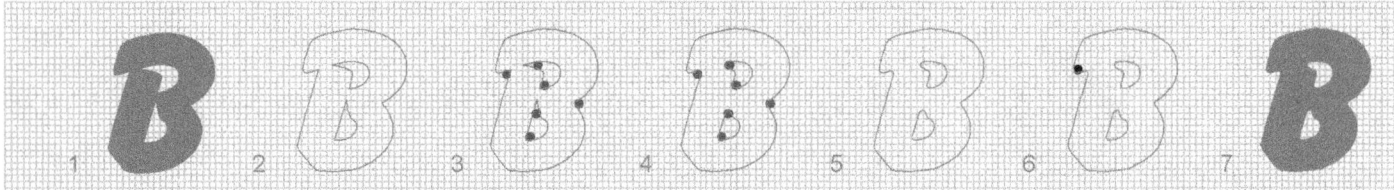

Figure 5-7 – *Steps in the conversion of a text letter into an outline drawing that can be used by a CNC router to cut an inlay and the pocket into which it will be glued. 1. The printed letter is chosen in part because no area of the inlay is narrower than the bit that will be used to cut it, and because it doesn't have too many sharp corners that will need to be rounded. 2. The text is converted to a series of drawn outlines. 3. Small circles with the same diameter as the bit that will be used to cut out the inlay are drawn and placed at all sharp points of the outline of the inlay. 4. The outline is modified to eliminate these sharp points so the cutting bit can reach all places on the outline. 5. The resulting outline. 6. The operations described in 3 and 4 are repeated, but this time for all points or narrow places that would appear in the pocket. 7. The final outline is filled with color so the modified letter can easily be visually compared with the original.*

printers provide instructions for preparing your artwork on their websites, and these instructions should guide the drawing of the design.

CNC Inlay Option

This option makes use of one or more pieces of shell or other inlay material fitted into a matching pocket or pockets. CNC cut inlays can be done in the shop if it is equipped with an appropriate CNC machine, or this work can be contracted out. In either case, the starting point is a drawing of the outline of the design, which will serve as the outline of the inlay itself and also that of its pocket. There are various types of machines capable of doing this work. Some, like laser cutting machines, can cut sharp lines and points. The most common type of machine is the CNC router, and this type of machine can only cut a line as narrow as the diameter of the bit used. As mentioned previously, high precision machines can make use of very small diameter bits. The diameter of the smallest bit that can be used should be determined before attempting to do any drawing, because this diameter imposes limits on how thin features of the design can be, and also on how pointy they can be.

I like to preview designs over a grid with lines ruled at the diameter of the smallest bit that can be used. So in the drawing, the first thing I do is draw such a grid. In the following examples, the design is just a single letter. I'll preview the desired letter in various fonts, drawn over the grid, as shown in **figure 5-6**. The grid makes it easy to do a rough visual check for parts of the letter that are narrower than the grid spacing, or for points on the letter that are too pointy to machine. I select a design that looks like it will work as is, or looks like it will require a small amount of modification (usually rounding of points) to work.

A step-by-step description of the drawing process is provided here, but making use of that drawing to actually cut the inlay and pocket are out of the scope of this book. It is generally the case that software that is used to turn a drawing into instructions for operation of the CNC machine requires the drawing to use the DXF file format, but most commercial CNC shops can deal with most drawing file formats.

☐ **Drawing the Design**

1. A box representing the area that can be decorated is drawn, using the dimensions from the box that has been drawn on the headstock template in a previous operation.

2. A grid is drawn with line spacing equal to the diameter of the smallest bit that will be used to cut out the design.

3. The decoration text is sized to fit in the area that can be decorated.

4. The text is converted to a drawing of its outline. Some drawing software has tools for doing this easily. The function is usually named "explode" or something like that. If no such facility is available, the view of the text is magnified and an outline is drawn over the text using multipoint curves. See **figure 5-7.1**, **2**.

5. Small circles are drawn, with diameters the same as the grid spacing. Using high magnification, these are moved into any inside corners on the outline as far as they will go without actually touching the outline. These are used to determine how much rounding over of these points is needed. This is shown in **figure 5-7.3**. Note that in some letters like the "B" shown in the figure, the inside corners inside the outline of each cutout in the letter must also be treated in the same manner.

6. Using high magnification, the outline is modified so all the points are rounded over to a radius that is slightly greater than that of the little circles. The outline is also modified to widen any narrow parts to a bit wider than the diameter of the little circles (**figure 5-7.4**). The little circles are now deleted (**figure 5-7.5**).

7. The steps above are necessary to modify the outline so the inlay can be cut out using a cutting bit of a certain diameter. Now a similar process is used to modify the outline so the pocket for the inlay can also be cut using that same bit diameter. Here, the little circles are used *inside* the outline of the letter. In the example, the only such point is at the top left of the letter, as shown by the little dot in **figure 5-7.6**.

8. Again, the outline is modified under high magnification to round over any marked corners so they are a bit wider than the indicator circles.

9. An indicator circle is drawn and moved around inside the outline to be sure there are no narrow places that the cutting bit will not be able to get through. In the original example letter, the space between the two cutouts in the letter was suspect, but

it has already been widened as a consequence of other editing of the outline. But if any narrow areas are found, the outline must be edited to eliminate them. After all modifications, the indicator circles can be deleted.

10. The finished outline should be aesthetically compared to the original. It is sometimes the case that modifications yield a letter which is not acceptable. In this case the whole process is repeated using a different candidate font as the starting point.

Hand Cut Inlay, Marquetry Style Option

This option makes use of one or more pieces of shell or other inlay material fitted into a matching cutout or cutouts. The inlay and the cutout are cut at the same time using a jeweler's saw. The sawing operation is a lot like that used to make and fit pieces of veneer together in the woodworking technique known as marquetry. The shell blank is tacked down onto the headplate and shell and headplate are cut through with the same cut. It is ideally suited for inlay that doesn't have too many pieces too close together, and that doesn't involve tiny cutouts in letters.

Because the inlay and the space for it in the headplate are cut out at the same time, the resulting piece fits in the cutout with a gap all around that is the width of the kerf of the jeweler's saw blade used to make the cut. For this reason, good-looking results can really only be had when a black headplate is used.

I'm not providing step-by-step details of the drawing process here, but do recommend two things. First, that the design be simple and not contain tiny cutout areas such as the "eyes" of the letter "B." It is not that this and similar letters cannot be accommodated by this technique, only that the design should make the eyes big enough so they can be accurately sawn out with a jeweler's saw. The second thing is that the design should not contain long strokes with parallel sides. It is difficult to accurately cut parallel kerfs with a jeweler's saw, and humans are very good at noticing when lines that are supposed to be parallel are not. It is better to chose a design that contains strokes that are not uniform in width. Considering the letters in **figure 5-6** for example, the two letters on the right are more suitable for hand sawing, because the strokes that make up these letters are not uniform in width.

The design should be drawn with lines that are approximately the same thickness as the blade of the jeweler's saw that will be used. This makes it a lot easier to keep the saw in the right place while cutting. The drawing should also include a vertical centerline, which will be used to orient the design on the headplate. Multiple copies of the design should be printed out on white paper before proceeding.

Photo 5-12 – *A sheet of laminated shell material and a slice of mother of pearl are shown on either side of the printed design. A rectangular piece of shell must be selected or cut that is big enough to accommodate the design.*

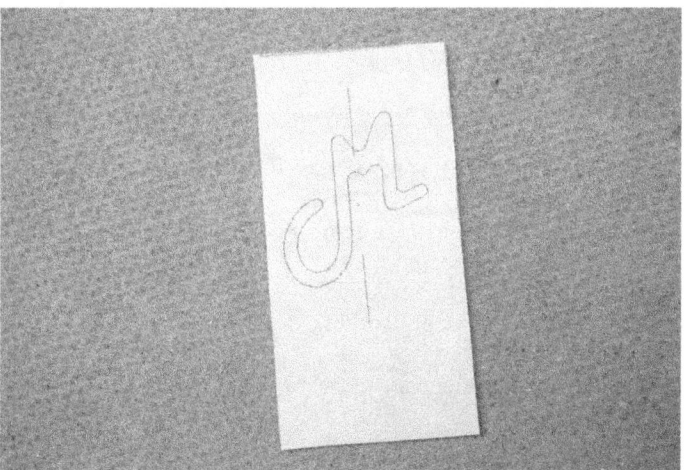

Photo 5-13 – *The paper with the design printed on it is trimmed to the size of the shell piece, and then glued onto it using wood glue. Note the centerline on the design, which will help to position the design on the headplate.*

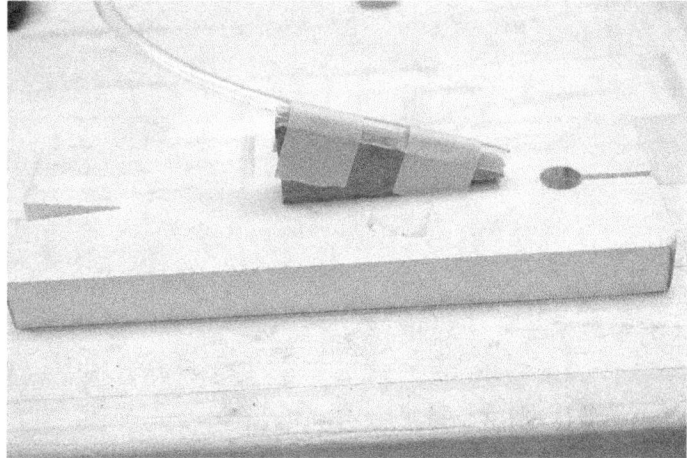

Photo 5-14 – *A small board is used as a jig to hold the piece while sawing. The hole and slot in one end, or the bird's beak cut in the other, are used to support the piece close to the saw blade while sawing. A small wedge of wood holds the end of a piece of tubing connected to an aquarium pump, which will blow enough air to keep the cutting area clean and the lines visible.*

Photo 5-15 – *The end of the wedge is undercut so the work can slide in there.*

☐ Constructing the Inlay

Materials
    Shell slices or sheets of laminated shell material, 0.05″ (1.3mm) thick
    Black ebony or phenolic impregnated wood headplate
    The design, printed on paper
    Wood glue
    Block of beeswax or paraffin
    Epoxy
    Ebony dust or black furniture powder
    Tape
    Double sided tape
Tools
    N95 or similar fine particle respirator
    Foam lined goggles or safety glasses
    Magnifying visor
    Small aquarium pump and tubing
    Small jeweler's saw frame
    Assorted blades, 0.025″ (0.64mm) to 0.018″ (0.46mm)
    Micro drill bit handle (pin vise), assorted micro drill bits
    Assorted small needle files

1. A slice of shell material big enough to accommodate the design is selected or cut from a larger sheet (**photo 5-12**).

2. The paper onto which the design is printed is trimmed to the size of the slice of shell, and then glued onto the shell with wood glue (**photo 5-13**). Not a lot of glue is required, but the entire surface of the shell slice must be covered in glue. The glue is allowed to thoroughly cure.

3. A simple jig to support the piece while sawing is made from a short length of flat board. The board is wide enough to support the top end of the headplate and must be long enough to be held in a vise. A board approximately 3″ (76.2mm) wide by 12″ (304.8mm) wide works fine. There are two ways to provide maximum support under the blade while sawing. One is to notch one end of the board with a V-shaped notch. The other is to drill a small hole near the end and bandsaw a slot so the jeweler's saw blade can reach the hole. The jig pictured in **photo 5-14** shows both of these options.

4. The jig uses a small aquarium pump to blow air at the cutting area, to keep the sawing dust away and give a clear view. The pump is connected to a length of clear flexible tubing. The end of the tubing is supported by a small wedge of wood so it

Photo 5-16 – *The shell piece is positioned in the right place on the headplate.*

Photo 5-17 – *The shell piece is glued in place with wood glue.*

Photo 5-18 – Setup to begin sawing. The jig is held in the vise, and the work is positioned over the hole and so air provided by the aquarium pump will blow away any sawing dust.

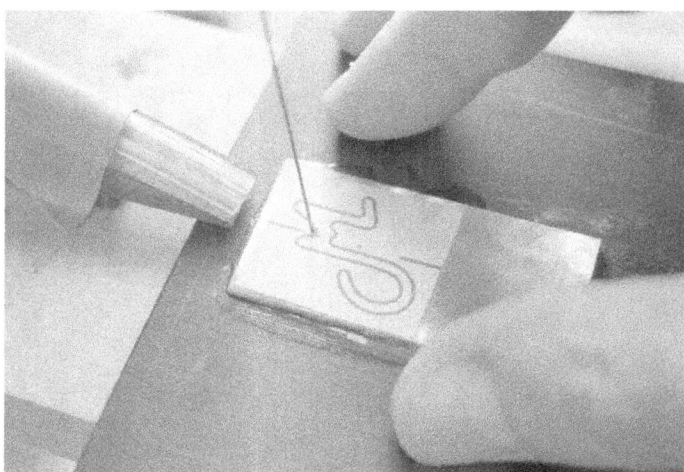

Photo 5-20 – The saw blade is threaded through the entry hole so it will cut on the down stroke.

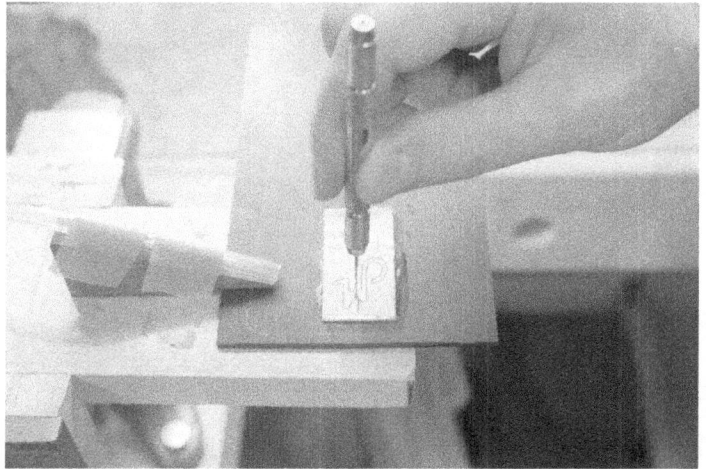

Photo 5-19 – An entry hole is drilled on the outline with a micro drill bit of the same diameter as the width of the saw blade to be used. The bit is held in a pin vise here, but can be held in a small power drill as well.

Photo 5-21 – The blade is clamped in the saw frame and tensioned, then sawing commences.

can be aimed at the cutting area. Note that the front of this wedge is undercut a bit, so the work can be positioned under the front of the wedge (**photo 5-15**). Although more permanent mounting is possible, I usually just tape the tubing end down to the wedge and use double-sided tape to stick the wedge in place on the jig board. Doing so aids repositioning of the tubing end, something that needs to be done often, depending on the piece being cut.

5. The shell slice with attached drawing is glued to the headplate. Wood glue is applied to the back of the shell, the piece is positioned in the proper place relative to the outline of the headstock penciled on the headplate (**photo 5-16**), and the slice is clamped in place (**photo 5-17**). The glue is allowed to thoroughly cure.

6. The holding jig can be clamped to the bench top or clamped in a vise. I find the latter puts the thing at a better elevation for sawing. The nozzle end of the tubing is placed to be out of the way and to provide a good stream of air where the sawing will take place (**photo 5-18**).

7. The work must be pierced with a hole drilled right on the outline, so the saw blade can be pushed through it. The hole is drilled with a micro bit that is the same diameter as the thickness of the saw blade to be used. Selection of which saw blade to use is a trade-off: The finer the blade, the finer the pattern that can be cut, but the work will proceed slowly and there will be a lot of blade breakage. Some experimentation will be required. The micro drill bit can be held in a holder (pin vise) as shown in **photo 5-19** and twirled to drill the hole. If a power drill is used it should be a very small one, and it will need a chuck that can hold the small bit. As is the case with the jeweler's saw blades, it is easy to break these small bits, so it is wise to always have extras on hand. The design shown in the photos has no "eyes" so it can be cut out from a single piercing on its outline. For letters like "B" with eyes, the eyes should be cut out first. Each outline must be started from a drilled hole. The eyes should be saved.

8. The teeth of the blade are drawn across the wax block for lubrication. The blade is oriented to cut on the down stroke, and then the blade is threaded into the drilled hole (**photo 5-20**) and

Photo 5-22 – *The design completely cut out.*

Photo 5-23 – *Heat is applied with a clothes iron to the remaining shell to melt the glue.*

Photo 5-24 – *After the shell is removed from the headplate, the area is gently scraped clean of any remaining glue. The paper covering the inlay piece is heated and removed, too.*

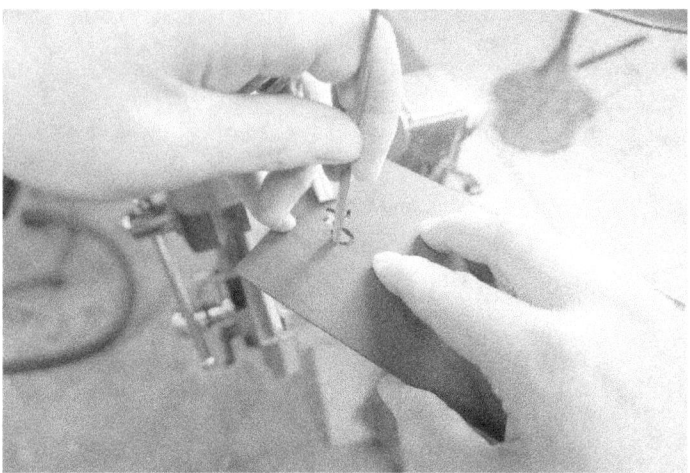

Photo 5-25 – *The edges of the cutout are cleaned up and smoothed, using needle files with vertical strokes. The headplate is supported on the sawing jig.*

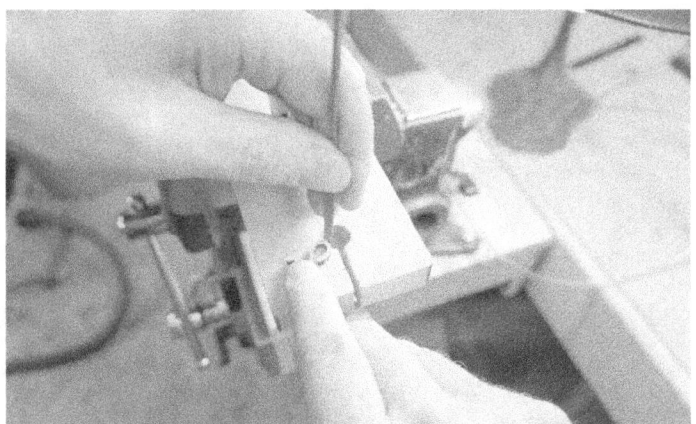

Photo 5-26 – *The edges of the inlay piece(s) are cleaned up and smoothed in the same manner.*

clamped into the saw frame. Blade tension is tightened, and sawing proceeds.

9. Accuracy of the cut is paramount, and so sawing is done while using an optical visor. This puts the luthier's face very close to the work, so protective equipment is needed to avoid breathing in the shell particles or getting them in the eyes. If the lines of the drawing were made the same width as that of the blade, sawing is done right on top of the printed outline. It is easy to see if the saw is wandering if any of the printed line remains behind the current sawing location (**photo 5-21**). Short, careful, and smooth strokes will help with accuracy and help prevent blade breakage. It also helps to regularly wipe the saw teeth with the wax block. Much care must be taken to support the work when the piece is mostly cut out, to avoid simply breaking it.

The final cutting should be done with very light strokes, and the saw angled forward a bit, to avoid chipping out the shell when the saw blade breaks through (**photo 5-22**). If the piece has eyes, they *must* be saved.

10. A clothes iron is set to low heat and used to melt the glue attaching the rest of the shell to the headplate. The iron is just pressed onto the shell (**photo 5-23**) for a few seconds, until the glue is melted enough so the shell can be removed with a chisel and gentle scraping (**photo 5-24**). Any excess glue is carefully scraped off the headplate surface. Then the iron is pressed to the paper covering the inlay piece(s) just long enough so the paper can be easily removed. The piece is not heated so much that the shell separates from the wood behind it.

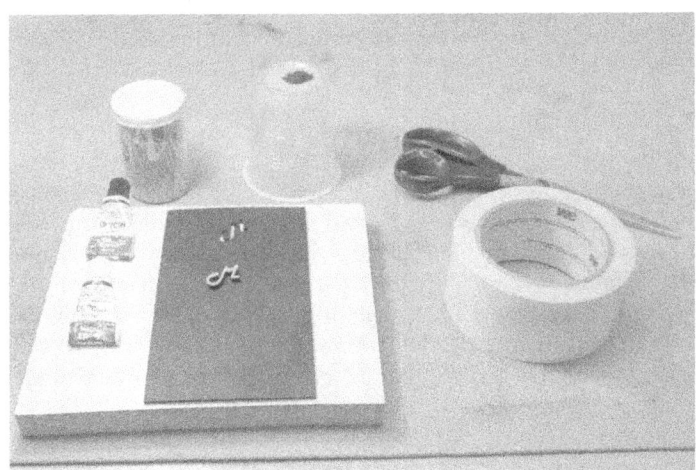

Photo 5-27 – *Ready to glue inlay into the cutout. The work is done on a melamine board. Double-stick tape holds the pieces in place while black pigmented epoxy is used to fill the gaps between inlay and cutout.*

Photo 5-28 – *A small piece of double-sided tape is stuck down to the board, then the headplate is positioned face down so the tape is under the cutout.*

Photo 5-29 – *The inlay piece is inserted, and then positioned using tweezers so the gap between cutout and inlay is uniform in width.*

Photo 5-30 – *Epoxy is mixed with black pigment to use as the filler.*

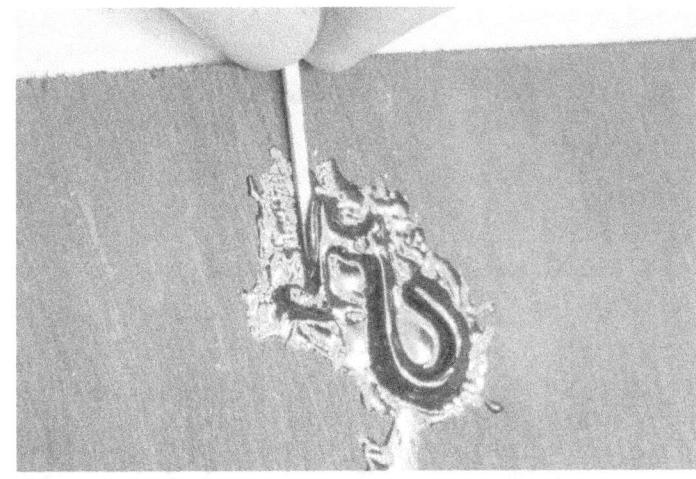

Photo 5-31 – *The filler is packed into the gap all around, and allowed to fully cure.*

Photo 5-32 – *The black filler is hardly visible next to the black headplate.*

11. The edges of the cutout in the headplate are filed smooth and continuous using needle files (**photo 5-25**). The area currently being filed is supported over the support jig used when sawing. The file is held vertically and moved up and down. The headplate should be regularly moved in front of a white background to better assess the smoothness of the edges and to indicate areas that need more filing.

12. The edges of the inlay are smoothed in the same manner (**photo 5-26**). The edges of any eyes that were removed should also be smoothed to the extent possible. Due to their small size they will be difficult to hold.

13. The inlay is glued into the cutout in the headplate using black-colored filler. The operation is performed on a piece of melamine board as shown in **photo 5-27**. A small piece of double-sided tape is stuck down to the surface of the melamine board, under where the inlay cutout will be. The backing paper is removed and the tape surface is touched a few times with a rag to reduce its tack. Then the headplate is placed on the board *face down* so the cutout is directly over the tape (**photo 5-28**).

14. The inlay is placed gently in the cutout, face down, and then manipulated with tweezers until it is centered in the cutout. Once centered, it is pressed in place so it is fixed by the tape (**photo 5-29**). The inlay has a layer of headplate wood attached to the shell, so it is thicker than the headplate.

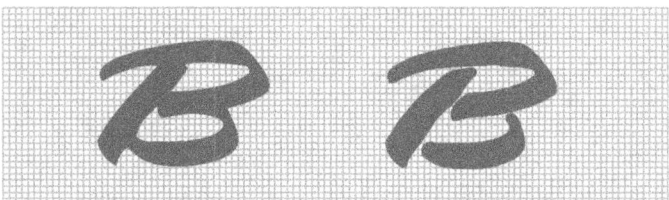

Figure 5-8 – The "B" on the right has been redrawn to separate it into three discrete strokes: an upper curve, a lower curve, and a vertical bar. Doing this makes it easier to saw out the inlay, because the eyes of the letter don't have to be pierced for cutting.

Photo 5-33 – The cut in the shell begins at an edge, and moves toward the drawn outline. Tilting the saw forward a bit helps to prevent chipping of the shell material when a cut is started or finished.

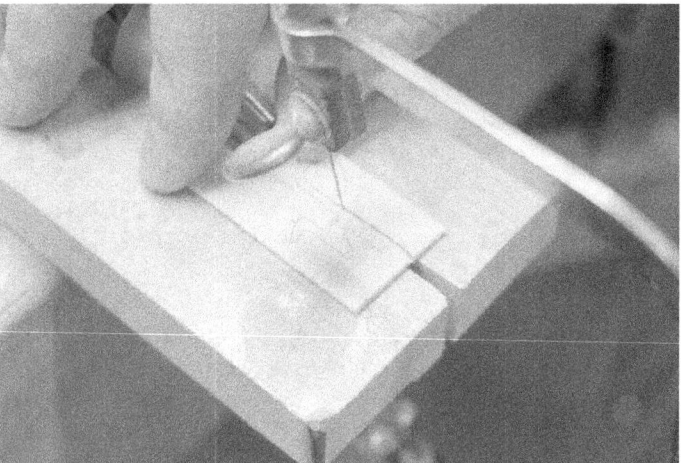

Photo 5-34 – Short vertical saw strokes are used to keep the saw on the outline, and to help prevent blade breakage. The area directly under the cut must be fully supported by the support fixture at all times.

15. A small amount of epoxy is mixed with a small amount of black furniture powder, to make an opaque black filler (**photo 5-30**). This is generously troweled into the space between the inlay and the cutout, using a wood toothpick or small stick (**photo 5-31**). The epoxy is allowed to cure overnight.

☞ Care should be taken when selecting something to mix epoxy on or in. There are some plastic cups that contain a substance which prevents epoxy from curing. Any cup that has not been successfully used in the past for this application should be checked before using it to mix epoxy for lutherie.

16. The headplate is removed from the melamine board, and the double-sided tape is removed. Excess wood and epoxy are now removed from the back surface of the headplate by sanding. Because the inlay is only held in place at its edges, the headplate should be placed face down on a flat hard surface like the melamine board while the back is sanded. A small hard sanding block that is a bit bigger in size than the inlay, with 80 grit PSA sandpaper attached, makes quick work of bringing the back of the inlay and the filler level with the back surface of the headplate.

17. The headplate is now ready for attachment to the headstock (**photo 5-32**).

Hand Cut Inlay, Cut and Pocket Option

This option makes use of one or more pieces of shell or other inlay material fitted into a matching pocket or pockets. The inlay piece is cut out of the shell first, and then it is traced onto the headplate, and a small special-purpose router is used to excavate a pocket to the outline. Although it is theoretically possible to make a tight-fitting pocket, it is more usually the case that the pocket will end up only roughly approximating the shape of the inlay piece. Pigmented filler is used to fill the gaps. For this reason, good-looking results can be difficult to achieve unless a black headplate and filler is used.

I'm not providing step-by-step details of the drawing process here. See the previous option for some suggestions about the drawing, and I'll make one more suggestion here. It is often convenient to separate the design into discrete strokes, as shown in **figure 5-8**. Doing so may make it easier to saw out the inlay. The eyes of the letter are no longer closed, and so it is not necessary to pierce the shell to saw out each eye. The space between the strokes should be at least the width of the jeweler's saw blade that will be used to cut the pieces out. Also, it may be easier to support each stroke piece while sawing, which in turn may make it more likely the pieces can be sawn out without breaking them. Plus, if a piece is broken while sawing, only that piece needs to be re-sawn.

☐ Constructing the Inlay

The sawing and shaping of the inlay pieces is similar to the process used in the previously described option. Construction details of that option should be read as background. Tools and materials used are generally the same, and so will not be specified here.

Excavation of the pockets in the headplate for the inlay pieces makes use of a small router, which is composed of a general purpose high speed grinder and a special router base for it. The router base is available from lutherie suppliers, and it is quite expensive. Note that the most important feature of such a router base is that it has a bird's beak-shaped cutout in it, which allows an unobstructed view of the bit during use. See **photo 5-38** to see what the base looks like.

The operations described invariably need to be performed under magnification.

1. A slice of shell material big enough to accommodate the design is selected or cut from a larger sheet (**photo 5-12**).

2. The paper onto which the design is printed is trimmed to the size of the slice of shell and then glued onto the shell with wood glue (**photo 5-13**). Not a lot of glue is required, but the entire surface of the shell slice must be covered in glue. The glue is allowed to thoroughly cure.

3. The same jig described for the previous option and pictured in **photo 5-14** is built to support the shell material while it is being cut. The holding jig can be clamped to the bench top or clamped in a vise.

4. A blade is clamped into the jeweler's saw frame, oriented so it cuts on the down stroke, and tensioned. The teeth of the blade are drawn across the wax block for lubrication.

5. The cut is started from an edge of the shell piece and moving toward the drawn outline. The saw blade is angled forward a bit when starting the cut to prevent chipping out the shell at the edge (**photo 5-33**).

6. Sawing proceeds, following the outline of each piece as closely as possible (**photo 5-34**). It is important that the shell be fully supported as close to the cut as possible, as the piece will be moved about on the support fixture during sawing, to be sure there is always good support directly under the cut. When a piece is almost completely cut out, the saw blade is again tilted slightly forward to avoid chipping on the top surface when the blade breaks through.

7. The paper on the inlay is removed either by dropping the inlay into a cup of boiling water, or by applying heat with a clothes iron set to low heat and then scraping the paper off.

8. The edges of the inlay are smoothed using needle files. The work is supported on the fixture just as for sawing, and the file is used vertically (**photo 5-26**).

9. The inlay piece is placed in position on the headplate and held in place while the outline is scribed onto the headplate, using an engraving scriber or a machinist's scriber (**photo 5-35**). It is often impossible to hold the inlay piece(s) in place with the fingers and scribe at the same time. In this case, the inlay is glued in place on the headplate using a light coating of wood glue. A light coating of glue is necessary so there will not be any glue squeeze-out around the edges of the inlay, which would interfere with scribing the outline. After the glue is fully cured the outline can be scribed easily. The heat from a clothes iron is applied to the inlay to soften the glue so it can be removed. Glue on the back of the inlay should be removed by dropping the inlay in a cup of boiling water and then rubbing softened glue from the surface.

10. The scribed outline is difficult to see, especially on a black headplate. To aid visibility, chalk or paint is rubbed into the scribing (**photo 5-36**).

11. The scribed outline is deepened using a sharp tipped knife. The knife tip is repeatedly drawn around the scribed outline

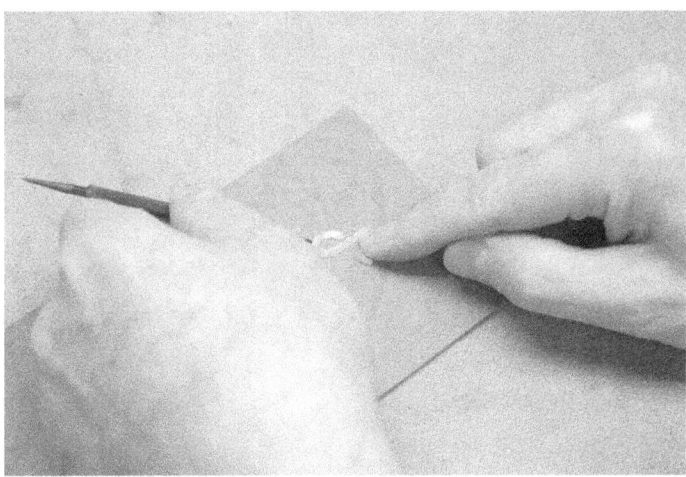

Photo 5-35 – *The outline of the inlay piece is scribed onto the headplate. This is often easier to do if the piece is tack glued down first. In the photo I am using a light colored headplate, only so the details of the operation can be seen.*

Photo 5-36 – *Chalk is rubbed into the scribed outline to make it more visible.*

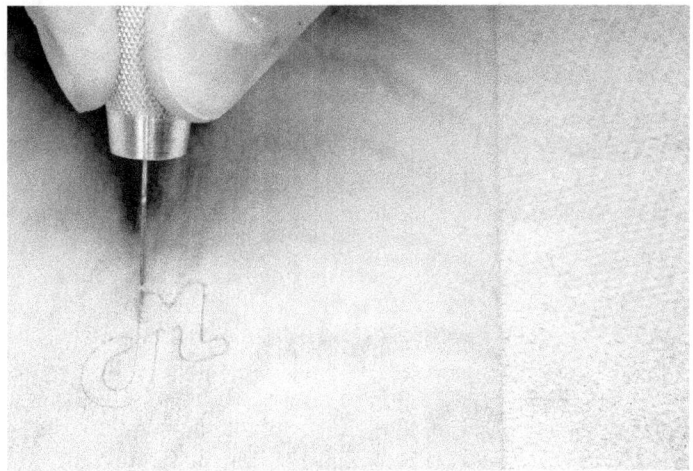

Photo 5-37 – *The scribed outline is deepened using a sharply pointed knife.*

with the knife pressed lightly, so the tip doesn't jump out of the scribed channel (**photo 5-37**). In this way the channel is gradually deepened with each pass. There is no need to attempt to cut the channel to the full depth of the pocket, but this deepening is done until the outline is clearly visible. Any chalk or paint will be gone at this point. It will help when routing the pocket to reapply chalk or paint to the outline.

12. The pocket is routed to a depth of the thickness of the shell inlay, typically 0.05″ (1.3mm) using the special-purpose router

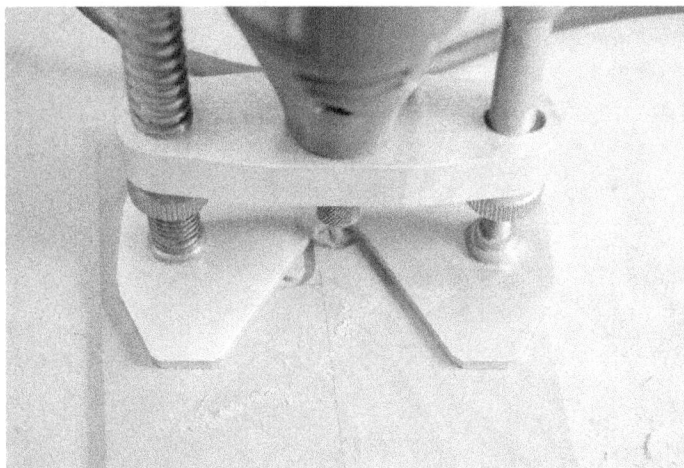

Photo 5-38 – *A small grinder with a special router base is used to rout the pocket.*

and an assortment of small diameter bits (**photo 5-38**). Useful bit sizes range from 0.125″ (3.2mm) down to 0.032″ (0.8mm). Bits at the small end of the range are expensive and easily broken. A good general strategy is to hog out as much material as possible using the bigger bits, getting close to but not right on the edge of the outline. Then, smaller diameter bits can be used to trim right up to the outline. Because the outline has been channeled with the knife, when the router bit approaches close to it, the final piece of waste tends to peel away visibly.

This routing work is tedious and must be done with some care. It is imperative while doing this that the headplate is oriented and reoriented so that the luthier's eyes can always see the cutting surface of the bit.

This means the opening in the router base plate should always be facing the luthier. This also means that the eye, the part of the outline currently being cut, and the bit should always be in a line, and that the part of the outline currently being cut should always be kept between the luthier's eyes and the bit.

There are two approaches which may be taken when routing into sharp corners. The first is to stop before the corner is reached, and then finish the corner using knives and tiny chisels. The second is to just rout right up to the point of the corner using the smallest diameter bit that can be handled. This latter approach makes for a loose fit in the corner between inlay and pocket, but filler will generally hide that gap in the finished instrument.

13. Once the pocket is fully routed, the inlay piece can be test fitted. The pocket must be completely clean of debris. It is usually necessary to scrape debris out from the edges of the pocket using a knife or small chisel. The piece should drop into the pocket without pressure. Pressing a piece into the pocket increases the likelihood of breaking it when attempting to pry it back out of the pocket. Additional work with knife or router may be necessary to achieve an easy drop-in fit. In addition to dropping into the pocket, the top surface of the inlay piece should be flush with the top surface of the headplate.

14. Once a good fit is achieved, the inlay piece is glued into its pocket. Medium cyanoacrylate glue is ideal for this, because it cures quickly. A small amount of the glue is smeared around on the floor of the pocket, using a toothpick or small stick. Then the inlay is dropped in, and pressed in place until the glue is fully cured.

15. A small amount of epoxy is mixed with a small amount of ebony sanding dust or black furniture powder to make an opaque black filler (**photo 5-30**). This is generously troweled into the space between the inlay and the pocket walls, using a wood toothpick or small stick. The epoxy is allowed to cure overnight.

16. The excess filler is sanded back using 180 grit sandpaper on a small hard sanding block. The end result is an inlay which is flush with the top surface of the headplate, as in **photo 5-32**. The headplate is now ready for attachment to the headstock.

Attaching the Headplate and Veneers

The next construction operation is to attach the headplate and any veneers to the headstock. Positioning of the headplate must be done with some precision, because the mitered end serves as one side of the channel that will support the nut.

☐ Gluing the Headplate and Veneers to the Headstock

The headplate and veneers are positioned with the use of brads located outside of the outline of the finished headstock shape. At this point in assembly, the outline shape should already be marked on the headplate. To be sure there are no gaps between the headplate and the rest of the headstock in the finished instrument, a thick and flat gluing caul is used in this operation.

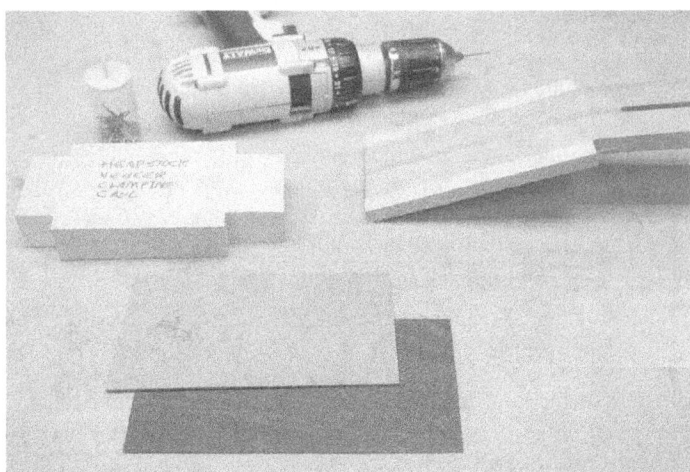

Photo 5-39 – *Tools and materials for gluing the headplate and veneers. A thick and flat caul is used to provide uniform clamping pressure during gluing.*

Photo 5-40 – *A stop is clamped down to the scribed line at the edge between headstock and fretboard surface of the neck. Note the centerline drawn on the end of the stop, aligned with the neck centerline.*

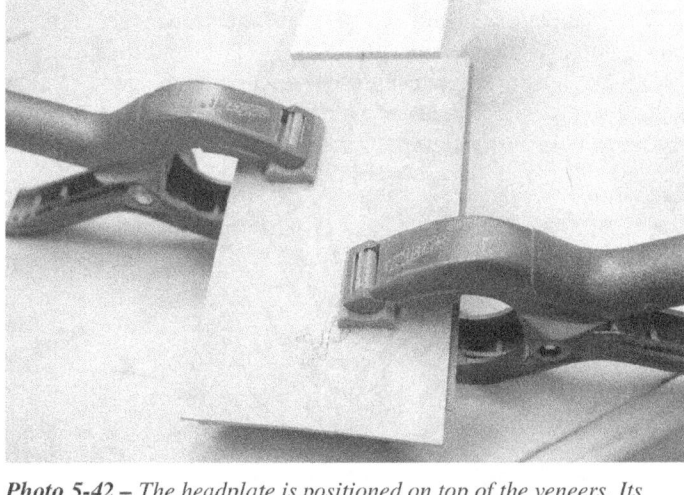

Photo 5-42 – *The headplate is positioned on top of the veneers. Its centerline is aligned with the centerline on the stop. Spring clamps are used to hold everything in place.*

Photo 5-41 – *The stop is used to locate the veneers and the headplate. Here a veneer is placed in position on the headstock and pressed against the stop.*

Photo 5-43 – *Holes are drilled outside of the outline of the finished headstock, in the corners of the headplate. The holes will be used for brads, which will keep everything in position. The holes must go through headplate, veneers, and just into the headstock underneath.*

Materials
    The neck assembly
    The headplate
    All headstock veneers that will be used
    #16 brads, approximately 1″ (25.4mm) long
    Flat board to use as a caul, at least ¾″ (19.1mm) thick
    Piece of scrap with a straight edge, to use as a stop
    Wood glue
Tools
    Hand drill with ¹⁄₁₆″ (1.6mm) bit
    Clamps
    Plastic soda straw

1. The tools and materials are collected together for this operation (**photo 5-39**). The veneers and headplate should be stacked in order on the bench. In the example shown in the photos, a single black veneer is used. The headplate and the headstock should have centerlines on their complete lengths. If these have been obliterated they should be redrawn now.

2. The caul should be cut slightly larger than the outline of the headstock of the finished instrument. The end of the caul that will be positioned at the nut end of the headplate must be cut straight. The corners of the caul are removed as shown, to provide clearance for the brads that will pin everything together during glue up. These brads will be located outside of the outline.

3. The centerline is marked on the end of a small piece of wood that will be used as a stop at the nut end. In the photos, a square of ¼″ (6.4mm) MDF about 2″ (50.8mm) square is used as the stop. The stop should be taller than the headplate and veneers. The stop is clamped to the neck using two clamps as shown in **photo 5-40**. The end of the stop toward the headstock is aligned on the scribed line on the edge between the fretboard surface of the neck and the top surface of the headstock. The centerline mark should align with the centerline of the neck.

4. The veneers are positioned on the headstock and pushed up against the stop (**photo 5-41**).

5. The headplate is positioned on top of the veneers and also pushed up against the stop (**photo 5-42**). The centerline of the headplate must meet the centerline penciled on the end of the stop. The nut end of the headplate must be fully in contact with the stop. Two spring clamps are used to hold everything in place. A straightedge aligned with the centerline on the headplate should also align with the centerline on the end of the headstock.

6. Holes for the locating brads are drilled near the corners of the headplate, *outside* the outline of the finished headstock

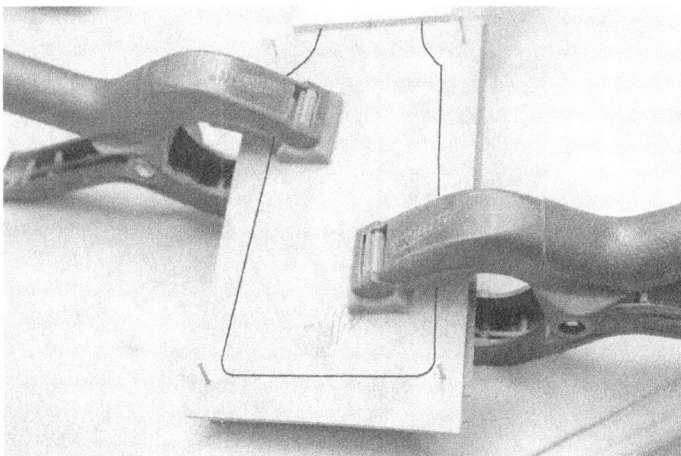

Photo 5-44 – *The brads are placed in the drilled holes.*

Photo 5-47 – *A plastic soda straw, snipped at an angle, makes a great tool to remove glue squeeze-out from inside edges.*

Photo 5-45 – *After glue is applied and the caul is placed on top, as many clamps as will fit are used to clamp everything in place while the glue cures.*

Photo 5-48 – *Brad pins used in gluing generally end up being glued in place. They can be removed by pushing a piece of scrap wood up against the brad, grasping the brad with pliers so the tops of the jaws are resting on the piece of scrap ...*

Photo 5-46 – *The stop is removed, and then the clamps that were holding it in place are used to further clamp down the nut end of the headplate and veneer pile.*

Photo 5-49 – *... then rocking the pliers toward the piece of scrap, levering the brad out of its hole. The scrap is important: It prevents the jaws of the pliers from denting the surface of the wood underneath.*

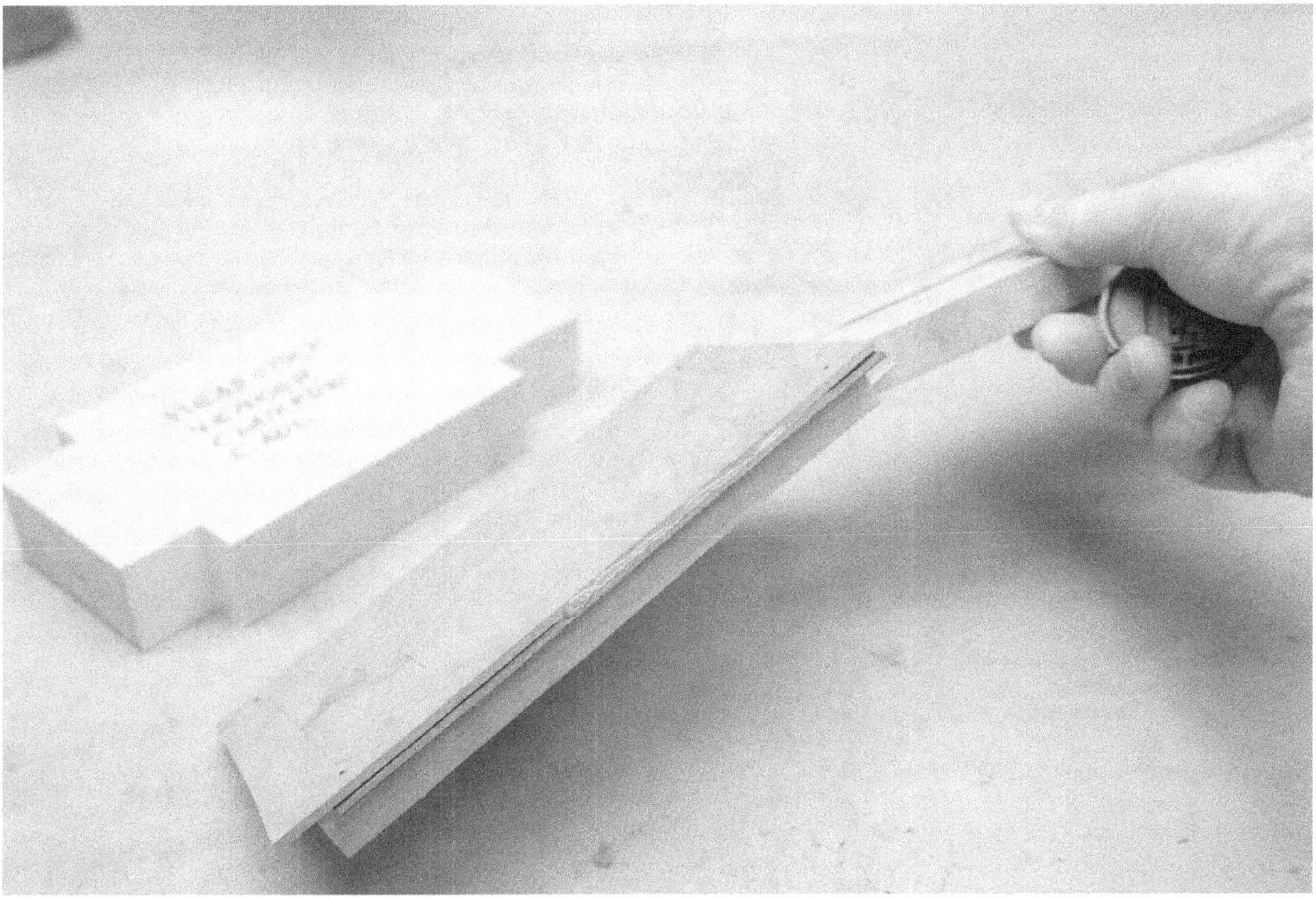

Photo 5-50 – *The headplate and veneer sandwich, glued in place.*

(**photo 5-43**). The holes should go through the headplate and veneers and part way into the headstock.

7. Brads are placed in the drilled holes to hold everything in place (**photo 5-44**). The spring clamps are removed. The gluing caul is test fitted, to be sure it clears the brads and its end can be positioned against the stop. The caul is modified as necessary if it does not fit.

8. The caul is removed, the brads are removed, and the headplate and veneers are removed as a unit and set on the bench, headplate up. The headplate is flipped off of the stack so it is now top down on the bench. A coat of wood glue is applied to

Photo 5-51 – *Any dried glue is cleared from the edge between headplate and fretboard surface of the neck using a chisel.*

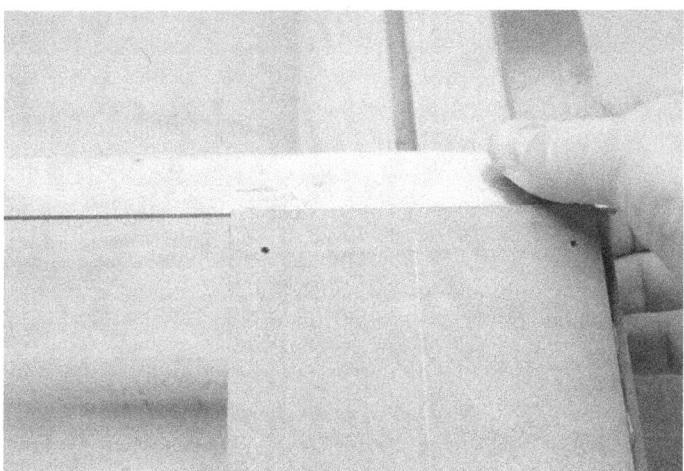

Photo 5-52 – *Using a square, the nut end of the headplate is checked to be sure it is perpendicular to the side of the neck.*

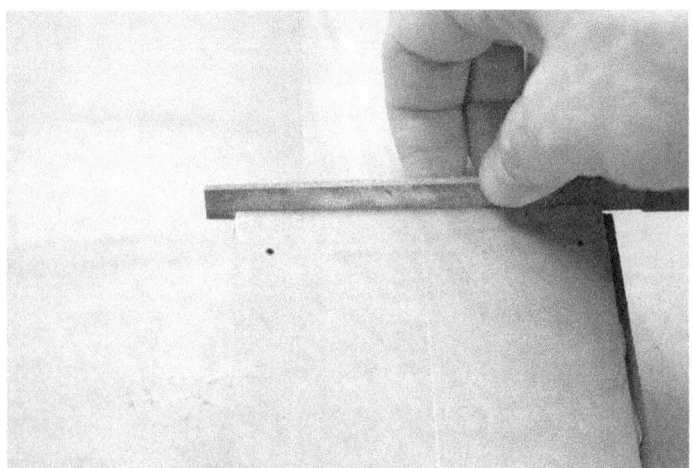

Photo 5-53 – *The nut end of the headplate can be squared up using a small file with a safe edge. The safe edge contacts the fretboard surface of the neck, so that surface is not filed.*

the headplate bottom, which is now face up. The brads are pushed through their holes in the headplate from underneath, so the points of the brads are pointing up. The veneer on top of the stack is flipped over onto the brad points and positioned so the brads go through the drilled holes in the veneer. Then the veneer is pressed into place into the glue on the headplate. A coat of wood glue is applied to the veneer. This must be done quickly because a veneer with glue applied to only one side will immediately begin to curl up.

The process of placing a veneer and applying glue is repeated until all veneers are on the stack and there is a coat of glue on the last veneer. Now the whole assembly is inverted onto the headstock, the brad points are positioned into the drilled holes, and then the brads tapped down into the holes a bit with a hammer. The headplate and veneer sandwich is slide down the shafts of the brads until it is fully in contact with the headstock. The gluing caul is applied, and as many clamps as will fit are used to hold everything in place (**photo 5-45**).

9. The clamps holding the stop in place are removed and the stop is removed, so it doesn't get glued down to the neck. Those clamps can be deployed to help clamp down the nut end of the headplate and veneer assembly if there is room for them (**photo 5-46**). Glue squeeze-out at the nut end is removed using a plastic straw snipped at an angle (**photo 5-47**), a great general-purpose technique I learned from Australian luthiers and authors Trevor Gore and Gerard Gilet. The glue is allowed to cure overnight.

10. The clamps and caul are removed. The brads can be pulled out by being grasped with pliers and then levered out against a scrap of wood on the surface of the headplate. The wood scrap is needed, to protect the surface of the headplate from being dented by the pliers. See **photos 5-48** and **5-49**. Note this is a general-purpose technique for pulling out pins, and will be referenced in subsequent operations. If the pins can't be pulled out because they are glued in place, they should be heated with a soldering iron. This melts the glue, and the pins can then be removed easily.

11. The headstock is examined for any slippage of the component pieces during the glue up step (**photo 5-50**). Any remaining glue in the inside edge between the headplate and the fretboard surface of the neck is scraped out using a chisel (**photo 5-51**).

12. The nut end surface of the headplate is checked to be sure it is square with the side of the neck (**photo 5-52**) and to be sure it is straight and perpendicular to the fretboard surface of the neck. If it is not, the end surface can be trued up using a flat file with a *safe edge* (toothless edge) in contact with the fretboard surface (**photo 5-53**).

13. The distance between the nut end surface of the headplate and the line scribed on the fretboard surface of the neck that represents the nut end of the fretboard is measured. It should be ¼″ (6.4mm), but filing in the previous step may have moved the headplate end back a bit. If the distance is less than or equal to ¼″ (6.4mm), then all is well. If it is greater than ¼″ (6.4mm), the line representing the nut end of the fretboard should be re-scribed so it is exactly ¼″ (6.4mm) from the end of the headplate.

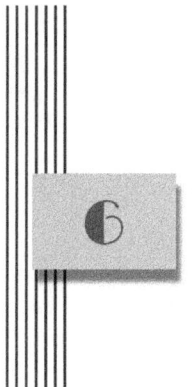

6 Further Refinement of the Neck

Previous chapters have provided upfront introductory descriptions of features to be implemented in the chapter, and also offered and explained construction options. In contrast, this chapter describes only continuing construction of the neck. The neck will be further refined, starting with the attachment of the fretboard, continuing with the shaping of the headstock, and ending with the trimming of the sides of the neck shaft and heel. The construction operations are all simple and straight forward.

Installing the Trussrod and the Fretboard

The slot for the trussrod has been cut in a previous construction operation. Likewise, the fretboard has been slotted for frets and cut to shape and is ready for attachment to the neck assembly. The fretboard will be located using brads as locating pins, the same technique used to locate the headplate while it was glued in place. Fretboard gluing will make use of a gluing caul too, to distribute clamping pressure and to be sure the resulting structure is nice and flat.

☐ Installation

Before the operation is started, the neck assembly and fretboard should be checked to be sure they still contain patent centerlines and other reference lines. The fretboard surface of the neck should have a scribed line indicating the location of the nut end of the fretboard. That surface should also have a centerline extending from the nut edge of the headplate to the nut end of the trussrod slot. The body contact end of the heel should have a marked centerline. The fretboard should have a centerline marked on both playing and gluing surfaces, and also on both ends. If any of these lines are missing, they should be redrawn in preparation for this construction operation.

Materials
    Neck assembly
    Fretboard
    Trussrod
    ¾″ (19.1mm) thick MDF
    Wood glue
    Silicone sealer/adhesive, any color
    1″ (25.4mm) wide masking tape
    #16 brads
Tools
    Clamps
    Large spring clamps
    Hand drill with ¹⁄₁₆″ (1.6mm) drill bit
    Side cutting pliers or end nippers
    Small hammer
    Plastic soda straw

---

1. A gluing caul is constructed out of MDF material. The caul should follow the taper of the sides of the fretboard and it should be as long as the fretboard from the nut end to the 14th

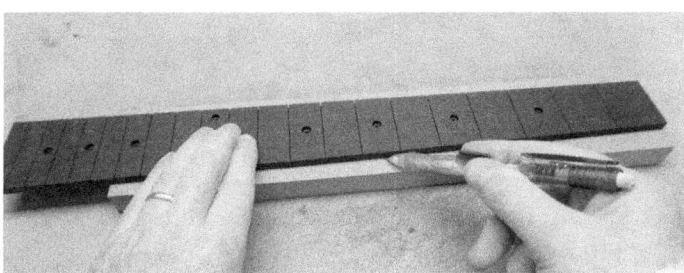

Photo 6-1 – *The part of the fretboard from nut to 14th fret is traced onto MDF. This will be cut out to make a gluing caul.*

Photo 6-2 – *The finished gluing caul on top of the fretboard.*

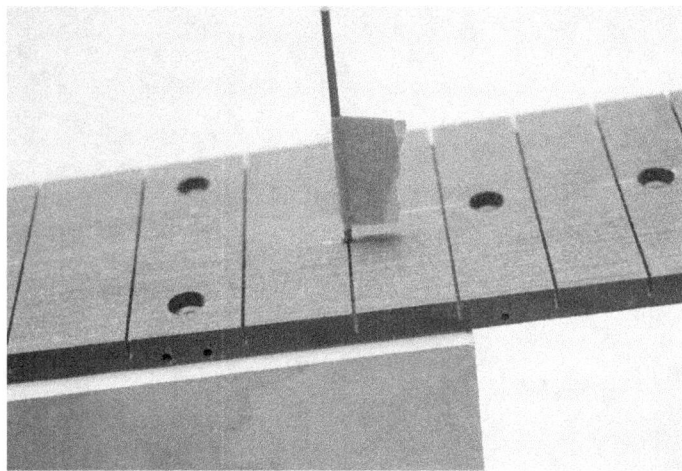

Photo 6-3 – *A 1/16" (1.6mm) hole is drilled through the fretboard at the slot for the 13th fret, and 1/2" (12.7mm) to one side of the centerline. Note the tape used as a depth mark for the hole.*

Photo 6-4 – *A #16 brad is tapped into the hole and a bit into the neck. There should be padded support under the heel when this is done.*

Photo 6-5 – *A similar hole is drilled at the 1st fret slot, but here on the other side of the centerline. A brad is tapped into this hole too, using a padded block as support under the neck.*

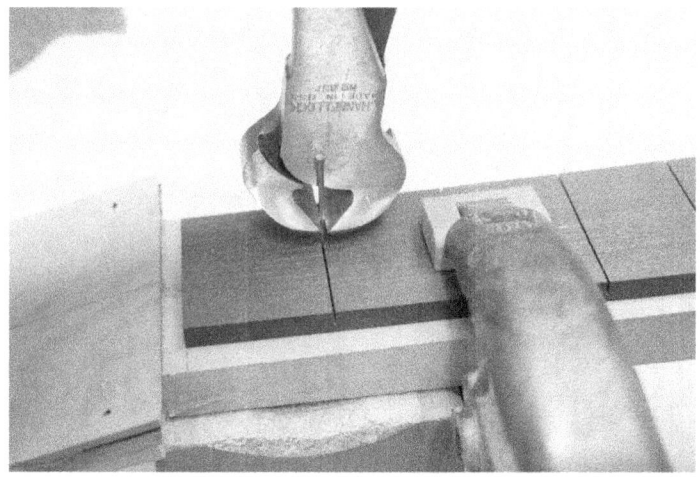

Photo 6-6 – *The tops of the brads are chopped off approximately 1/2" (12.7mm) from the top surface of the fretboard ...*

2. The fretboard is put in place on top of the neck assembly, with its nut end aligned with the scribed line on the fretboard surface of the neck indicating that location. The centerline on the nut end of the fretboard is also aligned with the centerline on the neck, and the fretboard is held in place using a large spring clamp at the 2nd fret position. The assembly is flipped over so the underside of the fretboard extension (that portion of the fretboard that overhangs the neck) can be seen. The centerline on the underside of the fretboard extension is aligned with the centerline on the body end of the heel. Another large spring clamp near the heel end at the 9th fret position is used to hold this end in place. Alignment is re-checked and modified until the fretboard is positioned as specified.

3. It is useful to trace the sides of the fretboard onto the fretboard surface of the neck in pencil at this time. These lines will make it easier to realign things if the fretboard is inadvertently moved.

4. A 1/16" (1.6mm) hole is drilled through the fretboard and a short way into the neck underneath, right at the 13th fret, and 1/2" (12.7mm) to one side of the centerline. It is useful to mark the depth of the hole to be drilled using masking tape on the drill bit (**photo 6-3**), to avoid the hole being drilled too deep. Note that the drilled hole will not be visible in the finished instrument, because the bead of the fret that will be installed here will cover the hole. If the drilling operation pulls some chips of wood out of the fretboard, these are glued back in place using cyanoacrylate glue.

5. The bottom of the heel is supported on a folded rag on the bench. A brad is inserted in the hole and hammered in just enough so it will stay in place (**photo 6-4**).

6. Steps 4 and 5 are repeated at the 1st fret, but 1/2" (12.7mm) to the *other* side of the fretboard centerline (**photo 6-5**). The underside of the neck shaft must be supported with a padded block of wood while the brad is tapped into place.

7. Using side cutting pliers or end nippers the brads are cut off approximately 1/2" (12.7mm) from the top surface of the

fret. The fretboard is placed on top of a piece of MDF, traced (**photo 6-1**), and then cut out (**photo 6-2**). When cutting the caul out, the saw blade should be kept just to the *inside* of the lines. This will result in a caul which is slightly smaller in width than the fretboard.

Photo 6-7 – ... leaving stubs of about ½″ (12.7mm) long.

Photo 6-8 – The caul is placed in position over the fretboard and tapped over each of the brads. This will make center marks for clearance holes to be drilled through the caul.

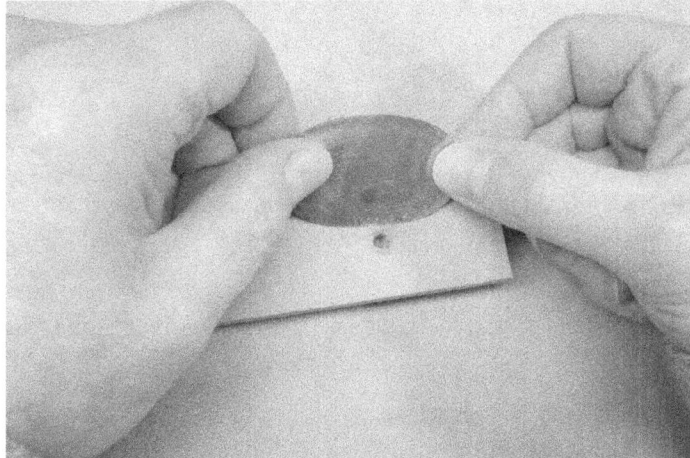

Photo 6-9 – The edges of the holes are scraped or sanded clean.

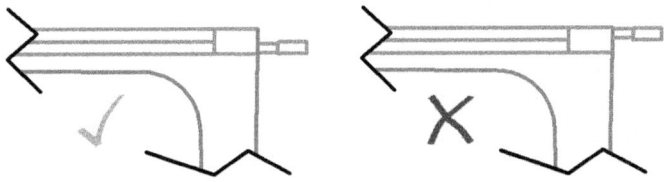

Figure 6-1 – The trussrod is inserted in its slot with the adjuster nut down, as in the left hand drawing.

Photo 6-10 – Dots of silicone sealer are placed on the floor of the trussrod channel.

fretboard (**photo 6-6**). The exposed ends of the brads will be sharp (**photo 6-7**).

8. The gluing caul is put in place on top of the fretboard. The ends of the brads will prevent it from contacting the fretboard. The top of the caul over the brads is tapped with the hammer (**photo 6-8**). The sharp brad ends will leave marks in the bottom surface of the caul.

9. Clearance holes for the brads of approximately ¼″ (6.4mm) diameter are drilled through the caul, at the marks made in the bottom surface of the caul. Any blowout around the drilled holes is cleaned off by sanding or scraping (**photo 6-9**). The caul is placed back on the fretboard so the brads are in the drilled holes, and checked for fit. The brad ends should not extend above the top surface of the caul.

10. The caul is removed and the fretboard is carefully lifted off the neck so the brad pins remain in the neck. The fretboard is now put back in place to check that the pins provide correct placement. Then it is removed again.

11. Any exposed threads on the trussrod are lightly oiled, and excess oil is wiped off with a rag. This will prevent any glue that may find its way to the threads from preventing operation of the trussrod.

12. If the trussrod is not straight, its adjusting nut is turned until it is straight.

13. The trussrod slot is carefully vacuumed clean of debris. The trussrod is laid in position but next to the trussrod slot. Small dots of silicone sealer (approximately ⅛″ (3.2mm) in diameter) are placed on the floor of the trussrod slot approximately every 3″ (76.2mm) (**photo 6-10**). These will prevent rattling of the trussrod in its slot in the finished instrument. No silicone adhesive dots should be placed where they could interfere with the threads of the trussrod. It is important that these dots of sealer be kept *small*.

14. The trussrod is placed in its slot.

Photo 6-11 – *The trussrod is covered with masking tape, in preparation for gluing.*

Photo 6-12 – *Glue is applied, then the tape is removed. The tape leaves a margin without glue on both sides of the trussrod. When the fretboard is applied and clamped, glue will squeeze into that margin, but not so much that it reaches the trussrod slot.*

Photo 6-13 – *The fretboard is fitted over the brad pins and pressed into place. Then the caul is fitted on top.*

Photo 6-14 – *Clamps are applied, as many as are available and will fit.*

Photo 6-15 – *Glue squeeze-out is scraped out of the inside edge between the underside of the fretboard extension and the body end of the heel, using a snipped plastic straw.*

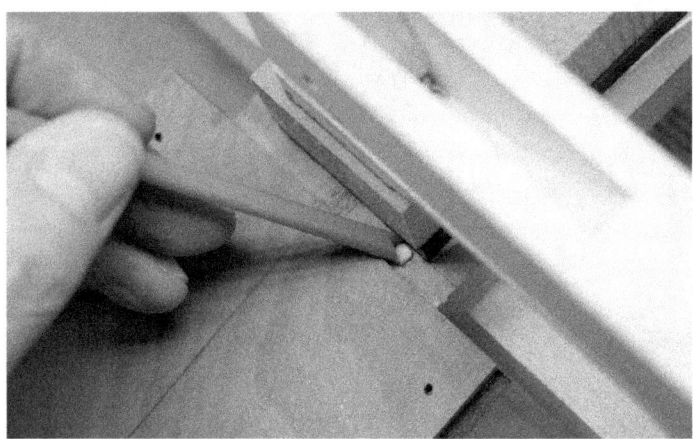

Photo 6-16 – *Glue squeeze-out is also scraped out of the nut slot, using the snipped plastic straw.*

Note that the trussrod is oriented so the adjusting nut is *down*, and hangs out of the heel end of the slot (**figure 6-1**). The trussrod is pressed firmly into place to seat it in its slot.

No part of the trussrod should end up sticking up out of the slot.

15. A piece of 1″ (25.4mm) wide masking tape is placed over the entire length of the trussrod, from the end of the headplate to the adjustment nut end of the trussrod (**photo 6-11**). The tape is centered, so that an area approximately ¼″ (6.4mm) wide is masked off on both sides of the trussrod.

16. Wood glue is applied to the entire exposed fretboard surface of the neck. The glue should come near to, but not quite up to where the nut will be located. Then the masking tape is removed (**photo 6-12**). Additional small dots of the silicone sealer are quickly placed on the top of the trussrod.

17. The fretboard is positioned into place, with its drilled holes lined up with the brads, and pressed into place. The caul is

placed on top of the fretboard (**photo 6-13**). As many clamps as are available and will fit are applied, evenly spaced. Care should be taken to position clamps directly over the nut end of the fretboard, and over the heel (**photo 6-14**). Bias the position of the clamps toward the sides of the fretboard.

18. The snipped plastic straw is used to clear glue squeeze-out from the inside edge between the underside of the fretboard extension and the body end of the heel (**photo 6-15**), and also from between the nut end of the fretboard and the surface of the neck (**photo 6-16**).

 Glue squeeze-out along the sides of the fretboard should be left alone. Attempts to clear it may end up packing glue in the holes drilled for the side marker dots and in the fret slots, and may also glue the caul to the fretboard.

19. The glue is allowed to cure overnight. Then clamps are removed and the caul is removed and discarded. The brads are removed with pliers and a scrap of wood to protect the surface of the fretboard, using the same levering technique that was used to remove the pins after the headplate was glued on in the previous chapter. If the brads are thoroughly glued in place, they can be heated with a soldering iron to melt the glue, and then easily removed.

20. A small chisel is used to remove any dry glue remaining in the nut slot, which is the space between the nut end of the headplate and the nut end of the fretboard.

Refining the Headstock

At this point in construction, if the neck is held up and viewed from the side, its profile will be much the same as that of the finished neck, except for the length of the headstock. But if the neck assembly is viewed from the front (looking directly at the playing surface of the fretboard) it is apparent that wood still needs to be removed from the sides of the neck and from the headstock. Shaping the headstock and drilling the holes for the tuning machines will be approached first.

 The bandsaw is a useful tool for trimming the headstock and the transition curves from the headstock to the neck to shape. But the fact that the headstock is angled relative to the neck presents a safety issue which must be dealt with before using the bandsaw. It is of absolute necessity that any piece that is sawed on the bandsaw be in solid and complete contact with the saw table at all times. Failure to do this can result in the blade of the saw violently yanking the work down into the table, with the possibility of serious injury to the luthier and damage to the work.

One obvious way to deal with this is to flip the neck assembly over so the headplate is flat on the bandsaw table. But doing this work looking at the back surface of the headstock is difficult, because the work will require cutting near to but not into the fretboard, and the fretboard is not readily visible in this orientation.

The approach described here involves temporarily building up the thickness of the back of the headstock with sacrificial layers of MDF. These can be glued together, but taping them

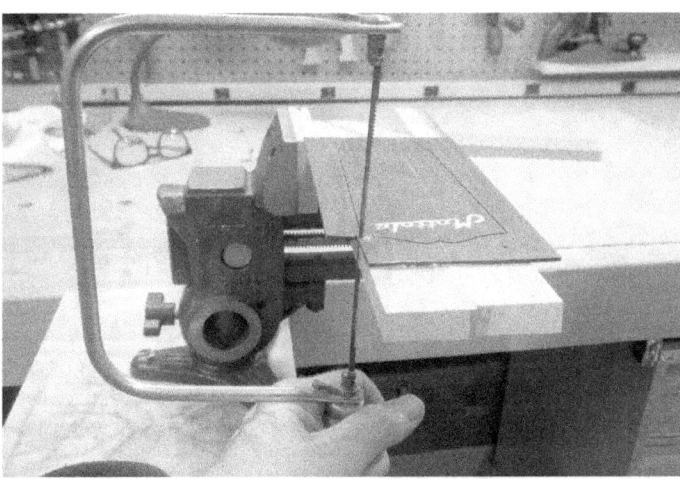

Photo 6-17 – The headstock can be trimmed to its rough shape using the coping saw. The neck is held in the vise with the top of the headplate horizontal, and the saw blade is maintained in a vertical attitude.

Photo 6-18 – A riser block made of a number of pieces of MDF material is used to safely present the headstock to the bandsaw.

together using double-sided tape is also effective and quicker. With enough thickness added, the headstock can be safely trimmed, with the bottom surface of MDF resting securely on the saw table. The accompanying assembly photos make clear how this works.

Of course the headstock shape can also be sawn out using a coping saw, which is a safer and less complicated method. Both options are presented.

The outline of the headstock has been penciled onto the headplate in an earlier assembly step. If it is not currently visible, it should be refreshed using the headstock template. The headstock template will also be needed for drilling the holes for the tuning machines, so it should be on hand in any case.

☐ Trimming the Headstock Using the Coping Saw Option

1. The neck assembly is held in the vise so that the top surface of the headstock is horizontal and the entire outline of the headstock is available to the saw (**photo 6-17**).

Photo 6-19 – Double-sided tape is applied to one side of each of the pieces of wood.

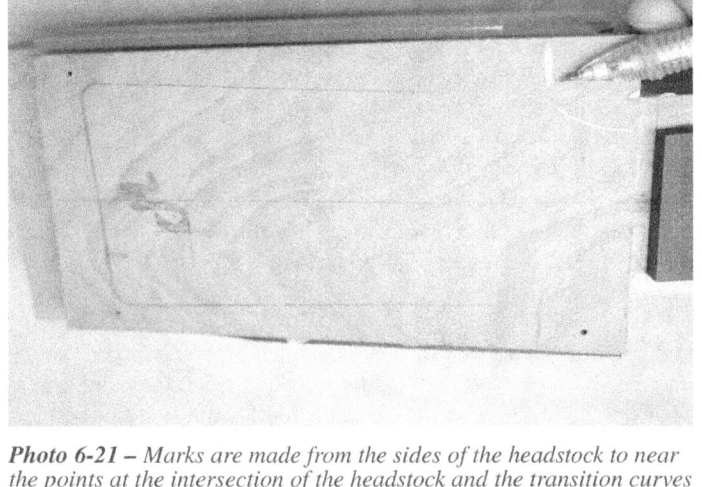

Photo 6-21 – Marks are made from the sides of the headstock to near the points at the intersection of the headstock and the transition curves to the neck.

Photo 6-20 – The pieces of wood are stuck together to form a riser block for the back of the headstock. The block is attached to the back of the headstock using double-sided tape, and the whole sandwich is compressed in the vise, to set the adhesive of the tape.

Photo 6-22 – Cuts are made along the lines.

2. The outline of the headstock and the transition curves between headstock and neck are roughly trimmed, using a coping saw and a blade of approximately 10 TPI. Care should be taken to keep the saw blade vertical, and to stay far enough away from the lines.

☐ **Trimming the Headstock Using the Bandsaw Option**

1. Rectangular pieces of ¾″ (19.1mm) MDF are cut (**photo 6-18**). These will be used as sacrificial "thickeners" for the headstock. The pieces must be larger all around than the headstock in its current state. The pieces should all be the same size. How many pieces are needed will depend on the size of the bandsaw table. Three pieces are generally needed.

2. Double-sided tape is affixed to one surface of each of these pieces. The tape should roughly cover the entire surface (**photo 6-19**).

3. The pieces are stuck together to form a riser block, which is in turn attached with double-sided tape to the back of the headstock (**photo 6-20**). Note that the back of the headstock must be perfectly flat for the tape to stick securely. If it is not, it should be sanded flat at this time, using sandpaper on a flat block that is wider and longer than the headstock. When doing this, it helps to round over the leading edge of the sanding block, so it fits into the transition curve between the back of headstock and the back of the neck. Once the riser block is stuck to the headstock, the entire assembly is temporarily clamped with clamps or squeezed together in the wood vise, to thoroughly set the adhesive of the tape.

4. Pencil lines are made on the headstock, from the sides to near the points between the headstock and the transition curve to the neck (**photo 6-21**). The bandsaw is used to make cuts along these lines, stopping close to the outline of the headstock (**photo 6-22**). When cutting the line on the right side of the headstock, the line can be followed exactly. Making the cut on the left side requires the neck to hang off the back of the bandsaw table, and the bandsaw frame will get in the way of making

this cut exactly on the line. The cut should be made as close to the line as possible.

👉 Care is taken when making all cuts with the bandsaw on thick stock to keep the MDF riser block flat against the table, and to avoid tipping the work, which could result in the blade grabbing the work and yanking it down into the table.

Photo 6-23 – The headstock is cut out to the previous saw cuts. The transition curves should not be cut out using the band saw, because these areas are not fully supported by the sacrificial riser block.

Photo 6-24 – The transition curves are shaped using a spindle sander or a drill press-mounted drum sander.

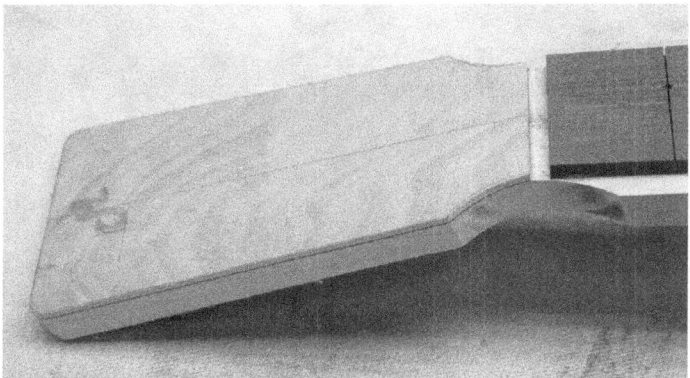

Photo 6-25 – The headstock and transition curves shaped to final dimensions.

5. The outline of the headstock is cut out to the cuts made in the previous step (**photo 6-23**). Although it is tempting to use the bandsaw to remove the waste in the transition curves, this should not be attempted because there is no support under these curves.

6. The riser block is left in place for subsequent trimming steps.

☐ **Further Refining of the Headstock**

1. The outline of the headstock, and the headstock-to-neck transition curves, are further refined and smoothed using a spindle sander, drill press-mounted drum sander, or by hand, using sandpaper on flat and round blocks. If either of the power tool options are used, the headstock top surface must be maintained in a horizontal position. If previous trimming was done using the bandsaw, then the still attached riser blocks will do that. If the outline was initially trimmed using the coping saw, then a thick block of wood should be used to raise the headstock up and keep it horizontal during sanding. Care must be taken when refining the transition curves to be sure the sander does *not* touch the corner of the fretboard (**photo 6-24**). If a sacrificial riser block was used, it is now removed.

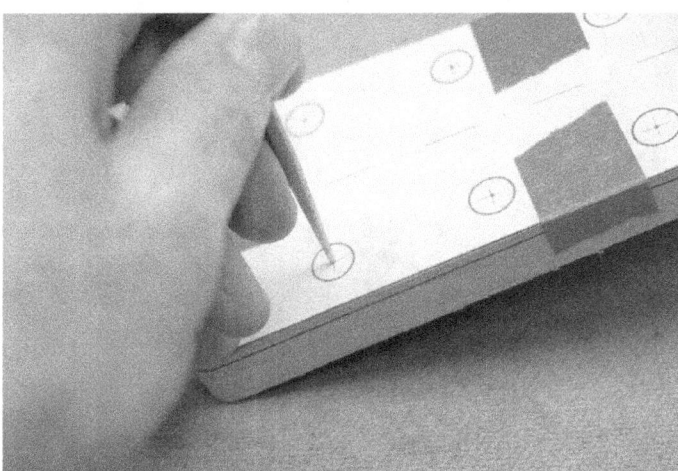

Photo 6-26 – The centers for the drilled holes for the tuning machine posts are pricked right through the template.

Photo 6-27 – The tuning machine holes are drilled at the pricked centers, using a brad point bit in the drill press. A hardwood block is used to back up the headstock, to help avoid blowing out the grain at the back of the headstock.

2. The straight sides of the headstock are further straightened by hand, using sandpaper on a hard block. The outline of the entire headstock should at this point match the template (**photo 6-25**).

Photo 6-28 – All the tuning machine holes drilled.

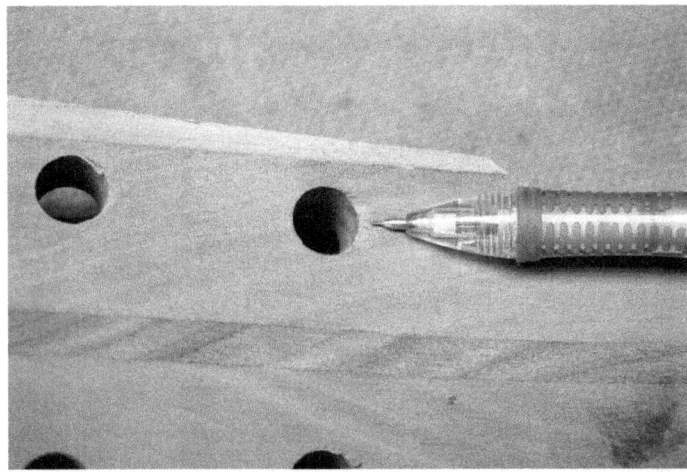

Photo 6-29 – A bit of wood has been blown out where the bit exited the back of the headstock on this hole.

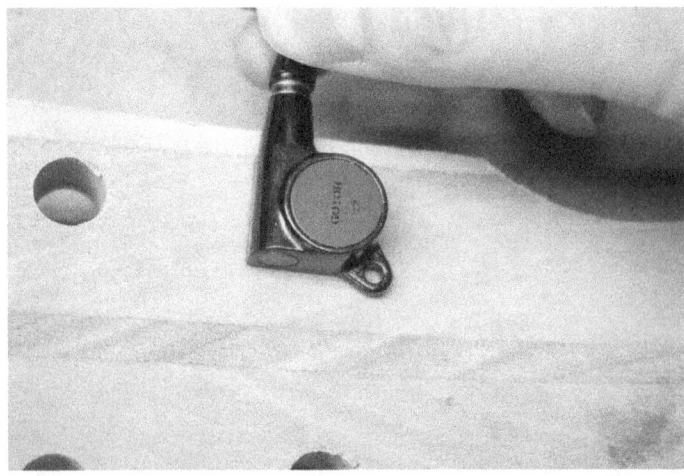

Photo 6-30 – The tuning machine will often cover the defect. If not, it will have to be repaired by gluing the blown out wood back in place (if it is available) or by puttying.

3. The template is taped to the top surface of the headstock, aligned with the nut end of the headstock and the centerline. An awl is used to prick the centers of the holes for the tuning machines. Centers are pricked right through the template and into the wood (**photo 6-26**). Then the template is removed and discarded.

4. Holes for the tuning machine posts are drilled at these pricked centers using the appropriate size brad point bit and the drill press (**photo 6-27**). The diameter of the holes needed is specified by the manufacturer or supplier of the tuning machines to be used. After all holes are drilled, the headstock looks like **photo 6-28**.

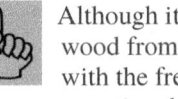 When drilling the holes, the back of the headstock must be supported on a smooth piece of *hardwood* scrap, as shown in the photo. This, and a light touch on the drill press lever as the bit exits the back surface of the headstock, will help prevent blowing out the grain (**photo 6-29**). Before each hole is drilled, any debris on the surface of the hardwood scrap should be cleaned off, so the back of the headstock will make clean contact with it. Minor blowout is usually not a problem, because it will covered in the finished instrument by the tuning machine (**photo 6-30**). Major blowout of the grain can be fixed by simply gluing the blown out piece back in, if it is available. If not, the divot can be puttied using a putty made from sanding dust of the wood species used for the headstock, mixed with wood glue or epoxy. This is mounded into the divot, allowed to cure, then sanded flush with the back of the headstock.

Removing Excess Wood From the Neck and Heel

Now that the headstock has been trimmed to its final shape, the sides of the neck shaft and heel need to be trimmed flush to the sides of the fretboard, and then the taper of the heel needs to be established. The side trimming can be done using a variety of tools, including rasps, spokeshaves and various saws (such as the coping saw, saber saw, etc.). The method described here makes use of a router and top bearing pattern bit. This is quick and easy, and keeps the sides of the shaft square to the top surface of the fretboard.

 Although it may be tempting to try to strip off excess wood from the sides of the neck using the bandsaw with the fretboard pointing up, this is an extremely dangerous operation, because the neck is unsupported underneath the cut.

Trimming the sides of the heel can also be performed using a variety of tools. The method described here makes use of a small plane.

☐ **Trimming the Sides of the Neck Shaft**

Before any trimming is done, the scribed centerline down the back of the neck shaft and down the back of the heel should be examined and refreshed if necessary. This is simple to do at this point, because the reference surface of the neck is still intact, but the reference surface will be trimmed off in the following steps.

1. The neck is clamped in the wood vise in the same manner and orientation as used previously to support it for routing the trussrod slot in Chapter 2. The heel is held by the vise, the top surface of the fretboard is kept horizontal, the headstock points toward the right. A piece of wood is set across the tops of the vise jaws, bridging them. Wedges of wood are used between this piece of wood and the underside of the neck shaft to support the shaft and the weight of the router.

2. A top-bearing pattern bit with a cutting length of at least 1″ (25.4mm) long is mounted in the router. I'm using a small trim router in the accompanying photos, but any router that will sit on the fretboard without danger of tipping can be used.

3. In operation, the bearing will ride on the side of the fretboard, so a check is made to be sure there is no hardened glue squeeze-out that will get in the way of the bearing. If there is, it can be removed using a chisel held vertically with its back against the side of the fretboard, and pressed down to chip away the glue.

Photo 6-31 – Excess wood is trimmed off the side of the neck using a router and pattern bit, with its bearing running against the side of the fretboard. A stop should be used to prevent the router from moving past the nut end of the fretboard.

4. The depth of cut is set on the router so that the top of the cutting edge is aligned with the seam between the fretboard and the neck wood.

☞ Some pattern bits have a lot of space between the bottom of the bearing and the top of the cutting edge. If a bit like this is used it may be possible that setting the depth as stated doesn't leave enough of the height of the bearing in contact with the side of the fretboard. There is a danger in this situation of the bearing slipping off during routing, which could damage the work. In the case where there is not enough contact between bearing and fretboard side, a straight piece of ¼″ (6.4mm) thick MDF can be attached to the top of the fretboard using double-stick tape, so its edge is aligned with the edge of the fretboard. This will provide additional depth for the bearing to run on.

5. As was the case when routing the trussrod slot, a clamp should be clamped to the headstock to serve as a stop, to prevent the router from cutting into the transition area between neck shaft and headstock. The location of the stop should be adjusted so the cutting bit will stop just short of the nut end of the fretboard.

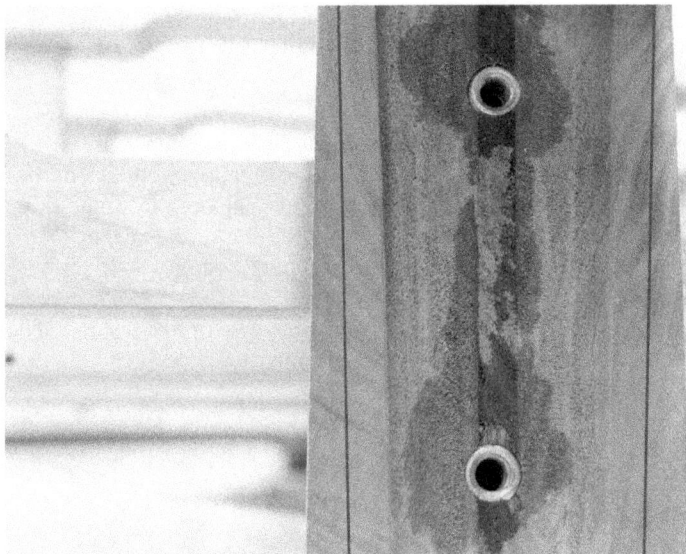

Photo 6-32 – Lines denoting the sides of the heel were drawn on the body contact surface of the heel in a previous assembly step. If they are no longer visible, they should be refreshed.

6. Cutting the right side (the side currently facing the luthier) proceeds with the router moving from left to right (**photo 6-31**). Because the full depth of the cutting edge of the bit is cutting, multiple shallow passes should be made. Only during the final pass will the bearing be riding on the side of the fretboard.

☞ Note that the fretboard extension is flexible and easily broken. It *cannot* support the weight of a heavy router. The cut should begin with the router positioned right over the corner of the heel.

7. If there is enough clearance for the router bit, the left side of the neck (the side currently facing away from the luthier) can be cut by leaving the neck in the vise and repeating steps 5 and 6 with the router working the other side.

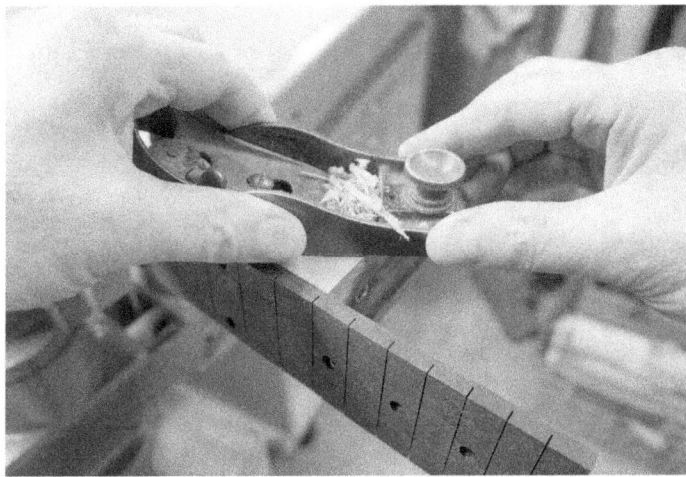

Photo 6-33 – The sides of the heel can be quickly trimmed down to the lines using a block plane.

 Note that on this side, the router is making a climb cut. These are inherently dangerous, because the router is trying to move with the cut, and can be pulled from the luthier's hands.

☐ Trimming the Sides of the Heel

Trimming the sides of the heel using a sharp block plane is quick and precise and yields accurate results.

1. The heel tapers in width from the fretboard to its end. Pencil lines indicating the finished location of the sides were marked on the body contact surface of the heel in a previous construction step (**photo 6-32**). If those lines have been obliterated, the template for the heel should be used to refresh them.

2. It is easiest to work one side of the heel at a time. The neck is held in the vise so that the side of the heel to be worked is facing up.

3. Excess material is planed off the side of the heel down to the line, using a small block plane (**photo 6-33**). Care is taken not to touch the side of the fretboard with the plane blade.

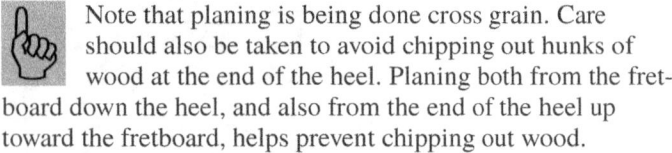 Note that planing is being done cross grain. Care should also be taken to avoid chipping out hunks of wood at the end of the heel. Planing both from the fretboard down the heel, and also from the end of the heel up toward the fretboard, helps prevent chipping out wood.

4. The other side of the heel is planed down in like fashion. The neck is now ready for carving of the shaft and heel.

Carving the Neck

The back and side surfaces of the necks and heels of most guitars are rounded and smooth. The cross section of the neck of the instruments under construction in this book is at this point of rectangular cross-section. In this chapter the neck will be carved to its final shape. There are a few construction operations that novice luthiers generally find particularly daunting, and neck carving is one of them. It makes perfect sense that this is the case. The process of visualizing the transformation of the rectangular cross-section shaft and heel into a smooth rounded continuous surface requires some three-dimensional visualization skills that most people have not fully developed or don't have at all.

Despite many years of lutherie experience, I have limited abilities in this regard myself. When I watch people like Portland, Oregon, luthier John Greven carve a neck freehand, using the stationary horizontal belt sander as the carving tool, I am in absolute awe at the skill involved. I just don't have, and probably never will attain, the level of skill necessary to do that. But not possessing this skill is by no means a barrier to successfully carving a guitar neck. It is just that a different carving technique is required.

Engineers are often asked how it is possible to solve complex engineering problems. The fundamental answer to this question is to first break down the complex problem into a number of smaller, less complex, and more easily solvable problems. This is the approach that will be taken here to the transformation of the current state of the neck to its finished state. I'll call the process to be employed *successive approximation*. The neck in its current state already roughly approximates its final shape. If the neck is viewed looking directly at the fretboard, it already looks pretty much the way it will look when done. Same goes if it is viewed directly from the side. What will be described in this chapter are a small number of simple layout and construction operations, each of which is simple to do (and simple to do precisely) and gets the neck closer to the desired shape.

The first few neck carving steps involve cutting facets (flats) onto the neck. This approach to guitar neck carving has been well described in the guitar construction literature. Good examples of this appear in work by William Cumpiano and Jonathan Natelson[1] and by one of my *American Lutherie* author colleagues, Greenville, Virginia, luthier John Calkin[2]. After this initial carving, the surface of the neck is further refined using some specialized techniques. Successive approximation by faceting is described in general terms here in this introduction, so the description of the construction operations will make better sense when they are encountered later on in this chapter.

Figure 7-1 shows the neck in its current state of construction and shows the locations of two cross sections on the shaft of the neck, the first at the position of the 1st fret, and the second at the position of the 11th fret. These cross section locations will be used to demonstrate the faceted approach to successively approximating the final shape of the shaft.

Figure 7-2 shows the steps involved in the transition of the two cross sections on the neck shaft from its current

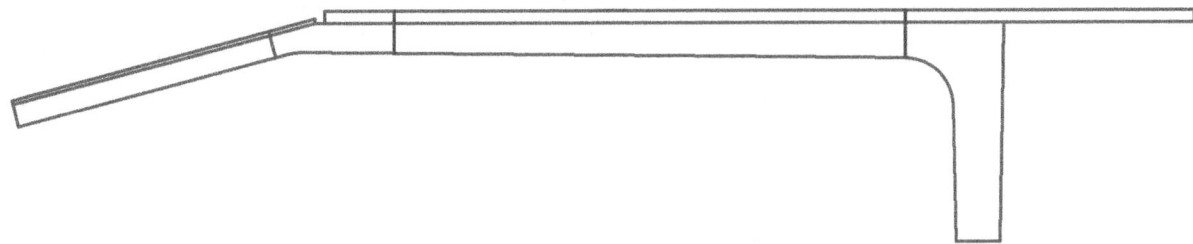

Figure 7-1 – Side view of the neck. The vertical lines represent the locations of cross sections that are useful in demonstrating how neck carving will proceed. The leftmost cross section on the shaft is located at the 1st fret, and the other one on the shaft is located at the 11th fret, just before the curved transition from shaft to heel.

rectangular shape to a shape near the desired shape of the finished shaft. To aid in seeing where we are headed, the target curves of the finished neck shaft are shown in **figure 7-2.2**. Note that these are the typical oval curves found in most guitar necks. After the target curves are established, the locations of the primary facets are drawn. These facets are angled at 45° from vertical and they just touch the target curve (that is, they are tangent to the target curves). After this layout operation, the waste wood outside the facet lines is removed (**figure 7-2.4**). At this point the cross sections more closely approximate the final shape.

Now the locations of the secondary facets are drawn. These are shorter in length than the primary facets, are angled at 22.5° from the primary facets, and they also just touch the target curve. After this layout operation, the waste wood outside the facet lines is removed (**figure 7-2.6**). At this point the cross sections closely approximate the final shape, so close in fact that further faceting is really not necessary. Construction will proceed from here by simply scraping off the remaining facet edges, and continue with surface-smoothing operations.

Although here the 1st and 11th fret cross-sections were used just to demonstrate how the successive approximation approach to neck carving works, in practice these are the locations that will be used when actual layout and construction work is done. The locations of the edges of the facets will be marked on the sides and bottom of the neck at each of these fret positions, then a straightedge will be used to connect these marks. The heel is marked and carved similarly and at the same time. The transition areas between shaft and heel and also between shaft and headstock are marked in a more informal manner. Details of this will be discussed in the following sections.

Layout and Construction

Most of the layout operations will require the use of straightedges that are flexible. Although thin and flexible metal and plastic rulers are available, a reasonable substitute is a strip of flexible hard plastic cut out using scissors. Even strips of cereal box cardboard will serve as useful alternatives to purchased rulers in this application. In fact, because shop-built straightedges can be made in any length desired, they are easier to use than purchased flexible rulers.

Although there are many different tools that can be used to perform the following carving operations, the descriptions are for the use of rasps and a flat-bottom spokeshave. These tools are easy and quick to use, and provide good control of the carving as it progresses. They are also commonly found in most wood shops, and are relatively inexpensive if they must be purchased. Coarse rasps and medium rasps (sometimes called wood files) are used. Good quality cabinet rasps are expensive, but inexpensive rasps of the "cheese grater" variety work well. Cabinet rasps should have the conventional profile, with one flat side and one curved side. If the "cheese grater" style of rasps are used, one curved and one flat rasp will be needed, or a single rasp with interchangeable blades can be used.

☐ **Building the Holding Fixture**

A simple holding fixture is constructed that presents the neck upside down, for easy access to the areas that must be worked during the carving process. If the fixture is secured in a vise when used, it also raises the work high enough so the luthier has better lines of sight. This helps with maintaining accuracy of the work. If the fixture is gripped by the vise near the

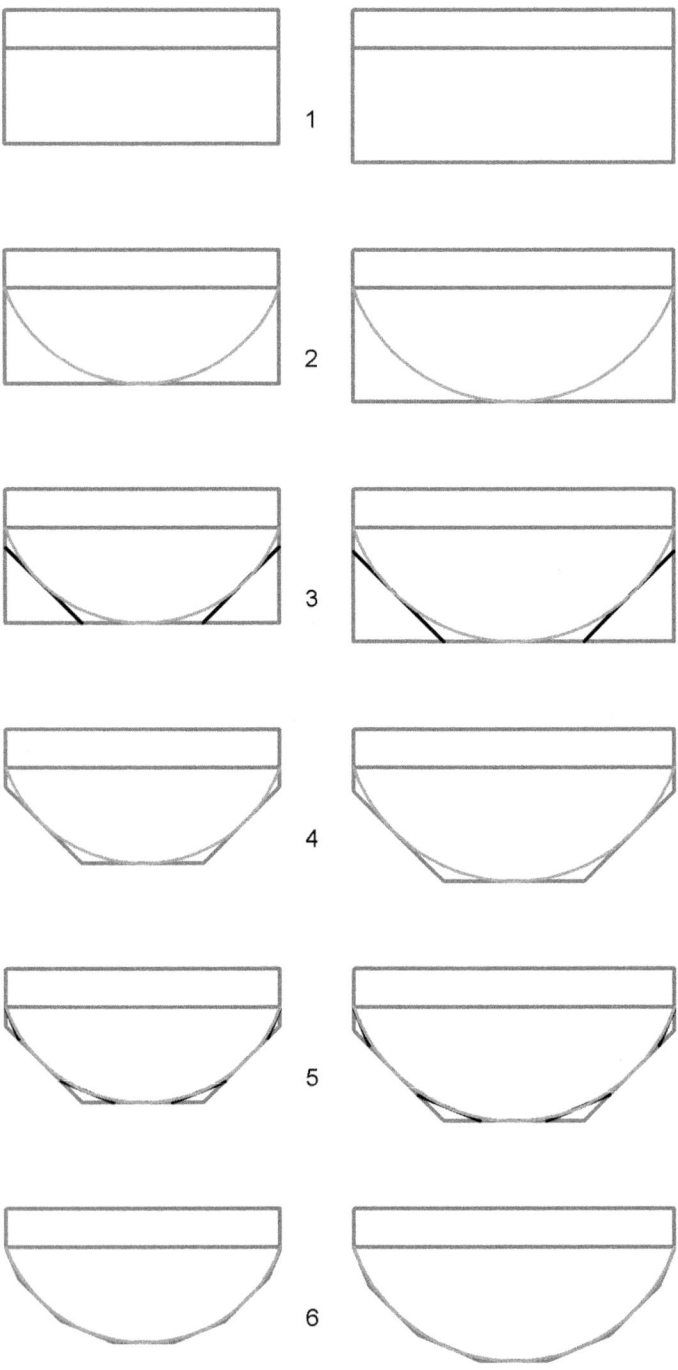

Figure 7-2 – *Transformation by successive approximation of the rectangular shaft cross sections (1) from the previous figure. The cross sections on the left are those at the 1st fret. The cross sections on the right are those at the 11th fret. Each step is simple to lay out, and removal of material requires no special skills. The desired curves of the finished neck are added in step 2. The primary facets are drawn (3) and then the excess material is removed (4). The secondary facets are drawn (5, but difficult to see at this scale) and then the excess material is removed (6). At this point, the shape of the shaft is so close to the desired finished shape that only minor scraping of the remaining sharp edges is needed.*

headstock end, this will provide easy access to the entire length of the neck. The fixture is built from a piece of 2×8 construction lumber or any other piece of wood that is approximately 1½″ (38.1mm) thick by 7½″ (190.5mm) wide. A piece 26″ (660.4mm) long is needed.

1. If a 2×8 is used, one edge is planed or ripped to remove the roundover edges. This will be the top surface of the fixture.

2. A protractor is used to measure the angle between the headstock top surface and the fretboard playing surface of the neck under construction. A mark is made on the bottom surface of the fixture 7″ (177.8mm) from one end. The protractor is placed at this mark and an angled line is drawn to the end of the fixture (**photo 7-1**).

3. A cut is made on this line, yielding a triangular-shaped piece (**photo 7-2**). The rough surface of this piece is planed or sanded smooth and flat, and perpendicular to the sides.

4. The piece is attached to the top surface of the fixture, opposite from where the cut was made, as shown in **photo 7-3**. In the photo it is being nailed on with finishing nails that will then be countersunk.

5. In use the fixture is secured in a vise (**photo 7-4**). The neck is positioned upside down on the fixture and secured with one clamp holding down the fretboard extension (**photo 7-5**) and another holding down the headstock (**photo 7-6**). Shims must be used between the fixture and the headstock for a good fit.

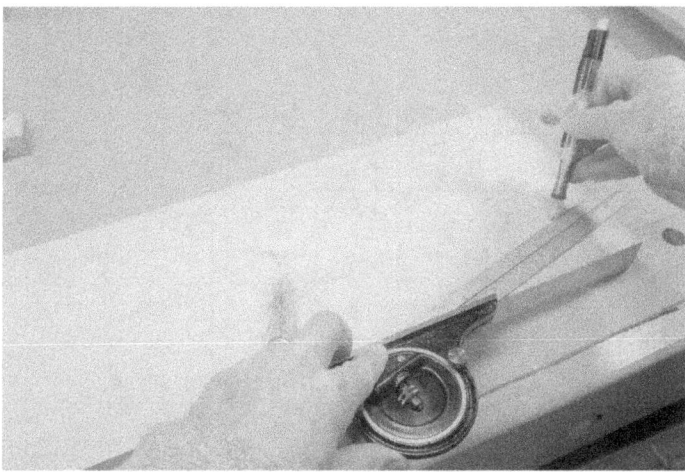

Photo 7-1 – *Building the holding fixture. A wedge with the same angle as the headstock is drawn at one corner of the board.*

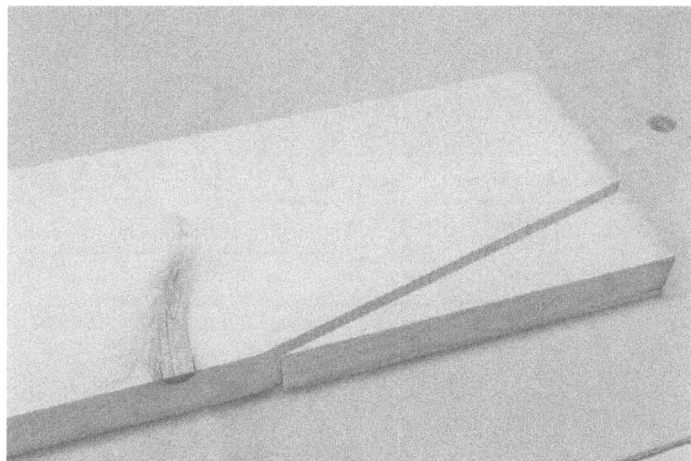

Photo 7-2 – *The wedge is cut out and its rough surface smoothed.*

Photo 7-3 – *The wedge is attached to the board opposite the cut corner. If it is nailed on as shown, the heads are set below the surface.*

Photo 7-4 – *The fixture in use. Here it is holding a classical guitar neck.*

Photo 7-5 – *A thin board or wedge of wood serves as a shim between headstock and fixture.*

Given the simple construction of the holding fixture, there will be space between the top surface of the fixture that is under the headstock, and the headstock itself. This must be filled with a flat piece of wood or a thin wood wedge, before attempting to clamp the headstock to the fixture. If this is not done, clamping pressure may break the headstock off.

☐ The Primary Facets

The borders of the primary facets will be marked out first, and then the facets will be cut. Marking out can be done with the neck on the bench or in the holding fixture, whichever is easier. The borders of the primary facets are based on measurements of the cross sections of the shaft at frets 1 and 11, as shown in **figure 7-3**. Note that in this figure and subsequent figures, the neck is presented upside down, because this is the orientation in which the carving of the facets will be done. The borders for the primary facets are drawn on the sides of the neck first. Then the borders for the primary facets are drawn on the back of the neck.

1. Drawing the borders of the primary facets on the sides of the neck. Referring to **figure 7-3**, the facet offsets are marked on the sides of the neck. A small ruler is used to measure at fret 1 on one side of the neck from the fretboard/neck shaft seam, up ⅛″ (3.2mm). A mark is made in pencil here (**figure 7-4**, top, left). The same is done on the other side of the neck.

2. Again referring to **figure 7-3**, the ruler is used to measure at fret 11 on one side of the neck from the fretboard/neck shaft

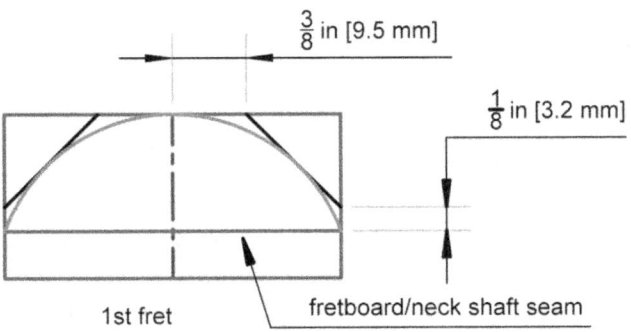

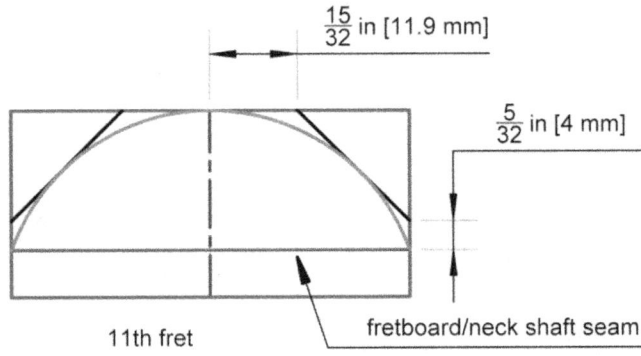

Figure 7-3 – *Offsets to the edges of the primary facets at frets 1 and 11. Offsets on the sides of the neck are measured from the fretboard/neck shaft seam. Offsets on the back of the neck are measured from the centerline. The cross sections are presented with the neck upside down, because this is the orientation that will be used when the facets are carved.*

Photo 7-6 – *The fretboard extension is clamped to the fixture on the other end.*

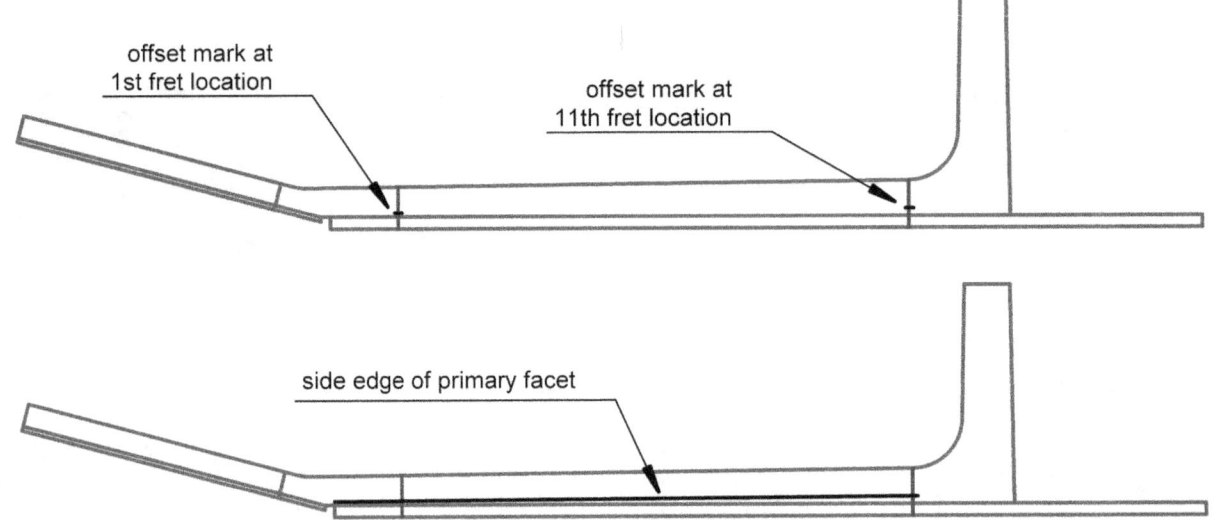

Figure 7-4 – *In the top drawing, offset marks are made on the side of the neck. The values of the offsets are taken from figure 7-3. These marks are connected with a straight line (bottom drawing), which marks the side edge of the primary facet of the neck shaft.*

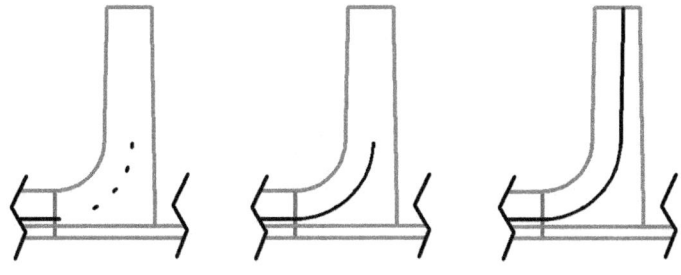

Figure 7-5 – The line marking the side edge of the primary facet is extended around the curve of the transition from shaft to heel, and then down the heel to its end.

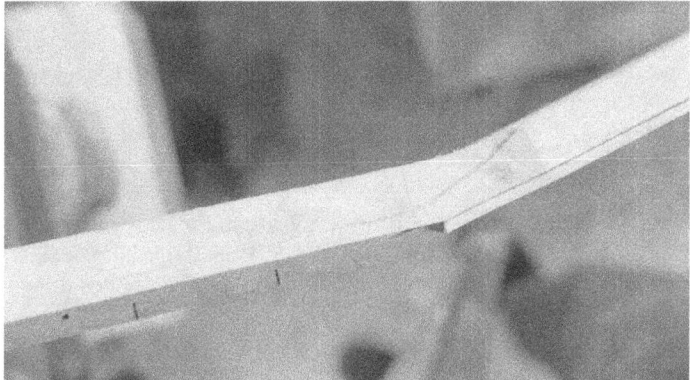

Photo 7-7 – The line marking the side edge of the primary facet is extended around the curve of the transition from shaft to headstock, as a freehand arc that ends at the lower corner of the headstock.

seam, up 5/32″ (4mm). A mark is made in pencil here (**figure 7-4**, top, right). The same is done on the other side of the neck.

3. On each side of the neck, the straightedge is placed on the marks at fret 1 and fret 11, and a straight line is drawn. The line is also extended to stop at the nut end of the fretboard (**figure 7- 4**, bottom).

4. The ruler is used to measure the offset from the mark on one side at fret 11 to the edge of the shaft. This offset is used to make a series of marks parallel to the curved edge of the part of the neck that transitions from shaft to heel (**figure 7-5**, left). These marks are connected freehand to make a smooth curve parallel to the curved edge (**figure 7-5**, center). The same is done on the other side of the neck.

5. A straightedge is positioned on one side of the heel, at the end of the arc made in the step above and parallel to the inside edge of the heel (not the body contact edge). A straight line is drawn, extending to the bottom of the heel (**figure 7-5**, right). The same is done on the other side of the neck.

6. A freehand arc is drawn in the shaft-to-headstock transition area on one side of the neck, extending from the nut end of the line previously drawn on this side, to the bottom corner of the headstock (**photo 7-7**). Small variations in the shape of this arc are not an issue. As long as the distance from the fretboard increases at each point along this arc as it proceeds from the nut end of the line to the bottom corner of the headstock, all will be well. Folks that are not comfortable drawing the curve freehand can make use of a flexible French curve template.

The same is done on the other side of the neck. Every attempt should be made to make these curves mirror images of each other. One way to do this is to draw one arc, put a clear computer printer label over it, trace the curve with a marker, remove the label, cut it out on the drawn curve using a knife or scissors, and then use one of the cut out pieces as a template to trace the curve on the other side.

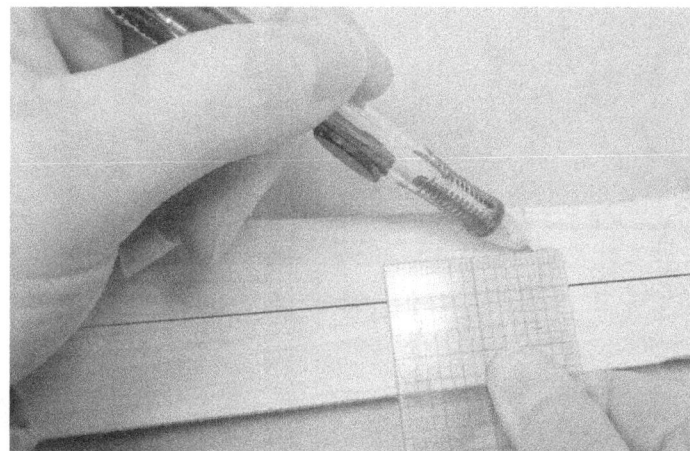

Photo 7-8 – Marks made to indicate the locations of primary facet borders on the back of the neck are measured from the centerline. Here the second of the two marks opposite fret 1 is made.

Photo 7-9 – Marks opposite fret 1 and fret 11 are connected on both sides of the centerline using a flexible straightedge.

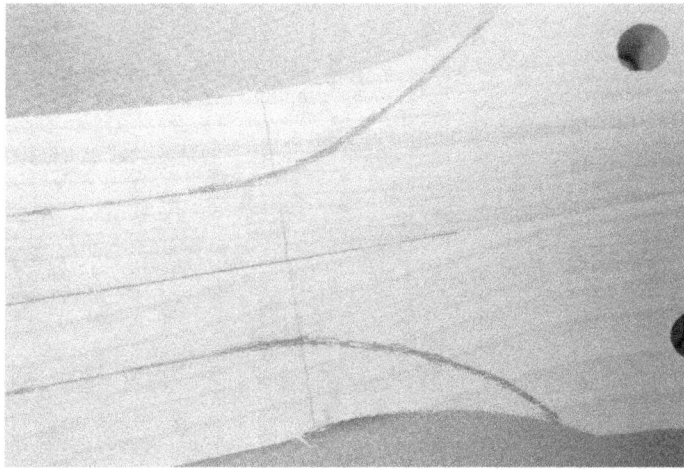

Photo 7-10 – Symmetrical freehand curves are drawn from the nut ends of the previously drawn lines, and ending at the corners of the headstock.

7. Drawing the borders of the primary facets on the back of the neck. Referring again to **figure 7-3**, the primary facet offsets are marked on the back of the neck. A small ruler is used to measure opposite fret 1 on the back of the neck, from the centerline out ⅜″ (9.5mm). A mark is made in pencil here (**photo 7-8**). This is repeated on the other side of the centerline as well.

8. The ruler is used to measure opposite fret 11 on the back of the neck from the centerline out ¹⁵⁄₃₂″ (11.9mm). A mark is made in pencil here. The same is done on the other side of the centerline.

9. A flexible straightedge is used to join the two marks on each side of the centerline. The resulting lines are shown in **photo 7-9**. The lines are extended to end opposite the nut end of the fretboard.

10. The lines are extended from the nut ends as freehand arcs, ending at the corners of the headstock (**photo 7-10**). Every attempt should be made to make these curves mirror images of each other. The same duplication technique described in step 6 can be used here.

11. A flexible straightedge is used to extend the heel ends of the lines into the shaft-to-heel transition curve and onto the heel, and continuing down to the bottom of the heel. The lines drawn on the heel should be parallel to the side edges of the heel.

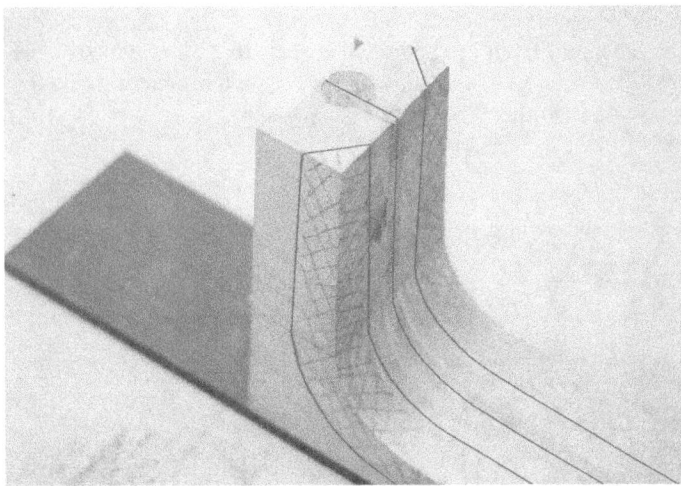

Photo 7-11 – *The primary facet lines on the back of the neck are continued through the shaft-to-heel transition. Then these lines are continued onto the heel, keeping them parallel to the side edges. The areas between the facet lines on the back and sides of the shaft and the heel are cross hatched, to indicate the material that must be removed.*

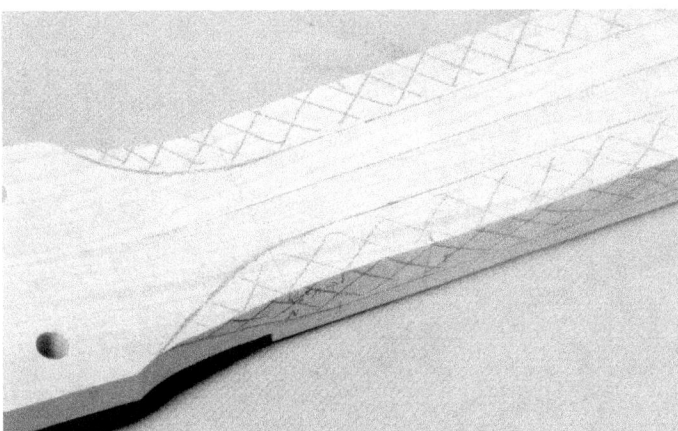

Photo 7-12 – *Cross hatching of areas where wood will be removed for the primary facets at the headstock end of the neck.*

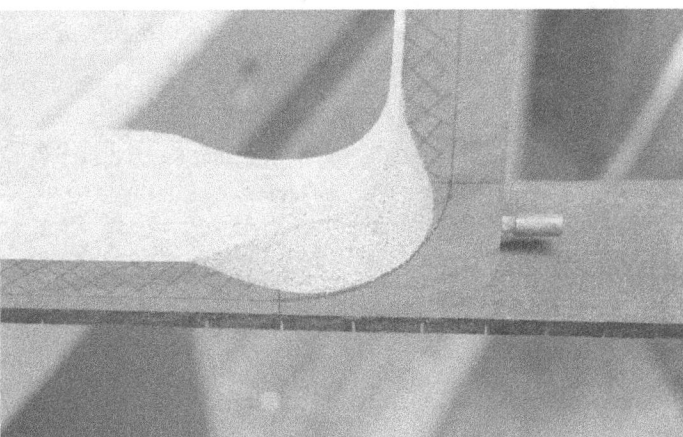

Photo 7-14 – *The finished primary facet, cut at the shaft-to-heel transition.*

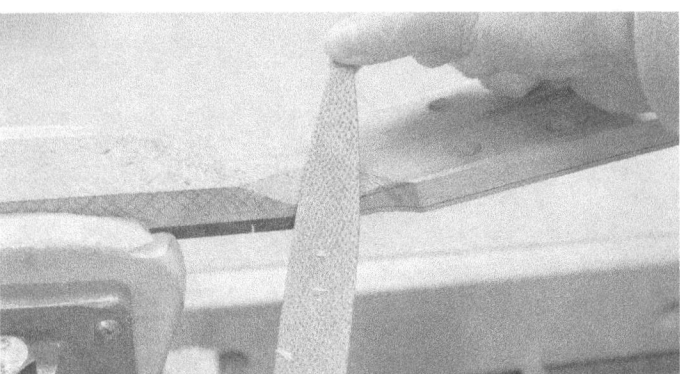

Photo 7-13 – *The curved side of the rasp is used to remove wood for the primary facet at the transition between shaft and headstock. The lozenge-shaped cut has to be worked from both ends, to avoid working into the grain. Here the neck is held in a pattern maker's vise just to make the photography a bit easier for me. This work can be done with the neck clamped to the holding fixture.*

Photo 7-15 – *To avoid banging up the delicate corner of the headstock when using the spokeshave, that area is heavily padded with tape.*

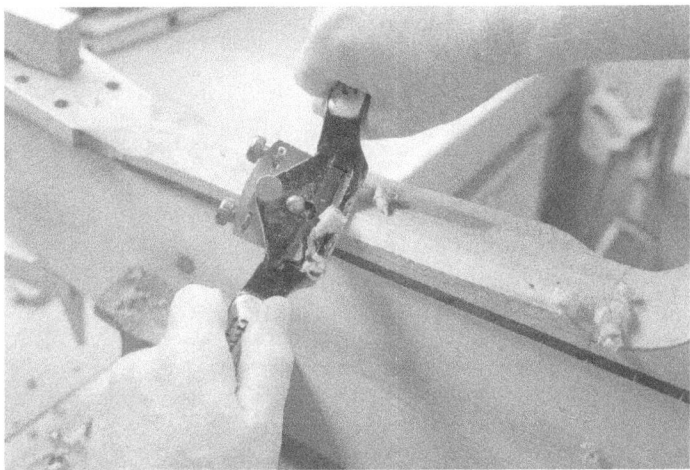

Photo 7-16 – Cutting the primary facet on one side of the shaft, using a spokeshave.

Photo 7-17 – Finishing up the facet, using a rasp.

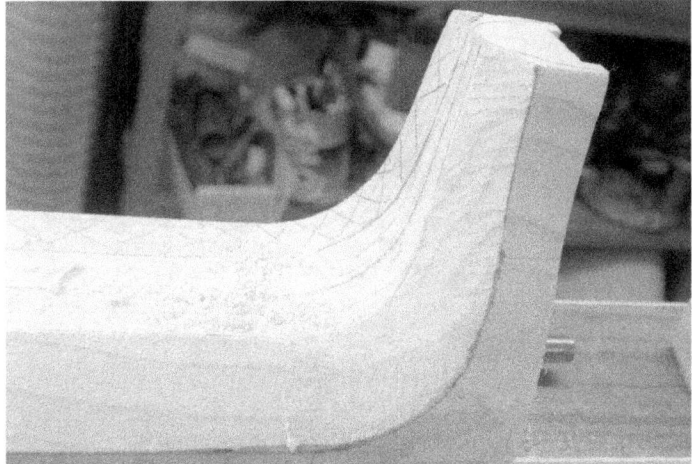

Photo 7-18 – The primary facet extended up the heel.

12. The area between the drawn outlines of each facet are cross hatched in pencil, to indicate where wood will be removed during the carving steps that follow (**photos 7-11, 7-12**).

13. The primary facets are carved. The neck is clamped onto the holding fixture. A coarse rasp with a curved surface is used to remove waste material between the lines in the transition area between shaft and headstock. The cut will have a lozenge shape and a flat floor (**photo 7-13**). It is generally necessary to move the rasp from the headstock into the center of the cut, and also from the shaft into the cut, cutting deeper at the center of the cut. The pencil lines should be avoided. As the width of the center of the cut approaches the pencil lines, the coarse rasp should be replaced by a medium one. These cuts are made at both sides of the neck. The resulting cut is as shown in **photo 7-14**.

 Much care should be taken to avoid rasping the actual corner of the headstock. This feature must remain sharp in the final shape of the neck.

14. Similar lozenge-shaped cuts are made using the curved rasps, in the transition areas between shaft and heel, on both sides of the neck (**photo 7-14**).

15. A spokeshave with a flat bottom, or a coarse flat rasp is used to remove the waste wood for the facet between the two lozenge-shaped cuts on each side of the neck. If the spokeshave is used, it is a wise idea to apply a few layers of tape or other padding to the shaft-to-headstock transition areas (**photo 7-15**). Doing so will help prevent the spokeshave from running into and denting this area at the end of each cutting stroke. In general, the cutting strokes are made moving from the heel end of the shaft toward the nut end, but in some cases cutting in the other direction works better (**photo 7-16**). Care should be taken to stay between the marked outlines of the facet, and to keep the facet flat.

16. A rasp with a finer cut is used to flatten and smooth the facet along its entire length, and to integrate it into the parts of the facet previously cut at the transitions (**photo 7-17**).

17. The flat coarse rasp is used to cut the facet on both sides of the heel. Results are shown in **photo 7-18**. Again, the finer rasp is used to flatten and smooth this part of the facet and to integrate it cleanly into the shaft to heel transition.

The ultimate curve of the neck profile has now been approximated with five flat surfaces. These are the two sides, the two primary facets just cut, and the back of the neck.

☐ The Secondary Facets

The procedures for marking out and cutting the secondary facets are similar to those used for the primary facets, but there are a few small differences. The borders of the secondary facets are based on measurements of the cross sections of the shaft at frets 1 and 11, as shown in **figure 7-6**. Note that the borders of each secondary facet are measured as offsets from one of the edges between the primary facets. There are four of these edges. Note also that the offsets at a given location are the same on both sides of the edge. When the borders for the primary facets were laid out, the borders on the sides of the neck were done first, followed by the borders on the back of the neck. Because there are four secondary facets and eight borders to be laid out, it is just simpler to lay out all the borders at the same time.

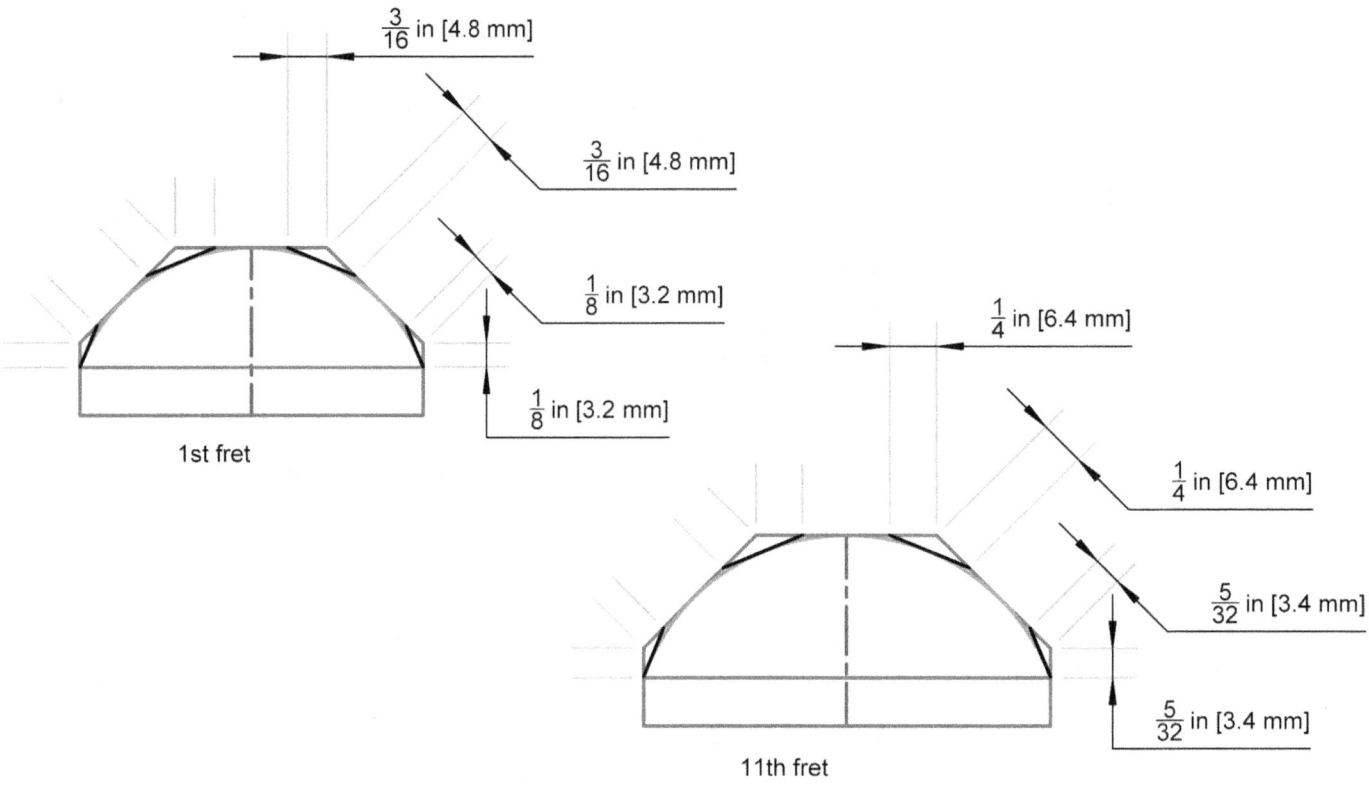

Figure 7-6 – *Offsets to the edges of the secondary facets at frets 1 and 11. All offsets are from one of the edges between the primary facets, and the offset values are the same on each side of an edge.*

Photo 7-19 – *The location of the 1st fret is transferred to the neck.*

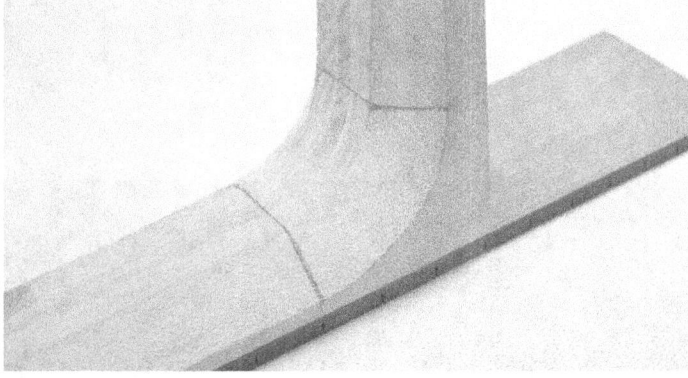

Photo 7-21 – *The location of the 11th fret is also transferred to the neck. A similar mark is made on the heel. This mark is located at a distance from the fretboard that is the same as the distance from the 11th fret to the body end of the heel.*

Photo 7-20 – *The marks indicating the boundaries of the secondary facets at the 1st fret are marked.*

1. Offsets are measured and marks are made at the position of fret 1 first. Because eight marks need to be made, it is convenient to first mark the position of fret 1 all around the shaft (**photo 7-19**).

2. The offsets for all borders of all secondary facets are measured, and marks are made, based on the values given in **figure 7-6**. Again, offset measurements are made from each edge between the primary facets, and are the same on both sides of the edge. There is one important special case when drawing these marks. When marking an offset near the seam between the fretboard and the shaft, the mark should *never* end up on the side of the fretboard, even though that's where the measurement says it should go. In this case the mark is *always* made right on

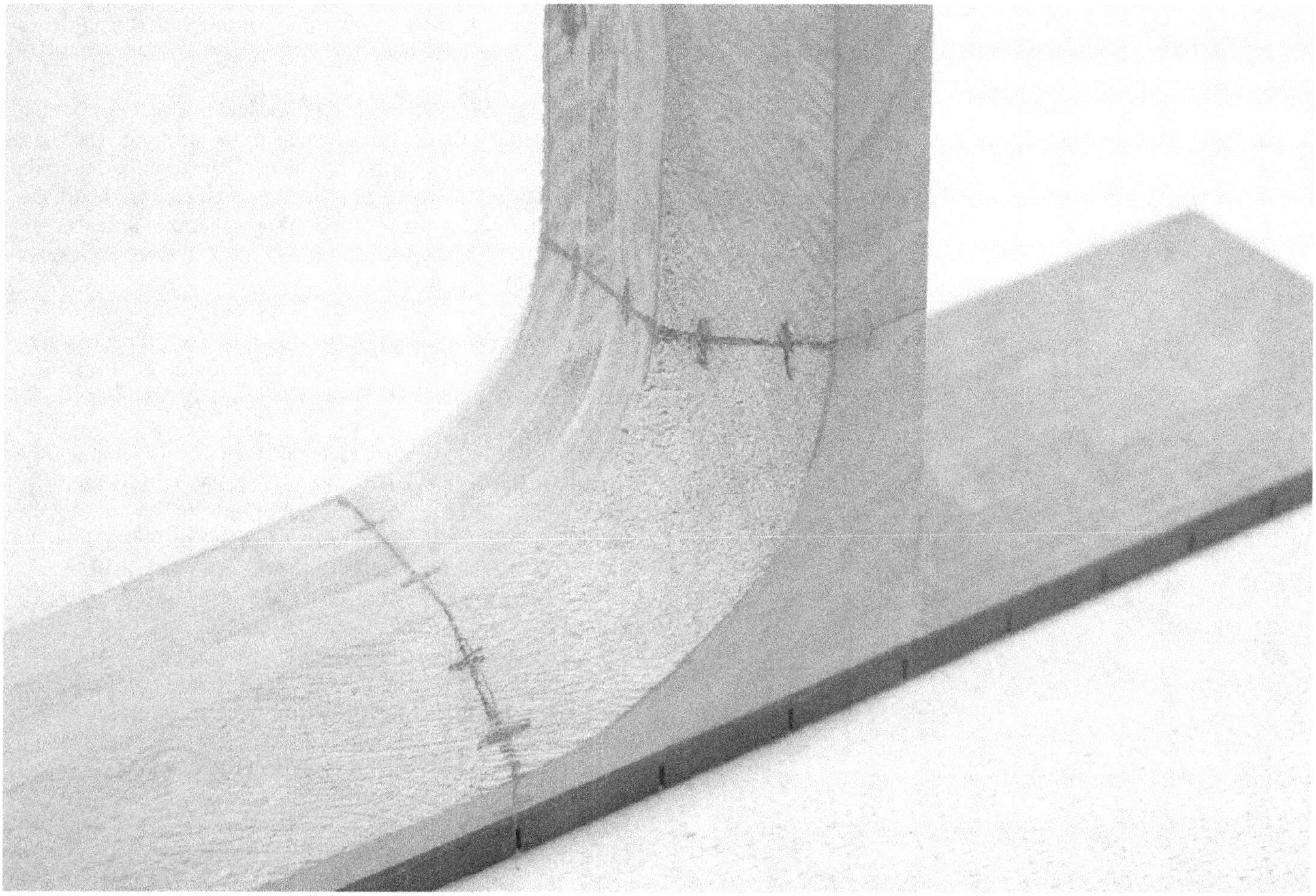

Photo 7-22 – The marks indicating the boundaries of the secondary facets at the 11th fret and on the heel are marked.

the seam instead. We do not want to cut into the sides of the fretboard at this stage of shaping. If the plan and templates were followed exactly, and if the primary facet was accurately marked and cut, this should not be an issue. Complete markings for the secondary facets at fret 1 are shown in **photo 7-20**.

3. Based on the values given in **figure 7-6**, offsets are measured and marks made at the position of fret 11 (**photos 7-21, 7-22**). Marks are also made on the heel where it is as wide as the shaft is at the 11th fret.

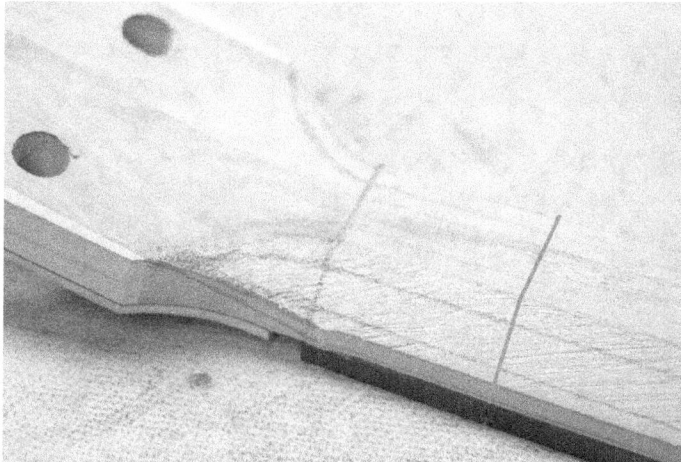

Photo 7-23 – The previously made marks are connected together using a flexible straightedge and extended to opposite the nut. The boundaries in the shaft to headstock transition are done freehand.

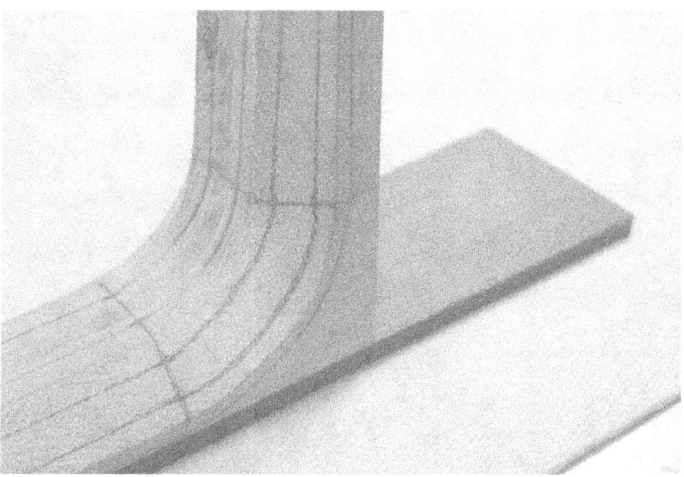

Photo 7-24 – The boundaries of the secondary facets are extended onto the heel.

4. Marks made in the previous two steps are connected using pencil and a flexible straightedge. The lines are extended to opposite the nut end of the fretboard.

5. The lines are extended from the nut ends as freehand arcs, ending at the corners of the headstock (**photo 7-23**). Although every attempt should be made to make these curves mirror images of each other on the two sides of the centerline, this can generally just be eyeballed.

6. A flexible straightedge is used to extend the heel ends of the two lines that are on the back surface of the neck into the shaft to heel transition curve and onto the heel, and continuing to the bottom of the heel. The rest of the lines are extended using the same drawing technique detailed in steps 4 and 5 of the previous operation, and shown in **figure 7-5**. The results are shown in **photo 7-24**.

7. The space between the drawn boundary lines of each of the secondary facets is filled with cross hatching, to guide carving of the facets (**photos 7-25, 7-26**).

8. Carving of the secondary facets is done using the same tools, techniques, and sequence as were used to carve the primary facets. Note that the edges being cut off are shallow and narrow, so more care, less effort, and less aggressive tools will be required. The areas of the facets in the headstock-to-shaft transition area are done first. Because the distance between the outlines is so small here, a rasp with a medium cut is used right from the start. Again, care is taken to avoid touching the corners of the back of the headstock, which should remain sharp. The areas of the facets in the shaft-to-heel transition area are done next. Carving with the rasp continues onto the heel and right down to the heel bottom edge. Finally the flat part of each facet over the shaft is carved, using either spokeshave or rasp.

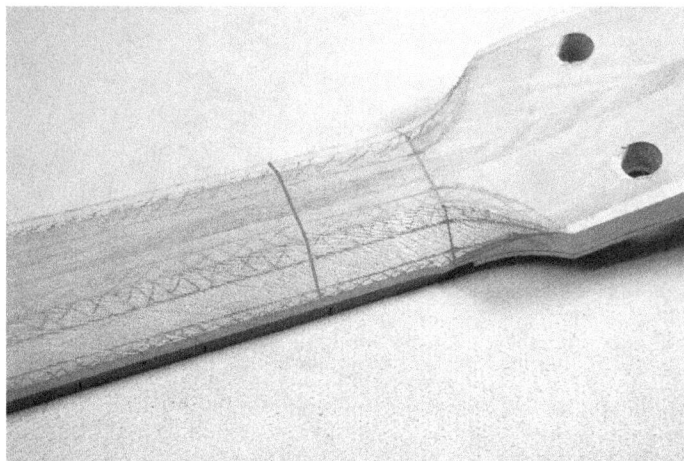

Photo 7-25 – *The secondary facets are cross hatched for visibility. Here's the view at the headstock end ...*

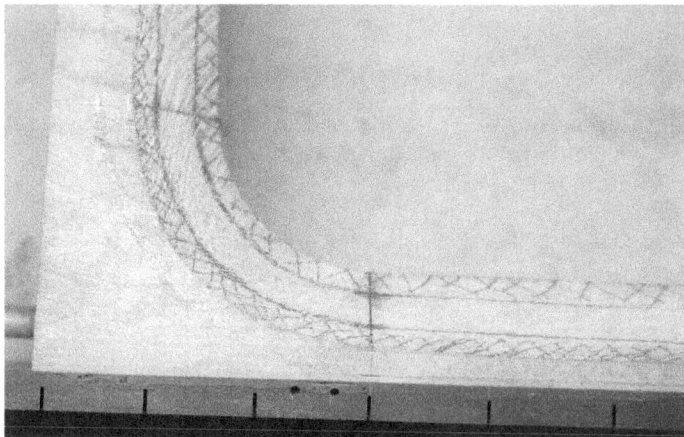

Photo 7-26 – *... and here is the view from the heel end.*

Care must be taken when carving the secondary facets located on the sides of the neck shaft, to avoid cutting into the sides of the fretboard. Keeping a sharp eye on the edge of the fretboard when rasping or shaving is a good idea. Lutherie is an activity that involves all the senses, and the ears and hands can help the eyes in this situation. Because of the glue at the fretboard seam, rasping or shaving with the spokeshave will make a slightly different sound, and provide a slightly different feel, while cutting on the seam.

Results of carving of the secondary facets are shown in **photos 7-27** and **photo 7-28**. The curve of the neck surface is now approximated by nine flat surfaces, so the ultimate shape is much more obvious at this point.

Photo 7-27 – *The secondary facets are cut flat using rasps and spokeshave. The results are shown here.*

Photo 7-28 – *A closer look at the completed secondary facets, at the heel end.*

☐ Smoothing the Carved Surface

After the secondary facets are cut, it would be possible to go on and mark out and cut tertiary facets, but these would be so narrow that they would be difficult to mark. Anyway at this point the neck is so close to its desired shape that all it requires are successive smoothing steps. These are done using medium rasps and 80 grit sandpaper. Much care is taken in the final steps to be sure the entire surface is smooth, with no obvious humps or valleys.

1. At this point in the process, there are noticeable edges between the flats of the secondary facets. A medium rasp is used to flatten these edges a bit, creating what can be considered to be tertiary facets (**photo 7-29**). Only a few light strokes are necessary to cut the edges down. The flat of the rasp is used on the shaft and on the heel, and the curved surface of the rasp is used in the transitions. When the edges near the fretboard are rasped, care should be taken to avoid rasping the sides of the fretboard. Rasping right down to the seam between neck shaft and fretboard is fine.

2. The rasp is now employed to round over the entire surface of the neck. Light strokes should be taken. As the rasp is pushed, it should also be moved sideways along the length of the shaft, and at the same time its handle lifted to change its angle. This complex movement is done to keep the rasp moving along and across the surface, to prevent digging any holes in the surface. The end result is shown in **photo 7-30**.

3. A sheet of 80 grit sandpaper in ripped into thirds lengthwise. One of these pieces is grasped at both ends, and used to sand the shaft (**photo 7-31**) by pulling the sandpaper back and forth over the surface. This operation is generally called shoeshine sanding. The purpose is to take down any high spots across the surface, and to smoothly round over the surface of the neck from side to side. While doing this, the sandpaper should be simultaneously kept moving along the length of the shaft. Again, the object of the longitudinal movement is to avoid sanding too much in one place. There should be as much sanding at the

Photo 7-29 – *The edges between the secondary facets are knocked off with the medium rasp.*

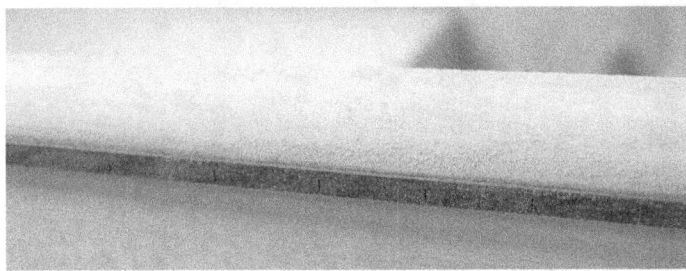

Photo 7-30 – *... The medium rasp is used to round over the entire profile of the shaft.*

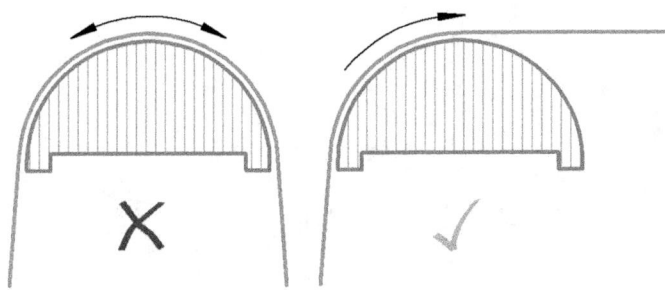

Figure 7-7 – *Shoeshine sanding of the heel should be done with the sandpaper wrapped only halfway around the heel, and sanding only in one direction, toward the center.*

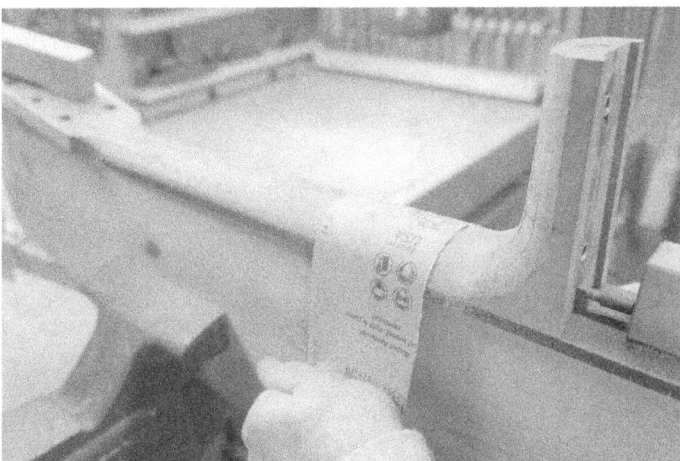

Photo 7-31 – *The shaft is shoeshine sanded with 80 grit sandpaper to refine the surface.*

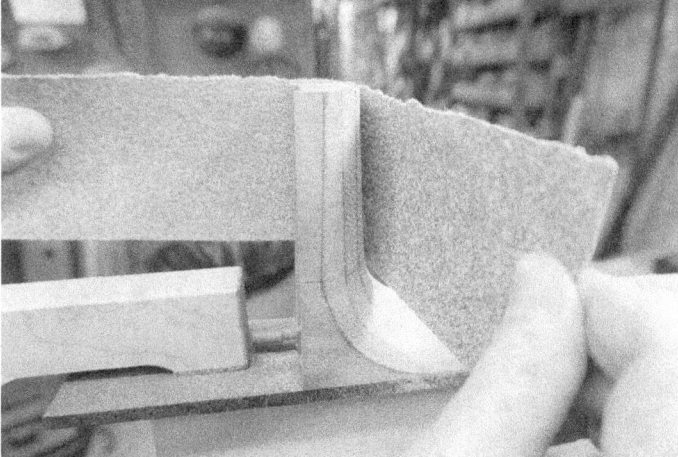

Photo 7-32 – *The heel is shoeshine sanded as well, but with a shallower wrap of the paper.*

Photo 7-33 – 80 grit sandpaper on a block is used to sand the shaft with the grain.

fretboard, and to particularly avoid touching the playing surface edges of the fretboard.

4. The heel is also shoeshine-sanded but using a slightly different technique. Here sanding is being done across the end grain, so it is generally more effective to wrap the sandpaper around only about 90° and sand in one direction only, from the edge toward the centerline (**photo 7-32**, **figure 7-7**).

 When shoeshine sanding the heel, care is taken to avoid touching the edges between the sides of the heel and the body contact surface. These edges should remain sharp.

Note that shoeshine sanding leaves cross-grain scratches on the wood of the shaft. These will be fully removed by subsequent sanding steps.

5. Next, 80 grit sandpaper is used on a hard flat sanding block to sand the shaft longitudinally, with the grain (**photo 7-33**). The block should be simultaneously moved across the width of the shaft, at the same time it is moved back and forth, again to avoid sanding too much in one place. During this sanding step, the sides of the fretboard can be integrated into the curve of the shaft, but the edges of the fretboard at the playing surface must still be avoided. Sanding is paused every now and again, to examine the work. Sanding dust collects in any hollow areas, so a

ends of the shaft as near the middle. Care should be taken to avoid digging a groove in the heel with the edge of the sandpaper while sanding the shaft near the heel.

 Much care should be taken when wrapping the sandpaper around the shaft to avoid touching the sides of the

Photo 7-34 – The block is used to sand the heel, also with the grain.

Photo 7-35 – *A sanding block with a curved profile is used to sand the transition area between shaft and heel ...*

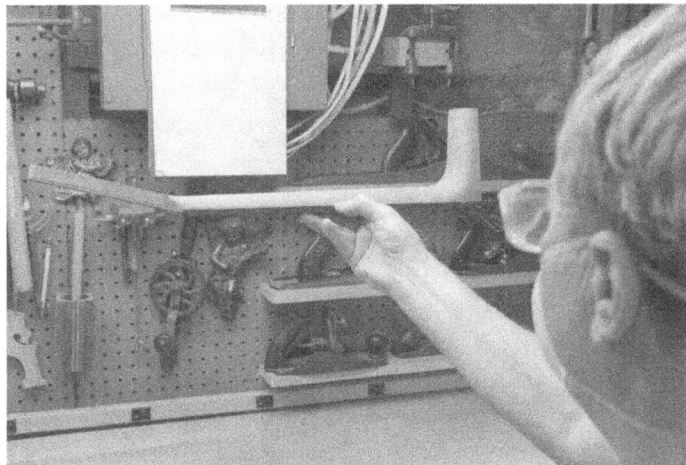

Photo 7-38 – *Another view of the initial sighting.*

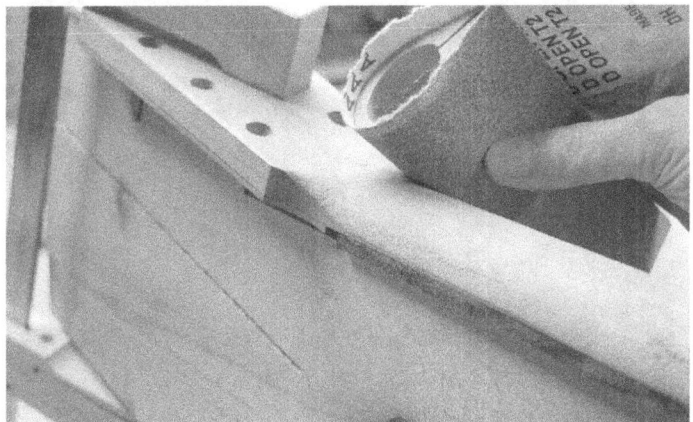

Photo 7-36 – *... and also the areas between shaft and headstock.*

the surfaces of the shaft and heel (**photo 7-35**). Sanding should be with the grain. Note there are two small areas here that require special attention. One of these is right on the centerline. This small area may be missed by most of the previous sanding operations, and so might remain flat at this point. Additional work with the round profile sanding block is often needed to attain a nice rounded shape throughout. The other small area that often needs special attention is the side of the heel, just under the fretboard. It helps to scribble some pencil marks over these areas. When the pencil marks have been sanded off, it will be known that these areas were at least touched by the sandpaper. It is often possible to identify small flat areas by touch, using the fingertips.

It is wise to always keep in mind while shaping the neck that there is a trussrod that is not far below the surface under the first fret, and that there are threaded inserts that are not far beneath the surface of the heel.

8. The round profile block is also used to smooth and round the shaft-to-headstock transition areas (**photo 7-36**), sanding with the grain. The points at the bottom corners of the headstock must remain sharp.

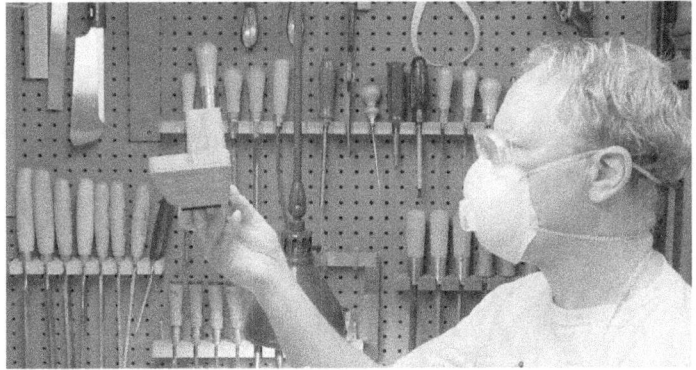

Photo 7-37 – *Visual assessment of the carving job begins by sighting over the shaft at the centerline.*

9. After the entire neck has been sanded as described, the shape of the neck is critically assessed visually, and reworked as necessary. Due to the complex shape of the neck and the subtleties of the irregularities that may be found, a specific technique is used to visually examine the work. This technique takes advantage of the ability of human sight to notice small discrepancies in the straightness of a two dimensional object, if it is presented against a sharply contrasting background. The neck is of course a three dimensional object. But if it is held at eye level so that the surface of the shaft presents as a horizon, and if the luthier focuses just on that horizon, then for all practical purposes it is a two dimensional object that is being inspected.

collection of sanding dust in one place may indicate more sanding work is needed around that spot.

6. The sanding block is also used to round the profile and straighten the lines of the heel, sanding with the grain (**photo 7-34**). The edge all around the bottom of the heel should remain sharp.

7. A round profile sanding block (or any cylinder that will serve the purpose) is used to smooth and round the surfaces in the transition area between shaft and heel, and blend this area into

The shaft is examined first. The neck is held horizontally at eye level, with the fretboard facing down. It is held in front of a contrasting background. In **photo 7-37** and **photo 7-38** I am

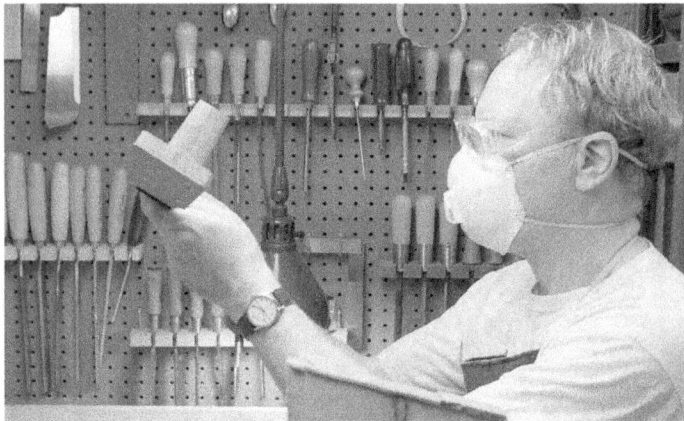

Photo 7-39 – *Inspection continues by incrementally rotating the neck toward the luthier.*

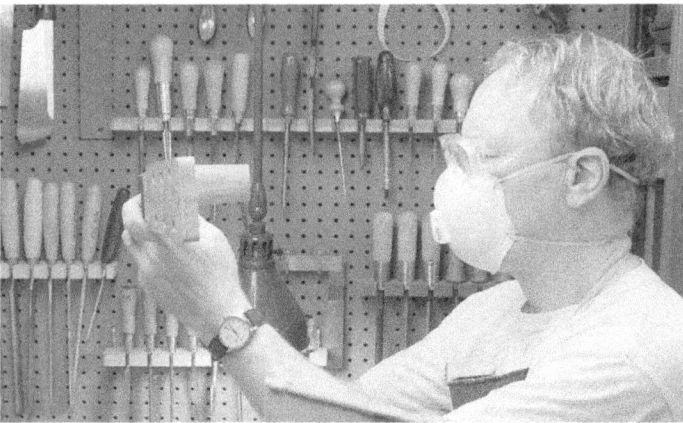

Photo 7-41 – *Rotation stops when the side of the fretboard is being examined.*

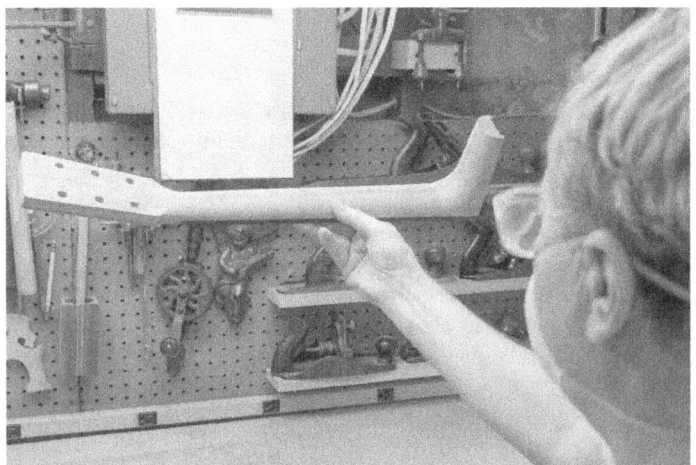

Photo 7-40 – *Another view of inspection of the neck when slightly rotated.*

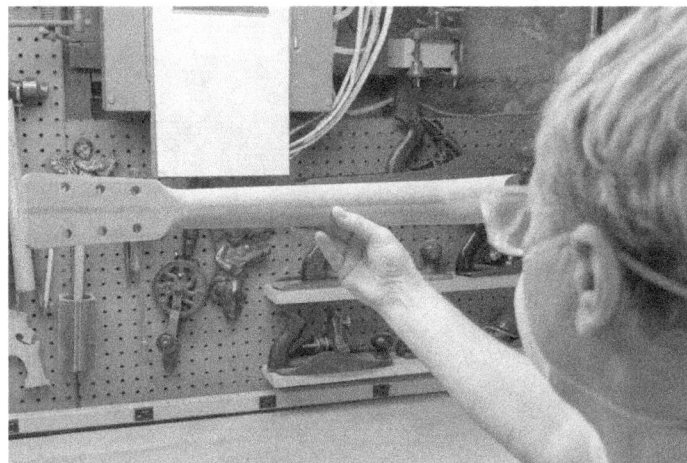

Photo 7-42 – *Another view of sighting over the side of the fretboard.*

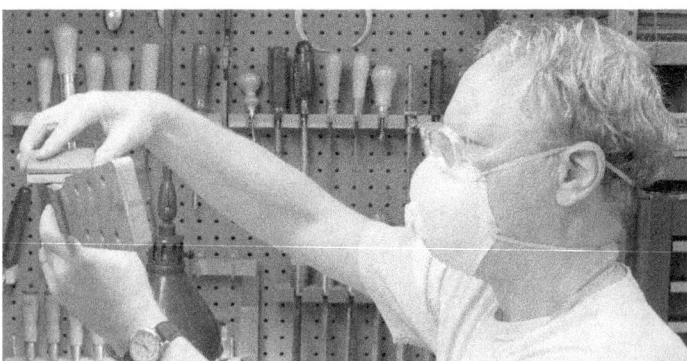

Photo 7-43 – *It is convenient to sand away imperfections with the neck held at eye level so sanding progress can be immediately seen.*

holding a light colored neck in front of the darker pegboard behind the workbench. If an appropriate background is not readily available in the shop, a large piece of paper or cardboard can be temporarily taped in place to serve as a background.

The horizon formed by the bottom of the shaft is sighted over along its entire length. Any imperfection such as a hump or a valley appearing on the horizon will be easily seen when the shaft is examined in this manner. If an imperfection is found, it is immediately sanded out. A good way to do this will be explained in step 11.

 Of course, a straightedge is a useful tool to use when examining the neck shaft for straightness. It must be short enough to fit between heel and headstock.

10. If no imperfections are found on the horizon with the neck in the fretboard down orientation (or if such imperfections have been sanded out), the neck is rotated slightly toward the luthier as shown in **photo 7-39** and **photo 7-40**. Actually in those photos the neck has been rotated toward the luthier quite a lot, but that is just so the direction and rotation will be obvious in the photos. The actual amount of rotation should be subtle. The visual assessment described in step 8 above is repeated at this rotation and any imperfections found are sanded out.

11. The above two steps are repeated (**photos 7-41, 7-42**) until the neck has been rotated to the point where the horizon is on the side of the fretboard. Then the neck is returned to its fretboard down orientation, and the entire assessment and refinement process is repeated, but this time with the neck being incrementally rotated *away* from the luthier.

12. During steps 9 through 11, any imperfections found are immediately sanded out. The imperfections are likely to be so small as to be invisible when viewed from any other perspective than the one described. A good way to sand out an

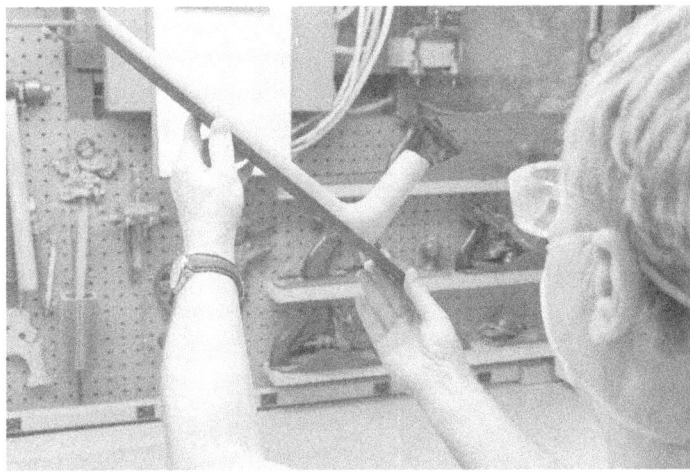

Photo 7-44 – *The best way to assess smoothness of the transition between shaft and heel is to hold it in an orientation that resembles the letter "V."*

imperfection is to keep the neck in the same position in which that imperfection was found, and use the sanding block to sand, while keeping the imperfection in sight (**photo 7-43**). This position is not a particularly efficient way to sand, holding everything up in the air like that, but in general not a lot of sanding is required to flatten each imperfection found.

13. After the shaft is assessed, the same procedure is used to assess the heel. The starting position is with the shaft pointing up and the body contact surface of the heel pointing down.

14. The transitions between headstock and shaft, and between shaft and heel, are assessed and refined in the same manner. But in these areas, the starting position is with the neck held up at eye level so the transition area can be viewed as a "V", as shown in **photo 7-44**. What is being sought is a clean "V"-shaped horizon, with straight arms and an evenly rounded valley. As the neck is tilted (**photos 7-45, 7-46**) the shape of the "V" will widen and flatten out. But the qualities of straight arms and an evenly rounded bottom should be persistently evident throughout rotation of the neck. When imperfections are found, they are dealt with using the flat sanding block when the imperfections are located on the arms, and the round profile block when they are found in the valley.

15. The neck is put aside for a day, and then the entire assessment and refinement process is repeated with a fresh view. It is useful to hold the neck with the headstock pointing the other way this time, too. If the previous steps were performed with the headstock to the left, this time around it should be pointed to the right. If no imperfections are found, then the neck is put aside for another day. If no imperfections are found two days in a row, then the assessment and refinement task is done. If one

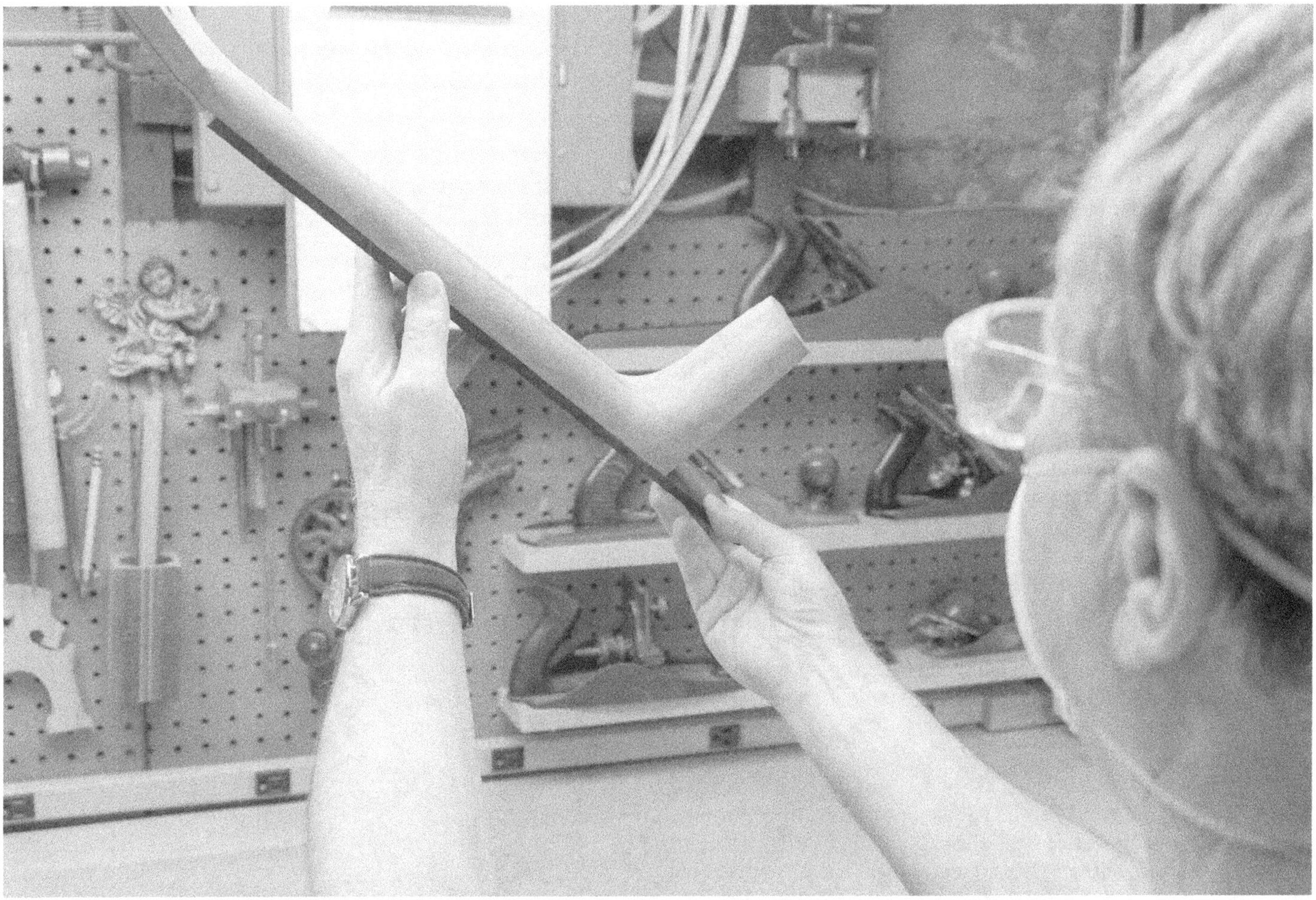

Photo 7-45 – *Inspection proceeds by slightly rotating the neck toward the luthier then sighting again.*

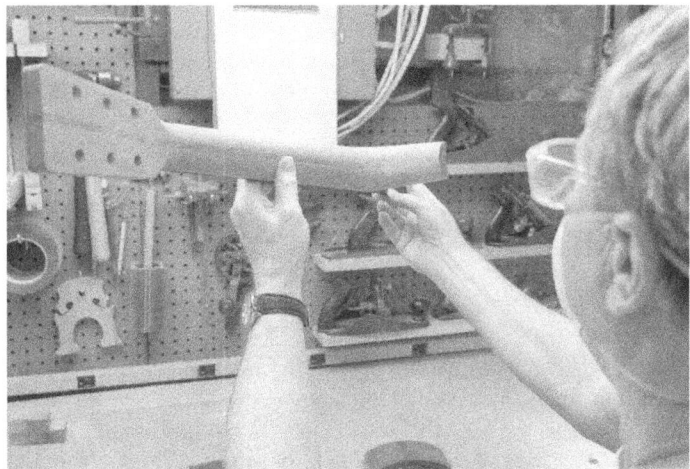

Photo 7-46 – *The process ends when the side of the fretboard and the side of the heel is reached.*

reason additional work on the neck will be postponed, is my observation that a number of lutherie novices are more motivated if work begins on the body of the guitar at this point. There are no technical reasons that neck work cannot proceed until completion.

---

1. Cumpiano, William; Natelson, Jonathan. (1993) *Guitarmaking Tradition and Technology.* Chronicle Books.

2. Calkin, John. (1993) Carving Neck Facets. *American Lutherie #33*, p.48

or more imperfections are found and sanded out, the neck should be put aside for another day and the process repeated.

Note that the described process of determining when the task is done is of general utility for all assessment and refinement operations. It should be considered to be a general principle of lutherie. It will appear again for other guitar construction operations described in this book.

16. The visual inspection process is extremely useful in locating imperfections, for luthiers with good visual acuity who are also perceptually sensitive to visual input. People who are more sensitive to touch may find it useful to use the fingers to probe the surface of the neck for imperfections. In fact, a tactile assessment is a useful final inspection step in all cases. The neck can be held in playing position and the fingers (mostly the thumb) are moved along the surface, in a manner that emulates playing. Then the process is repeated using the other hand. So, if this was originally done right-handed, it is now done left-handed.

17. With the exception of the top surface of the headstock and the playing surface of the fretboard, the entire neck is sanded, using 100-grit sandpaper. The flat and rounded profile sanding blocks should be used where appropriate. Following this sanding, the entire neck is rubbed briskly with a rag to remove all sanding dust. The sanding of the surface can be assessed to see if additional sanding at this grit is required.

The top surface of the headstock is not sanded because it has already been sanded to a finer grit, and if it contains shell material then sanding with coarse grit may put deep scratches in it. The playing surface of the fretboard is not sanded because it still needs to be cambered, an operation that is described in a following chapter.

Additional Work on the Neck

At this point, the neck will be put aside while work begins on the body of the guitar. The neck should be put is a safe place, out of the way of continuing construction work. Tasks still to be done on the neck include cambering the fretboard, installing the marker dots and the frets, and adding the heel cap. The

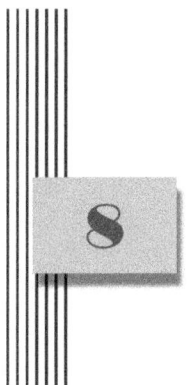

8 The Body Mold

The previous chapter covered one of the guitar building operations that novices find most difficult, carving the neck. That task was made much more understandable and reliable by breaking it down into small steps, easy to understand and implement. Another lutherie construction process that novices find difficult is bending the sides of the guitar to shape. This book will deal with side bending in exactly the same way that neck carving was dealt with, breaking it down into a series of small and simple steps. Doing so will make it possible for lutherie novices to get reliable and accurate results when bending the instrument sides. Another thing that will aid in this operation is the use of a body mold. Construction of the mold is described here.

The ribs (sides) of guitars and other stringed instruments are permanently bent into shape using heat. There are a number of commonly used methods for bending the sides of a guitar into their curved shape. The most common methods are as follows:

• The luthier bends the sides to shape by hand using a heated bending iron and a simple workboard, which provides a simple visual template for the ultimate shape of the sides.

• The luthier bends the sides to shape by hand using a heated bending iron, then inserts the warm and damp sides into a mold (also sometimes spelled *mould*) so they can cool and dry to their exact ultimate shape.

• The sides are bent to exact ultimate shape using a purchased or shop built side bending machine.

Different luthiers use different tool and fixture combinations, depending on a number of factors. Probably the two most common factors include the extent to which instruments are built on a production basis, and also which of these tools each builder is most familiar and comfortable with. It is worth noting that in a personal lutherie instruction environment (that is, in a formal

***Photo 8-1** – A simple solid body mold. Each half of the mold is made of identically shaped pieces of some sheet material, in this case MDF, glued and doweled together. The halves are bolted together with bolts through the large tabs at the ends of the mold. This mold uses 5 layers of ¾" (19.1mm) MDF and 1 layer of ¼" (19.1mm) MDF for a total depth of 4" (101.6mm).*

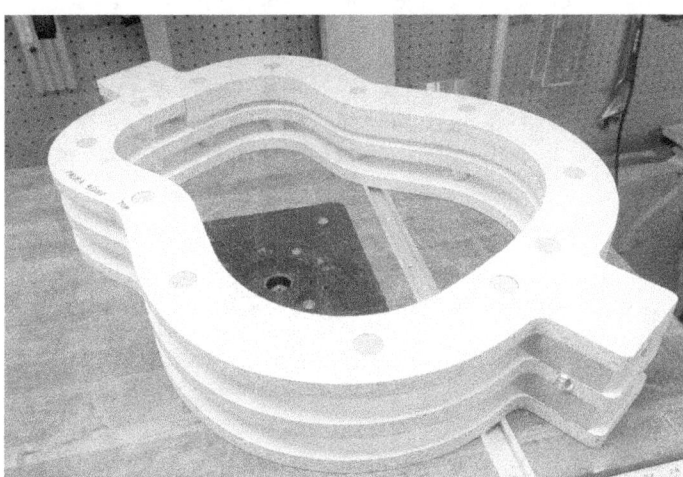

***Photo 8-2** – An "open frame" body mold. Only three pieces are really needed for each side of the mold, one each at the top and back edges of the guitar sides, and one near the middle. This mold, made of melamine board, adds an extra layer near the top of one side, which helps when the mold is used to bend the guitar's bindings. Notice the spacer blocks in the lower right corner that accurately separate the pieces.*

guitar building class), novice luthiers tend to be successful no matter the combination used. This makes perfect sense, because an expert teacher is directly available to the lutherie class students. In my observation, novices building without the aid of a teacher are far less successful when attempting to use the first method. As a result, I know of many top notch luthiers that learned to bend sides on a bending machine (the third method) and never learned how to bend sides using a bending iron.

The construction process described in this book makes use of the second combination listed. A heated bending iron is used to bend the sides by hand, then the sides are clamped into a shop-built mold while they cool and dry. The mold is a large jig, which is also used as an assembly fixture for a number of construction operations of the guitar body. Its construction is so important that it gets its own chapter.

In the introduction to the book I mentioned that there were many different ways to perform each lutherie construction operation, and that the ones I chose for inclusion in the construction process described in this book all met a number of criteria, the most important of which is likelihood of success when performed by a lutherie novice, working from a book in a self directed construction project. Another criterion mentioned is simplicity of the shop-built jigs and fixtures needed during construction. Although easy to build, the body mold is big and it does take some time to construct. The reason it is included in the construction process is that doing so makes it so much more likely that the lutherie novice will be successful in the construction of a guitar.

As mentioned, there are ways to build a guitar that do not require a mold. But in fact, most ways require some sort of body construction fixture. Some of these can be quite simple, such as the simplest form of the assembly workboard, traditionally used in Spanish guitar construction, called a *solera*. Unfortunately, in my observation and experience, the successful use of such a simple workboard requires either a side bending machine to bend the sides of the guitar, or if the sides are bent by hand on a simple iron as will be done in a later chapter of this book, it requires considerable side bending skill. This is something which the lutherie novice by definition does not have. There do exist variations on the basic solera that provide support in the process of bending the guitar sides by hand, but for the most part the simplest of these require almost as much time to build as the body mold that will be described here. Use of the body mold is well worth the time it takes to build it, because it greatly enhances the likelihood of success of the guitar construction project.

The mold of the type to be used is pictured in **photos 8-1** and **8-2**. It is what is generally called in North America an outside mold, that is, a mold that in use, is positioned around the outside of the guitar body. Interestingly, in some places this style of mold is called an inside mold, because the body goes inside it. As seen in the photos, the mold has a cavity that is the exact shape of the outside surfaces of the sides of the finished guitar.

The mold is as deep as the sides of the guitar are at the tail end, before the top and back plates are glued on. The mold is made in two pieces which are bolted together. Other features of the mold will be explained as its construction is explained.

Layout and Construction

Although the plans for the example guitars do not contain templates for the pieces of the mold, the critical part of the layout of the mold is the body outline, which *is* in the plans. The rest of the outline of the mold is not at all critical, and the construction description here explains how the layout is done.

As can be seen in the photos, the mold is made of a number of identical pieces of some sheet material, glued and doweled together. The number of pieces required depends on the depth of the mold, which in turn depends on the depth of the guitar under construction. It also depends on whether the mold is made using solid construction or if an "open frame" mold is built. I would generally recommend solid construction for the lutherie novice, because it makes the construction simpler. But in cases where the luthier just can't face cutting out so many pieces, the open frame mold does save some construction time, and makes more frugal use of materials. But it is more fragile and it is a bit more difficult to insert a tight-fitting *garland* (the subassembly consisting of the guitar sides, blocks, and linings) into it. Construction of each type is explained in the following operations.

Note that for purposes of identifying the different areas of the mold, the end of the mold containing the neck end of the body outline is called the neck end of the mold, and the end containing the tail end of the body outline is called the tail end of the mold.

Materials

Three common sheet materials can be used for the pieces of the mold. Each will work just fine in this application, but there is a tradeoff between the cost of the material and construction time associated with each one. Two of these, melamine covered particle board and MDF, have already been used for jigs described previously.

High quality void free exterior plywood with either "A" or "B" grade surfaces works well. Its major advantage is that it is dimensionally stable if it gets wet, which it is likely to do during the process of bending the guitar sides. Because it is stable when wet, a mold made out of plywood needs minimal sealing after it is built, and this can be a big saver of effort and total construction time. This material is the most expensive of the options presented, but is the one I recommend.

Melamine covered particle board can also be used. This is a good material when open frame construction will be used, because only the edges of the pieces will have to be sealed after the mold is built. It can also be used to build the pieces for a

Example Guitar	Rib Depth	# ¾" pieces	# ¼" pieces	Mold Depth
Tripletta OM	4" (101.6mm)	10	2	4" (101.6mm)
Paura Dreadnought	4¹¹⁄₁₆" (119.1mm)	12	2	4¾" (120.7mm)

Table 8-1 – *Total number of ¾" and ¼" thick pieces needed to build the solid mold for each of the example instruments. Half the total of the pieces of each thickness is used for each side. The combined thicknesses of the pieces on a side add up to the guitar body depth, or just a bit more.*

solid construction mold, but the advantage of the melamine covering will only be realized on the outside pieces in this case. Although the broad surfaces are covered in melamine, the edges are raw particle board which must be well sealed to prevent water from changing the shape of the completed mold. This sealing will require a number of coats of varnish or other finish. Melamine board is fairly inexpensive.

The least expensive material is MDF. It is probably not a good option to use for an open frame mold, because sealing the broad surfaces of the inside pieces of the finished mold is difficult to do. MDF absorbs water like a sponge and distorts badly when wet, so a mold made of this material will have to be well-sealed with a number of coats of varnish.

There are other more esoteric options for materials, but cost can be an issue. Tim Shaw, chief engineer – guitars, for Fender Musical Instruments, mentioned in a GAL Convention lecture the use of a frighteningly expensive plywood, clad in a phenolic composite. Materials like this hold up well in a production environment, but where the mold will be used to produce a limited number of guitars, more humble materials are certainly appropriate.

Materials
    Full sheet of ¾″ (19.1mm) sheet material (see text)
    ¼ sheet of ¼″ (19.1mm) sheet material
    3 ea. 36″ (914.4mm) lengths of 1″ (25.4mm) hardwood dowel
    2 ea. ¼″ - 20 × 5″ hex head bolts, flat washers
    Oil base varnish
Tools
    1″ (25.4mm) Forstner bit
    Hand held jigsaw
    Compass

Number of Pieces Needed

If an open frame mold will be made, then no matter which of the example instruments is being built, the number of mold pieces required is seven, each ¾″ (19.1mm) thick. For a mold of solid construction, the number of pieces and their thicknesses are as shown in **table 8-1**. Note that the values in the table assume pieces that are truly ¾″ (19.1mm) thick. Most domestic MDF and melamine board of nominal ¾″ (19.1mm) thickness is truly that thick. This is not always the case with plywood, which may have a true thickness of 18mm. It is important that the depth of the mold be exactly the same as the depth of the guitar sides at the tail end, as indicated in the table. A small fraction deeper is also fine.

Layout and Construction of the Template Piece

A single ¾″ (19.1mm) thick piece is built and carefully shaped first. This piece is then used as a template to build the remaining pieces.

☐ **Layout and Construction**

1. One half of the outline of the body is carefully cut out of the plan, using a knife or scissors. Note that one side of the body outline on the plan has the various segments of the guitar ribs marked out, with the points between segments indicated by letters. This is the half of the outline to cut out. The cut should be made along the outside of the outline and then along the centerline. Note that the top of the body, where the neck is attached, is flat and perpendicular to the centerline.

2. The ¾″ (19.1mm) thick material sheet can be cut into two to four pieces for easier handling. If it is cut up, care should be taken to keep the cut edges straight and perpendicular. One piece should be positioned so one of the straight and perpendicular 48″ (1219.2mm) long edges is facing the luthier. The half body outline, cut out from the plan, is placed with its centerline aligned with this edge, and so the top of the outline is 6″ (152.4mm) from the end. The paper is taped down to the sheet material as shown in **photo 8-3**.

3. The half body outline is carefully traced onto the sheet material in pencil. It is often necessary to tape down the traced edge in a few places to make the tracing, then go back and remove one piece of tape at a time, and pencil in that part of the outline previously covered by the tape. An accurate tracing is important. In addition to the outline, the locations of lettered points between the segments of the outline are also penciled onto the sheet material (**photo 8-4**). Only the location of the point labeled B is needed to construct the mold, but I routinely just pencil them all in.

4. The paper piece is removed but retained for future use. It may aid in reading the plan at a later time if the piece is taped back into the rest of the plan.

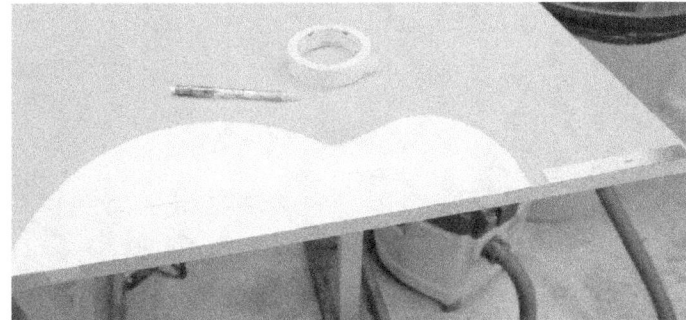

Photo 8-3 – Half of the outline of the guitar body is cut out of the plan and taped down to a straight edge of the mold material.

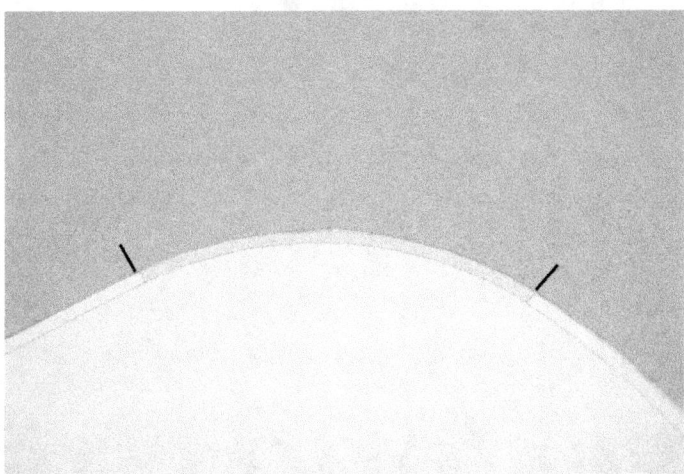

Photo 8-4 – The outline is traced onto the material. Marks are also made indicating where the segments of the outline are located.

5. The half outline of the body, traced in step 3 above, is also the inside edge of the mold half. The outside edge of the mold half is now penciled in, parallel to the inside edge and 3″ (76.2MM) from it. This will make the walls of the mold 3″ (76.2MM) thick, which works out well when using the 4¼″ (108MM) luthier's cam clamps that are recommended. Great accuracy is not required here. An easy way to do this is to open the compass to 3″ (76.2MM) and use it to "scribe" the outline of the mold by keeping the point of the compass in contact with the outline of the body, while moving the compass along the outline so it is approximately perpendicular to each curve of the outline (**photo 8-5**). Note that some fudging may need to happen around the waist of the outline, but as long as the penciled

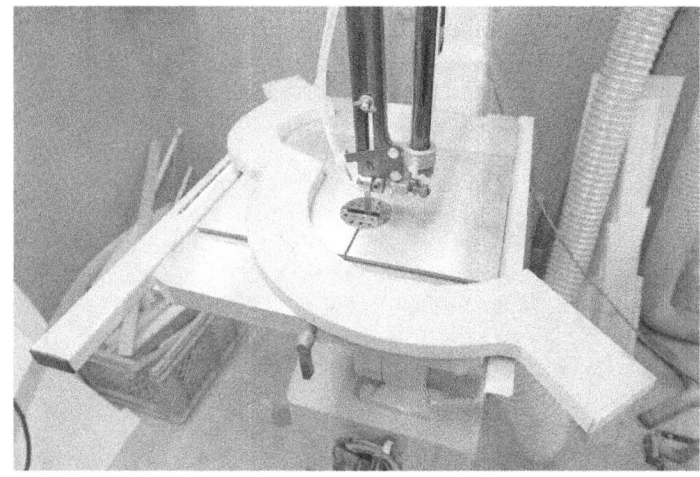

Photo 8-8 – *... then more accurate sawing is completed using the bandsaw.*

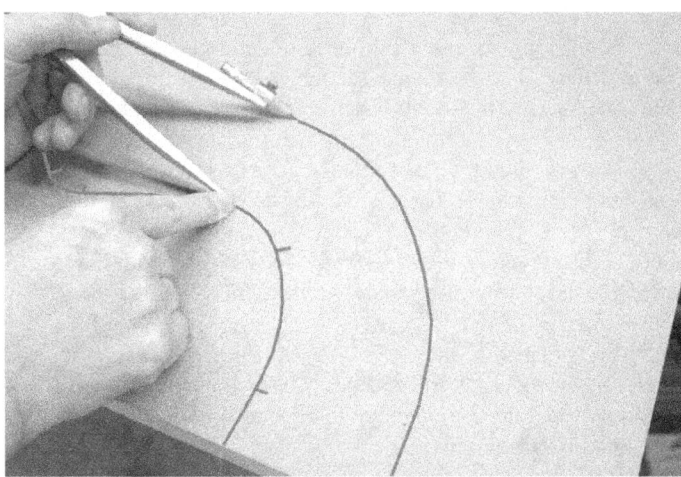

Photo 8-5 – *The outside of the mold is drawn by "scribing" a line parallel to the outline of the guitar body.*

Photo 8-9 – *Final trimming to the line is done using a sanding drum in the drill press or the spindle sander.*

line is generally parallel to the body outline and is no farther from it than 3″ (76.2MM) at any point, all will be well.

6. A tab 2″ (50.8MM) wide and 3″ (76.2MM) long is added to each end (**photo 8-6**). On one end of the material, that length happens automatically due to the original placement of the half body outline template. A similarly-sized tab is drawn at the other end as well.

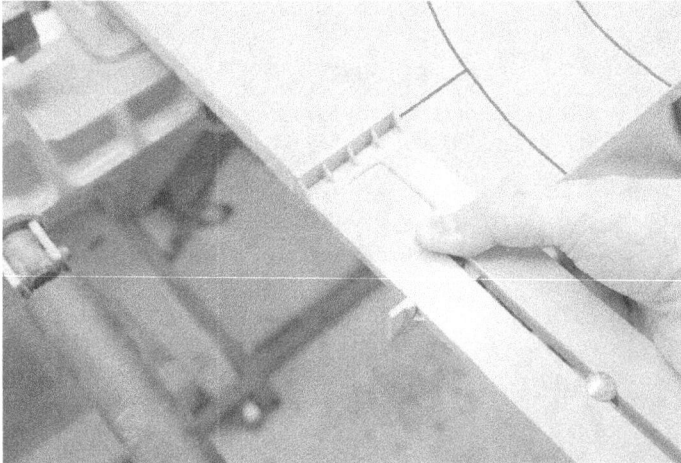

Photo 8-6 – *A tab is drawn at each end of the mold template drawing.*

7. The tabs are integrated into the drawing. The inside corners between tabs and the rest of the mold should be rounded over, to a diameter that is a bit larger than that of the pattern router bit that will eventually be used to cut out the rest of the pieces of the mold. The completed drawing of the mold piece template appears in **photo 8-7**.

8. The template piece is roughly cut out from the sheet, using a hand held jigsaw. Sawing is refined using the bandsaw (**photo 8-8**). Then the edges are sanded right up to the marked lines and the curves are smoothed, using either a sanding drum mounted in the drill press, or the stationary spindle sander (**photo 8-9**). Much care should be taken when sanding the inside part, to keep the curves smooth and flowing. From this point on, this template will define the shape of the guitar body outline.

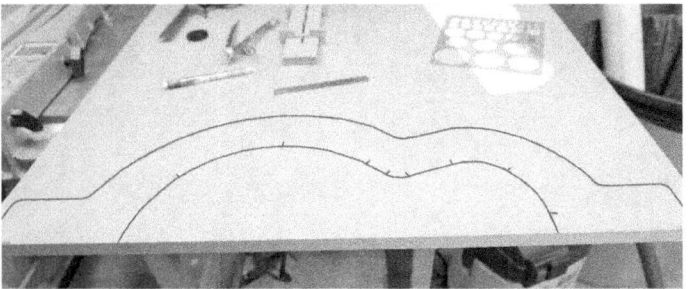

Photo 8-7 – *The completed drawing of the mold template piece looks like this. It is roughly sawn out using a jigsaw ...*

9. The topmost segment of the body outline must be made perpendicular to the flat part of the top tab (**photo 8-10**). Referring

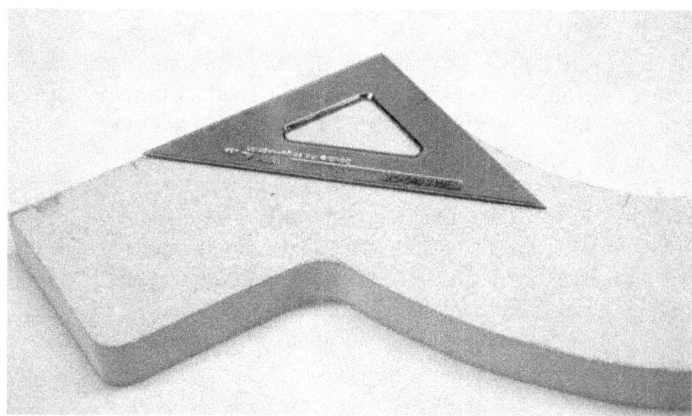

Photo 8-10 – The first 1¼″ (31.8MM) segment at the top of the outline must be square with the inside edge of the tab.

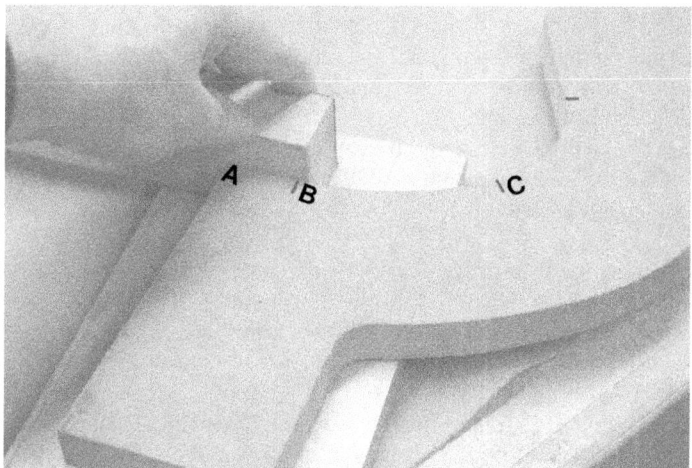

Photo 8-11 – If it is not square with the inside edge of the tab, segment AB must be made square. Here a sanding block is used.

Photo 8-12 – Holes are drilled for the lengths of dowel that will hold the pieces of the finished mold together.

Photo 8-13 – Five or six holes are drilled along the length of the template piece, centered across the width.

to the plan, this segment of the body outline is where the neck joins the body. It spans between the topmost point of the body at the centerline (point A) and point B, and is 1¼″ (31.8MM) long. If it is not perfectly square, this segment should be marked then sanded square, using a square profile sanding block with one surface covered with 80 grit PSA sandpaper (**photo 8-11**). The sanding block should be *exactly* 1¼″ (31.8MM) high, and approximately 12″ (304.8MM) long. Although this may seem overly long, this same block will be used to square up this same area of the assembled mold, and the extra length will be needed for that. If sanding this segment square caused the body outline to become jagged at point B, then segment BC should be carefully reworked on the drum or spindle sander to make that part of the outline smooth.

10. A 1″ (25.4MM) diameter Forstner bit is fitted in the drill press (**photo 8-12**), and five or six holes are drilled, approximately evenly spaced along the length of the template, and approximately in the center of its width. One hole should be near the intersection of each of the tabs, and the rest spaced appropriately in between these (**photo 8-13**). Care should be taken to be sure the bit does not break out any material when it exits the bottom surface of the template. Any raised lips caused by the drilling should be sanded flat, using a flat sanding block (**photo 8-14**).

Construction of the Mold Halves

The template piece just built is used to trace out the remaining pieces needed. It is also used as a router template to trim these pieces to exactly duplicate the template piece, and also finally as one of the pieces itself. During routing, the template is connected to the piece under construction by short lengths of the same dowel material that will be used to hold the finished mold halves together.

☐ Cutting the Pieces

1. The dowel pieces needed to hold the finished mold halves together are cut first. The number of pieces required depends on the number of holes that were drilled in each mold half. The length of the dowel pieces depends on the instrument being made. Refer to the **Mold Depth** column of **table 8-1** for the

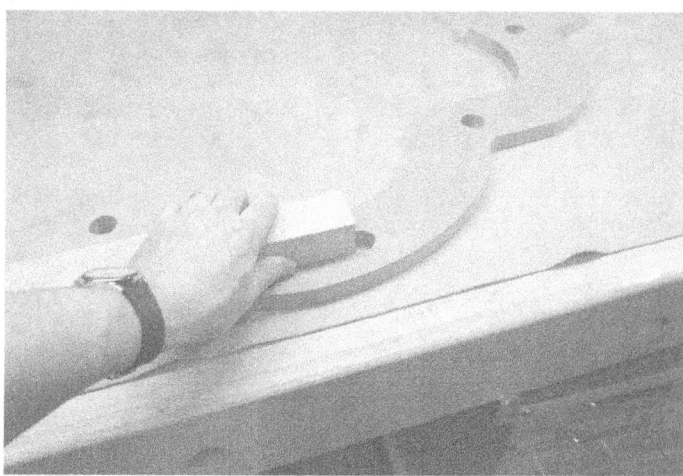

Photo 8-14 – Any ridges caused by drilling are sanded smooth, using a flat sanding block and PSA sandpaper.

Photo 8-15 – *Assembly dowel pieces (back) are cut to the depth of the mold. Short pieces (front) are used during routing to mate pieces.*

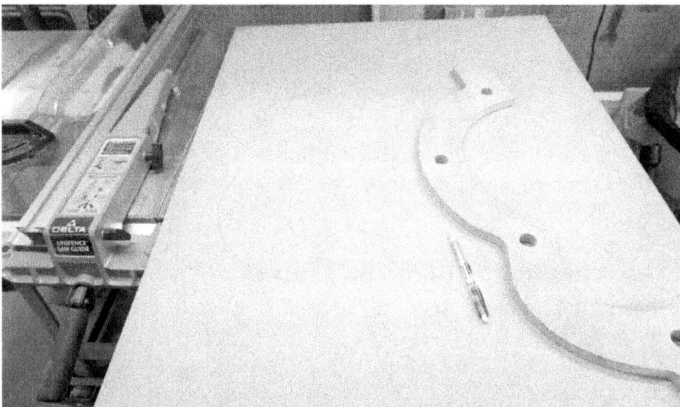

Photo 8-16 – *The template outline is traced multiple times onto the sheet material. These pieces are cut out with a jigsaw.*

Photo 8-17 – *The cut pieces are marked for drilling using the template and a Forstner bit, tapped with a plastic mallet.*

Example Guitar	Short Spacer	Tall Spacer
Tripletta OM	⅛″ (3.2mm)	⅞″ (22.2mm)
Paura Dreadnought	½″ (12.7mm)	1¼″ (31.2mm)

Table 8-2 – *The thicknesses of the spacers needed to build an open frame mold for each of the two example instruments.*

lengths for the example instruments. After the pieces are cut, the edges on both ends should be lightly chamfered. Retain leftover dowel material. This will be used to cut additional short pieces, which will be used during routing (**photo 8-15**).

2. The template piece is placed on the sheet stock and multiple additional pieces are traced in pencil (**photo 8-16**). With careful orientation of the template, it is usually possible to mark out pieces so there will not be too much waste. The pieces will be cut out using a hand held jigsaw, so enough space between the marked out pieces should be left to accommodate that tool.

3. The pieces are cut out, staying as close to the lines as is prudent.

4. Each piece must be marked and drilled with holes for the assembly dowels. A piece is placed on the bench and the template is placed on top and aligned with the penciled outline of the piece. Two clamps are used to clamp the assembly down to the bench top. The same 1″ (25.4mm) diameter Forstner bit that was used to drill the holes in the template is inserted in each hole, and tapped with a plastic mallet so its center point will make a center mark on the piece below (**photo 8-17**).

5. Using the drill press, 1″ (25.4mm) diameter holes are drilled through all the pieces at the marked centers. A flat sanding block is used to sand flat any lips that may result from the drilling (**photo 8-18**).

6. Each piece is routed flush to the template using a router with a flush trim router bit. A large router and a large diameter bit makes this task go quicker. Either a top bearing or bottom bearing bit can be used.

If a bottom bearing bit is used, the setup to rout each piece is as follows: The template is put on the bench and the piece to be cut is placed on top of it. The two pieces are held together, using two of the assembly dowels inserted into the holes near the ends of the pieces. The dowels are driven all the way through the assembly, so their tops are just below the top surface of the piece to be cut. The assembly is mounted for routing as shown

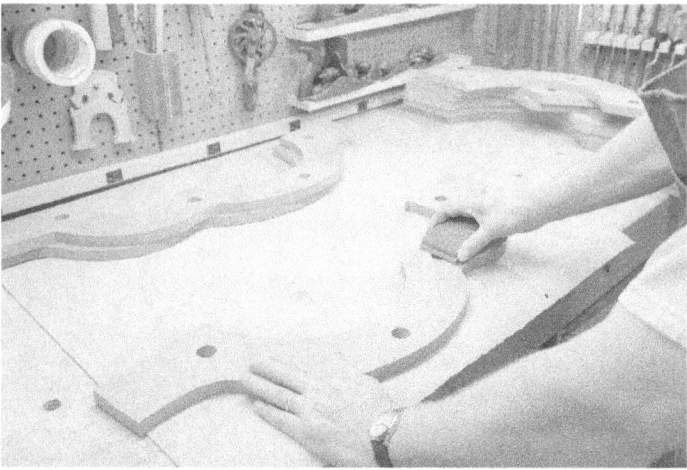

Photo 8-18 – *After the holes are drilled in a piece, a sanding block is used to remove any lip created during drilling.*

in **photo 8-19**, with one of the dowels clamped in the vise and the other dowel clamped to the front of the bench. The assembly can also be gripped in a tool of the style of the Stanley Black and Decker Workmate.

Note that if the dowels slip into the holes easily and can be rattled around once in, it is a good idea to first swell the dowels by wetting them and then letting them sit around for an hour until the surface water has evaporated. Then they can be test fitted again, and the wetting repeated if necessary. Dowels that present too tight a fit should be sanded gently on a sanding board, until a good fit can be achieved.

Additional lengths of dowel are cut and inserted into the rest of the holes. These pieces should be just short of the combined thickness of the template and the piece to be cut, so they don't stick up above the surface and catch the edge of the router base. The waste is routed off the piece, then the assembly is unclamped and the template is removed.

If a top bearing router bit is used, the setup procedure is almost the same. In this case, the template is mounted on top of *two* pieces to be cut, and the depth of cut is adjusted so that the middle piece will be completely trimmed flush (**photo 8-20**). This arrangement prevents the bit from touching the bench top. After a piece is cut, the piece underneath it is promoted to being the next piece to be cut.

 Note that each time the template is used to trim another piece, the depth of the router bit should be changed just a little, so the bearing contacts a new part of the template. The bearing of the pattern bit will compress the walls of the template a little where it rolls against it. If the bearing always contacts the template in the same place, it will soon wear a groove there. This is particularly an issue with a template made of MDF.

☐ **Assembling the Solid Mold Halves Option**

1. The pieces are divided into two piles, one pile each for the two halves of the mold. Each pile should be checked for total thickness before the pieces are glued together. If melamine board is used, the melamine of all but the two surfaces that will end up being the top and back of the finished mold are roughed

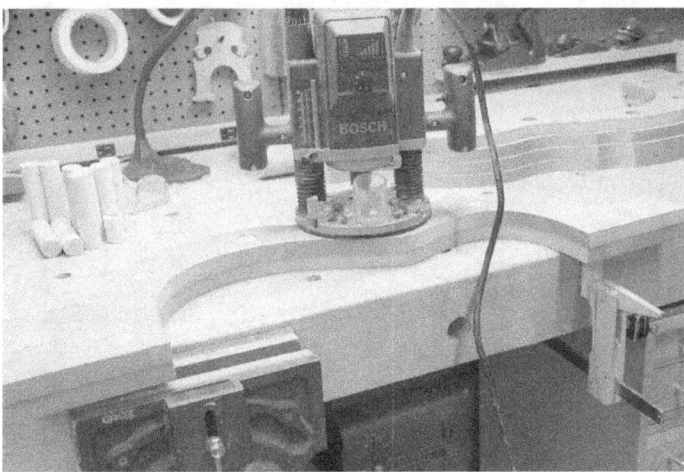

Photo 8-19 – *The setup for routing using a bottom bearing bit. The template is on the bottom. One long dowel is clamped in the vise, and the other is clamped to the front of the bench. Short dowel pieces fill the remaining holes.*

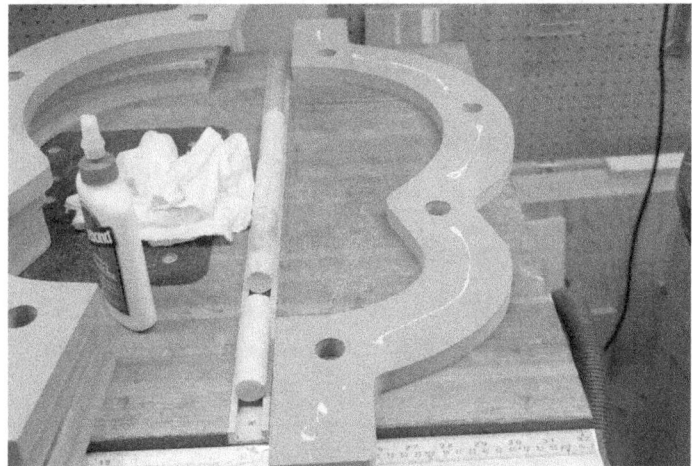

Photo 8-21 – *A thin line of wood glue is applied down the center of one of the pieces, avoiding the holes.*

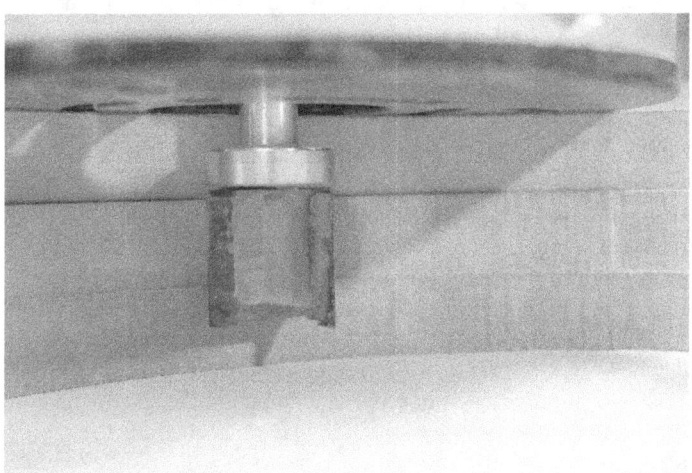

Photo 8-20 – *If a top bearing bit is used, the template goes on top and an additional piece is added to the bottom of the stack, to protect the top of the bench.*

Photo 8-22 – *After the mold side is assembled, it is clamped down to a flat surface until the glue cures.*

Photo 8-23 – *Spacers are used to locate the pieces of the side of the open frame mold that has three pieces. All spacers are the same height.*

Photo 8-25 – *Beginning assembly of the open frame side that has three pieces. The assembly dowels are glued into the drilled holes.*

Photo 8-24 – *On the side of the mold with four pieces, two different sizes of spacers are used, tall and short.*

Photo 8-26 – *Tall spacers are placed on top of the first piece, then the second piece is tapped into place using a block and mallet.*

up with 50 or 60 grit sandpaper on a flat block. This is necessary to get the wood glue to stick to the melamine.

2. One piece is placed flat on the bench. A thin bead of glue is run down the middle of the piece (**photo 8-21**). Care is taken to not get any glue in or near the drilled holes. Not a whole lot of glue is required here, and it is convenient to be able to glue up the mold half without any glue squeeze-out.

3. Another mold piece is placed on top of the first, and the assembly dowels are inserted into the holes and tapped with a mallet until they are in contact with the bench top.

4. Another piece is placed flat on the bench, and glue is applied as in the previous step. The assembly is placed on top of this piece and aligned, then the dowels are tapped with the mallet until they contact the bench top.

5. Step 4 is repeated for all remaining pieces for the mold side.

6. When the stack is complete, it is clamped to a flat surface with multiple clamps while the glue cures (**photo 8-22**). The glue should be allowed to cure overnight.

7. Steps 2 through 6 are repeated for the other half of the mold.

☐ Assembling the Open Frame Mold Halves Option

With the solid mold, the depth of the mold is equal to the total thickness of all the pieces that make up a side of the mold. The open frame mold makes use of one side assembly with three pieces and the other with four pieces. If each piece is ¾″ (19.1mm) thick, this will account for 2¼″ (57.2mm), and 3″ (76.2mm) of the total thickness respectively. The rest of the needed thickness for the mold sides must be made up with spacers that will be used to keep the pieces at a certain distance from each other. Refer to **photos 8-23** and **8-24**. The thickness of the spacers needed to make the side assemblies of an open frame mold for each of the example guitars are specified in **table 8-2**.

1. One or more lengths of MDF are ripped to the width (or planed to the thickness) of the tall spacers needed for the mold for the guitar under construction. The lengths should be long enough so they can be cut into 30 spacers, each approximately 2″ (50.8mm) long. Before cutting the lengths into pieces, it is

wise to mark them so it will be clear which dimension will be the spacer thickness when in use.

2. One or more lengths of MDF are ripped to the width (or planed to the thickness) of the short spacers needed for the mold for the guitar under construction. The lengths should be long enough so they can be cut into 10 spacers. The spacers are cut.

3. The mold side with three pieces will be assembled first. Assembly should be done on a glue-proof surface, like a piece of melamine board. One of the side pieces is placed flat on the glue-proof surface. Wood glue is wiped on the walls of each of the holes in the piece. The assembly dowels are inserted in the holes, then tapped with a mallet to be sure their bottoms are flush with the bottom of the piece (**photo 8-25**).

4. Ten of the tall spacers are distributed on the piece. Glue is wiped around each dowel just above the level of the tops of the spacers.

5. Another mold piece is positioned over the dowels, and tapped into place using the mallet and a block of wood (**photo 8-26**). The block is necessary to distribute the force, so it always ends up close to one of the dowels. This prevents the mallet blows from snapping the piece between the dowels. The piece is tapped all over its top surface, until its bottom surface is completely seated on the tops of the spacers (**photo 8-27**). The bottom of the piece should be carefully inspected to be sure it is in firm contact with *all* the spacers.

6. Steps 4 and 5 above are repeated for the final piece of this side of the mold.

7. The side of the mold with four pieces will be assembled next. This side is assembled upside down, also on a glue proof surface. Two of the mold pieces are placed one atop the other on the assembly surface and aligned. The insides of the drilled holes are wiped with glue. The assembly dowels are inserted in the holes, then tapped with a mallet to be sure their bottoms are flush with the bottom surface of the bottom piece.

8. The ten short spacers are distributed on the piece. Glue is wiped around each dowel just above the level of the tops of the spacers.

9. Another mold piece is positioned over the dowels, and tapped into place using the mallet and a block of wood, as in step 5 above.

10. Ten of the tall spacers are distributed on the piece. Glue is wiped around each dowel just above the level of the tops of the spacers.

11. The final mold piece is positioned over the dowels and tapped into place.

12. The glue is allowed to cure overnight. The spacers can be removed once the glue is cured.

13. It is useful if the tabs at the ends of each half of the mold are reinforced by gluing some of the spacers between the pieces (**photo 8-28**).

Photo 8-27 – *The second piece fully in place. Its bottom surface is in contact with the tops of all the spacers.*

Photo 8-28 – *Some of the spacers are glued between the pieces at the end tabs to reinforce the tabs.*

Photo 8-29 – *The inside surfaces of the tabs of the mold halves are flattened and squared up by sanding, using PSA sandpaper on a flat surface. Here the table saw extension table is used.*

Completing Construction

☐ Assembling the Mold

The process of assembling the mold halves is straightforward. The inside surfaces of the tabs must be made square and the critical top segment of the body outline must be squared again, just as it was when the template piece was built. Although the assembly dowels hold the pieces in fairly good alignment, the body outline surfaces are also sanded smooth, to eliminate any variation among the pieces.

1. The inside surface of the tabs of the halves of the mold must be squared up. The simplest way to do this is to stick down some 60 grit PSA sandpaper to a flat surface in two places, so these surfaces can be sanded flat and square in a single operation. **Photo 8-29** shows this done on the extension table of my table saw. Sanding is performed by pushing the mold half back and forth over the sandpaper.

Before sanding, the inside surfaces of the tabs should be covered in pencil marks. During sanding these are regularly checked. Once all the marks are removed, the inside surfaces of the tabs are flat.

While sanding, it is important to regularly check that the inside surfaces of the tabs are also square (**photos 8-30** and **8-31**). If they are not, sanding proceeds with the amount of tilt necessary to make them square.

After the tab surfaces of both halves are flattened, the fit is checked by putting them down on a flat surface, and pressing the tabs together. They should contact each other perfectly.

2. The top segment of the body outline must be squared up on both mold halves. In a previous operation, the top segment AB of the body outline was squared up in one dimension with the mold half template piece. This squaring up must be done again, this time in two dimensions (**photo 8-32**). That is, segment AB must be made square to the top and back surfaces of the mold, and also to the inside surface of the tab. The same sanding block used in the previous operation is used for this one (**photo 8-33**). Progress should be checked regularly while sanding.

Photo 8-30 – *While the tab surfaces are sanded, they must remain perpendicular to the top and bottom surfaces of the mold half. Note the PSA sandpaper under the tab.*

Photo 8-32 – *The short segment AB at the top of the body outline must be square in two dimensions. It is checked with a square ...*

Photo 8-31 – *During sanding, the surfaces of the tabs are regularly checked for flatness as well as squareness.*

Photo 8-33 – *... and sanded as necessary, using the same square profile sanding block used to perform this same operation on the template.*

The reason it is so important that this area of the mold is square is that, when the mold is used to assemble the guitar body, this part of the mold will support the neck block (**photo 8-34**). If the mold is not square here, the neck block won't be square to the centerline of the body and that in turn will make it difficult or impossible to attach the guitar neck to be in line with the body centerline. Time taken now to be sure this part of the mold is square is time well spent.

3. The two halves of the mold are now fitted together. Assembly should be done on a truly flat surface. This will align the halves in elevation. The flats at the neck end of the body outline (segments AB) are aligned, using a flat piece of wood that is clamped in place against the flats (**photo 8-35**). Another clamp is used to clamp the tabs together. A hand drill fitted with a 9/32″ (7.1mm) diameter drill bit is used to drill a hole through both tabs.

4. The tabs are bolted together before the clamps are removed. Note that if a long bolt is not readily available, a length of threaded rod with nuts and washers can be substituted (**photo 8-36**). When assembling an open frame mold, care must be taken to avoid crushing the tabs.

5. To aid in reassembly if the bolts are loosened in the future, it is wise to scribe a couple of lines across the center seam on top of the tabs. The scribed lines can be made more visible by

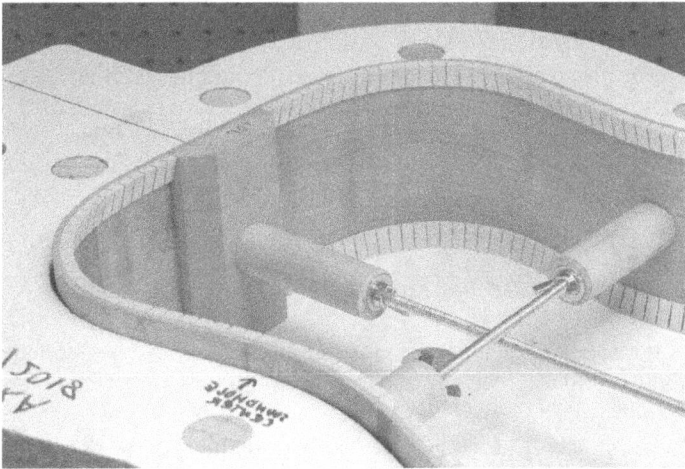

Photo 8-34 – *Keeping this part of the mold square is important, because in use it will position and support the neck block of the guitar during assembly.*

Photo 8-35 – *The two halves of the mold are clamped together at the neck end and the tabs are drilled through ...*

Photo 8-37 – *The seam between tabs should be scribed across, to aid in reassembly of the mold if it is ever taken apart.*

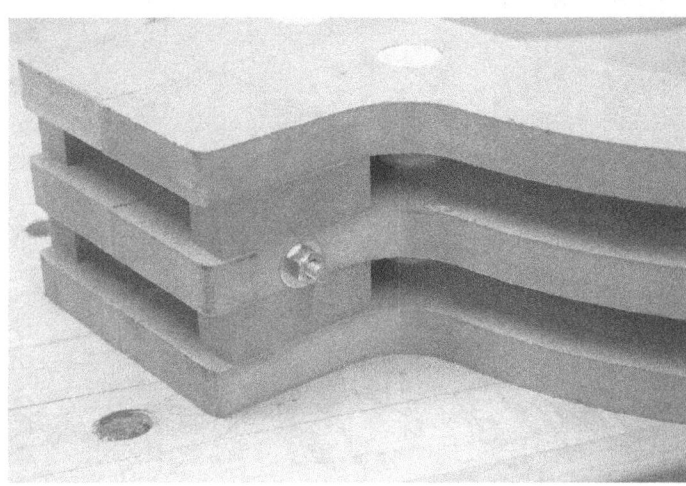

Photo 8-36 – *... for a bolt that will hold them together.*

Photo 8-38 – *A long sanding block with one curved side ...*

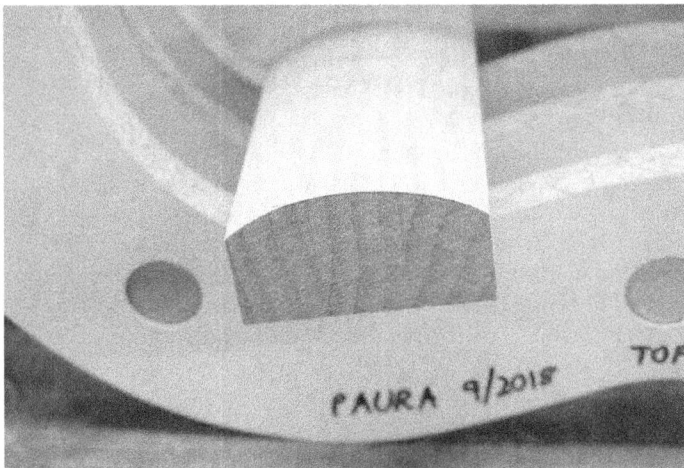

Photo 8-39 – ... *and one flat side is used to smooth the body outline surface.*

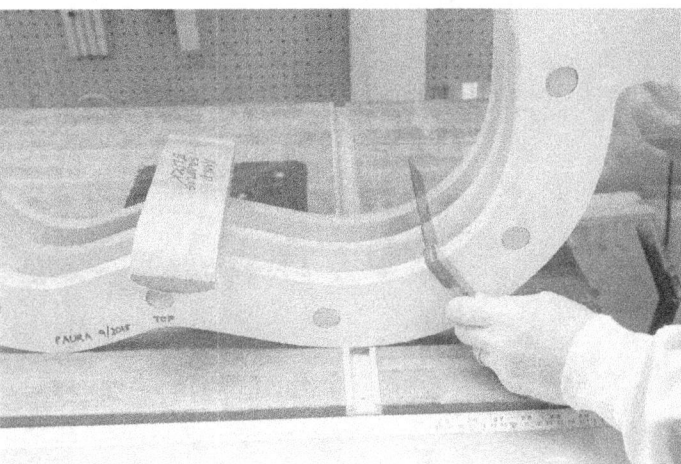

Photo 8-40 – *While sanding, the body outline surface should be checked for square with the top surface.*

being marked over with permanent marker (**photo 8-37**). The clamps are then removed.

6. The tabs on the tail end of the mold are bolted together and scribed in similar fashion. No special alignment is done at this end at this time. If the body outline is not smoothly continuous at the tail end, that will be fixed in the next step.

7. The body outline surface of the mold is smoothed, leveled, and squared. This is most easily done with a sanding block approximately 12″ (304.8mm) long, with a rounded surface on one side (**photo 8-38**) and a flat surface on the other (**photo 8-39**). The rounded surface can be made using a plane or belt sander, and the radius should be just a bit smaller than the radius of the upper bout curve of the guitar outline. The sanding surfaces are covered with 60-grit PSA sandpaper. The body outline surfaces of the mold should be marked up with pencil before sanding. It is easiest to sand with the mold standing up on one side, and with one of the luthier's hands holding one end of the sanding block and the other hand holding the other end. This is one of those situations where the old carpenter's advice to "use sandpaper like someone else is paying for it" applies. While sanding, the surface should be regularly checked to be sure it is square to the top surface of the mold (**photo 8-40**). Any discontinuities in the outline near each of the body ends should be sanded smooth. Sanding should proceed until all pencil marks are removed from the body outline surface. Note that any dings in the surface that might have been made by accidentally tipping the router when the mold pieces were pattern routed should be ignored. Trying to sand out really deep imperfections like this will just distort the outline of the guitar.

8. The sharp edges of the mold pieces should be taken off using a card scraper or sandpaper (**photo 8-41**). This is particularly important for the edges of the inner pieces of an open frame mold. Sharp edges here can catch the edges of the guitar sides when they are being inserted into the mold, unless these edges are chamfered.

☐ Sealing and Marking the Mold

It has been previously mentioned that sealer must be applied to the mold to prevent it from swelling if it gets wet. The sealer also provides a glue-proof surface. Conventional oil based polyurethane floor varnish is readily available, and works well as a sealer, but brushing lacquer and shellac work fine also. Thin casting epoxy works great as a sealer.

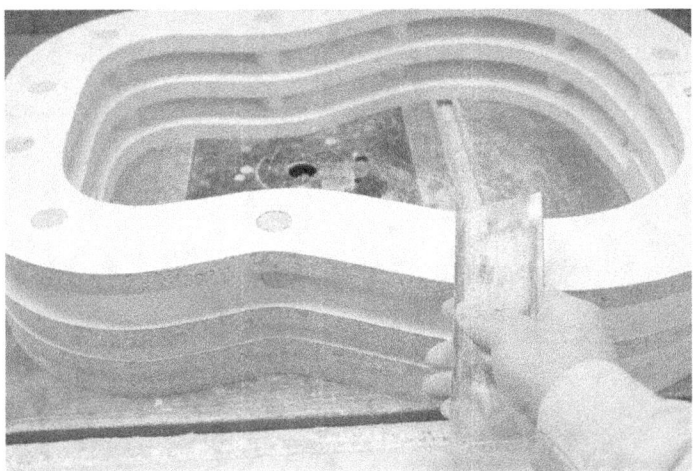

Photo 8-41 – *All sharp edges should be lightly chamfered, using a scraper or sandpaper.*

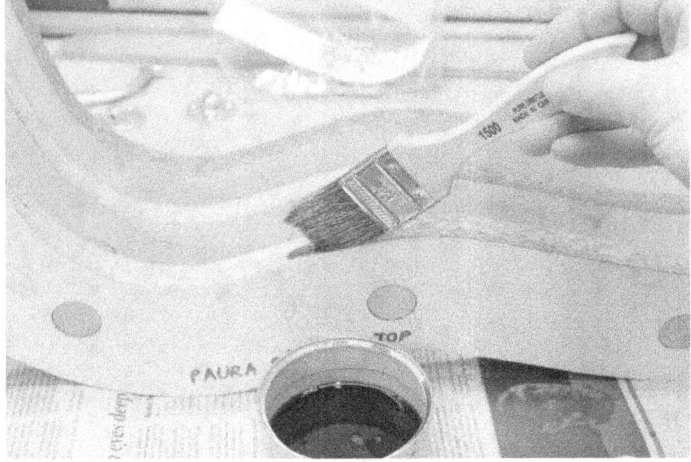

Photo 8-42 – *The entire surface of the mold must be well sealed. If melamine board is used then just the cut edges need additional sealing.*

It is important that water-based finishing products *not* be used for sealing, for obvious reasons. Just about any solvent-based finishing material can be used instead.

The body outlines of the example instruments are made up of a number of individual segments. After the mold has been sealed, the top surface is marked with the locations of the segments of the outline. These will be valuable guides when bending the sides of the guitar. More information on the segments of the outline and how they are used when bending the sides appears in another chapter.

1. The mold is sealed. The number of coats of sealer, and where those coats need to be applied, depends on what material was used to make the mold. If plywood was used, one coat of sealer should be applied all over. Additional coats are always helpful. If the mold is made of MDF, then at least three coats of sealer should be applied to the entire mold. If the mold is constructed of melamine covered particle board, then at least three coats of sealer should be applied to the exposed particleboard of the mold (**photo 8-42**). The sealer should be allowed to dry thoroughly before proceeding.

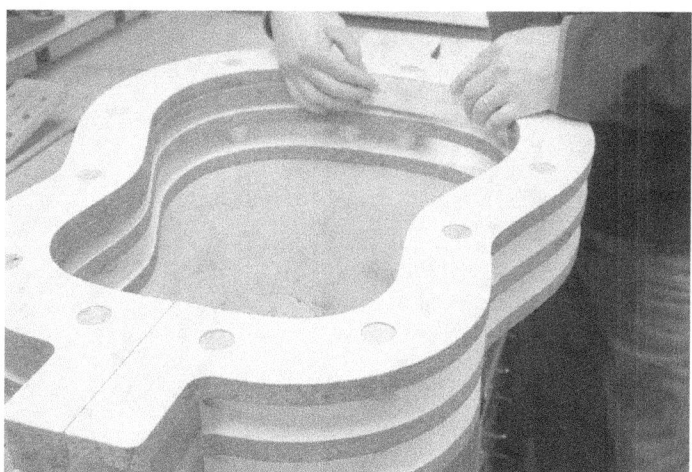

Photo 8-43 – *The guitar side segments "tape measure" is used to be sure the sides are the correct length.*

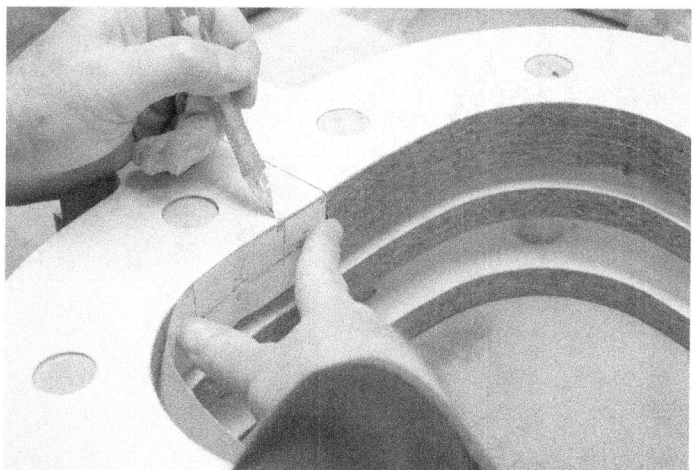

Photo 8-44 – *The individual segments of the body outline are transferred onto the top of the mold from the tape.*

Photo 8-45 – *The marks are permanently scribed, highlighted with a permanent marker, and the letter names are written in marker, too.*

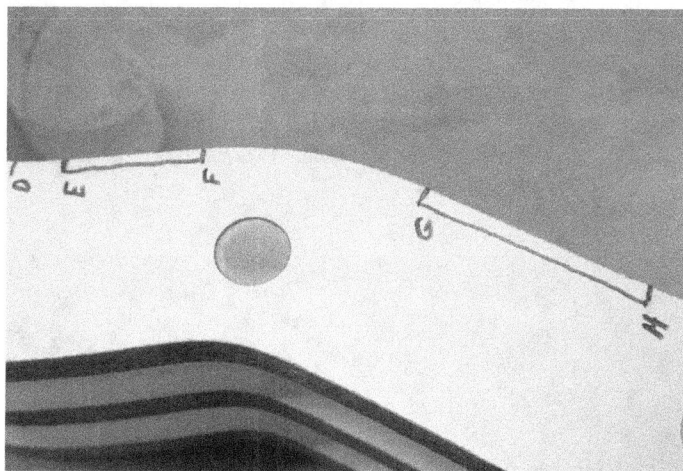

Photo 8-46 – *The two straight segments next to the waist curve segment are marked with straight lines.*

2. The plans for the example instruments have printed a scale printed on them, which shows the lengths of the individual segments of the sides of the guitar. This scale is printed on the plan between the front view and the side view. This scale is cut out of the plan using scissors, in the form of a long and narrow tape, like a cloth tape measure. After the tape is cut out, it should be covered with clear shipping tape on both sides. This will make it stronger and easier to handle.

3. If it has not already been done, one surface of the mold is identified as the top surface, and the mold is placed on the bench with the top surface up. For solid construction molds, either surface can be the top. For open frame molds, the top is the surface that has two mold pieces in contact on one side of the mold.

4. The length of the body outline of one side of the mold is checked using the tape made in step 2. Point A on the tape is aligned with the center seam of the mold at the neck end of the outline, at the top edge of the mold. The tape may be taped in place here. Then both hands are used to press the tape into contact with the inside surface of the mold, moving from the neck end down to the tail end. Point K on the tape should end up aligned with the center seam of the mold at the tail end, or at

least be no more than a small fraction of an inch from it (**photo 8-43**). A radical difference means some major error occurred during layout and construction of the mold.

5. The same procedure of working the tape in contact with the inside surface of the mold from neck to tail end is performed, but this time a pencil is used to mark the location of each of the lettered points on the tape onto the top of the mold (**photo 8-44**). When all points have been marked, their locations should be double checked with the tape.

6. After the locations of all the marks have been verified with the tape, an awl is used to scribe the location marks permanently into the top surface of the mold. A permanent marker is then used to highlight the scribed marks. It is also used to label each mark with its letter name (**photo 8-45**).

7. All of the segments that make up the outline of the body are circular arcs, with the exception of the segments on both sides of the waist arc, which are straight lines. These straight segments are labeled EF and GH. The marker is used to draw straight lines on the mold top for these segments (**photo 8-46**). This helps to identify them when the sides are being bent.

8. All of the marking steps have been done on the top of the mold for one of the sides of the guitar body outline. Although not necessary, the other side can be similarly marked if desired.

 The tape with the segments of the guitar sides printed on it is saved. It will be needed for a later construction step.

☐ Building the Floor and Insert

In addition to aiding in the bending of the sides, the mold is also used in the operations of shaping the edges of the sides and clamping on the top plate. For these operations, it is useful for the mold to have a floor, and also an insert which will raise the guitar sides up a bit above the top of the mold. These parts are made of the same material that the mold is made of.

1. The floor is built first. The mold is placed on top of a sheet of the desired ¾″ (19.1MM) thick material, and traced onto that material (**photo 8-47**). The floor is cut out using a jigsaw.

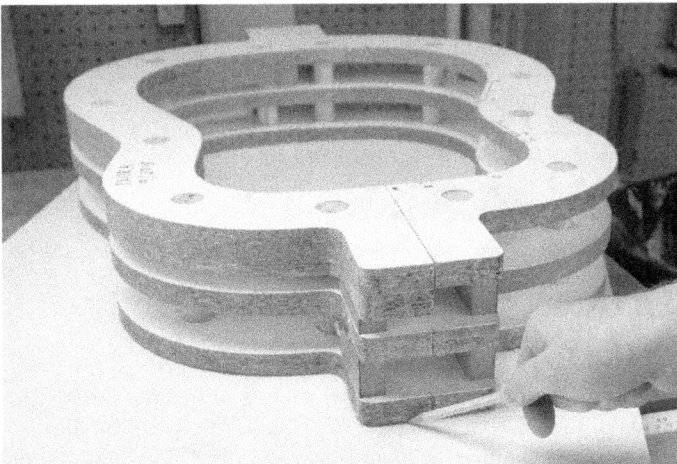

Photo 8-47 *– The outline of the mold is copied onto sheet stock and then cut out to form the floor of the mold.*

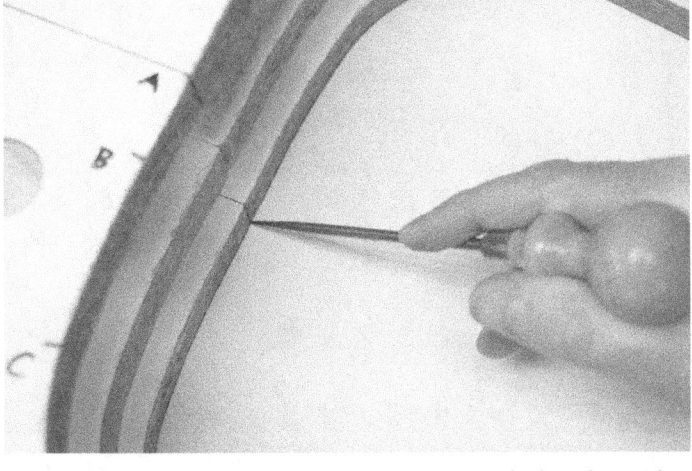

Photo 8-49 *– The location of the center seam is scribed on the inside of the floor at both ends of the mold ...*

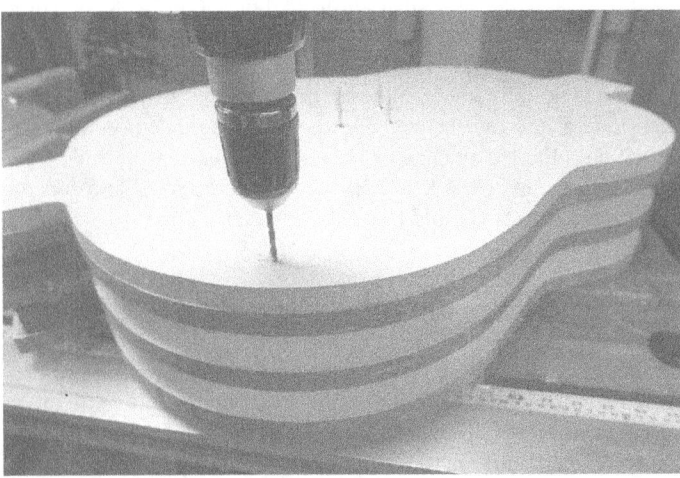

Photo 8-48 *– The floor is attached to the bottom of the mold using a few countersunk wood screws.*

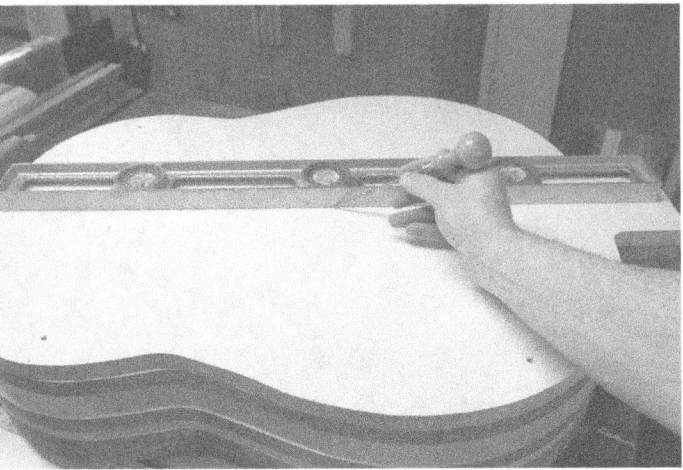

Photo 8-50 *– ... then the floor is removed, and the two scribed marks are connected to form the body centerline.*

2. The floor is attached to the bottom of the mold, using countersunk wood screws (**photo 8-48**). Then it is trimmed flush with the outsides of the mold, using the router and pattern bit.

3. A centerline scribed onto the inside of the floor is useful when assembling the body of the guitar. The location of the center seam of the mold is transferred onto the inside of the floor at the neck end, and the tail end (**photo 8-49**).

4. The floor is removed from the mold, and the two marks are joined with a straightedge, so a centerline can be scribed down the center of the floor (**photo 8-50**).

5. Two large holes are cut in the floor, to provide access to the insides of the mold through the floor (**photo 8-51**). The holes are easily cut with a large diameter hole saw, but can be cut with whatever tools are convenient. No specific size is required, but the holes should be big enough for the luthier to put his or her hand through them.

6. The floor is sealed, in the same manner as the mold. Note that the floor must be sealed on both sides, not just the inside surface. If only one surface of the floor is sealed, the piece will absorb moisture from the air at different rates on each side, and that will cause it to warp. If the floor is made of melamine board, no sealing is necessary, because no cut edges appear inside the mold. The floor should not be reattached to the mold just yet.

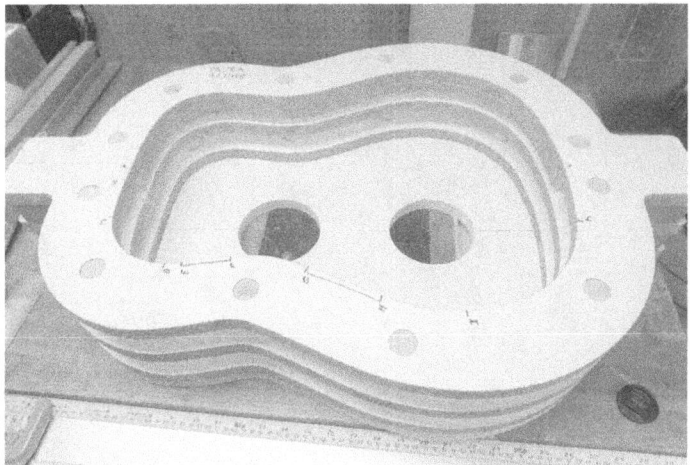

Photo 8-51 – *Two big holes are cut in the floor, to provide access to the inside of the mold through the floor.*

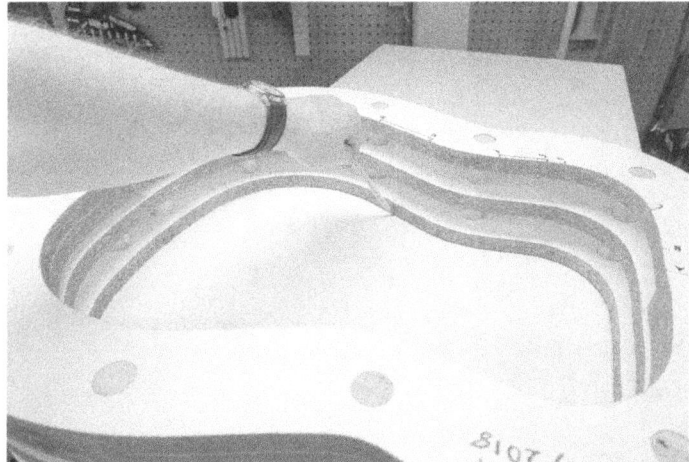

Photo 8-52 – *The mold without its floor is placed on top of sheet stock, and the inside is traced onto the stock to form an insert.*

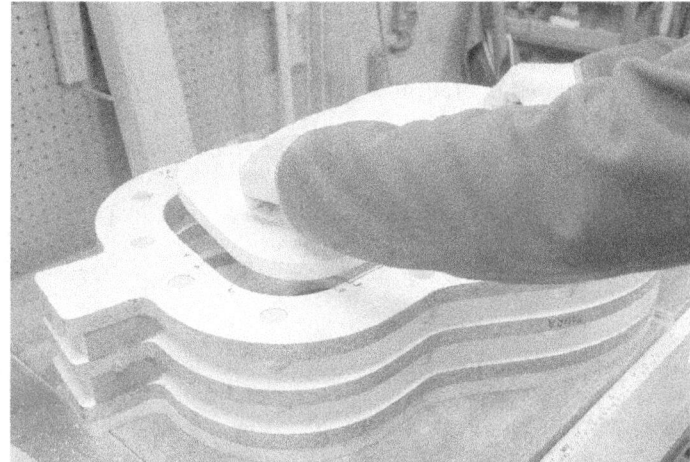

Photo 8-54 – *Fitting the insert into the mold.*

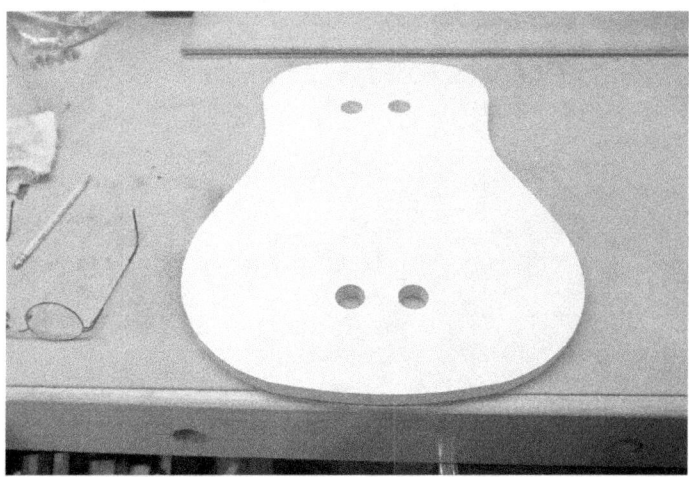

Photo 8-53 – *The insert is cut out, then holes are drilled to use as finger holes when installing and removing the insert.*

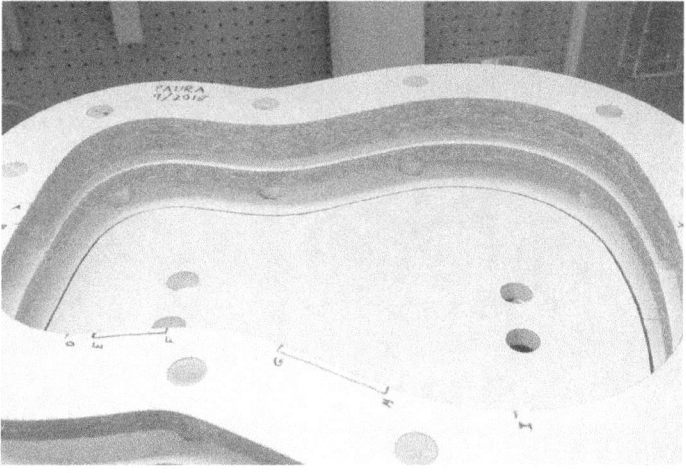

Photo 8-55 – *The insert in place, and fully in contact with the floor of the mold.*

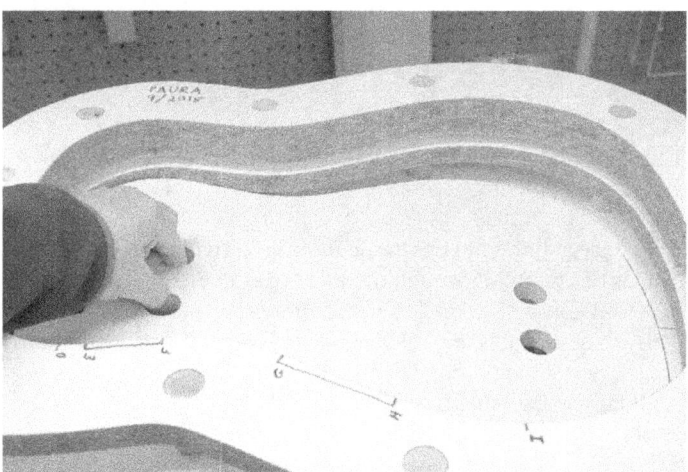

Photo 8-56 – *The insert must fit well, but be loose enough so the neck end can be lifted just a little bit.*

7. The insert is made next. The mold is placed on top of a sheet of the desired ¾″ (19.1MM) thick material, and the inside is traced onto the material (**photo 8-52**). The insert is roughly cut out using the jigsaw. Then the bandsaw is used to finely cut the outline. The bandsaw blade should be run right on top of the penciled line, instead of the usual practice of cutting just outside the line. This will make the insert slightly smaller than the inside of the mold. The insert must not be made grossly smaller than the insides of the mold. In use, the thin edges of the guitar sides will sit on top of the insert.

8. The floor is reattached to the bottom of the mold.

9. To aid in inserting and removing the insert, four holes of approximately 1″ (25.4MM) diameter are drilled through the insert, as shown in **photo 8-53**. These will be used as finger holes (**photo 8-54**).

10. The insert is trimmed as needed, so it sits flat on the floor of the mold, and so it can be inserted and removed without binding (**photo 8-55**). The neck end of the insert must be able to be lifted approximately ¼″ (6.4MM) as well (**photo 8-56**).

11. The insert is removed and sealed in the same manner as the floor. If the insert is made of melamine board, no sealing is necessary, because no cut edges will be in contact with the wet guitar sides when the insert is in use. When the sealer is fully dry, the insert is placed back inside the mold and the mold is set aside for future use.

Bending the Sides of the Guitar

Our attention turns now to the body of the guitar, its materials and construction. The large components of the body are composed of thin pieces of wood, the back and sides of hardwood, and the top of softwood. As far as construction goes, the sides are unique in that they are bent to shape using heat. Heat bending of wood is not something most lutherie novices have experience with. As a consequence, this chapter contains much background information on this process, as an introduction to the description of construction that follows.

The tool used to bend the guitar sides (also referred to as the ribs) into shape is called a bending iron. It is also sometimes called a hot pipe, because historical and some simple modern versions of this tool are little more than that. The really historical versions of the bending iron were heated with charcoal, and later versions were often heated with propane. Modern commercial bending irons are heated with electricity, and have thermostats to control the temperature. This tool was selected for use because it is relatively inexpensive, and can yield excellent results, with a bit of understanding of the wood bending process and how the bending iron works, and also a bit of practice with using it.

It has already been mentioned that lutherie novices often have the most trepidation about the operations of carving the neck and bending the sides. The concern that novice luthiers have about bending sides is completely understandable. I know of no readily available source of information on this process that explains it so that novices would have confidence in their ability to reliably perform this operation.

In the chapter on neck carving, the complex task of transforming the rectangular cross section neck assembly into its ultimate shape was reduced to a series of simple and familiar woodworking operations. The fact that these primary operations, the cutting of flat facets, are inherently familiar to all woodworkers, results in confidence on the part of the luthier that success can be had. In the case of guitar side bending, few novice luthiers have experience heat bending wood. For that reason, in addition to reducing the task of bending a guitar side to a series of simple operations, this chapter will also include some useful theoretical background information, and provide some practice exercises that can be employed to gain familiarity and confidence performing the operations, before committing to work on an instrument under construction.

The background information to be provided is on the subjects of heat bending wood; how bending irons work; and how guitar body outlines are typically designed. All of this background information converges on three simple principles of guitar side bending, the understanding of which will completely demystify the bending operation, and reduce it to a single fundamental task. This task is repeated multiple times, resulting in accurately bent guitar sides.

Wood Selection

Lutherie wood suppliers sell wood for the sides as a set which also includes the wood for the back. It is almost always the case that the back and sides of a guitar will be of the same wood species. Wood dealers put together guitar back and side sets (also called simply, guitar sets) out of two long *bookmatched* pieces for the sides, and two shorter and wider bookmatched pieces for the back plate. Because of the size differences needed, the side pieces are generally cut from a different piece of wood than the back pieces are cut from. This requires that the wood dealer select a pair of side boards that have a good visual match with the selected pair of back boards.

The term bookmatched above means that two pieces of wood are the result of successive slices off a board. If the two slices are stacked one on top of the other just as they came off the saw, and then the top one is flipped off in a motion similar to opening a book, the grain pattern of the two pieces will be near mirror images of each other (**figure 9-1**). At least they will be if the board from which they were cut was reasonably well quartered.

Sets sold by lutherie wood dealers usually contain pieces that have been planed to a thickness between ⅛″ (3.2mm) and ¼″ (6.4mm). Different luthiers have different target thicknesses for the sides (and backs), sometimes depending on the wood species, but in the context of the construction process described in this book and the woods likely to be used, a uniform target thickness of 3⁄32″ (2.4mm) is specified. Although this is a detail which should be brought up later, in the section on construction, it is mentioned here because not all lutherie novices have the facilities to easily thin backs and sides to thickness.

Figure 9-1 – *Bookmatched side pieces. The pieces are successive slices sawn from a board. When the pieces are opened up like a book, the grain pattern of a piece will be a near mirror image of that of the other.*

Woodworkers that have extensive hand plane skills can often manage this. But the stationary power tool most appropriate for doing this work is the wide drum sander, an expensive tool that not all shops have. Note that the stationary planer cannot be used to plane wood anywhere near this thin. But all lutherie wood suppliers can supply guitar sets sanded to the desired thickness upon request.

Suppliers often provide guitar sets in different sizes suitable for the different sizes of guitar to be constructed. There is no standardization at all with this. Every supplier denotes sizes differently, so it is always best to check the actual sizes of the pieces of wood that are on offer. The sizes needed for the example instruments are shown in **table 9-1**. I highly recommend that lutherie novices purchase the largest size available from the supplier, no matter which instrument will be built. This may provide some extra wood which can be used for other purposes. For example, wider side pieces may provide enough wood to cut strips from them that can be used for the guitar's bindings, and still leave enough for the sides themselves. The larger sizes may also provide additional length for the sides, and this can make bending of the sides a bit easier.

Lutherie wood suppliers offer back and side sets in different species and, to some extent, different grain orientations. Just as was done earlier in the book on the subject of selecting wood for the neck blank, I'll begin the discussion of wood species for guitar backs and sides with historical information.

For most of the 20th century, the wood species used for the backs and sides of steel string acoustic guitars made in the USA were small in number. The highest priced instruments used Brazilian rosewood (*Dalbergia nigra*), while instruments at a price point below that may have used East Indian rosewood (*Dalbergia latifolia*) instead. More moderately priced guitars were made of Honduras mahogany (*Swietenia macrophylla*). Budget priced instruments used any number of light in color domestic species including white oak (*Quercus alba*), unfigured soft maple (basically *Acer* spp. with the exception of *Acer saccharum*), birch (*Betula* spp.), and tulip poplar (*Liriodendron tulipifera*). These were invariably stained a dark color to resemble the higher priced woods.

Things began to change during the latter part of the 20th century, due to two different economic forces. The first was a move away from the use of domestic species for low priced instruments. These species had been associated with cheaper instruments for so long that they had negative appeal to customers. Manufacturers substituted higher priced solid woods, or domestic woods veneered over with more desirable tropical species for the low end instruments. The other economic force that affected wood choices for backs and sides was the increasing scarcity, and increasing price, of some of the traditional woods. This forced guitar makers to consider and use a number of alternate tropical wood species. These trends continue. But domestic species began to get a second look early in the 21st century, as will be detailed below. The upshot of all this is that the modern luthier has a wide variety of species to chose from when selecting wood for guitar backs and sides.

So how does the luthier decide? One way to consider this decision is to list the general properties that are desirable, and then to see how each available species stacks up for each of those. General desirable properties include sonic, structural, and visual properties. For the lutherie novice, we should add bendability to that list, because some species are more difficult to bend than others. There are other properties of course, and one more I'll add to the list is species endangerment, something which is an important consideration for more and more people. Each of these will be discussed in some detail below.

Sonic Properties

Everyone wants their guitar to sound good, so this is by far the most important consideration. Wood species that enhance or at least support good sound are preferred, while species that reduce sound quality should be scrupulously avoided. Given the small number of species used historically, and their

Example Guitar	Dealer's Size	Min. Side Width	Min. Side Length	Min. ½ Back Width	Min. Back Len
Tripletta OM	OM	4″ (101.6mm)	32″ (812.8mm)	8″ (203.2mm)	21″ (533.4mm)
Paura Dreadnought	Dreadnought, D	5″ (127mm)	32″ (812.8mm)	8¼″ (209.6mm)	22″ (558.8mm)

Table 9-1 – *Minimum widths and lengths for the pieces of guitar back and side sets needed to build the example instruments. Note that in the chart, the width of the back is expressed as the width of each of the two pieces of the back. Some wood dealers do it this way, others provide the width of both pieces put together. Note also that there is no standardization among wood dealers about what dimensions the "named" sizes refer to.*

associations with instruments at different price points, for a long time it was simply assumed that the use of Brazilian rosewood for guitar backs and sides was required for the best sound, since it was used on the best instruments. This assumption came under question as that wood became scarce and its price kept rising. There was never any scientific research that supported this assumption. But on the other hand, scientific research on lutherie matters is pretty sparse, and this was just one of many areas that had not been thoroughly investigated. There has always been anecdotal evidence that countered the assumptions about the superiority of Brazilian rosewood. To me one of the most compelling bits of such evidence is that the late Robert Ruck, one of the most highly regarded guitar luthiers of the late 20th century, did not typically use this species.

My own early investigations on this subject focused on comparing domestic species with similar density and stiffness to the commonly used tropical hardwoods. A far more comprehensive effort to compare traditional tropical hardwoods with domestic hardwoods was performed by a European organization, The Leonardo Guitar Research Project (https://www.leonardo-guitar-research.com). This was quickly followed up by formal scientific work by a group led by Samuele Carcagno.[1] These research efforts indicate that the species of wood used for the back and sides of a guitar has no relationship to the perceived goodness of the sound of the guitar. This being the case, the novice luthier can ignore this as an issue, and is free to consider whatever other qualities are desirable when selecting wood for backs and sides.

Structural Properties

The acoustic guitar is a delicate structure, so a highly desirable property is physical robustness. Since physical impacts resulting from knocks and falls are common, wood species with high impact resistance would be desired. Another issue is resistance to cracking due to dimensional changes as a result of changes in humidity. Many instruments end up suffering worse effects from the latter than from the former.

It is the case that most of the woods available for guitar backs and sides will offer similar impact resistance. However one wood does stand out, Honduras mahogany (*Swietenia macrophylla*).

As far as stability with changes in humidity goes, it is generally the case that the denser woods are more problematic. It is also the case that grain orientation is an important factor. For maximum stability, back and side wood should be quartersawn. In this orientation, most of the shrinkage and swelling will be in the thickness of the side, where it has the least detrimental effect. There is one wood species that has superior stability with changes in humidity, and that species is once again Honduras mahogany. Another advantage mahogany offers in this regard is that grain orientation really doesn't matter. It is just as dimensionally stable when flat sawn as it is when quartersawn.

Visual Properties

What looks good is highly subjective of course, but some visual qualities are fairly universal. For example, historically acoustic guitars have had dark colored backs and sides. So if a traditional look is desired, the wood used for the back and sides should be dark in color. Fashion changes though, and many modern instruments are making use of lighter colored woods.

Hardwoods are generally quite boring to look at, but there are some qualities which offer more visual appeal. These include color variation and grain variation, generally referred to as *figure*. It is also the case that most hardwoods look better when flat sawn as opposed to quartersawn. Note that with the possible exception of color variation, it may be prudent to reject wood with these visual qualities, because all of them make the wood less stable and more difficult to bend.

I recall reading a conversation in an online lutherie discussion group, where a soon-to-be guitar builder posted photos of the materials he collected for his first guitar, and asked for advice from experts for how to start his project. The experienced participants in that group universally suggested that he ditch the beautifully figured, flat sawn back and side set he had purchased, because they could tell how much trouble it would be to bend the sides, just from looking at the photos.

Bendability

The subject of how bendable wood is, is a fascinating one. Because the bending of wood has broad commercial application, there are good general data on the subject. One excellent source is a handbook published by the U.S. Dept. of Agriculture entitled *Bending Solid Wood to Form*.[2] Bendability is a function of wood species, and also of the thickness of the piece to be bent. There are variations in bendability within each wood species too. For most commercial applications, the major concern is how tight a bend can be made in a given piece of wood. For lutherie purposes we generally don't have to worry about this. Because we are working with such thin pieces, we can pretty much bend any species to the broad curves needed for the typical acoustic guitar. The tightest bend is typically the waist curve, but given the thinness of the sides, achieving this bend is rarely an issue. Guitars with cutaways are another story. Some of the curves associated with a cutaway are quite tight. But the example instruments constructed in this book are non-cutaway guitars.

Another issue of bendability for luthiers bending sides over a bending iron, is the amount of pressure needed to effect a bend. Although most people have the strength to be able to bend any wood species that a guitar would be made from, this is an issue that the lutherie novice may want to consider. Lutherie novices have greater success in bending sides when easier to bend wood is used.

The amount of pressure needed to bend the wood roughly follows the density of the wood. The domestic hardwood species typically used for guitar backs and sides are generally easy to bend. Although not all that dense, mahogany puts up more resistance to bending than do similarly dense domestic woods. The rosewoods bend well, but not as easily as domestic species. The very dense woods like ebony are difficult to bend, and should probably be avoided for use in a novice luthier project.

One last issue of bendability is the tendency for wood to crack under bending pressure. Wood with a lot of runout is usually more prone to cracking. Cracking is a big problem with highly figured woods, because the figure is the result of changes in direction of the grain. Highly figured wood has areas of very short grain, and bending stress can cause the wood to fracture in these areas. Highly figured wood may look great, but it is best avoided by lutherie novices.

Species Endangerment

As is always the case with natural resources, at one time the supply of tropical hardwoods that were traditionally used for guitar backs and sides was considered to be stable and inexhaustible. This view lasted right up until it was obvious that it was no longer true. The response of guitar builders to the increasing cost and reduced availability of our preferred wood species was to look for alternatives that looked and worked the same, or as closely as possible. As mentioned, this opened up for consideration a number of tropical species that were not as commonly used, and eventually it also led to increased interest in domestic species as well.

In recent years it has become obvious that this general way of doing business is not sustainable. During the course of my own lutherie career the rosewoods from Madagascar have gone from abundantly available and cheap to less available and more expensive, and then on to their current state of being all but wiped out. We simply cannot just move on from species to species, wiping one after another out of existence.

The *Convention on International Trade in Endangered Species* (CITES) is an international agreement, designed to reduce species endangerment due to overuse. Woods are listed by the organization in various categories, which impose restrictions limiting trade, or in some cases imposing a strict ban on importation. A number of luthiers including some large guitar factories are guided by this agreement when considering their use of certain wood species. The U.S. government is a member of this organization. Responsible lutherie wood suppliers follow the trade rules established by CITES.

Some Thoughts on Selecting Back and Side Material

As mentioned, modern lutherie wood dealers offer a lot of choices. Lutherie novices would be well advised to choose common, unfigured or lightly figured, and moderately priced wood for the back and sides of a project guitar. By far the most important consideration for a novice guitar-making effort is the likelihood of success. Using readily available materials will help to this end.

Novice luthiers with a preference for the use of domestic species will find excellent back and side sets available in birch (*Betula* spp.), black walnut (*Juglans nigra*), claro walnut (*Juglans hindsii*) and black cherry (*Prunus serotina*). Most of the photos in this book are of a guitar made of curly black cherry, and one made from a beautiful black walnut set given to me by Bell Buckle, Tennessee, luthier and lutherie supplier Kevin Waldron.

Practice Sides

The bending of the guitar sides can be accurately performed by any novice luthier with just a bit of experience with the fundamentals of bending, and a bit of practice going through the motions of actual side bending. Exercises that are appropriate for novice luthiers are detailed later in this chapter. Some material is needed to do those exercises however, so it is a good idea if some practice sides are ordered at the same time the actual back and side set that will be used in the guitar is ordered. All lutherie wood suppliers can supply practice sides, even if these are not listed on their websites. Practice sides are collected from orphaned sides, or sides with visual flaws in them. These should be thinned to the same thickness as for the real sides, 3⁄32"

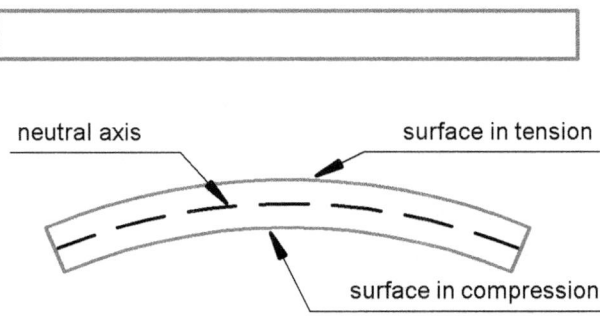

Figure 9-2 – *When a cold piece of wood is bent and held in position, the outside convex surface is in tension, and the inside concave surface is in compression. Somewhere between the surfaces is the neutral axis, which is under no stress. When the piece is released, internal stresses return the piece back to its original straight shape.*

(2.4mm). I recommend ordering four practice sides for use in the exercises that follow.

Heat Bending Wood

Understanding the bending characteristics of wood is fundamental to understanding how to bend the sides of the guitar to shape. First, let's consider what happens when a thin, dry length of wood is bent at room temperature. Force is applied to the wood to bend it into a curved shape, as in **figure 9-2**. The length of wood is bent and held in the bent shape. In this state, the outer convex surface of the wood is under tension, and the inner concave surface is under compression. In fact most of the wood throughout the piece is under tension or compression to some extent. There is only a thin line somewhere within the

---

What is "Tonewood?"

One doesn't have to look too deep into the world of lutherie information to come across the term "tonewood", used to identify wood suitable for use in musical instruments, and by exclusion and inference, wood that is not suitable for this application. But as should be obvious from the discussion about wood selection in these pages, the list of wood species generally considered to be tonewoods changes constantly, and has changed constantly throughout history. These changes are usually more readily explained by factors other than any effects a wood might have on the sonic qualities of an instrument.

My favorite definition of tonewood comes from Brampton, Ontario, luthier Charles Tauber, who states:

"A 'tonewood' is simply any wood that someone has used twice to make an instrument. Somebody tried it once, found it worked well enough for the purpose and used it again."

Charles says that his definition follows from fellow Canadian luthier Sergei de Jonge's response to being asked what his favorite tonewood is: "The kind that grows on trees."

wood that is under neither tension or compression. This is called the *neutral axis*.

In this example, the length of wood is being held in the bent shape. As soon as that hold is released, the tension and compression of the wood will force it to return to its straight, pre-bend shape. The property described in this example is called *elastic deformation*. The wood is deformed (bent), but when the bending force is released, the wood behaves elastically and returns to its original shape.

To the end of forming the curved sides of the guitar, the property of elastic deformation doesn't help us. Assuming it was possible to force the wood into the desired shape by clamping it into the mold, as soon as the clamps are released the wood would return to its unbent shape. Fortunately wood can be plasticized, that is, made so that if it is bent, it will retain the shape it is bent into. When this plasticization is done while the wood is bent, instead of undergoing elastic deformation, it will undergo *plastic deformation*. Wood is most readily plasticized using moisture and heat. We'll look at each of these individually.

It is clear that wet wood bends more readily than does dry wood. Green wood, which contains a considerable amount of water, bends easier than dry wood does. This is taken advantage of in the process of making wood baskets. Baskets are woven out of green wood. The woven structure holds the bends in the wood in place while the wood is still wet, but when the wood dries it retains its bent shape. It may be possible to thoroughly wet wood for guitar sides, clamp them into the mold, and then allow them to air dry or kiln dry them to set the bends. Although this may be possible, the process would be time-consuming, and it has the added disadvantage that the wood would tend to straighten back into its original shape if it got wet again.

What is needed is a relatively quick way to bend the guitar sides into shape, and in a manner in which they will retain that shape with changes in moisture level. Heat bending satisfies those requirements. Understanding how heat bending works requires just a bit of knowledge about the cellular structure of wood.[3]

Wood is composed of rigid cells that are long and thin. The cells are primarily oriented along the length of the wood. The walls of the cells are composed mostly of *cellulose* and related molecules. The outer parts of the walls also contain *lignin*. This substance is also concentrated between the cells. If wood was an engineered material, the lignin would be the glue that holds the cells together, and helps to stiffen the walls of the cells. Although lignin is rigid at normal temperatures, the application of heat plasticizes it. This allows the cells of the wood to move in relation to each other, and makes it easier for the walls of the cells to deform when under compression. This means that, at elevated temperatures, bent wood will undergo plastic deformation in the areas of the wood under compression. If the temperature is not too hot, when the wood cools the lignin returns to its rigid state. So, wood bent under heat, and then held in the bent shape while it cools, will retain its bent shape once it cools.

This process is also repeatable. After wood is bent and cooled, it can be reheated and bent some more. This is useful in the process of bending the sides of guitars on a bending iron. If a bend is made, but it turns out that it was not deep enough, the wood can be returned to the iron for additional bending.

Photo 9-1 – *A typical domestic commercial bending iron. The cross section of the iron itself is ovoid in shape, which makes it ideal for bending sides for various sizes of stringed instruments. It is electrically heated, and the temperature is thermostatically controlled. Note that the iron pictured has an optional small diameter extension on the top. This is used for bending tight curves on the sides of small instruments, and is not needed for guitars.*

Likewise if a bend was made too deep, the wood can be reheated and then unbent a little.

When bending the sides of the guitar to shape, we take advantage of heat and moisture. The wood to be bent must be heated on the side under compression to an internal temperature of 212°F (100°C) or a bit higher. Although guitar sides can be bent dry, bending is aided by the application of some amount of water. It turns out just a bit of water on the surface of the side under compression works almost as well as a thorough soaking, which could take days to accomplish. In addition to helping make the wood more plastic, the water also helps keep the surface of the wood from getting scorched during heating. More details on heat and moisture are presented in the following section.

The Bending Iron

There are a few options when it comes to procuring a bending iron for use in bending guitar sides. I use and recommend a domestic bending iron, such as the type pictured in **photo 9-1**.

Photo 9-2 – *The thermostat on the pictured iron is not calibrated in degrees. The knob just has numbers on it.*

Photo 9-3 – *An inexpensive magnetic contact thermometer, of the type used for the flue pipes of wood burning stoves, is used to measure the temperature of the iron.*

Photo 9-4 – *The iron can be oriented horizontally for use, as well as vertically. Orientation is a matter of personal preference.*

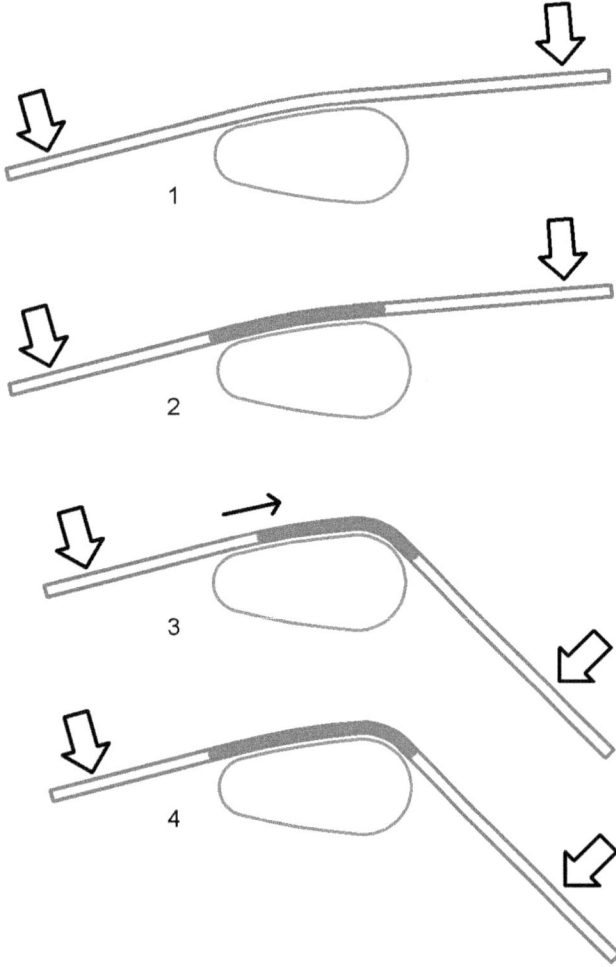

Figure 9-3 – *Discrete steps in bending wood on the bending iron. 1. The dampened piece is held in place against the iron with pressure near both ends. 2. The part of the piece in contact with the iron heats up. 3. The piece is slid over the surface of the iron to the right. Bending force bends the heated area of the wood overhanging the right side of the iron. 4. Again, the part of the piece in contact with the iron is heated, while the previously hot part on the right that is no longer in contact with the iron cools down and stiffens.*

It is readily available from lutherie suppliers. Irons of this type are moderately expensive, but they are robustly constructed and are quite reliable. The cross section of the iron is ideally shaped for the bending of guitar sides. The temperature of the iron is controlled by a thermostat. This is a feature I highly recommend in a bending iron to be used by a lutherie novice. There are a lot of variables associated with the bending process. Having a bending iron with accurately maintained temperature eliminates one possible source of problems.

One issue with the iron pictured is that its thermostat is not calibrated in degrees (**photo 9-2**). An easy, cheap, and highly recommended fix for this is to use a magnetic contact thermometer, of the type intended for use on the flue pipes of wood burning stoves (**photo 9-3**), to set the temperature the first time. These are readily available from various Internet sources.

Other options for lutherie bending irons include Asian bending irons. These are generally available from popular Internet auction websites, and are usually substantially less expensive than domestic irons. I have used some of these, and found them to be very good, with accurate temperature control and digital readout for the temperature. Another potential option which I'll mention just for completeness is a shop-built bending iron. There are numerous plans and descriptions of these in various places on the Internet. Most are quite inexpensive, but few offer thermostatic heat control. I can't really recommend any that I have come across though. None that I have seen offer accurate temperature control, and all had electrical and fire safety issues.

Bending irons can be used vertically or horizontally (**photo 9-4**). The orientation is a matter of personal preference. I prefer to use the iron oriented vertically, simply because it can be held securely in the vise. Some folks prefer the horizontal orientation because it is easier to apply bending force this way. In this orientation the wood is pushed down onto the iron. With the iron mounted vertically, bending force is applied by pulling the wood against the iron toward the luthier. This takes a bit more muscle, but I haven't found anyone that could not bend sides in this way. A vertically oriented iron generally makes the bend easier to see during bending, and this is a plus for some luthiers.

Basic Use of the Bending Iron

As mentioned, three things are needed to effect a permanent bend in wood. These are moisture, heat, and bending force. In use, the bending iron provides the heat, and the moisture and bending force are provided by the luthier. Because the bending iron is shorter in width than most of the bends that will be made in the wood, the wood must be moved over the surface of the iron to successively heat each part of a bend. **Figure 9-3** shows the bending process as a series of discrete steps. Pressing the wood to the bending iron heats up that part of the wood that is in contact with the iron. That portion is heated hot enough to plasticize the wood. The luthier slides the wood over the iron so a portion of the heated area now overhangs the iron. Pressure exerted near the ends of the wood by the luthier bends the hot and plastic portion. The movement of the wood brings more of the unheated part of the wood into contact with the iron on one side, and also brings the just bent part off the iron, where it can cool and harden the bend. Note that the more bending force is applied, the deeper the resulting bend will be.

The process just described could be repeated as many times as is necessary along the piece, to effect a long smooth curve. But in actual use a long smooth curve is bent by slowly and steadily moving the wood across the surface of the iron, while applying bending force all the while. This smooth, continuous bending process results in a smoother and more continuous bend. Note that the wood must be moved slowly across the surface of the iron. If it is moved too fast, the wood in any one place won't get heated enough while that place is in contact with the iron. More specific practical details about using the bending iron will follow in later sections.

The Construction of the Guitar Body Outline

In the beginning of this chapter, it was mentioned that background information on wood bending, the bending iron, and on how guitar body outlines are constructed would lead to some simple and easy-to-apply basic principles of guitar side bending. In this final background section we'll look at the construction of guitar body outlines.

When the guitar body outline is viewed, it looks like one continuous smooth curve. The idea of bending a straight piece of wood to duplicate the complex curve of one side of the instrument is indeed daunting. But the vast majority of guitar body outlines are actually composed of a number of circular arc segments placed end to end. At the point that one segment ends and the next one begins, the two arc segments are tangent to each other. This gives the appearance of a single smooth curve. That this is so is an interesting product of the way the human vision system works. We are particularly bad at identifying individual tangent arcs, unless we have a close reference to compare them to. The result is that in most cases, a series of tangent circular arcs looks like one continuous smooth curve.

Guitar outlines have been made in this way since guitar outlines were first drawn. This is a consequence of the tools available for traditional drafting, which rely heavily on the straightedge and compass. It is interesting that the majority of guitar outlines, from historical instruments to modern ones, were originally drawn using just five or seven circular arcs, plus two or three short straight lines, per side.[4,5] Not all modern guitar bodies are drawn using circular arcs, but even those that were not drawn this way originally can be accurately rendered as a series of tangent circular arcs. See the sidebar.

The body outlines of the two example instruments were drawn in this manner, and the lengths and locations of each circular arc segment are included on the plans. This is the tape that was used to mark the ends of segments on the top of the mold in the previous chapter. **Figure 9-4** shows a half body outline of the Tripletta OM style guitar, and includes the circles from which the upper bout, waist, and lower bout arcs are

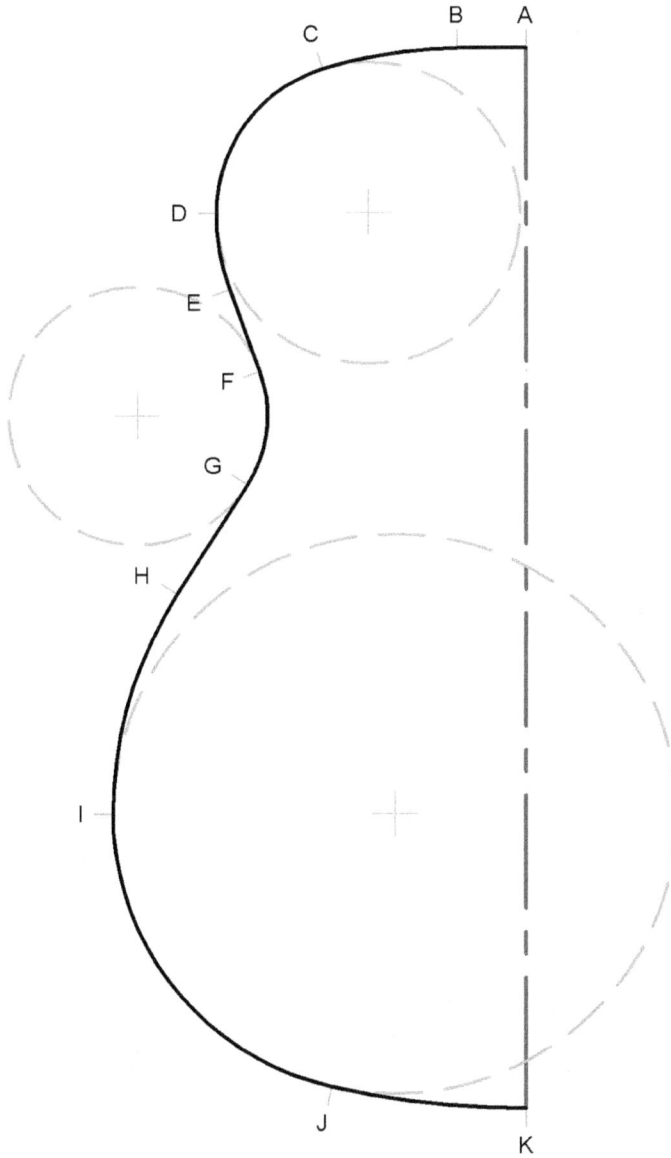

Figure 9-4 – *What looks like a single, continuous, smooth curve representing one side of a guitar body, is actually composed of individual circular arc and straight line segments. The full circles that define the upper bout arc (segment CD), the waist arc (segment FG), and the lower bout arc (segment IJ) are shown. Note that other segments are also circular arcs, but they are so shallow that their defining circles are too big to show in this figure. These are the neck arc (segment BC), the upper bout secondary arc (segment DE), the lower bout secondary arc (segment HI), and the tail arc (segment JK). There are also short straight line segments on both sides of the waist, segment EF and segment GH. The example instruments are flat at the neck end, and this flat is the straight line segment AB. The fact that guitar body outlines are composed of a number of circular arc segments means that the process of bending a side can be divided into a number of discrete bending operations, one per arc segment.*

Reverse Engineering the Body Outline

Although the plans for the example instruments clearly show the component segments of the body outline, it is usually not the case that this information is included on drawn plans. But it is *always* possible to figure out the location and radius of each of these curves, using simple trial and error drawing techniques. Details of this process are contained in a previously referenced article.[4] Here, a rough outline of the process is presented.

The first step is to draw horizontal lines representing the width of the body at the bouts and waist. The center points of the circles for each of the bout and waist curves will be located on the respective line somewhere. Trial and error will quickly produce the circles.

The second step is to locate and mark the points on the upper and lower bout curves where they diverge from their defining circles. A radius is drawn from each of these points to the center of the defining circle, and then this line is extended. The defining circles of the remaining four arcs are also drawn by trial and error. Because the neck arc BC is tangent to the upper bout arc CD, its center point will be somewhere along the extended upper radius line of the upper bout circle. Likewise, the center point of the upper bout secondary arc DE will be somewhere along the extended lower radius line of the upper bout circle. The remaining two arcs are tangent to the lower bout arc and their defining circles are determined in similar manner.

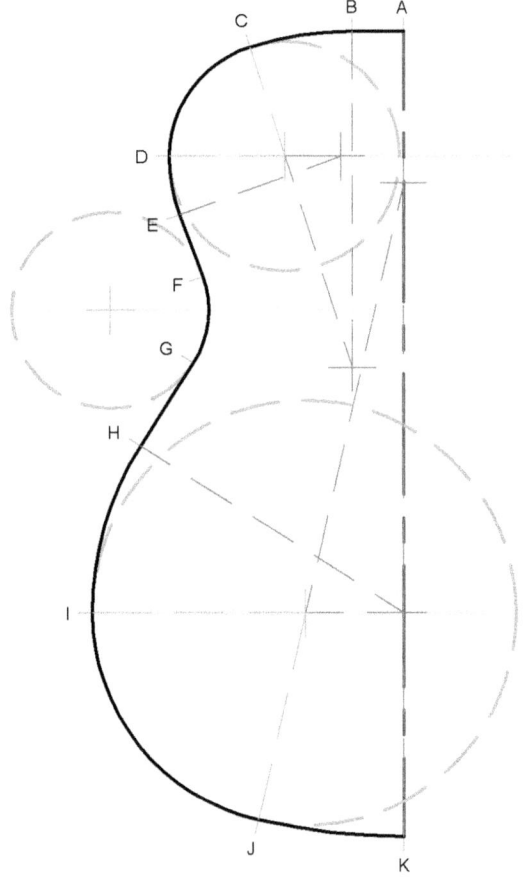

taken. There are four other circular arcs in this outline, but they are so shallow (i.e. their radii are so long) that it is not possible to fit their defining circles into the figure.

It should be obvious why the fact that the outline of a guitar side is composed of a series of individual arcs is important to the task of bending the side of a guitar to shape. In bending a guitar side, the luthier can first mark the location and length of each segment on the unbent side. Then the arc segments can be bent, one at a time. In this way, the complex task of taking a flat piece of wood and bending it accurately to the curves of the guitar side, is reduced to a series of small and easy-to-accomplish tasks.

Essential Principles of Guitar Side Bending

From the background information in the previous sections, we can now state the three essential principles that make it possible for lutherie novices to successfully bend guitar sides using a bending iron.

1. Each segment of the side is bent as a separate operation.

Given a flat unbent side on which the locations and lengths of the segments have been marked out, each segment can be bent as a simple, easy to understand, and easy to accomplish operation.

2. Constant pressure and constant speed yield a circular arc.

The curved segments of the guitar outline are all circular arcs. Given a bending iron with constant temperature, if a segment is bent on the bending iron using constant bending pressure throughout the bend, and if the wood is moved over the surface of the bending iron at a constant rate of speed, the resulting bend will be a curve of constant radius, that is, a circular arc.

3. If a bent segment does not match the mold it can be re-bent.

Although a segment can reliably be bent into a circular arc, that arc may end up shallower or deeper than is required for that

Photo 9-5 – An ordinary spray bottle is used to dampen the area to be bent. The surface that will contact the iron, and the surface opposite should be sprayed. During bending, the heat from the iron will evaporate the water. The area should be re-sprayed as needed. Note that spraying is done away from the iron, to avoid spraying water directly on the iron itself.

segment to match the mold. If a segment is too shallow, it can be bent again, which will make the resulting arc deeper. And if a bent segment is too deep, it can be unbent as much as needed to match the mold.

Specific Side Bending Techniques, and Exercises

 Exercises are provided here which reflect those techniques which generally require some repetition for novices to fully master.

Heating the Bending Iron

An electric bending iron needs to be preheated for at least 20 minutes before use. Before turning it on, the iron should be securely mounted in the position in which it will be used. The temperature of the iron should be set in the range of 260°F to 280°F (127°C to 138°C). If the thermostat control of the iron is not calibrated in degrees, a magnetic contact thermometer can be used to help set the temperature. The thermometer is attached to the top of the iron and the temperature control is turned to approximately 75% of maximum. After the iron warms up thoroughly, the temperature can be checked and adjustment made. This process can take some time. It is worthwhile to mark the thermostat dial once the correct temperature is achieved, to make it easier to set the iron the next time it is used.

Note that the indicated temperature is considerably higher than the internal temperature necessary to plasticize wood for bending. A higher iron temperature is necessary, because in use the wood is not held immobile against the iron, but instead is moved across its surface, and so will have limited time for the wood to reach the appropriate internal temperature.

The luthier may want to drop the temperature of the iron a bit if bending causes the wood to become deeply scorched. Some amount of scorching is common, particularly on wood that is light in color and wood that is oily. The scorching is generally only on the surface, and can be easily sanded out. But if scorching is chronic and deep, the temperature of the iron can be reduced.

On the other hand, if the wood has to be moved extremely slowly over the iron to get it to heat up enough to bend, or if it just won't bend at all, then the iron will have to be turned up a bit. Temperature changes should be made in small increments, and time should be allowed for the iron to settle at the new temperature.

Safety

The two hazards associated with the use of the bending iron are burns and smoke, and appropriate safety equipment to deal with each is appropriate. For the most part, the bending of guitar sides does not require touching the iron, but it is often the case that the hands must be positioned close to it. Standard cotton gardening gloves work well enough to provide burn protection in most cases, but heavier gloves may be necessary for some.

As far as smoke goes, in an ideal world the sides will be bent with no scorching of the wood at all. This is not always achievable though. In cases where the smoke associated with side bending is a problem, a suitable respirator and eye protection will be advantageous.

A hot bending iron should never be left unattended. The iron should be unplugged immediately following a bending session. A wise safety precaution is to set a timer that will produce an audible reminder to turn the iron off.

Wetting the Side for Bending

Before bending a segment of the side, it is wetted on both surfaces, using an ordinary pump spray bottle with the nozzle on the mist setting (**photo 9-5**). The wood should be moved away from the iron while spraying it, to avoid spraying water directly on the iron. Any surface water should be allowed to drip off the wood, before the wood is applied to the iron.

Note that very hard water and light colored wood may result in mineral staining of the wood. If this happens, it is best to use distilled bottled water in the spray bottle.

As a consequence of bending, the surface water will quickly dry out. If a segment needs to be bent more than once, it should be re-sprayed if the surface is dry.

It is not technically necessary to spray the back surface of the wood, the surface that will not contact the iron. It is the iron contact surface that will actually compress and bend. However it is useful to wet the other side as well, because doing so provides a visual clue that the wood is thoroughly heated internally, when it can be seen that the surface water on the side opposite the iron is drying out.

Applying Bending Pressure

Bending guitar sides using the bending iron requires the luthier to do two things – apply bending pressure, and move the wood across the surface of the iron. If these are studied and practiced individually, it will be much easier to do them both at the same time.

Bending pressure is applied by applying the wood to the opposite side of the vertical bending iron from where the luthier is standing, and pulling it toward the luthier. The basic form is shown in **photo 9-6**. The amount of bending pressure applied is dependent on how hard the luthier is pulling, and also where

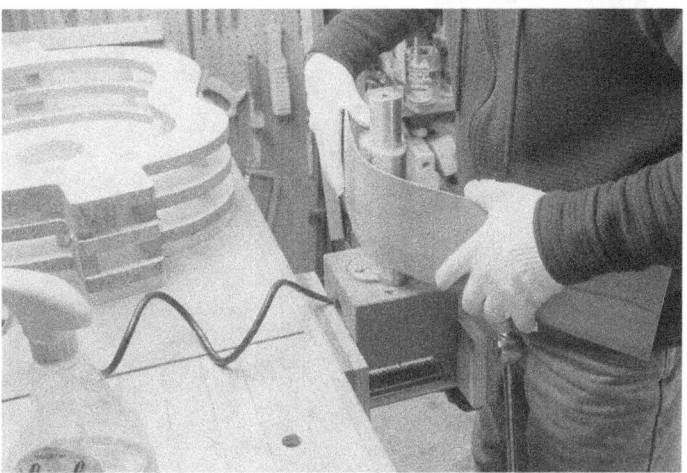

***Photo 9-6** – The basic side bending position when using a vertical bending iron. Note the use of cotton gloves for protection against the heat of the iron. The piece is always kept perpendicular to the iron. Bending of a short segment is being done here, and the hands are positioned approximately 6″ (152.4mm) from the ends of the segment. Pulling on the piece is done with the arms, shoulders, and back, not by leaning the luthier's weight backwards. The body position must be stable, in case the piece being bent snaps unexpectedly, so the luthier does not fall.*

the luthier's hands are on the wood. The farther apart the hands are, the more leverage there is. So for some amount of bending pressure, more pulling effort is required the closer the luthier's hands are to each other.

The luthier can apply a range of bending pressure. The more bending pressure, the tighter the resulting bend will be. For practical purposes the minimum pressure that can be applied is the amount needed to press the wood down to the side of the bending iron. The maximum pressure that can be applied is a little less than is required to snap the piece being bent.

It is a good idea to have some feel for all of this before performing actual bends.

Bending Exercises #1: Getting a Feel for Bending Pressure

Getting a basic feel for exerting and holding bending pressure is best done with the iron cold. The bending iron is positioned in the vise with the wide end to the right, but is not plugged in.

1. One of the practice sides is marked on the upper edge about 10″ (254MM) from one end. This will serve as the bending point. The hands are placed approximately 6″ (152.4MM) from

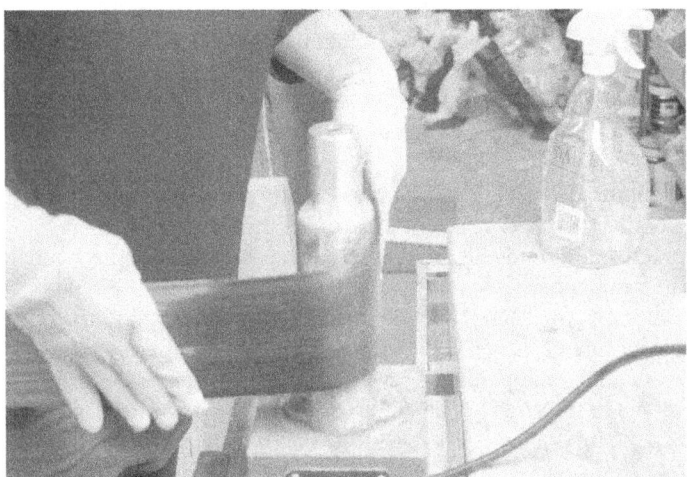

Photo 9-7 *– The wood is bent over the right (wide) end of the bending iron, while maintaining constant bending pressure. When the unbent ends of the practice side form a right angle, the side is removed from the iron.*

Photo 9-8 *– The bend is maintained by the continued application of bending pressure while the wood cools down. The luthier is waving the side around, to encourage air circulation.*

the mark, as in **photo 9-6**. The side is brought into contact with the bending iron so the mark is roughly centered on the wide side of the iron. Bending pressure is applied by pulling on the side until it fully contacts the wide side of the iron. This position is held, to get a feel for what minimum pressure feels like with the hands this far apart. This sequence is repeated a few times until this amount of pressure can be duplicated by feel.

2. The above is repeated, but this time a bit more pressure is applied and held. This represents the likely bottom of the range of useful bending pressure that will be employed during actual side bending. The amount of bending pressure is a function of the angle to which the flat, unplasticized side is bent. The rough angle that the side has been bent to is visually noted, and the feel of the pressure is also noted. This is repeated a few times.

3. The hands are moved so they are each approximately 3″ (76.2MM) from the mark and the bend above is repeated until the angle of the bend is the same as before. Note how much harder the side must be pulled to achieve the same angle of bend (and thus the same bending pressure), when the hands are closer to the bend and leverage is reduced. It is sometimes necessary when actually bending a side, to position one or the other hand quite close to where the bend is being made.

4. The hands are moved back to the original positions, and the bend above is duplicated. Now bending pressure is slowly increased. As this is done, careful attention should be paid to the sound of the wood. If at any point small cracking sounds are heard, bending pressure should be backed off a little, until it stops. If no such sound is detected, then bending pressure is slowly increased until the practice side snaps. Not everyone is capable of applying enough pressure in this way to actually break the side. The point just before cracking noises were heard approximates the maximum possible bending pressure that can be used to perform an actual bend. It is rare to apply this much pressure, for obvious reasons, but it is important to experience what this much pressure feels like.

Bending Exercises #2: Maintaining Bending Pressure

Maintaining bending pressure is simple when the iron is cold. But with a hot iron, pressure will be released by the plastic bending of the wood. Maintaining a fixed amount of bending pressure requires the luthier to continuously close the angle the side forms over the iron, in response to the plastic bending of the wood. This is done by feel, and that is the reason for the cold bending feel exercises previously done. For these next exercises, the iron is first preheated. Once up to temperature, the exercises can be performed.

1. One of the practice sides is marked on the upper edge about 10″ (254MM) from one end. This will serve as the bending point. Both surfaces of the side are sprayed with water around the bending point. The hands are placed approximately 6″ (152.4MM) from the mark as in **photo 9-6**. The side is brought into contact with the bending iron, so the mark is roughly centered on the wide side of the iron. Bending pressure is quickly applied by pulling on the side until it fully contacts the wide side of the iron, and then a little more pressure is applied with the right hand. When it begins to bend, the wood will be bent over the right end of the iron. The wood will begin to relax, and

this relaxation will be felt as diminished pressure on the right hand. In response, the right hand should be pulled in farther, to maintain bending pressure.

2. The wood can generally be bent right around the wide end of the iron in this way, until the right end of the practice side is now perpendicular to the left end (**photo 9-7**). Bending really far will require repositioning the luthier's body, so the right hand can continue to apply constant pressure.

3. When the bend is done, the side is removed from the iron, while bending pressure is maintained on the side. This requires

Example Guitar	Segment CD Length
Tripletta OM	3½" (88.9mm)
Paura Dreadnought	4⁵⁄₃₂" (105.6mm)

Table 9-2 – *Length of upper bout body segment CD for each of the example guitars.*

grasping the side where the hands are currently placed and pressing the hands toward each other. It is necessary to maintain bending pressure when the side is removed from the iron and for some seconds afterwards, while the side cools. If pressure is not maintained while the side cools, the wood will spring back to near its original unbent shape while it cools. It helps to cool the wood down by waving it around a bit, to circulate air around it. The side should usually be held under bending pressure about 15 seconds after it is removed from the iron (**photo 9-8**).

4. This exercise is repeated, at different places down the length of the practice side. After each bend, the side is flipped around so the next bend is made on the opposite surface. This will eventually give the practice side an undulating appearance.

5. The iron is unplugged.

Moving the Side Over the Bending Iron

It has been mentioned that to effect a bend that is longer than the length of the bending iron, the side must be moved over the surface of the iron during bending. And to achieve bends that are circular arcs, constant bending pressure and consistent speed of movement of the side are required. For the most part, the ability to move the wood over the bending iron at a regular rate of speed is easily achieved with the smallest amount of practice.

When bending guitar sides, it is generally advisable to move the side across the surface of the iron at a rate approximately in the range of ½" (12.7mm) to 1" (25.4mm) per second. It is quite easy to approximate the time interval by the familiar counting of "one one thousand, ...". About the only real issue is getting the movement started. The surface of the iron is not particularly smooth, and the wet wood may stick, more so because it is being forced in contact with the iron with some pressure. So some shove is required to get the wood to start moving. Once it begins moving, it must be kept moving. The thing to be avoided is a series of small, jerky, stick-slip moves. The desired result is movement that starts cleanly and quickly, followed by steady movement at the specified rate across the iron surface. As with the previously mentioned techniques, just a little practice is needed to fully master movement of the wood across the iron.

Bending Exercises #3: Moving the Side While Bending

For these exercises the iron is first preheated. Once up to temperature, the exercises can be performed.

1. One of the practice sides is marked on the upper edge about 6" (152.4mm) from what will be the left end. This will serve as the ending point for the bend. Another mark is made 6" (152.4mm) from the first one. This will serve as the starting point of the bend. Both surfaces of the side are sprayed with

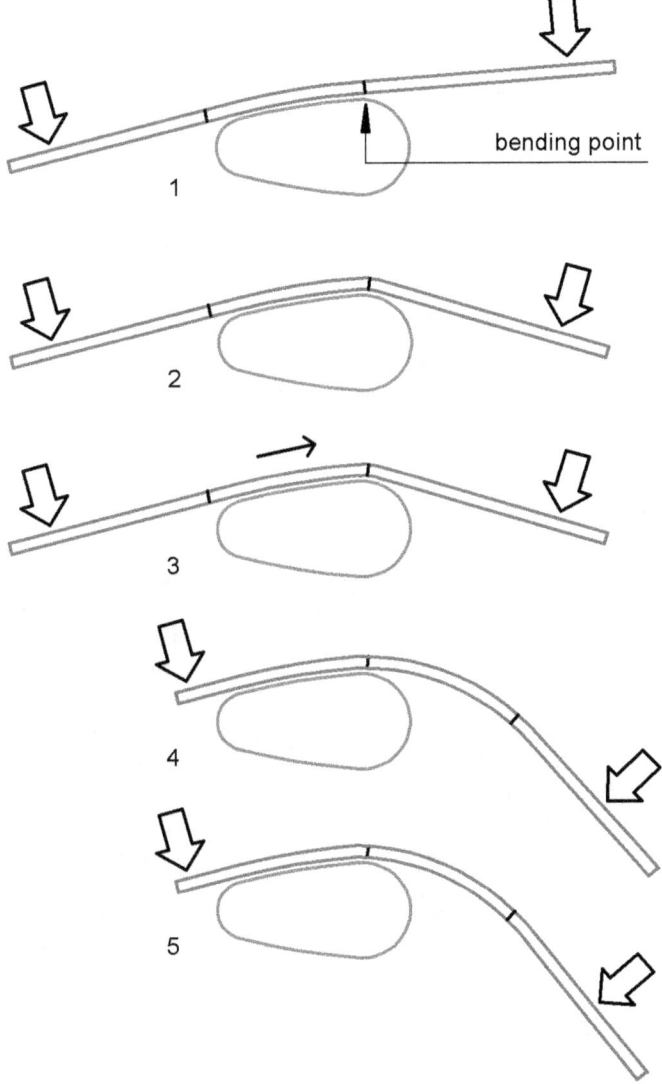

Figure 9-5 – *Moving the side across the bending iron while exerting bending pressure. 1. The side is positioned on the bending iron with the starting point for the bend aligned with the bending point of the iron. 2. Bending pressure is quickly applied. 3. When relaxation of the wood just begins to be felt in the hands, bending pressure is brought back up and maintained, and movement of the side from left to right is begun and maintained at a constant rate of speed. 4. Movement of the side is stopped when the ending point for the bend is aligned with the bending point of the iron. 5. The side is held here just long enough to feel the wood relax. Then the side is removed from the iron and bending pressure is maintained, while the wood cools.*

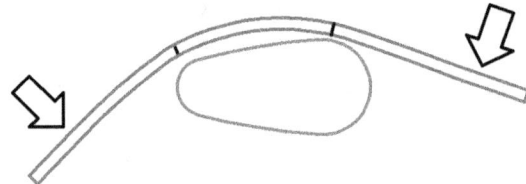

Figure 9-6– When re-bending a segment to make the bend deeper the current bend may make it impossible for the side to contact the broad side of the iron. This lack of contact reduces preheating of the wood. This in turn necessitates reducing the speed of the wood over the iron, to allow the wood to be heated enough at the point of the bend to be plasticized.

water around the segment to be bent. The hands are placed approximately 6″ (152.4mm) outside of the marks.

2. The side is pressed to the bending iron so the marked starting point contacts the iron at the point where the broad side of the iron meets the start of the wider right end of the iron. This is the bending point of the iron (**figure 9-5.1**). Bending pressure is quickly applied and held (**figure 9-5.2**).

3. When relaxation of the wood is just felt in the hands, bending pressure is maintained by pulling harder with the right hand. At the same time, the side is moved to the right at the specified rate of speed (**figure 9-5.3**).

4. Bending pressure is maintained, and a constant rate of speed is maintained, until the marked ending point reaches the point on the iron where the broad side of the iron meets the start of the wider right end. Movement of the wood across the iron stops here, but bending pressure is maintained (**figure 9-5.4**).

5. When relaxation of the wood is just felt in the hands at the end mark (**figure 9-5.5**), the wood is removed from the iron while continuing to exert bending pressure. The side is waved around a bit while it cools as in **photo 9-8**, then pressure is released.

6. This entire sequence can be repeated between these same marks to increase the depth of this bend, and also along the length of the practice side for additional practice.

7. The iron is unplugged.

Sequence for Bending a Circular Arc Segment

This is the essential bending procedure which will be used to bend the segments of the sides of the guitar. It is the culmination of all of the bending procedures described so far. For each segment, the side is bent, the bent segment is checked against its corresponding segment on the body mold, and the segment is re- bent as necessary until the segment perfectly matches the mold.

Bending Exercises #4: Bending a Body Segment

For these exercises the iron is first preheated. Once up to temperature, the exercises can be performed. The segment CD, the upper bout of the guitar outline of the mold, will be used as the target in this exercise.

1. One of the practice sides is marked on the upper edge about 6″ (152.4mm) from what will be the left end. This will serve as the ending point for the bend. The location of the starting point for the bend will depend on the length of the segment, which in turn depends on which of the two example guitars is being built. The length of segment CD is taken from **table 9-2**, or from the segment length tape that was previously cut out from the plan. A mark is made at this distance to the right of the previously made ending point mark. This new mark will serve as the starting point of the bend. Both surfaces of the side are sprayed with water around the segment to be bent. The hands are placed approximately 6″ (152.4mm) outside of the marks.

2. The segment is bent as described in the previous exercise, attempting to bend the segment to match the target segment CD on the mold. Care should be taken to be sure the entire length of the segment is involved in the bend. It is generally better to err on the side of bending too deep rather than too shallow, if this is possible.

3. After the segment has cooled for a few seconds with bending pressure maintained, it is placed on top of the mold, with its end points aligned with the segment CD on the inside edge of the mold, and checked for accuracy. It will be apparent if the curve of the segment matches that on the mold, or if it is too shallow, or if it is too deep.

4. If the curve of the segment is too shallow, the segment will have to be bent again, to increase the depth of the bend. The process for re-bending the segment is exactly the same as for

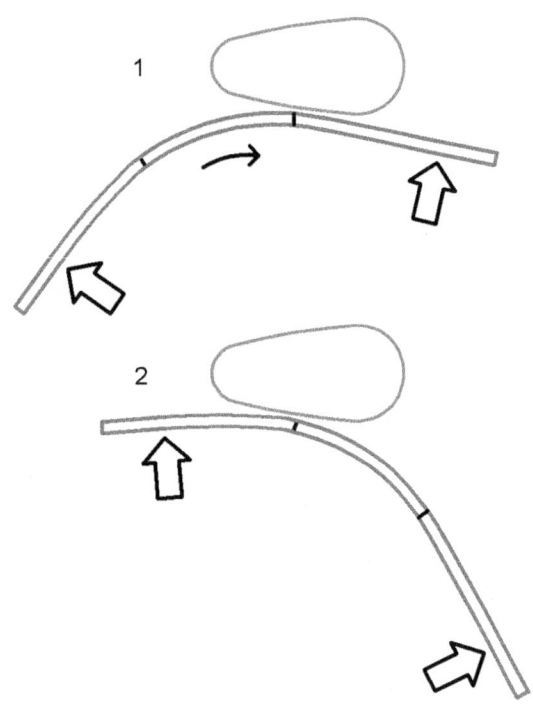

Figure 9-7– Taking some of the bend out of a bent segment is easy. The convex surface of the segment is dampened, and then the segment is moved evenly across the front side surface of the bending iron while applying pressure as shown.

Photo 9-9 – Bending near the end of the side is made a lot easier when the end is gripped with locking sheet metal pliers. If the jaws of the pliers are not as wide as the side, wood cauls can be used.

the initial bend. Note though that for segments that require a tight bend, it may not be possible for the initial contact of the side with the iron to fully contact the broad side surface of the iron. The now-curved segment may prevent this contact. In this case, the side is rotated clockwise a bit, so the marked starting point of the bend can contact the iron. If this has to be done, it is likely that the speed of movement over the iron will have to be reduced, because the lack of contact with the broad side of the iron will reduce preheating of the wood. See **figure 9-6**.

5. If the curve of the segment is too deep, the segment will have to be unbent some. Unbending is described in the following section.

6. After the curve of the segment exactly matches that of the mold, the curve should be examined closely to be sure the entire length of the segment has been bent, and that the bend imparted does not continue past either the starting or ending marks for the segment. In the former case the bend will have to be continued to the marks; in the latter case the bending past the marks will have to be removed by unbending.

7. Practice making this bend can be continued over the entire length of the practice side.

8. The iron is unplugged.

Unbending a Segment

If a segment is over bent it will be necessary to take some of the bend out. This is accomplished by evenly heating the convex surface of the side on the front side of the iron, while applying pressure. Not a lot of pressure is required. In order to maintain the circular arc, it is necessary that the full length of the segment be exposed to the iron, and that even pressure is applied throughout the procedure (**figure 9-7**).

Bending Near the End of the Side

For a long time, lutherie wood suppliers would always supply sides that were 6″ (152.4mm) or so longer than needed for the guitar to be built. But in recent years the amount of extra length has in some cases gotten much shorter. This means that sometimes there is not enough extra length around the first or last segment of a guitar side to provide enough leverage to allow easy bending of that segment. Locking sheet-metal pliers are useful in these cases (**photo 9-9**). They can be used with or without narrow wood cauls. They should generally be set up to provide the minimum amount of clamping pressure needed to securely grip the end of the side, so the blades of the pliers don't put dents in the wood.

Common Bending Problems and How to Fix Them

There are some general issues which come up from time to time when bending guitar sides over a bending iron. In general their identification and repair are straightforward, so no exercises are presented here.

Spring Back. It has been mentioned in various places in the chapter that wood that has been plasticized with heat and bent must be held in the bent position until it cools down enough to harden. If this is not done, the wood tends to unbend while it cools. This unbending is called *spring back*. Some wood species are more prone to it than others. It is also the case that even if a bend is held in position until it cools down, it may spring back to some extent anyway. If spring back is noticed, the most straightforward way to deal with it is to slightly over bend the segment in anticipation of some spring back. A certain amount of spring back will be unavoidable and will simply require additional bending of the segment.

Kinking. Wood that is easy to bend is subject to kinking, especially if it is bent under high bending pressure and low speed of the wood across the iron. It happens most often when attempting a tight bend. Kinking is basically a localized tight bend in the wood, possibly including damage to the fibers on the back surface of the bend. Kinking should be avoided, and the way to do that is to try to avoid high bending pressure and low speed movement at the same time. If a kink occurs, it should be removed by unbending it completely. In some cases the wood is weakened at the location of a kink to the extent that any attempt to re-bend it after it has been straightened out will cause it to kink again at that spot. This can often be fixed by backing up the wood to be bent with a thin piece of metal, generally

Photo 9-10 – Applying so much bending pressure that a side breaks is rare, except when highly figured wood is used. But if a break does happen ...

referred to as a *bending strap*. Often a small piece of wood veneer of the same width as the side can be used as a bending strap in a pinch.

Twisting. While a bend is being made, it is critical that the wood be kept perpendicular to the bending iron at all times. This prevents twisting of the side. Following each bend, the side can be placed on edge on the bench top. If no twisting is present, the entire length of the edge will be in contact with the bench top. Twisting is prevented by making sure the side is perpendicular to the bending iron. Another technique that helps prevent twisting can be applied to any segment that needs to be bent more than once. Each time the segment is bent, the side can be flipped over, alternating the edge of the side that is facing up during the bend. This is also the fix for a twist. The segment is unbent, then re-bent but with the side flipped over.

Scorching. Scorching of the wood often happens with light-colored wood, or wood that is particularly oily. It is only really an issue for the waist bend of a guitar side, because that is the only bend where the side contacts the bending iron on what will be the outside surface of the guitar. Minor scorching can be ignored, because it can be sanded out when the body is sanded. But deep scorching must be avoided. Scorching can be reduced or eliminated by lowering the temperature of the iron, or raising the speed at which the wood moves across the surface of the iron. Keeping the surface of the wood that is in contact with the iron wet at all times, and re-wetting when needed, will help reduce scorching. Keeping the number of repeated bends required to get a segment to match the mold will also help prevent scorching.

Breaking. It is usually difficult to actually break a side while bending it, unless the side is made of highly figured wood, or it is made of a very dense wood that is difficult to bend. As pointed out in one of the exercises, it is good practice to listen carefully for sounds of breaking or tearing, especially whenever bending pressure is increased, and to back off the pressure immediately if any such sounds are heard. Small tension failures are easy to fix, and tiny ones may not need to be fixed at all. But major shattering of the sides may result in the need to abandon the sides and to get replacements for them. This is another argument for using readily available wood for the backs and sides of an instrument. A lutherie wood supplier is much more likely to be able to provide replacement sides, if the back and side set is of a commonly available wood species. If a side breaks during bending (**photo 9-10**) it can usually be repaired by gluing it back together using cyanoacrylate glue, and then clamping it with glue proof clamps or cauls for a few minutes (**photo 9-11**). Bending of the side can continue after the clamps have been removed.

Layout and Construction

Practice sides have been used in the previous exercises, but here the process of bending the sides of the actual guitar is detailed. Although the exercises should provide adequate exposure to the general side-bending operations, it may be prudent to go through the following procedures with one or two additional practice sides, before committing to the sides of the guitar under construction.

Preparing the Sides

The sides as delivered by the lutherie wood supplier as part of a back and side set are two bookmatched pieces that are oversize in both width and length. Preparing the sides for bending involves first arranging the pieces in the orientation that will be used in the guitar, planing them to thickness, and then trimming them to width. In the finished guitar, the depth of the instrument is less at the neck end than it is at the tail end. This means that the width of the sides will taper from the tail end to the neck end. But this tapering will be done *after* the sides are bent to shape. Now, the sides will be trimmed to uniform width and bent that way. It is simply easier and less complicated to bend the sides on a bending iron while they are still in rectangular shape.

Note that if the sides are wide enough and clear of defects at the edges it may be possible to cut strips from them that can be used as bindings for the guitar. This assumes that wood bindings of the same material as the sides are desired for the guitar under construction. Whenever I have sides that are wide enough to do this I will always cut binding strips, even if I have no current plan to use them in the guitar under construction. Doing so provides another option for a change of design plan later, and doesn't take much additional effort at this time.

The sides will be trimmed to length *after* they are bent. The extra length of the sides while they are being bent affords greater leverage when making the bends at the ends of the sides.

□ **Orienting and Planing the Sides to Thickness**

The sides must be examined to determine which surface will be on the outside of the guitar, which of the edges will be at the top and bottom, and which of the ends will be at the neck and tail of the instrument. It is often the case that there is no real issue when it comes to orientation, but with some sides a little effort put into this examination now will result in a better looking finished instrument.

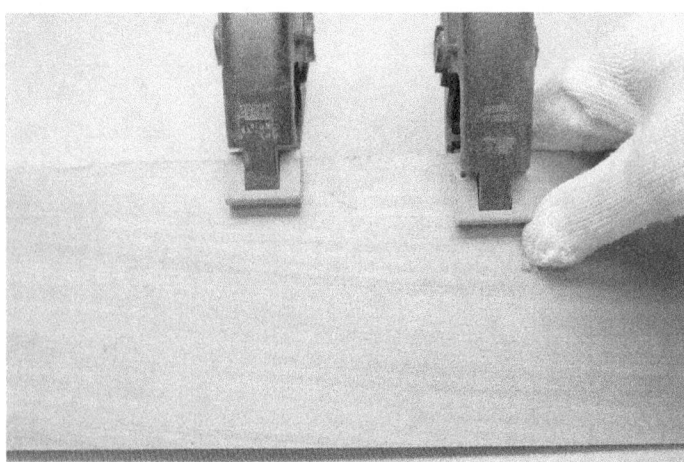

Photo 9-11 – ... *the side is immediately glued back together using cyanoacrylate glue and clamped for a few minutes while the glue cures. There is no need to dry the side before applying the glue and clamping.*

1. It is rare for back and side sets to come rough cut these days, but if this is the state of the set then all surfaces should be planed to the extent that they can be examined for defects.

2. The first examination step is to determine which surface of the sides will be on the outside of the guitar. The sides are laid out on the bench in bookmatch fashion, so the grain pattern on one side is a mirror image of the other, as in **figure 9-1**. The surfaces of the sides that are face up are carefully examined for defects like small knots and knot shadows. If any are found, they are circled in pencil. Then both sides are flipped over in a way that maintains the bookmatch orientation, so the surface that was previously facing the bench is now facing up. The same inspection is performed on this surface. The surface with the fewest number of imperfections is chosen as the outside surface of the guitar. It is almost always the case that the two surfaces that faced each other before the sides were opened up like a book will be the best looking surfaces. It is highly likely that there is no visible difference, in which case either surface will do. In any case, the pieces are placed on the bench, still in bookmatch orientation, so the surface that will be the outside of the guitar is facing up.

3. The sides must be planed or thickness sanded to a uniform thickness of ³⁄₃₂″ (2.4mm). If this has already been done, either by the wood supplier or in the shop, then this doesn't need to be repeated. Otherwise, the word "outside" is penciled onto the up facing surface of each of the sides, and the sides are planed or thickness sanded to spec, with all material removed from what will be the *inside* surface of the guitar. This operation can be performed using a stationary thickness sander, or by hand using hand planes, if the luthier has the skills to accomplish this, or using the thickness planing jig described in Appendix B. Following the thicknessing operation, the sides are again placed on the bench, outside surface up, and oriented in bookmatch fashion.

4. The sides are again examined, this time to determine which edge will be at the top of the guitar and which will be at the back, and which end will be at the neck end of the guitar body and which will be at the tail end. Note when doing this that the sides are currently oversize in both width and length. There are no hard and fast rules for making these selections, and for a lot of side sets there won't be any difference. But here are some simple pointers which may be of some use:

• if the grain pattern is wider at one end, then that end should be the tail end;

• if the grain is straighter on one edge, then that edge should be the top edge;

• if the bookmatch pattern looks better when the ends of the pieces are butted together on one end, then that end should be the tail end;

• if the sides look better near one end, then that end should be the neck end, because it is closer to the player's face when the guitar is held in playing position;

• if there is a flaw only on one side, then that side should be the right side of the guitar (if the guitar will be played right-handed), because that side is not visible to the player when the guitar is being played. As with all designations in this book of left and right on the guitar, the perspective is of the guitar when viewed from the front with the neck pointing up.

5. When the desired selections are made, the sides, still in bookmatched orientation, should be rotated and positioned on the bench so that the side closest to the luthier is oriented with the edge selected as the back closest to the luthier, and the end selected as the neck end to the left. The orientation information of this close side should be unambiguously penciled onto the side, near but not right at the tail (right) end, and near the center of the width. The side of the guitar (left/right) that this piece will be used for is also penciled on it.

Then the sides are rotated 180° on the bench, and the same orientation notes are penciled on the other side. The end results look like **figure 9-8**. This is done to be sure that the correct orientation of the sides is maintained during building. Note that all of these notes are made on what will be the outside of the guitar, where they will eventually be removed during final sanding.

6. The top edge of each of the sides is planed straight. This can be done using a variety of tools, including the jointer, the table saw fitted with a fine tooth blade and zero clearance insert, or the hand plane and straightedge.

7. The sides are ripped to width. Cutting is performed on the back edge. If the sides are wide enough and if it is desired, two or more ¼″ (6.4mm) wide binding strips can be ripped from each side first. Widths for the sides of the two example instruments are shown in **table 9-3**.

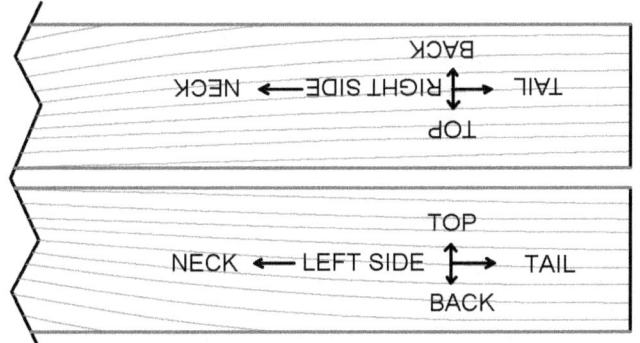

Figure 9-8 – *The orientation of the sides in relation to the finished instrument is unambiguously marked in pencil on the outside of each.*

Example Guitar	Side Width
Tripletta OM	4″ (101.6mm)
Paura Dreadnought	4¹¹⁄₁₆″ (119.1mm)

Table 9-3 – *Width to rip the sides pieces to, for each of the example guitars.*

***Photo 9-12** – The outline segment tape, cut from the plan and first used in the construction of the mold, is taped down to the sides so the segment end points can be transferred to them. The sides and the tape are oriented neck end to the left, tail end to the right. The tape is positioned centered along the length of the sides.*

***Photo 9-13** – Segment end marks are transferred from the tape to the sides. The letter names are written on the side, too.*

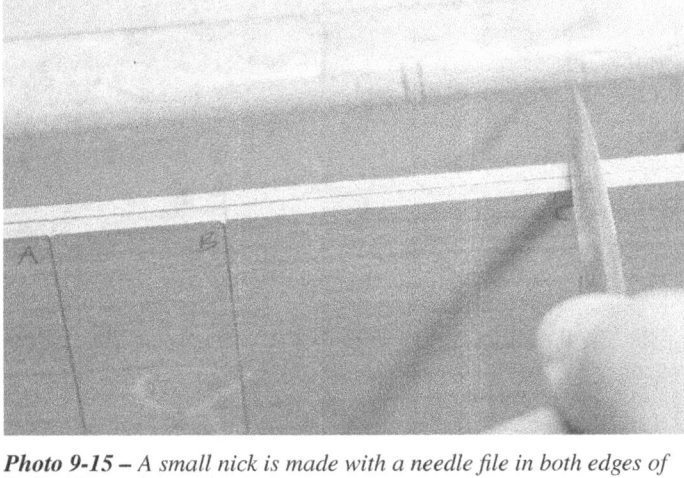

***Photo 9-15** – A small nick is made with a needle file in both edges of both sides at the marks.*

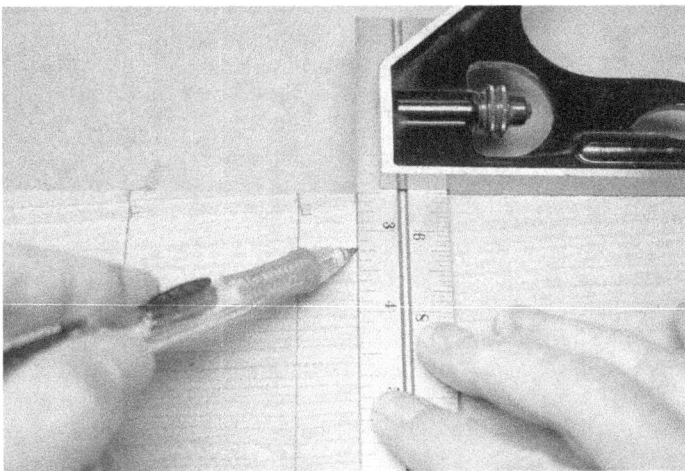

***Photo 9-14** – A square is used to make a line across the surface of the side at each mark.*

 It is prudent to save the off cuts. Doing so provides some matching wood which may be needed to perform some repair at some point during construction.

8. If cutting the sides to width obliterated any of the penciled markings done in step 3, these are refreshed now.

Bending the Sides

The process of bending the sides includes marking up them up with the locations of each of the segments, actually bending the sides, and then clamping them into the mold to cool and fully dry. Up to twelve clamps and special purpose cauls are needed to clamp each side into the mold. In cases where the number of available clamps is limited, it may be necessary to bend, clamp, and dry one side at a time.

☐ Marking the Segments on the Sides

Before bending, the segments are marked on the outside surfaces of each of the sides. Because the heat and water associated with the bending process can obliterate these markings, the segment ends are also physically marked on the edges of the sides using a file.

Materials
    The side pieces, marked and trimmed to width
Tools
    The outline segment tape, retained from mold construction
    Square
    Small triangular needle file
    The mold, with floor attached but without the insert

1. The sides are positioned on the bench in bookmatch orientation with the tail ends to the right. The outline segment tape is positioned near one of the edges. The tape is oriented with the neck end point, labeled "A" on the tape, to the left. The sides

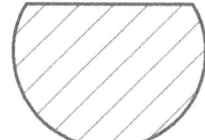 

Figure 9-9 – Approximate cross sections for cauls used when clamping bent sides into the mold for cooling and drying.

will be longer than the tape, so the tape is located along the length so there is an approximately equal amount of extra length on both ends. The tape is taped down at its ends using masking tape (**photo 9-12**).

2. Each of the segment end points A through K are transferred to the side in pencil. The letter names are written near these marks as well (**photo 9-13**).

3. A square is used to extend the marks completely across the outside surfaces of both of the sides (**photo 9-14**). The letter names are written next to the lines near each edge of both of the side pieces.

 The outline segment tape is retained. It will be used again during construction of the guitar body bindings.

4. The ends of each of the marked lines are filed into both edges of each of the side pieces, using a small triangular profile file (**photo 9-15**). The marks should be shallow but clearly visible. This is done because it is likely that the pencil markings will get eroded or obliterated during the bending process.

□ Making the Side Clamping Cauls

Cauls are needed for clamping the sides into the mold for final cooling and drying. The number of cauls needed depends on the number of clamps that can be deployed at a time. Clamping each side will require up to 12 clamps and cauls. If only 12 clamps are available, then 12 cauls should be made. If 24 clamps are available then both sides can be cooled and dried in the mold at the same time, so 24 cauls should be made. The cauls are either made from 1″ (25.4MM) diameter dowel stock or from 1½″ (38.1MM) wide strips ripped from any ¾″ (19.1MM) thick solid wood or plywood stock. Individual cauls are cut from the stock, each to the same length as the width of the sides. The side widths for the example instruments are shown in **table 9-3**.

If dowel stock is used, a flat should be cut on each caul, as shown in **figure 9-9**. This is most easily done with a belt sander. The width of the flat is not critical. It is just a convenient place to apply the clamp when the cauls are used. If flat stock is used, then one of the broad surfaces of each caul should be sanded or planed to a curve, also shown in **figure 9-9**. The radius of the curve is not critical.

□ Bending the Sides

The sides are bent by sequentially bending each of the arc segments in turn, starting with the waist segment, following the techniques described in the previous sections. After each successive segment is bent to shape, that segment is checked against the mold, then the entire length of the side that has been bent so far is checked for accuracy against the mold as well. If each of the segments bent so far are accurate when individually

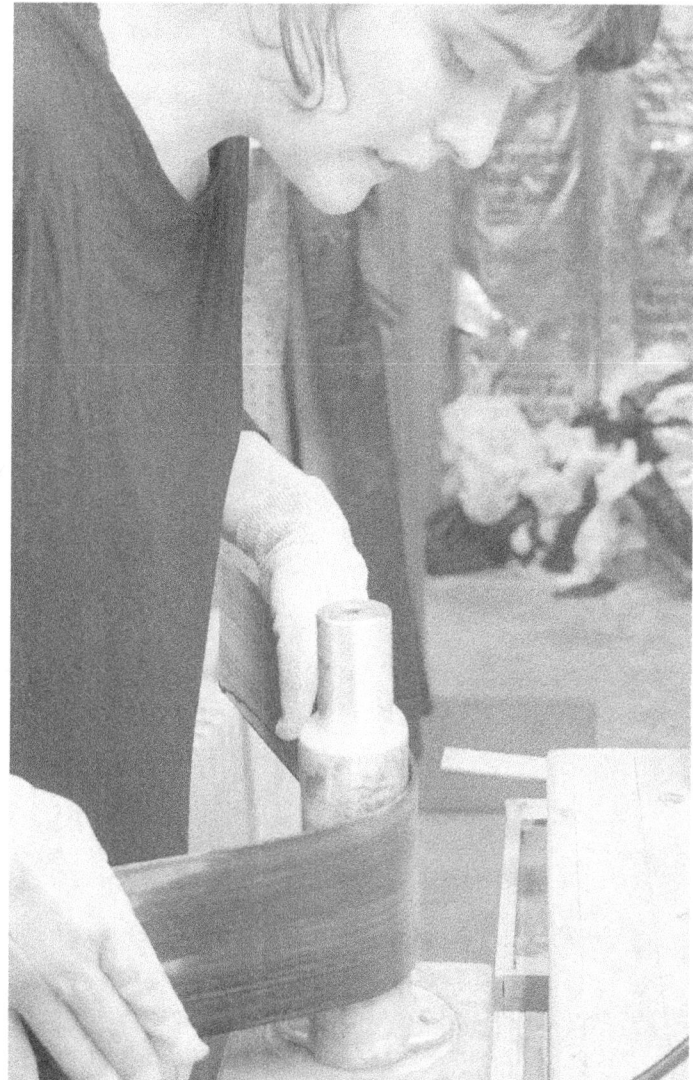

Photo 9-16 – Bending the waist of a guitar side.

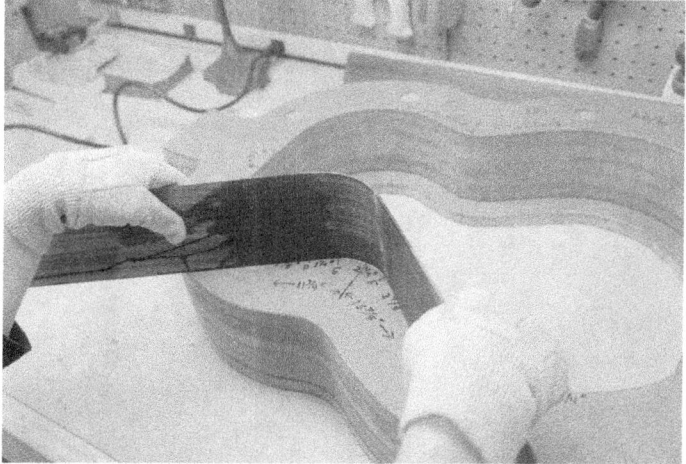

Photo 9-17 – The bend of the waist segment is checked against the mold.

Photo 9-18 – *The entire segment sequence from the waist to the tail end is checked.*

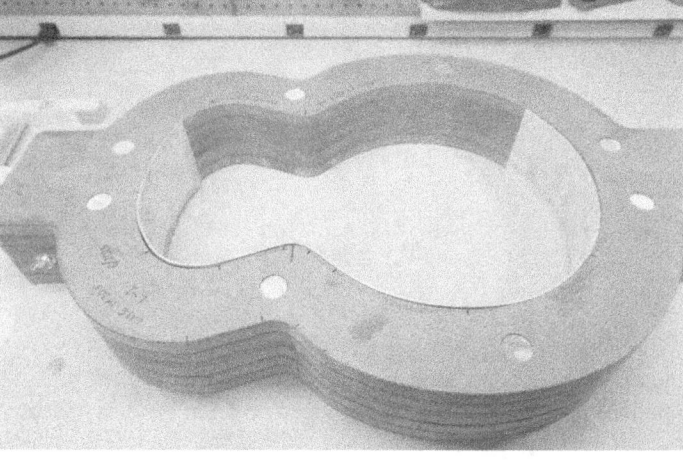

Photo 9-20 – *The entire side fits snugly in the mold when all segments have been bent.*

compared with the mold, but the entire length of the side that has been bent so far does not match the mold, the issue is with one or more of the transitions between the segments. It is usually easy to identify a faulty transition and fix it up.

It is often the case that the waist segment must be re-bent, because subsequent bending of other segments tends to open the waist up, making it more shallow. Once the entire side is bent, it is fitted into the mold and further checked and touched up as needed.

1. The iron is mounted as in the exercises and preheated.

2. The first segment of a side to be bent is the waist segment FG. The primary reason this segment is bent first is because it is the only segment where the outside surface of the side will

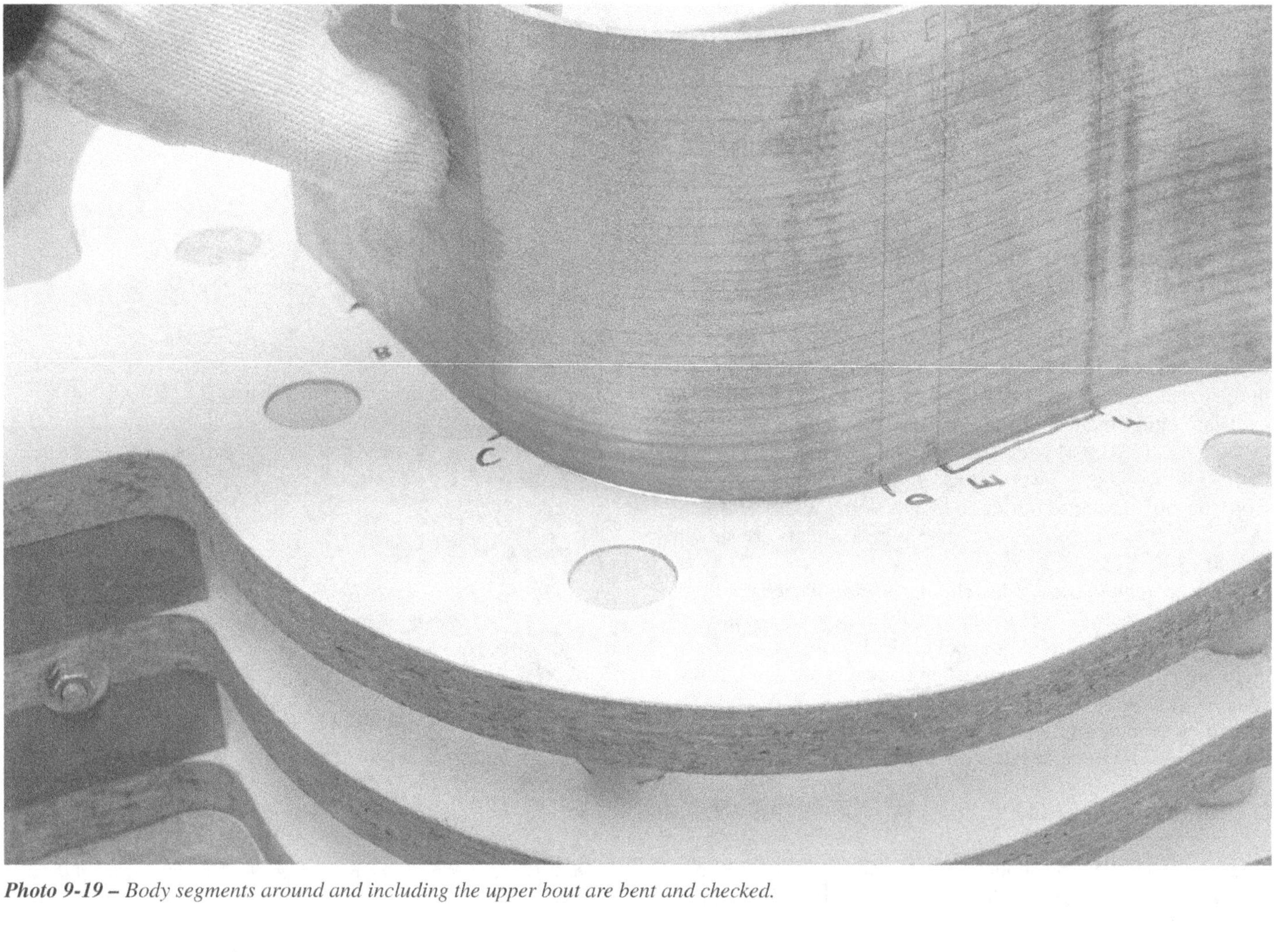

Photo 9-19 – *Body segments around and including the upper bout are bent and checked.*

Photo 9-21 – *The side is clamped into the mold using clamps and cauls. As many clamps and cauls as are necessary are used. The side is allowed to cool and fully dry in the mold. At least 48 hours should be allotted for this.*

be contacting the bending iron during the bend. When all the rest of the segments are bent, it is the inside surface of the side that will contact the iron. To avoid confusion, the waist is bent first. The side is sprayed with water around the waist segment FG on both outside and inside surfaces, excess water is allowed to drip off, and then it is bent as per the exercises (**photo 9-16**). It is checked against the mold (**photo 9-17**) and then re-bent or unbent as necessary for a perfect fit.

 If a curve needs additional bending passes over the iron, flipping the rib over top-to-bottom each time helps to avoid twists in the rib and aids in consistency.

3. The segments heading toward the tail end of the side are sequentially bent next, starting with the lower bout secondary arc segment HI. Note that segment GH just below the waist is straight, and so will not be bent. Segment HI and all subsequent segments are bent with the inside surface of the side in contact with the iron. This means that the curve of the waist will be pointing toward the luthier for these bends. It is usually best to orient the side so the waist segment is held in the right hand while making the bend. This puts the right hand close to the iron at the start of the bend. Holding the side in this manner helps to prevent opening up the waist curve while bending segment HI and subsequent segments.

The bend is performed, checked against the mold, and re-bent or unbent as needed. After this is done, the entire segment sequence from points F to I is checked against the mold, and any adjustments that need to be made are done.

4. Continuing toward the tail end, the lower bout segment IJ is bent next. Checking and rebending or unbending is done as in the previous steps.

5. When segment JK is bent, the bend is continued past point K and right to the end of the side. When working at the end of the side, it is often necessary to use the locking sheet metal pliers to grasp the end of the side.

6. The segment sequence from points F to K is checked against the mold (**photo 9-18**). Note that it is fine if the end of the side past point K is bent more deeply than the mold, as long as a good fit is had right up to point K.

7. Now the segments heading from the waist toward the neck end of the side are sequentially bent, starting with the upper bout secondary arc segment DE (**photo 9-19**). Note that segment EF just above the waist is straight, and so will not be bent. Segment DE is bent with the inside surface of the side against the bending iron. It is usually best to orient the side so the waist segment itself is held in the right hand for this bend. This

means the bend starts at point E and ends at point D. Note that for the example instruments, this segment is quite short, so the actual bend will be quite subtle. When the bend is checked against the mold, the bend of the waist is checked too, to be sure it did not get opened up.

8. Segments CD and BC are bent next, in the same manner as segment DE.

9. Note that segment AB is straight and so will not be bent. However, if the extra length on this end of the side is too long, the end of the side will contact the curve at the other side of the mold, and this will prevent segment AB from conforming to the mold when the side is placed inside the mold. The easiest way to deal with this situation is to simply bend that part of the side that is between point A and the end of the side so it is out of the way.

10. The side is placed into the mold and all of the segments of the side are aligned with their equivalent marks on the mold (**photo 9-20**). The side should fit snugly in the mold with no pulling away from the walls of the mold anywhere. Deviations that are less than approximately ⅛″ (3.2MM) can be ignored, as can any deviations where the side can be pressed into place using just light pressure from the pinky finger. Any adjustments necessary should be performed starting at the waist and moving outward from there.

 Knowing that the next step will be clamping the side into the mold, there is a natural tendency to assume that this clamping will just force the side into permanent shape. It will not. If the side does not accurately fit the mold, and then it is clamped in place, it will just spring back once the clamps are removed. A good fit as described above is required. The better the fit, the less distorting stress will be in the completed instrument.

11. When the side accurately fits in the mold, it is removed for a final wetting and heating. The entire side is sprayed with water on both surfaces and excess water is allowed to run off. Starting at the neck end, the entire concave surface of the side is slowly slid across the surface of the bending iron to heat the side. No bending pressure is applied. The purpose of this step is to wet and heat the side before it is clamped into the mold for final cooling and drying. When the waist is reached, the side is flipped over so the waist can be heated on its concave surface as well. After the waist is heated, the side is again flipped over for heating of the remaining length of the side down to the tail end.

The side is quickly placed in the mold and aligned with the segment marks on the mold. Then clamps and cauls are applied, starting at the waist and working out in both directions. The cauls are generally used with their curved side toward the inside of the guitar side, but on the apex of the waist curve, and also on the neck flat segment AB, the flat side of the caul is positioned towards the inside surface of the guitar side. As many clamps and cauls as are needed to clamp the side into contact with the inside of the mold along its entire length are used. The clamps can be repositioned as necessary. When complete the clamping will look like **photo 9-21**.

The side is checked all around to be sure the bottom edge is fully in contact with the floor of the mold. If it gaps in some places, the clamps in that area are loosened and the side is pressed down to the floor. Then the clamps are tightened. If it is not possible to keep the edge on the floor and also the segment marks on the side lined up with those on the mold, it is likely that there is a twist in the side, the result of one or more of the segments not bent perpendicular to the length of the side. This will be apparent by comparing the segment to its end marks on both edges. A bend that is not perpendicular to the length of the side will have to be re-bent so it is perpendicular.

12. The iron is unplugged if the other side will not be immediately bent.

13. The side is allowed to cool and dry, clamped into the mold for at least 48 hours. If enough clamps and cauls are available, the other side can be bent following the same steps, and then clamped into the mold with its ends overlapping the ends of the first side. If there are not enough clamps and cauls to do this, then the first side should be removed from the mold after thoroughly drying, before the second side is bent. After the side is removed from the mold, it should be reinserted to check to be sure it has not sprung back in any places. If it has, these places are touched up on the iron as described in earlier steps.

14. If there will be some time before work continues on the guitar, the bent sides should be kept clamped in the mold.

---

1. Carcagno, S., Bucknall, R., Woodhouse, J., Fritz, C., & Plack, C. J. (2018). Effect of back wood choice on the perceived quality of steel-string acoustic guitars. *The Journal of the Acoustical Society of America*, 144(6), 3533-3547

2. Peck, E.C. (1957). Bending Solid Wood to Form. *U.S. Department of Agriculture, Handbook NO. 125.*

3. Forest Products Laboratory, USDA Forest Service (1999). *Wood Handbook: Wood as an Engineering Material.*

4. Mottola, R.M. (2009). A Method for the Design of the Guitar Body Outline. *American Lutherie #97*. p. 52.

5. Mottola, R.M. (2010). A Method for the Design of the Guitar Body Outline, Part 3, Compound Radius Curves. *American Lutherie #103*. p. 60.

10   The Garland

The *garland* is the subassembly of the guitar consisting of the sides, blocks, and *linings*. The components of the garland are shown in **photo 10-1**. The blocks and the linings essentially provide for attachment of other parts of the guitar. The *neck block* provides attachment for the neck, and the *tail block* provides secure mounting for the *end pin*. The linings provide gluing area necessary to attach the top and back of the guitar. They also provide additional stiffness to the sides. Also seen in the photo are shop-built assembly tools called *rib jacks*, which are used to secure the garland in the mold during trimming operations on the edges of the sides.

Not a lot of background information is necessary before presenting the construction details of the garland, but some information about how and why the edges of the sides are trimmed is needed before diving into construction. It has been mentioned in the previous chapter that the sides of the steel string acoustic guitar generally taper in depth from the tail end to the neck end. When viewed from the side, the body of the guitar is slightly tapered. An exaggerated view of this is shown in **figure 10-1**. The sides were bent to shape while dimensionally rectangular, because it is easier to perform that operation with the sides in that shape. But at this point in construction, the taper must be marked onto the sides where they will contact the guitar back, and then the sides must be trimmed to that taper.

Also indicated in **figure 10-1** is a slight beveling down of the top, near the neck end. When the neck was constructed, the body contact surface of the heel was trimmed to a small angle. In the construction of the garland, that small angle is cut into the sides where the top of the guitar will contact the sides, in the area that will be under the fretboard extension in the finished instrument. This will help in fitting the neck to the guitar body during a later construction process.

Wood Selection

The wood species used for the blocks and the linings of guitars varies considerably. Violin family instruments use spruce (*Picea* spp.) for the blocks, as did a number of early guitars. Honduras mahogany (*Swietenia macrophylla*) is commonly used, as are other hardwoods that are fairly light in weight. These same species are often used for the linings as well.

Grain orientation for the linings is generally the same as that for the sides themselves. But the guitar lutherie literature is all over the map when it comes to grain orientation for the blocks. Australian luthier, author, and educator Graham McDonald covers this topic nicely in his comprehensive book on ukulele construction.[1] Probably the most conventional grain orientation is with the end grain on the sides of the blocks, and with the grain lines oriented parallel to the grain lines of the sides. In this orientation, expansion and contraction of the blocks with changes in humidity will tend to match that of the sides. But due to the small size of the blocks (and assuming they are made of a light hardwood), differential change with humidity is unlikely to be much of an issue with any grain orientation.

Lutherie wood suppliers offer blanks for the blocks and also *kerfed lining* strips in a limited number of species. My personal preference is for Honduras mahogany, but I also regularly use spruce, black cherry (*Prunus serotina*), or tulip poplar (*Liriodendron tulipifera*), if that is what I have on hand. Often off-cuts and other odd scraps can be laminated together to form a blank suitable for fashioning blocks. If the neck was cut from a rectangular blank, the saved off-cut can be repurposed as material to make a blank for the blocks. Yet another excellent material for blocks is void free Baltic birch (*Betula* spp.) ply.

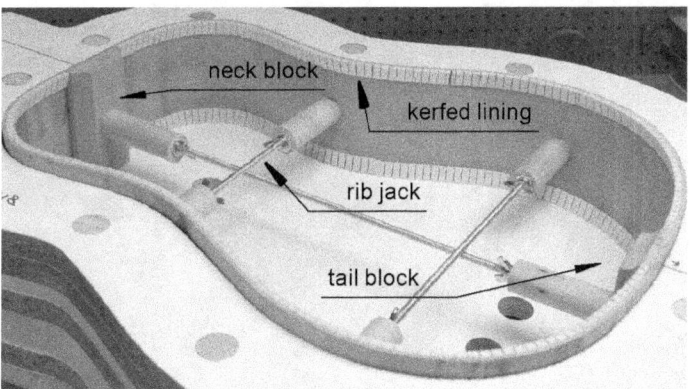

Photo 10-1 – *Component parts of the garland, the subassembly of the sides of the guitar. Also pictured are the rib jacks, which secure the sides in the mold during some construction operations.*

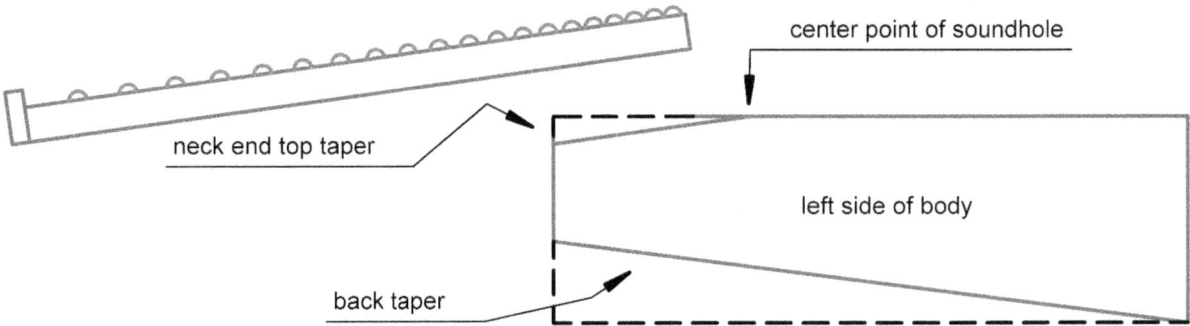

Figure 10-1 – Cartoon side view diagram of the guitar body and the fretboard. In the current state of construction, the sides are the same depth along their length. The finished guitar will be tapered at the back, with the depth of the sides tapering from tail end to neck end as shown here in exaggerated form. A small beveling of the sides at the top, near the neck end will also be done, this to accommodate the pitch angle of the neck.

The ¾″ (19.1mm) thick material needed for the blocks is readily available.

Layout and Construction

Making and Fitting the Blocks

The neck and tail blocks are constructed, and then fit to the sides. Templates for the cross sections of the blocks for the example instruments are found in the template books associated with the plans for those instruments. The sides are trimmed in length to create a butt joint at both ends, then the blocks are glued in place.

Terminology Describing Locations of Features of the Blocks

In the following sections, the terminology used to describe the locations of the features of the blocks and the sides always refer to locations of the finished guitar. So, the outside surface of the block is the surface that will contact the sides, and faces toward the outside of the guitar. The inside surface faces toward the inside of the guitar. The inside side edges are the long edges extending from top to back that face the inside of the guitar. The top and back surfaces of the block will contact the top and back plates of the finished guitar, respectively. Edges are named accordingly. For example, the inside top edge is the edge between the inside and top surfaces. See **photo 10-2**.

About the Shape of the Blocks

For the purpose of mounting the neck and securing the end pin, blocks of rectangular cross section would work fine. But as can be seen from the block template, the cross section of the neck block features sides that are heavily chamfered. This helps to prevent fractures along the grain of the top of the guitar. If the sides of the block were parallel to the grain of the guitar top, a blow to the top next to the block would concentrate the force of the blow right on the grain. The chamfering helps reduce concentration of such forces. The chamfering doesn't extend right to the surface that contacts the sides of the guitar, but stops short by about ¼″ (6.4mm). This provides a flat side for the block that is the same depth as the linings will be (**photo 10-3**).

The tail block is roughly rectangular in cross section, but the surface that mates with the sides is curved to the same radius as

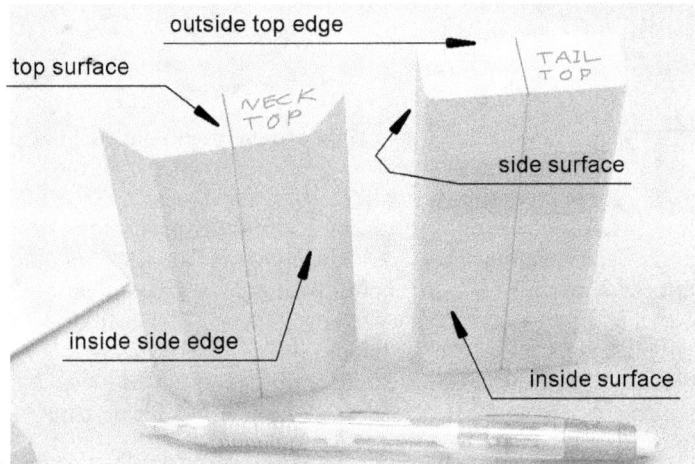

Photo 10-2 – Names of the surfaces and edges of the blocks.

the curve of the sides at the tail end of the guitar. The inside edges of the tail block are rounded over slightly. Top and back ends of the tail block have a concave cut in them, which will leave contact surfaces for the block with the top and back plates that is the same as the depth of the contact surface of the linings (**photo 10-4**). If this is not done, there is a tendency for the

Photo 10-3 – The sides of the neck block are chamfered so they will not run parallel to the grain of the top and back plates. This helps prevent cracking along the grain.

Dimension	Value
Thickness (all)	¾″ (19.1mm)
Neck Block Width	2½″ (63.5mm)
Tail Block Width	2″ (50.8mm)
Tripletta OM Neck Block Length	3¾″ (95.3mm)
Tripletta OM Tail Block Length	4″ (101.6mm)
Paura Dreadnought Neck Block Length	4¹³⁄₃₂″ (111.9mm)
Paura Dreadnought Tail Block Length	4¹¹⁄₁₆″ (119.1mm)

Table 10-1 – Rectangular dimensions for neck and tail blocks for the example instruments.

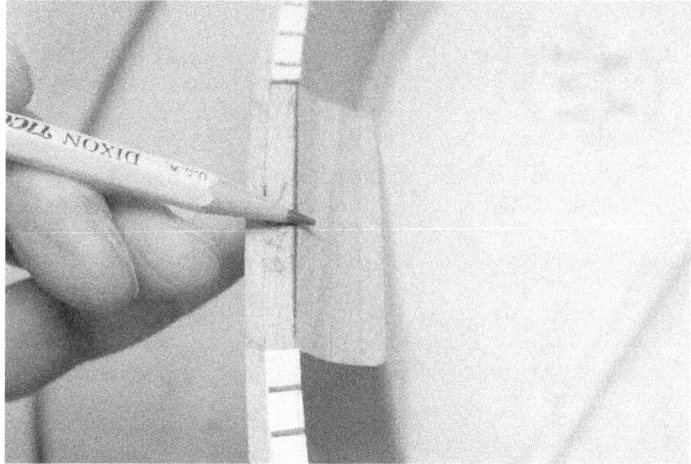

Photo 10-4 – The ends of the tail block are cut back, to leave a flat that is only as deep as the tops of the linings. This helps prevent depressions from forming in the top, next to the tail block.

Photo 10-5 – The blank for the blocks can be made of pieces of wood stacked together. Here, three pieces of wood have been stacked and glued together, then planed to thickness.

top to develop noticeable dips next to the location of the tail block. The dips are caused by expansion of the top wood due to absorbing water from the glue used to glue the top to the tail block. This dipping is not generally a problem on the back of the guitar, but both ends of the block are cut in this manner anyway.

☐ **Making the Blocks**

As mentioned in the introductory material, blanks for the blocks can be purchased from lutherie suppliers or fashioned out of other materials. The finished blank should be rectangular and exactly ¾″ (19.1mm) thick and at least 5″ (127mm) deep, with the end grain at the sides. Commercially available blanks are generally 3″ (76.2mm) wide, which is wide enough to provide enough wood for a single block. A shop-made blank that is approximately 6″ (152.4mm) wide will provide enough material for both blocks.

Details are not provided here for the construction of blanks in the shop. But it can be seen in **photo 10-5** and some of the other accompanying photos in this section that the example blocks have been made from blanks laminated from available wood.

1. If not already done, the blank(s) should be planed to ¾″ (19.1mm) thick.

2. The neck block is cut to the width specified in **table 10-1**. Note that if the blank is made of solid wood or stacked laminated wood, then the end grain will be at the side surfaces of the block. See **photo 10-6**.

3. The neck block is cut to the length specified in **table 10-1** for the instrument under construction. The lengths of the blocks must be accurate.

Photo 10-6 – After the blocks are cut to width and length, they are marked with centerlines on their inside, back, outside, and top surfaces. Note the orientation of the grain.

Photo 10-7 – The outside surface of the tail block is shaped to fit the curve of the tail end of the body. This can be done with sandpaper and the solid mold.

4. The tail block is cut to the width specified in **table 10-1**. Note that if the blank is made of solid wood or stacked laminated wood, then the end grain will be at the side surfaces of the block, as in **photo 10-6**.

5. The tail block is cut to the length specified in **table 10-1** for the instrument under construction.

6. Centerlines are drawn in pencil across inside, outside, top and back surfaces of the blocks. The blocks, cut to width and length and marked, are shown in (**photo 10-6**).

7. The block cross section templates are cut out from the template page for the instrument under construction.

8. The template outlines are traced onto the top and back of their respective blocks.

9. The surface of the tail block that will contact the sides at the tail end is shaped to the template lines. This can be planed using a small plane, or sanded using a sanding board. If a solid mold is used, PSA sandpaper can be applied to the inside of the mold at the tail end, and used to shape the curved surface of the tail block (**photo 10-7**).

10. The inside edges of the tail block are lightly rounded over. This can be done on the sanding board or on the belt sander (**photo 10-8**).

11. Using a spindle sander, sanding drum mounted on the drill press, or a gouge, the top and bottom surfaces of the tail block are scalloped back as shown in **photo 10-9** until only a flat about ¼″ (6.4mm) deep remains.

12. Using a saw, plane, belt sander, sanding board or some combination, the inside edges of the neck block are chamfered down to the template lines (**photo 10-10**).

13. The new inside edges of the neck block are lightly rounded over (**photo 10-11**).

The finished blocks are shown in **photo 10-2**.

Photo 10-8 – *The inside edges of the tail block are slightly rounded over.*

Photo 10-10 – *The inside edges of the neck block are chamfered to the template lines.*

Photo 10-9 – *Both the inside top and inside back edges of the tail block are scalloped, so only a ¼″ (6.4mm) deep flat portion remains at the outside top and back edges.*

Photo 10-11 – *After chamfering, the new inside edges are lightly rounded over.*

☐ Fitting the Blocks

This process includes trimming the guitar sides to length, and gluing in the blocks. This work is done using the mold as a construction fixture. Trimming the sides to length is described using a thin blade Japanese back saw, which makes for a quick and accurate job. Other tools may be useful for this task. The main issue is that in their bent state, the sides are unwieldy when positioning them for the cuts.

1. The sides are removed from the mold in which they were stored. The pencil markings denoting the sides of the guitar and the top and back edges may have been obliterated during bending. If so, the sides are re-labeled on their outside surfaces in pencil before proceeding.

2. If it is not already installed, the floor of the mold is installed on the mold now. The insert is not inserted in the mold.

3. One side is inserted in the mold, top edge up. The segment end points of the side are aligned with the corresponding marks on the mold, and the side is clamped into the mold using clamps and cauls. The back edge of the side must be in contact with the floor of the mold all along its length (**photo 10-12**).

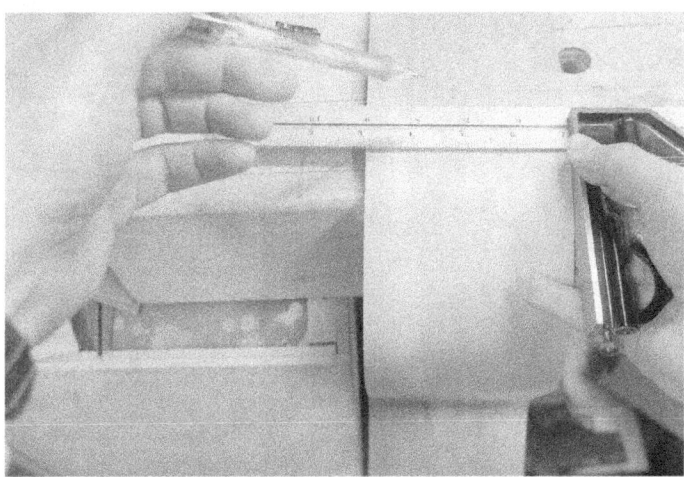

Photo 10-14 – The mark is extended across the outside surface of the side using a square. This is the mark for the cut to trim the tail end to length.

Photo 10-12 – One side is clamped into the mold, top edge up, aligned with the segment marks on the mold. The back edge of the side must be in contact with the floor all the way around.

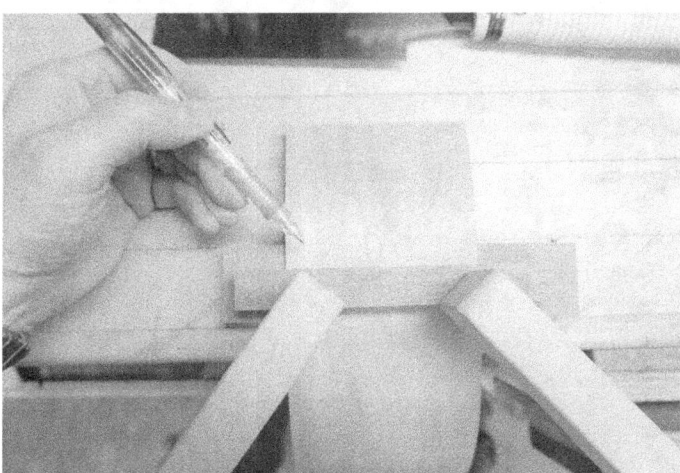

Photo 10-15 – The side is clamped to the bench with the tail end on a piece of scrap, and a fence on top with its far side aligned with the cut mark (not visible, but the pencil points at it).

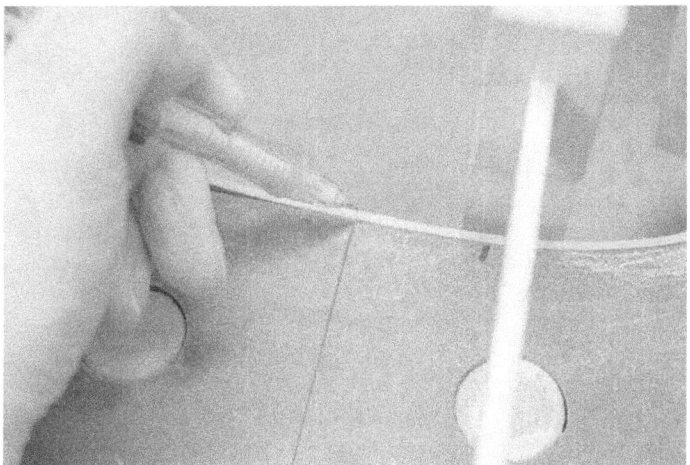

Photo 10-13 – The location of the tail seam is transferred from the mold to the side.

Photo 10-16 – The Japanese back saw will cut against the fence, as shown. The clamps must be positioned so they don't interfere with the saw during cutting. Light clamping pressure is required to avoid breaking the side.

154 Chapter 10: The Garland

Photo 10-17 – Another scrap of wood is used to back up the flexible blade of the saw, to keep the cut straight. The saw blade is lightly clamped between this piece and the fence, using hand pressure only while cutting.

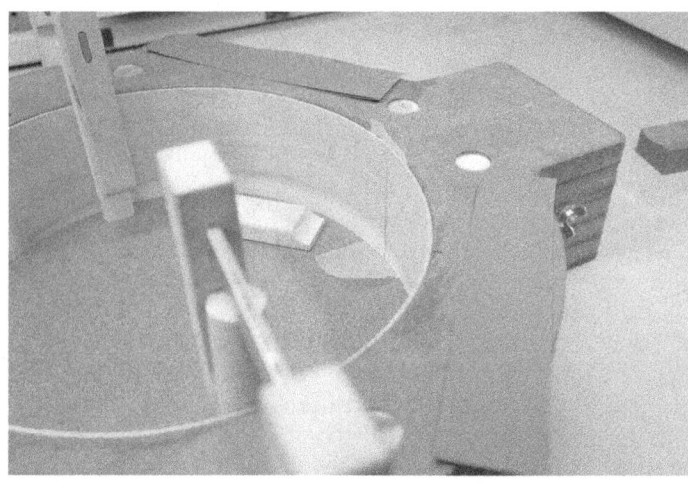

Photo 10-19 – Preparing to glue the tail block. Wax paper is placed between the mold and the sides, and where the tail block will sit on the mold floor. Clear packaging tape can be used instead. No clamps are used from the lower bout down to the tail end.

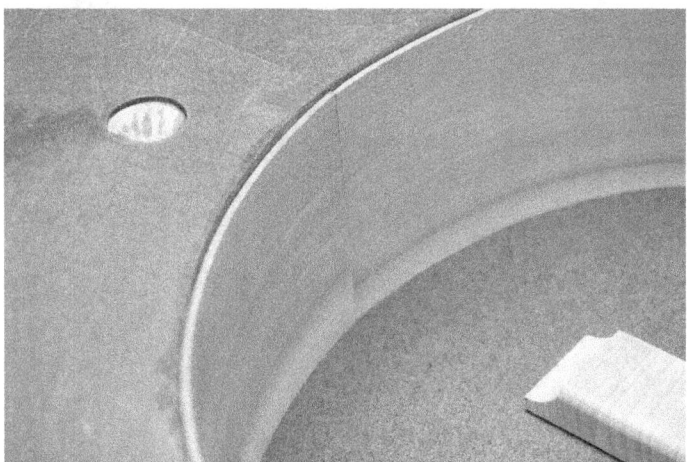

Photo 10-18 – After the sides are trimmed to length on both ends, they are returned to the mold, but top edge down, to assess the fit of the butt joints.

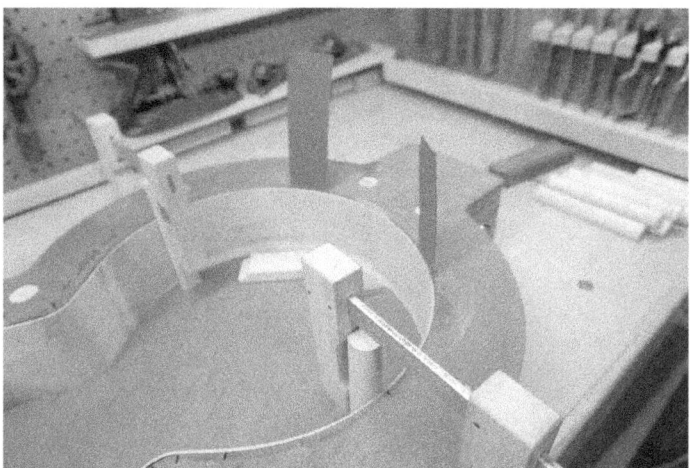

Photo 10-20 – Card stock shims are inserted between the mold and the sides, to squeeze the tail end butt joint together.

4. A pencil mark is made on the side at the tail end seam of the mold (**photo 10-13**).

5. The side is removed from the mold. A square is used to extend the mark made in the previous step, across the outside surface (**photo 10-14**). Note the orientation of the side with respect to the bench in the photo. The tail end is placed on the bench, with the rest of the side hanging down below the bench top.

6. The tail end of the side is lightly clamped down to the bench top as shown in **photo 10-15**. A scrap of wood or MDF approximately 1½″ (38.1mm) wide is placed under the side to protect the bench top while sawing. A rectangular scrap of wood or MDF approximately 1″ (25.4mm) wide is placed on top of the side as pictured, and clamped in place. This is used as a fence for the cut. The side of the fence that is away from the luthier is carefully aligned with the penciled line on the guitar side before the clamps are tightened. Note that the clamps must be positioned so they will not interfere with the saw (**photo 10-16**).

Neither of the wood scraps should be too wide, and the clamps should not be tightened any more than is necessary to keep everything in position for sawing. This will prevent breaking off the end of the curved side while clamping it between flat surfaces.

7. A third rectangular cross section stick of wood is used to back up the other side of the saw, while making the cut. Trapping the saw blade loosely between the fence and this piece will prevent it from flexing while cutting, ensuring that the resulting cut is straight (**photo 10-17**). The side is cut through, then unclamped.

8. Steps 3 through 7 are repeated for this side, but the marking and cutting are done at the neck end this time. When the side is clamped into the mold, the tail end is aligned with the tail end seam of the mold first, and clamping proceeds toward the neck end.

9. Steps 3 through 8 are repeated for the other side of the guitar.

Photo 10-21 – *The tail block is clamped in place using two clamps. The bottom clamp must not obscure visibility of the centerline on the mold floor, or the centerline mark on the block.*

Photo 10-23 – *Wax paper in place, in preparation for gluing on the neck block. Clear packaging tape works well too, and provides a clear view of the centerline on the mold floor.*

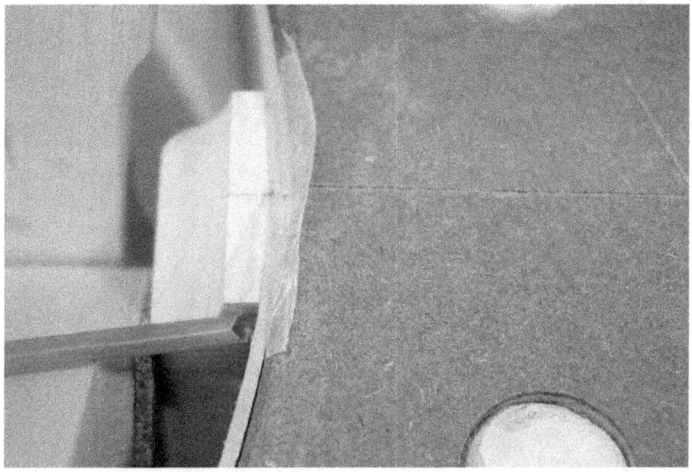

Photo 10-22 – *After clamps are in place, the snipped plastic straw is used to clear glue squeeze-out from between the tail block and the guitar sides.*

 When the other side of the guitar is marked, this must be done in the other side of the mold. The mold sides may be slightly different.

10. Both sides are fitted into the mold, top edges *down* this time, and the tail and neck seams are aligned with those of the mold (**photo 10-18**).

 Note that the top edges of the sides are down against the floor of the mold for this and all subsequent steps in this section.

The sides are temporarily clamped into the mold, using as many clamps and cauls as are needed and available. The fit of the butt joints at tail and neck ends are assessed. If either side is a bit too long, the sides may gap away from the mold at the waist if not clamped. If the gapping cannot be relieved by light finger pressure with the pinky finger, one or both of the sides may need to be trimmed a bit shorter.

11. The sides are unclamped and removed from the mold, in preparation for gluing in the tail block. A piece of clear plastic packaging tape is placed on the mold floor so it will be under the tail block. Another piece is placed so it completely covers the tail seam of the mold, where it will be behind the ribs at the tail seam. This will prevent the garland from being glued to the mold. If clear packaging tape is not available, wax paper may be substituted. Then the sides are replaced in the mold, again top edges down, and clamped in place, with the tail seam aligned with the tail seam of the mold. The guitar top edges of the sides must fully contact the mold floor. When clamping this time, no clamps are placed from the widest part of the lower bout down to the tail end (**photo 10-19**).

12. The hands are used to press the sides firmly against the insides of the mold where they are not clamped below the lower bout. If the tail seam gaps at all when this is done, shims made of card stock are used to close the gap. The shims are forced between the sides and the mold as shown in **photo 10-20**.

13. The centerline on the tail block is extended down into the concave cuts near the ends of the block. This is done so the centerline of the end of the tail block that will contact the floor of the mold will be visible with the block in place. The tail block is dry fitted in place, aligned with the centerline on the mold floor at one end, and with the top of the tail seam of the sides at the other end. Note that if wax paper is used instead of packaging tape, it may need to be trimmed back at one or both ends to provide visibility.

14. Gluing the tail block. A dry run is always prudent. The tail block is removed, glue is applied to its outside surface, then the block is pressed into place, again aligned with the centerline on the mold floor and with the tail seam of the guitar sides. The block *must* be in contact with the mold floor. Two clamps are used to lightly clamp the block in place (**photo 10-21**). The lower clamp is placed to allow visibility of the centerline mark on the block and on the mold floor. Alignment with the centerline is checked, contact of the block with the mold floor is

Photo 10-24 – Close-up of clamping of the neck block. Note the wax paper to prevent gluing the sides to the mold, also that the block is shorter than the sides.

Photo 10-25 – Another view of clamping the neck block, showing the arrangement of the clamps.

checked, and adjustment is made if necessary. The clamping pressure is increased and alignment checked again.

Cam clamps pull the piece being clamped toward the bar of the clamp. When used in this application, cam clamps may pull the block up and out of contact with the mold floor. The block *must* be kept in contact with the mold floor.

The snipped plastic straw is used to clear glue from the sides of the tail block (**photo 10-22**). The glue is allowed to cure at least four hours before clamps are removed.

Although the goal is to yield a perfect butt joint of the sides at the tail end, it is not a big deal if this doesn't happen. A later construction operation will inlay a *tail graft* (also called an *end graft*) here, so any gapping of this joint will be removed in that operation. See the following sidebar about this.

15. Steps 11 and 12 are repeated for the neck block (**photo 10-23**). If the garland can't be removed easily, it is possible that it got glued to the mold. In this case, the mold floor is removed and the tail block is tapped with a piece of wood and a mallet to free it up. Then the mold floor is reattached. It is important that the garland be inserted into the mold *top edges down*.

16. The neck block is dry-fitted in place, aligned with the centerline on the mold floor at one end, and with the neck end seam of the sides at the other end. Note that if wax paper is used instead of packaging tape to prevent gluing of the garland to the mold, the wax paper may need to be trimmed back at one or both ends, to provide visibility. The block *must* be in contact with the mold floor. Note also that the neck block is shorter than the guitar sides here: The sides will eventually be trimmed down to the level of the block.

17. The neck block is removed, glue is applied to its outside surface, then the block is pressed into place, again aligned with the centerline on the mold floor and with the neck end seam of the sides. The block *must* be in contact with the mold floor. It is

"I Meant to Do That" Dept.

It is not the case that everything goes completely according to plan every time, even for the most experienced luthiers. One example of this is when an instrument is planned to have a simple butt joint at the tail end, as in the photo of the Gibson L-1 style guitar pictured below, but when the tail block was glued on, the butt joint ended up less than perfect. It is at this point that we refer the issue to the "I Meant to Do That Dept." and "decide" that we really wanted the instrument to have a tail graft, as in the photo of the Paura Dreadnought style guitar.

The tail end of a guitar in the style of the Gibson L-1, which has a simple butt joint of the sides, here in the process of having its end pin installed.

The tail end of one of the example instruments, the Paura Dreadnought style guitar, features an end graft, which would cover any mistakes made in the butt joint of the sides

clamped in place using two clamps in the same manner as for the tail block (**photo 10-24**). Contact of the block with the mold floor, and alignment of the block with the centerline (**photo 10-25**) must be ensured before clamping everything firmly into place. The glue is allowed to cure at least four hours before clamps are removed.

18. When the glue is cured, the garland can be removed from the mold, and any wax paper or packing tape removed as well. The garland should be returned to the mold for storage.

19. The inside surfaces of the sides are cleaned up as necessary to remove any glue, pencil markings, and scorching from side bending. This can be done using 80 grit sandpaper on a cylindrical block, or using a card scraper. It is usually easier to do this if the floor is removed from the mold first. It should be noted that the sides are thin, so care should be taken not to thin them further. If there is doubt, the insides are left alone. The inside surfaces can be smoothed to any level desired. I generally stop at 100 grit.

Tapering the Sides

From this point on in the construction, the garland must be held in place in the mold in such a way that does not interfere with access to its edges, as would be the case when clamps are used. For this purpose, a set of rib jacks are fashioned, and these will first be used to secure the garland in the mold when tapering the sides. As mentioned the major tapering of the sides happens on the edges that will contact the back plate of the guitar. But a small beveled area is also cut into the neck end of the side edges that will contact the top plate.

☐ Making the Rib Jacks

Two or three rib jacks as shown in use in **photo 10-1** are constructed out of 1″ (25.4mm) or larger diameter hardwood dowel stock, ¼″-20 threaded steel rod and wing nuts, and ¼″ flat washers. One jack that spans the distance between the blocks is needed, as well as one which spans the distance between the sides at the waist. A third jack that spans the width of the lower bout is also useful.

In use, the jacks are positioned to press the garland against the inside surfaces of the mold, and securely hold it there.

☞ Note that the threaded rod of the diameter used is somewhat flimsy, but using flimsy rod is a safeguard to prevent the jacks from being used to force the ribs to comply to the shape of the mold. At this point in assembly, the garland has its own shape, and forcing it into the mold will cause problems. Care should be taken when using the jacks to not tighten them to the extent that they distort the shape of the mold. If an open frame mold is used, care should be taken when using the waist and lower bout jacks to be sure there is some part of the mold behind the place on the sides where the jack ends are pressing. If this is not the case, the jacks may crack the sides.

1. The following lengths of ¼″-20 threaded steel rod are cut: 6½″ (165.1mm), 12¼″ (311.2mm), and 16″ (406.4mm).

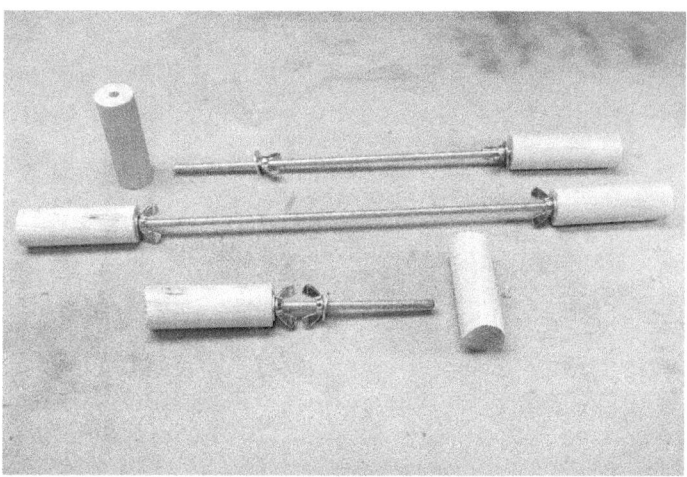

Photo 10-26 – *The completed rib jacks.*

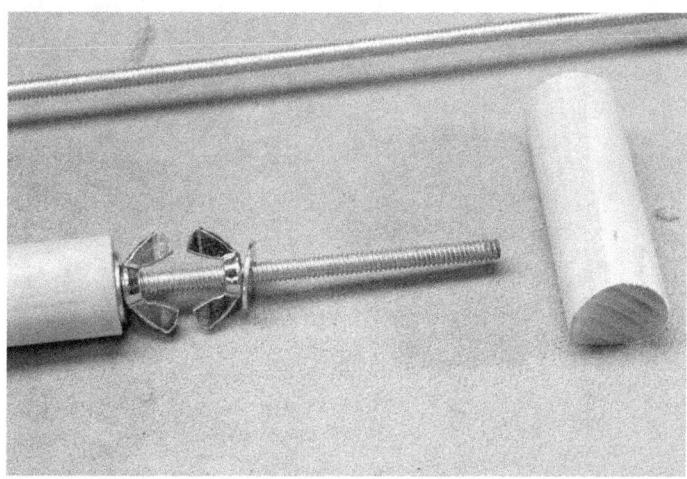

Photo 10-27 – *Close-up of the waist rib jack. Note the placement of the wing nuts and washers, and the concave cut in the dowel end.*

2. Two ¼″-20 wing nuts are threaded onto each rod so the wings are facing each other. ¼″ flat washers are added to each wing nut.

3. Six lengths of the 1″ (25.4mm) or larger diameter hardwood dowel stock are cut, each 3″ (76.2mm) long.

4. The drill press is used to drill a ¼″ (6.4mm) diameter blind hole into the center of one end of each of the dowel pieces, 2½″ (63.5mm) deep.

5. The undrilled ends of two of the dowel pieces are left flat. These pieces will be used as the ends of the longitudinal jack, and are placed on the ends of the longest piece of threaded rod. The undrilled ends of two pieces are cut to a slight concave shape, using a rasp or spindle sander or drill press-mounted sanding drum. These pieces will be used as the ends of the waist jack, and are placed on the ends of the shortest piece of threaded rod. The concave ends engage the curves of the sides at the waist. The undrilled ends of the remaining two pieces of dowel are cut to a slight convex shape, using a rasp or sanding board or belt sander. These pieces will be used as the ends of the lower bout jack, and are placed on the ends of the remaining piece of threaded rod.

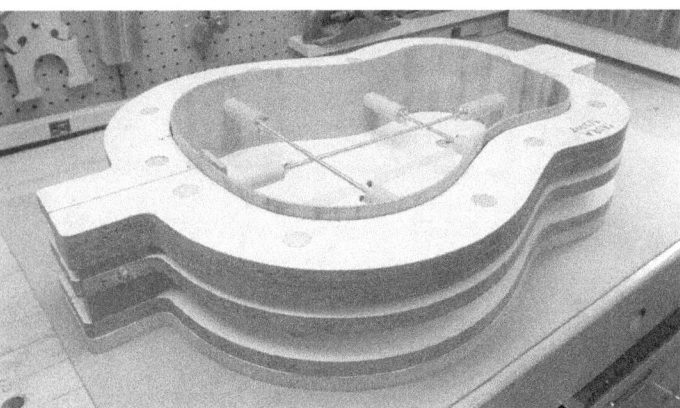

Photo 10-28 – *The garland in the mold, and held in place by the rib jacks. The garland extends above the top of the mold because it is sitting on top of the mold insert.*

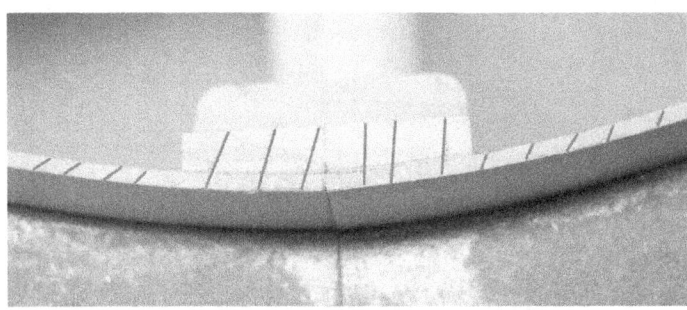

Photo 10-29 – *In preparation for level sanding the top edges of the garland, pencil marks are made all along the edge of the sides, and on top of the blocks.*

Photo 10-30 – *A sanding board that is longer and wider than the garland is used to level sand the top edges.*

Photo 10-31 – *The sanding board is used to scrub the top edges of the garland until all the pencil marks are removed.*

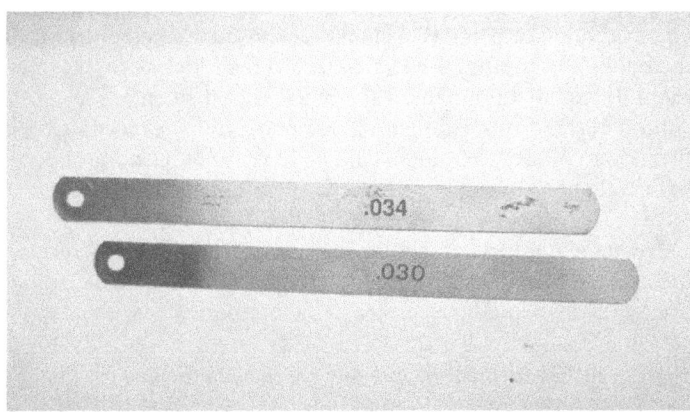

Photo 10-32 – *A stack of feeler gauges are used to mark the neck end of the garland for the top taper.*

6. Because the ends of the jacks are not permanently attached, it is a good idea if the name of each jack is written on each end piece. Finished rib jacks are shown in **photo 10-26** and **photo 10-27**.

☐ Trimming the Sides for the Neck Angle Bevel

This shallow bevel of the top edges of the garland starts in line with the center of the soundhole of the finished guitar, and ends at the neck end. It is implemented primarily by sanding. Before the bevel is marked out and cut, the top edges of the garland are sanded flat. After the bevel is cut, the subtle edge between the bevel and the rest of the flat top edges is gently rounded over.

1. The top edges of the garland are sanded flat, using the following steps. The floor is attached to the mold if it is not currently installed. The insert is placed on the floor.

2. The garland is inserted into the mold, top edges up. The insert will raise the top edges above the top of the mold. The center seams at the neck and tail ends are aligned with the center seams of the mold. The back edges of the garland should be in contact with the insert all the way around. The rib jacks are positioned and tightened enough to secure the garland in the mold (**photo 10-28**). Alignment is again checked and adjusted if necessary.

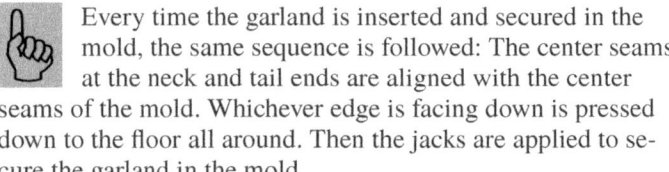 Every time the garland is inserted and secured in the mold, the same sequence is followed: The center seams at the neck and tail ends are aligned with the center seams of the mold. Whichever edge is facing down is pressed down to the floor all around. Then the jacks are applied to secure the garland in the mold.

3. In preparation for sanding the top edges of the garland flat, the edges of the sides and the top surfaces of the blocks are marked up with pencil marks (**photo 10-29**).

4. A large 80-grit sanding board that is at least a few inches wider and longer than the top of the garland is used to level sand the top of the garland (**photo 10-30**). The board is scrubbed back and forth or moved in a circular pattern (**photo**

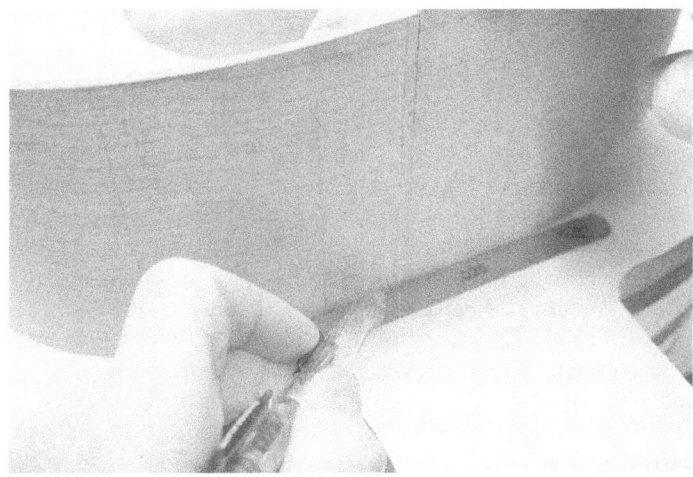

Photo 10-33 – *The garland is flipped top edge down on a flat surface, and a line is drawn across the top of the stack of feeler gauges.*

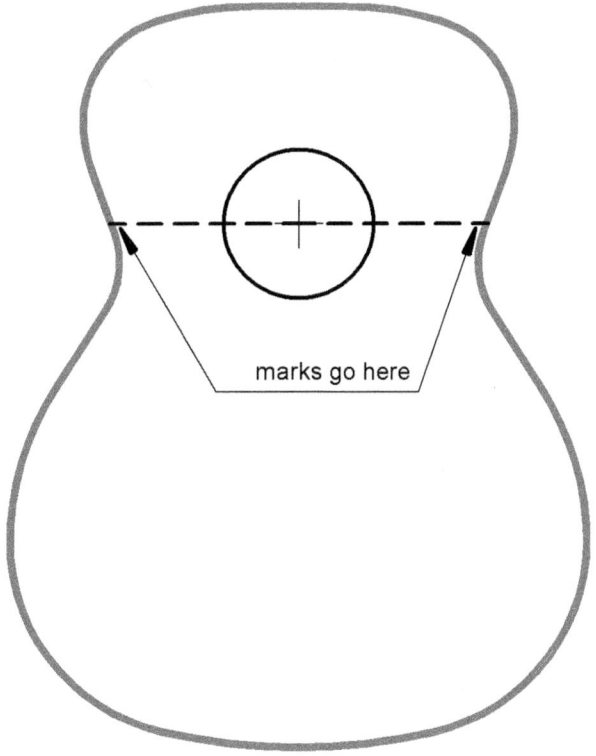

Figure 10-2 – *Marks must be made on the sides, opposite where the center of the soundhole will be in the finished instrument. These mark the end of the neck bevel.*

10-31), using the weight of the board to apply sanding pressure. The sanding board is removed regularly to check progress. When all the pencil marks are gone, the step is complete. Examination of partially removed pencil marks will show up low areas, and may give an indication that sanding pressure is being biased more to one side (or one end) than the other. In the latter case, this can be compensated for by rotating the mold 180° before proceeding.

5. The top bevel is marked out, first at the neck end. The jacks are removed and the garland is removed from the mold. The garland is placed top edges down on the bench or other flat surface. A stack of automotive feeler gauges adding up to a value in the range 0.062″ (1.6MM) to 0.064″ (1.6MM) is selected (**photo 10-32**) and placed on the bench, against the neck end of the garland. The garland is pressed flat to the bench at the neck block with one hand, and the other hand is used to make a pencil line approximately 2″ (50.8MM) long at the neck end seam on top of the feeler gauges (**photo 10-33**). The sides will be trimmed down to this mark at the neck block end in a later step. The stack of feeler gauges is retained for the next operation.

6. Now the ribs must be marked opposite where the center of the soundhole will be in the finished instrument (**figure 10-2**). The garland is returned to the mold with its insert in place. The garland is inserted top edges up. It is aligned and jacked in place. A board longer than the garland, and with one edge ripped straight, is used to locate and mark the center of the

Example Guitar	Neck End to Soundhole Center
Tripletta OM	5²³⁄₃₂″ (145.3MM)
Paura Dreadnought	5²⁵⁄₃₂″ (119.1MM)

Table 10-2 – *Distances from the neck end of the body to the center of the soundhole for the example guitars.*

Photo 10-34 – *A board with a ripped edge, marked with the distance between the body neck end and the center of the soundhole of the finished instrument, is aligned with the centerline of the garland.*

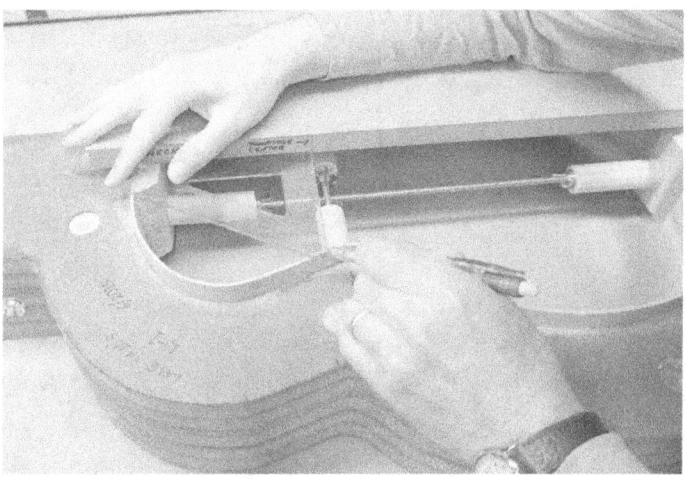

Photo 10-35 – *A drafting square, or anything with an accurate right angle, is used to transfer the soundhole center location to the edge of the garland.*

soundhole. If the board is approximately 24″ (609.6MM) long and 6″ (152.4MM) wide, it can later be used as a sanding board to cut the taper. A mark is made on the ripped edge of the board near one end. This mark corresponds to the neck end of the guitar body. A mark corresponding to the center of the soundhole is measured down from that body neck end mark. The distance between these marks for the example instruments are shown in **table 10-2**.

7. The board is positioned on top of the garland with the ripped edge on the centerline, and the neck end mark aligned with the neck end of the garland, as shown in **photo 10-34**.

8. A drafting square, or just a rectangular piece of wood, is aligned with the soundhole center mark on the marked board and used to mark that distance on the top edge of one side of the garland (**photo 10-35**). The mark should be extended down the outside of the side a bit too, in case the mark on the top edge gets obliterated during sanding. It is useful to transfer these marks to the top surface of the mold as well.

9. The marked board is flipped over and steps 7 and 8 are repeated to mark the other side of the garland.

10. Cutting the bevel. An 80-grit sanding board of approximately 24″ (609.6MM) long and 6″ (152.4MM) wide is ideal for cutting down the bevel. The goal is a flat facet, extending from the top of the penciled line at the center seam at the neck end of the garland, to the two marks indicating the soundhole center. The mold is oriented on the bench so the neck end is pointing toward the luthier. The sanding board is held perpendicular to the centerline of the mold. Sanding starts at the neck block end, since this is where most of the material that needs to be removed is located. After sanding down to very near the top of the neck end line, sanding proceeds to include more and more of the top edge of the sides, approaching but never actually touching the soundhole center marks. The bevel should be checked for flatness by resting the sanding board on it and viewing it critically from both sides (**photo 10-36**).

11. The sanding board is used to lightly round over the edge between the bevel and the rest of the top edges of the garland (**photo 10-37**). Because the angle is so small, doing this takes only a few gentle strokes. The visible result will be the elimination of the two soundhole center marks on the top edges of the garland.

Photo 10-36 – *The flatness of the facet is checked by resting the sanding board on top, and viewing from both sides. The facet should be flat, and should not quite touch the soundhole center marks.*

Photo 10-38 – *The saved cutoff from construction of the fretboard can be used for spacer material.*

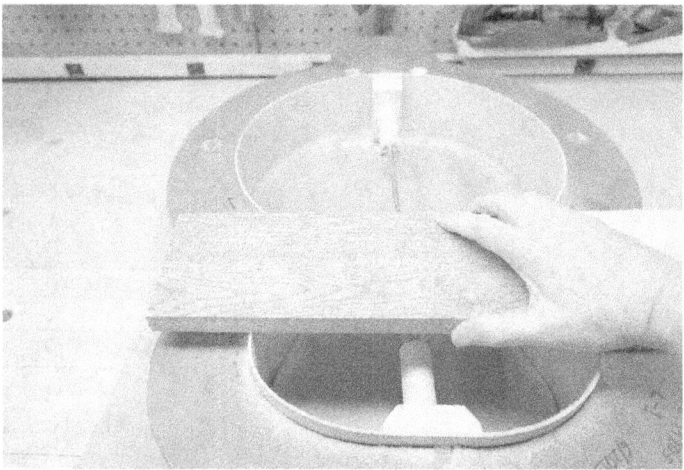

Photo 10-37 – *Using the sanding board to gently round over the edge between the flat top surface and the flat facet of the taper of the top.*

Photo 10-39 – *The spacer is tucked between the mold and floor, right next to the garland at the tail block.*

The sanding boards are saved for use in leveling the edges of the sides again, after the linings have been installed.

12. It is useful to write the word "top" on the top surfaces of both blocks at this time.

☐ **Trimming the Sides for the Back Taper**

1. Marking the taper. The jacks are removed and the garland is removed from the mold. The insert is removed and the mold floor is unscrewed from the bottom of the mold.

2. The mold floor is placed on the bench, and the mold is placed on top of it, just like if the floor was screwed on. The garland is inserted into the mold, top edges up, aligned, pressed into contact with the floor, and jacked in place.

3. A small piece of wood to use as a spacer is needed. The spacer must be ¼" (6.4MM) thick. This is the difference in the depth of the finished example guitars from tail end to neck end. Any piece of wood this thick will do. If the cutoff from the fretboard was retained (**photo 10-38**), that is a good source for the spacer. The spacer should be approximately ½" (12.7MM) wide and 2½" (63.5MM) long.

4. The tail end of the mold is lifted slightly, and the spacer is put between the bottom of the mold and the floor, right next to the tail end of the garland (**photo 10-39**).

5. With the spacer in place, the line of taper of the sides is scribed on the inside surfaces of both sides, from block to block. Scribing can be done in the traditional way, using the compass opened to ¼" (6.4MM), and dragged around the perimeter, with the leg resting on the surface of the mold floor, as shown in **photo 10-40**. It can be somewhat difficult to maneuver the compass around the rib jacks though. Another approach is to make and use half pencil, placing the half pencil on a ¼" (6.4MM) thick scrap of wood (**photo 10-41**). The half pencil is a generally useful shop-made tool. It is made by sanding down a sharpened pencil stub, using the belt sander or a sanding board, until its cross section is a semicircle. The half pencil will be used again in later construction operations.

Yet another approach to scribing is to make a one-time-use scribing tool, by gluing the conical part of a pencil stub down

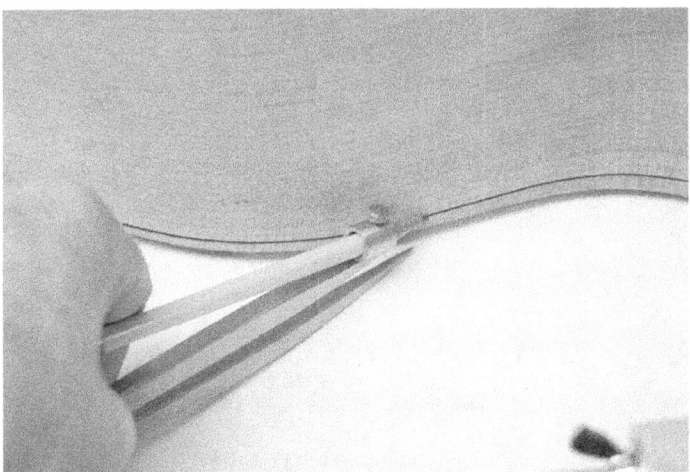

Photo 10-40 – *Scribing the taper on the inside surfaces of the sides using the compass.*

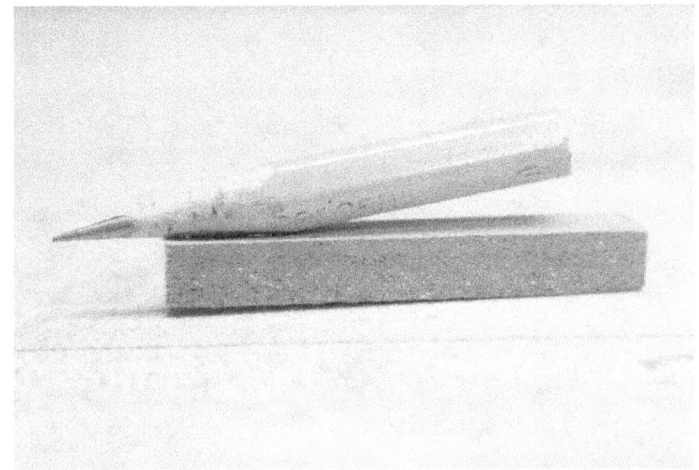

Photo 10-42 – *A one-time-use scribing tool can be made by gluing a pencil stub onto a spacer as shown.*

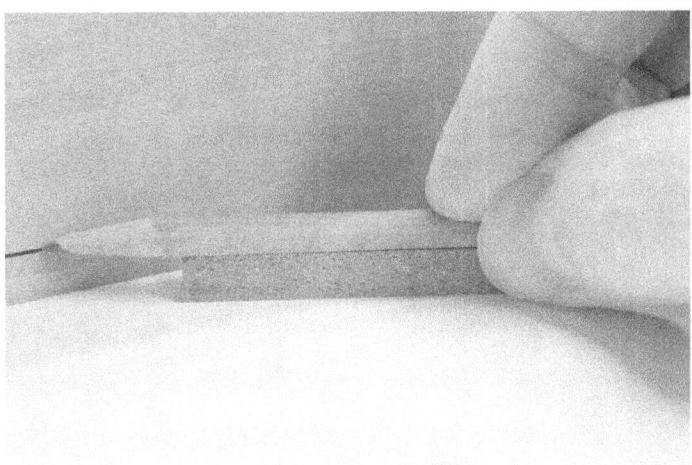

Photo 10-41 – *Scribing the taper on the inside surfaces of the sides using a half pencil resting on top of a spacer.*

Photo 10-43 – *The back edges of the sides (currently face up in the mold) are trimmed to the marked lines, using a block plane. Note the stack of feeler gauges under the neck block.*

Photo 10-44 – Individual triangular glue blocks are sometimes used as linings, usually in antique instruments, but also in some modern classical guitars.

Photo 10-45 – Solid linings are narrow strips of wood that are glued to the inside surfaces of the sides. They must be bent to shape first on the iron. This style of linings is not frequently used for steel string guitars.

to a ¼″ (6.4mm) thick scrap of wood, using cyanoacrylate glue (**photo 10-42**).

Because the tail end is raised up, the scribing process will result in lines that begin at the level of the back surface of the tail block, and end at the level of the back surface of the neck block.

6. The jacks are removed and the garland is removed from the mold. The spacer is removed, but retained for a subsequent operation. The floor is screwed on to the mold, and the insert is inserted. The garland is inserted into the mold, back edges up. The garland is aligned with the seams of the mold as usual. The stack of feeler gauges, used when marking the top taper, is placed under the neck block, before the garland is pressed down to the top surface of the insert. Note that, because of the short bevel on the top at the neck end, the edges of the garland cannot be pressed to the top surface of the insert all the way around. The neck block top surface will be raised above the surface of the insert by the thickness of the stack of feeler gauges.

When all is aligned, the garland is jacked in place with the rib jacks.

7. A block plane, spokeshave, or other small plane is used to trim the back edges down to the lines marked in a previous step (**photo 10-43**).

 When using the plane, care should be taken concerning the direction of the cut. Since the ribs are so thin, an accidental cut into the grain could easily split a hunk off the ribs well below the scribed line. Also, care should be taken to avoid running into the ribs with the front or back of the plane. Since the ribs are unsupported above the mold, it is easy to crack a rib by bumping into it.

8. The back edges of the sides, and the back surfaces of the blocks, are marked up with pencil in preparation for level sanding. The large sanding board is used to level the back edges in exactly the same way that it was used to level sand the top edges.

9. The garland is left in the mold, back edges up, for a subsequent operation.

The Linings

The linings provide a larger area for gluing the sides to the top and back plates, and also provide additional stiffness to the structure of the guitar body. There are three basic types of guitar body linings. Individual glue blocks, generally referred to by their Spanish name *peones*, are small triangular-profile wood blocks (**photo 10-44**). These are often found in early guitars, and are still used in some modern classical guitars, but are rarely found in steel string acoustic guitars. They are tedious to

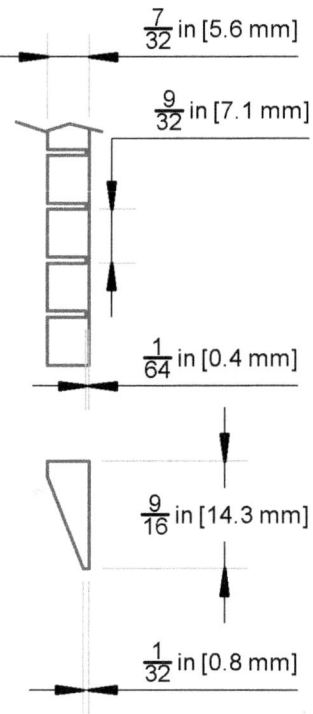

Figure 10-3 – Dimensions of typical kerfed lining material.

apply, and can only be used when attaching whichever plate is glued onto the garland first.

Solid linings are narrow strips of wood that are glued onto the sides at the edges. These are first bent to shape in the same way the sides were bent (**photo 10-45**). Solid linings are not commonly used in modern steel string acoustic guitars either, but some builders do use them.

The most commonly used linings for steel string instruments are called kerfed linings, and are made of strips of wood with triangular cross-section, that are cut almost all the way through with saw kerfs, at a small and regular interval. These can be seen in **photo 10-1**. Kerfed lining strips can be purchased from lutherie suppliers, or can be made in the shop. Lutherie suppliers will often have them available in one or maybe two wood species. When made in the shop, they can of course be made of any species desired. Any relatively lightweight hardwood works well for linings. I will often make them out of whatever scrap blocks of wood I have on hand.

Either of the example instruments will require about 120″ (3048mm) of kerfed lining material.

□ **Making Kerfed Lining Material**

Making kerfed lining strips is a good use for the large waste piece removed when making the guitar neck from a rectangular neck blank. In the construction steps that follow, I am starting with this piece of wood from a laminated neck blank. When squared up, it is approximately 2½″ (63.5mm) wide, 3″ (76.2mm) high, and 12″ (304.8mm) long. I am using the bandsaw and the table saw to fashion the lining strips. The dimensions of typical kerfed lining are shown in **figure 10-3**. The profile is not critical, but should be approximately that of a right triangle.

1. The bandsaw is used to resaw boards from the block, that are 2½″ (63.5mm) wide and approximately ⅜″ (9.5mm) thick (**photo 10-46**). The boards are planed or thickness sanded to 7⁄32″ (5.6mm) thick.

2. A 2½″ (63.5mm) high wood fence is attached to the bandsaw miter gauge. A stop block is clamped into the miter gauge slot in the bandsaw table, to limit travel of the miter gauge toward the bandsaw blade. The stop block is set so the miter gauge stops when the teeth of the blade are 1⁄64″ (0.4mm) from the face

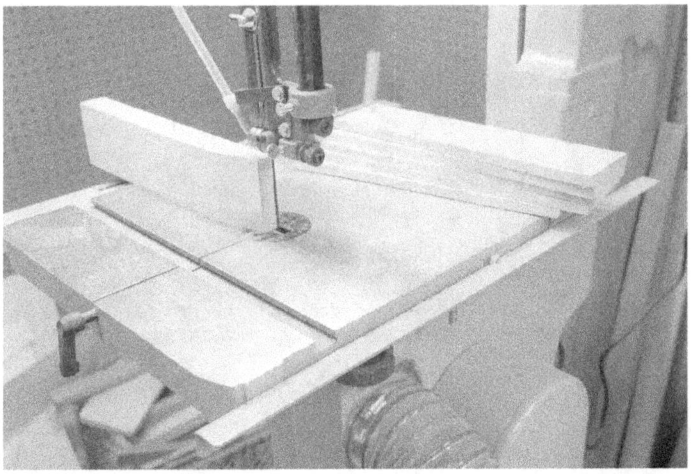

Photo 10-46 – *A block of waste wood, saved from construction of the neck, is used to make kerfed linings. The block is first resewn into boards.*

Photo 10-48 – *Two marks are made on the top of the fence, which will define the distance of the saw kerfs from each other.*

Photo 10-47 – *A wood fence is screwed to the bandsaw miter gauge, and a stop block is clamped into the miter gauge slot in the table, to stop the gauge just before the blade contacts the fence.*

Photo 10-49 – *Kerfs are made across the entire surface of the board.*

Photo 10-50 – The previously-cut kerf is lined up with the rightmost pencil mark, to position for the current kerf cut.

Photo 10-53 – Cutting the strips can also be done on the band saw using the fence.

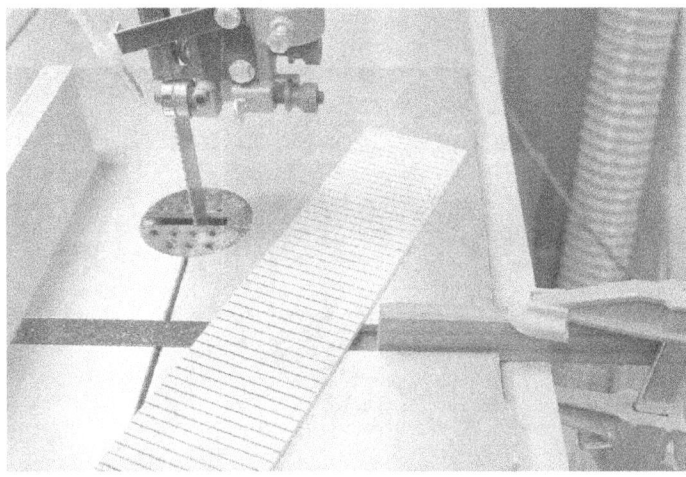

Photo 10-51 – One board, completely kerfed across its surface.

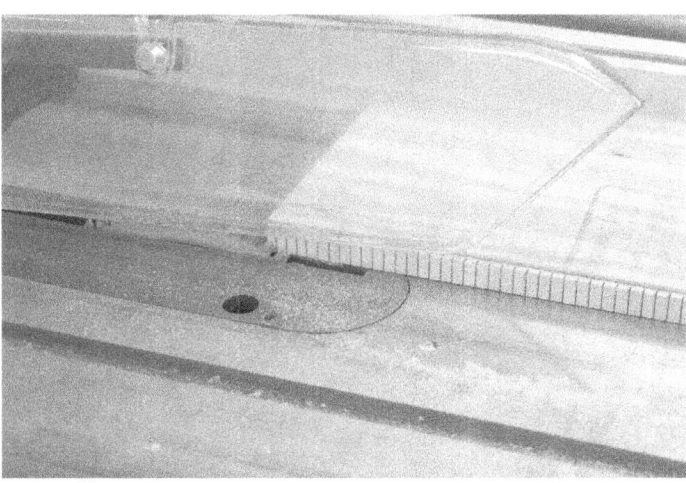

Photo 10-54 – A strip is double-stick taped to a board, to cut the taper on the front of the strip, using the table saw with tilted blade.

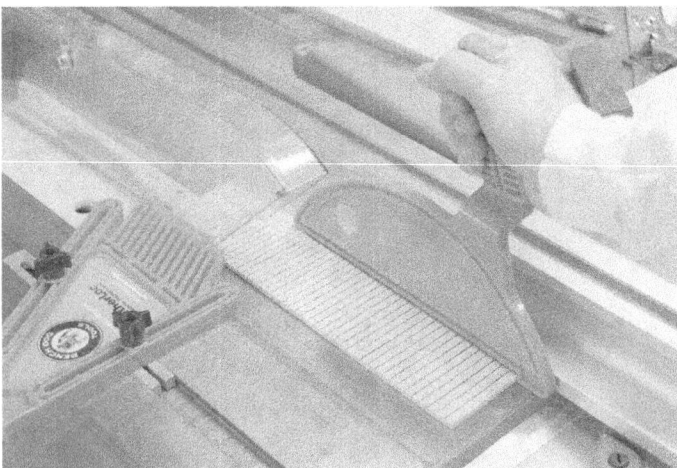

Photo 10-52 – The table saw setup for cutting the kerfed boards into strips. A fine blade and zero clearance insert are required.

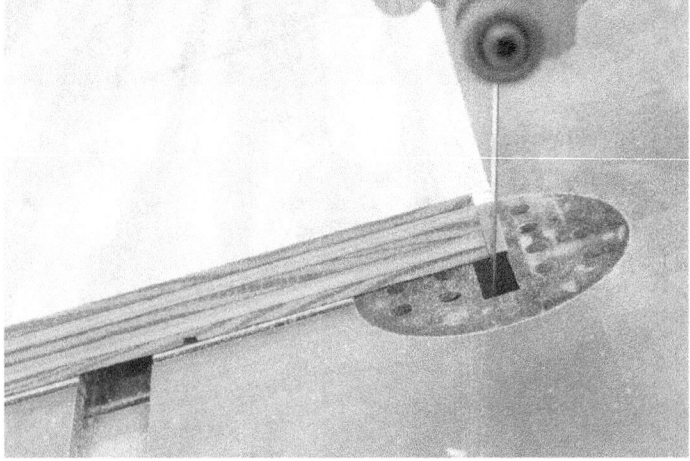

Photo 10-55 – The beveling operation can also be done on the bandsaw with the table tilted.

of the fence (**photo 10-47**). A feeler gauge can be used to measure this.

3. A pencil mark is made on top of the fence, in line with the blade. Another pencil line is made 9/32" (7.1mm) to the left of the first line (**photo 10-48**).

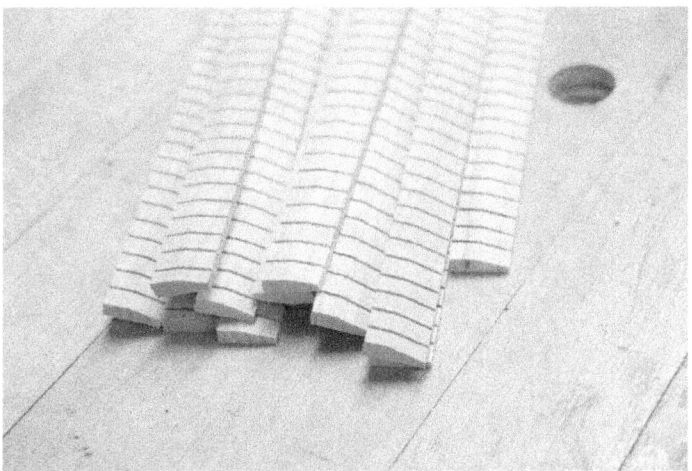

Photo 10-56 – *A bundle of kerfed lining strips, ready for use.*

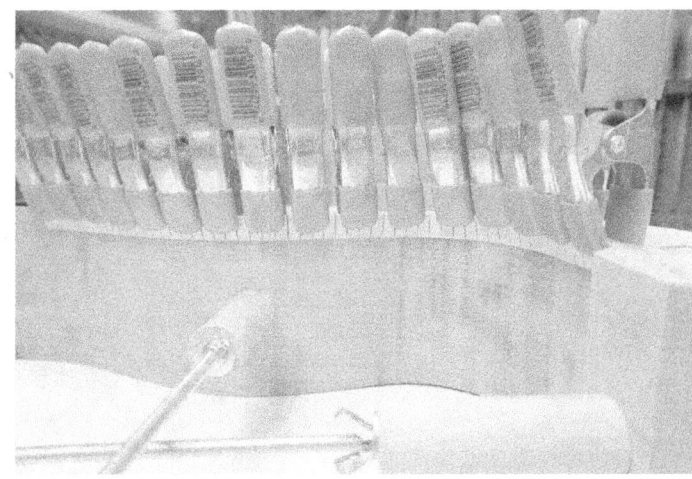

Photo 10-58 – *The spring clamps are placed right next to each other, or as we say here in Boston, "side by each."*

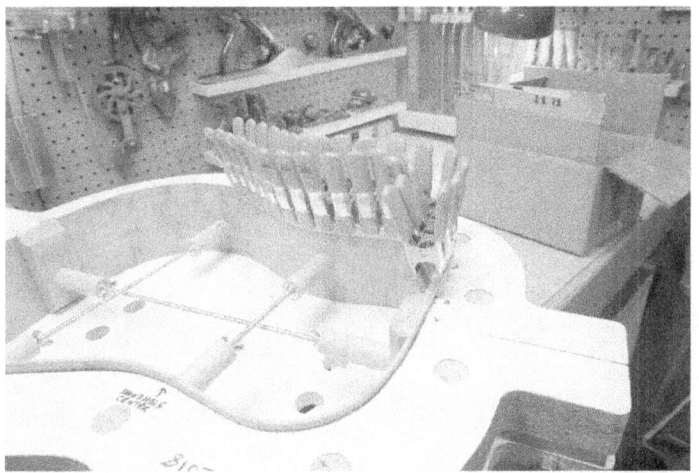

Photo 10-57 – *One strip of kerfed lining is glued down, starting at the side of the neck block.*

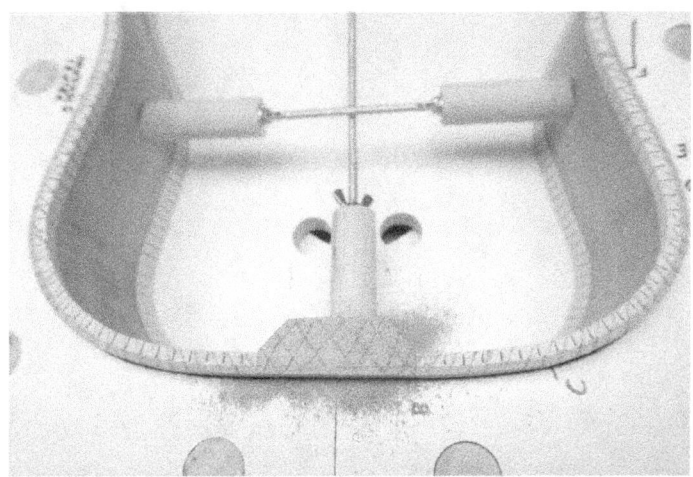

Photo 10-59 – *After the linings are glued in, the edges of the garland must be level sanded again. Here they are marked in preparation.*

4. The bandsaw is used to make a series of evenly spaced kerfs across the surface of each board. The board is fed from right to left. The right end of the board is aligned with the leftmost pencil mark on the fence, the board is clamped to the fence, and a kerf is cut. The board is unclamped, slid down the fence until the just-cut kerf is in line with the leftmost pencil line, clamped in place, and then another kerf is cut. Cutting continues in this manner (**photos 10-49, 10-50**) until the entire surface of the board is kerfed (**photo 10-51**).

5. The table saw is set up with a fine tooth blade and zero clearance insert, to safely rip the kerfed boards into ⁹⁄₁₆″ (14.3mm) wide strips (**photo 10-52**). This can also be done on the bandsaw (**photo 10-53**).

6. To support each strip for cutting the bevel on the front surface, a rectangular piece of ½″ (12.7mm) plywood is used as a base (**photo 10-54**). Double-stick tape is used to secure the strip to one long edge of the plywood. The table saw blade is tilted, and the fence is adjusted to make the cut as shown. Beveling can also be performed using the bandsaw and fence, with the table tilted (**photo 10-55**).

7. The kerfed lining strips are collected for use in the next operation (**photo 10-56**).

☐ **Installing the Linings**

The linings are glued to the inside surfaces of the sides, and clamped in place using 1″ (25.4mm) spring clamps. How much of the linings can be installed at a time depends on the number of spring clamps available. In use, the clamps are placed right next to each other, so 12 clamps will suffice to clamp a length of lining approximately 10″ (254mm) long. Strips of lining can be sawed to the length needed, or simply broken off at one of the kerfs.

Although spring clamps are individually inexpensive, the cost adds up when a lot of them are needed. Some luthiers substitute spring clothespins, adding a rubber band near the jaw, to provide extra clamping pressure. If wood clothespins are used, the jaws should be lightly waxed, to prevent them from being glued down. Or plastic clothespins can be used, as they are at the École-atelier Lutherie-Guitare Bruand, a lutherie school in Montreal headed up by luthier and educator André Brunet.

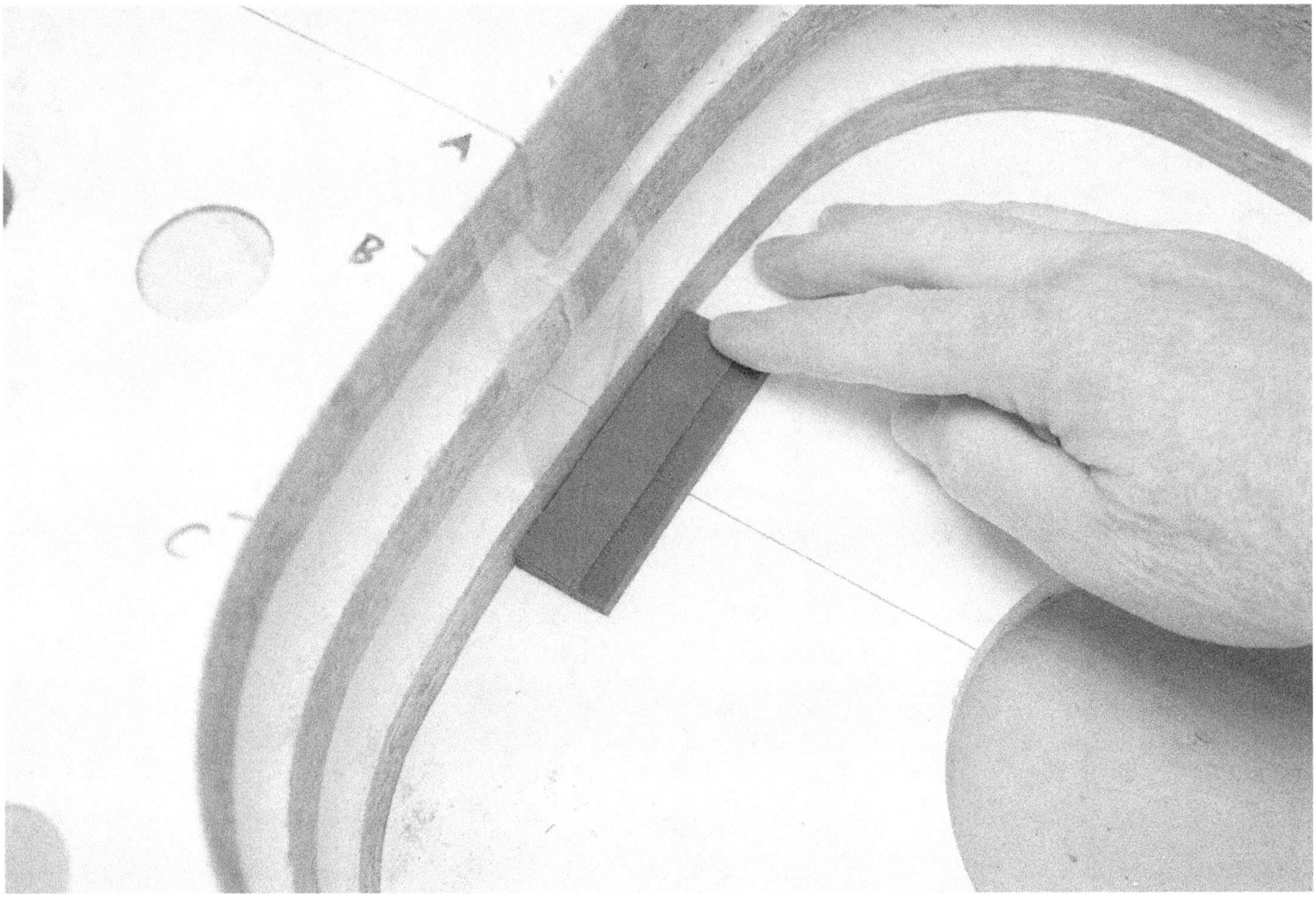

Photo 10-60 – The spacer is taped down to the floor at the neck end seam, using double-stick tape ...

1. The garland is already mounted in the mold, back edges up, following a previous operation. The lining strips are glued in place, starting at the neck block. The thinnest bead of glue possible is run down the center of the back (un-kerfed) side of a strip of lining. The strip is pressed into place, so the end butts against the side of the neck block. One hand is used to press the lining in place, while the other hand is used to apply the clamps. The thumb of the hand holding the lining is placed on top of the lining and the side during this operation. The thumb is used to locate the lining so its top surface and that of the side are level with each other. If the top surface of the lining is a bit higher than the edge of the side, that is OK. Clamps are placed

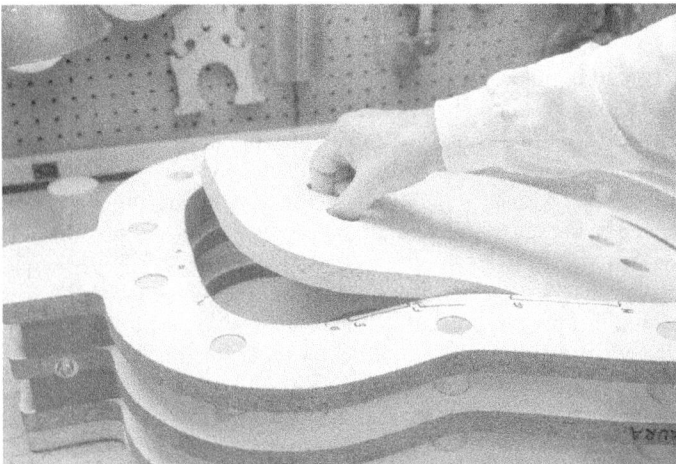

Photo 10-61 – ... then the insert is inserted. The spacer will raise the neck end, matching the taper of the back.

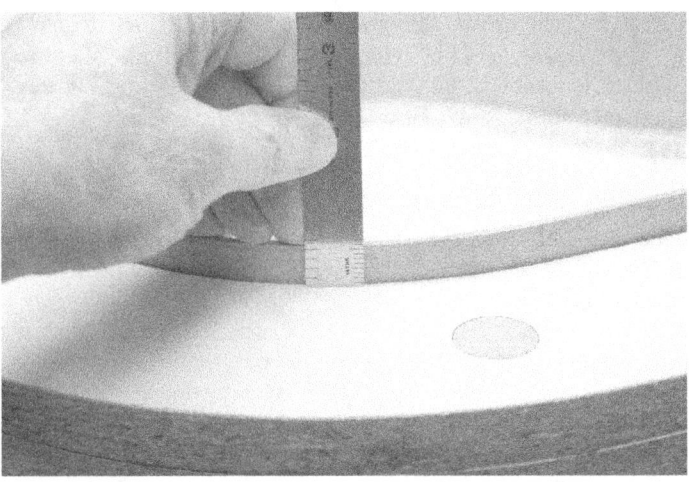

Photo 10-62 – The exposure of the ribs above the mold is measured and made uniform all around, from the soundhole center mark on one side, around the tail end, to the soundhole center mark on the other side.

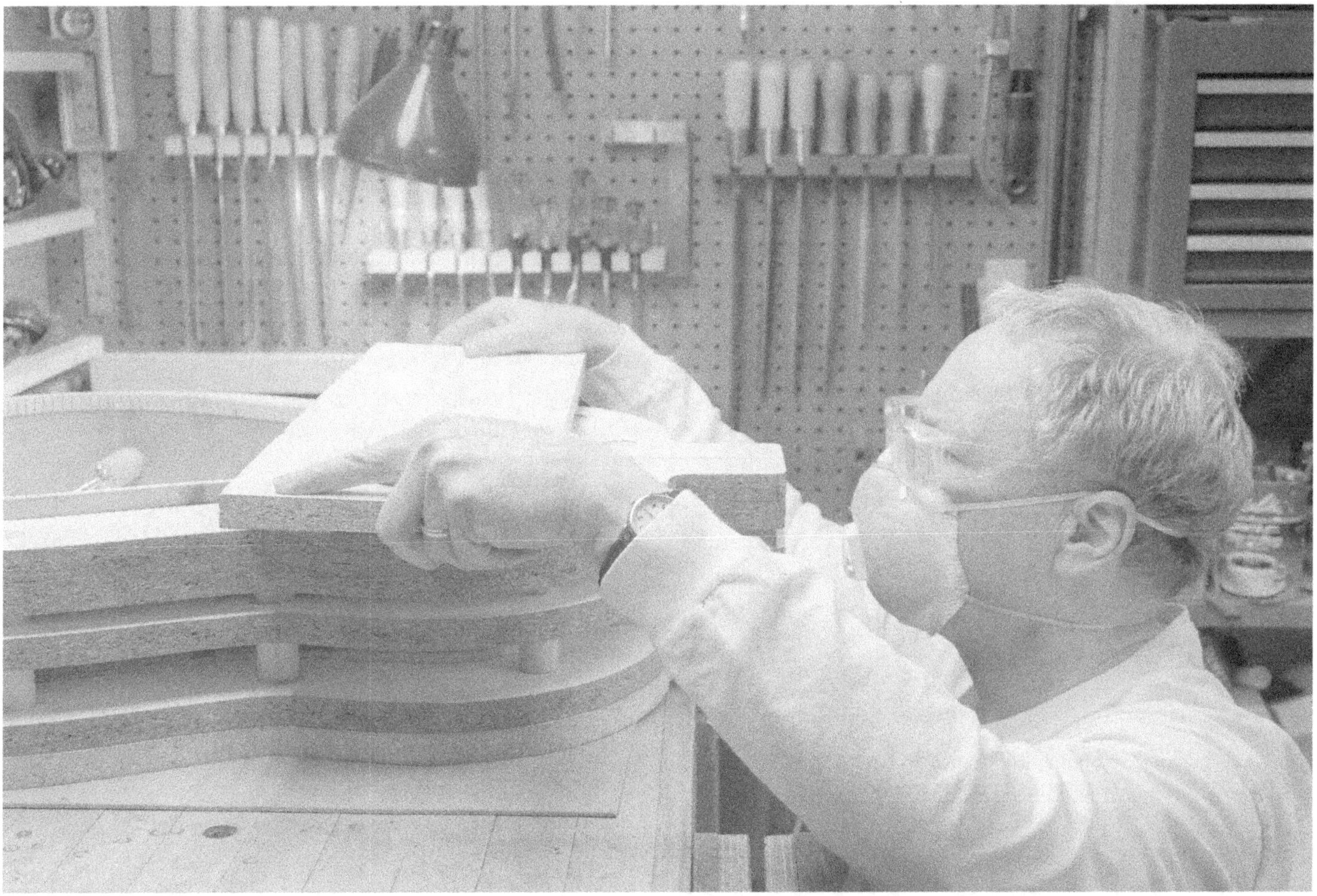

Photo 10-63 – *Flattening the beveled neck end of the top of the garland, using the narrow sanding board.*

in the center of the height of the lining, and right next to each other (**photos 10-57, 10-58**). Glue squeeze-out under the linings should be wiped up immediately. Squeeze-out on top of the lining can be ignored. That surface will be sanded smooth in a later step.

Although the luthier should always strive for neat work, this is particularly the case for parts of the guitar that will be visible in the finished instrument. Note that the back end of the neck block, and the linings of the back from the neck block down past the waist will be visible through the soundhole of the finished instrument.

2. Additional lining strips are applied in the same manner, butted against each other end to end. When nearing the tail block, the final strip of the side is placed dry, and marked for cutting to length. The strip is sawed to length, then glued in place. The glue is allowed to cure for one hour before clamps are removed and application of lining is continued.

3. The other side is lined in the same manner.

4. The edges of the sides, the tops of the linings, and the face-up surfaces of the blocks are marked all over with pencil, in preparation for a final level sanding (**photo 10-59**).

5. The large sanding board is used to flatten the back side edges and linings until all pencil marks are removed. The label "back" should be written in pencil on the ends of the blocks to aid in later orientation.

6. The jacks are removed, the garland is removed from the mold, and the insert is removed as well. The saved spacer that was used when scribing the taper of the back in a previous operation is then attached to the floor at the neck end seam of the mold, using double-stick tape (**photo 10-60**). The insert is then replaced in the mold (**photo 10-61**). The spacer raises the insert at the neck end to match the taper of the back.

7. The garland is inserted back into the mold, top-edges-up this time. It is possible that the garland has distorted enough so it will no longer easily fit into the mold. It is also a lot stiffer with linings, so it should not be forced – it could crack. If it won't go, the halves of the mold are separated a bit, and then reassembled with shims of veneer or card stock between the tabs. The distance from the top surface of the mold to the top edge of the garland should be measured, from the soundhole center mark on one side, down to the tail end, and then up to the soundhole center mark on the other side (**photo 10-62**). It should be the same all around. If it is not, the sides are pushed down and pulled up until the measurement is the same all

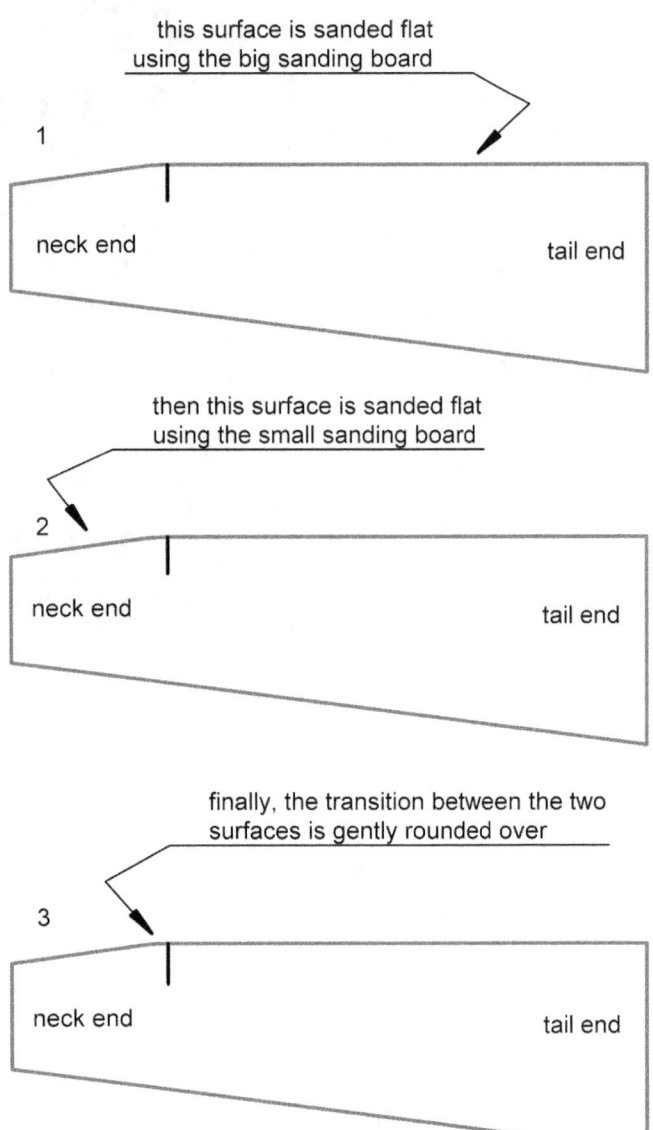

Figure 10-4 – *Cartoon side view of the garland, showing the sanding of the top surface that is needed after the linings are installed. 1. The main part of the top, from the center of the soundhole to the tail end, is sanded flat. 2. The surface of the neck end bevel is sanded. 3. The transition between these two surfaces is gently rounded over.*

10. The same sanding board that was used to initially level the surface of the neck end bevel is used again for that purpose (**figure 10-4.2**). Care should be taken to sand *only* as much as is needed for leveling, and to maintain the angle of the bevel (**photo 10-63**). A quick roundover of the edge between bevel and top surface is done, in the same manner as was performed previously (**figure 10-4.3**).

11. The label "top" should be written in pencil on the ends of the blocks to aid in later orientation. The garland should be stored jacked into the mold.

---

1. McDonald, Graham. (2019) *The Ukulele: An Illustrated Workshop Manual.* MusicBooks Press.

around as described. Once that is the case, the jacks are applied to fix the garland in position in the mold.

8. The linings are glued at the top edge, in the same way that they were glued in at the bottom edge.

9. The edges and blocks are marked up with pencil, and the large sanding board is used to level the top edges and linings, from the tail block to the marks on the outsides of the sides indicating where the center of the soundhole will be located (**figure 10-4.1**).

Note that because of the short bevel at the neck end, the goal here is not to eliminate *all* of the pencil marks, only those from the tail end up to the marks on the outsides of the sides indicating where the center of the soundhole will be located.

11 The Back Plate

The steel string acoustic guitar has two broad plates, the top and the back. From a construction sequence point of view, either can be built first, but in the context of a single guitar construction project I propose building the back plate first, for a couple of small reasons. The first is that it may be possible to make use of some of the off-cut material from the back, when fashioning the top plate. If the outline of the back is judiciously cut, it is usually possible to retain an off-cut large enough to use as the bridge plate for the top plate (**figure 11-1**). The second reason is that each plate is constructed from two bookmatched pieces joined together, and it is important to get this joint right for the top, if for no other reason than it will be visible in the finished instrument. Building the back plate first provides some experience in joining plate halves, and the back joint will be well reinforced and entirely invisible in the completed guitar.

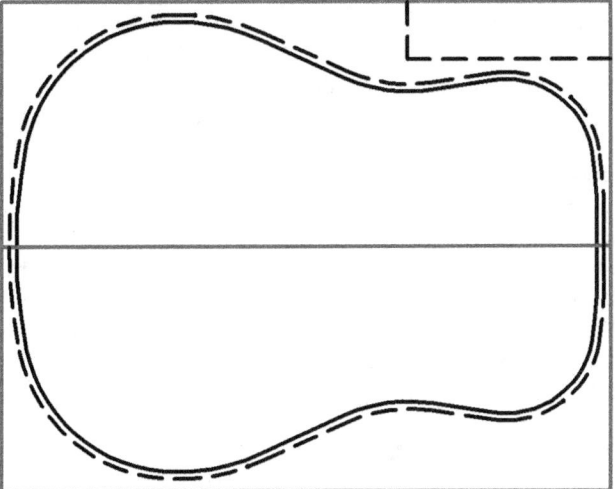

Figure 11-1 – *Diagram of the back plate outline. The dashed line represents a cutout margin. If the cutoff material near the upper bout is removed as a single piece, it can be used as the blank for the bridge plate of the top plate, or the tail graft in a later construction operation.*

As mentioned, the back comes from the lutherie wood supplier as two bookmatched pieces, in a set which includes the sides. The pieces are oriented bookmatch fashion in the finished instrument. In most cases a decorative *back strip* separates the two halves. I won't go into much more detail here about wood selection for the back, as that has already been covered in the chapter on bending the sides. One thing I will point out is that it is becoming common for steel string guitars to be built with back pieces that include some of the generally lighter color sapwood. The choice to use such sets is an aesthetic consideration only.

As is the case with the sides, guitar back pieces are supplied thicker than will be used in the instrument, and must be thinned before use. But there is an issue about just when this thinning is done. It is generally the case that it is preferable to join the two halves of the back first, and then to thin the back to its target thickness. This sequence tends to make the jointing of the edges and the gluing of the back halves easier and more accurate. The issue is that, based on extensive polling I have done, a substantial number of novice luthiers do not have the power tools or the hand tool skills necessary to accurately thickness the joined back plate. For this reason, the construction description here will first thin the plate halves to the target thickness for the back, and then join those halves together. Doing it this way allows the novice luthier to have the back plate halves thinned to the target thickness by the lutherie wood supplier. The jointing and joining construction techniques described here are well suited to dealing with pieces that are already thinned to target thickness.

I will point out here that this issue is becoming moot, because lutherie wood suppliers are more frequently supplying wood that is so close to the ultimate target thickness that there is little if any advantage to joining the halves first and thinning the entire plate afterwards.

So, lutherie shops that do not have the facilities to thickness the plate halves should have the plates sanded to thickness by the lutherie wood supplier. The back halves should be thinned to 3/32″ (2.4mm) at 100 grit for use, either by the supplier or in the shop.

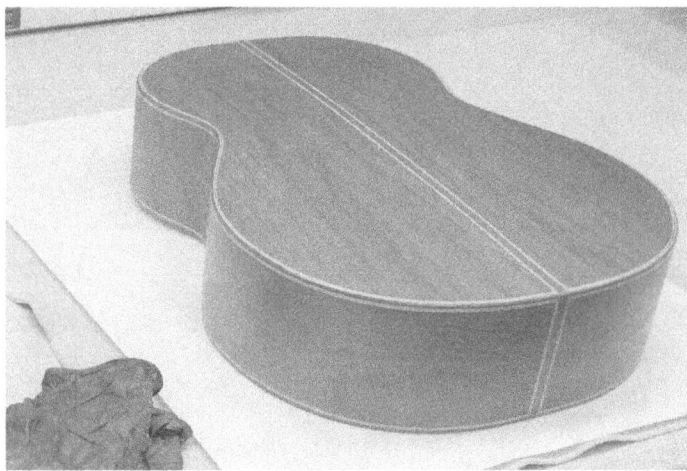

Photo 11-1 – *The back strip of a parlor guitar body. This back strip is made of the same material as the bindings, and has purfling lines that are the same pattern used for the bindings.*

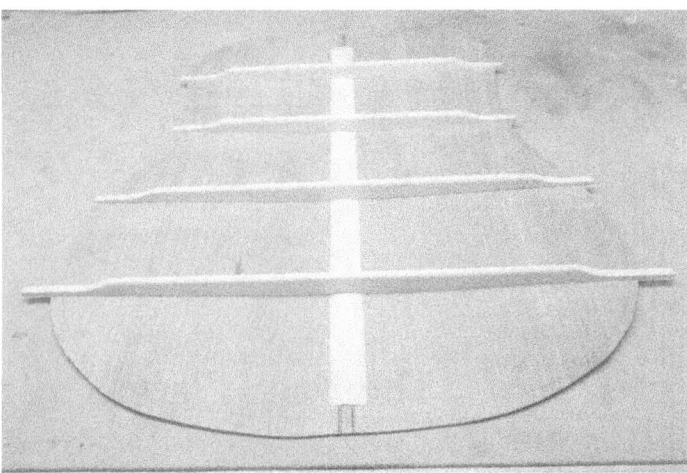

Photo 11-2 – *The inside surface of the back has a long shallow cross-grain strip made of spruce, that completely covers the joinery of the back center. This is called the back reinforcement strip. Also seen are the four transverse back braces typical of most steel string acoustic guitars. The arching of the surfaces of the braces that contact the back plate is higher for the two centermost braces and lower for the two braces near the ends. This forces the plate to be arched along its length as well as across its width.*

Jointing the Back

There are a number of ways to effectively joint the plate halves for joining. The construction details include the three most common methods– using a stationary jointer, using a hand plane and *shooting board*, and using a flat bar with PSA sandpaper attached. It is not unusual to find information on jointing from lutherie or general woodworking sources that asserts the superiority of joints that were planed with a hand plane. I have done some informal experiments using all three methods on thin spruce samples, and then subjecting the joints to tensile stress (i.e., pulling the joints apart) and to shearing stress, and the wood around the joint always fails before the joint does, no matter which jointing method was used. This suggests that all of these jointing methods are functionally equivalent for the purposes of joining guitar plate halves. That being the case, the novice luthier is free to make use of whichever method best suits his or her skills and available tools.

The Back Strip

Almost all steel string acoustic guitars made these days have a back strip that visually separates the two halves of the back in the finished instrument (**photo 11-1**). These are commonly made using a strip of wood that is of the same species as the bindings, along with some decorative purfling lines, as seen in the photo. Another approach is to use a decorative marquetry strip as the back strip. These are available from lutherie suppliers in a number of patterns, and are usually not expensive. There are two ways to construct the back with a back strip. The first is to join the back halves, then inlay the strip into a routed channel. The second method is to construct a back strip that is as thick or thicker than the back halves, and then laminate it between the halves as part of the back halves joining process. These options are discussed in the construction details and are shown in **figure 11-2**.

No matter the approach taken with the back strip, the joint is reinforced on the inside surface of the back with a *back reinforcement strip*. This is a shallow length of cross-grain wood that completely covers and reinforces the back joinery (**photo 11-2**).

About Plate Arching

Although the steel string acoustic guitar is often referred to as a flattop guitar, neither the top nor the back plates of modern instruments are actually flat. Both plates are arched or domed a bit, and the arching of the back plate is generally more pronounced than that of the top. Plate arching is included in the side view in the plans for the example instruments, but the

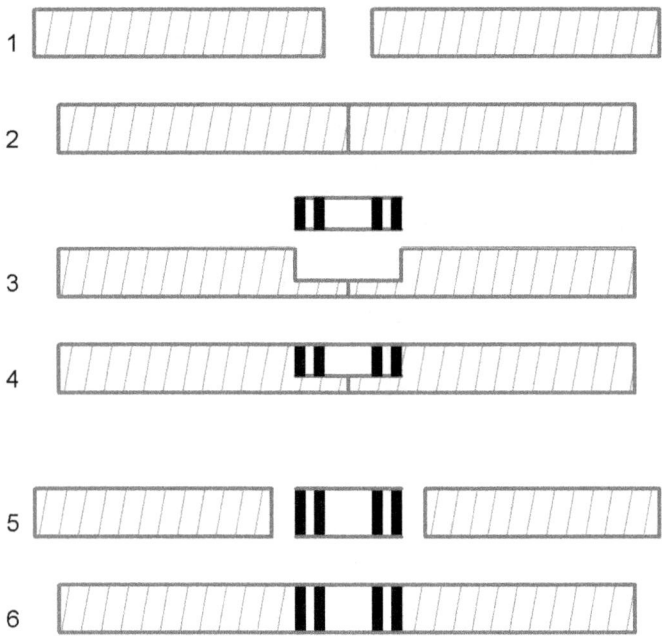

Figure 11-2 – *The most basic treatment of the back is to simply join the two halves (1, 2). A shop-built or purchased back strip can be inlaid into a channel routed into the back over the center seam (3, 4). This method is necessary for strips that are thinner than the back. For strips that are at least as thick as the back, the two halves of the back and the strip can be assembled as in 5 and 6.*

Figure 11-3 – *The general arching profile used in the construction of the example instruments, exaggerated in height so the details of the profile are visible. The profile is domed up in the center, but the ends are flat.*

arching is subtle, so it can be easy to overlook. Arching the plates provides some structural stability for an instrument under constant stress of string tension and changes in humidity. This is quite important for such a lightly constructed structure as the guitar.

Considering just the back plate, if it was built flat, then an increase in humidity would swell the plate across the grain to some extent, while the braces glued to it would not change much at all in length. The result would be that the plate may dome up. This doming has little structural consequence. But a decrease in humidity would have the opposite effect, shrinking the wood of the plate across the grain and dishing the plate into the body. This puts the plate wood in tension across the grain, increasing the likelihood it will develop cracks.

But if the plate is constructed with a dome already in it, a decrease in humidity will flatten the doming a bit, but usually not to the extent that the wood is in tension across the grain, reducing the chance of developing cracks. Note that this desired effect of back plate doming is never a sure thing, but we do it to decrease the likelihood of cracks developing if the instrument dries out. It also means that small impacts to the plate tend to compress the wood instead of pulling it, which also makes the structure more robust.

The mechanism used to dome the plates is pretty simple. The contact surface of each brace that will be glued to the plate is arched. Then, when the thin plate is glued to the arched brace, the plate will assume the same arched shape, at least it will in the area of the brace. Since the gluing surface of each brace of a plate will be arched, it is possible to effect a doming of the entire plate.

There are two broad approaches taken to plate arching in guitar lutherie. In one of these the plates are arched like the surface of a sphere, right to the edges. Doing this requires spherical molds, generally called *dished workboards*. The plates must be molded to shape, and the edges of the garland must be shaped to accept the spherical shape of the plates.

The other plate arching approach arches the plates to a complex shape that is humped up in the middle but is flat at the edges (**figure 11-3**). This approach requires no special molds. The edges of the garland can remain flat. As can be seen in **photo 11-2** and **figure 11-4**, the height of arching of the braces near the center of the back is higher than those of the braces near the ends of the plate. This produces a back plate that is arched both across its width and along its length. Note that in order to make the arching visible, the arching in the figures is quite exaggerated. The arching of the plates of real guitars is quite subtle.

The construction details presented here are for the latter method: arched up in the middle and flat at the edges. Although infrequently used for steel string guitars manufactured in a production environment, this method is commonly used in the construction of classical guitars and it is ideally suited for the construction of a single instrument.

About Plate Bracing

Guitar construction has evolved to make use of thin top and back plates that are stiffened with the addition of lightweight braces. The resulting plates are light in weight, stiff enough to withstand the effects of string tension on the guitar body, and strong enough to withstand a certain level of bumping and knocking. That the braced plates are light in weight helps to keep the instrument light in weight, which improves ergonomics. Lightweight plates also vibrate more freely than heavier structures, an important feature for the plates of a musical instrument, particularly the top, but also important for the back as well.

A number of bracing patterns have evolved for guitar plates. The most common bracing pattern for guitar back plates is called *ladder bracing*. This bracing pattern consists of several parallel transverse braces across the inside of the plate, which look something like the rungs of a ladder. Steel string guitars typically make use of four such braces. Some instruments make use of back braces that are different in width and height from each other. I have never found doing so to make for either a better sounding or a more physically robust guitar, so in most cases I'll use back braces that are all the same width and height, just because it makes preparing the brace blanks a little easier. The example instruments make use of back braces that differ from each other only in length. In fact, the bracing of the example instruments has been rationalized so that the blanks needed for the back braces and most of the top braces are all of the same width and height.

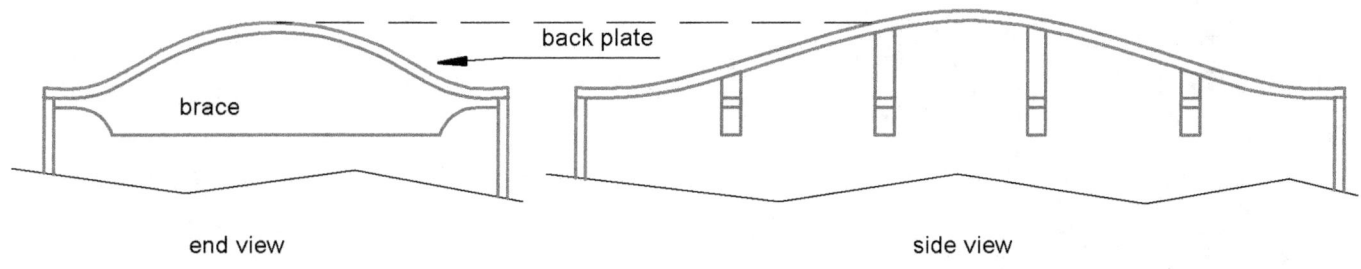

Figure 11-4 – *Orthographic representation (end and side views) of an exaggerated and inverted back, showing how arching of the braces effects arching of the back plate across the width of the plate and along its length.*

The previous section mentioned that the plates will be arched without the use of any special shaping molds. When the braces are glued to the back plate, they will be clamped in place using regular clamps. Since the arching of the plate will follow the arching cut into the gluing surfaces of the braces, it is necessary that the braces be kept as stiff as possible during gluing. For this reason, in the accompanying construction descriptions the braces will all be cut to their basic rectangular cross section shape, the bottoms arched, and then glued to the plate. After the glue cures and the plate is arched, the braces will be carved to their final shapes.

About Wood for Braces

Braces need to be light and stiff, and they must be made from a wood that is easy to carve. For these reasons, braces are almost always made out of some species of spruce (*Picea* spp.). Every luthier has their own preference for spruce species, but I find that all available species work about about the same for making braces. Brace wood is available from lutherie wood suppliers in quartersawn boards that are typically approximately ¾″ (19.1mm) thick and 22″ (558.8mm) long. The widths of the boards vary. Some suppliers sell bracewood only in narrow pieces. I generally prefer wider boards, because it allows ripping most of the brace blanks off the board using the table saw.

There are a few pieces of bracing needed for the top and back plates that are quite thin. One of these is the back reinforcement strip already mentioned. To fashion these thin pieces, I find it useful to buy a low-grade spruce guitar top blank. These are thin, quartersawn, and can be had cheaply from most lutherie wood suppliers.

Layout and Construction

Jointing the Back Plate Halves

☐ **Preparing the Back Halves for Jointing**

The halves of the back are planed to thickness, then the pattern of the back is checked for approximate position on them. After they are *patterned*, the inside edges (the edges that will be joined together at the centerline of the back) are jointed, and the outside edges are trimmed parallel to the inside edges. The half body outline that was cut from the plan in the process of building the mold is used as an aid in determining where the outline of the back should be on each back half. It is generally the case that the outline will be right in the middle of the plate, with the centerline aligned with the inside edges of the plate halves, but sometimes the pattern needs to be positioned to avoid defects in the plate.

1. If the back plate halves have not previously been thinned to a thickness of ³⁄₃₂″ (2.4mm) and sanded on both surfaces to 100 grit, either by the wood supplier or in the shop, that work is done now (**photo 11-3**).

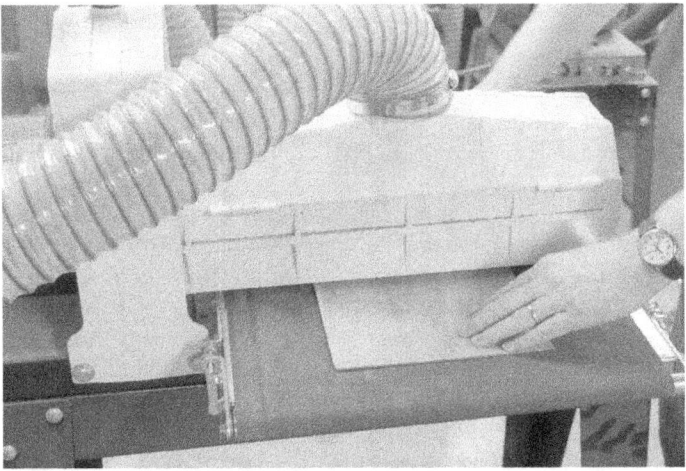

Photo 11-3 – *The back halves can be thicknessed by the supplier or in the shop, using a thickness sander as shown, or using more traditional hand planing methods, or using a router planing jig like the one described in Appendix B.*

2. The two halves are positioned against each other so the end grain lines up, and then they are opened bookmatch fashion on the bench. As was done with the sides, the surfaces of the back are examined, to determine which surface will be on the outside, and which end will be the neck end of the finished back. The half body outline cut from the plan while building the body mold is useful here, to get an idea what parts of the back halves will fall inside the pattern of the back. The outline of the back is not penciled on the wood just yet. But when a suitable outside surface is identified, both halves are marked in pencil on the outside surfaces with the word "outside." The neck ends are also marked "neck" and the tail ends "tail."

☐ **Jointing Using the Jointer Option**

Jointing of the inside back plate half edges can be performed quickly and accurately on a well set up stationary jointer. It should be noted though, that the term "well set up" has different meanings depending on the type of woodworking the machine is used for. For lutherie purposes, we need an extremely accurate joint along the entire length of the plate halves. The general machine instructions for setting up a jointer rarely include the fine tuning necessary to achieve such an accurate joint. Although instructions for doing this are outside the scope of this book, the process basically involves setting all knife edges dead level with the outfeed table, then making test

Photo 11-4 – *Jointing of the thin plate halves, using the stationary jointer, using a flat stiffening board to keep the halves flat against the fence.*

joints, assessing them, and making fine additional adjustments to the jointer outfeed table if necessary.

1. If the inside edges of the back halves are not approximately straight they should be planed or ripped straight at this time. Care should be taken to take the same amount of material off each half, to preserve the mirror image effect of bookmatching.

2. When running the thin plate halves across the jointer, care must be taken to be sure the halves are in firm contact with the jointer fence at all times. One way to do this is with the use of a flat sacrificial board that is thicker than the plate pieces. A piece of ¾″ (19.1mm) MDF that is the same length as the plate halves and a bit less wide, works well (**photo 11-4**). Both halves are jointed at the same time. With the halves placed outside surface up and bookmatched on the bench, the halves are closed like a book, with the inside edges now down on the bench. The two plate halves are held in this orientation, and transferred to the infeed table of the jointer and pressed to the fence. Then the stiffening board is placed in front of the halves as in the photo, and the whole sandwich is run across the jointer. The pieces are run across the jointer as many times as is needed for the entire length of the bottom edges of both pieces to be planed.

3. The joint is assessed by holding the jointed edges together by hand over a strong light and looking for light shining through the joint anywhere. In **photo 11-5** I'm using a tube drop light, which is ideal for candling the plate joint. During the day, the joint can be assessed by holding the plate halves in front of a big window. If the joint gaps at the center of the length or at the ends, the jointer will need to be adjusted. If adjustments are needed, it is wise to put the back aside while making these adjustments, returning to the back pieces only after the jointer has been adjusted for a straight cut. Steps 2 and 3 are then repeated.

4. The outside edges of the plate halves are ripped parallel to the inside jointed edges (**photo 11-6**).

□ **Jointing Using the Hand Plane and Shooting Board Option**

Although detailed discussions of the use of hand planes in performing the various lutherie construction operations are generally not provided in this book, the use of a plane and shooting board is esoteric enough to warrant a more complete description. In keeping with the general idea of using simply constructed jigs and fixtures, the description that follows includes the construction of a simple temporary shooting board, made out of different size pieces of MDF. The shooting board positions and fixes the two plate halves so their inside edges can both be jointed at the same time, using a hand plane on its side.

In the accompanying photos, I am using a #5 jack plane to joint the edges. When properly set up for this task, this size plane is perfectly suitable. It is probably the shortest plane that can be used to reliably joint guitar plate edges. In point of fact, I actually use the much longer #7 jointer plane for this work, but chose the #5 plane here, simply because it is easier to photograph.

Successful jointing of plate edges using a hand plane requires the plane to be *precisely* set up. The sole of the plane

Photo 11-5 – *No matter how the plate halves are jointed, the joint is examined by holding the halves together over a strong light source and looking for gaps where light shines through.*

Photo 11-6 – *After the inside edges of the back plate are jointed, the outside edges are trimmed parallel to the inside edges.*

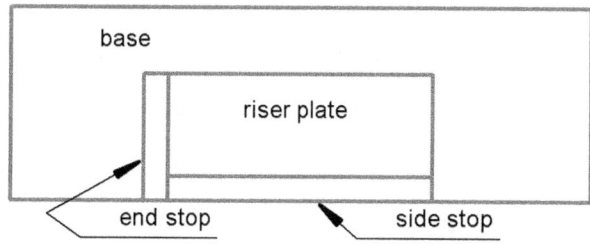

Figure 11-5 – *Schematic top view drawing of the base components of the shooting board. For left-handed use, the end stop goes on the right end of the riser plate.*

must be lapped flat and then polished. The blade must be freshly honed and polished. The plane must be able to be finely adjusted to take shavings that are translucent ribbons of wood, that are as long as the board being planed. A less than perfect state of tuning of the plane will always yield less than the desired results for this demanding planing operation.

1. Constructing the shooting board. The base of the shooting board is a rectangular piece of ¾″ (19.1mm) thick MDF about

Photo 11-7 – *The base of the shooting board and the side stop, are clamped down to the front edge of the bench. The clamp bars are down and out of the way.*

Photo 11-9 – *The inside edges of the plate halves are planed straight and smooth at the same time, to prepare for jointing.*

Photo 11-8 – *The end stop is clamped down square to the side stop using one short and one long clamp. Then the riser plate is placed on the base, against the stops.*

Photo 11-10 – *The setup for jointing the plate halves. The halves are on top of the riser plate, and captured by the stops. The edges to be planed overhang the riser plate. The plane will be used on its side.*

48″ (1219.2MM) × 16″ (406.4MM) for conventionally sized back halves and the #5 plane. The length is actually the length of the back halves, plus 2 times the length of the plane. The width of the base is the width of the back halves, plus the height of the side walls of the plane, plus another 4″ (101.6MM).

2. From the same MDF material is also cut a rectangular side stop 2″ (50.8MM) wide by as long as the halves; an end stop 2″ (50.8MM) wide by as wide as the halves plus 1½″ (38.1MM); and a clamping bar 6″ (152.4MM) wide by as long as the halves.

3. A rectangular riser plate is cut from ¼″ (6.4MM) thick MDF or plywood. The riser plate is as long as the halves, by ½″ (12.7MM) less than the width of the halves.

4. The base is aligned with the front edge of the bench, and clamped down at the front edge. The side stop is aligned with the front edge of the baseboard and positioned at its center, then clamped down, as shown in **figure 11-5** and **photo 11-7**.

5. The end stop is aligned with the front edge of the base and with the end of the side stop, as shown in **figure 11-5** and

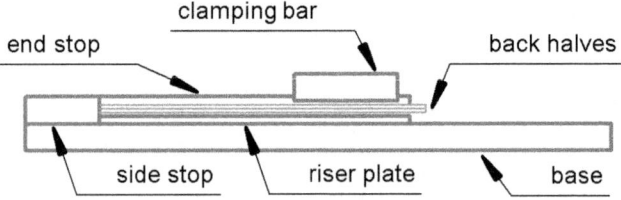

Figure 11-6 – *Schematic side view drawing of the components of the shooting board. Note the back halves overhang the riser plate.*

photo 11-8. A carpenter's square is used to be sure the two stops are square to each other, before the end stop is clamped down. The riser plate is placed on the base, against the stops. The riser plate will hold the back plate halves above the base, so the plane blade can fully engage them.

 When the shooting board is set up with the end stop on the left, the plane will be held in the right hand during jointing. For luthiers that want to hold the plane in the left hand, the end stop is instead positioned on the right.

6. Jointing the edges of the back halves. If the inside edges of the back halves are not approximately straight, they should be planed or ripped straight at this time. Care should be taken to take the same amount of material off each half, to preserve the mirror image effect of bookmatching. This is readily accomplished by planing both edges at the same time (**photo 11-9**). The direction of planing should be noted and retained by marking the halves in pencil. When the edges are jointed on the shooting board in a subsequent step, the halves will need to be oriented so the plane moves in the same direction as noted here.

7. The plane is finely set, with the edge of the blade square to the throat, and to take the thinnest continuous shavings possible, then put aside for the next few steps.

8. The outside edges of the plate halves are ripped parallel to the inside edges (**photo 11-6**). Both halves are ripped at the same time, or at least with the same fence setting. This will make both halves the same width.

9. The ends of the back halves are trimmed square to the inside edges. Both halves are trimmed at the same time. This will make both halves the same length.

10. The back halves are positioned on top of the riser plate and against the stops, so that the edges to be planed overhang the riser plate and point toward the back of the bench, as shown in **figure 11-6**. The clamping bar is placed on top of the back halves, near the edges to be planed (**photos 11-10, 11-11**). Note that nothing should be in the way of the movement of the plane across the edges to be planed.

11. If the shooting board is set up as described for right hand use, the left hand is used to press down on the clamping bar, and the right hand is used to smoothly slide the plane across the edges of the back halves from right (**photos 11-12, 11-13**) to left (**photo 11-14**). The stops hold the halves in position during planing. The operation is repeated until the resulting shavings are two ribbons that are of equal thickness, and as wide and as long as the edges planed. Then the joint is candled as described in the previous section and shown in **photo 11-5**. If the joint is not perfect, it is shot again and checked again.

Note that pressure with the hand on the clamping bar is generally all that is needed to hold the back halves still during shooting. This is because the plane is set so finely, so it doesn't drag the planed pieces around. But if the halves move at all during planing, the shooting board components can be modified to hold things together more securely. The underside of the end stop and the clamping bar, and both surfaces of the riser plate can be covered with PSA sandpaper. This will provide more grip to prevent movement while planing.

Photo 11-11 – *Another view showing the ends of the edges to be planed. The riser block raises the halves above the base so the plane blade can cut them. The clamping bar will prevent the halves from moving.*

Photo 11-13 – *This is the luthier's view of the starting position for shooting the edges. The plane is held flat to the base, and will be moved from right to left in one smooth steady stroke.*

Photo 11-12 – *The starting position for jointing right-handed. The left hand presses down on the clamping bar. The plane is positioned so the part of the sole in front of the blade is flat on the edges to be planed.*

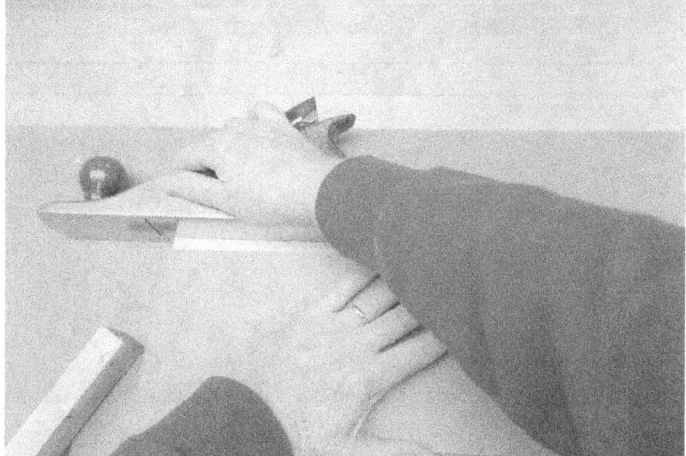

Photo 11-14 – *The shooting stroke ends after the plane blade has cleared the other end of the plate halves.*

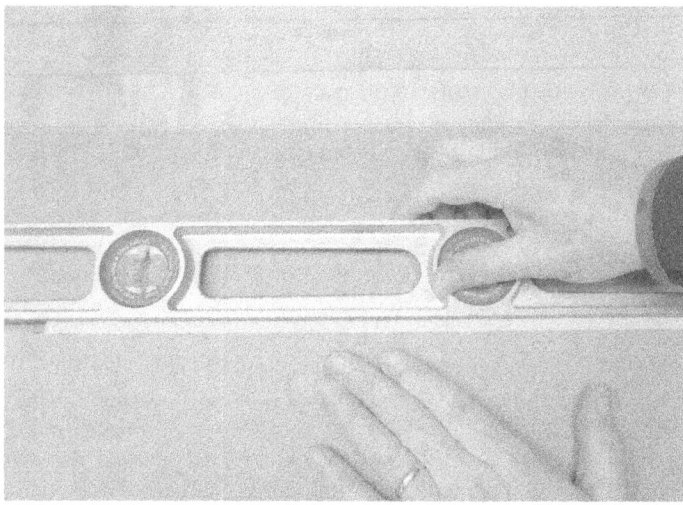

Photo 11-15 – *A construction level with PSA sandpaper can be used with the shooting board to sand the edges straight and flat for joining. The sandpaper should fully contact the entire length of the edges during sanding.*

Photo 11-16 – *The table saw with fine toothed blade, zero clearance insert, and feather boards is used to cut a thin wood strip to be used as the core of the center strip for the back.*

Photo 11-17 – *Preparing to apply glue to the purfling lines. The lines are placed together in order, and taped down to a glue proof surface. Glue will be applied quickly with a brush.*

☐ Jointing Using Sandpaper and Shooting Board Option

A third option for jointing the edges of the back plate is to use a 24″ (609.6mm) or 36″ (914.4mm) construction level with its narrow sides covered with PSA sandpaper. The level used must have narrow sides which are straight, and the broad sides must be flat. High quality levels will have flatness and squareness specifications which can be relied upon. Cheaper home center levels will not, so it is a good idea when buying one of the latter specifically for this purpose, to check them against each other while in the store. One narrow side of the level is covered with 100-grit PSA sandpaper and the other narrow side is covered with 150-grit sandpaper.

1. All steps but the last one of the previous section are followed to make and prepare to use the shooting board.

2. The edges to be "planed" are marked up with pencil marks along their entire lengths.

3. The level is placed flat on its side, so that the 100 grit sandpaper surface contacts the plate edges. The level is scrubbed back and forth to flatten the plate edges (**photo 11-15**). Straight strokes in both directions are taken. The entire length of the plate edges must be in contact with the sandpaper at all times. Care must be taken to keep the cut flat. It is helpful to use a clamp or two to clamp the plate halves in place. This allows both hands to be used to handle the level. Progress is checked by watching for complete removal of all the pencil marks.

4. The plate edges are marked up again with pencil.

5. Step 3 above is repeated with the 150 grit side of the level. The joint should be checked for even pencil mark removal after every few strokes.

6. Then the joint is candled, as described in the previous sections and shown in **photo 11-5**. If the joint is not perfect, it is sanded again and checked again.

The Back Strip

As mentioned in the chapter introduction, the back strip is typically either a purchased marquetry strip or a strip of wood that matches the bindings, the latter possibly surrounded with purfling lines that will also match those of the bindings. A decision that must be made at this point in construction is if the back strip will be inlaid into a channel, or if it will be laminated between the two halves of the back. In my own work I generally make that decision as follows.

If the back strip is the same thickness as the back halves, I will usually laminate the strip in. If the strip is either thicker or thinner than the back halves then I'll inlay it. Purchased marquetry strips are usually thinner than the back plate pieces, so they are always inlaid. I also laminate the strip in if I don't have a router bit that matches the width of the strip. It is possible to cut the channel for the strip in multiple passes of course, but I find that if I do this I often end up with a channel that is slightly wider than necessary. Another way to put this is that I often screw this up. So if I don't have a router bit that matches the width of the strip, I laminate it in.

Purchased marquetry strips come in common widths, so matching a router bit to them is never an issue. Shop-made plain wood strips are easy to accurately cut to width as well. But things get a little dicey when purfling lines are added to the strip. Purfling lines are available from lutherie wood suppliers in various wood species and colors. They are cut from 0.5MM thick veneer sheets and so are nominally 0.02″ (0.5MM) thick. When it comes to matching fractional inch router bits, this is an odd size. The issue is further complicated by the fact that the purfling strips swell in thickness when glue is applied to them. This swelling adds approximately 0.002″ (0.05MM) to 0.003″ (0.08MM) per glued surface. This means the effective thickness of each purfling line will be from 0.024″ (0.61MM) to 0.026″ (0.66MM).

Although it is possible to use the effective widths above to calculate the total width of a shop-built back strip composed of a strip of wood and surrounding purfling lines, or to determine the width the wood strip needs to be to meet a total width, I generally find it easier to just pick a width for the wood strip that is the same as what will eventually be used for the guitar's bindings, nominally ¼″ (6.4MM), then glue on the purfling strips, then laminate the assembly between the two back halves.

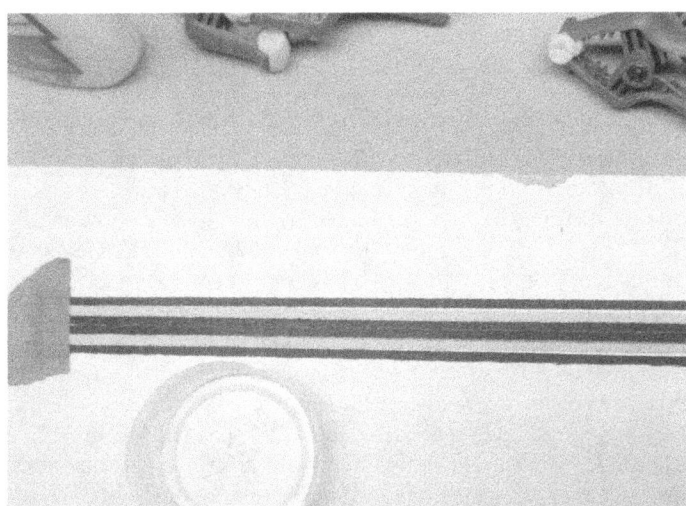

Photo 11-18 – *Close-up of the purfling lines, taped down and ready for glue to be applied.*

☐ Making the Back Strip

The following steps detail the construction of a simple back strip made of the same wood as the bindings of the guitar, sandwiched between Black/Maple/Black (BMB) purfling lines, that will match those of the back bindings. The results are seen in **photo 11-1**. This is a common and traditional approach to the back strip. If binding strips will be purchased from a lutherie wood supplier, an additional strip can be purchased for use as the back strip. Likewise if binding strips will be ripped from other stock, an additional piece can be cut for the back strip. It is often possible to cut a back strip from the outside edge of one of the halves of the back if the halves are wide enough.

1. A piece of wood for the strip is cut (**photo 11-16**) or procured from a lutherie wood supplier. The piece should be ¼″ (6.4MM) wide and as long as the back halves, generally about 22″ (558.8MM) long. If a piece of purchased binding is used, it will usually be 0.08″ (2MM) thick, suitable for making a back strip to be inlaid. If the piece is cut from excess width of the sides or the back, it will be ³⁄₃₂″ (2.4MM) thick, and suitable for either inlaying or laminating.

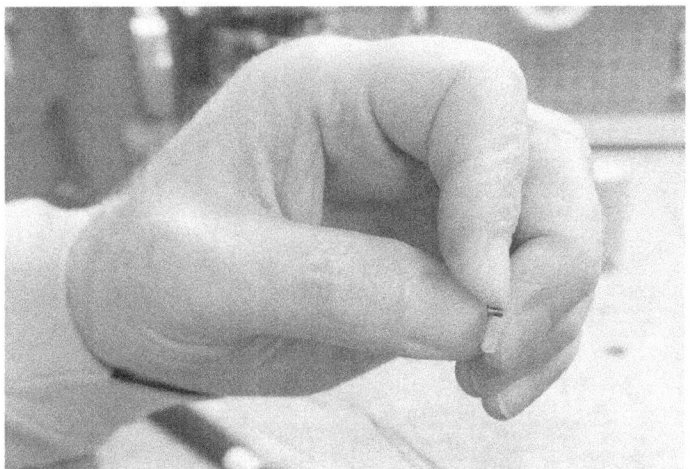

Photo 11-19 – *The fingers are used to align the purfling lines and the wood strip, and to press everything together. The fingers are maintained in this position and then moved down the entire length of the strip.*

2. Purchased veneer purfling lines will be used on both sides of the wood strip in a BMB sequence. The lines are ³⁄₃₂″ (2.4MM) wide and approximately 32″ (812.8MM) long. For this pattern, four black lines and two maple or white lines are needed. These are cut to the length of the back halves.

3. The easiest way to apply glue to the lines is to tape them down to a glue-proof surface, like a piece of melamine board (**photos 11-17** and **11-18**), and then to apply glue generously with a brush. The lines are first dampened on both surfaces by pulling them through a damp rag held in one hand. This helps to prevent them from curling. The lines are then taped down to the melamine board, next to each other in sequence, BMB, BMB, with just a bit of masking tape at the very ends of the

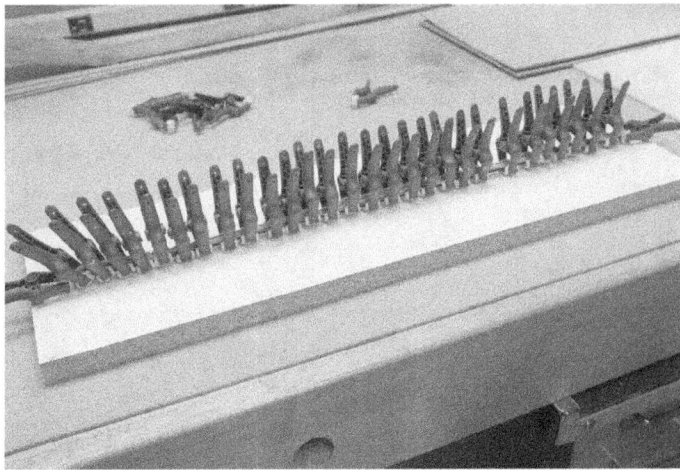

Photo 11-20 – *Many small spring clamps are used to clamp the lines to the strip. It will usually be necessary to adjust the alignment of the purfling lines as the clamps are applied.*

lines. Wood glue is poured into a cup and then quickly applied to the lines with a brush.

4. The tape holding the ends of the lines is removed. One BMB group of lines is picked up with the fingers and placed into BMB order. Note that there is glue on only one side of each line, so the lines have to be ordered so there is glue between all lines and also on one side of the gathered bundle. The glue side of this bundle is pressed onto one side of the wood strip, using the first three fingers to apply pressure, and to keep all the pieces together. The thumb and second finger are placed against the top and bottom surfaces of the wood strip, and are used to hold the pieces in alignment, while the first finger presses the lines together and to the side of the wood strip (**photo 11-19**). The fingers are run down the length of the strip in this manner, to press the pieces together and squeegee out excess glue.

5. The above step is repeated for the other three lines on the other side of the strip. The assembly should be looked over to be sure none of the lines are sticking up higher than the others, and that none of the lines have submarined under any of the others.

6. Small spring clamps are used to hold everything in place while the glue cures (**photos 11-20** and **11-21**). The plastic clamps pictured are ideal because they are glue proof. Ordinary wood spring clothes pins can be used, as long as their clamping surfaces are made glue proof with the application of a bit of wax. It is generally best to place one clamp approximately every 2″ (50.8mm) along the entire length, then fill in the spaces with additional clamps. The glue is allowed to cure for at least one hour before removing the clamps.

7. The strip is now carefully examined. It is likely that one side or the other will have the lines slightly raised above the surface of the center part. This side will be used as the *outside* of the strip. Glue is removed from this surface of the strip, and the lines are made flush. This can be done quickly and easily using a card scraper, as shown in **photo 11-22**. Then the word "outside" is penciled on it. The other surface is also scraped clean and flush. If it is intended that the strip will be laminated between the back halves, then the strip is scraped to a uniform $\frac{3}{32}″$ (2.4mm) thick.

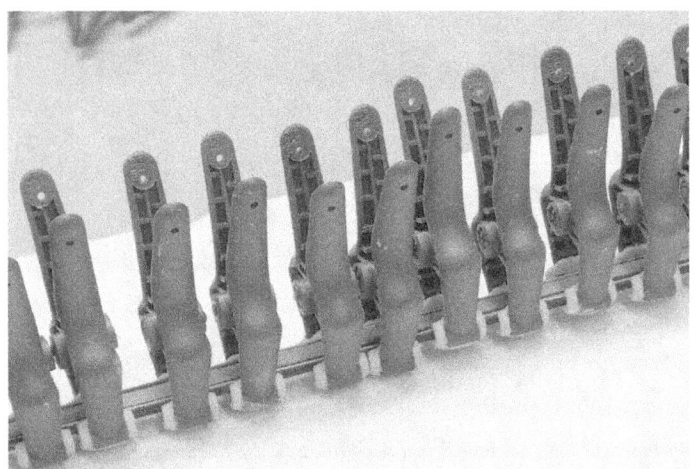

Photo 11-21 – Close-up of the clamping arrangement.

Photo 11-23 – A simple sanding fixture is made and used to remove excess glue from the sides of the finished center strip.

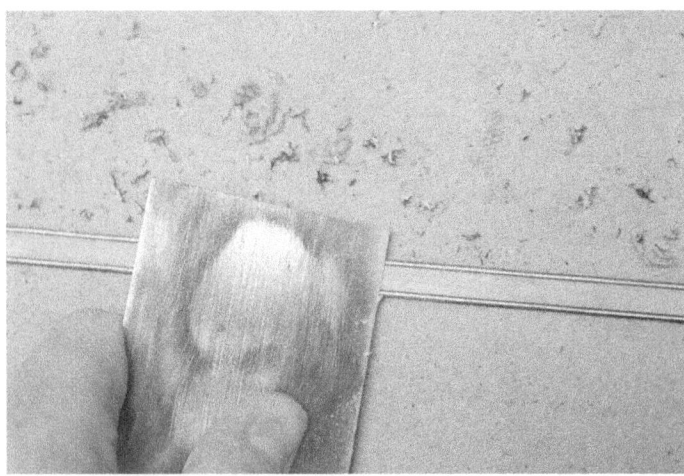

Photo 11-22 – After the glue is cured, a card scraper can be used to level everything and remove excess surface glue.

Photo 11-24 – The two back halves are trapped between two side stop pieces, which are clamped to the bench or to a large flat melamine board. There is a piece of wax paper under the joint.

8. Surface glue is removed and the sides of the back strip are squared up, using a simple sanding fixture consisting of a rectangular profile block of wood with 80-grit PSA sandpaper on the front surface. This is clamped to the bench or a piece of melamine board, and used to sand the sides of the strip, as shown in **photo 11-23**. Care is taken to not remove any of the thickness of the outside purfling lines when doing this.

☐ Inlaid Back Strip Option

With this option the back halves are first joined, then a channel is routed along the center seam, then the back strip is glued into the channel. The strip is then planed and scraped down to the level of the surface of the back.

There are many different schemes for joining the halves of a guitar plate. The one thing they all have in common is that just the smallest pressure on the joint is sufficient to close it. Because the sides of the back halves are parallel to each other, a simple clamping setup can be used to reliably join the halves. This can be done on a narrow bench, or a piece of melamine board approximately 24″ (609.6MM) wide and approximately 12″ (304.8MM) longer than the combined width of the back halves. In the accompanying photos I am doing this on the extension table of the table saw.

1. Joining the back halves. Two boards or pieces of MDF are cut approximately 24″ (609.6MM) long and approximately 6″ (152.4MM) wide. These will serve as side stops.

2. One of the side stops is clamped down to one end of the bench or the large melamine board. A sheet of wax paper at least 24″ (609.6MM) long is placed on the bench or board. One back half is placed outside surface up, on top of the wax paper

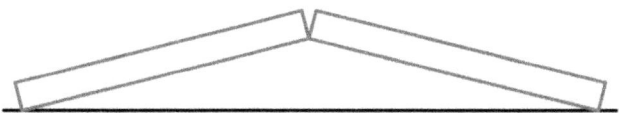

Figure 11-7 – *Because the space between the stops is smaller, the removed piece can no longer be dropped into place, but must be fitted by tenting the two halves, by raising them both where they meet.*

Photo 11-25 – *One of the halves is removed. A couple of thicknesses of masking tape are applied to the side of the side stop. This makes the distance between the stops smaller, and supplies clamping pressure for the joint.*

Photo 11-27 – *One of the halves is raised like a draw bridge, and glue it applied to the edge.*

Photo 11-26 – *This photo shows the tenting, but it is quite subtle.*

Photo 11-28 – *The half is lowered, both halves are tented, then the halves are pressed down to the underlying surface.*

so the side's outside edge is flat against the edge of the side stop. The other half is placed next, so its inside edge is flat against the inside edge of the first back half. The wax paper is repositioned if necessary so it is under the entire length of the inside edge joint.

3. The other side stop is positioned in contact with the outside edge of the second back half, and clamped into place. The entire setup is shown in **photo 11-24** on the table saw extension table. The joint should be closed all along its length, so that it is not possible to lift one of the halves without the other half coming up too. If the two halves do not contact along the entire length, lightly tapping the back side of one of the stops with a mallet will press things together.

4. One of the halves is lifted and temporarily removed. Two layers of masking tape are applied to the side of the side stop that was in contact with the outside edge of the removed back half (**photo 11-25**). This makes the distance between the two stops a few mils smaller, which will provide the clamping pressure when gluing the joint.

5. The removed half is replaced. In order for the two inside edges to meet now, both halves will have to be "tented" up in the middle (**figure 11-7**, **photo 11-26**). Then the halves are pressed flat down, to check that there is clamping pressure on

Photo 11-31 – *A construction level or other flat object is used to press down on the entire joint. The edges of the halves must be aligned over their entire length.*

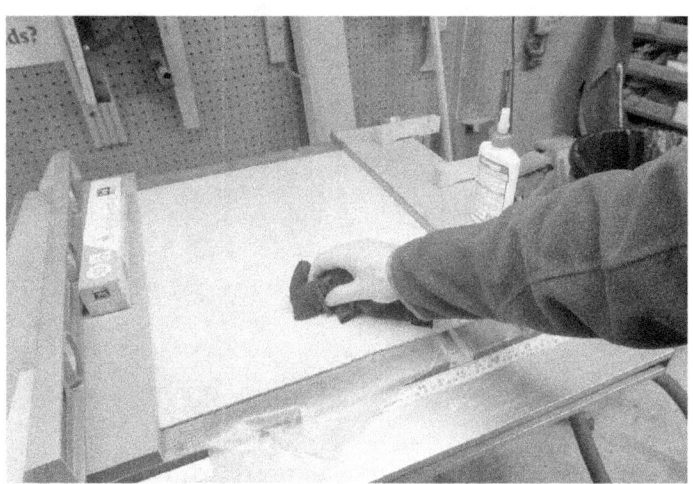

Photo 11-29 – *A rag is used to wipe glue squeeze-out from the joint, and to press both halves down to the bench surface.*

Photo 11-32 – *A weight is placed on top of the entire length of the seam. Here a long plane is used.*

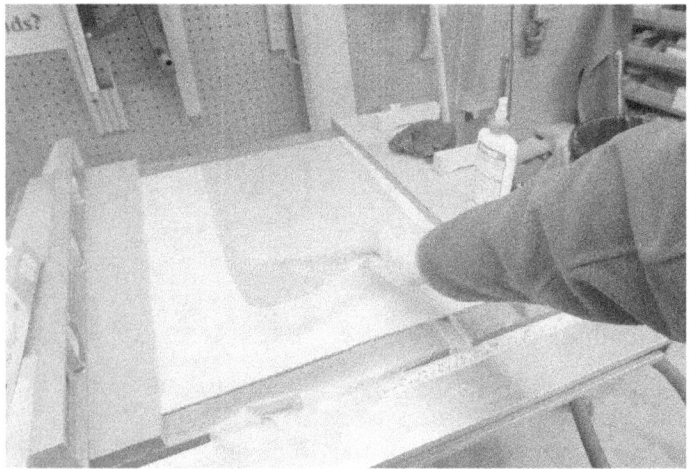

Photo 11-30 – *Wax paper is placed over the joint, to prevent glue from contacting anything placed on top.*

Photo 11-33 – *A fence is clamped down parallel to the seam and used to guide the router to route the channel for the inlaid back strip.*

the joint. If not, more masking tape will have to be applied to one or both of the stops.

6. The halves are tented up in the middle, then one of the halves is raised up like a draw bridge, so its inside edge is up. The thinnest continuous bead of glue that can be managed is run across the entire length of the edge, then smoothed down to completely cover the edge with glue (**photo 11-27**).

7. The half is lowered again, and the two halves are tented so their inside edges meet. Then both pieces are pressed completely flat to the bench or board underneath (**photo 11-28**). It is critical that neither half raises up higher than the other anywhere along the joint.

8. A rag is used to wipe excess glue from the joint area and to further press the entire joint area down in contact with the bench or board (**photo 11-29**). A sheet of wax paper is laid over the joint (**photo 11-30**).

9. A construction level or the straight side of a board is used to press the joint again, flat against the bench or board underneath (**photo 11-31**). Then the joint is weighted down to keep it in place while the glue cures. In **photo 11-32** I am using a #7 plane for this purpose, but any moderately heavy object or objects that will not mar the surface of the plate can be used.

10. The glue is allowed to cure at least one hour before releasing the back from the fixture. This is performed by unclamping one of the side stops, then removing the weight(s) and the wax paper, and then removing the joined back. Glue squeeze-out on both sides of the back is removed. This can be done quickly and cleanly using a card scraper.

11. Inlaying the back strip. The distance from the edge of the baseplate to the center of the collet of the router to be used is measured or taken from printed specifications. That distance is measured from the center seam on the outside surface of the back plate at both ends of the plate, and marked in pencil.

12. The back plate is clamped down to the end of the bench, with the side of a straight fence board aligned with the penciled marks made above, as shown in **photo 11-33**. One of the previously-used side stops can be repurposed as the fence board.

Photo 11-34 – *With the fence behind the router, the router is moved left to right. This presses the router against the fence.*

Photo 11-36 – *Glue is applied to the channel with a brush. It is important that the walls of the channel be completely covered with glue.*

Photo 11-35 – *If the strip doesn't fit the channel, the channel can be widened a few mils by putting a layer of tape on the fence then running the router by again.*

Photo 11-37 – *The strip is pressed into the channel by hand, and seated all along its length.*

Photo 11-38 – *After the glue is cured, the strip is leveled with the surface of the back. Here a card scraper is used.*

Photo 11-40 – *The mold is used to mark the outline of the back plate.*

Photo 11-39 – *A strip that is the same thickness as the back halves can be laminated between the back halves. The joining process just glues the strip in between the halves.*

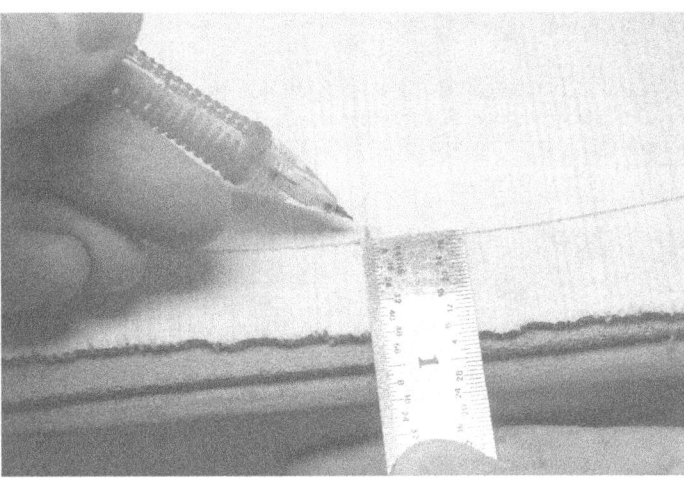

Photo 11-41 – *The distance from the edge of the plate to the outline, at both the neck end and the tail end, is measured then transferred to the other surface of the plate. These marks help to align the mold, so the plate outline can be traced onto the other surface.*

13. The router is fitted with a bit that is the same diameter as the width of the back strip to be inlaid. If the strip is thinner than the thickness of the back, the depth for the cut is set to the thickness of the strip. Otherwise the depth is set to $1/16''$ (1.6mm), which is $2/3$ the thickness of the back plate. The cut is checked at both ends of the plate, to be sure it will be *exactly* centered over the center seam, over the entire length of the seam.

14. With the fence behind the router as shown in **photos 11-33** and **11-34**, the cut is made by moving the router left to right, while keeping the side of the baseplate against the fence.

15. The fit of the inlay in the channel is checked. It should be easy to insert and to remove. A really snug fit must be avoided because the wood will swell when glue is applied and this may make it impossible to insert the strip. If the test fit is tight, the strip can be gently thinned using the edge sanding fixture as shown in **photo 11-23**. When doing this, care must be taken to avoid excessive thinning of any purfling lines on the outside edges of the strip. If this is an issue, the channel can be widened slightly instead, by applying one thickness of thin tape along the front surface of the fence (**photo 11-35**), then running the router across again.

16. Glue is applied to the channel with a brush (**photo 11-36**). Care is taken to be sure there is glue on the walls of the channel along its entire length.

17. The strip is pressed into the channel and seated well (**photo 11-37**). Excess glue is wiped off with a rag. Wax paper and weights are applied to the joint while the glue cures. The glue should be allowed to cure for at least two hours.

18. If the top surface of the strip is above the surface of the back, it is planed down to near the surface of the back, using a small plane. A block plane or smaller flat bottom plane is ideal for this. Planing should stop once the plane sole gets near to the surface of the back, to avoid gouging the back.

19. A card scraper is used to scrape the top of the strip flush to the top surface of the back, and to remove any remaining glue from the surface (**photo 11-38**).

☐ Laminated Back Strip Option

If the back strip is the same thickness (or can be made the same thickness) as the back plate halves, then the strip can be laminated between the back halves. The process of doing this is just a slight modification of that used to join the back halves, outlined in the section about that operation. The only difference is that the strip is sandwiched between the halves (**photo 11-39**). This means glue must be applied to the edges of *both* halves of the back.

After the glue has cured, both surfaces of the back must be scraped clean and flush.

☐ Cleaning Up and Cutting the Outline

1. Both surfaces of the back are checked to be sure they are smooth. A sanding block with 100-grit sandpaper can be used with the grain, to smooth any rough places. Note that as components are added to the inside surface, it will become increasingly difficult to smooth that surface, so it should be brought to the desired level of smoothness at this time.

The level of smoothness of the interior surfaces of the guitar has no perceivable effect on the tone of the finished instrument. Every luthier smooths the interior surfaces to whatever level he or she feels is appropriate.

2. If the pencil marks indicating which is the outside surface have been eradicated by any of the previous steps, they are refreshed now.

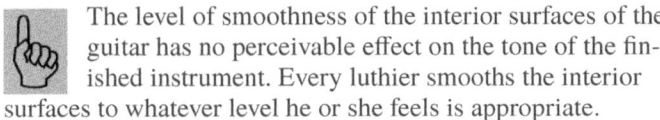

Figure 11-8 – *Schematic end view of back plate center seam, showing inlaid back strip, and the crescent-shaped cross section of the back reinforcement strip.*

3. The back is placed on the bench, outside surface up. A centerline is drawn in pencil down the center of the plate, which at this point is defined as the center of the back strip. The centerline should be continued onto the edge of the plate at both the neck and tail ends. Then the centerline should be continued onto the *inside* surface of the plate as well. The plate is again placed on the bench outside surface up.

4. Any debris on the back plate is carefully removed. The floor is removed from the mold, and the mold is carefully placed on top of the back plate. The seams at the ends of the mold are aligned with the back plate centerline. While keeping the mold seams aligned with the back plate centerline, the mold is moved to identify the best looking outline for the plate. Neither end of the inside of the mold should be closer than ½″ (12.7mm) to either end of the plate. When a satisfactory location is achieved, the inside of the mold is traced onto the back plate in pencil (**photo 11-40**).

5. It is useful to also draw the outline on the inside surface of the back plate. To do this, the distance from the neck end of the plate at the centerline down to the outline is measured (**photo 11-41**). That distance is transferred to the inside surface of the plate, and marked in pencil. Then, the distance from the tail end of the plate at the centerline down to the outline is measured, and that distance is also transferred to the inside surface and marked. The plate is placed on the bench inside surface up. The mold is placed on top of the plate, aligned with the plate centerline, and slid down until the two marks just made are just visible at the inside of the mold. The inside of the mold is traced onto the inside surface of the back plate in pencil.

6. The outline is cut out using the bandsaw, with the outside surface up. A generous ½″ (12.7mm) margin or more should be left around the outline. Because this plate is tilted a bit, due to the taper of the back and also because it will be arched, its actual dimensions will need to be slightly larger than the outline.

It is a wise idea to retain the two wide cutoff pieces from outside the upper bouts and waist. These may be of use for subsequent construction steps.

Photo 11-42 – *Strips of spruce are cross cut off a spare spruce guitar top half. These will be used to assemble the back reinforcement strip.*

Photo 11-43 – *The materials needed to glue down the back reinforcement strip include, masking tape, the pieces of the strip, two straight boards, and a long clamping caul.*

The Back Reinforcement Strip

The back reinforcement strip is a cross grain strip that reinforces the center seam and back strip of the back plate. It is usually made of spruce. It is cut and glued down as a number of pieces with rectangular cross sections, then it is sanded to a crescent cross section as shown in **figure 11-8**.

☐ Making and Installing the Reinforcement Strip

The strip is most easily made from pieces cut from one half of an inexpensive spruce guitar top blank. These generally come planed to a thickness of approximately 0.125″ (3.2mm), which is ideal for the reinforcement.

1. The width of the reinforcement is determined by adding ¼″ (6.4mm) to ½″ (12.7mm) to the total width of the back strip. The back strip in the photos is approximately ⅜″ (9.5mm) wide, including the purfling lines. Adding ½″ (12.7mm) to that yields a back reinforcement strip width of ⅞″ (22.2mm). Note that the back reinforcement strip should not be made any wider than 1″ (25.4mm). Doing so may make it difficult to bend the back into an arch.

2. The long sides of one half of an inexpensive guitar top set are ripped straight and parallel to each other. The ends of the plate half are cut square to the long sides. This piece will be used to make various braces and patches.

3. A few strips, of the width calculated in step 1 above, are cross cut off the plate half (**photo 11-42**). When placed end to end, the total length of the strips should exceed the length of the back plate. The remainder of this top half is put aside for use when the top is constructed.

4. The materials needed to glue down the reinforcing strip are gathered together. These are shown in **photo 11-43**. There are two boards with straight edges, each at least as long as the back; an MDF clamping caul strip that is a bit narrower than the reinforcing strip; and some masking tape.

5. The distance from the neck end of the guitar body to the inside surface of the neck block is measured on the garland (**figure 11-9**). This distance is transferred to the neck end of the inside surface of the back, and a pencil mark is made. The mark indicates the starting point of the back reinforcement strip. Note that for both of the example instruments, this distance is ²⁷⁄₃₂″ (21.4mm), assuming the rib thickness and neck block thickness are as specified in the plans.

6. One half the width of the reinforcing strip is measured from the centerline on the inside surface of the back, and marked in pencil at both ends of the plate (**photo 11-44**).

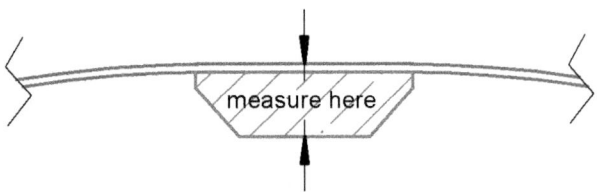

Figure 11-9 – *The measurement from the neck end of the garland down to the inside surface of the neck block is taken and transferred to the inside of the back. This indicates where the back reinforcement strip will start.*

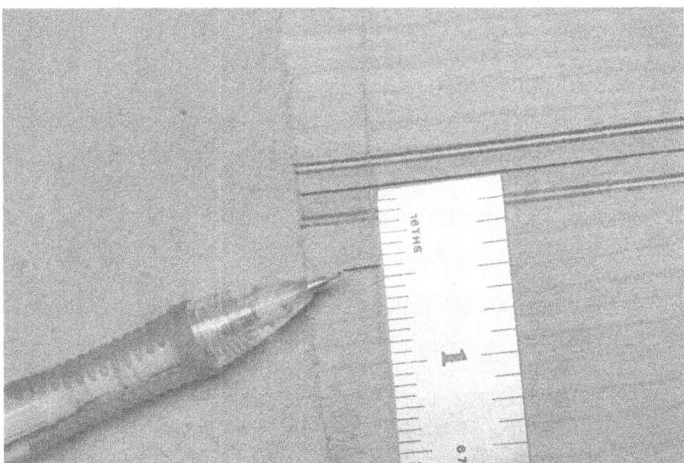

Photo 11-44 – *The location of one side of the back reinforcement strip is marked on the inside surface at both ends of the back plate.*

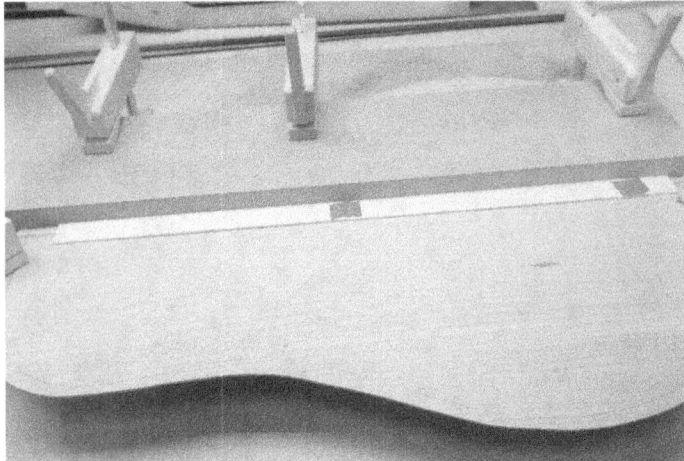

Photo 11-45 – *A fence board is clamped down where the side of the reinforcement strip will go. The pieces of the strip are taped together and pressed against the fence for gluing.*

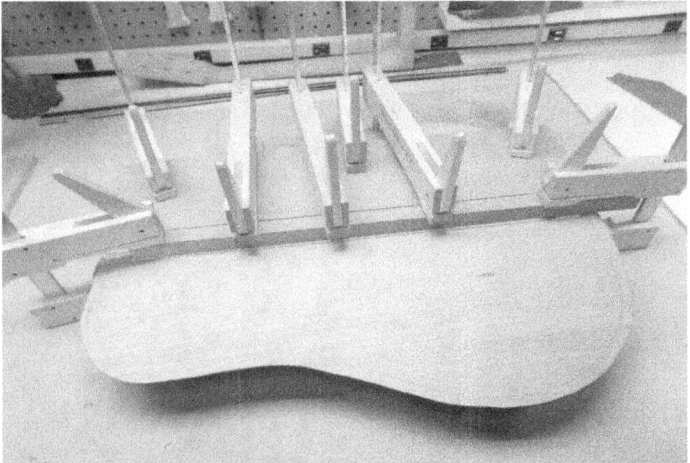

Photo 11-46 – *A long clamping caul is placed on top of the strip and clamped down while the glue cures.*

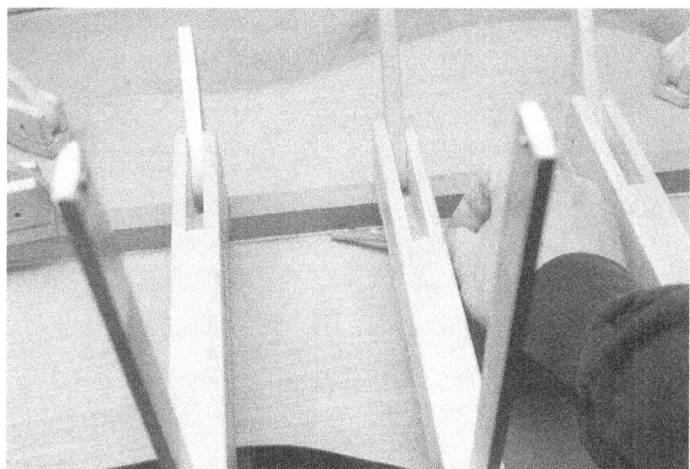

Photo 11-47 – Glue squeeze-out is removed between the back plate and the back reinforcement strip, using the snipped plastic straw.

Photo 11-48 – The back reinforcement strip after gluing.

end aligns with the start mark. The caul is placed on top of the reinforcement strip and clamps are used to clamp it in place (**photo 11-46**). Note in the photo that long clamps are used, placed on the fence side. Doing so pulls the reinforcing strip into contact with the fence. If the reinforcement pieces are not right up against the fence, a small block of wood and a mallet can be used to tap the pieces into place against the fence.

Photo 11-49 – A special sanding block is fashioned to sand the strip to a crescent-shaped cross section. A cylindrical channel is sanded into the center of a wood block using a thick dowel wrapped in coarse grit PSA sandpaper.

Photo 11-50 – The channel of the special sanding block is lined with 80-grit PSA sandpaper.

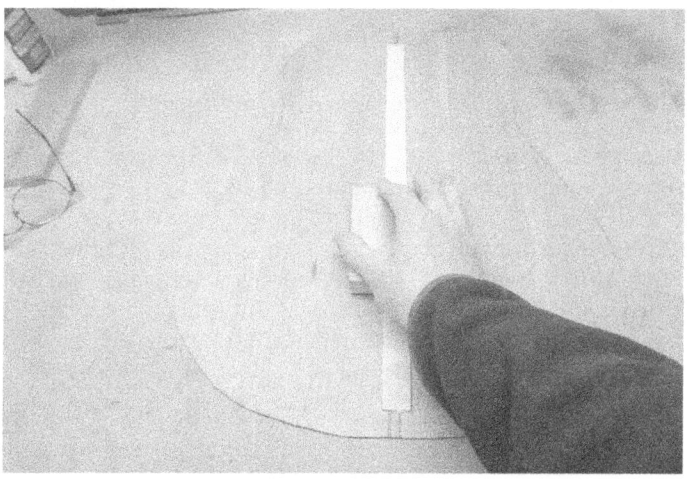

Photo 11-51 – The special sanding block is used to round over the back reinforcement strip.

7. One of the two boards is placed on the bench and the back is placed on top of it, inside surface up. This board will be used to back up clamping, to keep the back plate flat, so it goes under the middle of the plate. Note that the mold insert can alternatively be used to back up the plate for gluing. The other board is placed on top, with its straight edge aligned with the two marks made in the step above. The bottom board is oriented to be directly under the top board, and the boards are clamped in place (**photo 11- 45**).

The edge of the top board will serve as a fence, to locate the back reinforcing strip directly on the centerline of the back. The neck end piece is aligned with the start mark made in step 5 above and pressed against the fence. As each piece is placed down, it is taped to the previous piece with a small length of masking tape. The last piece should end at the tail end of the body outline. If it is too long, it may be snapped off at the appropriate length. Although the neck block end of the reinforcement will be accurately positioned now, the tail block end will be trimmed to fit perfectly in a later operation.

8. The entire length of reinforcing strip is flipped over, and glue is applied to the underside of the strip. The strip is flipped back over, pressed into contact with the fence, and moved so its neck

Photo 11-52 – *Close up of the back reinforcement strip at the neck end.*

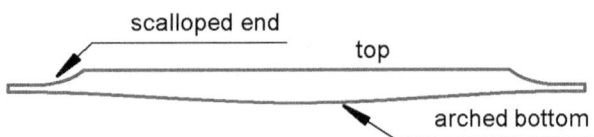

Figure 11-10 – *The features of the back brace.*

Figure 11-11 – *When finally carved to shape, the tops of the back braces can be shaped to (left to right) a rectangular shape, a rounded shape, or a pointed cathedral arched shape. Note the orientation of the grain.*

9. The fence piece is now unclamped and removed, and cleaned of any glue squeeze-out, so the board can be used again for another purpose.

 If the fence is not removed now, it will get glued to the side of the back reinforcement strip. This will make it quite difficult to remove later.

The snipped plastic straw is used to clear glue from around the reinforcing strip (**photo 11-47**). The glue is allowed at least one hour to cure, before clamps are removed (**photo 11-48**). The caul may get slightly glued to the top of the strip by a little glue squeeze-out. It can be tapped with a mallet to free it if necessary.

10. A sanding block approximately 4″ (101.6mm) square is fashioned, for use in sanding the reinforcing strip to a crescent shaped profile. The block has a cylindrical concave channel running down its length, which is as wide and as deep as the reinforcing strip (**photo 11-49**). The channel is marked out on both ends, and cut with a large diameter dowel covered in coarse grit PSA sandpaper. A spindle sander, sanding drum, or gouges can also be used to shape the channel. The channel is lined with 80-grit PSA sandpaper for use in sanding the profile of the reinforcing strip (**photo 11-50**).

11. The channel is aligned with the reinforcing strip, and the block is rubbed back and forth to profile the strip (**photo 11-51**). After the strip is profiled, it is sanded freehand using 100-grit sandpaper. Care is taken to be sure the thickness of the sides of the strip taper down to near nothing. The finished back reinforcing strip is shown in **photo 11-52**.

12. Any glue that may have hardened on the plate on either side of the strip is cleaned up, with some 80-grit sandpaper on a flat block, followed by 100-grit sandpaper. Any glue squeeze-out at the neck block end of the back reinforcement strip is cleaned up carefully with a chisel. This end will butt squarely against the neck block in the finished instrument.

The Back Braces

The blanks for the back braces will be ripped from a plank of quartersawn spruce that has been planed to thickness. Some

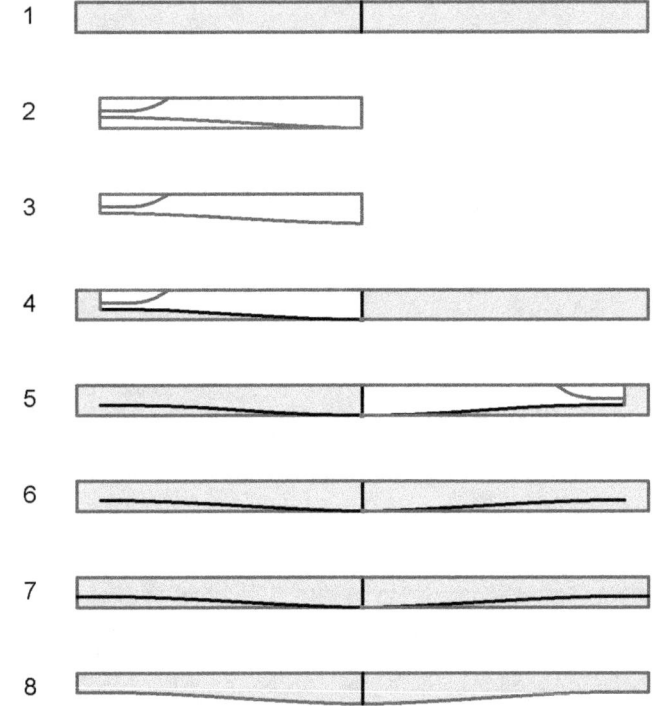

Figure 11-12 – *The stages of shaping the back braces in preparation for gluing them to the back plate. 1. The brace blank is cut over long, and its center is marked. 2. The half template for the brace is cut out to the brace blank outline. 3. The brace bottom of the template is cut. 4. The template is aligned with the brace at the centerline and top edge, and the bottom arching is traced onto the brace on one side. 5. The tracing of the bottom arching is repeated on the other end of the brace center. 6. The marked arching. 7. The ends of the arching lines are extended to the ends of the over-long brace. 8. The bottom of the brace is cut and sanded to the line.*

Brace#	Tripletta OM	Paura Dreadnought
B1	12″ (304.8mm)	12⅜″ (314.3mm)
B2	10½″ (266.7mm)	11¾″ (298.5mm)
B3	15″ (381mm)	15½″ (393.7mm)
B4	15¼″ (387.4mm)	16⅛″ (409.6mm)

Table 11-1 – *Over long lengths for the back braces of the example instruments.*

Photo 11-53 – *Four back brace blanks are ripped from the planed brace material board.*

Photo 11-54 – *After each brace blank is trimmed to over long length, the transverse centerline of each is measured and marked.*

Photo 11-55 – *The half back template for each brace is used to mark the arching curve for the brace bottom.*

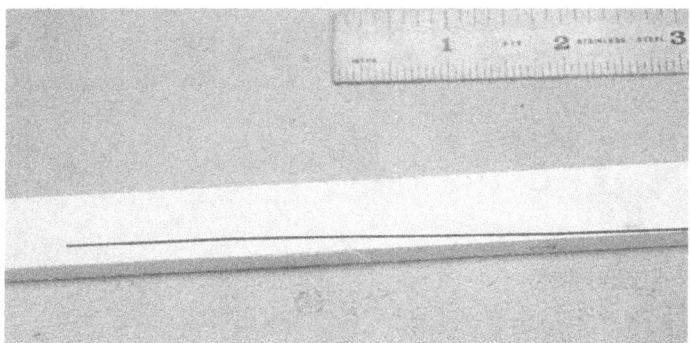

Photo 11-56 – *The arching curve marked on half of the brace.*

luthiers will split brace blanks off the plank rather than rip them. Depending on the state of the grain of the plank, this may result in brace blanks with straighter grain, and this in turn will make the braces easier to carve with edge tools. But bracewood planks from lutherie wood suppliers are generally sawn from split billets, so the grain is usually quite straight. Also, in the context of the construction process described in this book, there will be only minor carving operations, so this is not really an issue. Ripping the brace blanks rather than splitting them off eliminates the need to plane each blank to rectangular cross section individually.

After the blanks for the braces are made, they are cut to length a bit over long, and then the arching of the brace bottoms is transferred to the braces from the brace templates for the instrument under construction. Refer to **figure 11-10** for the descriptive terms for the parts of the brace. The brace bottoms are arched, and then the braces are glued to the back plate. Finally, the ends and tops of the braces are carved and sanded to final shape.

The brace ends are carved down in a distinctive curved ramp shape called a *scallop*. This is done so the ends of the braces can be poked into pockets cut in the linings before the plate is glued to the garland. The top surfaces of the back braces can be left in more or less rectangular cross section, with the edges rounded over a bit, or they can be rounded over, or carved to a pointed cathedral arch shape (**figure 11-11**). Removing material from the braces, especially from around the top surface, makes them less strong and less stiff, and also makes them a bit less massive. There are really no structural issues associated with the brace top shape. All shapes will result in braces stiff enough and strong enough for their purpose. Although changing stiffness and mass of back braces can produce measurable changes in the frequency response of a guitar, it is not at all clear if such changes result in any audible effect, and if they do, if those audible effects are desirable or not. That being the case, lutherie novices can shape the brace tops as desired for purely aesthetic reasons.

☐ **Initial Shaping of the Back Braces**

The step-by-step process for shaping each brace prior to gluing it down is shown schematically in **figure 11-12**.

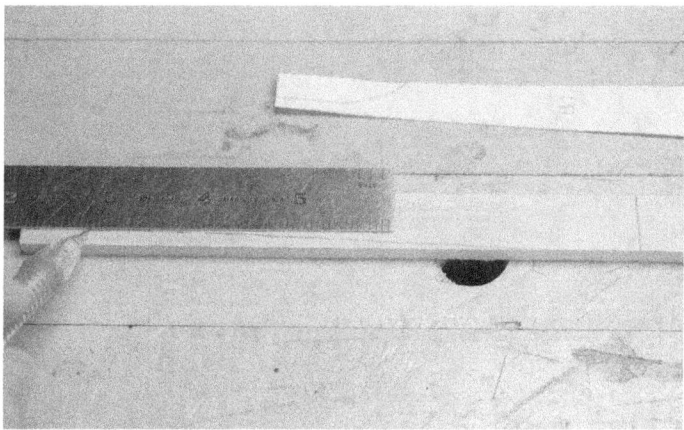

Photo 11-57 – *The ends of the arching curves are extended to the ends of the brace blanks, using a straightedge.*

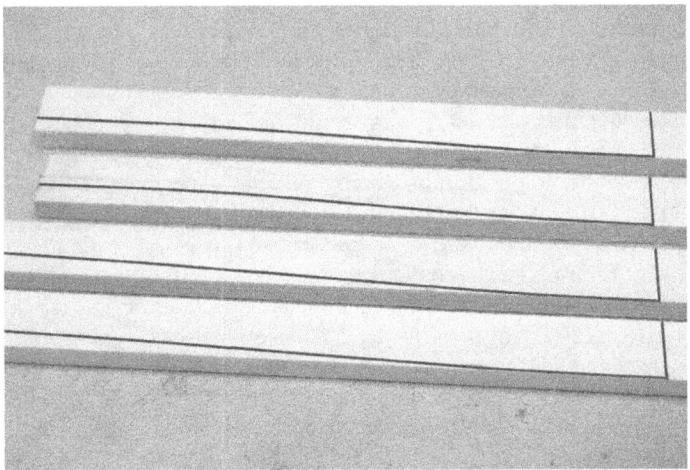

Photo 11-58 – Arching curves marked on each of the brace blanks.

Photo 11-59 – The brace bottoms are readily shaped to the arching lines using a spindle sander, or drill press-mounted sanding drum.

Brace#	Location
B1	3 5/16″ (84.1mm)
B2	7 5/16″ (185.7mm)
B3	11 11/32″ (288.1mm)
B4	15 19/32″ (396.1mm)

Table 11-2 – Location of each back brace for the example instruments, as the distance from the neck end of the body outline at the centerline, down to the side of the brace that is closest to the neck end.

1. The board of quartersawn spruce bracing material is prepared for use. If the edge of the board is not parallel to the grain, a new edge is sawn that *is* parallel to the grain. The board is planed smooth on both surfaces, to a thickness of 5/8″ (15.9mm). A planer or thickness sander can be used for this task.

2. Four pieces, each 1/4″ (6.4mm) wide are ripped from the board of bracing material (**photo 11-53**). These are the blanks for the four back braces. The board of bracewood is retained. It will be used for the braces of the top plate as well.

3. The brace blanks are cut to the lengths indicated in the plan, but over long. That is, approximately 1″ (25.4mm) is added to the length of each back brace in the plan, and the brace blanks are cut to those lengths. The over-long lengths for the braces of the example instruments are given in **table 11-1**. It is wise to mark each brace blank with its number as it is cut.

4. The measured centers of each of the brace blanks are marked in pencil (**figure 11-12.1, photo 11-54**).

5. The back brace half templates are cut out of the templates page for the instrument under construction. The templates are cut out on their rectangular brace blank lines (**figure 11-12.2**).

6. The arched bottoms of the back brace half templates are trimmed to the lines. The resulting template shape is shown in **figure 11-12.3**.

7. For each brace, the half template is used to mark the curve of the arched bottom on the brace blank. The half template is positioned against the center line of the brace blank and also against the top edge of the brace blank, and then the bottom arching is traced for one side of the brace (**figure 11-12.4, photos 11-55, 11-56**). The template is flipped over to the other end of the blank, and the arching for the other end is traced (**figure 11-12.5**). The templates are retained for later brace-shaping steps.

8. Because the brace blanks are over long, the ends of the bottom arching curves will not extend all the way the ends of the blanks. A straightedge is used to extend these curves straight to

Photo 11-60 – Marking the locations of the back braces.

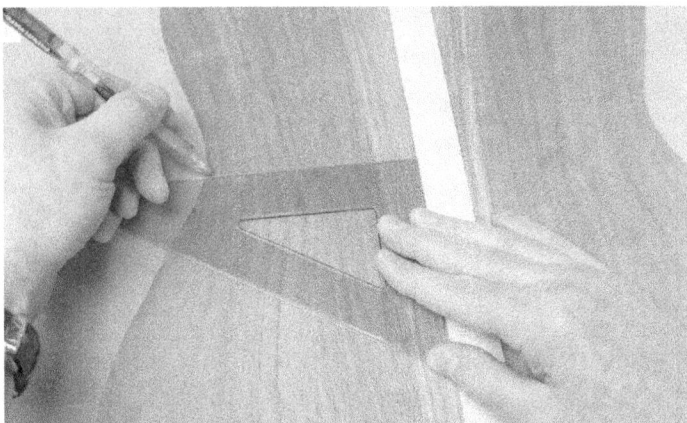

Photo 11-61 – A drafting square is used to transfer the location of a brace to the back plate, where the brace end will be.

the ends of the blanks (**figures 11-12.6, 11-12.7**; **photos 11-57, 11-58**).

9. The bottom of each brace is trimmed to the marked lines (**figure 11-12.8, photo 11-59**). Excess material can be removed using a number of tools. Probably the easiest way to do this is to saw off as much of the waste as is possible, and then use either the spindle sander or the drill press-mounted drum sander to trim the brace bottoms exactly to the lines. Note that if hand tools such as chisels or curved-sole spokeshaves are used, it is a good idea to mark the bottom arching on both sides of the brace blanks.

□ **Installing the Back Braces**

The process of installing the braces is straightforward. The location of each of the braces is marked on the inside of the back plate. Then a slot is cut in the back reinforcement strip for each brace. Finally, each brace is glued and clamped in place.

1. Marking the locations of the back braces. The location of each brace is indicated as a distance from the neck end of the body outline at the centerline, down to the side of the brace closest to the neck. These distances can be measured on the plan for the instrument under construction. For the example instruments, these distances are provided in **table 11-2**. Note that the neck end of the body outline at the centerline will be the reference point from which most braces will be located throughout this book.

An easy way to mark the brace locations is to place a long ruler against the back reinforcement strip with the zero end of the ruler at the neck end of the body outline. The locations of the braces can be marked on the back reinforcement strip in pencil (**photo 11-60**).

2. Those location marks must also be transferred to where the ends of the braces will fall as well. A drafting square against the back reinforcement strip at each mark made in the previous step, can be used to place these marks, as in **photo 11-61**. Another excellent tool for this job is the carpenter's framing square. Note that the brace end marks are made *outside* the body outline, and both to the left and to the right of the center of the plate.

3. The back reinforcement strip is cut through at each of the marks. A small rectangular block of wood, in contact with one side of the strip, is used as a fence to guide the cut. A Japanese

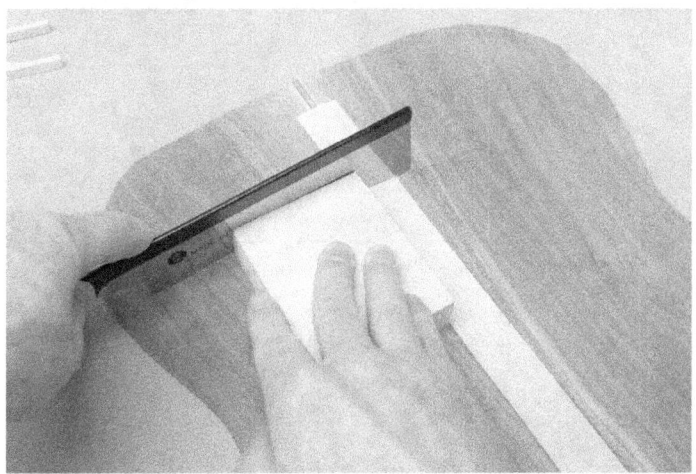

Photo 11-62 – Sawing through the back reinforcement strip, using a razor saw and a rectangular fence block.

Photo 11-64 – Chiseling out the channel in the back reinforcement strip for one of the back braces.

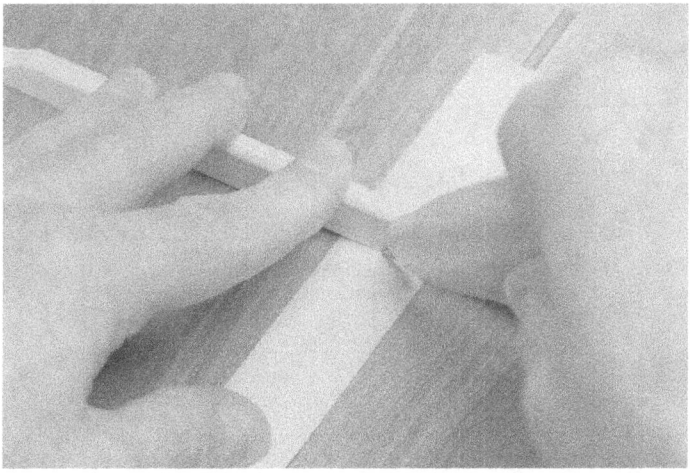

Photo 11-63 – Marking the other side of the channel, using a knife.

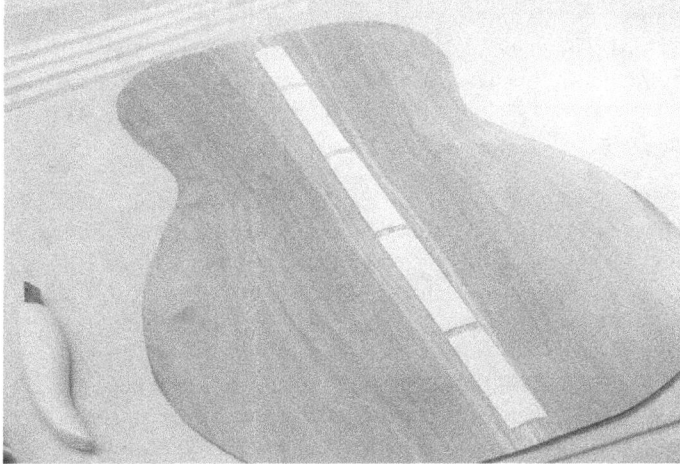

Photo 11-65 – Channels cut through the back reinforcement strip for each of the back braces.

Photo 11-66 – *The back braces are clamped down one end at a time, starting near the center of the brace.*

Photo 11-68 – *Back brace B1 fully clamped for gluing. Two long clamps are needed to reach the center of the brace.*

Photo 11-67 – *The clamps are arranged herringbone fashion along the end of the brace, to provide space for them all.*

Photo 11-69 – *Eight clamps are used when gluing down the longer back braces.*

razor saw with a blade with a curved tip is a good tool to use to make the cut (**photo 11-62**). Care is taken to not cut into the back plate.

4. The location to make the cut for the other side of each brace channel is marked by holding the brace against the first cut and making a mark on the reinforcement strip using a knife (**photo 11-63**). The fence block and razor saw are used to make this cut at the mark. It is desirable that the braces fit snugly in these channels, so it is generally a good idea if they are sawn a bit narrow.

5. The waste material is chiseled out using a ¼″ (6.4MM) chisel (**photos 11-64, 11-65**) and the brace is test fitted into the channel. The piece that is chiseled out is saved temporarily. If the brace won't fit, the channel can be widened a bit by carefully chiseling one or both of its sides. Snugness of fit here is a matter of artisanship and lutherie aesthetics. There will be no structural issue if the braces don't fit snugly, but it does look better when viewed through the soundhole of the finished instrument. Note relative to that, that only the joints at the tail side of the first brace and the neck side of the second brace are visible through the soundhole of a finished instrument.

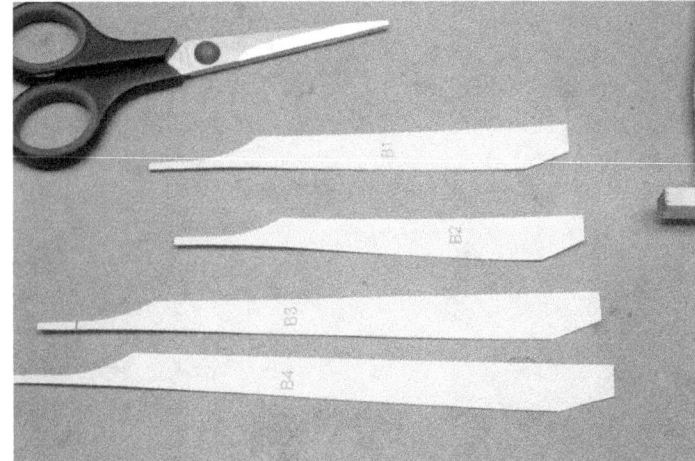

Photo 11-70 – *The back brace half templates are cut on the end scallop marks, and the inside bottom corners are cut off, to clear the back reinforcement strip.*

 If the channel is too wide for a snug fit of the brace, a small slice can be cut from the waste piece that was chiseled out of the channel, and then glued in. The glue

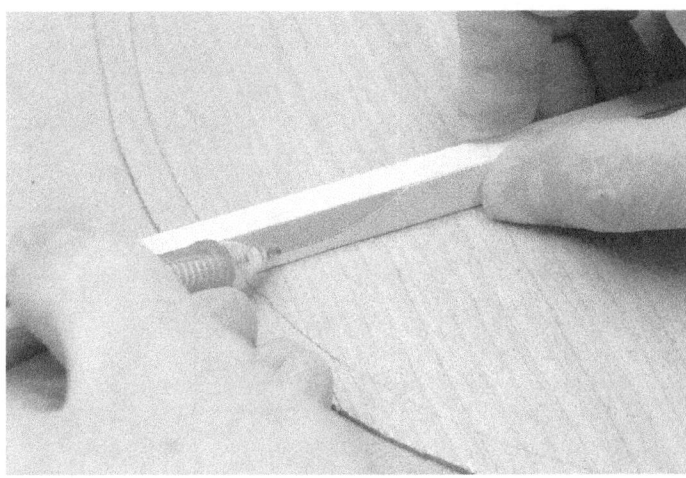

Photo 11-71 – *The curve of the scalloping at the end of each brace is traced onto both ends.*

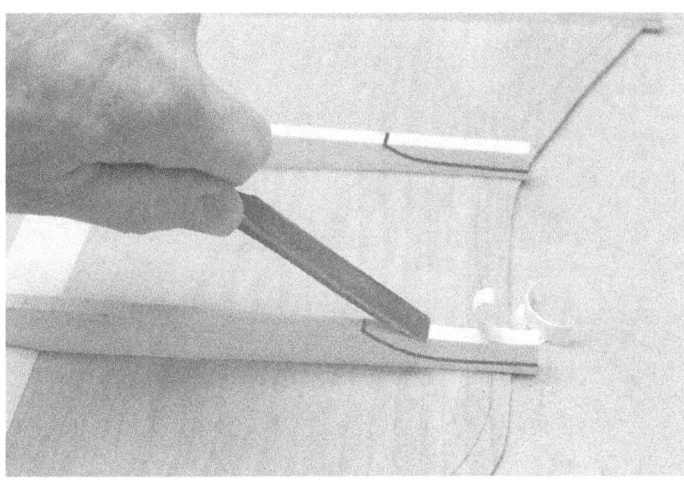

Photo 11-73 – *The brace ends are carved down to the lines.*

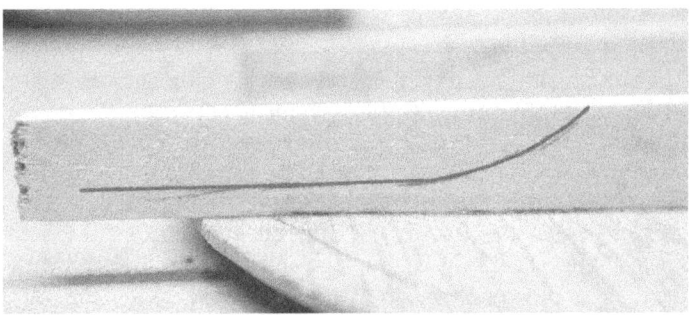

Photo 11-72 – *The end of the curve is extended parallel to the inside surface of the plate to past the edge of the plate.*

should be allowed time to cure before additional fitting work is attempted.

6. The braces are glued down and allowed to cure one at a time. As with most gluing operations requiring multiple clamps, it is always a good idea to do a dry run before committing to glue. Glue is applied evenly to the bottom of the brace, and the brace is fitted into its channel on the back reinforcement strip, with the brace centerline aligned with the center of the reinforcement strip. A single long clamp is used to lightly clamp near the middle of the brace (**photo 11-66**).

7. At one end of the brace, the side of the brace nearest the neck end of the plate is aligned with the penciled end mark. The brace is held in position while the next clamp is placed. The clamp is placed a bit down the length of the brace from the first clamp, and approaching the brace from the other side. The clamp is lightly clamped down. A third clamp is added, again approaching from the other side from the previous clamp. This alternating side-of-approach of the clamps gives the clamps the appearance of a herringbone pattern (**photo 11-67**). This is done because cam clamps tend to pull the work toward the clamp, and this pattern balances out that pulling. As the clamps are applied, the plate will bend to the arching of the brace.

Clamps are applied to the other end of the brace, starting near the center and moving out toward the end of the brace, in the same manner as the first end was done. The shorter braces each get six evenly-spaced clamps (**photo 11-68**). The longer braces get eight clamps (**photo 11-69**). Long clamps are used when needed near the center of the brace. Shorter clamps are used where they will reach.

Care should be taken to be sure the bottom of the brace is in contact with the plate along its full length. Clamps may have to be rearranged to make this happen. The clamps are tightened

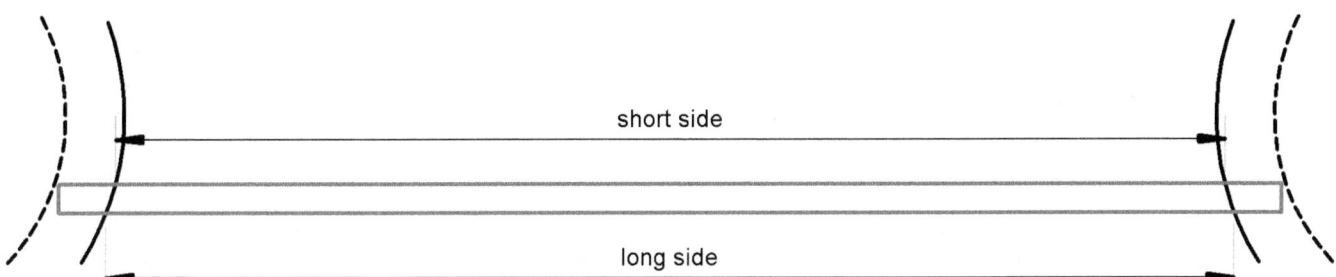

Figure 11-13 – *Because the outline of the plate is never perpendicular to the sides of the braces, the distance between where the brace crosses the outline at one end to where it crosses the outline at the other end of the brace is different for each side of the brace. When positioning the template to mark for the scallop at the end of the brace, the end of the template should be aligned with the outline on the short side of the brace.*

Photo 11-74 – The brace end scalloping is cleaned up and smoothed, using sandpaper on a round profile block.

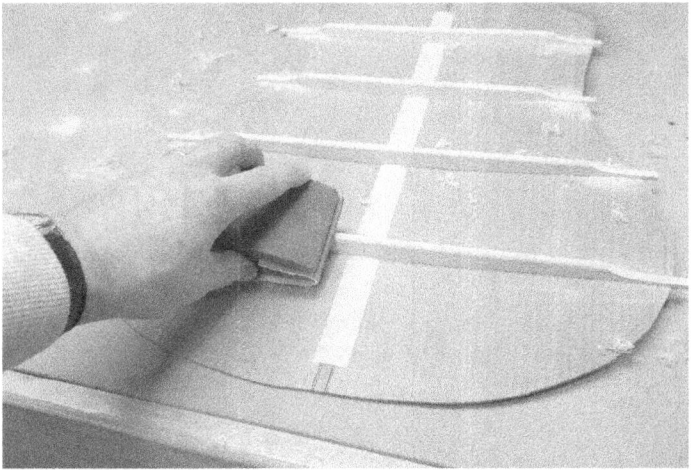

Photo 11-76 – Sandpaper on a flat block is used to clean up and smooth any shaping of the brace tops.

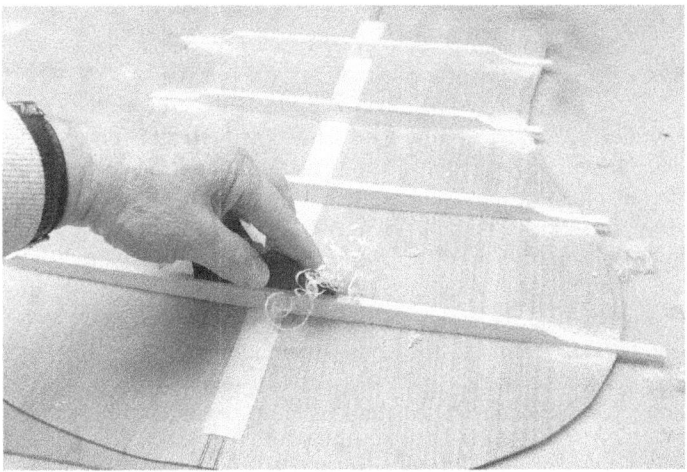

Photo 11-75 – The tops of the braces can be left flat, rounded over, or shaped to a cathedral arch, using a small plane.

only enough to maintain good contact between brace and plate. Too much clamping pressure will distort the brace.

The snipped plastic straw is used to clear glue squeeze-out from between brace and plate on both sides of the brace.

8. The glue is allowed at least two hours to cure, before removing the clamps.

9. The steps above are repeated for each of the four back braces.

□ **Final Shaping of the Back Braces**

The brace ends are scalloped, and then the tops of the braces are shaped as desired.

1. The scalloped ends of the back brace half templates are trimmed to the scallop lines, using scissors or a knife (**photo 11- 70**). Because the braces are now glued to the back plate, the corner of each template between the centerline end and the bottom must be cut off, so the template can clear the back reinforcement strip.

2. The templates are used to mark the scalloping onto the sides of the braces (**photo 11-71**). The template end is aligned with the plate outline for marking. Note that because the outline crosses the end of the brace at an angle, the distance along the brace from where it crosses the outline on one end to where it crosses on the other end will be different on each side of the brace (**figure 11-13**). The template end should be aligned with the plate outline on the *shorter* side of the brace. Then the scallop is marked.

3. A straightedge is used to extend the end of the scallop mark, parallel to the inside surface of the plate, and past the end of the plate (**photo 11-72**). This line should be ⅛″ (3.2MM) above the inside surface of the plate.

4. The brace ends are pared down to the marks (**photo 11-73**). A sharp chisel can be used bevel side down to do this work. The knife or a small hand-held sanding drum can be used as well.

5. Sandpaper on a round form is used to finish shaping and smoothing the surfaces of the scallops (**photo 11-74**). The brace ends should end up ⅛″ (3.2MM) thick from inside the body outline to the end of the brace.

6. The tops of the braces are shaped as desired. If the tops are left flat, the top edges are lightly rounded over. If the brace tops are to be completely rounded over or shaped to a cathedral arch, a small plane, such as a #100, can be used to do the shaping (**photo 11- 75**). Once the desired shaping is accomplished, the braces are sanded with 100-grit sandpaper, to smooth all surfaces and to remove any remaining pencil marks (**photo 11-76**).

7. The entire back is checked over for flaws, and is cleaned up and sanded to 100-grit wherever needed. The back is put aside in a safe place for a later assembly operation.

12 The Top Plate and Its Rosette

The top plate of the acoustic guitar is fundamentally similar in construction to the back plate. It is made of two thin bookmatched pieces, joined together at the center. But the top plate is almost always made of a softwood species. Like the back, the top plate is also stiffened with the addition of braces, but the typical bracing pattern of modern steel string acoustic guitar tops is more complex than the simple ladder bracing typically used for the back (**photo 12-1**). As such, bracing of the top is covered in its own chapter. Like the back plate, the top plate is generally arched, but the arching for the top is more subtle, and this arching generally does not extend above the soundhole. The soundhole is typically round, and this is usually surrounded by some sort of decoration called the soundhole *rosette* (**photo 12-2**).

The top is the most important acoustic component of the guitar. The vibrating strings drive the bridge, which in turn drives the top, which directly drives the air to produce sound. The other parts of the instrument vibrate too, and everything contributes to the sound, but the top's contribution is much more pronounced that those of the other components. For this reason the top must be constructed to be light enough to readily vibrate. But because the strings are pulling on the top via the bridge, the top must also be stiff enough so it doesn't deform so much from the effects of string tension that the instrument is made unplayable. The two desirable qualities of lightness and stiffness are generally at odds, and the construction of the guitar top has evolved to adequately provide both of these qualities. The materials used for the top, and the configuration of the plate and braces, make for a plate which is light enough to readily vibrate and stiff enough to counteract the destructive effects of string tension.

Wood Selection

As mentioned, guitar tops are almost always made of softwoods, which are generally lighter in weight than hardwoods. Historically the most commonly used wood for guitar tops has been spruce (*Picea* spp.). The species of spruce used depended on where in the world the guitar was made. European made instruments usually used *Picea abies*, commonly called European spruce, German spruce, or Norway spruce. Guitars built in the USA generally made use of local spruces such as red spruce (*P. rubens*), Sitka spruce (*P. sitchensis*), and Engelmann spruce (*P.*

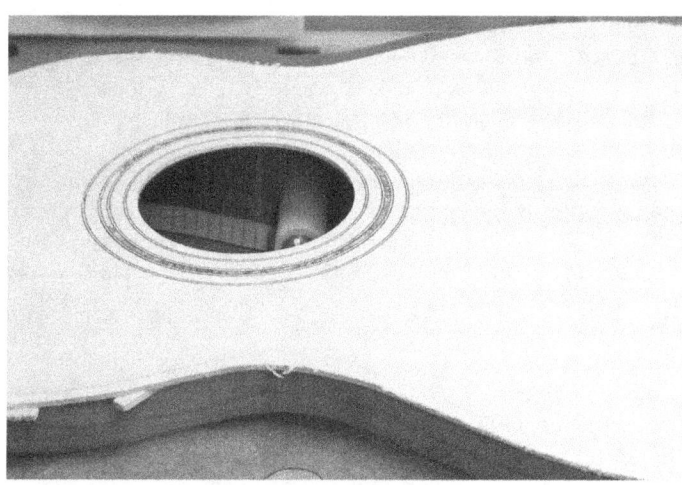

Photo 12-1 – *Typical bracing of the top of a modern steel string guitar is more complex than the simple ladder bracing typically used for the back plate.*

Photo 12-2 – *The soundhole of most acoustic steel string guitars is decorated with a rosette. The typical configuration consists of three concentric rings, with the center ring being wider than the other two. The center ring pictured has an inlay of abalone shell.*

engelmannii). All of these species are commonly used for guitar tops today. Red spruce, which grows in the eastern part of the USA, was used for a long time by C.F. Martin. Martin's strong influence on steel string guitar making in this country is evidenced by continued use of this species by a number of guitar makers, even though supplies of quality top sets are greatly diminished, and prices are quite high. It should be noted that Martin's initial use of this species is likely to have been a simple matter of convenience and expense. Red spruce was abundant in the area, and so it was likely the least expensive option at the time.

Spruces are particularly good at meeting the requirements of lightness and stiffness. Spruce tends to have a high *stiffness to weight ratio* (also called *specific modulus* or *specific stiffness*) and is also easy to shape using woodworking tools, and so it is ideal for use in guitar tops.

Another factor that must be considered when selecting materials is availability, and it was availability of spruce, or actually lack of it, that was responsible for guitar luthiers including western red cedar (*Thuja plicata*) as a suitable wood for guitar tops. During the 1970s, guitar makers in the USA found that abundant supplies of inexpensive spruce were no longer available, due to extensive purchases by large Japanese guitar manufacturers. This led to the consideration and eventual acceptance of western red cedar as an appropriate wood for guitar tops. This in turn led to the consideration of additional wood species for guitar tops.

There is not a single value for lightness or for stiffness for each wood species. For each species, the values for these qualities fall within a fairly wide range. Furthermore the range of values for each species will largely overlap those of other species. The upshot of this for wood selection is simply that there are a number of species which can be used to make the top plates of great sounding guitars.

In the context of the construction process described in this book, I'll focus on three top woods that are currently in good supply, are readily available, and can be reasonably priced, depending on grade. These are Sitka spruce (*Picea sitchensis*), Engelmann spruce (*Picea engelmannii*), and western red cedar (*Thuja plicata*). They are the most common species used by the large guitar factories building acoustic steel string guitars in the USA.

I must mention that at the time of writing of this book, a number of lutherie wood suppliers are offering top wood that has been heat processed. This is generally referred to as *torrefied* wood. Torrefied wood is more dimensionally stable with changes in humidity than unprocessed wood. It *may* also be more stable over time, and it *may* behave more like naturally aged wood in general. It takes special care to build using torrefied wood, and for this reason alone I am not recommending it for use by lutherie novices. But it is good to be aware that this heat processed wood exists.

As for guitar back wood, top wood comes as a set of two bookmatched pieces. The wood is always quartersawn and completely free of obvious defects within the pattern of the outline of the top. Guitar top sets are available from lutherie wood suppliers and from general lutherie suppliers as well. There are a number of lutherie wood suppliers that deal only in top wood. As with wood for guitar backs and sides, suppliers generally offer top sets in sizes for different guitars. The example instruments are of typical sizes. One is an OM size instrument, the other is dreadnought size.

About Top Wood Grading

The cost of a guitar top set varies greatly, depending on appearance grade. Guitar top wood grading is a fraught subject, because there are really no standards for it. Although there are common grade designations, in reality each supplier uses their own grading system, which is only really consistent for tops purchased from that supplier. To make matters more confusing, grading will usually vary over time, as a function of supply. A top set of a certain grade now will usually not look the same as a top of the same grade purchased from the same supplier 10 years ago. And to further muddy the waters, top grading will differ depending on the availability of the wood species, sometimes by a lot. For woods in short supply such as red spruce (*Picea rubens*) a high grade top will generally not compare favorably to a top of the same grade of the more readily available Sitka spruce (*Picea sitchensis*), for example.

It is important to understand that guitar top grading is based on appearance only. Higher grade tops may look better than lower grade tops in some ways, but they will not sound better nor perform better in any significant way. But higher grade tops will be more expensive, sometimes considerably so.

Most lutherie wood suppliers use some variation of the "A" grading system, where the more A's, the higher the grade. So an A grade top would be the lowest grade, and an AA grade top would be a higher grade than A. Some suppliers grade tops from A to AAA. Other suppliers will grade tops from A to AAA but also add a "master grade" on top. Still others will grade tops from A to AAAAA. All reputable suppliers will provide information about how they grade, and what characteristics they consider when grading. Here are the most common characteristics.

Grain Straightness. The straighter the grain, the higher the grade. But even the lowest grades usually have very straight grain.

Closeness of Grain Lines. The closer together the grain lines, the higher the grade.

Consistency of Grain Line Spacing. The more consistently spaced the grain lines are, the higher the grade.

Verticality of Grain. Guitar tops are quartersawn, which results in grain that is near vertical. The more vertical, the higher the grade. Note that this is a visual characteristic because *medullary rays* (characteristic cross grain structures in the wood), often called *silking*, are more visible if the grain is close to vertical.

Lack of Runout. If a board is viewed from the side, it is possible to assess how parallel the broad surfaces of the board are to the grain. Deviation of the broad surfaces of the board from exactly parallel to the grain is called *runout*. The less runout, the higher the grade. The two halves of a guitar top look more similar when runout is low. Lack of runout makes for easier machining, but that is not really an issue for a guitar top.

Photo 12-3 – This instrument made use of an excellent but inexpensive AA grade Sitka spruce top. The wide variation in color across the width of the top is apparent.

Photo 12-4 – Rosette of a guitar by the Spanish luthier Luis Reig, built in the mid-19th century. The central part of the rosette is made of wood veneer with a decorative vine design made of inlaid shell pieces.

Lightness of Color. Lighter colored top wood is generally graded higher than darker wood.

Consistency of Color. Wood that is consistently even in color is graded higher than wood with color variability.

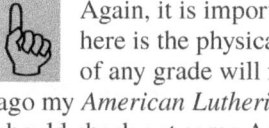 Again, it is important to note that what is considered here is the physical *appearance* of the wood. Top wood of any grade will make a fine instrument. Many years ago my *American Lutherie* colleague John Calkin suggested I should check out some AA-graded tops from a certain wood supplier. These tops were excellent in every way, but the grain was a bit wide and the color was quite dark and varying. They were amazingly inexpensive. I have built some of my best sounding instruments using this top wood, and I thank John every time I use it (**photo 12-3**).

The Soundhole Rosette

The top plate of the acoustic steel string guitar has a soundhole which is surrounded by a decorative rosette. A number of different styles of rosette have been used historically. Many early guitars had rosettes consisting of a wide band made of inlaid wood veneer or filled with *mastic*. This was inlaid with decorative pieces of shell or other substances (**photo 12-4**).

Spanish guitars in the style and of the lineage of Torres also have wide band rosettes, but these are filled with a decorative mosaic made of tiny squares of wood (**photo 12-5**). A common European style of rosette featured three inlaid rings around the sound hole. The inner and outer rings of this style are generally thin, and composed only of veneer lines, while the center ring is generally wider and contains some central decorative core (**photo 12-6**). Common materials for that core are wood marquetry strips, shell strips, and plain wood strips.

The latter three ring style was the one most commonly used by C.F. Martin. Since modern steel string acoustic guitars are from the Martin lineage, this style is commonly used. Construction of this style of rosette will be discussed in the construction section.

Photo 12-5 – Rosette of a classical guitar by Colombian luthier Alberto Paredes, shown during construction of the top plate. The central core of the rosette is a mosaic of tiny wood squares.

Photo 12-6 – The rosette of this late 19th century European guitar by an unknown maker is of the three ring style. The outer rings are made of inlaid veneer lines, and the inner ring is made of an inlaid marquetry strip.

Figure 12-1 – If the grain of the top plate is straight enough, it is a nice practice to be sure the jointed edges of the plate halves are parallel to the grain. The actual seam of a well-executed joint will be nearly invisible. If the joint is not parallel to the grain, as in the left side figure, the location of the seam is implied by the grain, and thus attention is drawn to it.

Layout and Construction

Many of the construction details of the top plate are similar enough to those of the back plate that they will be mentioned here only by reference. The descriptions, photos, and figures in the previous chapter should be referred to as needed.

 The softwood of the guitar top is easily dented. It is important during all construction operations involving the top that any surface on which the top is placed be cleaned of debris that might dent the top.

Preparing, Jointing, and Joining the Top Halves

☐ Preparing the Top Halves

As with the back, guitar top pieces are supplied thicker than will be used in the instrument, and must be thinned before use. Lutherie shops that do not have the facilities to thickness plate halves should have the plates sanded to thickness by the lutherie wood supplier. The top halves should be thinned as described below, either by the supplier or in the shop. If the luthier's shop has the facility to thickness the joined top, it is usually preferable to join first and then thin to thickness. Since some shops do not have this capability, the construction details that follow will thickness the halves first, and then join them.

1. The top halves are planed or sanded to thickness in the same manner as was done for the back. This can be done by the lutherie wood supplier or in the luthier's shop if it is equipped to do so. In the context of the construction process described in this book, I suggest a top thickness of 3/32" (2.4mm) at 100 grit for a top of any species of spruce, and a thickness of 1/8" (3.2mm) at 100 grit for a red cedar top.

2. As with the back, the halves are examined to determine which surface will be the outside surface. That information is marked in pencil near the corners of the two halves. Much care is taken when marking the outside surface of the soft top, to avoid denting it with the pencil. It is generally safest to limit markings to outside the pattern of the top outline.

☐ Jointing the Top Halves

1. When constructing the back plate, the edge to be jointed was selected based on the best look for the joined halves. For the top plate, it is traditional that the jointed edge is the one with the narrowest grain. So this means that "opening the book" for the top halves will be done so the narrow grain will end up at the centerline of the joined plate. Although there are rationalizations about why this is done this way, this orientation is primarily a visual thing. It puts the wider grain at the edges of the lower bout, where it will be less obvious in the finished instrument. The edge to be jointed is marked in pencil on both halves.

2. The grain for the wood of the top is generally straight, and the joint between the two halves of the top will be visible in the

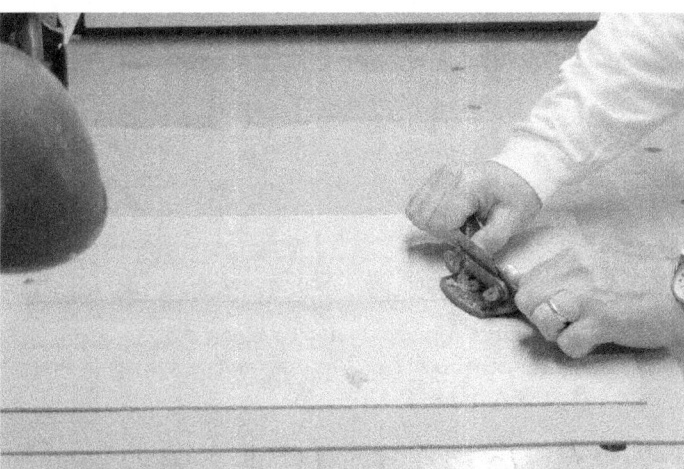

Photo 12-7 – Surface glue is scraped or sanded off both outside and inside surfaces of the top plate. Here a veneer scraper is being used, but a card scraper or sandpaper on a block can be used as well.

finished instrument, in the part of the top below the sound hole. In general, a well-executed joint will show no glue line at all, so if the joint is parallel to the grain it will be all but invisible (**figure 12-1**). A traditional technique which helps to hide the center seam is to cut the edges to be jointed so they are parallel to the same grain line on both halves. This is done by picking out one grain line near what will be the jointed edge of one of the plate halves, using a straightedge that is at least as long as the plate half. If it turns out that the grain is not straight enough so that the straightedge can be positioned as described, this construction step is abandoned. Otherwise, a mark is scratched using an awl or knife along the straightedge, and the edge is sawn or planed to this mark. A sanding board is often useful to do the final trimming to the mark.

3. The trimmed edge is positioned overlapping the inside edge of the other top half now, so that the two halves form a perfect mirror image about that edge. The edge is transferred to the second half using awl or knife, and the second half is trimmed in the same manner as the first.

4. The plate edges that will form the centerline are now jointed, using whatever tools and techniques were used to joint the edges for the back plate.

□ **Joining the Top Halves**

1. The outer edges of the plate halves are ripped parallel to the jointed edges, and so the two plate halves will be the same width. This step is done identically to the way it was done for the back plate.

2. The plate halves are joined in the same manner as used to join the halves of the back plate as well. Any remaining glue or unevenness of the levels of the plate halves is scraped or sanded away on both surfaces (**photo 12-7**). If the scraper is used to do this, much care should be taken to avoid scraping a hollow along the glue line.

Constructing the Rosette and Soundhole

Unless a luthier is making a copy of a historical instrument, the design of the rosette will usually be unique to that builder. Novice luthiers may want to stick to a proven design, and the following construction operations provide that: a typical three ring rosette pattern that can be implemented using readily available tools and materials.

Ring	Inside Dia.	Outside Dia.	Width
Inner	4¹⁹⁄₆₄″ (109.1mm)	4²⁹⁄₆₄″ (113.1mm)	⁵⁄₆₄″ (2mm)
Center	4⁵¹⁄₆₄″ (121.8mm)	5¹⁷⁄₆₄″ (133.8mm)	¹⁵⁄₆₄″ (6mm)
Outer	5³⁹⁄₆₄″ (142.5mm)	5⁴⁹⁄₆₄″ (146.5mm)	⁵⁄₆₄″ (2mm)

Table 12-1 – *Diameters of the three rings of the example rosette and the widths of their channels. The unfortunately awkward dimensions are the result of the dimensions of available precut shell pieces, and also the specific tools to be used to rout the channels with a router.*

Example Guitar	Neck End to Sound Hole Center
Tripletta OM	5²³⁄₃₂″ (145.3mm)
Paura Dreadnought	5²⁵⁄₃₂″ (146.8mm)

Table 12-2 – *Distance from the neck end of the top plate outline to the center point of the sound hole for each of the example instruments.*

The layout of the typical three ring rosette is fairly straightforward. The inner ring is spaced at an offset from the edge of the sound hole, typically at least ⅛″ (3.2mm). The outer ring is spaced approximately ¾″ (19.1mm) from the first ring, with the center ring spaced roughly evenly between the other two.

Each ring consists of inlaid material in a circular channel. The inner and outer rings are typically composed of veneer lines in a Black/Maple/Black sequence. The center ring is usually wider than the inner and outer rings, and includes veneer line borders on both sides of a central core. The central core is often made of wood, shell material, or a decorative marquetry strip. There are a lot of options available for the material of the central core from lutherie suppliers these days. Curved reconstituted stone strips are available, as are flexible abalone strips.

The construction operations below are for a specific three ring rosette pattern that works for either of the example instruments. The example pattern makes use of readily available materials. Three different techniques are generally used by luthiers for cutting the rosette channels: a traditional method using a knife blade circular cutter and a chisel; a power tool approach using a router and circle-cutting baseplate; or a power tool approach using a fly cutter. In the context of the construction process described in this book, only the first two will be described. Three different central core materials and the construction techniques applicable to each are specified.

Note that construction of the rosette requires high precision, but it involves materials that are not always dimensioned to high precision. The component parts are small. There are a lot of measuring and fitting steps involved in the construction. Digital calipers will be necessary to make most of the measurements.

Construction is further complicated by the fact that the various wood components used will swell in thickness when glue is applied to them. The dimensions appearing in the tables include a glue and swelling allowance of approximately 0.002″ (0.05mm) per wood surface. For example, the inner and outer rings of the rosette pattern each consist of three 0.02″ (0.5mm) veneer lines. The total thickness for the three lines is 0.06″ (1.5mm). These are inlaid into a ⁵⁄₆₄″ (0.078″, 2mm) wide channel. The extra space is required for the glue allowance of eight wood surfaces, two each for the three lines, and two for the walls of the channel.

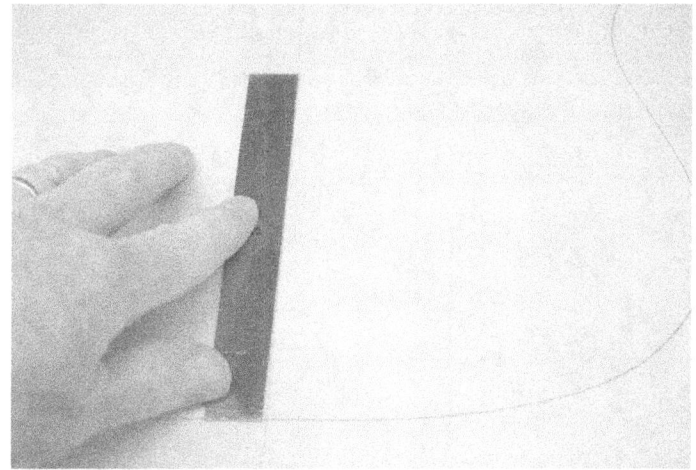

Photo 12-8 – *The center of the soundhole is located by measuring down along the centerline from the neck end of the plate outline. A mark is made at the center point, then it is pricked with an awl.*

The dimensions of the example rosette pattern are a bit awkward, but these are necessary to accommodate the dimensions of available precut shell pieces, the thickness of available veneer lines, and the diameters of available micro router bits. The diameters and widths of the rings of the example rosette pattern are shown in **table 12-1**.

☐ Preparing to Cut the Rosette Channels

1. The outline of the top plate is transferred from the mold to the outside and inside surfaces of the plate, using the same techniques described in the previous chapter for marking the outline on the back plate.

2. The center point of the soundhole is marked on the outside surface of the top. The distance from the neck end of the outline at the centerline, down to the center point of the soundhole, is taken from **table 12-2** and measured along the centerline using a ruler (**photo 12-8**). A mark is made at the sound hole center point, and carefully pricked with an awl.

3. A glue-proof workboard, approximately the same dimensions as the top plate, is cut from melamine board. The top plate is clamped, outside surface up, to the workboard using one clamp at each corner (**photo 12-9**).

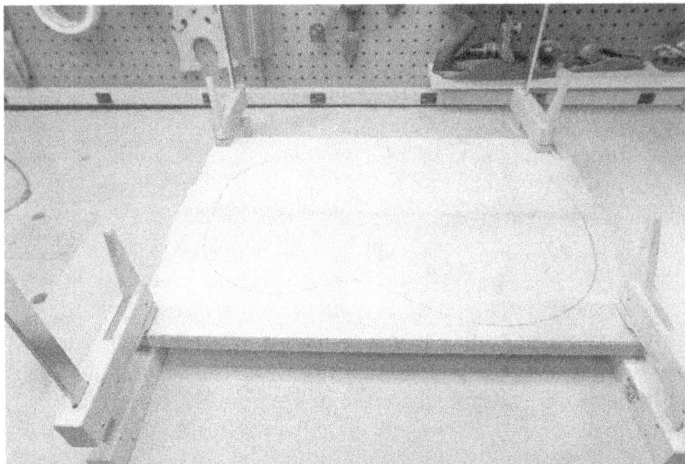

Photo 12-9 – A melamine workboard is used when cutting the rosette channels. The top plate is clamped to the workboard using one clamp at each corner. This keeps the clamps out of the way of subsequent work.

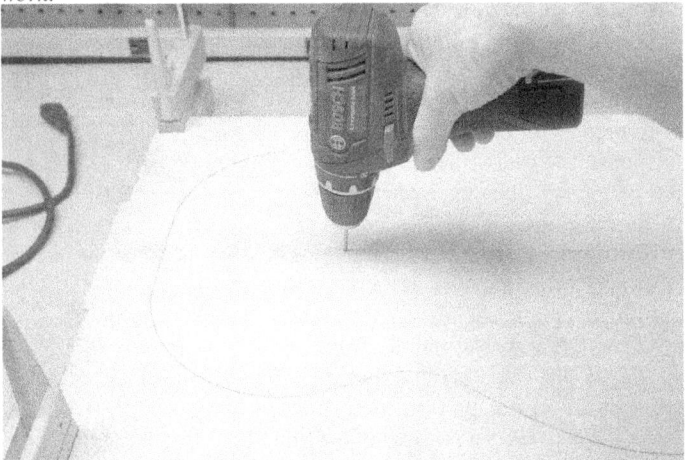

Photo 12-10 – Drilling a hole through the top plate at the center point of the soundhole and rosette. The hole will support a pivot pin, used when cutting the rosette channels.

Photo 12-12 – The business end of the compass gramil, showing the blade and pivot pin, and the screw used to adjust exposure of the blade.

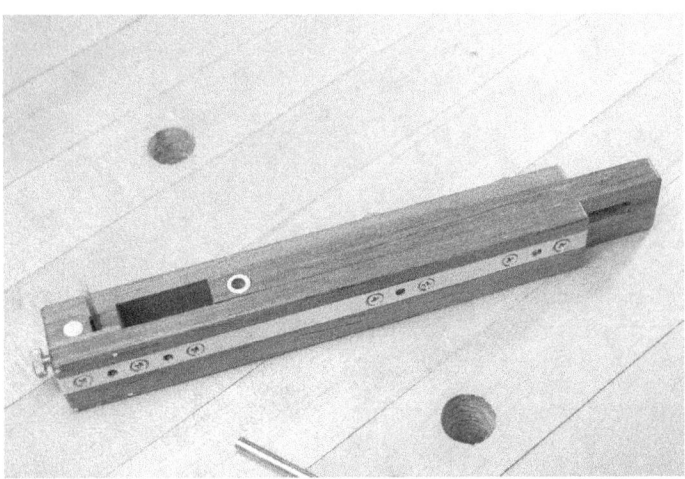

Photo 12-11 – A shop-built compass gramil, also called a circle cutter. The distance between the pin and the cutting blade is adjustable, and the blade can be mounted with its bevel toward the pin or away from it.

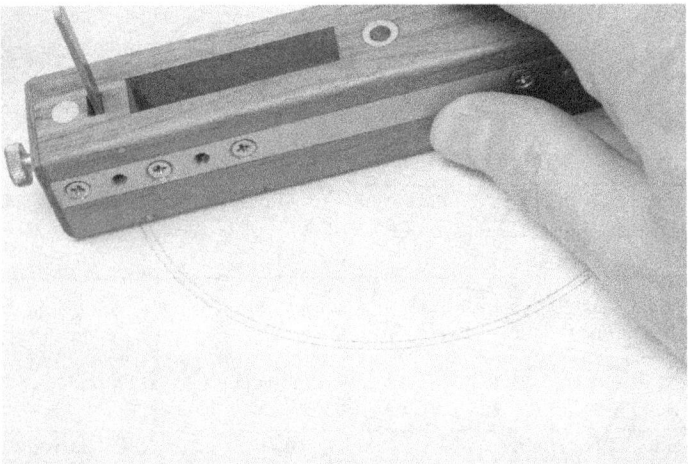

Photo 12-13 – As the compass gramil is spun around its pivot pin, the cutting blade cuts the walls of the channel.

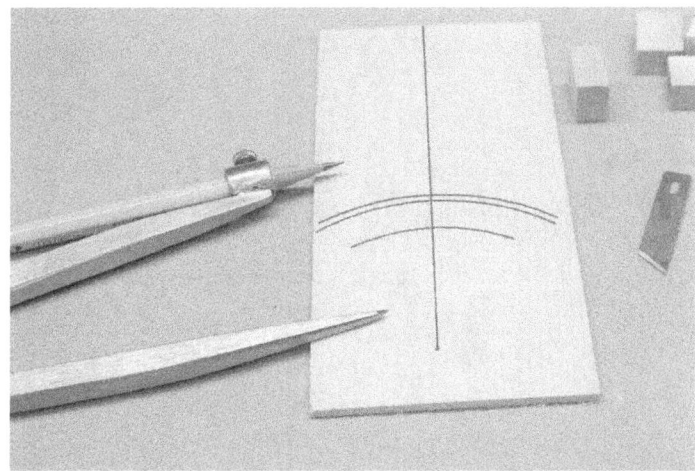

Photo 12-14 – *An arc is drawn on the baseboard of the disposable compass gramil for the sound hole, and for each wall of each rosette ring.*

4. An ⅛″ (3.2mm) brad point drill bit is fitted into a hand drill and a vertical hole is drilled through the top and the workboard at the center point of the soundhole (**photo 12-10**). This will support the pivot pin, used to cut the rosette channels and the soundhole itself in the following construction descriptions. A piece of duct tape or other sturdy tape is used to cover the drilled hole on the bottom of the workboard. This will prevent the pivot pin from being able to drop right through the hole.

Traditional Construction of the Rosette Channels Option

The channels are traditionally cut using edge tools. The walls of the channels are cut using a *compass gramil*, also sometimes called a circle cutter. This is a relatively simple device that supports a knife blade at an adjustable distance from a center pin. The compass gramil produces a very clean edge. In use, a hole is drilled at the center of the channels to be cut to accept the center pin, as described in the previous operation. The tool is adjusted to produce a cut of the desired depth and diameter of one wall of the channel, and is then fitted onto the pin and rotated around it by hand. Each rotation cuts a bit deeper, until a cut of the desired depth is cut. The other wall of the channel is cut in like manner. Then the waste wood between the cuts is removed using a chisel, to complete the channel. Waste wood can also be removed using a router with a circle cutter attachment of some kind.

It is interesting and somewhat surprising that compass gramils for use in cutting rosette channels are not readily available from lutherie suppliers, and the few that are available are quite expensive. Most luthiers I know that use this tool built their own. My own shop-built compass gramil is shown in **photos 12-11** through **12-13**.

The instructions that follow make use of an easy-to-assemble and disposable shop-built compass gramil, modeled after one used by James Buckland.[1] It is made of scrap wood and a hobby knife blade.

☐ **Building and Using the Disposable Compass Gramil**

Materials
    Hardwood board, approximately 3″ (76.2mm) × 5″ (127mm) × ⅛″ (3.2mm) thick
    Scrap of MDF
    Small wood blocks, approximately ½″ (12.7mm) high
    Hobby knife blade
    ⅛″ (3.2mm) diameter metal pin or drill bit
    Medium cyanoacrylate glue
Tools
    Compass
    Plastic mallet
    Micro chisels

---

1. A straight line is drawn down the longitudinal center of the thin board. A mark is made approximately 1″ (25.4mm) from one end of the board on the line. The mark is pricked with the awl. This mark represents the center point of the soundhole and rosette rings.

2. Arcs representing the circumference of the soundhole and each of the rosette channel walls are drawn on the board with a

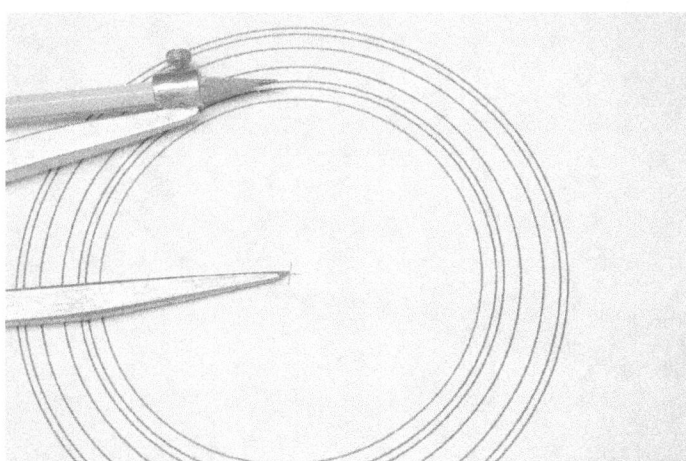

Photo 12-15 – *The radii for the arcs can be transferred to the compass directly from the plan.*

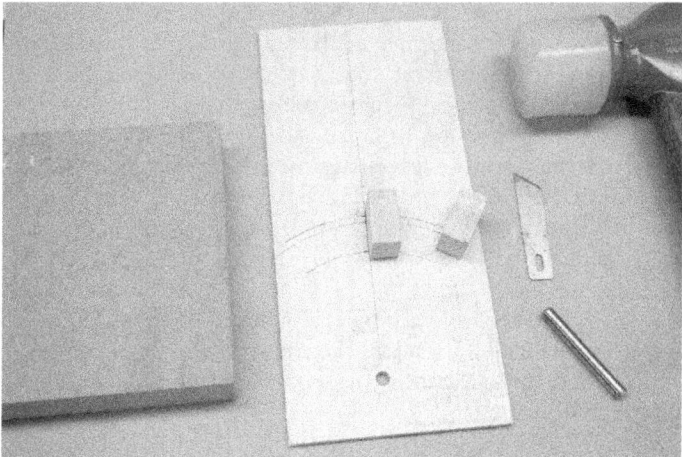

Photo 12-16 – *The parts of the disposable compass gramil include the depth gauge board, the baseboard with drilled pivot hole, the pivot pin, the cutting blade, and some small wood blocks to support the blade.*

Photo 12-17 – The hobby knife cutting blade is driven through the baseboard, until the exposed point underneath is the depth needed for the cut.

compass, using the center point as a reference (**photo 12-14**). The radii of the arcs can be transferred to the compass directly from the plan (**photo 12-15**).

 Although the soundhole will not be cut out at this time, an arc representing its circumference is made on the board now, so the disposable compass gramil can be used to perform that operation later.

3. An ⅛″ (3.2mm) brad point drill bit is fitted into the chuck of the drill press, and a hole is drilled through the board at the center point mark (**photo 12-16**). The hole will be used to engage the pivot pin.

4. The scrap of MDF will be used as a depth gauge for the cutting blade. A line representing the depth of the rosette channels is made 5/64″ (2mm) from the top surface of the scrap on one side of the scrap. This is most easily done by placing the scrap top down on the bench, stacking up feeler gauges to that amount, then making a pencil mark across the top of the gauges.

An additional depth mark is made, representing the actual thickness of the top plate. There should be some difference between the two marks.

5. The board is placed on top of the piece of MDF, with the pivot hole toward the luthier. The point of the hobby knife blade is placed somewhere along the arc representing the inside wall of the inner rosette ring, so the blade is in line with the arc (tangent to the arc), and the cutting edge is pointing to the right. The mallet is used to drive the blade into board until its point just protrudes a bit from the underside. The depth of protrusion of the point is checked against the channel depth line on the side of the MDF piece. Additional hammering with the mallet is done until the point protrudes to the channel depth mark (**photo 12-17**).

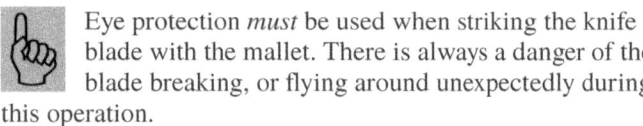 Eye protection *must* be used when striking the knife blade with the mallet. There is always a danger of the blade breaking, or flying around unexpectedly during this operation.

6. Medium cyanoacrylate glue is used to glue one of the wood blocks to the board, so it is butting against the cutting edge side (right side) of the knife blade (**figure 12-2**). The side of the block against the blade should be perpendicular to the penciled

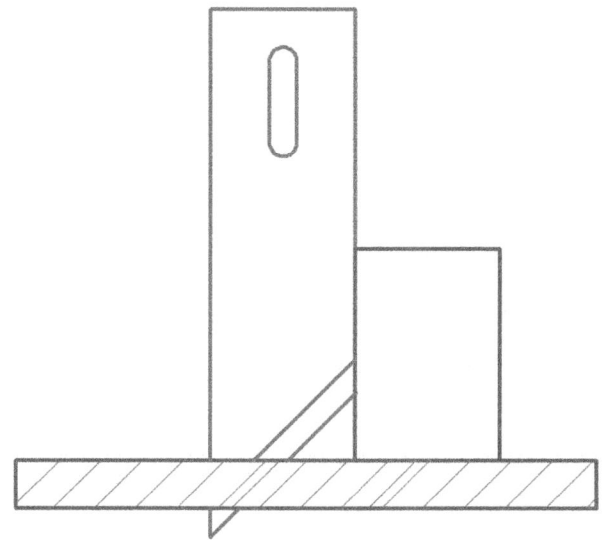

Figure 12-2 – Schematic of the cutting parts of the disposable compass gramil. The cutting edge of the blade points to the right, and the right side of the blade rests against the support block. The block prevents the blade from tipping to the right during cutting.

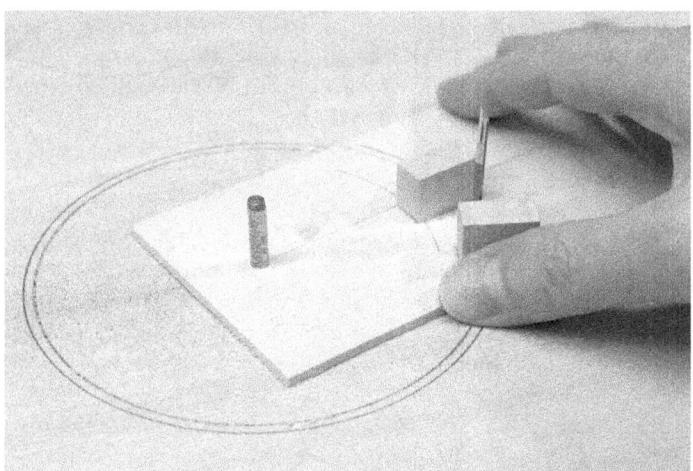

Photo 12-18 – The disposable compass gramil is used by rotating it around the pivot point clockwise. Successive rotations increase the depth of cut.

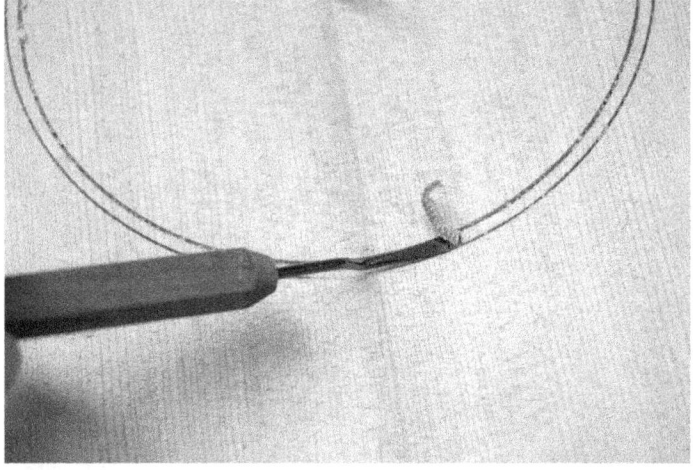

Photo 12-19 – A micro chisel is used to chisel the waste from the channel. Care must be taken to keep from damaging the edges and floor of the channel.

arc. In use, pressure on the cutting tip of the blade will make the blade lean over to the right. The block prevents the blade from leaning during cutting.

7. A short length of ⅛″ (3.2mm) metal rod can be used as a pivot pin, but the butt end of a drill bit of that diameter can also be used. The pin is fitted into the hole drilled into the top and the workboard at the sound hole center point. The hole in the compass gramil base board is slipped over the pin. Before the blade point touches the top plate, it is rotated on the pin so the blade point is on the top centerline on the neck side of the sound hole. Cutting *always* begins and ends here. It is desirable that any measurement or cutting mistakes will show up here, because this area will be covered by the fretboard extension in the finished instrument, and so those mistakes will not be visible.

8. The cutter is rotated clockwise about the pin, to make the cut in multiple shallow passes (**photo 12-18**). The lightest pressure should be used when cutting each pass. This is especially important when the blade is moving along the grain, where it tends to cut deeply. It is also important to use very light pressure because the blade is only held in place in the base board by friction. The entire cut should take no fewer than 10 passes. Cutting is complete when the base board is in firm contact with the top surface of the top plate. The feel of cutting also changes when the bottom of the cut is reached. Three more rotations are done for good measure, then the cutter is removed from the pivot pin. A check is made to be sure the blade is still at proper depth.

9. Steps 5 through 8 above are repeated for each of the walls of the rosette channels. The soundhole will not be cut out at this time. After each cut, the blade is pulled out of the baseboard using pliers, and then repositioned on the baseboard for the next cut. The blade should not be positioned directly in line with its location for the previous cut. Doing so will not result in firm seating of the blade in the base board. The blade support blocks do not have to be removed. It is often easiest to locate the blade for subsequent cuts by butting its right side against an existing block.

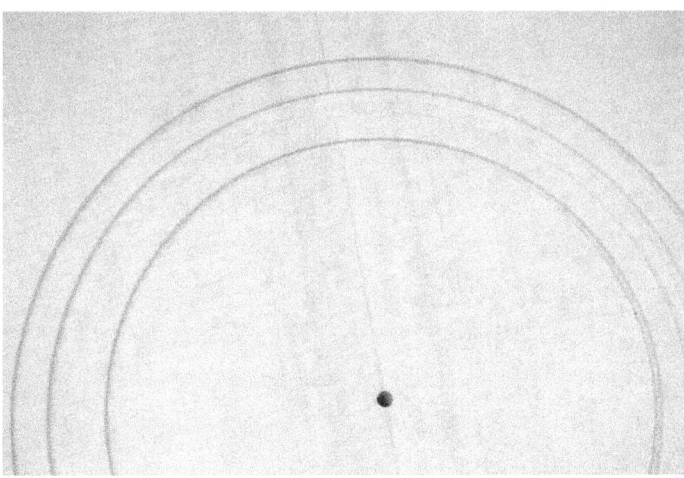

Photo 12-20 – *The finished channels for the example three ring rosette.*

10. An appropriately sized micro chisel is used to remove the waste wood from each channel. This is a slow and tedious process, that requires a lot of care and concentration to avoid bunging up the edges of the channels (**photo 12-19**). Note also that the floors of the channels are quite thin, so care must be taken to avoid breaching them. The channel floors should be scraped level and clean. All debris should be removed by brushing and vacuuming. The finished channels should appear as in **photo 12-20**.

11. The compass gramil is retained for later use in cutting out the soundhole.

Construction of the Rosette Channels Using a Router Option

The router is a natural tool for cutting the rosette channels, and is used by lutherie shops small and large. By way of example, the techniques described here are essentially those used in the early days by the Huss & Dalton Guitar Company, founded by luthiers Jeff Huss and Mark Dalton.

Router bits of appropriate diameter are readily available, but unfortunately when straight or conventional *upcut router bits* (also called *up spiral* or *right hand spiral*) are used to rout spruce and other softwoods typically used for guitar top plates, they leave a rough and hairy edge. This is because the tough grain fibers near the top surface do not get cut by the bit, but simply get pushed up. These fibers can be trimmed off with a sharp knife, but the process is so tedious and time consuming, and so likely to result in the edge of the channel getting nicked, that it is really not practical to do this.

Fortunately *downcut router bits* are available, specifically for the purpose of leaving cleaner edges. But their use is not without a complication. Whereas the action of an upcut bit tends to pull the router down to the work, the action of a downcut bit tends to lift the router away from the work. This causes considerable chatter unless the router is heavy enough to prevent it.

Lutherie suppliers sell circle cutting router bases or attachments for small hobby grinders. These bases range in price from expensive to *very* expensive. Use of such a base to avoid chatter requires either very shallow passes, or cutting the channel initially using an upcut bit and then switching to a downcut bit for a final finishing pass. Both prospects are tedious and time consuming.

Fortunately, "universal" circle-cutting router base plates that will fit most routers are available for full size plunge routers. These will cut circles in the diameters needed for guitar top

Cut	Bit Dia.	Pin Hole	Depth
Inner Ring	5/64″ (2mm)	4⅝	5/64″ (2mm)
Center Ring 1st	5/64″ (2mm)	5⅛	5/64″ (2mm)
Center Ring 2nd	5/64″ (2mm)	5¼	see text
Center Ring 3rd	5/64″ (2mm)	5⅜	see text
Center Ring 4th	5/64″ (2mm)	5 7/16	5/64″ (2mm)
Outer Ring	5/64″ (2mm)	5 15/16	5/64″ (2mm)

Table 12-3 – *Critical dimensions for each cut of the channels of the example rosette. Note that the center ring is formed from four separate cuts. The pin holes indicated here specify the base plate index hole to use for each cut. Note also that the depth of cut for the 2nd and 3rd cuts of the center ring can be the same as for the other cuts. If a thin inlay piece will be used for the central portion of the center ring, then the depth of cut here can be the thickness of that piece.*

rosette rings. The weight of the full size router, plus the thin diameter of the bits that will be used, means the channel cuts can be made in a couple of passes will no danger of chatter. Since a full size router is a necessary tool for lutherie work, the cost of the tools needed to use the router to cut the channels is usually only the cost of the base plate, bit adapter, and the required bits.

Although I try hard to avoid specifying particular brands of products in this book, here I must specify a particular model circle-cutting base plate. It is the Jasper M400 Pro from Jasper Tools. There may be other such base plates that work equally well for this application. If I find any, they will be included in the Appendix A Online Annex, in the Specific Tools Referenced in the Book section.

The base plate will attach to most modern plunge routers. As with all such products, this base plate contains a number of drilled holes. A pivot pin is placed in the hole for the diameter of the circle to be cut; this pin is placed in the center hole drilled through the top plate; and the router is rotated around the pin to make the cut.

Calculating which pin hole to use in the base plate for each cut requires some tedious arithmetic, which is based on the diameter of the router bit and whether an inside or outside edge is being cut. Instructions for doing the math are included with the base plate. To eliminate the need for these calculations, the pin hole to use for each cut required to make the channels of the example rosette is specified in **table 12-3**. For purposes of cutting channels of other diameters, I also provide a general-purpose calculator on my website at

LiutaioMottola.com/formulae/jasperRosette.htm

Jasper Circle Calculator

which will do all the math required.

The following operations include the construction of a simple cover plate for the router base plate, necessary to prevent the pivot pin from being inadvertently pushed up into the router base, and also instructions for using the router to cut the channels.

☐ **Making the Cover Plate for the Router Base Plate**

The circle cutter router base plate is made of thick plastic, with a lot of holes drilled through it. The holes are for the pivot pin, one for each circle diameter in the range that can be accommodated. The actual base of most routers is a casting which contains a number of pockets. When the base plate is in use, the pivot pin is placed in the appropriate hole in the baseplate, then the router is positioned so the pivot pin can be pushed into the center hole drilled through the top plate. But for some diameters, if the pin is not positioned perfectly over the center hole of the top plate, when the router is lowered onto the top, instead of the pivot pin entering the center hole, it will be pushed through the router base plate and into one of the pockets in the router base behind it. And this will not be at all visible. Attempting to use the router to cut a circle if this happens will result in the router slipping off the center hole, ruining the top plate.

To make sure this never happens, a cover plate should be made that prevents the pivot pin from pushing through the base plate (**figure 12-3**).

Materials
    ⅛″ (3.2MM) or thinner sheet plastic
Tools
    Circle cutter router base plate (Jasper M400 Pro)

1. Before the base plate is attached to the router, it is placed on top of a piece of ⅛″ (3.2MM) sheet plastic. Thinner plastic can be used. The outside of the base plate is traced in pencil onto the plastic (**photo 12-21**). The oddly shaped inside hole of the base plate is also traced, as are whichever of the mounting holes will be used to mount the base plate to the router.

2. The outline is cut out on the band saw and sanded to the line using whatever sanding tools are preferred. A critical fit is not required.

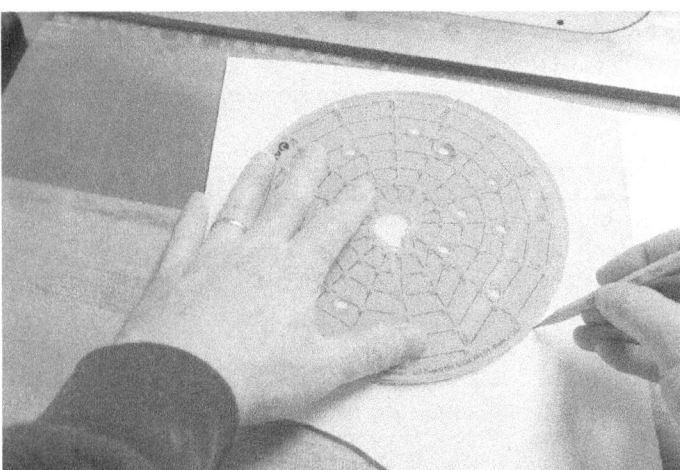

Photo 12-21 – *The outline, center hole, and the mounting holes for the router that will be used, are all traced from the circle cutter base plate to a sheet of thin plastic.*

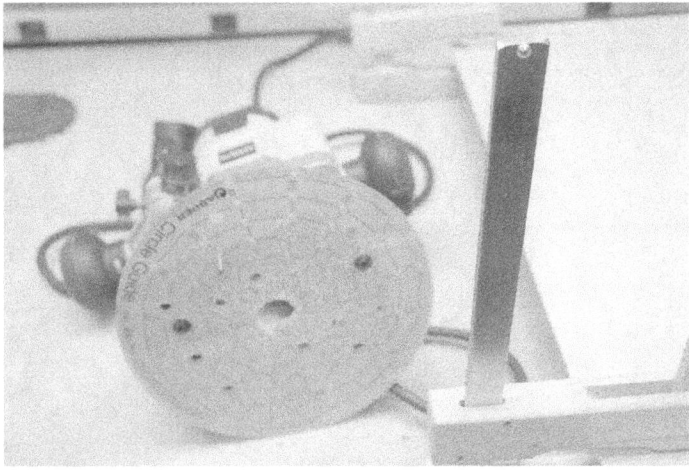

Photo 12-22 – *The router with circle cutter base plate and cover plate attached.*

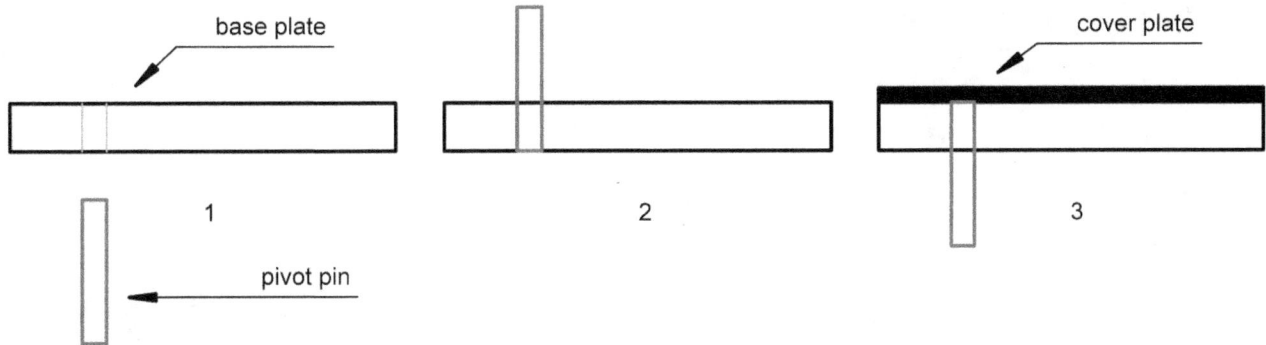

Figure 12-3 – 1. The circle cutting router base plate has index holes drilled through it. These accept the pivot pin. 2. Unfortunately, it is possible to accidentally push the pivot pin right through the base plate. 3. Constructing a cover plate and installing it over the base plate prevents the pivot pin from being accidentally pushed through the base plate.

3. The largest bit that will fit within the outline of the inside hole is used in the drill press to drill a hole in the center of the cover plate.

4. Appropriately-sized drill bits are used to drill out the mounting holes in the cover plate.

5. The base plate is attached to the router, with the cover plate sandwiched between the base plate and the router base (**photo 12-22**), and centered according to the instructions accompanying the base plate.

☐ **Cutting the Rosette Channels Using the Router**

Channel cutting with the router and circle cutting base plate is straightforward. Note in the following list of tools needed for this operation, that a collet adapter is used. This is because few full size routers come equipped with a ⅛″ (3.2MM) collet, and this is the shank size of the bit to be used.

 Note also the tools list includes a ¹⁄₁₆″ (1.6MM) diameter downcut router bit. This is not used to cut the rosette channels, but will be used in a later operation to cut out the soundhole. This appears here only so that all these special-purpose bits can be ordered at the same time.

Further note that it is a good idea to order more than one of each size of these bits. They are of small diameter, and made of solid carbide, and are thus prone to breaking.

Tools

    Router with circle cutter base plate and cover plate attached
    ¼″ (6.4MM) to ⅛″ (3.2MM) collet adapter
    ⁵⁄₆₄″ (2MM) diameter downcut router bits, ⅛″ (3.2MM) shank
    ¹⁄₁₆″ (1.6MM) diameter downcut router bits, ⅛″ (3.2MM) shank

---

1. The router is fitted with a ¼″ (6.4MM) collet and the collet adapter, and the ⁵⁄₆₄″ (2MM) diameter downcut router bit is inserted and the collet tightened.

2. Each cut is performed as a separate step. The cut for the inner ring of the rosette is done first. The router depth stop is set to the depth specified for the inner ring cut in **table 12-3** and

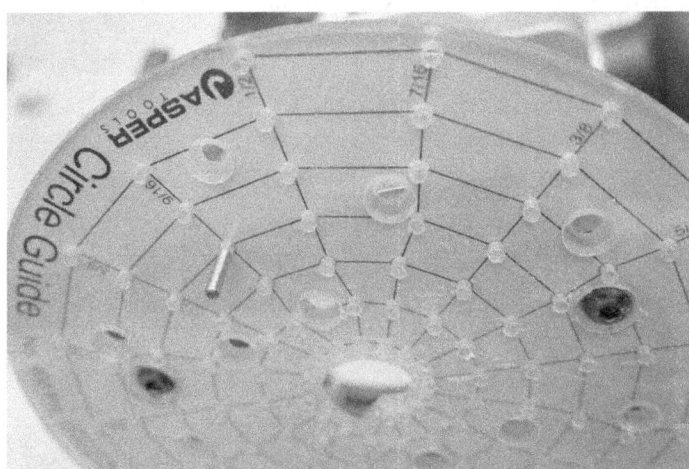

Photo 12-23 – The pivot pin is inserted in one of the indexing holes in the base plate. The cover plate prevents the pin from being pushed through the base plate.

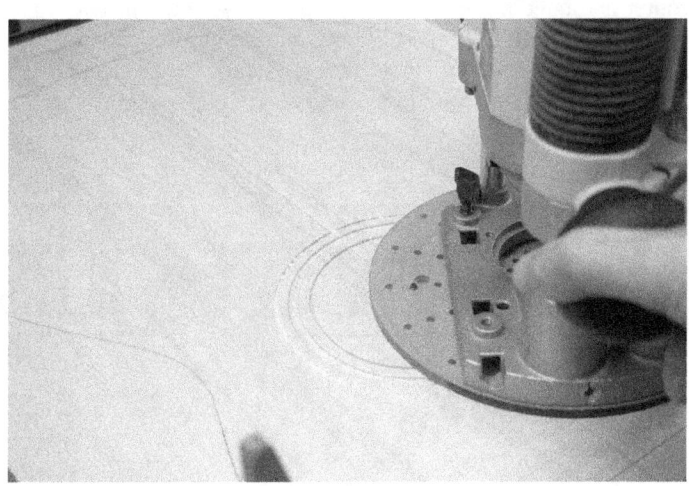

Photo 12-24 – The router being used to cut the rosette channels. In use, the router is rotated around the pivot pin to make a cut.

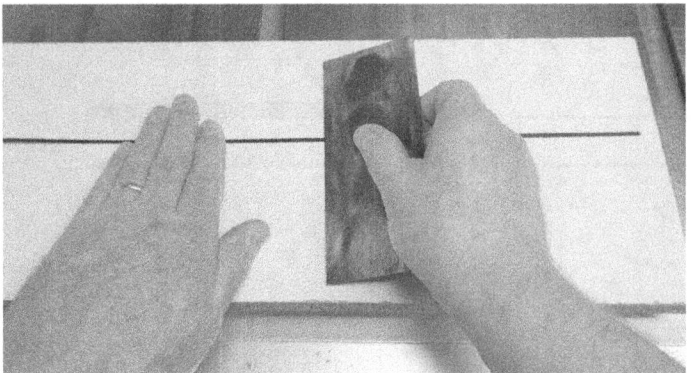

Photo 12-25 – *The veneer lines can be carefully scraped with a card scraper to uniformly reduce their thickness.*

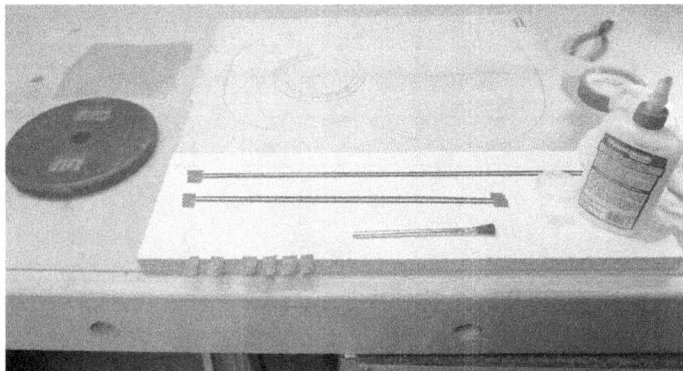

Photo 12-26 – *The setup for gluing. The groups of veneer lines for each channel are taped down to a glue-proof board so glue can be applied.*

locked in place. This must be done accurately to avoid plunging right through the top plate. It is a good idea to check the actual depth against one edge of the top plate, just to be sure the cut will not go through the plate.

3. The pin hole to use for the cut is also selected from the table. The pivot pin that comes with the base plate is inserted into that hole on the router base plate (**photo 12-23**).

4. The router is placed on top of the top plate, with the pivot pin aligned with the center point hole drilled in the top plate, and then carefully dropped into place so the pin is inserted in the hole, and the router base plate is resting squarely on the top plate.

5. The router is rotated around the pin until the bit is positioned so that it is on, or very close to, the centerline of the top plate on the neck end. The cut will start and stop here, because plunging sometimes distorts the channel a bit and this area of the top will be covered by the fretboard extension in the finished guitar. Any routing issues here will not be visible in the finished instrument.

6. The router is started and the trigger is locked. The router is plunged to its depth stop and the depth is locked. Then the router is rotated around the pivot pin clockwise to make a full circle cut (**photo 12-24**). The router must be moved fairly slowly. There is a lot of stress on a downcut router bit, and this bit is of small diameter and made of easily-broken solid carbide. A full circle should take about 30 seconds. After this is done, it is rotated full circle counter clockwise. The plunge lock is released and the bit raised, and the trigger lock is released and the motor turned off.

7. The router is removed from the work by lifting it straight up off the top plate to disengage the pivot pin. The cut channel is gently brushed and vacuumed of debris, and then inspected to be sure the cut was made all the way around.

8. Steps 3 through 7 above are repeated for each of the cuts appearing in **table 12-3**.

 If the instructions above are followed, the center channel will have a flat bottom of uniform depth. When the core of the center ring is to contain material that is thinner than the depth of the channel, a spacer of some sort will need to be placed in the channel during assembly, to raise that material up to the level of the top surface of the plate. An alternative to using a spacer is to raise the depth of cut for the two cuts in the middle of the center ring. See **figure 12-4**. These are named **Center Ring 2ⁿᵈ** and **Center Ring 3ʳᵈ** in **table 12-3**. For example, the thickness of most curved shell pieces intended for this purpose is 0.05″ (1.3mm). So the depth of cut can be set to this value for the two cuts in the middle of the center ring, and then returned to its original depth for the remaining cuts.

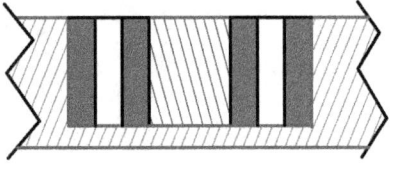

1

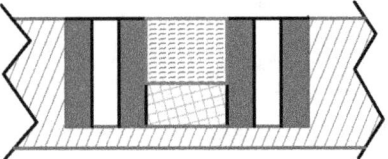

2

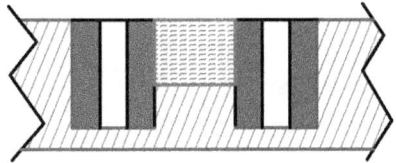

3

Figure 12-4 – *Cross section diagrams of the center rosette ring of a finished guitar. Example 1 contains three veneer lines on each side of a central wood core. The wood piece fills the entire depth of the channel. Example 2 shows a typical configuration for a central core of shell material. The shell is typically not as thick as the channel is deep, so installing it requires some spacer material under the shell. Example 3 shows an alternative to using spacer material under the shell. Here, the center part of the channel was made shallow enough to raise the shell material to the level of the top surface of the top. This construction option is really only available if the channels are cut using a router and a small diameter bit.*

Inlaying the Outer and Inner Rings

The outer and inner rings of the example rosette are each inlaid with three 0.02″ (0.5mm) thick veneer lines. These are readily available from lutherie suppliers and specialty wood trim suppliers. Note that lutherie suppliers also have pre-made black/white/black 0.06″ (1.5mm) thick purfling strips. Using these instead of individual veneer lines can save some time and trouble.

☐ Preparing the Veneer Lines

1. The veneer lines for the outer ring are done first. Digital calipers are used to measure the width of the outer channel in a number of places. If the channels were cut with the router, the width should be accurate, but there is often some deviation from the target width of the channel when it is cut using the compass gramil.

2. Three veneer lines are selected and cut to approximately 18″ (457.2mm) in length.

3. The calipers are used to measure their thicknesses. These are nominally 0.02″ (0.5mm) thick but are often a bit thicker. The thickness values are added together. Added to this sum is a glue allowance of 0.016″ (0.4mm).

4. If the resulting value from step 3 is less than or equal to that of the measured width of the channel, then the lines will fit in the channel and the rest of this step is skipped.

Otherwise the veneer lines are too thick to fit in the channel. It is extremely difficult to accurately enlarge the channel width to fit the lines, so the veneer lines are instead shaved down in thickness to fit the channel. This is most easily done using the card scraper. Each line is held down to a flat workboard using one thumb at one end of the line, then gently scraped with the card scraper (**photo 12-25**). A few gentle and uniform strokes, from near the holding thumb, down past the other end of the line are made. Then the line is reversed and the part that was under the holding thumb is also scraped. This is done to the other two veneer lines as well.

5. Steps 3 and 4 are repeated, until the resulting value from step 3 is less than or equal to that of the measured width of the channel.

6. The three lines are bundled together and a short length of the bundle is dry fitted into the channel. The fit should be loose, with space left of about half of the thickness of one line. The lines are put aside.

7. Steps 1 through 6 are repeated for the inner ring, but here the selected lines are cut to approximately 16″ (406.4mm) in length.

☐ Gluing the Veneer Lines Into the Channels

As with any gluing operation, it is prudent to do a dry run before committing to the application of glue.

Materials
    The veneer lines
    A melamine covered board (see text)
    Wood glue
    Glue brush
    Small cup to hold glue
    Masking tape
    A sheet of wax paper big enough to cover the rosette
Tools
    Cutting pliers
    A flat weight big enough to cover the rosette (see text)

---

1. The top plate can be un-clamped from the workboard for the gluing operation. This gets the clamps out of the way. The plate can be left on the workboard, or placed on any clean, flat glue-proof surface. The top is rotated so the neck end is pointed at the luthier.

 Note a glue-proof surface is needed because the floors of the channels are very thin, and it is possible for glue to squeeze through the floors and glue the top to the surface underneath.

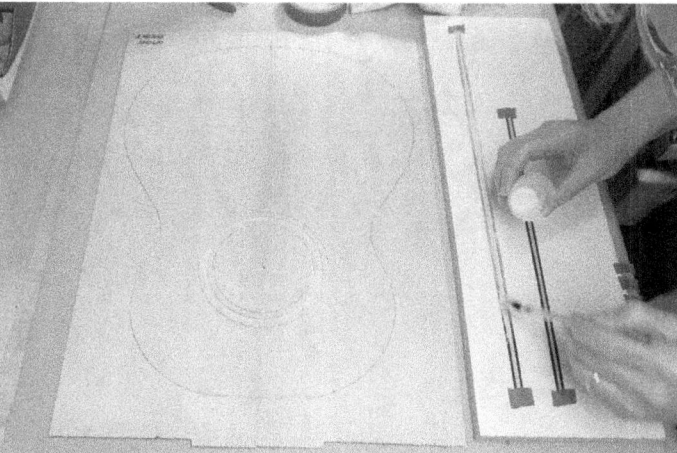

Photo 12-27 – Glue is quickly brushed onto the veneer lines for the outer channel.

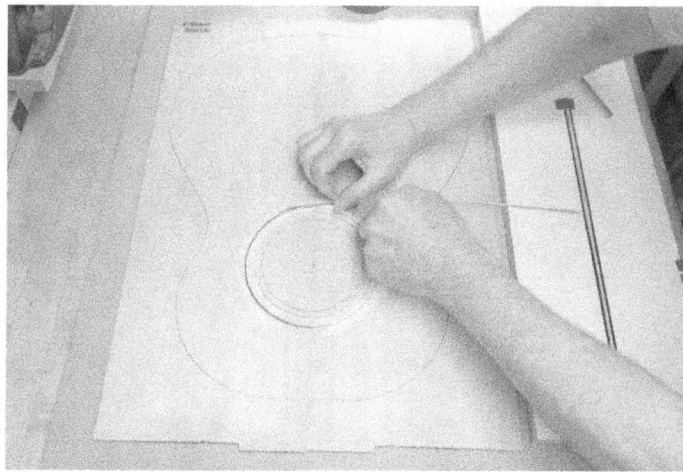

Photo 12-28 – The bundle of veneer lines is pinched together with one hand and pressed into the channel with the other.

If it will not be used here, the workboard should be retained for use in cutting out the soundhole in a later operation.

2. A length of melamine covered board is used to support the veneer lines while glue is applied. The three lines for the outer ring should be taped down to the board, in order as a group, using just a bit of tape on the ends. The same is done for the three lines for the inner ring. **Photo 12-26** shows the lines taped down and ready for the application of glue. The tools and materials needed for this operation are also shown in the photo.

3. Glue is poured into the cup. The brush is used to quickly apply glue to the exposed surfaces of the veneer lines for the outer ring (**photo 12-27**). Glue is also quickly brushed into the outer channel, avoiding getting glue in the center channel if possible. Speed is more important that complete coverage.

4. The tape is removed from the ends of the lines, and glue is smeared over the ends. Each line is quickly picked up with the fingers and placed on top of the next one, to form a bundle of the lines in their proper order. The bundle is picked up off the board and quickly pressed together. One side of the bundle will have glue on it, but the other will not. Glue is quickly applied to the side without it. This is most easily done by simply smearing that side of the bundle in the glue that is left on the surface of the board.

5. Both hands are used to insert the bundle into the outer channel. Insertion begins at the centerline on the neck end of the channel. Right-handed luthiers generally find it most effective to proceed clockwise from here (**photo 12-28**), using the nails of the first finger and thumb of the left hand to pinch the bundle together, and the fingers of the right hand to guide the bundle

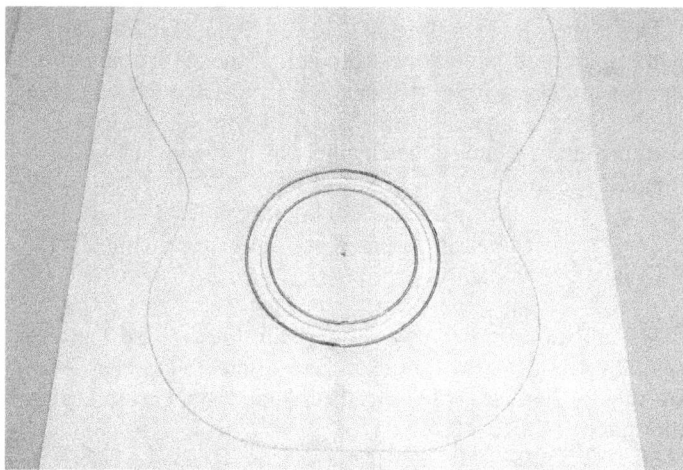

Photo 12-31 – *Insertion completed for both outer and inner rings.*

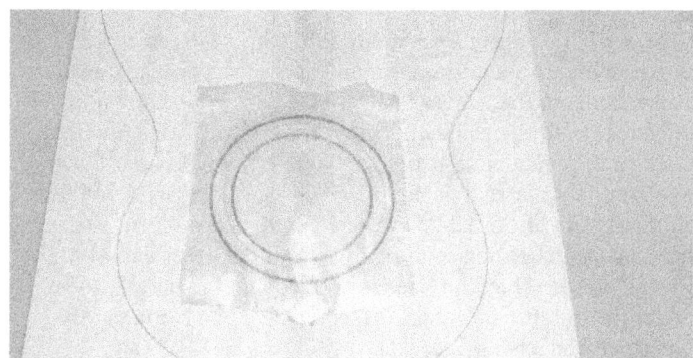

Photo 12-32 – *The rings are covered with a piece of glue-proof wax paper ...*

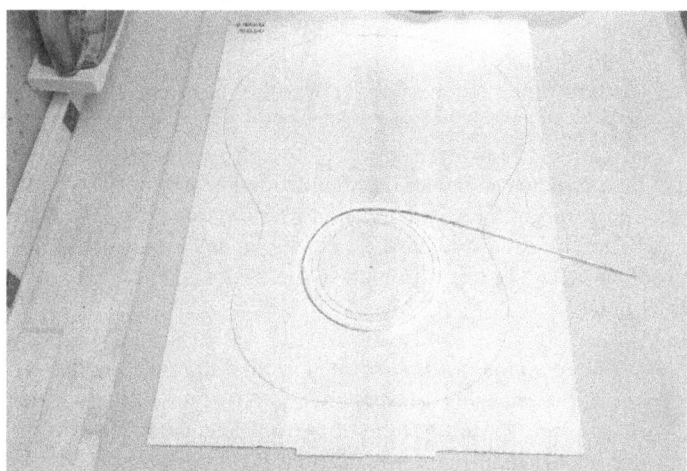

Photo 12-29 – *The veneer lines are a bit taller than the channel, so when they are fully seated in the channel their tops will be just higher than the surface of the top plate.*

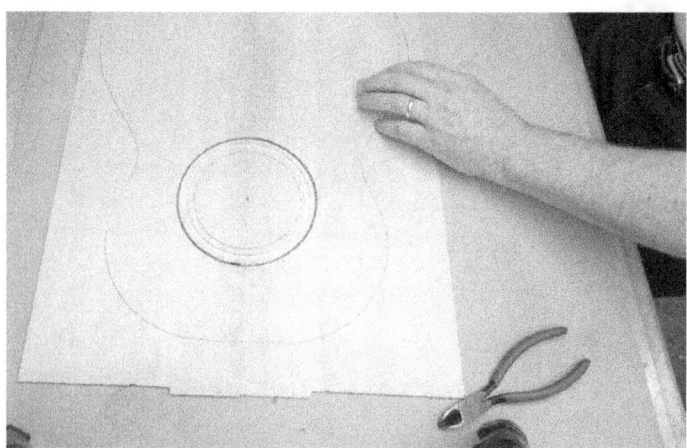

Photo 12-30 – *When insertion is complete, the excess part of the bundle is snipped off with diagonal cutting pliers.*

Photo 12-33 – *... and a weight is placed on top while the glue cures.*

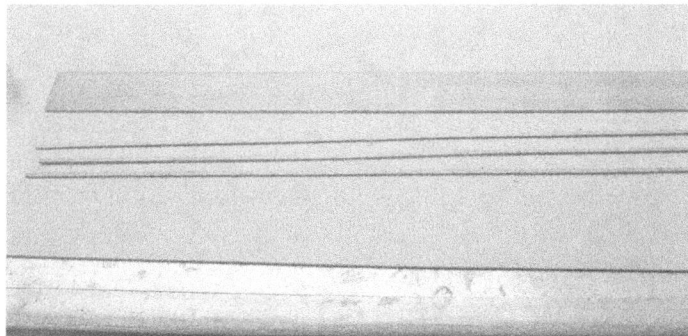

Photo 12-34 – *More than one solid wood core strip should be cut. They break easily when attempting to bend them on the bending iron.*

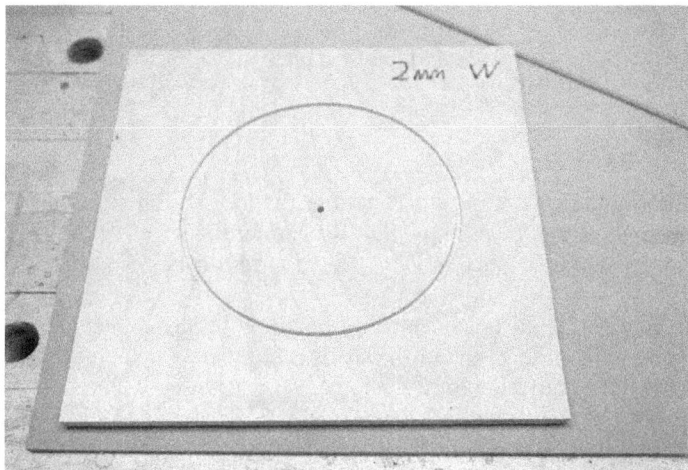

Photo 12-35 – *The completed mold, for use when bending a solid wood strip.*

and press it into place in the channel. The veneer lines are a bit taller than the channel, so they will stick up just a bit above the surface of the top when they are fully seated in the channel (**photo 12-29**).

Left handed luthiers usually find it most effective to proceed counter clockwise from here, using the nails of the first finger and thumb of the right hand to pinch the bundle together, and the fingers of the left hand to guide the bundle and press it into place in the channel.

Care must be taken to be sure the lines are actually fitting into the channel, and not simply being mashed down. The latter is possible, because the glue makes the lines quite soft.

If the lines just can't be cleanly inserted into the channel, it is best to abort this operation for now. The lines are pulled out, surface glue is wiped off the top, and remaining glue is allowed to thoroughly cure. Then the channel is re-cut or re-routed, and new lines are prepared, but this time additional glue allowance space is allocated when fitting the lines to the channels.

6. As insertion proceeds, the top is rotated, so that the section of the channel currently being worked on is near the luthier. When the starting point is reached, the cutting pliers are used to snip the bundle just before the final end is tucked into the channel (**photo 12-30**). A small gap between the ends of the bundle is not a problem, as this part of the top will be covered by the fretboard extension in the finished instrument.

7. The lines are glued into the inner channel in exactly the same manner (**photo 12-31**).

8. Attempting to remove glue-squeeze-out usually causes more problems than it solves, so squeeze-out should be left alone. But if any glue slopped into the center channel, it should be cleaned up. The rings are covered with a piece of wax paper (**photo 12- 32**), and that is covered with a weight while the glue cures (**photo 12-33**). I use a cast iron barbell plate for this purpose, but a flat piece of wood with any small amount of weight on top of it can be used instead.

9. The glue is allowed at least two hours to cure before removing the weight and wax paper.

Inlaying the Center Ring

The center ring for the example rosette contains veneer lines on both the inside and outside of a central core. Options for the central core include solid wood, a purchased marquetry strip, or commercially available curved pieces of shell material. The general assembly sequence is the core is prepared first, and then the materials for the whole ring are glued into the center channel.

An exception to this is when curved shell pieces are used for the core. The pieces are thinner than the channel. They are also delicate and hard to handle. So in this case instead of gluing in the shell at the same time that the veneer lines are glued in to the channel, a strip of PTFE plastic (one brand name is Teflon) is glued in place of the shell pieces. These strips are available from lutherie suppliers. After the glue is cured, the plastic strip is removed and the shell pieces are fitted and glued into the resulting channel.

☐ Preparing a Solid Wood Core Option

The solid wood core is too thick to be cold bent, so before it can be installed it must be heat bent, using the same tools and techniques that were used to bend the sides of the guitar. Any attractive piece of wood can be used for the core, but the piece should have straight grain and little runout. Wood for the core can be cut off a board. A good source for the material for a solid wood core is a length of wood binding strip, which is available from lutherie suppliers. This presents the opportunity to have the wood core of the rosette match the wood of the guitar binding if desired.

1. The wood for the core must be at least 20″ (508mm) in length. The piece is first planed to a thickness of 3⁄32″ (2.4mm), which is the same thickness as the width of the veneer lines that will surround the core. Then 5⁄64″ (2mm) wide strips are ripped from the stock. If wide enough stock is used, the strips can be ripped using a table saw with zero clearance insert, a fine blade, and appropriate featherboards and push sticks. The spindle sander or the drill press-mounted sanding drum can be used with a fence to dimension this wood core piece. Digital calipers are used to measure width and thickness of the prepared strips,

Photo 12-36 – *Bending the strip on the bending iron requires a light touch.*

Photo 12-38 – *A standard baking half sheet pan is used to hold the marquetry strip while it is soaked in boiling water. Soaking makes the glue elastic and the strip somewhat pliable.*

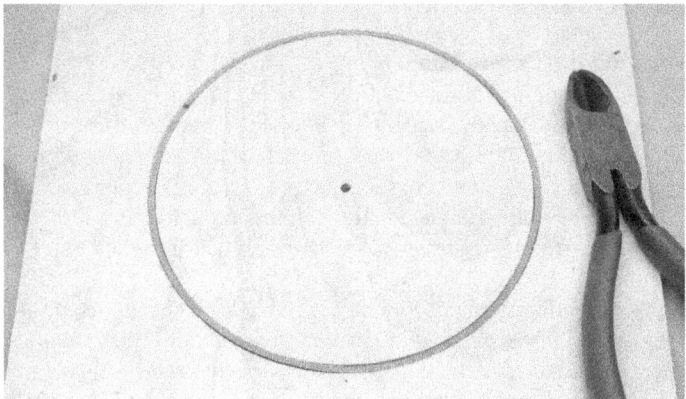

Photo 12-37 – *The solid wood core, bent into the mold, and snipped to length.*

and the strips are planed or scraped to accurate dimensions as necessary.

More than one strip should be prepared (**photo 12-34**), because the strips will be heat bent, and they are quite delicate and prone to breaking during bending.

2. A mold is made to aid in bending the wood core. The mold is made from a piece of ¾″ (19.1mm) or thicker plywood, approximately 8″ (203.2mm) square.

3. A ⅛″ (3.2mm) hole is drilled through the plywood at its center using the drill press. This hole will accept the pivot pin for cutting a circular channel.

4. A circular channel ³⁄₃₂″ (2.4mm) deep, ⁵⁄₆₄″ (2mm) wide, and approximately 4⁵⁹⁄₆₄″ (125mm) in inside diameter is cut in the surface of the plywood square. The same tools that were used to cut the rosette channels in the top plate are used to cut this channel. If the Jasper Tools circle cutter router base plate is used, the router is fitted with a ⁵⁄₆₄″ (2mm) diameter bit, and the pivot pin is inserted into the hole marked 5¼. The end of one of the strips is test fitted into the channel. It must be a loose fit. If the fit is tight, the channel should be widened a bit by sanding with a piece of folded sandpaper held in the hands vertically in the channel, and moved back and forth along the channel walls. Sandpaper can be used to slightly chamfer the edges of the channel. The finished mold is shown in **photo 12-35**.

5. The bending iron is heated for bending the strip. Once it is up to temperature, one of the strips is dampened by being drawn through a damp rag.

6. The strip is oriented so one of the ⁵⁄₆₄″ (2mm) wide surfaces will be the top. It is carefully and gently bent into a uniform circle, starting approximately 2″ (50.8mm) from the end, and continuing to approximately 2″ (50.8mm) from the other end (**photo 12-36**). The circle is compared to the mold channel and is reworked on the bending iron as needed. It need only approximate the diameter of the mold channel, but it should be carefully checked for kinks. Any of these should be carefully ironed out, using the same techniques used during side bending.

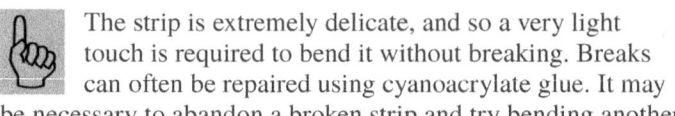 The strip is extremely delicate, and so a very light touch is required to bend it without breaking. Breaks can often be repaired using cyanoacrylate glue. It may be necessary to abandon a broken strip and try bending another.

7. The short straight end of the strip is chopped off using diagonal cutting pliers, and the strip is inserted into the channel of the mold, starting at the snipped end and working around to the starting place. The excess is clipped off using the cutting pliers. The strip should be fully seated in the channel (**photo 12-37**). It should be carefully checked again for any kinked places. These are easier to spot with the strip in the mold. Kinks should be worked out on the bending iron and the strip returned to the mold.

8. The strip is left in the mold for at least an hour to cool and dry. The strip should be stored in the mold if the center ring will not be immediately assembled.

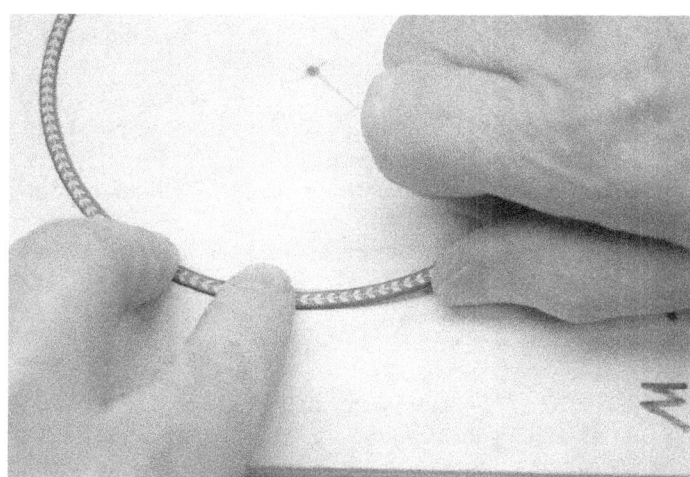

Photo 12-39 – After soaking, the marquetry strip is pliable enough so that it can be bent and fit into the mold.

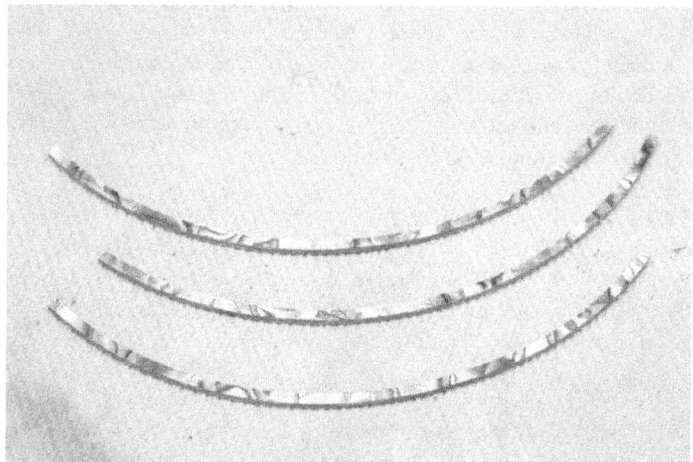

Photo 12-40 – Precut curved abalone strips for use in a rosette core. Three pieces are needed for the example rosette.

□ **Preparing a Marquetry Strip Core Option**

Commercially available marquetry strips are a good option for a decorative core. They are available in a number of patterns and widths. These strips cannot be cold bent, but strips that are no more than 1/8″ (3.2MM) wide can be bent using hot water. The strip should be at least 5/64″ (2MM) thick. A strip that is thicker than 3/32″ (2.4MM) should be thinned down to that thickness before using it.

1. The following instructions are for preparing a 1/8″ (3.2MM) wide marquetry strip. Sometimes such strips actually measure a bit wider than that, and if so they should be thinned in width, using the card scraper as discussed previously for the veneer lines. Note that it is wise to purchase more than one strip because it is possible to damage the strips during the bending process.

2. A mold is made to aid in bending the wood core. The mold is made from a piece of 3/4″ (19.1MM) or thicker plywood, approximately 8″ (203.2MM) square.

3. A 1/8″ (3.2MM) hole is drilled through the plywood at its center using the drill press. This hole will accept the pivot pin for cutting a circular channel.

4. A circular channel 3/32″ (2.4MM) deep, 1/8″ (3.2MM) wide, and approximately 4 59/64″ (125MM) in inside diameter is cut in the surface of the plywood square. The same tools that were used to cut the rosette channels in the top plate are used to cut this channel. If the Jasper Tools circle cutter router base plate is used, the router is fitted with a 1/8″ (3.2MM) diameter bit, and the pivot pin is inserted into the hole marked 5 1/4. The end of one of the strips is test fitted into the channel. It must be a loose fit. If the fit is tight, the channel should be widened a bit by sanding with a piece of folded sandpaper held in the hands vertically in the channel, and moved back and forth along the channel walls. Sandpaper can be used to slightly chamfer the edges of the channel.

5. A length of the strip approximately 18″ (457.2MM) long is cut using cutting pliers. The strip is placed in a shallow pan that is long enough to hold it. Note that a strip of this length will fit diagonally in a standard half sheet baking pan.

6. Boiling water is poured into the pan to cover the strip. The strip is allowed to soak for one minute (**photo 12-38**).

7. The strip is removed with tongs. One end is inserted in the mold at the point in the circle closest to the luthier and held in place with the fingers of the dominant hand while the fingers of the other hand are used to bend the strip so it can be further inserted into the mold channel (**photo 12-39**). As when inserting the veneer lines into their channels, right-handed luthiers usually find it easier to bend and insert the strip in a clockwise direction.

If the strip will not bend into the mold, it may need to be soaked in boiling water for a longer period of time. Marquetry strips with a diagonal pattern bend easier in one direction than the other. If the strip falls apart during bending, the soaking and bending should be attempted with a new strip, but soaked for a shorter period of time. Some iteration may be necessary to get the bending just right.

Core Material	Veneer Lines	Glue Allowance	Filler Strip?
5/64″ (2MM) wide solid wood	6	≥ 0.032″ (0.8MM)	no
1/8″ (3.2MM) wide marquetry strip	4	≥ 0.020″ (0.5MM)	no
5/64″ (2MM) wide curved shell	6	≥ 0.028″ (0.7MM)	5/64″ (2MM) wide PTFE plastic strip

Table 12-4 – Critical dimensions for the three options for the central core of the example three ring rosette. Note that when shell is used, the shell pieces are not glued in when the veneer lines are. A plastic strip is glued in instead. This will be removed and the shell installed in a later construction operation.

8. The strip is cut to length using diagonal cutting pliers. A weight is placed on top of the bent strip as was done when gluing in the veneer lines. This should be left in place while the strip cools and dries, overnight.

☐ **Preparing a Shell Strip Core Option**

As has been mentioned, the simplest way to implement a core for the center ring of the rosette made of shell material is to purchase precut curved abalone strips from a lutherie supplier (**photo 12-40**). Various widths are available, but for the example rosette, the pieces should be 5/64″ (2MM) wide, and have an inside diameter of 4⁵⁹⁄₆₄″ (125MM). The shell pieces are not glued into the channel at the same time as the veneer lines. Instead, a flexible piece of PTFE plastic of the same width as the shell strips is glued in, then later that is removed for insertion of the shell.

Materials
   3 pcs precut curved abalone strips, 5/64″ (2MM) wide
   5/64″ (2MM) wide PTFE (Teflon) filler strip material

---

1. A length of 5/64″ (2MM) wide PTFE filler strip material is cut approximately 18″ (457.2MM) long.

2. Digital calipers are used to check the width of the plastic. If it is wider than the width of the shell strips, the card scraper is used to thin the plastic strip down to near the width of the shell.

3. The plastic is bent into a circle approximately the diameter of the center of the center rosette channel.

☐ **Preparing the Veneer Lines**

Now that one of three optional cores has been prepared, the process of inlaying the center channel can commence. The first step is preparing the veneer lines that will go inside and outside the central core. This is exactly the same procedure that was used to do this for the lines of the inner and outer channels. Measurements are taken to ensure a good fit, and the lines are thinned as necessary. As was mentioned in the section about installing the lines in the inner and outer channels, luthier suppliers generally sell purfling strips made up of pre-glued veneer lines in limited sizes and color combinations. Use of these in place of individual veneer lines can make the job of preparing and installing the lines easier.

1. Digital calipers are used to measure the width of the center channel in a number of places (**photo 12-41**). If the channels were cut with the router, the width should be accurate, but there is often some deviation from the target width of the channel when it is cut using the compass gramil.

2. If a solid wood or marquetry core will be used, the core is gently removed from its mold, using a dental pick or similar tool (**photo 12-42**). Care must be taken to remove the core without breaking it.

3. The veneer lines are selected and cut to approximately 18″ (457.2MM) in length. If the core will be 5/64″ (2MM) wide solid wood or shell, then six lines are used, three on each side of the core. If the core will be a 1/8″ (3.2MM) wide marquetry strip, then four lines are used, two on each side. See **table 12-4**.

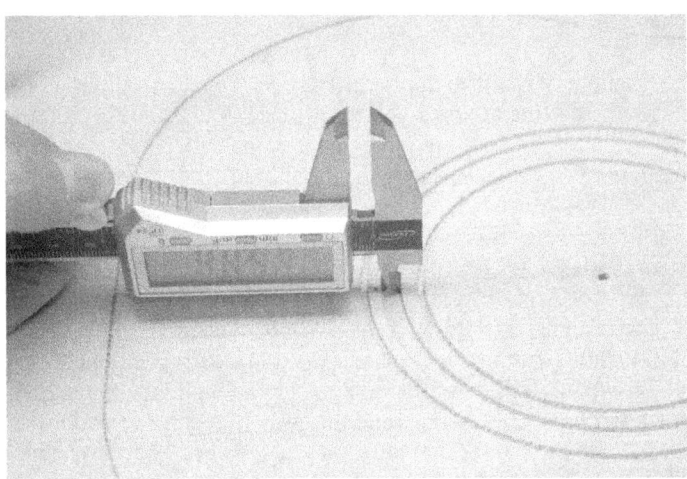

Photo 12-41 – Measuring the width of the center channel, using digital calipers.

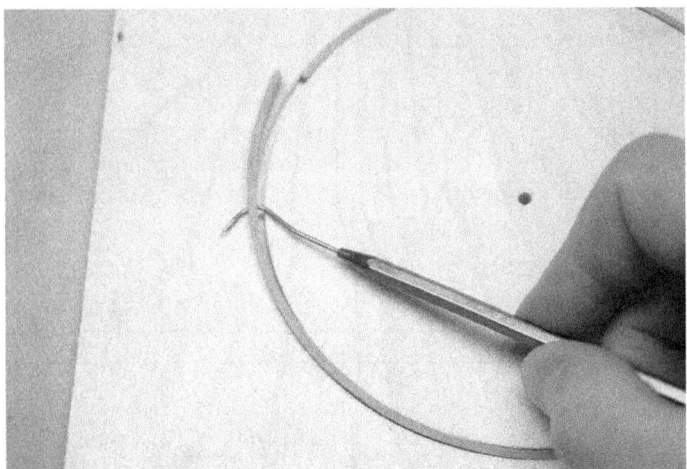

Photo 12-42 – The solid wood or marquetry strip core is carefully removed from the mold, using a dental pick or similar tool.

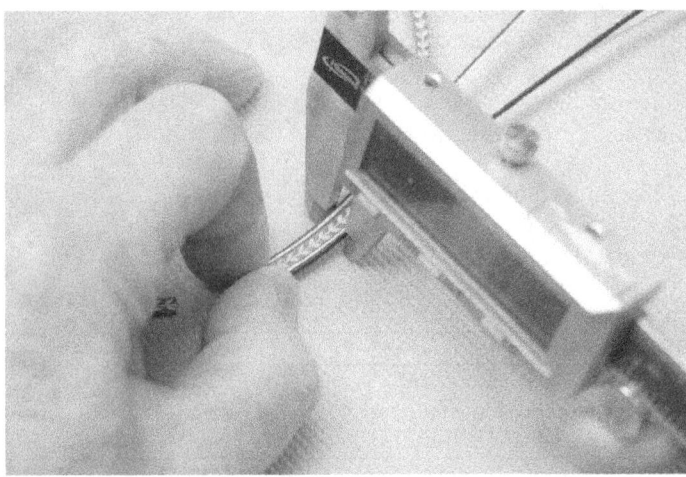

Photo 12-43 – The width of the bundle of center ring pieces is measured using digital calipers.

4. The veneer lines and the core are dry-fitted together, near one end of the core, held together with the fingers. Note that if the core will be shell strips, then the plastic strip is used as a stand-in for the core here. The calipers are used to measure the thickness of the entire bundle of pieces (**photo 12-43**). Added to this sum is a glue allowance taken from **table 12-4**.

5. If the resulting value from step 4 is less than or equal to that of the measured width of the channel, then all the components will fit in the channel and the rest of this step is skipped.

Otherwise, the components won't fit in the channel. If the width value is grossly larger than the width of the channel then it may be necessary to remove one or more veneer lines. Usually though, the width can be trimmed down by scraping the veneer lines thinner, as was described in the operation for preparing the lines for the inner and outer channels.

Steps 4 and 5 are repeated until the resulting value from step 4 is less than or equal to that of the measured width of the channel.

6. As a final check, the end of the bundle is dry-fitted into the channel. The fit should be loose, with the additional space approximately equal to the glue allowance specified in **table 12-4**.

□ **Gluing the Materials Into the Center Channel**

This operation proceeds in much the same manner as the previous operation to glue veneer lines into the inner and outer channels. Refer to the descriptions and photos for those operations. But there are more pieces to keep together in the process here, so it takes more concentration to execute this successfully.

1. If the top plate is still clamped to the workboard, it can be unclamped for the gluing operation. It can be left on the workboard or placed on any clean, flat surface. The top is rotated so the neck end is pointed at the luthier.

2. A length of melamine-covered board is used to support the lines while glue is applied. The outside lines should be taped down to the board in order as a group, using just a bit of tape on the ends. The same is done for the inside lines.

3. Glue is poured into the cup. The brush is used to quickly apply glue to the exposed surfaces of both groups of veneer lines. Glue is also quickly brushed into the center channel. Speed is generally more important that complete coverage.

4. The core material is placed approximately centered in the channel, with one end at the centerline on the neck end of the top plate.

5. The tape is removed from the ends of the lines and glue is smeared over the ends. For each bundle, each line is quickly picked up with the fingers and placed on top of the next one, to form a bundle of the lines in their proper order. The bundle is picked up off the board and quickly pressed together. One side of the bundle will have glue on it, but the other will not. Glue is quickly applied to the side without it. This is most easily done by simply smearing that side of the bundle in the glue that is on the surface of the board.

6. One of the veneer line bundles is picked up and its end is aligned with the end of the core. The bundle is pressed and

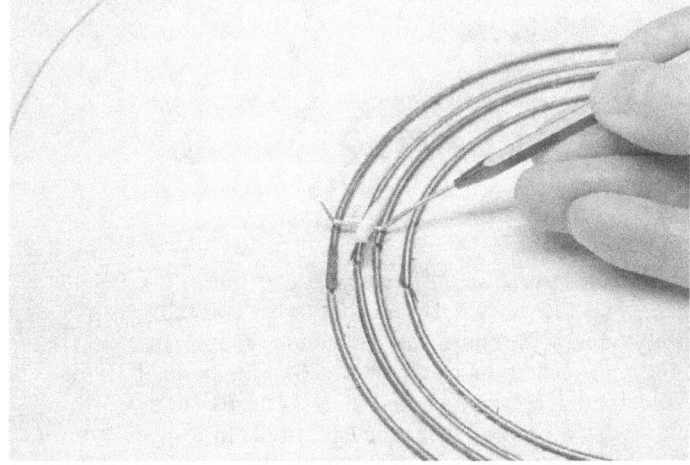

Photo 12-45 – *The end of the plastic filler strip, used as a substitute for the abalone pieces during gluing, is lifted using a dental pick.*

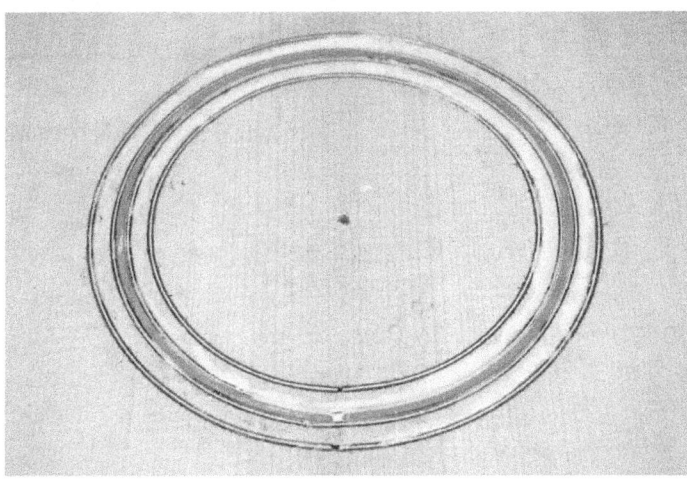

Photo 12-44 – *The pieces of the center ring glued into place. The glue squeeze-out is left alone.*

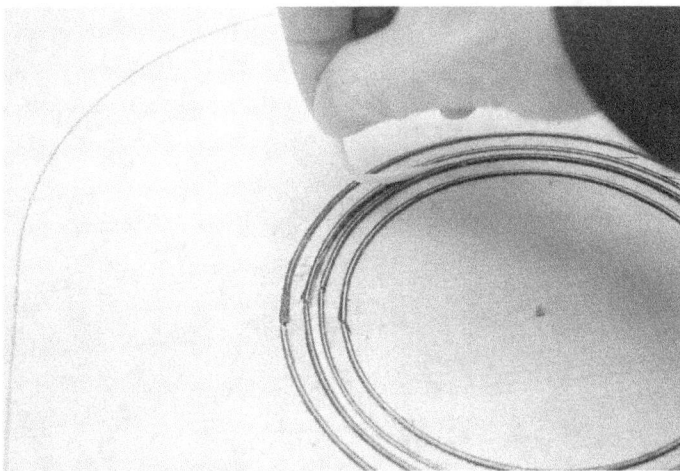

Photo 12-46 – *The plastic filler strip is removed.*

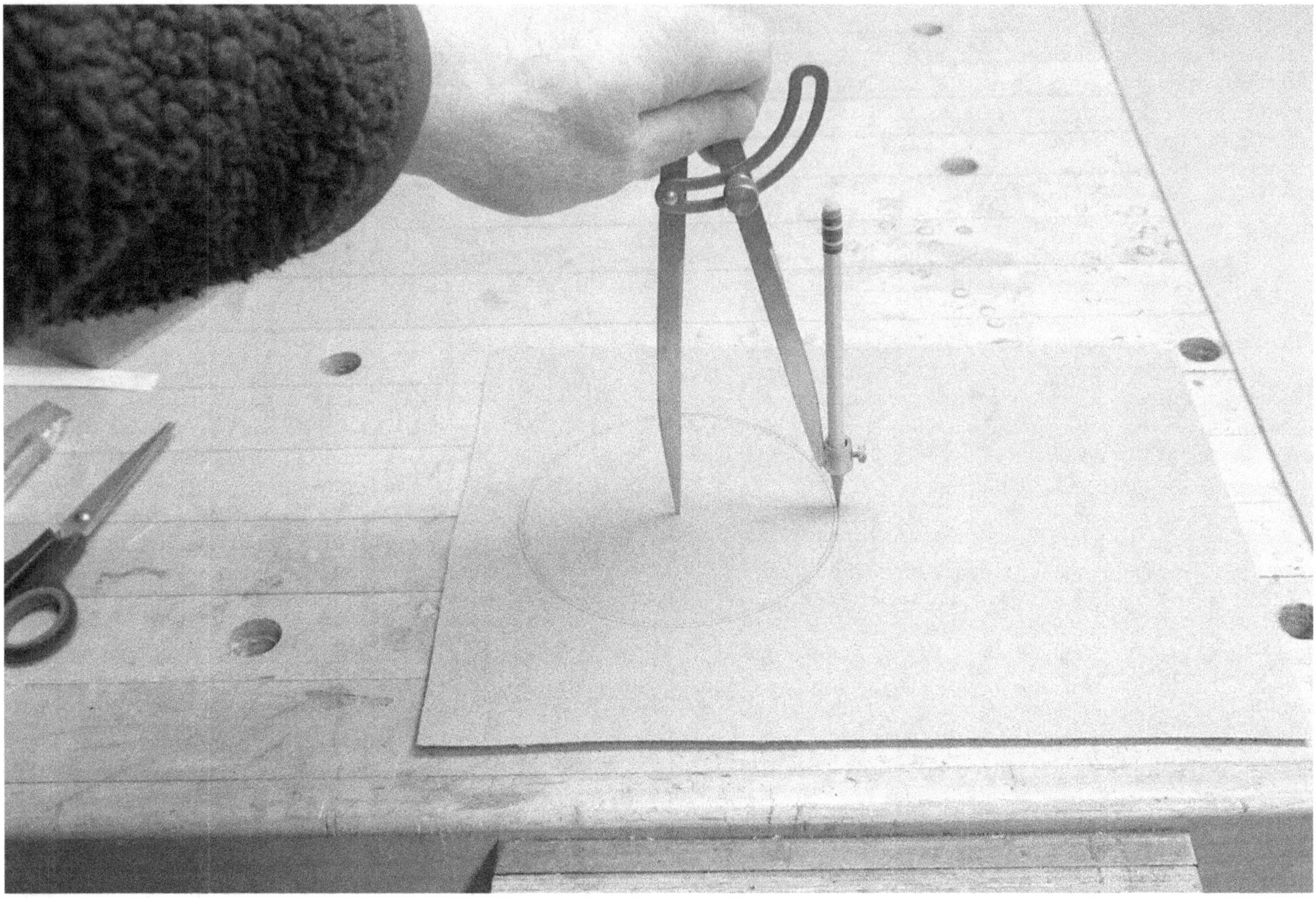

Photo 12-47 – *The outline for the spacer ring is drawn on the spacer material using the compass.*

held to the outside of the core. The other veneer line bundle is picked up and pressed to the inside of the core. Both hands are used to insert the entire bundle into the channel. Insertion begins at the centerline on the neck end of the channel. Right-handed luthiers generally find it most effective to proceed clockwise from here, using the nails of the first finger and thumb of the left hand to pinch the bundle together, and the fingers of the right hand to guide the bundle and press it into place in the channel.

If the bundle just can't be cleanly inserted into the channel, it is best to abort this operation for now. The components are pulled out, surface glue is wiped off the top, the core is thoroughly cleaned of glue, and remaining glue is allowed to thoroughly cure. Then the channel is re-cut or re-

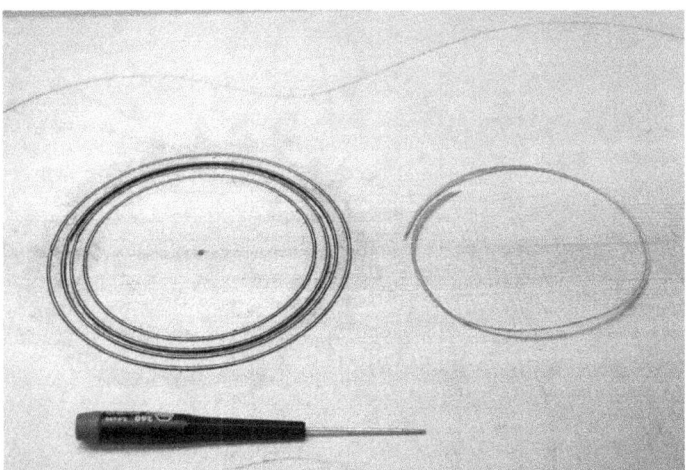

Photo 12-48 – *The spacer ring (right) ready to install in the channel.*

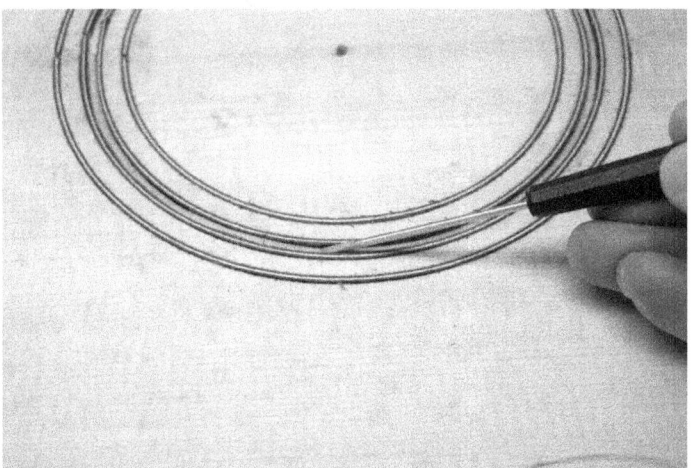

Photo 12-49 – *The spacer ring is glued to the bottom of the channel; and pressed in place all around.*

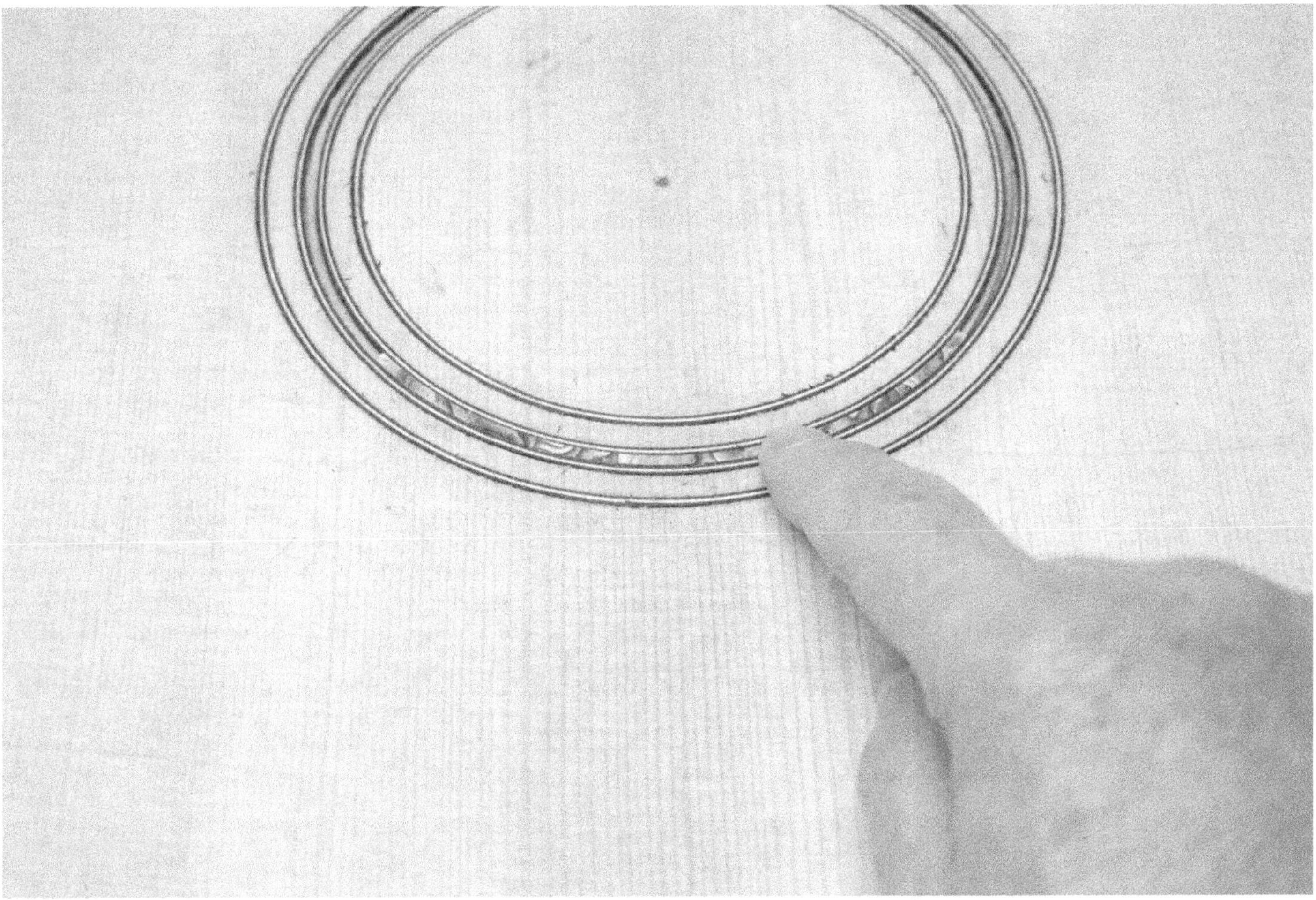

Photo 12-50 – One curved shell piece is placed so the center of its length is aligned with the top plate centerline.

routed, and new lines are prepared, but this time additional glue allowance space is allocated when fitting the lines and core to the channel.

7. As insertion proceeds, the top is rotated so that the section of the channel currently being worked on is near the luthier. When the starting point is reached, the cutting pliers are used to snip the bundle just before the final end is tucked into the channel.

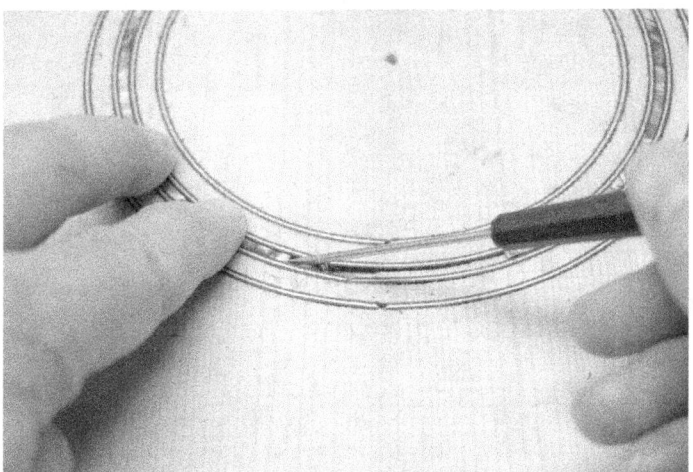

Photo 12-51 – After the other two shell pieces are installed, their ends are gently pressed to be sure the butt joints between pieces are closed.

The work is inspected to be sure the core and all lines are well seated in the channel (**photo 12-44**).

8. The rosette is covered with a piece of wax paper, and that is covered with a weight while the glue cures. The glue is allowed at least two hours to cure before removing the weight and wax paper.

☐ **Gluing In a Core of Precut Shell Pieces Option**

When the center ring was glued up, a strip of PTFE plastic was substituted for the curved abalone pieces. These will be glued into place now. The abalone pieces are thinner than other material used for the core. If the central part of the center channel was not routed shallower to compensate for this when the channel was cut, a spacer will have to be made to go under the abalone pieces, to raise their top surfaces up to the level of the top surface of the plate. Pretty much any sheet material that is 0.02″ (0.5MM) thick and can be glued can be used. Chipboard (also called cereal box cardboard) of that thickness can be obtained readily from cereal boxes. An excellent material to use for making the spacer is 0.02″ (0.5MM) thick black fiber veneer. This material is available from lutherie suppliers. It is easy to cut it cleanly using scissors.

1. The PTFE plastic strip is picked out of the channel using a dental pick or similar tool. One end of the strip is pulled up

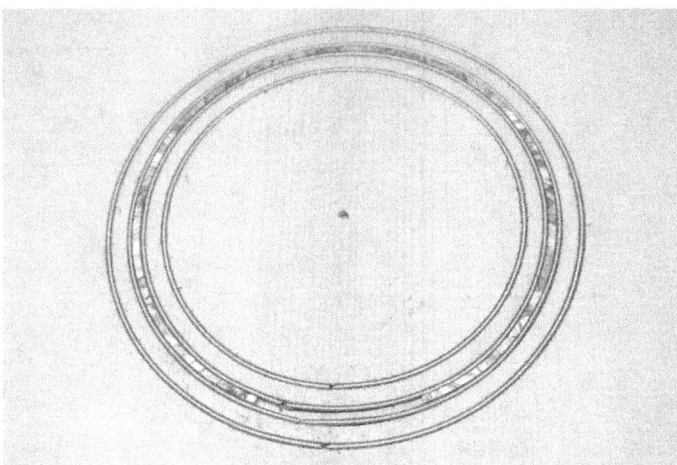

Photo 12-52 – *The completed abalone core, shown here with the top plate neck end toward us. Note the large gap at the neck end.*

with the pick (**photo 12-45**) then it is grasped with the fingers and the entire strip is removed (**photo 12-46**).

2. If the central part of the center channel was routed shallower when the channel was cut, this step and steps 3 through 5 are skipped. Otherwise a spacer will have to be made. The compass is positioned with one leg on the center of the center hole in the top plate, and the other leg is extended until it points at the *inside* edge of the channel for the shell material. The compass is used to draw a circle on the 0.02″ (0.5mm) thick material that will be used for the spacer.

3. Step 2 above is repeated, but with the compass opened so the second leg points at the *outside* edge of the channel for the shell material. Then the compass is used to draw a circle around the first circle (**photo 12-47**).

4. The thin spacer band marked out by the pencil lines is cut out, using scissors or a knife. The ring should be kept a bit thinner than the channel. There is no need to keep the ring in one piece. The finished spacer ring is shown in **photo 12-48**.

5. The spacer is dry-fitted into the channel, to be sure it fits without binding or folding up at the edges. Its width is thinned as necessary. A thin coat of wood glue is applied to only the floor of the channel. The spacer is placed into the channel, starting at the centerline on the neck end. A small screwdriver or splinter of wood is used to press the spacer into place all around (**photo 12-49**). The glue is allowed to cure for one hour.

6. One of the pieces of abalone is test fitted into the channel. The pieces are quite delicate and easily broken. Ideally the piece will drop into place or require just a bit of a push to press it down into the channel. The top surface of the piece should be

Photo 12-53 – *All gaps at the fretboard end are filled with epoxy.*

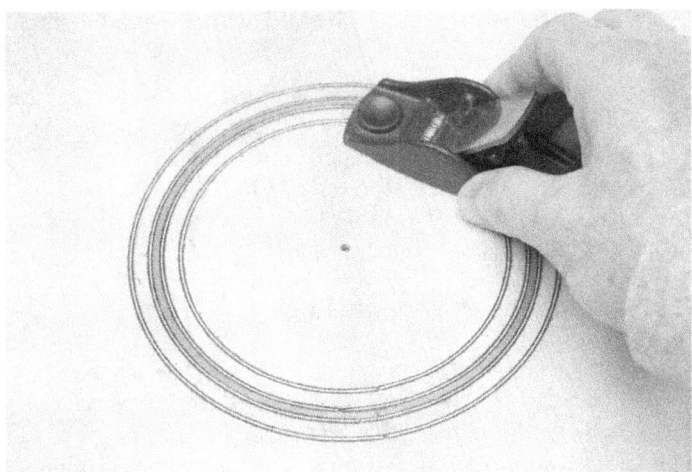

Photo 12-54 – *The rosette can be quickly leveled with a few tools, starting with a small plane.*

8. A second piece of abalone is butted against one end of the piece already inserted, and then inserted in the channel and pressed into place. The third piece is butted against the other end of the first piece, and then pressed into place. The small screwdriver can be used to gently press into the two free ends of the abalone pieces, to be sure the butt joints between the abalone pieces are tight (**photo 12-51**).

Note that a section of the channel at the neck end of the rosette is not filled (**photo 12-52**). This section will be under the fretboard extension in the finished instrument, and so will not be visible. It will be filled with an inexpensive material in the next operation.

Finishing Up the Rosette

Various pieces may be higher than the top surface of the top plate at this point. These will be leveled down flush to aid in subsequent operations on the inside of the top.

☐ **Filling and Leveling the Rosette**

1. There are small gaps in the veneer line channels at the neck end at this point. If abalone pieces were used as the core material of the center channel, then there is quite a wide gap there. The gaps are most easily filled using epoxy (**photo 12-53**). The epoxy is drop-filled into the gaps, and allowed adequate time to cure.

2. The top of the rosette is cut down flush to that of the top plate, using a small plane (**photo 12-54**), then a carder scraper (**photo 12-55**), followed by sanding with a hard sanding block or a sander with a hard backing plate (**photo 12-56**). This work must be done with the top backed up by a smooth, hard, flat surface, like the original workboard, to prevent pushing the rosette right through the thin floors of the rosette channels. Care is taken when using the plane not to gouge the top. The

at the same level as the top surface of the top. Note that the tops of the veneer lines will usually be a bit above that of the top plate. If the level is correct, the piece is carefully removed.

Note that abalone is unique in that if it breaks, it can still be used. The break ends up looking just like part of the pattern of the abalone itself and is easily filled with a drop of medium cyanoacrylate glue. Still, care should be taken when handling the pieces.

7. Glue is carefully applied on top of the spacer and on the walls of the channel. The center of the length of one of the abalone pieces is marked on the piece in pencil. This piece is placed in the channel with the center mark on the centerline of the top at the *tail end* of the rosette. It is pressed into place so it fully contacts the glue beneath it (**photo 12-50**).

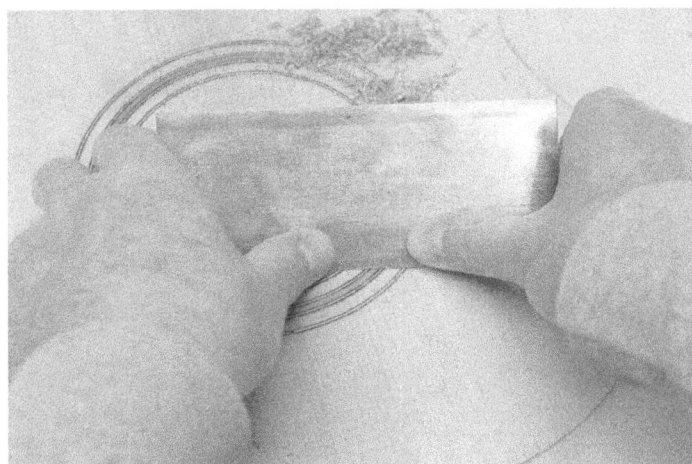

Photo 12-55 – *Leveling continues, using a card scraper.*

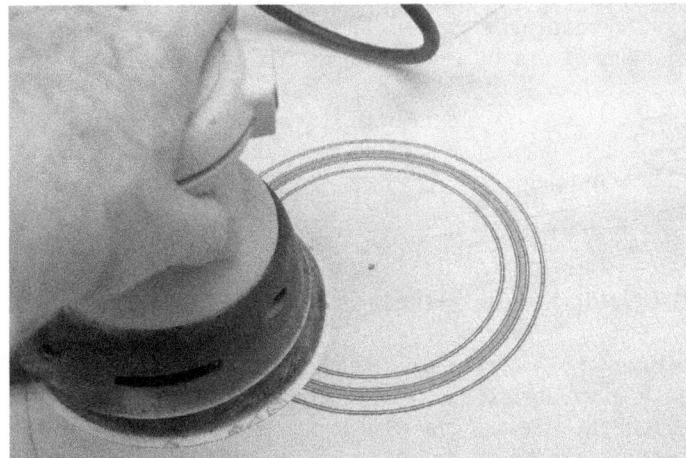

Photo 12-56 – *Leveling of the rosette is finished up using sandpaper on a hard block or a sander with a hard pad.*

Example Guitar	Soundhole Diameter	Router Bit Diameter	Baseplate Pin Hole
Tripletta OM	3⅞″ (98.4mm)	1/16″ (1.6mm)	4 1/16
Paura Dreadnought	4″ (101.6mm)	1/16″ (1.6mm)	4 3/16

Table 12-5 – *Diameters of the soundholes of the example guitars. Also included here are the bit diameter and pivot pin hole to use to cut out the soundhole using the Jasper Tools circle cutting router baseplate.*

Photo 12-57 – Sanding the edge of the soundhole smooth and square, using a chunk of a large diameter dowel as a sanding block.

plane is used to get the material down to *near* the top surface only. The card scraper can then be used to scrape right down to the top surface, but care should be taken to not scrape directly across the grain of the top. Doing so creates a washboard effect, which will be difficult to remove by sanding. Leveling the rosette is finished up using sandpaper on a hard sanding block.

 When switching to sanding, if the core of the center ring is made of wood, 100-grit sandpaper is used. But if the core is made of shell, 180-grit or higher sandpaper must be used, to prevent putting deep and difficult-to-remove scratches in the surface of the shell.

Cutting the Soundhole

The soundhole is cut out using the same tools and techniques used to cut the rosette channels. The top plate is first mounted on the workboard used when cutting the rosette channels. The pivot pin is used to align the holes drilled in the plate and workboard, then the plate is clamped to the workboard using four clamps, exactly as was done for cutting the channels.

 The clamps are necessary to prevent the plate from moving around at the moment the soundhole is cut through.

☐ **Using the Disposable Compass Gramil Option**

If the disposable compass gramil was used, it has been previously marked with an arc representing the circumference of the soundhole. That tool can be used in the same way that it was used to make the cuts for the walls of the rosette channels. The only difference is that the exposure of the point of the blade must be deep enough to cut right through the top plate.

 Note that when using the compass gramil to cut out the soundhole, it is usually better to cut only halfway through the plate from one side, then flip it over and cut the rest of the way through from the other side. The blade is less likely to bind in the deep cut this way.

☐ **Using the Router and Circle Cutting Base Option**

If the router and circle cutting router base was used to cut the rosette channels, then that combination can be used to cut the soundhole. For this purpose though, a $\frac{1}{16}''$ (1.6mm) diameter downcut router bit is used. The setup of the router and base for this operation is detailed in **table 12-5**. The soundhole should be cut out in three or four shallow passes.

☐ **Sanding the Soundhole Edge**

After the soundhole is cut out, the edge must be sanded smooth and square. This is easily done using a short piece of a large diameter dowel with PSA sandpaper attached to the circumference (**photo 12-57**). Care must be taken when sanding the thin softwood top to avoid distorting the round shape of the hole. The soft and thin wood sands quickly, but wood removal is greater when sanding the sides of the soundhole than when sanding its top and bottom.

---

1. Buckland, James (2010). 19th Century Guitar Making Techniques. *American Lutherie #103*, p.16

13 Bracing the Top Plate

It was mentioned in the chapter about the back plate that the purpose of plate bracing is to provide stiffness, while keeping the plate light enough to vibrate freely. This is because braces add considerably more stiffness than weight. The guitar top must directly support the tension of the strings. The strings terminate at the bridge, and are pulling directly on the top. And the guitar top must vibrate freely, as well as support string tension. It is certainly true that a plate could be made stiff enough to support the tension of the strings by simply making it thicker. But doing so would increase the weight of the plate as well. A number of different bracing patterns for the guitar top plate have evolved over time. All provide the stiffness needed to counteract string tension, and the lightness needed for free vibration of the top.

Bracing Patterns

There is great variety in the bracing patterns used for the tops of guitars, although most are variations on a small number of conventional patterns. Experimentation with bracing seems to have happened throughout the history of the guitar, but only a few basic patterns have persisted.

The top bracing for early plucked string instruments such as the lute and the oud made use of a simple ladder bracing pattern, the same basic pattern of parallel transverse braces that was used to brace the back plate in a previous chapter. There are many variations on the ladder bracing theme, but the basic pattern consists of one transverse brace above the soundhole, another below the soundhole, and a third transverse brace at the neck end of the bridge (**figure 13-1.1**). This pattern was used extensively on early guitars, and was used on many guitars built during the 20th century.

Another conventional bracing pattern is called *fan bracing*. This pattern is characterized by a number of braces that extend from just below the soundhole down to near the tail end of the top (**figure 13-1.2**). These braces are arranged much like the folds of a paper fan. Fan-braced guitar plates generally have a transverse brace above the sound hole and one below it as well. Additional braces near the tail end, called *cutoff bars*, appear in some fan bracing patterns. Although the originator of this bracing style is not reliably established, the earliest known use is by Spanish luthier Francisco Sanguino in the mid to late 18th century. The bracing style has been used by a number of luthiers since. It is now generally associated with the Spanish guitars of Antonio de Torres Jurado, the 19th century Spanish luthier who is considered to be the father of the modern classical guitar, and of the guitars of many luthiers who came after him. Fan bracing is used extensively in modern classical guitars.

A third conventional top bracing pattern is known as *X bracing* (**figure 13-1.3**). The name comes from the shape of the two main braces, which are in the pattern of the letter "X." As with the origins of fan bracing, we really don't have definitive information on who was the first person to make use of this pattern. But X bracing is closely associated with guitars made by C.F. Martin, who used this bracing pattern extensively. The company bearing his name still uses this pattern today. Because the modern steel string acoustic guitar is essentially derived from the guitars of C.F. Martin, this bracing pattern is commonly used for steel string guitars built by many luthiers. This is the bracing pattern that is used for the top plates of the two example instruments discussed in this book.

Function of Bracing

It has been mentioned that bracing is applied to top plates as a way to make them stiff enough and light enough. But braces perform other functions as well. Understanding a little about these helps to understand how the common bracing patterns evolved. Braces distribute the loads imposed by string tension on the bridge to a wider area of the plate. Braces add stiffness across the grain of the top. And braces cross grain lines of the top, which helps to prevent cracking along the grain.

If the only functional requirement for bracing was to support string tension, then the simplest bracing pattern would be a single longitudinal brace, down the centerline of the top. One issue with this construction is that it would encourage cracking of the plate along the sides of this brace, which would be parallel to the grain of the top wood. Small blows to the top near the sides of the brace could easily result in a crack, as could more subtle events such as a difference in string tension during string changing, or even differences in humidity over time.

It is desirable that the bracing of the guitar top should not encourage cracking along the grain. Actually, given that cracking

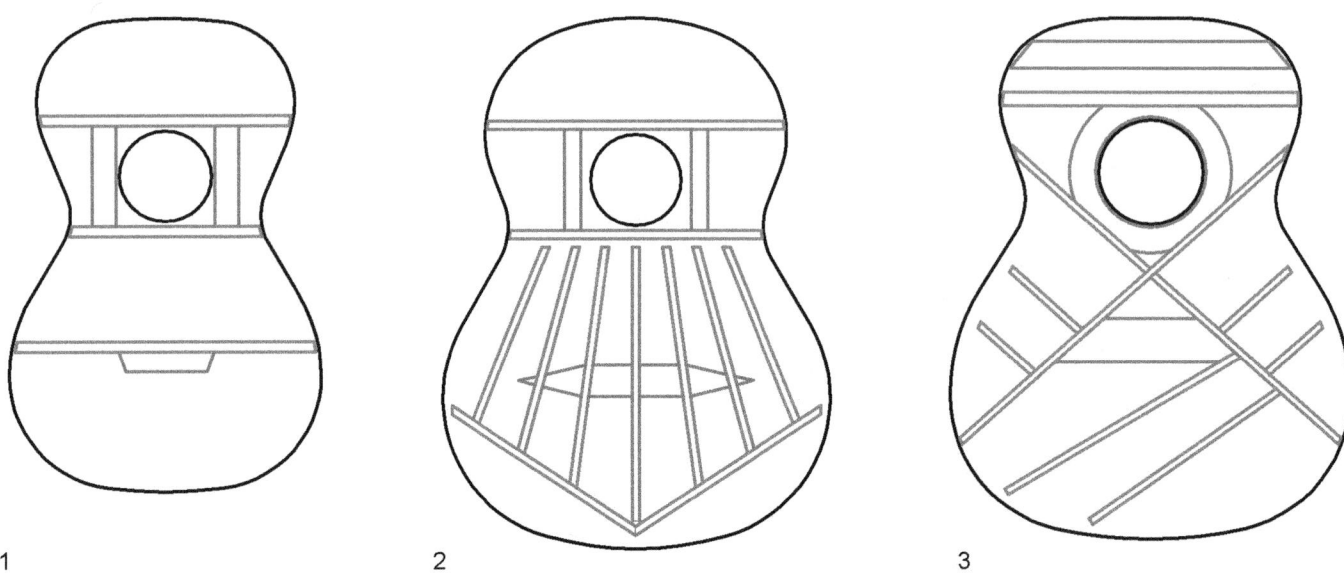

Figure 13-1 – *Typical guitar top bracing patterns, shown as x-ray views looking through the top. Ladder bracing, shown in example 1, is typical of most early instruments, and was used well into the 20th century. The pattern uses three or more braces positioned horizontally across the top plate, and these look somewhat like the rungs of a ladder. Fan bracing, shown in example 2, is now typically used in classical guitars. The fan braces below the soundhole are arrayed like the ribs of a small paper hand fan. X bracing is shown in example 3. It is typically used in steel string acoustic guitars. Its name comes from the pattern of its main braces, located under the soundhole, which form the pattern of the letter "X."*

in a thin plate as a result of humidity changes over time is a real and major issue, it is desirable that the bracing pattern help to discourage cracking, or at the least help to limit the extent of any cracks that do develop. For this reason, bracing patterns have evolved that orient some or all of the braces across some or all of the grain of the top plate.

This is readily seen in the ladder bracing pattern, where all of the braces span the entire width of the top. But looking at the other patterns in the figure, it can be seen that all the braces in all the patterns span the grain of the top to some extent. Although a crack may develop along the grain, it will generally stop when it reaches one of the braces. Not orienting braces parallel to the grain also helps to eliminate cracking from blows to the top near the sides of the braces.

Bracing patterns with a small number of big braces that are positioned obliquely tend to distort the thin top a bit around the braces. This gives the top of the guitar an unsightly rippled look. This is greatly reduced by using a larger number of thinner braces rather than just a few big ones. Both the fan bracing pattern and the X bracing pattern make use of a larger number of smaller braces.

For many experienced luthiers, there are few things more enjoyable than tinkering with bracing patterns. This is true for large guitar factories as well as for one-person lutherie shops. An example of the former can be seen in the guitar lines of Taylor Guitars, which make use of a number of different bracing designs, including traditional X bracing and less traditional patterns designed by luthier Andy Powers.

We do this experimentation as part of our constant quest for a better guitar. Sometimes we do this in an attempt to change the way the guitar sounds. It may be counterintuitive, but it generally takes quite radical bracing changes to effect even subtly noticeable changes in the sound of the instrument. For this reason, combined with the primary function of the top bracing which is to prevent the top from collapsing, lutherie novices are encouraged to follow the bracing pattern of the plan for the guitar under construction.

It should be noted that the X bracing pattern that is used in the example guitars is asymmetrical, containing two oblique braces near the tail end, that extend from one of the X braces down to near the tail. The positioning of these braces causes a bit of confusion during construction, because the plans for the example instruments and **figure 13-1** show the bracing for a right-handed guitar as if looking through the top plate, and during construction the luthier will be looking at the top plate from its inside surface. Although care should be taken to get this positioning correct (and the following construction details take care to point out how to do this), there are really no sonic consequences for reversing this positioning. As far as sound radiation goes, there is no bass side of the guitar top, nor is there a treble side.

Brace Carving

Many plans for acoustic guitars specify quite complex three dimensional scalloped shapes for the various braces of the top plate. Although the side profiles of the top braces of the example instruments are each unique in shape, and all have scalloping of their top surfaces, the cross-sections of all of the braces remain essentially rectangular. This simplifies the descriptions of construction and also the construction itself. There is no downside to this simplification. Many of the best sounding guitars employ braces with simple cross-section shapes. These include guitars from large companies such as Seagull, as well as those by individual luthiers.

Other Bracing Components

In addition to the braces, the top plate contains a number of thinner pieces. These are generally used to provide some

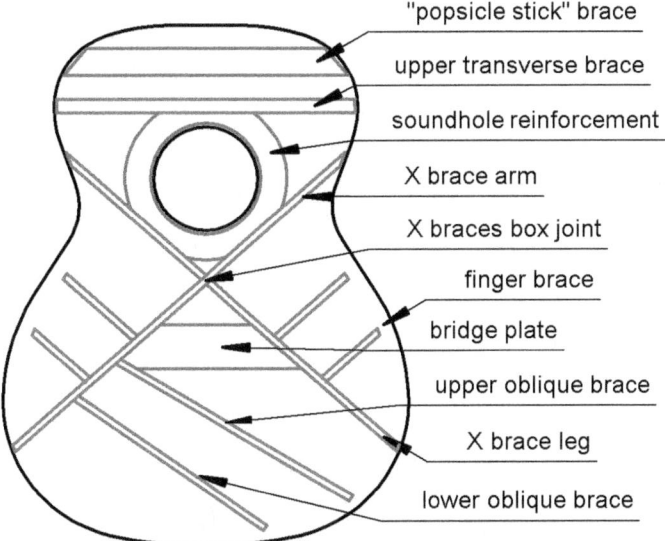

Figure 13-2 – The names of the braces of the X bracing pattern used to brace the top of the example instruments. Not shown is the box joint cap, which is described in the text. Note that the view here is looking at the inside surface of the top. This is the way the bracing will look to the luthier during construction of a right-handed guitar..

localized reinforcement. The names of all of the braces of the X bracing pattern that will be used in the example instruments are shown in **figure 13-2**, and the function of each of these will be discussed in the construction section.

Wood for Top Braces

For the most part, the same woods used to brace the back will be used to brace the top. The board of spruce brace wood previously used for the back will again be the source of the braces for the top. The additional spruce guitar top set which was the source of the wood for the center reinforcement strip of the back will also be used to provide material for bracing the top plate. One additional piece of wood is needed for the top though, a hardwood bridge plate. The details of this will be discussed in the construction section for that component. Blanks for the bridge plate are readily available from lutherie wood suppliers, and one of the cutoffs saved from the back may be big enough to use for this purpose.

"Tuning" the Top

Because the weight and the stiffness of the top wood and that of the braces can vary, it makes intuitive sense that an optimal-sounding guitar would require some sort of individual adjustment to its top. As mentioned in the introduction, there are a wide variety of such top tuning techniques in use. Some involve tapping the braced top and listening to the sounds it makes, then adjusting the shapes of braces. Others involve using instrumentation to tune sections of the top or the entire top to specific notes. Still others attempt to adjust the natural modes of vibration of the top or the completed instrument to specific frequencies.

As mentioned in the introduction to this book, I have observed no correlation of the perceived goodness of the tone of a guitar to any particular tuning method. Some of the very best sounding guitars I have heard were not tuned in any way at all. No large guitar manufacturers perform any individualized tuning. Some well-regarded luthiers include some sort of individual instrument tuning as a part of their personal construction techniques, and these techniques clearly provide excellent results. Some of those luthiers have described their construction methods in books, articles, and instructional videos, so anyone that desires to duplicate those methods can do so. But here, for simplicity and because there appears to be no downside to doing so, the construction methods described in this book do not include any kind of individual tuning techniques.

Layout and Construction

Aside from the difference in bracing pattern, the process of bracing the top plate is much the same as was used for the back plate. The major braces will be cut approximately rectangular in cross-section and their gluing surfaces will be arched, so that when the braces are glued to the plate, they will force the plate into an arch as well. Arching for the top is not as pronounced as for the back. The main braces will be shaped after they are glued on, using templates to specify the contours. Other braces are shaped before being glued in place.

Fashioning and Attaching the Top Braces

As was described in the chapter on the back plate, the width and height of the blanks for the major braces of the example instruments have been rationalized and made uniform. This greatly simplifies the construction of the bracing, and also of the description of that construction. The same 22″ (558.8mm) long spruce bracewood board, planed ⅝″ (15.9mm) thick, from which were cut the brace blanks for the back braces, will provide the material for the top braces as well. It is convenient to rip all the pieces needed to brace the top from that board beforehand. Five pieces each ¼″ (6.4mm) wide and one piece ½″ (12.7mm) wide are needed. Also required are the templates for the soundhole reinforcement ring, bridge plate, and the top braces, from the template book of the example instrument under construction.

The Soundhole Reinforcement Ring

The function of the soundhole reinforcement ring is to reinforce the part of the top under the rosette. Due to the thin floor of the rosette channels, the top plate is quite fragile in this area. Traditional instruments would usually use two thin pieces of wood near the sides of the soundhole to perform this function, as seen in **figures 13-1.1** and **13-1.2**. A full ring provides better support here, and is also useful in positioning the primary braces. As can be seen in **figure 13-2**, the soundhole reinforcement ring has flats on its outline that contact the upper transverse brace and both of the X braces.

The ring can be made of a wide variety of materials. Thin hardwood in the range of ³⁄₃₂″ (2.4mm) to ⅛″ (3.2mm) thick works well in this application, and it is sometimes possible to make use of off-cuts from the back plate to fashion a blank big enough for this ring. I am fond of 2mm Baltic birch plywood for this application. This material is not normally found at luthier wood suppliers, but hobby and model suppliers generally carry it. Spruce is traditionally used for the soundhole reinforcements. The same low-grade top wood that was used to build the center reinforcement strip for the back, can be used to make this ring. This wood will be assumed in the following construction section.

Although the outline of the top can be roughly cut out (leaving a generous margin) at this time, I will often wait to cut the plate outline until after the X braces have been put on. It is a bit easier to hold the plate when it is still rectangular in shape when carving those braces, but this is not a big deal one way or the other.

Note that most of the operations on the top will require the top to be placed inside-surface-up on the bench. It is important that the bench top be cleaned of all debris before the top is placed on the bench outside-surface-down, because any little piece of debris can put a dent in the top that may be difficult or impossible to remove.

☐ Construction of the Soundhole Reinforcement Ring

1. The template for the soundhole reinforcement ring is cut out, using knife or scissors (**photo 13-1**). Care is taken to be sure the straight sides are cut accurately.

2. The template is traced onto the stock to be used. If solid wood stock is used, the grain orientation should be horizontal. The centerline marked on the template is also transferred to the stock.

3. The reinforcement is cut out and sanded to the lines (**photo 13-2**). The inside hole will have to be drilled and then cut out using a coping saw. An alternative is to simply hog out the waste using a large diameter Forstner bit in the drill press and then sand to the line using a sanding drum or sandpaper on a cylindrical block. Care is taken to be sure the straight sides are cut accurately and are perpendicular to the top surface. The straight parts of the soundhole reinforcement ring are used to position the primary braces and so *must* be accurate.

4. The ends of the centerline penciled on the reinforcement ring are nicked, using a knife or a triangular needle file. These marks will be used to orient the ring to the centerline of the top when the ring is glued on.

5. The outline of the ring is composed of three straight lines and three circular arcs. The top edges of the ring at the arc segments are rounded over. The straight line segments are left flat

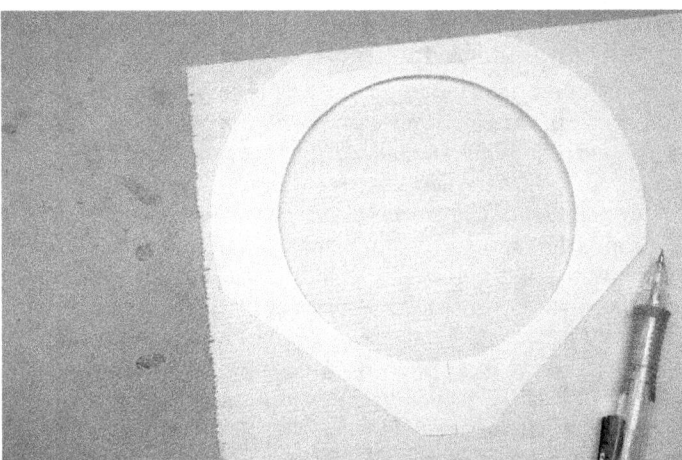

Photo 13-1 – *The soundhole reinforcement ring template is cut out and taped to the material that will be used for the ring. Here a piece of spruce is used.*

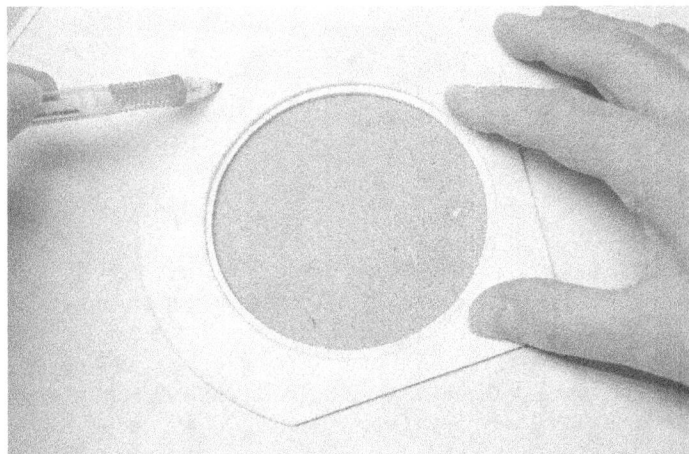

Photo 13-3 – *Tracing the flat parts of the ring's outline onto the top plate. Note that all curved top edges have been rounded over.*

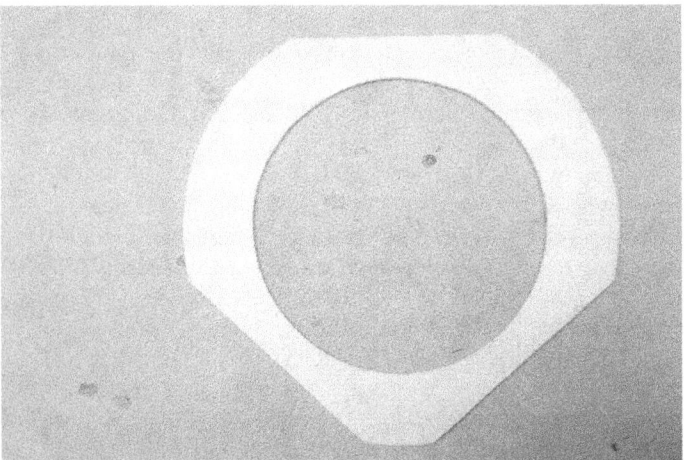

Photo 13-2 – *The reinforcement ring cut out and sanded.*

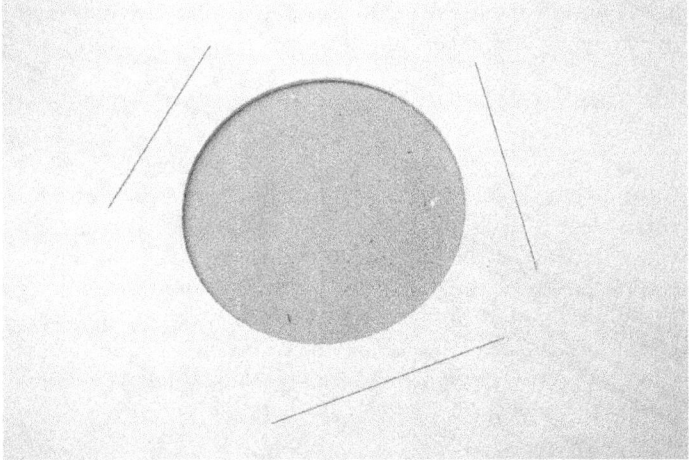

Photo 13-4 – *The top plate, showing the three pencil marks locating the three straight parts of the outline of the soundhole reinforcement ring.*

and perpendicular to the top surface of the ring. The edge of the inside circle of the ring is also rounded over. This rounding over can be seen in **photo 13-3**.

 Note here and in the rest of the discussion on construction, the terms "top edge" and "top surface" are relative to the manner in which the plate and braces are viewed during construction. That is, with the plate on the bench with its inside surface facing up. In this orientation, the top surface of a brace is the surface closest to the luthier's face. Likewise the bottom surface of the brace is the surface which contacts the inside surface of the plate.

☐ Gluing the Soundhole Reinforcement Ring

1. The process of gluing in the rosette may have caused the area on the inside surface of the top plate behind the rosette to bulge out slightly. In this case, this area is flattened using 100-grit sandpaper on a flat block.

2. The distance along the centerline from the neck end of the body, down to the neck end of the soundhole reinforcement ring, is transferred from the plan to the inside surface of the top and marked in pencil. Although it is not needed just yet, the distance along the centerline from the neck end of the body, down to the neck end of the bridge plate, is also transferred from the plan to the inside surface of the top and marked in pencil.

These measurements for both of the example instruments are 3¹⁷⁄₆₄″ (83MM) from the neck end of body to the neck end of the ring, and 11⁵⁄₃₂″ (283.4MM) from the neck end of the body to the neck end of the bridge plate.

3. Making a gluing caul. The outline and hole of the ring are traced onto ¾″ (19.1MM) thick MDF to fashion a gluing caul. The outline of the caul is cut out, keeping the saw blade just *inside* the line, to make the caul just a bit smaller all around than the ring. The caul is then cut into two pieces. This provides access to cut out the hole. The hole is cut out from both halves, keeping the blade just to the *outside* of the line, again to make the caul just a bit smaller all around than the soundhole reinforcement ring. All edges are sanded smooth.

4. The ring is positioned for gluing. The ring is placed in position so the nicks on its edges line up with the centerline of the top plate, and the hole in the ring and the soundhole are approximately concentric. The neck end edge of the ring should line up with its locating pencil mark. If not, the position of the locating mark is moved up or down until it is. All three of the flat parts of the ring outline are traced onto the top plate (**photo 13-3**).

5. The ring is removed (**photo 13-4**). A straight stick (one of the brace blanks can be used) is lined up with the pencil line corresponding to the neck end of the ring, and used to extend that line to outside of the body outline on both sides. A drafting square is used to check to be sure this line is perpendicular to the top plate centerline.

6. Setting up for gluing the ring. One of the brace blanks is clamped on its side onto the top at the marks indicating the neck end of the ring. One clamp is used at each end and one long clamp is used in the middle, approaching from the neck

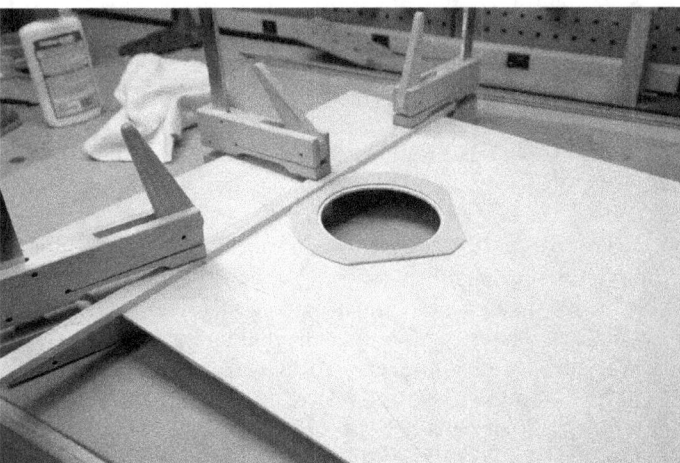

Photo 13-5 – *One of the brace blanks is clamped down to serve as a positioning stop, to prevent the ring from sliding toward the neck end of the top when glue is applied.*

Photo 13-6 – *Cauls are placed on top of the ring, and two clamps are positioned, approaching from the neck end. When the clamps are tightened they will pull the ring toward the positioning strip.*

Photo 13-7 – *All six clamps used to clamp down the ring. Four long clamps are used. The two short clamps in the center are fitted in the soundhole.*

end (**photo 13-5**). This brace blank will be used as a temporary stop when gluing the ring down. If the middle clamp won't reach because the plate is just too big, the outline of the plate can be cut out at this time, leaving a good ½″ (12.7mm) margin outside the line. The end of a ruler and a pencil is used to extend the top plate centerline up the soundhole side of the brace blank a bit. The mark should go up the side of the brace blank high enough so it will be visible above the top of the reinforcement ring. This mark will be used to center the ring. The ring is put back in position, and checked for fit again, to be sure the holes in the ring and the soundhole are as concentric as possible.

7. Gluing the ring. As usual, it is wise to do a dry run for unfamiliar gluing steps. The ring is picked up, glue is applied to its bottom surface and spread to cover the surface evenly, but a ¼″ (6.4mm) margin around the soundhole is left with no glue on it. This is done to try to avoid squeeze-out around the soundhole, which is difficult to clean up. The ring is replaced in position against the temporary stop, and aligned with the centerline. The cauls are placed on top of the ring, being sure that the edges of the cauls do not obscure the edges of the ring. Two long clamps are used on either side of the centerline and approaching from the neck end, to lightly clamp the ring caul so the pulling action of the clamps pulls the ring into the temporary stop (**photo 13-6**). A check is made to be sure that the ring is still correctly positioned, before tightening the clamps, and after tightening them too. It is critical that this piece is accurately positioned.

8. Two more long clamps, approaching from the sides and a bit from the tail end, are used to clamp the cauls on each side of the centerline on the tail end of the ring. Again, the ring position is checked as the clamps are tightened. The snipped plastic straw is used to clear glue from the soundhole edges of the ring.

9. Now two shorter clamps are inserted inside the soundhole, one pointing left and the other right. These are positioned to clamp the cauls at each side of the soundhole (**photo 13-7**).

10. The three clamps holding the temporary stop are removed, as is the stop itself. This must be done now, to prevent the stop from being glued to the top. The snipped plastic straw is used to clear any glue squeeze-out that can be reached.

11. The glue is allowed to cure overnight before the clamps and cauls are removed (**photo 13-8**). If there is any hardened glue next to any of the straight edges of the ring, it is carefully removed using a chisel.

The Bridge Plate

The bridge plate is a thin hardwood plate located directly under the bridge of the finished instrument, and spanning between the two legs of the X braces. Its purpose is to provide a bearing surface for the balls of the strings. Acoustic steel string guitars generally use bridge pins to anchor the ball ends of the strings at the bridge. In a properly functioning guitar, the bridge pins push the string balls over so the balls pull up against the bridge plate. The bridge plate prevents the balls from pulling right through the soft top wood and bearing up against the bottom of the bridge, a situation which usually leads to the bridge being torn up.

The material used for the bridge plate must be able to withstand pressure from the string balls without splitting or even getting much dented. Dense hardwood has been the choice material for bridge plates for quite some time. Rosewood (*Dalbergia* spp.) is a traditional material, but even less dense hardwoods such as the maples (*Acer* spp.) work well. Bridge plate blanks are available from lutherie wood suppliers, but can certainly be sawn from available lumber. Cutoffs from the back plate may be used if they are big enough. The wood should be quartersawn for stability. The grain should run more or less in the direction of the length of the blank. Some luthiers will purposely orient the grain so it is skewed a bit, to help eliminate cracks to the bridge plate caused by ill-fitted bridge pins.

☐ **Construction of the Bridge Plate**

1. If not done by the supplier, the bridge plate blank should be thinned to a thickness between ³⁄₃₂″ (2.4mm) and ⅛″ (3.2mm), and sanded on both surfaces to 100 grit. I prefer the thickness to be on the thin side of that range for heavy woods like rosewood,

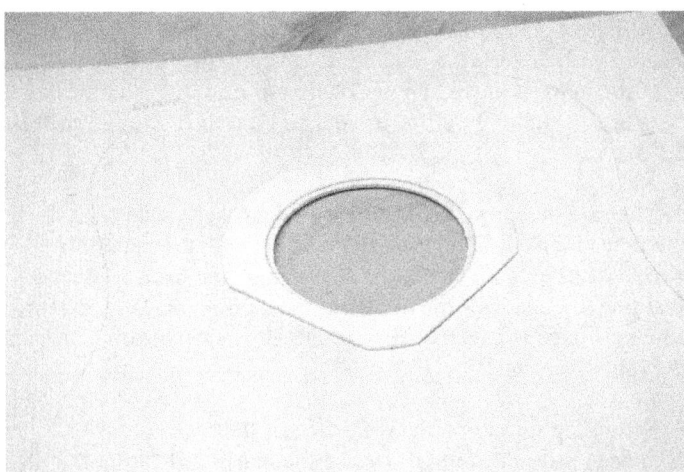

Photo 13-8 – *The finished soundhole reinforcement ring, glued to the top plate.*

Photo 13-9 – *The bridge plate template and the finished bridge plate.*

and on the thicker side of the range for medium density hardwoods like maple.

2. The template for the bridge plate is located in the template book and cut out using knife or scissors. Care is taken to be sure the angled sides are cut accurately.

3. The template is traced onto the blank. The grain orientation should be horizontal. The centerline marked on the template is also transferred to the blank.

4. The bridge plate is cut out, and its sides are sanded smooth and straight (**photo 13-9**). Care should be taken to be sure the angled sides accurately follow the template. These surfaces will be used to locate the X braces in a subsequent assembly operation.

5. The centerline on the plate is continued onto both of the long edges and also onto the other side of the plate.

6. The bridge plate is trapezoidal in shape, with one of the lower corners cut away. During assembly of a right-handed guitar, the bridge plate will be oriented with the cut corner to the bottom left.

 And during assembly of a left-handed guitar, the bridge plate will be oriented with the cut corner to the bottom right.

The bridge plate should be placed on the bench in the appropriate orientation at this time, and then marked in pencil to indicate the surface which will be inside the guitar and the surface to which glue will be applied. The long edges *not* on the gluing surface are lightly chamfered.

7. The bridge plate is not glued on at this time, but will be used in the construction and gluing of the X braces.

The X Braces

The X braces are the main braces of the guitar top. They stiffen the top longitudinally to resist the distorting effects of string tension, and they also provide additional cross-grain stiffening. The two braces are joined together in a box joint, just to the tail end of the soundhole.

When the back plate was braced, the braces were first arched on their gluing surfaces but otherwise left rectangular in profile, and then glued to the plate to arch the plate. Then the braces were carved to their final shape. This sequence keeps the braces as stiff as possible while they are being glued to the top, which helps to make the arching of the plate more accurate. The same sequence will be used here, and for the same reason.

□ **Layout of the Box Joint**

1. Three of the ¼″ (6.4mm) wide brace blanks are selected. Two pieces each at least 4″ (101.6mm) long are cut from one of these. These pieces will eventually be used to make the finger braces, but here they will be used to help lay out the box joint for the two X braces. All the pieces needed for the following assembly steps are shown in **photo 13-10**.

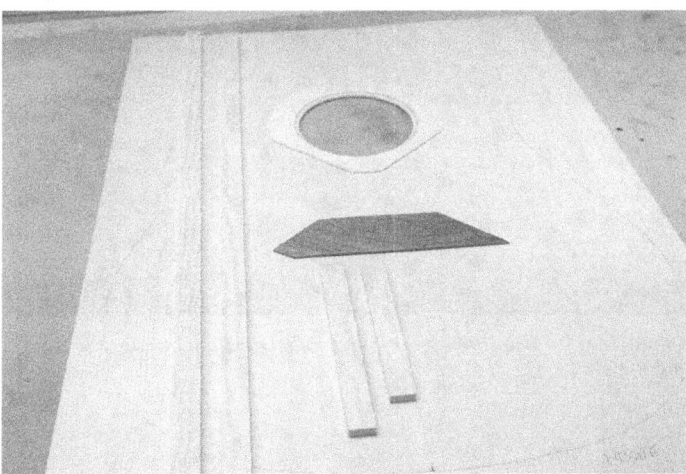

Photo 13-10 – The components needed to lay out the box joint of the X braces include two brace blanks, two short lengths of brace blank, and the bridge plate.

2. The number "4" is penciled on the side of one of the selected full length brace blanks, corresponding to the number of the brace on the plans for the example instruments. Then the blank is positioned so that it is flush against the left diagonal side of the soundhole reinforcement ring, and so its ends extend at least 1″ (25.4mm) beyond the outline of the body. Note the brace blank should be standing up, taller than it is wide (**photo 13-11**).

3. Using the mark on the centerline of the top for the location of the bridge plate, and the bridge plate centerline, the bridge plate is placed into position (**photo 13-12**). In position, the right end of the bridge plate should butt against the brace.

4. Now one of the short finger brace blanks is placed flush against the right diagonal side of the soundhole reinforcement ring. The other finger brace blank is placed against the left diagonal end of the bridge plate, so the two finger brace blanks are in a line (**photo 13-13**).

Photo 13-11 – One of the brace blanks is positioned flush against the soundhole reinforcement ring, and so its ends are outside of the body outline.

5. The number "3" is penciled on the side of one the remaining full length brace blank, and it is placed right on top of and

Photo 13-12 – *The bridge plate is positioned at the mark made on the top plate for that purpose. Its right end is flush against the brace blank.*

Photo 13-14 – *The remaining brace blank is placed on top of the two short pieces. The short pieces allow the brace blank to "fly" above the first brace.*

Photo 13-13 – *The two short pieces are placed in line as shown. They serve as spacers.*

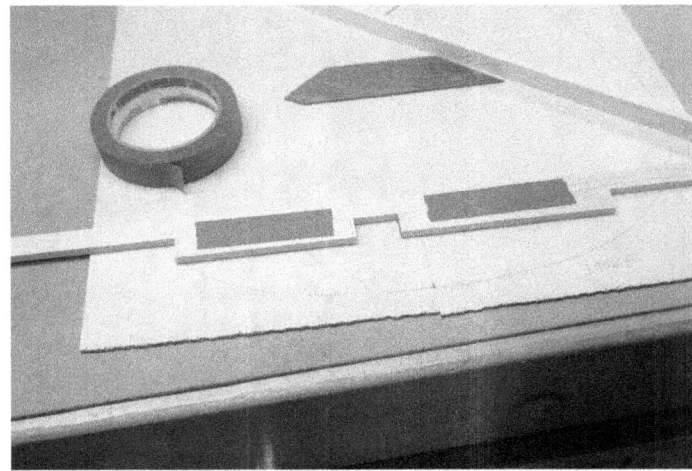

Photo 13-15 – *The short spacers are taped down to the sides of the brace blank.*

aligned with the two finger brace blanks, and so its ends extend beyond the outline of the body. The finger brace blanks just serve as spacers to allow this second long blank to "fly" over the first long blank (**photo 13-14**).

6. The flyover blank (#3) and both its spacers are removed without moving them in relation to each other. This assembly is placed on its side on a flat surface, and a piece of masking tape is used to tape one spacer/finger brace blank to the long blank, and another piece is used to tape the other spacer. The tape should not go right down to the bottoms of the finger brace blanks – space is left for these to directly contact the ring and bridge plate (**photo 13-15**). This assembly is flipped over and two more pieces of tape are used on this side.

7. Now the assembly is put back in place on top of the existing long brace, so it is flush against the left diagonal side of the ring and flush against the bridge plate right end, and so its ends extend past the body outline. All the pieces are examined carefully, to be sure everything is in contact with ring sides and bridge plate ends, and that the bridge plate is located where it should be. Now the X braces are held down to the top plate and the sides of the upper brace are traced in pencil onto the top of the lower brace where it passes over (**photo 13-16**). While still holding everything in place, the pencil is positioned so the sides of the lower brace can be traced onto the bottom surface of the top brace. It will not be possible to trace it right across because the work is being done upside down in a tight space, but marks are made as well as possible from both ends of each side.

8. A small pencil mark is placed on the top plate centerline, where the tail end side of the lower brace blank crosses it, to mark the location of the box joint on the top. The top brace is removed, and tape and spacers are removed from it. That brace is flipped over and the partial marks made in the previous step are connected using a straightedge and pencil (**photo 13-17**). This surface is also marked "bottom" in pencil.

9. Using a small square and ruler, the ends of these lines are extended exactly halfway down both sides of the brace. Then the ends of those lines on each side are connected, to fully mark the cut for the box joint (**photo 13-18**). The volume enclosed by all these pencil marks will be removed when making the box

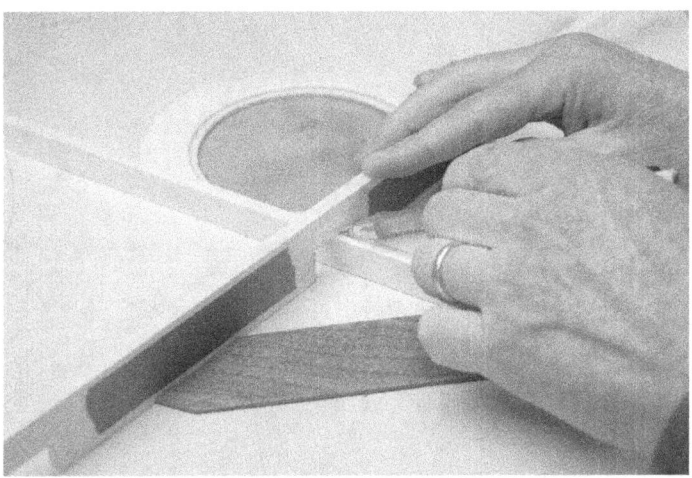

Photo 13-16 – The brace assembly is returned to its original position, and its sides are traced onto the top of the bottom brace. The sides of the bottom brace are marked on the bottom of the upper brace too.

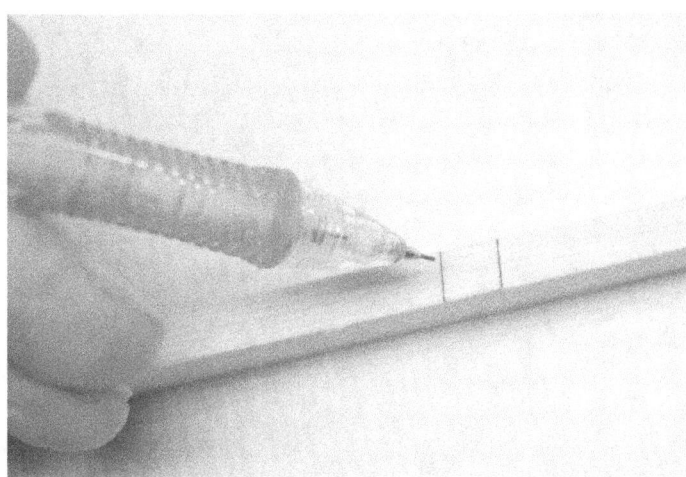

Photo 13-17 – A pencil and straightedge are used to continue marks straight across the brace surface.

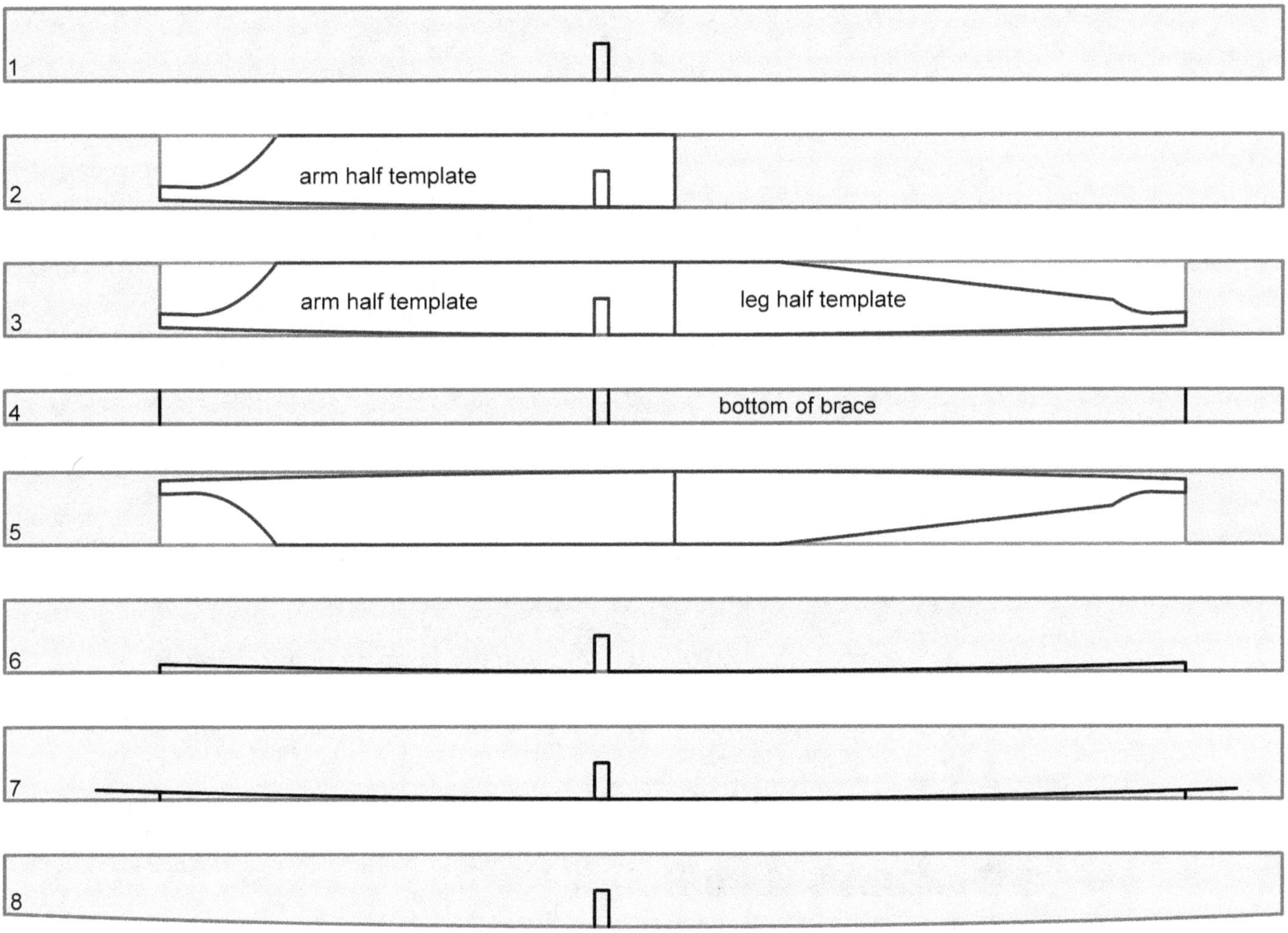

Figure 13-3 – The general sequence for arching the bottoms of the X braces begins with one of the brace blanks with box joint notch marked (1). The arm half template is aligned with the box joint mark, and taped in place on the blank (2). The leg half template is also positioned on the blank (3), and the arching contour is traced onto the blank in pencil. The templates are removed and the blank is turned over, bottom up, and the ends of the contour just marked are continued across the bottom of the blank (4). The blank is turned over again so the other side is now facing up, and the templates are attached, with their ends aligned to the end marks made on the blank bottom (5). The arching contour is traced from the templates, the templates are removed, and the blank is returned to its initial orientation (6). The ends of the arching contour line are extended a bit on both ends (7). Finally the bottom is cut down to the arching contour lines, extending the cuts right to the ends of the blank (8).

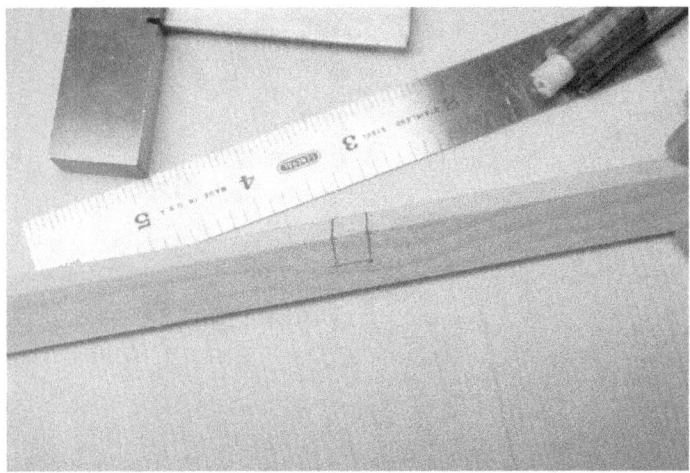

Photo 13-18 – *The lines are also continued halfway down the sides of the braces, and these lines are connected at their ends to form the complete outline of the cut for the box joint.*

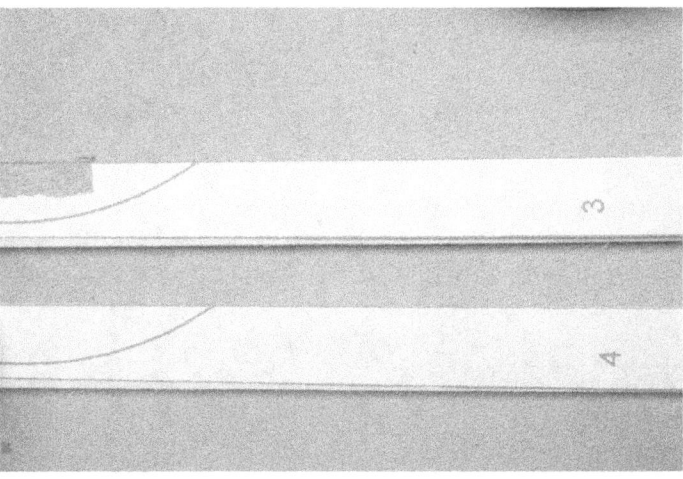

Photo 13-21 – *The templates have been cut out on their bottom gluing surfaces but not yet on their top surfaces.*

Photo 13-19 – *The waste is hatch marked for the cuts.*

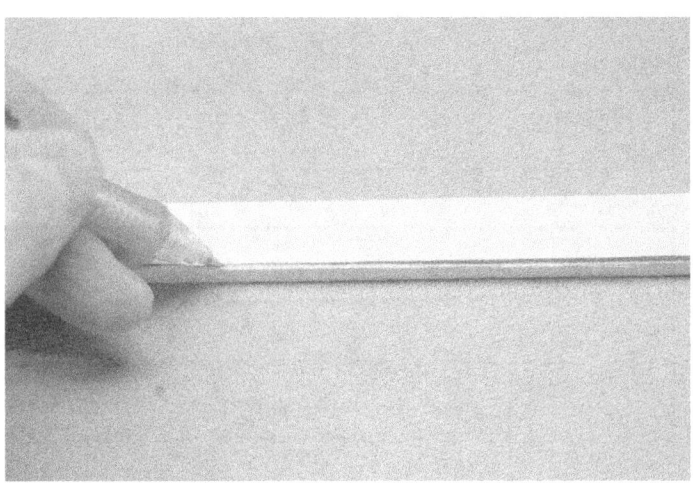

Photo 13-22 – *The arching curve on the bottom of the template is traced onto the brace blank.*

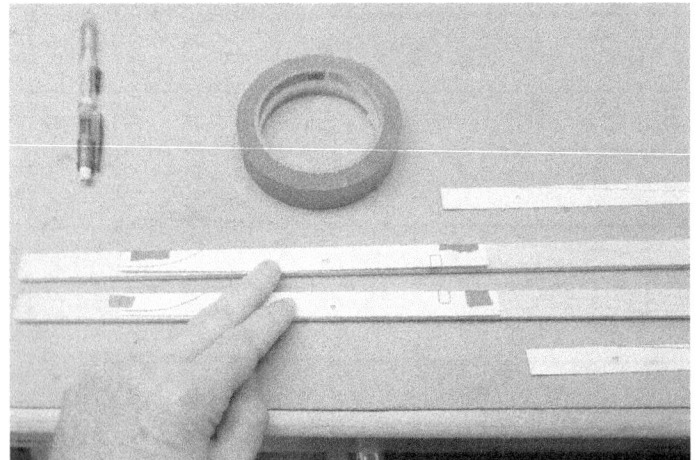

Photo 13-20 – *The arm half of the brace templates are taped to the side of the braces aligned with cut marks for the box joints.*

joint. It is a good idea to cross hatch inside the marks, to clearly indicate the waste to be cut away (**photo 13-19**).

10. The other X brace is similarly marked up for the cut for the box joint, marking down its sides from the lines marked on its top surface. Then this brace is also flipped over and "bottom" is penciled on its bottom surface. Note that brace #4 will be notched for the box joint on its top surface, and brace #3 will be notched on its bottom surface.

◻ **Arching the Bottoms of the X Braces**

The construction sequence for arching the bottoms of the X braces is shown schematically in **figure 13-3**.

1. The profile templates for the X braces are cut out, but the top surfaces are left rectangular. Only the arched bottom surfaces are trimmed at this time. Note there are two half templates for each brace.

2. The markings on the templates for the box joint are located on the "arm" halves of the templates– that is, on the upper halves. For the arm half of each brace, the appropriate template is taped to the side of the blank, so the straight top edge of the template is aligned with the top edge of the blank, and the drawing for the box joint cutout on the template is aligned with the pencil marks for the box joint made in the previous operation (**photo 13-20**, **figure 13-3.2**). The arching of the template

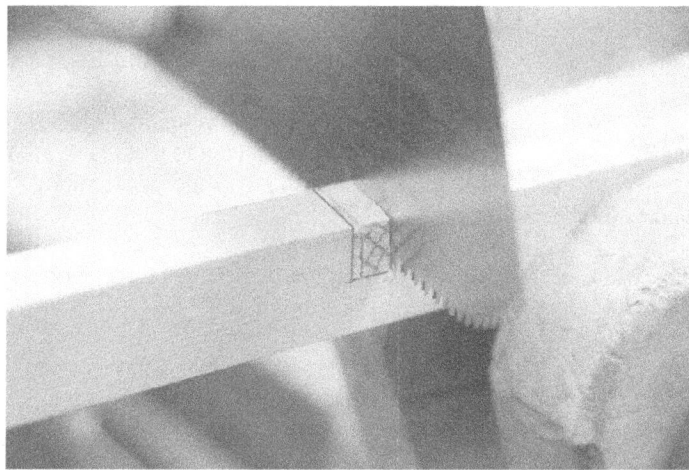

Photo 13-23 – *The markings on the braces are aligned, the braces are held in the vise, and the initial cuts are made with a razor saw.*

bottoms should be clearly seen, relative to the bottom edges of the brace blanks (**photo 13-21**). Note that the end of the template should not reach the end of the brace blank. There should be some excess material there.

3. Similarly, the templates for the "leg" ends are taped to the brace blanks, butting these half templates up against the arm template halves already in place, and keeping the top edges of the templates and the blanks aligned (**figure 13-3.3**). The two template halves can be temporarily taped together using small pieces of masking tape. Here too, the end of the template should not reach the end of the brace blank.

4. The bottom curved edge is carefully traced in pencil from the templates onto the blanks (**photo 13-22**). Near each end of each brace blank, a mark is placed on the bottom of the blank,

aligned with the end of the template. These marks are continued right across the bottom of the blanks, using a pencil and small square (**figure 13-3.4**).

5. Now the other sides of the blanks are marked for arching in similar fashion. The templates are removed from the blank and then the blank is flipped over, exposing the other side. When placing the templates on this surface, the printing on the templates will be facing the blank, and so is not visible. The top edges of templates and blanks are aligned, but instead of aligning the template arm half to the penciled box joint, it is aligned to the end of template marks made on the brace bottom (**figure 13-3.5**). The templates are taped in place, and the bottom curve is traced in pencil onto the blank. The templates are removed from the brace blanks (**figure 13-3.6**).

6. To accommodate small variations in the dimensions of the outline of the top plate, the ends of the brace bottom edge tracings just made must be extended in length about 1″ (25.4mm), while retaining the curve of the tracings (**figure 13-3.7**). This is most easily done by positioning one of the templates so the curve of the brace bottom tracing follows the curve of the bottom of the template, while the end of the template extends about 1″ (25.4mm) from the end of the tracing. The extension is made by tracing the template (**figure 13-4**). This is done on both sides of both ends of both braces.

7. Each brace blank is placed one at a time in position on the top plate, flush against the soundhole ring, and with its box joint mark lined up with the location mark made for that on the top plate centerline. This is done to check to be sure that the extended ends of the pencil lines representing the bottom edges of the blanks extend beyond the outline of the body.

8. The bottoms of both brace blanks are carved down to the traced curves. This can be done with plane or spokeshave set to take a very fine cut, or with spindle or drum sander, or just by dragging the pieces across a coarse grit sanding board. Depending on the length of the brace blanks, the traced curves might not extend right to the ends of the blanks. In this case, when carving down to the lines, the basic shape of the curves should just be continued freehand right to the ends of the blanks (**figure 13-3.8**).

9. When done, the carved surface is evaluated with the fingers, to be sure it is smooth and represents a continuous curve. Additional sanding is done if necessary to remove any peaks or valleys.

□ **Cutting the Box Joint and Gluing the X Braces**

1. Brace #3 will have the pencil marks for the box joint on its bottom obliterated by the shaping of the bottom curve, so these lines are restored now, using a pencil and straightedge.

2. The waste of the box joint is easily removed with a razor saw and chisels. The marks for the saw cuts on both braces can be aligned so the saw cuts can be done for both braces at the same time. The marks are aligned and both braces are held in a vise. Saw cuts are made inside the lines and just down to the pocket

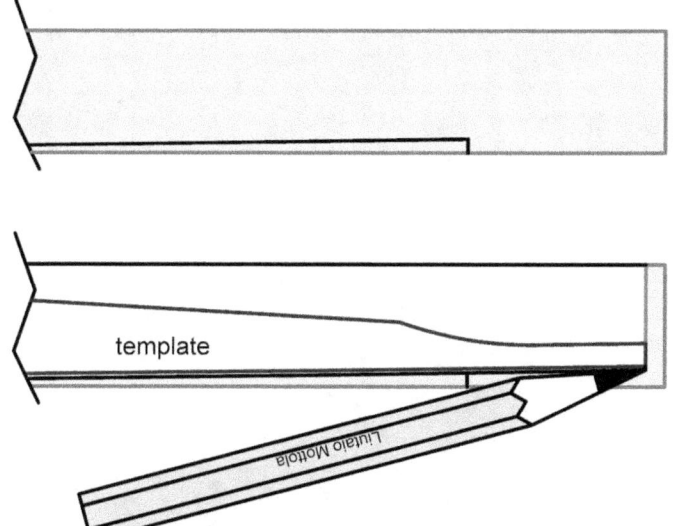

Figure 13-4 – *The original tracing for the brace bottom (top figure) must be extended in length. The template bottom is aligned with the curve and used to extend the mark as shown in the bottom figure.*

bottom lines, being careful to check both sides of the braces while sawing (**photo 13-23**).

3. A thin (≈⅛″ (3.2MM)) chisel can be used to chisel the waste out of the pockets. One brace is done at a time (**photo 13-24**).

 While chiseling, it should be kept in mind that the box joint connects the two braces at an angle from perpendicular, and so the saw cuts do not go perpendicularly across the braces.

The waste is chiseled out down to the floor lines of each pocket. Test fitting the braces together is attempted.

 Note that the braces can fit together two different ways! Properly fit together, the angle between the arms is wider than the angle between an arm and a leg.

A snug fit is ideal, but a forced fit risks splitting a brace. Excess material is trimmed away using a sharp knife (**photo 13-25**) or small chisel (**photo 13-26**). Test fitting and trimming is continued until a snug joint is achieved. It is critical that the bottoms of the braces line up (**photo 13-27**), that is, that one brace is not higher than the other. If this is the case, the floors of the notches are not deep enough.

Photo 13-24 – *A thin chisel is used to clean out some of the waste and to trim the floor of the notch.*

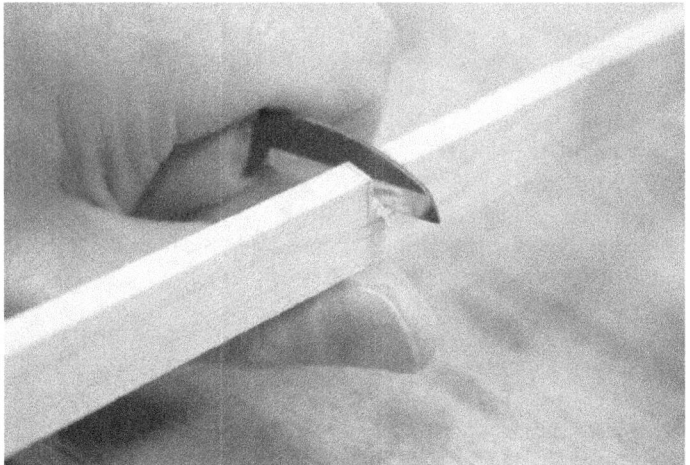

Photo 13-25 – *Excess material can be trimmed from the walls of the notch using a sharp knife.*

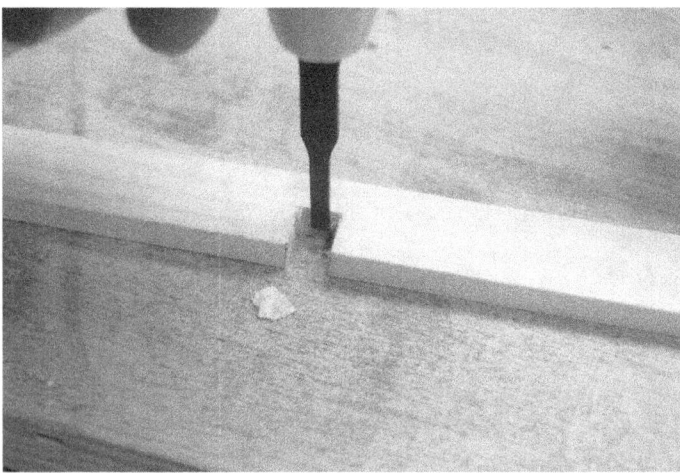

Photo 13-26 – *The floor of the notch is further refined using a small chisel.*

Photo 13-27 – *Test fitting the joint should result in the bottoms of the two braces being at the same height.*

Photo 13-28 – *The fit of the X brace assembly to the top plate is checked with the bridge plate positioned in its place. The brace ends are clamped down using spring clamps.*

4. When a good fit of the box joint is achieved, the braces are test fitted to the top plate. The braces are positioned in place over the top plate, snug with the soundhole ring sides, and with the tail end of the box joint aligned with its mark on the top plate centerline. It often happens that the cutting of the box joint changes the angle a bit. The angle is critical - more critical than is a snug box joint. If the braces cannot be made to fit snug against the sides of the ring and also against the ends of the bridge plate placed in its proper place, they can be bent just a little to make them fit. But if they need anything more than just a bit of minor tweaking, then the box joint will have to be loosened up so that they will fit perfectly to the soundhole reinforcement ring and the bridge plate.

5. Once this fitting is done, each of the four brace ends are temporarily clamped into place using spring clamps (**photo 13-28**). The fit with the soundhole reinforcement ring and the bridge plate is checked again, then the locations of the ends of the braces on the top, outside of the body outline, are marked for gluing. If the brace ends extend past the edges of the top plate then the bottoms of the braces are marked at the plate edges instead. It is also a good idea to write "arm" or "leg" on each brace end. These marks, plus the mark previously made on the top plate centerline indicating where the two braces cross, will accurately locate the X brace assembly while gluing. The arm and leg markings are so it is clear how to put the joint together correctly.

6. The brace assembly is unclamped from the top plate and the two braces are carefully taken apart.

7. Gluing the X braces to the top. A dry run is always a good idea. Since the top will be bent into a gentle arch by clamping it to the arched brace bottoms, clamps are applied from the center toward the outside. In addition to four long and 10 short clamps and four spring clamps, four wood wedges approximately 3″ (76.2mm) long by ½″ (12.7mm) thick at the thickest part are needed. If these are not already on hand they should be fashioned before proceeding.

8. Glue is spread on all three surfaces on the insides of both box joint pockets, and the two X braces are connected together, being careful that both bottoms are at the bottom, and the angle between arms is wider than the angle between arm and leg. The assembly is placed bottom down on the bench, and the top of the joint is tapped with a mallet to make sure the bottoms of the two braces are level with each other.

A thin bead of glue is applied along the bottom surfaces of both braces, and the glue is lightly spread to cover the surfaces. The brace assembly is fitted to the top plate, using the joint mark on the plate centerline, the diagonal sides of the soundhole ring, and the marks at the end of one arm, and a spring clamp is used to clamp down that arm end. The same is done for the other arm, followed by one of the legs, and then the other. If there are major amounts of glue anywhere on the surface of the plate, it should be wiped off at this time.

9. The bridge plate is temporarily fitted, and a check is made for appropriate fit. The spring clamps and the locations of the leg ends are adjusted as necessary (**photo 13-29**).

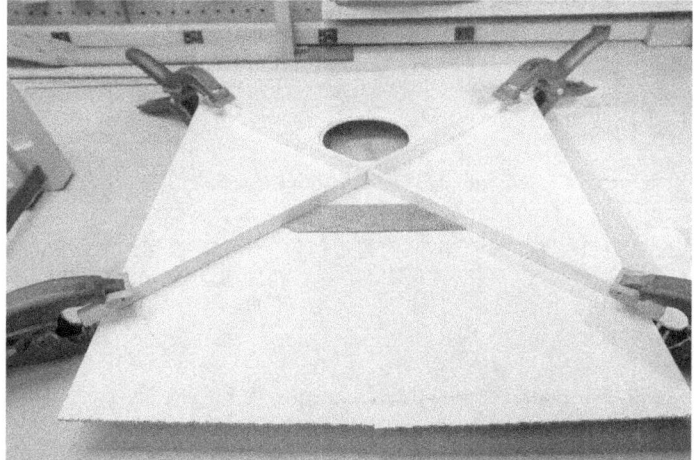

Photo 13-29 – After glue is applied, the brace assembly is positioned and held in place using spring clamps, just like when it was test fitted to the top plate.

Photo 13-30 – Clamps are applied starting near the box joint and working down the arms and legs toward the ends. Gentle clamping pressure is used to avoid distorting the top.

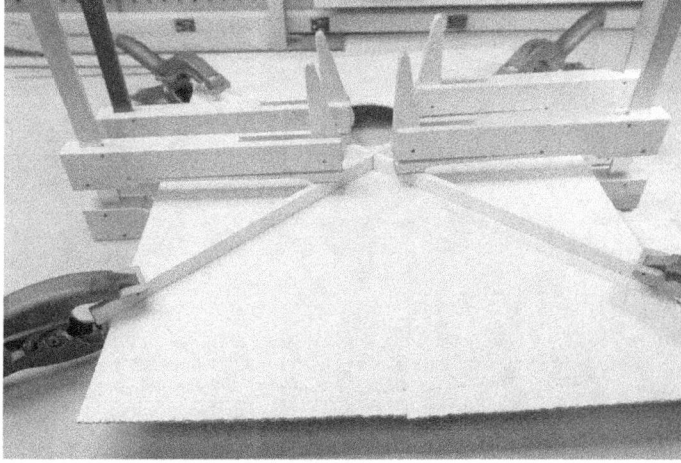

Photo 13-31 – Two more clamps are added near the joint in this photo.

Photo 13-32 – *All the clamps in place. The spring clamps are replaced with cam clamps at the brace ends.*

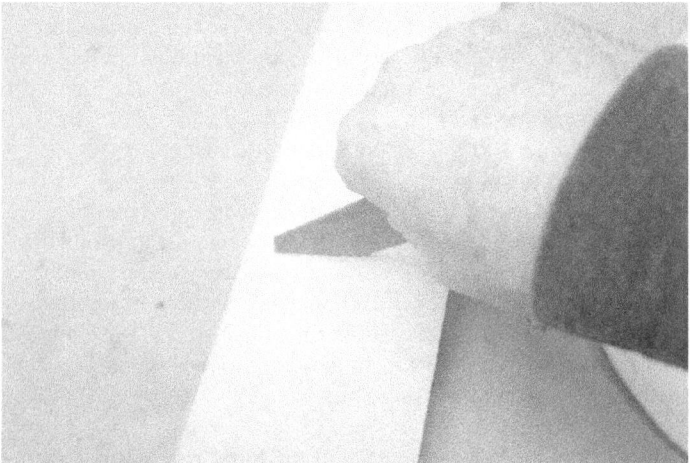

Photo 13-35 – *The ends of the bridge plate can be trimmed by rubbing them across the sanding board.*

Photo 13-33 – *The four clamps at the brace ends are elevated off the bench top using small wedges. This is necessary because otherwise the weight of these clamps will flatten the arching of the top plate.*

Photo 13-34 – *The bridge plate is fitted so its ends fully contact the sides of the X braces and so it meets (or comes close to meeting) its locating mark.*

10. Clamping of the braces is begun by applying and *lightly* clamping the four long clamps to each of the two arms and each of the two legs, each clamp about 1″ (25.4mm) from the box joint (**photos 13-30, 13-31**). The bridge plate is removed to avoid having it accidentally glued down by glue squeeze-out, and cleaned of any glue on it. More clamps are applied, evenly spaced down the arms and legs, working from the center toward the ends, and clamping lightly. The last clamp at the end of each arm and leg should replace the spring clamp (**photo 13-32**). The clamps will be mostly sitting on the bench.

11. One of the wedges is pushed under the last clamp of each arm and leg, raising the clamp off the bench by about ¼″ (6.4mm) (**photo 13-33**). The purpose of these wedges is to prevent the weight of the end clamps from straightening out the subtle arch that is imposed on the top plate by the arched bottom surfaces of the braces.

12. The snipped plastic straw is used to remove glue squeeze-out. Particular care is taken to remove any glue that would interfere with the placement of the bridge plate. The glue is allowed to cure at least four hours before the clamps are removed.

☐ **Fitting and Gluing the Bridge Plate**

1. The outline of the bridge plate is traced onto ¾″ (19.1mm) thick MDF, to be used as a gluing caul. The outline of the caul is cut out, keeping the saw blade just *inside* the lines, to make the caul just a bit smaller than the plate. Any rough edges left by the sawing are cleaned up. The edges of the caul can be waxed, or masking tape can be applied to them. This will help prevent the caul from being glued on if there is excessive glue squeeze-out.

2. The bridge plate is test fitted, to be sure it can be fitted at its mark on the top plate centerline, and that the ends of the bridge plate fully contact the sides of the X braces. Minor differences from the mark (**photo 13-34**) can be ignored, but the ends of the bridge plate must fit well against the sides of the X braces. Minor trimming can be done using the sanding board (**photo 13-35**).

Photo 13-36 – *The bridge plate is clamped down using a caul. Here, two clamps through the soundhole will pull the bridge plate in tight against the X braces.*

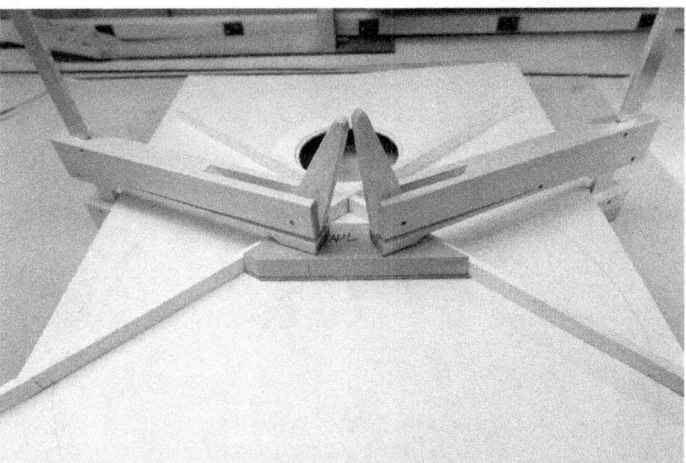

Photo 13-37 – *An alternative clamping arrangement uses two long clamps, approaching from the sides and angled from the neck end. This also pulls the bridge plate against the X braces.*

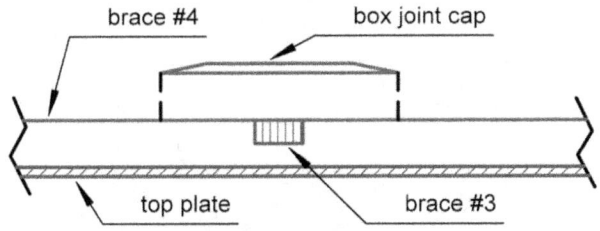

Figure 13-5 – *The box joint cap bridges the notch in the brace that has its notch facing up. This helps to prevent the box joint from opening up if the bracing structure is severely flexed.*

3. Glue is applied to the back side of the bridge plate and it is pressed into place. The caul is placed on top. Either of two clamping arrangements can be used. Either two clamps through the soundhole can be used, if they will fit and also reach the top of the caul (**photo 13-36**); or two long clamps approaching from the sides but angled in from the neck end can be used (**photo 13- 37**).

Photo 13-38 – *The ends of the top surface of the box joint cap can be quickly tapered by pulling them across the surface of the sanding board.*

Both of these clamping configurations tend to pull the bridge plate snug up against the X braces.

4. Glue squeeze-out is cleared with the snipped straw. The glue should be allowed to cure overnight before removing clamps.

 The bridge plate caul is retained, for use when the bridge itself is glued on in a later operation.

Any remaining hardened glue squeeze-out is scraped or chiseled away.

☐ **Making and Gluing the Box Joint Cap**

The box joint cap (top brace #5 in the plans for the example instruments) is a short cap used to strengthen the box joint. It is fashioned and glued down onto the #4 brace, over the box joint (**figure 13-5**). This piece is fashioned from some of the spruce soundboard material used to make the soundhole reinforcement ring.

1. The blank for the box joint cap is cut from thin spruce. It should be ¼″ (6.4MM) wide and ≈4″ (101.6MM) long. The ends are quickly tapered down using the sanding board (**photo 13-38**).

2. The tops of the X braces at the box joint are flattened a bit by sanding them with 100-grit sandpaper on a flat block. This is done just to be sure one of the braces is not a bit higher than the other one.

3. A thin bead of glue is applied to the underside of the box joint cap, spread a bit, and then the cap is pressed firmly in place, bridging the two parts of brace #4, and aligning it with the sides of the brace using the fingers (**photo 13-39**). Glue squeeze-out is gently wiped away with a rag held with three fingers, so that two fingers wipe the glue and keep the sides of the X brace and the cap aligned, while the middle finger of the three presses down on the top of the cap.

4. Two long clamps are applied with very gentle pressure (**photo 13-40**). The cap and brace are squeezed into alignment with two fingers while increasing clamping pressure a bit on one clamp. Then the same is done for the other clamp. Any remaining squeeze-out is wiped up. The glue is allowed to dry two hours before the clamps are removed.

□ **Shaping the Tops of the X Braces**

1. The templates for the X braces currently have only their bottom edges cut out. Now it is time to cut out the top edge profile of both template halves for one of the X braces (**photo 13-41**). These will be used to trace the profile onto both sides of both braces. Since the finished profile of the arm is rectangular except at the very end where it tapers down to ⅛″ (3.2mm) thick, all but the part of the template where it tapers down can be cut off. This will make it easier to handle the template, and also the soundhole reinforcement ring will not get in its way. It should be noted that, because the ends of the braces do not cross the body outline at a perpendicular, that one side of each end of each brace will be longer than the other. The brace end of the arm template half is aligned to the body outline on the *longest* side of an arm brace end (**photo 13-42**). The profile is then traced onto the side of the brace (**photo 13-43**). Now the location of the end is marked on the top surface of the brace, perpendicular to the length of the brace. This line is used instead of the body outline to position the end of the template on the other side of the brace (**photo 13-44**). Then the profile is traced onto that side of the brace, too.

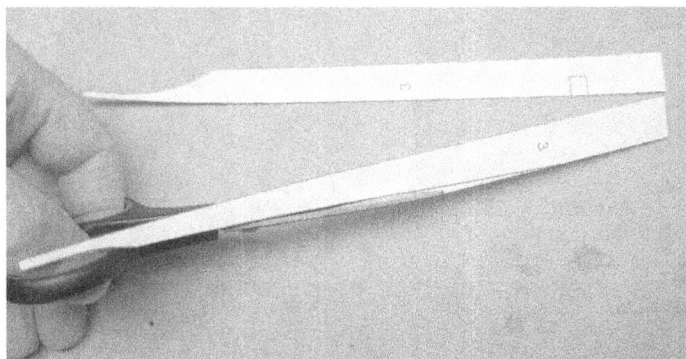

Photo 13-41 – *The top edge profiles of the template halves for the X braces are cut out, here using scissors.*

Photo 13-39 – *The box joint cap glued down, awaiting clamping.*

Photo 13-42 – *At the ends of the X brace arms, the only thing needed from the template is the profile of the scalloping at the end, so the template is just cut short. The template end is aligned with the plate outline.*

Photo 13-40 – *The box joint cap is clamped down during gluing.*

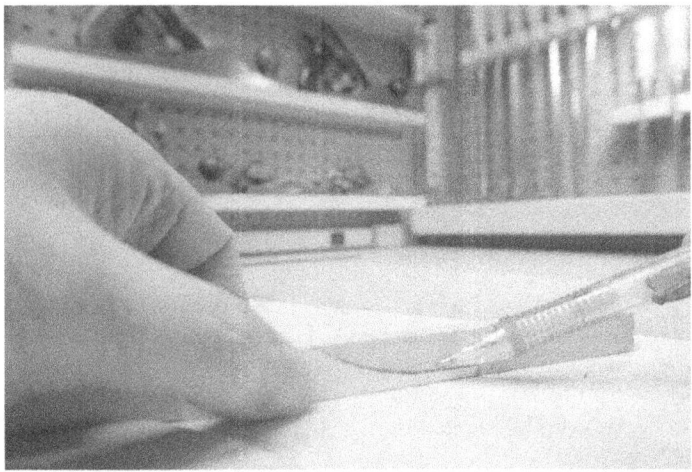

Photo 13-43 – *The top edge profile is traced from the template.*

2. That same template half is used to mark the other arm on both sides as described above.

3. The leg template will also have to modified a bit – a section of the bottom edge must be cut out so the template can hop over the bridge plate (**photo 13-45**). Then the leg template half is used in the same manner as in steps 1 and 2 to mark the profile on both sides of both legs.

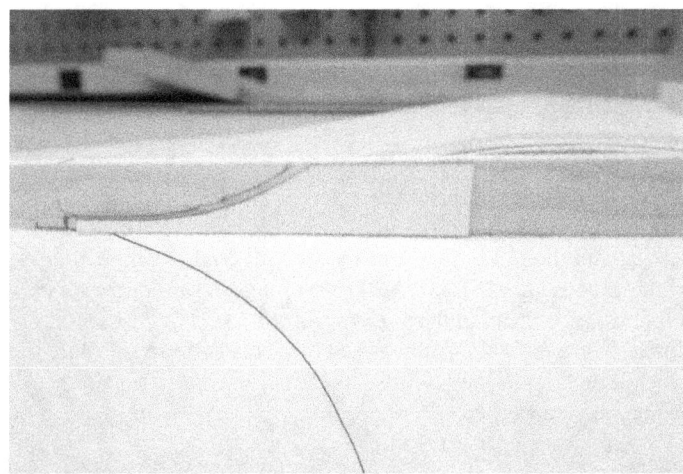

Photo 13-44 – *The template is flipped over to do the end of the other arm.*

Photo 13-47 – *... or a small plane.*

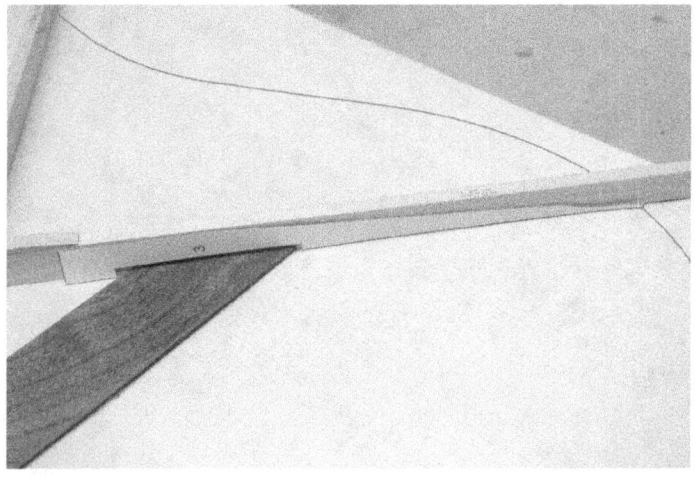

Photo 13-45 – *The leg end template must be notched on the bottom, to hop over the bridge plate.*

Photo 13-48 – *The scallops at the ends of the arms can be rasped or cut with a chisel.*

Photo 13-46 – *The top profiles of the legs can be shaped using a spokeshave ...*

Photo 13-49 – *The shapes of the scalloped ends are refined and smoothed using sandpaper on a cylindrical form.*

4. The braces are trimmed down to the lines, staying away from the area of the braces around the box joint and cap. Various tools can be used to do this including chisels, spokeshaves (**photo 13-46**), small planes (**photo 13-47**), and rasps. Cutting the concave surface near the brace end is best done with a chisel (**photo 13-48**) or rasp, and then finished up with sandpaper on a round sanding block (**photo 13-49**), or a section of dowel. Sanding here proceeds cross grain at first, to establish the curve and eliminate the pencil lines. Then finish sanding is done along the grain. Note that the ends of the braces must be ⅛″ (3.2MM) high for a distance of ⅜″ (9.5MM) or a bit more from the body outline. Measuring and sanding the brace ends to dimension now will help make subsequent assembly steps a lot easier.

5. The tops of the braces are sanded too, using sandpaper on a block (**photo 13-50**), until all plane or rasp marks have been removed and the brace tops are smoothly curved. The top edges of the braces are also rounded over a bit with sandpaper on a small block or held in the fingers (**photo 13-51**), but not too much, just to take the sharp edges off. This is done all along the brace length, from end to end, including the cap. The sides of the braces are sanded where necessary to remove any

Photo 13-50 – *The entire surface of the brace is sanded smooth to 100 grit.*

Photo 13-51 – *The top edges of the brace are rounded over slightly as well.*

Photo 13-52 – *The finished X braces.*

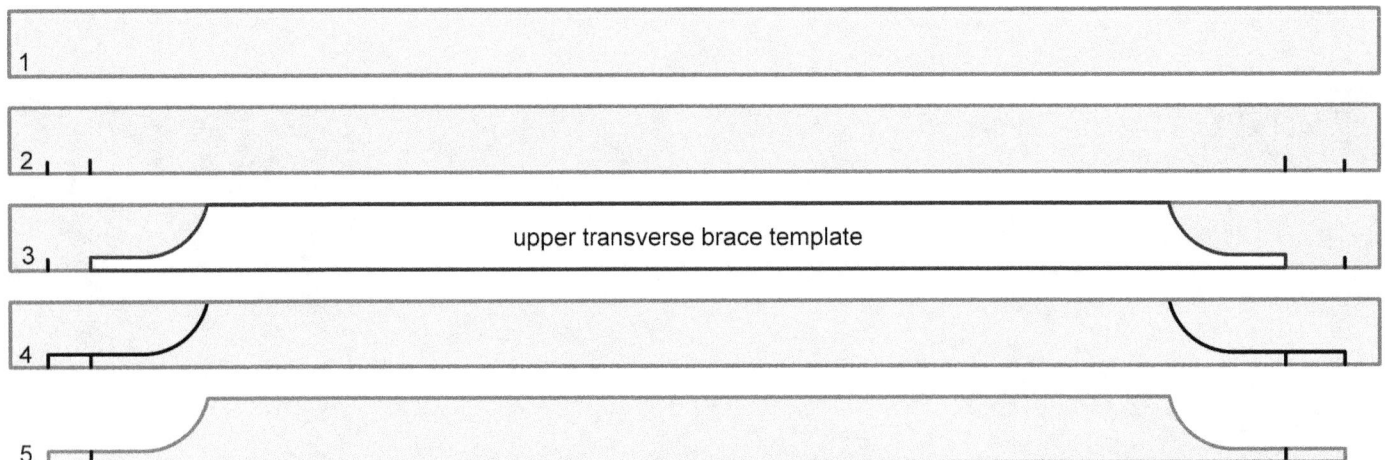

Figure 13-6 – *The sequence of steps to shape the upper transverse brace. The brace blank (1) is placed in position on the top plate. Marks are made where the blank crosses the plate outline and the edge of the plate (2). The template for the brace is aligned with the outline marks and is used to trace the scallops (3). A straightedge is used to extend the ends of the scallop tracings straight to the marks for the edge of the plate (4). The brace is cut to length at the plate edge marks and the scallops are cut out and refined (5).*

remaining pencil lines. The finished X braces appear as in **photo 13-52**.

☐ **Cutting the Top Plate to Size**

If this has not already been done, now is a good time to do it. A generous margin of about ½″ (12.7mm) is left outside the outline all the way around.

The Upper Transverse Brace and the "Popsicle Stick" Brace

The upper transverse brace is a heavy brace that is just to the neck end of the soundhole. Its purpose is to support the end of the fretboard and to prevent the sides of the instrument from caving outward due to the levering force of the neck.

The "Popsicle stick" brace (also sometimes called the tongue depressor brace) is a thin and wide transverse brace that is located just to the tail end of the neck block. Because it is thin, it does not offer much stiffness, but it does serve to help prevent cracks from forming and elongating in the top plate at the sides of the fretboard (**photo 13-53**).

Photo 13-53 – *Cracks eventually develop along the sides of the fretboard, as seen here in an old guitar, unless there is some support underneath to prevent this.*

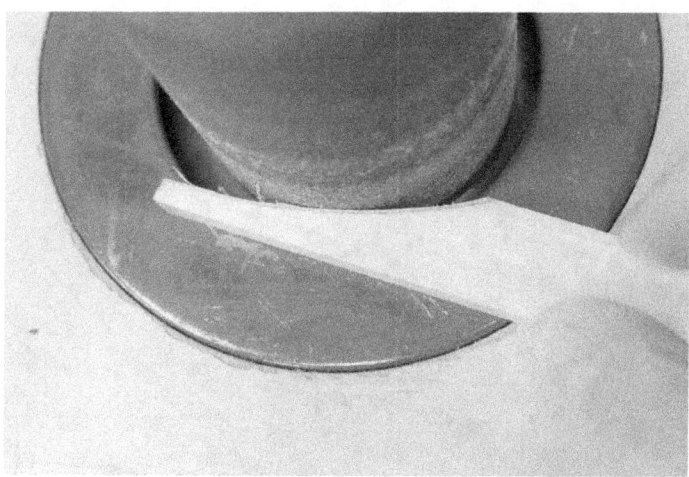

Photo 13-54 – *The brace end scallop can be readily cut or refined using the spindle sander or sanding drum.*

☐ **Shaping and Installing the Upper Transverse Brace**

Two things should be pointed out about construction of this brace. The first is that the brace will be fully shaped before it is glued to the top plate, for this and all subsequent top braces. Although it was useful in shaping the top to an arch to keep the tops of the X braces uncarved while they were glued on, this is no longer an issue, because the top has already been arched. So the rest of the braces will be fully shaped first, because it is much easier to shape the braces before they are glued to the top.

The second thing to be pointed out is that the bottom surface of this brace and also of the "Popsicle stick" brace is flat, not arched. This is because we want the area of the top plate above the soundhole to be flat. This makes it much easier to mate the fretboard extension to the top plate in a later operation.

The general sequence of steps for shaping, locating, and gluing down this brace is similar to that used for the back braces, with the exceptions that the bottom of the brace is not arched, and the brace is fully shaped before gluing. The descriptions and photos in the chapter on the back should be referred to as background for the construction operations presented here. The construction sequence for this brace is presented in schematic form in **figure 13-6**.

1. The brace blank to be used for this brace is the one that is ½″ (12.7mm) thick. This blank is selected and placed in position flush with the neck end flat of the soundhole reinforcement ring. Note the brace is taller than it is thick.

2. Viewing the brace from the soundhole side, the locations where the brace crosses the plate outline, and where it crosses the current edge of the plate, are marked on the side of the brace, at both ends of the brace (**figure 13-6.2**). The brace is removed from the top plate.

3. The upper transverse brace is labeled #2 in the plans for the example instruments. The half template for the brace is fully cut out using scissors or a knife.

4. The template is placed on the marked side of the brace blank, oriented so the tapered down end of the template is aligned with one of the marks indicating where the plate outline crossed. The curve of the end scalloping is traced from the template onto the brace. The other end of the brace is similarly marked by flipping he template over and aligning and tracing it on that end (**figure 13-6.3**).

5. The ends of the tracings are extended to the plate edge marks, using a straightedge to make these extensions straight and parallel to the bottom edge of the brace (**figure 13-6.4**).

6. The ends of the brace blank are cut off at the plate edge marks. The scallops at the brace ends are also cut out and sanded to the lines (**figure 13-6.5**). The latter is readily done using a spindle sander or drill press-mounted sanding drum (**photo 13-54**). Note that the ends of the brace must be ⅛″ (3.2mm) high for a distance of at least ⅜″ (9.5mm) from the body outline marks.

Photo 13-55 – *The first two clamps used to clamp down the upper transverse brace pull in against the soundhole reinforcement ring.*

Photo 13-56 – *One clamp is applied at the center of the brace, and two more clamps are applied to clamp down the ends of the brace.*

7. The entire surface of the brace is sanded to 100 grit, using a sanding block. The edges along the top of the brace are slightly rounded over, using sandpaper held in the hand.

8. Gluing the brace. Note that the bottom surface of this brace is flat; to be sure the area of the plate under this brace is flat, a flat board is used as a caul under the plate when gluing. It is important that no debris gets between the caul and the top plate. Glue is applied to the brace bottom and spread to cover its surface. Then the brace is aligned with the flat edge of the soundhole reinforcement ring and the plate outline marks, and pressed in place.

9. The brace is gently clamped with two clamps near the ends, approaching from the sides and angled toward the tail end. The clamps should clamp the caul in place as well. When these clamps are tightened, they will draw the brace in tight against the soundhole ring (**photo 13-55**).

10. Another clamp is added in the middle of the brace, approaching from the neck end, and then two more to clamp down the thin ends of the brace (**photo 13-56**). The snipped straw is used to remove glue squeeze-out (**photo 13-57**).

11. The glue is allowed 2 hours to cure before removing clamps.

☐ **Shaping and Installing the "Popsicle Stick" Brace**

This brace is wide and only ≈⅛″ (3.2MM) high. In the finished instrument it will butt against the inside surface of the neck block, so its location and its perpendicularity are critical. There is no template for this brace in the template pages for the example instruments because its shape is so simple.

1. A strip of wood 1″ (25.4MM) wide and at least 12″ (304.8MM) long is ripped from the extra top material used to make the soundhole reinforcement ring. This will serve as the blank for this brace.

2. On the plan, the distance from the neck end of the body at the centerline down to the inside edge of the neck block is measured. Note that for both of the example instruments this distance is 27⁄32″ (21.4MM). This distance is marked on the centerline of the top plate. A drafting square set to this mark and with one leg lined up with the centerline is used to extend this mark to outside of the body outline on both sides, making marks there.

3. The brace blank is aligned with the marks made above, and then marked for rough length. This is done by tracing the edges of the plate onto the bottom surface of the blank, at each end of the blank. The centerline of the top plate is also transferred to the brace blank.

4. The brace is removed, flipped over, and cut to length at the marks.

5. The top edges of the blank are rounded over. The radius of the roundover should be the same as the thickness of the brace.

6. Using the centerline marks as a guide and using a gouge, half round rasp, or sandpaper on a dowel, a 1⁄16″ (1.6MM) deep round bottom channel is cut down the center of the top surface of the brace (**photo 13-58**). This will provide clearance for an

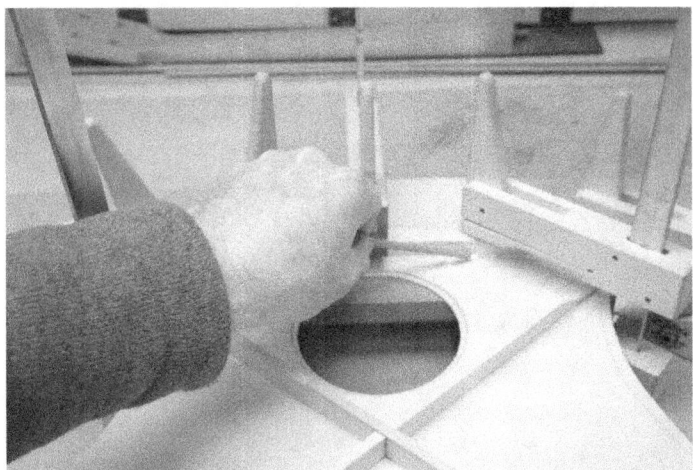

Photo 13-57 – *Glue squeeze-out is removed with the snipped plastic straw.*

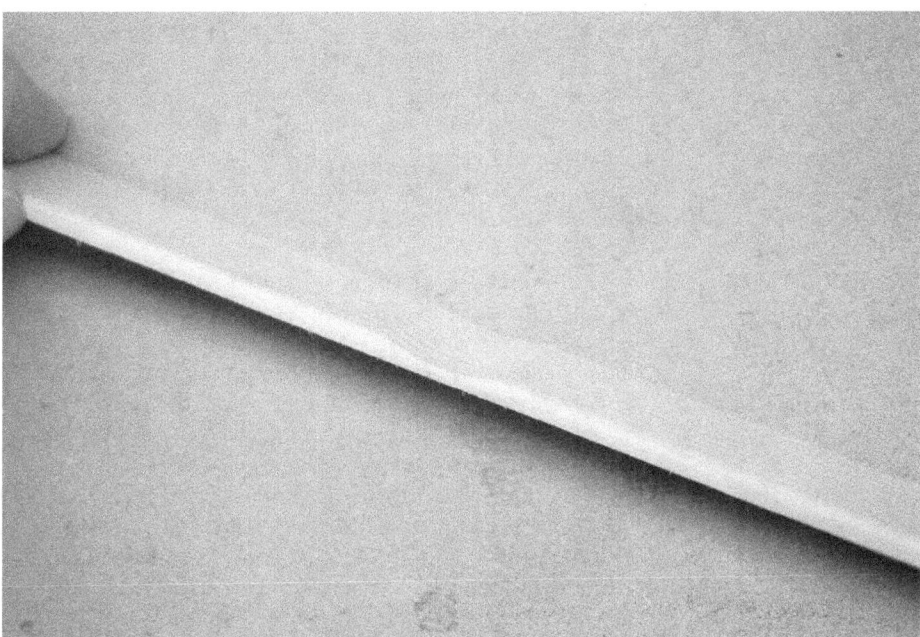

Photo 13-58 – *A shallow channel is cut across the center of the "Popsicle stick" brace, to provide access to the trussrod adjustment nut.*

Allen key to get to the trussrod adjustment nut in the finished instrument.

7. As when gluing the upper transverse brace, a flat caul is used under the top plate to keep this part of the plate flat during gluing of the "Popsicle stick" brace. Glue is applied to the brace bottom and spread to cover the surface, then the brace is pressed into place. Two clamps are gently applied near the ends approaching directly from the brace ends. The clamps should clamp the caul in place as well. The brace is kept in alignment with its locating marks as the clamps are tightened. The alignment is checked again and if the position of the brace has slipped, it is repositioned and the clamps tightened.

8. Two more clamps are added near the middle of the brace, approaching from the neck end, and two more are added on either side of those (**photo 13-59**).

9. The snipped straw is used to remove glue squeeze-out. There is a lot of gluing area here, so the glue is allowed to cure overnight before removing the clamps.

The Finger Braces and the Oblique Braces

The finger braces extend from the legs of the X braces toward the sides and toward the neck. There are four of them, two on each side, the one closer to the waist a bit longer than the other one. On the plans for the two example instruments these are numbered #6 and #7. The finger braces add a little cross-grain stiffness and they help to prevent cracks in these otherwise unsupported parts of the top.

The oblique braces extend from the left leg of the X braces and extend toward the tail end and toward the right, for a right-handed guitar, when the top is viewed from the inside surface. If the guitar under construction is left-handed, the oblique braces extend from the right leg toward the tail end and toward the left. These braces represent the only asymmetry of the typical X bracing pattern. These braces stiffen the area of the soundboard between the bridge and the tail end. This area tends to hump up due to string tension pulling the bridge toward the neck end of the body. These braces help to control this humping.

It is not known why these braces are asymmetrical to the rest of the braces of the top plate. Modern explanations and rationalizations abound, most often asserting that they induce different vibration characteristics on the bass and treble sides of the top.

☐ Shaping and Installing the Finger Braces

The finger braces are not very long or tall, and so it is often useful to cut them from off-cuts from the ¼″ (6.4mm) wide brace blank stock. Two braces can be cut from one length of stock, but be aware that due to their small size it may be safer

Photo 13-59 – *Five clamps are used to clamp the brace while gluing.*

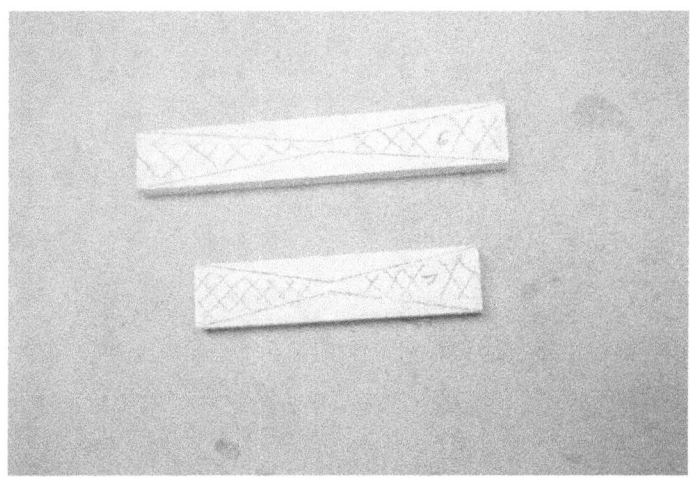

Photo 13-60 – *The four finger braces can be cut from small pieces of the brace stock.*

to cut these from longer pieces if they will be sawed out using the bandsaw.

1. The templates are cut out and used to mark the outlines of the braces on the stock (**photo 13-60**). Two braces of each length are needed. Note that the braces are triangular in profile, and it is not easy to trace against the thin ends, so it is usually easier to not use the templates, but to just mark off the length of the brace and mark the point of its peak, and then join ends and peak with lines drawn with a straightedge.

2. The braces are cut out and the top surfaces are sanded smooth to 100 grit (**photo 13-61**). The top edges are rounded over slightly with 100-grit sandpaper.

3. After the braces are cut to shape (**photo 13-62**) the bottoms must be arched. The bottom surfaces of the finger braces are slightly arched in an ad hoc manner, by dragging them over a sanding board, alternating one half the length of the brace at a time. The sanding sequence starts with half of the brace hanging over the end of the sanding board and one finger pressing down a bit on the end of the brace that is on the sandpaper (**photo 13-63**). The brace is pulled across the sandpaper (**photo 13-64**) and eventually completely off the end of the sanding board (**photo 13-65**), while increasing the pressure on the end throughout the sequence. Then the brace is flipped around and the sequence is repeated for its other end. This is repeated about 10 times. The goal is to impart just the slightest arch, not really even visible for braces this short.

4. The finger braces are positioned parallel to the arms of the X braces, with one end butted against a leg of the X braces. On the plan, measurements are taken perpendicularly down from the tail end side of the arm of the X brace to the neck end side of each finger brace. These measurements are transferred to the top by placing the end of a ruler flat against the arm of the X brace, so the ruler is perpendicular to the arm. For each brace, two small marks are made on the top plate, one near the X brace leg (**photo 13-66**) and one about 1″ (25.4mm) from the body outline (**photo 13-67**). The braces are each put in place, aligned with these marks.

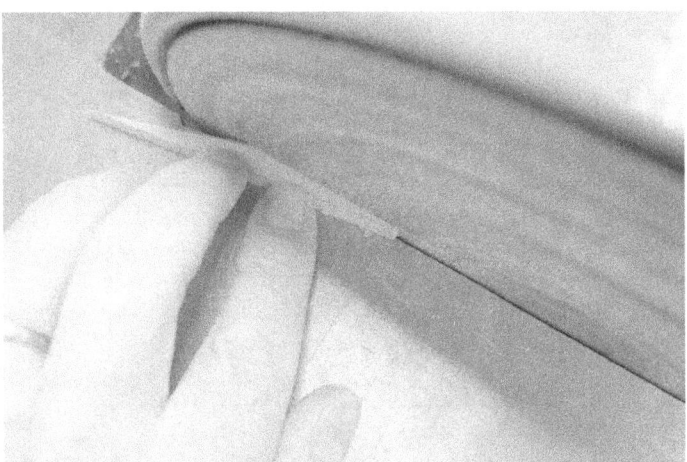

Photo 13-61 – *The tops of the finger braces are straightened and smoothed using a disk sander. A sanding board can also be used.*

Photo 13-63 – *To arch the bottom of the finger brace, the brace is pulled across the sanding board, starting in the middle of the brace. The finger pressing down on the top increases pressure as the brace is pulled.*

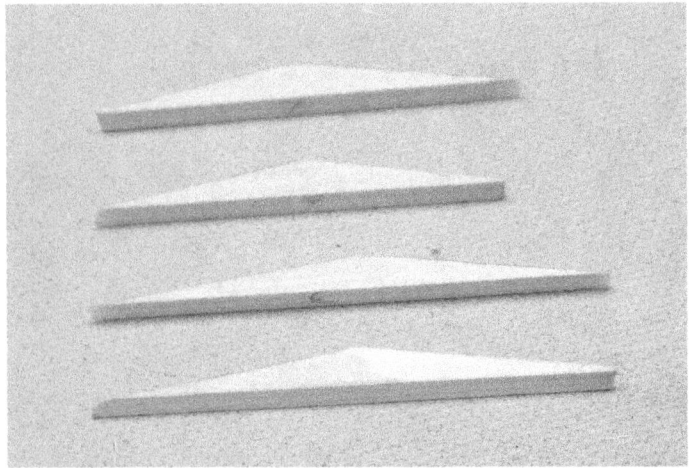

Photo 13-62 – *The four finger braces, ready to have their bottoms arched.*

Photo 13-64 – *This photo shows the halfway point of the brace bottom arching sanding stroke.*

The longer finger braces are located closer to the neck end of the top plate and the shorter ones closer to the tail end.

5. Note that the ends of the finger braces that butt up against the leg of the X brace do not meet the side of the X brace on a perpendicular. That end is trimmed with a knife to the appropriate angle (this is done by eye alone) and then sanded, so the entire finger brace end butts against the leg.

6. One of the finger braces is picked up and its *top* surface is wiped with a damp rag. This will help prevent the thin ends of the brace from curling up when glue is applied (see sidebar).

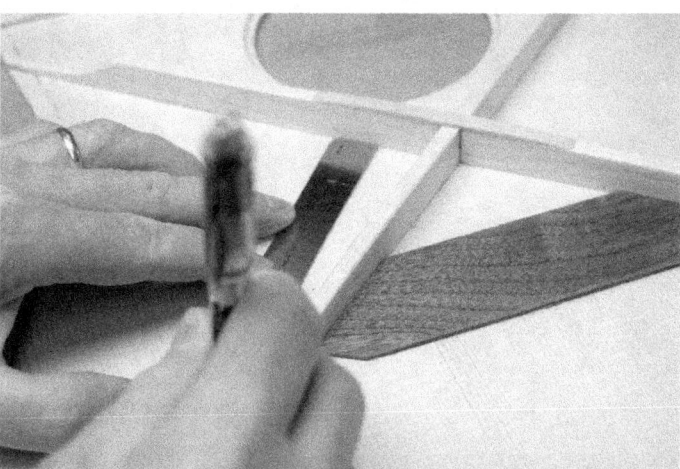

Photo 13-66 – *The finger braces are positioned parallel to the arms of the X braces. The location of the brace end that butts against the leg of the X brace is being marked in this photo.*

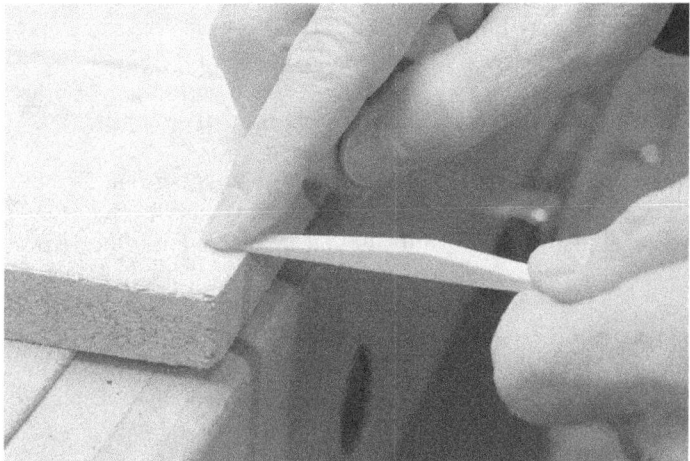

Photo 13-65 – *This photo shows the end of the brace bottom arching sanding stroke. After one stroke, the brace is flipped around and the other side of the bottom is sanded in the same manner.*

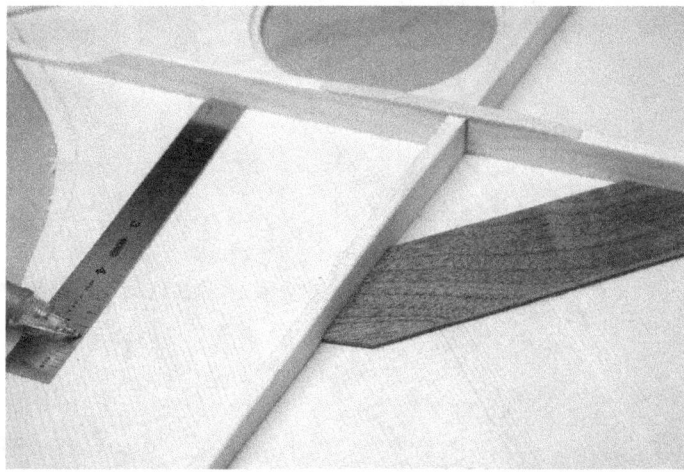

Photo 13-67 – *The location of the free-floating end of the finger brace is also marked.*

Gluing Thin Pieces of Wood

Whenever thin pieces of wood are glued down, the surface opposite the surface to which the glue will be applied must be dampened too. If this is not done, the water in the glue will cause the surface to which the glue is applied to swell, and this will bend the thin piece of wood upward. This is generally an issue with the application of veneer. Although guitar lutherie generally does not involve the application of veneer, the issue is the same for any part that is thin, or that has thin areas. A case in point is the end of the finger brace, which is very thin. If glue is applied directly to the bottom surface, the ends of the brace will bend up as in the figure below. But if the top surface of the brace is dampened first, then its swelling will counteract the swelling of the bottom surface when glue is applied.

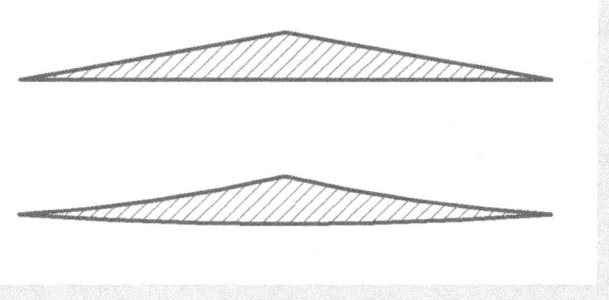

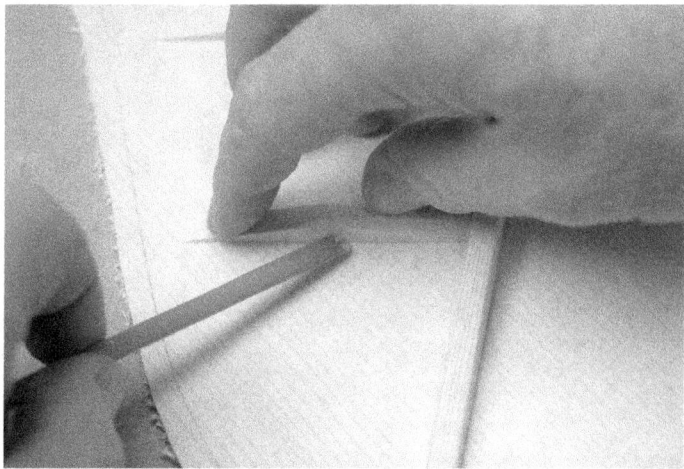

Photo 13-68 – *After glue is applied, the brace is pressed firmly in place, and then the glue squeeze-out is removed.*

Photo 13-69 – *The finger braces can usually be clamped down using a single clamp each.*

Glue is applied to the bottom of the brace and spread evenly, then the brace is put back in position and pressed firmly into place. Pressure is maintained on the brace with one hand and the snipped straw is used to clean up the glue squeeze-out (**photo 13-68**). A single clamp is applied with gentle pressure right at the peak of the brace (**photo 13-69**).

7. The rest of the finger braces are glued down in like manner. Glue is allowed to cure two hours before removing clamps.

8. A ruler is used to check to be sure the floating ends of the finger braces will clear the linings of the finished instrument. These ends should be no closer than 5/16″ (7.9mm) from the penciled plate outline. Any that are closer should be carefully trimmed back using a chisel.

☐ **Shaping and Installing the Oblique Braces**

The oblique braces (#8 and #9 on the plans for the example instruments) are fashioned and attached in much the same manner as for the finger braces. It should be noted that the orientation of these braces will be different depending on if the instrument under construction is right-handed or left-handed.

1. The templates for these braces are cut out. Note that the bottoms of these braces will be slightly arched, but the arching is so small that it is really difficult to trim the bottoms of the templates accurately, and then transfer those curves to the braces accurately. For that reason, the bottom edges of the templates are cut straight. The bottoms of these braces will be arched in the same ad hoc manner as was used to arch the bottoms of the finger braces. Again, the template bottoms are cut out using the straight, non-arched lines.

Photo 13-70 – *The oblique braces, cut out and smoothed, ready to have their bottom surfaces arched.*

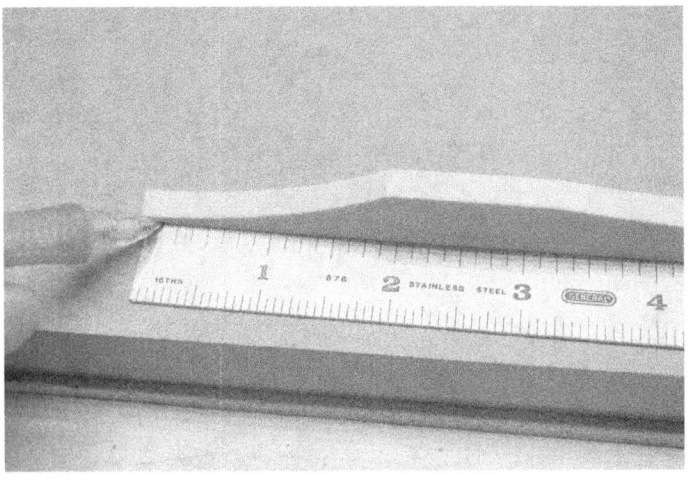

Photo 13-71 – *The arching elevation at the end of the brace is traced from the thickness of this metal ruler.*

2. The profiles are traced from the templates to some of the brace blank material. The braces are cut out and smoothed in the same manner as the other braces (**photo 13-70**).

3. The brace ends must be marked for arching. Each brace is placed bottom down on a flat surface and a 0.031″ (0.8mm) feeler gauge is placed on the flat surface next to the side of the brace near one end. In **photo 13-71** I am instead using a 6″ steel ruler which is the appropriate thickness. The side is marked just near the end, using the top of the feeler gauge (or ruler) as a guide (**photo 13-72**). This is done at both ends and both sides of both braces.

4. The bottoms are arched in the same manner as for the finger braces, starting in the middle of the brace on the sanding board and pulling the brace off the end of the board while increasing

pressure near the end. But for the oblique braces the pencil marks on the sides near the ends of the braces indicate just how much to arch the bottoms. When this step is complete, the arching of the brace bottoms will be apparent when the braces are resting on a flat surface (**photo 13-73**). This arching will result

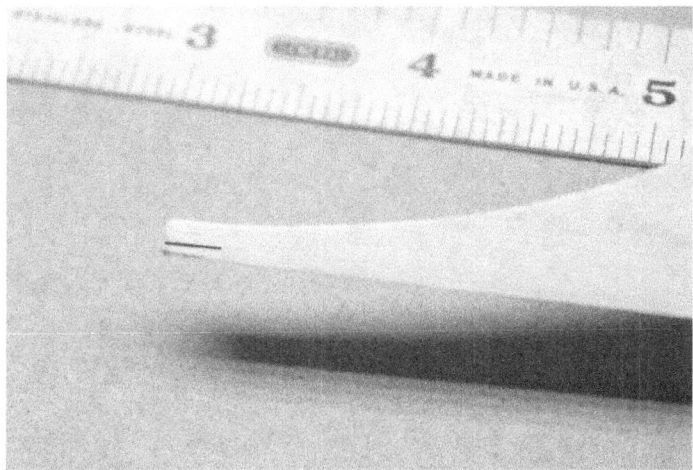

Photo 13-72 – *The arching elevation line penciled near the end of one of the oblique braces.*

Photo 13-73 – *The bottoms of the oblique braces are arched in the same manner as was used for the finger braces.*

Photo 13-74 – *The upper oblique brace clamped during gluing. The long clamp on the left is applied first.*

Photo 13-75 – *When clamping down the end of the oblique brace that butts against the X brace leg, it may be necessary to use a small caul if the leg gets in the way of the clamp.*

in sharp edges on the brace ends that will be positioned near the edge of the top plate.

5. Locating the position of the upper of the two oblique braces (#8) is easy. The thicker end of the brace goes in the notch in the bridge plate, butt against the leg of the X brace, and also butt against the side of the notch. The brace is put in position. It will be clear that the end of the brace that is in the notch will have to be cut a bit at an angle so the brace can butt fully against the leg of the X brace. That cut is made, and the brace is checked again for fit.

6. When all is well, the *top* surface of the brace at the thin end is wiped with a damp rag, glue is applied and spread on the bottom of the brace, and the brace is pressed into place firmly with the fingers. Glue squeeze-out is removed, then the brace is lightly clamped starting at the bridge plate end with a long clamp pulling the brace into the notch (**photo 13-74**). A small block may be needed sitting on the thin end of the brace to provide clearance for the clamp (**photo 13-75**). The position of the brace is checked to be sure the brace is butt against the side of the notch. Clamps are added, down to the end of the brace, clamping lightly. One more long clamp, and two regular clamps are needed.

7. Glue squeeze-out is removed. A wedge is pushed under the last clamp, as was done when clamping the X braces, to maintain the arching of the plate. The glue is allowed to cure for two hours before the clamps are removed.

8. The leg contact end of the lower oblique brace is located by measuring down the leg from the center of the X, to the point where the brace contacts the leg on the plan, and then transferring this measurement to the top plate. To locate the other end of the brace, the coordinates (horizontal, vertical) from the tail end of the outline on the centerline to the end of the brace are measured on the plan, then transferred to the top plate. It helps to use a drafting square and a ruler to measure and then mark the coordinates (**photo 13-76**). The brace is positioned in place and checked for positional accuracy (**photo 13-77**).

9. As with the upper oblique brace, the end of the lower brace that will contact the leg of the X brace must be cut at an angle so the brace fully contacts the leg.

242   Chapter 13: Bracing the Top Plate

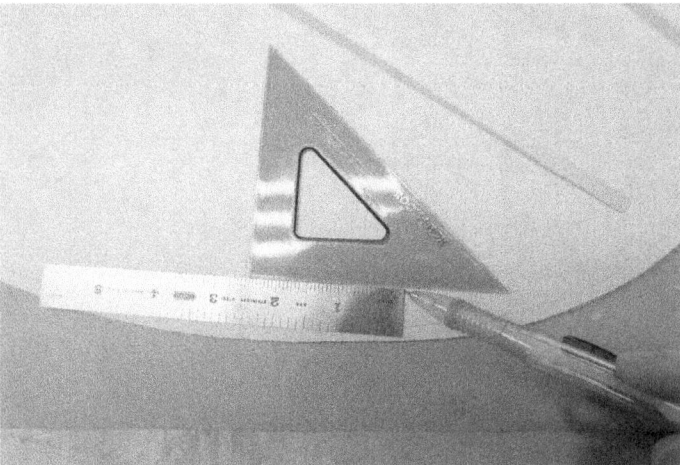

Photo 13-76 – *The coordinates of the floating end of the lower oblique brace are transferred to the top using a ruler and a small drafting square.*

Photo 13-77 – *The lower oblique brace in position, ready to glue down.*

10. The brace is glued and clamped as per the upper oblique brace.

11. A ruler is used to check to be sure the floating ends of the oblique braces will clear the linings of the finished instrument. These ends should be no closer than 5/16" (7.9MM) from the penciled plate outline. Any that are closer should be carefully trimmed back using a chisel.

Photo 13-78 – *The inside of the top with all braces attached and everything cleaned up.*

Photo 13-79 – *Some luthiers sign and date the inside of the top plate for future identification of the instrument. This optional step can be done in many different ways, the simplest of which is to use a permanent marker. I use a rubber stamp in my instruments.*

Cleaning Up the Inside of the Top Plate

It has been mentioned that the level of tidiness in which the insides of the guitar are left is a matter of personal taste. As a general rule I like to remove all pencil marks on the surfaces of the inside of the top, and excessive surface glue is sanded or scraped clean. The entirety of the inside can be scraped or sanded to whatever level of finish is desired. Luthiers commonly will sand at least to 100 grit, but many will finish the insides to higher grits. While doing this, every effort should be made to keep from obliterating any of the penciled outline of the plate, as this will be difficult to redraw now that the plate is covered with braces.

The finished bracing and cleaned up inside of the top plate is shown in **photo 13-78**. Some luthiers like to sign and date the underside of the top plate, so the instrument can be identified even if its paper label gets removed at some time during its life. In my own instruments I use a rubber stamp for this purpose (**photo 13-79**).

14 Assembling the Body

All of the major subassemblies of the guitar body are now complete. In this chapter the garland, top plate, and back plate will be assembled. Much of the work involves fitting the plates, and in particular fitting the ends of those braces that will be pocketed into the linings in the finished instrument. The pockets in the linings support the ends of the braces. This makes for robust construction for the finished instrument. The pockets also help to keep the plates and the ribs in alignment while they are glued together.

Attaching the Top

The top plate will be attached to the garland first, followed by the back plate. That order is not really important, but it is marginally easier to do it this way given the features of the mold that is being used.

Photo 14-1 – *A length of brace stock is attached to the neck-facing edge of the "Popsicle stick" brace using double-stick tape. Another length of stock serves as a fence to align it accurately with the edge. The taped-on piece will butt against the inside surface of the neck block, when the top plate is initially aligned with the garland to mark the brace ends and their pockets.*

☐ Marking and Trimming the Brace Ends

Looking at the inside of the top plate, it can be seen that a number of the braces currently extend beyond the plate outline. These ends must be trimmed so that they will end up just inside the sides of the garland. At this point in construction the actual perimeter of the ribs may be slightly different than the outline of the top plate traced onto the plate from the mold in an earlier construction step. So the construction steps that follow will mark the ends of these braces relative to the sides of the garland.

1. The mold is set up for this operation. If it is not already in place, the floor is attached to the mold. In the chapter on the construction of the garland a ¼" (6.4mm) thick spacer was taped to the floor at the neck end to raise up the neck end of the insert slightly. If that spacer is not still taped to the floor there, that should be done now. Then the insert is place into the mold.

2. The garland is placed into the mold, top edges up. Its end seams are aligned with the seams of the mold and it is jacked in place using the rib jacks.

3. When placed on the garland, the top plate will have to be positioned so the neck side edge of the "Popsicle stick" brace butts against the inside surface of the neck block. But when the top is positioned on top of the garland, the brace ends sticking out raise the "Popsicle stick" brace above the top of the neck block. So the height of that brace must be temporarily increased for this positioning. To do this, a cutoff of brace stock is temporarily attached to the surface of the "Popsicle stick" brace, so its neck side surface is aligned with the neck surface of the "Popsicle stick" brace.

Two pieces of brace stock or similar sized wood are cut about 6" (152.4mm) long. Double-stick tape is applied to one thin surface of one of these pieces. The other one is pressed down to the inside surface of the top and also to the neck side surface of the "Popsicle stick" brace. This piece is just used as a fence to stick the cutoff with the tape on it right on top of the "Popsicle stick" brace, aligned with the neck side surface (**photo 14-1**).

The fence piece is removed, and clamps are applied in a few places along the length of the brace stock to set the adhesive of the tape and firmly stick this cutoff down. The result is shown in **photo 14-2**.

4. Four clamps evenly spaced around the mold are used as "feet" to raise the bottom of the mold off the bench top. This allows additional clamps to be more easily placed, without having to lift the heavy mold.

5. The top is flipped over, placed on the garland, and gently slid into place until the cutoff applied above touches the inside surface of the neck block. The centerline of the top at the neck end is aligned with the seam of the garland. This requires looking at the centerline on the underside of the plate. While holding that in place, the same is done at the tail end. Two long clamps are used to lightly clamp the top in place at neck and tail end (**photo 14-3**). The clamps are placed just to the far side of the centerline, so the clamps don't obscure the centerline (**photo 14-4**). Alignment is checked again on both ends and adjusted as needed.

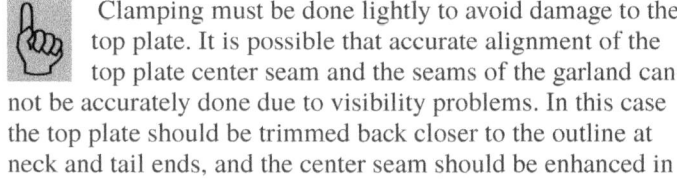

Clamping must be done lightly to avoid damage to the top plate. It is possible that accurate alignment of the top plate center seam and the seams of the garland cannot be accurately done due to visibility problems. In this case the top plate should be trimmed back closer to the outline at neck and tail ends, and the center seam should be enhanced in pencil on the inside surface of the plate at both ends as well. Then alignment can be attempted again.

6. The brace ends are now marked to the outside surface of the ribs. Because the clearance between the top of the mold and the underside of the brace ends is so small, doing this requires a very short pencil (**photo 14-5**). The ribs are traced onto the undersides of the brace ends (**photo 14-6**). The sides of the braces are also traced onto the top surface of the ribs and linings (**photo 14-7**). This latter operation might not be possible if the top is cut substantially bigger than the garland. In this case, the locations of the sides of the brace can be marked onto the outside of the ribs. To do this, the luthier must kneel down to look

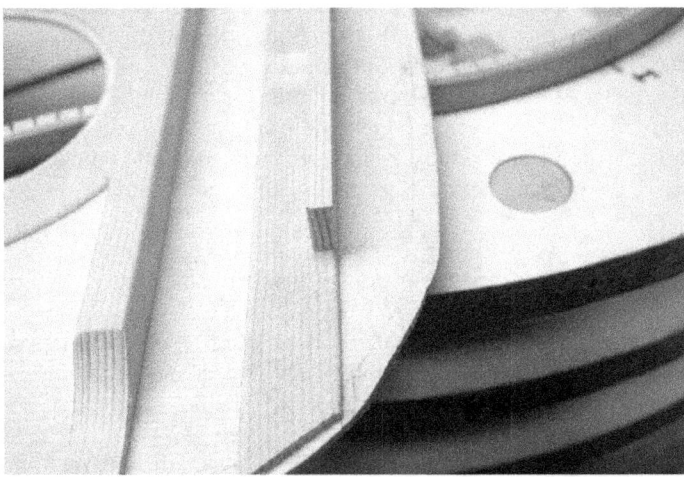

Photo 14-2 – The temporary height extender for the "Popsicle stick" brace, taped in place.

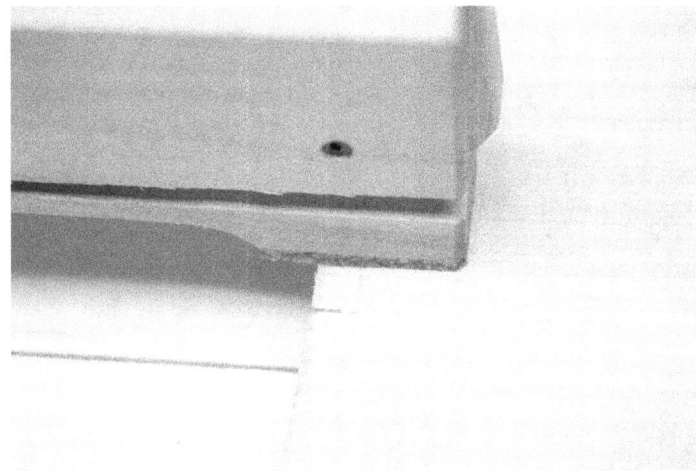

Photo 14-4 – The long clamps are placed just a bit behind the centerline so the luthier's view of the seams and their alignment is unobstructed.

Photo 14-3 – Four clamps serve as "feet" for the mold, to make it easier to apply additional clamps. Two long clamps hold the top in alignment with the garland.

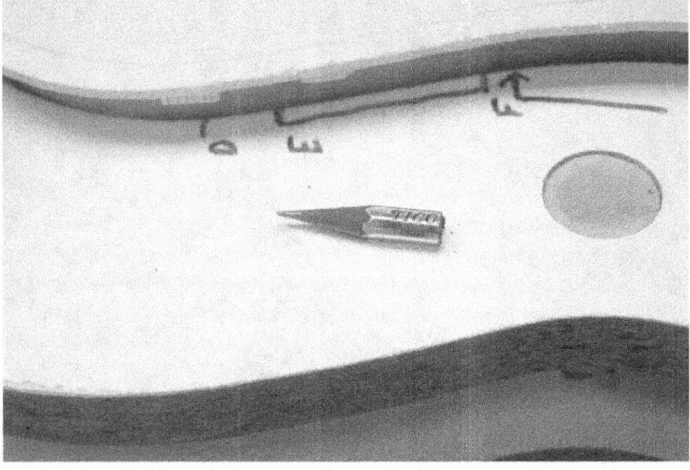

Photo 14-5 – A very short pencil is needed to mark the brace ends and the tops of the linings. The pencil is sharpened and then cut to length with a razor saw.

directly at the brace end and mark the location of each side of the brace onto the outside of the rib.

7. The top plate is unclamped and removed. A check is made to be sure all brace ends are fully marked. If the sides of the braces were marked on the outside of the ribs then those marks should be continued a bit onto the top surface of the ribs.

8. It should be noted that, because the garland may not be exactly the same shape as the inside of the mold at this point, the locations of the marks just made on the brace ends may be somewhat inside of the penciled body outline. If there is any doubt that the marks are accurate, the steps above should be repeated.

9. The top plate is placed on the bench, inside surface up. A pencil mark is made inside of each brace end pencil mark and parallel to it. The distance between the original and this new mark is the thickness of the ribs, nominally 3⁄32″ (2.4mm). See **photo 14-8**. Note that because the "Popsicle stick" brace is so wide, the original traced end marks will be visibly curved. When the new "parallel" marks are made they should be straight, so that the ends of the new marks are offset by the thickness of the ribs.

10. A razor saw is used to carefully saw through the brace ends at these new marks, until each brace end is just cut through (**photo 14-9**). Every attempt is made when doing this not to saw into the top. A Japanese razor saw with a curved end works great for this cut. The cuts should be made right on the lines, which will make the braces just a tiny bit shorter in length. This will aid in fitting the top plate to the garland.

11. Once all the brace ends are sawn through, a chisel is used to carefully remove the excess wood from the end of each brace (**photo 14-10**). The chisel or a scraper is used to scrape right down to the surface of the top (**photo 14-11**).

12. The thickness of each brace end is measured about ¼″ (6.4mm) back from the end. They should be exactly ⅛″ (3.2mm) thick from this point to the end. If any are thicker, a chisel and sandpaper are used to trim them down to proper thickness.

Photo 14-6 – The outside surface of the ribs is traced onto the bottoms of the brace ends that will be pocketed.

Photo 14-8 – Lines are drawn parallel to the outline markings on the brace ends. These are located at a distance that is the same as the thickness of the ribs, and mark where the brace ends will be cut. In the finished instrument, the brace ends will butt against the inside surface of the ribs.

Photo 14-7 – The sides of the brace ends are traced onto the top surface of the ribs and linings as well as possible.

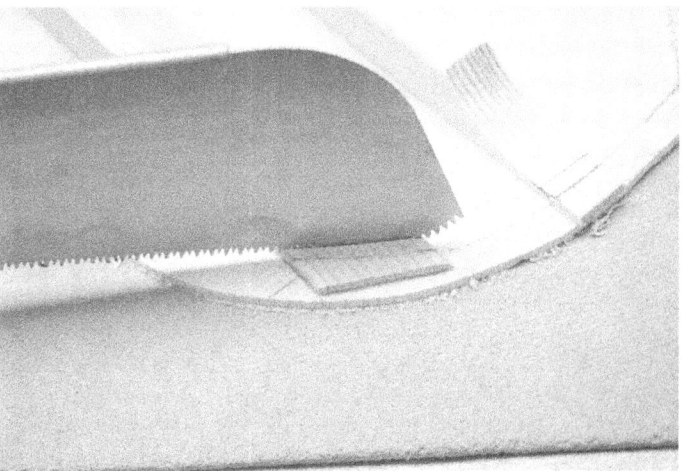

Photo 14-9 – The brace ends are cut to length using a razor saw with a curved end. The cuts should be just a bit on the short side.

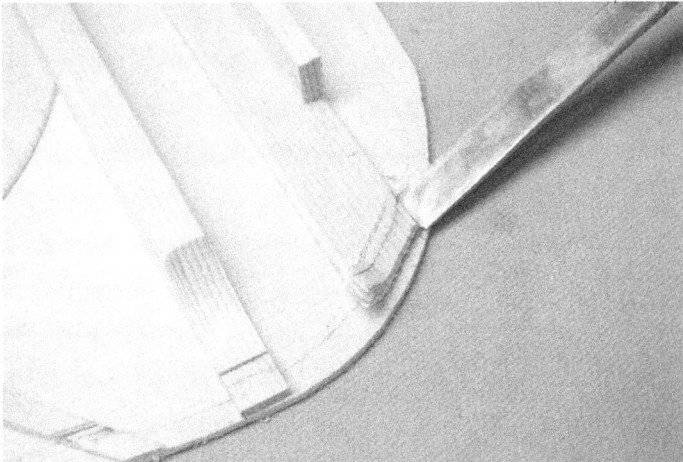

Photo 14-10 – Waste material from the brace ends is removed with a chisel.

Photo 14-12 – A straight stiff stick is used as a straightedge to fully mark the walls of the brace end pockets onto the tops of the linings.

Photo 14-11 – The surface of the top plate where the waste was removed is scraped clean of all remaining wood and glue.

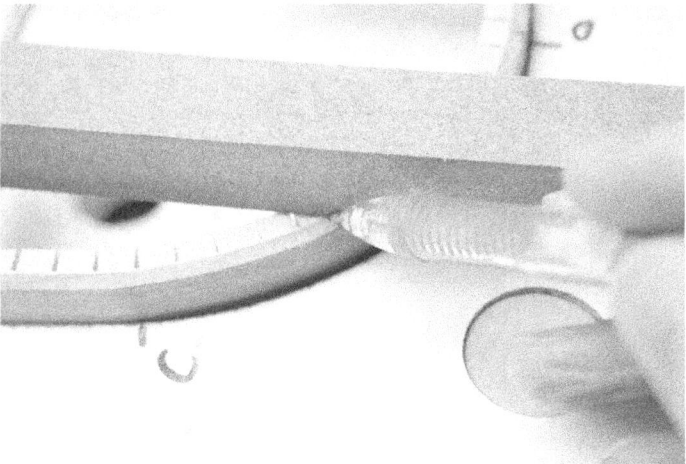

Photo 14-13 – Here the wall of one of the pockets on the neck end of the "Popsicle stick" brace is marked.

13. Now the top is returned to its place on the garland, checking again to be sure the location of the brace ends have been accurately marked on the top of the ribs and that the brace ends have been trimmed so they will clear the ribs of the garland. When all looks good, the piece of brace stock currently taped to the "Popsicle stick" brace is removed.

☐ **Pocketing the Brace Ends**

Each brace end will fit into a small pocket cut into the linings. All the pockets will be laid out first, and then cut. When cutting these pockets, we strive to make them accurate and tight fitting. There is an issue with cutting the pockets into kerfed linings, when the cuts come close to one of the kerfs. Dealing with this is explained in detail in the appropriate construction step.

The pocketing operation is fussy and tedious work that must be done with great care. I have found that lutherie novices get good at doing this quickly though. It is generally easier to do clean work when using mahogany (*Swietenia macrophylla*) linings, but if care is taken, good results can be had with any material. Careful paring, making use of small cuts, is a key to success.

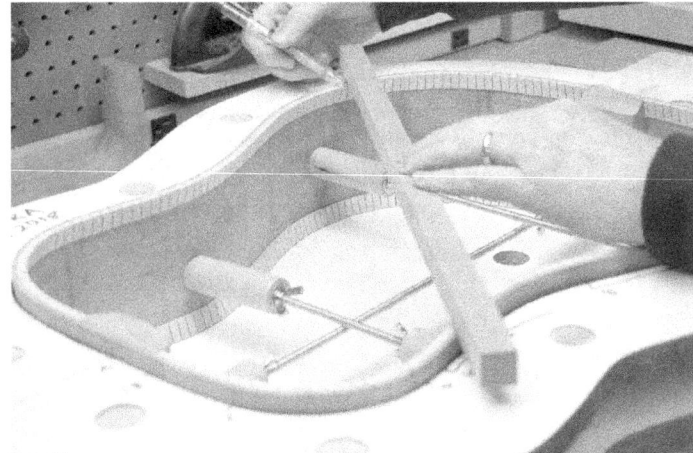

Photo 14-14 – One of the walls of the tail end pocket of one of the X braces is marked.

1. The first step is marking the outlines of the tops of the pockets on the tops of the linings. It is desirable to do this in a manner that keeps the walls of the pockets parallel to the sides of the braces. A stick or board with a straight side that is at least as long as the body is cut and used as a rigid straightedge.

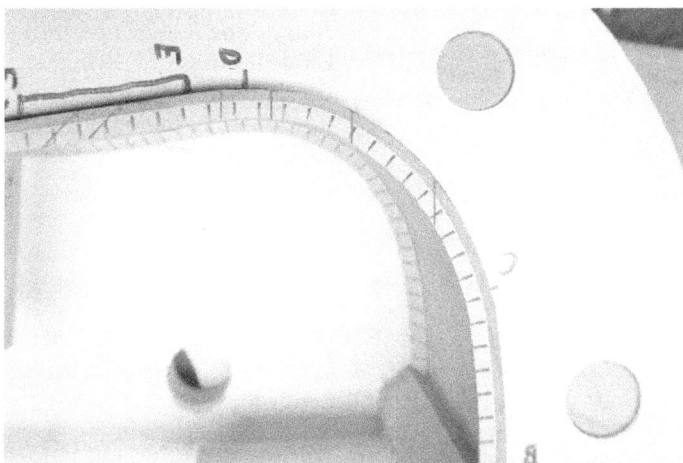

Photo 14-15 – *Marks for the walls of brace end pockets of the "Popsicle stick" brace, upper transverse brace, and X brace.*

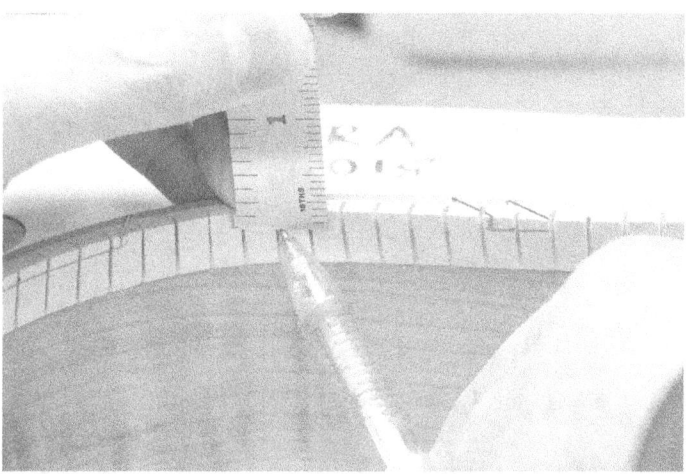

Photo 14-17 – *The depth of each pocket can be marked with a small ruler. Note one of the fingers behind the ruler serves as a depth stop.*

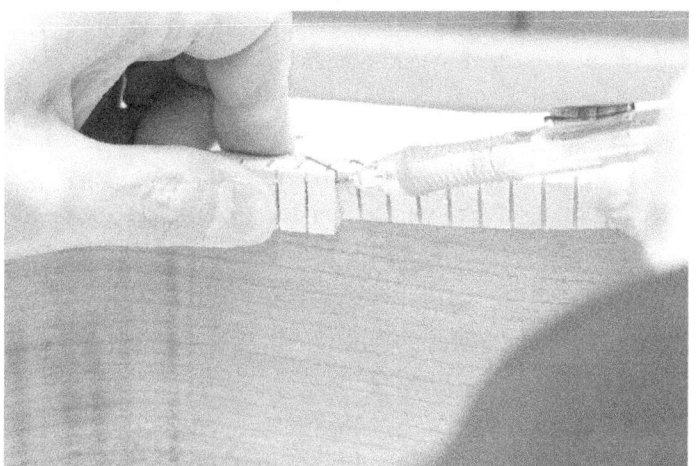

Photo 14-16 – *It is useful to use an inverted piece of lining material as a fence when marking the fronts of the walls on the linings.*

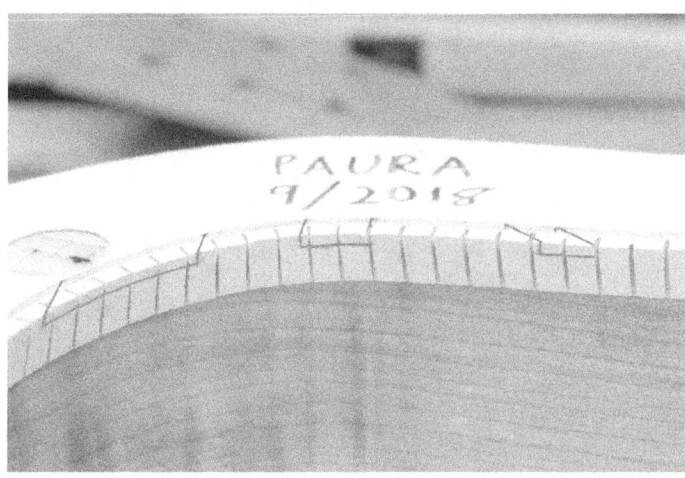

Photo 14-18 – *A few of the brace end pockets, fully marked out.*

2. The tops of the pockets for the "Popsicle stick" brace are marked first. There is currently a small mark on each side of the top of the ribs, indicating where the sides of the brace ends are located. These will be extended to mark the tops of the pockets on the tops of the linings. The straightedge board is placed across the garland, aligning the edge of the board with the two marks for the side of the "Popsicle stick" brace that is closest to the neck end of the body (**photo 14-12**). The edge of the board is traced onto the tops of the linings on both sides of the body (**photo 14-13**). Then the board is positioned to line up the edge with the two marks for the "Popsicle stick" brace side that is farthest from the neck block, and the lining tops are marked here in the same manner.

3. Step 2 above is repeated for all the other braces that pocket into the linings: the upper transverse brace, and the X braces. Note that marking the tops of the pockets for the ends of the X braces will result in diagonal marks (**photos 14-14, 14-15**).

4. Now the fronts of all the pockets are drawn, by extending each pocket top-side line down the inside surface of the linings a bit. Then, a three- or four-section length of kerfed lining material is used as a guide to draw lines from each of these marks down the inside surface of the linings ⅛″ (3.2MM). The piece of lining material is flipped over thick side down, its top edge is aligned with the top edge of the lining, and its side edge provides a nice square surface to use to guide the pencil (**photo 14-16**). These marks represent the sides of the pockets on the inside surface of the linings. Note that it often happens that one of these side lines falls right on a kerf in the lining, in which case it cannot be marked.

5. Finally, the end of a ruler is used to mark the floors of the pockets on the inside surface of the linings, down ⅛″ (3.2MM) from the top surface for the upper transverse brace end pockets, and those for the X brace end pockets (**photos 14-17, 14-18**). The floors of the pockets for the "Popsicle stick" brace are marked at whatever the thickness of that brace is.

6. Adjusting some of the pocket wall locations. The next construction step will be to saw down the sides of the pockets. But before that is done, it should be noted that some of these wall marks may come very close to the side of one of the teeth of the kerfed lining. Although it *should* be possible to saw a tooth in half, any sawing that leaves pieces thinner than half a tooth are quite delicate and will not hold up to the subsequent chisel

work needed to excavate the pocket. There are two ways to deal with this situation. The first is to simply enlarge the width of the pocket to the next kerf between teeth. This will make for a wider pocket, but much cleaner chisel work when the pocket is cleaned out.

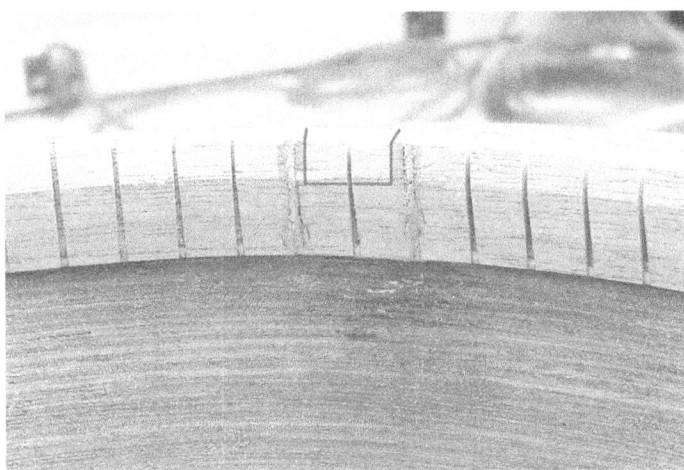

Photo 14-19 – If a wall is very close to a kerf in the lining, the kerf can be filled with wood before making the cuts for the pocket walls.

Photo 14-20 – The pocket walls are cut using a razor saw. Cutting is done with the saw tipped so it does not cut the ribs.

Photo 14-21 – A board is clamped to the top of the mold, in contact with the rib, behind a pocket, in preparation for chisel work. This prevents accidental splitting of the rib.

The second way to deal with this is to fill the kerf that is close to the marked location of the pocket wall (**photo 14-19**). This can be done with multiple pieces of veneer, or with a thin slice sawed off the end of a piece of lining material. Filling the kerf will reinforce the lining. When the glue dries and excess material is trimmed away, the wall can be sawn in its marked location. This takes more work, but results in tighter, neater pockets.

7. Sawing the sides of the pockets. Using a razor saw, the side line of each pocket is cut diagonally down from the top (**photo 14-20**). Sawing is done in the direction of the rib, that is, from the inside of the guitar toward the outside, to prevent blowing out the grain on the delicate linings. Note in the photo that I am using a pull saw to make the cut. The cut should not touch the outer top edge of the rib, but should go down to the floor line on the inside surface of the lining. Care is taken to be sure to accurately follow the lines penciled on top of the lining when making these cuts. And of course for those pocket outlines that fall directly on a kerf in the lining, no sawing is necessary.

8. Now each pocket can be excavated, using a short ¼″ (6.4mm) wide chisel and a small skew knife. Chiseling is done toward the ribs from the inside of the guitar. To avoid splitting the ribs, the part of the ribs above the top of the mold should be backed up with a heavy block of wood, clamped to the mold (**photo 14-21**).

9. The first step of excavation is scoring the floor line of the pocket, using the chisel or a knife held horizontally (**photos 14- 22, 14-23**). The temptation to simply jam the chisel into the wood at the floor line, and pop the waste out in one piece should be avoided. Doing so, it is just as likely that the bottom part of the lining will split off. During excavation, if any part of the lining splits away that was not intended, it can be glued back with cyanoacrylate glue before continuing excavation.

10. Shallow paring cuts are taken with the chisel, working from the inside of the linings toward the ribs, working the depth of the pocket gradually down to the floor. The bevel side of the chisel is kept up. The floor of the pocket is kept horizontal and

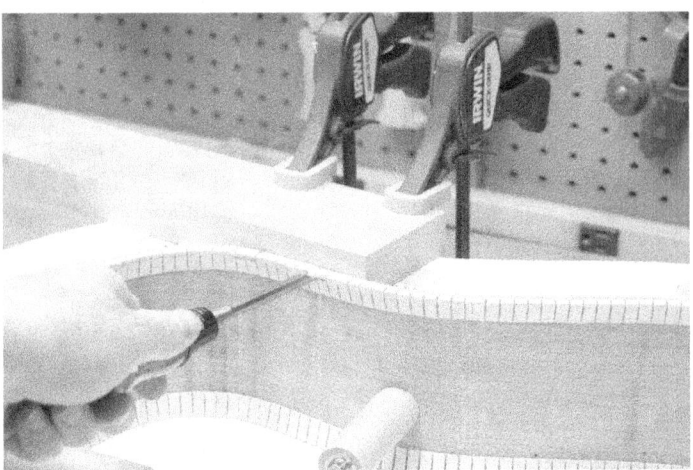

Photo 14-22 – A short butt chisel is needed to chisel out the waste from the brace end pockets.

flat. At this point some lining wood will remain glued to the inside of the ribs. This can be removed with vertical paring strokes with the chisel (**photo 14-24**). When doing this, the bevel side is kept toward the inside of the guitar.

Note that the walls of most of the pockets will not be perpendicular to the body outline. Fussy excavation is needed where there is an acute angle between the pocket side wall and back wall. This is the case for the pockets for the ends of the X braces. The skew knife is used here to carefully carve away material in these corners (**photos 14-25, 14-26**).

11. The pocket is scraped clean after it has been fully excavated (**photo 14-27**). The pocket is measured to be sure it is ⅛″ (3.2mm) deep (**photo 14-28**). If it is too shallow additional trimming of the floor is needed.

12. Steps 8 through 11 are repeated for each brace end pocket. The excavation debris should be vacuumed up after all the pocket excavation is done.

Sometimes excavation of one or more of the pockets doesn't go as planned to the extent that a do-over would be a good thing. It is possible to do this by simply cutting out a section of the lining, using knife, chisel, and scraper, and then cutting and gluing in a replacement piece of lining. Then the pocket can be attempted again. For an alternative to pocketing, see the sidebar about bracketing.

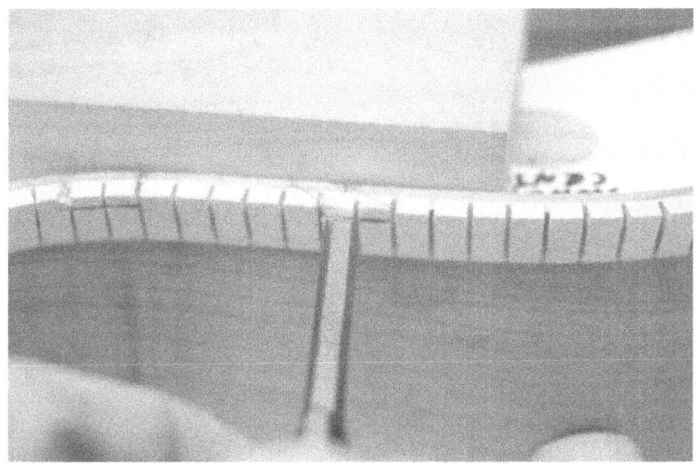

Photo 14-23 – *Excavation begins by scoring the pocket floor line with the chisel. Then the waste can be pared off, top to bottom.*

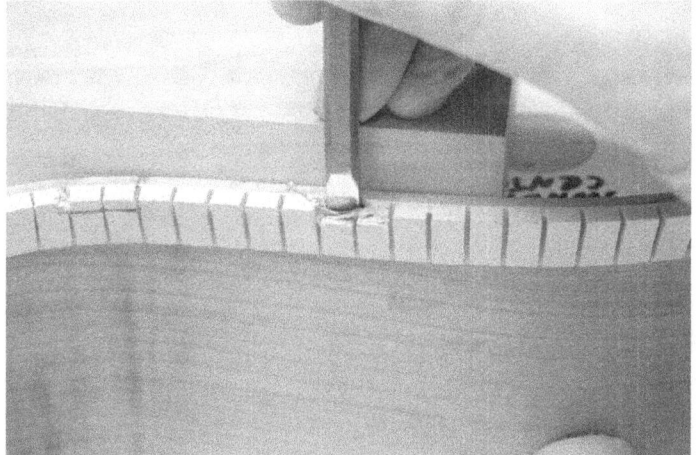

Photo 14-24 – *Vertical cuts are made to shave the waste wood off the inside surface of the rib.*

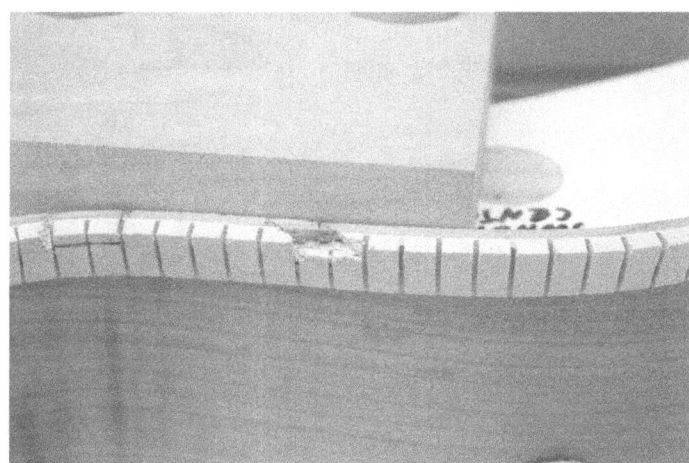

Photo 14-26 – *A pocket completely excavated, before it is scraped clean.*

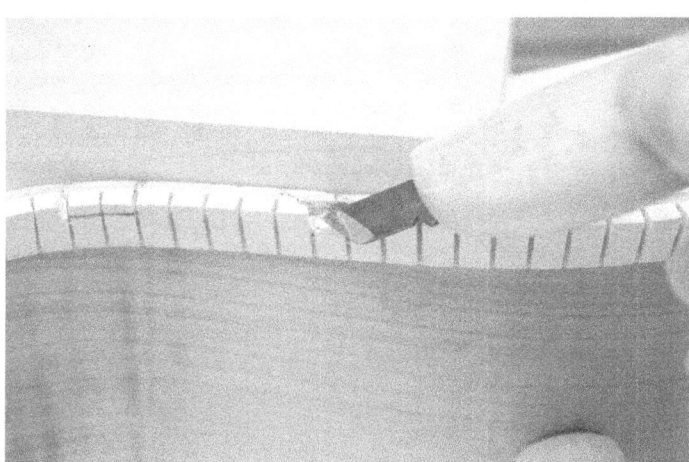

Photo 14-25 – *The highly angled pockets of the X braces require some finicky work with the knife.*

Photo 14-27 – *Some excavated and scraped brace end pockets at the neck end of the garland.*

☐ Fitting and Gluing the Top

1. The top is fitted to the garland. If all of the brace end cutting and pocketing of the linings was done accurately, the top should now sit snugly on the garland so that all the brace ends drop into their pockets, the underside of the top plate rests directly upon the top edge of the ribs all around, and the center seam of the top plate aligns perfectly with that of the garland at neck and tail ends. If not, some fitting will be required. Some specific things to look out for:

- if one or more of the floating brace ends on the finger braces or the oblique braces is too long and doesn't end short of the linings;

- if any of the pocketed brace ends are a bit too long they may not allow the top to drop down onto the ribs. But it may also push the entire top over to the other side and mess up the center seam alignment. The fix is to locate and trim the brace end;

- if a pocket is not wide enough for the brace end, it will prevent the top from dropping down onto the ribs. The fix is to trim the pocket a bit wider;

- if a pocket is not quite deep enough, the top will not fully drop down over that brace end. The fix is to deepen that pocket;

- if all brace ends drop into their pockets but the neck end of the top will not drop down fully, then the "Popsicle stick" brace is partially sitting on top of the neck block. The cause of this is usually one or more pockets are positioned a bit too close to the neck end of the garland. The fix is to identify the pocket(s) and trim the wall on the tail side a bit.

It is important that the seam of the top align with the seam of the ribs at both ends of the garland. If it does not, the luthier

---

Bracketing: An Alternative to Brace End Pockets

Pocketing of the brace ends provides a number of advantages when fitting the plates to the garland in the style of building that is presented in this book. There are other common ways to support the brace ends. One of them is with brackets that are glued to the sides of the garland and are positioned to support the brace ends. The photo below shows such brackets used in a reproduction of a 19th century guitar. A simple method of implementing brackets when kerfed linings are used is to cut out a section of lining where the brace end will be located, then glue in a new section of lining material in that space, dropped down by the thickness of the brace end. The sequence is shown in the figure below.

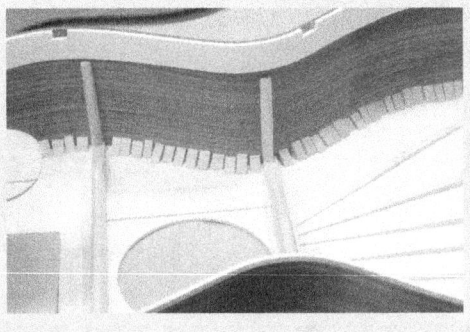

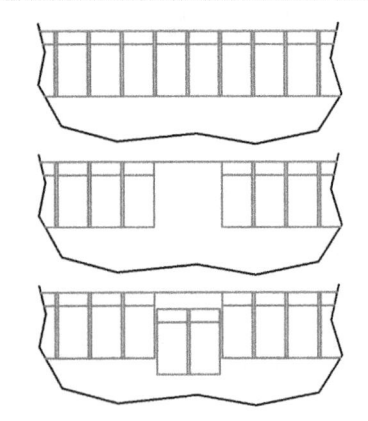

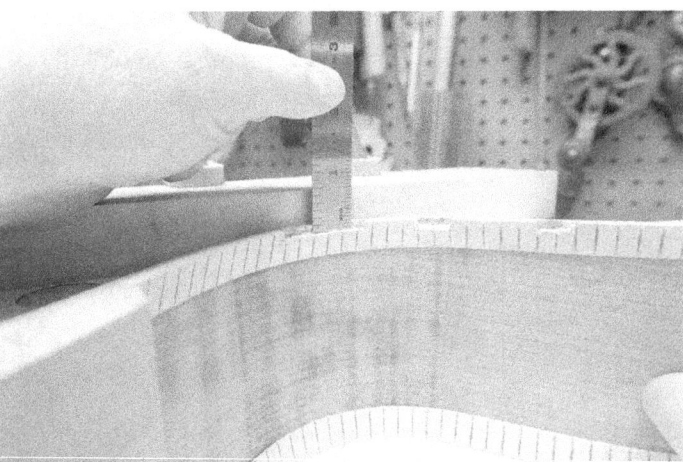

Photo 14-28 – The depth of the pockets is checked with a ruler.

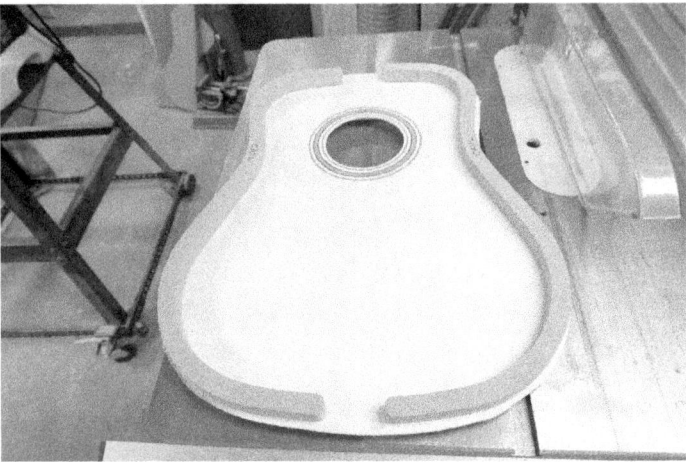

Photo 14-29 – Two long clamping cauls are cut from MDF. Use of the cauls allows clamping of the top with fewer clamps.

Photo 14-30 – *The edges of the cauls that will contact the top must be rounded over to avoid denting the soft top during clamping.*

must identify what is preventing this alignment and fix the problem.

When the top fits and is aligned well it should be removed, and then fitted back on the garland and the fit checked again.

2. Make gluing cauls. The minimum clamp set for construction described in this book includes 12 regular length and four long clamps. With only 16 clamps, cauls will be needed when gluing down the top plate. One caul for each side of the top is made from ¾″ (19.1mm) MDF (**photo 14-29**). The insert for the mold can be used as a template to draw the outside lines of each caul onto a piece of MDF. Repetitive marks are made ¾″ (19.1mm) inside the outline, then these lines are connected and the cauls are cut out. Each caul should end 1½″ (38.1mm) from the centerline of the top plate at both ends.

3. A sanding drum mounted in the drill press or a spindle sander is used to smooth the saw marks from inside and outside surfaces of the cauls. The end corners at the ends of the cauls are rounded over too. 80-grit sandpaper is used on a cylindrical form to round over the bottom edges (edges that will contact the top plate) on both sides of each caul (**photo 14-30**).

Note that the cauls are used to clamp soft spruce and it is imperative that the cauls don't dent the top. All sharp edges that will be in contact with the top must be smoothly rounded over.

4. Gluing the top plate. A dry run is always a good idea. If the garland has been removed from the mold so that the mold insert could be used as a template for the cauls, the insert, with its spacer, should be reinstalled; the garland inserted again, top edge up, and tugged around so the seams at the ends of the garland are aligned with those of the mold; and the garland jacked

Photo 14-31 – *The top clamping configuration. Six clamps are applied to each side. Two long clamps are applied to each end.*

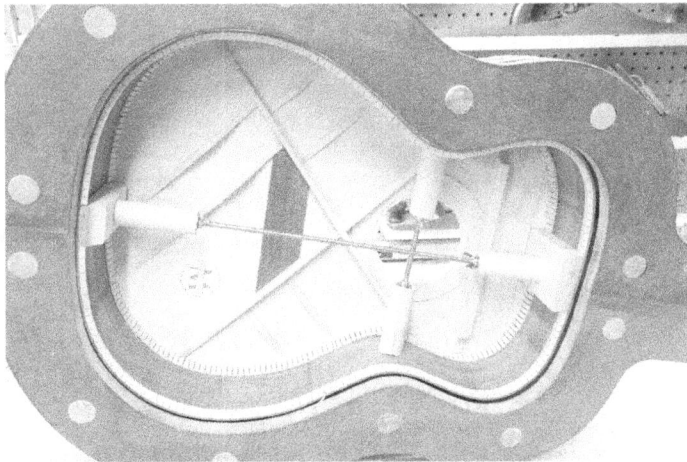

Photo 14-32 – *After gluing, the floor and insert are removed from the mold. The mold is positioned on its side to do this.*

attempt should be made to get a thin continuous bead all the way around. The tops of the blocks get glue as well.

6. The top is positioned onto the garland, lining up the centerline marks at both ends with the seams in the ribs. If there is any wiggle room in the fit, the top should be pressed toward the neck block, so the "Popsicle stick" brace is in contact with the neck block. The top is pressed into place all around, to be sure all brace ends are in their pockets and the entire perimeter of the top is in good contact with the tops of the ribs.

7. As was done when marking the brace ends, one long clamp is positioned next to the neck end centerline mark but on the other side from where the luthier is, so the center seam alignment can be seen when the clamp is lightly clamped. Another long clamp is applied similarly at the tail end. The alignment is checked once more, and any fitting adjustments are made.

in place. The top should be test-fitted to the garland one last time.

5. A thin bead of glue is applied onto the top surface of the garland, being sure to get some glue into the bottoms of each of the brace end pockets. Too much glue should be avoided, because the squeeze-out will run down into the body, but an

8. Now the gluing cauls are placed onto the top so their outer edges are aligned with the penciled outline on the top, and six clamps per side are arranged evenly around each side. That number will include the two clamps on each side that are currently just being used as feet to raise the mold up off the bench top. The clamps are thrown to clamp lightly, and a check is made to be sure the top is securely in place all around. It will probably be necessary to lift and turn the whole affair around to see the other side. Finally, two more long clamps are added,

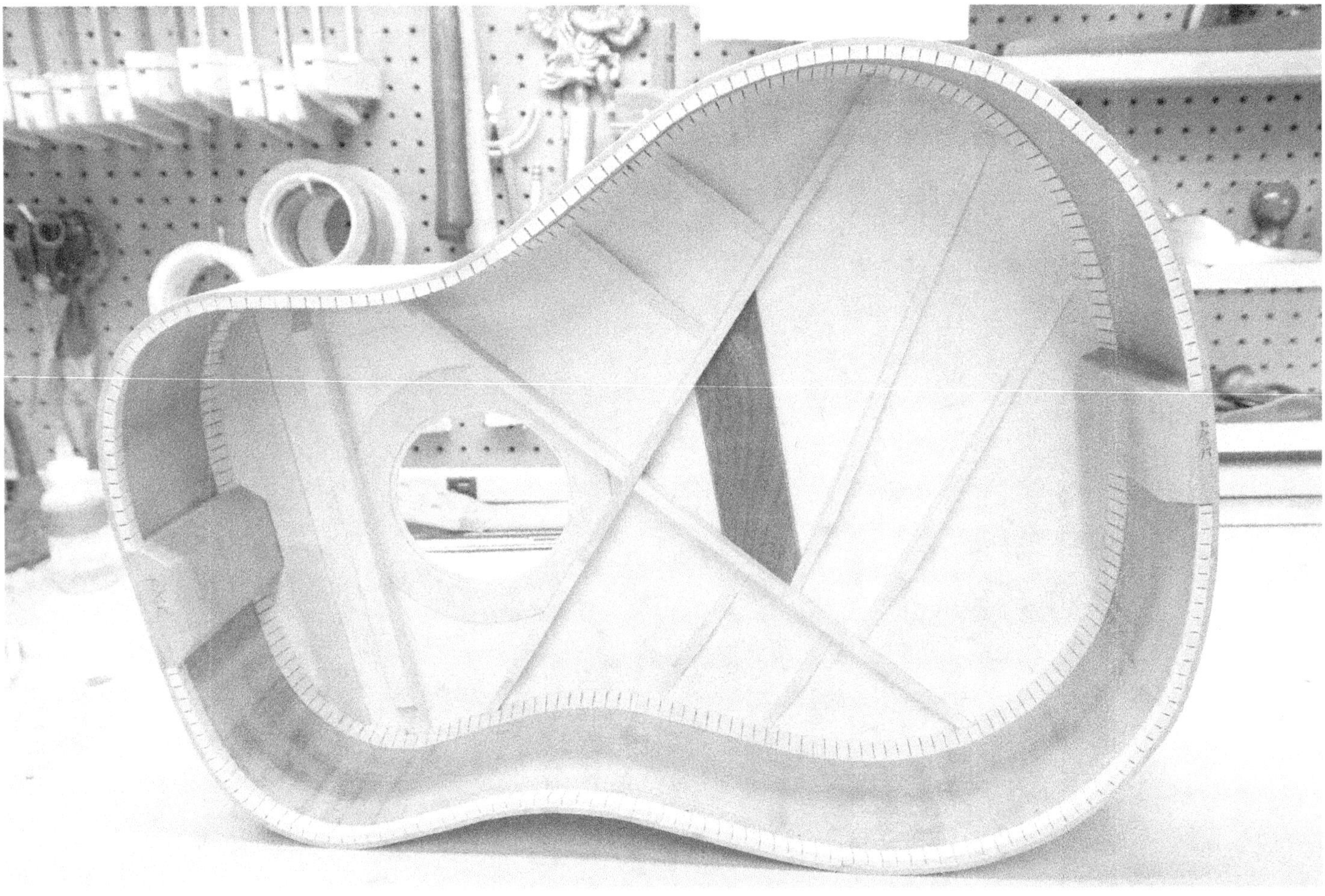

Photo 14-33 – *With the top attached to the garland, it is appropriate to start referring to the assembly as the body.*

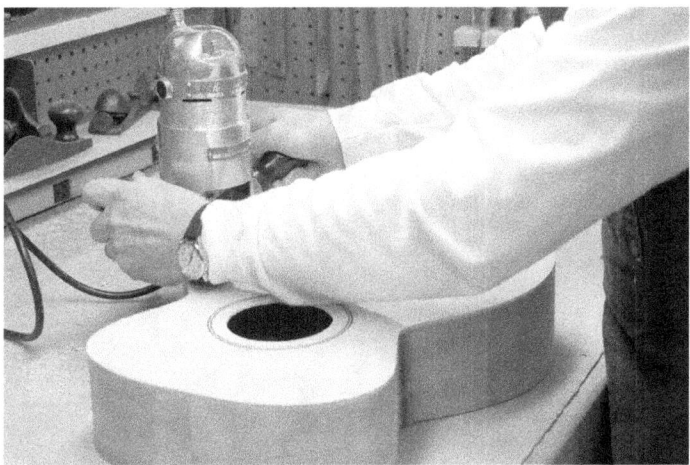

Photo 14-34 – Using a small router to trim the top flush to the sides. Note the position, with forearms on the top, to steady the body and the router.

Photo 14-35 – Measuring the width of the trussrod adjuster nut.

one to each end, next to the two already there (**photo 14-31**). Clamping is done with moderate clamping pressure only, to avoid damaging the top plate.

9. The glue is allowed to cure for 4 hours before removing clamps and cauls.

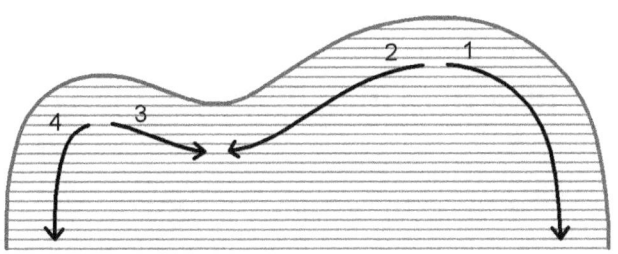

Figure 14-1 – Excess material is routed off each side of the top in four separate passes. This prevents the router from cutting into the grain, which would yank big chunks of wood off, damaging the top in the process. Note that two of these cuts (#1, #3) are climb cuts, so the router must be handled particularly carefully for these.

10. The body is removed from the mold. The ribs are held in place in the mold by the rib jacks. These can be disassembled and removed through the soundhole, but it is easier if the back is taken off the mold. This is done by carefully setting the mold on its side on the bench, removing the screws attaching the floor of the mold, and removing the floor and the insert (**photo 14-32**).

 Note that the mold should *not* be flipped over with the top plate resting on the bench to remove the floor of the mold. The delicate top cannot support the weight of the heavy mold.

The jacks are removed. The mold is placed on the bench back side down, and the body is carefully lifted out. The body now looks as pictured in **photo 14-33**.

11. The edges of the top plate are trimmed flush to the sides of the body. This can be done with plane, chisel and scraper; or using a bottom bearing pattern bit in a small router (**photo 14-34**). In either case it is imperative that planing or routing be done "down hill" to avoid splitting the grain of the spruce and yanking off big pieces of the top (**figure 14-1**). Note that performing this step using a router will involve some *climb cutting*. If using a router, only as much of the cutting edge needed to trim the top is exposed. This will help avoid gouging the ribs.

 A router with a small baseplate should be used if at all possible for this task. A laminate trimmer is ideal. Because the plate is slightly arched, the larger the router baseplate, the more the router will be tilted by the plate arching. Tilting is reduced when a small base router is used.

12. The amount of squeeze-out from gluing on the top is assessed. If there is a lot of squeeze-out or if glue has dripped down between the kerfs of the linings onto the insides of the ribs, it should be remembered when it is time to glue on the back plate to use a thinner bead of glue. Any excess hardened glue is scraped off the insides of the body now.

Preliminary Fitting of the Neck

The gross fitting of the neck to the body is done in the following operations. Final fitting will be done after neck and body are fully assembled.

☐ Cutting the Access Channel for the Trussrod Adjuster

A short channel must be cut in the top at the neck end to provide clearance for the trussrod adjuster nut, and to provide access to it for adjustment from within the body. In the finished instrument, the trussrod will be adjusted using an Allen key inserted into the trussrod adjuster nut through the soundhole. This channel can be cut using a router with a round bottom bit, but the instructions here make use of simple hand tools to drill, saw, and chisel the channel. The width, depth, and length of the channel are determined from measurements taken directly from the trussrod adjuster nut.

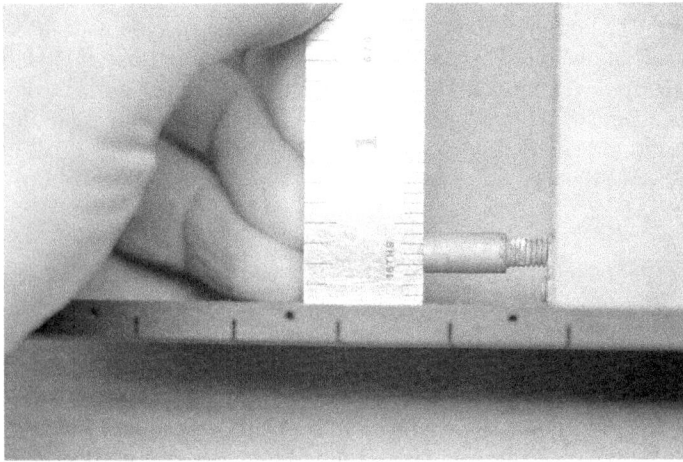

Photo 14-36 – *The distance from the underside of the fretboard to the other side of the trussrod adjuster nut is measured with a ruler.*

Photo 14-38 – *A shallow hole is drilled on the centerline at the inside edge of the neck block. The hole just goes through the top.*

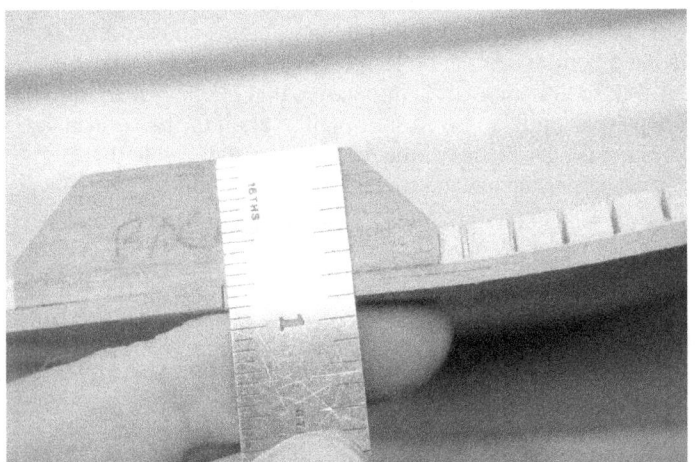

Photo 14-37 – *The combined thickness of the ribs and the neck block is measured with a ruler.*

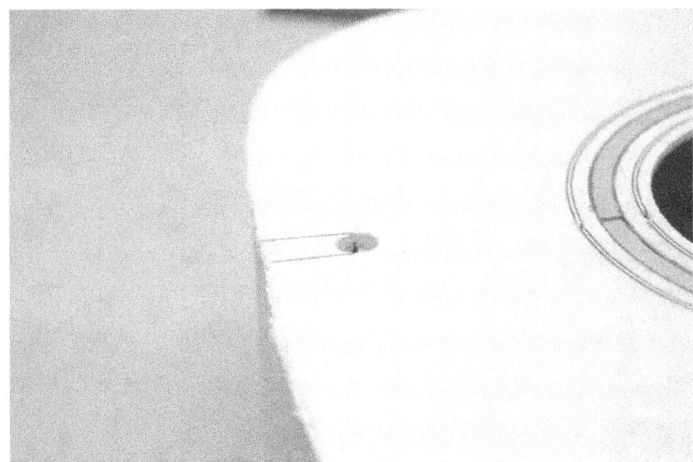

Photo 14-39 – *The walls of the channel are laid out in pencil using a straightedge inline with the diameter of the hole.*

1. The width of the widest part of the trussrod end and adjuster nut is measured (**photo 14-35**), and ⅛″ (3.2mm) is added to that measurement. This will be the width of the channel.

2. The distance is measured from the underside of the fretboard to the other side of the trussrod nut (**photo 14-36**), and ¹⁄₁₆″ (1.6mm) is added to that measurement. This will be the depth needed for the channel.

3. The distance from the outside of the ribs at the centerline to the inside edge of the neck block is measured (**photo 14-37**). This distance is transferred to the top and a mark is placed on the centerline there. Using a brad point bit of the diameter of the width of the channel in a hand drill, a hole is carefully drilled at the mark, just through the top into the block and just through the edge of the "Popsicle stick" brace (**photo 14-38**).

4. Pencil lines are drawn from the width of this hole and parallel to the centerline to the neck edge of the top (**photo 14-39**). The depth of the channel is transferred to the neck end of the ribs at the center seam and marked in pencil. The side lines of the channel are extended down the neck end of the ribs. A razor saw is used to saw down through the top on the inside of the

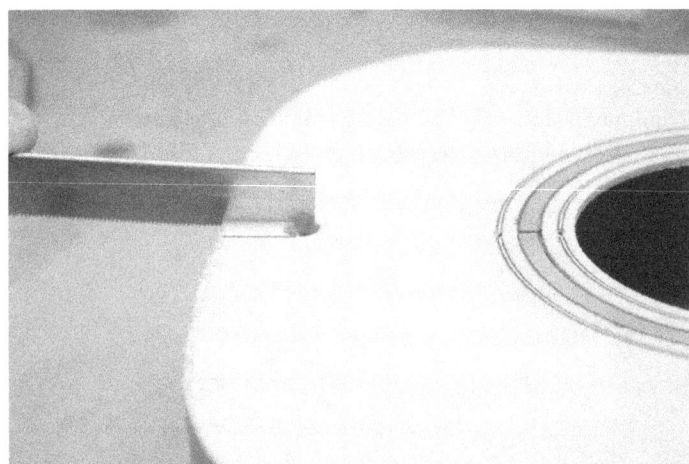

Photo 14-40 – *Cuts are made at the wall lines using a razor saw. The cut go almost as deep as the target depth of the channel.*

marks (**photo 14-40**). Sawing stops at half the width of the channel above the penciled depth mark on the ribs. This provides space so the bottom of the channel can be rasped round.

5. The waste is chiseled out from the channel to the bottoms of the saw kerfs, being careful not to split or mar the top while paring the spruce (**photo 14-41**). The bottom of the channel is rasped with a round rasp down to the marked depth (**photo 14-42**). The finished channel appears as in **photo 14-43**.

6. Clearance is checked by holding the neck in place. There should be nothing obstructing the trussrod end and nut, and there should be no contact between it and the neck block. If there is, the channel is trimmed as needed.

☐ **Drilling Holes for the Neck Bolts**

Materials
  2 ea. ¼″ – 20 × ⅜″ (9.5MM) long cone point set screws
  2 ea. ¼″ – 20 × 1½″ (38.1MM) long cap screws
  2 ea. ¼″ lock washers
  2 ea. ¼″ flat washers

1. One ¼″ – 20 × ⅜″ (9.5MM) long cone point set screw is inserted *backwards* into each threaded insert in the neck heel. The points will be facing out (**photo 14-44**). They should not be screwed in so far that it won't be possible to get them out again. (If this does happen, flats will have to be filed on the sides of the point, so the screw can then be turned with pliers.)

2. The neck is placed in position on the body, pressing the fretboard down to the top. The heel is wiggled back and forth

Photo 14-43 – The completed channel, ready for test fitting and possible adjustment.

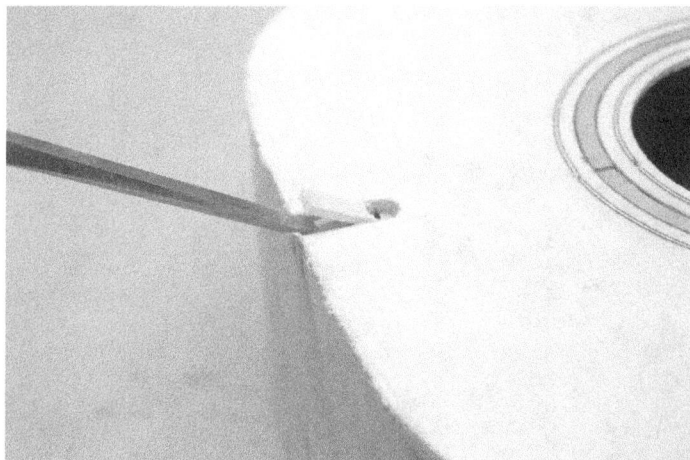

Photo 14-41 – Waste is chiseled out of the channel down to the depth of the wall cuts.

Photo 14-44 – Two cone point set screws are used to mark the locations of the centers of the neck inserts onto the body.

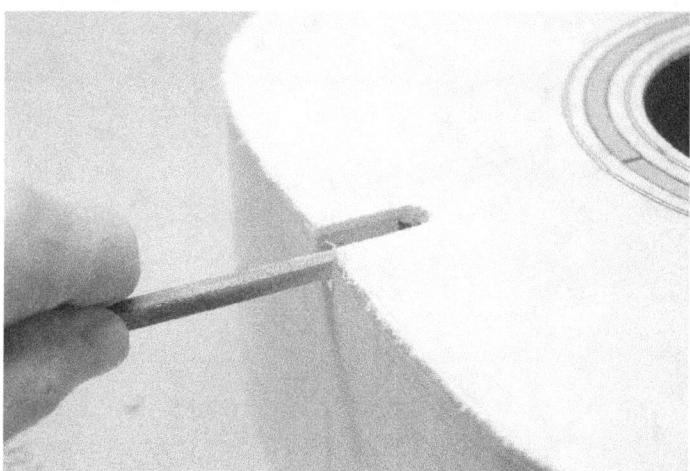

Photo 14-42 – The bottom of the channel can be rasped to the target depth using a round rasp.

Photo 14-45 – The pricked centers for the bolt holes are enhanced with pencil for visibility.

Photo 14-46 – A block of wood is clamped to the inside surface of the neck block, to back up the drilled hole so the exit comes out clean.

Photo 14-47 – The disposable drilling guide block is slipped over the drill bit ...

Photo 14-48 – ... and the point of the bit is centered in the pricked center mark for the hole.

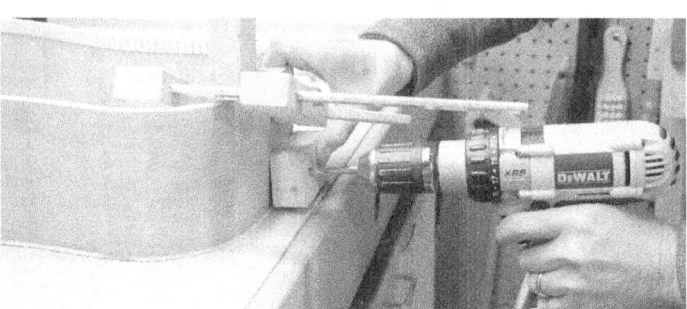

Photo 14-49 – The guide block is pushed along the drill bit to contact the body, which will force the bit perpendicular to the body surface.

Photo 14-50 – The finished neck bolt holes, drilled through the neck block.

Photo 14-51 – The neck is bolted in place to check its gross fit to the body.

while pressing it into the body, so the points of the set screws mark the body at the centerline. The neck is removed, and the set screws are removed from the inserts. An awl is used to prick center marks where the marks made by the set screw points cross the center seam. The pricked marks are made more visible with pencil (**photo 14-45**).

3. A scrap of hardwood board at least ¾″ (19.1mm) thick is cut 2″ (50.8mm) wide by about 10″ (254mm) long. This is cut in half lengthwise, yielding two 5″ (127mm) long pieces. Using a ⁵⁄₁₆″ (8mm) bit and the drill press, a through hole is drilled near the centerline of one of these pieces and about 1″ (25.4mm) from one end. This piece will be used as a disposable drilling guide to keep the drilled holes straight.

4. The other piece of wood will be used to back up the neck block, to prevent the grain from being blown out when the drill exits the inside surface of the neck block. This piece is clamped against the inside surface of the block so that the clamp is out of the way enough to provide clearance for drilling one of the holes (**photo 14-46**).

5. The body is oriented on the bench top down and neck end facing out, and it is lightly clamped or blocked in place to prevent it from moving around. Note in the photos that I am using a router pad on top of the bench, which helps considerably to keep the body in place. A ⁵⁄₁₆″ (8mm) brad point bit is chucked

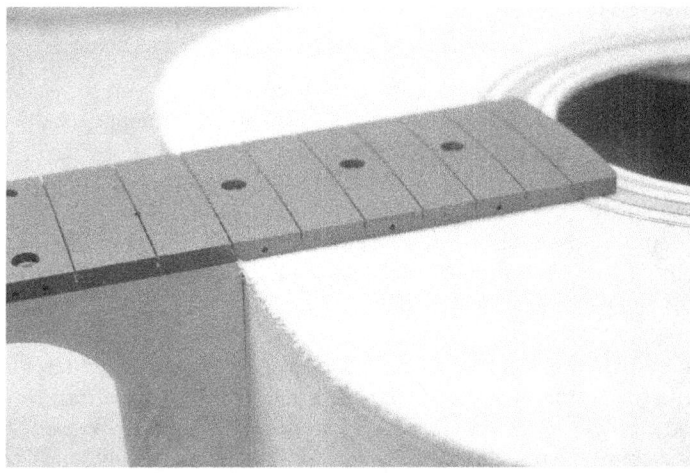

Photo 14-52 – The intersection of fretboard and heel should be in contact with the top edge of the top plate.

Photo 14-53 – The bolt holes may need to be elongated using a round profile rasp.

into the hand drill. The bit is slipped through the hole in the drilling guide (**photo 14-47**). The point of the bit is located into one of the pricked centers (**photo 14-48**), then the drilling guide is slid down the bit so it is flush with the neck end of the body (**photo 14-49**), all while keeping the bit point in the center hole. The drilling guide is pressed firmly into place against the body, and the hole is drilled. It may be easier to drill it only part way, then remove the guide and replace the brad point bit with a standard twist bit to finish the hole.

6. The clamp on the backup board is moved if necessary to provide access to the other hole center. This hole is drilled in the same manner as the first one. The clamp and backup board are removed (**photo 14-50**), and debris inside the body is vacuumed up.

7. Using 2 each ¼″ – 20 × 1½″ (38.1mm) long cap screws, ¼″ lock washers, and ¼″ flat washers, the neck is bolted to the body, hand tight (**photo 14-51**). A check is made to be sure that the neck can be positioned so the junction between fretboard and heel is firmly in contact with the edge between the top and the body (**photo 14-52**). If the fretboard sits high, whatever is preventing it from sitting down is determined and corrected. It is possible the channel cut for the trussrod adjustment nut is too shallow, and it is possible that the bolt holes just drilled are slightly high. In either case, a round rasp is used to increase the depth of the channel or the holes (**photo 14-53**) until the fretboard junction sits easily on the edge of the top.

Note that the heel should mate fairly well to the body. The underside of the fretboard extension may be a bit higher than the body at the its end, or the extension may need to be bent up a bit to make it fit. These conditions are normal at this point in construction and will be dealt with later. A check is made to be sure the flat washer on the bolt near the back end of the neck block will clear the back plate and the back plate center reinforcement strip. If it will not, a washer with a smaller outside diameter must be used, or a flat must be ground on that washer for clearance.

8. A check is made to be sure an Allen key can be fitted into the trussrod adjustment nut (**photo 14-54**). If not, the shallow channel in the center of the "Popsicle stick" brace is cut deeper to provide clear access.

9. The hardware and the neck are removed. The hardware is retained for attaching the neck in a subsequent operation.

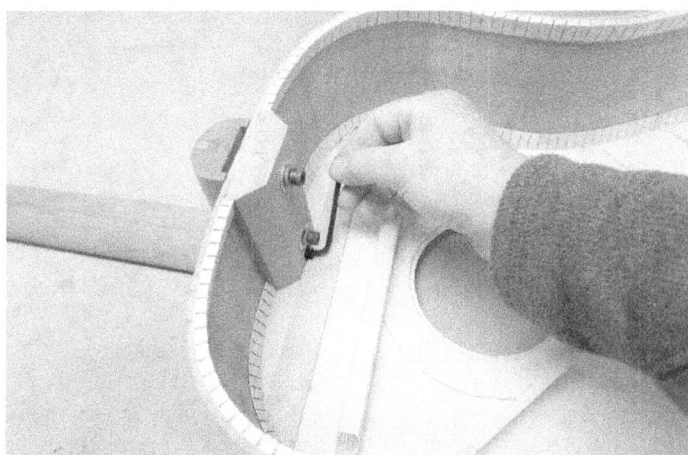

Photo 14-54 – Access to the trussrod adjuster nut is checked. The channel in the "Popsicle stick" brace may need to be modified to provide clearance.

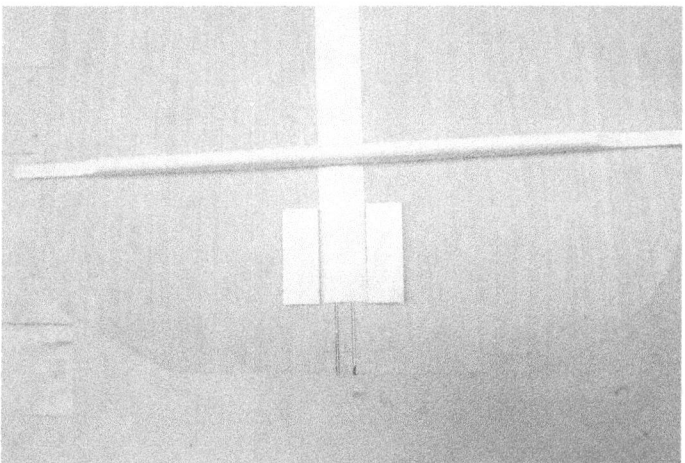

Photo 14-55 – Two thicker scraps of wood are taped down on either side of the neck end of the back reinforcement strip, flush with its end, so they will contact the neck block.

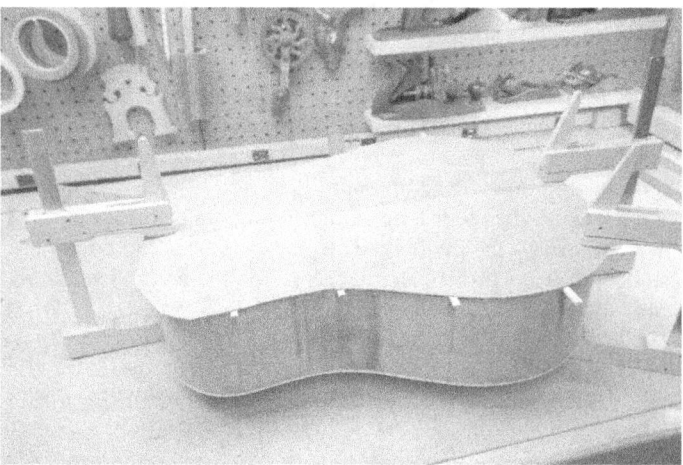

Photo 14-56 – When fitting the back, it is clamped on using two clamps, in the same manner as was used for the top plate.

Attaching the Back

The general procedure for fitting and gluing the back is the same as for fitting and gluing the top plate, but with a couple of variations. The back plate is aligned with the garland using the neck end of the back reinforcement strip against the neck block. Usually the back plate is attached with the body not in the mold, but in some cases the mold must be used. The construction steps which follow assume the mold will not be used. Determining if the mold should be used must be done before proceeding.

The body is placed on the mold as if it is going to be inserted into the mold, and checked to see if the shape of the back edge of the garland is approximately the same as the inside of the mold. If the body can be inserted into the mold without having to squeeze the back edges considerably to make it fit, then assembly can proceed without the use of the mold. This is almost always the case. By the time the blocks and the linings and the top plate have been glued to the ribs, the structure is generally rigid enough that it will accurately retain its shape without the mold. But if the ribs were not accurately bent and have been forced to fit into the mold using the rib jacks, sometimes the shape of the outline at the back edges of the garland is distorted

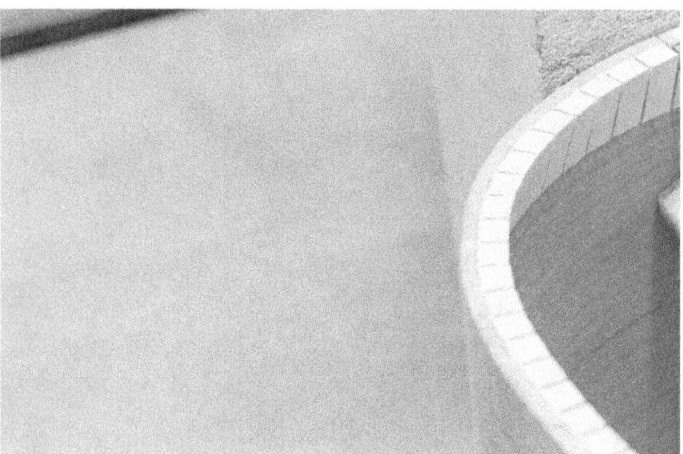

Photo 14-57 – A tall block of wood is clamped directly to the outside of the ribs to back up the ribs when chiseling the pockets.

enough that the mold must be used to support the body while the back is fitted and glued.

If the mold must be used, the floor must be removed from the mold and the two halves of the mold separated. The body will no longer fit in the mold top down, and the only way it will fit is if the mold is bolted together with some spacers between the halves. Some experimentation will be required with spacers to configure the mold so the body can be easily slipped top down into the mold. It is important that it not be forced. Doing so will surely break the delicate top plate.

Once the mold has been reconfigured to accept the body top down, the floor is attached and the insert is put in, but without the spacer that was used to raise up the neck end of the insert when the body was in the mold top up. The rib jacks are used to secure the body in the mold for all the operations involving the fitting of the back plate.

☐ Attaching the Back Plate

1. The top plate was positioned so the "Popsicle stick" brace was flush against the inside surface of the neck block. On the back plate it is the neck end of the back reinforcement strip that is butt against the inside surface of the neck block. Because the strip is shallower than the brace ends, some temporary substitute blocks must be attached to the back with their ends flush with the end of the strip. A couple of 2″ (50.8mm) long pieces of brace blank material are cut and double-stick taped down on both sides of the strip, so the end of the strip and those of these pieces are all aligned (**photo 14-55**).

2. As was the case at this point in fitting the top plate, the brace ends will prevent the back plate from sitting right down on the ribs and linings. With the body positioned back edges up on the bench, the back plate is slid into place until the taped-on stop pieces contact the inside surface of the neck block. Note that the back is more arched than the top, and so it may be necessary to bend the plate down so these pieces will make contact. The centerline of the plate is carefully aligned with the neck end seam of the body. One clamp is used to lightly clamp this end in place. The clamp is positioned so it does not obscure the view of the centerlines. Then the tail end of the back plate is positioned and clamped in like fashion, aligning centerline with seam. The neck end is checked again for alignment and to be sure the temporary stop pieces are still in contact with the neck block. When all is well, another clamp or two is added and lightly clamped, just to prevent the assembly from rocking on the bench (**photo 14-56**).

3. The brace ends and the locations of the brace ends on the body are marked just as was done for the top braces. The clamps are removed and the back is removed. The two pieces of scrap that were taped down next to the end of the center reinforcement strip are removed. The brace ends are checked to be sure they are no more than ⅛″ (3.2mm) thick. The brace ends are trimmed, and the pocket outlines are drawn in the same fashion as for the top. The pockets are excavated and cleaned up in the same manner as well. The difference here is that the body is no longer held in the mold, and so backing up where the chiseling is being done requires a tall, heavy block of wood clamped directly to the side of the body (**photos 14-57, 14-58**). Note that lutherie novices invariably cut cleaner brace end

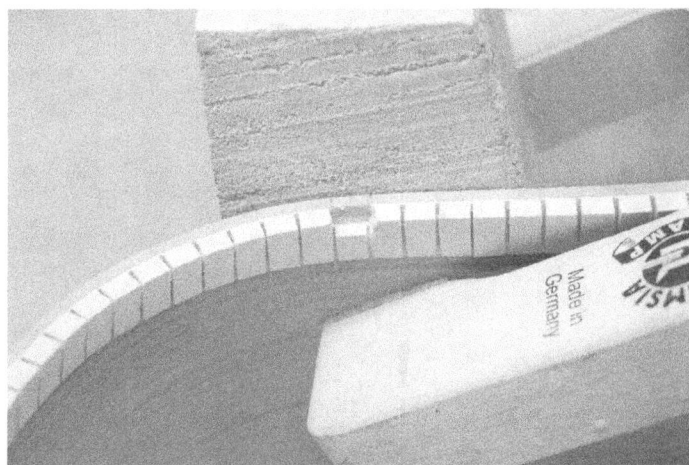

Photo 14-58 – Here is a finished pocket for one of the back braces, and a close-up of how the back up block is clamped.

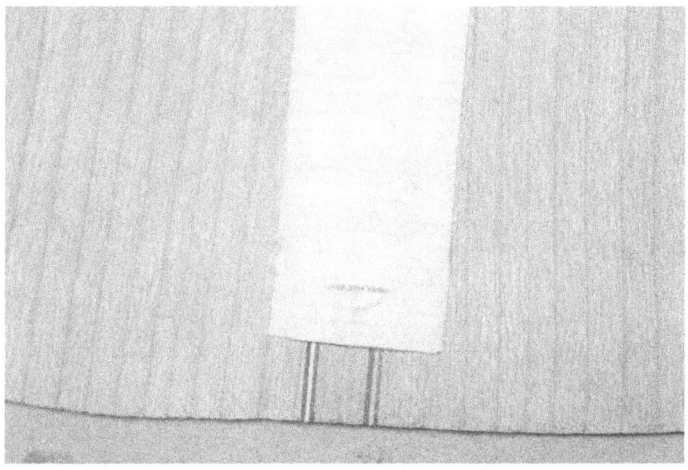

Photo 14-60 – Some of the pencil lead gets rubbed onto the center reinforcement strip, locating the end of the tail block.

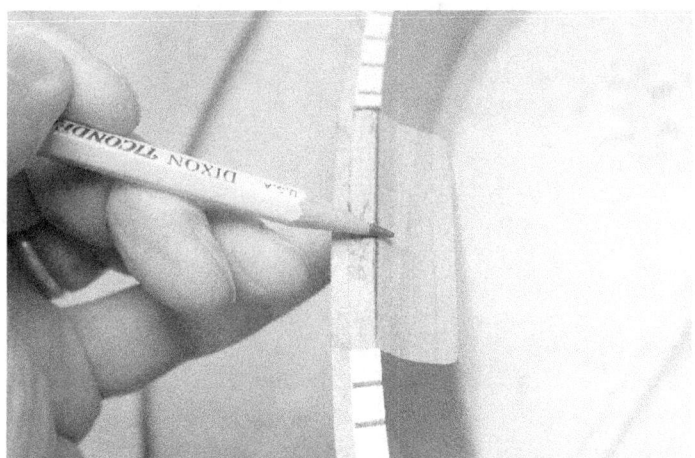

Photo 14-59 – The inside edge of the tail block is heavily rubbed with pencil lead. This will get transferred to the back reinforcement strip.

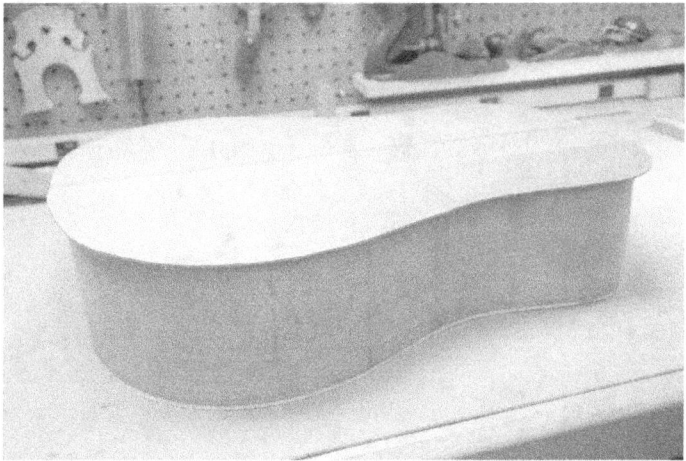

Photo 14-61 – The back is put in place and checked for fit. This one fits so well it stays in place with no clamps.

pockets on the back, probably because they have recent practice on the top. This is a good thing, because at least some of the pockets in the back linings will be visible through the soundhole of the finished instrument.

4. The back is test fitted to the garland. Be aware that the tail end of the back reinforcement strip is currently too long to clear the tail block, and this will prevent the tail end braces from fully fitting into their pockets. To trim the tail end of the back reinforcement strip to length, a soft pencil is used to heavily mark the inside back edge of the tail block (**photo 14-59**). A lot of lead is used. The back plate is put back in place so all brace ends are in their pockets (even though the tail end ones still won't go in all the way) then the back plate is pressed down firmly, right over the tail block. Doing this transfers some of the pencil lead to the back reinforcement strip. The back is again removed. The location of the inside edge of the tail block will be transferred to the back strip (**photo 14-60**). The strip is sawn at this mark with a razor saw, being careful to not mar the surface of the back plate. The waste is chiseled off in the same manner used to do so for the brace ends.

5. Fit is checked again, and any adjustments necessary to achieve a solid fit all the way around between the back plate and the ribs are made (**photo 14-61**).

6. Gluing on the back plate is the same as for the top, but with one important exception. The body is (usually) no longer in the mold, so the bottoms of the clamps will be clamping directly onto the top plate. It is *extremely* important that the clamps *only* contact the edge of the top, right over the ribs and linings. It is equally important that the clamps are only *gently* tightened. The same number of clamps are used and in the same locations. The cauls are used as well (**photo 14-62**). A thin bead of glue is applied all around onto linings and blocks, the neck end of the top plate is positioned and aligned, and then lightly clamped in place with a single clamp. The back is pressed into place from neck to tail end so all the brace ends engage their pockets, then the tail end is aligned and lightly clamped. The neck end is checked again for alignment. The cauls are positioned, and six clamps are applied per side, lightly clamped, being careful to only clamp over the very edge of the top. The joint is checked for solid contact all around. The glue is allowed to cure for two hours before removing clamps. The clamps should be removed in a timely fashion. The body is immediately flipped over and the intersection of the linings and

Photo 14-62 – *The clamping arrangement for the back. Note that the clamps must be placed right over the ribs to avoid cracking the top.*

the back plate is examined through the soundhole. If there are obvious glue blobs present, they are probably still soft enough to remove using a short chisel, scraper, or short knife through the soundhole.

7. Excess wood is trimmed from the edges of the back plate. This is done in the same manner as for the top.

☞ If trimming is done using a router with a bottom bearing flush-trimming bit, care should be taken to be sure the bearing will not fall into the lower neck bolt hole. If the cutting depth cannot be adjusted to avoid this, this small part of the trimming will have to be done by hand, using a chisel or knife.

15 Body Decoration

At this stage of construction the body is functionally complete. But there are some decorative elements that are added to most guitars: the tail graft, and bindings and purflings. The tail graft is a piece of wood that covers the tail seam between the ends of the sides. As was mentioned in the chapter on construction of the garland, the tail graft is traditionally a feature of higher end flattop guitars. It was generally not found on inexpensive manufactured steel string guitars in the past, its deletion being a cost-saving measure. It should be noted that violin family instruments, archtop guitars, and mandolins don't traditionally have a tail graft, so its appearance does not universally denote an instrument of higher price. These days though, nearly every steel string or classical guitar will have a tail graft.

There are two basic styles of tail graft. For steel string guitars the most common style is the tapered tail graft, which has an elongated keystone shape – a trapezoid that is a bit wider at the top than the back (**photo 15-1**). The other style is rectangular (**photo 15-2**). Although there are no hard and fast rules, this style is more common on classical guitars.

As a decorative element, each individual luthier will dimension the tail graft to suit their own aesthetic taste. There are some practical limits to the size and shape of the tail graft though. Because the tail graft will be inlaid into the body at the tail end of the guitar, it must be narrower than the tail block. Otherwise, making the cut in the body for the graft would simply cut the sides off of the tail block. Another limit is that, if the guitar will have an end pin, the width of the tail graft at the center of its length (where the end pin will go) will probably be at least a bit wider than the end pin is. This last one is an aesthetic issue only.

The construction details that follow are for making a tapered tail graft. As mentioned this style is more commonly used for steel string guitars, and it is also easier for lutherie novices to build this style and achieve a nice tight fit.

Any wood can be used for the tail graft. A common decoration theme makes use of a tail graft that is made out of the same wood as the bindings. This makes for an integrated look, and is the approach taken in the guitars in the photos. But some luthiers use a different wood here, sometimes matching the wood used for the headplate. The effect can be quite dramatic,

Photo 15-1 – *The tapered tail graft is wider at the top than the back. It is generally a good idea to make it wide enough at the middle so it is a bit wider than the end pin.*

Photo 15-2 – *The rectangular tail graft. This one is as thin as the bindings and made of the same wood.*

Photo 15-3 – Top purflings are between the binding and the top plate. Side purflings are between the binding and the sides of the guitar. When alternating color purfling lines are used, light-colored lines are generally positioned next to dark-colored wood, and vice versa.

Photo 15-4 – The back purflings are between the binding and the back plate. Note that fewer purfling lines were used here than were used for the top purflings.

depending on the species used. In general, lutherie wood suppliers do not sell wood cut specifically for tail grafts, but wood sold for use as headplates and bridge plates can be used. Because the piece of wood needed is so small, it is often possible to make use of an off-cut from the back plate as the basis for the tail graft.

The body bindings and purflings are the other decorative elements that are addressed in this chapter. Although there have been guitars built without bindings, doing so is quite rare. The bindings perform structural functions as well as being decorative. They cover the end grain of the plates, and in so doing, prevent, or at least greatly slow down, much of the transfer of water into and out of the wood. The bindings are usually made of a material that is more tolerant of physical abuse than the wood of the top plate, and so they help protect the edges of the body from damage from physical blows.

Bindings may be made of either wood or plastic. Plastic bindings tend to be used for less expensive guitars. They are easier to install than wood bindings. Wood bindings are usually made of some robust hardwood. Two common approaches to selecting the wood species include using the same species that is used for the back and sides for the bindings, or using a wood for the bindings that contrasts with the wood of the back and sides. Wood and plastic binding strips are available from lutherie wood suppliers. Most suppliers will offer wood binding strips in a number of species. Commercially available wood binding strips generally are dimensioned approximately 0.25˝ (6.4mm) high, 0.08˝ (2mm) thick, and approximately 32˝ (812.8mm) long. Four such strips will be needed to bind a guitar.

The construction details in this chapter are for the use of wood bindings. For the most part, the construction operations are similar when plastic bindings are used. The big difference is that wood bindings must be heat bent, in the same manner that was used to bend the guitar sides.

The final decorative elements that will be dealt with here are the purflings. These have been introduced already in the chapter on the construction of the back plate. There, the solid wood back strip was decorated on both sides with alternating black and maple purfling lines. Purfling lines were also used to decorate the sides of the central core of the soundhole rosette. The purflings associated with the bindings are named depending on where they are located with respect to the bindings. Those that are between the bindings and the body sides are called *side purflings*. Purflings between the bindings and the plates are referred to as either *top purflings* (**photo 15-3**) or *back purflings* (**photo 15-4**), depending on the plate.

Other materials besides veneer lines are used for purflings. Two common such materials have already been introduced when construction of the soundhole rosette was discussed. These are marquetry strips and shell material. These tend to be used only with the most fancy decoration schemes. Examples of these can be found in the work of California luthier Howard Klepper, among others. The construction operations detailed in this chapter will deal exclusively with purflings made of veneer lines.

A common technique for dealing with the ends of purflings is to miter them into other purflings. For example, the ends of the purflings along the sides of the back strip are often mitered into the back plate purflings, and the ends of purflings on the sides of the tail graft are often mitered into the side purflings of the top and back bindings (**figure 15-1**). This makes for a clean look. The construction operations that follow will describe how to do this. It takes a little planning ahead, but it is not difficult to do.

Note that mitering the ends of purflings together requires the pattern of purfling lines to be the same. So, if the purflings of the tail graft are of three lines in a black/maple/black sequence for example, the side purflings of the top and back bindings should have this same sequence. Likewise if the purflings of the back strip are of three lines in a black/maple/black sequence, the back plate purflings should have this same sequence.

It is not necessary to miter the purfling ends as described above. The choice to do so is an aesthetic one. When the purflings associated with the bindings are not mitered as described, they are simply butt joined at the body centerline. This is also shown in **figure 15-1**.

A couple of final notes on the subject of purfling color sequences. In general, light-colored lines will be placed next to dark woods, and dark-colored lines against light woods. Because the top plate is usually a light-colored wood, if the back

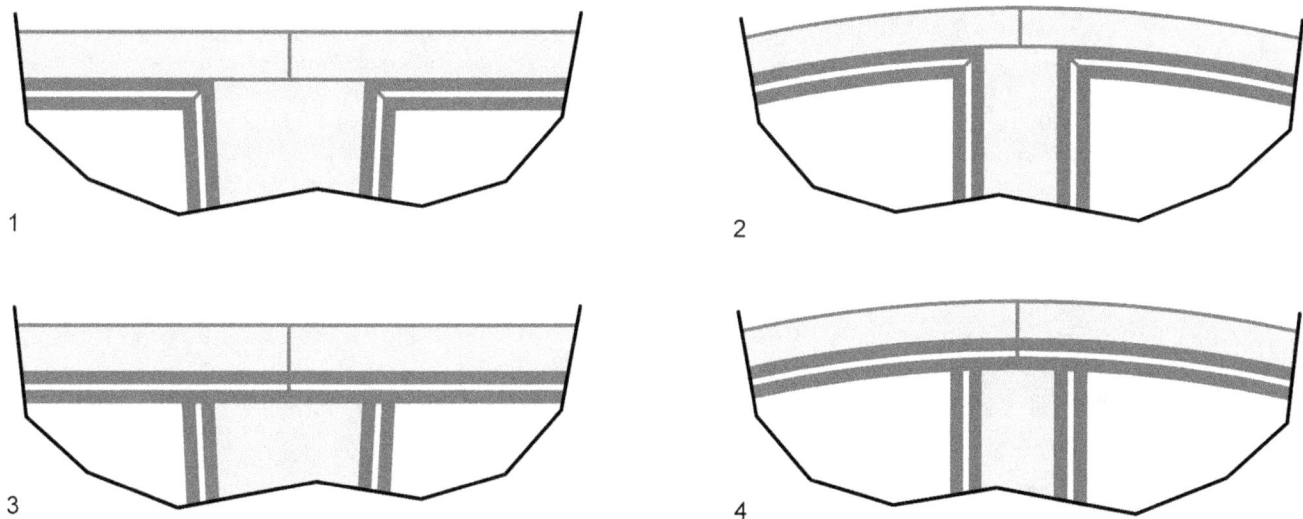

Figure 15-1 – *Purfling lines can be mitered into adjoining purfling lines or not, depending on preference. Mitering of purfling lines gives a clean look. No mitering provides a 3D effect, making one part look like it is inset. In 1, the side purfling lines are mitered into the purfling lines of the tail graft at the tail end of the body. In 2, the back plate purflings are mitered into the purflings along the back strip. In 3, the side purfling lines are not mitered into the purfling lines of the tail graft at the tail end of the body. In 4, the back plate purflings are not mitered into the purflings along the back strip.*

plate is made of a dark wood then it is likely that the top will use one more line in the purfling bundle than will be used for the back. It should also be born in mind that whatever the width of the top or back purfling bundle is, it should not exceed the thickness of the tops of the linings. If it did, cutting the channel for the purflings could cut the plate right off the guitar.

Layout and Construction

The Tail Graft

As mentioned, the width of the tail graft can be whatever looks good, but because installing it involves cutting away some of the rib material over the tail block, the width must be less than that of the tail block. I like to keep a margin of at least ½″ (12.7mm) on either side. The example instruments use a 2″ (50.8mm) wide tail block, so this means the maximum width of the graft for these instruments should be 1″ (25.4mm). The minimum width can be anything that looks good, down to a minimum of what is workable, which is about ¼″ (6.4mm). As also mentioned, the width at the center should be wider than the diameter of the end pin that will be used for the instrument.

☐ Making the Tail Graft

1. If it is not already, the blank for the tail graft should be planed to the same thickness as the ribs, nominally ³⁄₃₂″ (2.4mm). The piece should be cut 2″ (50.8mm) longer than the body is deep at the tail end, so for the example instruments the blank will be about 6″ (152.4mm) long for the Tripletta OM style guitar, or about 7″ (177.8mm) long for the Paura dreadnought style guitar. The full-sized template in **figure 15-2** tapers from 1″

Photo 15-5 – *The tail graft is marked out. Here a cutoff from the back plate is used as the blank.*

Photo 15-6 – *The sides of the piece are trimmed straight and square to the broad surfaces. Here a sanding board and a fence are used.*

(25.4mm) to ½″ (12.7mm) over 6″ (152.4mm) and can be used for either example instrument.

2. The outline is marked on the blank, with the grain following the length (**photo 15-5**), and then cut out. This is conveniently done on the bandsaw.

3. The side edges must be smoothed and straightened, and they must be made perpendicular to the outside surface. This can be done using a plane on its side with a bench hook, or it can be done on a sanding board, using a flat board as a fence to keep the sides perpendicular to the top surface (**photo 15-6**).

4. The sides of the tail graft can now be decorated with purfling lines. If these purfling lines will be mitered into the side purfling lines, then the same pattern of purfling lines that will be used for the side purflings of the bindings should be used here. All purfling lines are cut to about 1″ (25.4mm) longer than the length of the graft.

5. An assembly board is fashioned. A piece of melamine-covered particle board, longer than the graft and about 6″ (152.4mm) wider is selected or cut for use as a base. Also cut are two plastic pieces from ⅛″ (3.2mm) thick sheet stock, about 3″ (76.2mm) wide and about 6″ (152.4mm) longer than the graft. One of the plastic pieces is clamped down to the melamine board using two clamps.

6. The purfling lines for one side of the tail graft are bundled in order, then placed against the edge of the plastic, then the graft is placed against the bundle of purfling lines, then the bundle of lines for the other side are placed against the graft, and finally the other piece of plastic is placed against the bundle, pressing everything together. The second piece of plastic is clamped in place using two clamps (**photo 15-7**).

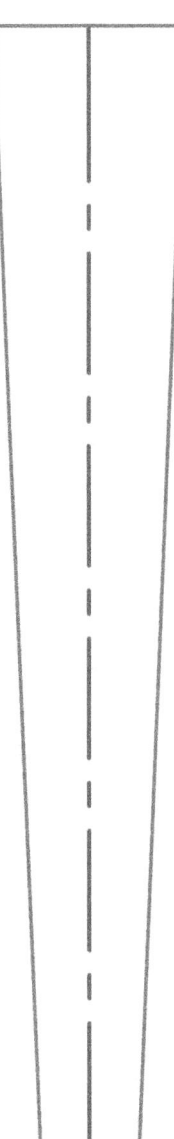

Figure 15-2 – *Tapered tail graft template.*

7. The graft and the purfling lines are slid out from between the plastic pieces and removed for gluing. Glue is applied to the purfling lines for one side of the graft in the same manner as was used to glue and laminate lines for the back strip and the rosette. The lines are gathered together in order and the bundle is positioned against one of the plastic pieces, near the fat end of the gap between the two pieces. The graft is positioned against the lines and pressed into place. The other bundle of lines are glued and bundled up and then pressed to the other side of the graft.

8. The whole tail graft assembly is slid farther into the gap, being sure the graft and all lines are still seated on the surface of the melamine board. This will clamp everything together. It is unlikely that the assembly will slide back out, but just in case, a scrap piece of wood is butted against the fat end of the assembly and then clamped down to the melamine board.

9. The glue is allowed to cure two hours before removing the plastic pieces and removing the tail graft assembly from the melamine board (**photo 15-8**). It is likely that the assembly will have to be lifted from the board using a putty knife. Once removed, it is flipped over to allow the glue to fully harden on the back side for another hour.

10. Excess purfling material is trimmed from the ends, and the lines are scraped flush with the surface of the graft on both sides (**photo 15-9**). Any glue is scraped off the outside purfling lines. Care is taken not to reduce the thickness of the lines while this is done.

11. A centerline is penciled down the center of the graft on both sides.

Photo 15-7 – *The fixture used to glue purfling lines to the sides of the graft includes a glue-proof base and two pieces of plastic. Pressing the graft into the space between the plastic pieces clamps the lines in tight.*

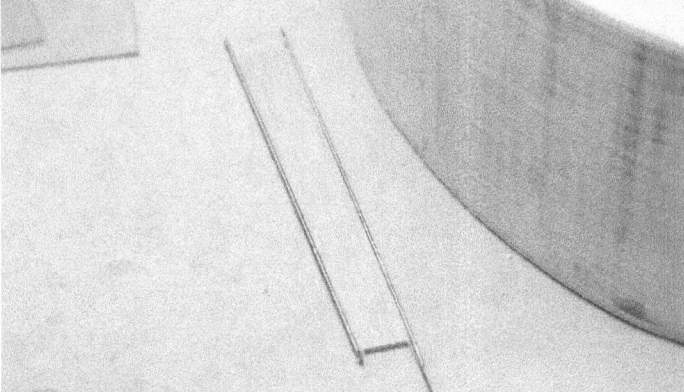

Photo 15-8 – *The tail graft with glued on purfling lines.*

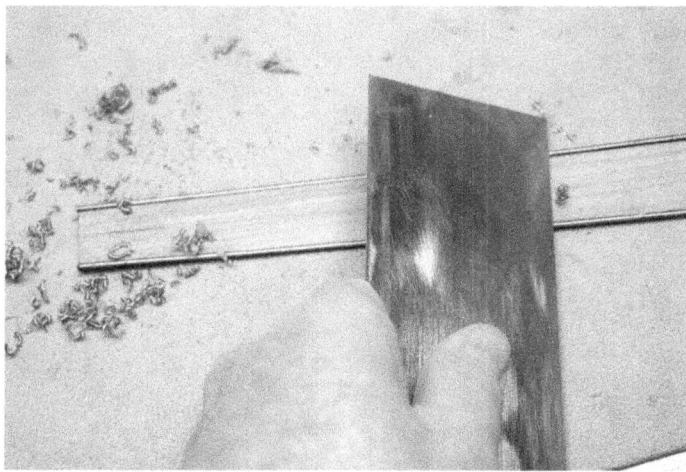

Photo 15-9 – *A card scraper is used to scrape the surfaces of the lines flush with the surfaces of the graft.*

Photo 15-11 – *The layout for the sides of the pocket that will be cut for the tail graft.*

Photo 15-10 – *With the thin end of the graft positioned at the back plate, the graft is traced onto the ribs at the tail centerline.*

Photo 15-12 – *The side lines are extended up onto the top plate and then a piece of rib cutoff is used to mark what will be the floor of the pocket.*

☐ Inlaying the Tail Graft

The outline of the pocket for the tail graft is traced from the tail graft itself, then the pocket is excavated using knife, chisel and rasp. The side walls of the pocket are straightened, then the tail graft is glued in place.

1. The body is placed on the bench so it is sitting on the neck end area and the tail end is up.

 A hand is kept on the body at all times – it is not stable in this position and can easily fall, and that fall can do serious damage.

The tail graft is placed on the tail end of the body, aligned with the body centerline and so the short end of the graft is flush with the surface of the back. It is held in place by hand and a pencil is used to trace the sides of the graft onto the ribs (**photos 15-10, 15-11**).

2. The graft is removed and the pencil lines are extended a bit onto the back and top plates. A cutoff from the sides or back is

Photo 15-13 – *The same marking of the pocket sides and floor that was done on the top plate is also done on the back plate.*

used as a thickness gauge to pencil the thickness of the ribs at the tail block onto top and back plates (**photos 15-12, 15-13**).

3. The waste at the ends of the pocket is removed first.

 It is important that before starting to chisel the waste out at the tail end, chunks of the top and back plates corresponding to the ends of the tail graft are first removed. If this is not done, it is easy to splinter the plates as the chisel exits the cut.

A straightedge and knife are used to deeply score the penciled lines of the pocket ends that are perpendicular to the grain of the plates (**photo 15-14**). Deep scoring is done by making repeated cuts, each a little deeper. In the photos I am using a straightedge made from a piece of the same ⅛″ (3.2mm) thick clear plastic that was used to make the gluing fixture for the graft. The plastic is a bit flexible. It is also slippery, so a piece of PSA sandpaper is applied to the back of the plastic so it will stick to the wood without shifting around when it is held in place.

4. The little side lines of the pocket ends are also scored with the knife. These should not be scored deeply, because they are on the grain and doing so may split the plate. These are just gently marked with the knife (**photo 15-15**). The fully scored pocket end is shown in **photo 15-16**.

5. A small narrow chisel is used to carefully, slowly, and gently excavate the wood from top and back plates inside these scored lines (**photo 15-17**). Care is taken to chisel perpendicular to the grain, stopping well short of the end line, then chisel in the other direction. Once the pocket has been chiseled down to the

Photo 15-16 – *The same scribing is done for the top end of the tail graft pocket.*

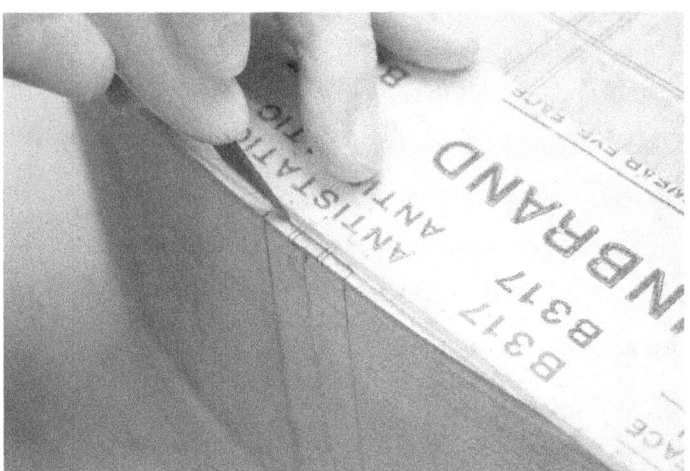

Photo 15-14 – *A straightedge and a knife are used to scribe the pocket floor line on the back plate. The straightedge is a piece of plastic with PSA sandpaper attached to the bottom.*

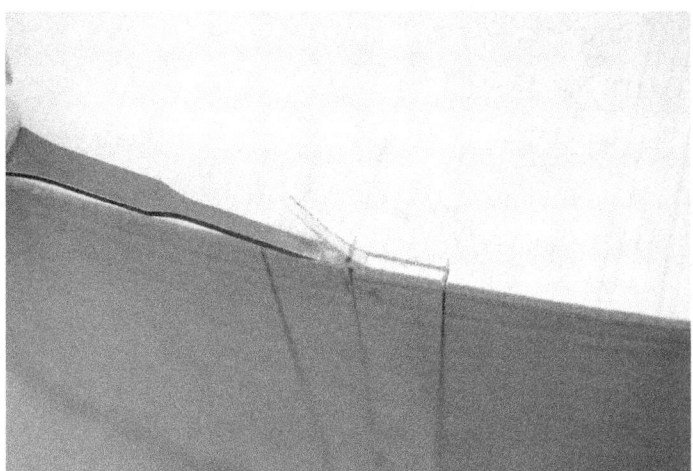

Photo 15-17 – *The waste wood is carefully excavated from the pocket ends using a small chisel. Shallow cuts are made ...*

Photo 15-15 – *The side lines are shallowly scribed. Attempting to scribe too deep here will split the back.*

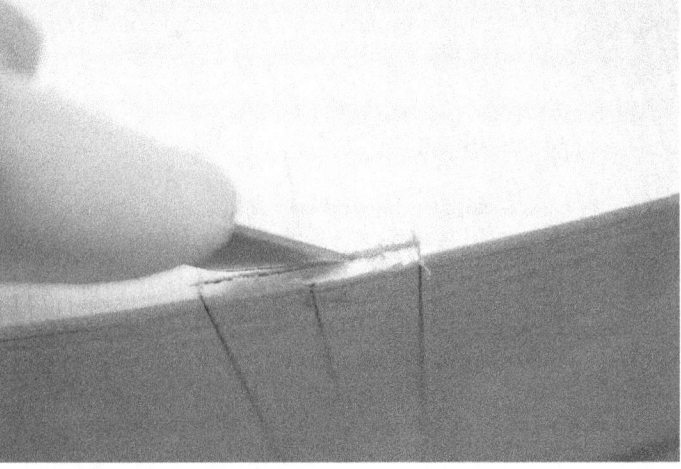

Photo 15-18 – *... then the borders of the cut are scribed again with the knife ...*

depth of the scribed lines, the lines are deeply scribed again (**photo 15-18**). Scribing and chiseling (**photo 15-19**) is continued until the surface of the ribs is reached (**photo 15-20**).

6. The waste in the rib pocket for the tail graft is excavated in the same manner. When scribing the side lines of the pocket, the body must be held securely and in a manner that provides access to the tail end. With padding hanging over the edge of the bench, and the luthier sitting on a stool facing the bench, the neck end of the body is rested on the padded stool top, trapped between the luthier's legs, and the side of the body is rested gently against the padded edge of the bench (**photo 15-21**). The side lines are scribed using the knife and straightedge in the same manner as was used to scribe the pocket ends (**photo 15-22**).

7. A fixture to securely hold the body tail-end-up is extremely useful when chiseling the waste out of the pocket, but not strictly necessary. Construction of such a jig, called a guitar body vise, is detailed in Appendix C. If such a vise is available, the walls of the pocket can optionally be cut using a back saw with a depth stop. In **photo 15-23** I am using a fret slotting saw for this purpose.

Photo 15-21 – Holding the body while scribing the walls of the pocket in the body ribs. The body is resting on the stool, clamped between the knees, and resting against the padded edge of the bench.

Photo 15-19 – ... for more chisel work. The pocket ends are cut down are far as the thickness of the plates.

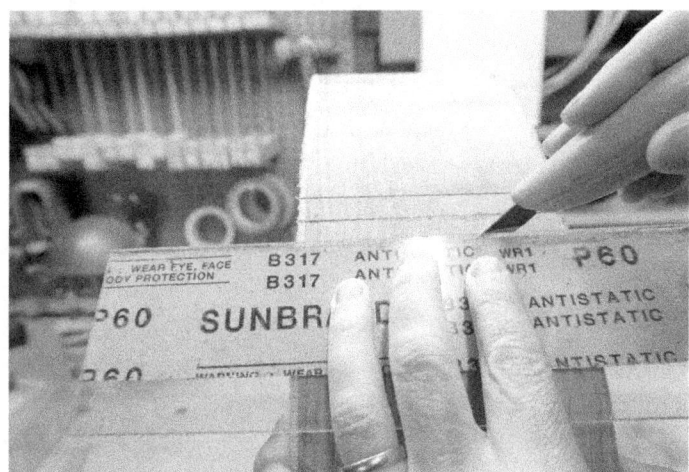

Photo 15-22 – Scribing is done with the knife against the plastic straightedge.

Photo 15-20 – The end of the tail graft pocket completely excavated.

Photo 15-23 – If the body can be securely supported (here a special guitar body vise is used) then the side walls can optionally be sawn with a back saw.

8. If a guitar body vise is not available, the same basic hold that was used when scribing the pocket walls is used when chiseling out the waste, but in this case the top or back of the guitar is leaned against the padded edge of the bench. The chisel is held in a back hand stabbing grip in one hand while the other hand guides the blade. The forearms rest on the body to provide stability (**photo 15-24**). For a graft of the dimensions described, I use a short ½″ (12.7mm) chisel. The first cut is used to carefully remove wood along one side of the pocket, right next to one of the scribed lines (**photo 15-25**). I'll cut on the side opposite the hand I am holding the chisel with, to provide a good view of the scribed line. I try to take shallow cuts and strive for uniformity of depth, never going deeper than the scribed side line.

9. The body is then flipped over, top for back, so the other side of the pocket can be chiseled in like manner. Then a third pass is used down the middle to flatten the floor of the channel.

10. Steps 6, 8, and 9 are repeated until the pocket is as deep as the tail graft is thick. The goal is a flat bottom channel, because eventually the flat bottom tail graft will be glued into it. A pass with a wider chisel helps to see if the pocket bottom is really flat. The result should be a fairly flat-bottomed but shallow pocket. It usually takes 3 to 4 passes to excavate the channel so the graft fits flush to the channel edges.

Photo 15-24 – *The position used to chisel out the waste when a body vise is not available. The body rests on the stool and is supported by the knees and held against the padded bench edge with the forearms.*

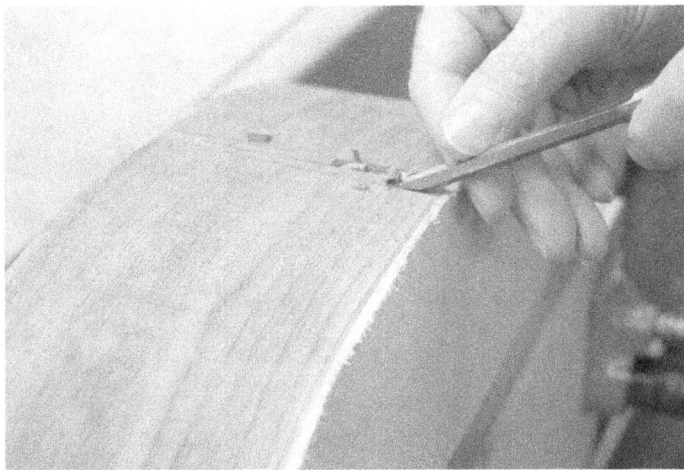

Photo 15-25 – *Beginning the excavation of the tail graft pocket using a chisel.*

Photo 15-27 – *The graft is test fitted by sliding it into the pocket. The walls are rasped until the graft fits completely and tightly.*

Photo 15-26 – *The floor of the pocket is flattened and the walls are straightened using a rectangular profile rasp.*

Photo 15-28 – *When the graft finally fits the pocket nicely, the end often extends past the back plate.*

11. The sides and bottom of the pocket are now cleaned up, using a flat rectangular profile rasp (**photo 15-26**). The graft is test fit to see if the sides of the graft and those of the pocket are straight and parallel (**photo 15-27**). If not, the angle of the walls of the pocket can be carefully changed a bit at a time to effect a perfect fit (**photo 15-28**). Note that at this point the graft probably fits deeper (from the body top to the body back) into the pocket, so its thin end sticks out a bit from the back of the body. This is why the graft was constructed to be a few inches longer than the body.

12. The graft is glued into the pocket. The body is held tail-end-up on the bench, using two clamps that clamp over the neck block as a base (**photo 15-29**). Glue is applied to the floor and walls of the pocket, and the graft is wedged into place. If the body can be safely maintained in the tail-up orientation, a small weight can be placed on top of the graft (**photo 15-30**), but if the fit is tight this really isn't necessary. The glue is allowed to cure for at least two hours.

13. Excess wood is trimmed off the ends of the graft (**photo 15-31**). In the photo I am using a flush cutting Japanese razor saw, intended for flush trimming plugs. Other tools can be used. If necessary, the ends of the graft are sanded flush with the surfaces of the top and back plates using a hard sanding block.

14. The tail end of the body is sanded so ribs and graft are flush, and so the curve of the body is again established. A random orbital palm sander makes quick work of this task (**photo 15-32**), but sandpaper on a block can be used as well.

Photo 15-30 – A piece of wax paper is placed over the glued-in graft, and a small weight is applied while the glue cures. Here a block plane is used.

Photo 15-31 – After the glue cures, the ends of the graft are cut off flush with the surfaces of the plates. Here a flush cutting Japanese razor saw is used.

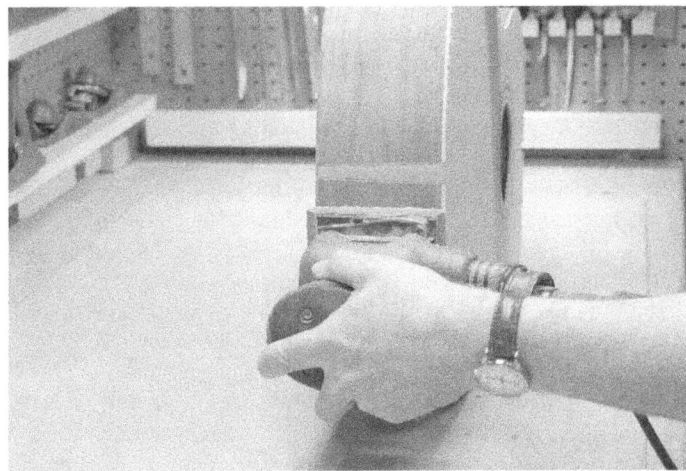

Photo 15-32 – The tail graft is sanded flush with the surrounding ribs of the guitar body.

Photo 15-29 – The body can be supported tail up for gluing the tail graft, using a couple of clamps clamped over the neck block to serve as a base.

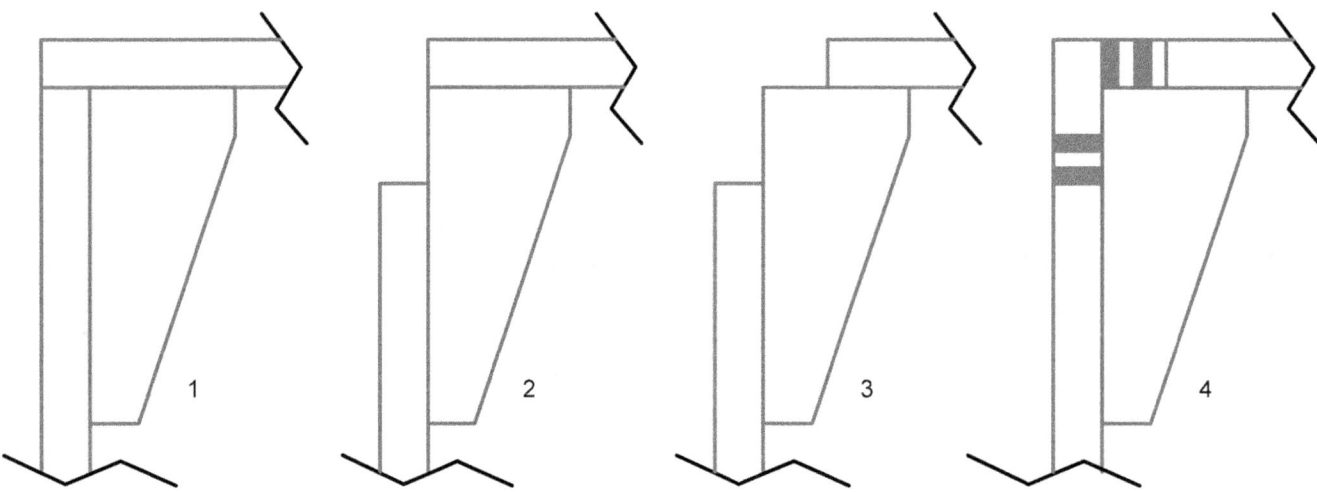

Figure 15-3 – *The basic binding sequence, shown as cross sections of the top left edge of the body. 1. The current state, showing top plate, body side, and linings. 2. The binding channel is cut. 3. The purfling channel is cut. 4. Binding and purflings are glued into the channels.*

Body Bindings and Purflings

The rough sequence for assembling and installing the bindings and purflings is as follows. First, the side purflings are glued to the binding strips. This operation is identical to that used to apply purflings to the back strip in the chapter on the back. Then, the binding strips are gathered together into a flat bundle and heat bent, using the bending iron and the body mold, in much the same manner as was used to bend the body sides. Next, the ledges for the bindings and the plate purflings are cut into the edges of the body, using either a small router and rabbeting bit, or a special cutter called a *gramil* and a chisel. Finally, the bindings and purflings are fitted to the ledges and glued in place. **Figure 15-3** shows the basic sequence of cutting the ledges and applying the binding and purflings. Note that since bindings and purfling lines are fragile and prone to breaking during bending, it is a good idea to have some extra on hand.

Of course, the ledges have to be cut to fit the bindings and the purflings, so the dimensions of these must be based on the dimensions of the bindings and purflings and the number of purfling lines to be used in each location.

As mentioned in the introduction, commercially available wood binding strips are generally dimensioned 0.25″ (6.4MM) high, 0.08″ (2MM) thick, and approximately 32″ (812.8MM) long. That length is appropriate for binding most common guitar sizes and is right for the two example instruments. The thickness is also appropriate for all guitars. If the binding were thinner, its edge could not be rounded over very much in the finished guitar, and if it were thicker it would be difficult or impossible to bend to shape. The height of the binding is something that the luthier may want to vary for aesthetic reasons, but there are practical limits to how much this can be varied. The combined height of the bindings and the side purfling lines must be greater than the edge thickness of the plate of the guitar. And it must be less than the height of the linings used, otherwise cutting the ledges for the bindings will simply cut the plate right off the guitar. My general recommendations for lutherie novices is to use binding strips of the dimensions noted above, unless there is some compelling aesthetic reason not to.

Veneer purfling strips are available from lutherie suppliers, and these are also fairly uniform in size. They are generally dimensioned 0.02″ (0.5MM) thick, 3/32″ (2.4MM) wide, and approximately 32″ (812.8MM) long.

The dimensions of the available binding and purfling strips allow the luthier to estimate the approximate dimensions of the ledges that will be cut. In point of fact I will always size these cuts based on the actual dimensions of the binding and purfling pieces I am about to install. But having some idea of the dimensions needed will allow the luthier to procure the appropriate tools for making the ledges. This is particularly important if the ledges will be cut using a router and a rabbeting bit set. Look ahead to **figure 15-6** for typical dimensions of the rabbets when commercially available components are used.

Photo 15-33 – *The binding strip and the purfling lines are placed on a glue-proof workboard, in preparation for application of glue.*

Construction of the Bindings

There are two basic operations here. The first is gluing the side purflings to the binding strips and cleaning things up. After this is done, the bindings are heat bent in the same manner as was used to bend the guitar sides.

☐ Gluing Side Purflings to the Binding Strips

As mentioned above, this operation is nearly identical to that used to attach purfling lines to the sides of the back strip, so a review of how that was done is probably a good idea. The number and colors of the strips should be determined before proceeding. Usually one to three side purfling lines are used. The side purflings should fit in aesthetically with the overall purfling scheme that was devised for the instrument.

 Note that some lutherie suppliers stock binding strips that have purfling lines glued to them already. If these are used, this construction operation is skipped.

1. A binding strip is placed on its side on a length of melamine board and then lightly taped down at the ends. The side purfling lines are placed in order on the assembly board right next to what will end up as the bottom surface of the binding and also taped down at their ends (**photo 15-33**).

2. Glue is quickly applied to the entire top surface of each of the purfling lines, using a cup of glue and a glue brush.

3. After glue is applied, the tape is removed and the purfling line closest to the binding strip is lifted up, turned, and pressed against the bottom of the binding strip, gluing it in place. Each remaining line is lifted and pressed in place in the same manner. Note that this will end up with the surface of the last purfling line with no glue on the showing surface. Wipe this entire surface with a damp rag. This will help prevent the last line from curling away from the rest.

4. The stack is squeezed together with the fingers at one end. A rag held in the other hand is run down the length of the stack, pressing everything together and removing excess glue at the same time. The stack is eyeballed to be sure all purfling lines are flush with the surface of the binding all along the length.

5. A pile (50 to 60) of clothespins (plastic is best) or other small plastic spring clamps is applied all along the strip. If wood clips are used, the jaws should be lightly waxed before use to keep them from getting glued to the work. It is generally a good idea to apply every other clamp, and then when done with the entire length, to go back and fill in from the other side. The clamps will form a herringbone pattern (**photos 15-34, 15-35**).

6. Excess glue is wiped from the assembly board with a wet rag. The glued binding and purfling strip is allowed to cure at least one hour before removing the clamps.

7. Steps 1 through 6 are repeated for the other three binding strips.

8. Excess hardened glue is removed from the binding strips and the purflings are made flush with the side surfaces of the binding. This is easily done with a card scraper (**photo 15-36**). It is most important to provide smooth and straight gluing surfaces.

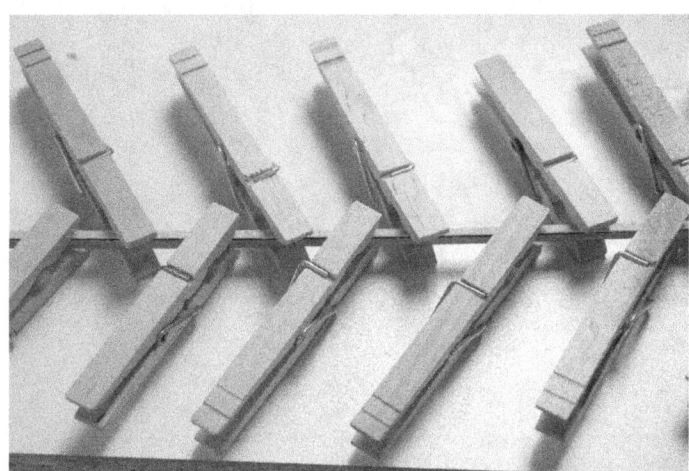

Photo 15-35 – *Here is a close-up of the clamping arrangement.*

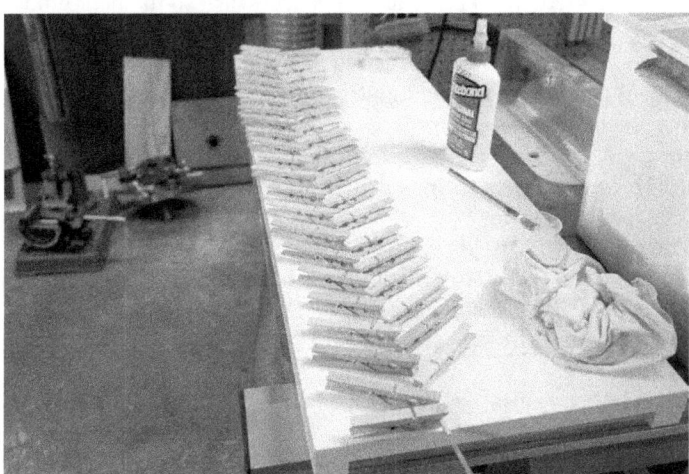

Photo 15-34 – *After glue is applied, a lot of spring clamps are applied to press purflings to binding. Here, waxed wood clothes pins are used.*

Photo 15-36 – *After the glue dries, the purfling lines are scraped flush with the binding strip and all surface glue is removed.*

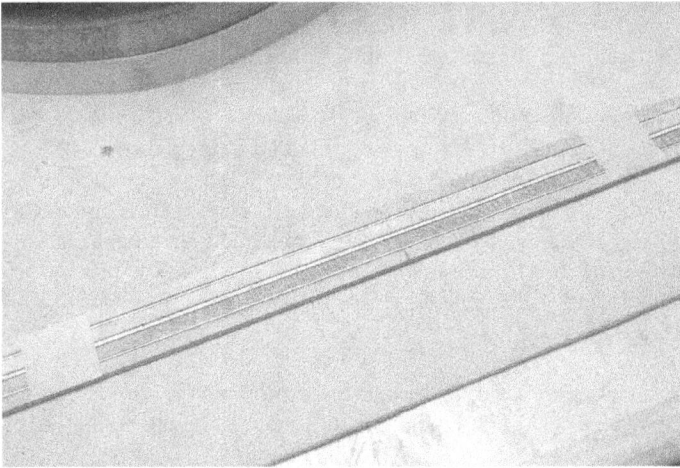

Photo 15-37 – *The binding strips with side purfling attached are bundled and taped for bending. Note the orientation of the purflings.*

Photo 15-39 – *The binding strip bundle is clamped into the mold to cool and dry.*

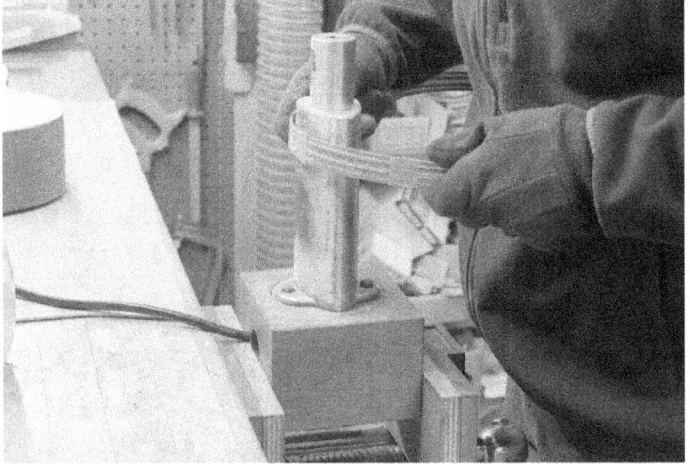

Photo 15-38 – *The bundle is heat bent in the same manner as was used when bending the sides.*

Photo 15-40 – *The binding strip bundle on top of the guitar body to be bound and purfled.*

The strips are carefully checked for spots where the purflings are sunk in from the surface. If these are too deep to scrape out, the sunken side can be simply designated as the inside gluing surface of the strip, that is, the surface that will contact the guitar body when the strip is installed. But if there are sunk-in purfling lines on *both* sides of the binding it is usually best to just make a new strip, although repair may be possible by heating the purfling strips with an iron until the glue melts, quickly repositioning the strips, and then clamping.

□ **Bending the Bindings**

The body binding strips are heat bent in the same manner and using the same tool set as was used to bend the sides. It is worthwhile reviewing the chapter on side bending in preparation for bending the binding strips. The descriptions in this section assume familiarity with side bending. Because the individual binding strips are delicate and easily broken, they will be ganged together for bending. This makes them behave even more like one of the guitar sides during bending.

1. The four binding strips are laid out across the bench so their ends are all aligned and their top and bottom surfaces are in contact. Two of the strips should have the side purflings oriented so they are toward the luthier, and the other two strips are oriented so the side purfling lines are away from the luthier.

Note that this orientation is necessary so the bent binding strips will be appropriately oriented for both sides and both plates of the finished guitar. One way to visualize this is, if the finished guitar is sitting top up on the bench, two of the bindings strips (the ones at the top plate) will have their side purflings at the bottom edge of the strips, and two will have the side purflings at their top edges.

The collection of strips is taped down to the bench with a piece of tape at each end. Note that the surface of the collection that is visible will be the outside surface of the individual strips in the finished instrument.

2. The body outline segment tape that was used to mark segments onto the sides before they were bent is used to mark the segments onto the collection of binding strips in pencil. The tape is shorter than the binding strips, and before marking, the tape should be positioned so there is an equal amount of extra length on each end. A small square is used to continue the

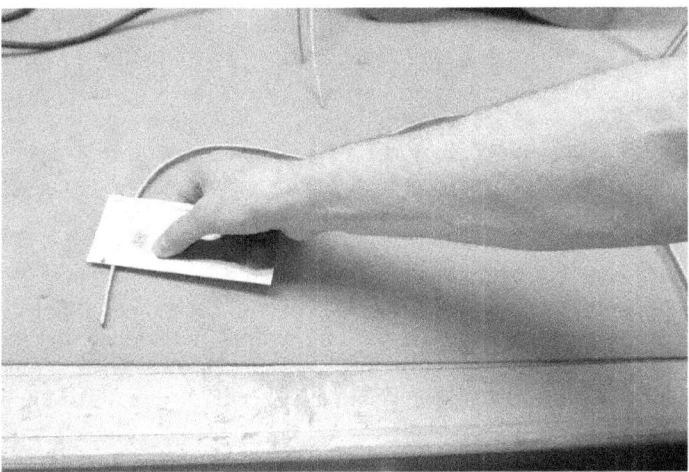

Photo 15-41 – *The card scraper is used to remove any glue from the bottom surface of the binding strip and to flatten it.*

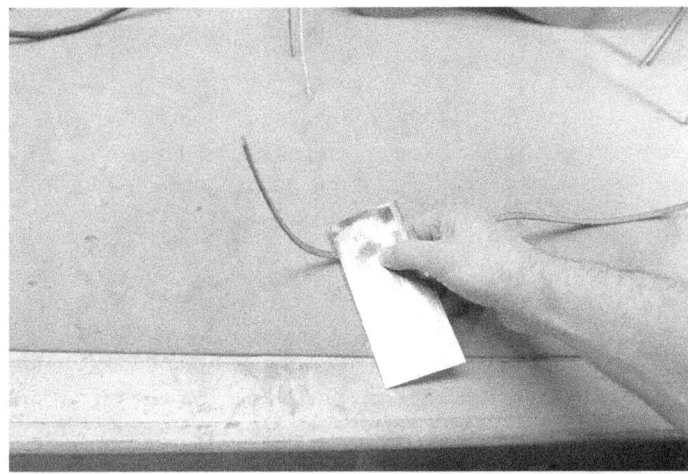

Photo 15-42 – *The card scraper is used to clean up and flatten the inside gluing surface of each binding strip.*

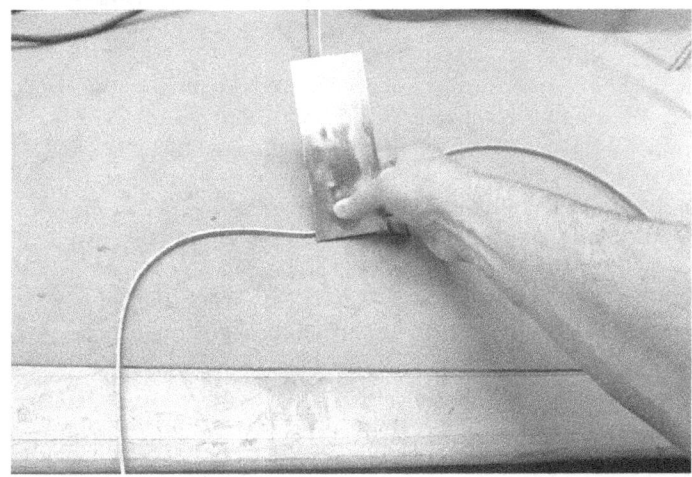

Photo 15-43 – *The scraper is used to chamfer the inside bottom edge of each strip.*

markings completely across the surface of the collection of binding strips. The segment end letters are also written near the marks in pencil. It is not necessary to notch the binding strips with a small file as was done when the sides were bent. In fact, this should explicitly *not* be done here, because such notches would be visible in the finished instrument.

3. All four strips are taped together with pieces of tape placed approximately every 4″ (101.6mm). See **photo 15-37**. Excess tape length is cut off, not folded over and around the bundle. The back side of the bundle will (mostly) contact the bending iron, and tape there would cause problems. Tape *is not* applied over segment FG, which is the waist. This is because, when the waist is bent, the bending iron will contact the bundle on this surface, and if there is tape here the iron will cook it right to the wood surface, making it difficult to remove after bending.

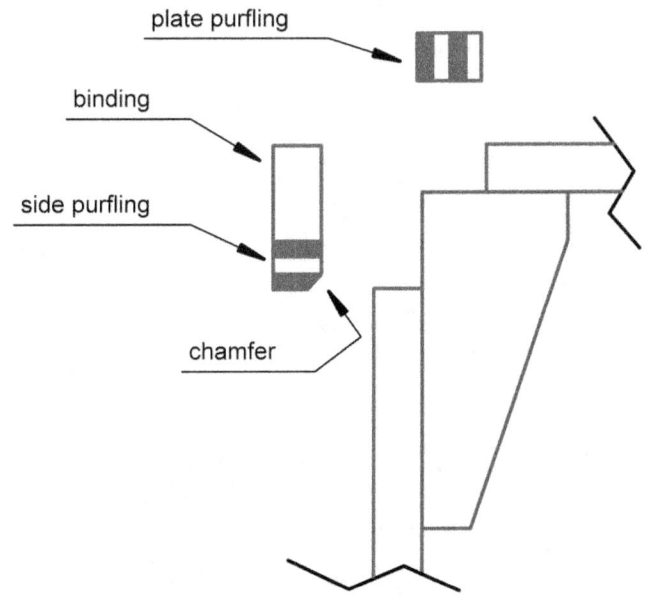

Figure 15-4 – *The components of the bindings and purflings. Note the chamfer on the bottom inside edge of the side purflings attached to the bindings.*

4. The bundle of binding strips is bent to shape in the same way that the guitar sides were bent (**photo 15-38**). If any of the tape comes off during bending, more tape can be applied to hold the bundle together. The waist must be bent quite accurately, but the rest of the bending does not have to be nearly as accurate as was necessary when the sides were bent.

The bundle is about ¼ the width of a rib and so is more delicate than a rib, so it should be bent very gently. If a strip is broken, it can usually be glued back together with cyanoacrylate glue. Too many breaks and repairs that are too visible will require new strips to be made and bent.

5. After bending, the binding strip bundle is clamped into the mold and allowed to cool and dry overnight (**photo 15-39**). Note that if an open frame mold is used, the bundle is clamped over that part of the mold that has two thicknesses of mold pieces.

6. The fit is checked against the sides of the guitar body (**photo 15-40**). For the most part the fit does not have to be perfect, but it should fit well at the waist. If not, the bend of the bundle is touched up dry on the bending iron. When the fit is accurate,

the tape can be removed and the bundle separated into its component binding pieces.

7. It is possible that the side purfling lines got separated from the bindings in places during bending. The binding pieces should be checked carefully for this, and the purflings glued and clamped wherever they are separated from the bindings. These small gaps will be visible in the finished instrument, and it is a lot easier to fix this now than it is to do so later.

8. The bottom and inside surfaces of each piece should be scraped flat and clean of any remaining surface glue. These will be the gluing surfaces when the bindings are installed. The bottom surface can be scraped clean using the card scraper (**photo 15-41**). This should be done with the strip sitting on and supported by the bench. The scraper can be used to quickly scrape the inside surface clean as well. Note that the part of the strip that is being scraped must be supported underneath, to prevent the scraper from breaking the strip (**photo 15-42**).

9. The bottom inside edge of each piece is chamfered (**figure 15-4**), using the scraper or sandpaper (**photo 15-43**). This is necessary to attain a good fit between the binding pieces and their channels when the bindings are installed on the guitar body. The chamfer compensates for the fact that the inside corner of the channel into which the binding will fit will never be perfectly sharp. The chamfer also provides a bit of space for glue squeeze-out to go. Note that for each piece, the bottom surface is the surface with the side purfling lines attached.

Cutting the Binding and Purfling Ledges

As mentioned, two different methods for cutting the ledges are provided, one using power tools and the other hand tools. Both methods use the surface of the guitar sides as the reference surface for determining the width of the ledges. For this reason the first step that must be done is to sand the guitar sides smooth of any rippling, a certain amount of which is inevitable for sides bent by hand.

After that is done, the ledges are cut. The deeper outside ledge for the binding is cut first, followed by the shallower ledge for the plate purfling. In preparation for each of these cutting operations, the dimensions of the ledge to be cut are determined. This will be done by setting up the cutting tool using the actual binding and purflings to be used. Given conventionally sized binding and purfling strips, general dimensions for the ledges are shown in **figure 15-6**.

Once the dimensions of the ledge are determined and transferred to the cutting tool, a test cut is made in wood scrap and the fit is checked. Fine tuning of the dimensions of the cut is done here, before cutting of the actual guitar body is done.

Cutting of the binding ledges in the guitar body is straightforward, except when the side purflings will be mitered into the purflings of the tail graft. In this case, a change in the depth of the binding channels is made at the tail end. Cutting of the purfling ledge for the top plate is always a simple task. Cutting of the purfling ledge for the back plate is also straightforward, except when the back plate purflings will be mitered into the purflings of the back strip. In this case the cutting of the purfling ledge must be interrupted on each end, so that it does not cut across the back strip or its purflings. The specifics of how these alterations are accomplished are given in the construction operations.

☐ Sanding the Sides

In preparation for binding, the guitar body sides are sanded up to 100 grit. This work is done now, before the bindings are installed, because it is desirable to make clean channels for the bindings to fit into, and because it is not desirable to thin the bindings too much with a lot of sanding later.

 In all sanding operations on the body from now on, it is critical to keep in mind that everything that will be sanded is only 3/32″ (2.4mm) thick. So all sanding must be done judiciously, to remove only the noted flaws and no more wood than that. The box is closed at this point, so it is difficult to keep an eye on how thin the ribs and plates are getting. Because of this, it is prudent to regularly test for thin spots by gently pressing on different areas with the thumbs.

Some woods are easier to sand than others. Rosewood and other oily woods tend to corn up the sandpaper when power

Photo 15-44 – *The guitar body sides are sanded free of ripples and other defects in preparation for binding.*

Photo 15-45 – *The neck end of the ribs must remain flat for attachment of the neck.*

sanded. An eye should be kept out for *corning* on the sandpaper. Most non-oily hardwoods sand out well though. When sanding the sides it is not always clear just how much scorching must be removed, and sometimes sanding scratches go unnoticed. It is often useful to rub alcohol, naphtha, or paint thinner on the wood with a rag to help see the scratches and visualize what the surface will look like under finish. If this is done, all of the solvent must evaporate before additional sanding is done.

1. The sides will contain a number of ripples and flats on the curves, scorched areas, and other imperfections resulting from the bending of the ribs and gluing up the garland. 80-grit sandpaper on a block (**photo 15-44**) or 100 grit on a random orbital sander (ROS) with hard platen is used first. Starting at the tail end, any remaining imperfections are removed in the transitions between the tail graft and the ribs, and this area is given a gentle rounding over. While sanding it is good to be aware of any areas that will need to be puttied, patched, steamed, or otherwise fixed up, and to make a note of them. That will be attended to later though. The work proceeds up toward and over the lower bout on one side, removing any peaks and valleys found, so the ribs describe a smooth continuous curve. Note that, if vacuum pickup is not used on a power sander, sanding dust will visibly accumulate in any hollows, making them much easier to see. Sanding is continued past the lower bout and approaching, but not into, the waist. Then, again starting at the tail end, the same thing is done on the other side of the body.

2. The waist must be sanded using sandpaper on a cylindrical form by hand, unless a long rolling pin type sander is available.

3. Following the waist, sanding continues up the sides using the ROS or flat sanding block to do the upper bouts approaching the neck end. The area where the neck will attach needs to be kept flat, and this is best achieved with a flat sanding board that is a bit wider than the body is deep at this point. Flatness here can be checked using a straightedge (**photo 15-45**). This flat extends approximately 1½″ (38.1mm) on both sides of the center seam. Not only does this area have to be flat, it must be kept perpendicular to the top centerline. It should be recalled that there is a 91° angle between the ribs and top at the neck end

Photo 15-46 – *A typical rabbeting router bit mounted on a trim router.*

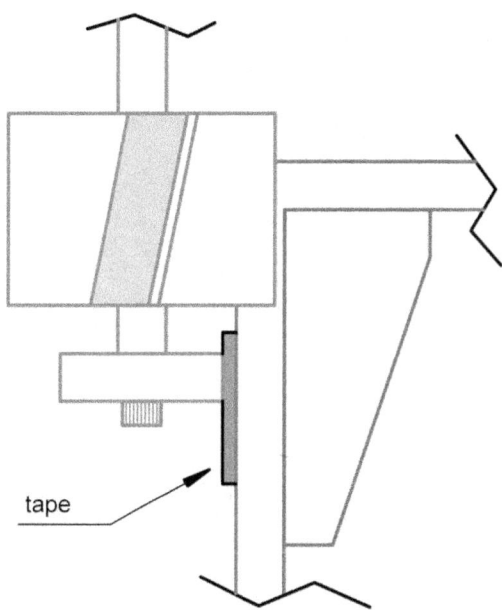

Figure 15-5 – *Tape applied to the body side can be used to shim out the cut when using a rabbeting router bit. The pilot bearing rides on the tape, which makes the width of the rabbet narrower by an amount equal to the thickness of the tape.*

centerline. This doesn't require measurement just yet, but it should be kept in mind that when checking for perpendicularity the bar of the square will not sit flush on the top.

5. If hand sanding was done using 80-grit sandpaper, it should then be repeated using 100 grit.

☐ **Routing the Binding and Purfling Ledges Option**

The ledges (also called channels or rabbets, or rebates if you are British) for the bindings and purflings are most easily cut into the edges of the body using a trim router and a rabbeting bit set (**photo 15-46**). These sets include a bottom bearing router bit, usually with a diameter of 1″ (25.4mm), and a collection of replaceable guide bearings of various diameters, but each smaller than the diameter of the bit. The smaller the bearing used, the wider the rabbet that will be cut. Rabbeting bit sets are available from general woodworking suppliers and also from lutherie specialty suppliers. Note that a cutter that provides a bit of down shear is preferred, because it leaves much cleaner edges. In general the sets available from the general woodworking suppliers are quite inexpensive, but unfortunately they do not come in the sizes or the gradations needed to cut the rabbets required for guitar bindings and purflings. The rabbeting bit sets available from lutherie suppliers are quite expensive, especially if they come with a large set of bearings which can accommodate purflings of different numbers of lines. But these sets have the distinct advantage that they are sized specifically for the dimensions needed to cut binding and purfling rabbets.

Note that it is possible to make use of the bit sets from the general woodworking suppliers for this task, but doing so requires adjusting the width of the rabbet by applying some hard tape (tape that cannot easily be compressed by the router

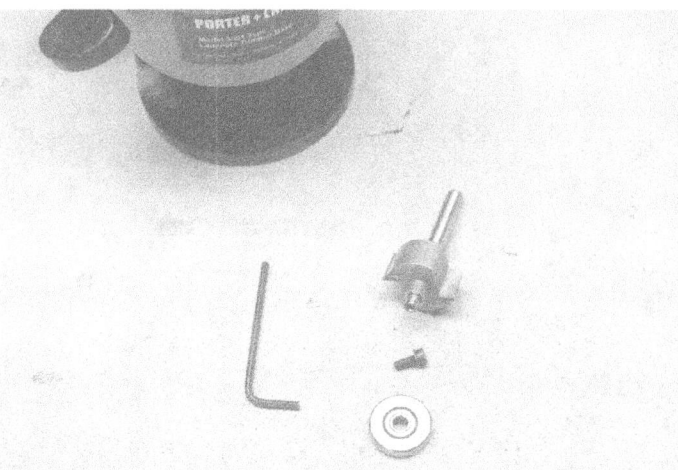

Photo 15-47 – *The rabbeting router bit has replaceable bearings. The smaller the bearing diameter, the wider the rabbet.*

cut. Construction details for doing this are not provided, but when this is done it is wise to experiment on scrap wood to achieve the desired width of cut.

Using the rabbeting sets from the lutherie suppliers is a far more reliable way to rout the ledges. It is possible to buy only those bearings that are needed to rout the ledges for the binding and purfling scheme to be used on the guitar under construction. **Figure 15-6** lists the bearing size to use for the binding ledge needed to accommodate bindings of typical thickness, and also the bearing sizes needed for purfling ledges for different numbers of purfling lines, assuming a bit with a diameter of 1″ (25.4mm).

Two rabbets are needed, one for the binding strip (with side purflings attached) and the other for the plate purflings (**figure 15-6**). The rabbet for the bindings is cut first. It must be as deep as the height of the binding strip with side purflings attached, and as wide as that strip is thick, nominally 0.08″ (2mm). The rabbet for the plate purflings is routed next. The width of this one will depend on the number of purfling lines to be used.

As was the case when the excess plate material was routed off the top and back in a previous chapter, the edge of each side of each plate is routed in a separate operation, and each of these operations are in turn performed as four separate cuts, each cut moving the router "down hill" relative to the grain of the plate. This avoids running the router into the grain, which prevents it

bearing) to the sides of the guitar. In use, the bearing of the router bit will run on the tape rather than on the side of the body, resulting in a channel which is thinner than would normally be cut (**figure 15-5**). Multiple layers of tape may be needed to space out the bearing to make the desired width of

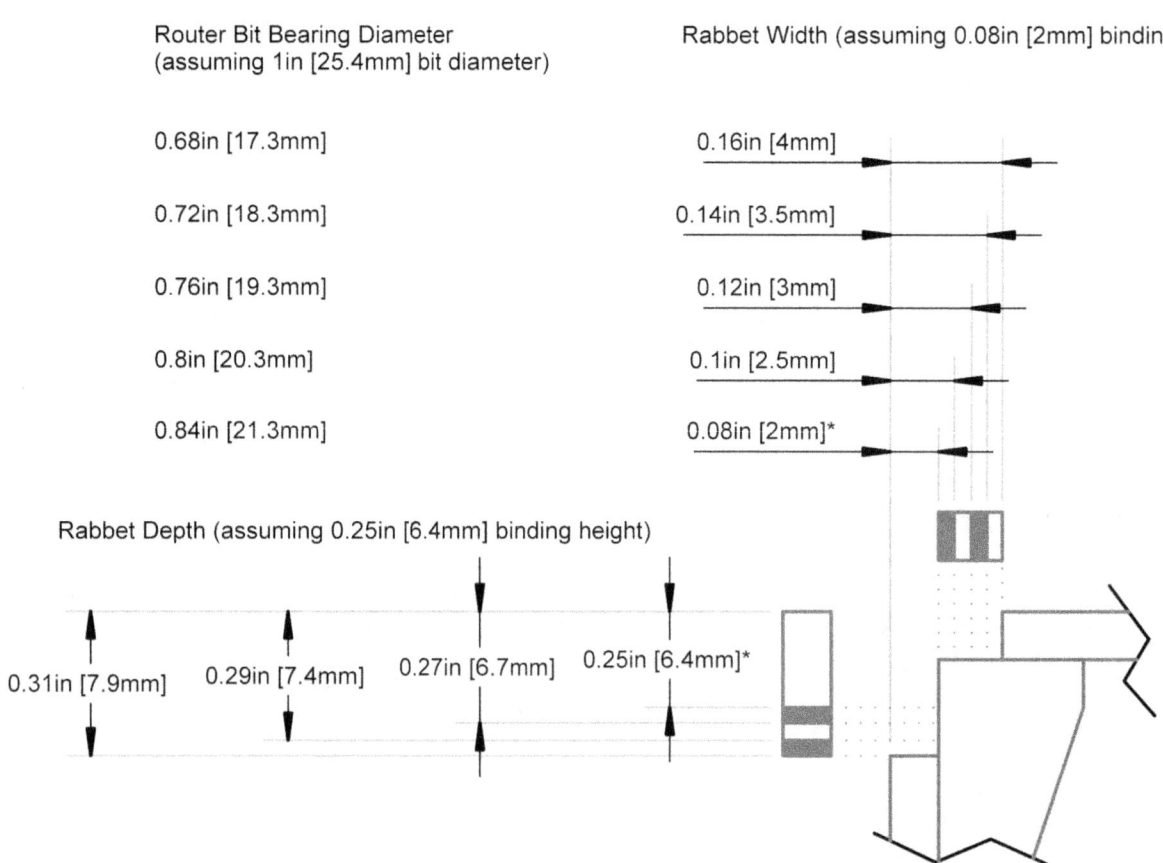

Figure 15-6 – *Binding and purfling rabbet depths and widths for bindings and purflings made up from typical commercially available binding strips and purfling lines. Note that the widths for the purfling rabbets also include the width of the binding rabbet, because the reference surface for the purfling rabbets is the side of the guitar body. Also included in the chart are the bearings needed to cut rabbets of the indicated widths, assuming the router bit has a 1″ (25.4mm) diameter.*

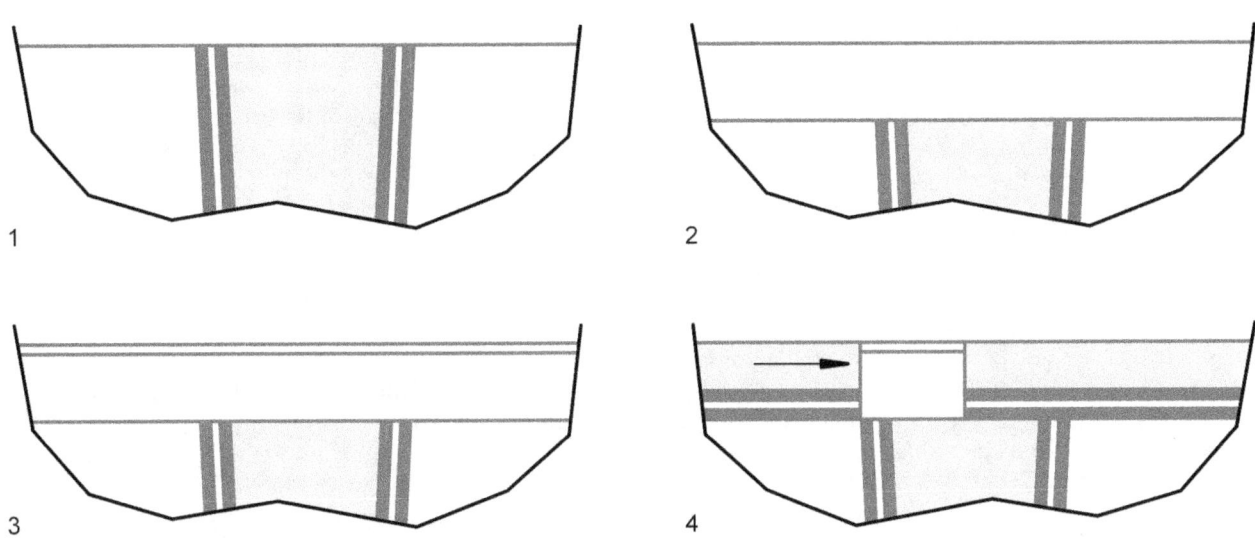

Figure 15-7 – *Cutting the binding and purfling rabbets when the side purflings will not be mitered into the tail graft purflings. 1. The tail end of the body, ready for cutting the rabbets. 2. The binding rabbet cut, straight across the top of the tail graft and its purflings. 3. The purfling rabbet is added. 4. Right side binding strip (and the top plate purflings, not visible here) already installed. The left side pieces are in the process of being installed.*

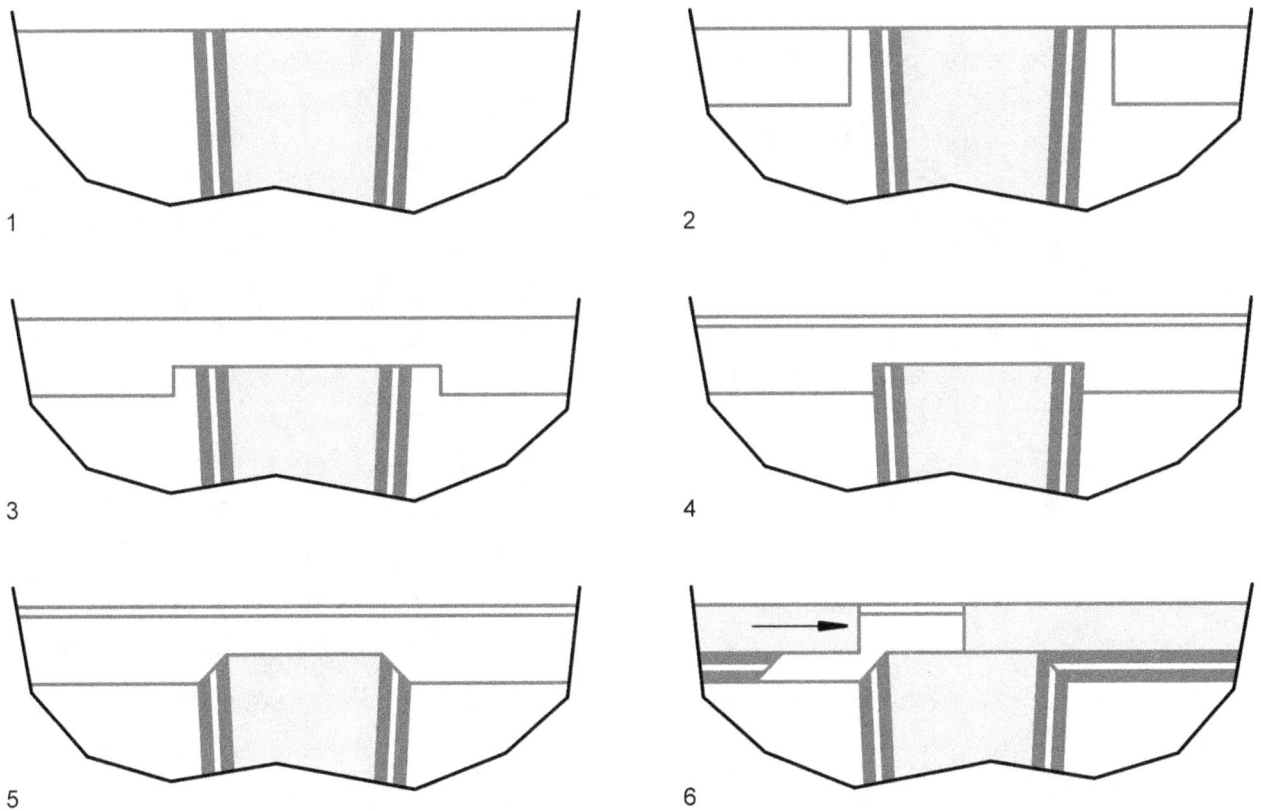

Figure 15-8 – *Cutting the binding and purfling rabbets when the side purflings will be mitered into the tail graft purflings. 1. The tail end of the body, ready for cutting the rabbets. 2. The binding rabbet is cut, but stopping on both sides of the tail graft and its purflings. 3. The top of the tail graft is cut at the height of the side purflings. 4. The floor of the binding rabbet continued right up to the sides of the tail graft purflings, and the purfling rabbet is cut. 5. The tail graft purfling ends are mitered. 6. Right side binding strip (and the top plate purflings, not visible here) already installed, with the side purflings mitered into the tail graft purflings. The left side pieces are in the process of being installed.*

from yanking big chunks of wood from the plate. Note also that care must be taken to avoid letting the router bit bearing fall into the trussrod slot or either of the neck mounting holes when routing across the neck end of the body. This was also discussed in the section on routing excess plate material from the plates in the chapter on assembling the body. That section on trimming excess material from the plates should be reviewed as background for the construction steps to be detailed here.

When the side purflings will *not* be mitered into the purflings of the tail graft, routing the binding ledge is straightforward. The binding ledges are routed to be as deep as the combined height of the bindings and attached side purflings, and they are routed all around the perimeter of the body (**figure 15-7**).

The desire to miter the side purflings into the tail graft purflings complicates routing of the binding ledges just a bit. For most of their length, the binding ledges are routed to be as deep as the combined height of the bindings and attached side purflings. But the ledges must be cut shallower over the ends of the tail graft and its purflings, to accommodate the mitering of the purflings. How this is accomplished is discussed in the construction steps, and is shown in schematic form in **figure 15-8**.

Routing the purfling ledges for the top plate is always straightforward. They are routed as deep as the purfling strips are wide, and as wide as is required for the number of purflings lines to be used. How the purfling ledges of the back plate are routed depends on if the back plate purflings will be mitered into the purflings along the sides of the back strip. If the back plate purflings will *not* be mitered into the back strip purflings, then routing the purfling ledges is performed exactly the same as for the purfling ledges of the top plate (**figure 15-9**). When it is desired to miter the back plate purflings into the back strip purflings, cutting of the purfling ledge for the back plate must be stopped before the ends of the back strip purflings are reached, on *both* ends of the body. The details of how this is done are described in the following construction steps, and are shown in schematic form in **figure 15-10**.

1. The rabbets for the bindings are cut first. The bearing is selected for the rabbeting bit (**photo 15-47**) that will result in a rabbet that is as wide as the binding strip is thick. For commercially available binding strips, the rabbet should be 0.08˝ (2mm) wide. The bearing is attached to the bit and secured with its mounting screw.

2. The bit is inserted in the collet of a trim router or other router with a small baseplate and the collet is tightened. A small diameter baseplate is necessary to accommodate the

Photo 15-48 – *The binding strip with its attached side purflings is used as a gauge to set the router depth of cut.*

Photo 15-50 – *The fit of the binding strip is checked in the test rabbet.*

Photo 15-49 – *A test cut is always made in scrap wood first.*

Photo 15-51 – *Care must be taken to be sure the pilot bearing does not drop into either of the neck mounting holes.*

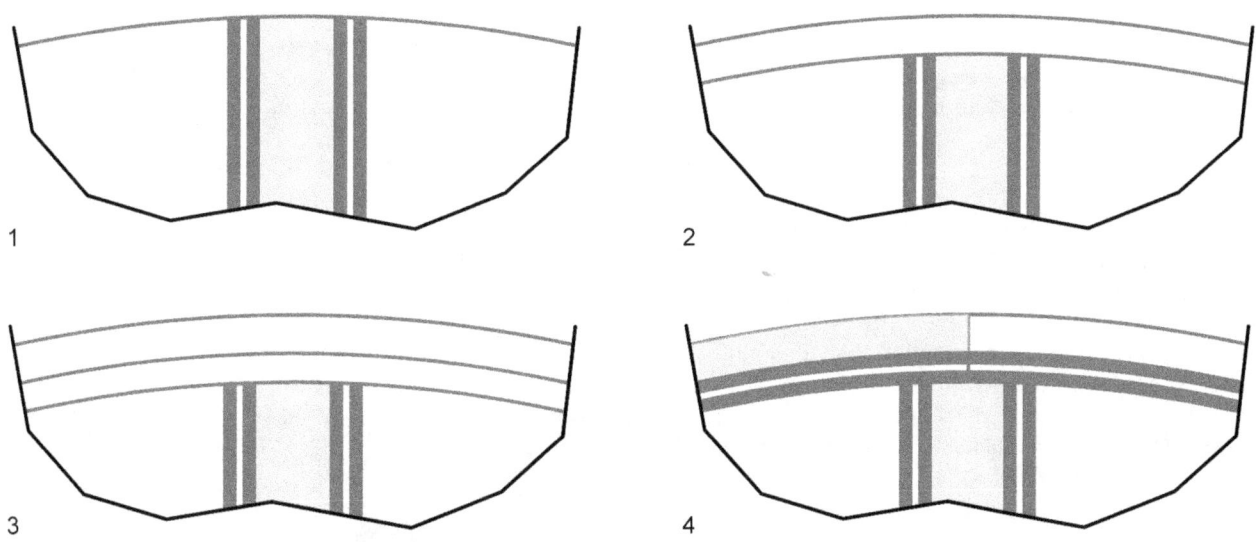

Figure 15-9 – *Cutting the binding and purfling rabbets when the back plate purflings will not be mitered into the back strip purflings. 1. The back of the body, at the tail end, ready for cutting the rabbets. 2. The binding rabbet cut, straight across the tail end of the back strip and its purflings. 3. The purfling rabbet is added. 4. One binding strip and both back plate purfling bundles already installed.*

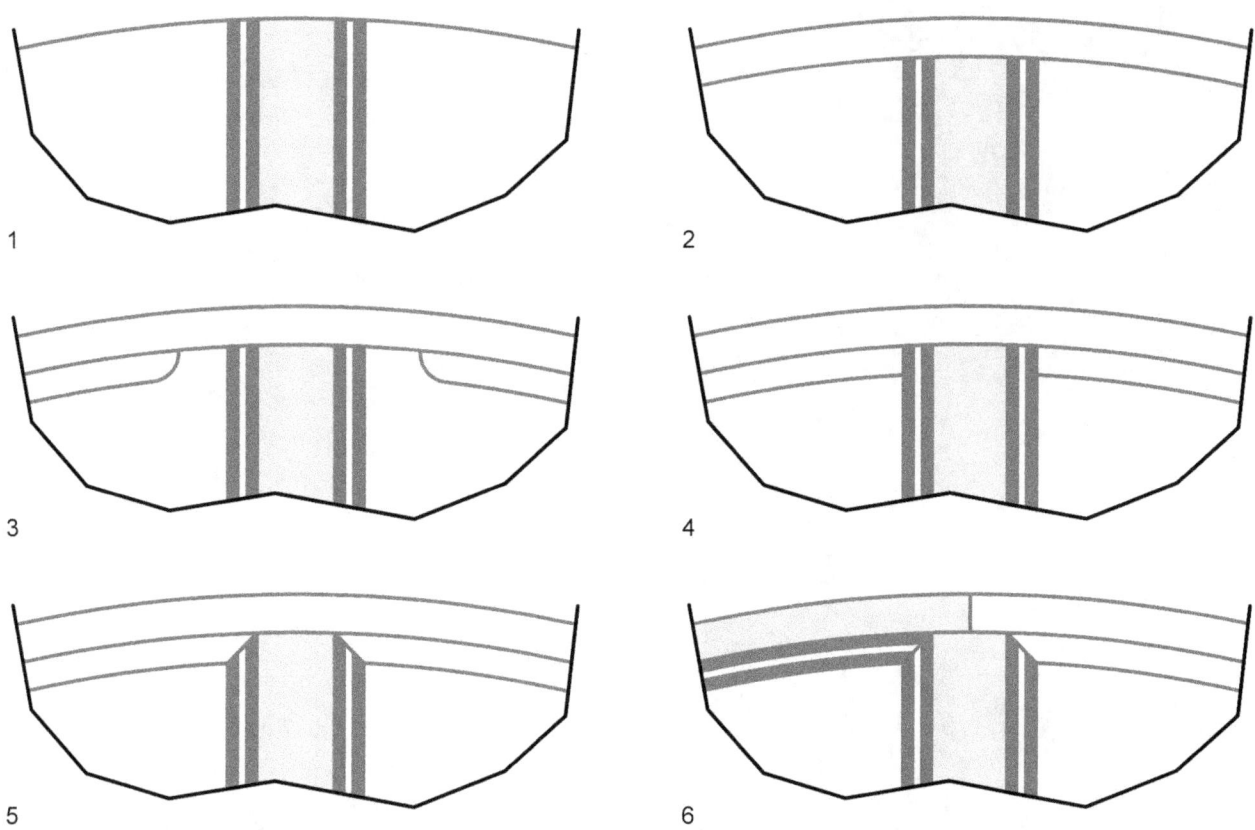

Figure 15-10 – *Cutting the binding and purfling rabbets when the back plate purflings will be mitered into the back strip purflings. 1. The back of the body, at the tail end, ready for cutting the rabbets. 2. The binding rabbet cut, straight across the tail end of the back strip and its purflings. 3. The rabbet for the back plate purflings is cut, but stopping on both sides of the back strip and its purflings. 4. The ends of the purfling rabbet trimmed flush against the back strip purflings. 5. The ends of the back strip purflings are mitered. 6. One binding strip and the back plate purflings on that side already installed, with the back plate purflings mitered into the back strip purflings.*

arching of the guitar plates. Because the plates are arched, a big router base will not sit securely on either the top or back plate.

3. Bit exposure (depth of cut) is set to be the same as the height of the binding strip with attached side purfling strips. This is best done by using the actual binding strip as a gauge (**photo 15-48**).

4. A test cut is made in a block of scrap wood (**photo 15-49**) and the dimensions of the rabbet are checked against the actual binding strip to be used (**photo 15-50**). If the depth of the rabbet is not correct, the depth of cut of the router is adjusted. If the width of the rabbet is not correct then a different size bearing will have to be fitted to the rabbeting bit. Fine tuning of a rabbet that is just a bit too wide that cannot be done using available bearings will have to be made using hard tape, as shown in **figure 15-5**. If any adjustments are made here, a new test cut should be made and checked.

5. The edge of one side and one plate of the guitar body will be routed at one time. Before routing, the router is moved all along the length of the rout to be sure the bearing will be in constant contact with the side all along the way. Care should be taken to note if the bearing will drop into either one of the neck bolt holes or the trussrod slot at the neck end of the body (**photo 15-51**). If so, the hole or slot will have to be temporarily filled to prevent this from happening, or a stop will have to be attached that will prevent the router from going far enough for this to happen, and then the routing continued using hand tools.

If the side purflings will be mitered into the purflings of the tail graft, then a stop will have to be positioned to prevent the router from moving close enough to the tail graft for the bit to cut into its purflings. In **photo 15-52** a clamp is used as a stop. This prevents the router from cutting into the tail graft purflings (**photo 15-53**). Note that the remainder of the rabbet will be cut by hand in a later construction step.

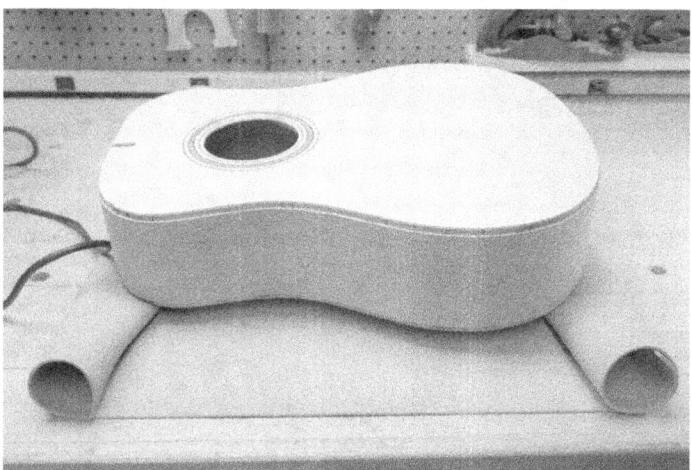

Photo 15-54 – If no stops are needed, the body can be simply supported for routing using a foam rubber router pad.

Photo 15-52 – A clamp is placed as a stop to prevent the router from routing into the tail graft purflings.

Photo 15-53 – Here the cut has been made and the router removed to show the stopped cut.

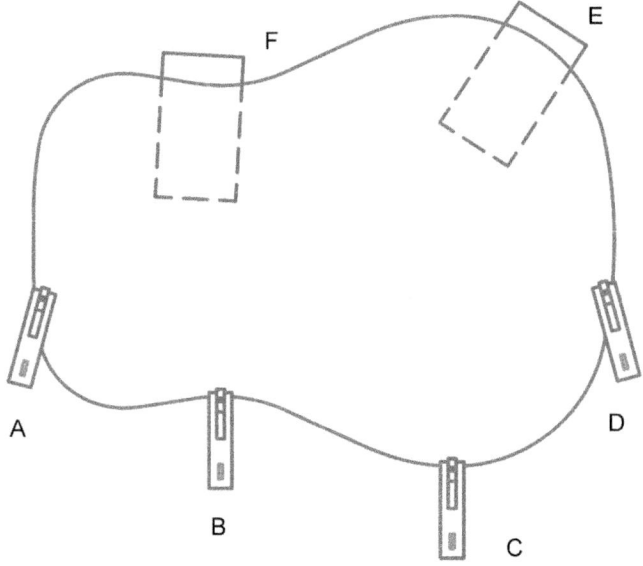

Figure 15-11 – If a clamp has to be placed as a stop to prevent the router from going too far (for example A), it will not be possible to simply rest the body on a router pad for routing. The body will have to be supported in a stable manner. Additional clamps can be applied around the perimeter of the side that will not be routed in the current operation (example B, C, D). These serve as "feet" to support the body. Wedges of wood are placed under the body (example E, F) on the side to be routed to support the body there.

6. The guitar body can often be simply supported for routing using a foam rubber router pad that will prevent the body from sliding around on the bench. Because the plates of the guitar are arched, a thick pad with some give should be used. If a thinner pad is used, it can be rolled up at the ends to support the arched plate (**photo 15-54**). The pad should be cleaned of any debris before use.

If clamps are used as stops, they will make the body wobbly on the router pad, so additional clamps are placed around the perimeter of the side that will not be routed, and wedges of wood are placed under the body on the side to be routed to support it securely (**figure 15-11**). Additional means of fixing the body in place for routing, such as bench dogs or other bench fixtures are always a good idea if they are available.

7. Routing of the binding rabbet for one side of one plate is done in exactly the same manner as was employed to rout off excess plate material in the previous chapter. The router is held in both hands, and the forearms are used to steady the body on the router pad (**photo 15-55**). The edge to be routed is always positioned on the opposite side of the guitar body from where the luthier is located. To prevent routing into the grain of the plate and possibly tearing out large hunks of wood, routing is divided into four distinct "downhill" cuts:

A. from the lower bout down to the waist;

B. from the lower bout down to the tail end;

C. from the upper bout down to the neck end;

D. from the upper bout down to the waist.

Note that, when the neck end of the body is toward the left, B and D are climb cuts. Particular care must be taken when these cuts are performed to prevent the router from getting out of control of the luthier.

Note also that for any routing operation where there is a possibility of unintentionally knocking off a hunk of wood that is needed, it is wise to operate the router without vacuum dust collection. It is possible that a piece of wood that was inadvertently torn out can be glued back in place, but only if it can be found.

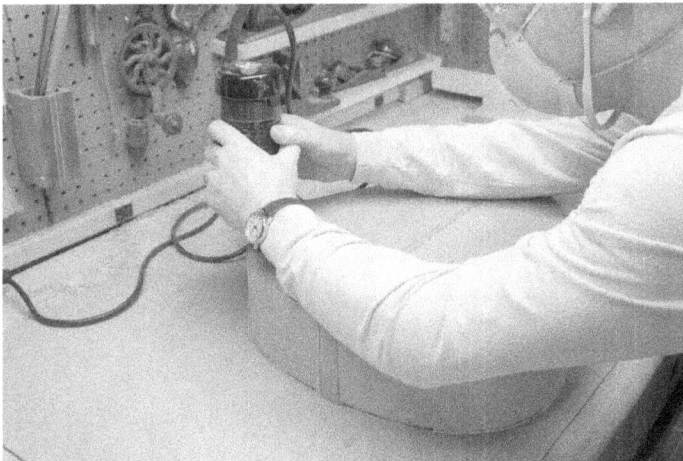

Photo 15-55 – *The forearms rest on the body to keep it from moving around during routing.*

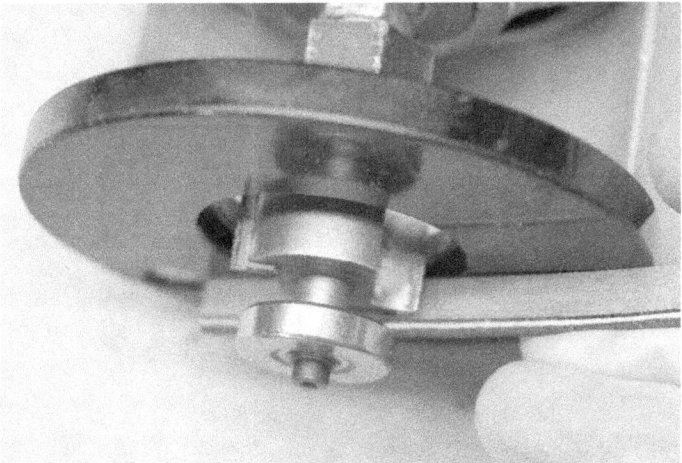

Photo 15-57 – *To trim the ends of the tail graft, the depth of cut is set to the height of the binding only, not including the side purflings.*

Photo 15-56 – *The finished binding rabbet will usually expose some of the linings underneath the sides and plates.*

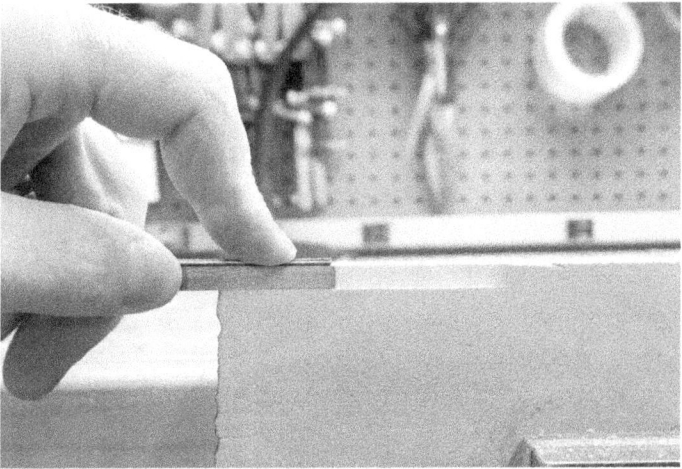

Photo 15-58 – *A test cut is made in scrap and the fit is checked.*

Photo 15-59 – *The tail graft ends are trimmed at what will be the level of the bottom of the binding.*

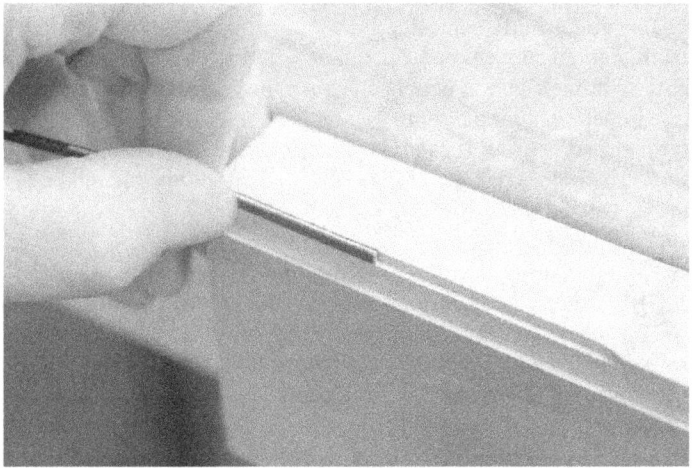

Photo 15-61 – *A test cut is made in scrap and checked for accuracy using the number of lines that will be in the actual purfling bundle.*

Photo 15-60 – *The depth of cut for the purfling channel is set using one of the purfling lines as a gauge.*

Photo 15-62 – *If the back plate purflings will be mitered into the back strip purflings, the rabbet must stop short of the back strip purflings.*

The entire channel is looked over carefully, checking for evenness of width and depth. Thin or missed places are touched up with another pass of the router.

If the body sides and the binding strips are of typical dimensions then the resulting rabbet will expose (or nearly expose) the linings underneath the sides (**photo 15-56**).

If a stop was placed to prevent the router from routing over the tail graft, it is removed now.

8. Steps 5 through 7 are repeated for each of the other three plate side edges. If the side purflings will *not* be mitered into the tail graft purflings, results are shown schematically in **figure 15-7.2**. If the side purflings *will* be mitered into the tail graft purflings, results are shown schematically in **figure 15-8.2**.

9. If the side purflings will be mitered into the tail graft purflings, the top and back ends of the tail graft must be trimmed to length. Each end is trimmed so the distance between the surface of the plate and the trimmed end is the same as the height of the binding strip alone, *without* the side purflings. The depth of cut is set to be the height of only the binding strip (**photo 15-57**).

A test cut is made in scrap wood and the depth of cut is checked before proceeding (**photo 15-58**).

The router is run over the tail end of the top plate and the back plate to trim the ends of the tail graft. The results are shown in **photo 15-59** and schematically in **figure 15-8.3**.

10. The ledge for the top plate purflings is cut next. A bearing is selected for the rabbeting bit to cut a rabbet wide enough for the number of top plate purfling lines desired. If conventionally dimensioned binding and purfling strips are used, and if a rabbeting bit of 1″ (25.4mm) diameter is used, the bearing diameter can be obtained directly from **figure 15-6**. The bearing is installed on the rabbeting bit.

11. The depth of cut is adjusted to be the same as the width of the purfling strips (**photo 15-60**). A test cut is made in scrap and checked (**photo 15-61**).

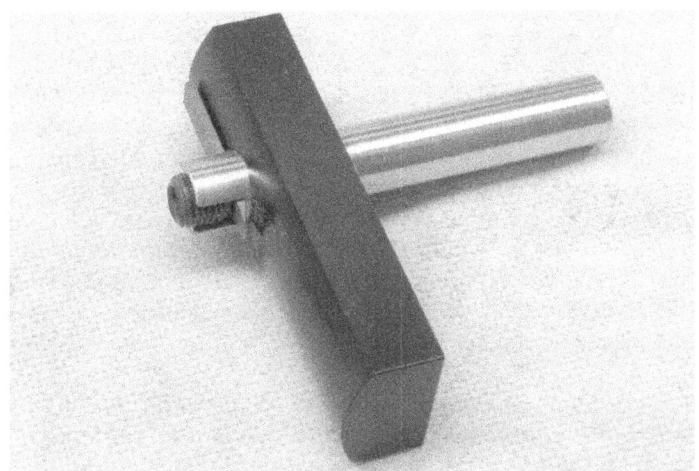

Photo 15-63 – *A gramil used to mark and cut binding and purfling rabbets.*

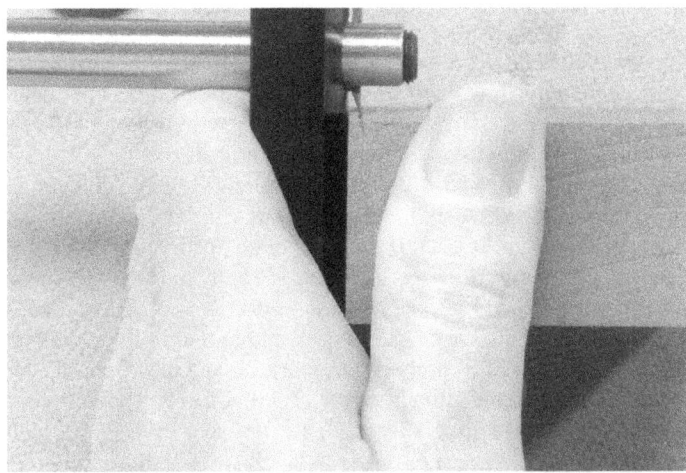

Photo 15-64 – *After the blade is set, the gramil is used to mark a cut in a piece of scrap wood. This will be used to check accuracy of the cut.*

12. Using the same routing techniques as described in step 7, the purfling ledge is routed into one side of the top plate, and then the other side of the top plate.

13. The ledge for the back plate purfling is cut next. A bearing is selected for the rabbeting bit to cut a rabbet wide enough for the number of back plate purfling lines desired. If conventionally dimensioned binding and purfling strips are used, and if a rabbeting bit of 1″ (25.4mm) diameter is used, the bearing diameter can be obtained directly from **figure 15-6**. The bearing is installed on the rabbeting bit.

14. The depth of cut for the purfling ledge is set (if necessary) and checked.

15. If the back plate purflings will be mitered into the purflings of the back strip, then stops will have to be positioned to prevent the router from moving close enough to the back strip for the bit to cut into its purflings. This is similar to how a stop was placed to prevent the router from cutting into the purflings of the tail graft during routing of the binding ledges.

☞ The difference here is that stops have to be placed on the neck end of the body *and* the tail end, to prevent the router from cutting into the purflings at either end of the back strip.

15. Using the same routing techniques as described in step 7, the purfling ledge is routed into one side of the back plate. If stops were positioned, they are repositioned to prevent routing into the back strip purflings when the other side of the back is routed. Then the other side is routed. If the back plate purflings will *not* be mitered into the back strip purflings, results for the tail end are shown in **figure 15-9.3**. If the back plate purflings will be mitered into the back strip purflings, results for the tail end are shown in **figure 15-10.3** and **photo 15-62**.

16. When all ledges have been routed they are cleaned up as needed with rasps and sandpaper on a cylindrical block, and then checked for fit, using a short stack of pieces of purfling lines and the binding strips. Note that any fuzzing at the edges of the channels in the top can be removed carefully with the card scraper, scraping "downhill", or with a knife using careful down strokes. The fuzz should not be simply pulled off. Doing so will result in deep and long fibers being pulled up out of the surface of the top.

☐ **Chiseling the Binding and Purfling Ledges Option**

The binding and purfling ledges can be cut using an adjustable cutting gauge called a gramil (**photo 15-63**) and a chisel. Gramils specifically designed for this operation are available from lutherie suppliers. In this section I am using a beautiful gramil designed by the late Richard Schneider, a well known builder of classical guitars from Washington state. The blade of the gramil is adjustable for the width of the channel and also the depth. The fence of the gramil has two surfaces, one curved and one flat. The curved surface is used when the fence must follow a curved surface, such as the sides of the guitar body. The flat fence surface is used when the surface to be followed is flat (or "flat-ish"), such as the surfaces of the plates.

The basic technique for cutting a rabbet using the gramil is as follows. The gramil is configured to use the curved fence surface. The blade depth is set to make a shallow marking cut. Then the distance of the blade tip from the gramil fence is adjusted to the desired width of the rabbet. The gramil is then used to mark what will be the inside wall of the rabbet, on the surface of each plate. To do this, the fence of the gramil will bear on the sides of the guitar body. Next, the gramil is configured to use the flat fence surface. The distance from blade to fence is again adjusted, this time for the depth of the rabbet, and the gramil is used with the fence bearing on the surface of the plate, to mark the depth of the rabbet with a cut on the sides of the guitar body. The waste wood is removed from the marked rabbet using a small chisel.

Additional cutting can be done with the gramil to keep the wall and floor of the channel flat and square. However, the gramil cannot be effectively used to trim the walls of the rabbets in the waist area of the guitar body. This is because the width of the gramil blade interferes with deep concave cuts (**figure 15-12**). A general technique for dealing with this is to simply carve out the waste as well as can be done using a chisel, and then clean up the width of the rabbet in the waist using sandpaper on a cylindrical form.

If the side purflings will be mitered into the purflings of the tail graft, then marking of the depth of the rabbet for the bindings and removing the waste must stop short of the purflings of the tail graft (**figure 15-8.2**). Otherwise, marking and chiseling of waste will proceed right across the tail graft and its purflings (**figure 15-7.2**). Likewise, if the back plate purflings will be mitered into the purflings of the back strip, then marking of the purfling rabbet and removal of waste must be stopped short of the purflings of the back strip at neck and tail end of the back plate (**figure 15-10.3**). Otherwise, marking and chiseling of waste will proceed right across the back ends of the back strip and its purflings (**figure 15-9.3**).

 A note on the descriptions of dimensions used when discussing the gramil. No matter how the gramil will be oriented while cutting, the adjustment for the distance between the fence of the gramil and the blade tip will always be referred to here as the width adjustment. The amount of blade exposure will be referred to as the depth of cut adjustment.

 A note on the orientation of the bevel of the gramil blade. The side of the blade that is beveled should *always* be the waste side of the cut. For all the cuts made in the following constructions steps, the blade should be attached so its bevel is pointing toward the gramil's fence.

1. The binding ledges will be marked and cut first. First, the width of the binding ledges will be marked. The curved fence surface of the gramil is used. The binding strip is used as a gauge to set up the width of cut to be the same as the width of the binding. The exposure of the blade (depth of cut) is set to be the same as the total height of the binding including attached side purfling strips.

2. The gramil is used on a rectangular scrap of wood to cut a shallow mark from one flat surface (**photo 15-64**). The fence of the gramil is held in contact with the side of the scrap when making this mark. The mark is checked for accuracy and the width of cut is adjusted if necessary.

3. The gramil is used to cut a *shallow* mark all around the perimeter of the top plate (**photo 15-65**) and then around the perimeter of the back plate.

4. Now the gramil will be used to mark the depth of the binding ledges. The flat fence surface is used. The binding strip is again

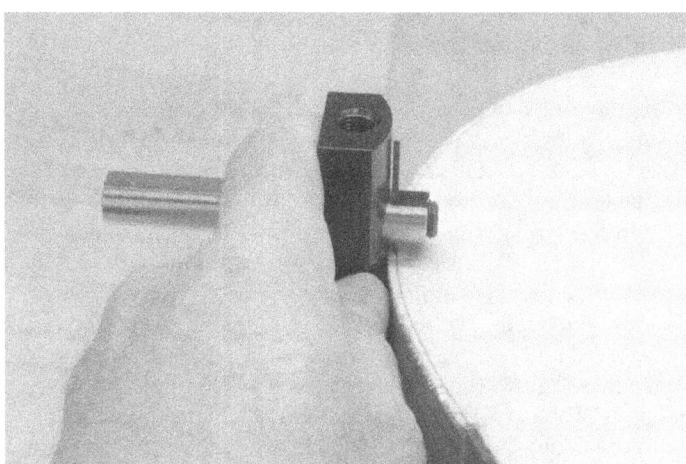

Photo 15-65 – *The marking cut for the binding rabbet is cut into the top plate using the gramil pressed to the body side.*

Photo 15-67 – *The test block, showing wall and floor trial cuts for the binding rabbet.*

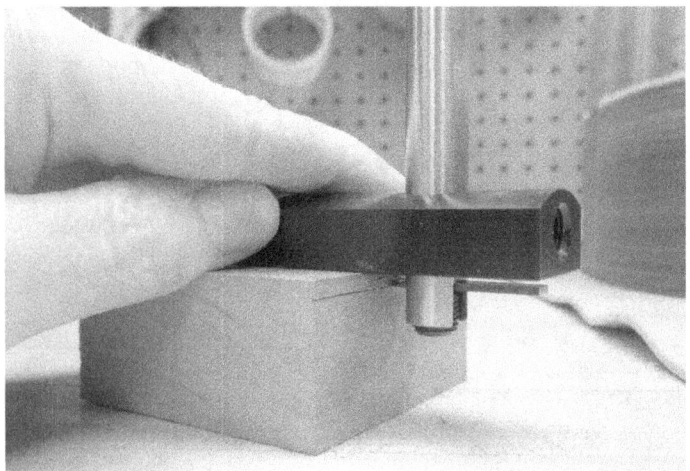

Photo 15-66 – *Here the gramil is set up to make a trial cut at the depth of the floor of the binding rabbet.*

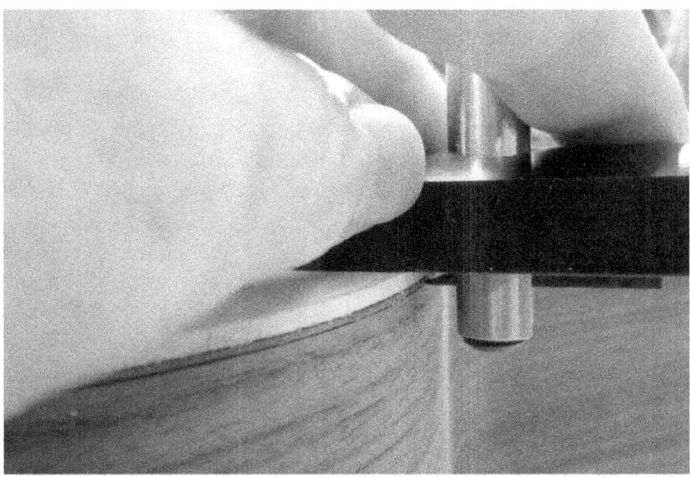

Photo 15-68 – *The gramil is used to mark the floor of the binding rabbet.*

Photo 15-69 – *Paring away the waste using a narrow chisel.*

Photo 15-70 – *Cleaning up the rabbet using a small square profile rasp.*

used as a gauge to set the width of cut of the gramil to be the same as the total height of the binding strip, including any attached side purflings. The exposure of the blade is adjusted to make just a shallow marking cut.

5. As configured, the gramil will be used to cut a mark representing the floor of the binding ledge. But first it is used to mark the same scrap block that was used in step 2. This time the fence of the gramil is held in contact with the top surface of the scrap (**photos 15-66, 15-67**). The mark is measured for accuracy and the depth of cut is adjusted if necessary.

6. The gramil is used with its fence held in contact with the top of the body to cut a mark around the guitar body sides just under the top plate (**photo 15-68**). If the side purflings will be mitered into the purflings of the tail graft, this marking cut should stop before cutting across the purflings of the tail graft on both sides.

7. Step 6 is repeated with the gramil fence held to the back plate. Again, if the side purflings will be mitered into the purflings of the tail graft, the marking cut should *not* continue across the tail graft or its purflings, but should stop just short on both sides of the tail graft and purflings.

8. If the side purflings will be mitered into the purflings of the tail graft, the gramil is set up to mark the depth of the binding ledge over the ends of the tail graft. The gramil is set up to use the flat fence surface, and the binding strip is again used as a gauge, this time to set the width of cut to be the same as the height of *just* the binding part of the binding strip, that is, *not* including any attached side purflings. Thus set up, the gramil is used with its fence held in contact with the top of the body to cut a mark just across the tail graft and its purflings. This is repeated with the fence held against the back plate of the body to mark the back end of the tail graft. These marks indicate where the tail graft ends will be.

9. A narrow chisel is used to pare a shallow cut to begin removal of the waste wood of the binding channels (**photo 15-69**). Extreme care must be taken to avoid cutting into the cut marks on the surfaces of the plates and the sides. This is slow and tedious work. The shallow cut is made for the binding channel on the top and back plates.

10. The blade of the gramil is again adjusted as in step 1.

11. The binding channels are cut to final depth as a series of shallow chiseled cuts as described in step 9. Following each shallow cut to remove some of the waste, the gramil can be used to cut down the wall of the rabbet a bit, in preparation for the next bit of work with the chisel. The gramil can be used in this way everywhere along the edge, with the exception of in the waist. As described in the introduction to this construction operation and shown in **figure 15-12**, this is because the width of the blade will gouge out the cut when used inside a concave

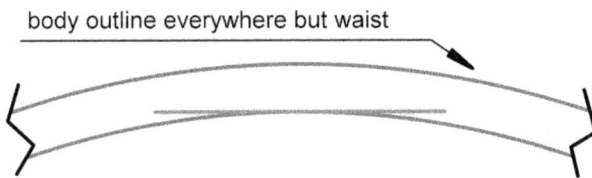
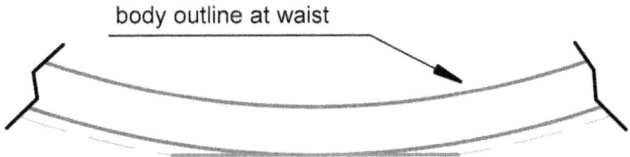

Figure 15-12 – *The gramil can be used for deep cuts, as long as the wall of the cut rabbet is either flat or convex, but it cannot be used for deep cuts if the wall is concave. As is seen in the drawing on the left, when the wall that is cut is convex, the width of the blade of the gramil ends up being in the waste of the cut, where it does no harm. But as can be seen in the right side drawing, if a deep cut is attempted where the wall is concave, the width of the blade ends up being deeper into the wood than is intended. The result is the cut ends up being deeper than intended here. The sides of the blade also tend to gouge the material, resulting in a cut that is not as smooth.*

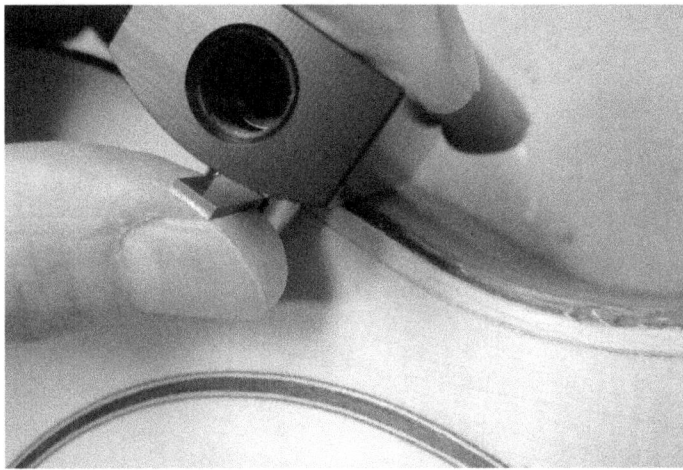

Photo 15-71 – *Marking the cut for the top plate purfling rabbet.*

Photo 15-73 – *The plate purfling rabbet, fully excavated.*

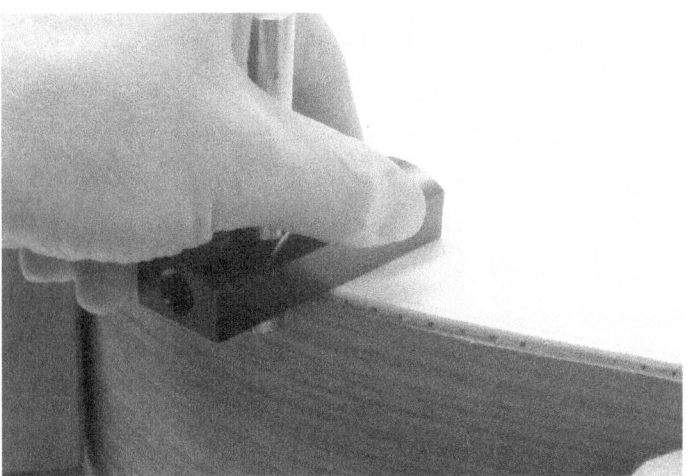

Photo 15-72 – *The gramil is used with the flat fence surface to mark the cut for the floor of the top plate purfling rabbet.*

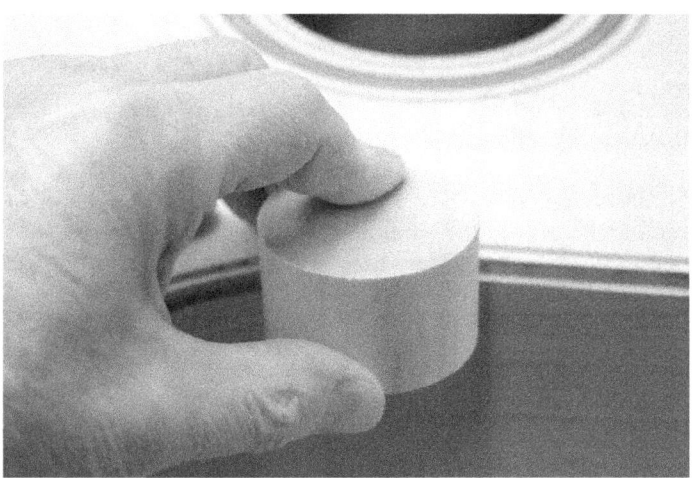

Photo 15-74 – *Straightening up the rabbets inside the waist curves can be done with sandpaper on a short length of dowel.*

curve and when the cut is deep. The effect of this is that the rabbet will end up wider and more ragged than desired if the gramil is used for deep cuts in the waist.

Because the gramil cannot be effectively used in the waist, it is prudent when working in the waist curves to use a chisel or shallow sweep gouge to remove waste wood and to stay a bit away from the marked wall line. The width of the rabbet can be cleaned up later using sandpaper on a cylindrical form.

☞ Care must be taken to avoid cutting the ledge too deep over the ends of the tail graft and its purflings, if the side purflings will be mitered into the tail graft purflings. Depth marks for the binding channel over the tail graft ends were made in step 8. The ledges should not be chiseled deeper than these marks here.

12. When the depth of the binding ledge gets close to the bottom mark, the gramil can be used to make the final cut that will establish the floor of the ledge. The gramil is adjusted for width of cut as per construction step 4, but the blade exposure is set to be the desired width of the binding channel. The gramil is then used as in steps 6 and 7, but here the cut is made a bit deeper for each of multiple passes around the body. Again, the area around the tail graft is not touched.

A schematic representation of how the finished binding ledge will look at the tail end of the body near the top plate if the side purfling will *not* be mitered into the tail graft purflings is shown in **figure 15-7.2**. If the side purfling will be mitered into the tail graft purflings then it will look like **figure 15-8.3**.

13. The rabbet can be cleaned up using a square profile rasp (**photo 15-70**) everywhere except inside the waist curves, where sandpaper on a cylindrical block can be used. Dimensions of the rabbet should be checked using a piece of the binding with attached side purfling lines.

14. The ledge for the top plate purflings is cut next. First, the gramil is used to mark the width of the purfling ledge. The curved surface of the fence is used. The width of cut on the gramil is adjusted to be that of the width of the binding ledge *plus* what is needed for the number of plate purfling lines to be

Photo 15-75 – *The purfling rabbet is checked using a few short pieces of purfling.*

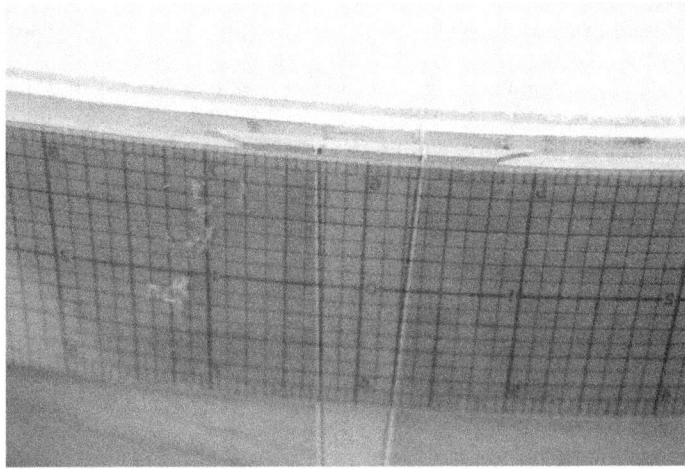

Photo 15-77 – *A flexible ruler is taped down with its edge in line with the floor of the binding channel, in preparation for trimming the ends of the channel.*

Photo 15-76 – *The binding rabbet is checked using one of the bent binding strips with side purflings attached.*

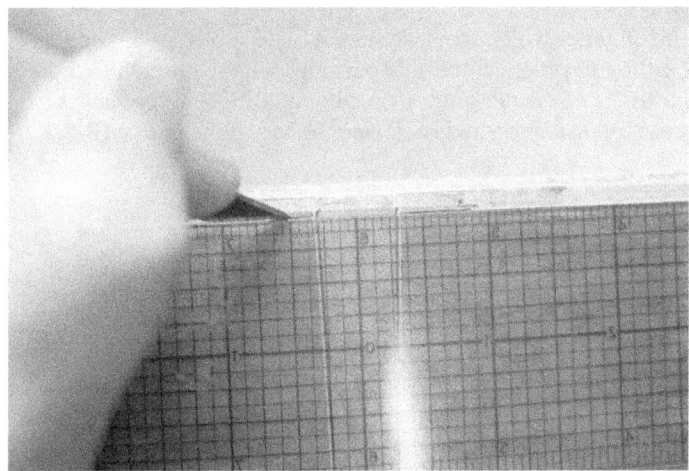

Photo 15-78 – *Deep repetitive cuts are made with the knife, from purfling outward, guided by the edge of the ruler.*

used for the top plate. Widths for bindings and purflings lines of conventional dimensions are provided in **figure 15-6**.

15. The depth of cut is adjusted to be the same as the width of the purfling strips. A test cut is made in scrap and checked.

16. The gramil is used with its fence held against the guitar body sides to cut a marking line for the top plate purfling ledge all around the perimeter of the top (**photo 15-71**).

17. Steps 14 through 16 are repeated for the back plate. Note that the number of purfling lines used for the back plate is usually different than the number used for the top plate, so the width of cut will have to be adjusted specifically for the back plate before proceeding. Note also that, if the back plate purfling lines will be mitered into purfling lines along the sides of the back strip, then this mark must *not* cut across the back strip or its purflings at either neck or tail end. The cut mark must stop just before the back strip purflings are reached.

18. The gramil will now be used to cut a mark denoting the floor of the top plate purfling ledge. The flat surface of the fence is used. The distance between the gramil fence and the tip of the blade is set to be the width of the purfling lines. The blade exposure has to be set deep enough so, when the gramil is positioned with its fence on the surface of the top plate, the blade point will be able to reach the wall of the binding ledge, so it can make a mark there. As usual, a test cut is made on the scrap block to be sure the gramil is correctly set before use on the guitar body.

19. The gramil is used to cut the mark denoting the floor of the top plate purfling ledge (**photo 15-72**). The mark is cut all the way around the perimeter of the top.

20. The gramil as set up is used to cut a mark denoting the floor of the back plate purfling ledge as well. Note again that, if the back plate purfling lines will be mitered into purfling lines along the sides of the back strip, then this mark must not cut across the back strip at either neck or tail end. The cut mark must stop just before the back strip purflings are reached.

21. The waste is chiseled out of these rabbets using the same tools and techniques used to perform this operation on the

binding ledges. A schematic representation of how the finished purfling ledge will look at the top plate near the ends of the back strip if the back plate purflings will *not* be mitered into the back strip purflings is shown in **figure 15-9.3**. If the back plate purflings will be mitered into the back strip purflings then it will look like **figure 15-10.3**.

22. After excavation of the waste is finished (**photo 15-73**), the purfling ledges are cleaned up with rasps and sandpaper on a cylindrical block (**photo 15-74**) and then checked for fit, using a short stack of pieces of purfling lines (**photo 15-75**). The fit should also be checked with purfling lines and the binding strip. If the binding strip fits well without plate purflings (**photo 15-76**) but bulges away from the body sides in places when purfling strips are added, it is likely that the plate purfling ledges are not wide enough where the check was made.

☐ **Cutting the Tail Graft Purfling Miters Option**

No matter which tools were used to excavate the binding and purfling channels, if the side purflings will be mitered into the purflings of the tail graft, then cutting of the binding rabbets was stopped at top and back near the tail graft (**figure 15-8.3**).

Now the remaining waste in the binding rabbets must be removed with chisel and knife (**figure 15-8.4**), followed by mitering the ends of the tail graft purflings (**figure 15-8.5**). This is an easy but fussy operation. As has been done with previous operations that required straight cuts to be made with a knife, the cuts are made next to a flexible straightedge. Here a clear flexible ruler is used.

1. Double-stick tape is used to stick a flexible straightedge onto the ribs at the tail end, so the upper edge of the straightedge is flush with the floor of the binding channel of the top plate (**photo 15-77**).

2. The straightedge is used as a guide to run a knife from close to the tail graft purfling out toward the rest of the binding channel (**photo 15-78**).

 This is an operation that may require the use of a headband magnifier, depending on the eyesight of the luthier (**photo 15-79**).

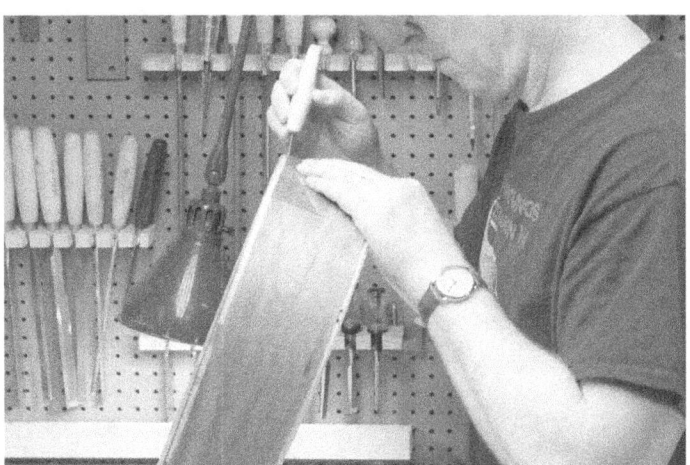

Photo 15-79 – *I need to use an optical visor to do this detailed work.*

Photo 15-81 – *When finished, the ends of the binding rabbet butt right up against the tail graft purflings.*

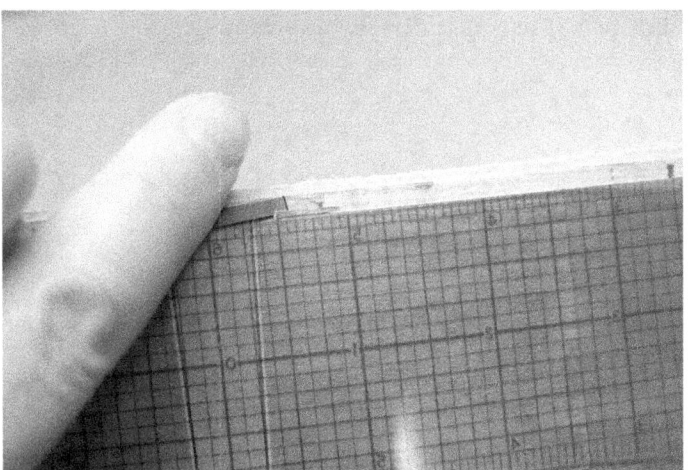

Photo 15-80 – *The waste wood is carefully pared away using a small chisel.*

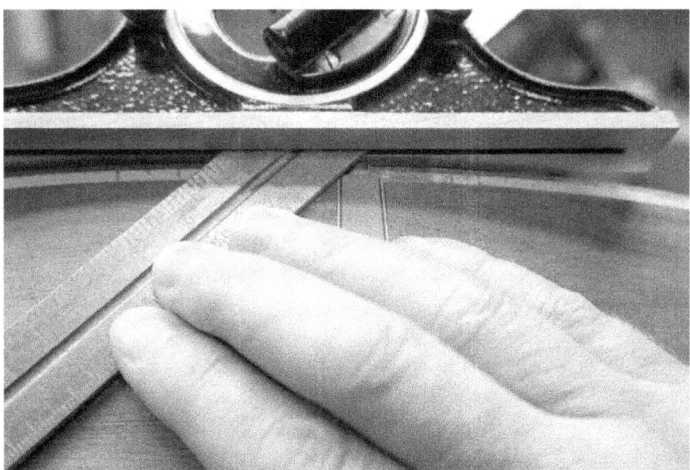

Photo 15-82 – *A protractor is used to mark the miters at the ends of the tail graft purflings.*

The cut is made multiple times on both sides of the tail graft in this manner, resulting in deep scoring. Care must be taken to not cut into the tail graft purfling.

3. The waste is chiseled away to the depth of the knife cuts using a small chisel (**photo 15-80**). Knife cutting and chiseling are repeated as necessary, until the binding channel has been extended to full width and depth, right up to the purfling of the tail graft. There will be some fussy work in the corners of the binding rabbet, up against the tail graft purflings. Results should look like **figure 15-8.4** and **photo 15-81**.

4. Steps 1 through 3 are repeated for the back plate end of the tail graft.

5. The purfling strip ends of the tail graft are now mitered. A protractor is set to 45° and then its fence is set on the back plate with the bar positioned against the end of the purfling on the appropriate side (**photo 15-82**). The miter cut to be made to the end of the purfling is carefully marked with a knife. Then a small chisel is used to cut the miter at the mark, right through the purfling (**photo 15-83**).

6. The protractor is flipped around to mark and then miter the purfling on the other side of the tail graft. The result of the mitering steps is as shown in **figure 15-8.5**.

7. Steps 5 and 6 are repeated to miter the tail graft purfling ends on the top plate end of the tail graft as well.

☐ **Cutting the Back Strip Purfling Miters Option**

If the back plate purflings will be mitered into the purflings of the back strip, then cutting of the back plate purfling rabbets were stopped at neck and tail ends near the back strip (**figure 15-10.3**). Now the remaining waste in the back plate purfling rabbets must be removed with chisel and knife (**figure 15-10.4**), followed by mitering the ends of the back strip purflings (**figure 15-10.5**) at both ends. This is an easy but fussy operation. As has been done with previous operations that required straight cuts to be made with a knife, the cuts are made next to a flexible straightedge. Here a clear flexible ruler is used.

1. Double-stick tape is used to stick a flexible straightedge across the back at the tail end, so the edge of the straightedge is flush with the wall of the purfling channel. Note that at the tail end the purfling channel is actually curved, not straight. But if the length to be cut is short enough then using the straightedge as a guide will work out fine. If in previous steps, cutting of the rabbet stopped far away from the back strip purflings, it may be prudent now to go back and cut these closer.

2. The straightedge is used as a guide to run a knife from close to the back strip purfling out toward the rest of the purfling channel (**photo 15-84**). The cut is made multiple times on both sides of the back strip in this manner, resulting in deep scoring. Care must be taken to not cut into the back strip purfling.

3. The waste is chiseled away to the depth of the knife cuts using a small chisel. Knife cutting and chiseling are repeated as necessary until the purfling channel has been extended to full width and depth, right up to the purfling on both sides of the back strip. There will be some fussy work in the corners of the

Photo 15-83 – *The marked miters are cut using a small palm chisel.*

Photo 15-84 – *Scoring the cuts to continue the ends of the purfling channel on the back is done using the flexible ruler, too.*

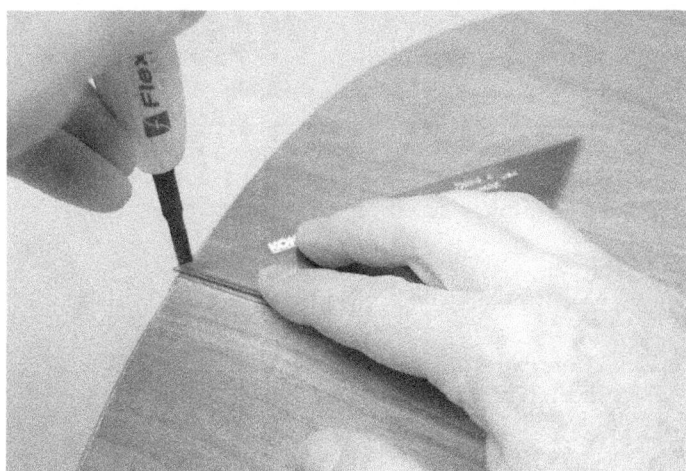

Photo 15-85 – *The miters at the ends of the back strip purflings can be cut against the side of a small drafting square.*

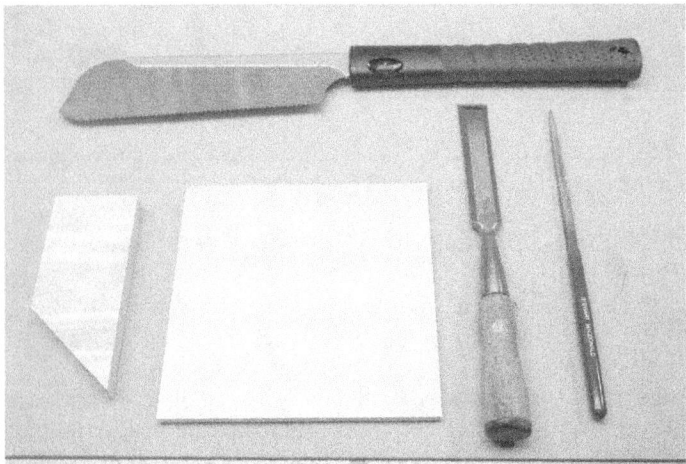

Photo 15-86 – The parts of the disposable mitering fixture, and the cutting tools that will be used with it.

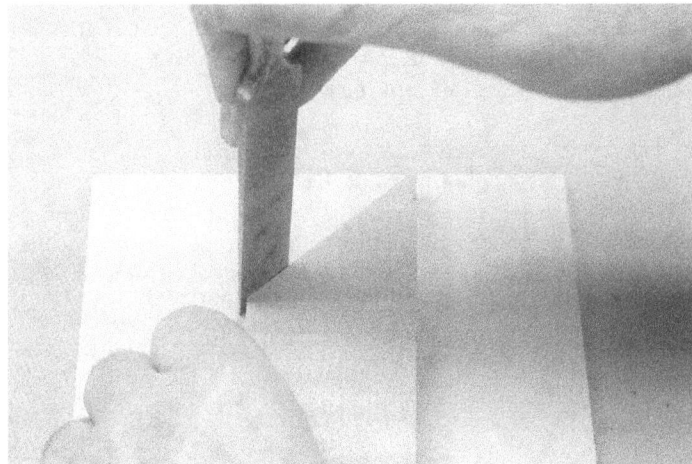

Photo 15-88 – The disposable mitering fixture is used to pare the end of a purfling bundle at a 45° angle using a chisel.

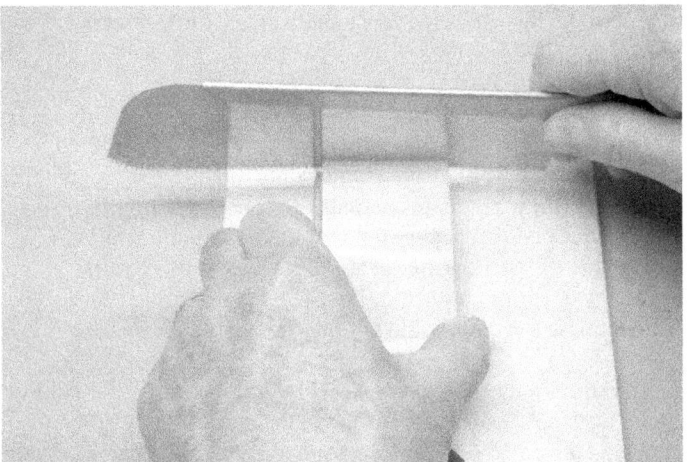

Photo 15-87 – Using the disposable mitering fixture to saw the end of a binding strip square.

purfling rabbet, up against the back strip purflings. Results should look like **figure 15-10.4**.

4. Steps 1 through 3 are repeated for the back plate purfling rabbets at the neck end.

5. The purfling strip ends of the back strip at the neck end are now mitered. A small 45° drafting square is set on the back plate aligned with the back strip and positioned to cut the miter of the purflings on one side if the strip (**photo 15-85**). A small chisel, resting against the square is used to cut the miter, right through the purflings.

6. The drafting square is flipped around to cut the miter of the purflings on the other side of the back strip..

7. Steps 5 and 6 are repeated to miter the back strip purfling ends at the tail end as well. The resulting back strip ends will look like **figure 15-10.5**.

Attaching the Bindings and Purflings

The bindings and purflings are glued onto the binding ledges in much the same manner as was used to glue the components of the soundhole rosette into their channels. There is a separate piece of binding for each side of each plate, so in the construction steps that follow, each piece of binding will be attached to the body as a single sequence.

Because there is a separate piece of binding for each side of each plate, the ends of the bindings of each plate must be joined together at the tail end. This is generally and most conveniently done using a simple butt joint. So in preparation for attaching a binding piece, the tail end is first fit and then cut square. When the side purflings will *not* be mitered into the tail graft purflings, the side purflings already attached to the binding strip are just cut off square as well. But when the side purflings will be mitered into the tail graft purflings, the side purflings at the tail end of the binding strip must be trimmed back at an angle for that miter joint. This is shown schematically in **figure 15-8.6**.

The purflings will be attached at the same time as the bindings, and they will be handled as separate lines which will be glued together at the same time they are installed. For convenience, the end of each purfling bundle will be glued and then trimmed beforehand. This makes it a lot easier to manage the purfling lines during gluing.

The bindings and purflings are held in place using tape while the glue cures. There are a number of different tools and techniques for holding the bindings in place, but tape seems to work well for novice luthiers. The tape I am using here is a 1″ (25.4MM) wide heavy brown kraft paper tape with a rubber adhesive. It is available from industrial suppliers and is often referred to as tear-able packing tape. Any tape will do, but tape that doesn't stretch (or doesn't stretch much) works best in this application.

The binding and purflings are initially attached at the tail end of the guitar body and are sequentially glued and taped into place, working toward the neck end. After the glue cures, the tape is removed.

☐ Building a Disposable Mitering Fixture

The process of preparing the binding strips and bundles of purfling strips for gluing to the body involves the accurate trimming of the ends of these. Binding strip ends are always

Photo 15-89 – *A binding strip is fitted to the waist and then taped in place, so the length of the strip can be ascertained.*

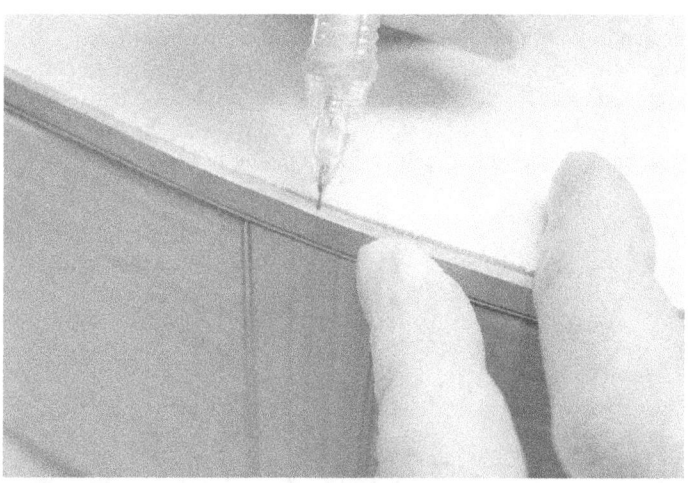

Photo 15-91 – *While it is held in place, the end of the binding is marked at the centerline of the top plate.*

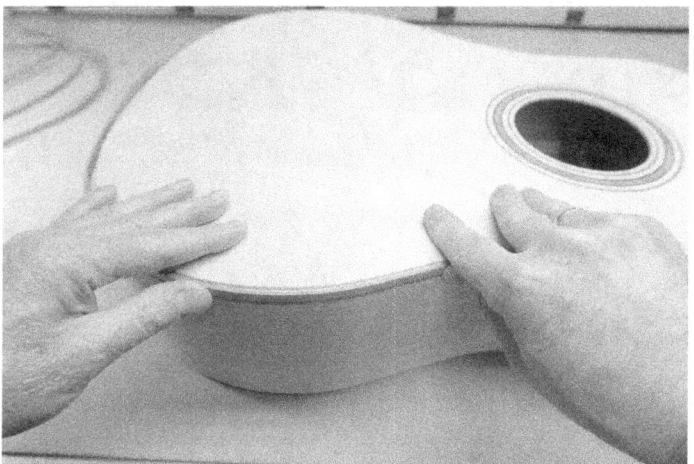

Photo 15-90 – *The binding is pressed and held in place while the hands move down to the tail end of the body.*

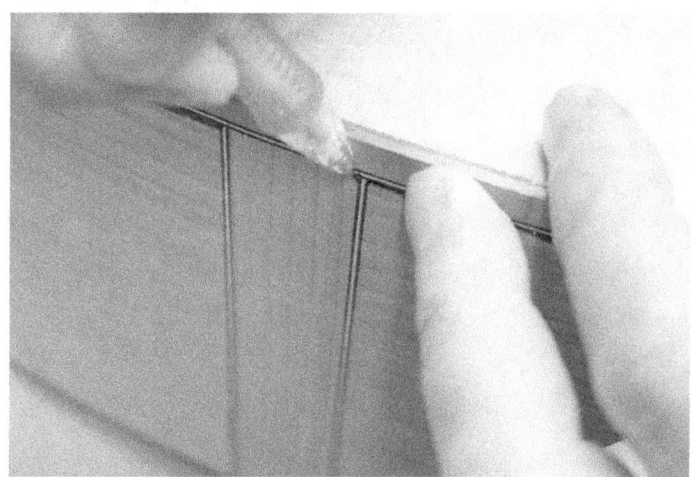

Photo 15-92 – *While the binding is held in place, the end of the side purfling is also marked.*

trimmed square to the sides of the strips. The ends of purfling bundles are either trimmed square or at 45°, depending on the purfling configuration. The cuts on the bindings are conveniently made using a razor saw, but the purfling bundles are generally too small to saw and so are cut using chisels. It is often the case that small fitting adjustments need to be made to these cuts, and these are conveniently done using chisels and small rasps.

Although some of these cuts are made before the part involved is attached to the guitar body, some of them have to be made while the part is already mostly attached to the guitar. This section describes construction of a disposable and extremely simple fixture that can be used for making these various cuts in the binding strips and purfling bundles, before they are attached to the body, or after they are mostly attached.

The fixture consists of a simple small base and a double ended fence piece that can be used to make 90° or 45° cuts. The components of the fixture are shown in **photo 15-86**. General usage is shown in **photos 15-87** and **15-88**. Specific use of the fixture will also be shown in some of the subsequent construction operations.

In use, the fence piece is generally just held in place while the cut is being made. It can also be attached to the base with double-stick tape, which will allow it to be moved if necessary.

1. The base of the fixture is cut from any ¼″ (6.4mm) thick stock. It should be cut approximately 6″ (152.4mm) square. The small size and thin thickness are needed so the fixture can be used resting on the top of the guitar body.

2. The fence part is made from stock that is at least ½″ (12.7mm) thick. It is cut 2″ (50.8mm) wide and 5″ (127mm) long. One end is cut off to an accurate 90° and the other end is cut off to an accurate 45°.

☐ **Gluing the Bindings and Purflings**

There are four binding strips, and they and their accompanying purflings will be glued to the body one at a time. The overall process of doing this is similar for all four, but there are some small but significant differences that are pointed out in the following construction steps.

1. Binding and purflings will be applied to the right side of the top plate first. One of the bent binding strips with side purfling attached is positioned in place on the right side of the top. Note that only two of the four strips will have the side purflings under the binding when positioned here. The fit at the waist is most important, so the binding is moved around until a good fit can be made between the strip and the ledge at the waist. Once this is achieved, the strip is temporarily taped in place with a single piece of tape (**photo 15-89**). If the strip cannot be easily taped into place and does not fit tightly everywhere along its

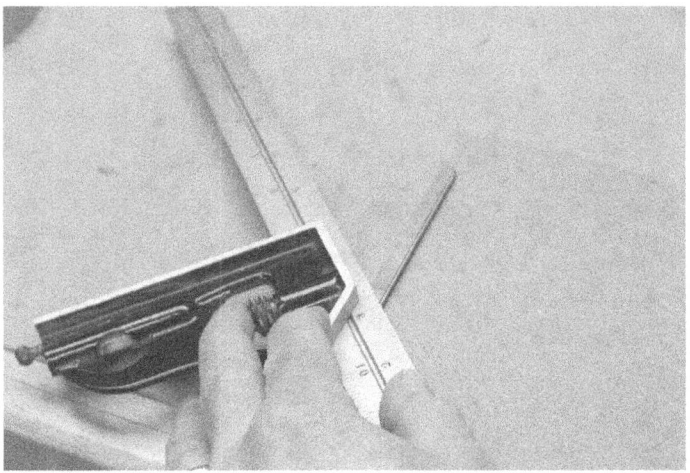

Photo 15-93 – *The miter for the side purfling end can be marked using a combination square.*

Photo 15-96 – *The fit of the purfling miter is checked. It may have to be trimmed a bit for a perfect fit.*

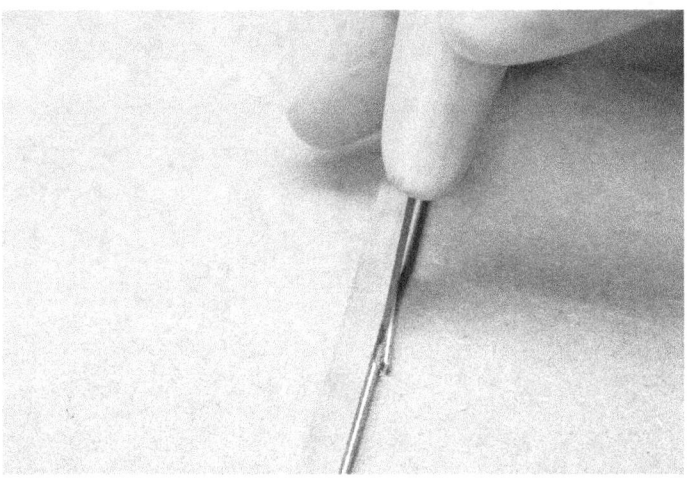

Photo 15-94 – *The side purfling is cut at the miter mark, then the waste is separated from the binding using a small chisel.*

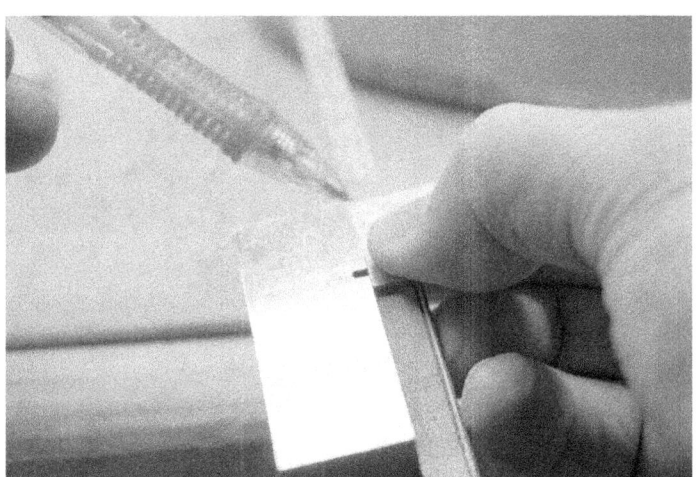

Photo 15-97 – *The end of the binding is marked off square.*

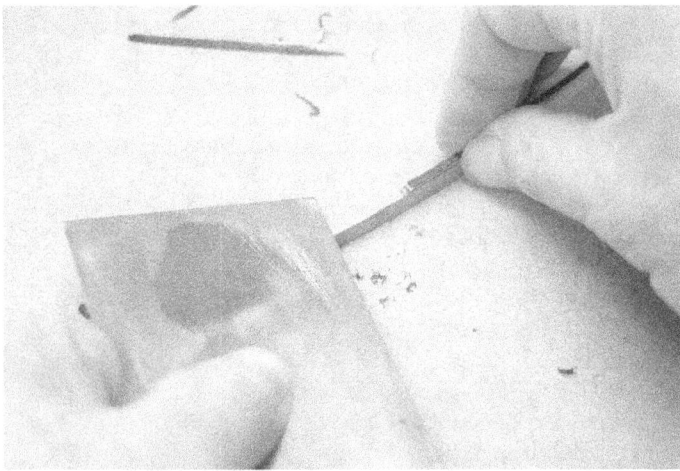

Photo 15-95 – *The bottom surface of the binding is scraped clean of any glue and residue of the side purfling.*

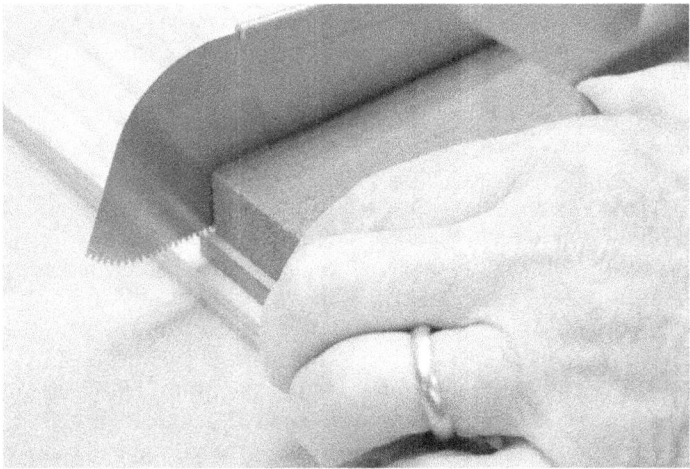

Photo 15-98 – *The end of the binding is cut off square using the disposable mitering fixture and a razor saw.*

length, it is prudent to touch it up dry on the bending iron before proceeding. Since the strips were ganged together when bent, it is likely the other strips will need to be touched up as well.

2. The binding is now marked for cutting at the top plate centerline at the tail end. Both hands are used to press and hold the binding in place, sliding the hands along the edge, from the tape at the waist, down to the tail end, pressing and holding the binding in place all the time (**photo 15-90**). The goal here is to get an accurate measurement of the length to cut the binding strip. While still holding the binding in place, a pencil mark is made on the top of the binding, in line with the center seam of the top plate (**photo 15-91**). If the side purflings will be mitered into the tail graft purflings, then, while the binding is still held in place, the location on the side purfling where it meets the purfling on the right side of the tail graft is also marked in pencil (**photo 15-92**). The piece of tape at the waist is removed, and the binding strip is removed from the body.

3. If the side purflings will be mitered into the tail graft purflings, the side purflings are marked for the miter using a combination square and a knife. The binding is aligned with the edge of a straight piece of scrap and held in place. The combination square is placed with its 45° fence against the scrap edge and the binding strip, at the mark made on the purflings in the previous step (**photo 15-93**). A knife is used to mark the miter cut, on the purfling only. A small chisel is used to cut the miter at the mark (**photo 15-94**). The excess purfling is carefully chiseled away from the bottom of the binding, and then a scraper is used to clean off any remaining purfling wood and glue (**photo 15-95**). The fit of the miter is checked (**photo 15-96**). Any final trimming for fit should be done carefully, removed only as much material as is needed to attain a perfect fit.

4. The end of the binding strip is cut off at the mark made at the body centerline in step 2. That mark is first extended across the outside surface of the binding strip using a small square (**photo 15-97**). The excess is sawn off at this mark, keeping the cut square (**photo 15-98**). The disposable miter fixture is used to keep the cut square. The fit is checked for alignment (**photo 15-99**) and trimmed as necessary.

 The binding cutoff is retained. It may be needed to patch up the bindings in a later operation.

Photo 15-99 – *The fully trimmed tail end binding and mitered side purfling.*

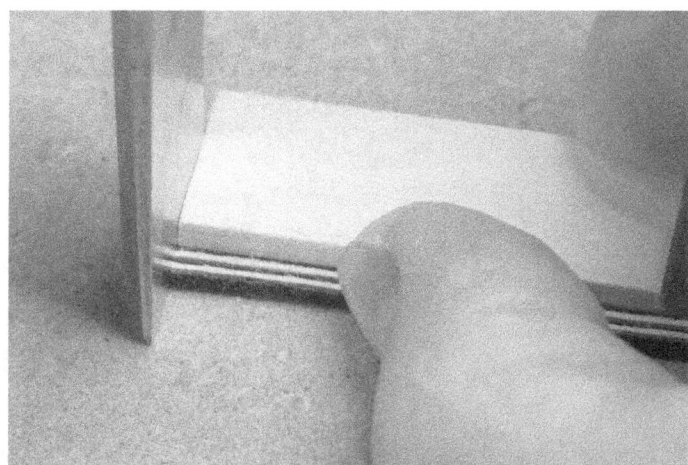

Photo 15-101 – *The mitering fixture is used with a chisel to trim the end of the plate purfling bundle square.*

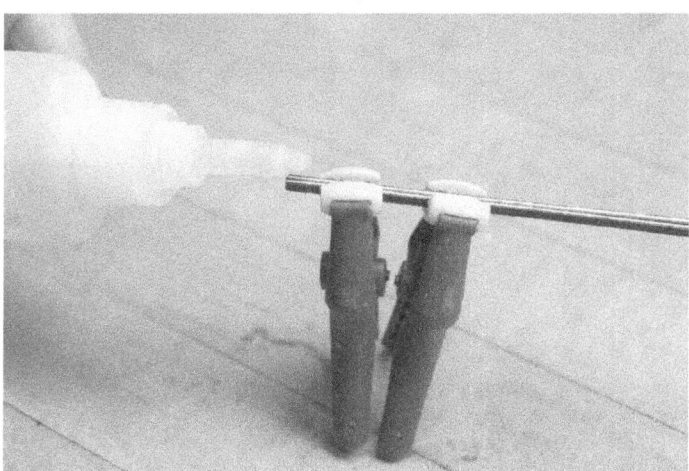

Photo 15-100 – *The plate purfling bundle is clamped dry with glue-proof clamps, and a drop of thin cyanoacrylate glue is applied to the end.*

Photo 15-102 – *If a sturdy tape dispenser is not available, 40 pieces of tape are torn off and hung from the edge of the bench.*

5. The purfling lines that will be used for the top plate purflings are bundled together in order, then clamped at one end of the bundle using small plastic glue-proof clips. One drop of thin cyanoacrylate glue is applied to the end of the bundle (**photo 15-100**) and allowed to cure for a minute. Then the end of the bundle is trimmed square using a chisel and the disposable miter fixture to keep the cut square (**photo 15-101**).

6. As mentioned, 1″ (25.4mm) wide kraft paper tape will be used to hold the binding in place during gluing. Because the binding process requires one hand to hold the binding in place while the other hand is used to fetch and initially apply each piece of tape, it is essential that the tape be held in a heavy tape dispenser that can reliably be used one handed. If such a dispenser is not available, before beginning the binding process

Photo 15-103 – Glue is brushed onto a length of the binding and purfling ledges.

Photo 15-106 – The binding strip is also pressed into place at the tail end. When all is aligned, a piece of tape holds everything.

Photo 15-104 – The lines of the purfling bundle are fanned with the fingers, then glue is applied to a length of the lines.

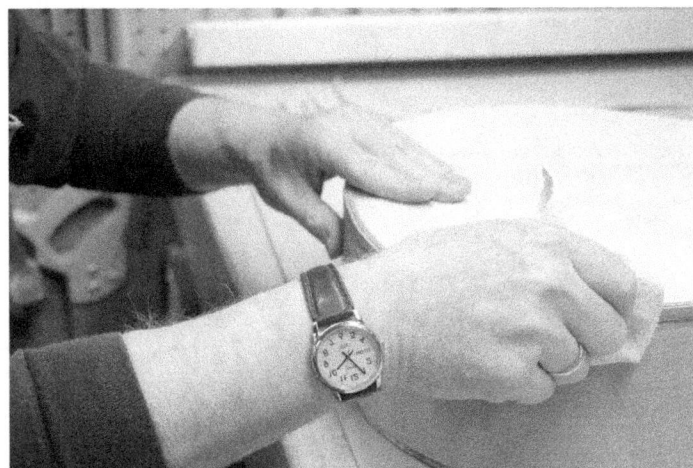

Photo 15-107 – A rag is used like a squeegee to press the purfling bundle and binding in place, and also remove excess glue.

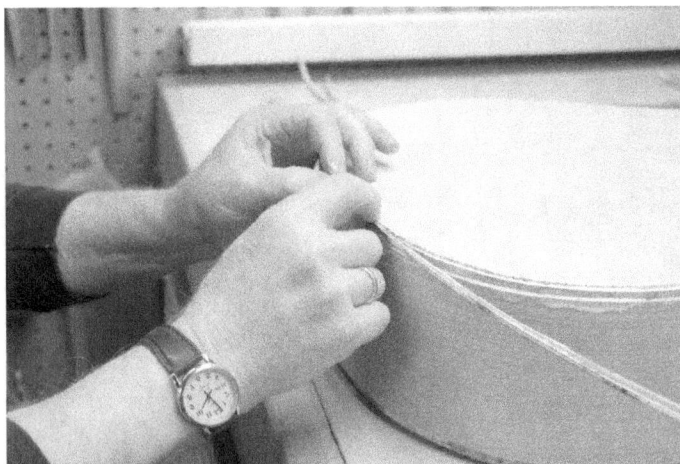

Photo 15-105 – The end of the plate purfling bundle is aligned with the top centerline, and the bundle is pressed into place.

Photo 15-108 – One piece of tape is placed to tack down the end of the section. Then additional pieces of tape are added from the end.

approximately 40 pieces of tape each approximately 4″ (101.6mm) long should be torn off the roll and stuck to the bottom edge of the bench so they will be readily available (**photo 15-102**).

7. The purflings and bindings will be glued and taped into place approximately 6″ (152.4mm) at a time. Glue is brushed into the ledges for this distance from the tail end centerline (**photo 15-103**), which is approximately to the widest part of the lower bout.

8. Starting from the glued and trimmed end, the purfling bundle is fanned with the fingers so glue can be applied that will stick the lines together (**photo 15-104**). Here too, glue is applied to approximately 6″ (152.4mm).

9. The glued and trimmed end of the purfling bundle is aligned with the centerline of the top plate and the bundle is inserted into the purfling ledge and pressed into place and held (**photo 15-105**).

Note that orientation of the purfling bundle may matter. When a dark-colored binding is used, it is traditional that a light-colored purfling line be in contact with the binding and a dark-colored line be in contact with the light-colored top plate.

10. The trimmed end of the binding is also aligned with the centerline of the top plate and pressed into place. If the side purflings have been trimmed so they will miter into the

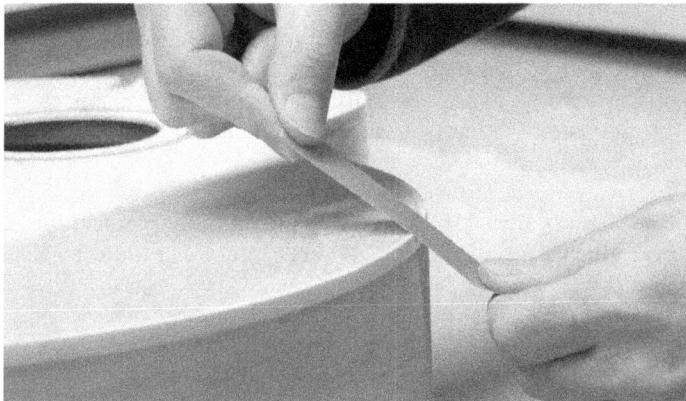

Photo 15-109 – *Each piece of tape is applied to securely hold everything in place without gaps. Taping starts like this ...*

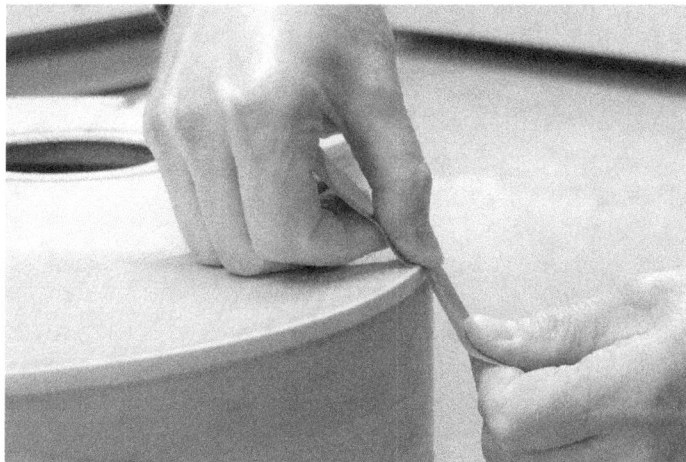

Photo 15-110 – *... then the thumb, positioned over the tape, is used to press and hold the binding in place.*

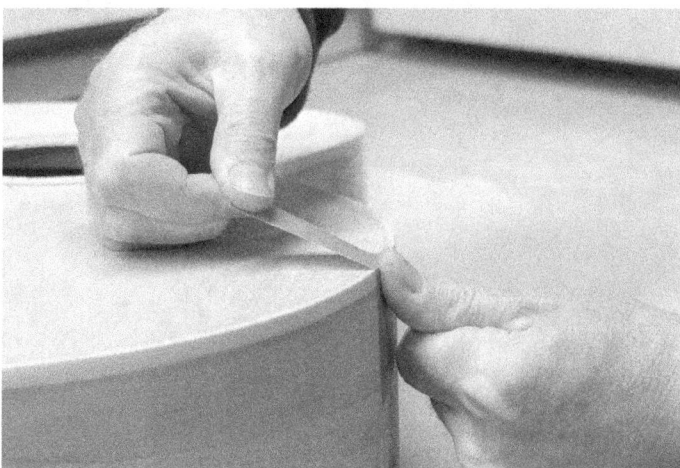

Photo 15-112 – *Then the other end of the tape is stretched across the plate tightly ...*

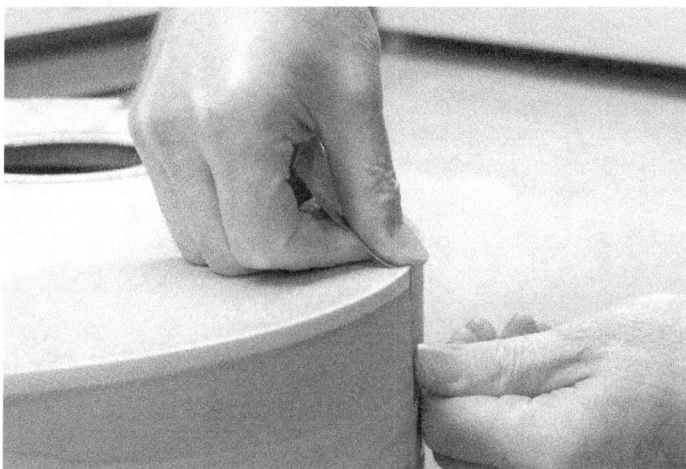

Photo 15-111 – *The tape is stretched downward tightly, and pressed to the side of the body.*

Photo 15-113 – *... and pressed to the surface of the plate.*

purflings of the tail graft, then the end of the binding is slid into place so that the purflings meet in a perfect miter. It may be necessary to wipe some glue out of the way to see the miter joint. When the end of the top plate purfling bundle and the binding are properly aligned, a piece of tape is applied to keep everything in place (**photo 15-106**).

11. A rag, pinched between the fingers, is slid from the body end and used like a squeegee to insert the purfling lines and the binding strip into place, and to remove excess glue (**photo 15-107**). This motion should seat purflings and binding tightly into their respective channels. This is done only up to the point where glue has been applied. Then a piece of tape is temporarily applied to keep everything in place (**photo 15-108**). Care is taken to be sure purfling strips are not submarining under each other or the binding. Taping down the purflings and binding tightly now continues from the body end, working toward this temporary piece of tape.

12. Each piece of tape is applied in such a way as to keep the purflings and binding strip firmly seated against the floor and wall of their respective ledge. The sequence of applying each piece of tape is shown in **photos 15-109** through **15-113**. The pieces of tape should be applied close together, but some space should be left between the pieces so that the tightness of the fit can be more easily seen.

13. After a section has been glued and taped right up to the temporary piece of tape at the end of the section, that temporary piece of tape is removed and discarded, and the glue application, purfling application, binding application, and taping described in steps 7 through 12 are repeated for the next section. The sections are roughly from the tail end to the lower bout; lower bout to near the waist; the waist itself; from near the other end of the waist to the upper bout; and finally from the upper bout to the neck end.

Note that it is always difficult to fan the purfling lines and to apply glue to the channels right at the start of a section. This is done as well as it can be done.

 Special care is taken when taping in the waist. This is the place where a perfect fit is the most difficult to achieve. Also, the pieces of tape here will often overlap

Photo 15-114 – *Binding and purfling have been applied to the entire side.*

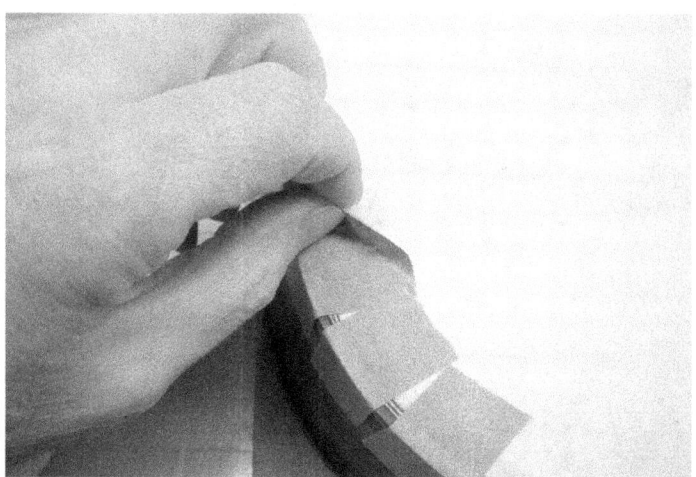

Photo 15-116 – *Tape is pulled off the top across the grain. Pulling it with the grain can yank up large fibers. If fibers get pulled up no matter how the tape is removed, heating the tape first with a hair dryer will help.*

Photo 15-115 – *The work is inspected for gaps. Any that are found may be pressed in place and taped again if the glue is not completely set.*

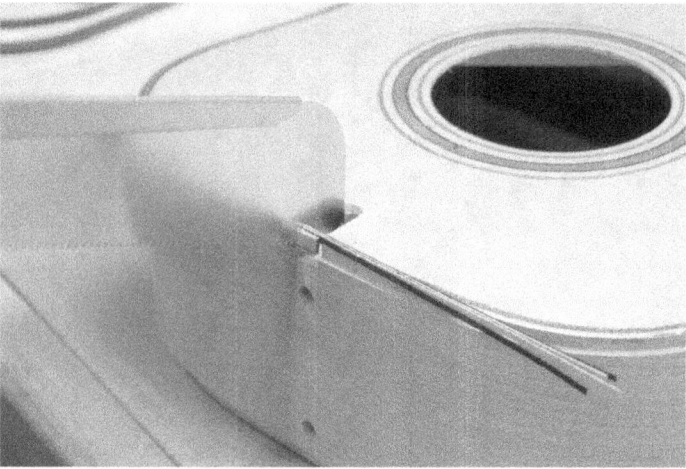

Photo 15-117 – *Excess binding and purfling are trimmed off flush with the trussrod adjuster slot.*

Photo 15-118 – If the side purflings are mitered in, fitting the left side binding and purfling requires a bit of picky fitting work.

each other, which makes it more difficult to assess the fit of the purflings and bindings.

As the neck end is approached, the ends of the purfling bundle and the binding can be snipped off a bit long, using cutting pliers. The ends will be trimmed flush to the sides of the trussrod channel after the glue is dry. A final piece of tape goes over the binding and purflings at the neck end. The completed application will look like **photo 15-114**.

14. The work should be critically inspected for any gaps that are visible between the pieces of tape (**photo 15-115**). If gaps occur anywhere, the tape is removed around the gap, the

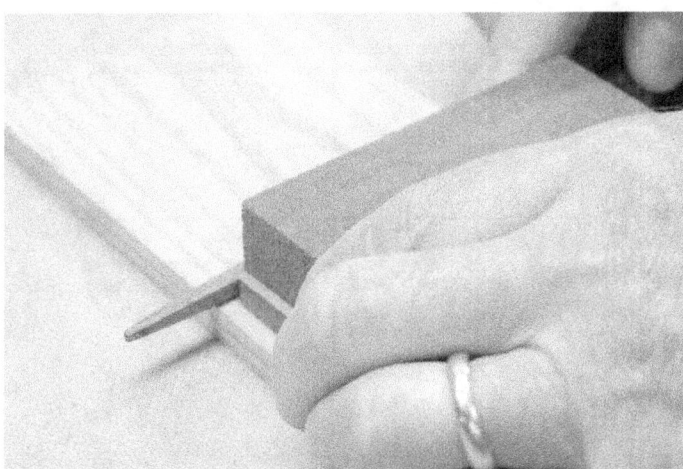

Photo 15-119 – The end of the binding strip can be lightly trimmed using a rasp and the mitering fixture.

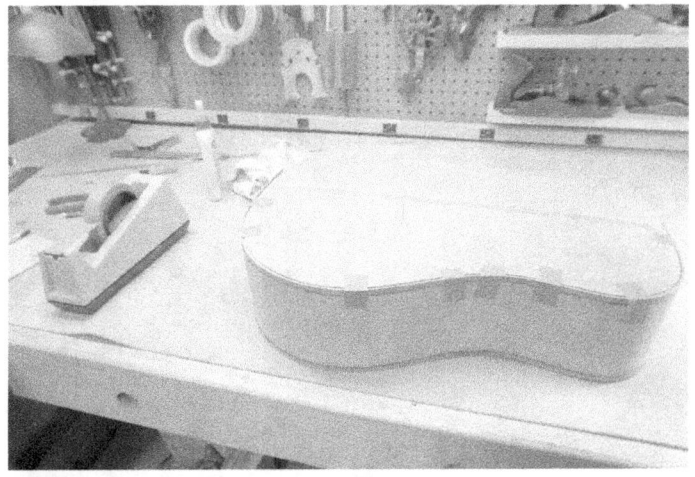

Photo 15-120 – After the tail end of the binding strip is fitted, the entire length of the strip is fitted and taped down ...

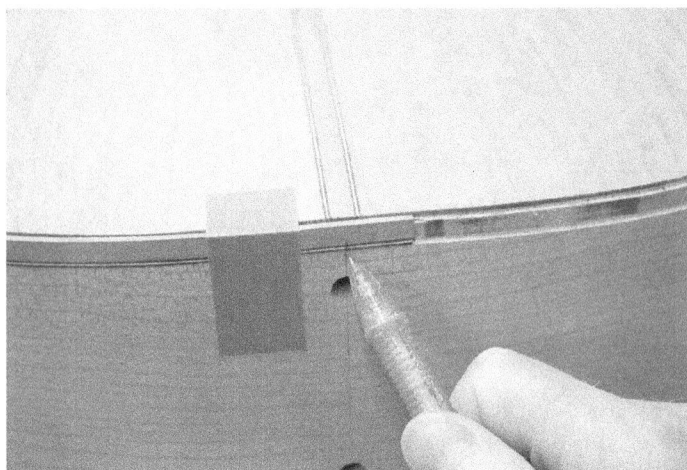

Photo 15-121 – ... *so the location of the neck end can accurately be marked for cutting.*

binding and purflings are pressed firmly into place, and tape is again applied.

15. The glue is allowed to cure for at least two hours before the tape is removed. The tape must be removed from the top plate in a particular way to avoid pulling up big fibers from the plate surface. The end of the tape that is on the top plate is picked with the fingers until there is something to hold on to. Then the tape is pulled 90° to the grain to remove it from the top (**photo 15-116**), and then it is pulled down to remove it from the sides. Pulling the tape in this way will be easy to do at the waist and bouts, but it will generally cause the tape to tear when this is done at the ends of the body.

If big fibers are pulled up while removing a piece of tape, this is most easily fixed before those fibers have been completely yanked away from the surface of the top. A bit of glue is smeared into the channels left in the top by the pulled up fibers, then the tape is carefully pressed back into place so the fibers end up right back where they came from. The glue is allowed time to cure before an attempt is made to remove the tape again.

Photo 15-122 – The tail end of the purfling bundle is trimmed.

A Tight Purfling Joint at the Neck End of the Back Plate

When the back plate purflings will not miter into the back strip purflings, the purfling bundles meet in a butt joint at tail and neck end. The neck end joint is particularly difficult to do because there is no margin for error. If the final purfling bundle is a bit too long, it won't fit, and if it is a bit too short there will be a gap at the end that will require filling. Substituting a slight vertical scarf joint for the butt joint makes the fitting a lot easier.

If the neck end of the first installed bundle is cut with a slight bevel (1), and if the end of the second bundle is cut a bit over long and also slightly beveled (2), the fit does not have to be perfect as long as the two ends are tightly wedged together. The end of the second bundle will stick up above the surface of the binding a bit (3), but the binding itself will cover the small gap under that end. After the glue is cured the top surface of the second purfling bundle end is scraped level with the top of the binding (4). The result is a tight joint with a lot less fuss.

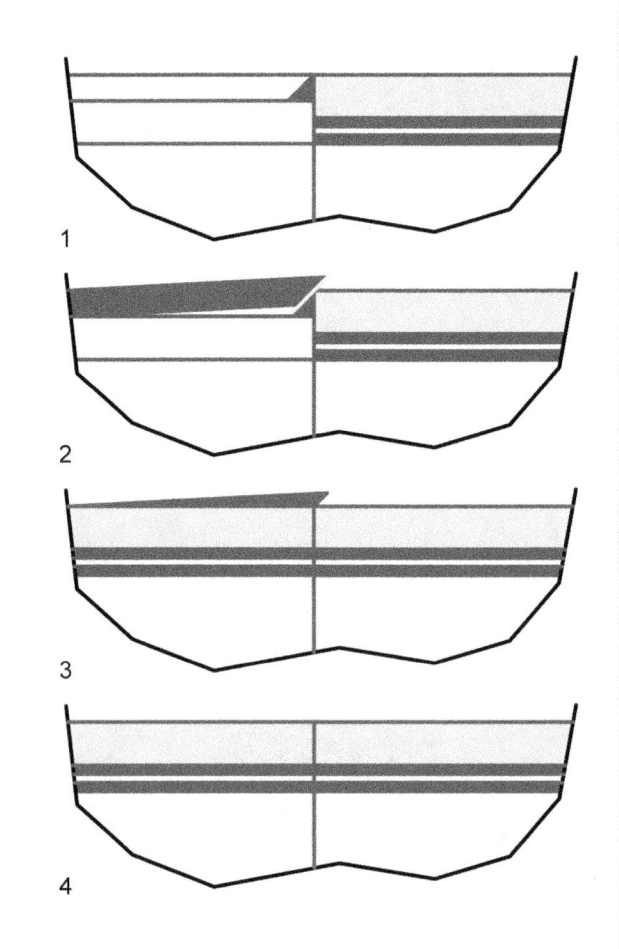

Photo 15-123 – *The bindings and purflings are scraped flush with the plates of the guitar body. Here a card scraper is used.*

16. Now that the tape is off, the fit of the binding and purflings to their ledges can be critically assessed. The primary defects that are possible here are gaps between binding or purfling, or between them and the wall of the purfling ledge or the floor of the binding ledge. Small defects of this sort can be repaired by filling them. This repair is discussed in a subsequent chapter. Gaps that are large enough that they are not appropriately repaired by filling can often be repaired using heat. The bending iron, or a clothes iron, or if one is available, a tacking iron can be used to heat the area over and around the gap enough to melt the glue. Then the binding and purfling can often be pressed into place and taped or clamped until the glue hardens again.

17. A razor saw is used to trim the ends of the purflings and binding flush with the wall of the trussrod channel at the neck end (**photo 15-117**).

18. The left side of the top is bound and purfled next. In preparation for fitting the tail ends of the left side purflings and binding, all dried glue squeeze-out remaining from when the right side of the top was bound must be removed from the ledges and the ends of the right side purflings and binding. This is best done using a knife and small chisel.

19. Applying binding and purflings to the left side of the top is done in the same manner as described in steps 1 through 17. If the side purflings will be mitered into the tail graft purflings, there is one small additional complication with mitering the end of the side purfling and trimming the binding to length. When the end of the binding was trimmed for the right side, it was only necessary to visually align it to the centerline of the top plate. But applying the left side pieces requires a perfect miter between the side purfling end and that of the tail graft purfling, and also a perfect butt between the binding ends. Initial cuts are made as described in steps 3 and 4, followed by picky fitting (**photo 15-118**). It is usually best to trim the binding end ever-so-slightly over long, and then to gradually trim back the cut end, using a fence to keep the end square (**photo 15-119**), followed by test fitting. The trimming can be done using the disposable mitering fixture, and either a sharp chisel or a small rasp with rectangular cross section.

20. The left side of the back plate will be done next. The first thing that was done when attaching each of the bindings of the top plate was to mark and trim the side purflings and the binding at the tail end, as described in steps 1 through 4. This is done here in the same manner.

21. After the tail ends of the side purflings and the binding strip are trimmed, the binding strip is temporarily taped in place so the neck end of the strip can be marked and cut. In order for the neck end to be accurately marked, the strip must fit accurately in its ledge all the way from the tail end to the neck end. To accomplish this, the tail end is fitted and taped down, the fingers

Photo 15-124 – *The bindings are also scraped flush to the ribs of the body. If the card scraper is used, it is held so it does not create a hollow in the middle of the rib.*

Photo 15-125 – *The bindings can also be sanded flush with the surface of the ribs using a hard sanding block that spans the ribs top to back.*

are used to pull and press the binding tightly in place and taped down at regular intervals, moving from tail end to neck end (**photo 15-120**). Then the neck end of the binding strip is marked (**photo 15-121**). The tape is removed and the binding is removed. Then the neck end is cut at the mark, using the disposable mitering fixture.

22. The bundle of purfling lines that will be used for the back plate purflings is assembled and its end is glued as per step 5. If the back plate purflings will be mitered into the back strip purflings, the glued end of the purfling bundle is mitered using the disposable mitering fixture and a sharp chisel (**photo 15-122**). Otherwise the end of the purfling bundle is trimmed square.

23. The binding and plate purfling bundle are glued in place as specified in steps 6 through 13. The purfling bundle neck end is now marked and trimmed. The neck end of the binding strip has already been trimmed in step 21. If the back plate purflings will *not* be mitered into the back strip purflings, the most convenient way to trim the plate purflings at the neck end is with a chisel with its back placed in contact with the end of the binding strip. A slight angle to the cut so the top edge is flush with the end of the binding but the bottom edge is just a bit longer can help improve the fit of the purfling butt joint. See the sidebar.

If the back plate purflings will be mitered into the back strip purflings, they are marked, then mitered using the mitering fixture propped onto the guitar body.

24. Binding and purfling are completed for this side as per steps 14 through 16.

25. The final binding strip to be applied is for the right side of the back. In preparation, all glue squeeze-out is carefully chiseled out of the channels at the ends of the binding and purflings of the left side.

26. The tail end trimming of the binding and side purflings is performed as described in step 20. The plate purfling bundle is assembled, its tail end glued and trimmed as per step 22. Marking and trimming the neck end of the binding strip can be done as in step 21, but here the plate purflings are also fitted dry into their ledge. Pressing and taping everything into place proceeds until the upper bout is reached. Then the purfling bundle alone is pulled into place and the neck end is marked. Trimming the purflings is a bit tricky because they are not glued together. My preference is to trim each of the lines ever so slightly over length at its mark, using flush cut pliers if these are available. If not, the lines can be individually cut using a chisel or knife and the mitering fixture, positioned in a convenient place on the guitar body. After the purflings are trimmed, the neck end of the bindings is marked and cut using the mitering fixture and a razor saw. Again, I like to make this cut ever so slightly over length, and then trim back as required just before the end is actually glued.

26. After dry fitting binding strip and purfling bundle, the tape is removed and the binding and purflings are glued in place as specified in steps 6 through 13. Note that it is wise to stop gluing and taping when the upper bout is reached, then check the fit of the purflings again, and trim as necessary. Then the binding is also checked for length and trimmed as necessary before proceeding. This strip is finished up as per steps 14 through 16.

27. There is generally a lot of dried glue around the bindings and purflings that needs to be removed at this point. Also the top and side surfaces of the bindings and purflings must be scraped flush with the surfaces of the guitar body. This is easily done using a card scraper (**photos 15-123**, **15-124**) or hard sanding block (**photo 15-125**). The edges of the bindings should be kept sharp for now. They will eventually be rounded over, but this must be done *after* the neck is fitted. The area of the guitar sides at the neck end where the neck will attach must be kept flat.

16 Installing the Frets

Construction of the neck is currently not quite complete. A few more things need to be done to finish it up. These include cambering the playing surface of the fretboard, installing the marker dots, installing the frets, and trimming the length of the heel and finishing it off. All but the last of these are discussed in this chapter.

The general topic of fretboard cambering was discussed in the chapter dealing with fretboard construction. It was brought up there because it impacts how deep the fret slots must be cut. Here, the actual cambering operation is described. Although there are a number of tools and jigs for doing this, the simplest way to camber the fretboard to a uniform radius is to sand it using a concave cylindrical sanding block. These are readily and inexpensively available from lutherie suppliers.

Installing the marker dots is a simple process. They are glued in and then sanded flush to the surfaces into which they are embedded. Selection of marker dot materials was also discussed in the chapter on fretboard construction and will not be repeated here.

Fret installation is the major operation that will be detailed in this chapter. As with most lutherie operations there are a number of common ways to do this. Almost all lutherie production shops make use of some kind of arbor press and special cauls to press frets into their slots (**photo 16-1**). This requires more specialized tools and fixtures than may be apparent at first. There are also special fret pressing pliers and clamps available from lutherie suppliers. In keeping with the general principles of the construction process described in this book, the operation described here makes use of considerably more humble tools and fixtures. A plastic mallet is used to hammer the frets into their slots (**photo 16-2**), and various simple holding fixtures are used while this is done. Even when special fret installation tools are used, sooner or later one or more frets will have to be hammered in anyway. This traditional style of fret installation is not difficult to learn.

About Fretwire

Fretwire is a standardized manufactured product. There are three qualities of fretwire that are of concern to luthiers. The first is the bead size. As was discussed in the chapter on fretboard construction, the tang of the fretwire, the part that fits into the slot cut into the fretboard, is standardized in

Photo 16-1 – *Fret installation using an arbor press and a fret installation caul. Each fret is pressed into place quickly using this technique. Some variation on this technique is used in most production shops.*

Photo 16-1 – *Fret installation using a hammer. This is the traditional method of performing this operation. It is not as quick but uses simple and inexpensive tools, and is easy to do.*

dimensions, but the bead of the fretwire comes in a wide array of heights and widths (fretwire cross section is shown in **figure 16-1**). It used to be, certain fretwire sizes were "for" certain instruments,. For example, electric guitars generally used fretwire that was wider than what was generally used for acoustic guitars. These days there is a trend toward the use of wide fretwire for just about all instruments. The fretwire should be chosen based on the preferences of the player, but if the player has no specific preferences, whatever the lutherie supplier offers as their standard size for modern acoustic steel string guitars is a good choice. These will generally be around 0.080˝ (2MM) wide.

There is a meme that says narrow wire provides better intonation but wears quickly, but in fact there are no credible formal studies that show the intonation is any worse when using wide wire. So this really is not something that has to be considered.

The second quality of fretwire that is of concern to luthiers is the alloy from which it is made. Some of these alloys are harder than others. The wire is generally made of nickel silver, an alloy that, oddly enough given the name, contains no silver. This alloy is hard enough to withstand the abuse of metal strings being pressed into it and rubbed across it for a good long time, but it is also soft enough to be easily worked during fret installation and dressing.

Nowadays you can also get beautiful gold colored fret wire, and also fretwire made of stainless steel. The former is harder than typical nickel silver, and the latter is considerably harder. Both of these are highly durable, but are a lot tougher to cut and shape. For stainless steel fretwire, special tools and special installation and dressing operations are required. Lutherie novices are advised to stick to nickel silver fretwire. The construction operations in this chapter assume nickel silver wire will be used.

The third quality of fretwire that is of concern to luthiers is the form in which it comes. The wire used to make modern instrument frets comes on a roll from the manufacturer. When you buy fret wire in small quantities it is usually just snipped off a larger roll. But some lutherie suppliers cut the wire into short 12˝ (304.8MM) lengths and straighten them out. I generally don't recommend buying it like this. The short lengths are wasteful – you always end up with pieces that are just a bit too short to make a fret. But the main thing is, the fretboards of modern steel string guitars have cambered playing surfaces, and it is a *lot* easier to install fret wire that has a bit of a curve to it on a cambered fretboard. The construction information in this chapter describes how straight lengths of fretwire are bent into the needed curves, but that is an extra step that is unneeded if the fretwire comes in its rolled-up form.

Construction

Although there are a number of construction operations that follow, I'm putting a common parts and materials list here. Some of the tools are special-purpose lutherie tools, and it may be convenient for these to be acquired at the same time. Each of these tools is discussed in the construction section in which it is first used.

Materials
    80 and 180 grit PSA sandpaper
    Marker dots, rods
    Medium cyanoacrylate glue
    Thin cyanoacrylate glue
    Cyanoacrylate glue solvent (acetone)
    Wax paper
    6´ (1.8M) fretwire, preferably cut from a roll
Tools
    Fretboard radius sanding block (see text)
    Fret slot cleaning tool (see text)
    Eye protection
    Nitrile gloves
    Micro transfer pipettes
    Diagonal cutting pliers
    Sandbag (see text)
    Plastic face mallet (see text)
    Flush-cutting end nippers (see text)
    Mill file or fret leveler file (see text)

Cambering the Playing Surface

As was mentioned in the chapter on fretboard construction, the radius of camber for most acoustic steel string guitars ranges from 12˝ (304.8MM) to 16˝ (406.4MM), with 12˝ (304.8MM) being the most common. The fret slots have been sawn to a depth suitable for any radius in this range. An 8˝ (203.2MM) long fretboard radius sanding block of the desired radius is purchased from a lutherie supplier for use in this operation. Note that suppliers offer these blocks in various lengths. Shorter ones are not useful for the construction described here. Longer fretboard radius sanding blocks are advantageous, but they are more expensive.

After the fretboard is cambered, the fret slots must be cleaned of sanding debris. This cannot always be done by vacuuming alone. A fret slot cleaning tool is useful to loosen the debris in the fret slots. Commercial tools are available from lutherie suppliers. But a hobby knife blade (or a utility knife blade, or even a hacksaw blade) can be fashioned into a fret slot cleaning tool by grinding off the edge. An unmodified hobby knife can be used as a fret slot cleaner simply by dragging it through the fret slot using the back of the blade.

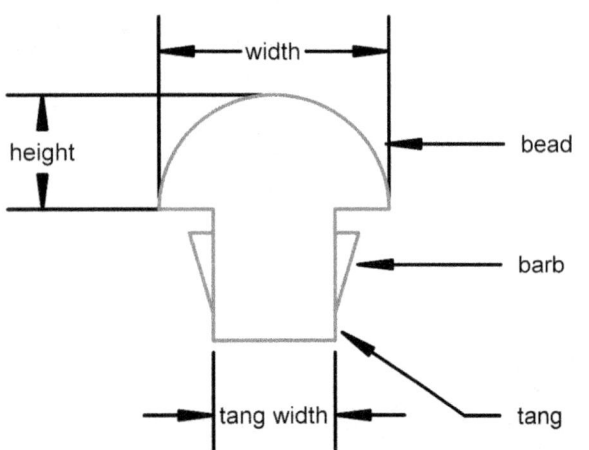

Figure 16-1 – *Cross section of fretwire, showing the component parts.*

Building the Fretboard Extension Support

The fretboard extension is quite delicate and easy to break off in its current state. To support it during sanding of the fretboard playing surface, a support block is built and installed. This can be made of any scrap wood that is approximately 2¼" (57.2mm) thick. If scrap this thick is not available, the piece can be made of laminated ¾" (19.1mm) thick stock. In the accompanying photos the support block is made of three pieces of MDF laminated together.

1. Stock used to build the support block for the fretboard extension is laminated together if needed.

2. A piece approximately 2¼" (57.2mm) wide is cut. One end of this is accurately cut to a 91° miter (**photo 16-3**). This angle matches the angle between the body contact surface of the heel and the fretboard extension of the example instruments. With the neck positioned fretboard down on the bench, the block is positioned on the underside of the fretboard extension to check for fit. It will have to be positioned to one side of the trussrod adjustment nut.

3. A notch is chiseled out of the center of the bottom surface of the block, on the end that contacts the heel, to provide clearance for the trussrod adjusting nut (**photos 16-4** through **16-6**).

4. Although the block can be drilled for a bolt that will thread into the upper threaded insert in the heel, it is easier to simply

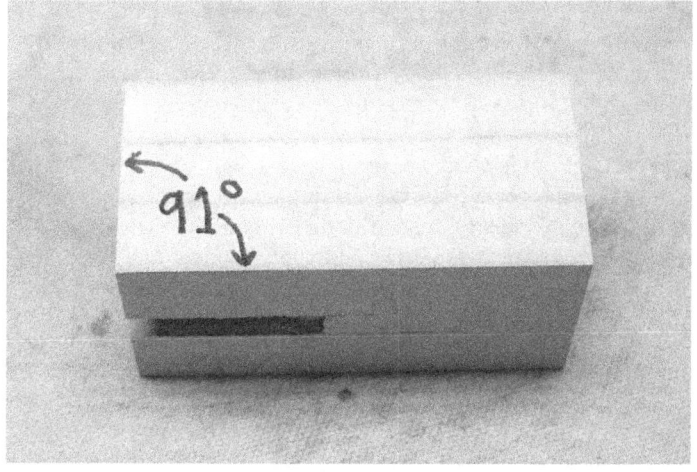

Photo 16-3 – The fretboard extension support block is mitered on one end to the same angle as that between heel and fretboard extension.

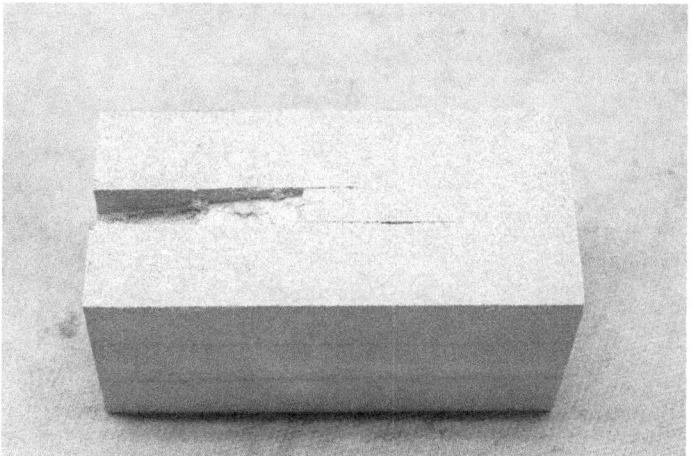

Photo 16-4 – A notch is chiseled into the bottom of the block to provide clearance for the trussrod adjusting nut.

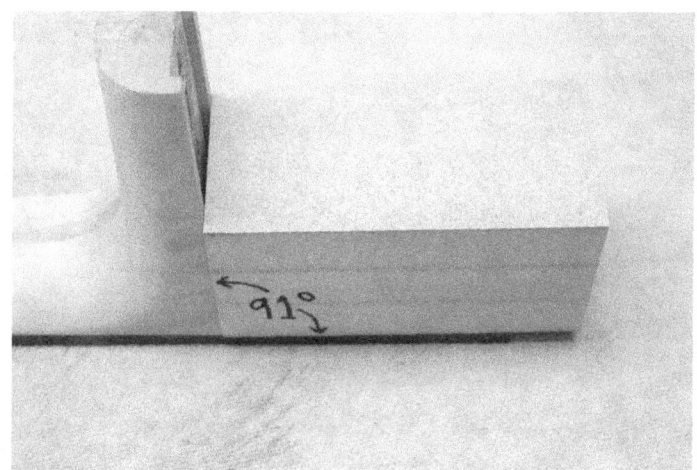

Photo 16-6 – The fitted block in place.

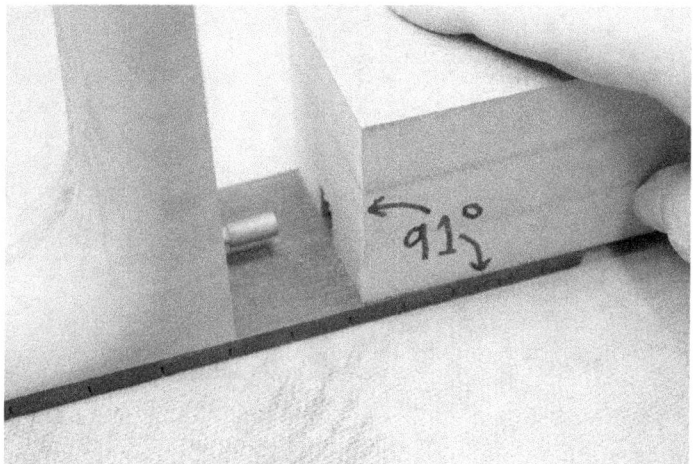

Photo 16-5 – The block is tested for fit and modified as necessary.

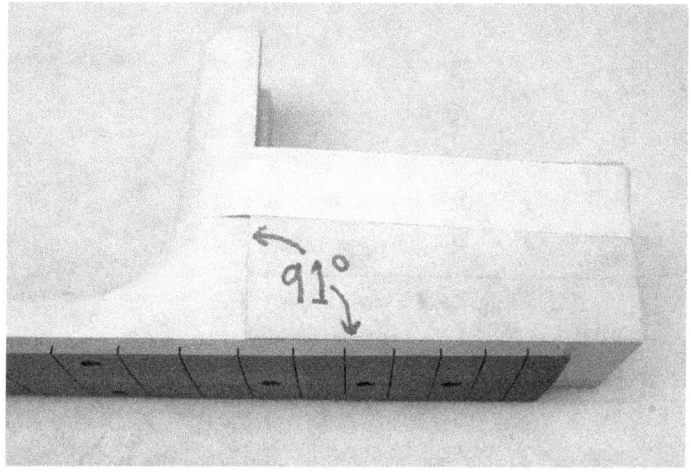

Photo 16-7 – To keep the block in place it can be simply taped to the heel with any stiff tape.

tape the block in place using any stiff tape (**photo 16-7**). Here the same kraft paper tape used to tape the bindings is used.

☐ Sanding the Camber

The camber is sanded using the radius sanding block clamped face up in the vise. The neck is held in the hands, with one hand on the headstock and the other on the heel and also pressing down on the top of the support block. This is not a delicate operation. Still, care must be taken to avoid pressing down on the headstock with enough force to snap it off. Likewise, care must be taken to be sure there is always some pressure on top of the support block, to prevent the fretboard extension from snapping off.

1. PSA sandpaper is applied to the radius sanding block (**photo 16-8**). 80 grit is a reasonable choice. Cutting will not be fast at this grit, but that allows the work to be regularly examined for uneven sanding. The block is clamped in the vise, face up (**photo 16-9**). Pencil marks all over the fretboard playing surface will help gauge sanding progress.

2. The fretboard playing surface is sanded by moving the neck back and forth across the sanding block (**photo 16-10**). The movement should be straight in line with the length of the sanding block. The neck should regularly be swapped end for end. This will help even out any tendency of the luthier to apply uneven pressure, which can result in uneven sanding. Care is taken to be sure of even sanding. The surface is examined regularly, looking for uneven sanding. Because the nut end of the fretboard is not as wide as the body end, sanding goes more quickly there. To compensate, more sanding strokes will be needed farther away from the nut end. If there is sanding unevenness from side to side, the pressure exerted on the neck while sanding should be modified to compensate.

The parts of the fretboard near the edges ends up getting sanded first, while the center part will be untouched by the sandpaper until sanding is nearly done. Sanding is complete when the entire surface of the fretboard is uniformly sanded. Only as many strokes as are needed to completely sand the surface should be applied. Over-sanding will thin the fretboard and decrease the depth of the fret slots.

The camber of the fretboard surface will be obvious when checked against a straightedge (**photo 16-11**).

Photo 16-8 – *A fretboard radius sanding block from a luthier supplier, with PSA sandpaper attached to the concave sanding surface.*

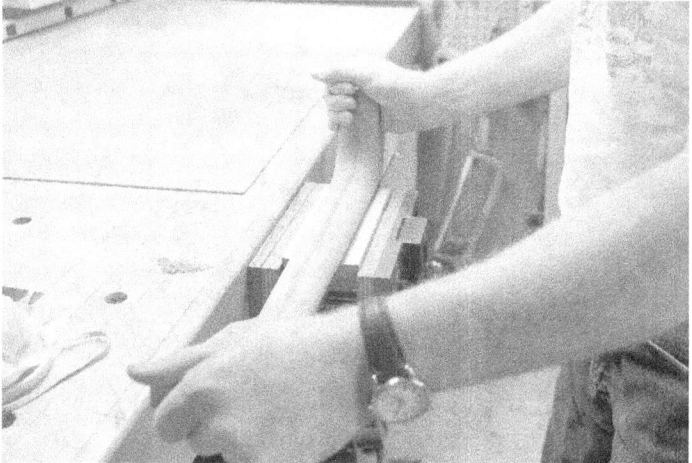

Photo 16-10 – *Sanding the camber on the playing surface of the fretboard.*

Photo 16-9 – *The fretboard radius sanding block mounted face up in the vise.*

Photo 16-11 – *A straightedge sitting on top of the fretboard shows the progress in forming the camber.*

3. The sanding process packs sanding debris into the fret slots. This is removed using a fret slot cleaning tool (**photo 16-12**). After cleaning the slots with the tool, the slots are thoroughly vacuumed of debris.

4. The playing surface of the fretboard is sanded up to 150 grit. This can be done using regular sandpaper on a flat sanding block if an assortment of grits of PSA sandpaper is not available. When sanding by hand, care is taken to keep the side edges of the fretboard sharp, and to avoid sanding any flat spots onto the now nicely cambered playing surface. If PSA sandpaper is available, it should be used on the radius block when doing this additional sanding. The fret slots should be cleaned of debris again once sanding is done.

5. The fretboard extension support block is left in place. It will be used in the following operation.

Installing the Marker Dots

The marker dots for the playing surface and the side of the fretboard (or the plastic rod to be used for side markers) will already be on hand at this time, having been used earlier in the process of drilling their mounting holes. The dots on the playing surface are glued in place using medium cyanoacrylate glue, which provides some gap filling between the sides of the dots and the walls of their pockets.

Side dots are installed using thin cyanoacrylate glue, applied using a micro transfer pipette. These little disposable applicators are available from lutherie suppliers, but they are much less expensive when purchased from scientific and medical lab suppliers.

☐ Installing Playing Surface Marker Dots

Eye protection and gloves are worn when gluing the dots in place. Cyanoacrylate glue is used to glue the close fitting dots into blind pockets. It is possible for glue to squirt out when the dots are inserted.

1. The holes for the marker dots are all thoroughly cleaned of any remaining sanding debris.

2. The playing surface marker dot holes are inspected to be sure they are still deep enough following cambering. This is not likely to be an issue, but if it is, it will most likely show up on the outside edges of the double dot holes. Any holes that have been sanded too shallow can be deepened using the drill press and the same bit originally used to drill the holes.

3. A small amount of medium cyanoacrylate glue is applied to the floor and walls of one of the playing surface marker dot holes (**photo 16-13**). The glue can be smeared around the walls using a toothpick.

4. The dot is placed approximately in the hole then covered with a small piece of wax paper. The wax paper is used to prevent squirting of glue when the dot is pressed into place. The dot is quickly manipulated into place through the wax paper then pressed into place. Care is taken to be sure the dot is sitting squarely in the hole and is not cocked. The wax paper is removed and discarded. Excess glue is removed with a rag.

5. Steps 4 and 5 are repeated for each playing surface dot marker.

6. After the glue cures, the tops of the dots are sanded flush to the playing surface. This is done using 180 grit PSA sandpaper on the radius sanding block. The physical motion used is exactly the same as was used to sand the camber on the fretboard. Progress is checked often. Sanding stops when the tops of all dots are flush with the playing surface, and all 150-grit sanding scratches have been removed from the playing surface.

7. Using regular sandpaper on a flat sanding block, the playing surface of the fretboard is sanded up to 320 grit.

☐ Installing Individual Side Dots Option

If individual side dots are used, they are glued in using a slightly different technique than was used to glue the playing surface dots. The side dots are so small they are difficult to manipulate into place, particularly into a hole containing fast drying glue. So they are inserted dry and then thin cyanoacrylate glue is wicked in around them.

Photo 16-12 – *Fret slots must be cleaned of sanding debris. A knife blade used backwards or a special purpose slot cleaning tool is used.*

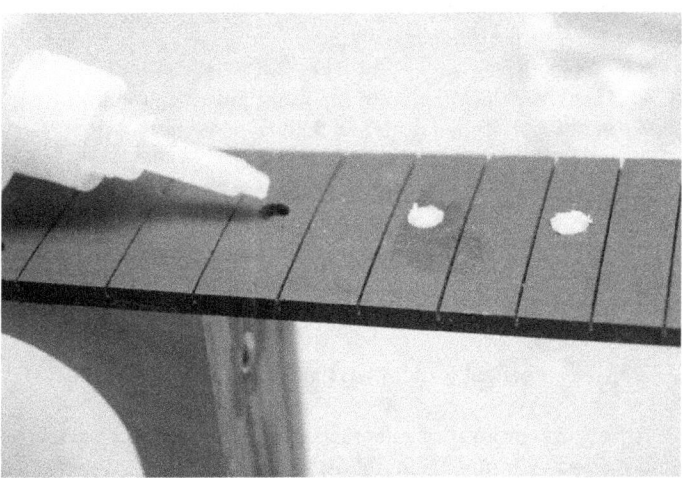

Photo 16-13 – *Playing surface marker dots are glued in using medium cyanoacrylate glue.*

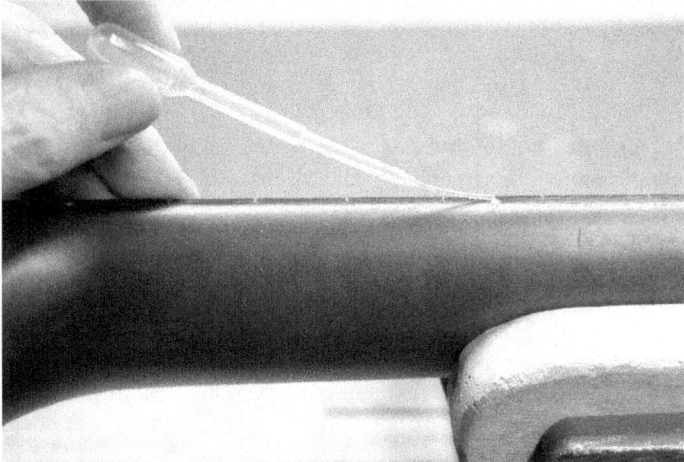

Photo 16-14 – Thin cyanoacrylate glue is wicked around the side marker dots using a micro transfer pipette.

Photo 16-16 – ... and then snipped off using diagonal cutting pliers.

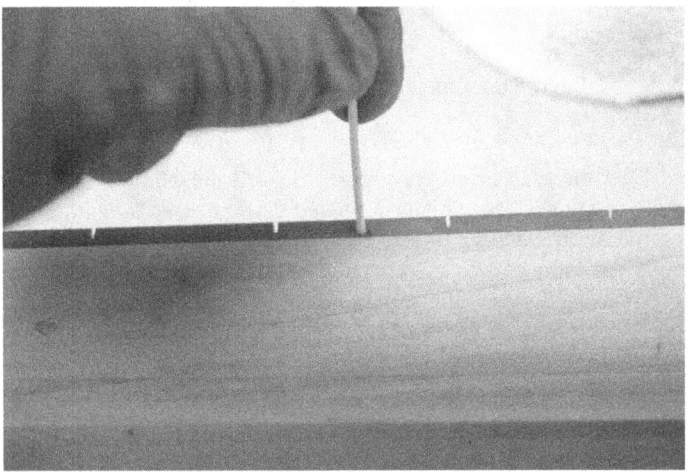

Photo 16-15 – Installing plastic rod side marker dots is easy. Glue is applied, the rod is pushed into the drilled hole ...

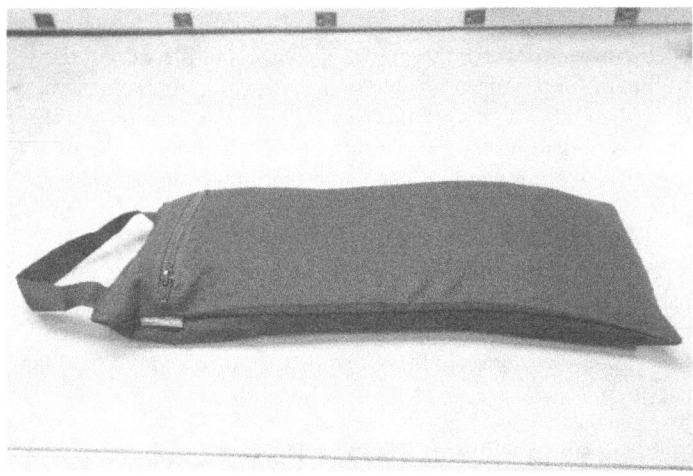

Photo 16-17 – An inexpensive yoga sandbag makes an excellent support for the neck shaft while inserting the frets.

☞ Eye protection and gloves are worn when gluing the dots in place. Thin cyanoacrylate glue is used in this operation. In addition to danger to eyes from splashes, thin cyanoacrylate wicks into any space and instantly glues the parts together, even if the "parts" are human fingers. Cyanoacrylate solvent (acetone) should *always* be on hand when using thin cyanoacrylate glue.

1. The neck is positioned with the fretboard side containing the side dot holes in it facing up and held in place in the vise.

2. A dot is placed in one of the drilled holes and manipulated into place. Tweezers or small needle nosed pliers may be needed to grasp the dot. Once in place the dot is pressed into the hole so its top surface is flush with the surface of the fretboard side.

3. Step 2 is repeated for all the other side dots.

4. A *tiny* amount of thin cyanoacrylate glue is carefully wicked into the space around each dot using a micro transfer pipette (**photo 16-14**). Any surface glue is wiped up with a rag. The glue is allowed a few minutes to fully cure.

5. The side of the fretboard is sanded using 180 grit sandpaper on a flat block, to remove any surface glue residue and to make the tops of the dots flush with the surface of the fretboard side.

❑ **Installing Plastic Rod Side Dots Option**

Installing side markers made from plastic rod is a lot easier than installing individual side dots. The rod end is glued into a hole, then snipped off.

1. A bit of medium cyanoacrylate glue is applied to the edges of one of the side marker holes. The hole should *not* be filled with glue.

2. The plastic rod is pressed into the hole as far as it will go (**photo 16-15**). Excess glue is removed with a rag. The rod is snipped off flush with the fretboard side surface using diagonal cutting pliers (**photo 16-16**).

3. Steps 1 and 2 are repeated for all the rest of the side marker holes. If snipping the rod distorts its end enough to make it difficult to insert in the next hole, the edge of the rod end can be lightly chamfered on a sanding board before each insertion.

4. The glue is allowed a few minutes to fully cure.

5. The side of the fretboard is sanded using 180-grit sandpaper on a flat block, to make the tops of the dots flush with the surface of the fretboard side.

Fret Installation

Fret installation requires some special tools which are not commonly included in the tool collections of most general woodworkers. All the tools that are mentioned here are readily and inexpensively available, although as far as I know not from a single source.

Sandbag

Luthiers use many different things to support the underside of the neck for fret installation. A sandbag is an excellent support for the neck when installing frets. It readily conforms to the contours of the neck shaft and provides solid support under the area where a fret is being installed. Sandbags can be shop made, but doing so requires sewing skills. One of the sandbags I use is made from a section of a leg of an old pair of blue jeans (**photo 16-2**). Inside is a heavy plastic zipper bag containing fine sand. Such sand is available from hardware stores and home centers as sandbox or play sand. Coarse sand should not be used.

Luthiers without sewing skills can simply purchase a sandbag. What are called yoga sandbags (**photo 16-17**) are readily available from yoga and exercise equipment suppliers. They are inexpensive. A double bag should be used. The inside bag is filled with fine sand, closed, and put inside the outer bag. One thing that must be considered when using a yoga sandbag for fret installation is the locations of the bag zippers. If the guitar neck is positioned on top of the zipper of the sandbag, the neck could easily be dented when fret hammering is done. An easy way to avoid this is to load the bag so inner and outer bag zippers are on the same end and the same side of the outer bag, then use the bag folded over (**photo 16-18**), with the zippers on the inside of the fold.

Plastic Face Mallet

A polyurethane plastic face mallet of approximately 12oz (340G) is ideal for use as a fret hammer. The plastic face helps

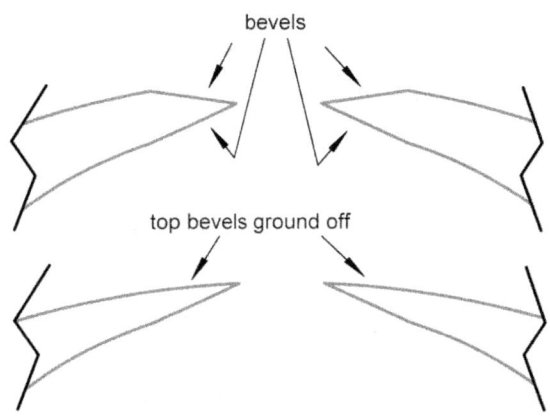

Figure 16-2 – *The cutting edges of conventional end nippers are beveled on top and bottom surfaces, as shown in the upper side view drawing of the jaws. Flush cutting end nippers are made by grinding down the top surface of the tool, resulting in edges that are beveled only on the bottom (lower drawing). The edges are more delicate, but they do cut flush.*

to avoid dents in the fretboard, and the weight is just about right for the fret installation task. These are readily available from hardware stores and home centers. Mallets of this type and size are also available with shot-filled dead blow heads, and these are even better suited to the job because the head does not bounce when delivering the blow.

Flush Cutting End Nippers

These are not essential but are highly recommended tools. They are used to cut the fretwire flush with the sides of the fretboard after the frets are installed. They are also useful for lifting a fret out of its slot. As far as I know, these are not available from typical tool suppliers. But any shop with the facilities to accurately grind metal can readily convert conventional end nippers to flush cutting end nippers. The blades of standard end nippers have been ground with a bevel on both sides of the nipper blades. If the top surface of the nippers is ground down, that removes the blade bevels from the tops of the blades (**figure 16-2**). **Photo 16-19** shows what this looks like.

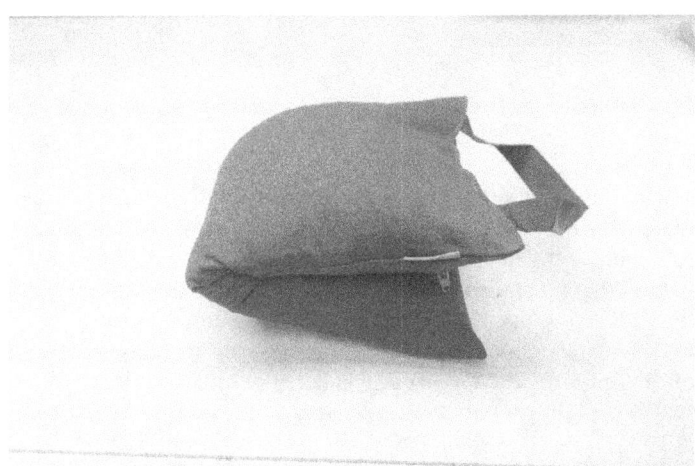

Photo 16-18 – *The yoga sand bag is used folded in half. This puts the zippers on the inside, where they can't damage the surface of the neck.*

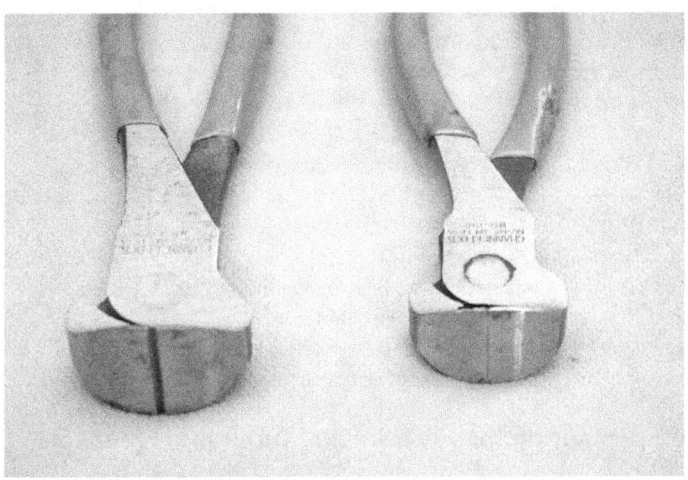

Photo 16-19 – *Conventional end nippers (left) have their top surface ground down to make them flushing cutting end nippers (right).*

Chapter 16: Installing the Frets

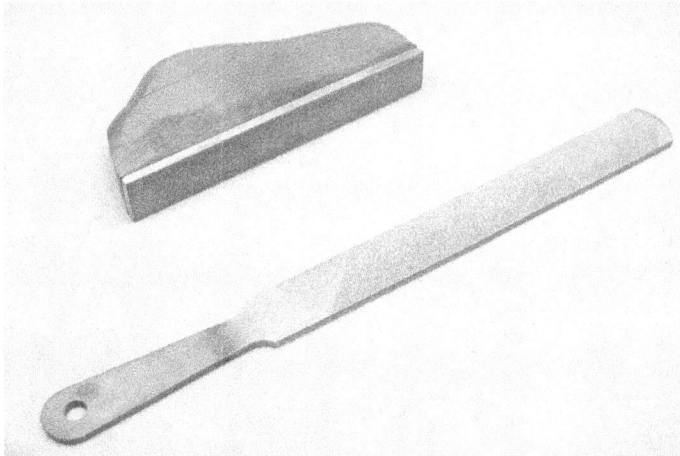

Photo 16-20 – A flat mill file (bottom) or a special-purpose fret leveling file (top) can be used for all fret filing tasks.

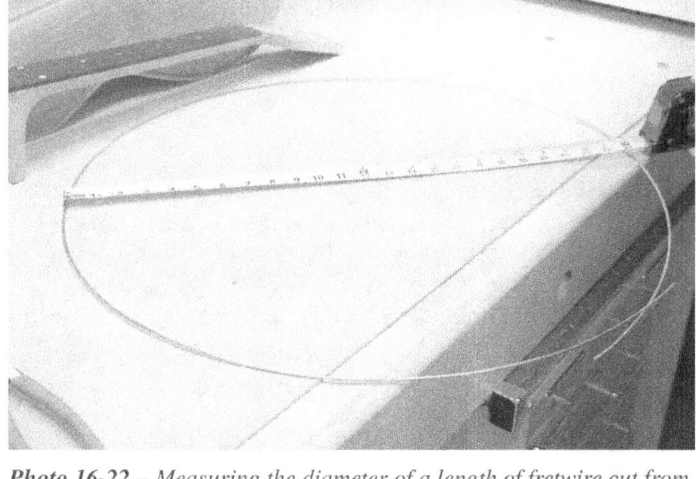

Photo 16-22 – Measuring the diameter of a length of fretwire cut from the roll.

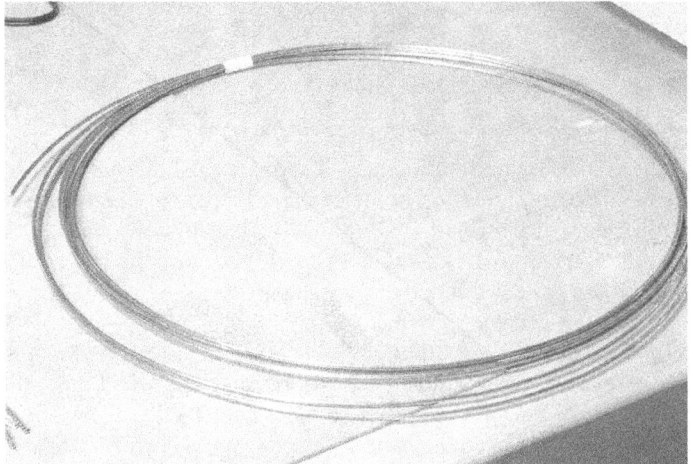

Photo 16-21 – A roll of fretwire.

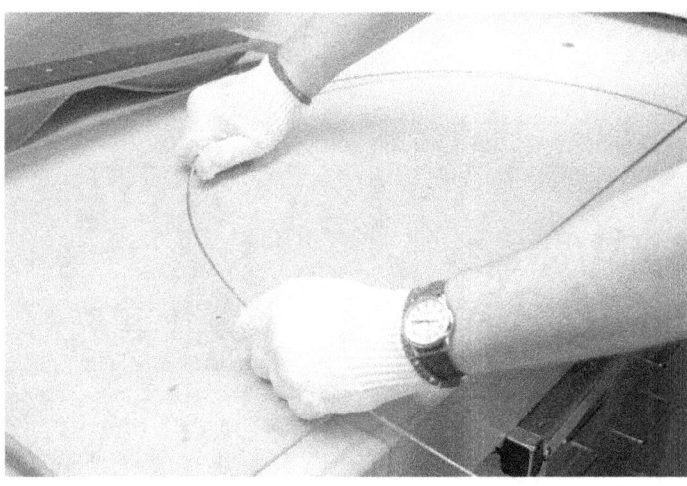

Photo 16-23 – Forming the fretwire to a smaller radius curve by hand.

Flush cutting end nippers are available from lutherie suppliers. They are more expensive than conventional nippers but not dramatically so.

Mill File or Fret Leveler File

A file is used to file the ends of the frets flush with the sides of the fretboard, and then it is used to bevel them. Any flat mill file between 6″ (152.4mm) and 10″ (254mm) works well for this, but the file can't have a handle, which would get in the way. It is useful if the file also doesn't have a tang, which is sharp enough to do damage if the file slips. I use a file that has one end shaped into a kind of flat handle (**photo 16-20**), and that works well in this application. Such files are readily available in hardware stores and home centers.

In use, a mill file without a handle must be held by its edges, which is a little uncomfortable. Lutherie suppliers sell special fret leveler files which have a handle attached to one side. These are easy to hold. These files are not too expensive. It is also possible for a luthier to epoxy a wood handle to a mill file,

☐ **Preparing the Fretwire and Cutting the Frets**

The fretwire has to be cleaned, curved, and cut into pieces before fret installation can proceed.

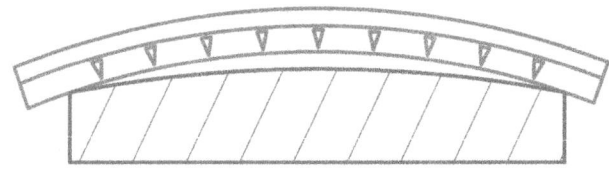

Figure 16-3 – For easiest fret installation, the radius of curvature of the fret should be a little less than that of the camber of the fretboard playing surface.

1. There is often oil of some sort on the fretwire which must be removed. If the fretwire is stored as a roll it is likely that the roll is taped together, and this may leave some tape adhesive behind that must also be removed. These contaminants are easily removed with a rag and some naphtha, paint thinner, or alcohol. Since doing this requires going over the entire surface of the fretwire, the opportunity is taken to look over the wire for dings, crimps, and deep scratches.

2. This step describes shaping fretwire that comes on a roll (**photo 16-21**). See the alternate step below for fretwire that comes in straight lengths.

Photo 16-24 – *A thick dowel with a slot cut into it can be used as a simple form to bend straightened fretwire into a curve.*

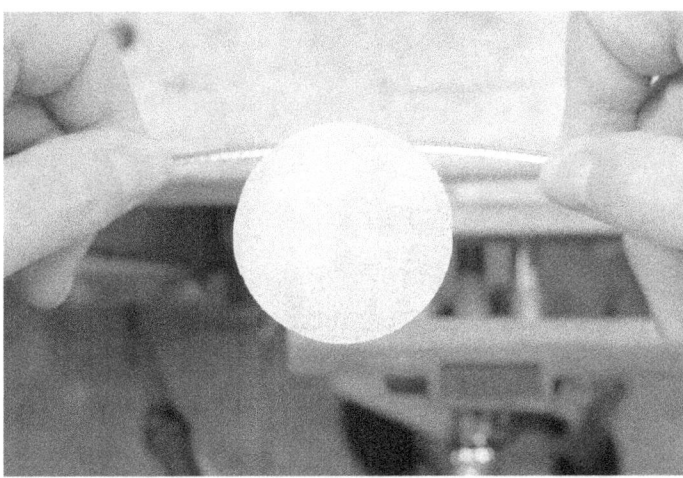

Photo 16-26 – *The dowel is held in the vise and the fretwire is worked in much the same way as the sides are bent over the bending iron.*

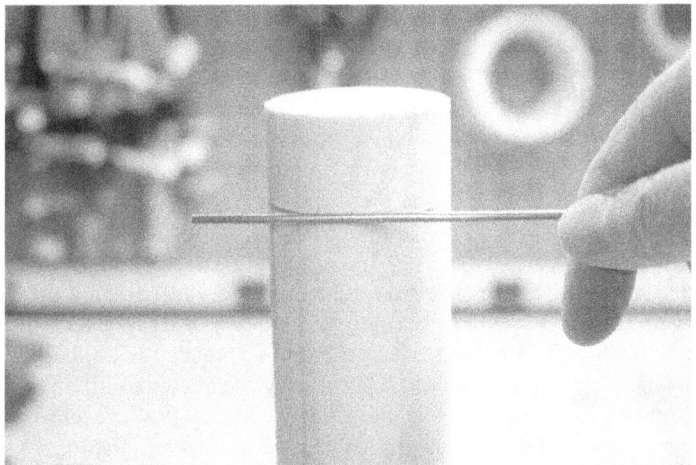

Photo 16-25 – *The slot provides relief for the tang of the fretwire.*

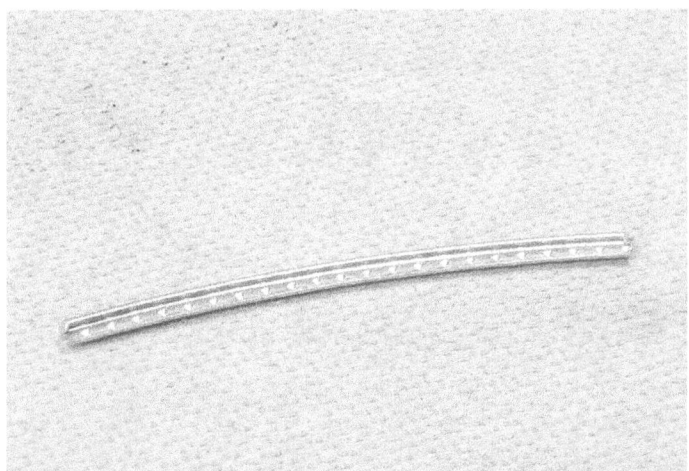

Photo 16-27 – *One piece of fretwire, chopped from the roll. It is a bit over-long.*

Fret installation is much easier if the radius of curvature of the fretwire is a little less than that of the fretboard surface (**figure 16-3**). In **photo 16-22** the diameter of the fretwire roll is 24″ (609.6mm), which makes its radius 12″ (304.8mm). If the radius of the fretboard camber is 12″ (304.8mm), it is desirable to bend the fretwire so the radius of the roll is approximately 11″ (279.4mm).

It is quite easy to make broad bends in the fretwire if it is in roll form. The wire is grasped near one end of the roll in one hand and the other hand grasps the wire at about shoulder distance (**photo 16-23**). The wire can be gently bent to increase or decrease the radius of curvature. The wire is moved through the hands, bending in a fluid motion all the way to the other end of the roll.

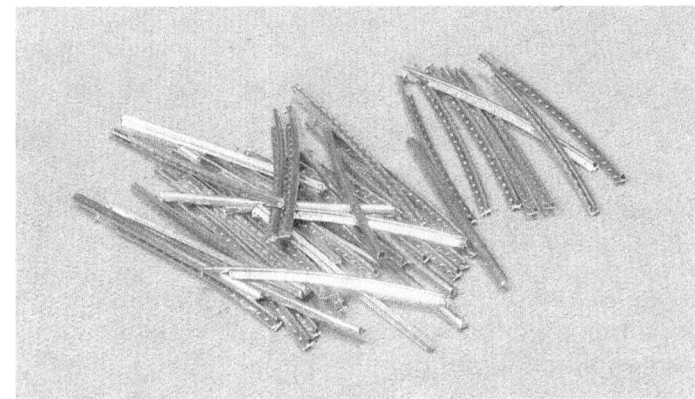

Photo 16-28 – *A pile of lengths of fretwire, ready to install.*

2. (Alternate) If the fretwire comes as straightened pieces, each piece must be bent to a radius slightly less than that of the fretboard surface. This is easily done using a dowel as a bending form, in much the same manner as was used to bend the guitar sides over the bending iron. Just as bending the sides right to the ends of the wood is difficult, it is also difficult to bend the fretwire as the ends of each piece are approached. The consequence of this is that the unshaped ends of the fretwire must be discarded.

A bending form is made from a large diameter dowel. A diameter of 2″ (50.8mm) works well, but even a 1″ (25.4mm) diameter dowel works fine. A single narrow cut is made near one end of the dowel, perpendicular to its axis, and about ¼ the way through (**photo 16-24**), using the bandsaw or a razor saw with a

Photo 16-29 – It is much easier to install the frets if the top edges of the fret slots are chamfered using a triangular needle file. The frets will fit better, too.

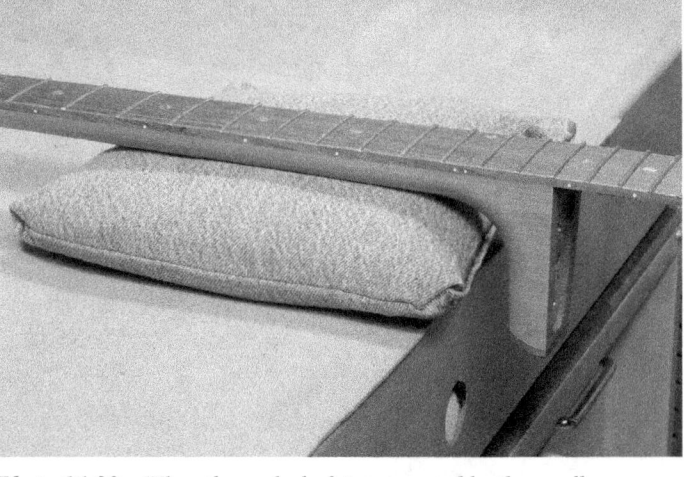

Photo 16-30 – When the neck shaft is supported by the sandbag, care must be taken to be sure there will be no pressure on the headstock or the heel. Here the heel is hanging over the front of the bench.

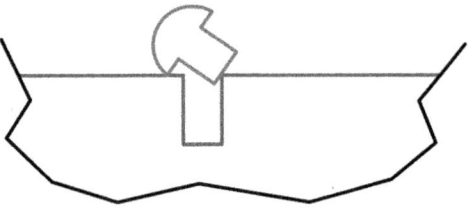

Figure 16-4 – When fret installation is started, care must be taken to prevent the fret from tipping over while hammering it. Hammering a tipped fret will result in a difficult-to-remove dent on the fretboard surface, caused by the edge of the bead of the fret.

☐ **Installing the Frets**

Eye protection is worn while installing frets. The fret ends are sharp, and pieces of the frets or the frets themselves can shoot off unexpectedly in any direction.

1. The fret slots are checked for adequate depth. Although they were originally sawn to an appropriate depth, the process of cambering the playing surface may have reduced the thickness of the slots. If this happens, it is usually at the edges at the body end of the neck. Any slots that are too shallow are sawn again, using the same sawing techniques used when the fretboard was originally slotted. Usually the entire slot does not need to be sawn, just a section near the edge. Care is taken to make the cuts only as deep as is necessary.

2. A triangular needle file is used to *lightly* chamfer the edges of each fret slot (**photo 16-29**). Doing this makes it much easier to insert the tangs of the frets, and it also ensures that the undersides of the fret crowns end up sitting right on top of the fretboard playing surface. Care must be taken not to mar the surface of the fretboard with the file.

3. Fretting proceeds from one end of the fretboard to the other. I like to start at the nut end. The neck shaft underneath the fret to be installed is supported by the sandbag (**photo 16-30**). Each blow of the fretting hammer will push the neck lower into the sandbag, so it is important that there is enough clearance under the headstock and the heel to prevent them from coming into

kerf a bit wider than the thickness of the fret tang and barbs. This slot provides relief for the fretwire tang while bending (**photo 16-25**). Each piece of fretwire is moved across the dowel from one end to the other while constant bending pressure is applied (**photo 16-26**). A few passes may be necessary to bend each piece to a radius slightly smaller than that of the fretboard camber.

3. The fretwire is cut into 2½″ (63.5mm) to 3″ (76.2mm) long pieces (**photos 16-27, 16-28**) using side cutting pliers or end nippers. One piece is needed for each fret slot. The example instruments have 20 frets. Note that the ends of the fretwire roll (or the ends of the individual lengths if the fretwire was purchased this way) will not be properly curved for use, and so must be discarded.

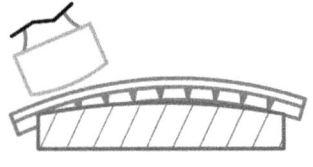 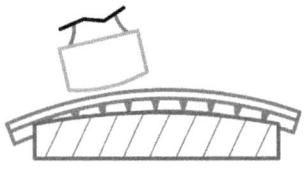 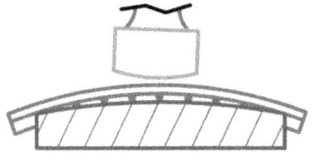 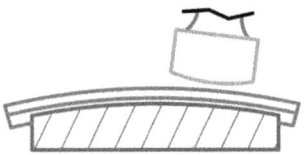

Figure 16-5 – Chasing the fret in, working left to right. This technique helps to encourage even insertion of the tang along the entire length of the fret, and discourages the tendency for the end of the fret opposite from where the hammering is going on from popping out of the slot.

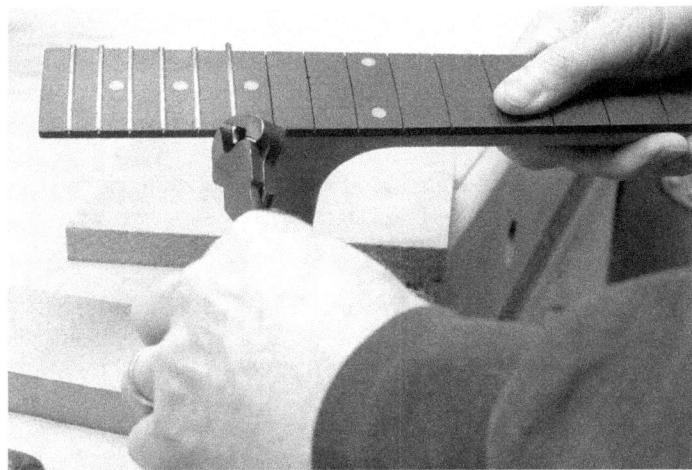

Photo 16-31 – After a fret is installed, its ends are cut flush to the sides of the fretboard using flush-cutting end nippers.

Photo 16-32 – The heel is supported on a pad on the bench when frets are hammered into the slots directly over the heel.

contact with the bench top during fretting. One way to be sure the heel is clear is to hang it off the front of the bench.

4. It is pretty simple to tap in the frets, but it is one of those operations that is a bit awkward at first. One tip about hammering. Most folks' only experience comes from hammering in nails, where the idea is to pound the suckers in with as few macho whacks as possible. A bit more finesse is required here, and a lot of small taps work better than trying to bludgeon the fret in with a couple of crushing blows. To get the fret started, it is held in position with one hand and tapped down with the mallet on one end to get the tang started in the slot. Once the tang is seated on one end, the luthier's fingers can be taken out of the way so the fret can be tapped all along its length.

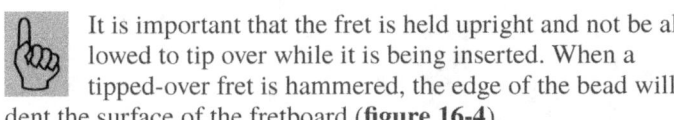 It is important that the fret is held upright and not be allowed to tip over while it is being inserted. When a tipped-over fret is hammered, the edge of the bead will dent the surface of the fretboard (**figure 16-4**).

I'm left-handed, so I start on the left side of the fretboard, but work can be started on whichever side is comfortable. Fret insertion involves tapping and moving the mallet with each tap toward the other side of the fret (**figure 16-5**). This process is called *chasing*. The fret should go deeper into the slot with each tap. If the starting end begins to pop out of the slot, it is hammered back down and chasing starts over again, tapping along the length of the fret. Once the other end is reached, direction is reversed, tapping back to the original end. This back and forth tapping is continued until the entire length of the fret is firmly seated in the slot. If at any time an end pops out or starts to pop out, it is knocked back in, held in place with a finger, and then chasing proceeds from that end. It doesn't take long to get the hang of this, and once this happens the luthier automatically starts to increase the strength of the mallet blows, resulting in a fully seated fret with fewer taps and in much less time. This is one of those mechanical skills where it doesn't take too long to become an expert.

Problems with frets not staying in are almost always caused by one of the following:

- the fret not being originally bent a little tighter than the radius of the fretboard. If the fret is originally curved shallower than the fingerboard it is nearly impossible to get the ends to stay in;

- lack of solid support under the neck, directly under where the hammering is happening;

- junk in the fret slot;

- pounding too hard.

5. Frets should be installed one at a time. After a fret is fully inserted, a good look at the fret is taken, along its length from both sides, to be sure it is well seated and fully in contact with the surface of the fretboard. Magnification may be necessary. Also looked at are the frets that have already been installed that are near the one just put in. These sometimes pop up, especially on the fretboard extension, which is quite flexible. If a fret is not fully seated, it is hammered some more. Particular attention is paid to the ends of the frets. If a fret won't go in all the way, it is looked at carefully while hammering it at that spot. If the hammer blows seat it, but it springs back out, chasing the hammer blows from side to side of that spot in an attempt to straighten that length of the fret may result in seating.

Another possibility is to glue down a lifting fret section with thin cyanoacrylate glue. The tiniest drop, delivered with a micro transfer pipette at the gap between fret bead and fretboard surface, will wick under the fret and into the slot, and a quick clamping will secure it for the minute it takes for the glue to cure.

If more hammering or gluing doesn't work, the fret can be removed using flush ground nippers; a new piece of fret wire can be cut, and installation can be attempted again. When a new fret is installed in a slot that previously had a fret in it, care must be taken to be sure the barbs of the new fret do *not* drop into the depressions left by the old fret's barbs.

If a fret won't go all the way in and mallet blows at that spot won't seat it at all, then there is debris in the slot or the slot is too shallow. In either case the fret will have to be removed and the problem corrected before insertion can be tried again, always using a new piece of fret wire.

If a fret will not stay seated because its slot is worn too wide, bottom of the tang can be widened by supporting the fret upside down on some hard surface anvil and lightly tapping the bottom of the tang with a ball peen hammer along its entire length.

6. The overhanging fret ends are chopped off flush to the sides of the fretboard after each fret is installed. This is done using flush cutting end nippers (**photo 16-31**).

7. The frets over the shaft of the neck up to fret 11 or 12 are all installed following steps 3 through 6.

8. When installing the frets that are over the heel (13, and possibly 12) the bottom of the heel must be supported. It can simply be rested on the bench top with some padding underneath (**photo 16-32**). The fret(s) is installed following construction steps 3 through 6.

Note that fret 14 is right at the edge of the heel. Attempts to install this fret with just the heel end supported is likely to snap the fretboard extension off. Step 9 below should be used when installing this fret.

9. Frets 14 through 20 are installed with support directly under the fretboard extension. Two pieces of MDF scrap can be used for this purpose (**photo 16-33**). Two pieces are needed here so they can be separated a bit to provide space for the trussrod adjustment nut. The MDF pieces are placed at the edge of the bench, so the heel and shaft of the neck can hang over the front of the bench during installation of these frets.

Note that frets over the extension may not seat well simply because the underside of the extension is not yet glued to anything and can bend down, opening up the fret slots a bit. If the frets over the extension can be hammered into place and stay in place while the extension is being held flat against the two supporting boards then they will likely stay in place once the fretboard extension is glued to the body, too.

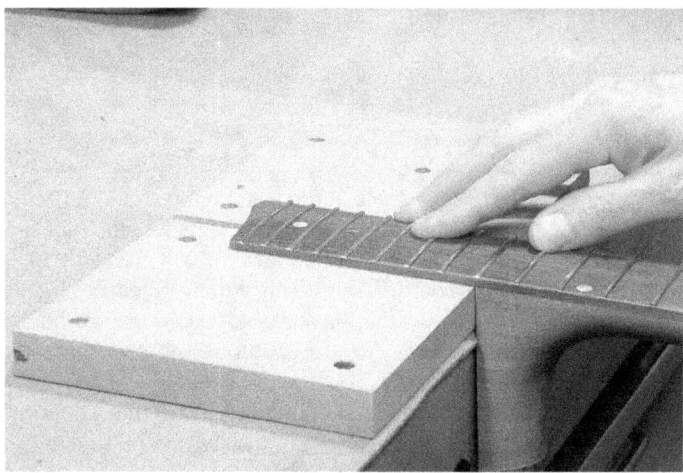

Photo 16-33 – Two pieces of MDF scrap are used to support the fretboard extension when frets are installed in the slots there.

Photo 16-35 – ... or a special fret leveling file with a convenient handle can be used for this and other fret filing jobs.

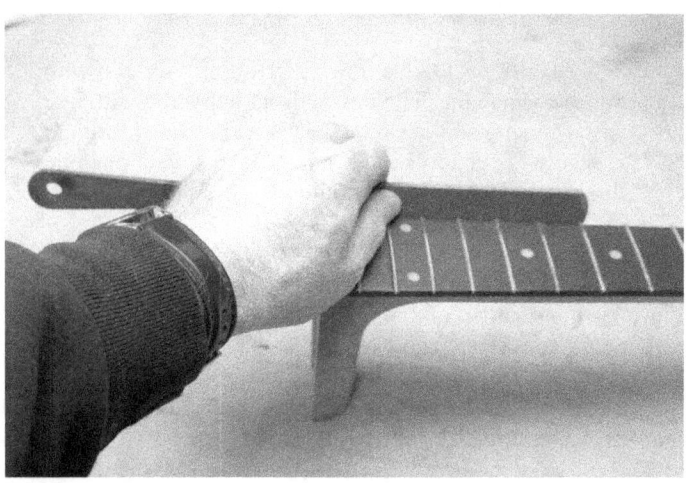

Photo 16-34 – After all frets are installed and checked, the ends are filed flush to the sides of the fretboard. Any flat mill file can be used ...

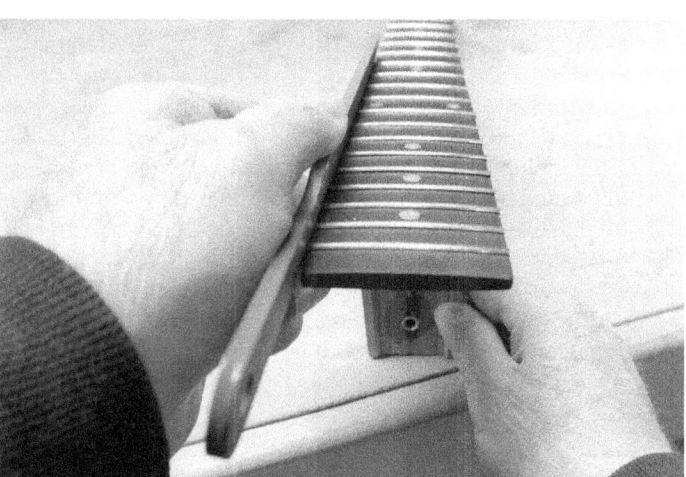

Photo 16-36 – The fret ends are beveled using the mill file or the special fret leveling file.

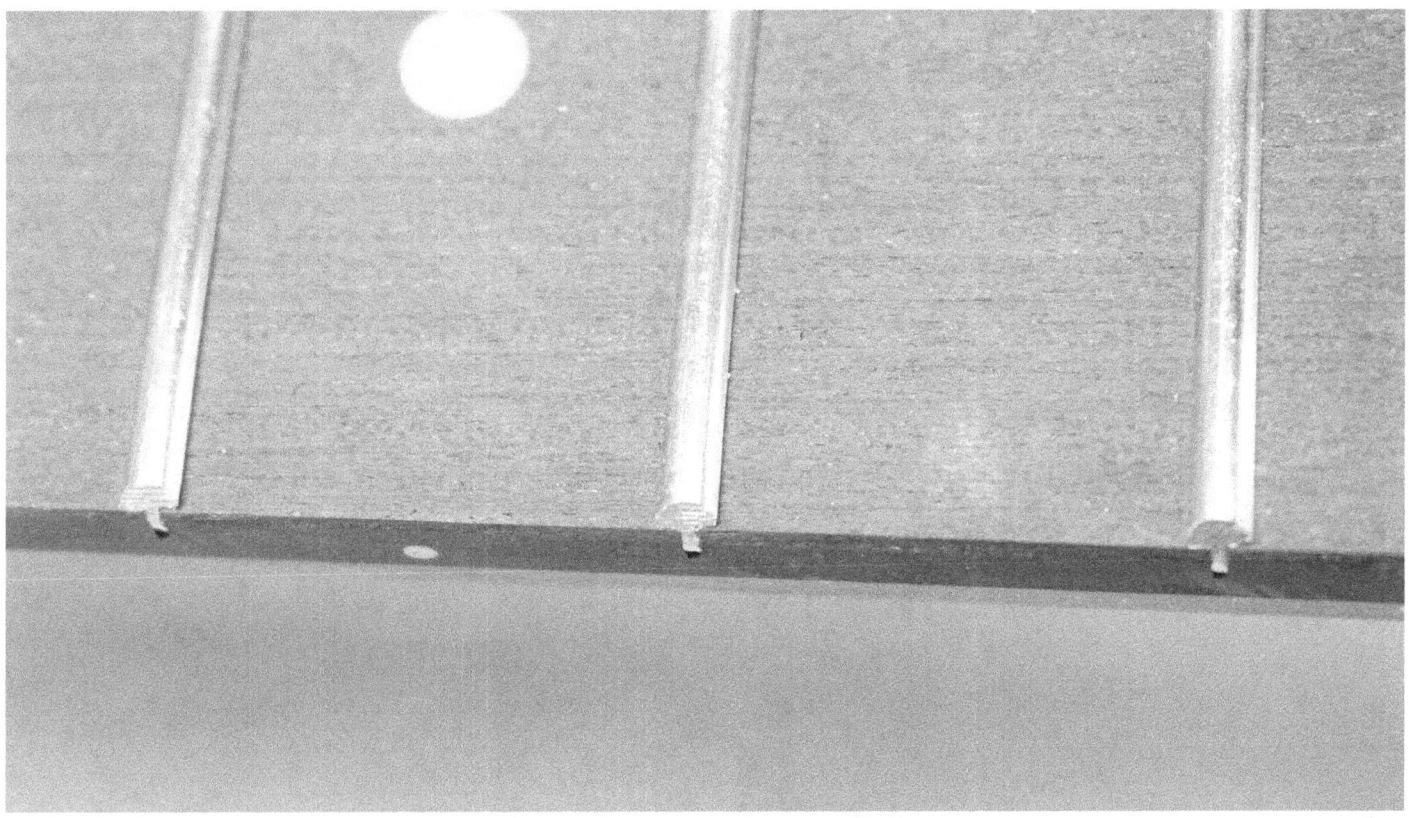

Photo 16-37 – Beveled fret ends. Note that beveling stops before the edge of the fretboard starts to get chamfered.

☐ Filing the Fret Ends

The ends of the frets are sharp and jagged, so the next step is to file them flush with the sides of the fingerboard and then bevel them a bit.

1. Either a flat mill file (**photo 16-34**) or a special fret leveler tool (**photo 16-35**) is used to file the fret ends flush with the fingerboard sides. In this step it is just the fret ends that are filed. Filing the sides of the fretboard is avoided. Luckily, mill files don't work too well when they are in broad contact with a flat surface like the side of the fretboard, so there is little chance of abrading the wood. But even if this happens, it can always be cleaned up with a little sandpapering. It's actually easy to know when the file is no longer just filing fret wire but is also in contact with the wood. While filing only metal, the file can be felt chattering in the hand as it crosses over the fret ends, and it makes a kind of chirpy sound while it does it. Once the fret ends are flush with the fretboard sides, the chattering sensation and the chirpy sound stop.

2. After the ends are filed flush, they are filed again, this time to put a slight bevel on the fret ends. The operation is the same as filing the ends flush, only the file is held tipped into the fretboard at a slight angle (**photo 16-36**). Different luthiers use different angles of fret end bevel. Anywhere from 15° to 40° from vertical is common. My preference is to keep the angle small. Beveling too much makes for an instrument that is difficult to play. It is easy to bend the string right off the side of the fret if the bevel is too great.

More care must be taken here not to file the wood. The file is coming down on the edge of the fretboard, and it is not desirable to file a flat here. Again, the technique to know when to stop filing is to sense the way the file feels, and to listen to the sound it makes. When the chattering and chirping stop, it is time to stop filing. Filed fret end bevels are shown in **photo 16-37**.

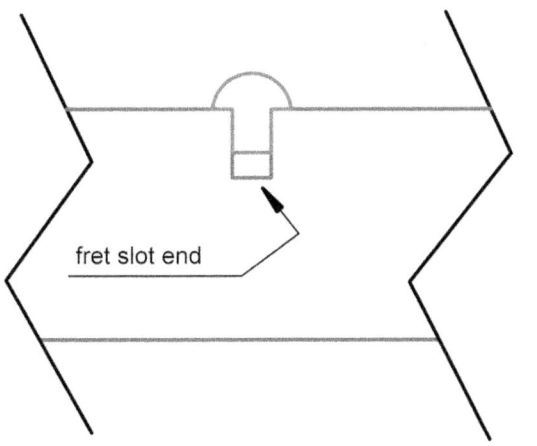

Figure 16-6 – The hole at each fret end between the bottom of the tang and the floor of the fret slot must be filled with putty of the same color as the fretboard.

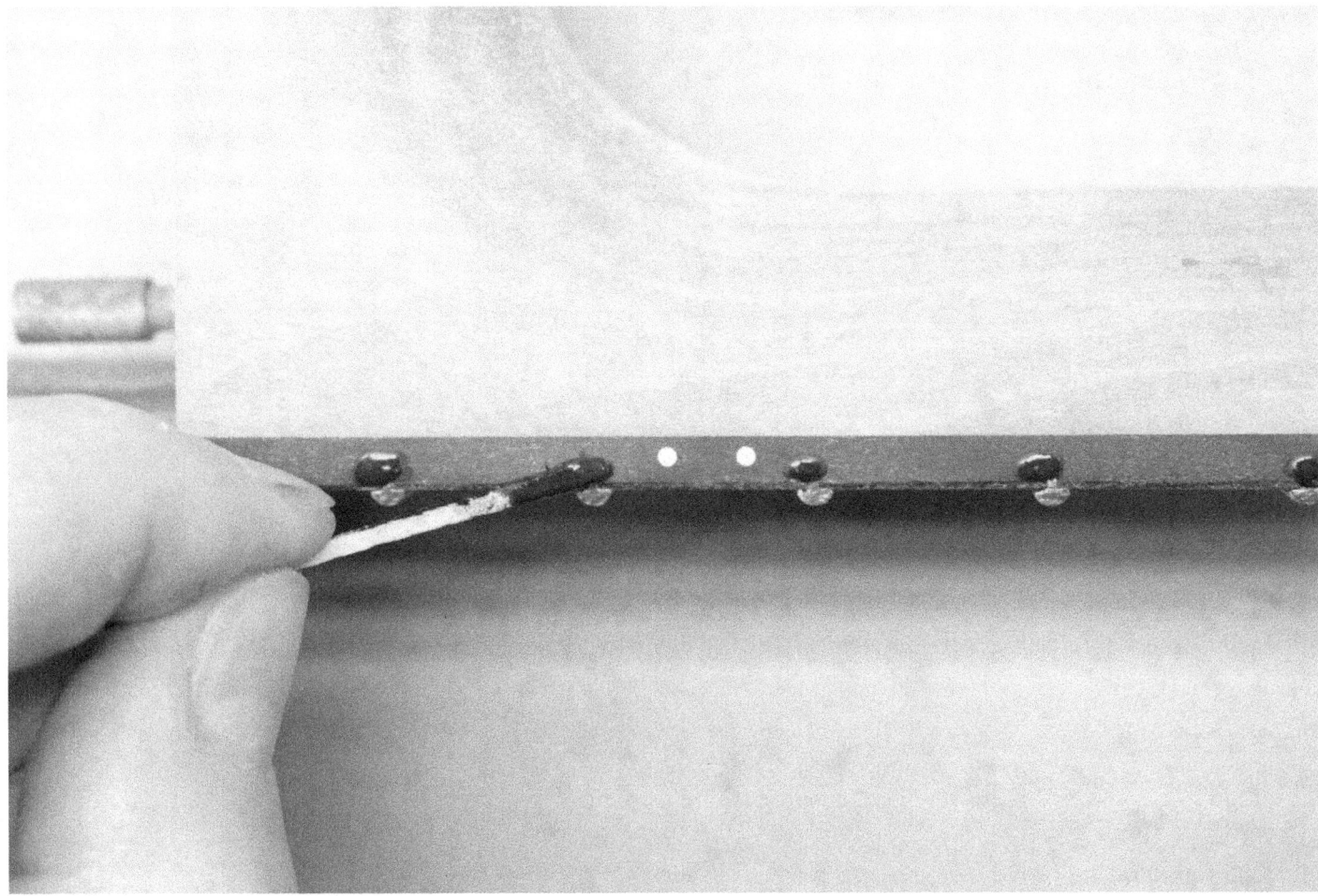

Photo 16-38 – *The fret slot end holes are filled with a putty made from wood glue and sanding dust or dry pigment.*

☐ **Filling the Fret Slot Ends**

The fret slots in the fretboard were sawed a little deeper than the depth of the tang of the fretwire. The holes under each fret end are visible (**figure 16-6**), so these will be filled with putty that matches the wood of the fretboard.

1. A small quantity of sanding dust from the species of wood of the fretboard is mixed with 5 minute epoxy with a toothpick to form a stiff putty. If such sanding dust has not already been collected, it is generated now, by sanding an off-cut of the fretboard on a sanding board. If the fretboard is made of ebony or black phenolic impregnated wood, dry black pigment can be used instead of the sanding dust.

2. The toothpick is used to pack the holes at the fret slot ends with putty (**photo 16-38**). The putty should be mounded up a little over each hole as well. The putty is allowed to cure for at least two hours.

3. The dried putty is sanded flush with the sides of the fretboard using a small flat sanding block and 180 grit sandpaper.

With the exception of trimming the heel and installing the heel cap, construction of the neck is now complete. Those final operations will be done after the neck has been fitted to the guitar body. The frets still need to be leveled and dressed, but this will wait until after finish has been applied to the guitar.

17 Fitting and Attaching the Neck

The fitting of the neck to the guitar body is one of the most critical tasks of guitar construction. It is also one of the things that are most troublesome to the novice luthier. The type of neck joint used in this book was selected specifically because it is easier to fit than a lot of other neck joint types. The fitting method described in the construction section of this chapter makes the task quick and precise.

At this point in construction of the guitar the neck should fit pretty well. The surface of the heel that contacts the body, and the area of the body where that contact is made should be flat, and the angle between heel and fretboard extension should be the same as that between the body at the neck end and the top at the neck end. The reason additional fitting is needed is because small variances in angles of contact between the neck and the body can result in larger variances when the top and the edges of the fretboard are projected over the body to the location of the bridge. Because the physical relationship of the strings to the bridge is *so* critical in the finished guitar, those aspects of the fitting of the neck that affect that relationship are also critical.

The fact that the guitar neck does not always just fit perfectly to the body at this point, and that final fitting is necessary, should not be a source of concern to the luthier. All guitar necks, made by all guitar luthiers, require fitting to the body. It should be noted that even Taylor guitars, built substantially by robots, require some final fitting of neck to body. Large adjustments are rarely necessary. If the neck was constructed with careful consideration of its neck angle, the mold was built with the appropriate flat for the neck block, and the top was braced according to construction descriptions, minimal adjustment will be necessary.

The physical positioning of the neck in relation to the body is succinctly described using the conventional terms used to describe the orientation of any 3D object in space. There are three axes around which the neck can be rotated, and rotation about those axes are denoted by the terms *roll*, *pitch*, and *yaw*. Roll is rotation about the longitudinal axis of the neck and is demonstrated in **figure 17-1**. This is the simplest fitting adjustment to make, because all that is really required here is to be sure the underside of the fretboard extension is parallel to the top surface of the guitar top.

Pitch is rotation about an arbitrary transverse axis, coinciding with the edge of the top plate binding at the neck end of the top (**figure 17-2**). The requirement here is that the projection of the tops of the frets down the centerline of the fretboard must be within a critical distance from the surface of the top at the location of the bridge. In the finished guitar, this will provide a reasonable string height over the frets for ease of playing. The fitting involved is changing the angle of the contact surface of the heel to make that happen. Note also that it is highly desirable that this fitting also result in the underside of the fretboard extension being in perfect contact with the guitar top. Although

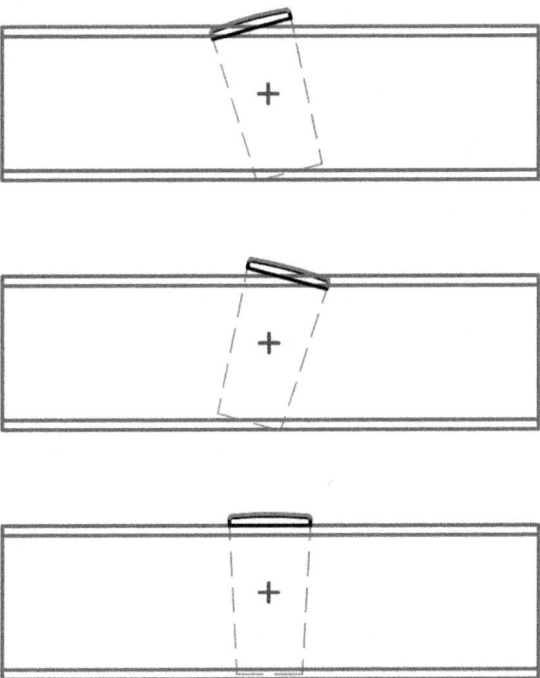

Figure 17-1 – *Examples of differences in* roll *of the neck relative to the guitar body are shown in this x-ray drawing, looking through the guitar body from the tail end. When the neck is properly adjusted for roll, the underside of the fretboard extension will be parallel with the top of the guitar body, as in the lowest figure.*

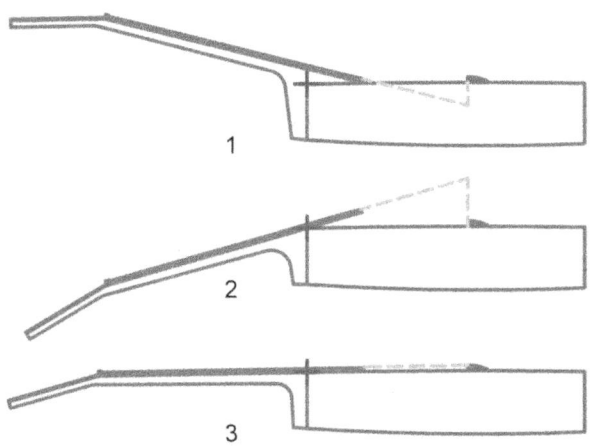

Figure 17-2 – *Examples of* pitch *of the neck relative to the guitar body. The dashed lines show the projection of the tops of the frets to the bridge location. In example 1 the neck is pitched too far forward, which will result in string action that is too high for playability. Example 2 shows a neck which is pitched too far back. This will result in the strings being in firm contact with the frets, unless a high bridge is used. Example 3 shows an appropriate pitch for the neck.*

the ribs of the guitar body (**figure 17-5**). The requirement here is that the projection of the edges of the fretboard must each be the same distance from the guitar top centerline. This guarantees that the centerline of the fretboard is in line with that of the guitar top. The practical consequence of this alignment is that the strings will end up going over the saddle of the bridge.

When discussing changes in yaw in this chapter, the perspective is looking at the front of the guitar, as shown in **figure 17-5**. Steering the fretboard extension to the left side of the guitar results in the strings also moving toward the left, and the headstock moving toward the right. Steering the fretboard extension to the right results in the strings also moving toward the right, and the headstock moving toward the left.

In theory each of these fitting adjustments is completely independent from the other two, but in practice, because pitch and yaw will be adjusted by removing wood from the body contact surface of the neck heel, making one of these adjustments tends to have some effect on the other. That being the case and also in theory, it would be good to order the adjustments to do the one that is most out of whack first. In practice though, the adjustments will proceed in the order they are presented here – roll, pitch, and yaw. The roll adjustment really is independent from the others and so is performed first, just to

it usually is, this is actually a secondary consideration that will be dealt with separately if it is not.

When discussing changes in pitch in this chapter, the orientation of the guitar is sitting on the bench, top plate up, as shown in **figure 17-2**. Increasing the pitch (forward pitch) results in the headstock being farther away from the bench. Lowering the pitch (back pitch) results in the headstock being closer to the bench.

The pitch examples in the figure are of course exaggerated. The actual range of pitch differences likely to be encountered is quite small. In theory, one way that this could be dealt with is by raising or lowering the height of the bridge or the bridge saddle. It turns out this is not really an option. Conventional bridge height is quite critical. Significantly lowering or raising bridge or saddle height will cause structural problems.

The problem with raising the height is demonstrated in **figure 17-3**. **Figure 17-3.1** shows the side view of a bridge of typical height, with the strings breaking over the saddle and string tension pulling on the bridge. The simple mechanical equivalent as shown in **figure 17-3.2** is a simple lever to which the strings are attached. String tension pulls on the lever. The specific construction of the top plate, including its thickness and the thicknesses, widths, and orientations of the braces is sufficiently rigid to prevent levering by the bridge to significantly distort the top. But if the bridge/saddle height was to be increased, the leverage also would increase. Given a fixed amount of string tension, increasing bridge/saddle height increases the leverage, and doing so will result in more distortion of the top (**figure 17-3.3**).

Lowering saddle or bridge height is also problematic. In addition to playability issues caused by a too-short bridge, reducing bridge height can result in reduction of the angle at which the strings break over the top of the saddle, called the *breakover angle* (**figure 17-4**). This can cause buzzing of the strings against the saddle and other problems.

The final possible rotation of the neck is yaw, which is rotation about an arbitrary axis aligned with the neck end seam of

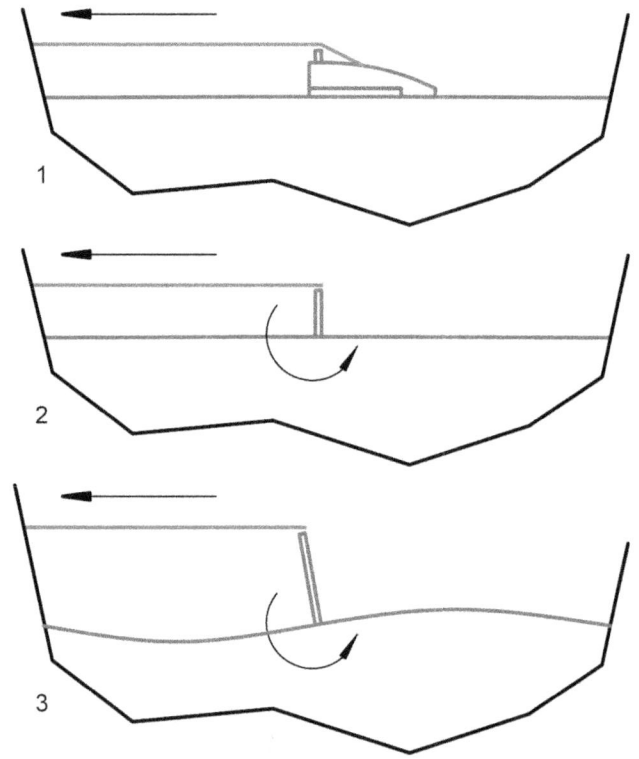

Figure 17-3 – *Although it is theoretically possible to compensate for some range of neck pitch by adjusting bridge height, there are practical restrictions to doing this. Example 1 shows a normal bridge and saddle height. In example 2, that is reduced to its simple mechanical equivalent, which is a short lever with the strings pulling on the top of it. Example 3 shows what happens if the bridge height is dramatically raised to compensate for a neck pitched too far back. Raising the bridge height makes the lever arm longer, which proportionally increases the effect of the lever. Since the top and top bracing isn't designed to handle this much leverage, the bridge gets pulled forward and the shape of the top gets distorted.*

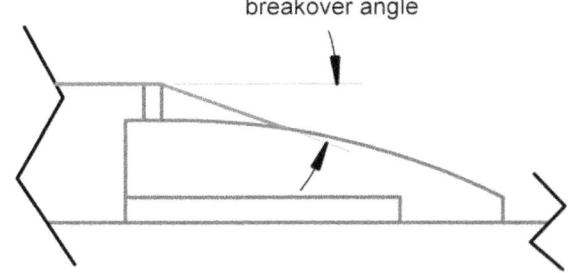

Figure 17-4 – Attempting to compensate for a neck that is pitched too far forward by lowering the saddle height will result in a smaller breakover angle of the strings over the saddle. This results in less string pressure on the saddle, which can result in string rattling and other problems.

Figure 17-5 – Examples of yaw of the neck relative to the guitar body. Proper yaw adjustment aligns the body and neck centerlines and positions the projections of the fretboard sides evenly over the bridge, which in turn will make the strings lie evenly over the bridge saddle.

get it out of the way. Pitch is adjusted next because it is so critical and because it involves not only optimal bridge height but also the fit of the fretboard extension to the guitar body top. Yaw is rarely out of adjustment much, and so it is done last.

Construction

Fitting of the neck to the guitar body is performed using a set of three simple shop-built sanding boards, each board for one or two particular fitting functions. The sanding boards make the fitting process simple, fast, and accurate. After the neck is fully fitted, a decorative heel cap is attached to the bottom of the heel. Finally, the neck is permanently attached to the body.

The Neck-Fitting Sanding Boards

The three neck-fitting sanding boards are made of melamine-covered particle board, to which 80-grit PSA sandpaper is applied in a specific pattern. As is seen in **figure 17-6**, the pattern is different for each board surface, and depends on the

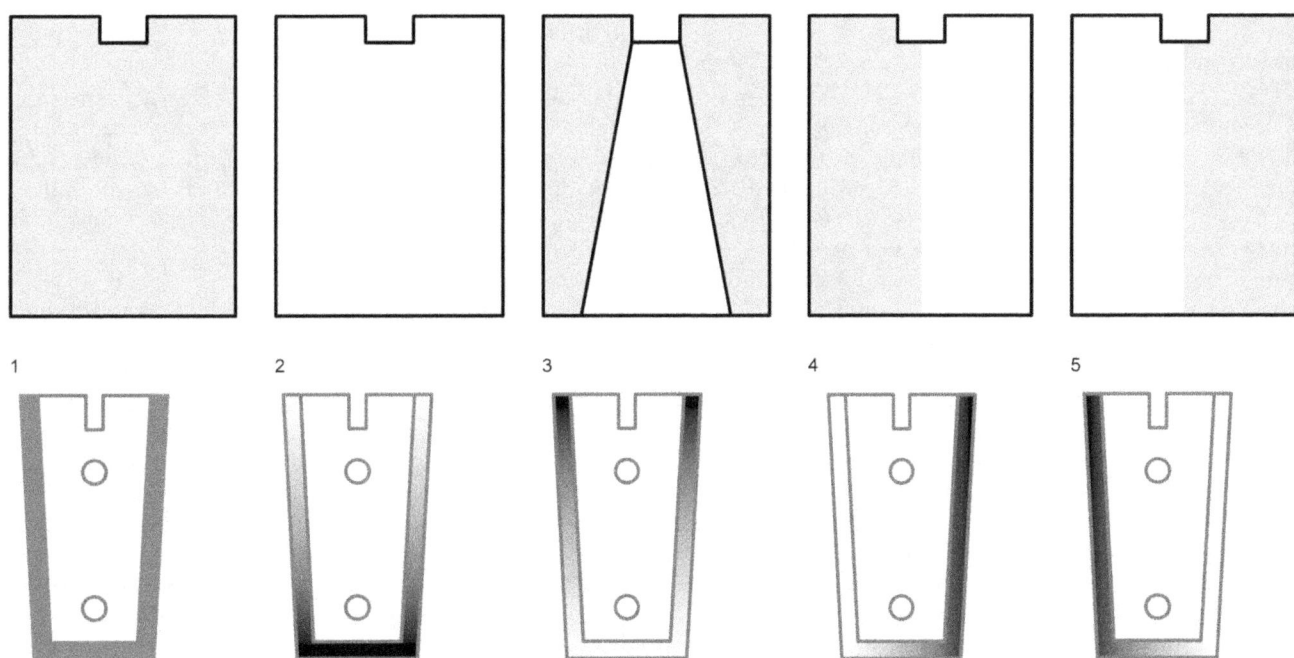

Figure 17-6 – The sandpaper patterns of the neck-fitting sanding board surfaces, and the way each one sands the body contact surface of the heel. Surface 1 is used to flatten the body contact surface of the heel. When the heel is rubbed back and forth across this one, it uniformly sands the entire contact surface and flattens it. Surface 2 is used to pitch the neck back. It has no sandpaper attached, but it is used with a separate piece of sandpaper. In use, more material is removed from the back end of the body contact surface than from the top end. Surface 3 is used to pitch the neck forward. When the heel is rubbed back and forth across this one, more material is removed from the top end of the body contact surface than from the back end. Surfaces 4 and 5 are used to adjust yaw, steering the fretboard extension either to the left side of the guitar (4) or to the right (5). When the heel is rubbed back and forth across either of these, material is removed only from one side of the body contact surface.

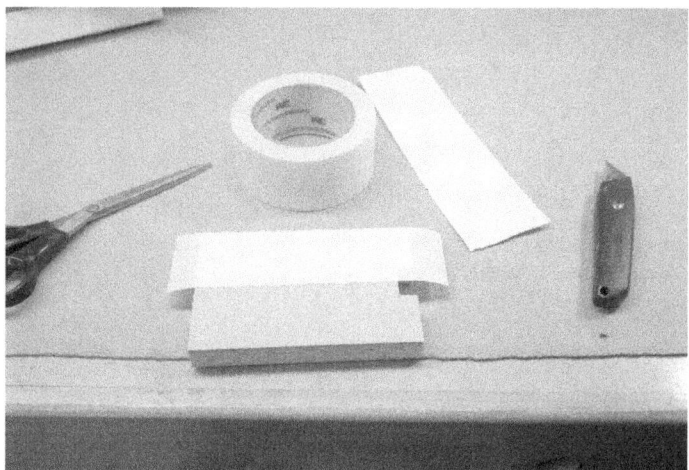

Photo 17-1 – *The part of the surface of a neck-fitting sanding board that is not covered in sandpaper is covered with smooth plastic of approximately the same thickness as the sandpaper. Double-stick tape is used to attach the plastic.*

Photo 17-2 – *When constructing the neck-fitting sanding boards it is a good idea to identify the function of each surface.*

particular adjustment for which the board is designed. In use, each board will sand a particular pattern, removing only some of the wood from the body contact surface of the heel, thus effecting the adjustment. For example, the sanding board used to adjust yaw has two sanding surfaces, one to steer the fretboard extension to the left and the other to steer it to the right. Each of these is covered in sandpaper in a pattern which will only sand one side of the heel's body contact surface but not the other. This means material is only removed from one side during sanding, and this in turn steers the direction of the fretboard extension toward the other side of the guitar.

☐ **Making the Sanding Boards**

1. A set of templates for the neck-fitting sanding boards is available for download for each of the example instruments. These were probably already downloaded along with the plans and templates. If not, these can be downloaded from the Plans and Templates section of the Online Annex in Appendix A. The sanding board templates are printed onto card stock and cut out. Note that these templates are designed specifically for the example instruments. Instructions for designing sanding boards like this for any instrument are available elsewhere.[1]

2. Three boards, each 4½″ (114.3mm) wide by 6″ (152.4mm) long are cut from melamine-covered particle board stock.

3. The notch at the top of each template is accurately transferred to each of the three boards and cut out. The dimensions of the notches are the same for each board. Location and dimensions of the notches are critical.

The notches provide clearance for the trussrod adjustment nut. In use, each board is held sandpaper-surface-up in the bench vise, the body contact surface of the heel is placed in contact with the sanding surface, with the fretboard hanging over and pressed against the top edge of the board, and the heel is scrubbed side to side across the surface of the board. The trussrod adjuster nut and the notch will limit just how far the heel can be moved in each direction.

4. PSA sandpaper is applied to the surface of each board as indicated in the pattern for each board. The patterns are also critical. The board used to flatten the contact surface of the heel is completely covered with sandpaper. This is the easiest board to cover, so it is done first. It is generally best to cut the sandpaper a bit oversize, apply it, then trim it to accurately fit the board, using a utility knife. The back surface of this board will be used to pitch the neck back, and it has no sandpaper on it.

A permanent marker is used to mark the function of each surface of the board somewhere on the edge of the board. See **figures 17-6.1** and **17-6.2**.

5. The sanding board used to steer the fretboard extension to the left and to the right is covered next. One surface of the board is used to steer left and the other surface to steer right. The sandpaper for each surface is applied to one half of the surface, with the inside edge of the sandpaper at the vertical centerline of the board.

If this sanding board was used at this stage in its construction, the movement of the edges of the neck heel over the edges of the sandpaper would quickly peel and tear the sandpaper. To prevent this, the portion of each surface that is not covered with sandpaper is covered with some slippery material of the same thickness (or slightly thinner) as the sandpaper used (**photo 17-1**). The PSA sandpaper I use is 0.036″ (0.9mm) thick. For the covering material I use 0.032″ (0.8mm) PVC sheet, available from hobby suppliers, attached with double-sided tape. The tape is 0.003″ (0.1mm) thick, for a total thickness of 0.035″ (0.9mm). Lots of other readily available materials can be used too. I have often just used file folder card stock, in as many layers as needed. It is even possible to simply use the backing material that comes on the double-sided tape.

The edges of the sandpaper and the covering material must be neatly butted together, without gaps and overlap.

A permanent marker is used to mark the function of each surface of the board somewhere on the edge of the board. See **figures 17-6.4** and **17-6.5**.

6. The sanding board used to pitch the neck forward is built next. This one has sandpaper on both sides of a central section, which must be covered with a covering material as indicated in the previous step. It is generally easiest to apply one of the pieces of sandpaper, cut out the covering material and apply double-stick tape to it, trim the double stick tape, apply the covering piece, then apply the other piece of sandpaper.

The back surface of this board is not used as a sanding surface. A marker should be used to mark the function of the front surface of the board on the board edge. See **figure 17-6.3**.

7. The top (notched) edge of each sanding board must be burnished to remove any sandpaper grit that overlaps the edge. This is done by briskly rubbing a piece of scrap wood back and forth over the top edge of each sanding board (**photo 17-3**).

This will prevent the edge of the sandpaper from cutting into the underside of the fretboard when the sanding board is used.

Fitting the Neck

The neck fitting process begins with checking and flattening of the mating surfaces of the body and the neck, followed by the three fitting adjustments in sequence. Because pitch and yaw adjustments can have an effect on each other, final checks are made and touch up work is done as necessary.

Preparing Body and Neck for Fitting

At this stage in construction the contact surfaces between the body and the neck should be quite flat, but these are checked and flattened if necessary.

☐ Checking and Flattening Contact Surfaces

1. The neck end of the body sides around the seam is checked for flatness using a straightedge and strong back light. The flat here needs to accommodate the width of the heel of the neck only. If this area is not quite flat, it is usually due to a slight

Photo 17-3 – *The notched top edge of each of the neck-fitting sanding boards is burnished by rubbing briskly with a flat block of wood. This removes any sanding grit from the edge of the sandpaper, and prevents that edge from cutting into the underside of the fretboard extension.*

Photo 17-5 – *If additional flattening is required in this area of the top, it is done using a hard sanding block.*

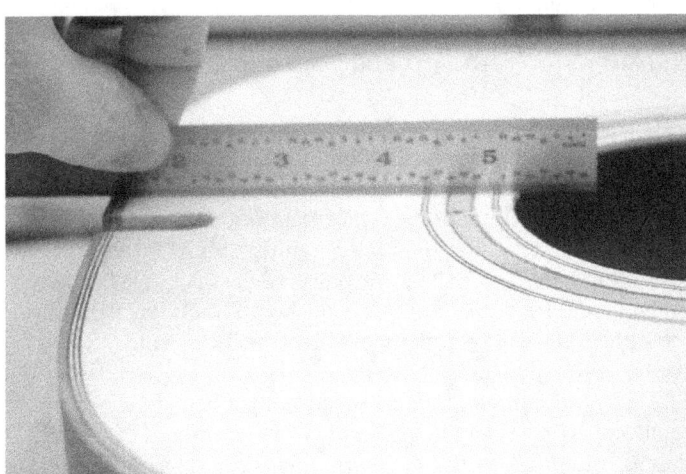

Photo 17-4 – *the area of the top plate that will be in contact with the underside of the fretboard extension is checked for flatness using a straightedge.*

Photo 17-6 – *Flattening the body contact surface of the heel using the flattening sanding board surface. The sanding board is clamped sandpaper surface up in the bench vise.*

Photo 17-7 – *The neck is positioned with the body contact surface of the heel flat on the sandpaper, with the trussrod adjusting nut in the notch at the top edge of the sanding board, and with the fretboard extension in contact with that top edge.*

Photo 17-8 – *In use, the neck is held in position and scrubbed back and forth across the sanding board.*

protrusion of the bindings. A hard sanding block should be used to flatten this area if necessary.

 This step is important. If the body is not flat here, a perfect fit of the neck to the body will not be achieved.

2. The part of the top above the soundhole that will be covered by the fretboard extension is also checked for flatness (**photo 17-4**) and sanded flat if necessary. Often the edge of the binding is raised a bit above the surface. Here again, if necessary, a hard sanding block is used to flatten the area (**photo 17-5**).

3. The body contact surface of the neck heel is flattened in preparation for the subsequent fitting adjustments, using the sanding board just built specifically for this purpose. The sanding board is clamped in the bench vise sandpaper-surface-up (**photo 17-6**). The heel contact surface is scribbled with pencil marks, and the heel is positioned on the sanding board with the fretboard extension hanging over the notched end (**photo 17-7**). Even pressure is applied down on the heel, and the fretboard extension is also lightly pressed into contact with the notched end of the sanding board. The heel is slid back and forth (**photo 17-8**) to uniformly sand and flatten the contact surface until the scribbled pencil marks are all gone. Regular checking of the remaining pencil marks will indicate where pressure needs to be applied for even sanding.

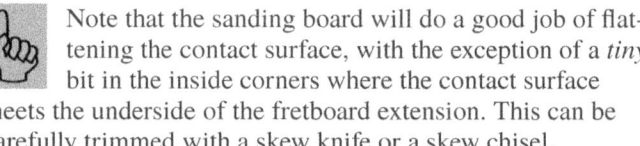 Note that the sanding board will do a good job of flattening the contact surface, with the exception of a *tiny* bit in the inside corners where the contact surface meets the underside of the fretboard extension. This can be carefully trimmed with a skew knife or a skew chisel.

About Roll and Centering Adjustment

This is a simple adjustment, to be sure the underside of the fretboard extension is essentially parallel to the surface of the top of the guitar body and is capable of seating flat. With the neck held in place against the body so the heel is approximately positioned and fully in contact with the body end, the neck can be rolled so the fretboard extension is parallel to the top plate. A check is made to be sure the bolt hole alignment allows the neck to be bolted down in this orientation.

While on the subject of bolts and bolt holes, this style of neck joint does not prevent the location of the neck from shifting side to side a bit. Travel here is limited only by the tightness of the neck attachment bolts in their holes. So another thing that will be done in this operation is to center the neck and mark its location so it can be repeatedly assembled to the body and retain that alignment.

☐ **Aligning Fretboard and Top, and Centering the Neck**

1. The neck is attached to the body using the mounting hardware, which is tightened snugly by hand. This hand tightening should allow for intentional adjustment of the position of the neck, but not be so loose that it can move around on its own. The intent here is that the positioning of the neck relative to the body should be stable, but the joint should not be so tight that the luthier can't intentionally move the neck around.

2. Because the pitch of the neck has not yet been adjusted, the relationship between the underside of the fretboard extension and the guitar top will look approximately like one of the examples in **figure 17-2**. If this looks like **figure 17-2.1**, then the heel is gently twisted to try to get both corners at the fretboard end in contact with the guitar top. If the relationship looks like

figure 17-2.2, then the heel is gently twisted to try to get the inside edge between the top of the heel and the underside of the fretboard extension to fully contact the top edge of the binding that is underneath it. If the relationship looks like **figure 17-2.3**, then the heel is gently twisted and pressed down, to try to get the underside of the fretboard extension to fully contact the guitar top.

3. If the twisting in the step above was able to effect the described fit, then no further roll adjustment is needed. But if the described fit cannot be obtained, it is because something is preventing the heel from being twisted far enough. The most likely cause is the neck bolts are up against the sides of their bores, preventing the heel from being twisted in that direction. In this case the bolt (or bolts) is identified by feel, then the neck is removed from the body and the bolt hole is enlarged as needed, using a round profile rasp. The other possibility is the trussrod adjustment nut hitting one of the walls of its slot. In this case the slot is rasped a bit wider on that side.

The neck is then bolted back on using all the mounting hardware, and checked again as per step 2. The process is repeated until the heel can be twisted to achieve the desired fit.

4. The neck is removed from the body. The width of the fretboard is measured at fret 14 with some precision (**photo 17-9**). The width is transferred to the top of the bindings on the top at the neck end of the body in pencil, so that the centerline of the top divides that width in half (**photo 17-10**).

5. The neck is again bolted to the body, hand tight. The heel is twisted into position as described in step 2, and the heel is also slid sideways so that the fretboard is centered between the pencil marks made in step 4. When the neck is accurately positioned, a knife is used to nick the edge of the top binding to more permanently mark the position of the sides of the fretboard (**photo 17-11**).

6. Without disturbing positioning of the neck, the guitar is flipped over and the knife is used to nick the back binding to mark the positions of the sides of the heel (**photo 17-12**). These marks will be used during subsequent fitting steps. They allow the neck to simply be held in position when checking progress of the remaining fitting steps.

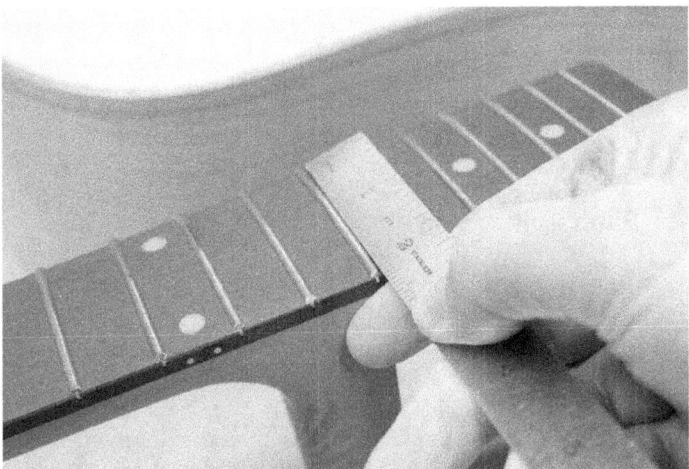

Photo 17-9 – Measuring the width of the fretboard at the 14th fret.

Photo 17-10 – The width of the fretboard at the body join is transferred to the body, centered about the centerline.

Photo 17-11 – The neck is attached and lined up between the marks, then the actual width of the neck is notched into the edge of the binding using a knife. This is done on each side of the fretboard.

Photo 17-12 – The width of the heel is marked on the edge of the back binding with a knife as well.

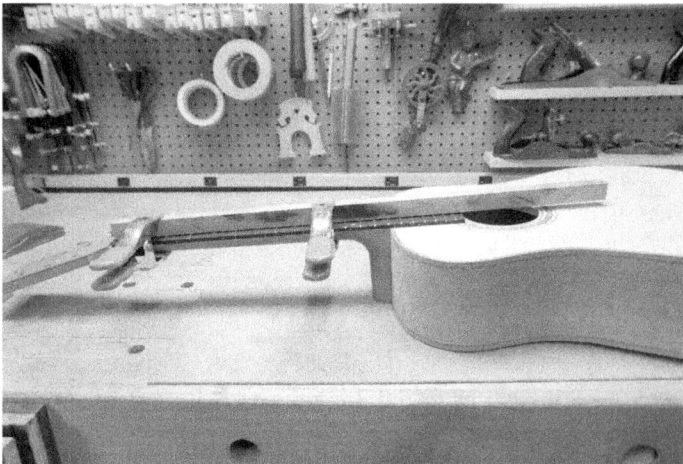

Photo 17-13 – *A straight stick is used to project the plane of the tops of the frets over the guitar top to the location of the bridge.*

Photo 17-14 – *The distance from the plane of the fret tops (represented by the bottom surface of the stick at its end) down to the surface of the top at the bridge location is measured. This distance will determine the amount and direction of pitch adjustment needed for the neck.*

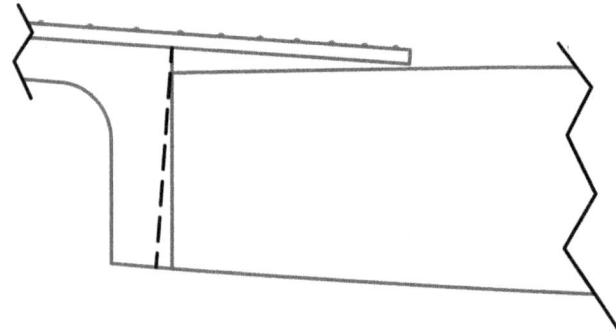

Figure 17-7 – *If the neck must be pitched back, a small wedge of wood must be taken out of the body contact surface of the heel as indicated by the dashed line in this exaggerated drawing. The bigger the wide end of the wedge, the more the neck will be pitched back. Material can be removed in this wedge shape with much precision using one of the special purpose neck-fitting sanding boards.*

 Each time the neck is fitted to the body hereafter, the nicks will be used to align the heel to the body.

7. The neck is removed from the body.

About Pitch Adjustment

As mentioned, the primary concern when adjusting the pitch of the neck is the height of the projection of the tops of the frets over the guitar top at the location where the bridge will be placed. Fitting is done using an actual measurement of that height as a guide. If the pitch needs to be changed, that is accomplished using the back pitch and forward pitch sanding board surfaces.

☐ **Pitch Adjustment**

1. A straight stick is constructed to help measure pitch. The stick should be straight, about 1″ (25.4mm) × 1″ (25.4mm) and the length of the scale length of the instrument. The example instruments have a scale length of 25.5″ (647.7mm).

2. The stick is held in contact with the centerline of the fretboard so one end is at the nut end of the fretboard, and the fretboard surface is visually checked for flatness. With the stick held in place, the trussrod adjuster nut is turned until the fretboard from the nut end to fret 14 is flat. Note that the fretboard extension may not be flat – it usually curls downward a little bit because the fret tangs in the fret kerfs exert a wedging force.

3. The stick is removed and the neck is temporarily bolted on, turning the bolts only hand tight. As is the case with all temporary attachment of the neck during fitting, the heel is located between the knife nicks made in the bindings, and the neck is pressed down so that some part of the underside of the fretboard extension (the end corners, the heel corners, or the whole thing) contacts the top of the body. The stick is installed again, this time using two clamps clamped at around frets 1 and 11 to hold it in place in the center of the fretboard, with one end aligned with the nut end (**photo 17-13**). Note that the fretboard extension may curl down a bit and may have to be gently wedged up in contact with the stick.

 The tops of the frets on the fretboard extension should always be in contact with the underside of the stick whenever measurements are taken. If only the end of the fretboard extension contacts the top, this will usually require just pressing the neck down until the frets on the extension all touch the stick.

4. A small ruler is used to accurately measure the distance between the bottom surface of the stick at its end and the top surface of the top at the centerline (**photo 17-14**). This is the nominal location of the bridge saddle. The target distance is between ⅜″ (9.5mm) and ⁷⁄₁₆″ (11.1mm) which will provide reasonable action with a normal sized bridge and saddle in the finished instrument. If the measured distance is within this range then no pitch adjustment is necessary. If the measured distance is smaller than ⅜″ (9.5mm) then the neck will have to be pitched back to bring this distance up. If the measured distance is greater than ⁷⁄₁₆″ (11.1mm) then the neck will have to be pitched forward to bring this distance down.

5. (Pitching the neck back option) To pitch the neck back, a small wedge of material needs to be removed from the contact surface of the heel. This wedge must be thicker at the back end of the heel and taper to nothing at the fretboard end (**figure 17-7**). Pitching the neck back is done using the back surface of the flattening sanding board. This surface has no sandpaper on it.

The technique used to do this is generally called the *sandpaper pull method*. The board is clamped in the bench vise with the surface without sandpaper up (**photo 17-15**). A strip of heavy 80-grit sandpaper approximately 4″ (101.6mm) wide by 11″ (279.4mm) long is cut, and its back surface is covered with clear packing tape. It is then notched at one end to provide clearance for the trussrod adjustment nut. The packing tape will help prevent tearing of the sandpaper around the notch. Then the sandpaper strip is positioned on top of the sanding board as shown in **photo 17-16**.

The heel is placed on top of the sandpaper, with the underside of the fretboard extension in contact with the notched edge of the sanding board and also with that edge of the sandpaper (**photo 17-17**). The notched edge of the sandpaper must be in

Photo 17-15 – *The flattening board is clamped in the bench vise with the back (sandpaper less) surface face up.*

Photo 17-17 – *The neck is placed on top of the sandpaper with the underside of the fretboard extension flush with the top edge of the board and sandpaper.*

Photo 17-16 – *A sheet of sandpaper is notched on one end to provide clearance for the trussrod adjustment nut. It is placed on the board with that edge aligned with the notched edge of the board.*

Photo 17-18 – *While even pressure is exerted on the heel, the sandpaper is pulled straight out from under the heel.*

Photo 17-19 – The sandpaper must remain flat to the board for the entire pull stoke to maintain a flat body contact surface of the heel.

Photo 17-20 – The pitch forward sanding board is placed face up in the bench vise. Note that the pattern of the sandpaper will result in more sanding at the top end of the heel than at the back end.

contact with the underside of the fretboard extension. Firm and even pressure is applied to the heel to press it onto the sandpaper. While pressure is maintained, the sandpaper is pulled straight out from under the heel (**photos 17-18** and **17-19**). It is important that the back of the sandpaper be in contact with the surface of the sanding board at all times during the pull. Doing this effects differential sanding of the contact surface of the heel. The part of the surface at the fretboard doesn't get sanded at all; the part of the surface at the end of the heel gets sanded a lot; and a point halfway between gets sanded half the amount as at the heel end. The result is a small wedge of material gets sanded away from the contact surface.

 Firm and even pressure on the back of the heel must be maintained throughout the entire sanding stroke to produce an even and flat cut.

This sanding stroke is repeated four or five times. Then step 4 is repeated to gauge progress. If no progress is indicated, then pressure can be increased or the number of strokes can be increased, or 60 grit sandpaper can be substituted.

The sequence of measurement and then repeating a group of some number of sanding strokes is repeated, until the target measurement is attained when step 4 is performed. It is a good idea to alternate the hands used to hold the heel and pull the sandpaper. This helps to even up any unintentional unevenness of pressure on the heel.

If at any time the heel contact surface looks like it is becoming less flat, it can be flattened using the flattening surface on the other side of the sanding board.

5. (Pitching the neck forward option) To pitch the neck forward, a small wedge of material needs to be removed from the contact surface of the heel. This wedge must be thicker at the fretboard end of the heel, and taper to nothing at the back end (**figure 17-8**). Pitching the neck forward is done using the pitch forward sanding board. The surface of this board has sandpaper on it in a pattern that will differentially sand the contact surface of the heel more at the fretboard end than at the back end. The board is clamped in the bench vise with this surface up (**photo 17-20**).

Figure 17-8 – If the neck must be pitched forward, a small wedge of wood must be taken out of the body contact surface of the heel as indicated by the dashed line in this exaggerated drawing. The bigger the wide end of the wedge, the more the neck will be pitched forward. Material can be removed in this wedge shape with much precision using the special purpose forward pitch neck-fitting sanding board

Photo 17-21 – The neck is placed on the sanding board with the heel pressed firmly down and the underside of the fretboard extension fully contacting the top edge of the board. Then the heel is scrubbed side to side.

Photo 17-23 – Here is the end of a sanding stroke. The top end of the body contact surface gets sanded a lot, but the back end doesn't get sanded at all. The middle of the heel gets sanded half as much as the top end.

Photo 17-22 – Here is the heel in the center of a scrubbing stroke. It can be seen that in this part of the stroke only the top half of the body contact surface of the heel is getting sanded.

The heel is placed on top of the sandpaper, with the underside of the fretboard extension in contact with the notched edge of the sanding board. While the heel is held in contact with the surface of the sanding board with even pressure, it is scrubbed back and forth to perform the sanding (**photos 17-21** through **17-23**).

This sanding stroke is repeated four or five times. Then step 4 is repeated to gauge progress. If no progress is indicated, then pressure can be increased or the number of strokes can be increased.

The sequence of measurement and then repeating a group of some number of sanding strokes is repeated, until the target measurement is attained when step 4 is performed. It is a good idea to alternate the position of the hands used to hold the heel while sanding. This helps to even up any unintentional unevenness of pressure on the heel.

If at any time the heel contact surface looks like it is becoming less flat, it can be flattened using the flattening surface on the other side of the sanding board.

6. The pitch adjustment may have changed the way in which the fretboard extension contacts the guitar top. In most cases at this point, the extension will sit fully in contact with the top or close to it. If there is now a noticeable wedge-shaped gap between the underside of the fretboard extension and the guitar top, it will be filled in a subsequent operation.

About Yaw Adjustment

Following pitch adjustment, the yaw of the neck is adjusted. In theory, this should be a simple matter of adjusting the yaw of the neck so its longitudinal centerline is aligned with that of the body. Unfortunately there is no conveniently marked centerline for the neck at this point in construction, so this adjustment is made by projecting the sides of the fretboard to the bridge location on the guitar top, and adjusting the yaw until these are equidistant from the guitar top centerline. Measurements are made in the same general way as was done when the pitch was

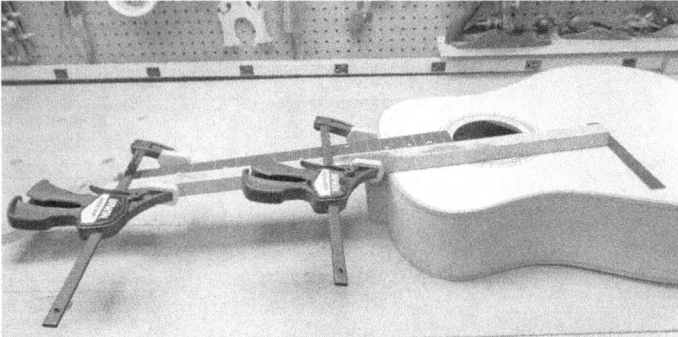

Photo 17-24 – Setting up to measure yaw. The straight stick is clamped to the left side of the fretboard so it extends over the guitar top to the bridge position. The inside surface of the stick projects the plane of the fretboard side. The distance between that surface and the centerline of the top is measured at the end of the stick.

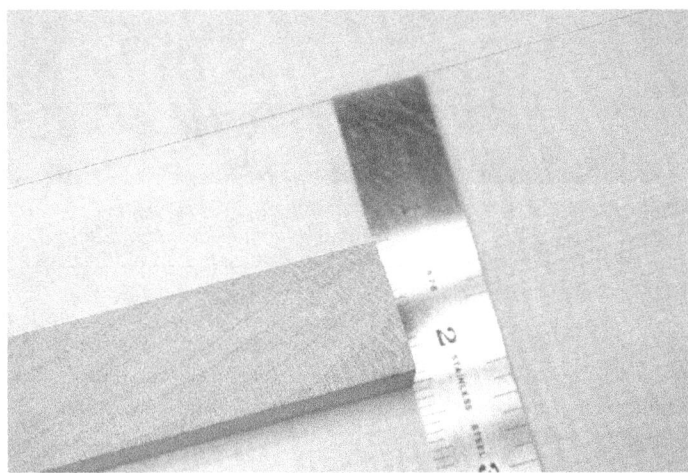

Photo 17-25 – Close-up of measurement of left side of fretboard projection to the centerline of the top. In the photo the location of the top centerline has been enhanced for visibility.

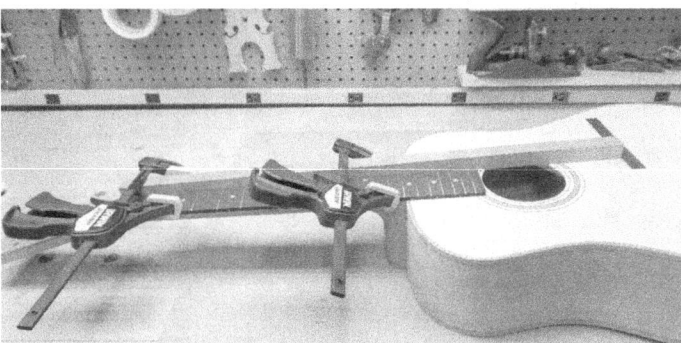

Photo 17-26 – After the left side is measured, the stick is clamped to the right side of the fretboard for measurement there.

adjusted, using the straight stick and a ruler. Adjustments will be made using the yaw adjustment sanding board, which has two surfaces, one to steer the fretboard extension toward the left side of the guitar body, and the other to steer it toward the right.

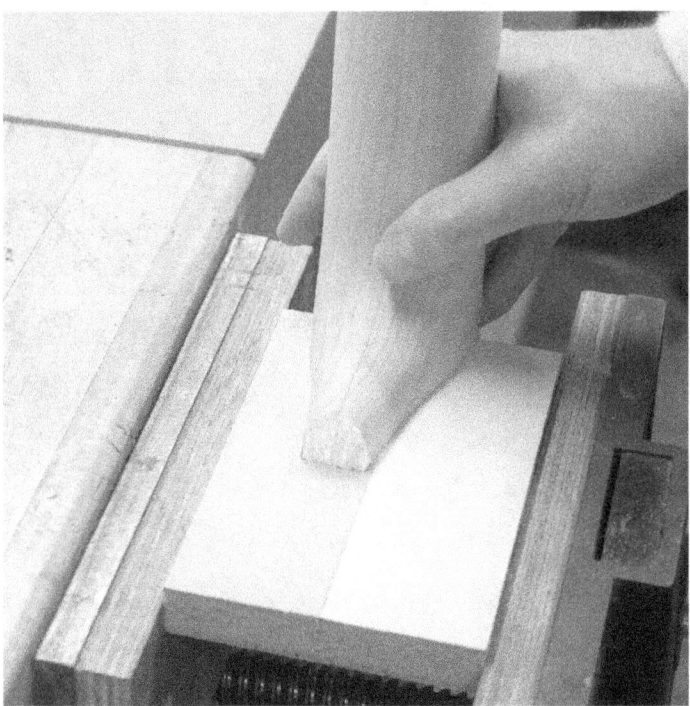

Photo 17-27 – Steering the fretboard extension to the left side of the guitar using one of the yaw adjustment sanding board surfaces. The pictured surface of the sanding board only removes material from the right side of the body contact surface of the heel.

☐ **Yaw Adjustment**

1. If it is not currently, the neck is bolted onto the body and bolts tightened hand tight.

2. The straight stick used when adjusting neck pitch is clamped to the left side of the fretboard, with one end aligned with the nut end of the fretboard and the other end over the body and touching the top (**photo 17-24**).

3. A short precision ruler, placed square with the body end of the stick, is used to measure from the inside edge of the stick to the centerline of the top (**photo 17-25**). The value of this measurement is written down.

4. The stick is unclamped, then similarly clamped against the right side of the fretboard (**photo 17-26**). The ruler is used to measure from the inside edge of the stick on this side to the centerline of the top.

5. The two measurement values are compared. If they are within $1/16''$ (1.6MM) of each other then no yaw adjustment is needed. The rest of the steps in this operation are skipped.

6. Otherwise, the fretboard extension must be steered toward the side of the guitar that had the lower value of the two measurements. Another way to state this is that material must be removed from the body contact surface of the heel, but only on the side where the *higher* measurement was taken. The stick is removed, the neck is removed, and the body contact surface of the heel is scribbled with pencil marks *only* on the side where the higher measurement was taken.

Photo 17-28 – The heel in the center position of the scrubbing movement.

Photo 17-29 – The heel in the rightmost position of the scrubbing movement.

7. The yaw adjustment sanding board is clamped in the vise with the appropriate surface up. The scribbled side of the body contact surface of the heel is the one that needs to be sanded. So when the heel is placed on the sanding board in sanding position, that side of the body contact surface of the heel will have sandpaper under it.

8. While applying uniform pressure to the back of the heel and also pressing the underside of the fretboard extension to the notched end of the sanding board, the heel is scrubbed back and forth a few times to remove some material (**photos 17-27** through **17-29**).

9. Steps 1 through 8 are repeated until the neck is aligned as indicated in step 5.

10. Yaw adjustment may have modified pitch adjustment a bit, so the steps in the previous section are performed to reevaluate and, if necessary, readjust pitch. And of course any pitch adjustment made could also affect yaw adjustment. If pitch adjustment is made, yaw should be reevaluated and adjusted again as needed.

11. The heel should sit flat and in full contact with the guitar body. If is does not, then pitch or yaw adjustment may have distorted the body contact surface of the heel. The flattening sanding board should be used to make this surface flat again. But of course anytime any sanding on the body contact surface of the heel is performed, pitch and yaw must again be evaluated and, if necessary, adjusted.

About Fretboard Extension Fitting

In all likelihood after fitting is done, the fretboard extension will sit in full contact with the top as in **figure 17-2.3**. If it does not but the fit is close, it is possible that the fretboard extension will still fit well when it comes time to finally attach the neck to the guitar body. If that is not possible then a wedge of wood will have to be constructed to fill the space between the underside of the fretboard extension and the top surface of the top.

☐ **Checking the Length of the Fretboard Extension**

The fitting adjustments made are always quite small, so it is highly unlikely that any of them have taken enough material off the heel to effect a change in the relative length of the fretboard extension. But it is worthwhile to check this at this point in construction, because the opportunities to trim it will shortly run out. The neck should be attached to the guitar body and bolted hand tight. A check to see if the end of the fretboard extension overhangs the soundhole is made. If it does, the end of the fretboard is trimmed back to exactly meet the edge of the soundhole.

☐ **Checking the Fit of the Fretboard Extension**

1. The neck is attached to the guitar and bolted on hand tight. The stick used when adjusting the pitch is clamped to the center of the fretboard in the same way as it was when pitch was adjusted. As a sanity check, the distance from the body end of the stick to the top of the guitar is measured again. It should be within the specified range.

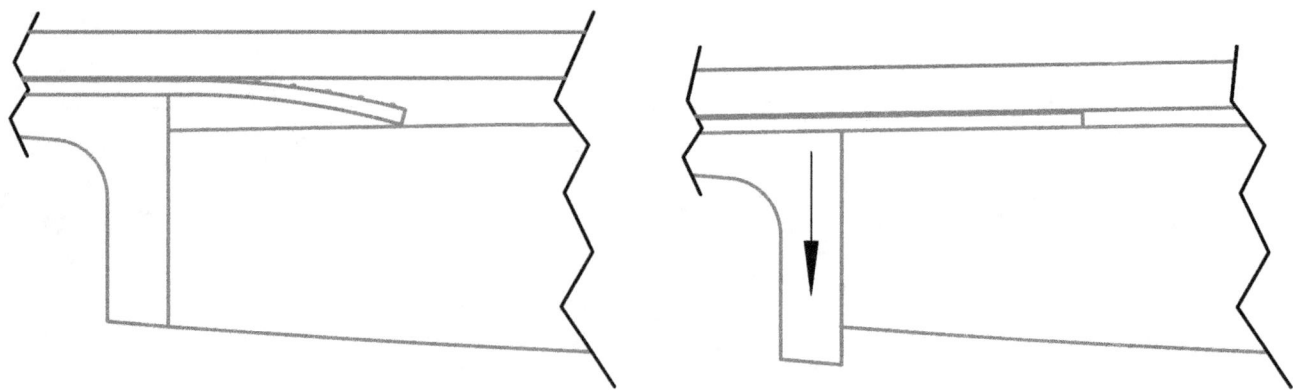

Figure 17-9 – *If the fretboard extension is raised above the neck and that distance is small, and if the extension is bending down toward the top, it may be possible to gently press the neck down onto the body to straighten and fully seat the extension.*

2. If the fretboard extension is fully in contact with the guitar top and the frets on the extension are fully in contact with the underside of the stick, then no further fitting is needed and all subsequent steps in this operation are skipped.

3. If the relationship between the extension and the guitar top looks like **figure 17-2.1** and the end of the extension is bending down toward the guitar top, the entire neck is gently pressed down toward the top, sliding the heel down the body a bit toward the guitar back, until the extension straightens out and all the frets on it are contacting the underside of the stick (**figure 17-9**). If the neck cannot be slid down, then its travel is being limited by the neck bolts contacting the bottoms of the bolt holes. The bottoms of the holes should be rasped out a bit to provide clearance for this movement, and this step performed again. If pressing the neck down in this way eliminates the gap between extension and guitar top at the heel, then no further fitting is needed and all subsequent steps in this operation are skipped.

4. If the relationship between the extension and the guitar top looks like **figure 17-2.1** and step 3 above left a gap between extension and guitar top at the heel, then the height of the gap is measured using a stack of feeler gauges. The measurement is written down. If the gap is less than or equal to 0.020″ (0.5MM) high, the stick is removed and a further attempt is made to close the gap by gently pressing the neck down toward the top. If it will close by doing this, then no further fitting is needed and all subsequent steps in this operation are skipped.

Note that eliminating the gap in this way actually bends the end of the fretboard extension up a bit, and it will no longer be on the plane of the rest of the fretboard, but this will be compensated for during a subsequent fret leveling operation.

5. If the relationship between the extension and the guitar top looks like **figure 17-2.1** and the gap measured in step 4 is greater than 0.020″ (0.5MM) high, or the gap failed to close, then a spacing wedge will have to made to fill the gap. This is described in the following construction operation.

6. If the relationship between the extension and the guitar top looks like **figure 17-2.2**, then the height of the gap between the end of the fretboard extension and the guitar top is measured

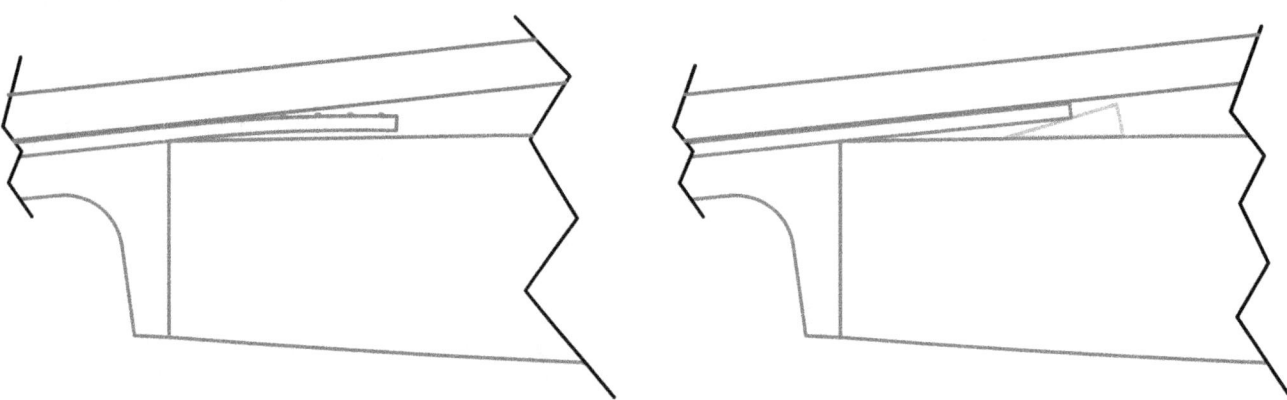

Figure 17-10 – *If the fretboard extension will not fully contact the top, a filler wedge will have to be made and installed. If the fretboard extension is bending down, a small temporary wedge of wood is used to wedge the extension straight up against the stick so that the thickness of the filler wedge can be determined.*

using a stack of feeler gauges. If the end of the fretboard extension is bending down toward the guitar top, a small wedge of wood should be used between the end of the extension and the guitar top, to gently press the fret extension straight, so the frets on the extension are all in contact with the underside of the stick (**figure 17-10**). This is done before the measurement is taken. If the gap is less than or equal to 0.032″ (0.8MM) high, the wedge is removed and an attempt is made to gently press the fretboard extension in place with the fingers. If this can be done, then no further fitting is needed and all subsequent steps in this operation are skipped.

Note that this will make the tops of the frets that are on the fretboard extension a bit lower than the rest of the frets. This is called *fall off*, and a small amount of it is not a problem and may actually be advantageous when setting the string action of the finished instrument.

7. If the relationship between the extension and the guitar top looks like **figure 17-2.2** and the height of the gap measured in step 6 is greater than 0.032″ (0.8MM) high, or the gap failed to close, then a spacing wedge will have to made to fill the gap. This is described in the following construction operation.

☐ **Constructing a Fitting Wedge for the Fretboard Extension**

If the previous construction operation resulted in a wedge-shaped space between the underside of the fretboard extension and the top of the guitar, a wedge of wood must be fashioned to fill this space. In general, this wedge will be made from the same species of wood that is used for the fretboard. If the blank used for the fretboard was generously long, there should be enough cut off material available from which to fashion a fitting wedge. It is also convenient to fashion the wedge from a headplate blank, because these are already quite thin. Because such wedges are thin, they are quite unobtrusive in the finished guitar. Such a wedge can be fashioned using a number of woodworking tools. The general scheme is to thin a piece of stock to the same thickness as the wide part of the wedge, and then taper the thickness of the stock to form the wedge.

Photo 17-30 – The setup for sanding the wedge shape for a filler wedge. A short stop is attached to the far end of the melamine-covered board in the vise.

Photo 17-32 – The piece and its backing block are placed on the sandpaper with what will be the thick end of the wedge against the stop. Even pressure is applied to the backing block.

Photo 17-31 – The piece of wood to be sanded into the wedge is taped to its backing block using double stick tape. The end of the sandpaper is placed against the stop.

Photo 17-33 – The sandpaper is pulled straight out from under the piece while even pressure is maintained. The sanded surface will not be sanded at all at the end against the stop, but is considerably sanded at the other end. After a number of strokes this differential sanding results in a wedge shaped piece.

Because such wedges are thin, work holding is always an issue. One simple work holding technique is to use small pieces of double-sided tape to stick the work to a thicker backing block while the taper is cut. The method described here makes use of the now familiar sandpaper pull method to fashion the wedge.

1. A headplate blank of the same species as the fretboard is selected and trimmed to be just a bit wider than the fretboard is at its widest part. It is cut to just a fraction longer than the length of the fretboard extension.

2. Double-sided tape is used to attach the piece to a thick backing block. The backing block should be the same dimensions as the piece, but if the block is a bit bigger, the work piece should be attached so one of its ends is aligned with one of the ends of the backing block. The double-sided tape should *not* be applied right up to the edge of the other end of the work piece. That end will end up being the thin edge of the wedge. When it comes time to remove what will be a delicate wedge from the backing block, that will be done using a putty knife, and a margin without tape will make it easier to remove the wedge without breaking its sharp edge.

3. The blank is marked in thickness all around its perimeter. The thickness should be the same as the thick end of the wedge needed.

4. A block plane, scraper plane, or a sanding board is used to carefully thin the blank to the marked lines.

5. The taper can be accurately cut on the blank using the sandpaper pull method, described in the step used to pitch the neck back. A flat melamine-covered particleboard board of the size of the special neck-fitting sanding boards is cut. A strip of wood that is a bit taller than the board is thick is attached to one end of the board to serve as a stop. A strip of 80-grit sandpaper is cut a bit narrower than the board. The board is clamped in the vise (**photo 17-30**).

6. The sandpaper strip is placed face up on the board with one end in contact with the stop (**photo 17-31**). The blank, attached to its backing block, is placed on top of the sandpaper with the end that will be the thick end of the wedge in contact with the stop (**photo 17-32**).

7. The backing block is pressed down with uniform pressure with one hand, while the other hand is used to pull the sandpaper strip straight out from under the block (**photo 17-33**).

8. Steps 6 and 7 are repeated until the blank has been sanded into a wedge. It is useful to change hands to help equalize differences in pressure applied to the backing block. The sanded surface should be regularly checked for evenness and flatness. Flatness can be maintained by sanding the surface on a sanding board. Evenness of sanding can be maintained by pressing down a bit harder over areas that appear to be sanded less.

Note that it is not possible to sand the sharp edge of the wedge down to nothing without distorting that edge. Some small thickness here will be necessary.

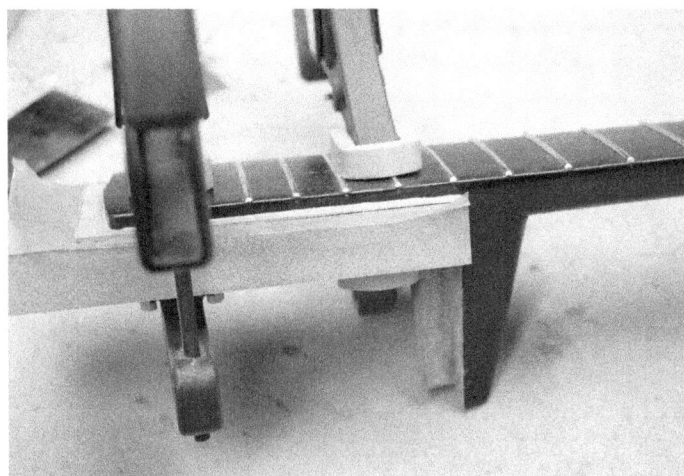

Photo 17-34 – *The filler wedge being glued to the underside of the fretboard extension. Note the use of wax paper and a flat caul when clamping. In new construction the wood species of the wedge will be the same as that of the fretboard. This photo was taken from a neck undergoing restoration. It was used here because the light colored wood of the wedge is visible in the photo.*

9. The wedge is carefully removed from the backing block using a putty knife that is wider than the wedge. The knife is started from the thick end of the wedge.

10. Once removed, the wedge is checked for fit by dry fitting it under the fretboard extension. A notch will have to be cut out from the appropriate end to provide clearance for the trussrod adjustment nut. This notch should have similar dimensions to the slot in the top used for the same purpose.

11. The fit of the neck should be checked once again with the wedge in place.

12. The wedge is glued to the underside of the fretboard extension using a clamping caul and a pierce of wax paper to prevent the caul from being glued on (**photo 17-34**).

Photo 17-35 – *The fully fitted neck bolted to the body.*

13. The sides and end of the wedge are trimmed and sanded flush to the sides and end of the fretboard extension.

14. The neck should now fit perfectly to the body when bolted in place (photo **17-35**).

Attaching the Neck

Now that the neck has been fitted, it is almost ready to be attached permanently to the guitar body. One final construction step that must be done before attachment is making and fitting the *heel cap*. The heel cap is a decorative cap of wood at the back end of the heel (**photos 17-36, 17-37**). After that is made and fitted, the neck will be attached to the guitar with the neck bolts, and the fretboard extension will be lightly glued down to the top plate.

About the Heel Cap

It may seem odd that the heel cap was not fitted to the heel before all the fitting of the neck to the body was done, but there is method to this particular madness. After the heel cap is attached, the length of the heel is pretty much fixed. Fitting the neck may have required making small changes to the vertical location of the neck in relation to the body, and these changes could result in the need for a slightly shorter or longer heel. Now that the neck is fitted, the length of the heel is established and the heel cap can be fitted.

The heel cap is a decorative element for which there are a lot of material options. It is commonly made from the same

Photo 17-36 – *A plain heel cap. This is made of the same wood species as the body. Its surface is flush with the surface of the back, and its thickness is roughly the same as that of the bindings.*

Photo 17-37 – *A heel cap with purfling lines. This one is made of the same species as the bindings. The thickness of the heel cap matches that of the bindings and the purfling lines line up with the side purflings.*

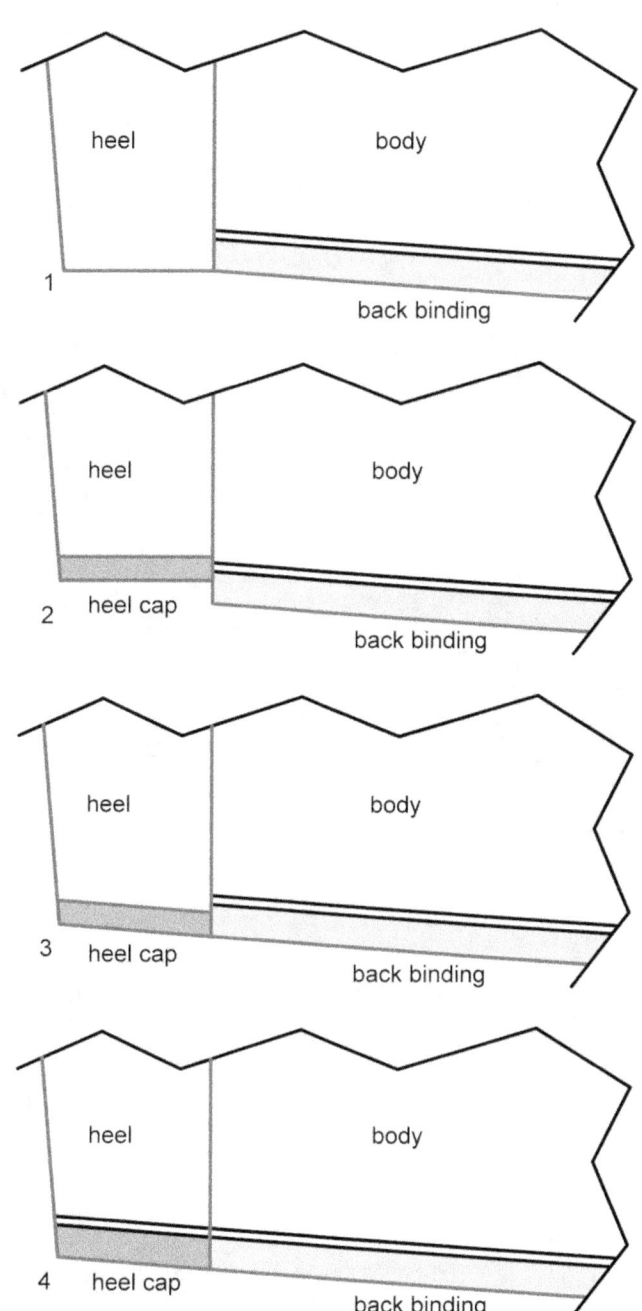

Figure 17-11 – *Various heel cap configurations. The diagrams show the heel cap area of a guitar that is sitting top up on the bench, with the neck to the left. 1. No heel cap, end of heel is cut square to the body. 2. Plain heel cap, also cut square to the body. The thickness of the cap does not match other features of the guitar, and the end surface does not align with the back. 3. Similar to 2, but the heel cap follows the angle of taper of the back, and its end surface is aligned with the back. 4. Similar to 3, but the thickness of the heel cap is the same as the height of the binding, and it has purfling lines which match and align with the body side purflings.*

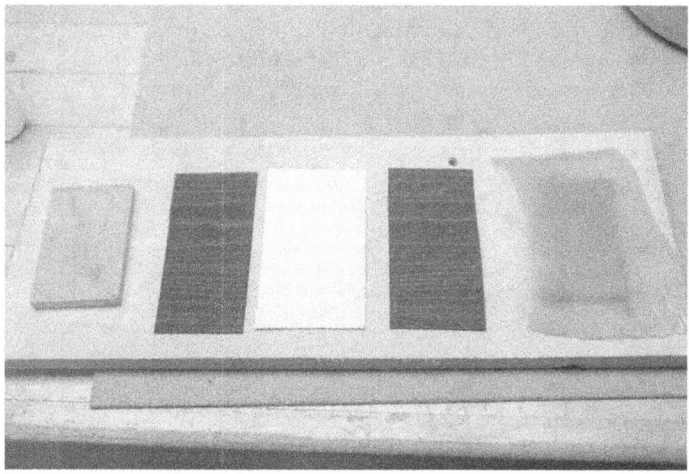

Photo 17-38 – *The components of a heel cap blank with purfling lines. From left to right are the heel cap blank, veneer sheets, and wax paper over a clamping caul for the veneers.*

Photo 17-40 – *The finished heel cap blank with purfling lines. This one has been squared up for the photograph, but there is no need to do this for actual construction.*

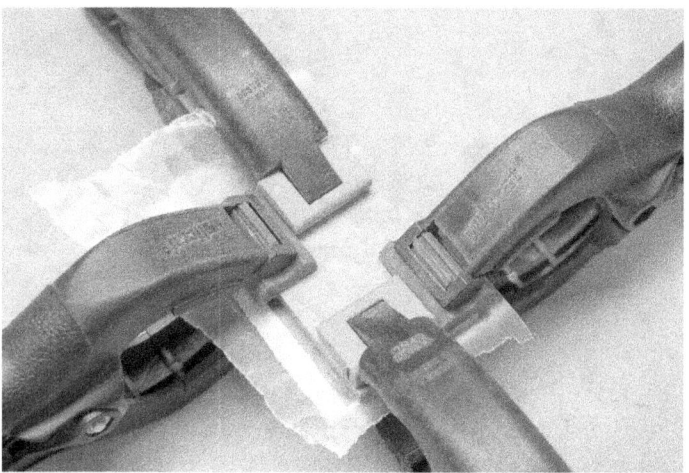

Photo 17-39 – *The heel cap components are glued and laminated together, then clamped while the glue cures.*

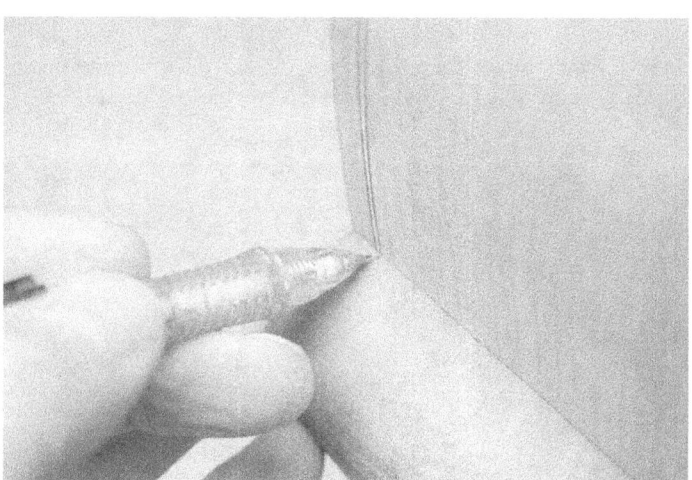

Photo 17-41 – *The location for the cut of the end of the heel is transferred onto each side of the heel from the body. Here the cut will be above the body side purflings.*

species as the fretboard, and if so a saved off-cut from the fretboard can be used to fashion it. It is also common to make the heel cap from the same species as used for the headplate or tail graft or bindings. If so it may be a bit more difficult securing a blank. Lutherie wood dealers rarely carry blanks specifically sized for heel caps.

There is no standard thickness for heel caps, but it is usually a good idea to make it thick enough to allow for a bit of final trimming. Starting with a blank that is approximately ¼″ (6.4mm) thick is common. There are also options for the angle at which the heel cap is placed relative to the back of the body, and the extent to which the surface of the cap matches that of the back (**figure 17-11**).

A common decorative treatment, particularly when the heel cap is made of the same species as the bindings, is to match the thickness of the heel cap to that of the bindings, and to use the same side purfling treatment (**photo 17-37**). This gives a nice integrated look, but it does require some precision when trimming the end of the heel to make things line up. As this is probably the most complicated heel cap treatment, this is what the following construction operation will detail.

☐ **Making and Fitting the Heel Cap**

The first step is putting together the heel cap blank. Then a simple fixture is constructed that is used to accurately cut the end of the heel at an angle, in preparation for attaching the blank. One of the neck-fitting sanding boards will be repurposed to use as the base of this fixture. The fixture will be used to guide the blade of a razor saw. The heel end is cut, then the blank is glued on. The final steps include shaping the heel cap to the profile of the rest of the heel.

1. The materials for the heel cap blank are selected and cut to size (**photo 17-38**). The blank should be roughly ¼″ (6.4mm) bigger all around than the end of the heel. If the heel cap will be decorated with purfling lines, these are implemented using sheets of veneer of the same materials and thickness as the side purfling lines. These lines are typically 0.020″ (0.5mm) thick. If veneers will be used, a caul is also needed for gluing everything up.

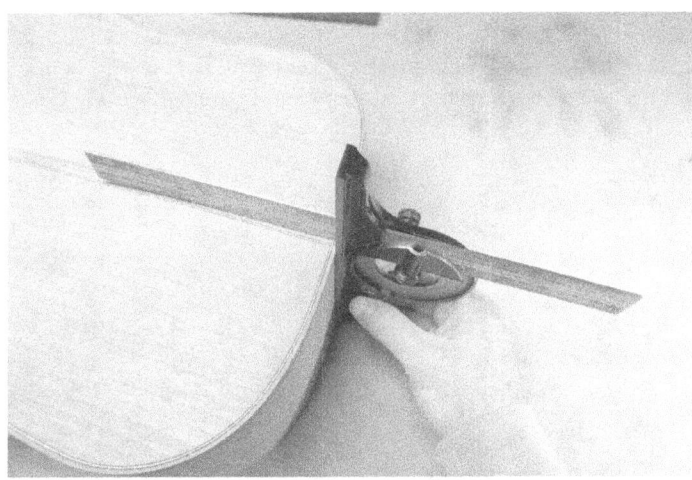

Photo 17-42 – The angle between the body sides at the neck end and the back plate is copied with a protractor.

Photo 17-44 – Cutting the MDF blank in half at the angled lines results in two rails with their ends cut at identical angles.

Photo 17-43 – The body neck end to back plate angle is transferred to the center of an MDF blank, which will be used as the rails to guide the saw cut.

Photo 17-45 – The heel is held in position on the baseboard and the end-of-cut marks are transferred to the surface of the board.

2. Glue is applied to the heel cap blank and the veneers, then all is sandwiched together, covered with a sheet of wax paper, and the caul is applied on top. Spring clamps can be used to clamp the stack together while the glue cures, about 3 hours (**photo 17-39**).

3. The caul and wax paper are removed (**photo 17-40**). There is no need to plane any straight edges. The blank will be trimmed down after it is glued to the heel.

4. With the neck bolted to the body, the location where the heel will be cut is transferred from the body to the heel. The heel cap to be installed here has veneers to match the side purfling, so the heel will be marked for cutting just above the topmost veneer line of the side purfling (**photo 17-41**). This marking is done on each side of the heel.

5. A protractor is used to measure the angle between the body at the neck attachment point and the back plate (**photo 17-42**). Since the back plate is arched it is not possible to get a completely accurate angle measurement, but a close approximation

Photo 17-46 – The marks are connected with a straight pencil line.

is good enough. After the measurement is taken, the angle of the protractor is locked.

6. A length of ¾″ (19.1mm) MDF is cut to be fashioned into rails that will guide the saw when cutting the heel to length. This should be approximately 9″ (228.6mm) long and 1½″ (38.1mm) high. The height must not be taller than the height of the blade of the razor saw that will be used to cut the heel to length. And the height must be at least ½″ (12.7mm) taller than the thickness of the heel near its back plate end.

7. The protractor is used to make a cut line near the center of the length of the piece of MDF (**photo 17-43**). The piece is cut in two on this line, and the cut edges are sanded straight (**photo 17-44**). The cut surfaces of these rails will guide the saw, so the angle should be accurate and identical on both pieces, and the surfaces should be smooth.

8. The back surface of the flattening neck-fitting sanding board will be used as a baseboard for the heel sawing fixture. The sanding board is clamped in the bench vise with the back surface up. The neck is placed on the sanding board in the same orientation that was used when fitting the neck, that is, with the body contact surface of the heel in contact with the surface of the board, and the underside of the fretboard extension in contact with the notched end of the sanding board. Then the pencil marks on the heel that indicate where the cut will be are transferred to the surface of the sanding board (**photo 17-45**).

Photo 17-49 – *The heel is placed in position, ready for the cut. If the heel cannot easily be held steady for the cut, PSA sandpaper can be put down on the baseboard, or the heel can be bolted to the baseboard.*

Photo 17-47 – *Double-sided tape is applied to the back (longest) edge of the two rail pieces.*

Photo 17-50 – *The saw blade is pressed against the angled ends of the rails to guide the cut.*

Photo 17-48 – *The rail pieces are stuck down to the baseboard with their angled ends on the line, and their sides aligned with the side edges of the baseboard.*

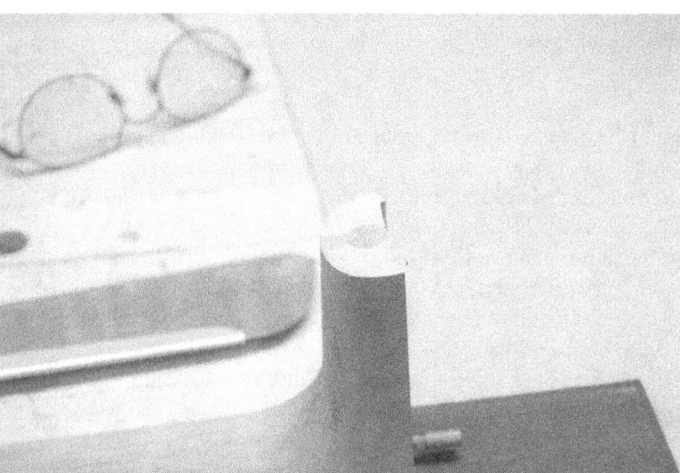

Photo 17-51 – *The trimmed end of the heel.*

9. The two marks are connected with a straight pencil line, made using a straightedge (**photo 17-46**).

10. Because one end of each of the two rail pieces is cut at an angle, the top of each rail will be shorter in length than the bottom. Double-sided tape is stuck to the bottoms of the two rail pieces (**photo 17-47**).

11. The rails are stuck down to the baseboard with their angled ends aligned with the pencil line across the baseboard, and with their sides aligned with the side edges of the baseboard (**photo 17-48**). After the rails are positioned, they should be clamped down tightly with a clamp in a few places along their length, to set the adhesive of the double-sided tape. The clamp is removed.

12. The heel is positioned on the baseboard and held in position (**photo 17-49**) for the cut. In the photos I am using a Japanese razor backsaw to make this cut. Because the blade is thin and sharp, this saw does not tend to yank the work around during cutting, so the heel can easily be held in position by hand. But there is no reason why the baseboard cannot be enhanced to hold the heel more securely. A piece of PSA sandpaper on the baseboard between the rails will prevent movement of the heel

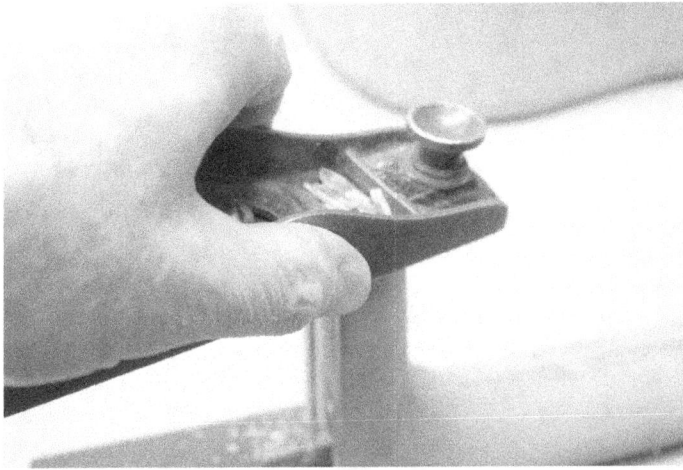

Photo 17-52 – *Small adjustments and flattening of the heel end can be made using a block plane …*

Photo 17-53 – *… or a small sanding board.*

Photo 17-55 – *The heel cap is now rasped to close to the contours of the heel.*

Photo 17-54 – *The roughly shaped heel cap blank is glued to the end of the heel. An overhanging margin must be maintained all around.*

Photo 17-56 – *A sanding block is used to finish shaping the heel cap to the contours of the heel.*

Photo 17-57 – *Care is taken to not disturb the body contact surface of the heel. Here a sanding block with just a strip of sandpaper is used to get that part of the heel cap close.*

Photo 17-59 – *The neck is bolted to the body and then a sanding block is used to sand the heel cap end flush with the guitar back.*

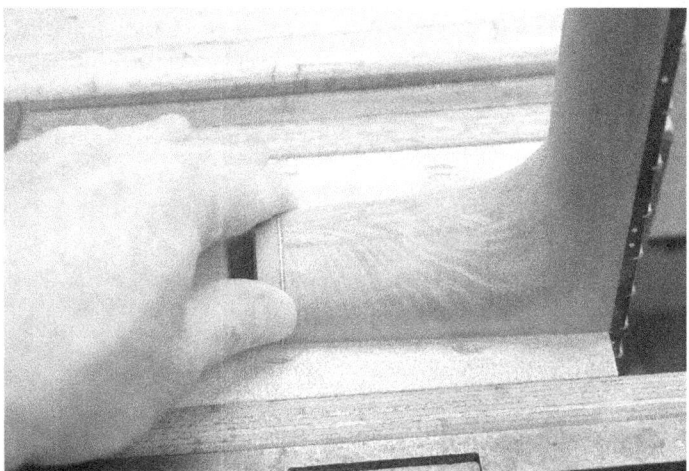

Photo 17-58 – *A few strokes on the flattening sanding board surface finishes flattening the body contact surface of the heel cap.*

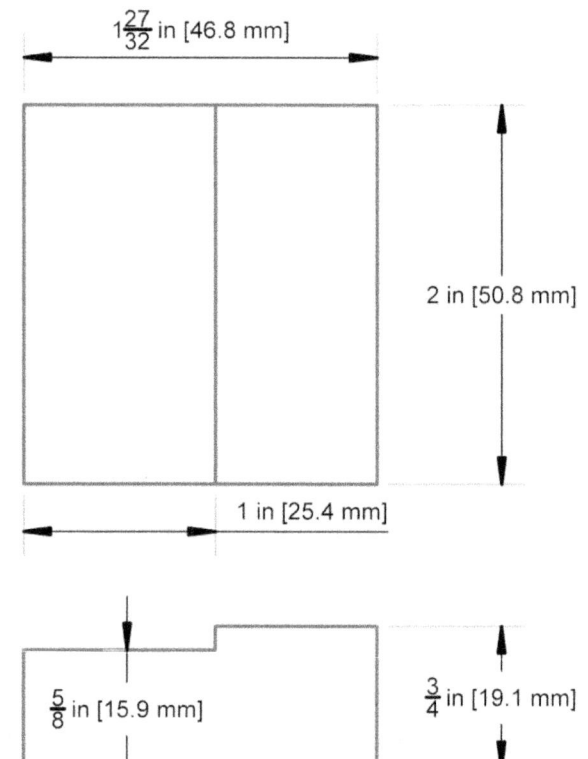

Figure 17-12 – *A template for the clamping caul used to glue the fretboard extension down to the guitar top. The rabbet on the top surface of the caul provides clearance for the "Popsicle stick" brace.*

to a great extent. Or if desired, the baseboard can be drilled and the heel bolted to it to mount it securely for the cut.

13. The heel is cut to length with the side of the saw blade *always* in contact with the ends of the rails (**photo 17-50**).

14. After the cut is made (**photo 17-51**), the cut surface is flattened as needed and the heel is finely adjusted for length before the heel cap blank is glued on. A sharp and finely set block plane (**photo 17-52**) or a sanding board (**photo 17-53**) can be used to do this.

15. The heel cap blank is roughly cut to shape, but leaving a margin on all sides. Glue is applied and the heel cap is clamped in place (**photo 17-54**). Note that due to the angle of the heel end surface, the edge of the heel cap blank *must* extend beyond the body contact surface of the heel.

16. After the glue cures and the clamps are removed, the heel cap is carefully rasped (**photo 17-55**) and then sanded (**photo 17-56**) to match the contours of the rest of the heel. Note that when sanding the body contact surface of the heel cap down to the level of the rest of the body contact surface of the heel, it is useful to use just a strip of sandpaper on a sanding block (**photo 17-57**). This will prevent inadvertently undoing any of the careful neck fitting work that was done in previous operations.

17. If needed, the reverse, flattening, surface of the sanding board that was used as the baseboard for the cutting fixture is

Photo 17-60 – *The fretboard extension gluing caul, ready for installation.*

Photo 17-62 – *Two thin beads of glue are applied to the underside of the fretboard extension, leaving generous margins all around so there will be no squeeze-out to deal with.*

Photo 17-61 – *The caul is taped in place inside the top, with the rabbet up and toward the neck block.*

Photo 17-63 – *One clamp is used to lightly hold the fretboard extension in contact with the top at the edge of the binding.*

used for final flattening of the body contact surface of the heel (**photo 17-58**).

18. The neck is mounted on the body, and all of the pitch and yaw measurements are taken again, to be sure nothing has changed as a result of the heel cap work. If anything is out of spec, the appropriate fitting operation should be done.

19. Sandpaper on a hard block is used to sand the end of the heel cap flush with the surface of the back plate (**photo 17-59**).

 The stick used in adjusting the fit of the neck is retained for use in future construction operations.

About Attaching the Neck

The actual process of attaching the neck is straightforward. Although it is one of those operations that must be performed with some speed before the glue starts to cure, at this point in construction after so many fittings of the neck, the luthier is usually quite comfortable with inserting and tightening the bolts and can do this quickly. As far as the neck bolts go, one small difference here is that some low-strength (purple) thread-locker fluid is applied to the threads before the bolts are installed this final time. This will help prevent them from working their way loose.

The fretboard extension will be glued down to the top, but this is accomplished using a minimum of glue. It is done this way for several reasons. The first is that using a lot of glue may distort the top, because the water in the glue is absorbed mostly by the top wood. The second reason is that this is one glued joint where it is highly desirable not to have any squeeze-out to clean up. An additional reason is to be kind to the future luthier who will need to remove the neck to perform a repair. To help spread out clamping pressure, a gluing caul is made and fit inside the top.

☐ Attaching the Neck

As with all complex gluing operations it is a good idea to do a dry run before actually committing to glue.

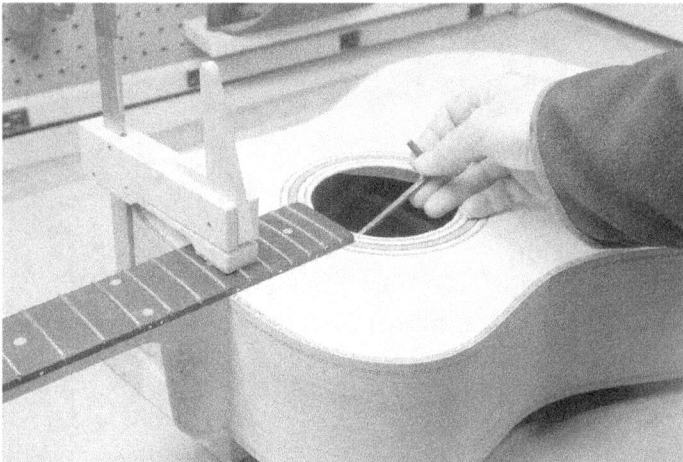

Photo 17-64 – *The neck bolts and their washers are installed and tightened.*

Photo 17-65 – *One or two clamps are used to clamp down the fretboard extension to the top.*

1. The gluing caul for use inside the body under the fretboard extension is constructed. The dimensions shown in **figure 17-12** can be used for the caul for either of the example instruments. The caul is conveniently made from MDF. The caul is made so it presses up the "Popsicle stick" brace and the underside of the top plate between that brace and the upper transverse brace. The dimensions in the figure should be used when constructing the caul. The rabbet can be made using any tools, but it is easily cut using a razor saw. After the caul is built it is checked by holding it in place to be sure it fits properly. It is inserted with the rabbet up and toward the neck block.

The caul is reshaped as necessary to fit. **Photo 17-60** shows the caul ready to be used.

2. One or two long pieces of tape are placed along the underside of the caul with tails of tape extending past the sides of the caul. The caul is inserted into place under where the fretboard extension will go and taped securely in place (**photo 17-61**).

3. Two thin beads of glue are applied to the underside of the fretboard extension. The beads run parallel to the side edges of the extension, about ½″ (12.7MM) from them. The beads start and end about ½″ (12.7MM) from the end of the fretboard

Photo 17-66 – *The guitar with neck permanently attached.*

Photo 17-67 – The edges of the body bindings are rounded over using sandpaper or a scraper.

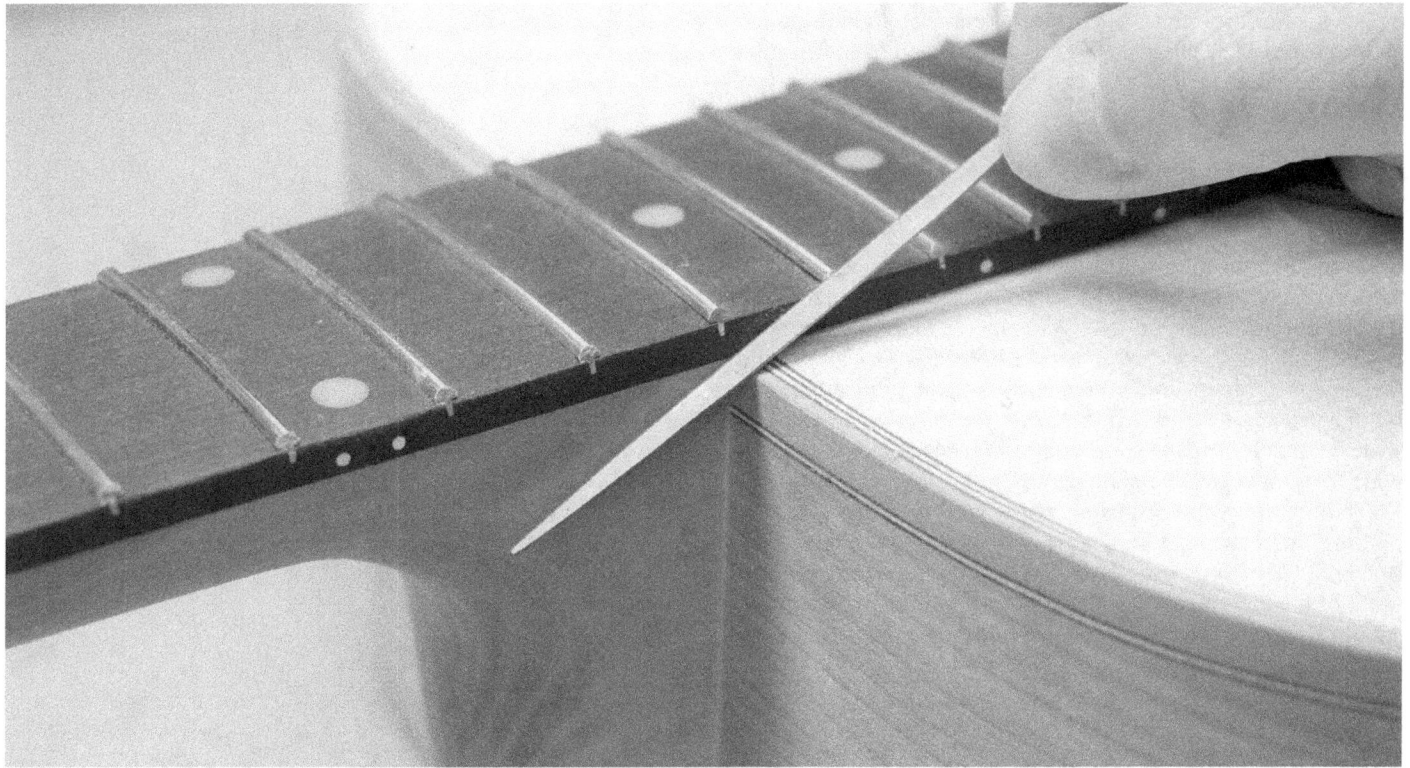

Photo 17-68 – Rounding over the bindings right at the heel can be troublesome. This can be done neatly using a small file.

extension and the heel as well (**photo 17-62**). The object here is to just *lightly* glue the extension down, and with no squeeze-out whatsoever.

4. The washers are slipped over the neck bolts. A small drop of low-strength (purple) threadlocker is placed on the threads near the end of each of the neck bolts.

5. The neck is attached to the body and bolted in hand tight. A lightly thrown clamp is used to be sure the heel end of the fretboard extension is firmly seated on the top plate (**photo 17-63**). The bottom pad of this clamp goes over the back, over where the neck block is located. The bottom pad of the clamp must *not* touch the bottom of the heel. The top pad of this clamp goes over the fretboard extension, over where the neck block is located.

6. The appropriate size Allen key is used to tighten the neck bolts (**photo 17-64**).

 Much care is taken to not over-tighten the neck bolts, which could strip the threaded inserts out of the heel. Once the bolts are snug they can be turned approximately ⅛ of a turn more to fully tighten them. To avoid over-tightening, it helps to insert the long arm of the Allen key in the bolt and twist the key by holding the short arm. This provides less leverage, and reduces the possibility of over-tightening.

7. One or two clamps are used to clamp down the fretboard extension (**photo 17-65**). The extension should be examined from all sides to be sure it is completely seated on the top plate. There should be no glue squeeze-out but if there is it is quickly removed with the snipped plastic straw.

8. The glue is allowed to cure for two hours before the clamps are removed. The caul and the tape are removed from the guitar body. The guitar with permanently attached neck is shown in **photo 17-66**.

☐ Filleting the Binding Edges

Although not technically a part of attaching the neck, rounding over the bindings must be done after the neck is attached. This is the last construction operation on the instrument proper. The operation can be performed with sandpaper held in the fingers or it can be done using the card scraper (**photo 17-67**). Care should be taken to apply a uniform roundover all along the length of the bindings. Care is also taken to be sure the radius of roundover is wide enough to provide some comfort for the player, but not so wide that it involves the plate purflings.

The only fussy part of this operation is at the points where the bindings meet the heel. It is often difficult to make a nice transition here. The scraper sometimes helps, but depending on the grain of the bindings it may also pull out splinters of wood. A small needle file can be use to good effect here (**photo 17-68**).

---

1. Mottola, R.M. (2016) Aligning the Bolt-on Butt Neck Joint. *American Lutherie #126*, p. 52.

18 Preparing for Finishing

The major construction of the instrument proper is at this point complete, the only remaining construction work being in the finishing of the instrument and the construction and installation of the *fittings*, including the bridge, nut, and end pin. Although the major construction is complete, there is work to be done to get the instrument ready for the application of finish. This includes sanding the entire guitar up to a suitably fine grit, but it almost always includes some touch-up work as well. Any dents in the body caused by inadvertent knocks during construction must be removed. Gaps appearing between various pieces of the guitar must be closed or filled. Any hollows that are deep enough so they cannot be effectively sanded out must be filled. And any issues with the ends of the purfling lines should also be addressed.

Much care should be taken with the preparation for finishing. A good finish is as dependent on the prep work as it is on the application of the finish. This process should not be rushed. Careful inspections should be made where required.

Because it can't be known in advance which of these touch-up operations will need to be performed, this chapter presents a number of the most useful such operations in cookbook form. These are selected and applied as necessary to the particular construction defects present in the instrument at hand. Of course a careful inspection of the guitar is the first order of business, to identify all the small flaws that need attention.

About Initial Sanding and Inspection

The current state of the guitar, as far as sanding goes, is that it has been sanded up to 100 grit, with the exception of any parts which have shell inlay. These have been sanded up to 180 grit. Although in theory the surface is refined enough for an inspection to identify touch-up work that needs to be done, it is my experience that it is often better to sand the entire instrument up to 180 before making the inspection.

Some people need a more refined surface for inspection than others. This is no fault of the individual, but appears to be at least partly related to the size of the woodworking objects that have been worked on in the past. Folks that have worked primarily on small objects in the past tend to be able to do an accurate assessment of touch-up work needed at this point of refinement. This may have to do with the fact that the size of the flaws that are considered to need attention are generally relative to the size of the object.

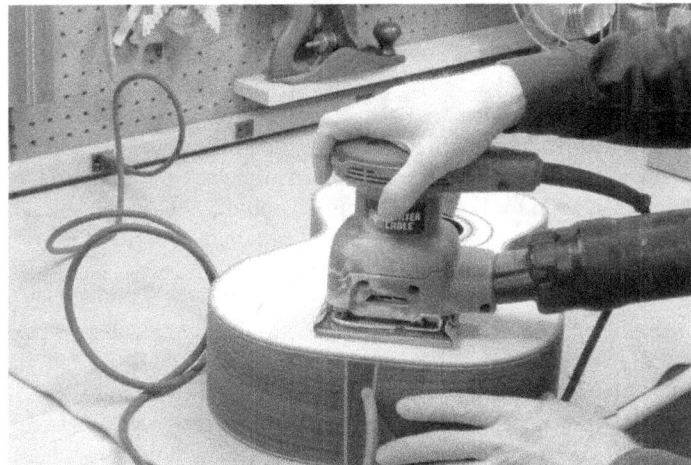

Photo 18-1 – *Sanding the top using a random orbital quarter sheet sander with a thin foam interface pad to back up the sandpaper.*

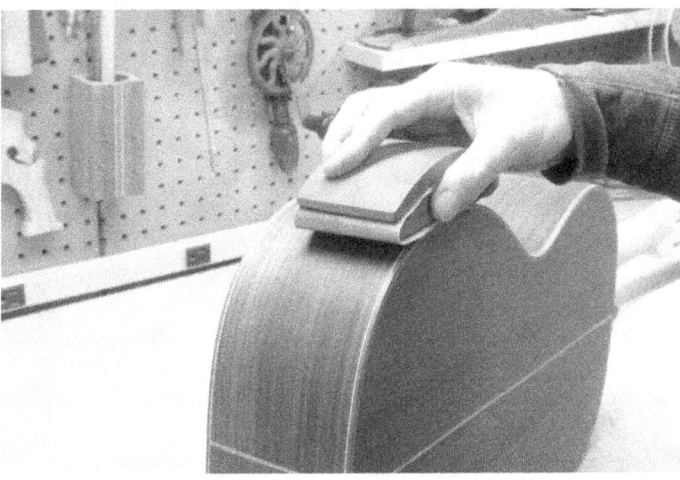

Photo 18-2 – *Sanding the ribs using a hard rubber sanding block.*

Photo 18-3 – *Sanding into the inside edge between the heel and the ribs using a teardrop shaped rubber sanding block. Any sanding block with a sharp edge can be used.*

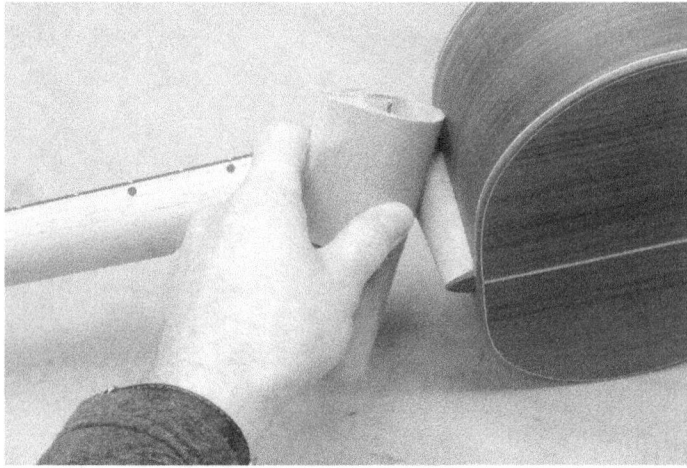

Photo 18-4 – *Sanding into the curves between the heel and the neck shaft using the round surface of a teardrop shaped rubber sanding block. Any sanding block with a cylindrical shape can be used.*

The general inspection scheme that is detailed here involves a number of individual inspection steps, each looking for a particular class of defects. Issues found are marked for later touch-up work, except for coarse sanding scratches, which are most readily fixed on the spot.

☐ **Initial Sanding and Inspection**

1. The entire guitar, with the exception of the fretboard playing surface and any areas that have shell inlay (such as the headplate and the fretboard sides) are sanded up to 180 grit. Sanding can be performed using a random orbital sander and a thin foam interface pad (**photo 18-1**) or using sandpaper on a sanding block (**photo 18-2**). Some areas, such as the inside edges where the heel meets the body sides, the waist, and the various curves of the neck and heel are done by hand using an appropriately shaped block (**photos 18-3**, **18-4**), no matter what tool is used for the rest of the instrument. It is important to avoid sanding areas that have shell inlay with the coarser grits, to avoid scratching the shell.

Care is taken to avoid getting hardwood sanding dust on the soft guitar top while sanding the top. Not only can the hardwood dust scratch the top, it can also cause discoloration that is difficult to remove. Care is taken to not over-sand and thin the bindings at the waist.

Some woods whisker up when sanded in one direction or the other. If this happens while sanding, it is prudent to determine which sanding direction causes the whiskers to be raised, and then only sand that wood in the other direction.

Starting at 120 grit, the sharp edges of the headstock and neck transition are ever-so-slightly rounded over. The luthier should strive for uniformity of the roundover here. Uniformity of the roundover of the bindings is also important.

 When using the sander, every other grit is used, so only 120 and 180 grits are used. Much care should be taken when sanding the top to only sand as much as is needed to remove the previous grit's scratches. The top is soft and is easily thinned by aggressive sanding.

Luthiers prone to sweating should be sure to position their heads so they are not directly over the guitar, to avoid dripping sweat on the wood. If sweat is dripped on the wood it will leave a stain which will be visible under finish, even though it will probably *not* be visible during sanding. Sweat dripped on the wood is removed by wetting and wringing out a rag, and wiping it over the sweat spots and then over the *entire* surface of the body or neck. The surface is allowed to dry completely before continuing sanding.

2. The entire instrument is rubbed briskly with 0000 steel wool, working with the grain. This is done to remove sanding dust that may be packed into gaps, obscuring them from view. After the steel wool, the same brisk rubbing is performed but this time using a soft clean rag.

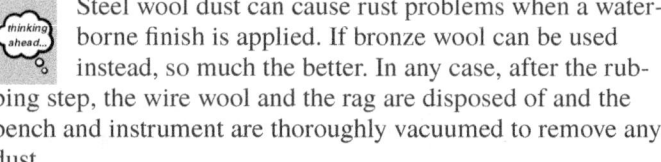 Steel wool dust can cause rust problems when a waterborne finish is applied. If bronze wool can be used instead, so much the better. In any case, after the rubbing step, the wire wool and the rag are disposed of and the bench and instrument are thoroughly vacuumed to remove any dust.

3. Inspecting for dents and coarse sanding scratches. These can be found anywhere on the surface of the guitar, and are most readily seen on the broad surfaces when viewed under raking light. To set up for this inspection, a lamp or other strong source of light is placed at the back of the bench and as low as possible, and pointing toward the front of the bench. The guitar is placed on the bench in front of the light. Inspection involves bringing the luthier's eyes down close to the level of the surface under examination, looking across the surface, not down onto it from above. The low position of the lamp will cast long shadows, even on the tiniest of defects, and these shadows will be most visible from a low angle. Examination in this way will show defects that are otherwise unnoticeable under normal lighting and viewing angles.

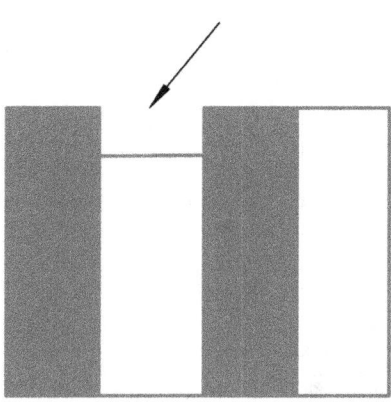

Figure 18-1 – *Schematic cross section of a purfling bundle with a small dip in the surface of one of the light colored lines.*

Photo 18-5 – *Steaming out dents in wood is done using a damp rag and a soldering iron. The rag is folded twice, placed over the dent, then the soldering iron is gently pressed and moved around in the dent to steam it out.*

Coarse sanding scratches are sanded out or scraped out with a sharp card scraper, as they are found. Dents are depressions where wood was compressed but not actually removed. These are caused by whacking the guitar into some blunt object or by whacking or dropping some blunt object on the guitar during construction. Dents appearing in the top plate are often caused when the guitar is placed top down on the bench without the bench top being cleaned of debris. Dents should be lightly marked in pencil for later repair.

4. Inspecting for gaps between parts. Gaps can appear anywhere that parts of the instrument butt against each other. For this reason the inspection for gaps involves carefully and methodically visually following joints, to be sure they are fully joined along their entire lengths. For example, the joints between each piece of binding, its surrounding purfling, and the body panels surrounding the purfling should be carefully checked all along the length of the binding piece. Any gap found is lightly marked in pencil for touch-up. Particular care is taken to identify gaps that have been fully filled by glue squeeze-out. These will not have the appearance of a hole, but they will need to be patched up just the same.

5. Inspecting for dips in purfling lines. Because the purfling lines may have been glued together by hand, sometimes a line will dip below the level of the rest of the lines for a short distance, creating a small hollow. This is shown schematically as a cross section in **figure 18-1**. Such dips are usually shallow and can be difficult to see. But careful examination with raking light of the surface of the purflings along their lengths will identify these dips so they can be marked lightly in pencil.

6. Inspecting for gaps in purfling end joints. Gaps that appear in the end joints of the purfling are generally easy to spot. Although these gaps will usually be filled with glue squeeze-out, the color difference between the glue and the colors of the purfling lines tends to make these stand out. They should be lightly marked with a pencil for subsequent repair.

The Touch-up Techniques

A number of common touch-up techniques are presented. Each one is used to touch up a particular type of defect.

Steaming Dents

Most small dents can be steamed out using a damp rag and a point source of heat. A pencil soldering iron of the type used for electronic work is ideal for this task. It is useful to do a trial run of dent steaming on a piece of scrap wood of the same species. The only potential issue is burning the wood. A trial run on the same wood species will provide good information on how long the iron can be left in contact with the wood before it starts to burn.

1. The soldering iron is turned on and allowed time to warm up. If the iron is adjustable for temperature, the lowest temperature setting is generally used.

2. A small rag of T-shirt or similar material is dampened and wrung out, then folded into four thicknesses. The rag is placed

Photo 18-6 – *If care is taken not to let the rag get too dry, a dent in soft wood can be completely removed without burning the wood.*

Photo 18-7 – *Sometimes gaps appearing between wood parts have been completely filled with glue squeeze-out. The glue must be carefully chipped out of the gap without damaging the wood edges. The gap should end up deep enough to take and hold putty.*

over the dent, then the soldering iron is gently applied to the rag over the dent and moved around so it covers the entire area of the dent (**photo 18-5**). It should be possible to feel the dent through the soldering iron. The heat of the iron will produce steam, which will swell the wood in the dent. Progress should be checked to be sure that the wood is not getting scorched. Each time the rag is applied, a different area of the rag should be used, because the process quickly dries out that part of the rag directly under the soldering iron.

3. If the dent has not been completely removed and there is no burning of the wood surface, the steaming process can be repeated a number of times until the dent is completely removed (**photo 18-6**).

Closing Binding Gaps Using Heat

Small gaps that appear around the bindings are sometimes repairable using heat. The area over and around the gap are heated on the bending iron enough to melt the glue. Then the binding is quickly clamped into place, removing the gap. Clamps are left in place for at least one hour while the glue hardens. This technique is not always successful but is always worth a try.

Puttying Gaps

Small gaps can be filled with a putty of the same or similar color as the surrounding wood. Various materials are available for this, including commercial putties and lacquer fill sticks. The main issue with the former is the availability of a limited number of colors. Lacquer fill sticks are used by melting the lacquer into the gap and smoothing it over. They usually come as part of a lacquer fill repair kit, which includes a number of colors of lacquer sticks, an iron to melt the lacquer, and the tools and materials to smooth the fill. These kits are useful but quite expensive.

Detailed here is a putty made from wood sanding dust and glue. This is a common and traditional putty, and has been introduced previously for the purpose of filling the gaps under the fret ends. Its advantages include that a good color match can be had, because the putty is made with the sanding dust of the actual wood to be filled. To enhance the color match and to provide rapid curing of the putty, I like to use 5 minute epoxy as the glue that binds the sanding dust. The epoxy is quite clear and so doesn't color the putty as do some wood glues. This is particularly an issue with putties made of light colored woods. Epoxy also has the advantage of not shrinking as it cures, as some wood glues do.

It is sometimes necessary to seal the wood around the gap before putty is applied, to prevent the color of the putty from staining the surrounding wood. This is generally only necessary when the putty is made from a dark wood and the gap is right against a light-colored wood. This is particularly necessary when using a putty made of rosewood dust right up against the wood of a spruce top.

Sealers have three important qualities. They provide a physical barrier, which in this application prevents the color of the

Photo 18-8 – *The gap is filled with a putty made from sanding dust from the same wood as (in this case) the back plate, mixed with 5 minute epoxy. It is packed into the gap using a wooden toothpick used as a tiny spatula.*

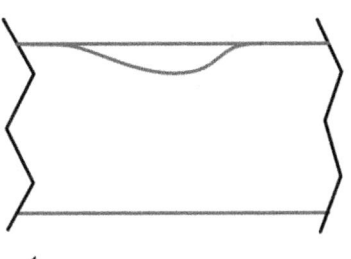 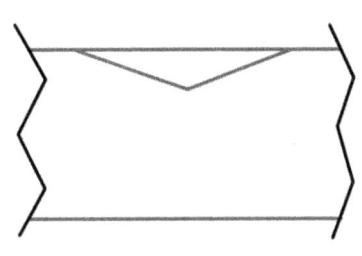 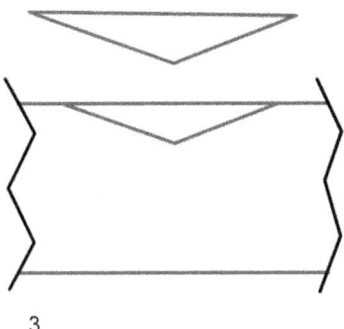

Figure 18-2 – *The first diagram (1) shows a dip in a purfling line at the outside of a purfling bundle. Dips in any of the lines in a purfling bundle that are too deep to drop-fill with clear filler can be fixed by patching in new wood. The dip is first chiseled to a shallow triangular shape (2), then a matching piece of purfling line is chiseled out of stock and glued in place (3). After the glue cures the patch is leveled.*

putty from staining the surrounding wood. They do not deeply penetrate the wood, so excess sealer is readily sanded off. And sealers dry quickly, so work can proceed without a long delay.

Various readily-available sealers can be used for this purpose. Blonde shellac of 2 pound cut, either mixed in the shop or from a can makes a great sealer. Another option is to use vinyl sealer. Although generally used as a sprayed sealer when spray finishing wood, this product works great as a wipe-on sealer for puttying touch-ups. It is clear in color. It is available from general woodworking suppliers and from lutherie suppliers as well.

Sometimes when larger gaps are puttied the repair remains visible, even if the color match between the surrounding wood and the putty is good. The detail that makes the repair visible is the absence of grain lines on the puttied surface. This is remedied by drawing in the grain lines, using special graining pencils or fine-tip graining markers available just for this purpose. These are generally available from wood finishing suppliers and may be available from some lutherie suppliers as well.

Note that the following gap-filling steps are used for general gap filling but not for filling gaps at the ends of purflings. The latter touch-up is discussed in its own section.

Materials
    2 pound cut blonde shellac, or vinyl sealer
    5 minute epoxy
    Sanding wood dust from variously used wood species
    Graining markers or pencils to match grain of wood used
    Flat wood toothpicks
Tools
    Hobby knife or scalpel or small skew knife

---

1. If the gap is filled with glue squeeze-out the glue must be removed to a depth that provides room for the putty. This is most easily done using a small knife (**photo 18-7**). It is often tedious work, and care must be taken not to damage the surrounding wood. The gap is thoroughly vacuumed out after chipping out the glue.

2. If a dark putty will be used against a light colored wood, the area around the fill should be sealed to prevent the color from the putty from bleeding into the light wood. A small piece of cotton T-shirt material is folded over twice and used as a pad to apply either vinyl sealer or 2 pound cut blonde shellac. Sealer is applied to the pad until it is wet but not dripping. Then the pad is quickly wiped *once* across the gap and the small area around it that should be sealed from the putty. The sealer must be allowed to cure at least two hours before puttying the gap.

3. If sanding dust for the particular wood species needed has not been previously collected, it is generated and collected now. An easy way to do this is to thoroughly vacuum the surface of a sanding board and then just sand a cut-off until enough sanding dust can be accumulated. It is a good idea to generate more than is needed for a single patch and to save it in a small labeled jar for future use.

 If there are a number of gaps on the guitar that will need to be filled with the same wood species of putty, it is generally a good idea to do them all at the same time. That way only one batch of putty needs to be mixed.

4. A small amount of opaque putty is mixed using 5 minute epoxy and some of the sanding dust. Because the quantities involved are usually so small, a flat wood toothpick can be used to mix and apply the putty. As a rough measure, there should be about as much sanding dust as there is epoxy. The proportions are not critical as long as the resulting putty is opaque and not so thick that it can't easily be worked into the gap.

5. The putty is packed into the gap and mounded over a bit (**photo 18-8**). The putty is allowed at least two hours to cure.

6. The putty is leveled off by sanding with 180 grit sandpaper on a hard block.

7. If the repair is obvious due to lack of grain lines, these can be added on top of the patch using a graining marker or pencil of the appropriate color. Use of these tools is always tested off the instrument on scrap to be sure of results before committing to use on the instrument.

Clear-Filling Gaps

Gaps that are shallow or so thin that they cannot be effectively filled with putty can be filled with a transparent material

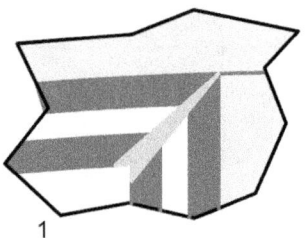 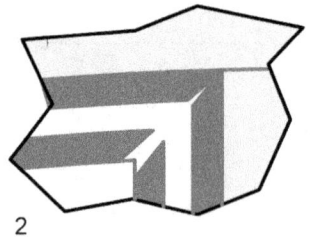 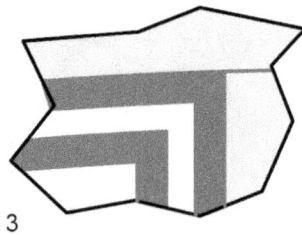

Figure 18-3 – *Repairing an inaccurate purfling miter joint using putty. Any glue squeeze-out in the gap between the purfling bundle ends is cleaned out (1), then the gap is filled with a putty that matches the wood of the light purfling lines (2). A graining marker that matches the wood of the dark purfling lines is used to fill in the missing parts of the dark wood lines (3).*

by *drop-filling*. The object of this technique is to fill those hollows that would be obvious after the finishing material is applied. The most readily available material for drop-filling is medium cyanoacrylate glue. The glue is dropped into place from the tip of a wood toothpick or using a micro transfer pipette.

Sometimes the glue gets wicked into the gap such that the gap remains. If so, additional applications can be made, or the gap can be filled with a more viscous clear material such as 5 minute epoxy.

If the drop fill results in a mounded fill after the glue cures, it can be sanded flush with the surface using 180 grit sandpaper on a block.

Repairing Dips in Purfling Lines

Shallow dips can usually be drop-filled to good effect. Deeper dips are best repaired by patching in some new purfling material. A useful tool for repairing purfling lines is a micro chisel that is exactly as wide as one purfling line. Such a chisel can be easily made from a hobby knife blade, which is the same

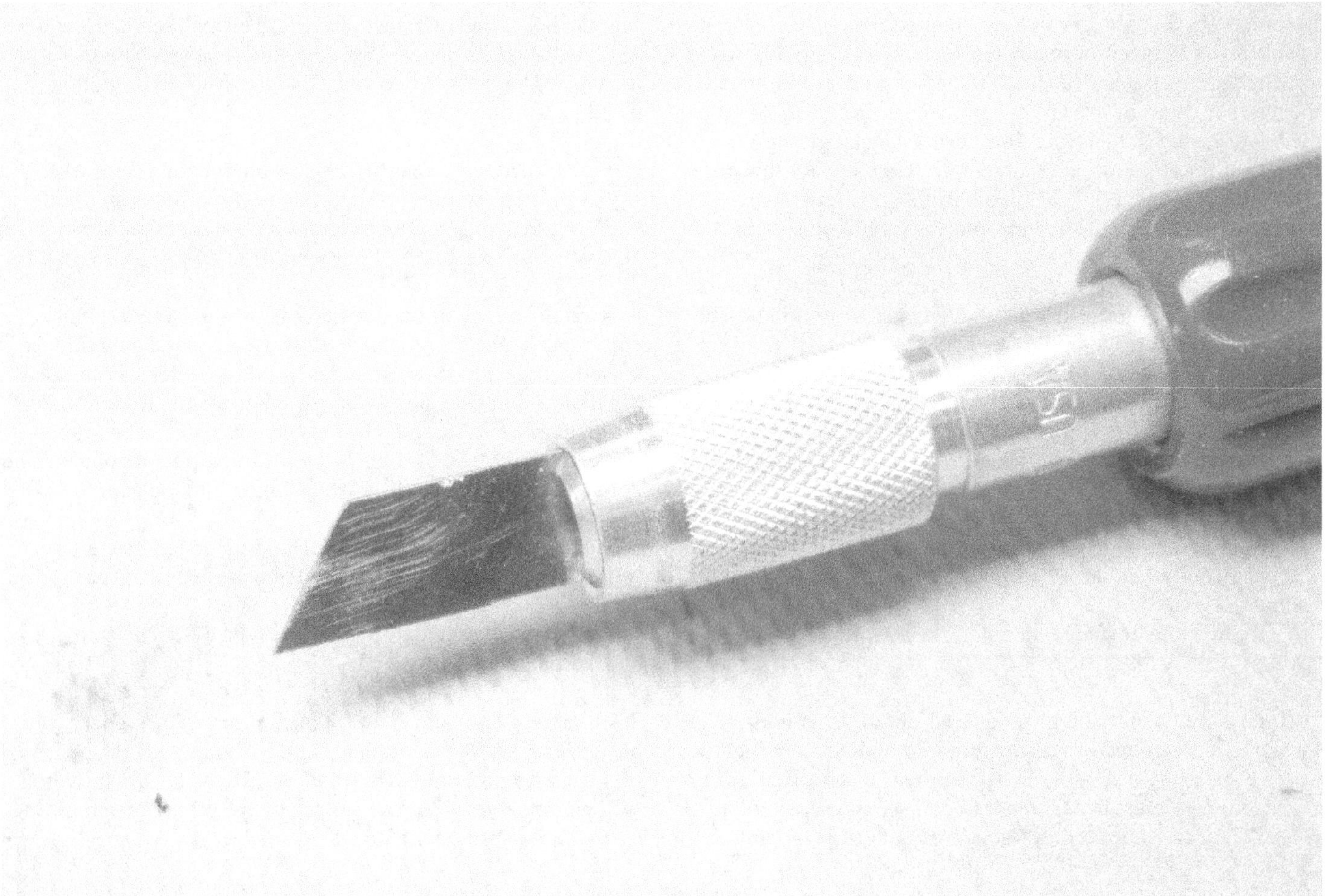

Photo 18-9 – *A purfling line chisel is made by grinding the edge off a hobby knife blade. The blade is the same thickness as a commercial purfling line.*

thickness as a commercial purfling line is wide, 0.020″ (0.5mm).

☐ Making a Purfling Line Chisel

1. The sharp edge of the hobby knife blade is ground off using stone, grinder, or sanding board. The new edge, which is now the bevel of the chisel, should be made square to the sides of the blade.

2. The back edge of a hobby knife blade comes rounded over. This should also be ground square to the sides of the blade.

3. The bevel and the back surfaces are honed and polished smooth, in the same manner used for any chisel.

4. The blade is fitted into a hobby knife handle for use (**photo 18-9**).

☐ Patching in Wood

The basic strategy is to reshape the dipped area of the purfling line to have a wedge shape, then glue in a similarly wedge-shaped piece of wood.

1. The purfling line chisel is used to trim the dip so it has two approximately flat surfaces that describe a wedge shape if they could be viewed from the side (**figure 18-2**).

2. A similarly shaped wedge of the same color purfling material is cut. This can be difficult to do, given the small size of the piece to be cut and the thinness of the purfling material. An easy way to do this is to secure a sandwich of purfling lines in a small vise, and use the purfling line chisel to chisel out a wedge shaped piece, using the same motions used in step 1 (**photo 18-10**).

3. The piece cut in step 2 is glued into the cavity made in step 1. It can be secured in place while the glue cures using tape or a small weight on top.

4. After the glue cures the patch is sanded flush to the surface.

Repairing Purfling End Joints

Butt or miter joints of the ends of purflings that do not meet properly can often be fixed by patching in material as described above. But this is sometimes a tedious process because it usually involves the width of a purfling strip containing multiple lines. In this case it is usually prudent to patch in pieces cut from multiple lines glued together.

Photo 18-10 – *The purfling line chisel being used to chisel a replacement piece of light colored purfling wood from a purfling bundle secured in a small vise. Note the grip on the chisel, with the thumb and first finger on the sides of the blade and up close to the cutting edge.*

It is also possible to achieve a good touch-up using putty and a graining pen. The general strategy here is to putty the gap using a putty that matches the light color wood of the purfling bundle, and then fill in the darker purfling lines using the graining marker.

1. The gap is cleaned of any glue squeeze-out (**figure 18-3.1**).

2. Putty matching the light color purfling line(s) is mixed and packed into the gap. After the putty cures, the patch is sanded flush with the surface (**figure 18-3.2**).

3. A graining marker or pencil matching the color of the darker purfling lines is used to fill in the darker lines (**figure 18-3.3**). When using a marker for this fine work, it is sometimes helpful to use the sharp edge of a single-edge razor blade as a dam to prevent the marker ink from flowing beyond its intended boundary. The razor blade is held in place until the ink dries, then lifted straight up and away from the patch. Any ink on the edge of the blade can be cleaned off, so the blade can be used again for this purpose.

Final Sanding and Inspection

Following any touch-up work, the entire instrument is examined once again. Any additional flaws found are touched up. As with other construction operations performed, it is wise to continue this inspection and touch-up loop until the final inspection reveals nothing more to touch up. Then the instrument is put aside for a few days and inspected once again, with fresh eyes.

In production woodworking, sanding usually proceeds through the grits no higher than 180. In the process described in this book, the instrument is sanded up to 320 grit. Although this extra sanding is unlikely to produce a smoother finish, the finer grits often reveal coarser grit sanding scratches that are not otherwise visible. This finer grit sanding also helps to bring up a better shine in plastic and shell material.

Any areas that contain plastic or shell, such as the top surface of the headstock or the side of the fretboard should be sanded some more, using 400 and then 600 grit sandpaper. This will eliminate any visible scratches in the surface of the inlay material.

19 Applying the Finish

Guitar finishing is an interesting topic, one that is not often covered in much depth in books and courses on guitar building. There are a number of perspectives from which to view the topic and the issues involved. Here, I am going to first provide a brief historical look, and follow that with the same kind of requirements analysis that was originally presented in the introduction to this book. There, the issue at hand was figuring out an optimal strategy for building the guitar, based on a set of requirements for the guitar but also related to the luthier's abilities and the tools and equipment at his or her disposal. Here, the issue at hand is figuring out one or more optimal finishing strategies to present, given that same basic set of requirements.

The finish on the guitar provides some amount of protection for the wood against dirt and liquids, and if the finish is tough enough it also provides some amount of additional abrasion resistance. All finishes enhance the look of the new wood, and because they help reduce staining they help to retain a clean look much longer than if the wood were left unfinished.

It is often surprising to find out that guitar finishing technology has historically followed wood furniture finishing technology, at least fundamentally. The 19th century saw the use of a number of finishes for guitars, including *oil varnish*, which is a mixture of a resin, a drying oil, and an evaporating solvent. Also used was shellac and other *spirit varnishes*, which dissolve resins and other ingredients in alcohol. All of these finishes were generally applied with a brush.

Two technologies introduced in the early 20th century would be quickly adopted for furniture and guitar finishing. These were nitrocellulose lacquer and spray application. Sprayed lacquer dramatically reduced the time and effort needed to finish a guitar, and this quickly became the conventional way to do it. But of course the equipment needed to spray was expensive, limiting its use to instruments built on an industrial scale. Hand built instruments, and in particular classical guitars were and still often are finished using the materials and techniques of the previous era.

Sprayed nitrocellulose lacquer is still used by many guitar finishers. But large guitar manufacturers mostly finish guitars today using sprayed UV-cured polyester finish, which offers great time and effort savings. This technology is even more expensive, and so is out of reach for most small shops.

All the time that finishing technology was advancing for use in industrial finishing operations, there have been people doing wood finishing by hand. Products for hand finishing have also been developed. Today the hand finisher can chose from a wide variety of finishing products. Wipe-on varnishes are quick and easy to apply. Brushed-on oil varnish is still available, but becoming less so, due to increasing environmental prohibitions of the solvents they release while curing. Shellac and other spirit varnishes are also still available. A number of waterborne finishing products are available that are easy to apply and are more environmentally friendly than their oil varnish predecessors. There are even UV-cured polyester finishes that can be applied by brush. Choosing among these is optimally accomplished taking into consideration a list of requirements for what the finish should do, and also what skills and equipment are possessed by the luthier.

Finishing Requirements

In this chapter two different finishing options are presented. This section presents the rationale for selecting these two for use in the construction process described in this book, from the many finishing options available. This was done primarily by considering how each finish rated in terms of some requirements. These requirements are listed here in order of my assessment of their importance, in the context of a guitar building strategy aimed at the novice luthier.

Effect of the Finish on the Tone of the Guitar

No matter the advantages provided by a guitar finish, if it degrades the tone of the instrument then it is not under consideration. Not being detrimental to the tone of the finished instrument is by far the most important requirement that was considered when selecting finishes to be presented here. Although there is not much formal research on this subject, one encouraging study done by Howard Stephens showed there was little difference in the tonal effects of different finishes as long as the thickness of the finish was held constant.[1] This finding is generally supported by anecdotal evidence, and by the stated preference of many luthiers for a thin finish.

Familiarity

This was considered to be a requirement of primary importance. If a luthier is familiar with and skilled in the application of a finishing material, then that is probably the best one for that luthier to use. The rationale here is simple. The application of most finishing products requires skill gained from practice, and usually some tools collected along the way. Making use of a known process will almost always produce better results than if a heretofore unknown process and material is used.

Unfortunately this requirement was of little help in selecting finishing options for the construction process described in this book, because there was no consensus among the luthiers polled in preparation for the development of that process, when it came to finishing materials and techniques. Still, put as advice for the novice luthier, it is probably better to ignore the finishes presented here if the luthier is already adept at applying some other finish and has the equipment to do so.

Application Equipment

It is a general philosophy of the construction process described in this book to make use of construction techniques that do not require extensive and expensive special-purpose tools, fixtures, and other equipment. This same approach is extended to finishing. Except when the novice luthier is already skilled at applying a sprayed finish and already has all the equipment to do so, it is difficult to justify the use of spray finishing in the process. At first glance the cost of such equipment may seem to be modest. Small spray guns of good quality may be had at reasonable prices[2]. But a capacious compressor is needed to power that gun, and exhaust fans and filters and personal protection equipment are needed for safe application. If the materials to be applied are flammable, then an additional level of safety equipment is required. And the list goes on.

For this reason, only finishing materials which are applied by hand were considered for inclusion here. These include most of the materials which can be applied by wiping or brushing, including various varnishes. Some hand-applied finishes were further eliminated from consideration based on their toxicity. Although the tools needed to apply such materials may be inexpensive and readily available, the equipment needed to provide adequate personal protection for the luthier can be quite expensive.

Safety

This is of course explicitly coupled to the requirement for minimal application equipment, above. Safety equipment is not considered to be optional. All equipment needed for safe application is an absolute requirement. Finishes which inherently pose fewer safety risks and so require less safety equipment were chosen over more dangerous substances.

Ease of Application

Hand finishing requires practice, but some finishes are trickier to apply than others. For example, brushed on UV-cured polyester requires only a single coat, but much care must be taken to be sure that one coat is of adequate thickness. In contrast, most waterborne varnishes can be built up in a number of easy-to-apply thin coats, that each *burn in* to the previous coats, resulting in a uniform coating of appropriate thickness. Easier-to-apply finishes were chosen over those that are more difficult to apply.

Environmental Considerations

One way to classify finishes is by the way they produce a coating on the surface of the wood. When available finishing materials are divided this way, there are three basic classes of finishes. *Evaporative finishes* contain solids dissolved in a vehicle solvent. As the finish cures, the solvent evaporates away, leaving the solids as a coating on the surface of the wood. For the purposes of this discussion I'll include oil varnishes in this category, even though they also undergo some chemical changes as they cure. *Coalescing finishes* contain small particles of solids held in suspension in a vehicle. As this class of finish cures, the vehicle also evaporates away, but as it does so the small particles of solids coalesce and link into a large and more uniform surface coating. *Catalyzed finishes* undergo chemical changes as they cure. These changes result from the addition of a chemical catalyst right before the finish is applied. There are also *UV-cured finishes* that behave in a similar manner, but instead of a chemical catalyst, exposure to ultraviolet light effects the chemical change.

Of these, the class of finishes that has the most direct adverse environmental effects is the class of evaporative finishes. These often contain substances that exhibit strong greenhouse effects in the atmosphere. As such, the availability of these finishing products has been increasingly limited by regulation. It is expected that this trend will continue. Although evaporative finishes were not completely discounted when considering finishes to describe in this book, the trend of increasing unavailability was a strong consideration.

Effectiveness of Presentation in a Book

Application details were ultimately going to be presented in this book. Finishes for which the presentation of application was better suited for a book were chosen.

Protection Provided

It may seem odd to list this requirement last. If the construction process described in this book were oriented toward large scale production lutherie, where equipment and training cost would be amortized over many instruments, this requirement would likely be one of the most important. Here though, luthier safety and the likelihood of the successful application of the finish were considered to take precedence.

Some Candidate Finishes

As mentioned there are a number of useful finishing materials for guitars, and any of these can be used to produce a fine finish. Candidate finishes were considered for application description in this book based on the listed requirements. Some significant finishes were not chosen to have their application described here. These are listed below.

Note that only the briefest descriptions of some of the generally available finishes are presented here. For more complete information a definitive reference should be consulted. Any of the wood finishing books by wood finishing guru and luthier Jeff Jewitt, for example, will provide much more detail on the various finishing products available.

Spray Finishes

These were all not chosen primarily due to the quantity of application equipment required and the expense of that equipment. Those finishes that use *volatile organic compounds*

(VOC) as vehicles were also not chosen due to safety considerations. Most available spray finishes do provide excellent protection and ease of application.

Spirit Varnishes

There are a number of hand-applied spirit varnishes that offer good protection and are relatively safe to use. The coats of most spirit varnishes burn in to each other, forming a solid mass of finish. But these were not chosen primarily because they are difficult to learn to apply, particularly from an application description provided in a book.

Brushing Lacquer

Although generally easier to apply than most spirit varnishes, brushing lacquer requires considerable work to rub out following application. With a vehicle composed of highly flammable VOCs, it was also not chosen for safety and environmental reasons.

Oil Varnish

Although brushed oil varnishes provide excellent guitar finishes they were not chosen for a number of reasons. Coats of oil varnish go on as discrete layers which do not burn into each other at all. This makes application somewhat difficult to learn, because cutting through the top layer of varnish during the rubbing-out process results in an unsightly visible border called a *witness line*, which cannot be removed. Although relatively safe, these varnishes do use a VOC vehicle, and for this reason manufacturers of oil varnishes have been dropping them from their product lines in recent years. I have used oil varnish as my primary guitar finish for many years, but it got to the point where I would just become comfortable with a particular varnish when the manufacturer would stop making it, requiring learning a new product, which would shortly be dropped as well.

French Polish

High end classical guitars are almost always finished using *French polish*, which is shellac applied with a pad. The finish is easy to apply but application is quite time consuming. The resulting finish is thin and quite delicate. There are a lot of steps to the finishing process, which make it somewhat difficult to describe in a book.

Catalyzed Finishes

This class of finish includes any varnish which comes in two parts which must be mixed together just before application, and also UV-cured finishes which must be cured under UV lights or in direct sunlight. These finishes are generally applied as one thick coat, which cures very fast, and is then rubbed out. Applied by hand, rubbing out these finishes takes considerable work. Catalyzed finishes are also not very forgiving because they must be applied quickly. Some present safety issues.

About the Selected Finishes

I've selected two finishes, the application of which will be described in detail in this chapter. One is a simple satin oil wiping varnish finish, most often erroneously called an oil finish due to the viscosity of the varnish. It is often referred to as wipe-on finish, finishing oil, or Danish oil. It is applied directly to the wood using a cloth pad. Application requires minimal equipment. The material is relatively safe. Oil wiping varnish is extremely easy to apply, and a description of its application lends itself well to presentation in a book. It is not a hard finish, so the protection it provides is minimal, but all of its other advantages make it a good choice for detailed application description in this book.

It should be noted that this finishing material makes use of a vehicle that is largely composed of VOCs, and these materials are subject to increasingly vigorous regulation. As of the time of publication of this book, oil wiping varnish products are not available in all US states due to environmental regulations. The number of states restricting its use can surely be expected to increase.

The other finish described here is a satin waterborne varnish applied with a foam brush. This is applied over clear waterborne pore filler, for woods that have pores. This also requires minimal equipment for application. The material is non-flammable and the vehicle used is primarily composed of water. As such it is a lot safer than most other finishing materials. It is generally considered to be more environmentally friendly than a number of other finishing materials as well. With some care, this material is quite easy to apply and it is relatively easy to describe its application in a book. Waterborne varnish provides good protection.

Note that both finishes have a satin gloss. Although both types of finishing products are available in gloss, these were not selected. Commercial "gloss" wiping varnish simply does not produce a gloss finish, despite manufacturers' product claims. And although gloss waterborne varnish can be rubbed up to a nice gloss, doing so requires additional finishing steps and equipment, and provides more opportunity for application errors.

In an ideal world it would be adequate to specify just the generic types of the finishing products used, and any specific products of these types would work fine, given the following application descriptions. Unfortunately this is not how it works in the world of wood finishing products, where product qualities, descriptions, and application instructions vary greatly, even within a product category. I am loath to actually recommend specific products here, but unfortunately the application details to be presented were developed for *specific* finishing products. But because the formulation and availability of specific finishing products change over time, the specific products that can be used with the accompanying application details are not specified in the book, but are listed in the Finishing Materials section of the Online Annex found in Appendix A.

Finish Application

As mentioned two different finish applications are described here. This is a good place to mention that another finishing option is to contract out the finishing to a professional. Guitar finishing specialists do exist, and excellent results can be had by going this route.

Preparing the Shop for Finishing Work

If the instrument will be finished in the shop, there are a number of steps which must be taken before finishing commences, no matter what finish is to be applied.

One of the major issues when applying any finish in the woodworking shop is dust. Reducing airborne dust and also dust from any surfaces that are above the areas of the shop where finishing will be performed is an absolute necessity. Everything in and around the finishing area should be vacuumed thoroughly and wiped down with a damp rag. Basically, when it comes time to begin finishing, the shop should no longer be considered to be a wood shop, but a finishing shop.

Adequate lighting is important to good finishing. The availability of raking light makes it much easier to see missed spots when applying finishing material. Point source lights reflect off the surface of the finish, and help indicate the degree of flatness and gloss. I recall a nice published photo of the finish rubbing-out shop at boutique guitar maker Huss & Dalton. The walls are festooned with tiny white Christmas lights. They are not there to celebrate the holiday, but to provide point sources of light to aid in the rubbing-out process.

Adequate ventilation and safety equipment are critical. All finishing material manufacturer's safety and ventilation requirements should be strictly adhered to.

Care is also taken to adhere to the manufacturer's recommendations for application temperature range. Most varnishes are quite balky to apply near the low end of the recommended temperature range. They are too viscous to flow out well and slow to cure. Additional heat in the shop is often useful. But there are issues at the upper end of the manufacturer's recommended application temperature range as well. Here, the finishing material may dry too fast for easy application, particularly on the larger surfaces.

Before beginning finishing, some arrangement is made for hanging the instrument while the finish cures. It is useful if the hanger includes a swivel so that the instrument can be rotated around while it is hanging. **Photos 19-1** and **19-2** show a simple hook arrangement that makes use of a ceiling hook, a swivel, and a sturdy hook for the guitar, the latter made of bent ⅛″ (3.2mm) × ¼″ (6.4mm) steel bar stock. In use the guitar is hung by one of the drilled tuning machine holes on the bent steel hook. Note that the bend in the hook must be shallow enough so, when the guitar is hanging from it, the shaft part of the hook does not contact the front or back surface of the headstock.

I like to cover the bench with a large clean piece of paper for finishing (**photo 19-3**). Unprinted newspaper is available from art suppliers, and plain wrapping paper is available in most

Photo 19-1 – *An overhead hook for supporting the guitar while the finish is curing. There is a screw hook in the joist, a swivel (here a small pulley with a swivel on it), and a big hook made of bent steel bar stock.*

Photo 19-3 – *The bench is covered with a clean sheet of paper in preparation for finishing. This provides a dust-free surface and also keeps finish drips off the bench top.*

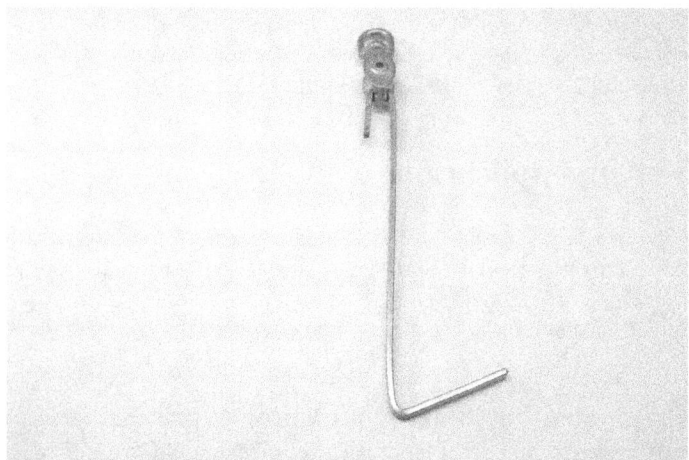

Photo 19-2 – *The swivel pulley and bent steel hook. Note the hook part is nearly flat, so when the instrument is hooked onto it no part of the hook shaft touches the instrument headstock.*

Photo 19-4 – *A sheet of wax paper is inserted into the guitar to prevent finish drips from marring the inside of the back.*

pharmacies and office supply stores. The paper provides a barrier between the work and any debris that may remain on the bench, and it also provides a plain background that makes it easy to see any drips of finish, so they can be wiped up before they do any damage. I learned this simple but substantial improvement to my finishing technique from Portland, Oregon, luthier Cyndy Burton, and it has saved me all manner of finishing aggravation over the years. The paper sheet can be removed or replaced as needed during finishing.

Preparing the Instrument for Finishing Work

There are a couple of things which are done to the instrument prior to the start of finishing. The first of these is to insert some material into the soundhole that will protect the inside of the back of the guitar from drips. My preference is to insert a sheet of wax paper about 10″ (254MM) square (**photo 19-4**), followed by three or four sheets of paper towels (**photo 19-5**). These are taped securely to the inside of the back, so they don't move around when the instrument is moved into different positions (**photo 19-6**).

It is also useful to plug most of the tuning machine holes to prevent finish from accumulating at their edges and then dripping through the holes. This is particularly an issue for a brushed finish. Careful work with either finish will eliminate this as a problem, but filling the holes is easy enough to do. Inexpensive foam earplugs (**photo 19-7**) are trimmed to a length

Photo 19-7 – *Foam earplugs are used to fill most of the tuning machine holes, to prevent finishing material accumulation there.*

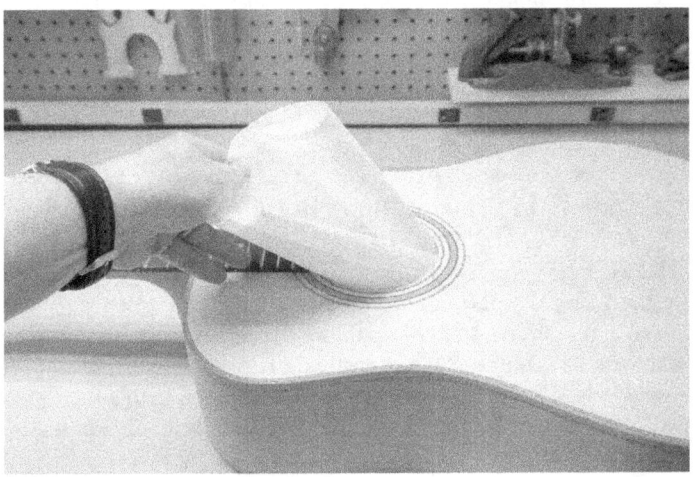

Photo 19-5 – *A wad of paper towels goes in on top of the wax paper.*

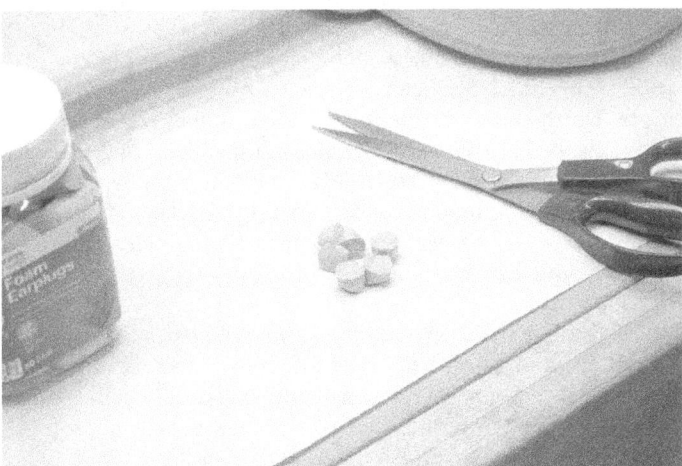

Photo 19-8 – *The earplugs are trimmed to a bit shorter than the headstock thickness.*

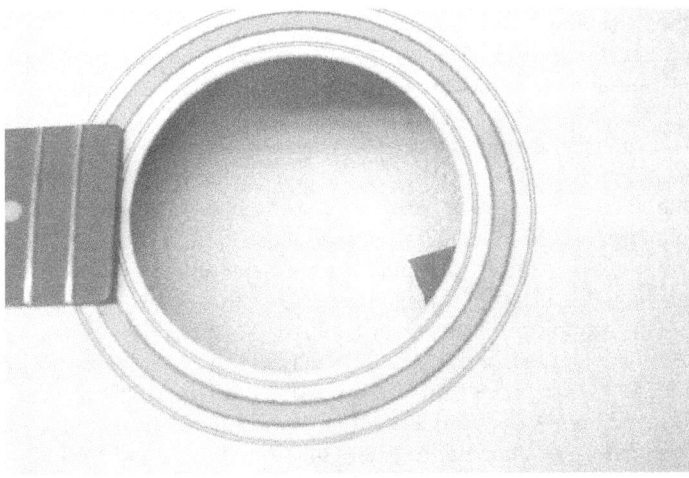

Photo 19-6 – *The protective materials are taped in place with masking tape so they don't move around.*

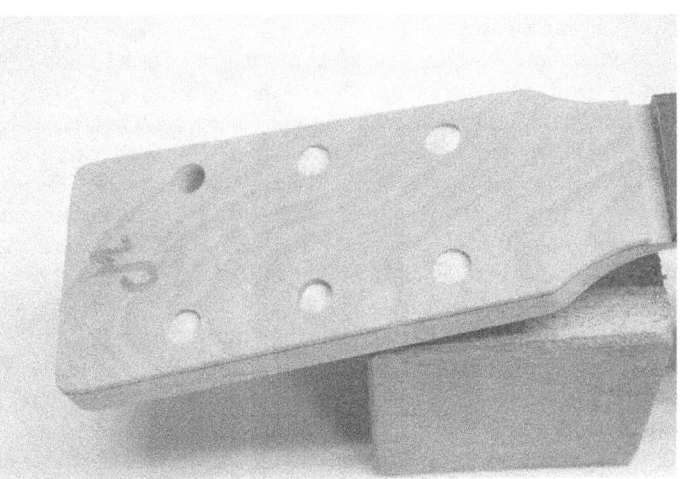

Photo 19-9 – *The trimmed earplugs in the tuning machine holes.*

a little less than the thickness of the headstock (**photo 19-8**). The trimmed pieces are inserted in the tuning machine holes so their ends are just below the surfaces of the headstock (**photo 19-9**). Foam earplugs are available from the pharmacy. Note that one of the top holes should be left unplugged, so the instrument can be hung up using this hole.

Some luthiers like to mask off the fretboard playing surface during finishing. I generally do not do this when using hand-applied finishes. Runs and drips on the fretboard surface are rare with careful application, and they can be quickly removed when they occur using a rag and thinner. If masking is done and a brushed finish is applied, ridges often form at the edges of the masking tape.

A guitar neck rest that supports the neck of the guitar when the instrument is sitting on the bench will be required for finishing and most of the rest of the construction operations. These are simple blocks with a padded concave channel at the top. They are available from lutherie suppliers, but simple shop-built neck rests like the one detailed in Appendix D are often used.

Finishing with Satin Oil Wiping Varnish

I have been using wiping varnish finishes since early in my lutherie career.[3] There was a vogue for this type of "oil" finish for electric basses in the late 1980's and early 1990's, especially for instruments that were built of the darker-colored woods. This finish has been perfected for use on acoustic guitars by North Devon, UK, classical guitar luthier Kevin Aram, who presented his finishing technique at the Guild of American Luthiers Convention in 2014. That presentation has since been written up as an article in *American Lutherie*.[4] The application techniques described here are fundamentally similar to those appearing in Kevin's article.

Note that although all oil wiping varnishes are composed of similar materials, their formulas are different and they can vary substantially in viscosity and drying time. The finishing details below are not necessarily appropriate for *all* oil wiping varnish products. See the Specific Finishing Materials section of the Online Annex, presented in Appendix A, for the products for which the finishing details here are known to work.

Application Strategy

The finishing material is applied directly to unfilled wood with a pad in multiple coats. Most of the application details concern the order in which the various surfaces are coated and how the instrument is held and positioned to do that. After the guitar is fully coated, it is hung up while the finish cures. Because varnish takes a while to dry tack-free, it is prudent to place the hook that will be used to hang the instrument in a dust-free location that is also not drafty. Steel wool is used to smooth the finish between coats.

One hand will be used to pad on the finishing material, and the other hand will be used to pick up and move the guitar. A nitrile glove is used on the application hand to protect it from contact with the material. A clean cotton glove is worn on the other hand to prevent fingerprints on the wood or finish surface.

Materials
   Tack rags
   Wiping varnish (see text)
   Clean, washed, 100% cotton T-shirt material
   0000 steel wool
   Single-edge razor blades
   Mineral spirits

☐ Wet Inspection

It is particularly important to check the surface for even the smallest sanding scratches and the tiniest dips and crevices, because the resulting thickness of the finish to be applied here will be so thin. *Wet inspection* is the application of alcohol or paint thinner to the surface to visualize what the surface will look like under finish. This is done as a preliminary inspection step here. One surface of the instrument at a time is wet with thinner using a rag, then examined under raking light. Any surface imperfections are filled or sanded as described in the previous chapter, before proceeding with finishing.

☐ Applying Headstock Decoration Label

If the instrument will use a printed stick-on label for headstock decoration, that label is applied now. The backing paper is carefully removed from the label and the label is carefully positioned and lightly pressed into place on the headstock. Once the label has been positioned properly, the label is pressed more securely to set the adhesive.

☐ Sealing to Prevent Pigment Bleeding

Bleeding of pigment from darker-colored wood onto adjacent lighter wood is a particular problem with hand-applied finishes, because the physical act of applying the finish picks up pigment and moves it around. This is particularly an issue with some rosewoods. The general solution to the problem is to apply a protective layer of finish that will prevent subsequent applications of finish from raising and smearing the pigment. A test for pigment bleeding can be done by dipping a small corner of a rag into mineral spirits and then rubbing it briskly on and around the back binding and purflings somewhere. If pigment is picked up and smeared onto lighter woods while this is done, then a sealing application should be performed on the bindings and purflings, and everywhere else the pigment-bleeding wood is directly in contact with a light-colored wood.

This of course leaves the problem of how to apply the protective sealer in the first place. The way this is done is to apply the sealing material so the application pad moves along the line of the seam(s) between adjacent pieces of wood, and to avoid moving the pad in any way perpendicular to those seams. Examining the pad and changing it for a clean one if it picks up any color is also useful to prevent pigment bleeding.

For example, an instrument with rosewood back, sides, and bindings and maple purfling lines is likely to be subject to bleeding of pigment from the rosewood onto the maple. A sealing operation can be performed prior to general finish application by applying finishing material only to and around the bindings, following the curve of the bindings with the pad as the finish is applied here. Similar sealing application is done in other places where pigment bleeding may be a problem.

These include along the back strip, at the edges of the tail graft, at the sides of the fretboard, and at the edges of the headplate.

Note that this may not be a problem with many woods. For example, two of the guitars frequently photographed in this book were made of black cherry (*Prunus serotina*) and black walnut (*Juglans nigra*). Neither showed any tendency to bleed color during finishing.

1. A few application pads are made up from T-shirt material. The cloth is cut with scissors into pieces approximately 3˝ (76.2mm) square (**photo 19-10**). The cloth is folded into a pad which has all edges either inside the pad, or at the back end of it. To do this, the piece is first folded vertically approximately into thirds, but so the free edge of the cloth is not on the edge of the pad (**photo 19-11**). This is then folded horizontally in half, so the edges are all inside (**photo 19-12**). In use, the pad is held so the remaining cloth edges are in the hand. (**photo 19-13**). This folding in of the edges is done to help prevent lint being pulled from the pad during use. Lint will generally come from the raw edges of the cloth, and this folding method keeps those edges away from the application area of the pad when it is used.

Two pads will generally be used, one for applying the varnish to the work, and the other for smoothing it out and absorbing excess.

Photo 19-10 – *Folding the application pad starts with a square piece of T-shirt cloth.*

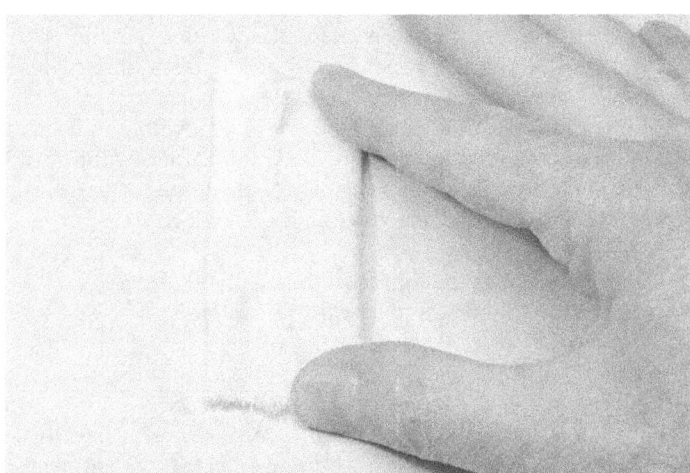

Photo 19-11 – *First, it is folded vertically in approximate thirds, but so the edge of the cloth is not at the edge of the pad.*

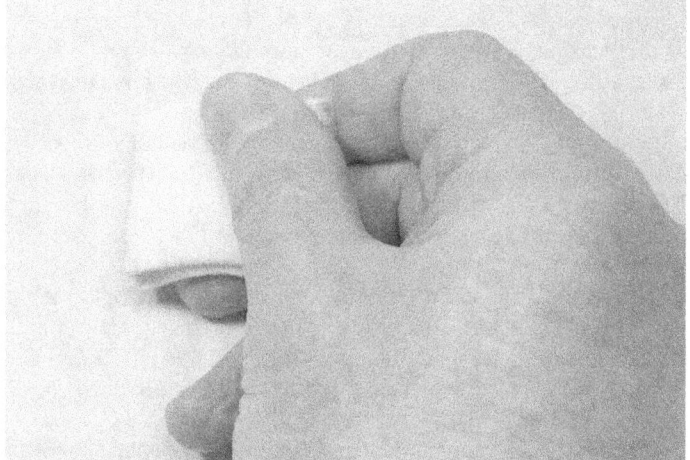

Photo 19-13 – *In use, the pad is held so the edges of the cloth are in the hand.*

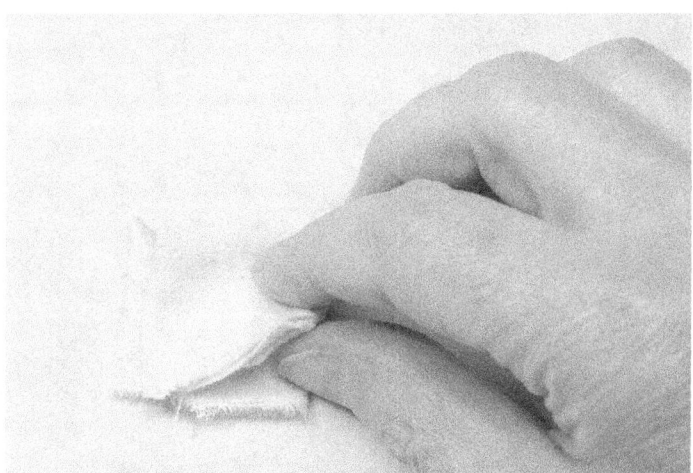

Photo 19-12 – *Then it is folded in half horizontally.*

Photo 19-14 – *A plastic storage container lid makes a nice clean place to put the pad down. Wiping varnish can be decanted into a small squeeze bottle for ease of use.*

2. The wiping varnish is decanted into a suitable container if it is not already in one. Most of the products come in small rectangular cans with a small opening on top. In use, the varnish can be applied to the pad by covering the opening of the can with the pad and turning it briefly upside down. If this can't be managed easily with one hand, some varnish can be decanted into a small plastic squeeze bottle (**photo 19-14**).

3. All of the surfaces to which a sealing coat will be applied are rubbed over lightly with a tack rag.

4. A sealing coat is applied to one length of binding or other area at a time. If the bindings will be sealed, then the top bindings are done first. One of the pads is wet with varnish. It should be wet but not dripping. This application pad is used to apply a ribbon of varnish in one continuous pass over the area to be sealed. For a length of binding, the pad is held in three fingers so it folds gently around the edge of the binding, applying varnish to the perimeter of the plate, the bindings and purflings, and a thin area of the guitar sides (**photo 19-15**). The areas adjacent to the application are checked for runs. Any found are cleaned up with a clean rag. Runs onto the playing surface of the fretboard are thoroughly cleaned off using a rag and mineral spirits.

5. Excess varnish is removed. A dry pad is run along the length of the binding, pressed gently to smooth the varnish and remove any excess. As a general application rule when using this material, unbroken coverage is required, but since the varnish is quite thin in viscosity and the instrument will be hung up vertically during curing, the coat should be quite thin as well. Removing excess varnish is important. This will always be done after any application of wiping varnish.

6. The application pad is checked for color bleeding onto the pad. If there isn't any, it is probably not necessary to continue the sealing application. If there is color here, the pad should be flipped over to a fresh surface for its next use, or replaced.

7. If sealing is continued, the back binding is done next. The guitar is flipped over on the bench, with the fretboard resting on a block that raises it off the bench. This means the top plate binding at the tail end will be in contact with the paper on the bench. This area has wet varnish on it, so this will have to be smoothed out after the back areas have been sealed. The back binding is sealed following steps 4 through 6.

8. If the back strip or the headplate edges will be sealed, this is done in like manner, with the guitar top-down on the bench with the fretboard raised on a block (**photo 19-16**).

9. The guitar is removed from the bench and hung up. The application and smoothing pads are used to touch up the varnish at the tail end of the top, where it was disturbed by contact with the paper on the bench.

10. If the sides of the fretboard will be sealed, this is done while the instrument is hanging up.

11. The varnish is allowed to cure for 24 hours. After it is cured the sealing is checked for runs. Any runs are carefully sliced off using a single-edge razor blade or a small and very sharp chisel. If runs have formed, this should inform the luthier that the application coat was too thick. Subsequent coats should be made thinner.

12. The sealing coat is also checked for any color staining of any of the light-colored wood. Anywhere there is staining, the varnish is cut back using either 0000 steel wool or a single-edge razor blade until all staining color is removed. These spots are touched up with a light additional application of wiping varnish and allowed to cure. This is repeated until all areas intended to be sealed are sealed with no color bleeding.

13. The sealed areas are lightly rubbed with 0000 steel wool with the grain, in preparation for finish coating.

☐ **Finish Coats**

Finish coats are applied in the same sequence as is used to apply the sealing coat. The only difference is that the varnish is applied to completely cover each broad surface.

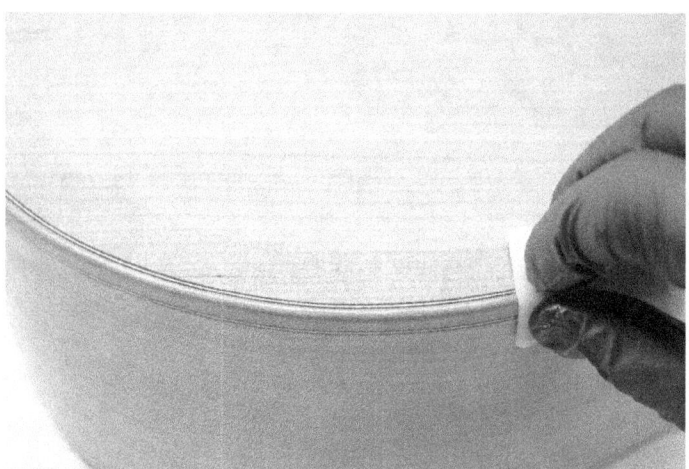

Photo 19-15 – *When applying a sealing coat to the bindings and purflings, the pad is held in three fingers and moved straight across the length of the bindings.*

Photo 19-16 – *Sealing the back strip. Notice the pigment on the pad that bled out of the rosewood back.*

1. Pads are made and the varnish is decanted if necessary, as described in the previous operation.

2. The entire instrument is lightly rubbed with a tack rag, turning the rag frequently to a new tacky area.

3. Varnish is applied to the top first. One of the pads is wet with varnish. It should be wet but not dripping. This application pad is used to apply varnish to the entire top and the edges of the fretboard extension. Application can be done using broad overlapping circular strokes or simple long overlapping stripes, as long as full coverage is achieved. Achieving full coverage is aided by the use of raking light, which helps to show any missed spots. Whenever the pad goes dry enough so full coverage cannot be achieved without going back over the work, the pad is recharged with more varnish.

The areas adjacent to the application are checked for runs. Any found are cleaned up with a clean rag.

4. Excess varnish is removed from the surface. A dry pad is run in straight, slightly overlapping strokes, with the grain, pressed gently to the surface to smooth the varnish and remove any excess (**photo 19-17**). Unbroken coverage is required, but since the material is quite thin in viscosity and the instrument will be hung up vertically during curing, the coat should be quite thin as well. To avoid runs during curing, it is prudent to err on the side of less varnish rather than more.

5. The headstock is coated next, using the same application techniques. All surfaces of the headstock are covered, as well as a small portion of the neck shaft and fretboard sides adjacent to it. It is generally easier to do this by picking the guitar up off the bench, grasping it near the middle of the neck shaft, and applying the varnish with a pad held in the other hand. Then a dry pad is used to remove excess varnish, as previously described.

6. The guitar is returned to the bench, top down, with the fretboard resting on a block. This angles the top so only one point at the tail end will touch the paper on the bench. Placing the instrument down like this will disturb the varnish only at that point and not across the entire top. That disturbed point will be cleaned up later. Varnish is applied to the back plate and the back of the heel cap in the same manner as for the top. Note that, supported only at two points, the instrument is quite wobbly. This is generally not an issue, because the varnish is applied so gently to the surface. Again, excess varnish is removed using a dry pad.

7. The guitar is again picked up off the bench. Varnish is applied to the ribs and the heel and to adjacent parts of the neck shaft and fretboard edges while the instrument is held by the neck in one hand. The small area at the tail end of the top that was touching the paper on the bench during the previous step is touched up as well. Excess varnish is removed.

8. The guitar is hung up on its hook. Care must be taken when positioning the guitar onto the hook to avoid messing up the varnish on the back of the headstock. With the fingers of one hand in contact with the fretboard playing surface, the currently unvarnished parts of the neck shaft and fretboard edges are varnished. When the dry pad is used to smooth and blot the varnish, it is also used to blend the just covered areas of the neck with those previously covered.

9. The guitar is carefully checked for complete coverage and for the formation of any runs. These are fixed up if found.

10. The varnish is allowed to cure for 24 hours. After it is cured it is checked for runs. Any runs are carefully sliced off using a single-edge razor blade or a small and very sharp chisel. If runs have formed, this should inform the luthier that the application coat was too thick. Also removed from the surface are any large pieces of dust that have adhered to the varnish during drying.

11. The entire surface of the guitar is *lightly* buffed using 0000 steel wool, working with long and light strokes with the grain (**photo 19-18**). The varnish coat is thin and soft. It is easy to damage it using aggressive strokes with the steel wool. The purpose of steel wool buffing here is to remove tiny surface irregularities and dust. If the surface of the steel wool begins to clog, another area on the pad (or a new piece) is used.

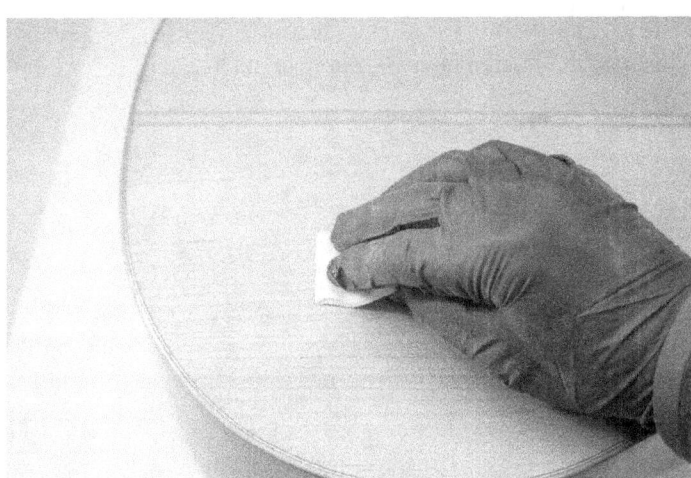

Photo 19-17 – *The dry pad is used to gently smooth the applied varnish, using gentle straight strokes.*

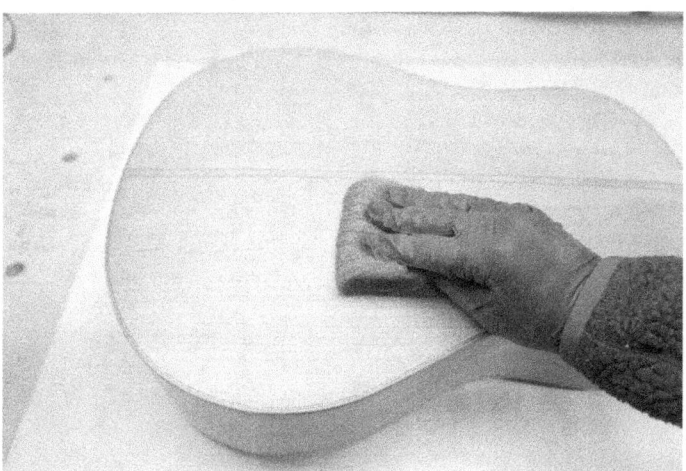

Photo 19-18 – *After a coat of varnish is fully cured, it is rubbed with long and light strokes using 0000 steel wool, to prep for the next coat.*

12. The guitar is rubbed with a rag with the grain and then thoroughly vacuumed in preparation for the next application.

13. Four to eight coats are applied to the guitar, following steps 1 through 12. It is generally advisable to use the minimum number of coats necessary for the surface to appear smooth. This is particularly an issue for porous hardwoods. More coats partially fill the pores with varnish, and this is generally not an ideal look. Note that in some cases it may be appropriate to apply more coats to the top than to other parts of the instrument.

14. The steel wool buffing for the final coat should leave the entire surface with a uniform satin finish. Following buffing with steel wool, the entire surface of the guitar is buffed with a clean dry cotton T-shirt material cloth, again with the grain, pressing down quite firmly. This burnishes the surface and brings up a bit of shine.

15. This type of finish is inherently soft, but it hardens up considerably with time. It is a good idea to hang the instrument up for two or three weeks before doing any more work on the guitar. This will cure the varnish enough to prevent a lot of surface blemishes that can result from additional construction handling.

Finishing with Satin Brushed Waterborne Varnish

The guitar finishing schedule I've used for the longest time made use of oil varnish grain filler and oil varnish. But in recent years, environmental restrictions have resulted in one after another of the fillers and varnishes I was familiar with being dropped from the product lines of their manufacturers. The transition to waterborne filler and top coats took a little time to work out, but at this point this is the finishing combination I use most often.

Waterborne fillers dry quickly and hard, and so they require a different technique than is used for oil-based fillers. I am particularly fond of clear fillers because there is no need to attempt to match the color of the filler to that of the wood. The particular filler mentioned in the Finishing Materials section of the Online Annex found in Appendix A, is amazingly forgiving in terms of application. It can be applied in just about any way imaginable and it works just fine. The filler and the application technique for it described here were first brought to my attention by Hawaii luthier Bob Gleason in 2016.[5]

Waterborne varnish is easy to apply, but its drying characteristics are not quite the same as those of oil varnishes, and this means the application method is not quite the same either. Although waterborne varnishes dry much more quickly, they do run easily until they begin to dry. This warrants application to a horizontal surface, where the varnish can flow out and then begin to dry. As is the case with any varnish, heat quickens drying. The varnishing method described here is somewhat similar to that detailed by Portland, Oregon, luthier John Greven in his classic series of guitar construction articles in *American Lutherie*.[6] The particular brand of varnish used is specified in the Finishing Materials section of the Online Annex found in Appendix A.

Application Strategy

Porous wood is grain-filled using the specified waterborne grain filler, which is applied in multiple applications with a rag, and then sanded smooth.

The entire instrument is varnished using the specified satin waterborne varnish, applied with a foam brush. Note that foam brushes have either small cell foam or *really* small cell foam. The latter is much preferred, because the varnish flows from it more slowly. Because the varnish runs easily on surfaces that are not horizontal until it begins to dry, and because the varnish burns in well, it is applied in a series of partial applications, each of which coats just one area of the guitar. These area applications proceed as fast as the varnish takes to dry. This means that one or two complete coats can be applied to the instrument per day. Although applying varnish to one area at a time increases the amount of time it takes to varnish the instrument, this also makes for a fairly foolproof hand-application process that does not require any special work-holding fixtures.

Complete finish coats are applied no more than a day apart, because subsequent coats will completely burn in to already-applied coats if the new coats are applied in this amount of time.

Note that all areas of the guitar cannot be made to be completely horizontal for application of the varnish. Areas that can't be kept horizontal are manipulated after application of the varnish to prevent runs from forming, and are also heated to hasten drying.

One hand will be used to brush on the finishing material and the other hand will be used to pick up, hold, and move the guitar. Nitrile gloves are used on both hands to protect them from contact with the material.

Following application and thorough curing of the varnish, the surface is wet-sanded to level the finish.

Materials
    Tack rags
    Waterborne grain filler (see text)
    Waterborne varnish (see text)
    1″ (25.4mm) and 2″ (50.8mm) foam brushes (see text)
    Clean, washed, white, 100% cotton T-shirt material
    Single-edge razor blades
    Masking tape
    600 and 1000 grit wet or dry silicon carbide sandpaper
    Heavy cut automotive polishing compound
Tools
    Neck rest (see Appendix D)
    Plastic scraper or old credit card
    Heat lamp
    Sandbag
    Clean board, approximately 6″ (152.4mm) × 24″ (609.6mm)
    Micro-tip transfer pipettes
    Gum rubber erasers, approx. 1⅛″ (28.6mm) × 2″ (50.8mm)

☐ Sealing to Prevent Pigment Bleeding

Bleeding of pigment from darker-colored wood onto adjacent lighter wood is a particular problem with hand-applied finishes because the physical act of applying the finish picks up pigment and moves it around. This is particularly an issue with some rosewoods. The general solution to the problem is to apply a protective layer of finish that will prevent subsequent applications of finish from raising and smearing the pigment. A test for pigment bleeding can be done by dipping a small corner of a rag into the waterborne varnish and then rubbing it briskly on and around the back binding and purflings somewhere. If pigment is picked up and smeared onto lighter woods while this is done, then a sealing application should be performed on the bindings and purflings, and everywhere else the pigment-bleeding wood is directly in contact with a light-colored wood. After the test area fully dries, it should be scraped clean of any color staining before proceeding.

Sealing is done in exactly the same way as described under the previous section on applying a wiping varnish finish, but instead of wiping on a sealer application of wiping varnish, a sealer application of the waterborne varnish is used. This is applied with a pad, exactly as described for sealing with wiping varnish.

☐ **Grain Filling Option**

Those parts of the guitar which are made of a porous hardwood will have their pores filled prior to varnishing. If there are no woods with pores used in the guitar, this operation is skipped. The guitar top does not need to be filled.

1. If the sides and end of the fretboard will be filled, masking tape is applied around the fretboard extension to prevent filler from getting onto the top around the extension.

2. The back is filled first. A small amount (about a teaspoon) of the filler is placed on the back. This is worked into the pores of the back with a rag made of white cotton, moving in a highly overlapping small circular pattern. Application moves in this way until the entire back has been covered with filler. More filler is added to the back if needed. The entire back can be covered in this way before the filler begins to dry. If at any point the filler remaining on the surface starts to stiffen up, it should be scraped cleanly off the back, using a plastic scraper or old credit card, and then discarded. If soft filler remains when the back is done, it is wiped off the back using the rag. Care is taken to leave no remaining surface filler.

3. The ribs of the guitar are done next, using the same application technique. If the bindings have pores, these are filled at the same time as the ribs are done. Care is taken to keep filler off the top of the guitar. It is difficult to prevent filler from building up in the inside edges between the ribs and the heel, so after filling here, these edges are meticulously scraped to remove any remaining filler. As in the previous step, excess filler is wiped or scraped off the surface before it fully hardens.

4. The neck, fretboard sides, and headstock are done next, again using the same application technique as described in step 2. There is no need to wait for the filler to completely dry before placing back or ribs down on the paper on the bench while positioning the guitar to fill the neck. Care is taken to avoid getting filler on the fretboard playing surface, on the top, or in the nut slot. Any filler applied to any of these areas should be quickly wiped off and then the area wiped with a damp rag to remove any traces of filler remaining. Filler in the inside edges of the nut slot can be removed using a chisel or single-edge razor blade. The nut slot can be masked if filler is repeatedly accidentally applied there.

5. The filler should be allowed to cure for one hour before another application. Before the next application, any obvious globs of hardened filler on the surface are spot-sanded off, using 220-grit sandpaper on a block. Then steps 2 through 4 are repeated for the next coat. Three filler coats should be applied in total. After the last coat, the filler is allowed to cure overnight.

6. Any masking tape used is removed. The filled surfaces are carefully and completely sanded with the grain using 220-grit sandpaper on a block to level them. This sanding must be

> ## Varnish and Temperature
>
> The recommended application temperature for most varnishes ranges from approximately 70°F (21°C) to approximately 90°F (32°C). Viscosity and drying time are critically affected by temperature. At colder temperatures, the varnish is more viscous and takes longer to flow out. At temperatures below the recommended application temperature range, the varnish may not flow out at all. And the varnish also takes longer to firm up and dry at lower temperatures too. At higher temperatures, viscosity is lower and drying time is faster. This improves flow-out and reduces runs and sags on surfaces that are not horizontal. Of course at temperatures above the recommended application temperature range, the varnish may dry so quickly that it makes application difficult.
>
> As a general rule, it is noticeably easier to brush varnish at temperatures near the higher end of the recommended application temperature range. In my experience 85°F (29°C) is about ideal. This is generally higher than is desired for human comfort, but if shop temperature can be maintained at a higher than normal temperature during varnishing, results will be improved. This applies to oil varnishes and waterborne varnishes, although the latter seems to be a little more forgiving about application temperature. If the temperature is to be elevated in the varnishing room, the guitar and the can of varnish should be in the room too, so that the room, the guitar, and the varnish all end up at the elevated temperature before finishing begins.
>
> Years ago we got a question in to the *American Lutherie* Questions Column about oil varnish application, which I referred to Orlando, Florida, classical guitar luthier Alfredo Velazquez for an expert answer. His varnishing skills are masterful. Having struggled myself with the application of oil varnish year round in New England, a task which requires considerable seasonal temperature-dependent doctoring of the varnish, as well as changes to technique, I was at first taken aback by the simplicity of his application recommendations. But of course he works in a place where ideal varnishing temperatures exist for most of the year. Varnishing truly is an easier job in Florida than it is in a lot of other places.

Photo 19-19 – An application container is made by drilling a hole in the lid of an airtight container, to provide tight clearance for the handle of the foam brush.

Photo 19-21 – The finished application container ready for use in varnishing the guitar.

Photo 19-20 – The lid supports the brush so it will be submerged in varnish when the lid is screwed on. If the hole is not tight enough it can be supplemented with a bead of silicone sealer.

complete enough to leave the surfaces uniform in appearance, but over-sanding is avoided, because this can expose new and unfilled pores.

7. The entire surface of the guitar is rubbed with a soft, clean, dry rag to remove any surface sanding debris. Then it is thoroughly vacuumed (including inside) in preparation for varnishing.

☐ **Making the Varnish Application Container**

Because the application technique to be described makes use of a number of short finishing sessions close together in time, it is useful to keep the brush suspended in varnish between these sessions. This eliminates the time and waste associated with cleaning the brush many times. To do this, an application container is put together that provides airtight storage for the varnish and an arrangement to suspend the brush in the finish. In the accompanying photos I am using a plastic jar for the container, but any jar or can that is wide enough to accommodate the brush and that is airtight can be used as well.

Photo 19-22 – The lamp on the bench behind the guitar will provide raking light during varnishing. This makes it easier to identify missed spots. Note also the heat lamp hanging from the joist at the top of the photo. This will be used to gently heat the instrument to aid flow-out and to speed drying.

A hole of the same diameter as the handle of the foam brush to be used is drilled in the center of the lid of the jar (**photo 19-19**). If the fit between hole and handle is tight enough (**photo 19-20**) the brush will be suspended by that friction alone, and the seal between hole and handle will be reasonably airtight (**photo 19-21**). If it is not tight enough, a bead of

Photo 19-23 – The brush is moving right to left like an airplane landing, and has just gently touched down near the tail end.

Photo 19-25 – The stroke continues right off the plate.

Photo 19-24 – The angle of the brush to the surface is raised to nearly vertical, as the edge of the back is approached.

silicone sealer can be run around the top of the hole. Once cured this will serve as a gasket.

☐ **Applying Headstock Decoration Label**

If the instrument will use a printed stick-on label for headstock decoration, that label is applied now. After it is applied, the surface of the label will have to be sealed to prevent the waterborne varnish from dissolving the ink on the label.

1. The backing paper is carefully removed from the label and the label is carefully positioned and lightly pressed into place on the headstock. Once the label has been positioned properly, the label is pressed more securely to set the adhesive.

2. A small amount of a sealer consisting of one part oil-based varnish (*not* waterborne varnish) and one part paint thinner is thoroughly mixed together is a small cup. A small pad is made from a piece of T-shirt material. This is dipped into the sealer then squeezed out. A single coat of sealer is gently and quickly applied to the entire surface of the label with a single wipe of the pad.

3. The sealer is allowed to cure for at least 24 hours before the instrument is varnished.

☐ **Varnishing the Guitar**

As mentioned, the instrument will be varnished with a number of coats, each of which is composed of a number of section applications, each on a specific section of the guitar. The varnish is allowed to cure so it is dry to the touch between these section applications. The sections, in order of application are: top, ribs, headplate, back, and the neck, including the back and sides of the headstock. The instrument will receive a total of 8 to 10 complete coats, with five section application sessions per coat. It is wise to keep track of coat and section, using a written check list of the form: 1T, 1R, 1H, 1B, 1N; 2T, 2R ...

In preparation for varnishing, a lamp should be placed at the back of the bench where it can provide raking light on the surface to be coated (**photo 19-22**). A heat lamp (or two) should also be placed overhead somewhere, so that a varnished surface can be held up to it to help speed curing. This is seen at the top of **photo 19-22**.

A few words about brushing technique. Most folks have experience with interior house painting, which involves a lot of working of the finish with the brush to attain even color and good coverage. Varnishing brush technique is *completely* different. The object here is to transfer varnish to the surface with as little brushing as possible. The general technique is to apply the finish to a horizontal surface, and to just let the finish flow off the brush during long, smooth, slightly overlapping strokes.

For the larger flat horizontal surfaces (the plates), the brush is gently dipped into the varnish, gently lifted and tilted so one corner of the brush edge points down, and then excess varnish in the brush is allowed to flow back into the jar. It flows back in a steady stream, but then begins to flow in a series of drips. The brush is *never* wiped off on the edge of the container. Doing this causes air bubbles, which will result in a rough textured finish. This is the same reason the brush is dipped and lifted gently, to prevent the formation of air bubbles.

When the flow of varnish out of the brush turns into a series of drips, the brush is fully loaded. The brush is then briefly turned upside down and flipped to examine its broad sides, to be sure it absorbs any remaining surface varnish. The surface varnish can be seen being absorbed into the brush. If it is not fully absorbed the brush is returned to its position over the application container and allowed to drain a bit more. Now the tip of the brush is gently but quickly applied at the centerline of the surface to be varnished and near to an edge, in a *landing stroke* (that is, with the tip of the brush approaching the surface like a plane coming in for a landing, *not* like a helicopter coming in for a landing), and then moved slowly and gently across the surface toward the edge (**photo 19-23**) until the edge is approached. The brush is angled to a more vertical attitude as the edge is reached (**photo 19-24**), and the edge is brushed off with light contact, so as not to squeegee material out of the brush at the edge (**photo 19-25**).

Now the brush moves in the opposite direction. The following pass again uses a landing stroke (to avoid brushing into the edge, as this would squeegee varnish out of the brush, resulting in drips down the side), touching down an inch or so after the edge, into the place just varnished (**photo 19-26**).

The brush is moved slowly and gently across the surface without pressing down on it. Pressing would squeeze varnish from the brush, causing bubbles and ridges. The varnish should simply be allowed to flow off the tip of the brush, which is just gently in contact with the surface (**photo 19-27**). The speed at which the brush is moved across the surface is governed by the Goldilocks principle. If the brush is moved too fast, the varnish will not be able to drain out of it at a rate fast enough to completely cover the surface. This will result in incomplete coverage behind the brush. If the brush is moved too slowly, a thick puddle of varnish will be deposited. This encourages the varnish to run if the surface is not horizontal. If the brush speed is *just right*, a thin and even coat that completely covers the area behind the brush is deposited on the surface.

When the opposite edge of the surface is reached, the same angling vertical of the brush is done (**photo 19-28**), so the brush brushes off the edge at a vertical orientation and with light contact between its tip and the surface (**photo 19-29**).

Successive stripes of varnish are applied in the same manner, each with a bit of overlap of the previous stripe. Varnish application continues in this manner until the brush begins to run dry. An eye is kept on the area just behind the brush, watching for an even application of finish as wide as the brush. The brush stroke is quite slow, and as it continues it slows down

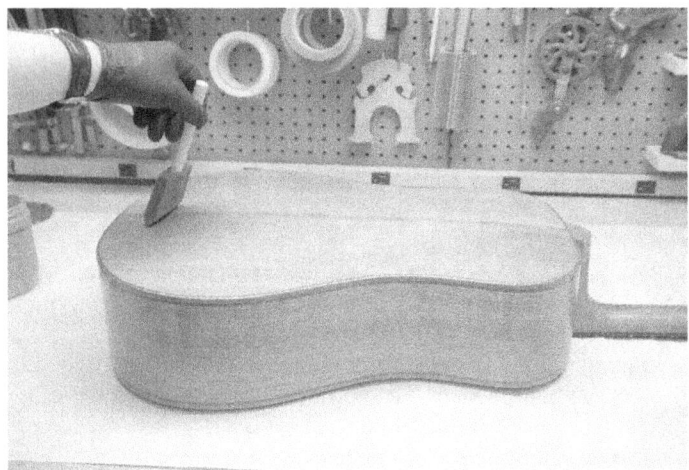

Photo 19-26 – *Now the brush is raised a bit and its direction is reversed. It is now moving left to right, coming in for a landing, and has touched down in the wet varnish a bit in from the edge.*

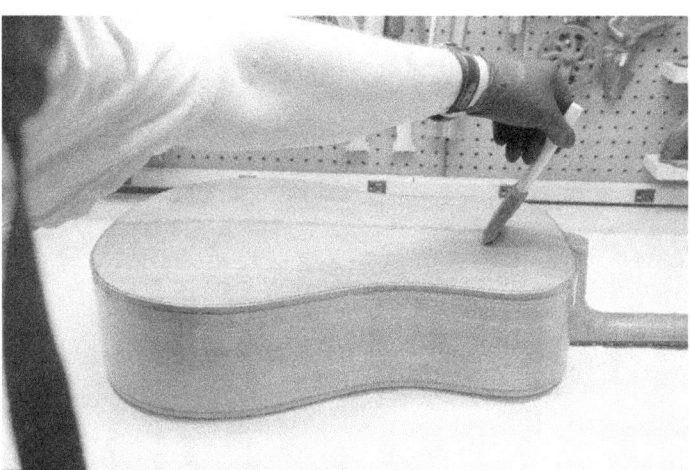

Photo 19-28 – *As the opposite edge is approached the angle of the brush begins to rise to more nearly vertical.*

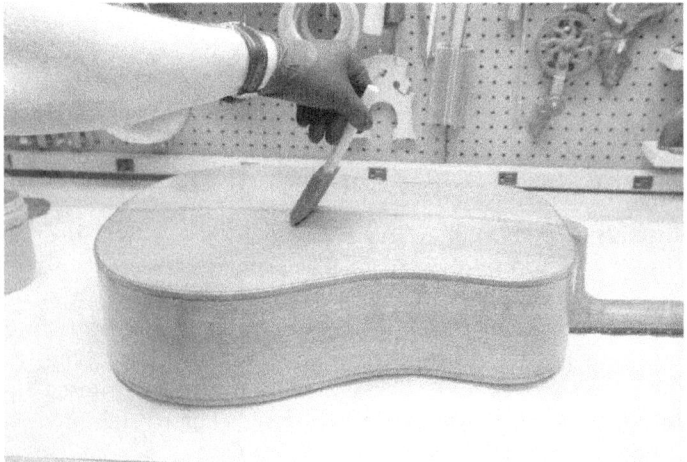

Photo 19-27 – *The gentle stroke continues across the surface of the plate, leaving a ribbon of varnish on the surface behind the brush.*

Photo 19-29 – *And the stroke ends with the brush gently brushing off the edge on this end.*

even more because there is less varnish in the brush so it takes longer to get complete coverage behind the brush.

A coat of even thickness is striven for. When spaces without varnish start to appear behind the brush, it is starting to dry out. The brush is dipped again as above and varnishing continues.

Specific brushing descriptions will be given for each of the areas of the instrument. It is important to varnish with raking light on the surface, as this allows missed spots to be easily seen. It is not always a simple matter to arrange for raking light that completely covers the area to be worked at one time, and if it can't be arranged then after a section is varnished the instrument can be held up to raking light to check the entire varnished surface for missed spots. These are touched up with a single simple stroke.

Note that horizontal positioning of the surface being varnished is critical. As long as the temperature is warm enough the varnish flows out level (or nearly so) when the surface is and remains horizontal while varnishing and during initial curing. This is easy to attain while varnishing the plates and headplate, but some special techniques are required to simulate this when doing the ribs and the neck.

A clean dry rag, a damp rag, and a dry foam brush are always kept on hand to clean up drips and runs during varnishing. Details for how and when to use these are in the following finishing steps.

1. Satin varnish contains flattening agents which settle out of (or float up from) the rest of the varnish. The varnish is slowly and gently stirred in the can using a clean stick, to mix it thoroughly but to also avoid bubbles. Before the first application session, the application container is filled with stirred varnish so the suspended brush will be fully submerged.

2. Prior to each application session, the area to which varnish will be applied is thoroughly tacked off using the tack cloth (**photo 19-30**).

3. Before each application session, nitrile gloves are fitted to the hand that will do the brushing, to protect the luthier from contact with the varnish, and also to the hand that will be used to manipulate and hold the guitar during finishing.

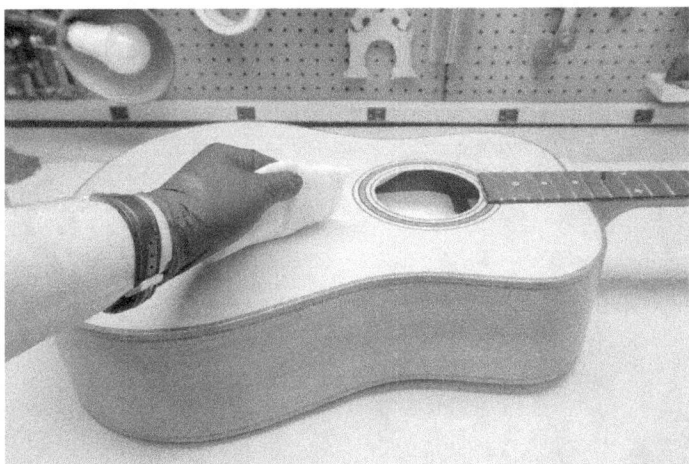

Photo 19-30 – *Immediately before varnish is applied to an area of the guitar, that area is cleaned of surface dust using a tack rag.*

Photo 19-32 – *The corner of a cloth pad is used to apply varnish to the sides of the fretboard extension.*

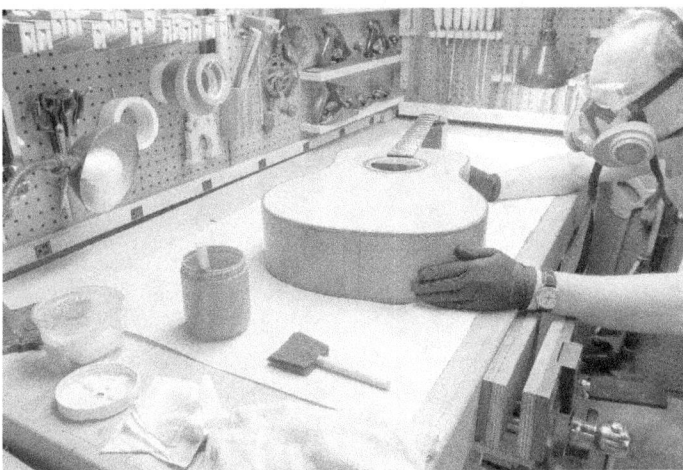

Photo 19-31 – *When varnishing the top, the guitar is placed top up on the paper with the neck pointing either left or right.*

Photo 19-33 – *The pad is also used to apply varnish to the end of the fretboard extension and to the part of the top between the fretboard end and the soundhole.*

4. Before each application session, the lid is removed from the application container, the brush is removed from the lid, and the varnish is slowly and gently stirred using the brush in the application container. The varnish in the container is also topped up at this time with stirred varnish from the can if necessary. The varnish is allowed to drain out of the brush back into the container as previously described. A clean rag is used to wipe any varnish off the handle near the top of the brush.

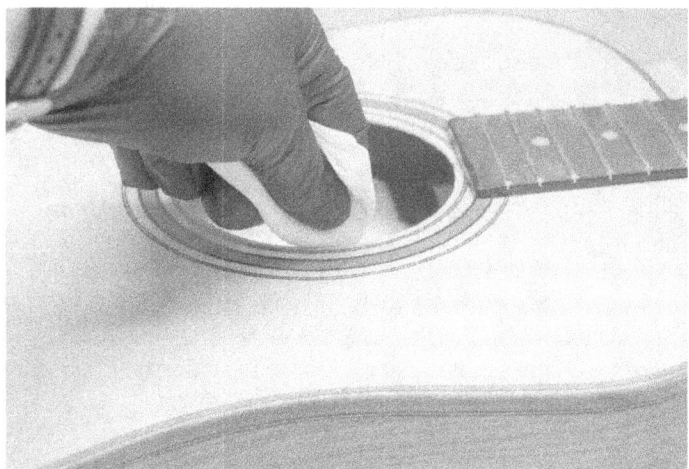

Photo 19-34 – *The pad is also used to apply varnish to the edge of the soundhole.*

Photo 19-37 – *... and goes off the edge.*

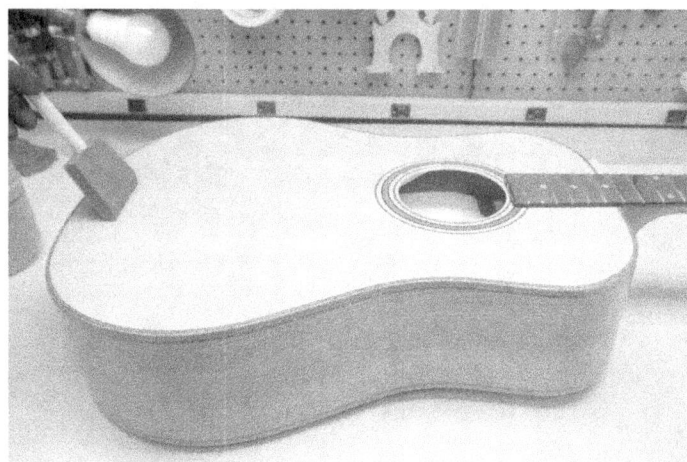

Photo 19-35 – *The first stroke begins with a landing at the centerline of the top. Here the brush is moving right to left.*

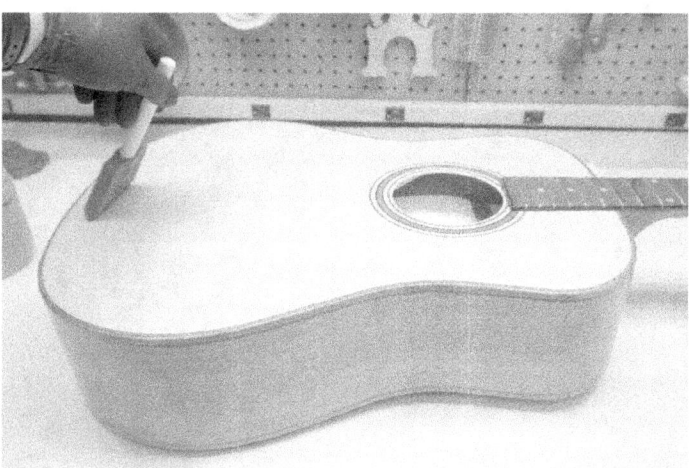

Photo 19-38 – *Now the brush moves left to right and lands in the wet varnish already applied.*

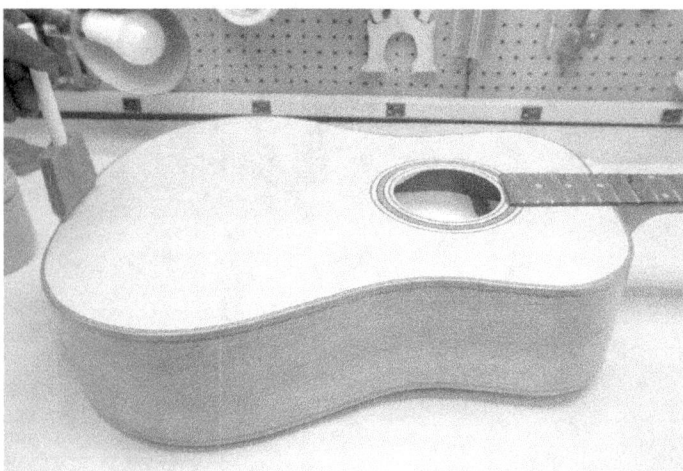

Photo 19-36 – *The stroke continues to the edge at the tail end...*

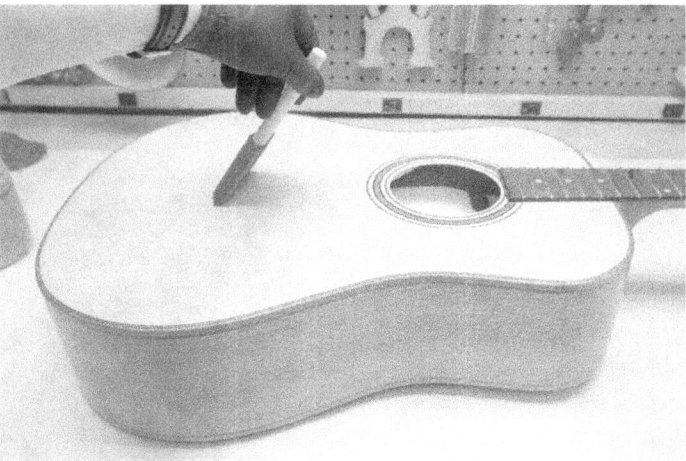

Photo 19-39 – *The stroke continues along the centerline of the top ...*

5. The first application session will apply varnish to the top plate. The guitar is oriented top up on the bench with the neck pointing to the right or left and supported on a padded block or neck rest (**photo 19-31**). Varnish will first be padded onto the fretboard extension. This is begun by folding a piece of the T-shirt material in half and then in half again. The corner that now has no outside edge is used as an applicator. This corner is dipped in the varnish about ½″ (12.7mm) and then squeezed between gloved fingers to remove excess. The gloves are wiped clean on a rag. This applicator tip is used to apply finish onto

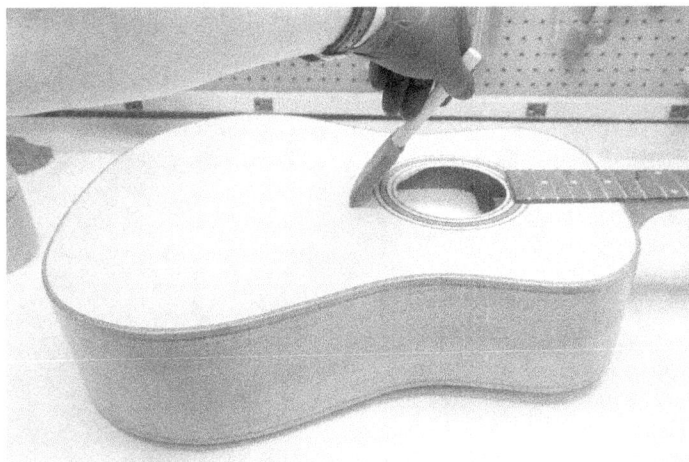

Photo 19-40 – *... approaching the soundhole. The angle of the brush is raised as the edge is approached...*

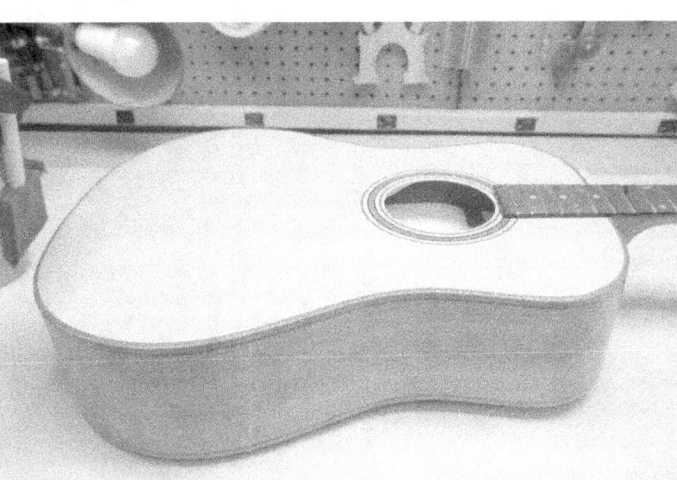

Photo 19-43 – *The stroke goes off the edge.*

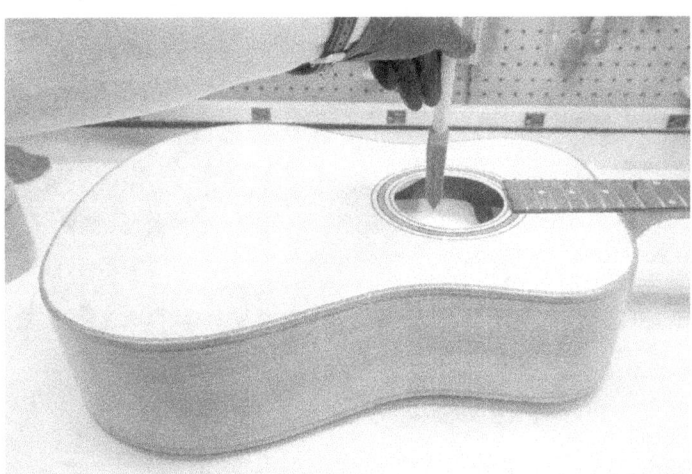

Photo 19-41 – *... and the stroke continues off the edge of the soundhole.*

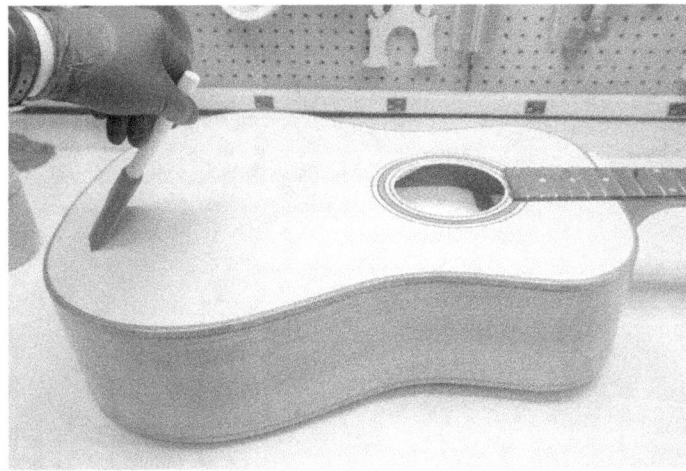

Photo 19-44 – *The second ribbon of varnish is applied in exactly the same way as the first one was, slightly overlapping the first one.*

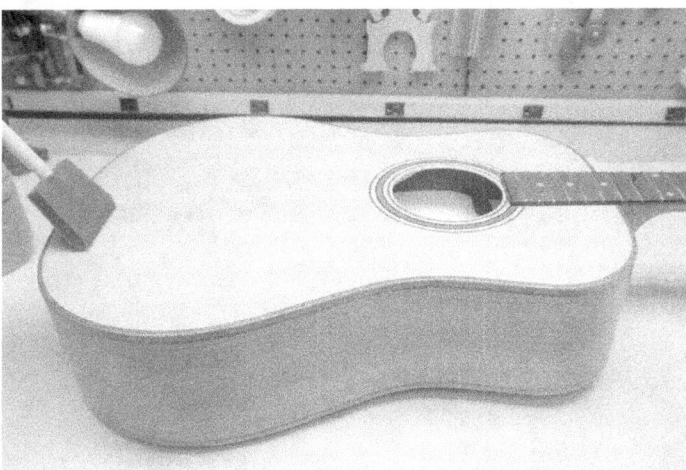

Photo 19-42 – *The next stroke is applied next to and slightly overlapping the previous stroke, on the side of the centerline closest to the luthier.*

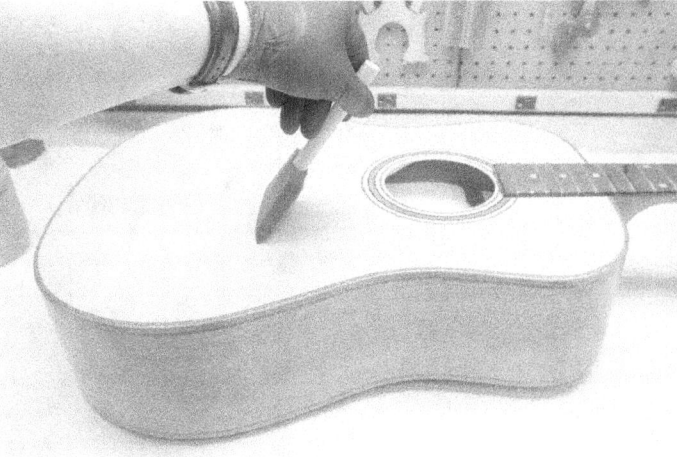

Photo 19-45 – *But on this one, rather than ending the stroke at the edge of the soundhole...*

the sides of the fretboard extension (**photo 19-32**), the end of the fretboard extension, and the top between fretboard end and soundhole (**photo 19-33**), and also around the inside edge of the soundhole (**photo 19-34**). During application, the corner can be dipped again if necessary, but generally this will not be needed. Any varnish that was mistakenly applied to the fretboard playing surface is removed using the damp rag.

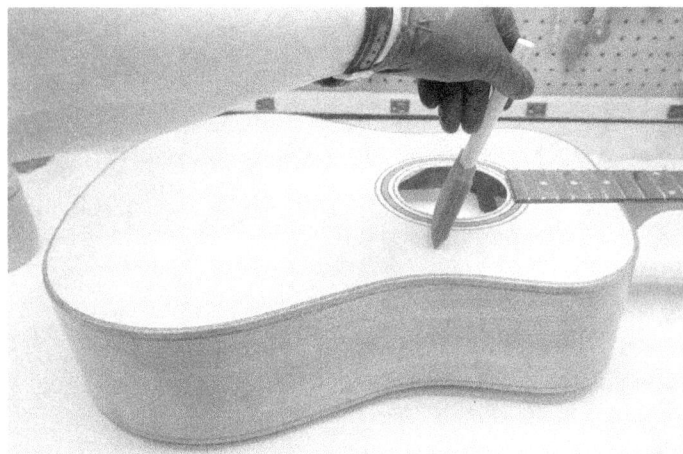

Photo 19-46 – ... *the stroke goes around the soundhole, applying varnish right up to its edge.*

Photo 19-49 – *A few cross-grain strokes are used to coat between the fretboard extension and the edge of the last stroke. Care is taken to not get a lot of varnish in the edge between the top and the side of the fretboard extension.*

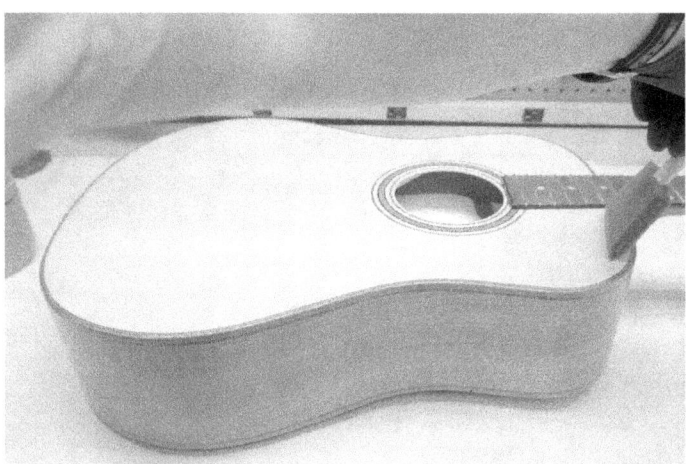

Photo 19-47 – *The stroke continues to the edge, and the brush angle rises as the edge is approached.*

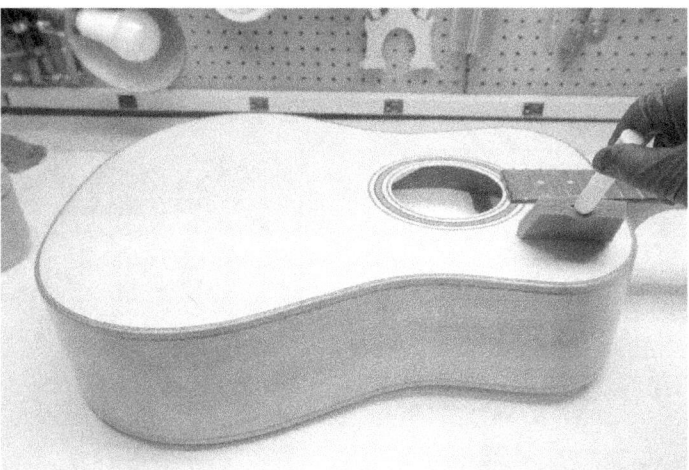

Photo 19-50 – *The brush is moved gently for these cross grain strokes. They will also coat right up to the soundhole edge and right up to the neck end edge of the guitar top.*

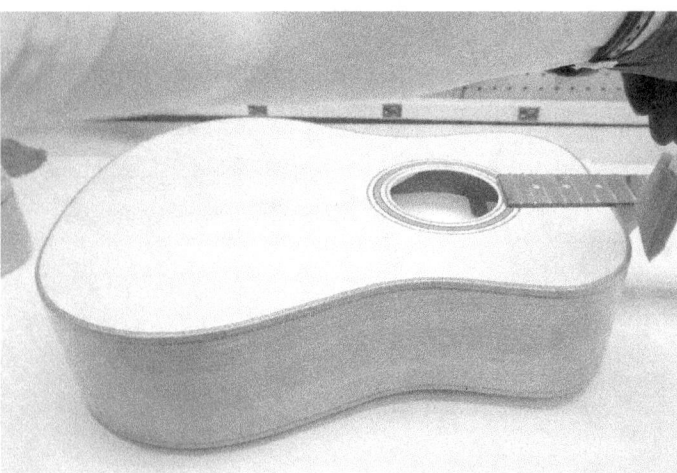

Photo 19-48 – *The stroke continues gently off the edge, next to, but not touching, the side of the fretboard.*

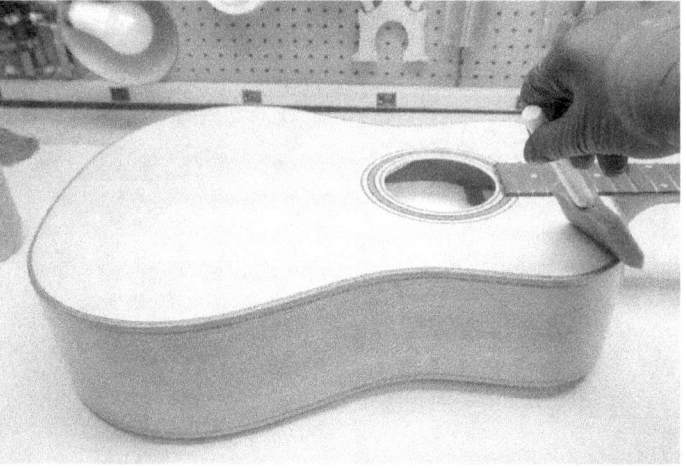

Photo 19-51 – *The final stroke on this side of the top follows the edge of the top.*

6. The remaining surface of the top will be done with the brush. The first brush stroke begins with a landing about 2″ (50.8mm) from the tail end on the centerline. Brushing proceeds toward the tail (**photo 19-35**), angling the brush to vertical (**photo 19-36**) as it lightly goes over the edge (**photo 19-37**). If any material drips down the side, now or at any time during application, the drip is removed with a clean rag or the dry brush. The brush is returned to the surface using a landing stroke, so the tip lands in a place already wet, about 1″ (25.4mm) from the edge (**photo 19-38**). This stroke is continued (**photo 19-39**), smoothly, slowly, not pressing the brush, but keeping it in gentle contact, until the soundhole is reached (**photo 19-40**). Brushing off the edge into the soundhole is done in the same manner as brushing off the tail edge, angling the brush to a vertical orientation (**photo 19-41**).

7. The next stroke is applied next to the one just laid down, closer to the luthier, overlapping it a bit, starting at the tail end (**photo 19-42**) and applying it in exactly the same manner as the first (**photos 19-43** through **19-45**). This stroke will not end squarely at the soundhole, and so should bend a little around the soundhole (**photo 19-46**). When working around the soundhole, the side edge of the brush should be right up to the soundhole edge, but not over the edge, because brushing over the edge will squeegee varnish out of the brush and form runs. The stroke is continued near to, but not touching the side of the fretboard extension (**photo 19-47**), and continues off the edge of the top (**photo 19-48**).

8. The small area next to the fretboard extension is covered next. It is best if this is done without dipping the brush again, using just the varnish remaining in the brush following the previous stroke. This small area is covered by pushing varnish into the inside edge between the top and the fretboard extension, using the tip edge of the brush (**photo 19-49**). Building up a lot of finish in this inside edge is avoided if at all possible. If there ends up being a lot of varnish here, the tip edge of the dry brush is used to remove some of it. If necessary, a gentle stroke can now be made in this area to help everything flow out (**photo 19-50**).

9. More slightly-overlapping strokes are applied to the length of the top, with each stroke applied closer to the luthier. Because the edge of the top closest to the luthier curves with the outline of the body, the last stroke is applied so the side of the brush follows the edge of the top (**photos 19-51** through **19-55**).

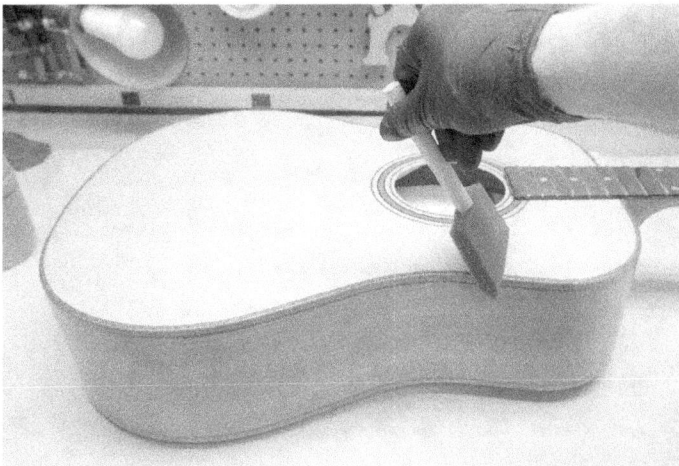

Photo 19-52 – The brush should just barely overhang the binding edge. Complete coverage of the edge is necessary...

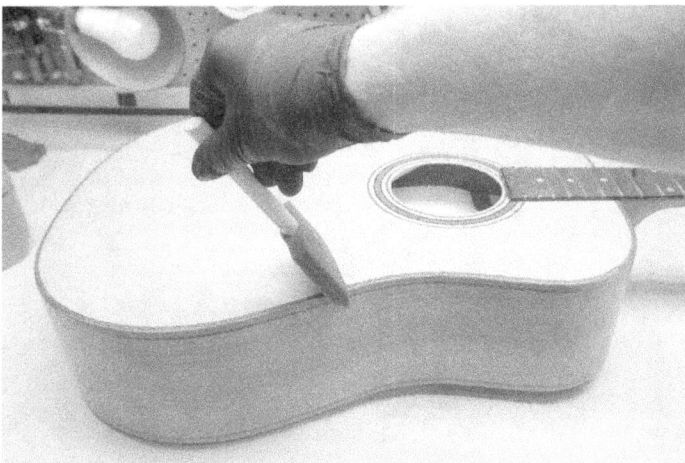

Photo 19-53 – ... but it is important to avoid drips down the side of the guitar, too.

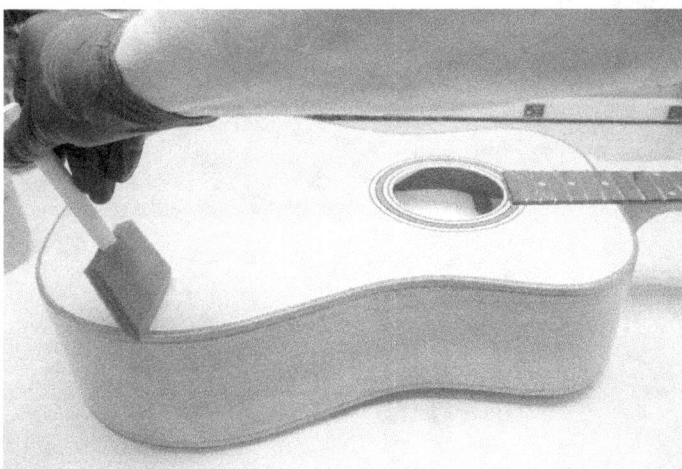

Photo 19-54 – This stroke should blend in with the previous longitudinal strokes.

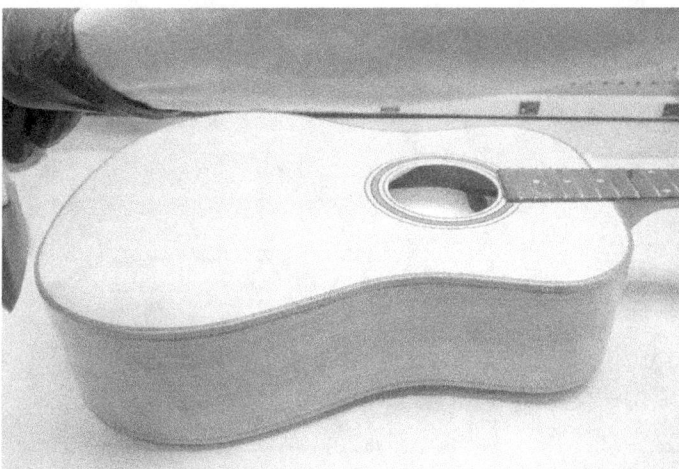

Photo 19-55 – The stroke finishes by going off the edge at the tail end. At this point this entire side of the top is completely covered.

Again, if any varnish drips down the side, it is removed immediately. It is important that application to the plates and ribs go right to the edges. This will ensure that the edges get adequately coated.

Photo 19-56 – *The guitar is grasped low on the neck with the thumb and forefinger down toward the body and the fingers on the fretboard. This grip will allow the guitar to be rotated while varnishing the sides, from this position to the position where the tail end is upright.*

Photo 19-59 – *Varnishing proceeds with the brush more or less held in position while the body is rotated under it.*

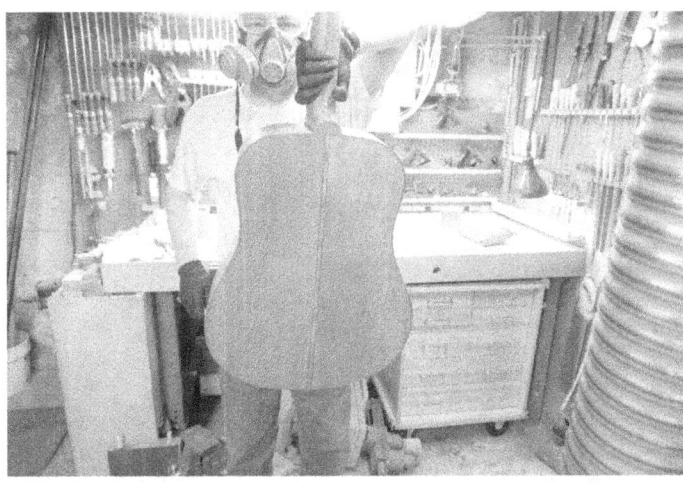

Photo 19-57 – *This grip allows varnishing the ribs to be started at the edge with the top.*

Photo 19-60 – *An attempt is made to keep the part currently being varnished as horizontal to the floor as possible.*

Photo 19-58 – *The stroke is started with the brush near but not right at the heel, with the side of the brush edge on the body edge with the top.*

Photo 19-61 – *Again, the specified grip on the neck allows the body to be rotated.*

Usually, the once-loaded brush will contain enough varnish to complete one half of the top before it needs to be dipped again.

But if at any time dry spaces in the applied varnish are noticed, the brush is going dry and so it should be dipped again.

10. Before proceeding on to the other half of the top, the varnishing is carefully examined for missed spots. Any that are found are quickly and gently touched up.

11. The guitar is spun around so the other side is facing the luthier. The neck is supported on a neck rest. The brush is dipped, allowed to drip out, and varnish is applied to this side of the top in the same fashion, applying longitudinal ribbons, starting near the centerline, slightly overlapping varnish already applied, and proceeding toward the edge nearest the luthier. Now the entire top is examined in raking light to be sure it is completely covered. Touch-up work is done where necessary, but avoiding excessive working of the varnish.

12. The varnish should self-level after a bit, although the first coat will end up fairly dry. The brush is returned to the varnish container lid and the lid is fitted on tightly. The small application rag is discarded. If the dry brush was used, it is thoroughly cleaned with water, squeezed out, and allow to dry. The surface that was varnished is allowed to dry to the touch before

Photo 19-62 – *The stroke continues onto the tail end of the ribs.*

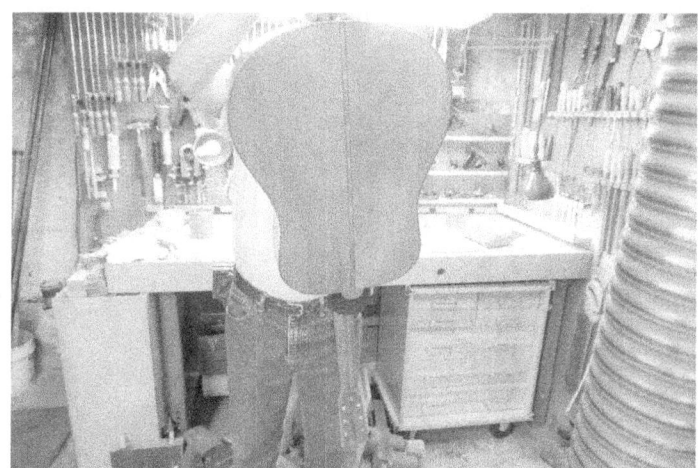
Photo 19-63 – *The stroke continues across the tail end of the guitar ribs. At this point, the wrist of the holding hand can't turn any further unless a new grip is taken.*

Photo 19-65 – *Varnishing proceeds up this side and along the top plate edge. As the guitar is lowered the place on the luthier's leg where the headstock is supported moves up.*

Photo 19-64 – *The headstock is rested against the leg and a new grip is taken that will allow the guitar to be moved down and away from the luthier.*

Photo 19-66 – *While the waist is being varnished the headstock is now pressing against the luthier's waist.*

proceeding. This can be hurried along with gentle heat from the heat lamp if the varnishing is being done in cooler ambient temperatures.

13. Varnish is applied to the ribs of the guitar next. This involves holding the guitar in the hand. Anytime there is a need to do this, before the guitar is grabbed, a check is made to be sure the luthier's gloves are clean. Steps 2 through 4 are repeated to ready the guitar, luthier, and varnish. The guitar is lifted vertically (neck up), holding the neck with the off hand, close to the heel and with the thumb and index finger down (**photo 19-56**), and so the front of the guitar is facing the luthier. This thumb down grip is important, because it allows the guitar to be held neck up and neck down with the same grip. Varnish application to the ribs begins about 1″ (25.4mm) from the heel on the right side (if the luthier is right-handed, otherwise on the left side), brushing toward the tail end in a single stroke, with the side of the brush aligned with the front edge of the guitar (**photo 19-57**). As this stroke proceeds, the guitar is rotated so that varnish is always being applied to a horizontal surface (**photos 19-58** through **19-62**). Brushing is done in a single stroke right to the tail end, if there is enough varnish in the brush to do so. Otherwise the brush is dipped when needed.

Photo 19-69 – *The guitar is slowly rotated on an imaginary axis going through the soundhole while the varnish on the sides cures. This helps prevent runs from forming. The neck is held in both hands.*

Photo 19-67 – *When the upper bout is varnished the headstock is against the luthier's chest.*

Photo 19-70 – *The instrument is slowly rotated so that one area of the sides after the other is horizontal.*

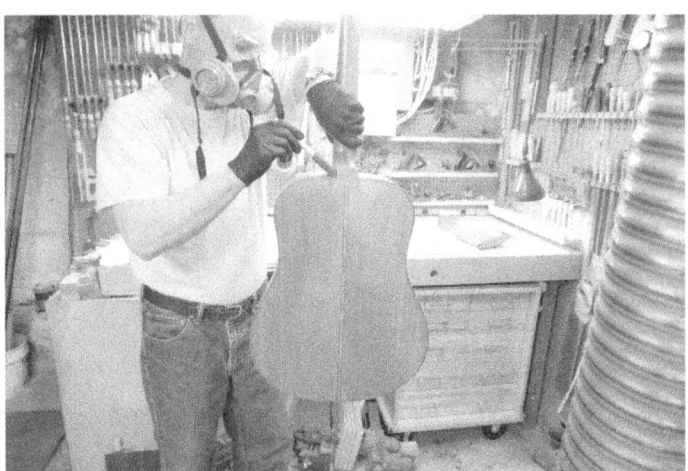

Photo 19-68 – *The stroke stops near the heel. Then the unvarnished areas on both sides of the heel are varnished.*

Photo 19-71 – *As the guitar is rotated, the ribs are examined for runs. Any runs that are found during rotation are picked up using the dry brush.*

14. At this point the guitar is being held like a lollipop (**photo 19-63**). What is desired is to keep going, rotating the instrument and continuing the stroke, but the holding hand can't turn anymore while maintaining the current grip. To rectify this, the headstock of the guitar is propped against the luthier's leg, and the guitar is angled a little away from the luthier (**photo 19-64**). By doing this the luthier can adjust the grip on the guitar and continue the stroke. As the stroke continues down the other side of the body with the head propped against the leg, the top of the guitar is no longer facing the luthier (**photos 19-65** through **19-66**). Now the rib being brushed is facing the luthier. But as long as the top can be seen (so any varnish drips can be seen) all is well. The stroke is continued to within 1″ (25.4mm) of the heel (**photo 19-67**).

15. At this point (most of) the front half of the ribs have been coated with varnish. The brush is dipped. Starting in the original starting position (neck up), but this time with the guitar back facing the luthier, steps 13 and 14 are repeated to coat (most of) the back half of the ribs. Depending on the depth of the ribs, a third stroke may have to be applied to completely coat the ribs, this one right down the center of the ribs.

16. After the previous step is performed the brush will not have a lot of varnish in it. This lightly loaded brush is used to carefully brush the currently uncoated areas of the ribs that are right next to the heel on both sides of the heel (**photo 19-68**). When doing this, care is taken to not build up a lot of varnish in the inside edge between rib and heel. If finish bridges the space between rib and heel, is it mostly wicked out using the tip of the dry brush.

17. Top and back plates are checked for runs using raking light. Any runs found are removed using the dry brush or clean rag. Raking light is also used to thoroughly examine the ribs, to be sure there are no missed spots. Any missed spots are fixed up using a single simple brush stroke to cover each one.

18. When the top was varnished, the varnish was allowed to cure with the top in a horizontal position. This enhanced flow-out and prevented any runs from forming. But due to their shape it is not possible for the entire surface of the ribs to cure in a horizontal position. To avoid runs on the ribs, the guitar is slowly rotated around an imaginary horizontal axis running through the center of the soundhole while it cures (**photos**

Photo 19-72 – *If a heat lamp is available, it is positioned so the sides are warmed as the guitar is rotated.*

Photo 19-74 – *Slow rotation continues until the varnish has set enough so it can no longer run.*

Photo 19-73 – *Sometimes it is easier to continue rotation with one hand on the neck and the other in the soundhole.*

Photo 19-75 – *The headstock is rested on a board in the bench vise so the headplate is horizontal for varnishing. Note the lamp directly behind. It is turned off for photography, but of course should be on while varnishing.*

19-69 through **19-74**). Each rotation should take about 3 minutes. This is best accomplished holding the guitar using both hands, and it helps to have the top facing the luthier, so that one hand can be used to grip the body inside the soundhole if necessary.

A heat lamp can be used to help speed curing of the varnish, and this also helps to prevent the varnish from running. If a heat lamp is used, as the guitar is rotated the part of the ribs exposed to the lamp is always kept at least 12″ (304.8mm) away from the lamp. It is necessary to avoid "cooking" the varnish. If vapor can be seen evaporating off the varnish surface then the lamp is too close or the rotation is too slow.

This slow rotation is done for between 10 and 30 minutes, depending on ambient temperature and heat lamp use. If any obvious runs are seen early in the process, these can be gently reduced on the wet varnish surface with the dry brush, but care must be taken to only absorb the run. The dry brush can easily mar the curing coat, especially if it is used late in the curing process, when the varnish is more viscous. The varnish does not have to cure completely dry, just dry enough so when the instrument is placed on the bench on its back it will not run or sag. Usually when the surface of the varnish begins to dull all over the coat is sufficiently cured. The instrument is placed on

Photo 19-78 – Brush direction reverses from left to right, and the brush lands in the wet varnish from the previous stroke.

Photo 19-76 – The sane basic strokes used when varnishing other horizontal surfaces are used here. The brush is moving right to left and lands near the headstock end. The side closest to the luthier is varnished first.

Photo 19-79 – The stroke continues the length of the headplate.

Photo 19-77 – The stroke goes off the edge of the headstock with the brush vertical.

Photo 19-80 – The brush goes off the nut end of the headplate. Care is taken to not get varnish on the end of the fretboard here.

its back on the bench and allowed to cure until the varnish on the ribs is dry to the touch.

19. As after varnishing the top plate, the brush is now returned to the varnish container lid, and the lid is fitted on tightly. If the dry brush was used, it is thoroughly cleaned with water, squeezed out, and allow to dry.

20. The headplate is coated next. Steps 2 through 4 are repeated to ready the guitar, luthier, and varnish. Since it is possible to brush and cure the headplate with it in horizontal orientation, that is the way it is done. The instrument is placed back down on the bench. Then it is grabbed by the neck and the neck end is lifted off the bench until the headplate surface is horizontal. The distance between the bench and the back of the headstock is noted. A board is clamped with one end sticking up in the bench vise, with the end of the board at the noted distance. The back of the headstock is rested on top of the board, with the body of the guitar sitting on the bench (**photo 19-75**).

21. A coat of varnish is applied to the headplate using the now familiar brushing techniques for coating a flat horizontal surface (**photos 19-76** through **19-80**). When doing this, much care is taken to avoid getting material in the nut slot or on the nut end of the fretboard, and to avoid any drips down the sides of the headstock. Any drips are cleaned up using the rag or dry brush. If varnish gets on the fretboard, it is thoroughly removed using a damp rag and then a dry rag. The brush may be wide enough to cover the width of the headstock in one stripe, but if not two stripes will be needed.

22. The headstock is left in this horizontal orientation (possibly gently heated under the heat lamp) until the varnish cures enough so that it won't run. This should take about 10 to 30 minutes. The brush is now returned to the varnish container lid and the lid is fitted on tightly. If the dry brush was used, it is thoroughly cleaned with water, squeezed out, and allow to dry.

23. Varnishing the back and heel cap. Steps 2 through 4 are repeated to ready the guitar, luthier, and varnish. This session can be started as soon as the top is dry to the touch and the instrument can be rested on the top, and the headplate surface is cured enough so it won't run. It is done in exactly the same manner as was the top, only without the complications of the

Photo 19-81 – *The guitar positioned for varnishing one side of the heel, neck shaft, and headstock. The sandbag resting on the waist prevents the guitar from falling off the bench. The headstock overhangs the front of the bench.*

Photo 19-83 – *Varnishing continues with the sides of the fretboard. The short strokes go off the edge toward the fretboard playing surface. Much care is taken to avoid runs onto the fretboard playing surface.*

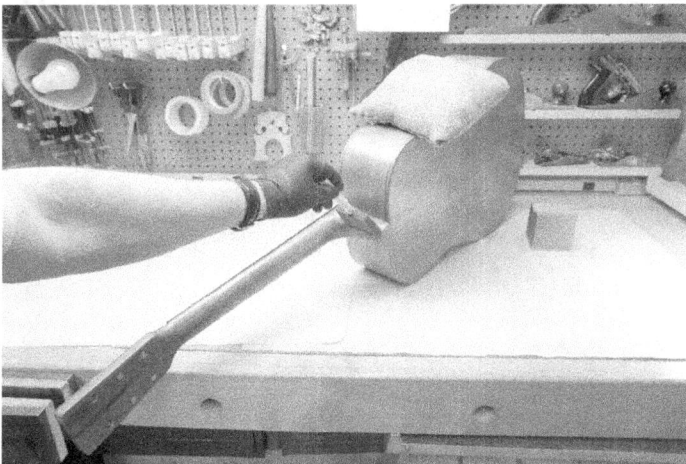

Photo 19-82 – *Varnishing proceeds with a lightly loaded brush, starting on the side of the heel.*

Photo 19-84 – *Going off the edge here is done with light contact.*

Photo 19-85 – *These strokes are continued for the entire length of the fretboard edge.*

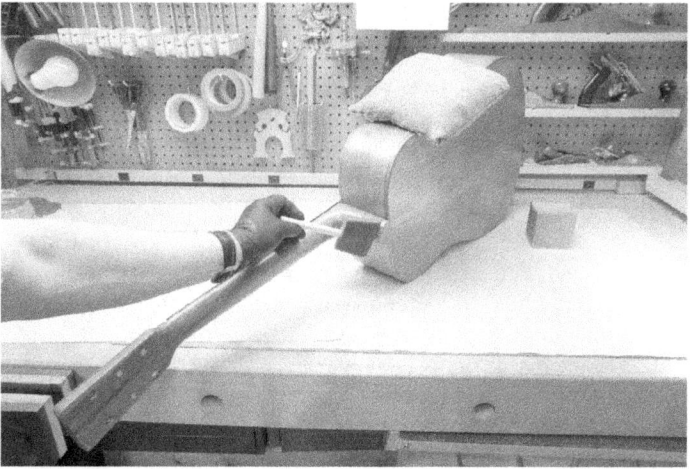

Photo 19-87 – *One varnish application stroke is made from the edge at the back of the heel...*

Photo 19-86 – *Again, going over the edge is done with light brush pressure.*

Photo 19-88 – *... around the heel to neck shaft curve...*

fretboard extension and the soundhole. The tricky areas are the inside corners between ribs and heel cap. Sometimes finish will collect here and drip down, so this area is examined carefully following brushing. Any pending drips are removed using the rag. In general the brush need only be dipped once per side of the back.

24. After the back is coated, the sandbag is rested on the back of the neck near the headstock. This will lift the entire top off the bench (because the instrument will be sitting only on the fretboard extension) so air can circulate to the top so it can more completely cure. The brush is returned to the varnish container lid and the lid is fitted on tightly. If the dry brush was used, it is thoroughly cleaned with water, squeezed out, and allow to dry. Top and back plates as well as the ribs are allowed to dry to the touch before proceeding to the next step, coating the neck.

Photo 19-89 – *... and down the shaft to the headstock. An additional overlapping stroke may be added as needed for full coverage.*

25. Varnishing the neck and headstock. The instrument will need to be held and manipulated by the body during this session, so the entire body must be cured enough so it can be handled. Steps 2 through 4 are repeated to ready the guitar, luthier, and varnish. The body is set on its side on the bench with the fretboard facing the luthier and the headstock slightly overhanging the bench. It will not balance in this position, so the sandbag is placed on the waist (**photo 19-81**). The sandbag prevents the guitar from falling off the front of the bench. Note that with the weight of the sandbag up high this is a precarious

Photo 19-90 – *A light stroke is used on the neck shaft to headstock transition.*

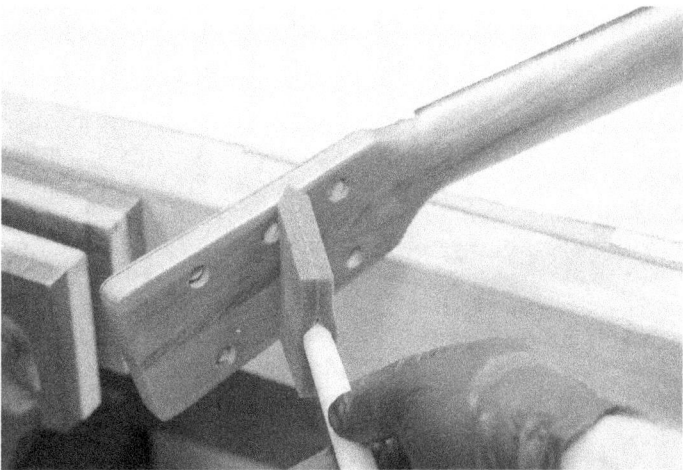

Photo 19-93 – *Varnishing the back of the headstock is done with a continuation of the stroke used to varnish the neck shaft.*

Photo 19-91 – *The side of the headstock is covered with a single stroke.*

Photo 19-94 – *The usual gentle movement off the edge is performed here.*

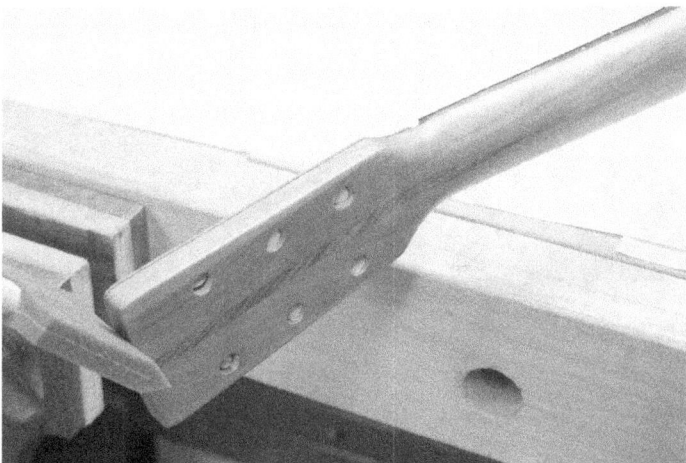

Photo 19-92 – *The end of the headstock is covered with a single stroke as well.*

balance, and caution must be used to avoid knocking the instrument over.

26. Because there is so little surface area to cover here, and because it is more difficult to avoid runs when varnishing the neck, it is highly desirable to work with a lightly loaded brush. After stirring the varnish, the brush is lifted and allowed to drip out well. Then the gloved fingers are used to gently squeegee some more varnish out of the brush toward its edge. After this there should be no dripping from the corner of the brush when it is held vertically over the can. The gloves are either wiped thoroughly to remove all varnish from them, or replaced. Varnish is first applied to the up-facing side of the heel, working from the edge formed with the ribs down to the centerline of the heel (**photo 19-82**). Care is taken to not get too much finish in the inside edge. If it builds up here, it is wicked out using the dry brush.

27. Varnish is next applied to the fretboard side in multiple short strokes. The fretboard edge is approached just like approaching the edge of the body. Each stroke moves from the shaft, toward the fretboard edge, coming off the edge with the brush vertical (**photos 19-83** through **19-86**). This is done all the way down the neck to the nut end of the fretboard.

28. Now smooth long strokes are used to apply varnish to the up facing half of the heel and the shaft (**photos 19-87** through

19-89). Runs must be carefully watched for. Any that are forming are carefully picked up with the dry brush.

29. A light and careful stroke is used to brush varnish onto the shaft to headstock transition (**photo 19-90**). It is easy to put too much varnish here, and easy to create runs into the nut slot. Now the side of the headstock (**photo 19-91**) and then the top of the headstock are carefully brushed (**photo 19-92**). It may be easier to use the narrower 1″ (25.4mm) brush to do these narrow parts of the headstock. The back of the headstock is then varnished (**photos 19-93** and **19-94**). Since this is a vertical surface at this point, runs are almost guaranteed. They are wiped from the bottom edge using the rag or dry brush.

30. One hand is placed on the side of the body to hold the guitar steady while the sandbag is removed, then the body is flipped over so the other side is facing up. The sandbag is placed on the waist, and varnishing is continued on this side of the neck, using the same sequence used for the first side. It is usually not necessary to dip the brush again for this side.

31. A check is made in raking light for complete coverage, then the brush is put aside. The paper on the bench is checked for any drips, and any found are wiped up. Any drips on the fretboard are wiped up with the damp rag and then the dry rag. The guitar is picked up by the body and slowly rolled from side to side, starting with the fretboard facing down and parallel to the floor. It is rolled through 180° from one side of the fretboard up to the other. Positioning the neck in the heat of heat lamps speeds drying (**photos 19-95** and **19-96**). While rolling the neck, everything is looked over carefully for drips, and any found are picked up with the dry brush. This slow rolling motion is continued for at least 10 minutes or until the varnish cures enough so it begins to dull and it will not run any more.

32. The brush is returned to the varnish container lid and the lid is fitted on tightly. If the dry brush was used, it is thoroughly cleaned with water, squeezed out, and allow to dry. The guitar is placed top down on the bench, handling it only by the body, and the varnish is allowed to cure to the touch before the next step.

33. Steps 2 through 32 describe the application of a complete coat of varnish to the guitar. This sequence will be repeated for a number of complete coats. But before the next coat commences there are a couple of between-coat steps that are performed. One of them is drop-filling, which follows the second and some subsequent coats, but is skipped following the first coat. The entire instrument is checked in raking light to identify any sinking spots in the varnish. These usually are seen at the bindings and purflings and other places where there are glue joints. They happen when there is a spot that is dry of glue. The finish gets wicked into the space before it is completely cured.

Drop fills are done with a micro-tip transfer pipette filled with varnish. When drop filling a sunken spot, an attempt is made to leave a blob or line of varnish that is slightly higher than the surrounding finish, because it will shrink as it dries. If it is found that a spot needs to be drop filled repeatedly after each coat (that is, the spot repeatedly wicks up the drop fill varnish),

Photo 19-95 – The instrument is slowly rolled about its longitudinal axis, to help reduce drips while the varnish is starting to cure.

Photo 19-96 – After varnishing the neck, the instrument is slowly rolled from this position to the position where the opposite side of the fretboard is on top. At the same time it can be moved back and forth under the heat lamp, to help flow-out and speed curing of the varnish.

Photo 19-97 – The remains of drips and runs that were not completely chiseled off, such as those inside the circled area, are removed by dry sanding with stearated paper on a block.

it is prudent to try drop filling it with medium cyanoacrylate glue, or to try troweling in some clear water-based grain filler. This will usually seal the spot and prevent it from further wicking of the varnish.

While checking for voids that need drop filling, the guitar is also checked for any spots that were simply missed by the brush. If these are tiny they can be drop filled, but if they are bigger a small brush is used to fill them in with varnish.

It takes some time for the drop fills to cure and they should be cured in a horizontal position. So it may take some time to do these if there are a lot of them or they are all over the guitar. The drop fills should be allowed to cure overnight so they are hard enough to withstand a little sanding the following day.

34. It is likely that there will be some runs and drips on the finish in various places, and also possibly some bulges left by the drop fills. These are chiseled off as close to flush as possible, using a very sharp chisel and a slicing motion. A single-edge razor blade can also be used. If the drips are really big there may still be liquid inside after chiseling, and this should be allowed to fully cure before subsequent work.

Note that if the finish has curtains or sags it may be a better bet to wait until these are fully cured and then sand them flush using *stearated* sandpaper on a block, as described in the next step. If sags or runs are found, it is a good idea to note where they are on the instrument. They will usually be on the ribs or on the neck and headstock. If there is finish sagging, this is an indication that either the varnish is being applied too thickly or that not enough time is being spent rotating the freshly varnished part around, before finally placing it back on the bench to fully cure. This should be remembered for subsequent applications and adjustments to varnishing technique made accordingly.

35. A *light* sanding with the grain, using 320-grit paper is useful after the first coat, because the waterborne finish raises the grain. The surface is not sanded smooth, but just enough to take off most of the roughness. Some luthiers find it useful to scuff sand a bit after each coat, to flatten any pimples left by bubbles or debris in the varnish. If this is done, stearated 320 grit (FEPA P400) grit paper is used. A little more localized sanding can be done to more nearly level any hardened drop fills or drips that were not quite chiseled off flush, and to level any sags in the finish (**photo 19-97**). And if cyanoacrylate or grain filler was used to fill sunken areas, then these will have to be sanded flush before proceeding.

Sanding helps to identify tiny voids. The sanding dust of the varnish is white and the dust will fill these voids, making them stand out. A fine abrasive pad can be used to remove the dust. If it resists being removed with the pad, it may have to be picked out using a dental probe or pin. Then the void is drop-filled as described in step 33.

36. If care is taken about airborne dust during varnish application, there should be no debris stuck in the finish. But sometimes things happen. Mosquitoes for example, *love* clear finishes and may get stuck in the finish before it dries. Any foreign particle like that needs to be removed using a dental pick or small sharp knife blade. The cavity remaining should be drop-filled and allowed to cure.

37. The inside edges between the heel and the body, and those between the top and the fretboard extension are checked to be sure there isn't varnish building up there. If there is too much varnish here, the excess can be scraped out using the corner of a card scraper or the edge of a chisel used as a scraper.

38. Subsequent coats. A total of 8 to 10 coats of varnish are applied. In general, waterborne varnish will fully burn in if coats are applied no more than a day apart. So it is a good idea to work on a one or two coats per day schedule, and to not wait more than a day between coats. As mentioned, after the first coat the grain may be raised and require some light sanding. After the third or fourth coat all drop filling should be done and the finish should be level. If not, before adding coats more drop filling and then sanding down those areas is done until the finish *is* level. The rest of the coats should go on smoothly. Generally, by coat number four the luthier has enough varnishing experience to know how long the rib and neck coats must be cured before the instrument can be set down without danger of sags.

After soaking in the finish for a few days, the edge of the foam brush will often distort into a twisted shape. If this happens, as much of the finish as possible is squeegeed out of the brush and back into the container, then the brush is thrown away. A new brush is used for subsequent applications.

39. Fully curing the varnish. The instrument should be hung to fully cure for one month before attempting leveling the finish. Shorter curing intervals are possible, but it is ever-so-much easier to do the leveling after the finish is fully cured. Before hanging the instrument up, it is examined carefully in raking light to be sure there are no major hollows that need to be filled. At this point they can still be drop-filled with varnish and

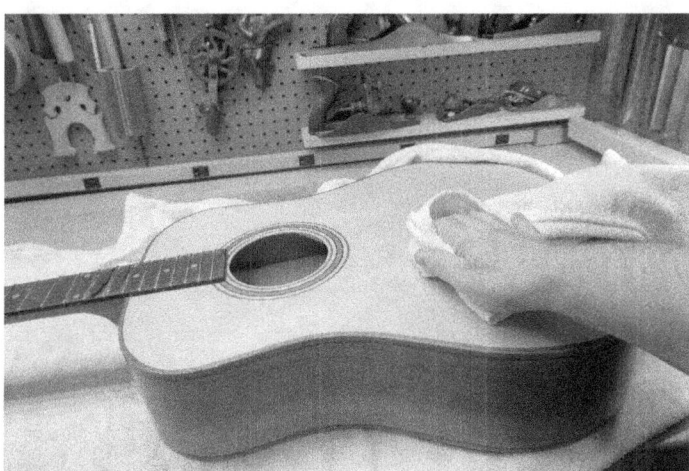

Photo 19-98 – *In preparation for wet sanding, the guitar is placed on a big towel, and another towel will be used to wipe off the sanding slurry.*

the drop fills will completely burn in. But if the hollows are not detected now, they will be difficult to repair later.

My vision is not that great and I do this checking and filling operation a few times. Any time I notice something that needs to be filled, I fill it and let it cure, then check again. I keep doing this until I've looked over the instrument completely three times without finding anything that needs filling. Then I'm confident it is ready for a full cure.

☐ **Leveling the Finish**

After the finish is cured for a month it can be rubbed out. Since this month is otherwise down time, it is often appropriate to skip ahead to the construction of the bridge and then return to the task of leveling the finish. Note that rubbing out is possible after as little as a week, but the job is generally *much* easier to do if a longer cure time is allowed.

No matter how smoothly the finish was applied to the instrument, there will always be irregularities in the finish surface. This is the case even for finely applied spray finishes. So after the finish is applied, the next step is to level it, to give the surface a smooth and consistent look. This step is absolutely critical when a gloss finish is used, as reflections in the finish will show all the irregularities in the surface. Leveling the finish is also necessary when applying a satin finish, as described in these pages.

The first leveling operation is wet sanding. Wet sanding is often used when sanding finish because the water cools the sanding surface, and this cooling reduces the tendency of the sanding dust to melt and fuse to the sandpaper, a process called corning. The finish is wet sanded with water and a few drops of dishwashing liquid, using fine grit silicon carbide wet or dry sandpaper, supported on a small gum eraser sanding block. A couple of grits are used. Note that the dishwashing liquid is necessary. Without it, the water forms a boundary between the sandpaper and the surface of the finish, and the sandpaper will just slide over the finish without sanding it at all.

Although the entirety of the finished surface will be leveled, there is a specific order I am proposing here for wet sanding the guitar. The reason for this order is that it introduces all of the

About Sandpaper Grit Systems

It was mentioned early on in this book that whenever sandpaper grits were specified, these would be in the grit grading system of the Coated Abrasives Manufacturer's Institute (CAMI). This is the system used primarily in North America. Sandpaper grit specifications in this system use a plain number, such as 220 or 320. The most common grading system used in Europe and in some other parts of the world is that of the Federation of European Producers Association (FEPA). Sandpaper grit specifications in this system use numbers preceded by the letter "P." For the most part, the two systems are interchangeable for those sandpaper grits normally used when sanding wood. Unfortunately these grading systems diverge dramatically for grits over about 320, and this is the range of grits that is used when wet sanding finishes. Fortunately only two of these fine grits are used here, CAMI 600 and 1000. The approximate FEPA equivalents of these grits are P1000 and P2000, respectively.

Although all abrasive manufacturers and specialty suppliers are well aware of these differences, I have noticed that some general woodworking and lutherie suppliers are not, sometimes even leaving the "P" off the description of sandpaper in their catalogs.

wet sanding hazards one at a time. These are things the luthier will need to be on the lookout for while wet sanding, to ensure that the finish is not sanded through to the wood. The back is done first because there is only one simple hazard with that plate. The neck shaft and heel are done last because there are a number of them to be aware of while leveling the finish there.

1. A big towel is put down on the bench, and the guitar is placed on top of that, back plate up. Another big towel is kept on hand. This one will be used to wipe off the sanding slurry (**photo 19-98**).

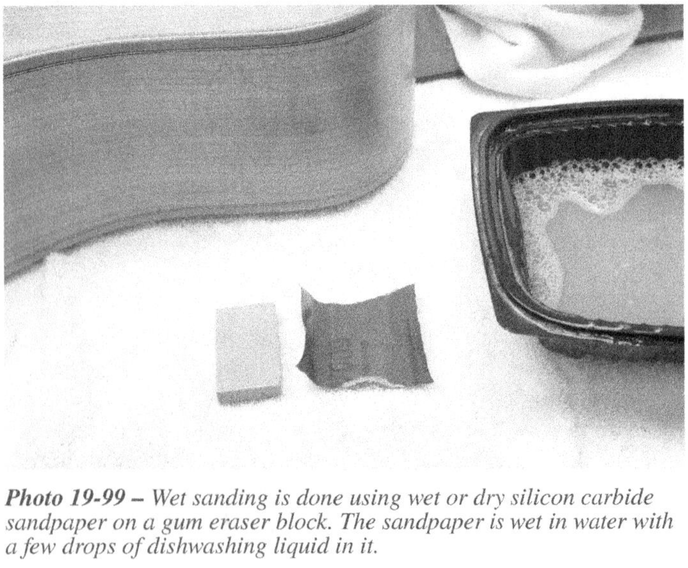

Photo 19-99 – *Wet sanding is done using wet or dry silicon carbide sandpaper on a gum eraser block. The sandpaper is wet in water with a few drops of dishwashing liquid in it.*

Photo 19-100 – *Wet or dry sandpaper is wrapped around the gum eraser sanding block for wet sanding.*

2. A small tray or takeout food container is half filled with water, and a few drops of dishwashing liquid are added and mixed in. A few pieces of 600-grit silicon carbide wet or dry sandpaper are cut to a size so they can be wrapped around a gum rubber eraser (**photo 19-99**). Note that this is CAMI 600 grit, *not* P600 grit (see sidebar). One of the pieces of sandpaper is soaked in the water for a bit.

3. Leveling the back. Before wet sanding, the surface of the back is "read" with the fingers. It will be noticed that the surface humps up a bit at the blocks and braces and dips down a bit other places. These peaks and valleys are generally so small that they don't matter but it is good to be aware of where they are. Although these variations may be visible under certain conditions, they can always be reliably felt with the fingers. It is useful to know where the high places are, to avoid inadvertently sanding off all the finish there.

4. The back is wet sanded in sections. About ¼ of the back is done at a time. The wet piece of sandpaper is wrapped around the eraser (**photo 19-100**), and then dipped in the water. Then the entire section is sanded using overlapping circular strokes (**photo 19-101**). If the film of water between the sandpaper and the surface makes things too "grabby" to easily move the block, a few more drops of detergent are added to the water in the tray. The detergent serves as a *wetting agent* (also called a *surfactant*) which reduces the surface tension of the water. Even sanding is striven for over the entire section. Care is taken to not round over the edges. The sanding block is kept flat on the back.

☞ Note that the issue with the body edges is that force is concentrated there. While sanding with the flat of the block, a certain amount of pressure is being applied. When a flat area is sanded, the force applied is distributed over the approximately 2 square inch area of the surface of the block. But when an edge is sanded, all that force is applied to a small area. The sandpaper cuts much faster under that condition. So it is easy to cut through the finish at the edges. Unless there is a particular lump or something on an edge, the edges will be avoided during most of wet sanding. While on the subject of the edges, it is good practice to avoid having a large amount of the sanding block overhanging the edge, because this may inadvertently round over the edge, endangering it.

If there are any noticeable nibs or other high spots to the finish, these are sanded down until they are flush with the rest of the surface. As the sandpaper dries out, it is dipped again in the water. Sanding like this proceeds for about one minute. Then the sanded area is wiped of slurry using the second towel, and the surface is allowed to dry. Drying takes only a few seconds. The surface is examined with raking light. Areas that did not get sanded can be seen. These stand out as shiny patches, even when a satin varnish is used.

Sanding is continued in one-minute sessions, wiping and assessing after each, until all the shiny spots are gone. This may take a number of sessions. The luthier should be aware of any areas that are deep enough to actually feel with the fingers. These are probably too deep to sand out without cutting completely through the finish, so these are left alone. As sanding progresses, larger and larger areas will be flat and dull in appearance, with only a few shiny spots remaining. At this point it is wise to concentrate sanding on just these shiny spots. Basically the goal is to sand just to the point of flatness and then stop, to avoid the possibility of sanding right through the finish.

The recommended varnish has some tint to it and if this material was used, any spots which may be getting thinner than the rest of the section will be slightly lighter in color as well. Those spots are best avoided for subsequent sanding.

Sanding near the edges takes some special care. The best approach is to use long oval sanding patterns here that follow the outline of the back.

Another area of the back that requires special attention is the back of the heel. This is generally smaller than the sanding block and there are edges all around that can easily be cut through. These edges are usually even sharper than those of the body, making it even easier to cut through here. If the back of the heel is flush with the rest of the back, then this can be

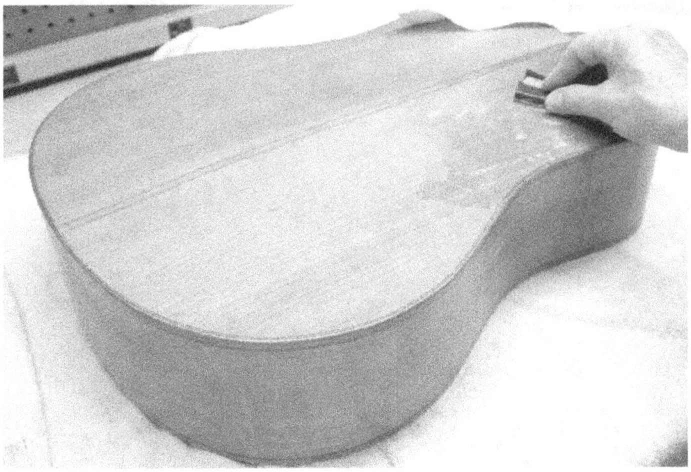

Photo 19-101 – Sanding is done in sections, using overlapping circular patterns. The slurry is regularly wiped off so the leveling can be assessed.

Photo 19-102 – When wet sanding into an inside edge, the edge of the sandpaper is aligned with the end of the block, and that edge of the block is used to work into the inside edge.

approached with a corner of the sanding block, being careful to never allow a large portion of the block to overlap the heel, which would sand the edges. If the back of the heel is lower than the rest of the back it can be sanded separately, using a smaller block made by cutting up an additional eraser.

5. Once one quarter of the back is done, the other quarters are wet sanded in like manner. The sandpaper is replaced after the back is done. It is replaced for each plate or other major part of the guitar to be sanded.

 If the entire instrument will not be wet sanded at one session, it should not be left sitting on the wet towel. Instead it should be hung up until the next session. The towel is hung up to dry, too.

 If at any time during wet sanding the finish is cut through to the wood, varnish will have to be applied again to that part of the guitar. See the sidebar.

6. Leveling the Top. The absorbent padding taped inside the soundhole is left in place. This will help prevent staining of the wood inside with water. Additional absorbing material such as

Cutting Through the Finish

If the specified wet sanding steps are followed and there are no dramatically thin spots to the finish, wet sanding should leave a uniform thickness of finish everywhere. If at any time sanding cuts right through the finish to the wood, it will become apparent that this has happened. If this happens at any time while rubbing out, more varnish must be applied to the entire affected area. So if the back is sanded through anywhere, then the entire back must be refinished. If an edge is cut through somewhere then finish must be reapplied to both surfaces that the edge borders. Here, the term "surface" refers to an area of the guitar that is completely bounded by hard edges. For finishing purposes the surfaces of the guitar are the top, back, ribs, headplate, and the neck, heel, and back and sides of the headstock. It is usually not necessary to remove all finish in an area when refinishing. This is assessed after the first refinish coat. If it can be seen where sanding through occurred after a refinish coat is applied, then all finish on the plate *will* have to be removed before reapplying all coats. If the sanded through spot is not visible through the first refinish coat, then the rest of the coats can be applied to the affected area without completely removing the finish on that area.

a small towel can be placed inside the soundhole for additional protection. Every attempt is made to not get water inside the guitar. The top is leveled in the same manner as the back. Special care must be taken around the fretboard extension. It is often best to sand into the inside edge between top and extension using just the end of the block (**photo 19-102**). Progress is checked often.

7. Leveling the ribs. This is similar to doing the plates but it should be kept in mind that most of the rib surface is convex and so pressure on the sanding block will be concentrated on a small area. Light pressure and an oval sanding pattern with the long axis parallel to the grain of the ribs are used. The ribs are

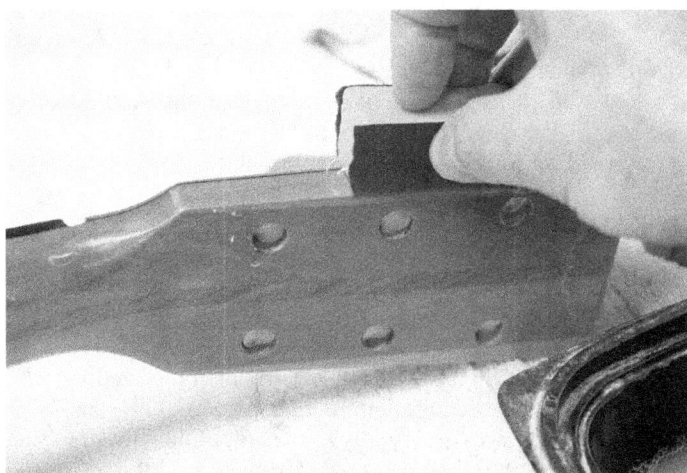

Photo 19-103 – Wet sanding the side of the headstock is done using a block that is just a bit wider than the headstock is thick.

Photo 19-104 – The flat back of the headstock is wet sanded using the usual circular motion, but care must be taken where the headstock transitions to the curves of the shaft.

Photo 19-105 – The transitions between the sides of the headstock and the neck shaft are wet sanded with the paper supported by a rod or one finger.

level sanded one side at a time, going from the tail end to the heel end. Areas that require special attention are the waist and the inside edge with the heel. Since the waist is concave, there is a natural tendency to press hard on the sanding block so it bends to conform to the curve. This added pressure removes material much faster. A softer foam rubber pad instead of the eraser sanding block is useful here, but the sandpaper can also be supported with the fingers. In any case, dwelling in the waist is avoided, and progress is checked often to prevent overdoing it. Sanding into the inside edge with the heel is done in a similar fashion to doing the inside edge between top and fretboard extension. The sandpaper edge is aligned with the short side of the sanding block, and this is pointed at the inside edge as sanding progresses using oval strokes, the long axes of which are perpendicular to the grain of the rib. Again, progress is checked frequently.

8. Leveling the headplate. The earplugs are left in the machine holes during wet sanding. The headplate is leveled just like the plates, but due to its small size and sharper edges additional care is taken not to move the sanding block much over the edges while sanding.

9. Leveling the headstock sides and end. Here, a smaller sanding block that is just a bit wider than the thickness of the headstock is a must (**photo 19-103**). It is often possible to use the long side of the eraser sanding block to level here. Straight strokes are used. The edges of the headstock are quite sharp and must be meticulously avoided. Exceptional care is used when sanding the rounded-over transitions from the sides of the headstock to its end. Also meticulously avoided are the sharp edges between the headstock sides and the transitional areas between the headstock and the neck shaft.

10. The back of the headstock is leveled in similar fashion to the headplate (**photo 19-104**), but it should be kept in mind that the concave curve where it transitions to the back of the neck shaft is subject to over-sanding. The transitional areas are fussy for a number of reasons which are familiar by now. They are small, and they are terminated on the top and the head ends by sharp edges. In addition they will have a more lumpy varnish surface, just because it is more difficult to let natural flow-out level the finish while varnishing the complex curves here. If there are any lumps which must be taken down, it is recommended to use a short length of dowel or, if it is on hand, a medium soft or medium (40A, 50A) neoprene rubber rod. Once this surface is lump-free it can be worked with sandpaper over a finger (**photos 19-105** and **19-106**), but much care is taken to avoid those two sharp edges. This is far more fussy work here than for any of the other areas worked so far.

11. Leveling the neck shaft and heel. This is the most difficult area to wet sand because all of the wet sanding hazards previously discussed appear here. It is essentially convex and so must be gently worked to avoid cutting through (**photo 19-107**). It has hard edges at the fretboard top and these must be carefully worked to avoid cutting through. The inside edges between the heel and ribs must be carefully worked with the sandpaper aligned with the end of the block. The inside edges between the sides of the fretboard extension (which is wet sanded now along with the rest of the fretboard sides) must be done carefully so as not to mar the surface of the top. This is best done with a specially-cut short sanding block or with the sandpaper carefully supported at the end of a finger. There are

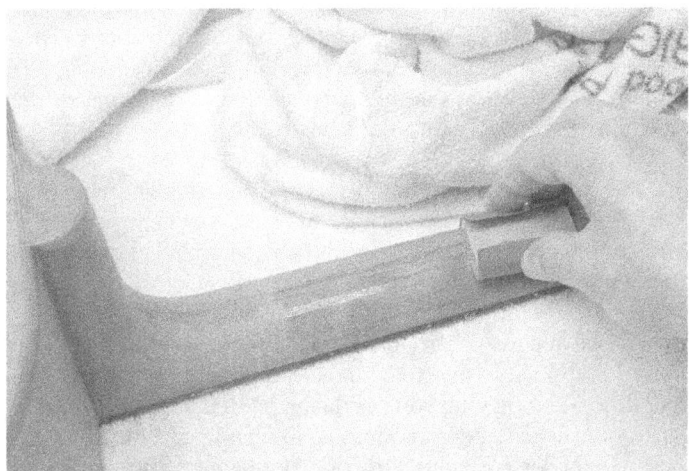

Photo 19-107 – *The shaft of the neck is wet sanded using the block and an overlapping pattern of long ovals.*

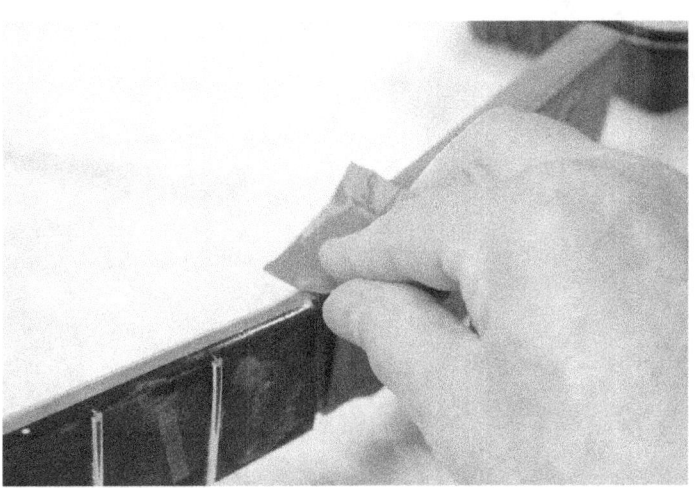

Photo 19-106 – *The transition areas must be carefully sanded to avoid cutting through the sharp edges.*

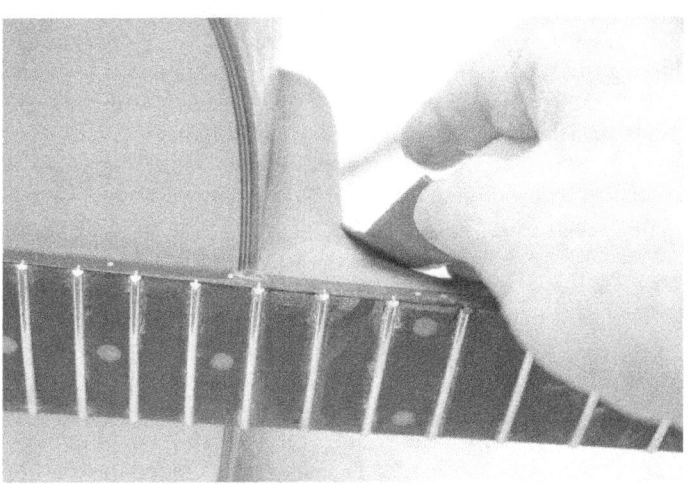

Photo 19-108 – *The curves of the transition from neck shaft to heel are wet sanded with the paper supported by the fingers.*

complex curves between the heel and shaft (**photo 19-108**) and also between the headstock and shaft. Lumps here are generally best leveled using a cylindrical rubber form of some kind or a length of dowel, followed by general sanding with the sandpaper supported over the fingers. And finally, this is an area that tends to be more lumpy than most others because it is not so easy to apply a lump-free finish here. Leveling work is done in small areas, and progress is checked often.

12. After the entire surface of the instrument has been leveled with 600 grit, the instrument is hung up and allowed to dry for a day before proceeding. The water in the tray is dumped and the tray and any sanding blocks used are thoroughly rinsed. The entire instrument is wiped down with a damp rag to remove all traces of sanding slurry and grit.

13. The tray is half filled with water again, and some detergent is added as before. Now the entire instrument is wet sanded as per the steps above, but this time using CAMI 1000 grit (FEPA P2000 grit) silicon carbide wet or dry sandpaper, and using straight long strokes following the grain instead of the circular and oval strokes. Sanding is done no more than what it takes to remove the 600 grit scratches, but note that at these fine grits it is difficult to actually see the scratches. It generally does not take more than a single short session per area if a thorough job was done with the previous grit. Note that sanding at this grit may turn up some areas that require additional wet sanding with the coarser previous grit. After sanding is done, the entire instrument is wiped with a damp cloth.

14. The last step for a satin finish is polishing the entire instrument with a coarse automotive compound. Any heavy cut automotive compound works fine. The compound comes as either a liquid in squeeze bottles or as a paste in cans. A clean rag made of terrycloth or the inside nap of sweatshirt material is dampened and then thoroughly squeezed out. A little compound is applied to the cloth, and the entire back is polished at one time, rubbing with soft overlapping circular strokes until a soft satin sheen comes up. Pressing too hard is avoided. It is possible to work up something of a gloss with harder pressure, even on satin varnish, but that gloss will be quite uneven. A uniform satin surface throughout is desired here. One plate/area at a time is worked, as was done while wet sanding, until the entire instrument is done. Before proceeding to a new surface, the rag is rinsed, squeezed out, and some compound is applied to it. Again, care is taken to not be too aggressive with the compound. It is possible to remove quite a lot of finish with it. After compounding, the entire instrument is polished up with a clean dry terrycloth rag, to remove all remaining traces of the compound.

No wax or polish should be applied to the instrument. Still to be done is gluing down the bridge and nut and affixing the pick guard, and waxes applied now may cause adhesion problems.

15. Now the entire instrument is carefully inspected for uniformity of the finish surface. Wet sanding and compounding is touched up as necessary. Care is taken to inspect all the inside edges. Two places that accumulate too much finish are the fretboard extension to top edges at the top to rib corner; and also the heel to rib edge at the back end of the heel. If there is too much finish in these places it can be carefully scraped out using a sharp knife, then sanded with CAMI 1000 grit (FEPA P2000 grit) paper, used dry, then polished with the automotive compound. If there are any small areas near edges that were sanded through it *may* be possible to polish a bit of the varnish onto those places with a rag. Any but the tiniest areas, in not so obvious places, where the finish has been cut through will have to be refinished as previously described.

16. The paper towels and wax paper taped inside the guitar are removed.

---

1. Stephens, H. (2015). The Effect of Finishes on the Vibration Properties of Spruce Guitar Soundboard Wood. *Savart Journal*, 1(5). Retrieved from https://www.savartjournal.org/index.php/sj/article/view/25

2. Mottola, R.M. (2002). Product Review: Asturomec Spray Gun. *American Lutherie #72*, p. 60.

3. Read, J., Mottola, R.M. (2002). Wiping Varnish – A Guide. *Guitarmaker #44*, p. 50.

4. Aram, Kevin (2016). A Rubbed-Oil Finish Method for Classical Guitar. *American Lutherie #127*, p. 38.

5. Gleason, Bob (2016). Aqua Coat Clear Wood Grain Filler. *American Lutherie #126*, p. 66.

6. Greven, John (2014). How I Build Forty Eight Guitars a Year- With Almost No Tooling. *American Lutherie #117*, p. 6; *#118*, p. 18.

20 The Bridge

The steel string guitar bridge provides a number of functions. It anchors the physical ends of the strings to the instrument. It also implements the body-end termination of the *vibrating length* of the string. In so doing, it also provides the mechanism by which the vibration of the strings is transferred to the guitar top plate.

The bridges of early guitars were simple affairs, which combined the string anchor and vibrating length termination functions at a single point. This was the same arrangement used for lutes and other early string instruments. The front of these bridges featured a series of drilled horizontal holes, one for each string. The strings were simply passed through these holes and tied (**figure 20-1**). Bridges of this style were used on guitars into the early 19th century.

The addition of bridge pins as the method for anchoring the string ends was most likely done for strictly aesthetic reasons. This feature does complicate the construction of the bridge significantly though. The tapered pins must be fitted into tapered bores, and a slot must be added to the bores to provide clearance for the strings (**figure 20-2**). Because the strings enter the tops of these slots at an angle that is close to the top surface of the bridge, the use of bridge pins requires the use of some separate facility to provide termination of the vibrating lengths of the strings. If this is not done, it is likely that the strings would buzz against the top of the bridge. This termination is provided by a *saddle*, over which the strings are stretched. The path of each string bends down from the saddle to its bridge pin, and this bending provides enough downward pressure from the string onto the saddle to effect good acoustic coupling of the string to the bridge, and also to prevent buzzing of the string over the top of the saddle.

In some mid 19th century guitars such as those made by Louis Panormo, the saddle was an integral part of the bridge, implemented as a simple raised lip at the bridge front (**photo 20-1**). But the modern implementation of the saddle is a separate component, usually made of bone or some other hard material, that fits into a slot on the top surface of the bridge. It

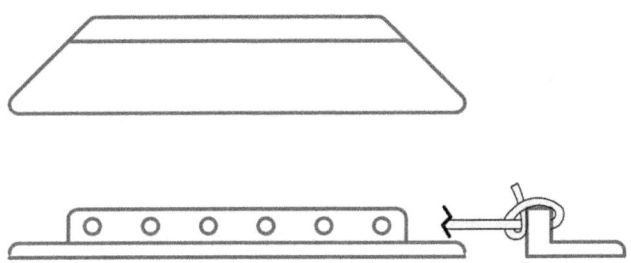

Figure 20-1 – Top, end, and side view diagrams of a typical early guitar bridge. The strings are run through the holes in the bridge and tied.

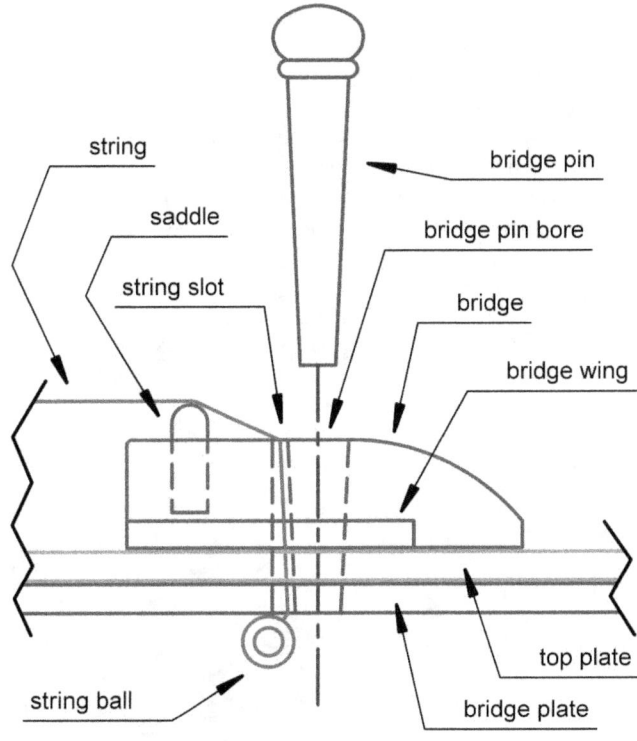

Figure 20-2 – Side view diagram of a modern steel string guitar bridge, with names of component parts.

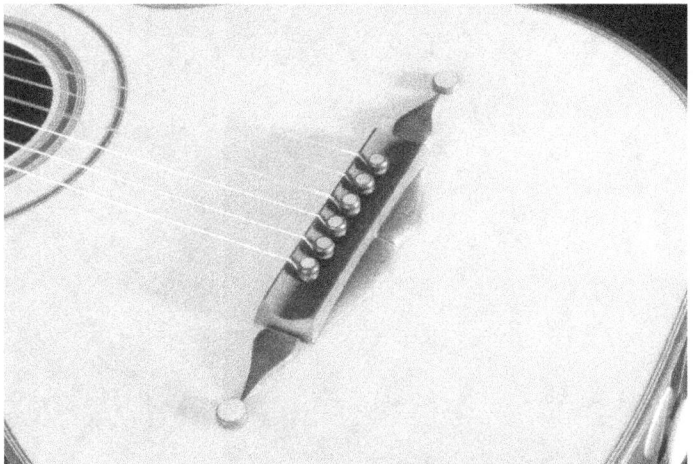

***Photo 20-1** – Pin bridge on a replica of a mid 19th century guitar by Louis Panormo built by the author. The bridge features bridge pins and a saddle, but the saddle is an integral part of the bridge, not a separate piece.*

***Photo 20-3** – Modern steel string guitar bridges use a separate saddle, mounted in a routed slot. The ends of modern steel string guitar bridges taper down to thin sections called bridge wings.*

is likely that the separate saddle was developed to help prevent the strings from wearing grooves into the top of the relatively softer wood of the integral saddle. The use of a separate saddle also provides for a small amount of height adjustment which can be used in adjusting the action (string height over the frets) when the instrument is originally set up.

Evolution of the bridge also involved the ends of the structure. In early instruments the central core of the bridge was often extended at the ends by decorative elements as seen in **photo 20-2**, which shows the bridge of a Stradivarius Sabionari baroque guitar replica made by Netherlands luthier Sjaak Elmendorp. This style of bridge is often referred to as a *mustache bridge*. The previously mentioned guitars of Louis Panormo also featured decorative bridge ends (**photo 20-1**). In more modern instruments these decorations are replaced by integral *bridge wings*, flat extensions to the ends of the bridge that are considerably thinner than the central part of the bridge. Typical modern steel string guitars feature bridges with smooth curved transitions from the central part down to the surfaces of the wings (**photo 20-3**). These bridges also have a central part that widens on the tail side to end up wider than the wings; and this central part also tapers down in thickness from just behind the bridge pin holes to the tail side of the bridge. This type of bridge is generally called a *belly bridge*, and this is the type that is used on the two example guitars in this book.

About Bridge Saddle Compensation

A look at the saddle of any steel string acoustic guitar shows that it is not positioned perpendicular to the centerline of the guitar top. Instead it is positioned at a slight angle (**photo 20-4**). Although it is not apparent from just looking at it, the saddle is also *not* located at a distance from the nut equivalent to the scale length of the guitar, but somewhat longer than that. The combination of angle and offset makes the distance from the nut to the saddle different for each string. The distance from nut to saddle along the string path of the high E string will be a bit longer than the scale length of the guitar. For each of the other strings in sequence down to the low E string, that distance will be a little longer than for the previous string.

Courtesy Sjaak Elmendorp

***Photo 20-2** – Decorative ends of the bridge of a Stradivarius Sabionari baroque guitar replica made by Netherlands luthier Sjaak Elmendorp.*

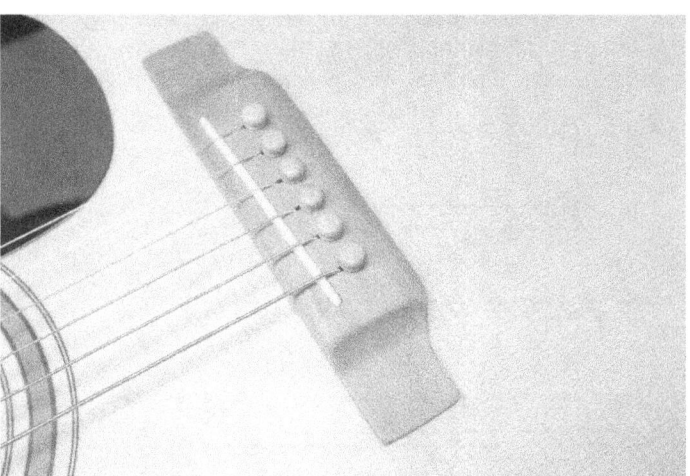

***Photo 20-4** – The slanted orientation of the saddle of this black cherry bridge provides compensation for sharp intonation of the fretted notes. The thicker strings require more compensation than the thinner strings do.*

This lengthening of the scale length is called compensation, and it is done to improve the intonation of the fretted notes. As was discussed in the chapter on the fretboard, the frets are positioned as a function of the twelfth root of two, which also defines the pitches of the musical notes in equal temperament. If the bridge saddle were located at a distance from the nut equal to the scale length of the guitar, and an open string was tuned to pitch, all of the fretted notes played on that string would be sharp.

Understanding why the fretted notes would play sharp and also how compensation works requires an understanding of the relationship of the pitch of a vibrating string to its weight per unit of length, its vibrating length, and its tension. This relationship is described by a mathematical equation, developed by a 17th century French monk named Marin Mersenne. Since this book is a math-free zone we'll skip the equation, but the basic principles can be simply described in a series of statements:

- If string weight per unit of length and length are constant and tension is increased, the pitch goes up, and if tension is decreased the pitch goes down;

- If string weight per unit of length and tension are constant and length is increased, the pitch goes down, and if length is decreased the pitch goes up;

- If string length and tension are constant and the weight per unit of length is increased, the pitch goes down, and if the weight per unit of length is decreased the pitch goes up.

Now, back to the explanation why, if the bridge saddle is located at a distance from the nut equal to the scale length of the guitar and an open string is tuned to pitch, all of the fretted notes played on that string would be sharp. There are two things which cause this sharping. The first is that the strings are located at a small distance above the tops of the frets, and the process of fretting a note requires pressing the string down to the fretboard. Doing so stretches the string a little, increasing its tension a little, which in turn raises its pitch a little, making the played note sharp. This tension increase during fretting causes most of the sharping, but there is another thing which contributes as well: the bending stiffness of the string.

The primary force that keeps a vibrating string vibrating is its string tension. But a small contribution is also made by the bending stiffness of the string. The math used to lay out the fret positions assumes a theoretical vibrating string that has no bending stiffness. All real strings have some amount of bending stiffness though, and that bending stiffness raises the pitch a little bit above its simple theoretical value.

It is desirable that all the fretted notes play substantially in tune, not just the open string. When considering what might be done to make that happen, the relationships among pitch, weight, length, and tension stated above are useful. One possibility might be to increase the weight of the string (that is, use a different string that weighs more per unit of length). Doing so would reduce the sharping of the fretted notes but it would also flatten the open string by the same amount. Another possibility might be to decrease the tension of the string, tuning it down so the fretted notes were no longer sharp. But doing that would also flatten the open string by the same amount. The last possibility is to increase the length of the string. Doing this, by moving the bridge saddle farther away from the nut, will flatten each note by a *different* amount, with the flattening effect being more pronounced for the higher frets and the least pronounced

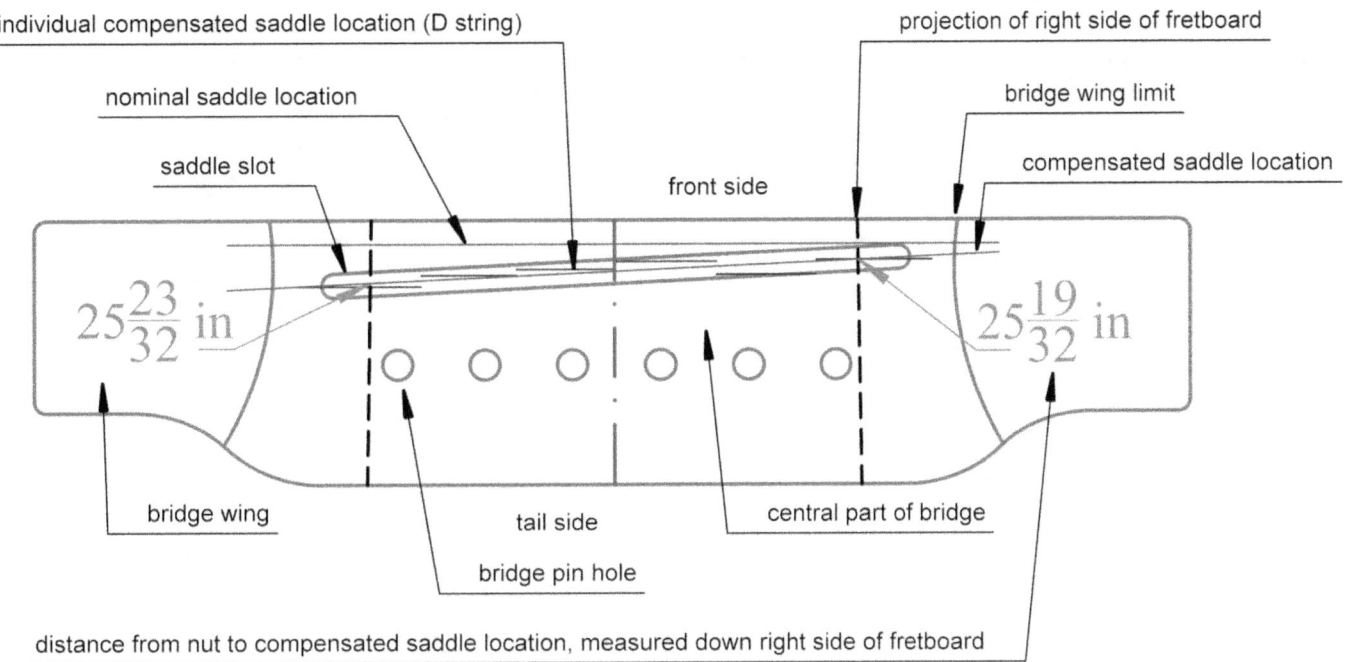

Figure 20-3 – *Diagram of top view of the steel string guitar bridge for a right-handed instrument, showing some of its features related to compensation and bridge pin hole spacing.*

for the open string. This difference of flattening effect is due to the fact that the new placement of the saddle will represent a smaller percentage of the vibrating length of the open string as it will for, say, the vibrating length of the string when fretted at the 12th fret.

This makes it possible to find some location for the saddle that will make the open string note and one of the fretted notes be the correct pitches. The most common method for bridge saddle compensation will locate the saddle so the open string note and the note fretted at the 12th fret are accurate in intonation. Although this compensation method will only provide perfect intonation for the open string and the 12th fret, doing this brings the rest of the fretted notes close enough to perfect intonation for most practical purposes.

The amount of repositioning of the saddle needed to do this can be calculated using math[1] or using a special purpose calculator.[2] It can also be determined by trial and error, and this is the method used historically to do this. Compensation is a function of scale length, action (string height above the frets), and string gauge. Shorter scale length or higher action or heavier gauge strings requires more compensation. But for the steel string acoustic guitar, a conventional amount of compensation will work just fine within the common ranges for scale length, action, and string gauge.

Figure 20-3 diagrams the top view of a typical steel string guitar bridge and names some of its features. Those features related to compensation are discussed here. Others that are related to construction of the bridge and its placement will be discussed later in this chapter.

The horizontal line near the front edge of the bridge represents the nominal location of the saddle, that is, the line is parallel to the nut and the distance from the nut to the line is the scale length of the instrument. Below that are a series of six short lines, each of which indicates the calculated compensated saddle location for one of the strings. The reason there is a different compensated saddle location for each string is because each string has a different amount of sharping due to fretting string stretch and bending stiffness.

The amount of sharping due to fretting string stretch and due to bending stiffness are related to the diameter of the string or, for wound strings, to the diameter of the string core. Everything else being equal, fretting a string with a large diameter (core) will result in a relatively sharper pitch than when fretting a smaller diameter string. This relationship is inherently obvious when considering the compensated saddle locations for the high E string and the B string in the figure. The high E string needs some amount of compensation, but the thicker B string requires more compensation than the high E string does.

This relationship is less obvious for the wound strings, because the amount of compensation needed is related to the diameter of the string *core*, and information on wound string core diameters is not readily available from string manufacturers' literature. A typical G string will have a core diameter that is a bit bigger than the diameter of the high E string and less than that of the B string, and it can be seen in the figure that this results in a compensation value for that string that is somewhere between those for the high E and B strings.

Some guitars will provide separate compensation for each string. This is the way most electric guitar bridges work, providing a separate saddle for each string. In an effort to improve intonation accuracy, some builders of steel string acoustic guitars will cut facets into the top surface of the bridge saddle to provide separate compensation for each string. Others will simply shape the top of the saddle to a ridge that runs right down the center of the thickness of the saddle, as represented by the slanted line in **figure 20-3** labeled "compensated saddle location." This is the approach that will be implemented in the construction operations which follow.

The location of the slanted line down the center of the thickness of the saddle in the figure is calculated to come as close to each of the individual compensation lines as possible. Thus it represents a kind of average compensation for all the strings. Although not indicated in the figure, this line is located 3/32" (2.3mm) along the path of the high E string from the red line representing the nominal location of the saddle, and 13/64" 5mm) along the path of the low E string. These are typical compensation offset values for a slanted saddle, and are used by many luthiers for steel string acoustic guitars.

Note that there are a lot of different approaches taken to intonation and compensation. In theory each represents some level of intonation accuracy, so at first blush it would seem appropriate to make use of whichever approach provides the most accuracy. But actually validating overall compensation effectiveness of a steel string guitar is not quite as simple a task as it may appear to be[3, 4], and musicians may not be able to hear the differences between some of the different approaches anyway.[5] The straight-slanted saddle approach described here is easy to implement and of proven effectiveness, so construction based on this approach will be described in the following construction section.

About Materials for the Bridge

Wood

The traditional woods for the bridges of steel string acoustic guitars are the ebonies (*Diospyros* spp.) and rosewoods (*Dalbergia* spp.). Some luthiers like to use the same species as is used for the fretboard. Others will use rosewood no matter the fretboard species. Recently a number of luthiers have rediscovered the lighter hardwoods often used before the evolution of the steel string guitar, such as walnut (*Juglans* spp.), beech (*Fagus* spp.), and hop-hornbeam (*Ostrya virginiana*). These are particularly of interest to those luthiers wanting to make use of domestic species. I have used each of these species and quite a

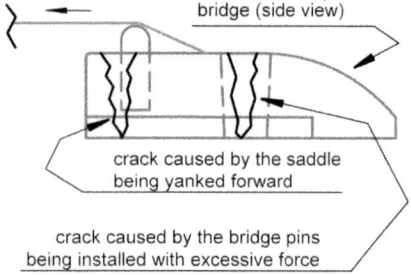

Figure 20-4 – *Abnormal stresses on the bridge that can occur when the strings are suddenly tensioned due to a fall of the instrument, or if badly fitted bridge pins are forced into the pin holes, can cause cracks in the bridge. This is more of an issue when the wood used for the bridge is quartersawn, because the cracks follow the grain.*

*Photo 20-5 – End pins are usually chosen to match the bridge pins. Here is the end pin of the guitar whose bridge is shown in **photo 20-4**.*

few others as well (**photo 20-4**), and find they all make excellent guitar bridges.

Lutherie wood suppliers and general lutherie suppliers generally stock bridge blanks for steel string guitars of the most commonly used species. Some suppliers stock more exotic species as well. Purchased bridge blanks are most often quartersawn. I am not particularly insistent about the use of quartersawn wood for bridges. In fact, I generally prefer to use wood which is way off quarter for this purpose, particularly if it is rosewood or a similarly "split-y" wood. This is because off-quarter grain orientation seems to help prevent a couple of bridge failure catastrophes that often happen as a result of physical abuse of the guitar (**figure 20-4**).

The first of these is a splitting of the bridge at the saddle slot, which can happen if the strings are suddenly tensioned, usually the result of a bad fall of the guitar onto the fretboard. The second of these is splitting of the bridge in line with the bridge pin holes, which happens when ill-fitting bridge pins are severely forced into their bores. Although prevention of these failures is by no means a primary concern of the luthier, anything which can help prevent them from happening will increase the usable life of the guitar.

Whether purchased or cut in the shop, the bridge blank should be at least 6½″ (165.1mm) long, 1½″ (38.1mm), wide, and 7⁄16″ (11.1mm) thick.

Bridge Pins

Bridge pins are manufactured items that are available from lutherie suppliers in a variety of materials, including a number of species of wood. Most of these are tropical hardwoods, but boxwood (*Buxus sempervirens*) pins are readily available for those looking for (European) domestic species. Bridge pins made of horn, bone, and various plastics are also available. Some bridge pins include shell dot decorations. The choice of material is primarily aesthetic. Some luthiers will use the same material for the bridge pins as for the end pin (**photo 20-5**). If this is desired, it is usually a good idea to buy them all at the same time.

Bridge pins are available with or without longitudinal slots cut in their shafts (**photo 20-6**). The slot provides clearance for the string in a bridge pin bore that does not have a slot cut in it for this purpose. It is a relatively recent invention. The descriptions of construction in this book include cutting slots in the bridge pin bores, so either slotted or unslotted bridge pins will work. The upshot is that this isn't something that needs to be considered when the pins are purchased.

One thing that does have to be considered when buying bridge pins is the angle of taper of their shafts. There are two common tapers, 3° and 5°. Each will require a special purpose reamer to taper the bridge pin bores. So whichever taper is used, a reamer of the same taper will also be needed.

Saddle and Nut Material

Saddle and nut materials have to be hard and tough. It helps greatly if the material is also easy to work by rasping and sanding. Traditional saddle and nut materials include bone and ivory. Ivory is essentially outlawed but bone (usually cow or water buffalo) is readily available and generally inexpensive. Lutherie suppliers sell bridge saddle and nut blanks made of bleached bone, solid surface counter top material (one popular brand is Corian), and usually some made of proprietary

Photo 20-6 – These bridge pins have slots cut in their shafts to provide clearance for the strings. Such slots are not needed if the bridge pin holes are slotted to provide the necessary clearance. Slotted bridge pin holes provide longer life for the bridge plate. Slotted pins can be used with slotted holes. If they are used, the slots in the pins are simply turned away from the slots in the holes.

materials specially formulated for use in this application. All of these materials are ideal for saddles and nuts (**photo 20-7**).

We luthiers often enjoy arguing about which nut and saddle material sounds the best, but informal experiments I did early on in my own building career indicate that for all practical purposes there are no audible differences attributable to nut and saddle material among the commonly used materials.[6]

Suppliers will usually also sell inexpensive blanks made of plastic. These are probably best avoided. Although the material is easy to shape, it is quite soft and does not hold up well to the strings moving over it. None of the recommended materials are particularly expensive, and all will provide much better wear than plain plastic.

Saddle blanks generally are available in two thicknesses, 3/32″ (2.3MM) and 1/8″ (3.2MM). The former is a traditional size and is still used for classical guitars, but most modern steel string guitars including the two example guitars in this book will use the 1/8″ (3.2MM) thick saddle blank. Nut blanks are available in a number of thicknesses as well. The two example guitars use nuts that are 1/4″ (6.4MM) thick. Purchased blanks come a bit oversize so they can be sanded to fit.

More options are available for luthiers that are willing to cut their own blanks. Solid surface counter top material is available in a range of colors, and free samples of this material can usually be repurposed for saddle and nut blanks. Another useful material for saddles and nuts is phenolic impregnated paper composite, which comes in a black color. One brand name is Garolite. This material has the look of ebony but it holds up much better than ebony does in this application.

Layout and Construction

Templates for the bridge for right and left-handed instruments are available in the template book for each of the example instruments. The general shape and size of the bridge, and the shape, size, and location of the saddle slot will not be changed from the template. But the spacing of the holes for the bridge pins may have to be changed, depending on the dimensional accuracy with which the fretboard was built. This will be checked and an alternate bridge template with appropriate pin spacing

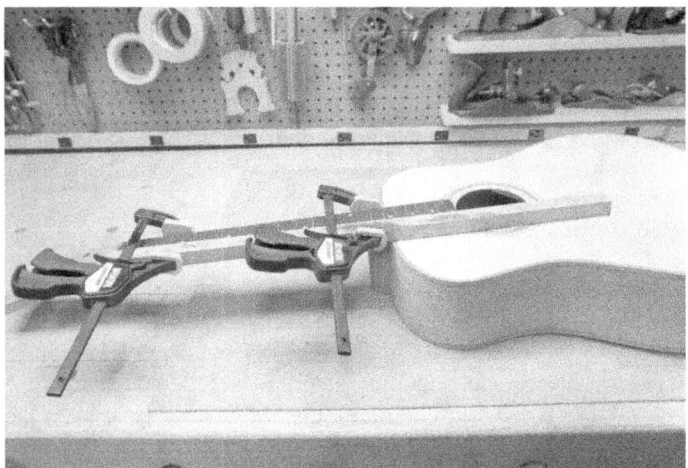

Photo 20-8 – *The scale length stick is clamped to the side of the fretboard as it was during fitting of the neck, shown in this photo.*

will be used if needed. The thickness of the bridge blank will be adjusted based on the set of the neck.

Before the bridge is glued down, its footprint on the guitar top must be scraped clean of finish so the glue can adhere there. This is tedious work, and I have not found any readily available commercial tool which makes it any easier. But a special-purpose scraper can be made by cutting down a small card scraper. Even better is a special purpose scraper made by turning the edge of an inexpensive wood chisel or plane blade or spokeshave blade. Appendix E describes making such a scraper. In a pinch, standard single edge razor blades with turned edges can be used as well. Construction of these tools will be described.

Special-purpose clamps are needed to clamp the bridge during gluing. These are available from lutherie suppliers and are called bridge clamps or soundhole clamps. They are deep C-clamps that are specially dimensioned for clamping guitar bridges. Two of these clamps, either 5″ (127MM) or 7″ (177.8MM) long, are needed.

Materials
    Bridge blank
    #16 × 1″ (25.4MM) long brads
    Sheet cork
    Bridge pins (see text)
    Guitar string set, 0.012″ (0.30MM) – 0.053″ (1.35MM)
Tools
    Scale length stick, retained from fitting the neck
    Bridge plate caul, retained from bracing the top
    2 soundhole bridge clamps (see text)
    Bridge pin reamer, same taper as bridge pins
    Countersink (hand held is preferred)
    Purchased or shop-built bridge slotting saw (see text)
    Small round-profile needle file

Checks and Adjustments

These are done prior to construction, to be sure the bridge pin hole spacing is appropriate for the string spacing imposed by the dimensions of the fretboard, and to be sure the bridge will end up being the appropriate thickness for the guitar.

☐ **Checking Projected Width of the Fretboard**

Sometimes the projection of the sides of the fretboard to the location of the bridge ends up a bit different from that of the plan. If the fretboard was built with care taken to its dimensional accuracy, then this difference will be quite small. But if the difference is significant, the string spacing at the bridge will be affected, and the spacing between the bridge pin holes on the plan and on the bridge template will not be suitable for that string spacing. A special gauge, included in the template books for the example instruments, is used to check the projection of the fretboard sides at the bridge location. If there is a significant difference from the plan, alternate bridge templates are available in the template books for use in building the bridge.

1. The page of the template book for the example instrument that contains the bridge pin hole spacing gauge and right-

handed alternate bridge templates is printed on card stock if this is not already done and the gauge is cut out using scissors.

2. With the guitar lying top up on the bench with the neck pointing to the left, the scale length stick saved from previous construction work is clamped against the left side of the fretboard (the side facing the luthier), aligning one end with the fretboard end of the nut slot (**photo 20-8**). If the stick is no longer handy, a ruler can be used instead. For the example instruments, the scale length is 25.5″ (647.7mm).

3. The gauge is placed on the guitar top so the inside corner of the end of the scale length stick is aligned with the dark green mark at the left side of the top edge of the gauge, and the lines at the center of the gauge are parallel with the center seam of the top plate (**figure 20-5**). Two small pieces of tape are used to tape the gauge in place to the top.

4. The scale length stick is unclamped and repositioned and clamped to the right side of the fretboard, with one end aligned again with the nut end of the fretboard. The inside corner will point to or near to one of the marks at the right side of the top edge of the gauge (**figure 20-6**).

5. If the inside corner of the scale length stick is approximately pointing at the shorter dark green mark at the right side of the top edge of the gauge, then the fretboard has been constructed accurately to the plan, and the plan bridge templates can be used. The plan bridge templates are found on the same page of the template book that contains the templates for the neck and tail blocks.

6. If the inside corner of the scale length stick is *not* pointing at the shorter dark green mark at the right side of the top edge of the gauge, then the fretboard has not been constructed accurately to the plan, and a bridge template with alternate bridge pin hole spacing must be used. The color of the closest line on the gauge that the inside corner of the stick is pointing at is noted. The alternate bridge template of that same color should be used to construct the bridge. So for example, if the inside corner of the scale length stick is pointing at the blue line on the gauge, then the blue alternate bridge template will be used. Alternate bridge templates for a right-handed guitar are found on the same page of the template book as the bridge pin hole spacing gauge was found.

 Alternate bridge templates for a left-handed guitar are found on another page of the template book.

7. Scissors and knife and straightedge are used to cut out the selected bridge template. The saddle slot is carefully cut out of the template using knife and straightedge.

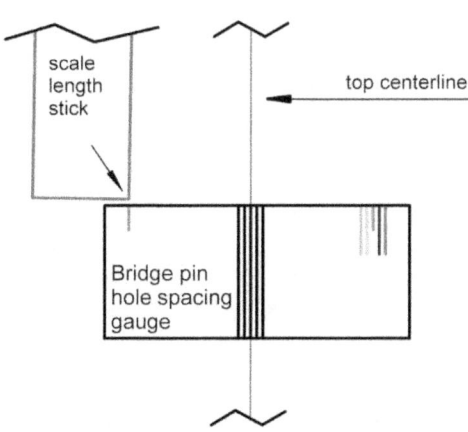

Figure 20-5 – The bridge pin hole spacing gauge is placed on the guitar top, with its center lines parallel to the centerline of the top, and the mark on the top left of the gauge lined up with the inside corner of the stick. The gauge is taped in place to the guitar top.

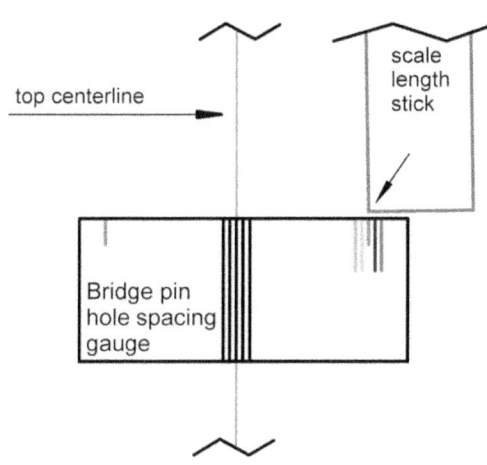

Figure 20-6 – The stick is transferred to the right side of the fretboard. If the inside corner points to the shorter line on the top right of the gauge, the standard bridge template is used. Otherwise the alternate template that is the same color as the line pointed to is used.

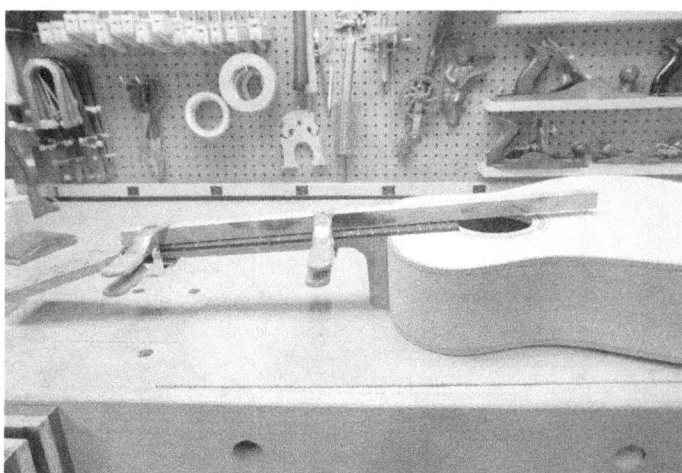

Photo 20-9 – The scale length stick is clamped to the center of the fretboard, as in this photo taken during neck fitting.

Photo 20-10 – *The distance from the bottom of the stick at its end to the surface of the guitar top is the target thickness of the bridge.*

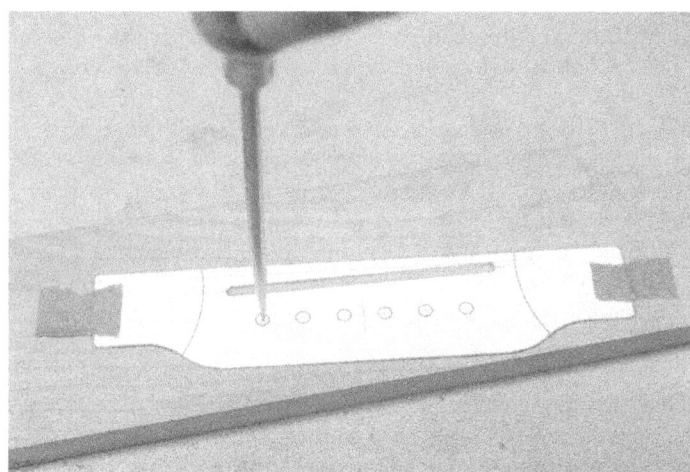

Photo 20-12 – *The template is taped in place on the bridge blank, then the centers of the bridge pin holes are pricked through the template.*

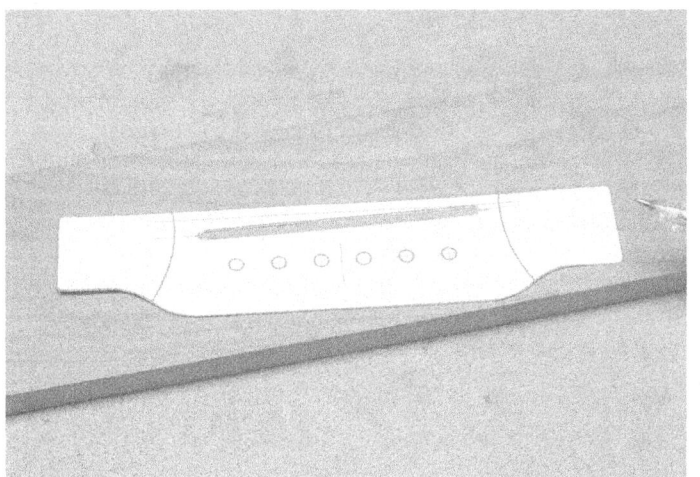

Photo 20-11 – *The bridge template is placed where desired on the bridge blank for tracing.*

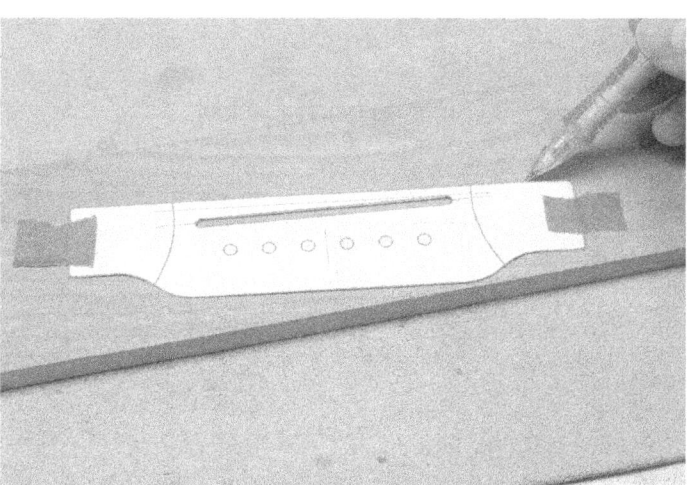

Photo 20-13 – *The outline of the template and also the outline of the saddle slot are penciled onto the bridge blank.*

☐ **Planing the Bridge Blank to Thickness**

The pitch of the neck was set to provide for a bridge of appropriate thickness for the guitar. For the example instruments the target thickness is ⅜″ (9.5mm). At this point in construction the distance between the projection of the tops of the frets at the bridge location and the guitar top will be checked again, and the bridge blank will be planed to a bit less than the measured value.

1. With the guitar lying top up on the bench with the neck pointing to the left, the scale length stick is clamped onto the tops of the frets, at the middle of the fretboard, aligning one end with the fretboard end of the nut slot (**photo 20-9**).

2. The distance from the bottom of the end of the stick down to the top is measured (**photo 20-10**).

3. The measurement obtained above is used as the target thickness for the bridge blank. The bridge blank is accurately planed to just a bit less than this thickness.

4. Step 1 is repeated. The bridge blank is placed on the guitar top and an attempt is made to slide one of its long sides a bit under the end of the stick. If this cannot be done, the thickness of the bridge blank is reduced just enough so a long side will *just* begin to slide beneath the end of the stick. This fine thickness reduction can be done on a sanding board.

Building and Installing the Bridge

☐ **Making the Bridge**

The bridge template selected and cut out in a previous operation is used to lay out the bridge.

1. The template is placed on the bridge blank where desired (**photo 20-11**) and taped down with two small pieces of masking tape at the wing ends.

2. The tip of a sharp awl is carefully located at the center of each bridge pin hole and pressed through the template to mark the centers of these holes on the bridge blank for subsequent drilling (**photo 20-12**).

Photo 20-14 – *The outline of the bridge is cut out and the edges are trimmed accurately to the lines. The inside curves can be shaped on a spindle sander or a sanding drum.*

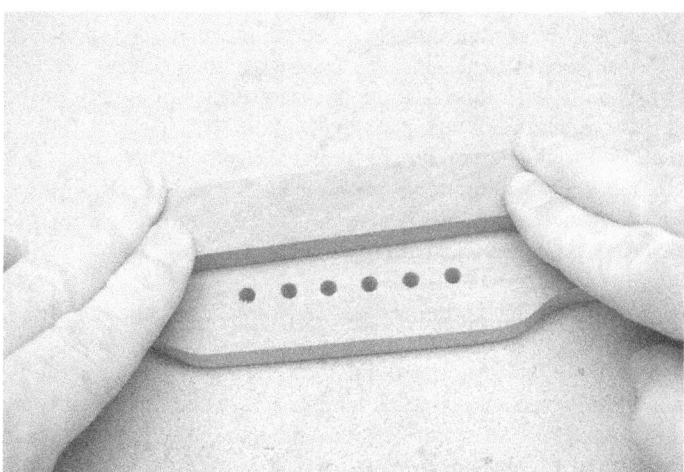

Photo 20-16 – *A cutoff with a straight edge and double-stick tape is aligned with the tail side edge of the saddle slot marks and stuck down.*

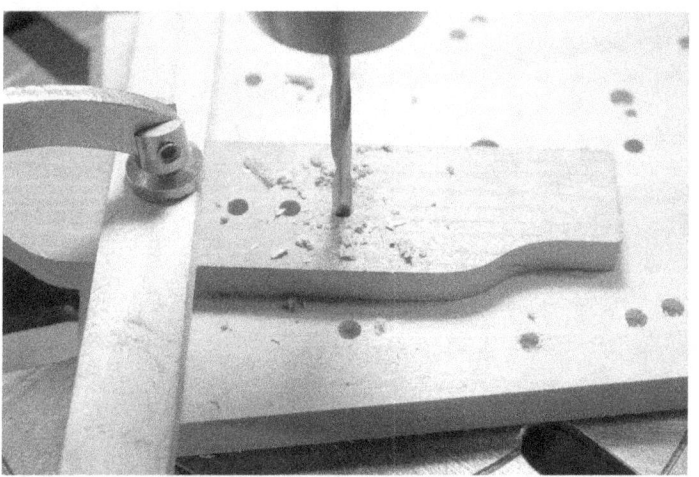

Photo 20-15 – *A brad point bit in the drill press is used to drill the bridge pin holes at the pricked centers.*

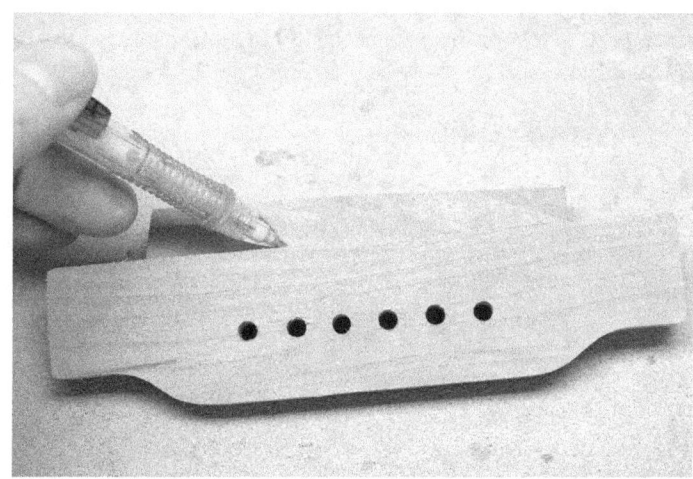

Photo 20-17 – *The bridge is flipped over, and the front edge of the bridge is traced onto the cutoff.*

☞ To accurately pierce hole centers, the awl is tilted away from the luthier so its point is pointing toward the luthier, with the point resting on the hole center mark. This orientation makes the precise location of the awl tip visible. Then the awl is tilted to vertical while maintaining the tip on the center mark.

3. The perimeter of the template and also the perimeter of the saddle slot are traced onto the blank with pencil (**photo 20-13**). The template is removed from the blank but retained for future construction steps.

4. The bridge outline is cut out using band saw or coping saw and then rasped or sanded to the lines. A spindle or drum sander can be used to do the inside curves (**photo 20-14**) and a sanding board with a fence can be used for the straight sections. The cutoffs are saved.

5. A ³⁄₁₆″ (4.8MM) brad point bit is chucked in the drill press and the bridge pin holes are drilled at the pricked centers (**photo 20-15**). The bridge is backed up with hardwood scrap while

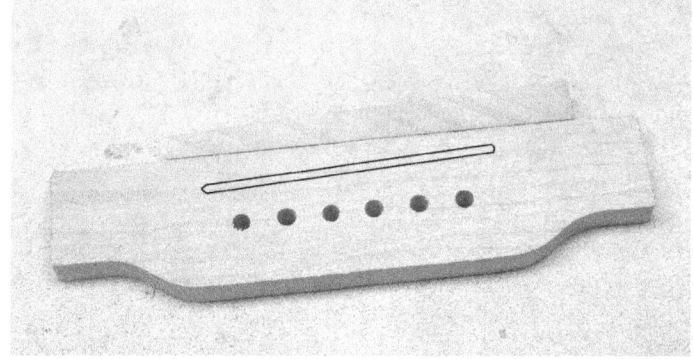

Photo 20-18 – *The angled spacer and the bridge. The top edge of the angled spacer is parallel to the angle of the bridge saddle markup.*

drilling, to avoid blowing out the grain when the bit exits the back of the bridge.

6. In the next few steps a simple fixture will be put together out of MDF to use to rout the slot in the top of the bridge for the saddle. This fixture will use a plunge router with an edge guide. Because the saddle slot is angled relative to the front of the

bridge, the first order of business is making an angled spacer out of the cutoff material saved from when the bridge was cut out. Double-stick tape is applied to one surface of a piece of the cutoff (or any thin piece of scrap) of about 4″ (101.6MM) long with a straight edge on it. The straight edge on the scrap is aligned with the penciled line on the bridge for the wall of the saddle slot nearest to the bridge pin holes, and then pressed into place so the tape sticks (**photo 20-16**).

7. Now the bridge is flipped over and a line is penciled on the underside of the scrap, tracing the front edge of the bridge (**photo 20-17**). The scrap and tape are removed and the scrap is cut and planed to this line. A sanding board and fence can be used to do the fine shaping right to the marked line. When the completed angled spacer is placed next to the front of the bridge, it can be seen that the outside edge of the spacer is parallel to the marks for the saddle slot (**photo 20-18**).

8. A piece of MDF approximately 24″ (609.6MM) × 8″ (203.2MM) is cut for the base of the routing fixture. Two additional pieces approximately 24″ (609.6MM) × 2″ (50.8MM) are also cut. These will form the platform on which the router will ride.

9. Using a few pieces of double-stick tape (**photo 20-19**), one of the 2″ (50.8MM) wide pieces of MDF is taped down to the base board so it overhangs the long edge of the base board just a bit. This will serve as the fence along which the router edge guide will run. Clamps are applied and then removed along the entire length of the fence to be sure the tape grabs securely.

10. The fixture is oriented so the fence side is away from the luthier on the bench. A piece of double-stick tape as long as the bridge is stuck down on the base about midway from end to end of the fence and up against the inside edge of the fence. The angled spacer is stuck down to the tape so one edge is fully in contact with the inside edge of the fence. For a right-handed bridge, the fat end of the spacer will be on the right.

 And for a left-handed bridge, the fat end of the spacer will be on the left.

Photo 20-19 – *To make the saddle slot routing fixture, a narrow piece of MDF is double-stick taped down to the baseboard, so it overhangs the edge of the baseboard a bit.*

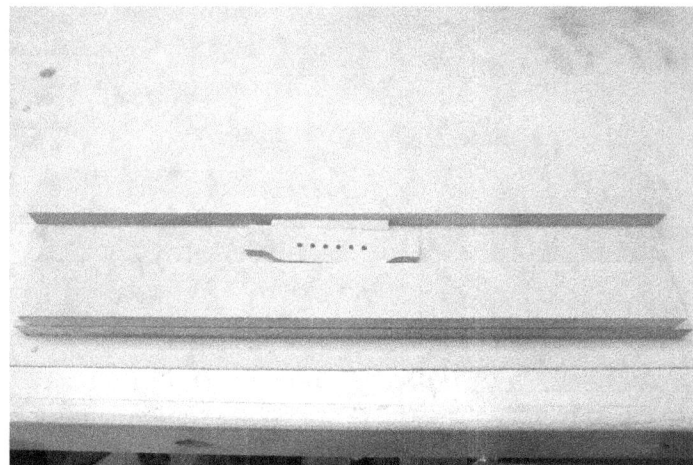

Photo 20-21 – *Another narrow piece of MDF is stuck down to the baseboard on the other side of the bridge. The router will sit on top of the two narrow pieces.*

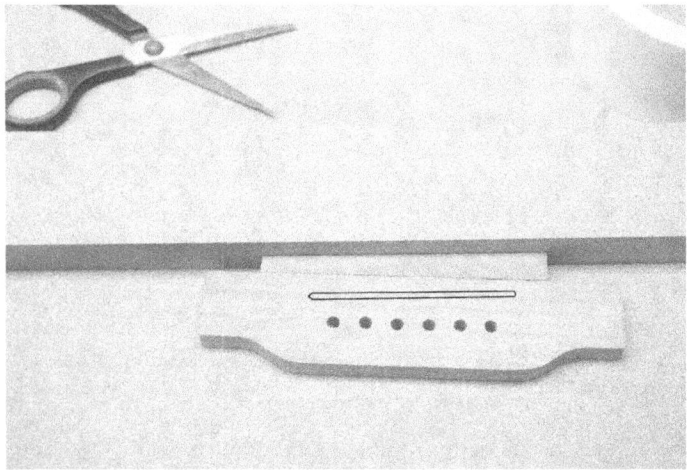

Photo 20-20 – *Double-stick tape is used to stick down the angled spacer and the bridge to the baseboard, and up against the fence piece.*

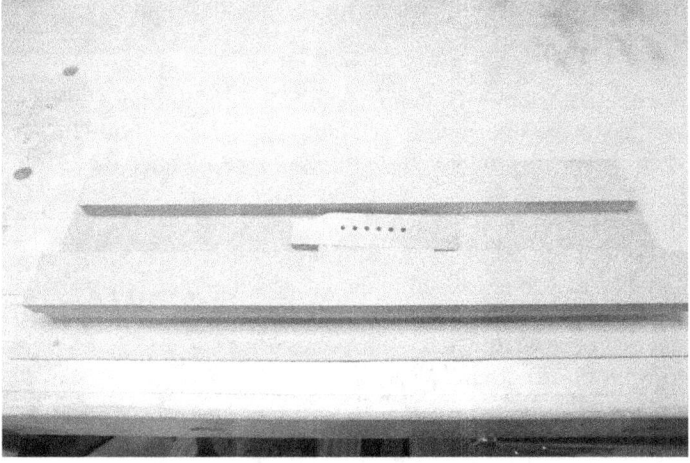

Photo 20-22 – *The assembly is flipped around so the fence piece is facing the front of the bench.*

The bridge is also stuck down to the tape so its front edge fully contacts the spacer (**photo 20-20**). A check is made to be sure the positioning is correct. A square is used to be sure the saddle slot lines are parallel to the outside edge of the fence. A clamp is used to apply pressure to the bridge to be sure it is securely stuck to the base.

11. A few pieces of double-stick tape are applied to the other 2″ (50.8mm) piece of MDF and this is stuck down to the base so it is just touching the back edge of the bridge (**photo 20-21**). The fixture is spun around again on the bench so the fence is facing the luthier (**photo 20-22**).

12. A ⅛″ (3.2mm) diameter bit is inserted into the plunge router and the edge guide is attached. The edge guide is adjusted so the bit will cut right between the pencil lines of the saddle slot. The bit is aligned with one end of the saddle slot and a small piece of scrap wood is clamped to the fence to serve as a stop for the edge guide. Then the bit is aligned with the other end of the saddle slot, and a stop is clamped to the fence here, too. The stops guarantee that the slot will be cut to exactly the

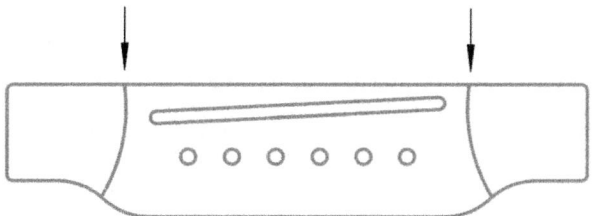

Figure 20-7 – *These are the marks on the template that indicate the limits of the bridge wings. These will be transferred to the top of the bridge in preparation for cutting down the bridge wings.*

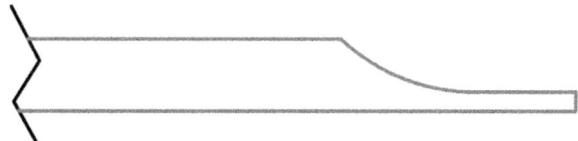

Figure 20-8 – *The bridge wings are initially cut down like this.*

Photo 20-23 – *The router is set up for the cut. The edge guide runs against the fence. The clamps hold stops which limit the travel of the router, so the saddle slot is cut exactly to length.*

Photo 20-25 – *Close-up of one of the edge guide stops.*

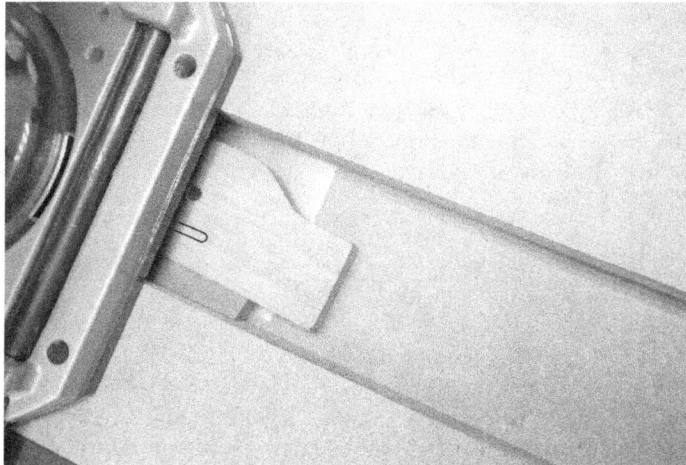

Photo 20-24 – *Close-up of the end of the bridge in the routing fixture, ready to be routed.*

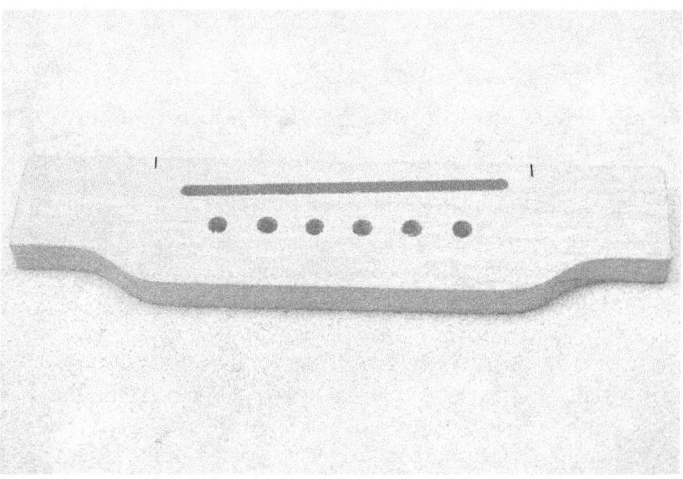

Photo 20-26 – *The limits of the bridge wings are transferred from the template and marked on the front of the bridge in pencil.*

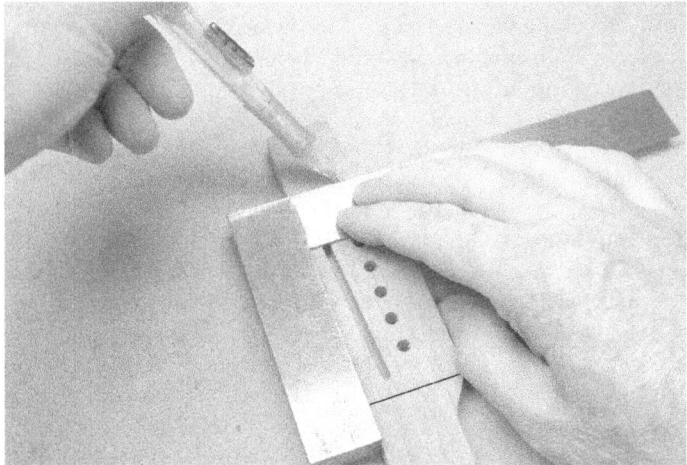

Photo 20-27 – *The marks for the limits of the bridge wings are extended across the width of the bridge using a square against the front side.*

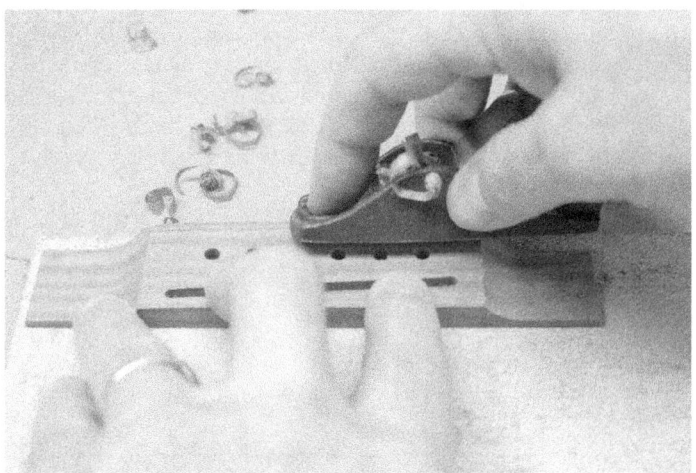

Photo 20-29 – *The tail side of the bridge is rounded over. Here a small plane is used to do the work.*

Photo 20-28 – *The wings can be cut down using a spindle sander and fence. Note the spindle turns counter clockwise, so it is* not *attempting to pull the work into the spindle!*

Figure 20-10 – *The front side roundover is cut down like this.*

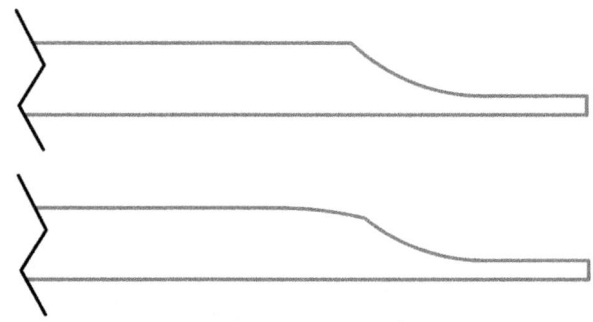

Figure 20-11 – *The transition edges between the central part of the bridge and the wing curves are rounded over like this.*

Figure 20-9 – *The tail side roundover is cut down like this.*

correct length. The setup of the router is shown in **photos 20-23** through **20-25**.

13. The final depth of cut stop on the router is adjusted so the slot will be $9/32''$ (7.1MM) deep from the top surface of the bridge. Movement of the router is checked to be sure everything will work right when actually cutting.

14. The router will move left to right for the cuts. Cuts of no more than $1/8''$ (3.2MM) deep each are used. For each cut, the edge guide is brought in contact with the left stop, care is taken to be sure the edge guide is fully in contact with the fence, the router is started, plunged to the depth of the cut, and moved from left to right, keeping the edge guide in contact with the fence at all times. When the right stop is reached, the plunge is retracted, the router is turned off, and then the router is set up for the next deeper cut. After the slot is cut to depth, the fixture is disassembled and the bridge is removed from the baseboard.

15. The template is repositioned onto the bridge and the tops of the lines indicating the limits of the bridge wings (**figure 20-3, figure 20-7**) are marked onto the front of the bridge (**photo 20-26**).

16. The bridge wings will be cut down to $3/32''$ (2.4MM) thick, with a semicircular transition from the surface of each wing up to the top surface of the rest of the bridge (**figure 20-8**). A square is used to extend the bridge wing limit marks across the top of the bridge (**photo 20-27**) and down the front and tail surfaces. The bridge tail view template from the template book can be cut out and traced and the tracing followed if desired. Material can be removed using rasps or gouges and sanding blocks, or using either spindle or drum sander and a fence (**photo 20-28**).

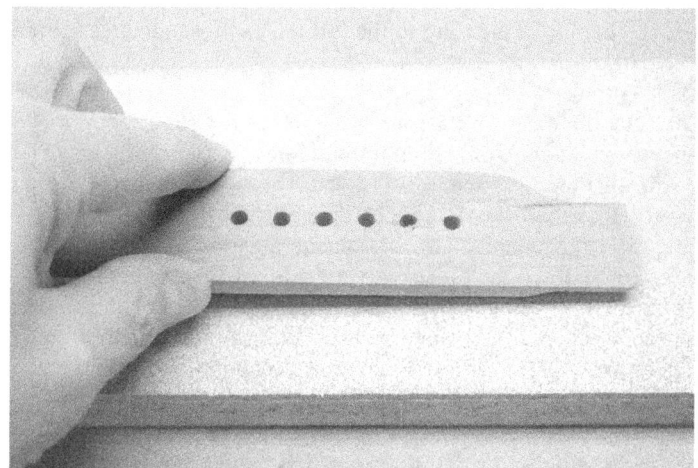

Photo 20-30 – The transition edges between the central part of the bridge and the curves of the wings can be rounded by pulling them across a sanding board.

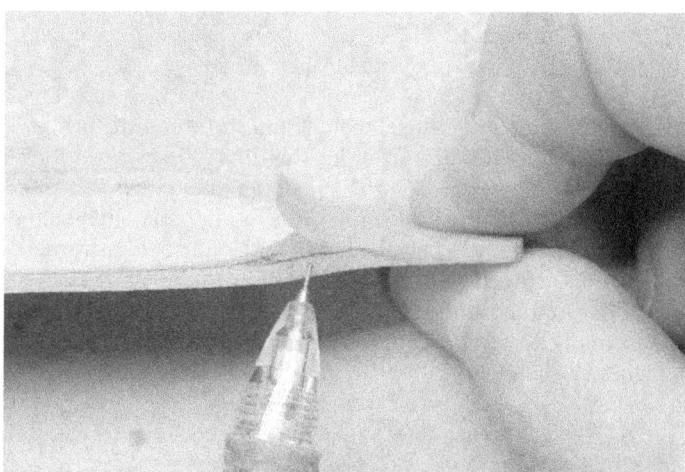

Photo 20-32 – The tail edge and wing edge thicknesses are continued across the tail corners. Here a corner is marked in pencil.

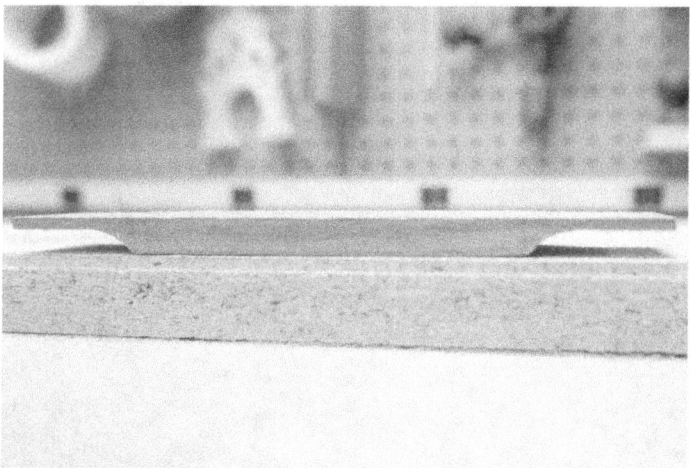

Photo 20-31 – The rounding over here is subtle, as can be seen with the bridge up side down on the sanding board.

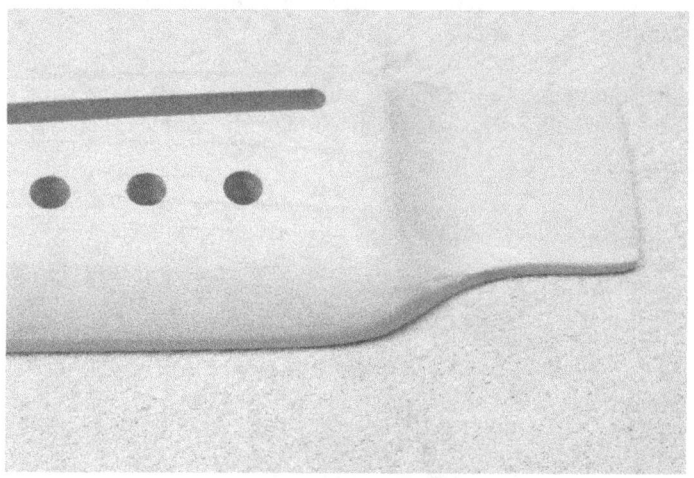

Photo 20-33 – The tail side corner, smoothed out so the thickness of the entire tail side edge is consistent.

17. The tail side of the bridge, from just a bit behind the bridge pin holes down to $3/32''$ (2.4mm) from the bottom, is rounded over in a gentle arc (**figure 20-9**). Using a straightedge, a line is penciled across the top of the bridge approximately $1/8''$ (3.2mm) on the tail side of the bridge pin holes. Another line is penciled $3/32''$ (2.4mm) from the bottom of the bridge on the tail side. This can be drawn using a marking gauge, or feeler gauges can be stacked up to the appropriate height and placed next to the bridge, and then the top surface of the gauges can be traced onto the bridge.

The roundover is cut between these lines, using whatever tools are convenient. For example, it can be cut using a small plane, with the bridge double-stick taped to a piece of scrap wood held in the vise, or simply held in place on a sanding board (**photo 20-29**).

18. Rounding over the top edge at the front side of the bridge. This is done in the same manner as the tail side was rounded over but there is no need to pencil in any guide lines. The top edge of the bridge from the end of the saddle slot closest to the edge and around to the front side of the bridge is simply rounded over (**figure 20-10**).

19. The transition edges between the central part of the bridge and the wing curves are rounded over next (**figure 20-11**). Using a straightedge, a pencil line is drawn across the top of bridge parallel to a wing end and approximately $3/32''$ (2.4mm) outbound of the outermost bridge pin hole on that end. A line is made next to the outermost bridge pin hole on the other end in like fashion. These guide lines are used to sand wide roundovers on the sharp edges between the bridge top and the curved transitions to the wings. There is no need to do this to any particular spec. A broad roundover is imparted on each end, limited by the two pencil marks.

An easy way to do this is to flip the bridge upside down and drag it across a sanding board (**photo 20-30**). Each sanding stroke starts with the bridge almost flat on the board; then the end opposite the one being sanded is picked up as the stroke progresses, imparting a nice smooth roundover. Care is taken not to cut too deep into the transition curves. About $1/32''$

(0.8MM) is fine (**photo 20-31**). Care is also taken not to touch the ends of the wings to the sandpaper as well.

The result of this rounding is that the top surface of the bridge remains flat but ends up sort of looking like it describes a long gentle curve. There are two goals in doing this. The first is that the surface around the bridge pin holes has to remain flat so the bridge pins will seat nicely. But also, in the finished instrument the top edge of the saddle will be curved, and this process of gently curving the ends of the central part of the bridge is done to just imply some bit of curve on the top surface to (sort of) match the saddle curve.

An additional subtle visual improvement can be had by taking a bit more off on the treble side of the bridge than the bass side when doing this shaping. In the finished instrument the saddle will end up a bit higher on the bass side, so lowering the top of the bridge just a bit at the treble side helps to make it appear that the saddle exposure is the same across the saddle.

After the roundover, there will still be a sharp edge at the wing transition curve. This edge can be sanded to round it over to the extent that looks pleasing to the luthier, using sandpaper held in the hand.

20. Shaping the corner between the tail of the central part of the bridge and the transition to the wings. The central part of the bridge tapers down to $3/32''$ (2.4MM) at the tail side and the wings are $3/32''$ (2.4MM) thick. But the corners between the wings and the tail roundover rise up considerably higher. A pencil is used to continue the line of the tail side across these corners (**photo 20-32**). Then a small file or small flat stick with PSA sandpaper is used to round these corners over so that they end up with a $3/32''$ (2.4MM) high flat edge to match those of the tail end and the wings (**photo 20-33**).

21. Other fillets and chamfers. There remain a few hard edges, mostly at the edges of the wings. These are gently rounded over or chamfered to taste. These should generally retain some sharpness, to give the curves of the bridge some definition. Note that the sharp edges all around at the bridge bottom should remain sharp.

22. The entire bridge is sanded up to 320 grit (**photos 20-34** through **photo 20-36**). When sanding, care should be taken to avoid rounding over any edges that are intentionally left sharp,

Photo 20-34 – *The entire surface of the bridge is sanded up to 320 grit. The sharp edges should remain fairly sharp.*

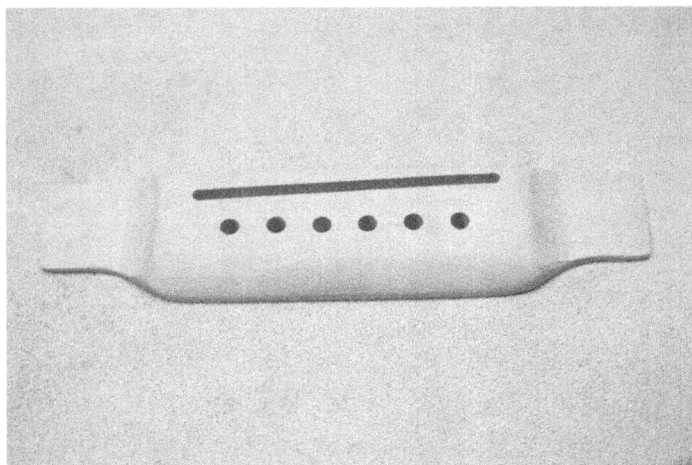

Photo 20-36 – *View of the fully sanded bridge from the tail side.*

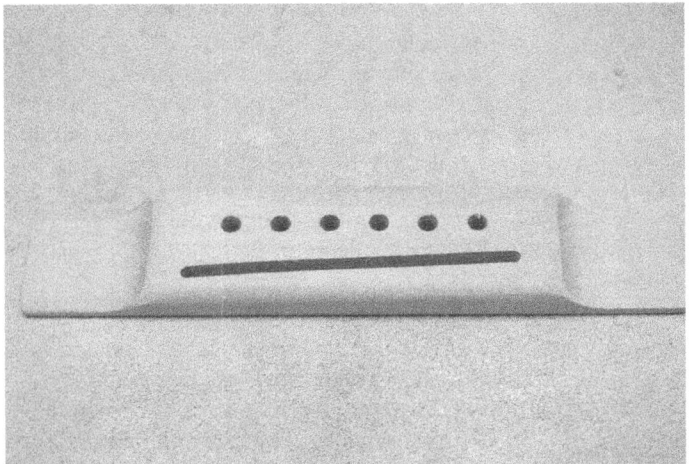

Photo 20-35 – *View of the fully sanded bridge from the front.*

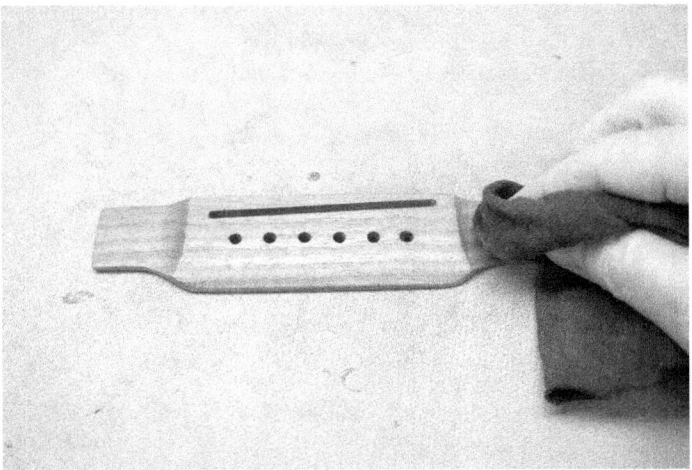

Photo 20-37 – *After sanding, the bridge can be polished up to a shine by rubbing briskly with a soft rag.*

like the top edges of the wings. Doing so makes the contours of the bridge look a little mushy. Also an attempt is made to keep the portion of the top of the bridge where the pin holes are located basically flat. These holes will be enlarged by reaming and will also be chamfered a bit when the pins are fitted.

Note that it is traditional that the bridges for steel string guitars are not finished. On factory instruments they are usually polished to give them some shine. If the bridge will be polished, I recommend doing this by rubbing it briskly with a clean dry rag (**photo 20-37**) or machine polishing it using a clean dry buff.

It is a good idea to avoid polishing compounds when polishing the bridge, because contamination of the gluing surface of the bridge with compound will adversely affect the glue joint.

23. Drilling location holes. A ¹⁄₁₆″ (1.6mm) diameter drill bit is chucked in the drill press and two holes are drilled through the floor of the saddle slot on its centerline and about ¼″ (6.4mm) from each end (**photo 20-38**). The bridge must be backed up with hardwood to avoid blowing out the grain when the bit exits the bottom. These holes will be used for location pins which will hold the bridge in place during gluing.

□ **Fitting and Locating the Bridge**

From this point in construction on, the instrument should be supported on the bench by a piece of carpeting or terrycloth or other material that will not scratch the finish.

The bridge must be carefully located on the top before it is glued down. Doing so will result in proper alignment of the bridge saddle to the fretboard, which will provide accurate positioning of the strings relative to the edges of the fretboard of the finished guitar. Careful location of the bridge will also ensure proper intonation of the guitar.

1. The scale length stick from previous operations is used to place the bridge in approximate position on the top of the guitar. The stick is placed on the centerline of the fretboard, on top of the frets, and can be clamped in place with spring clamps. One end of the stick is aligned with the nut end of the fretboard. The bridge is placed on the top so its front side is approximately at the other end of the stick (**photo 20-39**).

Photo 20-38 – Holes for the locating pins are drilled through the floor of the saddle slot.

Photo 20-40 – If the bottom of the bridge doesn't perfectly match the guitar top under it, it often must be fitted.

Photo 20-39 – The scale length stick is used to place the bridge in its approximate location on the guitar top.

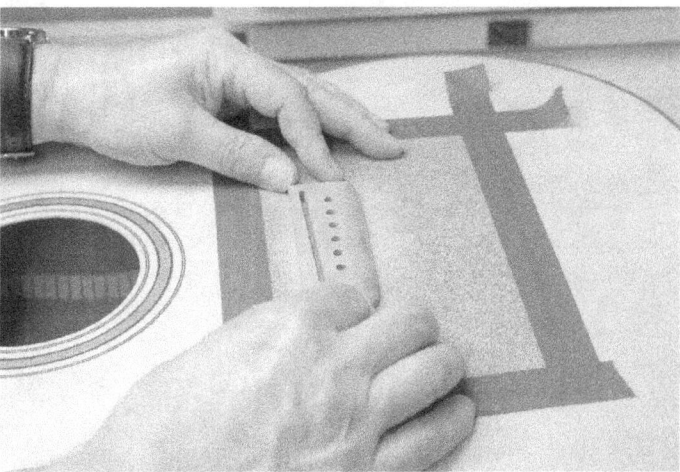

Photo 20-41 – A piece of coarse sandpaper taped to the guitar top is used to fit the bridge to the guitar top.

2. A check is made to see if the bridge sits flat on the top. Sometimes the wings bend up a bit, just as a consequence of shaping the bridge (**photo 20-40**). If they can be bent down with light finger pressure and the bridge sits cleanly on the top then no fitting work is necessary.

If the bridge does not sit in full contact with the top, it needs to be fitted to the top. A half sheet of 100-grit sandpaper is taped down, grit up, on the top in the area of the bridge location, using masking tape.

☞ Anytime something is taped to the finished surface of the guitar, it is a good idea to fold one end of each piece of masking tape over about ¼″ (6.4mm) before using it to tape that thing (in this instance, the sandpaper) down. This way there is a "handle" to use to easily remove the tape when the time comes to do that. Otherwise, the tape must be picked off the finished surface, and this often scratches it. For all subsequent operations involving taping things to the finished surface of the instrument, this handle-forming technique is used.

The bridge is placed in approximate position on top of the sandpaper and rubbed back and forth along the centerline of the top until it is uniformly in contact with the sandpaper surface across the entire width of the bridge (**photo 20-41**). The bottom surface of the bridge can be marked up with pencil marks, and when they have all been sanded off the job is done. Sanding progress can also be gauged by looking at the pattern of the sanding dust on the sandpaper. When the dust pattern is as wide as the bridge is, the job is done, and the bridge is removed. Then the bridge, the sandpaper, and the surrounding top are carefully and thoroughly vacuumed off, without touching anything with the vacuum nozzle (**photo 20-42**). Sanding loosens grains of grit from the sandpaper, and even one of these loose grains can scratch the finished surface. The tape is now pulled up and the sandpaper is removed. Then the top is vacuumed again.

3. Locating the bridge. As mentioned, the bridge position is critical for good intonation of the finished instrument. It has to be positioned accurately relative to the location of the nut. Although this can be done with a ruler and the bridge itself, it is tedious to do it this way. It is a whole lot less frustrating to

Photo 20-42 – All sanding dust is vacuumed off the sandpaper, the guitar top, and around the guitar before the sandpaper is removed.

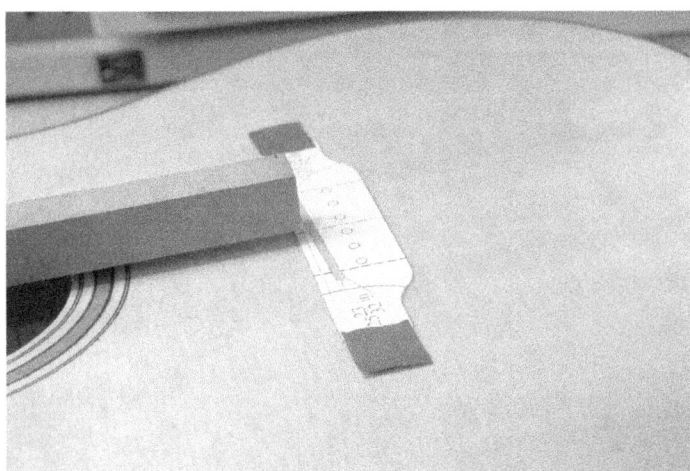

Photo 20-44 – The template is approximately located using the scale length stick and then lightly taped down.

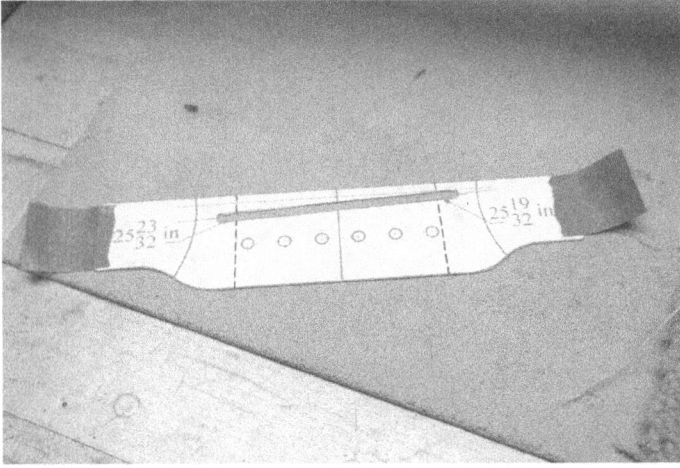

Photo 20-43 – The template, ready to be located at the position of the bridge on the top plate.

Photo 20-45 – A long ruler is used to measure down the left edge of the fretboard from the nut to the plan bridge location.

instead locate the bridge template, saved from an earlier operation, or reprinted on card stock and cut out anew. Once the template is located and fixed in position, the bridge will just be positioned on top of the template.

Since repeated measurements have to be made from the nut end of the fretboard, it is useful to put something into the nut slot to serve as a stop for the end of the ruler. Any short piece of scrap of about ¼″ (6.4mm) × ½″ (12.7mm) × ≈2″ (50.8mm) long will do. A sanding board is used to refine the thickness of this piece so it fits snugly in the nut slot.

4. A short piece of masking tape is put on each wing end of the bridge template (**photo 20-43**) so the tape does not obscure the target measurement values printed on the template. The scale length stick is clamped on the centerline of the fretboard with one end up against the nut stop. The bridge template is positioned in place with its centerline aligned with the top plate center seam, and so the line representing the nominal saddle location (see **figure 20-3**) is in line with the end of the measuring stick. The template is lightly taped in place with the two affixed pieces of tape (**photo 20-44**).

5. A 36″ (914.4mm) long ruler marked in ¹⁄₃₂″ (0.8mm) increments is placed on the fretboard so its zero end is butt against the nut stop and its edge is aligned with the left edge of the fretboard (**photo 20-45**). The ruler will cross over the template (**photo 20-46**).

6. **Figure 20-3** should be referred to for the following description. The bridge template is printed with dashed lines representing the projection of each edge of the fretboard. Also printed on the template are the distances from the nut to the centerline of the thickness of the saddle slot along those projections. The centerline of the saddle slot has been mostly removed when the slot was cut out of the template. But the ends of this centerline are still visible, and can be used as reference.

A check is made to see that the fretboard left side projection line printed on the template is in line with the edge of the ruler, and the distance from nut to the centerline of the saddle slot is the same as specified on that side of the bridge template. For the example instruments (if they are right-handed) the left side distance is 25²³⁄₃₂″ (653.3mm). See **photo 20-47**. If either one of

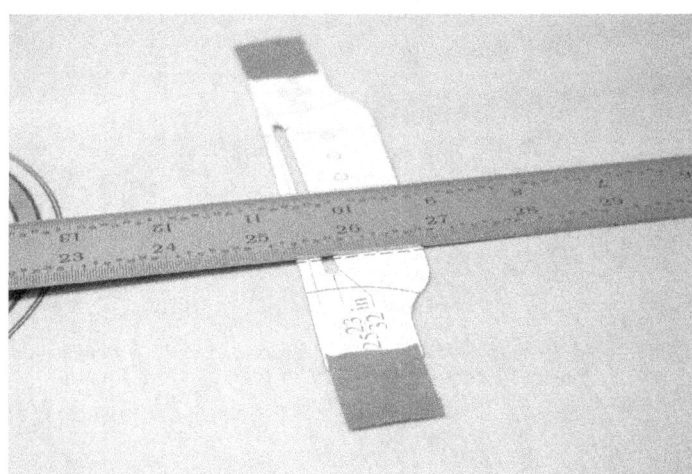

Photo 20-46 – *The fretboard projection line on the template must line up with the edge of the ruler. If it doesn't, the template is moved to where it does.*

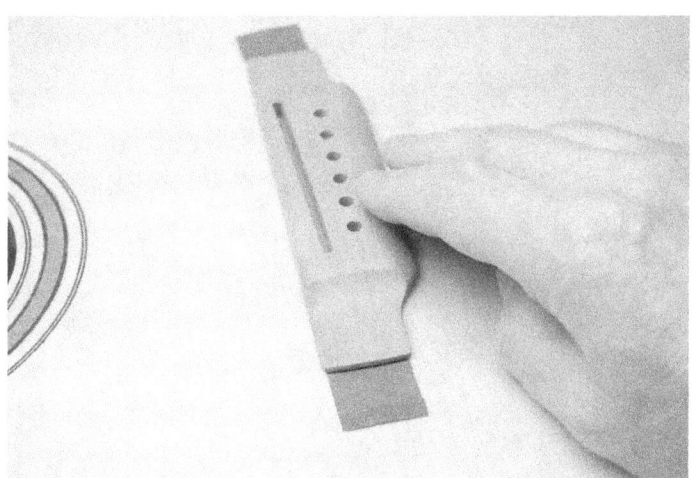

Photo 20-48 – *After the bridge template is accurately located, the bridge is placed on top of the template.*

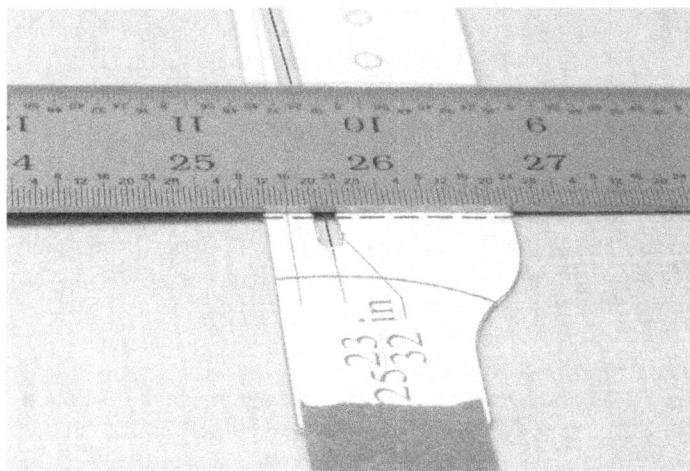

Photo 20-47 – *The centerline of the saddle slot must be located at the exact distance from the nut that is printed on the wing of the template. If not the template is moved.*

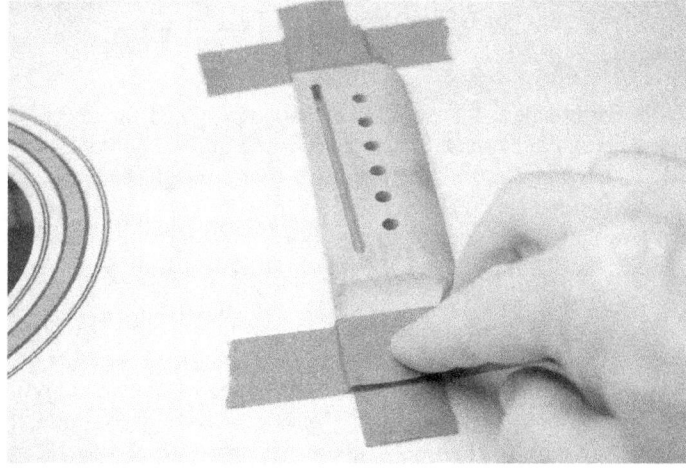

Photo 20-49 – *The bridge is taped in place.*

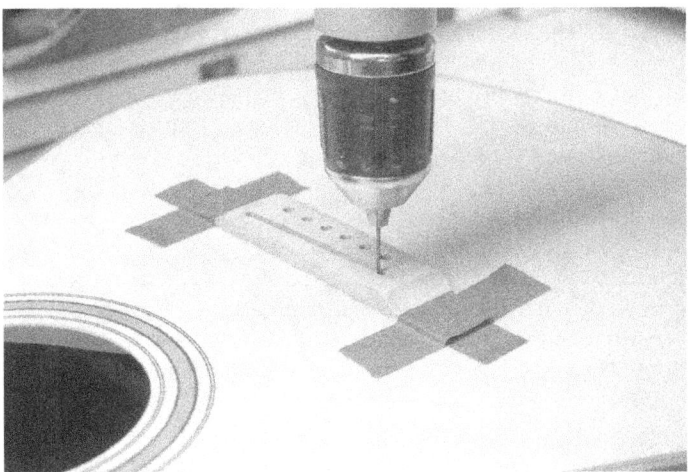

Photo 20-50 – *The alignment holes in the floor of the saddle slot are used as guides to drill through the top and bridge plate.*

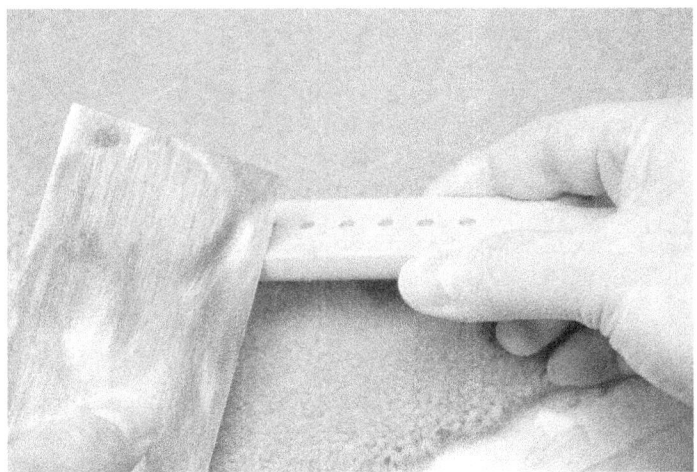

Photo 20-52 – *The edges at the bottom of the bridge are chamfered so the bridge bottom will contact the top after the finish is removed.*

Photo 20-51 – *After the bridge and template have been removed the bridge can be pinned into place using two brads and the alignment holes.*

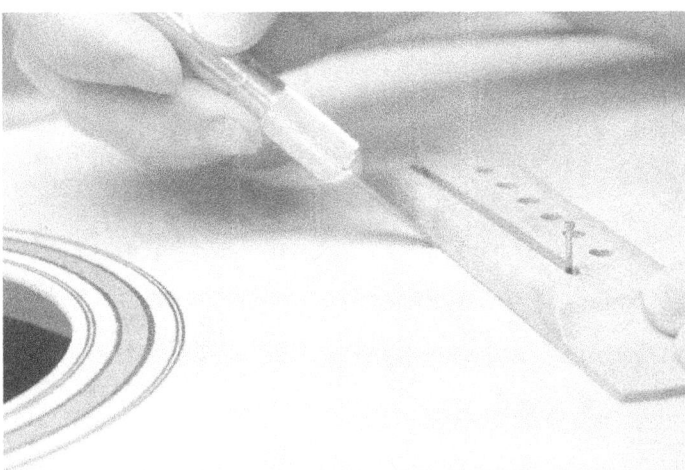

Photo 20-53 – *The outline of the bridge is scribed in the finish. Because of the chamfer at the bottom of the bridge, the scribed outline will be just a bit smaller than the bridge.*

these conditions is not met, the tape on the ends of the bridge is gently pulled up and the template is moved into the correct position. While doing this an attempt is made to keep the centerlines of the template and the top plate aligned, if possible. The tape is stuck back down when the template is in the correct position.

7. The right side is measured in the same fashion as in step 6: ruler against nut stop, ruler edge aligned with fretboard right edge. For the example instruments (if they are right-handed) the right side distance is 25¹⁹⁄₃₂″ (650.1mm). If the position of the template is not correct, the tape is lifted and the template position is corrected. Then the tape is stuck back down again.

8. Steps 6 and 7 are repeated until the position is correct when checked on both sides. Note that it is possible that the actual width of the fretboard edge projections at the bridge saddle will be a bit wider or narrower than what is marked on the template. If that happens, the template should end up positioned so the differences between the ruler edge and the projection line are the same on both sides.

9. The bridge is placed right on top of the template so it is aligned with the template all around (**photo 20-48**). Note it is possible to see through the bridge pin holes to the template, and this helps with alignment. The bridge is carefully taped down with a long piece of tape over and perpendicular to each bridge wing (**photo 20-49**). Care must be taken to be sure it is *securely* taped down. Additional tape may be needed. The location of the bridge is checked once more.

10. A ¹⁄₁₆″ (1.6mm) drill bit is chucked in a hand drill, which is used to carefully drill straight down into each of the two alignment holes in the floor of the saddle slot, drilling right through the top and bridge plate (**photo 20-50**). The tape and bridge are removed, and then the tape and template are removed as well.

11. Two #16 brads 1″ (25.4mm) long are used as locating pins to pin the bridge to the top, using these alignment holes (**photo 20-51**). The brads should not be pushed all the way into the saddle slot: they will be difficult to remove if they are. With the brads in place, it should be impossible to wiggle the bridge around. If there is some play, the brads are removed one at a time and they are hammered a bit square, using a hammer and

Photo 20-54 – *The scribed outline of the bridge is surrounded with tape, to help prevent scratches outside the bridge footprint while scraping off the finish.*

Photo 20-55 – *A scraper is used to slowly and methodically scrape off the finish. Scraping is always done from the edges inward.*

anvil, then they are inserted again. This is repeated until a solid, no-wiggle fit is achieved.

☐ **Gluing the Bridge**

Now that the bridge is located on the top it can be glued in place. This is one of the most critical gluing operations on the guitar, so it must be performed with care. Before the bridge can be glued down, the finish on the top in the footprint of the bridge must be scraped away, so the bridge can be glued to bare wood. This scraping operation is also critical for a good glue bond.

This is a good place to mention that there are two basic techniques for providing a clean gluing surface on the top. One is to apply an adhesive mask to the top in the shape of the bridge footprint before the guitar is finished. After finishing the mask is removed to reveal a clean surface. The other approach is the one described here, finishing the guitar, and then scraping finish away. This latter approach was chosen because the bridge mask interferes with hand finishing, and also because lutherie novices seem to have better success using it.

1. Although not specifically related to bridge gluing, now is a good time to remove protective materials used during finishing. The foam earplugs in the tuning machine holes are pushed out from the front, using a dowel that will easily fit in the holes. The absorption material and tape inside the soundhole is also removed.

2. Chamfering the bottom edge of bridge. A scraper is used to lightly chamfer the bottom edge of the bridge all around about ¹⁄₆₄″ (0.4MM) (**photo 20-52**). This is done so the edges of the bridge will clear the edges of the finish once it is scraped off, which will allow the bottom of the bridge to contact the bare wood of the top.

3. Removing finish from the top. The first step in this process is scribing the outline of the bridge into the finish. With the bridge securely pinned to the top, a scalpel or hobby knife held at a 45° angle is used with its point directed right into the small chamfer that is around the base of the bridge. The knife is held in one hand while the other hand presses the bridge down to the top (**photo 20-53**).

A few things to keep in mind while doing this are important. The first is that only enough pressure should be exerted on the knife to scribe the surface of the finish. A deep cut should *not* be made. The minimum pressure that results in a visible scribed outline is the goal. This is done for a couple of important reasons. The first is, if the finish is cut right through to the wood this invariably results in the wood being slightly cut as well. A cut in the wood, even a very shallow cut, will weaken the wood fibers that the bridge will be glued to, weakening this important glue joint. Cutting into the wood allows water from the glue to enter the end grain of the top wood, where it will bulge up the edge of the glue joint, further weakening it and also often resulting in a visible bulge.

The second reason is that a slip of the knife while gently scribing will usually result in nothing more than a shallow scratch in the finish that can usually be rubbed out, whereas if a heavy cut is being made, the slip will probably result in a deep scratch that may be impossible to remove.

While on the subject of slip ups, another thing to keep in mind is to always cut from a corner of the bridge toward the center, and once the center is reached, begin again at the opposite corner and scribe toward the center from there. So for example when scribing the side of the bridge closest to the soundhole, the knife point is initially placed at the left corner of the bridge and scribing proceeds along the edge toward the centerline of the top. Then the knife is lifted and the tip is placed at the right corner, and scribing proceeds toward the centerline, meeting the previous scribed line there. This helps to avoid slip ups. If scribing was done moving toward a corner, it is easy to scribe just a little too far, going past the corner.

When this step is complete, there should be a scribed outline of the entire bridge and it should be just a bit smaller than the bridge footprint, because the knife was held at a 45° angle and its point was placed right into the small chamfer all around the base of the bridge. The bridge is removed to check.

4. The finish material will be scraped off using a scraper, and it is a wise idea to apply tape around the scribed outline to protect that surface (**photo 20-54**). Without it, slips of the scraper can be disastrous to the finish.

5. There are a number of tools that can be used to scrape off the finish. Razor blade scrapers can be used. These are single-edge razor blades that have had their edges turned to form a hook. They work well to remove finish but the edge wears quickly, and so these must be regularly replaced.

A small rectangular card scraper of about 1½″ (38.1 MM) or 2″ (50.8 MM) is another good tool. Scrapers like this often come as part of scraper sets, available from woodworking and lutherie suppliers. It should be freshly sharpened for use in this application.

Another tool that is useful is a freshly sharpened butt chisel or plane blade about 1½″ (38.1 MM) wide, with its edge turned using the scraper burnisher, in the same manner as the edge is turned for a conventional card scraper. See Appendix E for information on constructing such a scraper.

Whichever tool is used, it should be sharpened (or for the razor blade scraper, replaced) as often as is necessary to retain a sharp edge. The process of scraping off finish is time-consuming and should not be rushed. Shallow scrapes are taken here. Each stroke is started with the scraper edge close to the scribed line and masking tape. Scraping is done in the direction of the grain (**photo 20-55**). Scraping proceeds toward and past the middle of the width of the bridge footprint but *not* right to the opposite side scribed line (**photo 20-56**). Some scraping strokes are taken from that side instead, scraping with the grain toward the middle. An attempt is made to scrape down uniformly over the entire footprint. It is not desirable to scrape down to wood in some places and have others still in need of a lot of scraping.

The goal is a smooth and cleanly scraped surface, with no gouges and no hollowing out of the top. Scraping away the finish has a distinctive feel. This feeling changes when scraping gets down to wood. There is also a distinctive sound when scraping finish, a kind of squeaking. That changes to a more

Photo 20-56 – *The entire area of the bridge footprint should be evenly scraped, and then this is repeated until the finish is evenly scraped down to the wood.*

Photo 20-58 – *The bridge plate caul is held in place inside with one hand and the other hand is used to prick it with a brad through the alignment holes.*

Photo 20-57 – *The fully scraped bridge footprint, ready for the bridge to be glued down.*

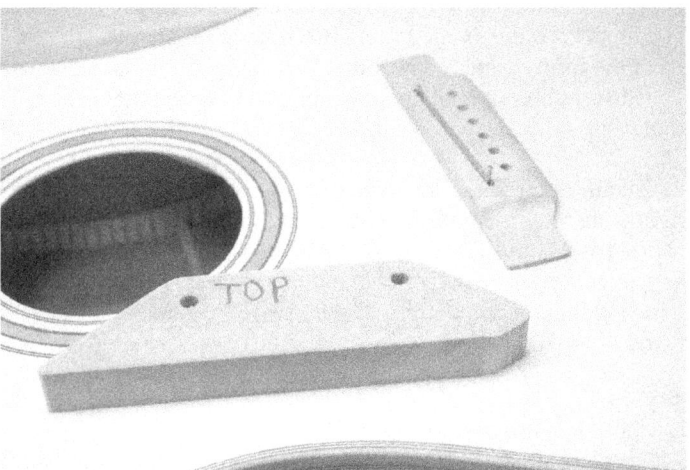

Photo 20-59 – *Larger diameter clearance holes are drilled through the bridge plate caul at the pricked centers, using the drill press.*

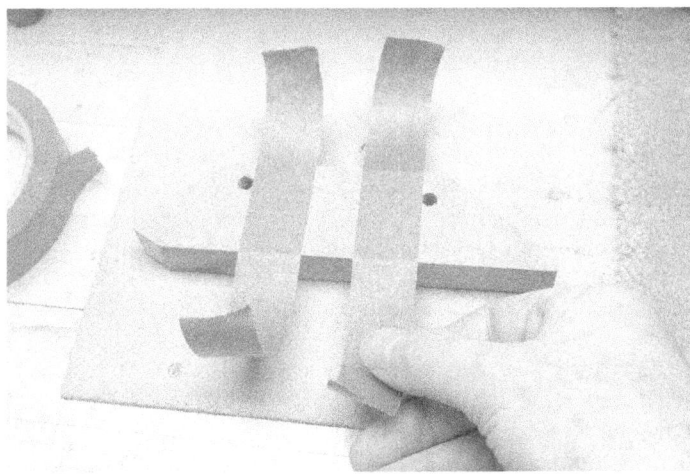

Photo 20-60 – Tape is applied to the bridge plate caul in preparation for taping it in place inside the guitar.

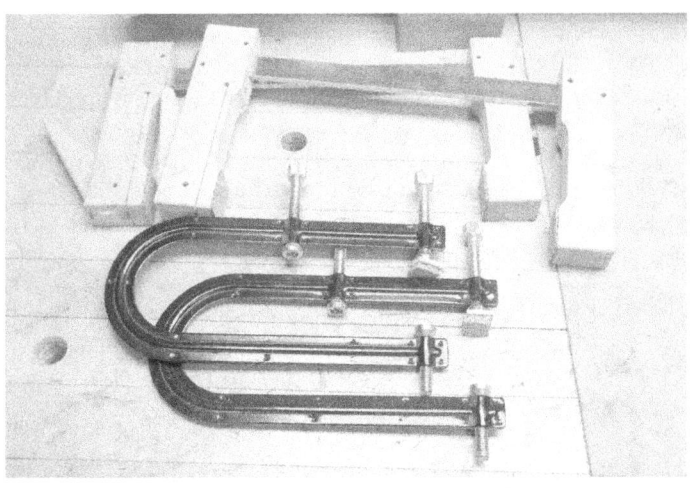

Photo 20-62 – In the foreground are two of a different style of bridge clamp. These have a leveling screw inbound of the clamping screw.

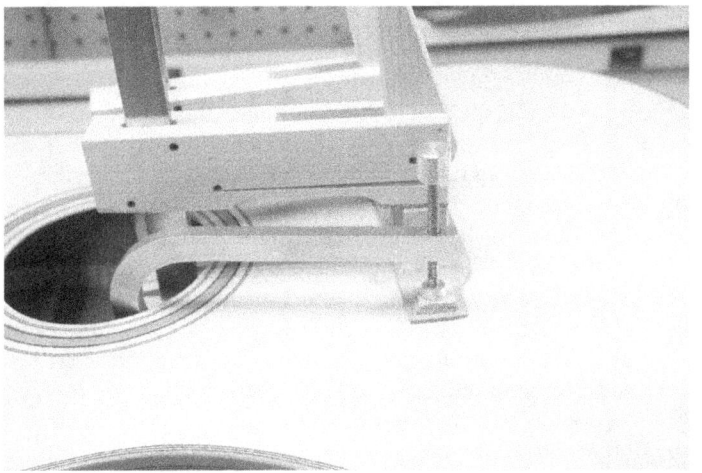

Photo 20-61 – Here is the arrangement of clamps. Two cam clamps are used on the central section of the bridge, and two bridge clamps are used on the wings.

Photo 20-63 – A close-up of the clamping arrangement. Note the tall caul on the central section of the bridge. This provides clearance so glue squeeze-out can be removed from the front side of the bridge. The special-purpose bridge clamp in the foreground has a short, small footprint caul double-stick taped to its screw pad.

saw-like sound when scraping reaches the wood. The smell changes, too. When scraping wood it smells like, well, wood. As scraping in one area approaches wood, attention should be turned to another area.

When the scraper is actually touching the wood of the top, it is wise to be aware of any runout in the wood. The scraping process may be smoother from one side of the footprint or the other on each side of the centerline. At this point, care is taken to clear all the finish away from the edges of the footprint. Again, the goal is to have the entire area scraped clear of finish but without hollowing out a cavity in the top wood.

6. When the scraping task is complete, the protective tape is removed, and all the scraping debris is vacuumed up (**photo 20-57**). A rag with some naphtha can be used to remove any adhesive residue left by the tape. Then the bridge is checked for fit. If the finish is removed right up to the scribed lines, the bridge should feel like it is nestling down into a slight socket. Because it is slightly beveled all around, this is actually what is happening.

7. The bridge plate caul originally used when bracing the top plate is repurposed here as a clamping caul. The caul is placed inside the guitar, in position up against the bridge plate. Fitting is done by feel. It will only fit in one orientation. It is held in place with one hand, while with the other hand one of the bridge locating brads is picked up and poked through the drilled location holes in the top, pricking the top surface of the caul (**photo 20-58**).

8. The caul is removed, and the pricked marks are used as centers to drill two ¼″ (6.4 mm) clearance holes for the brads through the caul, using the drill press. A countersink is used to lightly chamfer the drilled holes (**photo 20-59**).

9. The bridge is pinned in place, pushing the brads down until their heads are near the top surface of the bridge. The bridge plate caul is put back in place inside. It is easiest to locate one of the brads with a finger and then move the caul so the appropriate clearance hole fits over it, then do the other one. A check is made to be sure the caul ends up in the right place, provides clearance for the brads, and fully contacts the bridge plate. Any

modifications necessary are made to the caul to make a good fit. The caul is removed, some pieces of tape are placed on it (**photo 20-60**), and it is reinstalled and taped securely in place. Extra tape is used as necessary. The brads are removed and then reinstalled, to be sure this can be done without interfering with the caul. This is important. If inserting a brad misses the clearance hole and pushes down on the top of the caul, the caul must be repositioned.

10. Trimming the locating pins. If longer brads than the specified 1″ (25.4mm) were used, they should now be trimmed to 1″ (25.4mm) long. This will prevent the bottoms of the pins from interfering with the clamps.

11. Selecting clamps. Four clamps are needed to clamp the bridge in place. Two will clamp the center section of the bridge down, while the other two are used to clamp down the wings (**photo 20-61**). For the example instruments, the two center clamps are the standard 4½″ (114.3mm) luthier's cam clamps used throughout this book. The wings are clamped down with two special-purpose guitar bridge clamps (**photo 20-62**).

12. Making clamping cauls for the bridge. Cork-padded cauls are needed for this gluing operation. The cauls serve the usual purpose of spreading out clamping forces to a wider area, but in this operation they also serve to raise the clamps above the top surface of the bridge. This provides clearance under the clamps so the glue squeeze-out can be cleared from around the edges of the bridge.

Two relatively short cauls are used for the clamps that will clamp down the wings. One taller bar caul is used for the clamps that will clamp the center section (**photo 20-63**). The wing cauls are cut from ⅛″ (3.2mm) thick hardwood stock and are ⅝″ (15.9mm) square. The dimensions are fairly critical. If thicker stock is used it may be impossible to get the clamps into place through the soundhole. If the squares are bigger, the cauls may extend beyond the boundaries of the wings, and this will make it difficult (and maybe impossible) to clear the glue squeeze-out from around the bridge.

The center section caul is a 3¼″ (82.6mm) long length of ¾″ (19.1mm) × ¾″ (19.1mm) square wood or MDF. Here again the dimensions are fairly critical.

The surface of each of the cauls that will contact the bridge is lined with ⅛″ (3.2mm) or ¼″ (6.4mm) sheet cork. This can either be glued in place or taped using double-stick tape. Oversize pieces of cork are attached, and then trimmed to the dimensions of the caul. Then, double-stick tape is used to attach each wing caul to the upper pad of a soundhole clamp. Clamping down hard on a scrap piece of wood will achieve a good grip on the clamp pad with the tape.

13. Waxing or oiling the bridge. Steel string guitar bridges are generally left essentially unfinished. I like to apply a light coat of paste wax (if the wood doesn't have pores, or has small pores) or a light coating of oil. This will darken the wood a bit and give it a bit of shine. But also it helps to prevent glue squeeze-out from sticking to it while gluing the bridge on. A bit of oil (any kind – olive oil is fine) or paste wax is applied to a small clean rag and it is sparingly applied to all surfaces of the bridge *except* the bottom (**photo 20-64**). It is *extremely* important to avoid contaminating the bottom gluing surface of the bridge with oil or wax. Be aware that even a bit transferred from the fingers will have a bad effect on glue adhesion in this critical joint. The oil or wax is allowed to dry for a bit. Excess is rubbed off using a clean rag. Note that this operation may be repeated later after additional woodwork in done on the bridge, but it is done now primarily to prevent squeeze-out from sticking to the sides of the bridge.

14. The two bridge locating pins are rubbed with paste wax, or they are rubbed over the surface of a block of paraffin or beeswax. This will help prevent them from being glued in place while gluing the bridge.

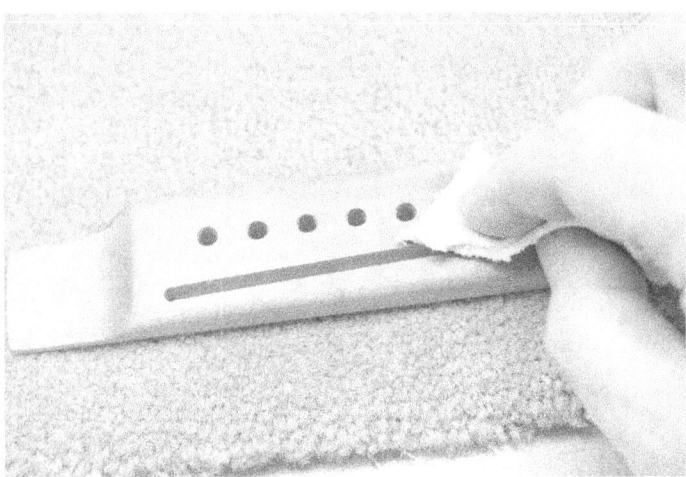

Photo 20-64 *– The top and sides of the bridge are carefully and lightly oiled or waxed in preparation for gluing it on. This will prevent the glue squeeze-out from adhering to the bridge when the glue is scraped off. Much care is taken to prevent any of the oil or wax from getting on the bottom gluing surface of the bridge.*

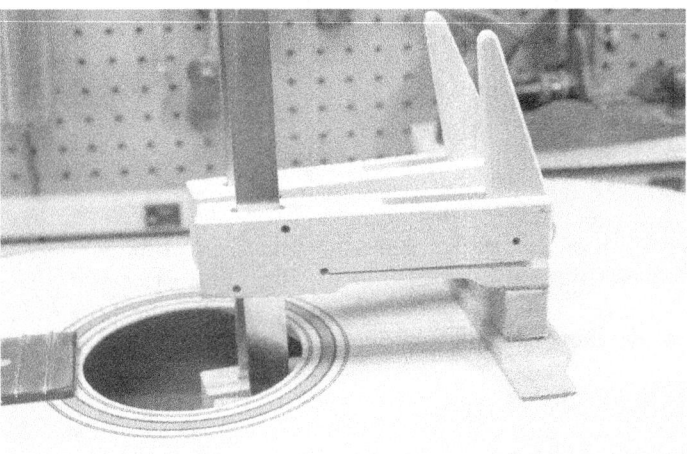

Photo 20-65 *– The two cam clamps are placed first, to clamp down the central section of the bridge.*

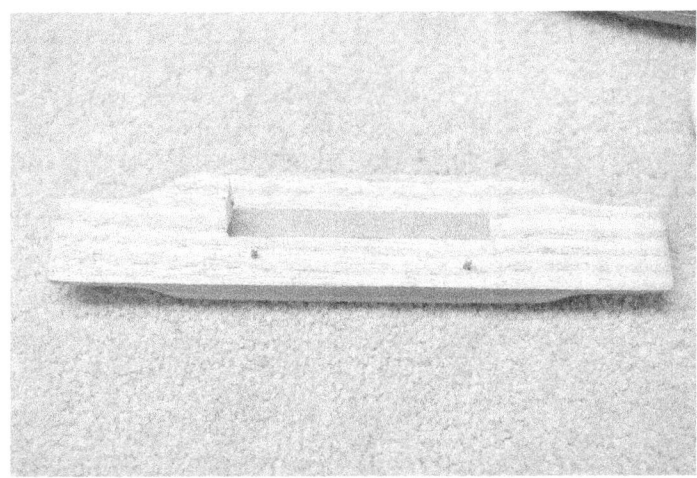

Photo 20-66 – *Before glue is applied, a piece of tape just big enough to cover the bridge pin holes is applied, to prevent glue from running through the holes as it is applied.*

Photo 20-68 – *After the glue cures, all the clamps are removed, then the cam clamps are reinstalled, but leaving clearance for the bridge pin holes.*

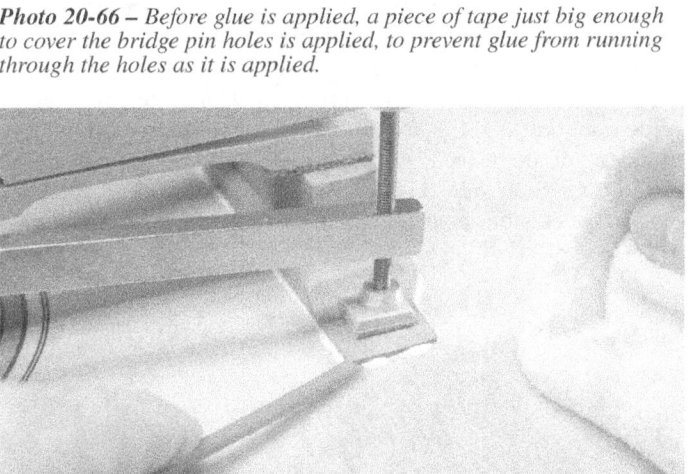

Photo 20-67 – *The squeeze-out is cleared using the snipped straw. Note that there is enough clearance under the clamps to get the straw all the way across the front edge of the bridge.*

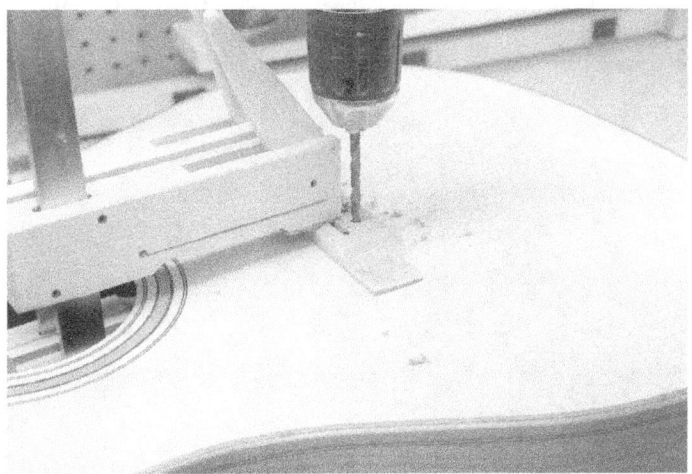

Photo 20-69 – *The bridge pin holes are drilled right through the top and the bridge plate, and just a bit into the caul. The clamps hold the bridge plate caul in place to back up the bridge plate during drilling.*

15. A dry run of gluing the bridge is critical to success. The soundhole clamps are set up by screwing their bottom pads all the way down, and screwing the top pads all the way up. This is necessary to provide enough clearance to get the clamps in place through the soundhole. Note that some longer soundhole clamps such as the ones pictured in **photo 20-62** have an additional top screw, used to level the clamp once it is in position. These should also be screwed all the way up at this time.

16. One locating pin is inserted partway through one of the holes in the saddle slot floor of the bridge. The bridge is tilted into position so the end of the pin can be seen, and it is guided into the appropriate hole in the top. The bridge is dropped in place, being careful to position it right on top of the bare wood area. When this operation is done with glue applied it is necessary to not smear glue all over the top while getting the bridge into position. The other pin is inserted and the bridge is wiggled around as necessary to find the hole in the top for it. The pins are pushed in so their tops are flush with the top of the bridge.

17. The bar caul is placed on top of the center part of the bridge. One of the cam clamps is carefully placed through the soundhole, avoiding bumping it into the edge of the soundhole. It is positioned over the caul to one end, and lightly clamped in place. The other cam clamp is placed in like fashion (**photo 20-65**). The clamps are tightened.

18. Holding one of the soundhole clamps in one hand, and with a finger of the other hand under the caul on the upper pad, the clamp is guided into position. The finger keeps the caul from being detached during positioning. When the clamp appears to be in position (upper pad right over the center of the wing) it is lifted straight up until it is felt that the bottom pad of the clamp is sitting squarely on the surface of the inside caul. The clamp is repositioned as necessary, held in position, and then tightened. When the wing caul touches the wing, care is taken to be sure it ends up square to the wing and doesn't overhang it, before tightening the clamp fully. If the clamp has a leveling screw, that is screwed down, with a piece of cardboard under the pad to protect the finish on the guitar top, until the clamp sits level relative to the top. The final soundhole clamp is installed in like fashion for the other bridge wing (**photo 20-63**).

Note that glue squeeze-out will have to be removed from all around the bridge using a snipped straw and a small rag. It is a good idea to practice this to be sure the clamp and caul arrangement provides access all around the perimeter of the bridge.

19. The clamping sequence specified in steps 15 through 18 should be practiced until it can be reliably accomplished in a couple of minutes. Then all clamps and the bridge are removed for actual gluing.

20. Gluing the bridge. A narrow piece of masking tape (with a "handle") is applied to the bottom of the bridge so it *just* covers the bridge pin holes (**photo 20-66**). A snipped plastic straw, a damp rag of about 3″ (76.2MM) square, a couple of pieces of damp T-shirt material about 1″ (25.4MM) square, and some dry clean rags are collected and placed within easy reach. Glue is applied to the bottom of the bridge and spread quickly to completely cover the bottom. The masking tape covering the pin holes is removed and discarded. The bridge is positioned and clamped as per steps 15 through 18.

21. The snipped straw is used to remove glue squeeze-out. This is done in a small section at a time, to avoid smearing glue up the sides of the bridge. The small damp rag is used to remove any traces of squeeze-out left on the surface of the top and the sides of the bridge (**photo 20-67**). It is difficult to reach under the clamps with the rag to completely clean the soundhole side of the bridge. Here, one of the small 1″ (25.4MM) square damp rags can be pushed with the tip of the snipped straw to mop up. A careful inspection is made all around, to be sure all glue squeeze-out has been removed. The glue is allowed to cure overnight. In addition to letting the glue in the joint cure, there will be some glue pooled in the bridge pin holes that must fully harden before the holes are drilled out.

22. Drilling bridge pin holes through. All clamps and the outside cauls are removed, then the two cam clamps are reinstalled so they will clamp the inside caul in place, but also provide clearance to drill out the bridge pin holes (**photo 20-68**). A 3⁄16″ (4.8MM) drill bit is chucked in a hand drill, and each pin hole is drilled out, keeping the drill bit straight up and perpendicular to the top of the instrument (**photo 20-69**). There is no need to drill too deep, about 5⁄8″ (15.9MM), just enough to clear out any glue in the existing hole, and then drill through the top and the

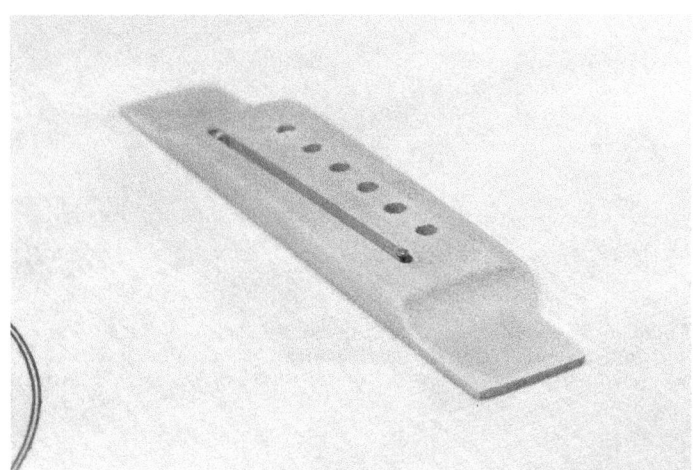

Photo 20-70 – *The locating pins must now be removed from the saddle slot.*

Photo 20-72 – *If the pins got glued in, they are heated with a soldering iron until the glue melts. Then they can be pulled with the pliers.*

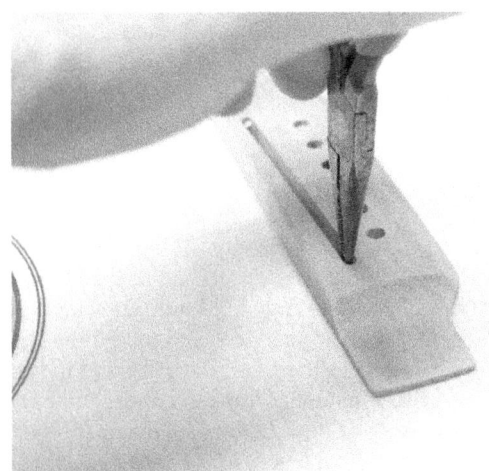

Photo 20-71 – *The locating pins are removed with needle nose pliers, being careful not to damage the edge of the saddle slot.*

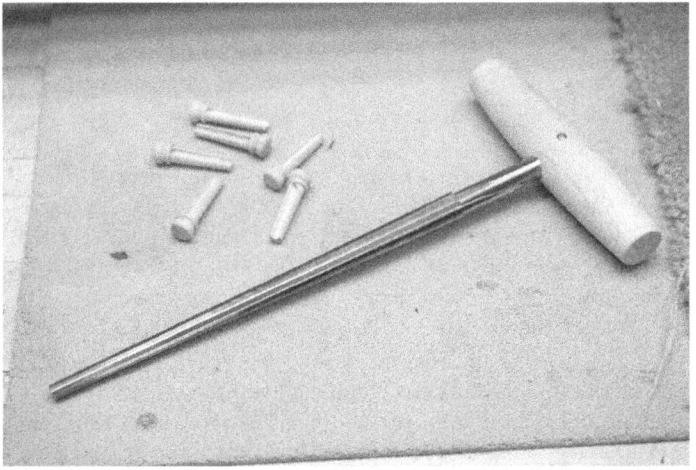

Photo 20-73 – *A bridge pin hole reamer and some bridge pins. The taper of the reamer must match the taper of the shafts of the bridge pins.*

bridge plate. The inside caul serves to back up the bridge plate to prevent the grain from being blown out when the bit exits the back surface of the plate. After all holes have been drilled out, the clamps are removed (**photo 20-70**). The inside caul and all the tape holding it in place are also removed. The top surface of the caul is examined to be sure all the pin holes were drilled all the way through. Debris is carefully vacuumed up from inside the instrument and from the top and bridge.

23. Removing the locating pins. The locating pins can usually be pulled straight up out of the saddle slot using needle nose pliers (**photo 20-71**). Attempting to lever these out is never a good idea, as this will definitely dent the top of the bridge and damage the walls of the saddle slot. The top of the pin is gripped with the pliers and the pin is pulled straight up. If the pin won't come out easily, the head of the pin is heated with a soldering iron for a few seconds. The soldering iron is held upright, lightly touching the head of the pin (**photo 20-72**). When the pin gets hot the glue holding it in place will melt and the pin can be removed easily with the pliers.

Care is taken to not press down on the pin with the soldering iron. If pressure is applied, once the glue lets go, the soldering iron tip will plunge into the saddle slot and possibly burn or otherwise damage the bridge.

After the pins are removed they are discarded. The floor of the saddle slot is cleaned of any debris there. A hobby knife or narrow chisel may be required. Much care needs to be taken when doing this, to avoid damaging the walls and top edges of the slot.

☐ Rough Fitting the Bridge Pins

As mentioned earlier, the bridge pins have tapered shafts which fit into tapered bores drilled through the bridge, top plate, and bridge plate. The bores will be roughly tapered now, with final fitting done later in construction. A special-purpose bridge pin hole reamer is used to do this (photo **20-73**). There is no special skill required to ream bridge pin holes, but care must be taken to not over-ream the holes.

1. The bridge pin hole reamer is fitted into any bridge pin hole. The hole is reamed a bit, keeping the reamer upright at all times (**photo 20-74**). When reaming, the reamer must be turned all the way around 360° in the direction of cut, usually clockwise,

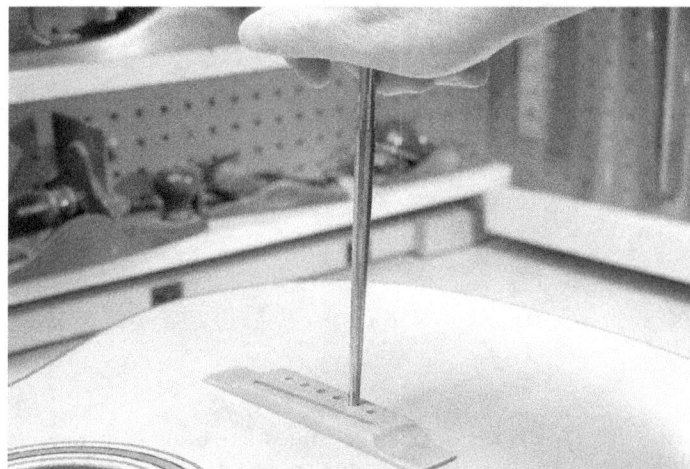

Photo 20-74 – *Reaming a bridge pin hole.*

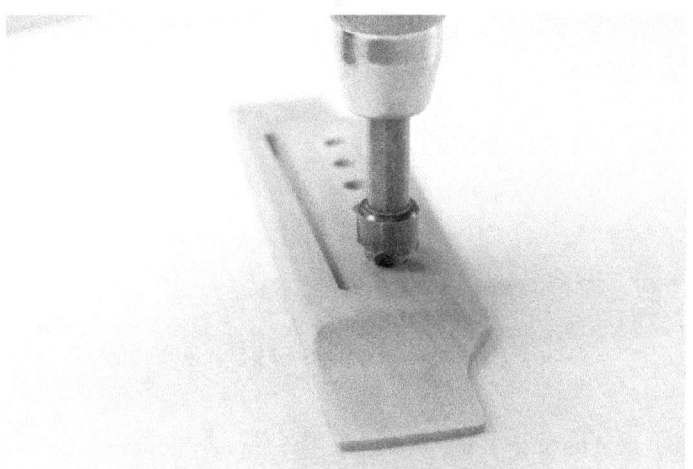

Photo 20-76 – *The edges of the bridge pins holes are chamfered using a countersink.*

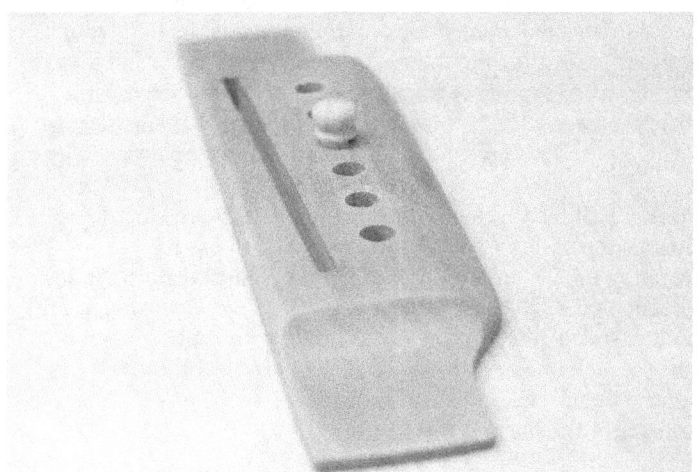

Photo 20-75 – *As reaming proceeds, a pin is test fitted. This one is almost fully seated.*

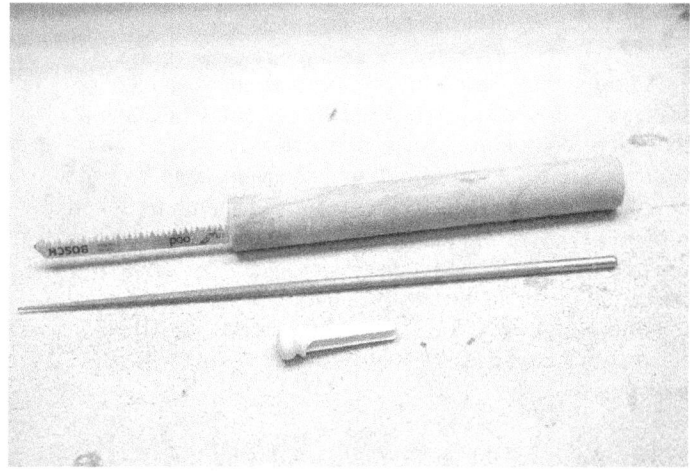

Photo 20-77 – *Tools needed to cut the string slots: a bridge pin hole slotting saw, a small round-profile needle file, and a bridge pin. Not pictured: a set of guitar strings.*

Photo 20-78 – *The saw is used to cut the slot on the saddle side of the bridge pin hole. Note the completely vertical orientation of the saw.*

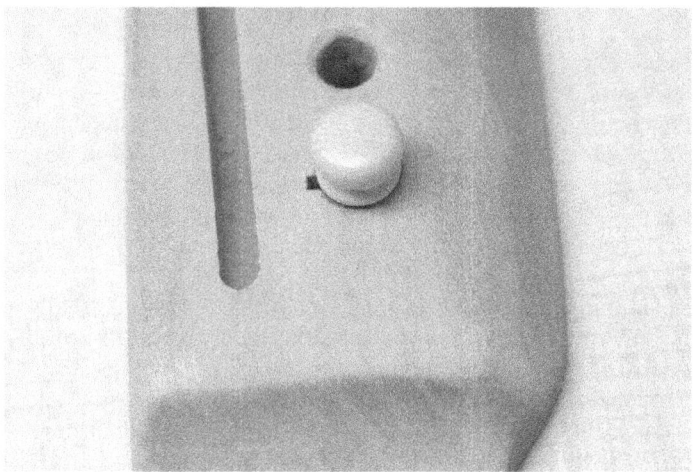

Photo 20-80 – *It can be seen here that there is just enough room for a low E string to clear the underside of the head of the bridge pin.*

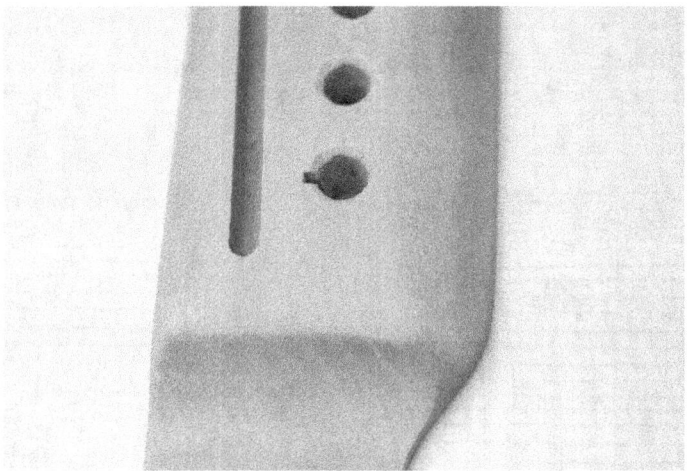

Photo 20-79 – *The sawn slot looks like this. It is just deep enough for the string to clear the underside of the head of the bridge pin.*

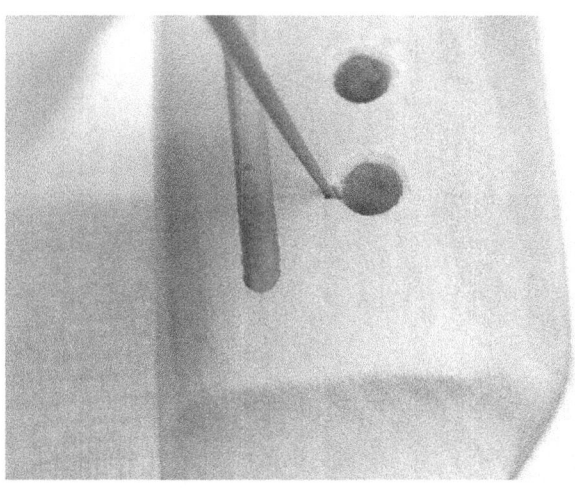

Photo 20-81 – *The end of the slot is rounded over a bit using the needle file.*

and kept turning in that direction. The reamer should *not* be rotated a little back and forth, because this will create a bore that is not round. The reamer should not be pressed into the bore while reaming. Instead, just the weight of the reamer will move it deeper into the hole as it is turned. The first time, the reamer should be turned just five rotations.

2. A bridge pin is test fitted into the partially reamed bore. The bridge pin should not be pressed in too hard. Doing so may make it difficult to remove the pin, and may even split the bridge. As the pin is inserted, some chirping sounds may be heard. One chirp is deep enough. The pin should be able to be removed easily by hand. If the bore is not reamed wide enough, the pin is removed and reaming continues, a little at a time, until the pin fits in the bore with about 1/16″ (1.6mm) of its shaft exposed (**photo 20-75**). As this is approached, it will take fewer turns to make progress. Usually a single complete turn is enough.

3. The rest of the holes are reamed in like fashion, repeating steps 1 and 2 above.

When the bridge pin is test fitted to a bridge pin hole that has been reamed too deep, the head of the pin will sit right on the top surface of the bridge, and the pin will be able to be rattled around in the hole. If the hole is not too badly over-reamed it can be repaired by wiping some medium cyanoacrylate glue all around inside the hole with a cotton swab, allowing the glue to thoroughly cure, and then test fitting the pin again, continuing reaming a bit if necessary. A badly over-reamed hole will have to be fitted with an oversize bridge pin. These are available from lutherie suppliers.

4. After all the holes have been reamed, they are chamfered using a countersink for wood screws. I like to use a hand countersink because it provides better control (**photo 20-76**). If a countersink chucked into a drill is used, the drill should turn at low speed and light pressure should be used. A chamfer of the same diameter as the base of the head of the bridge pin is applied to all holes. This is about 1/16″ (1.6mm) more than the diameter of the reamed holes.

☐ Sawing the String Slots

A slot to provide clearance for the string is sawn into the wall of each bridge pin bore on the side toward the bridge saddle. These string slots are sawn with a special string slot saw. Such saws are available from lutherie suppliers, and often come in various thicknesses to match the diameters of the strings. This matching is hardly necessary, and so one string slot saw that will saw a kerf about the width of the diameter of the typical guitar low E string can be used to cut string slots in the bridge for all strings.

A string slot saw can readily be fashioned from a small power jigsaw blade, set in a simple handle made from a piece of dowel. Instructions for constructing this simple tool appear at the beginning of the following series of construction steps.

A small diameter round-profile needle file is also needed to cut the string slots (**photo 20-77**).

Photo 20-82 – Sanding the saddle blank to thickness on a sanding board. Care is taken to be sure that sanding results in uniform thickness.

1. If a commercial string slot saw is available, steps 1 and 2 are skipped. If a commercial string slot saw is not available, such a saw can be made from a fine-tooth wood-cutting power jigsaw blade that is no higher than 3/16″ (4.8mm) (measured from the back of the blade to the tips of the teeth), and about 0.050″ (1.3mm) thick. A Bosch T101AO blade works perfectly in this application.

2. A length of dowel will serve as a handle for the saw. An axial hole is drilled in one end of the dowel, wide enough to accept the shank end of the jigsaw blade. The shank of the blade is inserted into this hole, and the hole is filled with epoxy. The epoxy is allowed to cure overnight.

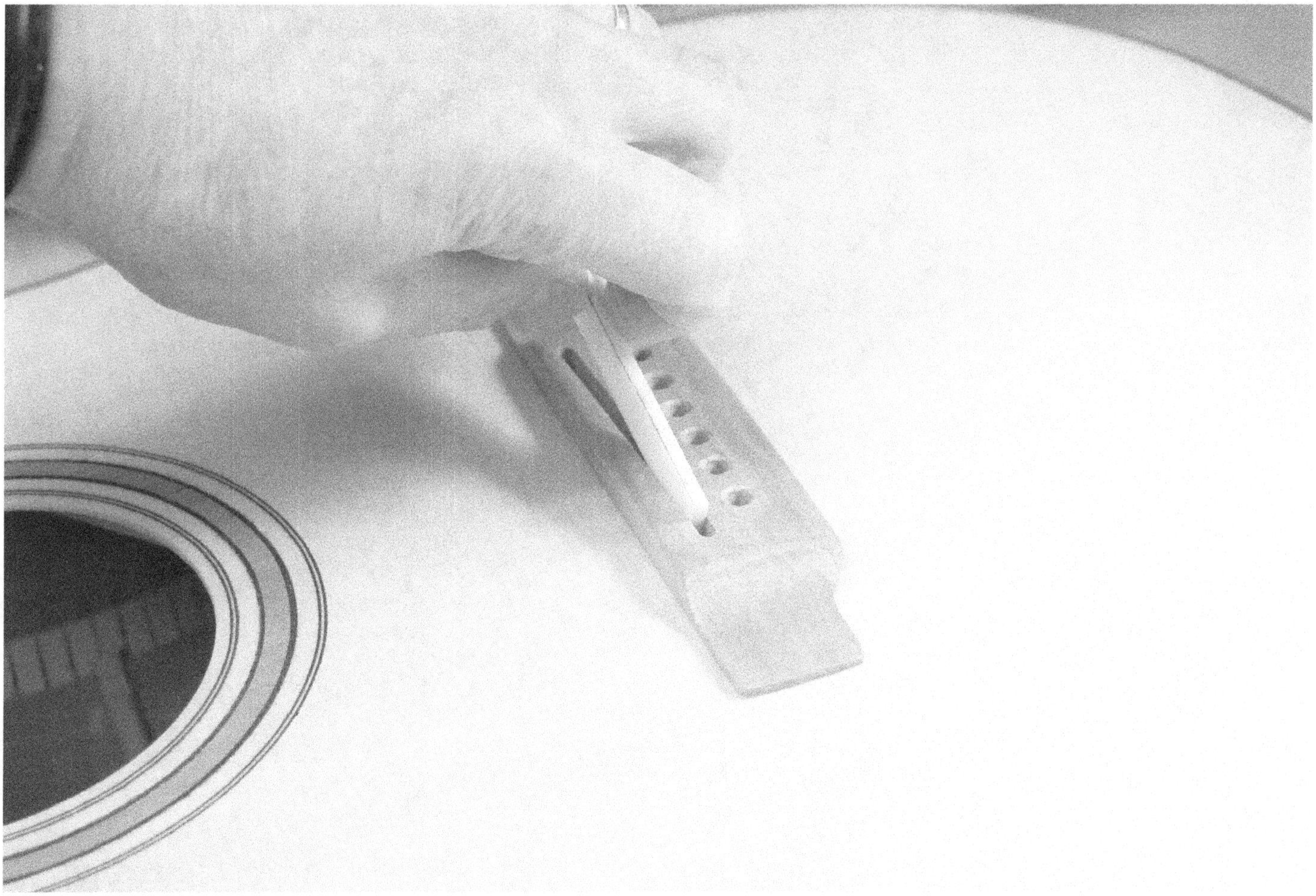

Photo 20-83 – The saddle is test fitted into the slot by attempting to insert one end. It should never be forced. Doing so may split the bridge.

3. The string slot saw is used to saw a shallow slot in the wall of the first bridge pin hole, on the side of the hole nearest the saddle slot (**photo 20-78**). The slot should be sawn as deep as the chamfer around the hole, plus a little more, the additional depth being about as deep as the kerf is wide. The slot should go the entire depth of the hole. Because the hole is tapered and narrower at the bottom, this means that most of the cutting will occur below the top surface of the bridge. The saw blade should be kept in a vertical orientation while sawing. The target slot is quite shallow (**photo 20-79**).

4. A bridge pin is fitted into the hole to check the depth of the slot. If the shaft of the pin is slotted, the slot on the shaft is positioned so it is *not* in line with the string slot just sawn in the bridge. The slot should be wide enough for a low E string and provide just enough room for a low E string to be able to exit without touching the underside of the head of the bridge pin. This can be spot checked visually (**photo 20-80**), but to fully check the entire length of the slot for fit, an attempt is made to install an actual low E string, and then insert the bridge pin. If the slot is not wide enough, it can be widened with a thin flat needle file. If it is not deep enough, it is sawn a bit deeper. If all looks good from the outside but the string still interferes with full insertion of the bridge pin, the slot is not deep enough at its bottom, so it should be sawed again with the saw kept vertical to deepen just the bottom.

5. A sharp small diameter round-profile needle file is used to round over the flat leading edge of the slot (**photo 20-81**).

6. The bridge pin hole is now checked and reamed to fully fit the bridge pin. The string is reinstalled and the bridge pin reinserted and gently pressed into place. If the pin does not seat so the underside of its head is in contact with the top of the bridge, the pin and string are removed and the hole is ever-so-gently reamed with a single light turn of the reamer. This step is repeated until the pin is well seated.

7. Steps 3 through 6 are repeated for the remaining bridge pin holes. Note that each slot needs to be no deeper than is required to accommodate the string that will go in that slot.

8. The strings used to test the fit of the slots are retained for later use.

9. Cleaning up the bridge. A small piece of 320 grit sandpaper is used to clean up the slots and the chamfers as necessary. The entire bridge is checked over and any dents or glue left by previous operations are cleaned up, being extremely careful not to scratch the guitar top. Sanding debris is vacuumed off the top and the bridge, and inside the guitar and around and under it are vacuumed too. The bridge surface is rubbed briskly with a rag, and then oil or wax is reapplied as in a previous step.

☐ **Rough Fitting the Saddle**

In this operation, the saddle will fitted into the saddle slot. The shape and height of the top of the saddle will be dealt with in a subsequent operation. Saddle materials and blanks have been discussed previously. At this point the saddle blank is a bit oversize in all dimensions.

1. The blank is first thinned so it will begin to fit in the saddle slot of the bridge. The saddle slot is checked to be sure it is

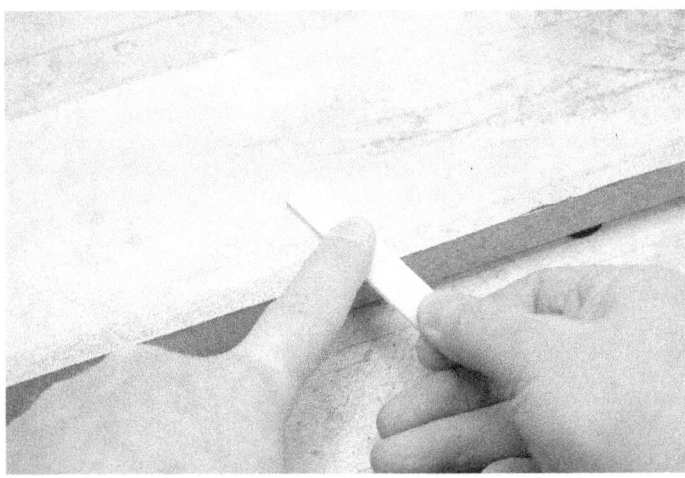

Photo 20-84 – If one end is thicker than the other, it can be selectively thinned down by sanding off the edge of the sanding board.

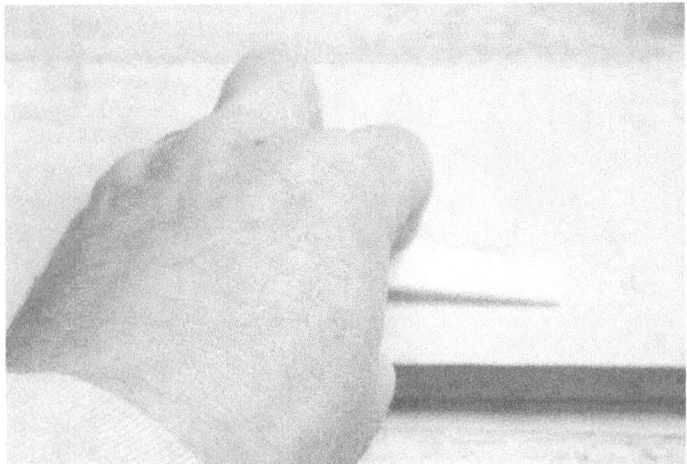

Photo 20-85 – Rounding over the end is done by dragging the end across the sanding board ...

Photo 20-86 – ... while at the same time lifting it to a vertical position. Both sides of the saddle end should be sanded in this way to round over the end.

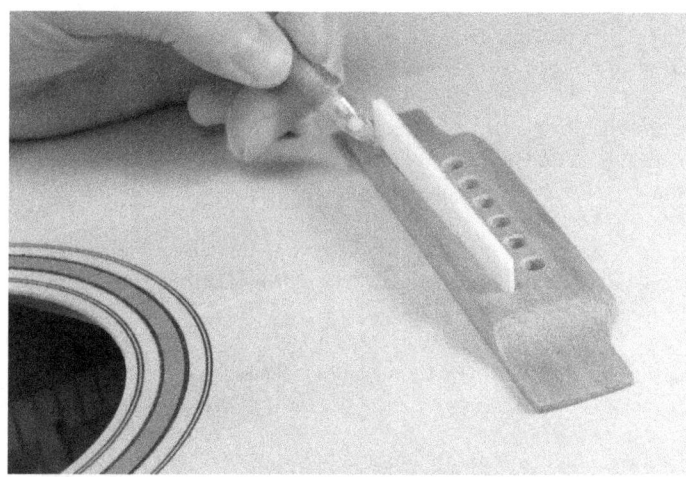

Photo 20-87 – After one end of the saddle is rounded to fit the saddle slot, the saddle is fitted into the slot so the rounded end is against one end of the slot, as pictured. Then the other end of the saddle is marked for cutting to length.

The blank is held down on the sanding board with the thumb and two other fingers. The thumb and middle fingers are positioned on the ends of the blank so that they apply downward pressure, and also grip the ends so the blank can be moved around. The middle finger provides downward pressure on the middle of the blank, which would otherwise end up a bit thicker than the ends. All of the following sanding techniques are aimed at maintaining even thickness of the blank while sanding. Sanding proceeds by moving the blank in a circular pattern over the sanding board.

The blank is sanded for 20 or so circles, then it is rotated 180° and sanded for 20 more circles. The blank is flipped over and another 20 circles are done. Then it is rotated 180° and 20 more circles are done. All of this rotation and flipping over helps to maintain even thickness while sanding.

 Rather than vacuum up the sanding dust from the sanding board, some of the dust should be collected and saved for future use in making repairs to the saddle or nut.

clean and that the floor is level with no debris on it. A sanding board with 180-grit sandpaper is used to gradually thin the saddle blank so it will begin to fit into the saddle slot (**photo 20-82**).

The blank is wiped clean with a rag, then test fitted by attempting to insert one or both of its ends into the saddle slot (**photo 20-83**). It should not be forced. Doing so may split the wood of the bridge. If it doesn't fit, sanding continues, using the

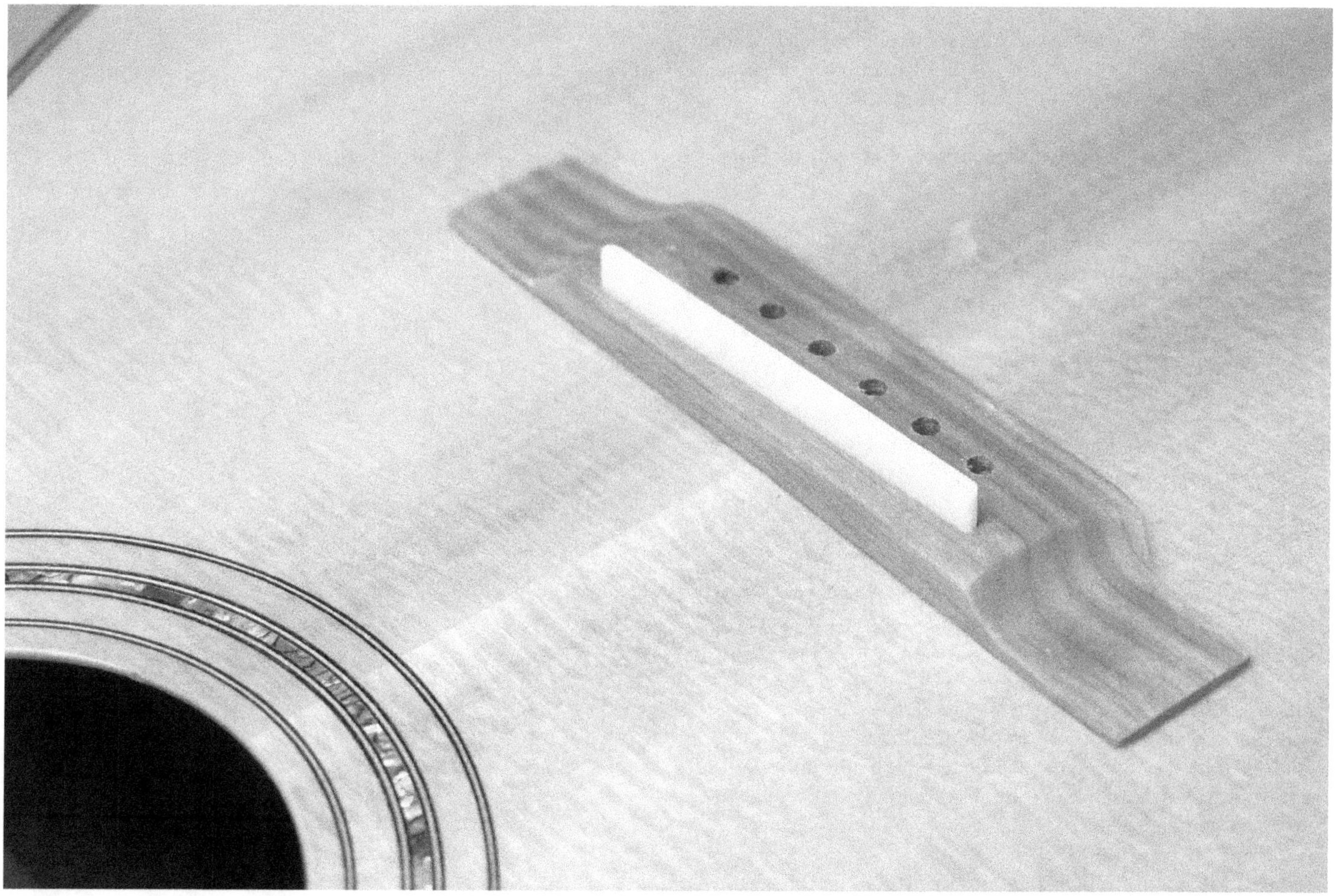

Photo 20-88 – The saddle fully fitted to the saddle slot. The top of the saddle will be shaped in a subsequent construction operation.

same sequence as above, but this time the circles are made in the other direction.

Sanding and fitting continue until one end or the other begins to go into the slot. At this point the object is to sand until the two ends of the blank begin to be able to be inserted into the slot. If one end begins to fit but the other does not, the thicker end is sanded with back and forth strokes with the thin end off the edge of the sanding board so it does not get sanded any more (**photo 20-84**). The blank is repeatedly flipped over while doing this, and test fitting continues until this end begins to fit.

2. Now the blank is fit to length. One end of the blank is rounded over by dragging the end across the sanding board, starting with the blank nearly flat with the board (**photo 20-85**) and tilting it up to a vertical position as the stroke proceeds (**photo 20-86**). A few strokes like this are done, then the blank is flipped over so the same thing is done on the other side of the same end. This is continued until the end is completely and evenly rounded over with a radius that matches the rounded end of the saddle slot.

3. The rounded end is fit shallowly into the slot, with the end of the blank against the end of the slot. Then the other end of the blank is marked for cutting to the length of the slot (**photo 20-87**). A small square is used to continue this mark, then the excess length is cut off using a razor saw.

4. The cut end is rounded over in the same manner as described in step 2. The blank is tested for length by attempting to shallowly insert it into the slot. If it doesn't fit, the length is decreased by continuing the rounding-over sanding of one end, checking, and rounding over some more until the blank is the correct length.

5. Now the saddle must be carefully sanded to adjust its thickness and length until the saddle has a clean slip fit into the saddle slot, and it sits squarely on the floor of the slot (**photo 20-88**). The saddle should never be forced into the slot. When it is properly fitted, it should be easy to remove from the slot using only the fingers.

If at any time the saddle does get stuck in the slot, it can be removed using flush cutting end nippers, but these will of course mar the surface of the saddle. It is also possible to use a machinist's scriber or a dental probe, pricked into the end of the saddle and then lifted up. No matter how a stuck saddle is removed, care should be taken to never pry it out with a tool that rests on the bridge. Doing this will surely dent the bridge.

With each test fitting, it is determined where the saddle needs additional sanding. It will often need thinning in the center, which is done by holding the saddle in both hands and sanding on the corner of the sanding board, so that only the center part of the saddle gets sanded.

6. The saddle is left in this state for now. It will be further shaped and refined in a later construction operation.

---

1. Elmendorp, Sjaak (2010). It's All About the Core, or How to Estimate Compensation. *American Lutherie #104* p. 56.

2. Mottola, R.M. Fretted Instrument Bridge Saddle Compensation Calculator. *Liutaio Mottola Lutherie Information Website*. Retrieved from https://www.liutaiomottola.com/formulae/compensation.htm

3. Mottola, R.M. (2018). Same-Fretted-Note Intonation Variability of the Steel String Acoustic Guitar. *OSFPreprints*. Retrieved from https://osf.io/45mtc

4. Mottola, R.M. (2019). Quantifying Player-Induced Intonation Errors of the Steel String Acoustic Guitar. *OSFPreprints*. Retrieved from https://osf.io/xrj52

5. Mottola, R.M. (2018). Blind Listening Evaluation of Steel String Acoustic Guitar Compensation Strategies. *OSFPreprints*. Retrieved from https://osf.io/udt79

6. Mottola, R.M. (2003). A Cheapskate's Sampler of Tools and Supplies. *American Lutherie #74* p. 36.

21 Fret Dressing

The frets have been previously installed and their ends have been beveled. But they are not quite ready for prime time yet. Still to be done is filing the tops of the frets so they are all on the same level relative to the strings of the guitar. This will create flat areas on the tops of the frets, and these flat areas must be reshaped into rounded fret crowns. The sharp edges at the fret ends must be rounded over a bit, too. Finally, the frets must be polished up with successively finer grits of abrasive paper and then with abrasive polish, until they achieve a nice shine. All of these operations will be described in this chapter.

It is also possible following finishing that the fretboard surface between the frets needs a little work. That will be taken care of here as well.

Fretboard and Fret Dressing Operations

Although much of the work to be described here is performed using conventional tools and also special-purpose tools that have previously been used when the frets were installed, there are a couple of special-purpose lutherie tools which are necessary for the following operations. Unfortunately there are really no alternatives to these tools. Fortunately they are readily available from lutherie suppliers and are not particularly expensive.

The first of these is a special-purpose file for re-crowning the frets after they have been leveled. A *fret crowning file* has a concave slot on one or both of its thin sides, and the slot contains either file teeth or coarse abrasive particles. The files generally come in different widths. If common wide fret wire is used then a wide fret crowning file is used.

The second special-purpose tool needed is a triangular profile *fret dressing file*. This is used to file the fret ends. It is a triangular profile needle file with all of the edges between the flat sides ground flat, so the edges don't cut. When shaping the ends of the frets, these flat edges are often positioned right on the surface of the fretboard. These "safe" edges will not cut the fretboard but allow filing the fret right down to where it contacts the fretboard surface.

Materials
    Cereal box cardboard
    Single-edge razor blades
    320-grit sandpaper
    400, 600, 1000-grit silicon carbide sandpaper
    Optional: 1500 and 2000-grit silicon carbide sandpaper
    Paste metal polish
Tools
    Flat mill file or special-purpose fret leveling file
    Fret crowning file (see text)
    Triangular fret dressing file (see text)

Cleaning and Preparing the Fretboard

The work to be done on the frets requires that the fretboard be as flat as it can be made. So adjusting it to be flat is the first order of business. Because the fret work requires the use of tools which are capable of scratching and denting the beautiful finish currently on the guitar, the top in the area around the fretboard extension is covered to protect it.

When guitars are spray finished the fretboard is usually totally masked before spraying commences. I don't generally mask the fretboard when a hand-applied finish is used, because

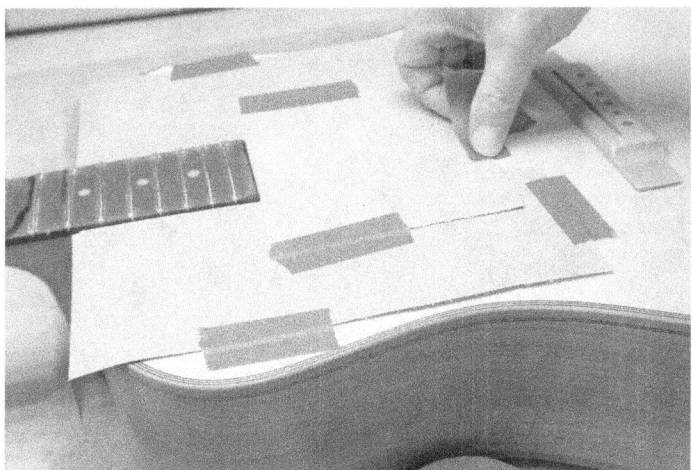

Photo 21-1 – To protect the finish, the top of the guitar is protected around the fretboard extension with cereal box cardboard. The cardboard folds down over the ribs next to the heel to protect that area as well.

runs of varnish across the masked fretboard usually manage to find their way under the masking tape next to the frets anyway. If any finish got on the fretboard during finish application it was likely cleaned off at that time, but residue will usually remain. And if the finish was wet sanded, there will almost always be some stains from the wet sanding slurry on the fretboard as well. All of this is cleaned off now.

Also dealt with here are the dry edges of the finish. The varnish was applied right up to the edges between the fretboard sides and the playing surface. The dry edges of the varnish usually overhang the fretboard playing surface somewhat, and these must be scraped flush to the playing surface.

After the fretboard surface is cleaned up it is masked to prevent it from getting damaged during the fret dressing operations.

☐ Setting Up for Fret Dressing, Cleaning Up the Fretboard

1. Adjusting the trussrod. A straightedge that is at least as long as the fretboard is used to check that it is as straight as possible. The straightedge is placed on top of the frets, on the longitudinal centerline. The trussrod is adjusted as necessary and the check made again. This process is repeated until the fretboard is as straight as it can be made along the entire length. If it can only be made straight from the 1st fret to the 14th (body join) fret and the fretboard extension falls off (i.e., bends downward toward the top) a bit, that is fine. But a note should be made of the fact that the fretboard exhibits this fall off. This will inform how the process of leveling the frets will go in a later step.

Adjusting the trussrod with a conventional Allen key is a major pain because the hand has to be placed in the soundhole. The orientation of the guitar that is generally most comfortable is with the luthier sitting on a stool, the guitar sitting on the luthier's legs with the guitar neck pointing down and between the legs. Note that ball end Allen keys are much easier to use.

2. Protecting the guitar top. Although this is technically not necessary, it really is a good idea to protect the top from accidental scratches while dressing the frets. Cereal box cardboard is taped down to the top around the fretboard extension to protect it from being scratched during these operations. One piece is placed on each side of the extension, with the ends folded over and taped to the ribs next to the heel. Then another piece is added to cover the soundhole and central section (**photo 21-1**).

3. Cleaning up the fretboard surface. Some amount of clean up is always necessary. The entire fretboard surface is wiped down with a rag and naphtha or paint thinner to remove any finish slurry. While this is being done, it is important to get into the edges between the frets and fretboard.

4. A razor blade scraper (see Appendix E) is used to scrape down the edges of the varnish at the edges of the fretboard; to scrape off any varnish that may have gotten on the fretboard surface; and to scrape off any recalcitrant wet sanding slurry. These scrapers dull quickly and are replaced as necessary when they get dull. Scraping down the edges of the varnish at the edges is a somewhat tricky operation, because it is easy to inadvertently chip pieces of the finish away from the sides of the fretboard. While scraping with the grain of the fretboard, the scraper is simultaneously moved toward the center of the fretboard (**photos 21-2** and **21-3**). This motion pulls the finish on the fretboard sides inward. If the scraper is accidentally moved the other way it may pull the finish away from the fretboard sides. The varnish edges should be scraped right down to the level of the top (playing surface) of the fretboard. Note that this usually needs to be done at the soundhole end edge of the fretboard, too. Here the scraper may not be the best tool because it would be used cross-grain, but 320-grit sandpaper on a soft rubber block like a gum eraser works well. The fretboard edges can be rounded over a bit if desired. The sequence of steps to scrape the entire fretboard surface goes like this:

• Scraping starts at the soundhole end and works toward the nut end. Because it is not practical to scrape onto the soundhole end of the fretboard, 320-grit sandpaper supported on an eraser is used to sand this first section of the fretboard smooth of any varnish.

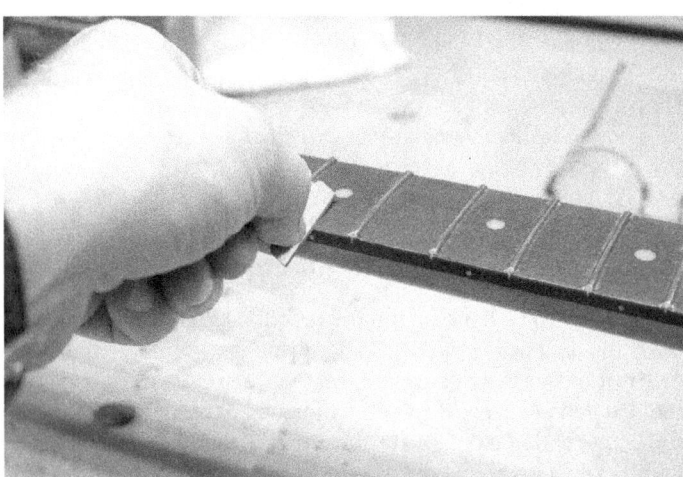

Photo 21-2 – *When scraping the edge of the finish flush with the playing surface of the fretboard, the scraper is moved in line with the edge ...*

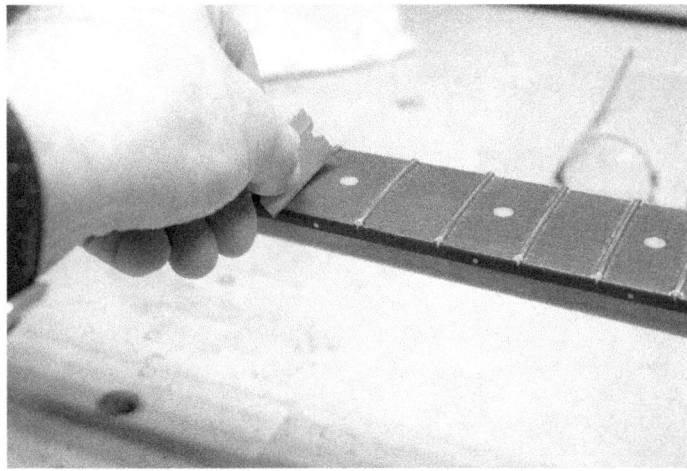

Photo 21-3 – *... while at the same time moving it toward the centerline of the fretboard. This "pulls" the edge of the finish inward, which helps prevent it from chipping away from the sides of the fretboard.*

- The razor blade scraper is used to scrape the next section of fretboard. Each scraping stroke starts with the edge right in the space between the fret closest to the luthier (**photo 21-4**) and scraping proceeds away from the luthier, right up to the next fret. Scraping each section starts on the left side, and the finish edge is scraped down flush with the fretboard surface. A little roundover of the edge is done if desired, but care is taken to avoid chipping away the finish from the side of the fretboard. Scraping of the section continues, moving from the left to the right, removing any spattered finish and debris. Then the finish edge on the right side is scraped down to the fretboard surface, and whatever roundover desired is done here as well.

- Scraping continues down the fretboard in this manner, working on each section of the fretboard in turn. Care is taken when scraping the last section not to slip and scratch the headplate. Installing the temporary wood nut stop used earlier will help prevent accidents.

- Now scraping turns around and work proceeds up the fretboard from the opposite direction. Going this direction is quicker because most of the scraping is already done. It is really only the edges between frets and fretboard that need work in this direction (**photos 21-5** and **21-6**).

5. All the debris is vacuumed away. The entire fretboard is briskly wiped with a rag, working it side to side to remove debris from the inside edges between frets and fretboard. A toothpick or the corner of the scraper may be necessary to remove recalcitrant debris. Brushing here with a toothbrush also works well to remove debris.

6. Each section of fretboard is sanded with the grain, using 320 grit sandpaper supported on the eraser. The side of the eraser is used so it will fit between frets (**photo 21-7**). The entire fretboard is wiped down with the rag again.

7. The entire fretboard surface is carefully checked and touched up as needed.

8. Installation of the frets is checked. Although this was done when the frets were installed, it is a good idea to carefully check over the frets again, to be sure none are raised out of their slots in places. This is best done with the eye level with the fretboard surface, looking down from each side of the

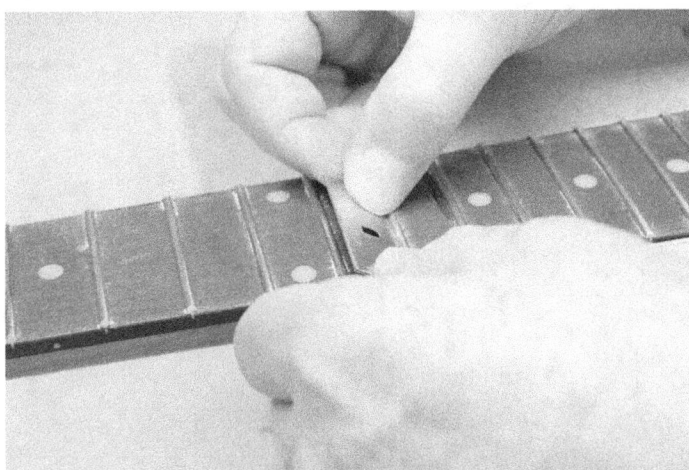

Photo 21-4 – When scraping the fretboard clean between frets, the scraping stroke begins with the edge right against the bead of one fret.

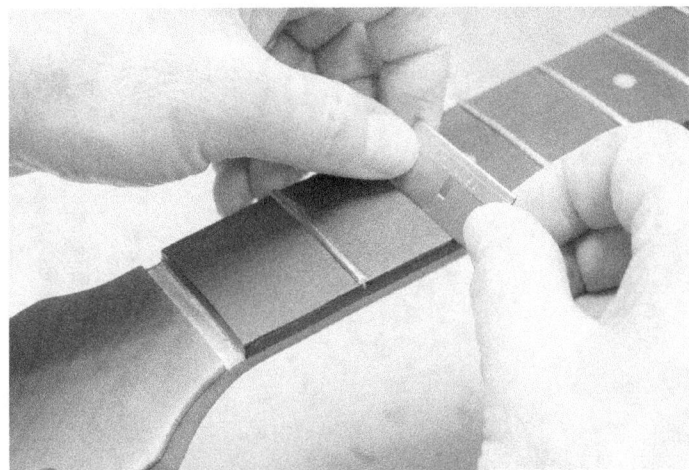

Photo 21-6 – There is usually not much to be done when scraping in this direction, as all the heavy work has already been done.

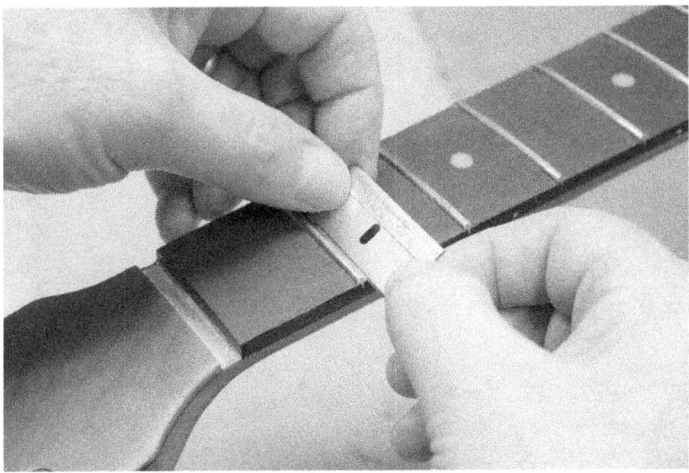

Photo 21-5 – After the fretboard is scraped moving toward the nut, the instrument is turned around and the fretboard is scraped toward the bridge.

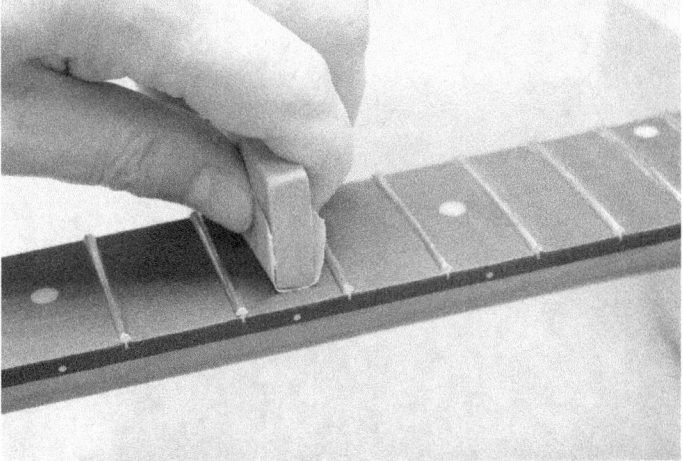

Photo 21-7 – A gum eraser on its side is used as a sanding block because it fits between the frets everywhere on the fretboard.

fretboard, one fret at a time. Then this examination is repeated from the other end of the fretboard. If any frets are raised up, the plastic hammer and the sandbag can be used as originally, but only for those frets over the shaft. Any popped-up frets on the fretboard extension will have to be clamped back down, using a bar clamp through the soundhole and some sort of caul inside. If a fret pops back up again after being hammered or clamped in place, a clamp is used to clamp it down, and then a small amount of thin cyanoacrylate glue is wicked between fret and fretboard, using a micro transfer pipette. The glue is allowed to cure, then the clamp is removed, and any excess glue on the fretboard surface is scraped off with a razor blade scraper.

9. Masking the fretboard. Although this is time-consuming, it is worth the effort for lutherie novices to carefully mask the fretboard to protect it from accidental scratches. The neck is supported under the shaft with a neck rest (Appendix D), or a padded block of wood, or anything that can support it securely and without scratching it. The body should be sitting on carpeting or some similar material. The temporary nut stop is inserted into the nut slot if it is not already there.

10. The fretboard in between the frets is covered with masking tape pieces long enough to cover the sides of the fretboard and a bit of the neck shaft too (**photo 21-8**). Two pieces of masking tape are used per section. The side edge of the first piece of tape goes right up against one fret. The second piece of tape overlaps the first piece and its side edge goes right up against the other fret. If 1″ (25.4MM) wide masking tape is used and taping starts at the nut end, a few sections of the fretboard can be taped this way, before the fret spacing gets smaller than 1″ (25.4MM) and narrower tape is needed.

If various small widths of masking tape are not kept on hand, a cut down the center of a length of masking tape can be made with a hobby knife to make lengths of tape that are approximately ½″ (12.7MM) wide (**photo 21-9**). Taping continues down the fretboard as before, using this narrower tape, making sure that the original, straight edges of the tape are butt against the frets (**photo 21-10**).

Eventually even the ½″ (12.7MM) wide tape will be too wide, and at this point the hobby knife is used to cut widths of tape that are ⅓″ (8.5MM) wide, by running two cuts down a length of

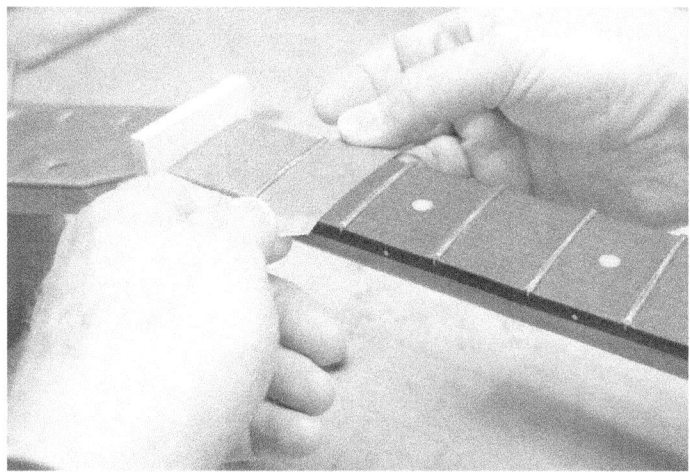

Photo 21-8 – *The space between frets is covered with masking tape. Two pieces are used on each space between frets.*

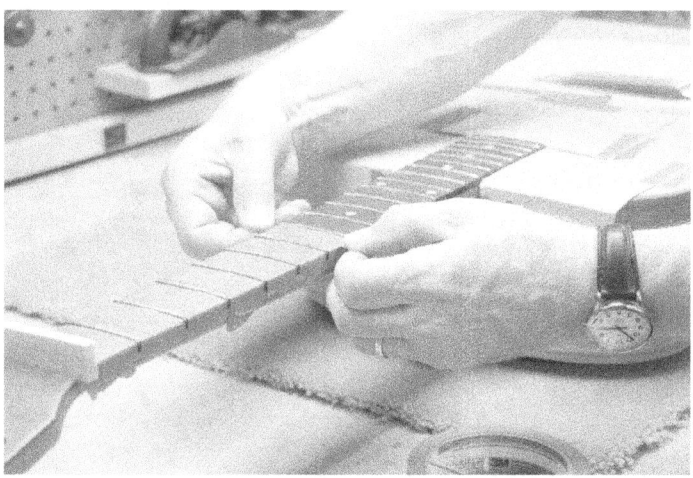

Photo 21-10 – *The cut pieces are applied between frets. Again, two pieces are used for each space between frets.*

Photo 21-9 – *The tape is too wide to fit between most frets. If narrower tape is not available, a length of tape can be cut in half lengthwise using a hobby knife.*

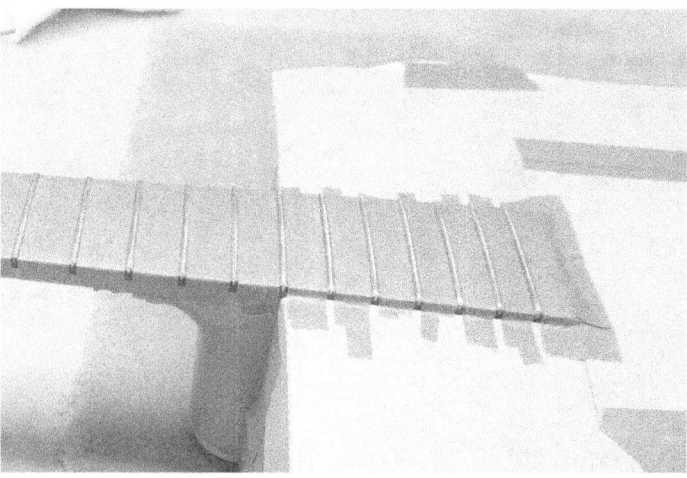

Photo 21-11 – *The soundhole end of the fretboard is covered with a single piece of tape.*

the tape. When cut in this manner, the center section of the tape is discarded, because both of its edges will be wavy due to the knife cuts. The two side lengths are used to continue masking between the frets.

The last section of fretboard, from the last fret to the soundhole end, is covered with a 1″ (25.4mm) wide piece of tape (**photo 21-11**).

11. Viewing the sides of the fretboard will show an exposed bit under each fret (**photo 21-12**). These are all covered with a single length of 1″ (25.4mm) wide tape on each side, so the straight top edge of the tape comes right up to the bottom of the fret bead at each fret end (**photo 21-13**).

Fret Leveling, Re-Crowning, and Fret End Dressing

☐ **Fret Leveling**

The purpose of fret leveling is to remove any planar discrepancies in the tops of the frets. Some frets have been installed a bit higher or lower than others. The fretboard itself will have some irregularities which will be reflected in the fret tops as well. Leveling the frets results in the potential for lower action for the strings and fewer fret buzzes in the finished guitar.

Fret leveling is done using the same tool that was used to file and bevel the fret ends when the frets were installed. The same flat mill file (**photo 21-14**) or special-purpose fret leveler (**photo 21-15**) is used here.

The body of the guitar should be supported on a soft pad. The neck should be supported on a neck rest or some sort of neck support with padding on top. The support should be moved during fret leveling so it is always under the area of the fretboard that is currently being filed.

1. Marking the fret tops. It is useful to mark the tops of the fret crowns all along their lengths with a permanent marker. This makes it easier to see any spots that have been missed by the file.

2. The fret tops in one section of the fretboard are leveled at a time. It is easiest to start with the upper frets, from the highest numbered fret to whatever fret is covered by the length of the file. The file is placed on top of the frets in this area, and is

Photo 21-12 – *Underneath each fret is a narrow exposed area of the fretboard and neck.*

Photo 21-14 – *The same tool that was used to file and bevel the fret ends is used for leveling the frets. A flat mill file can be used. Note the neck rest under the neck on the left.*

Photo 21-13 – *The exposed areas under the fret ends are all covered with a single length of tape that goes onto each side of the fretboard.*

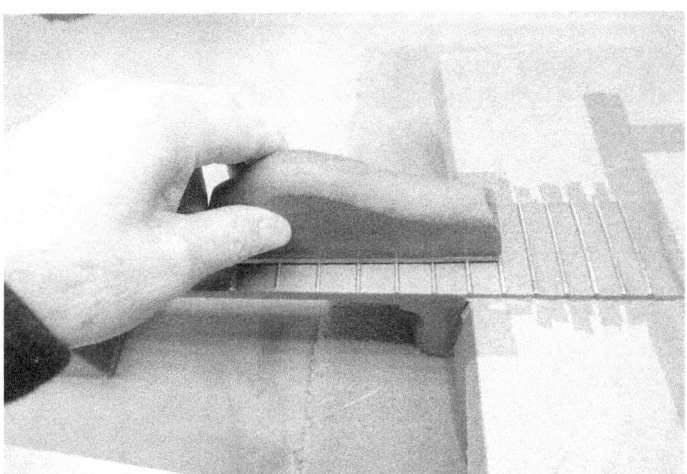

Photo 21-15 – *A special fret leveler file can also be used.*

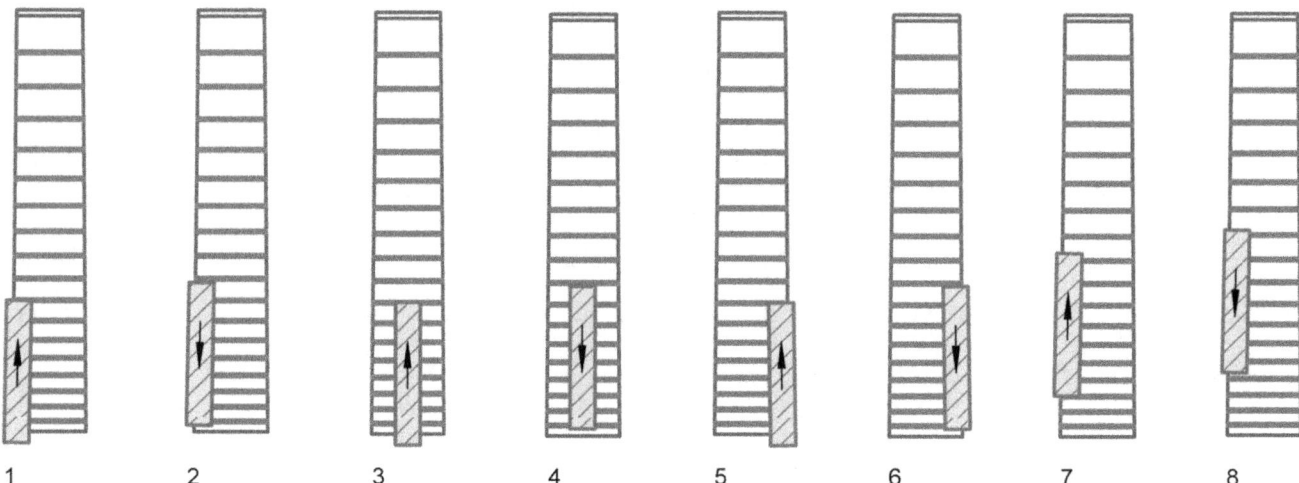

Figure 21-1 – *Diagram of file movement during fret leveling, starting at the soundhole end of the fretboard. 1. The file is placed at the left side of the fretboard on top of the frets at the soundhole end, aligned with the left side edge of the fretboard, and moved forward in a filing stroke. 2. The file is moved back. As back and forth filing is done, the file is simultaneously moved slowly to the right. 3. Eventually it ends up at the center of the fretboard and oriented along its centerline. 4 Back and forth filing continues, as does slow movement to the right. 5. Eventually the file ends up at the right side of the fretboard, aligned with the right edge. 6. And back and forth filing continues. Now as filing continues, the file begins to move slowly back to the left. 7. When it returns to the left side, if all fret tops of the frets in the area being filed have not been touched, filing continues back and forth and across the fretboard, until the tops of all the frets here have been touched by the file. Then the file is moved down the fretboard a few frets. 8. And back and forth filing continues here, with the file moved in the same manner to the right and then to the left, until all of the newly filed frets are also touched by the file. Progress continues in this manner,, blending in the new areas with those previously filed, until the frets on the entire fretboard have been filed.*

filed back and forth in line with the paths of where the strings will be. Filing starts with the file sitting on the fret tops on the left side of the fretboard with the file parallel to that edge (**photo 21-16**, **figure 21-1.1** and **21-1.2**), filing back and forth, using just the weight of the file and no additional pressure. As back and forth filing proceeds, the file is simultaneously slowly moved toward the centerline of the fretboard (**photo 21-17**, **figure 21-1.3** and **21-1.4**). As the file is moved, its angle is also changed so it is always filing along the paths of the strings. This movement while filing continues until the file is at and parallel to the right edge of the fretboard (**photo 21-18**, **figure 21-1.5** and **21-1.6**). Then filing continues, while slowly moving back toward the left side of the fretboard. It should be kept in mind that the fret tops are cambered and it is not desirable to flatten out the camber.

Control of the file should be maintained at all times. It should not be allowed to slip off the fret tops and damage the sides of the fretboard. An eye should be kept on the tang, if the file has one. Care is taken to know where the tang is, and to prevent it from bumping into anything. As filing moves from side to side, it must go right up to the ends of the fret tops on both sides, but care is taken to not file off the corners between the fret tops and the fret ends.

Photo 21-16 – *Fret leveling begins on the left side of the fretboard at the soundhole end. The file is moved back and forth, parallel to the fretboard side edge.*

Photo 21-17 – *At the same time the file is moving back and forth, it is slowly moved toward the center of the fretboard. When it gets here, the file will be in line with the fretboard centerline.*

While filing, an eye is kept on the tops of the frets. The tallest frets will develop a clear flat on their tops early on, while lower frets will not be touched by the file at first. Fret leveling persists in this area of the fretboard as described until *all* frets in the area have at least a tiny flat across their entire widths (**photo 21-19**). Note that it is unlikely that the width of this flat will be consistent across each fret. This is fine. It is important that the file touch each part of the top of each fret, not how wide the flat is at any given point.

Filing pauses in this area of the fretboard when the tops of all the frets here have been touched by the file. Then the file is moved down toward the nut a few frets, and filing in this new section continues as described, blending this new area of the fretboard into the one just done, until all of the frets of the new area have at least a small flat on them all the way across (**figures 21-1.7** and **21-1.8**).

3. This process continues down the neck until the nut is reached and all the frets on the fretboard have been leveled. Care is taken to not bang the file into the temporary nut stop, which could yank it out of its slot. The support under the neck should be moved so it is always more or less under the area currently being filed. This prevents the neck from springing up and down during filing.

4. Once the entire fretboard has been filed, the file is placed back on the highest numbered few frets, and a check is made for high frets with the file oriented along each of the paths of the strings. It is possible to identify a high fret in a range of frets because the file can be made to rock back and forth over that high fret. The file is moved a bit at a time down the neck toward the nut, checking continuously for high frets. Any that are high will need additional filing, but these should not be filed one fret at a time. The same filing and blending technique described above is used.

5. When things look good and the tops of all frets have been touched by the file, and when there is no obvious rocking of the file over high frets, a long straightedge is used to check each string path in turn for flatness of the fret tops (**photos 21-20** and **21-21**). If the fret tops are flat from the 1st through the 14th fret and then fall off above the 14th fret, that is fine. If there is

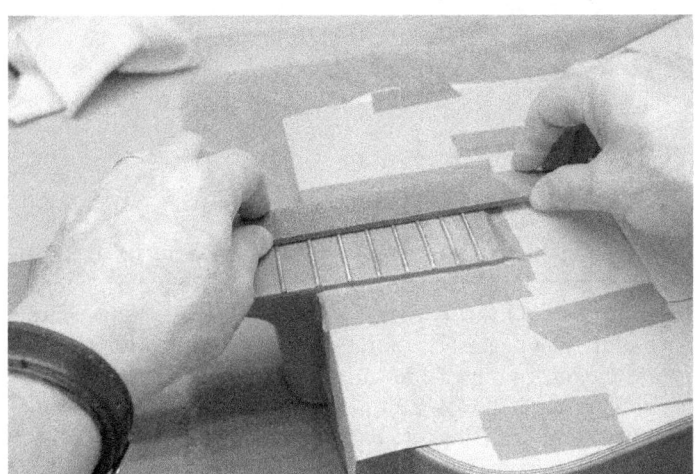

Photo 21-18 – Lateral movement continues to the right side edge of the fretboard. And here, file back and forth movement is in line with the right side edge of the fretboard.

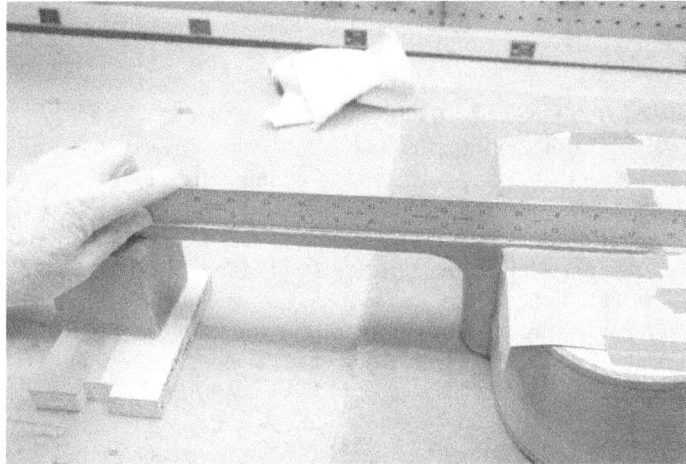

Photo 21-20 – Following fret leveling, the surface of the frets is checked for flatness at each of the string positions, starting at the low E position ...

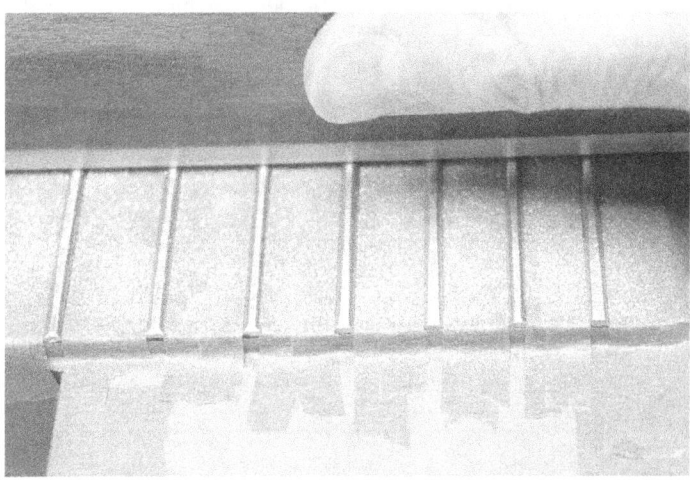

Photo 21-19 – Fret leveling in one area is complete when each of the frets have been touched by the file. Some frets and some areas will be filed more than others. This is normal.

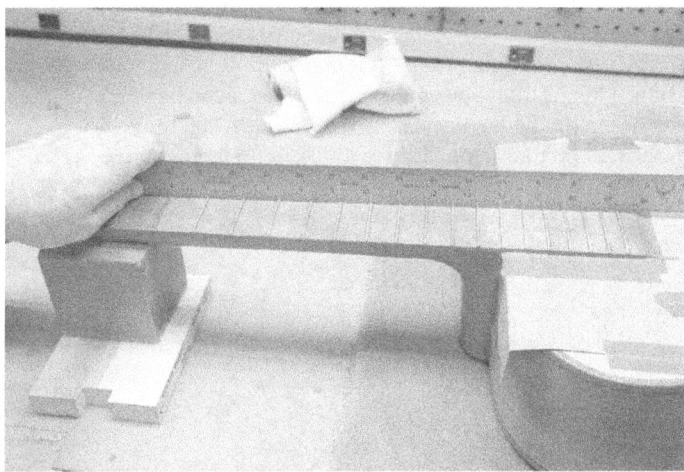

Photo 21-21 – ... and ending at the high E position. If the straightedge can rock at any of the string positions then more localized filing is needed to reduce the high point that the straightedge is rocking on.

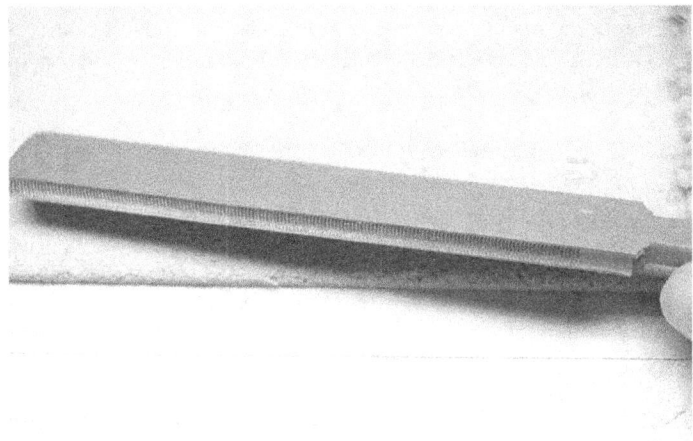

Photo 21-22 – *The concave filing edge of a fret crowning file.*

Photo 21-23 – *The crowning file is held upright, and filing proceeds across the entire length of the fret, pitching the file as needed to compensate for the camber of the fret.*

no fall off of the fretboard extension, then all the frets of the fretboard should be flat along each string path.

Any additional filing of high spots is done, and then the straightedge is used to check again. This sequence is repeated as necessary.

While leveling the frets, the filings should *not* be brushed off the fretboard. If they are brushed off, some of them will invariably end up under the guitar. They can easily scratch the finish. The filings should just be left where they land. They are useful there, because they indicate just where metal has been taken off of the frets. Any fret or part of a fret with no filings next to it has not yet had a flat filed there. When fret leveling is completed, the filings are vacuumed off the fretboard and off the bench under the neck and around the guitar.

An interesting thing happens once the frets have been leveled. The fretboard was originally cambered to a cylindrical shape. Because the fret beads are consistent in height, before they were filed the tops of the frets also described a cylindrical surface. But after filing following the string paths as described above, the tops of the frets now describe a surface that approximates a section of the surface of a cone. This just happens automatically, as a consequence of filing along the paths of the strings. Testing for flatness along what will be the string paths with the long straightedge verifies this. Such a surface provides for marginally more optimal action of the strings on the finished instrument.[1]

Much care is taken when checking the fret leveling job using the straightedge, and reworking as necessary. A well done fret leveling job will make it possible to achieve desired string action on the finished instrument.

☐ **Re-Crowning the Frets**

After the fret tops have been leveled they must be recrowned. At this point the fret tops each have a flat of some width. If the frets were to be left in this condition, during playing when a string was fretted it would be stopped on the sharp edge of the flat nearest the nut. For theoretically accurate intonation the crown must be restored so the stopped string is actually terminated closer to the longitudinal centerline of the fret (**figure 21-2**). There are three common ways to do this. Although only one of these will be described in detail, the other two are mentioned for informational purposes.

The frets can be re-crowned using a fret crowning file (**photo 21-22**). This is the recommended approach. The operation is simple and quick, and easy to describe in a book. Lutherie novices always obtain good results with this approach. It does require the special purpose fret crowning file, but this tool is readily available and not too expensive.

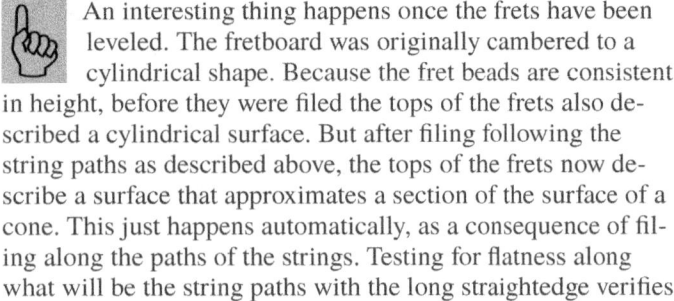

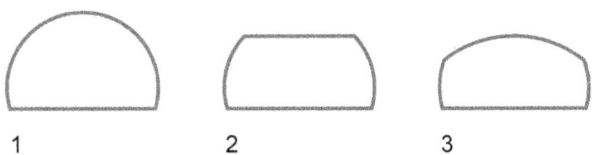

Figure 21-2 – *Cross-section of fret bead: 1. Before fret dressing. 2. Cross-section of bead after fret leveling. Cross-section after re-crowning.*

Figure 21-3 – *Schematic top view of fret: 1. Before fret dressing. 2. After fret leveling a flat of some shape will extend across the length of the fret. 3. After re-crowning the flat will be reduced to a thin and regular shape.*

Figure 21-4 – *While re-crowning a fret, the pitch of the fret crowning file must change to match the curve of the fret top.*

Frets can also be re-crowned using a triangular fret dressing file, a tool which is needed to dress the ends of the frets anyway. Although this technique is not difficult to learn, it is maddeningly difficult to describe and document because the results of the filing strokes are so subtle. For this reason, it is even difficult to photograph the process. So this technique will not be described in detail here.

The third common method for re-crowning frets following leveling is to implicitly re-crown them, as a part of later fret polishing steps. Although easy to do, this approach is particularly useful when fret leveling results in minimal flats on the fret tops, and this is not always the state of things. For this reason I generally consider this a more advanced technique, and recommend that lutherie novices make use of the fret crowning file instead, which will always yield reliable results.

1. Using the fret crowning file is easy. Starting at one end of a fret, filing is done back and forth along the length of the fret top, pitching the file to accommodate the camber of the fret along its length (**photo 21-23**). Filing is done until an evenly thin continuous line of flat remains on the fret. More filing will be required on those places where the flat left by fret leveling is wider (**figure 21-3**). It is best to err on the side of too little filing rather than too much, because the height of a fret can be lowered by filing it too much. As long as a thin line of flat remains across the length of the fret, its height will be maintained. Because the top of the fret is cambered, the pitch of the file must changed depending on its location along the fret (**figure 21-4**).

2. All frets are re-crowned in this manner. Filing debris is thoroughly vacuumed up when done.

☐ Dressing the Fret Ends

The length of each fret has been crowned, but there are sharp edges at the ends where the bead of the fret meets the bevels at the fret ends. These sharp edges are removed using a triangular fret dressing file with safe edges. Dressing each fret end is done in four quick strokes. Filing can be done into (toward) the fret end or away from it (off the edge of the fretboard). I prefer to

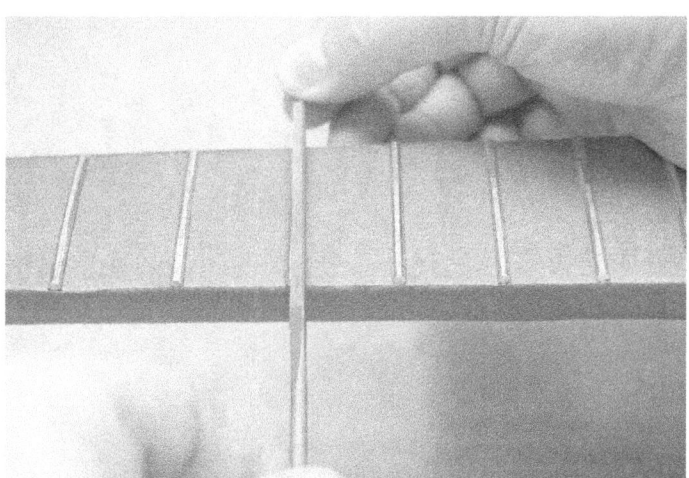

Photo 21-25 – As the file is pushed forward, it is also moved along the fret edge toward the apex of the fret. The first stroke stops here.

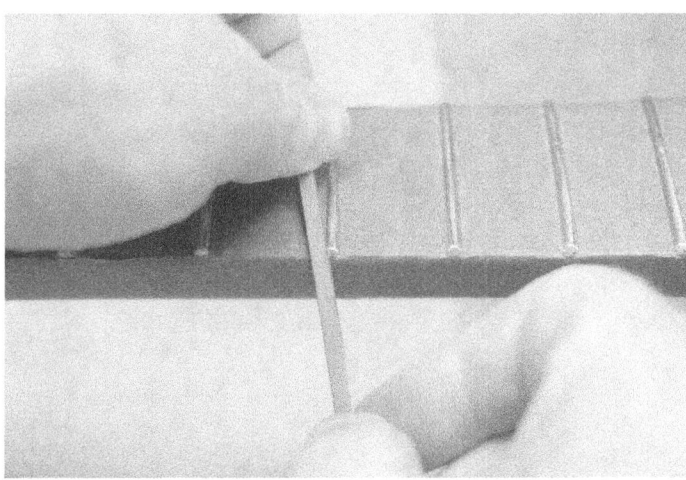

Photo 21-24 – The first fret end dressing stroke begins with the file on the fretboard with a cutting surface against the edge of the fret. Note that here I am filing toward the fret end.

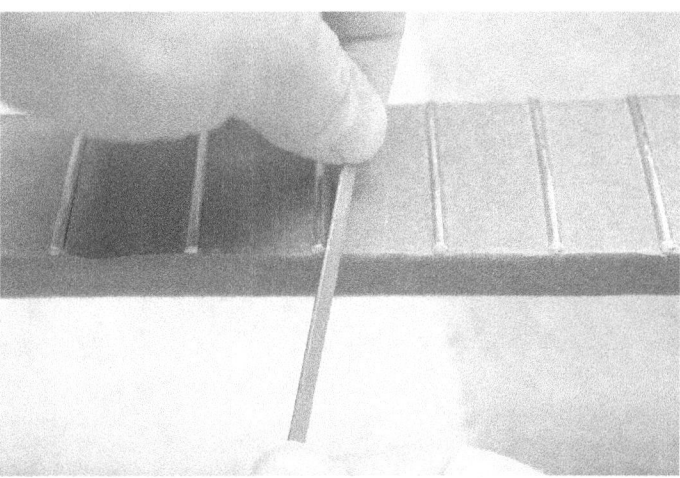

Photo 21-26 – The second fret end dressing stroke begins on the other side of the fret, but is otherwise identical to the first stroke.

file toward the fret end when possible, because doing so affords a better view.

Note that the ends of some of the frets will often have blobs of hardened finish left by the finishing process. These are either filed off with the file or chipped off with a knife as they are found.

1. The file is held with both hands, one on the handle and one at the tip end. It is positioned on one side of the first fret with a cutting side vertical and against the edge of the fret, and a safe edge resting on the tape on the fretboard (**photo 21-24**). As the file is pushed forward to file the edge, it is also rolled toward and past the longitudinal centerline of the fret (**photo 21-25**). This will file off the edge and leave a small facet. This stroke is repeated from the other side of the fret (**photo 21-26, 21-27**) to completely remove the edge from the entire end of the fret. Both strokes are repeated, for a total of four strokes, taking care to create a uniformly-sized facet all around. The facet created is tiny (**photo 21-28**). No attempt should be made to hog off a lot of material.

2. Step 1 is repeated for each fret on the side of the fretboard currently being worked. Note that the frets on the fretboard extension may require a number of shorter strokes and are easier to do filing off the end of the fret (**photo 21-29**). An attempt is made to keep the size of the facets about the same for all frets.

3. When done on this side of the fretboard, the instrument is turned around on the bench and the fret ends on the other side are dressed.

4. When all are done, a thumb and finger are run along the ends of the frets, feeling for any remaining sharp places (**photo 21-30**). If sharp places are identified, more filing is done there as needed.

Polishing the Frets

At this point the fret tops contain file marks from the leveling, re-crowning and end dressing operations. The flat ends of the frets contain file marks from when they were beveled. Now these file marks must be removed and the frets polished up, by the application of progressively finer abrasives, until the frets are smooth and shiny all over. This is done with wet or dry

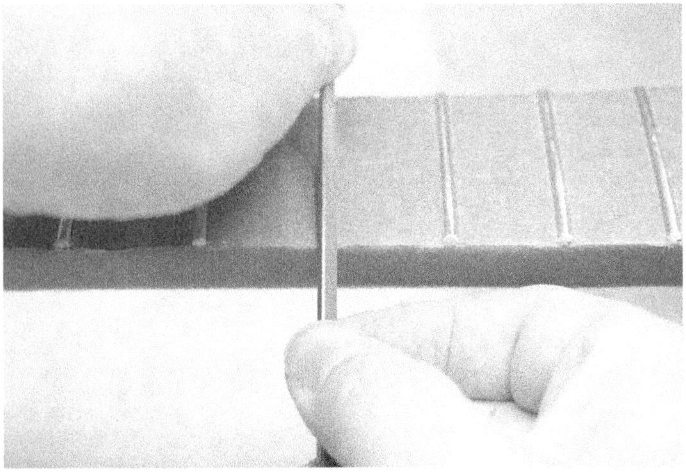

Photo 21-27 – *The second stroke also ends at the apex of the fret.*

Photo 21-29 – *Filing can be done away from the fret end as well as toward it. It is usually easier to file the frets on the fretboard extension with short strokes moving away from the fret.*

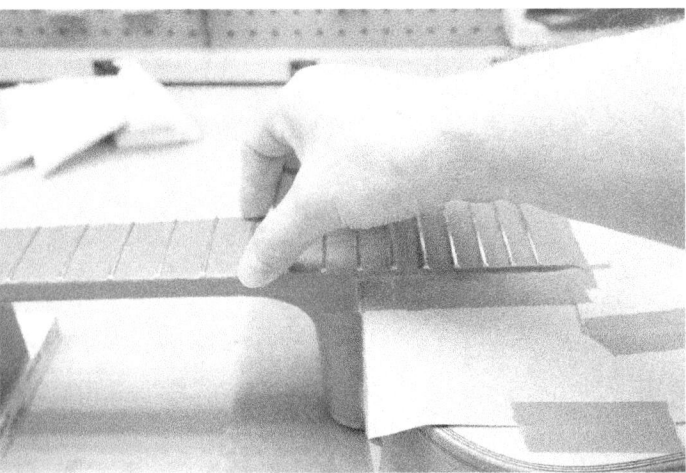

Photo 21-28 – *The result of fret end dressing is a small and even chamfer replacing what was the sharp edge at the fret end.*

Photo 21-30 – *The best way to check for successful fret end dressing is by feel. Two fingers are run down the fret ends, feeling for any remaining sharp edges.*

silicon carbide sandpaper, used dry, followed by application of a paste metal polish or by power buffing with buffing compound.

☐ Removing File Marks

1. The first step is to use small pieces of 320-grit sandpaper backed up either by one finger or the side of a gum eraser to remove all file marks left by the previous operations. The gum eraser is a lot easier on the fingers. Sanding is done back and forth along the entire length of a fret, until no file marks remain (**photo 21-31**). An attempt should be made to not round over the transition from fret top to fret end while doing this. Because the top of the fret is crowned, the eraser will have to be tilted sometimes to be sure the entire crown has been sanded (**photo 21-32**). Sanding debris is wiped off with a rag often, so that progress in removing the file marks can be seen. There are often one or two deeper pits that will need more sanding work, and that are only visible after the fret top has been rubbed briskly with a rag.

2. Step 1 is repeated for all the rest of the frets. A fresh surface of the sandpaper is used for each fret, as the metal readily clogs the sandpaper. When all fresh areas on a piece of sandpaper are used up, a new piece is used. After the fret tops are all smooth, the flat surfaces of the fret ends are sanded in similar fashion (**photo 21-33**). Only up strokes are used here. Down strokes will pull the masking tape away from the sides of the fretboard.

3. Sanding debris is vacuumed off the fretboard and from around the guitar, and the frets are wiped briskly with the rag.

☐ Polishing the Frets

Although fret polishing is performed using successively finer grits of sandpaper, the individual fret sanding technique used for removing the file marks is not primarily used here. A more efficient sanding technique is used to speed the process.

1. The first polishing step involves sanding the frets with 400-grit silicon carbide sandpaper. A different size piece of sandpaper is used, and a different sandpaper holding technique is used as well. A sheet of sandpaper is folded in the middle across its

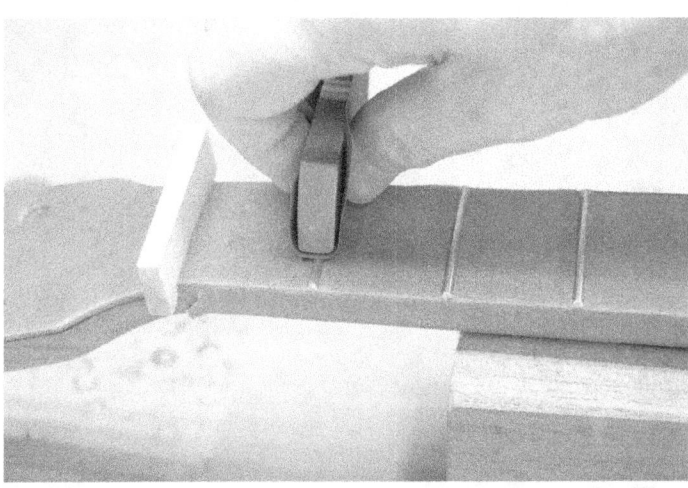

Photo 21-31 – File marks are removed from the fret surface using 320 grit sandpaper supported on the side of a gum eraser sanding block.

Photo 21-33 – The sanding block is used to remove file marks from the fret ends, left when the fret ends were beveled. These are removed with up strokes only to avoid peeling off the tape.

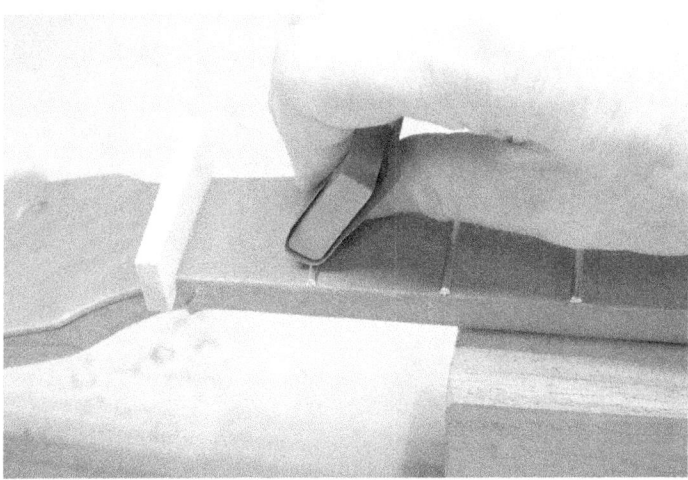

Photo 21-32 – The sanding block is tilted to remove re-crowning file scratches that are farther down the sides of the fret.

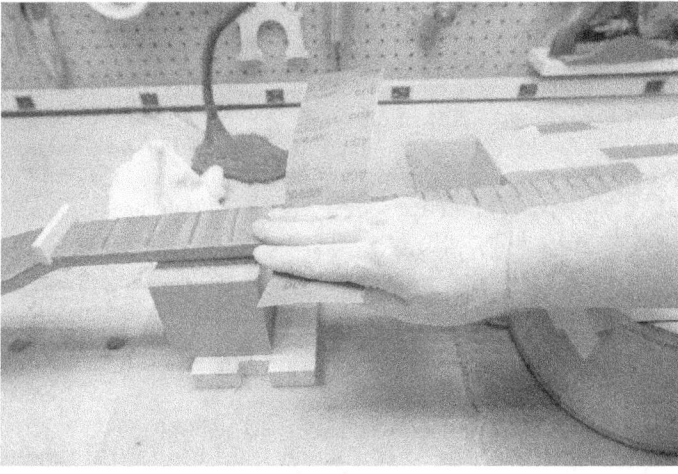

Photo 21-34 – When polishing the frets the strip of sandpaper is held near one end in a grip with the three middle fingers above the paper and the thumb and last finger below.

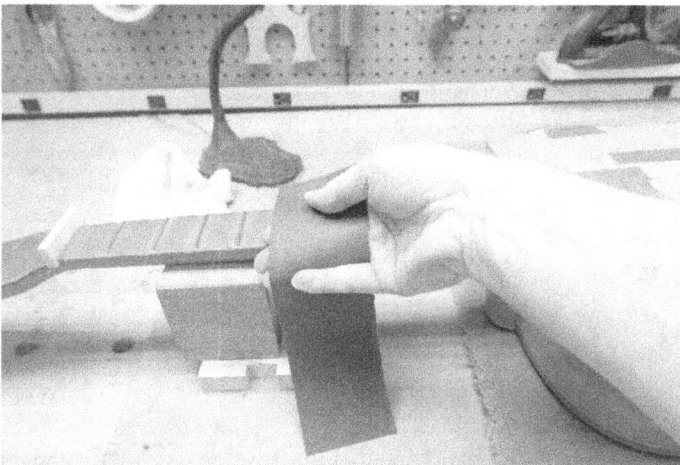

Photo 21-35 – *This is how the grip looks from the sanding side.*

Photo 21-37 – *Polishing progress should be checked regularly. Defects that may have gone unnoticed at a lower level of polish become visible when the level of polish is higher.*

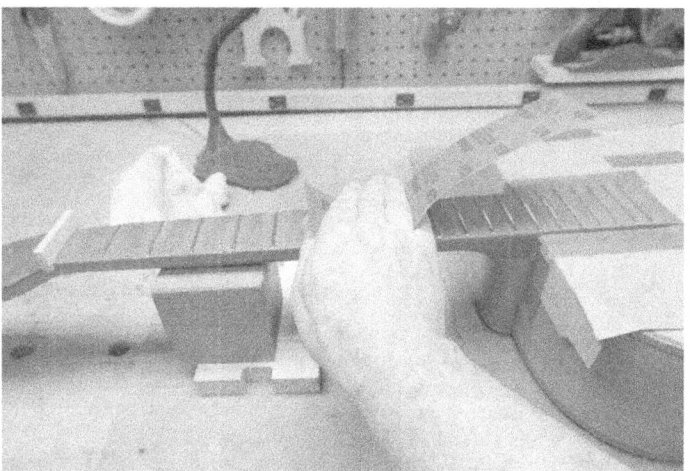

Photo 21-36 – *The tops of the frets are sanded using long strokes along the entire length of the fretboard. The relatively soft fingers are compliant, and allow the sandpaper to wrap around the fret crowns while sanding.*

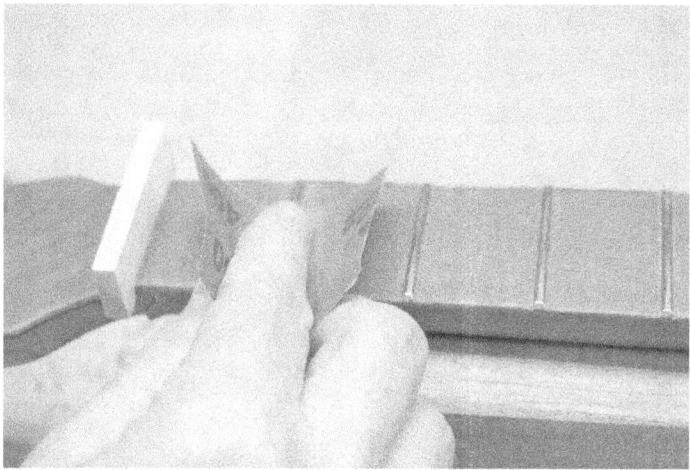

Photo 21-38 – *Sometimes individual frets will need attention. Here a small piece of sandpaper is supported by the tip of a finger.*

Photo 21-39 – *Work on individual frets can also be done with the sandpaper backed up by the gum eraser.*

width and then torn on the fold. Then one of the halves is also folded along the width of the full sheet and torn on the fold, yielding two quarter sheets that are 8½″ (215.9mm) long × 2¾″ (69.9mm) wide.

2. Any rings on the fingers of the hand that will hold the sandpaper are removed. One of the quarter sheets is held near one end so the sandpaper wraps under the three middle fingers and is held there by the thumb and last finger (**photos 21-34** and **21-35**). The tops of the frets are sanded with long back and forth strokes, with the fingers held parallel to the frets, pressing down firmly, going from one end of the fretboard to the other (**photo 21-36**). The sandpaper, supported by the fingers in this manner, hops over the tops of the frets and in the process rounds the crown and sands a little down the sides of each fret.

3. The fret ends of the frets over the neck shaft are sanded using the same hold. The hand is simply tilted to do the fret ends. When sanding the ends of the frets on the fretboard extension, the sandpaper must be slipped down so it is backed up by the fingertips. When the paper clogs, it is pulled through the fingers a bit to expose a fresh surface, and sanding continues. Sanding proceeds until the entire piece of sandpaper has been clogged up. The sandpaper is replaced whenever necessary.

Photo 21-40 – Sanding far down the side of a fret will often abrade the masking tape there. If this begins to happen, an additional piece of tape should be applied to protect the fretboard.

Photo 21-42 – A small buffing wheel charged with buffing compound and mounted on a drill can be used to quickly and easily polish all the frets.

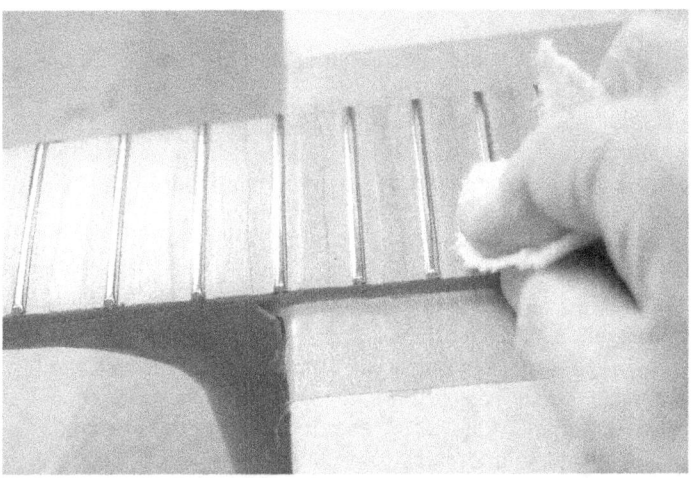

Photo 21-41 – Final polishing can be done using metal polish and a rag. The frets are individually polished.

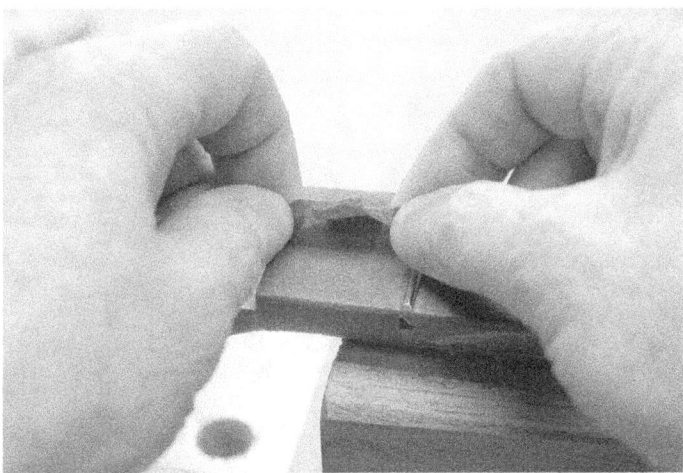

Photo 21-43 – To avoid pulling the finish off the fretboard sides, the masking tape between the frets is removed by pulling toward the center of the fretboard.

4. Sanding debris is thoroughly vacuumed up and the frets are rubbed across their lengths briskly with the rag so they can be examined. At this point it is important to carefully examine not just the tops and ends of the frets but their sides as well. This is done by sighting down the fretboard from the nut end (**photo 21-37**), and then from the soundhole end. Any roughness left by previous filing or sanding operations will be apparent as gouged lines, small pits, or obvious scratches. Places where the finish ran and coated the frets may also be found. These show up as dull and discolored areas on the sides of the fret. Using fresh sandpaper supported by a finger or the eraser, any of these defects are thoroughly sanded from the frets (**photos 21-38** and **21-39**). Note that if much sanding is required at the side of a fret (**photo 21-40**) it is possible to wear through the protective masking tape. If that begins to happen, another piece of tape is applied right over the previous one. A thorough vacuuming, rubbing with the rag, and inspection is performed again, before moving on to the next finer sandpaper grit.

5. Steps 1 through 4 above are repeated with successive grits 600, 1000, and if desired, 1500 and 2000. With each grit the shine on the frets will increase. Use of the two finest grits is not necessary, but their use will result in shinier frets, and will make it easier and quicker to do final polishing.

6. Finally, each fret is individually polished to a bright shine with paste metal polish and a rag (**photo 21-41**). If available, the frets can be quickly polished using a small buffing wheel in a power drill (**photo 21-42**). The wheel can be charged with any stick buffing compound. My preference for this task is green chromium oxide.

7. The frets are again inspected carefully, and touched up with sandpaper and polish anywhere needed. As with many such visual inspections, I usually inspect and touch up, and then wait a bit before inspecting again with fresh eyes. When two successive inspections can be done without finding anything that needs additional work, the job can be considered done.

Photo 21-44 – *After the tape is pulled from one side, it is pulled from the other side. Now it is only adhered in the middle.*

Photo 21-46 – *... and pulled off the fretboard.*

Photo 21-45 – *The ends of the tape are grabbed together ...*

8. When the frets look good, the protective tape can be removed. The two long strips down the sides of the fretboard are removed first. Then the pieces of tape between the frets are individually removed.

 It is important that the tape protecting the fretboard surface be removed by pulling it toward the center of the fretboard from each side toward the centerline (**photos 21-43** through **21-46**). That is, the tape is not pulled from one side of the fretboard and right off the other. Doing so may pull the varnish away from the sides of the fretboard.

9. After the fretboard tape has all been removed, the protective cardboard on the guitar body can be removed as well. The fretboard and guitar top surfaces are vacuumed well, without letting the vacuum nozzle touch the surfaces.

10. The fretboard surface is inspected carefully. If there were spots where the masking tape was worn through during fret polishing, those spots may show up as having a different texture. These spots are scraped to blend them with the fretboard surface around them.

11. A rag is dampened with naphtha or paint thinner and the fretboard, the neck, the guitar top, and the areas of the ribs and heel that had tape applied to them are thoroughly wiped down. Masking tape almost always leaves behind some areas of adhesive, and this will remove it. When the thinner dries all these surfaces are again checked carefully for any recalcitrant adhesive, and if found it is removed with the thinner-dampened rag.

12. The tips of the fingers are used to feel down along the fret ends again, as was done following fret end dressing, feeling for sharp edges where the corners of the frets meet the fretboard. Now that the tape has been removed, some sharp edges may be felt that were not felt before. The fret dressing file is used to carefully and gently remove any sharp edges found. Generally this can be done without leaving any noticeable marks on either the fret end or the fretboard, due to the angle at which the file is used. But if the operation does leave visible marks then the fretboard will have to be re-scraped here, or the fret end will have to be re-polished as necessary.

---

1. Jaén, F.A.(2010) Not Only Cones Make It– And Cylinders Almost Do. *American Lutherie #101*, p. 52.

22 The Final Details

There are a few unrelated operations which have to be done to complete the guitar. Most of these involve installation of the fittings. These operations are simple to do and simple to explain, like installing the end pin, the tuning machines, the label, and the optional *pickguard*. These are detailed in this chapter, along with the more complicated tasks of finishing the bridge saddle and constructing the *nut*.

Construction Operations

Installing the End Pin, Tuning Machines, Label

☐ **Installing the End Pin**

Materials
    End pin
Tools
    End pin reamer (see text)

The end pin is optional. For a guitar that is always played while seated it is not needed. It serves as the strap button on the tail end of the guitar, otherwise it is purely decorative. Note that a simple screw-on strap button is an easy alternative to the end pin. Installation of a strap button does not preclude installation of an end pin at a later time.

The end pin was already mentioned in the chapter on the bridge, because these are usually purchased at the same time and usually are made of matching materials. Installation of the end pin is similar to installation of the bridge pins. A mounting hole is drilled, the hole is reamed using a tapered reamer, and the pin is fitted into the tapered bore. Unlike the bridge pins which have to be removable, the end pin is permanently glued into its bore. Note that this is another case where a special-purpose tool is needed. The taper of the end pin hole must match that of the pin's shaft, and a special end pin reamer is needed to ream the hole. These are available from lutherie suppliers.

The mounting hole for the end pin must be drilled straight and perpendicular to the surface of the tail end of the guitar. To simplify this step, a guide block similar to the one used to drill the holes in the heel of the neck for the threaded inserts is used. Holding the guitar while this is done can be accomplished using a guitar body vise (Appendix C) but lacking that, the body can be held in position as described here.

1. Marking the center for the end pin. It is located in the center of the tail graft, halfway between top and back and halfway across the width of the graft. The distance from the upper right corner of the tail graft to the lower left corner is measured with a small ruler. This value is divided in half. The result is the location along the ruler edge where the center mark goes. The center mark is pricked using a sharp awl.

2. Making a drilling guide block. As mentioned, the hole must be drilled straight and perpendicular to the tail graft surface. To aid in this, a simple jig is made from cutoffs of ¾" (19.1MM) thick plywood and some cork. Two identical pieces are cut, each 2" (50.8MM) wide and as long as the body is deep at the tail end. The two pieces are stacked up and joined together, using double-sided tape, glue, screws, brads, etc.

Photo 22-1 – *The guide block is laminated from two pieces of plywood. Then a hole is drilled through it at its center, using the drill press.*

3. Using a straightedge, diagonal pencil lines are drawn on a broad surface of the block, from the upper left to lower right corners, and from upper right to lower left corners. These lines cross at the center of the surface. The center is pricked with the awl. Using the drill press and a brad point bit, a ¼″ (6.4mm) diameter hole is drilled through the piece (**photo 22-1**). Two strips of cork sheet are cut, ¼″ (6.4mm) wide and a bit longer than the jig. Double-sided tape is used to tape these along the long edges of one broad surface of the block (**photo 22-2**). The cork strips raise the block enough so it will sit squarely on the curved tail end of the guitar.

4. Drilling the end pin hole. If a guitar body vise is available, the guitar is secured in it, tail end up. If not, the guitar can be held by the luthier sitting on a high stool as shown in **photos 22-3** and **22-4**. A ¼″ (6.4mm) brad point bit is chucked into a hand drill. If the guitar is held in the luthier's lap, it is useful to use a compact drill for this operation. The guide block is slipped over the bit so the side with the cork is where the point of the bit is (**photos 22-5** and **22-6**). With one hand, the block is held up against the chuck. The bit is centered in the pricked center mark, keeping it as perpendicular to the tail surface as possible (**photo 22-7**). The guide block is carefully slid down the bit shaft until it is sitting on the tail of the guitar, all the while being sure the bit remains in its center mark (**photo 22-8**). This involves some adjustment of the angle of the drill, because the guide block forces the bit to be more or less perpendicular with the guitar's tail surface. The guide block is oriented so its narrow ends are parallel to the top and back edges of the guitar, and it is sitting flat on the tail surface.

Photo 22-4 – Side view of drilling the end pin pilot hole with the guitar held in the luthier's lap.

Photo 22-2 – Two strips of cork sheet are applied to the edges. These will allow the block to sit on the curved surface of the guitar's tail.

Photo 22-5 – The drill and guide block to be used. The components are shown positioned on the bench here just for photography.

Photo 22-3 – Drilling can be done with the guitar held in the lap of the luthier sitting on a high stool.

Photo 22-6 – The guide block is slipped over the bit so it is up against the drill chuck. The cork pieces will contact the guitar.

Again, this must be done without moving the point of the bit out of its center. The guide block is held in firm contact with the guitar and the hole is drilled about ½″ (12.7mm) deep. The drill and guide block are removed.

5. The brad point bit is removed from the drill and replaced with a conventional ¼″ (6.4mm) twist bit. The hole is finished up with this bit because it leaves a cleaner exit hole on the inside of the tail block. The hole is drilled through using the guide block as above. An attempt is made to control how fast the bit drills: a cleaner exit hole results if the bit exits the tail block with a slow feed rate. The drill and guide block are removed.

6. Reaming the end pin hole and fitting the end pin. Reaming and fitting proceeds in exactly the same way as for the bridge pins. The hole is reamed using the end pin reamer (**photo 22-9**). The fit of the end pin is checked as reaming proceeds. The pin does not fit in the hole at first. When it does fit in the hole, reaming and checking proceeds until the pin can be inserted about halfway down its shaft (**photo 22-10**). A check is made to be sure that the pin is perpendicular all around to the tail surface. If it is not, it is often possible to bias pressure to one side while reaming, to help reorient the hole to the perpendicular. Reaming and checking continue until the flange of the pin is just a tiny bit above the tail surface, about ¹⁄₆₄″ (0.4mm).

7. The end pin is removed, any surface debris is removed from pin and tail surfaces, and a tiny amount of glue is wiped on the

Photo 22-9 – *After the pilot hole is drilled through, reaming of the end pin hole is started.*

Photo 22-7 – *The point of the bit is engaged in the pricked center, then the guide block is moved in contact with the guitar.*

Photo 22-10 – *The hole is reamed until the end pin can be inserted approximately halfway. Then the pin is checked for perpendicularity.*

Photo 22-8 – *With the bit still engaged in the pricked center and the guide block in contact with the guitar, the hole is drilled.*

Photo 22-11 – *The hole is carefully reamed until the pin is just a hair above fully seated. Then glue is applied and the pin is fully seated.*

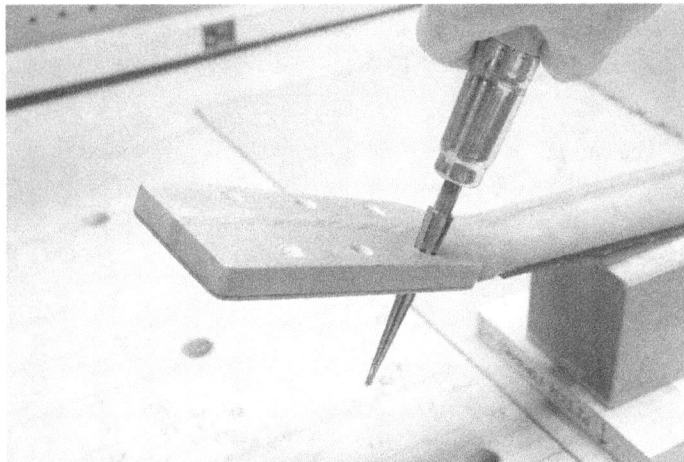

Photo 22-12 – *Tuning machine holes may have to be reamed a bit from the back of the headstock so the machines will fit.*

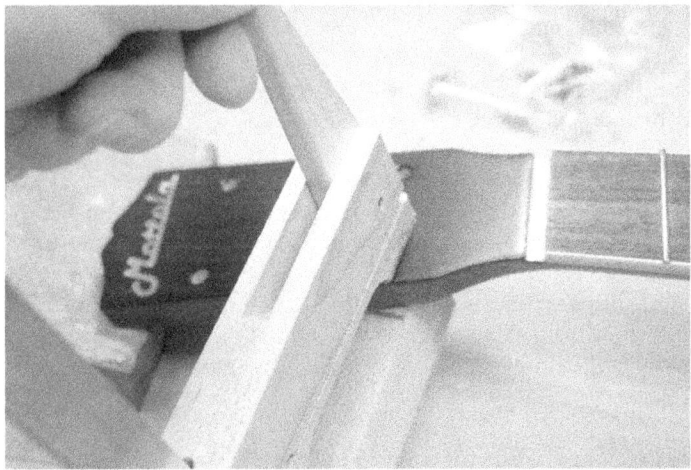

Photo 22-14 – *Then the bushing is fully pressed in place using a clamp.*

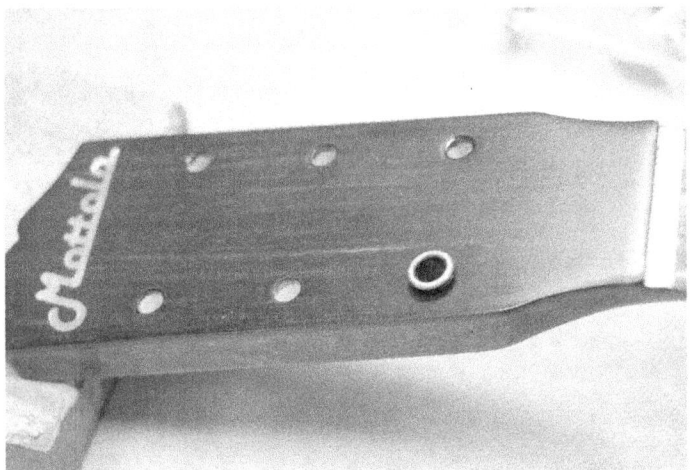

Photo 22-13 – *Machine holes are reamed from the front until a press-in bushing fits about halfway into the holes.*

Photo 22-15 – *All bushings are pressed into place in like manner. Bushings should be pressed in until they are fully seated.*

side of the pin shaft, near the tip. The pin is inserted in the hole and pressed firmly to seat it (**photo 22-11**). The glue is allowed to cure one hour before the guitar is moved.

8. The inside of the guitar is thoroughly vacuumed of any debris.

☐ **Installing the Tuning Machines**

Selection of the tuning machines was discussed early in the book. There are basically two types of tuning machines, as far as installation goes. One type uses bushings that press in from the front, and then the machines are screwed on from the back. The other type uses a threaded shaft and a long nut which screws on from the front. Both types are considered in the following installation steps.

1. The guitar is placed on the bench, top down, on carpeting and the neck is supported with some sort of padded supporting block. An attempt is made to fit the machines into their bores from the back. They often do not fit because varnish has built up around the edges of the bores during finishing. A few light strokes with a hardware store reamer or an end pin reamer from the back side of the headstock will take care of that (**photo 22-12**).

Tuning Machines with Press-In Bushings Option

2. The guitar is flipped over and an attempt is made to fit the press-in bushings into the holes from the front. The holes are carefully reamed using a hardware store reamer or an end pin reamer, with regular testing of the fit of the bushings. The goal is for the bushings to fit halfway into the holes without a lot of pressure, that is, without so much pressure that they can't be removed from the hole by pulling them out with the fingers (**photo 22-13**). When that target fit has been achieved, debris is blown from the holes, and the bushings are pressed into the holes by hand. Then they are pressed firmly into place using a clamp with cork lined pads (**photo 22-14**). The bushings are pressed in until their flanges are just flush with the top surface of the headstock (**photo 22-15**). Additional pressure may damage the finish on the surface.

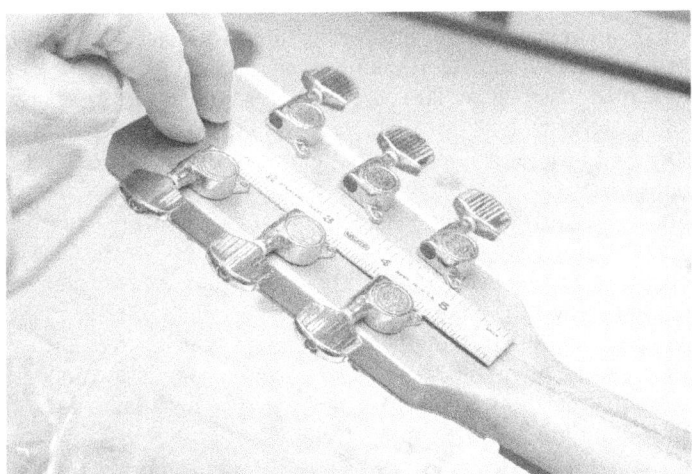

Photo 22-16 – *A small ruler or other straightedge is used to align the tuning machines on each side of the headstock.*

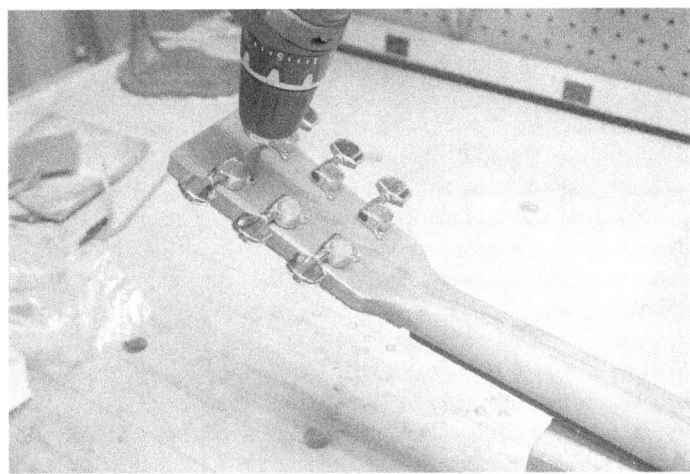

Photo 22-18 – *The pilot holes are drilled.*

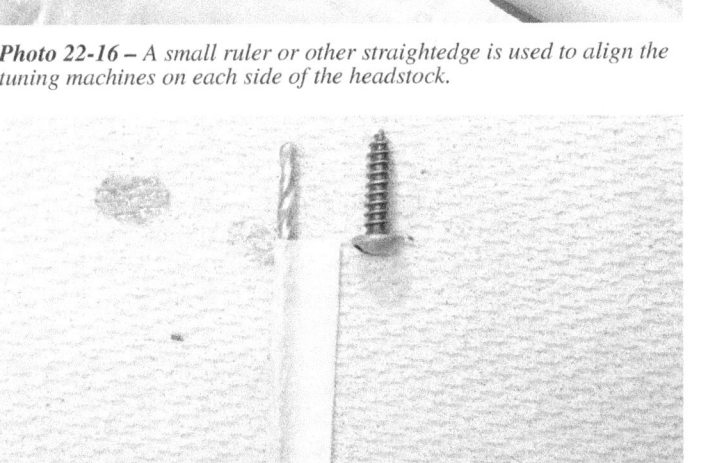

Photo 22-17 – *The drill bit used to drill the pilot holes for the mounting screws is marked for depth using tape.*

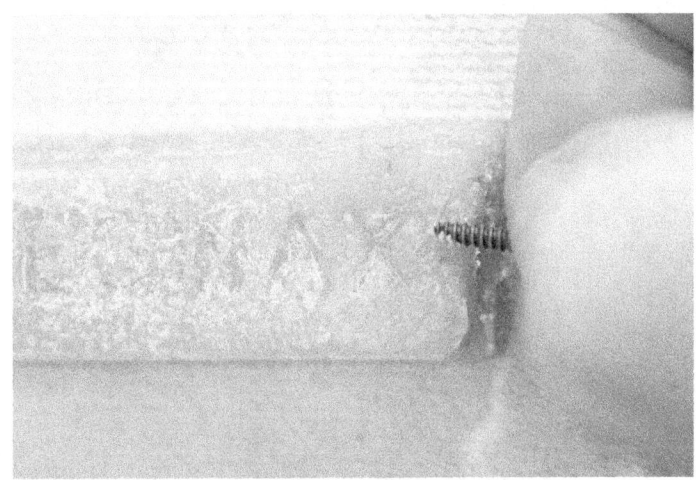

Photo 22-19 – *Screw threads are waxed for easy insertion by rubbing them across a block of beeswax or paraffin.*

Tuning Machines with Long Top Nuts Option

2. The guitar is flipped over and an attempt is made to fit the top nuts into the holes from the front. A few light strokes with a hardware store reamer or an end pin reamer from the front side of the headstock are made until the nuts fit easily in the holes. Each of the nuts has a decorative washer that fits over the shaft part of the nut. These washers are fitted to the nuts. Note that the washers often have distinct top and bottom surfaces.

Both Types of Tuning Machines

3. The guitar is placed on the bench, top down again. A tuning machine is inserted into its bore. Each machine has one or two holes used to screw the machine to the back of the headstock. For machines with a single screw hole, the small tab drilled for a small wood screw on each tuner points toward the nut and toward the headstock centerline. For machines with a front attachment nut, the nut and washer are screwed on hand tight from the front, and then slightly tightened using a small socket wrench or small open end wrench to just snug the nut. The rest of the machines are installed in the same manner.

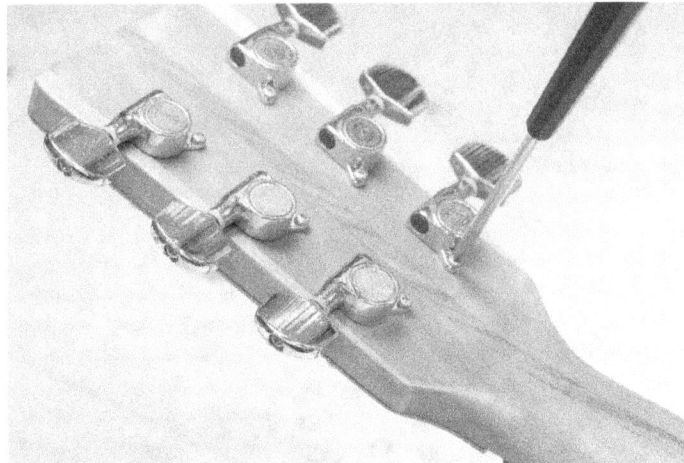

Photo 22-20 – *The mounting screws are driven into the holes and tightened just snug.*

4. A ruler or other small straightedge is used to line up the machine bodies on each side of the headstock, twisting them around a bit until the flats on the insides of the machines all line up (**photo 22-16**). For machines which use press-in

bushings, the straightedge may have to be kept in place for subsequent attachment of the mounting screws.

5. Pilot holes for the screws are drilled. A 1/16″ (1.6MM) bit is chucked into a hand drill and a piece of masking tape is placed on the bit to mark the depth of the small wood screws (**photo 22-17**). This should be done carefully. Using the screw holes in the tuning machines as guides, pilot holes are drilled for each of the small wood screws, stopping at the tape depth indicator (**photo 22-18**).

6. The threads of one of the screws are wiped across a piece of beeswax or paraffin (**photo 22-19**), and the screw is screwed in place using the appropriate size screwdriver (**photo 22-20**). Care is taken to prevent slipping that could scratch the finish. This is particularly a danger when screws with slotted heads are used. While tightening these, it is wise to grasp the screw head and the tip of the screwdriver between thumb and forefinger so the connection between the screw head and the screwdriver tip is completely surrounded by fingers. The screw is driven until it is just snug. It should not be over-tightened. The rest of the screws are installed in like manner.

7. If the tuning machines use press-in bushings then machine installation is complete. If the machines use nuts then these are tightened now. The guitar is turned over so the headplate is up, and a socket with its drive handle is used to tighten each nut (**photo 22-21**). It is important not to over-tighten the nuts. Doing so can crush the wood, which will crack and separate the finish. I like to choke up considerably on the ratchet handle so I am just grasping it with my fingertips right around its head. An open end wrench can be used instead but again, care is taken not to overdo it. On the other hand, the nuts must be tight enough to prevent rattling of the machines, which can be the source of an often difficult to track down buzzing in the finished instrument. Completed tuning machine installation is shown in **photo 22-22**.

☐ **Making and Installing the Label**

Guitars traditionally have a paper label glued to the inside of the back plate. A label of approximately 3¼″ (82.6MM) × 3¾″ (95.3MM) is made and glued inside the instrument so it is visible through the soundhole. A number of drawing and text document software packages can be used to make a label, and it can be printed out using any laser or ink jet printer. Rectangular, round and oval-shaped labels are popular. Information on

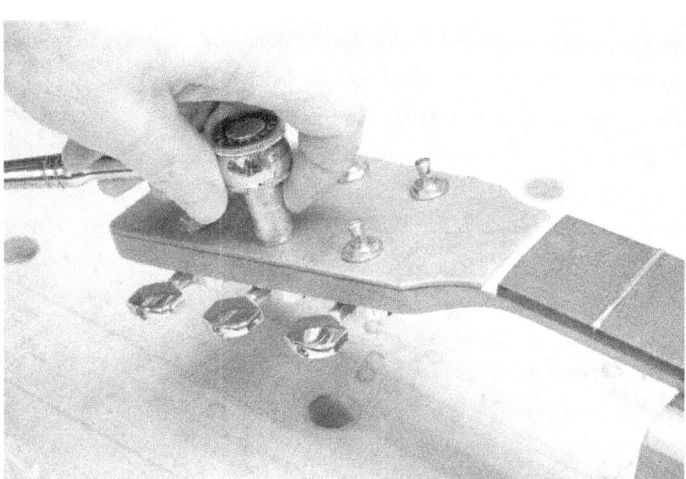

Photo 22-21 – *Tuning machine nuts are tightened using a socket wrench, choking up on the wrench so they are not tightened too much.*

Photo 22-23 – *The paper label is printed out, then cut out using scissors. Here an oval-shaped label is used.*

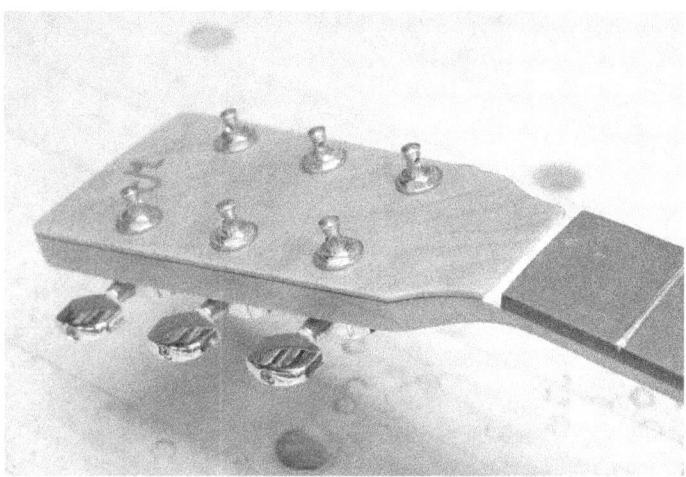

Photo 22-22 – *The complete set of tuning machines fully installed.*

Photo 22-24 – *The label will be glued into the guitar. Here a standard glue stick will be used.*

the label can include the luthier's name and the date the guitar was built as well as any additional information desired. I like to print labels onto 24lb (90GSM) 100% cotton rag paper, which is fairly strong and thick enough so that glue doesn't bleed through it.

 Luthiers that are likely to build more than one instrument may want to consider adding some sort of serial number to the label. This information may be useful in the future to the luthier and to instrument historians. It is interesting to note that a serial number was not a common label item for guitars until the middle of the 19th century, when they began to appear in guitars by Louis Panormo.

1. The label is designed using drawing software and printed out. The printed label should be allowed to sit for a few hours to be sure the ink is dry, then it is cut out with scissors (**photo 22-23**).

2. The label is placed face down on a clean piece of paper or cardboard, and glue is applied to the entire back surface (**photos 22-24** and **22-25**). Diluted woodworking glue applied with a brush works well, as does a glue stick.

3. The label is carefully pressed into place on the inside of the back through the soundhole (**photo 22-26**), being careful not to get any glue on the soundhole rim. The label is generally butted against the back brace just above the soundhole, and centered on the back reinforcement strip. Once it is in position, it is pressed down lightly with the fingers, then a rag is used to thoroughly stick it down. Pressing with the rag begins over the back reinforcing strip, then working outward, rubbing down and toward the edges of the label. Any glue that squeezes out will be picked up by the rag. The rag is turned as necessary to avoid getting any glue on the top surface of the label.

4. Any glue that got on the top or soundhole edge while getting the label inside the guitar is removed with a damp rag. Completed label installation is shown in **photo 22-27**.

The Pickguard

Acoustic guitar pickguards are simple thin plastic plates that are adhered to the guitar top. Their distinctive shape evolved to protect the general area of the top that is subject to scratching as a result of hard strumming with a pick. Guitars intended for flatpicking generally have them, and guitars intended for fingerpicking often do not. So the first choice to be made is to decide

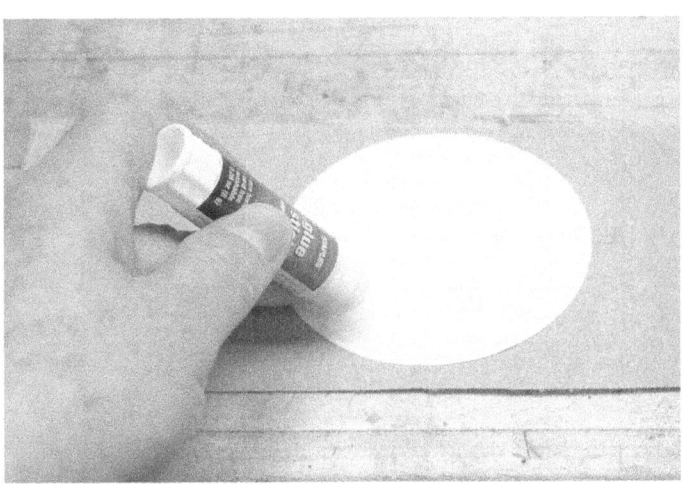

Photo 22-25 – The label is flipped over onto a piece of cardboard, and glue is applied to completely cover the back.

Photo 22-27 – The label is pressed in place on the inside of the back, usually in contact with the upper visible back brace.

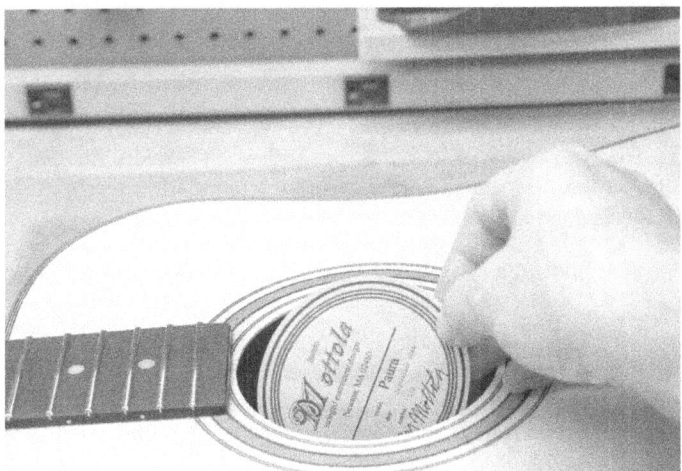

Photo 22-26 – The label is inserted into the guitar, without getting glue on the edge of the soundhole if possible.

Photo 22-28 – Guitars intended to be played finger style often do not have pickguards.

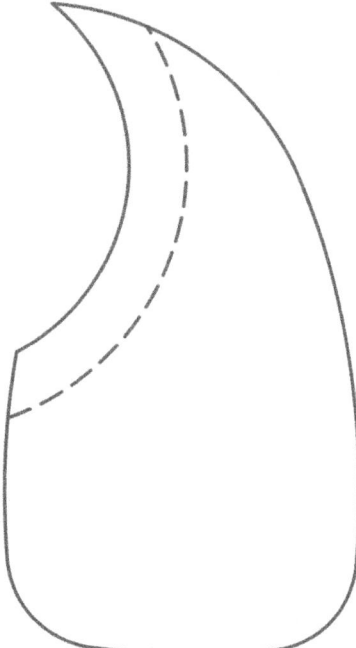

Figure 22-1 – *The template for the pickguard can be trimmed so the curve around the soundhole exposes some amount of the rosette.*

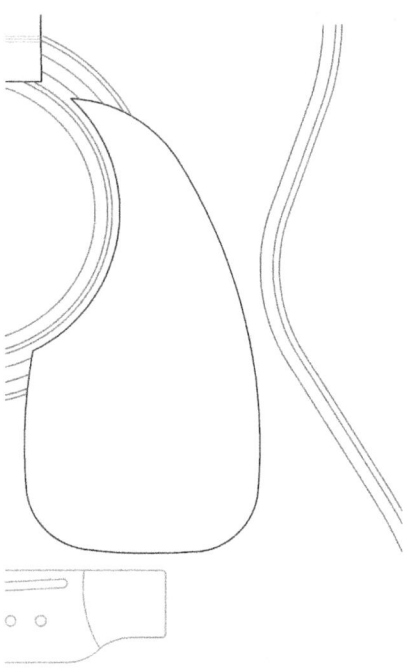

Figure 22-2 – *In this drawing, the pickguard has been trimmed to expose only the innermost ring of the rosette.*

whether or not to install a pickguard on the guitar (**photo 22-28**).

If a pickguard will be installed, it can either be purchased or made in the shop. Lutherie suppliers generally carry pickguards made of a number of different materials, and these are often available for different styles of guitars. The two example instruments in this book are of common styles. One is an OM style instrument and the other is a dreadnought style. Purchased pickguards are readily available for both of these. They are usually listed as Martin-style pickguards.

 Off-the-shelf pickguards are available for left-handed guitars from some suppliers, but choice of material is usually limited.

Another option is to purchase a custom-made pickguard from suppliers that specialize in these. Although more expensive, this option can provide a pickguard shaped specifically for the instrument under construction. And of course more options for materials for left-handed pickguards are available if it is custom made.

Making a pickguard is not at all difficult. Self-adhesive pickguard material is available from lutherie suppliers, and it is easy to cut out a pickguard from these materials using either scissors or a knife. Templates for traditional pickguards for the two example instruments are available in the template books for those instruments. Instructions are available elsewhere for drawing traditional pickguards as well.[1] If a pickguard is made in the shop, the radius of the curve of the pickguard can be adjusted to perfectly fit that of the soundhole or any of the rosette rings. How this is done is described in the construction description following.

☐ **Making the Pickguard**

The following construction description starts with a sheet of purchased self-adhesive pickguard material. This material is available in a number of color options including clear, from lutherie suppliers. It comes in thicknesses ranging from 0.012″ (0.3mm) to 0.020″ (0.5mm).

1. The template for the pickguard is printed on card stock and cut out using knife or scissors.

2. The template is placed in position on the top of the guitar. It is determined where the concave curve of the template outline should fall in relation to the soundhole and the rosette rings (**figures 22-1, 22-2**). For clear pickguards it is common that this curve is drawn to be just a bit outside of the soundhole, and inside of the innermost rosette ring. The entire rosette will be visible through the clear plastic.

For pickguards that will be made of opaque material, the curve is usually drawn so it falls between the second and third rings of a three ring rosette. This curve on the template is modified as desired, and the fit is checked again on the guitar top.

3. The outline of the template is transferred to the white covering on the back side of the pickguard material. This covering is what will eventually be removed to reveal the adhesive on the back of the pickguard. The pickguard material is placed on the bench so the white covering material is facing up. For a right-handed pickguard, the template is placed upside down on top.

For a left-handed pickguard, the template is placed upside up on top of the back of the pickguard material.

The template is traced onto the back of the pickguard material using a pencil or a thin black marker.

4. Cutting out the pickguard. This is done using scissors.

 It is important that cutting be done in a counter-clockwise direction around the pickguard outline. If cutting proceeds in a clockwise direction when cutting with the material bottom up, the edge of the pickguard will end up bent ever so slightly upward, and this will compromise adhesion of the pickguard to the guitar top. This happens due to the shearing action of the scissors.

5. The edge of the pickguard is sanded to smooth it and remove any facets left by the scissors. The easiest way to do this is with 320 grit sandpaper on a small block. The concave part of the outline is sanded with the sandpaper supported on a cylindrical form, like a chunk of a dowel. It is wise to use the sandpaper to slightly fillet the sharp peak in the outline at what will be the neck end of the pickguard. Sanding is most easily done with the pickguard placed upside up at the edge of the bench, so the part that is being sanded overhangs the bench a little.

6. The thicker pickguard material looks better if the edges are slightly beveled. This can be done using a razor blade scraper, again with the pickguard placed upside up at the edge of the bench, so the part that is being scraped overhangs the bench.

Installing the Pickguard

Precut and shop-made pickguards with an adhesive backing are installed in the same manner.

1. The pickguard is placed in position on top of the guitar, with care taken to be sure the concave edge of the pickguard is placed *exactly* where it should be in relation to the rosette rings. It is taped in place with a few pieces of masking tape. A longer piece of masking tape is used to tape down the tail end of the pickguard. This is positioned so half of the tape is on the pickguard and the other half is on the top (**photo 22-29**).

2. The position of the pickguard is checked again. If all is well, all of the tape is removed except for the long piece at the tail end (**photo 22-30**). This piece of tape is used like a hinge,

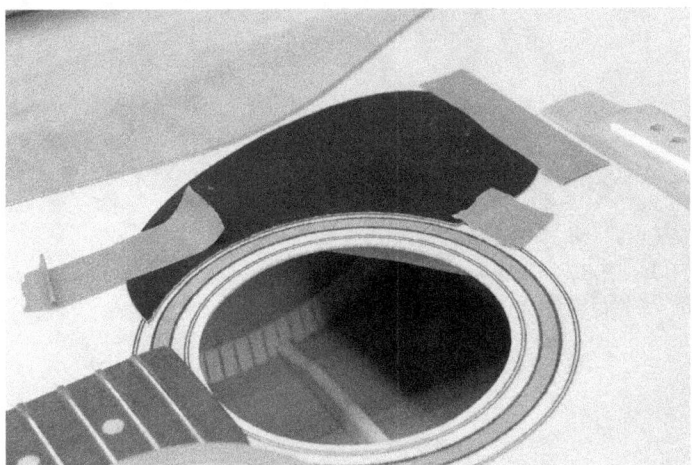

Photo 22-29 – The pickguard is taped in place so the concave curve is aligned with the soundhole and rosette.

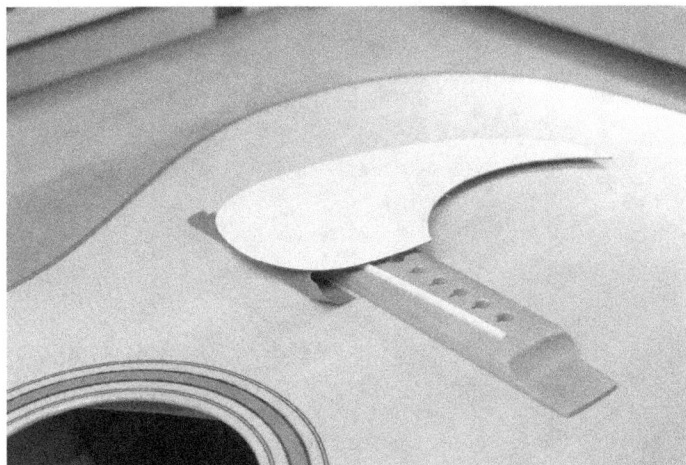

Photo 22-31 – The piece of tape serves as a hinge. The pickguard is hinged back, revealing the paper covering the adhesive.

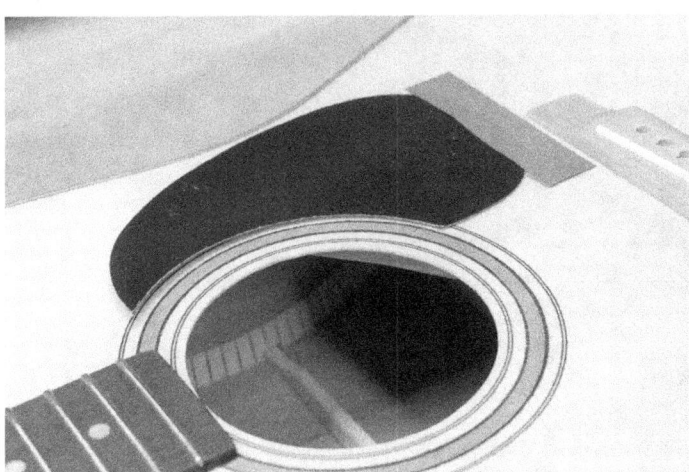

Photo 22-30 – One long transverse piece of tape is left at the bottom. This piece is half on the pickguard and half on the guitar top.

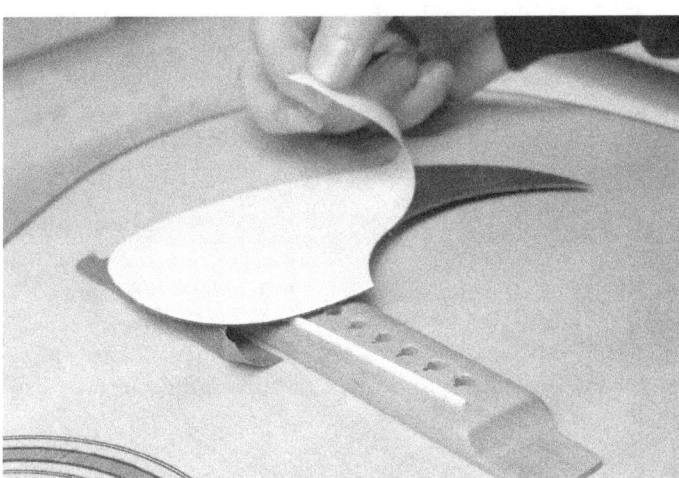

Photo 22-32 – The white paper covering the adhesive is peeled back and removed.

Photo 22-33 – *The pickguard is hinged back into place. Before pressing down on it, its position is adjusted if necessary.*

Photo 22-35 – *A chunk of dowel is used to burnish the surface of the pickguard, starting from the tail end …*

Photo 22-34 – *Now the pickguard can be smoothed down with the fingers.*

Photo 22-36 – *… and working up to the tip end. This sets the adhesive so it bonds strongly to the top.*

opening the pickguard like a trap door, until its top surface is contacting the top of the instrument (**photo 22-31**).

3. The backing paper on the back of the pickguard is carefully removed to expose the adhesive (**photo 22-32**). Then the "trap door" is carefully closed, adhering the pickguard *lightly* and positioning it as it contacts the top, to be sure the curve of the pickguard lines up appropriately with the rosette rings. The fingers are used to press the pickguard into place, starting at the tail end (**photo 22-33**) and working up toward the sharp tip near the fretboard (**photo 22-34**).

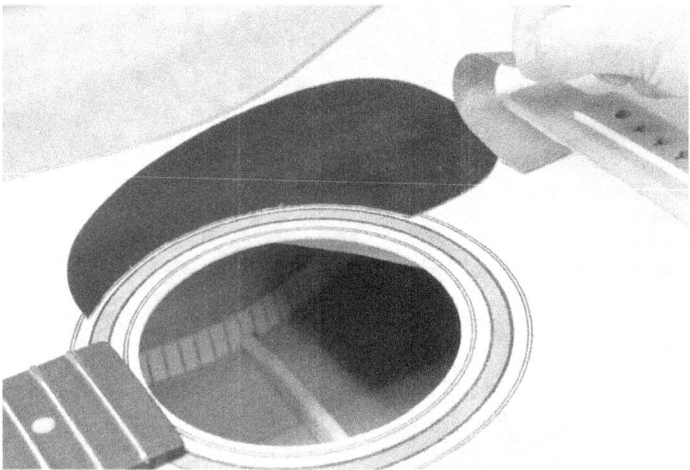

Photo 22-37 – *The piece of tape is then removed.*

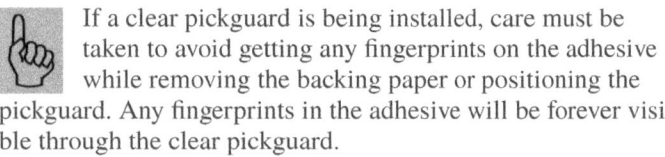 If a clear pickguard is being installed, care must be taken to avoid getting any fingerprints on the adhesive while removing the backing paper or positioning the pickguard. Any fingerprints in the adhesive will be forever visible through the clear pickguard.

4. The side of a length of dowel is used like a squeegee, moving from the tail end (**photo 22-35**) up to the tip (**photo 22-36**), to burnish the top surface of the pickguard, to set the adhesive.

5. The last piece of masking tape is removed (**photo 22-37**), and the clear protective film is removed from the top surface of the pickguard (**photo 22-38**). The installed pickguard is shown in **photo 22-39**.

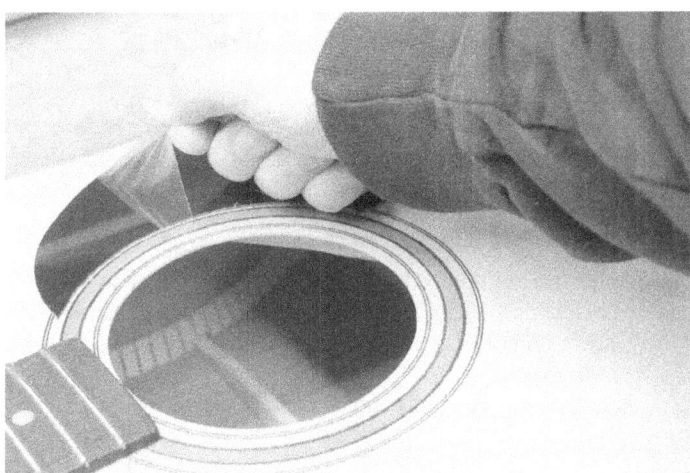

Photo 22-38 – *The clear plastic used to protect the top surface of the pickguard is peeled up and removed.*

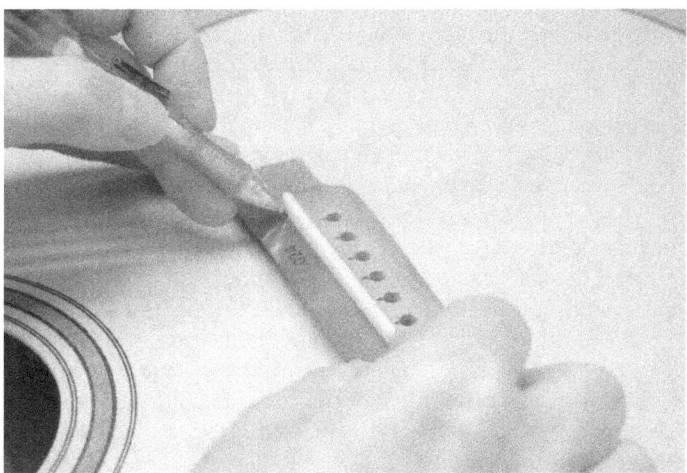

Photo 22-40 – *The top of a stack of feeler gauges is traced onto both ends of the front of the saddle, to indicate minimum exposure.*

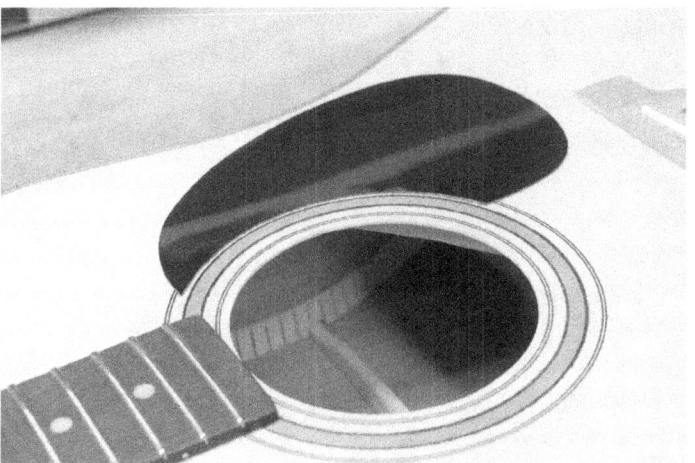

Photo 22-39 – *The finished pickguard, installed.*

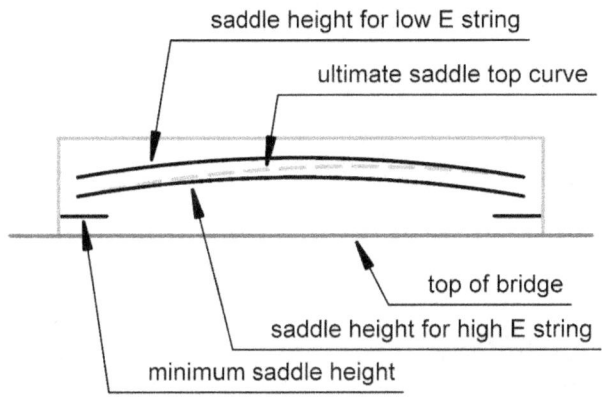

Figure 22-3 – *Marks on the front of the saddle, and what they represent.*

☐ Marking and Shaping the Bridge Saddle Top

The saddle has previously been sanded to thickness, cut to length, and its ends have been rounded to match the rounded ends of the saddle slot in the bridge. Now the saddle must be marked for approximate height and also to follow the camber of the fret tops. Then, the top surface of the saddle will be peaked along the saddle's longitudinal centerline, so the strings will contact a fairly narrow surface. Doing this improves intonation and helps to prevent buzzing.

1. The temporary nut is removed if it is installed. The saddle must be in the saddle slot and firmly seated on the slot floor. If there have been no changes made to the trussrod adjustment since the frets were dressed it is likely that the tops of the frets from 1 through 14 are still flat when checked with a straightedge. But if they are not then the trussrod should be adjusted to make the fretboard flat here.

2. The first step in this process is marking the minimum height for the saddle top above the top surface of the bridge. This *may* be used in a later operation. Feeler gauges are stacked up to 0.040˝ (1mm) and the stack is placed on the top of the bridge in

Photo 22-41 – *The gauge to scribe the saddle-height curves onto the front of the saddle is assembled, using the scale length stick, a thin extension stick, feeler gauges, and the half pencil.*

front of the saddle. Marks are made on the front of the saddle near both ends with pencil, tracing the top surface of the feeler gauges (**photo 22-40**). The top of the bridge is slightly curved at the ends, so the stack of feeler gauges must be kept in contact with the bridge top directly under where each mark is made. The minimum saddle height marks are shown in **figure 22-3**.

3. A simple gauge is built to mark the saddle for height (**photos 22-41** and **22-42**). This will be used to scribe the front of the saddle relative to the curve of the tops of the frets. The scale length stick used in previous construction operations is used as the base of the gauge. A short piece of wood is cut from ¼″ (6.4MM) thick scrap so it is about the same width as the scale length stick and 7″ (177.8MM) long. This is glued (or screwed or nailed with brads) to the bottom of the measuring stick near one end, with 1″ (25.4MM) overlap between this piece and the stick, so that this extension piece in effect extends the length of the stick by 6″ (152.4MM). If the pieces are glued together, they are clamped and the glue is allowed to cure. Cyanoacrylate glue is used to good effect here because it dries quickly.

4. The gauge will be used to mark the saddle at ³⁄₃₂″ (0.094″, 2.4MM) and also ⅛″ (0.125″, 3.2MM) above the surface of the frets. These marks correspond to the height of the saddle at the high E string end and the low E string end, respectively. When the gauge is laid on the frets so the extension piece is positioned between the end of the fretboard and the bridge, the underside surface of the stick is at the level of the surface of the frets, and the top surface of the extension piece is as well. Note that the fretboard extension may fall off a bit below the level of the rest of the fretboard. If it does, care is taken to be sure that the measuring stick is held flat to the tops of frets 1 – 14. Feeler gauges are stacked up to ³⁄₃₂″ (0.094″, 2.4MM) and the stack is taped down to the top of the extension piece. The half pencil is sharpened and then placed on top of the feeler gauges so it extends past the end of the extension and feeler gauges about ½″ (12.7MM). The half pencil is taped in place.

Note that the various components of the gauge may have to be moved around a bit to get everything to fit. The extension piece must be between the fretboard end and the front of the bridge, and the half pencil must extend over the bridge enough to draw a line across the entire front of the saddle.

With the stick held in contact with frets 1 – 14, and so the pencil point is touching the front of the saddle, the stick is slid across the fret tops from one side of the fretboard to the other, to mark the front of the saddle (**photos 22-43** and **22-44**).

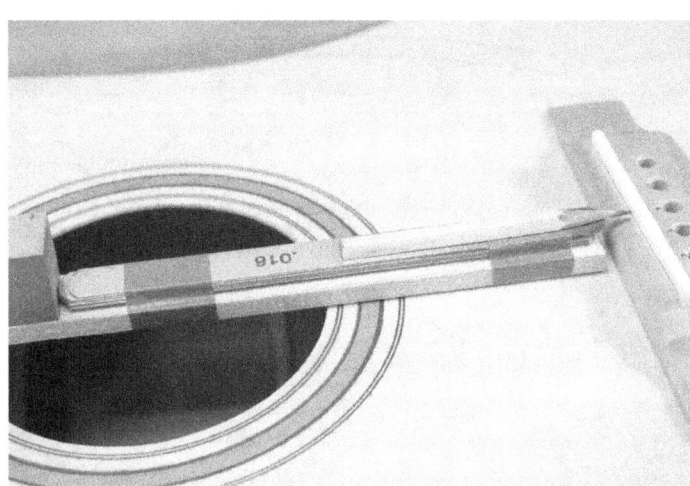

Photo 22-42 – Close-up of the business end of the gauge. The feeler gauges and (eventually) the half pencil are taped to the thin extension stick.

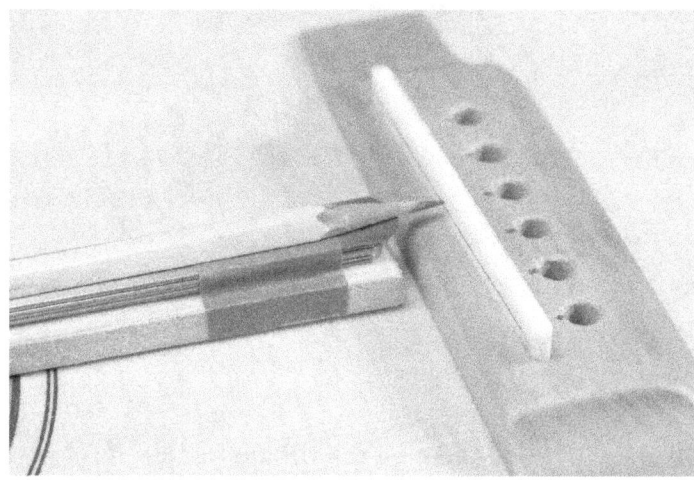

Photo 22-44 – The half pencil draws a mark on the saddle that is above the projection of the fret tops by the amount of the feeler gauges.

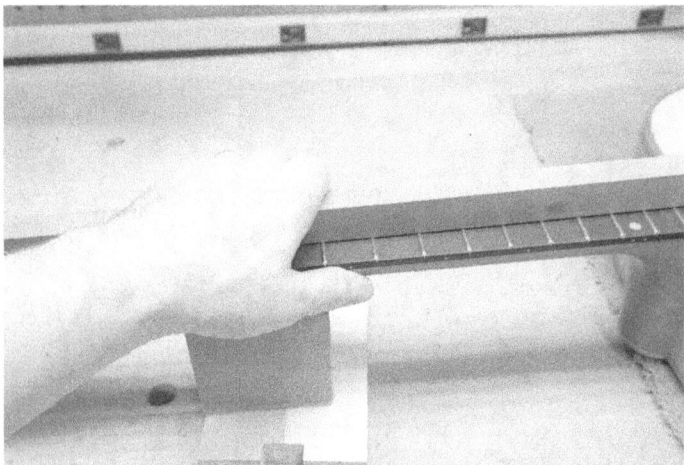

Photo 22-43 – In use, the gauge is held in contact with frets 1 through 14, and slid side to side across the frets.

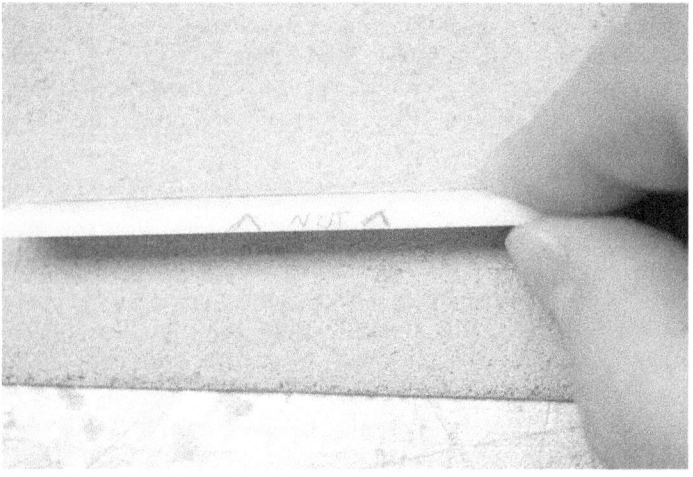

Photo 22-45 – The bottom of the saddle is marked to show its orientation. Placing the marks here means there is no danger of them being sanded off.

5. The pencil and feeler gauges are removed from the gauge. Feeler gauges are stacked up to ⅛″ (0.125″, 3.2mm). The stack of feeler gauges is taped down to the extension piece of the gauge as before, and the half pencil is taped on top. The gauge is used as in the previous step to mark the front of the saddle across its front. This mark will be ¹⁄₃₂″ (0.031″, 0.8mm) above the previously made mark. See **figure 22-3**. The marking gauge can now be disassembled.

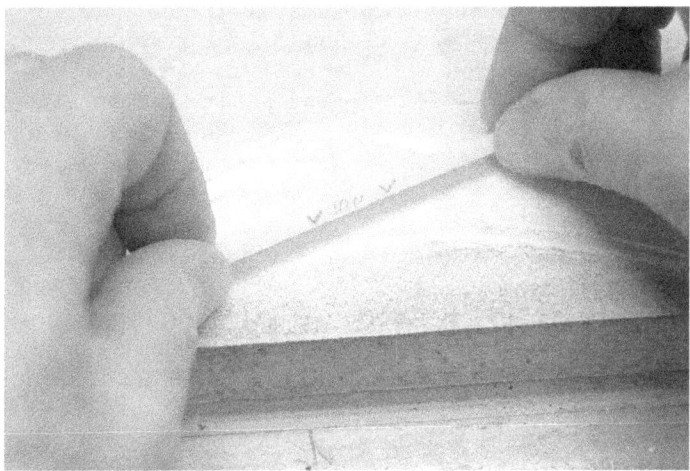

Photo 22-46 – *The top of the saddle is crowned by dragging it across a sanding board, to chamfer the two top edges. The result should be a thin flat line along the center of the top.*

6. The saddle is removed from its slot and the bottom of the saddle is marked in pencil with arrows pointing toward the nut (**photo 22-45**). This is done so the saddle can always be installed in its slot in the correct orientation, since marks made anywhere else on the saddle will eventually be sanded off.

7. There are now two curved pencil lines on the front of the saddle. As seen in **figure 22-3**, the bottom line indicates the target height of the top of the saddle on the treble side (high E string side) of the saddle. If the instrument is right-handed and the saddle is being viewed with the top of the saddle up, then this is the left side of the saddle. The upper line is the target height on the bass side (low E string side). If the instrument is right-handed and the saddle is being viewed with the top of the saddle up, then this is the right side of the saddle.

And if the instrument is left-handed and the saddle is being viewed with the top of the saddle up, then the treble side is the right side of the saddle, and the bass side is the left side of the saddle.

Now, the top of the saddle must be cut down so its bass side is at the upper line and the treble side is at the lower line, and with a smooth curved transition between these two points. The line to cut down to is shown for a right-handed guitar in **figure 22-3** as a dashed line. Cutting down the saddle top can be done with a file or rasp with the saddle held in a vise. It can be done by dragging the saddle over the sanding board (if there is a lot of material to remove, a coarse grit sanding board can be used first), or it can be done using drum or spindle sander, or disk or vertical belt sander. The saddle is first cut down uniformly to

Photo 22-47 – *The top of the saddle, after crowning has been done.*

Figure 22-4 – *The top of the saddle is cut down to retain the marked heights for the high E string and low E string, and to also retain the curve of the fret tops.*

Photo 22-48 – *The completed (for now) saddle in its slot.*

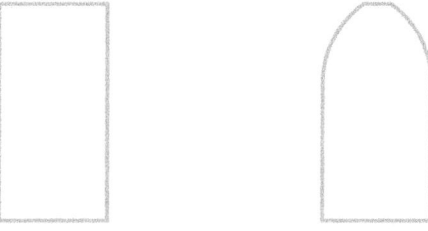

Figure 22-5 – *Cross section of the saddle, showing chamfering of the top edges, until the top of the saddle is reduced to a thin line.*

the upper bass side line, then the cut is made so its height on the bass side remains intact, but so it transitions to be deeper and deeper as the lower line on the treble side is approached (**figure 22-4**. This is all done by eye.

8. The two top edges of the saddle are chamfered, by dragging the saddle across the sanding board at an approximate 45° angle on each side (**photos 22-46** and **22-47**, **figure 22-5**). The target is a narrow flat down the middle of the saddle top that is 1/32″ (0.8MM) wide. Care must be taken to not let the chamfering drop below the minimum height marks.

9. The saddle is fitted into its slot and seated (**photo 22-48**). The saddle is not quite done but it is done to the extent needed to string up the guitar and check and adjust the action. The saddle will be shaped some more and then polished in a subsequent operation.

Building and Fitting the Nut

For such a small part of the guitar, shaping the nut requires a lot of steps and a surprising number of tools. Its dimensions are critical, too. A badly-built nut can result in an instrument that is difficult to tune, difficult to play, and that has poor intonation. Lutherie novices may be tempted to buy a pre-slotted nut, but these usually cannot be made to fit to a hand-built guitar as well as a nut built by hand, and fitting may require nearly the same amount of time and tools as would be needed to do the job from scratch. Nut materials and nut blanks have been discussed previously.

Roughing out the nut is done in the same manner and using the same tools as were used to rough out the saddle. There are no special tools involved.

Slotting the nut on the other hand *does* require special nut files or razor saws. The nut requires some very thin slots (0.012″ (0.3MM) is a common high E string diameter) and some which are considerably wider (the low E string of a typical string set is 0.054″ (1.37MM) in diameter). Usually general-purpose razor saws do not have blades that are thin enough to cut the thinnest nut slots. Likewise, the thinnest needle file in a typical assortment set is generally not thin enough to make the slots for any but the thickest strings.

Lutherie suppliers sell sized razor saws and special-purpose sized nut files made just for this operation. Although the unit price for these is not too high, a full set of six such saws or files is quite expensive. Although nut razor saws cut quickly and easily, it is far easier to cut a nut slot overly deep when using a saw. For this reason, if the novice luthier has to make a choice between these tools, I would generally recommend the nut files.

Nut files are thin and flat files that have cutting surfaces only on their edges. They are gauged in the same thicknesses as typical guitar string diameters. In theory one nut file is needed for each string size, but there is a filing technique that will be explained later that can be used to file a slot that is somewhat wider than the thickness of the nut file. Use of this technique reduces the number of nut files that are absolutely necessary. For builders who want to economize, I recommend purchasing just three sizes of nut files: 0.013″ (0.33MM), 0.024″ (0.61MM), and 0.042″ (1.07MM). Each of these can be used to cut two different width slots. But a full set of 6 nut files which includes

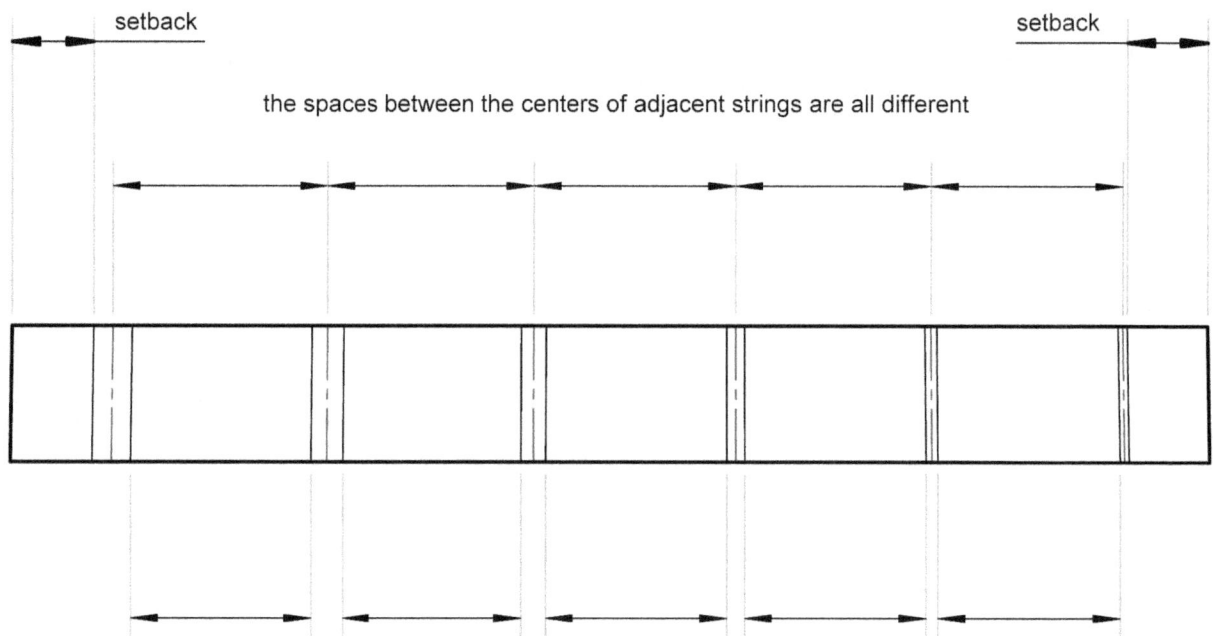

Figure 22-6 – *The layout of the nut, with proportionally spaced string centers. The two outer strings are set back from the ends of the nut by some amount. The distances between centers of adjacent pairs of strings are all different, farther apart for the bass strings than for the treble strings. The spaces between the edges of adjacent strings are all the same.*

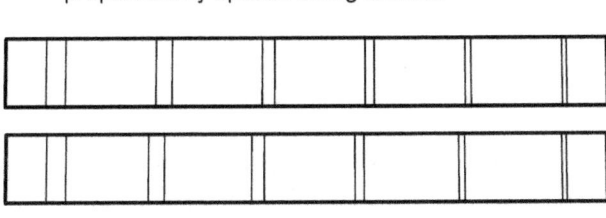

Figure 22-7 – *The difference between string slots with proportionally spaced string centers and slots with equally spaced string centers is readily seen when they can be compared close together.*

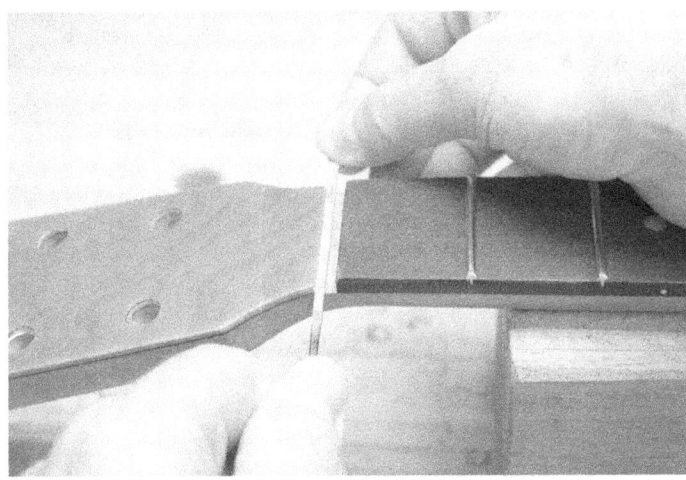

Photo 22-49 – *The slot for the nut is cleaned up using a square profile file. The walls and floor must be made straight and perpendicular.*

Photo 22-50 – *The nut slot, ready for fitting the nut.*

those widths mentioned plus 0.016″ (0.41mm), 0.032″ (0.81mm), and 0.050″ (1.27mm) makes nut slotting a lot easier.

The slotting geometry of the nut is interesting and is described with its own terminology (**figure 22-6**). The ends of the nut are flush with the sides of the fretboard. The two outer strings are set back from the edges of the fretboard and consequently from the ends of the nut. The amount each of the outer strings are set back from the ends of the nut is appropriately referred to as *setback*. The amount of setback varies as a matter of preference, but generally falls in the range of 0.10″ (2.5mm) to 0.16″ (4.1mm). Typical setback values for steel string acoustic guitars are 0.13″ (3.3mm) for the high E string and 0.16″ (4.1mm) for the low E string. These are the setback values used in the plans and templates for the example instruments.

Once the slots for the outer strings are located on the nut, it would seem that finding the locations for the other four strings would be simply a matter of measuring the distance between the centers of the outer strings and dividing that by five, to yield the distance from the center of any string to the center of the string next to it. In fact we do not use equal spacing to the string centers but instead use *proportional spacing* to the string centers. This means that the distance between string centers varies in proportion to the diameter of the strings, and that the amount of space between the adjacent edges of adjacent strings are all equal.

The reason proportional spacing is used is because it looks better. This is readily seen in a close proximity visual comparison of nuts with equal and proportional spacing (**figure 22-7**). The reason it looks better is a side effect of how the human visual system works. When looking down at the strings as they pass over the nut, we can only approximately visualize the locations of the string centers. But we can definitely identify the edges of the strings. As such, our visual system makes use of the edges when considering how close the strings are to each other. If the distances between string centers are all equal, the spaces between the edges of adjacent strings get smaller going from the high E string down to the low E string. This makes it appear that the string spacing is off.

Since our visual system makes use of the edges when considering how close the strings are to each other, the solution to the string spacing appearance problem is to space the strings proportionally, so the amount of space between the adjacent edges of adjacent strings are all equal.

It should be noted that this visual effect is a function of how long the nut is and the differential diameters of the strings. If the nut were just a bit longer than it is or if the differences in string diameters wasn't as big as it is, we would not be able to see this at all. In fact, luthiers rarely bother to fuss over string spacing at the bridge saddle, where the spacing is wider than it is at the nut. We also don't generally use proportional spacing when laying out the string slots for classical guitars, because the differences between the diameters of the strings of that instrument are not as great.

There are a number of ways to lay out the locations of the proportionally spaced string slots on the nut. All of these start with the measured length of the nut. One way to do this is arithmetically. If the two setback distances and the diameters of all the strings are all subtracted from the length of the nut, the result is the total length of all five of the spaces between the strings. Dividing this by five yields the space between any two adjacent strings. All these values can be used to lay out the string slots.

Another way to lay out the locations of the proportionally spaced string slots is with a special-purpose string spacing ruler. This is a special-purpose lutherie tool designed specifically for this application. These are available from lutherie suppliers.

The nut slotting operation below makes use of a special nut slotting template, which can be downloaded from the Plans and Templates section of the Online Annex of this book, found in Appendix A. The template is printed out on a sheet of matte clear address labels (Avery 8660 or equivalent) and cut out as specified below. This approach is quick and easy, free of math, and requires no expensive special-purpose tools. The template also takes care of the setback of the two outer strings.

☐ **Roughing Out the Nut**

Again, this is done in much the same manner as roughing out the saddle, so the descriptions should be familiar.

1. At this point, the nut blank is a bit oversize in all dimensions. If it is not already, the top and bottom of the blank are made parallel, and the broad surfaces are made perpendicular to top and bottom.

2. The nut slot on the neck, between the ends of the headplate and fretboard, must be cleaned up and squared. This is best done using a small flat needle file with a safe edge, but any rectangular or square profile file that will fit in the slot will do (**photo 22-49**). The objectives are to make the floor of the slot clean and flat, and to make the walls of the slot clean and perpendicular to the floor. Generally all that has to be done here is to use the file to level any finish that has built up around the ends of the nut slot during finishing, and to clean all accumulated debris out of the slot (**photo 22-50**). Care should be taken not to let the tip of the file exit the slot while filing. Doing so can chip finish off that side of the neck. So work should be done from one end of the slot and then the other. The file itself is used to check for flatness of the surfaces.

3. The nut blank is reduced in thickness using a sanding board with 180 grit sandpaper. This is done in exactly the same manner as when reducing thickness of the saddle blank (**photo 22-51**). Sanding the nut blank and attempting fit are done until it fits snugly in the nut slot, with its base sitting securely on the floor of the slot (**photo 22-52**).

4. The nut blank is cut to length next. The guitar is flipped over so the top is down on the carpet. The nut is held in its slot with

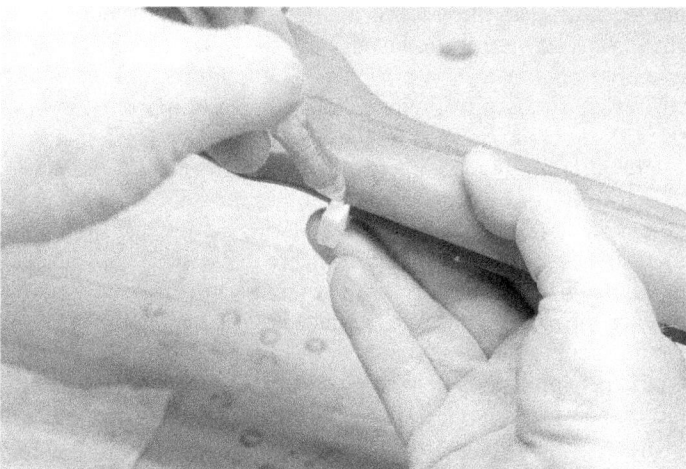

Photo 22-53 – The ends of the nut blank are marked for cutting to length.

Photo 22-54 – The nut with end marks. The nut is trimmed down to these marks.

one hand while the other hand is used to pencil the width on the bottom of the nut, with the pencil lead right against the wood at the ends of the nut slot (**photo 22-53**). The edges of the end of the fretboard are traced onto the nut, too, as are the short edges of the headplate. The guitar is flipped back over top up, and the nut is removed from the slot (**photo 22-54**). The ends of the nut are cut and shaped until the marked lines just barely disappear. If there is a lot of waste, it can be cut off using a razor saw or sander. A careful look should be taken at the pencil lines on the bottom of the nut. Often they are slightly concave. If so, the last bit of material has to be removed using a convex needle file or a small diameter drum or spindle sander. If the lines are straight then any tool that leaves a flat surface can be used.

As the pencil lines are thinned, the nut is test fitted. The fingers are used to feel how much more material has to be removed. A little material is taken off both ends at a time and then fit is checked again. Ideally the nut should end up just a hair longer than the slot (**photo 22-55**), so that subsequent sanding of the nut ends during final shaping and polishing will bring it down to the exact length of the slot.

5. Now the rough height is cut. The nut is installed in its slot so it is well-seated. The half pencil is sharpened, then placed flat down on the first two (at least) frets, with its point in contact with the front surface of the nut. The pencil is moved side-to-side across the fret tops, to transfer the curve of the fret tops to the nut (**photo 22-56**). This mark represents the approximate depth of the string slots.

6. Feeler gauges are stacked up to approximately 0.054″ (1.37mm), which is the diameter of a typical guitar low E string. The stack of gauges is placed on the frets near the nut, and the half pencil is placed on top. The feeler gauges and half pencil are moved side-to-side, to mark the approximate height curve of the nut (**photo 22-57**).

7. The nut is removed from the guitar (**photo 22-58**) and cut down using whatever tools are desired, until the top line just disappears. One way to do the final sanding here is to hold the nut upside down on the sanding board and sand the top in a rocking fashion (**photo 22-59**).

Photo 22-55 – *A perfect fit leaves the nut just a hair longer than the nut slot. This difference will be removed when the nut is further sanded.*

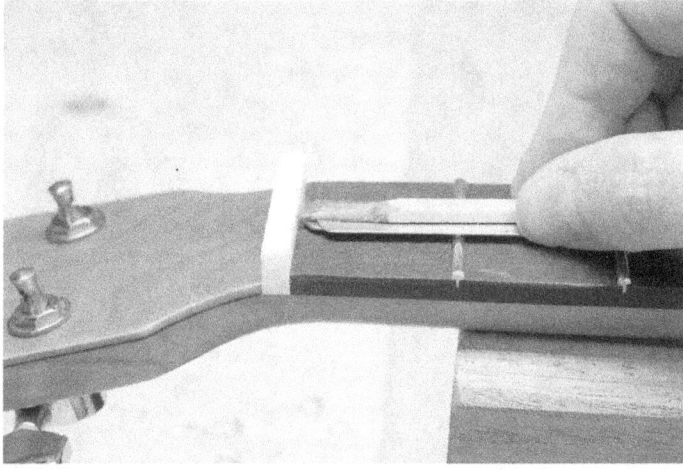

Photo 22-57 – *Feeler gauges are used to raise the pencil up, to mark the approximate top surface of the nut.*

Photo 22-56 – *The half pencil is used to mark the projection of the tops of the frets onto the nut. This line indicates the string slot bottoms.*

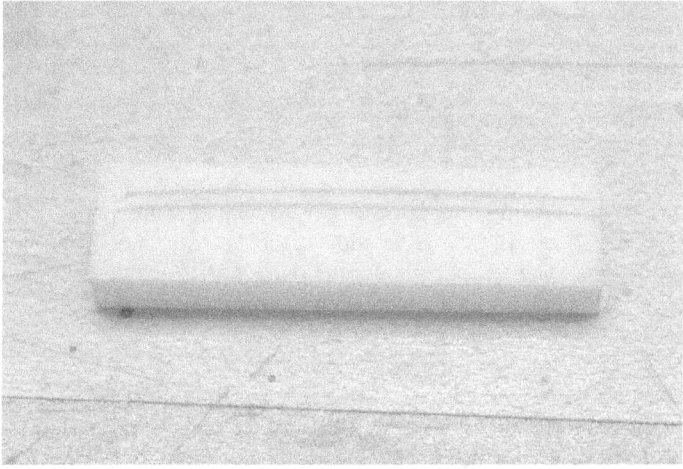

Photo 22-58 – *The nut top and string slot floor lines, penciled on the front of the nut.*

Photo 22-59 – The top of the nut is sanded down until the top line just disappears.

Photo 22-61 – A flexible ruler is used to measure the length of the nut across the top surface.

Photo 22-60 – The nut is clamped in the vise in preparation for applying the template and doing the slotting.

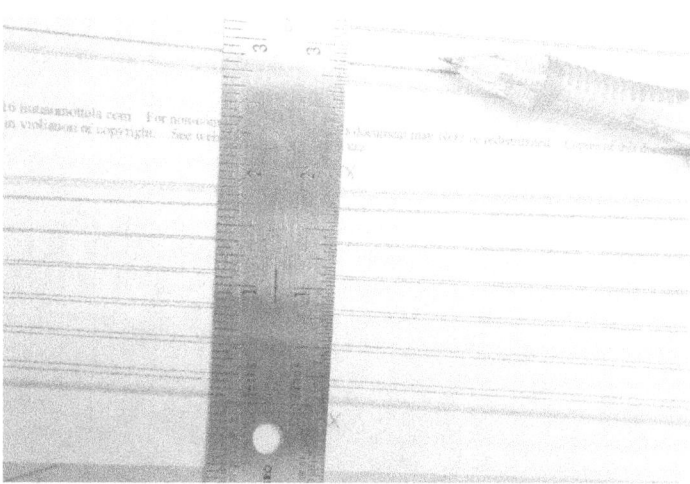

Photo 22-62 – The place on the template that is the same as the measured length of the nut is located.

☐ **Slotting the Nut**

Materials
    The roughed out nut
    Set of acoustic steel string guitar strings
Tools
    Set of 3 or 6 nut files (see text)
    Downloaded Nut Slotting Template (see text)
    Matte clear address labels, Avery 8660 or equivalent

1. The nut slotting template sheet is downloaded and printed out on a sheet of matte clear address labels, Avery 8660 or equivalent. The template is printed using a PDF viewer. When printing the template, care is taken to be sure the Actual Size button is selected in the PDF viewer.

The template sheet contains two templates, one for a right-handed guitar and one for a left-handed guitar. Each template consists of lines representing the string slots and the edges of the fretboard at various setbacks. The lines diverge from one

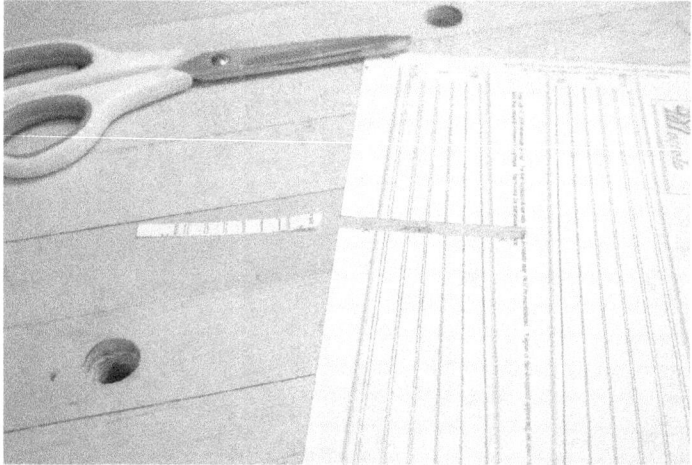

Photo 22-63 – That section of the template is cut out using scissors.

end of the template to the other. This means that the template represents a different nut width at each point along its length.

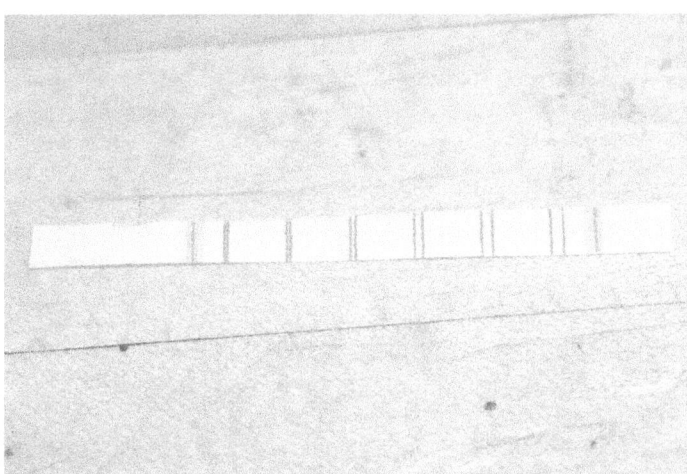

Photo 22-64 – *The cut out nut slotting template, ready for application on the top of the nut.*

Photo 22-66 – *The template is pressed firmly in place to set the adhesive.*

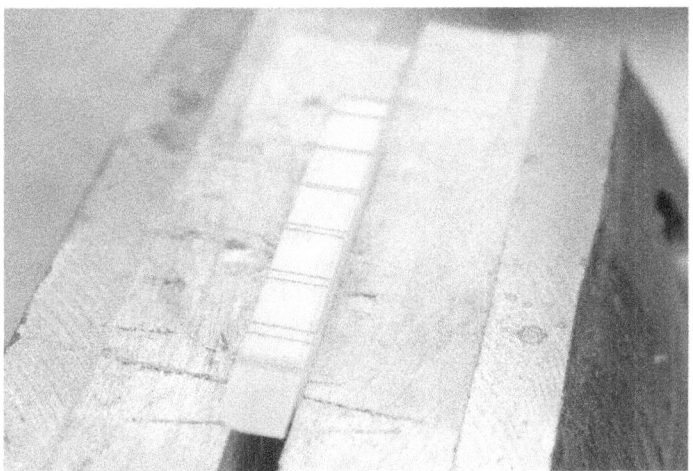

Photo 22-65 – *The template is applied with the red setback line aligned with the bass side edge and the green setback line aligned with the treble side edge of the nut.*

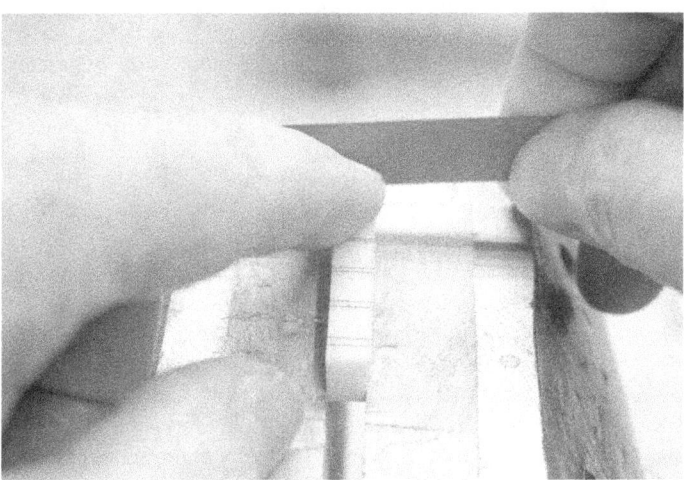

Photo 22-67 – *The file is positioned in between the lines for a string slot. A finger of the other hand is used to hold the file in lateral position while filing proceeds.*

2. The nut is held in a vise with smooth jaws, so that the top surface is up and most of the nut is exposed (**photo 22-60**). This is necessary to provide room for filing the string slots. The nut should be oriented with its headstock side to the luthier's left and its fretboard side (currently pencil marked with the bottom of string slots mark) to the right.

3. A flexible ruler with fine graduations is used to measure the length of the top of the nut (**photo 22-61**). The flexible ruler is needed because the top of the nut is arched.

4. The printed template sheet is oriented with its top of page to the luthier's left. For a right-handed instrument, the unmarked right-handed template is used. Starting from the narrow end of the template, the ruler is moved to the right, measuring at each of the gray lines across the template, from the red setback line on the bass side of the template to the green setback line on the treble side (**photo 22-62**). This process stops at the place on the template where this measurement equals the measured width of the nut. The nearest gray cross line is marked on the template.

Photo 22-68 – *The slot is filed with the file held at an angle pointing down toward the headstock side of the nut. The slot floor must be angled down and flat. Filing stops when the pencil line is reached.*

 For a left-handed instrument, the template marked "lefty" is used instead.

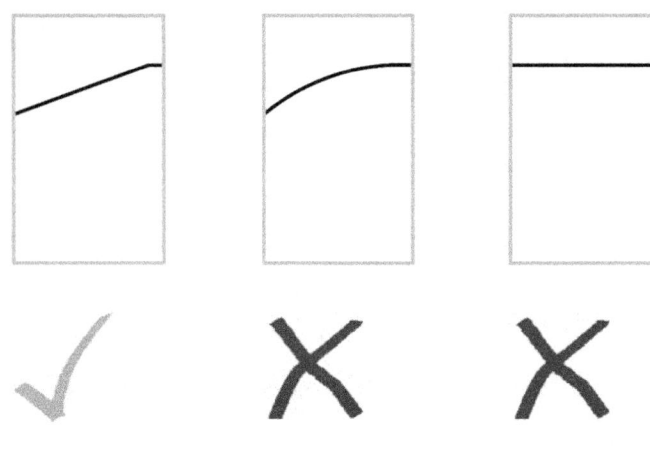

Figure 22-8 – *Schematic diagrams of the floor of the nut slot. The floor must be mostly flat and angled down toward the headstock, with just a bit at the fretboard side level with the top of the nut. This provides sharp termination of the vibrating length of the string at the front of the nut. The floor should not be fully rounded or fully level with the top of the nut. Either of these will cause intonation or buzzing problems.*

Photo 22-69 – *Widening a string slot begins with the nut file held at an acute angle against one of the slot walls.*

5. Scissors are used to cut out the section of the label containing this width (**photos 22-63**, **22-64**). Each section (between gray lines) is about ¼" (6.4mm) wide, the same as the width of the nut. The paper backing is removed from this piece of label and it is stuck down on top of the nut so the red bass side setback line is aligned with the bass side top edge of the nut, and the green treble side setback line is aligned with the treble side top edge of the nut (**photo 22-65**). For a right-handed guitar, the bass side of the nut is toward the luthier, and for a left-handed guitar the bass side edge is away from the luthier in the current orientation of the nut in the vise.

The top of the label is rubbed firmly to ensure good adhesion to the nut (**photo 22-66**). The nut is removed from the vise, and scissors or a knife are used to trim off excess label material. Then the nut is returned to the vise, oriented as before.

6. The slot for the high E string is cut into the nut using the template. The 0.013″ (0.33mm) thick nut file is used to cut the slot. The file is placed in position between the template lines for the high E string. The file should be angled down toward the headstock side at an angle slightly less than that of the headstock, to begin cutting the slot on the headstock-facing edge of the nut. With the file in position, a finger of the hand not holding the file is placed on top of the nut, so the nail of that finger contacts the side of the file (**photo 22-67**). This serves as a guide to keep the file between the lines as the cut is made. Filing proceeds a bit at this angle, keeping the file between the template lines. Positioning is corrected early, if necessary, while it is still possible.

Filing continues until a shallow slot is cut across the top of the nut between the lines. More filing is done, keeping the file lifted at an angle slightly less than that of the headstock, until the slot barely reaches the marked pencil line on the fretboard side of the nut (**photo 22-68**). A file brush is used to clean the cutting edge often. It clogs up fast. As the cut approaches the depth line, the file is removed, the slot is cleaned out, and its depth is checked. The depth often appears to be shallower than it really is, because filing dust builds up at the bottom of the slot.

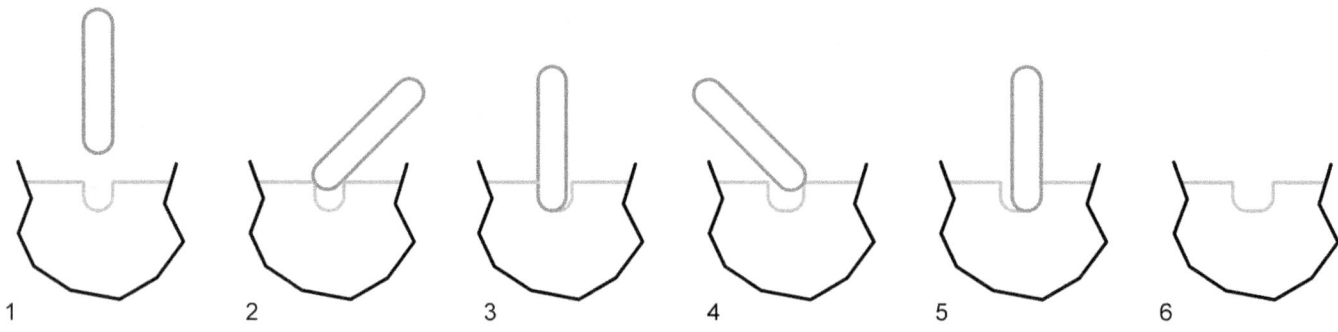

Figure 22-9 – *Schematic of the process of using a nut file to widen a string slot. 1. The initial slot is cut to the width of the file. 2. A stroke to remove material from one wall of the slot begins with the file in contact with the top edge of that wall. 3. The angle of the file changes throughout the filing stroke and ends vertical. This removes an even amount of material from the wall. 4, 5. Wall filing is repeated for the other wall. 6. The finished slot.*

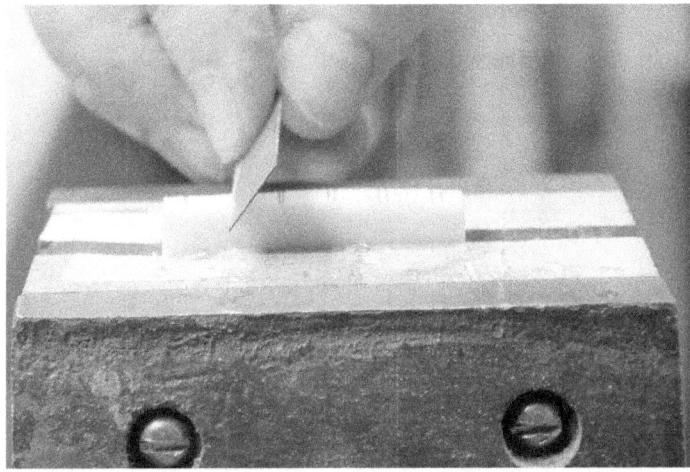

Photo 22-70 – As the filing stroke proceeds, the angle of the file is straightened out so an even amount of material is filed off the wall of the slot.

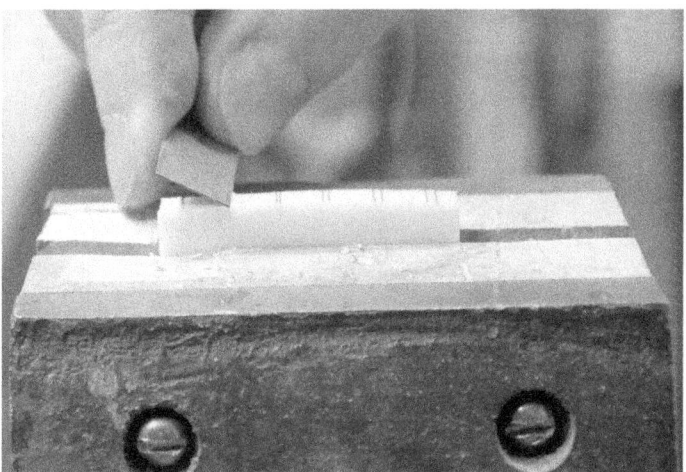

Photo 22-72 – Filing continues in the same manner but on the other wall of the string slot.

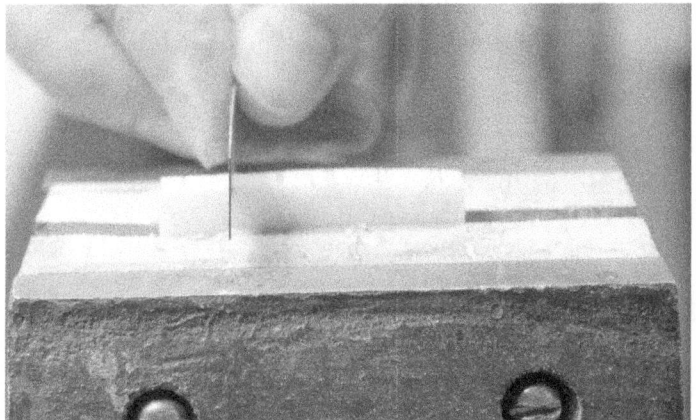

Photo 22-71 – The filing stroke ends with the file oriented vertically.

Photo 22-73 – As before, the angle of the file becomes more vertical as the filing stroke proceeds.

Now, just a bit of a flat is filed level with the top of the nut on the fretboard side of the nut (**figure 22-8**) and then blended in with the rest of the slot. This prevents undue wear of the fretboard edge of the slot, and also a characteristic "tink" sound when the wound strings are tuned up to pitch.

☞ While filing, care is taken to not twist the file. Doing so may break off a chunk of the nut on either side of the slot. If the file binds in the slot, the flat sides of the file are rubbed against a piece of beeswax or paraffin.

☞ When the slot is cut to depth, it is deeper on the headstock side of the nut than it is on the fretboard side, due to the angle of the cut (**figure 22-8**). This angle is important. Also important is that the floor of the slot is not rounded from one end to the other. A straight angled slot with just a bit of a flat at the fretboard side prevents intonation and buzzing problems in the finished guitar.

Photo 22-74 – The stroke ends with the file held vertically. The floor of the slot must be rounded following widening.

7. The slot is checked for fit using a high E string. It should fit in the slot without binding or pinching, and sit right at the bottom of the slot at both ends. Magnification may be needed to perform this check.

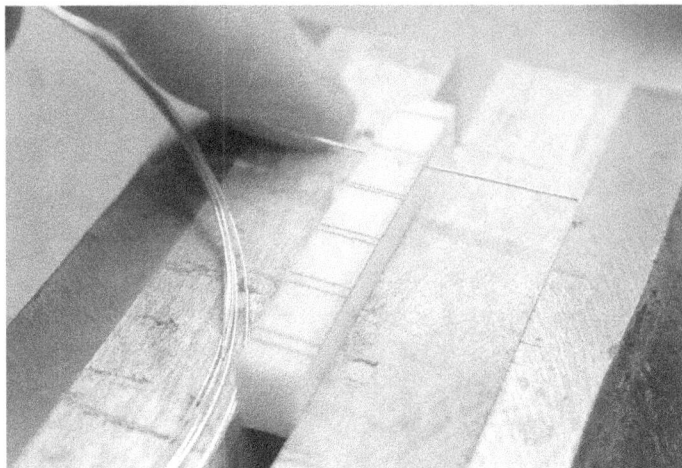

Photo 22-75 – *The string is used as a gauge to check the slot. It must fit well in the slot, with no binding or rattling, and sit cleanly on the slot bottom.*

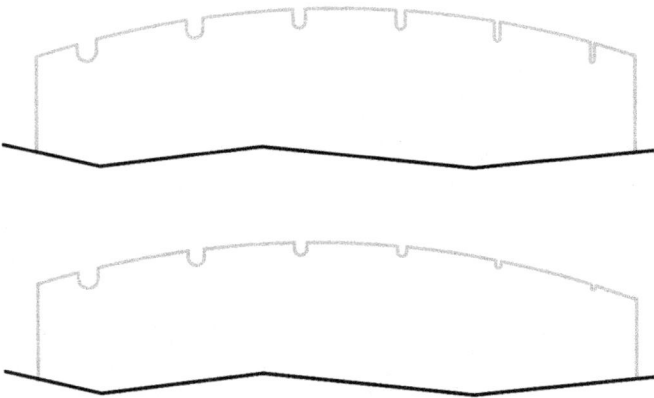

Figure 22-10 – *The top of the nut is cut down so the depth of each string slot is the same as the diameter of the string that will go in it. The slots for the thicker strings can be made a bit shallower, but care is taken to be sure all slots are deeper than half the diameter of their strings.*

Photo 22-76 – *The slotted nut. Final shaping, polishing, and installation of the nut will be done following the setup operation.*

8. The slot for the B string is cut next. If a full set of 6 nut files is available, this one is done in exactly the same manner as the high E string, but using the 0.016″ (0.41mm) wide nut file. If only the minimal file set is on hand, then this slot is also cut using the 0.013″ (0.33mm) file. This file is narrower than the slot has to be, as can be seen by the template lines for it. The cut is started as in step 6 above, but the file is positioned so the cut will be equidistant from the template lines for this slot. Filing continues until there is a shallow slot across the nut top. The file is removed and a sharp knife is used to cut right on each of the template lines for this slot, then the bits of template label between the lines are removed with the knife. Filing continues until the slot is cut to depth, as per step 6.

9. Now the slot must be widened by shaving down the side walls. This is done by starting the file cutting edge right near the top of the slot but so its cutting edge is directed to one of the sides (**photo 22-69**, **figure 22-9.2**). As the file is pushed it is kind of rolled down the wall of the slot to pare away material from the slot wall (**photos 22-70, 22-71; figure 22-9.3**). Shaving the side walls of the slot is done on one side then the other (**photos 22-72** through **22-74; figures 22-9.4, 22-9.5**). As this motion is repeated, the walls will be filed away and the slot will widen. The slot is cleaned and examined often as progress is made. Care is taken to be sure the slot is widening evenly on both sides and along its depth. After a few widening strokes are done, the B string is used as a gauge to check the slot width (**photo 22-75**). The floor of the slot must be rounded in shape and the string must fit in the slot all the way to the bottom, without binding. Widening is repeated as necessary until a good fit is achieved.

10. The remaining slots are filed in like fashion. If the three file set is used, the slots for the G and A strings are filed in the same manner as the high E string slot, and those for the D and low E strings are filed in the same manner as the B string slot. If a full set of six files is available, each slot is filed with the file matching the diameter of its string. The strings are used as gauges to be sure each slot is wide enough for its string. Slot widths are adjusted as needed using the slot side filing technique.

11. Any remaining template label material is removed from the top of the nut between the slots using a knife. Any adhesive remaining is removed with naphtha and a rag. The top of the nut must now be shaped so that all of the slots are only as tall as the strings that will fit into them. At this point, the slot for the low E string should be about as deep as the diameter of the low E string. But each successive slot is increasingly deeper than the diameter of its string, with the high E string slot being considerably deeper (**figure 22-10**). The top of the nut is selectively sanded down by rubbing it across the sanding board, just as was done when the top of the nut was originally shaped (**photo 22-59**). The strings are used as gauges indicating how deep each slot should be.

All slots are now at their approximate finish depths (**photo 22-76**). There is more shaping of the nut to be done, also some polishing, but this will wait until after the guitar is set up. Setup will involve additional checking and possibly additional filing of the nut slots.

---

1. Mottola, R.M. (2020) Drawing the Traditional Acoustic Guitar Pickguard. *American Lutherie #141*, p. 62

23 Stringing Up and Setup

Stringing the guitar up for the first time is probably the most significant construction milestone. It will be the first time the complex and lightweight structure will be subject to the stress of string tension. And it will be the first time the instrument speaks. If ever there is a moment during construction that can be considered magical, this is it.

All experienced luthiers recognize an interesting phenomenon that occurs when the newly constructed guitar is first strung up and played. The voice of the instrument changes rapidly while the first few notes are played, but settles down after a few minutes into what will be its true voice. I and other luthiers have made informal experiments to try to ascertain what is going on structurally and acoustically during these first moments of a guitar's life, but none of these investigations have been particularly fruitful in identifying any dramatic physical changes. Theories abound, mostly centering on the fact that the first application of string tension is stressing the structure and producing small physical changes to the instrument. The neck is bending upward, which in turn strains the trussrod. The neck block is tilting inward, which presses the top above the soundhole down. The bridge tilts forward, which further presses the top in front of it down, and also humps up that part of the top behind the bridge. These changes strain the ribs and the back in subtle ways. The strings directly press on the nut and saddle, pressing them into firmer contact with their mounting slots.

Of course, there is a distinct possibility that the reason no significant structural changes related to first stringing up have been found is that there are none. This suggests the possibility that the sound of the guitar is not actually changing, but it is the luthier's perception of the sound of the instrument that is changing.

As luthiers, our moment of joy at the birth of a new instrument is somewhat fleeting. Once the instrument settles down and can retain its tuning for more than just a few minutes, it is time to set it up. Setup involves making adjustments for optimal playability. Some of these adjustments are made to the nut and saddle. After these are made, the final shaping and polishing of those parts will be performed.

With any large and complex construction project there are always opportunities for things to go wrong. The construction steps of the process described in this book were particularly designed to reduce most of these, and to provide ample opportunities for correction. Although unlikely, remaining issues at this point in construction are various buzzes and rattles. Identifying some of the more common sources of these and fixing them are discussed at the end of this chapter.

Construction and Troubleshooting

Stringing Up and Setting Up

☐ **Stringing Up**

Some of the details which follow may seem a little picky, but the setup of a guitar has a big effect on how well it plays. During setup, the strings will be tightened and loosened repeatedly, and this often results in broken strings. It is a good idea to have more than one set of strings on hand. Stringing up is done with the guitar face up on the bench with the neck pointing to the left. The neck should be supported by a neck rest or padded block near the nut.

A string winder is helpful when stringing up but is not absolutely necessary.

1. A check is made to be sure neck bolts have not loosened during the latter stages of construction. The nut is placed in its slot if it is not there already, and centered.

2. The knobs on the tuning machines are turned so all the holes in the string posts are perpendicular to the guitar centerline. The two E strings will be strung up before the others. Doing so will prevent the strings from pulling the nut sideways out of its slot.

3. The low E string will be strung up first. The ball of the string is dropped into the bridge pin hole, and a check is made to be sure the fat part of the string at the ball will fit in the slot in the pin hole, so the ball can be pulled up against the bridge plate. If the slot is too narrow, it is widened a bit using a needle file until it is wide enough to accommodate the string. Bridge pins generally come slotted but since the pin holes were slotted

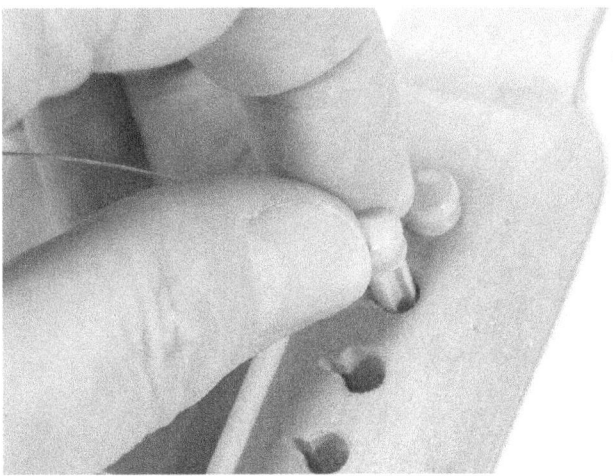

Photo 23-1– The bridge pin holes have slots for the strings, so if a slotted bridge pin is used its slot is oriented toward the tail of the bridge.

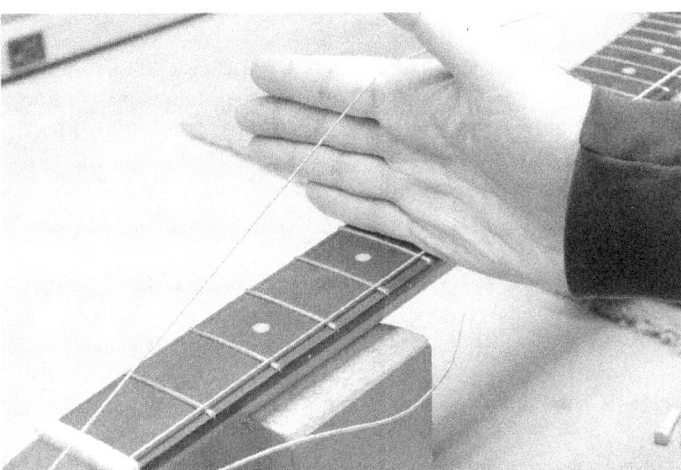

Photo 23-2– To determine how much slack is needed, the hand is placed on the fretboard, karate-chop style, and the string is run over it.

Photo 23-3– The string is bent sharply at right angles, where it enters the hole in the post and also where it exits the hole.

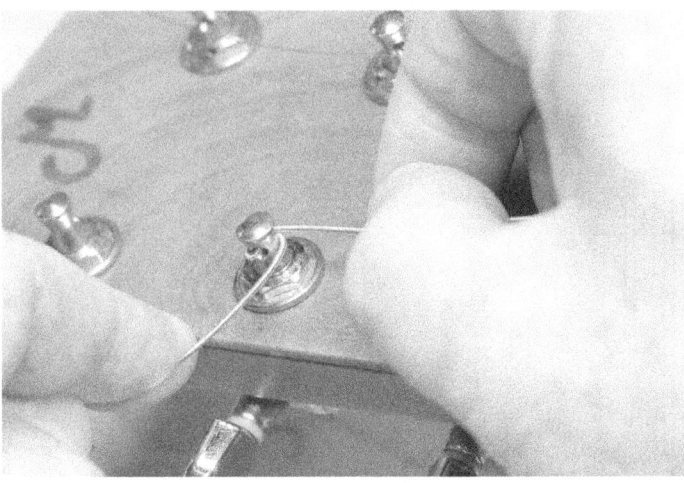

Photo 23-4– The tail end of the string is wrapped tightly around the top of the post, then passed under the string.

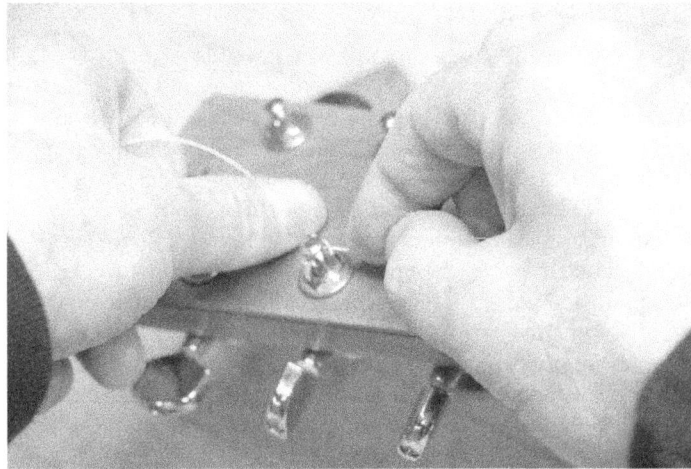

Photo 23-5– Finally, the tail end is wrapped tightly over the string so the tail will remain parallel to the surface of the headstock.

a tug on the string straight upward is given, to be sure the ball is set against the bridge plate.

4. The free end of the string is inserted into the hole in the tuning post. The string is always inserted into the end of the hole closest to the guitar's centerline. Some slack in the string is needed so the string will be able to wind around the post a few times when it is eventually tuned to pitch. The easiest way to estimate the amount of slack needed is to put the right hand on the middle of the fretboard, karate-chop style, with the string running over it (**photo 23-2**). The free end of the string is pulled taught with the left hand. Then the karate-chop hand is removed, and the string is bent to a sharp right angle where it enters the post hole, and in the opposite direction where it exits the post hole (**photo 23-3**).

5. The free end of the string is tightly looped around the post, going toward the end of the headstock. It is pulled under the string where it enters the post hole (**photo 23-4**), and then is tightly bent up and over that part of the string (**photo 23-5**). The free end should now be lying down against the headstock surface. With one hand, the string is gripped where it passes

during construction, the slots in the pins will not be used. So, when the pin is inserted, the slot in its shaft should face the tail end of the guitar (**photo 23-1**). The pin is inserted snugly, then over the nut to put some tension on it, while the other hand is used to tighten the tuning knob, making sure the windings around the post wind *down* the post. This is done until there is enough tension on the string to hold it in its nut slot.

6. The high E string is strung in like fashion. Because this string is so thin, there will probably be no need for adjustment to the bridge pin string slot. Since this string is on the opposite side of the guitar centerline, the dress of the string into and around the post will be a mirror image of that of the low E string.

7. Adjusting the setback. The strings are not tuned all the way up to pitch, but enough tension is put on them to hold the nut in place and so the strings will stay in place on the saddle. A check is made to be sure the nut is properly centered in its slot. If not, it is pushed into position. For one of the two E strings, setback is measured at the nut, from the outer edge of the fretboard to the outer edge of the string, using a small ruler.

Now at the saddle, the string is pushed and pulled into position on the saddle so that it is parallel to its edge of the fretboard (**photo 23-6**). Parallelism can be eyeballed, or the ruler can be used to measure the setback at the soundhole end of the fretboard. Note that the string may have to be held in position on the saddle with one hand. A sharp pencil mark is made on the top of the saddle on both sides of the string.

The string is pushed out of the way and a needle file or nut file is used to file a shallow nick between the pencil marks, just deep enough to locate the string. This is not a slot, but the tiniest of nicks. The string is slid back into position on the saddle. It is possible to feel when the string drops into the nick.

8. Step 7 is repeated for the other E string.

9. Calculating string spacing at the saddle. The distance between the centers of the two E strings is measured at the saddle using a flexible ruler (**photo 23-7**). That distance is divided by 5 and the result is written down. That will be the distance between string centers for all the strings. Note that proportional spacing is not necessary at the saddle, because the distance between strings here is wide enough so differences are not apparent when looking at the string spacing.

10. The remaining strings are strung up as described above, again not to pitch but with enough tension to hold their locations on the saddle. The remaining strings are pushed and pulled into approximate spacing on the saddle. The ruler and the string center spacing measurement, and also the luthier's eyes, are used to work the strings to equal spacing at their centers. When the spacing is satisfactory, pencil marks are made on both sides of each string, the strings are pushed out of the way, and the saddle top is nicked between each pair of pencil lines (**photo 23-8**). Then the strings are moved back into their places.

11. The strings are tuned to pitch. Excess string length is cut from the strings near the tuning posts, using diagonal cutting pliers. The length of the tails should be a bit less than the distance from the hole in the tuning machine string post down to

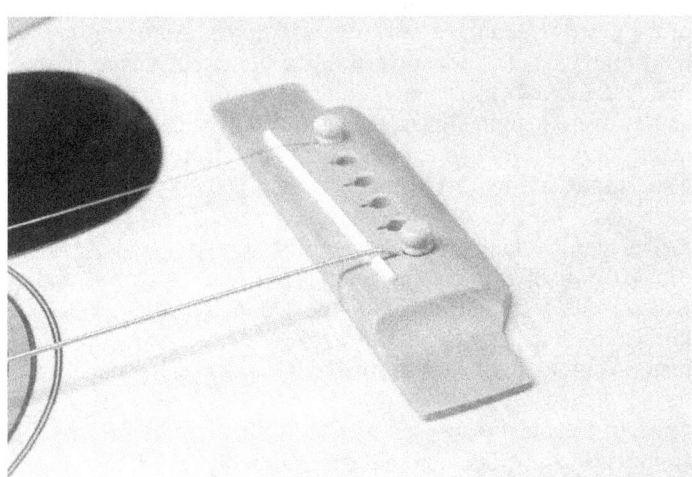

Photo 23-6– The two E strings are mounted first. The strings are pushed around on the saddle to make the strings parallel to their respective edges of the fretboard. This can be done visually or using a ruler.

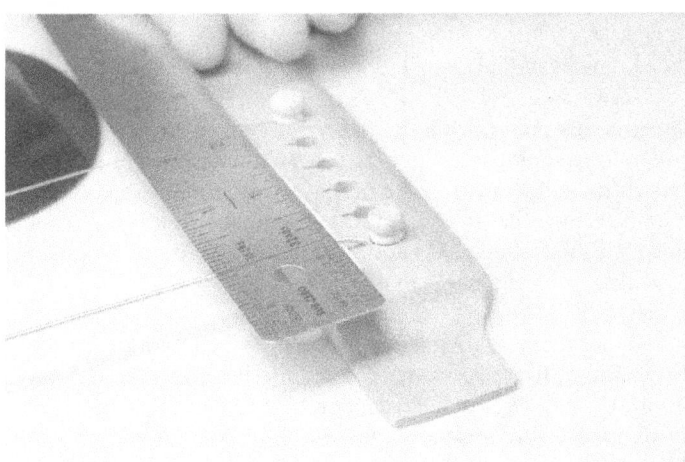

Photo 23-7– The distances between the centers of the two E strings is measured.

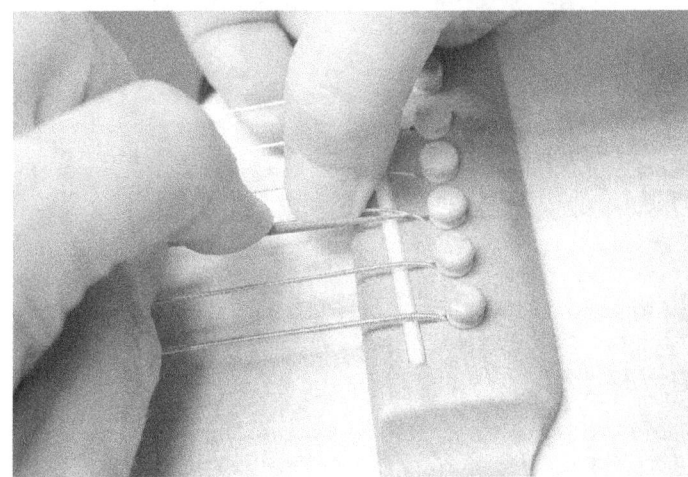

Photo 23-8– After every string's position on the saddle is determined and marked, each string is pushed aside and a tiny locating nick is made on the saddle using a needle file or nut file.

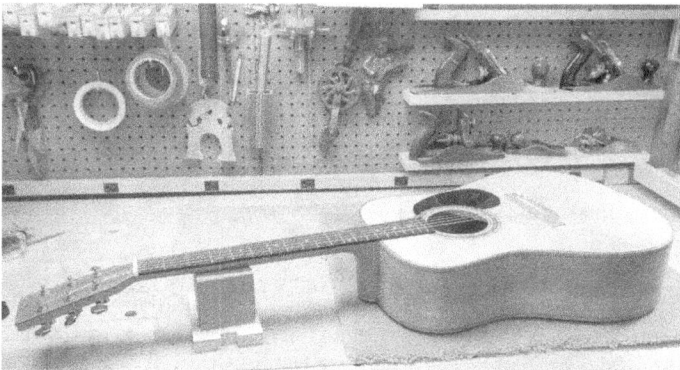

Photo 23-9– The setup for checking and adjusting relief and action, with the neck supported on a neck rest.

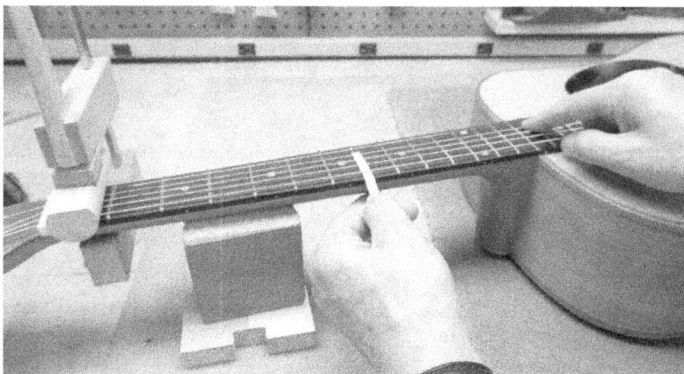

Photo 23-10– Checking the relief. A clamp and dowel are used to "fret" the strings at the first fret. One finger frets the G string at the fourteenth fret. The space between the top of the sixth fret and the underside of the string is measured with feeler gauges or thicknesses of paper.

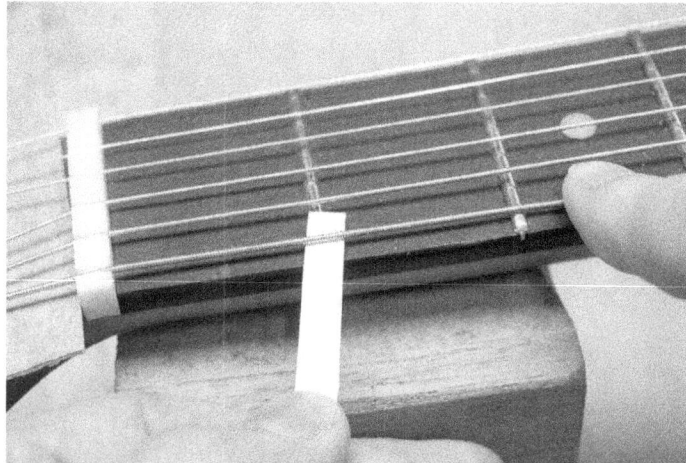

Photo 23-11– Checking the action at the nut. Here two thicknesses of paper are used to check the gap at the first fret, while a finger is used to fret the string at the third fret.

the top surface of the headstock. Then the tails are bent down using needle nose pliers, so their sharp ends are not likely to stab the luthier or the player.

The strings will need regular re-tuning to pitch as the structure of the guitar moves in response to string tension.

 The following setup operations are not performed until the guitar has settled down to the point where it can maintain its tuning for more than a few minutes.

▫ Adjusting Relief

A generally well-setup guitar will have a small amount of relief (also called up bow) to the fretboard. This allows for optimal action by providing some space for the vibrational displacement of the strings. Although back bow (negative relief) will invariably cause fret buzzing unless the string action is very high, and although way too much relief can cause audible intonation problems, there is quite a large range of relief values which will work well for an acoustic guitar. This is fortunate because relief adjustment affects string action and affords us one of the most straightforward ways to adjust the action, particularly if it is too low. But as a starting point in setting up a new guitar the relief will be set to nominal specs.

1. The guitar is tuned to pitch for the relief measurement.

2. Relief is measured by fretting at the first fret and the fourteenth fret, and then measuring the gap between the underside of the G string and the crown of the sixth fret. All of this requires three hands, so it is generally easier to put a capo on the first fret, fret the G string at the fourteenth fret with one hand, and measure with the other. If a capo is not available, a short length of dowel *lightly* clamped across the strings works fine as a substitute (**photo 23-10**).

3. The nominal target measurement for the gap is 0.012˝ (0.3mm), which will provide good action and intonation, and will also allow for adjustment to the action higher and a bit lower. This gap can be checked with a feeler gauge, or approximated with three thicknesses of 20lb (75gsm) printer paper.

Since there is really no one "correct" value, I find it easier to simply eyeball it. The nominal gap is roughly the same as the thickness of the high E string, so this check can be made with the guitar on the bench and the luthier crouched down and looking at the fretboard from the high E string side. For a right-handed guitar, the neck and headstock should point to the right.

 For a left-handed guitar, this check is done with the neck and headstock pointing to the left.

Done in this manner, it is easy to visually compare the gap between the underside of the G string and the crown of the sixth fret with the thickness of the high E string. If the gap is greater than that, then the trussrod must be tightened. If it is less than that or if the fretboard is back bowed, then the trussrod must be loosened.

4. It is not really known in advance how much tightening or loosening of the trussrod will be required to effect the change desired. On the example instruments, access to the trussrod adjusting nut is through the soundhole. If a conventionally-sized Allen key is used to adjust the trussrod, the strings will have to be slackened enough to get the luthier's hand and the wrench inside to make the adjustment. Luthiers with fat hands like mine may have to pull the bridge pins and unhook the strings at

Action	Low E String @ 12th	High E String @ 12th
Low	0.110″ (0.28mm)	0.080″ (2.03mm)
Medium	0.125″ (3.18mm)	0.095″ (2.41mm)
High	0.155″ (3.94mm)	0.125″ (3.18mm)

Table 23-1– Typical action measurements for acoustic steel string guitars.

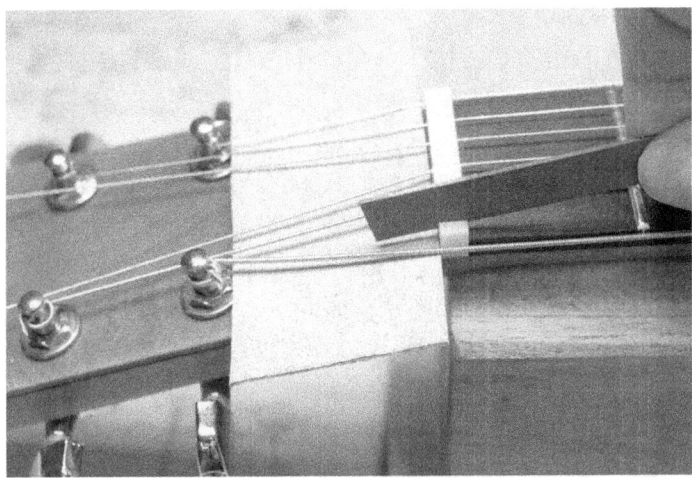

Photo 23-12– String slots in the nut are filed at an angle that is slightly less than that of the headstock. A piece of cardboard protects the surface of the headstock from the end of the file.

the bridge to provide access. The trussrod is tightened or loosened a bit as required.

Two things to note. If the trussrod is currently under tension one way or the other, then small movements of the adjusting nut will make for fairly big changes in relief. If the adjusting nut offers any resistance, I recommend turning it no more than ⅛ turn at a time in whatever direction is needed. When turning the adjusting nut it should be remembered that, when facing the adjusting nut, turning clockwise tightens it and will result in less relief, and turning counterclockwise "loosens" it and will result in more relief.

The other thing to note is that it is possible that the trussrod is in its neutral range right now. If it *is* in its neutral range it will not offer much resistance to turning, possibly for as much as a half turn. If so, it will first be necessary to take up this slack before any adjustment will have an effect.

After the adjustment, the strings are put back in place and the guitar is tuned up to pitch. The relief is checked again and any change is noted. The process of checking and adjusting the trussrod is repeated until relief is at approximately the specified value. Note that sometimes trussrod adjustments take a bit of time to settle down. It may be found the next day that the relief value is different. If so, it is adjusted again.

☐ **Adjusting Nut Slot Depths**

When the nut was originally slotted, the depths of the slots were left a bit higher than is required for optimal playing. The final depths are adjusted now.

1. The guitar is tuned to pitch.

2. The nut string slot depth check is simple to do. The low E string is fretted at the third fret, with the fretting finger close to the second fret. Then the height of the gap between the bottom of the string and the crown of the first fret is checked. The nominal target depth is between 0.008″ (0.2mm) and 0.004″ (0.1mm). Depth can be checked with feeler gauges if gauges this thin are available. If not, a doubled-over strip of plain 20lb (75gsm) printer paper is about 0.008″ (0.2mm) thick, and can be used as a gauge. The string is fretted as described, and the paper strip is pulled through the gap (**photo 23-11**). If there is just a bit of resistance to the pull then this gap is about right. If the paper strip pulls out with no resistance then the gap is too high and the floor of the nut slot must be lowered.

3. Lowering the floor of the string slot is done in exactly the same way as when filing the slot originally, except this time it is being done with the nut in place on the guitar. Before starting, a piece of cereal box cardboard is cut to fit between the headstock side of the nut and the posts of the first two tuning machines. This is slipped in place under the strings and is taped down if necessary. The cardboard will protect the top of the headstock from damage from an errant nut file.

String tension is slackened enough so the string can be removed from the nut slot, then the slot is carefully deepened just a bit with the appropriately sized nut file. Care is taken to be sure to maintain the angle of the slot floor (**photo 23-12**) and to add the tiny flat at the fretboard end. No more than a few strokes with the nut file are taken until a good feel is developed for how quickly it is cutting. Filing debris is thoroughly cleaned out of the slot. Then the string is put back in the slot and tuned up to pitch. A critical look is taken under the string, where it exits the slot on the fretboard side, to be sure the string is fully seated to the full depth of the slot. If the slot is too narrow at the bottom, the string may not touch the floor. The slot is touched up as necessary. Note that if tuning the wound strings back to pitch results in a "tink" sound as tension is increased, the tiny flat at the fretboard end of that nut slot should be lengthened just a bit.

4. Steps 2 and 3 are repeated until there is just a bit of friction when trying to pull the paper strip out.

5. Steps 2 through 4 are repeated for the rest of the strings. The protective cardboard is removed from the headstock.

 Despite all appropriate care taken, it sometimes happens that the floor of one or more of the string slots gets filed too deep. This can be readily seen during the string slot depth check– the string will be in contact with the top of the first fret. There are two options if one or more slots are filed too deep. The first is to discard the nut and construct a new one. The second option is to fill the offending slots and then refile them. This latter approach is described in the sidebar.

☐ Adjusting Action

The action is the height of the strings over the frets. Because the distance from string to frets varies along the length of the fretboard, it is the convention to take this measurement only at the 12th fret. When we consider the action of all the strings we usually express this in general terms, such as high action, medium action, or low action. When the guitar is being set up we must also consider (and measure and adjust) action for each individual string. **Table 23-1** shows typical action measurements for acoustic steel string guitars. Note that the table shows values for only the E strings. Note also that the values for the high E string are always 0.03″ (0.8MM) lower than those for the low E string. This differential is necessary because the low E string moves farther when it vibrates than the high E string does, so it needs more space between the string and the fret tops to prevent it from buzzing against them.

The table does not provide explicit values for the action of the other strings. In general, the action for these strings will be set up so it decreases evenly from the low E string to the high E string. Because the total E to E action difference is only 0.03″ (0.8MM), this means that the action of each successively higher pitched string will be 0.006″ (0.15MM) lower than that of the preceding string.

Experienced luthiers usually set up the relative action among the strings and the general action for all the strings at the same time. This is possible given experience in performing this operation, and a high degree of dimensional accuracy maintained during construction of the instrument. In my observation, lutherie novices following the construction process described in this book are best served by first setting up the relative action, followed by the general action.

Action is checked by measuring the gap between the underside of each string and the crown of the 12th fret directly below it. This can be measured with feeler gauges but is more often done using a ruler or digital calipers or a special-purpose string action gauge. Using any of these, it is necessary to get the eye down so it is level with the side of the string, so it is possible to sight the underside of the string and the measuring tool behind it.

Filling a Nut String Slot for Re-Filing

If a string slot in the nut is cut too deep, it is usually possible to fill the slot and then re-file it to the proper depth. The nut is removed from the guitar and clamped in a vise for this work. Small pieces of masking tape are applied over the slot on both sides of the nut. The top edges of the tape should come up to near the top of the slot (**figure 23-1**). The tape serves as dams to contain the filling.

Baking soda is packed into the slot and leveled off to the top edges of the tape. A flat wood toothpick is a useful tool for this. Then a single drop of thin cyanoacrylate glue is applied to the baking soda, using a micro transfer pipette.

Baking soda is an accelerant for cyanoacrylate glue, so the glue will cure instantly. The tape pieces are removed and the sides of the nut are cleaned up as necessary. The string slot is re-filed in the same manner as when it was first made.

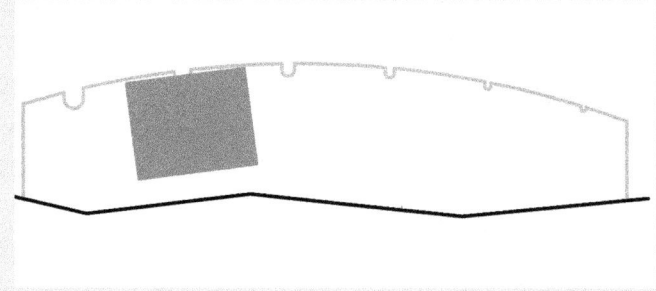

Figure 23-1– Tape pieces are applied over both ends of the string slot to serve as dams during filling.

If the ruler is used, it is simply positioned with its zero end on top of the 12th fret and behind the string (**photo 23-13**). It is tedious to read though, due to the fine scale needed.

Digital calipers are easier to use than a ruler here. The easiest way to use digital calipers for this measurement is to use the depth gauge. The probe is set on top of the 12th fret with the

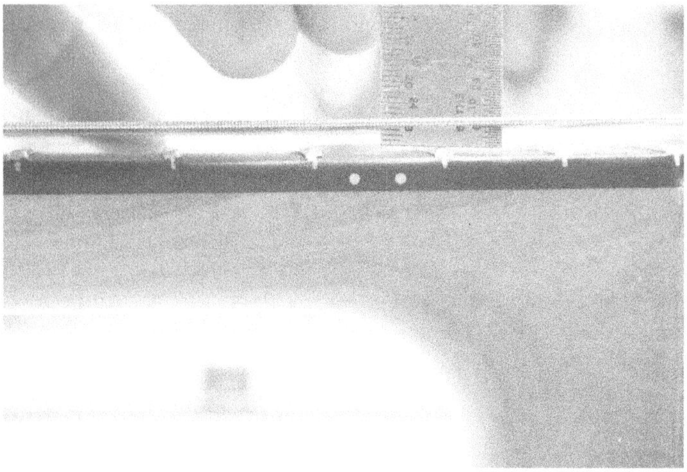

Photo 23-13– Action can be measured with a fine ruler, but the markings are difficult to see.

Photo 23-14– Action can be measured with the depth gauge of digital calipers. But keeping the end of the probe balanced on top of the fret is difficult.

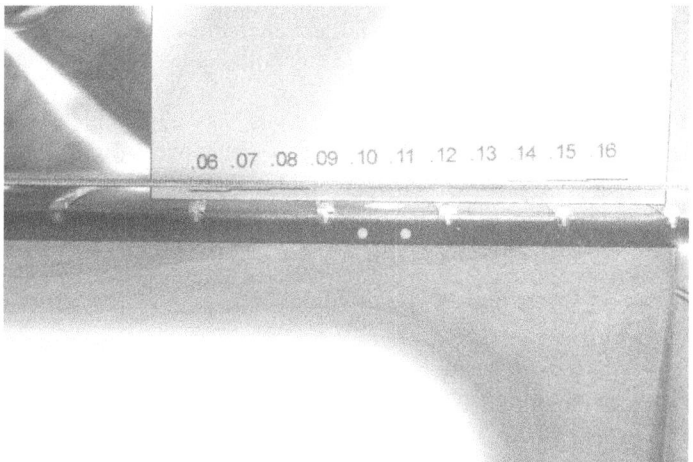

Photo 23-15– Action can be easily measured using a special-purpose string action gauge. The one shown is included in the template books for the example instruments.

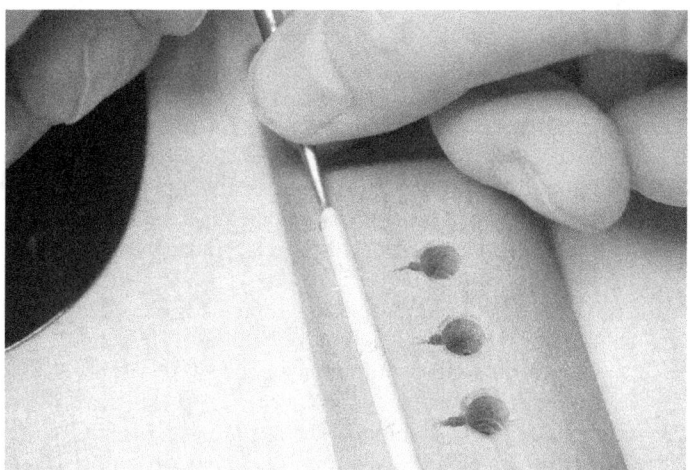

Photo 23-16– Removing the saddle. If it can't be grasped, the sharp point of an awl is stuck in the treble end (where the prick mark will be less noticeable to the player) and the saddle is lifted out of its slot.

gauge behind the string. Then the gauge is opened up until the base of the depth gauge just disappears above the bottom of the string (**photo 23-14**). Although a bit easier to manage than the ruler, measurements done with this tool are also tedious, because the tip of the narrow depth probe must be balanced on top of the fret.

The special-purpose string action gauge is the easiest tool to use for this measurement. Nice metal commercial gauges are available from lutherie suppliers. A gauge is also available in the template books for the example instruments. This can be printed on card stock and cut out with scissors. Gauges of this type consist of a card ruled in 100^{ths} of an inch but with the marks arrayed across the width of the card. The card is placed on top of the frets and behind the string and then slid along the frets until the mark closest to the string bottom is over the 12th fret (**photo 23-15**). The string action gauge ruler is simple and relaxing to use.

1. Setting the relative action among strings. As mentioned above, it is desirable that, starting with the low E string, the action of each successive string is 0.006˝ (0.15MM) lower than the string preceding it, and that the action of the high E string is 0.03˝ (0.8MM) lower than that of the low E string. In practice, given how small that string-to-string difference is, it is difficult to measure, mark, and cut such tiny differences with great accuracy. For all practical purposes, if the action of the high E string is 0.03˝ (0.8MM) lower than that of the low E string, and if each successive string is *somewhat* lower than the string before it, the result will be perfectly fine. If the top of the saddle was shaped according to the description of that operation in the

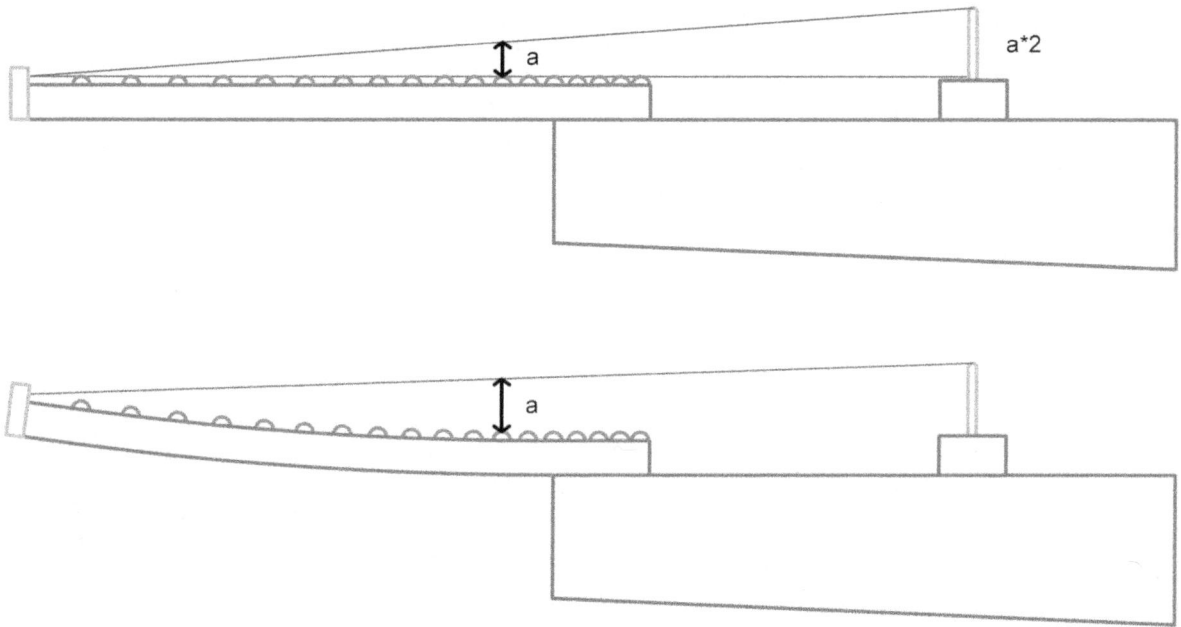

Figure 23-2– Action of the guitar strings is related to other aspects of the guitar's geometry. The upper figure shows the relationship between action (a) and bridge/saddle height. A change in action of any amount will require a change of bridge saddle height that is twice that amount. The lower figure shows how neck relief generally affects action. Increasing relief increases action.

previous chapter, usually little or no additional adjustment will be required here.

The action of the low E string is measured and recorded.

2. The action of the high E string is measured and recorded. If the difference between these measurements is approximately 0.03″ (0.8mm), then the rest of this step is skipped.

If the difference between these measurements is considerably less than 0.03″ (0.8mm), the action of the high E string will have to be lowered until the difference equals 0.03″ (0.8mm). This is accomplished by using the appropriate nut file to deepen the nick in the saddle that the high E string is sitting on. This should be done a little at a time, checking the action of the string often, until the desired action is achieved.

If the difference between these measurements is considerably more than 0.03″ (0.8mm), the action of the low E string will have to be lowered until the difference equals 0.03″ (0.8mm). This is done in exactly the same manner, using the appropriate nut file to deepen the low E string nick in the saddle.

3. Now the action of the A, D, G, and B strings are checked and adjusted if necessary. As mentioned, the action of each string should be 0.006″ (0.15mm) lower than the string preceding it from low E to high E, but this accuracy will be difficult to achieve. Action is lowered if necessary using a nut file to deepen the notch for that string on the saddle, as described in step 2.

4. If steps 2 and 3 resulted in anything other than minor filing of the nicks, the saddle must be removed and the top of the saddle must be sanded again to shape, as described in the previous chapter. Here, sanding is done until each nick is just barely visible. Sanding the top of the saddle will widen the width of the saddle top crown, so additional chamfering must be performed on the saddle top to maintain a thin and uniform crown.

 Because the saddle sits low in the slot it may not be easy to grab it to remove it. If so, an awl or machinist's scribe can be used to remove the saddle. The point of the tool is poked into the treble end of the saddle and then the tool is lifted (not pried), lifting the saddle with it (**photo 23-16**). A recalcitrant saddle can also be removed by holding one of the pins that were used to locate the bridge when it was glued on, and feeling around inside the guitar for one of the holes drilled through the bridge plate. The pin is inserted in the hole, and used to push the saddle up out of its slot.

5. After the relative action is set, the general action can be set, using the values for the high E string in **table 23-1** and the current measured action value for that string. Lutherie novices should probably not aim for the lowest action possible. Very low action is only achievable when precise fret dressing was done. At least for the initial setup, it is usually wise to aim for medium action.

If the current general action is approximately equal to the desired action as specified in the table, then no additional work needs to be done and the remainder of this step can be skipped.

If the action needs to be raised, there are two ways to do this. These can be used individually or in combination.

The first way to raise the action is to raise the saddle, either by building a new, higher, saddle, or by inserting hardwood shims under the saddle. It should be noted that doing this requires the total thickness of the shims to be twice the amount that action needs to be raised. The geometry involved is shown in **figure 23-2**. Appropriate shim material includes lengths of hardwood purfling lines. This material is 0.02″ (0.5mm) thick, so each piece of this material will raise the action by 0.01″ (0.25mm). The limit to which action can be raised by shimming is 0.04″ (1mm). Shimming any higher than this endangers the integrity of the saddle slot.

 Only small changes in height can be made in this manner. Larger changes made by shimming or otherwise raising the saddle will have adverse effects on the structure of the guitar which can easily result in damage.

The second way to raise the action is to increase the amount of relief by adjusting the trussrod. The geometry involved is shown in **figure 23-2**. This is accomplished by turning the trussrod adjustment nut counter clockwise by small increments, checking action after each adjustment, until the desired action is attained.

Note that this adjustment is made possible by the use of a double action trussrod. Although it can theoretically provide a wide range of adjustment, the adjuster nut should *never* be turned more than a total of ½ turn. Doing so can damage the neck or the rod.

If action needs to be lowered, there are two ways to do this. These can be used individually or in combination.

Action may be lowered by lowering the saddle height. This is the preferred method of doing this. This is done by removing the saddle and shaving down its bottom surface. The amount of material to be removed will be twice the amount that the action needs to be lowered. There is a limit to how much material can be removed here. This is based on a minimal saddle exposure

Photo 23-17 – *The half pencil is used to mark the level of the tops of the strings as they exit the slots on the back of the nut.*

(the distance between the top of the bridge and the lowest point on the top of the saddle) of 0.04″ (1mm). To determine the maximum amount of material that can be removed from the base of the saddle, the distance from the top of the bridge to the lowest point on the top of the saddle (usually under the high E string) is measured. Subtracting 0.04″ (1mm) from that yields the maximum amount of material that can be removed. And halving that value yields the maximum amount that action can be lowered in this way.

Action can also be lowered (but only a tiny amount) by decreasing the amount of relief, by adjusting the trussrod. Because the relief had previously been set up to near optimal, there is not much range available here for lowering action. This is accomplished by turning the trussrod adjustment nut clockwise by small increments, checking action after each adjustment, until the desired action is attained. Relief must also be checked after each adjustment, and care must be taken to be sure there is always *some* relief, even if that amount is small.

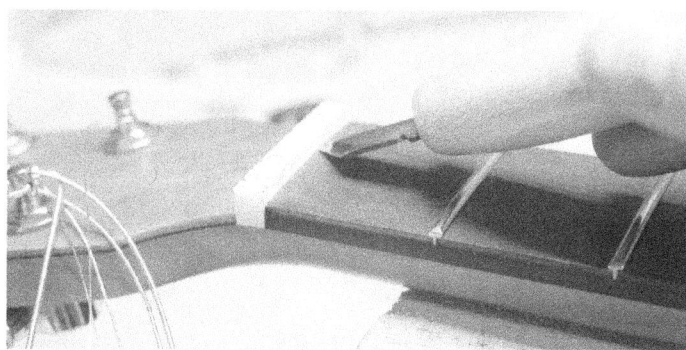

Photo 23-20– *The level of the top of the nut slot on the fretboard side is lightly scribed onto the nut using a knife.*

Photo 23-21– *The sanding board is used to chamfer the headstock half of the nut top down to the marked lines. Note the tilt of the nut toward the luthier.*

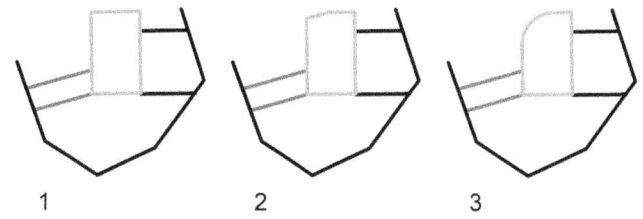

Figure 23-3– *End view of the shaping of the top surface of the nut. The profile begins rectangular (1). The back (headstock) half is chamfered to the same angle as the top surface of the headstock (2). Finally the back half is smoothly rounded over (3).*

Photo 23-18– *The half pencil is used to mark the level of the tops of the strings as they enter the slots on the front of the nut.*

☐ Checking for Rattles and String Buzzes

At this point the guitar is checked for the appropriate sounding of notes all over the fretboard. This is done methodically, playing each open and fretted note sequentially on each string, picking with up and down strokes, and picking soft and hard for each. This is done to detect any rattles or buzzes which will have to be attended to.

 If the instrument is right-handed, this check is made with the instrument in right-handed playing orientation. If it is a left-handed instrument, the check is made playing in left-handed orientation (neck to the right).

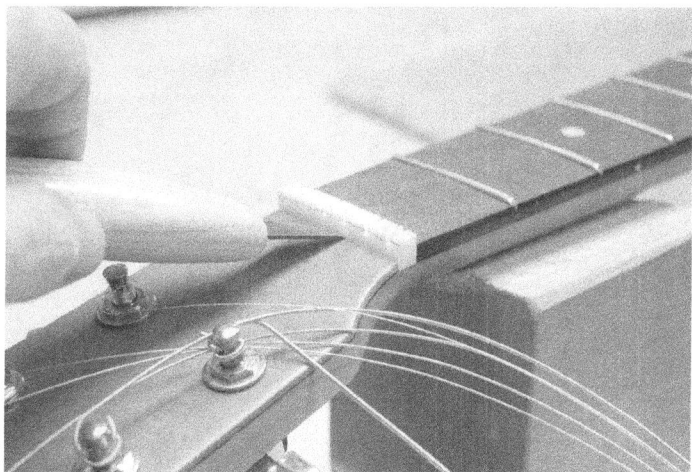

Photo 23-19– *The level of the top of the nut slot on the headstock side is lightly scribed onto the nut using a knife.*

Rattles are loud raspy sounds emanating from the guitar. These are the result of something that is loose. String buzzes are the result of some vibrating part of a string coming in contact with something while it vibrates. Tracking down and fixing the causes of rattles and buzzes is discussed in a subsequent section. If any rattles or buzzes are found, that section should be referred to at this point. Otherwise, attention can turn to the final finishing of the nut and the saddle, and installation of the nut.

□ **Finishing the Nut and Saddle**

1. The top of the nut must be cut down to the level of the tops of the strings. The half pencil is used with its flat sitting on a string to mark the back of the nut on both sides of that string (**photo 23-17**). The same marking is done for the rest of the strings. After the tops of the strings on the back of the nut have been marked, the same thing is done on the front of the nut (**photo 23-18**).

2. Marking the boundaries of the nut slot on the nut. In a later step the nut will be sanded up to fine grits and then polished. But it is undesirable to sand that portion of the nut that sits in the nut slot, because doing so will loosen its fit in the slot. The top edge of the slot on the back of the nut is lightly marked using a knife (**photo 23-19**). Then the same is done on the front of the nut (**photo 23-20**).

3. The strings are slackened and the bridge pins are removed. The strings are removed from the bridge. The top edge of the saddle slot on the saddle front and back are marked using the knife as described above. Then the saddle is removed.

4. Shaping the top of the nut. The top of the nut must be cut down to the pencil marks on the fretboard side of the nut that indicate the tops of the strings as they enter the slots. This step can be done quickly and accurately using the 180 grit sanding board. The nut is grasped top down with both hands so the luthier is looking at its front (fretboard) side. The top surface is sanded with the familiar rocking sanding motion that was used when rough shaping the top of the nut in a previous operation. Sanding is done until the string pencil lines almost disappear.

5. After the top of the nut has been sanded down to the marks on its front, the nut is flipped around so the back (headstock) side is facing the luthier. Sanding will be done again down to the pencil marks, but here the nut will be tilted back toward the luthier 15° while sanding (**photo 23-21**). The result will be a 15° chamfer across the back half of the top of the nut, as shown in **figure 23-3.2**.

6. The slots are thoroughly cleaned of debris using a toothbrush and a knife. A portion of each string is placed into its respective slot to check to be sure the top surface of the nut is level with or slightly below the tops of all strings (**photo 23-22**). This relationship is aesthetic only. But it is important that the slots don't end up being too shallow. If the slots are too shallow the strings will pop out when the strings are tuned to pitch, and the only solution to this will be to make a new nut.

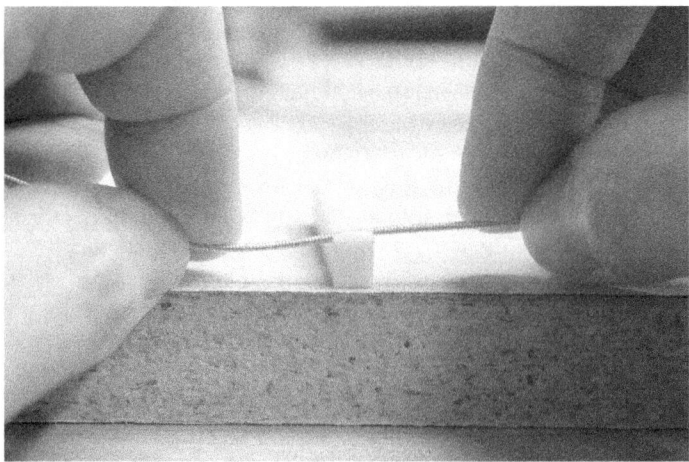

Photo 23-22– The strings are used as depth gauges to measure the string slots. The top surface of the nut should end up flush with the tops of the strings or slightly below the tops of the strings.

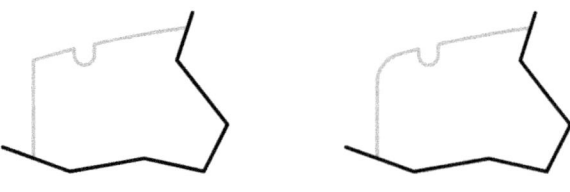

Figure 23-4– The corners of the nut are rounded over to taste.

Photo 23-23– The fully shaped nut and saddle with all the corners rounded over.

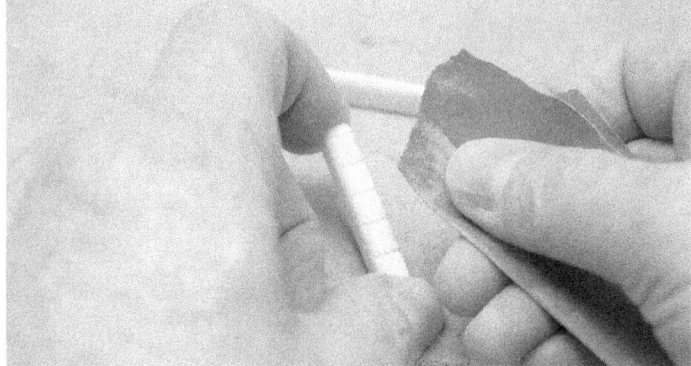

Photo 23-24– Nut and saddle are polished by first sanding with successively finer grits of sandpaper.

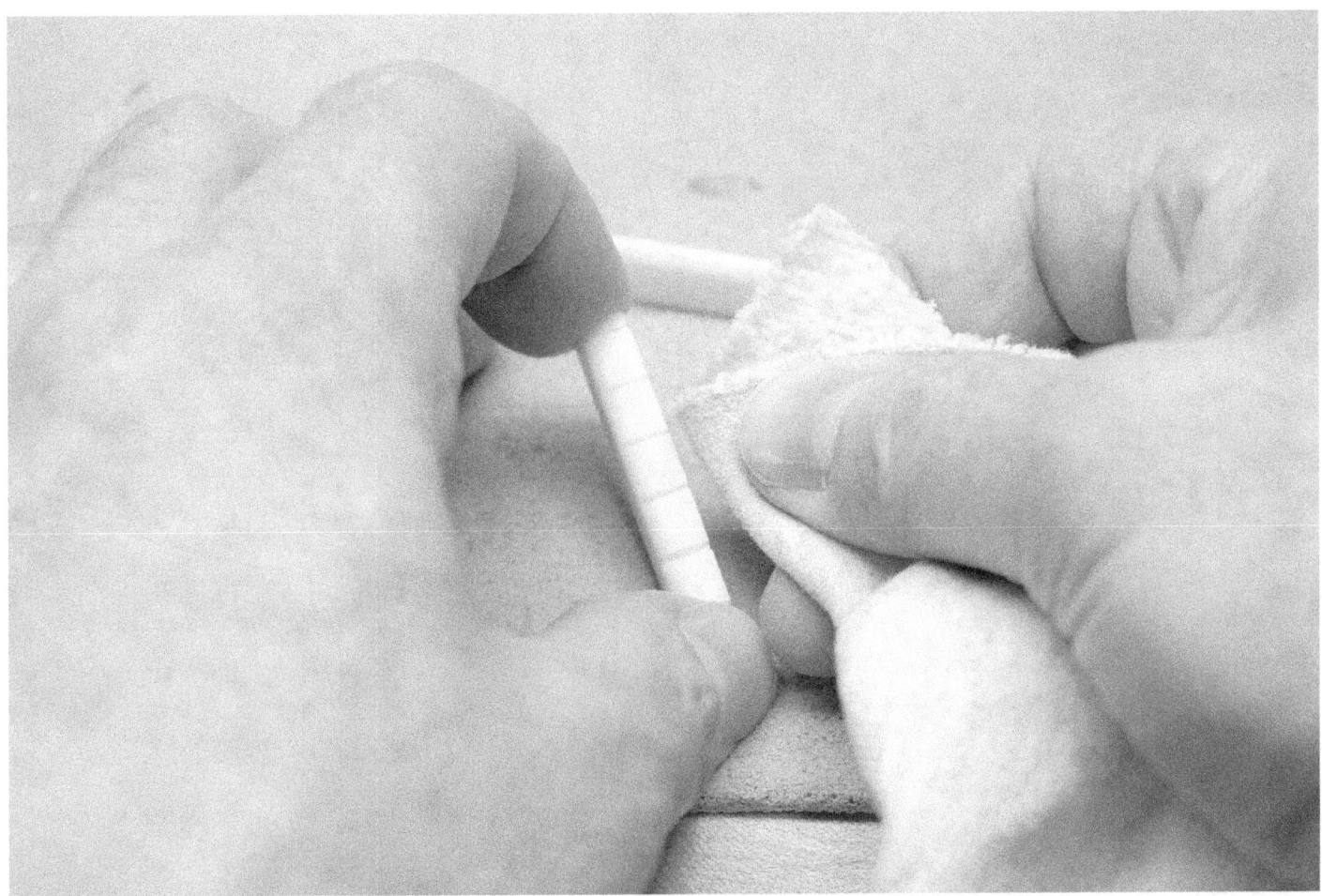

Photo 23-25– Following sanding, the nut and saddle are polished with automotive polishing compounds and a rag.

7. The sanding board and the now familiar sanding motion are used to put an approximately 1/16″ (1.6mm) chamfer along the top back edge of the nut. The nut is tilted at an approximately 45° angle when doing this. After this facet is sanded, the same sanding motion but with varying amounts of tilt is used to turn the chamfer into a fillet (roundover). The roundover covers the rear half of the top of the nut, as shown in **figure 23-3.3**.

8. A round needle file is used to *slightly* widen the back (headstock) ends of the nut slots and round over the slots' back edges. This rounding over of the edges makes it easier for the strings to slip through the slots. Most of the strings take a bend after exiting the back of their slots on the way to the tuning machine posts, and it helps if this bend does not coincide with a sharp edge on the slot.

9. Rounding over the nut and saddle top end edges. These edges are rounded over to taste, by dragging them across the sanding board while varying the tilt of the nut. The result for the nut is shown in **figure 23-4**. After this operation is complete, there will still be fairly sharp corners at the top back end intersections. These corners are smoothed and rounded over to taste, using the sanding board (**photo 23-23**).

10. Polishing the nut and saddle. The nut and saddle are now sanded successively with 220, 320, 400, 600, and 1000-grit sandpaper. This is most easily done with small pieces of sandpaper held in one hand, and the piece to be sanded held in the other (**photo 23-24**). Care should be taken on each piece to *not* sand below the scribed lines that indicate the tops of the respective mounting slots. Doing so, particularly with the coarser grits, will loosen the fit of the nut or saddle in its slot. After each grit, the edge of the piece of sandpaper is used to remove debris from the nut slots. After 600 grit, the fit of the nut is checked to be sure there are no sharp edges protruding, as would happen if the nut were a bit too long. This check is best done by feel, using the finger tips. If the nut is a bit long then it will be necessary to drop back to a coarser grit and then sand the ends to achieve a good fit. Sanding then proceeds up through the grits. When 1000 grit is used, the sharp edges on the top front and front edges of the nut are lightly chamfered just enough so they are not sharp to the touch.

On the saddle, the chamfers at the saddle top and the top edge itself are rounded over to the extent that there is not an obvious flat on the top surface. Every attempt is made to not obliterate the string nicks in the top of the saddle while sanding it. If this is about to happen, the nicks can be refreshed with a needle file, but a very light touch should be used when doing this.

11. When the sanding is complete, debris is cleaned out of the nut slots and saddle nicks. A clean rag with a bit of the heavy cut automotive compound on it is used to polish up what will be the exposed surfaces of nut and saddle (**photo 23-25**).

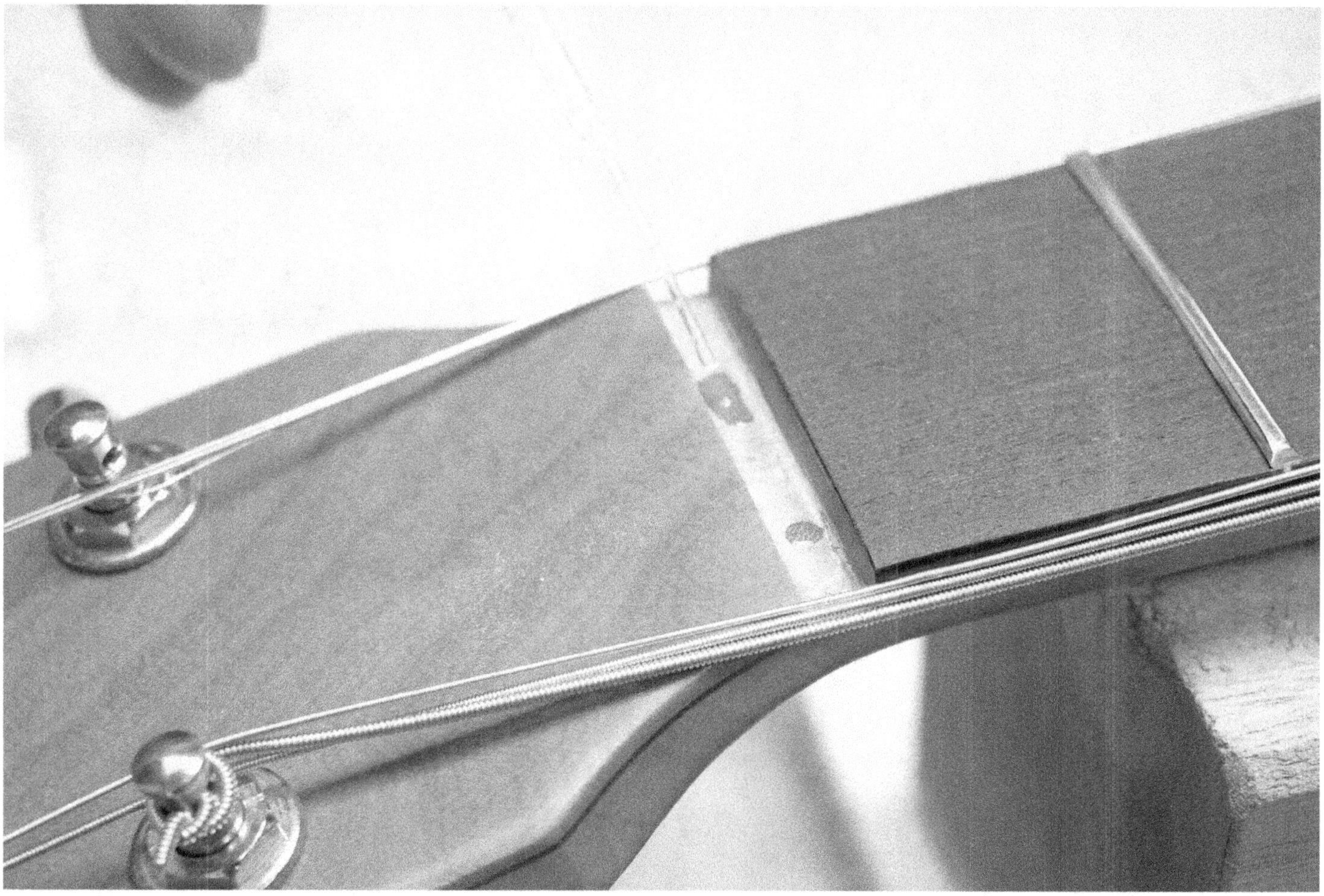

Photo 23-26– Two tiny drops of medium cyanoacrylate glue are applied to the floor of the nut slot, using a micro transfer pipette.

Following that, these surfaces are rubbed briskly with a soft dry rag to bring up some shine. The shine should reveal any sanding flaws, and if any are seen they are sanded out, followed again by the automotive compound, followed by dry buffing. All of the nut and saddle materials mentioned previously in the book rub up to a nice shine.

It is best not to get too carried away polishing up nuts and saddles made from synthetic materials. It is possible on some of them to buff up to a high gloss that looks downright plastic-y.

12. The nut and the saddle are thoroughly washed to remove any compound that collected in the slots and nicks. The compound residue can oxidize bronze string windings.

13. Installing the saddle and gluing the nut. The saddle is installed in its slot, being careful about its orientation. The nut is installed in its slot, dry, for now. The strings are installed and tuned up to loose tension. String tension will be used to press the nut in place during gluing. Tension should not be so high that the strings can't be pulled up out of the nut slots and laid to the sides of the nut. This is done now, and the nut is removed.

A transfer pipette is used to place two *tiny* drops of medium cyanoacrylate glue on the floor of the nut slot, each about ⅓ the way in from the ends (**photo 23-26**). The drops must be *tiny*.

Squeeze-out of the glue *must* be avoided here. The nut is placed in its slot and the strings are returned to their slots in the nut. With the fingers, the side-to-side position of the nut in its slot is quickly adjusted by feel, until it is dead center with no overhang of the nut at either end of the slot. The glue is allowed an hour to fully cure before the strings are tuned to pitch.

Troubleshooting

Methodically playing the guitar as described in the section above called *Checking for Rattles and String Buzzes* will generally elicit any such noises that require attention.

Rattles

As described previously, rattles are loud raspy sounds and are the result of some part of the guitar that is loose. The general technique for identifying a rattle begins by being able to reliably elicit the rattle. Rattles are rarely frequency-specific and can usually be elicited by hard playing.

Once the rattle can be reliably elicited it can be tracked down. The most common sources are a loose trussrod, loose tuning machines or tuning machine buttons, loose bridge pins, a sloppy fit of the saddle in its slot, and loose neck bolts. A rare possibility in a new guitar is a loose brace inside. An embarrassing possibility is a clamping caul left inside the guitar (ask me how I know). Tracking down most of these requires eliciting the rattle while selectively damping vibration of these individual components. Doing this is often most conveniently

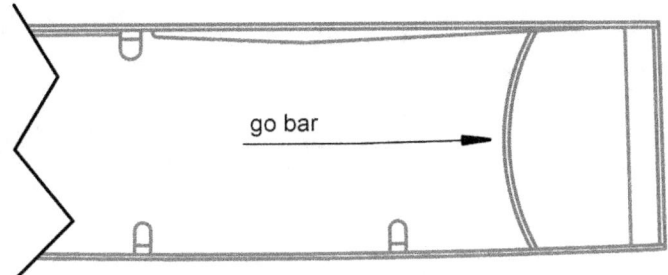

Figure 23-5– Clamping a loose brace while gluing it, using a flexible length of wood called a go bar. In this diagram the end of a brace close to the tail end of the guitar is clamped up, using a go bar spanning the underside of the end of the brace and the inside surface of the back.

done with the help of another person. If the rattle goes away while damping a component but can be reliably heard when that component is not damped, then the source of the rattle has been located.

The easiest way to damp vibration of a component is to grasp it firmly with the hand or fingers. For example, when selectively damping a tuning machine, it is held tightly in the fingers in such a way that any vibration of the machine against the headstock will be damped, and also so that any vibration of its component parts (tuning button, shaft, top washer, etc.) will also be damped.

Some components cannot readily be damped in this manner. These include the neck bolts and the trussrod. To eliminate these components from contention, it is usually best to simply tighten them a bit and then check again for the rattle. The trussrod presents something of a special case. When tightened one way it will force the neck to up bow, and when tightened the other way it will force it to back bow. But due to the backlash in the threads of the screws of the trussrod there is a fairly wide area between these two conditions, where the adjustment nut can be turned but the trussrod is loose. This area of adjustment can be felt. The adjustment nut is quite easy to turn when in this area. If the trussrod adjustment nut is loose, it should be turned clockwise just until resistance is felt. This puts tension on the trussrod and its component parts, effectively damping any vibration of the rod or its components.

A loose brace is a potential cause of a rattle. Although quite rare in a new instrument, if all other avenues have been looked into this should be checked. This is done by feel, reaching inside the guitar and grabbing each brace at various places along its length and attempting to gently pull it away from the plate to which it is glued. If a brace is loose it will usually be pretty obvious when tested in this manner.

After the source of the rattle is determined it can be fixed. Fixes for the potential rattle sources mentioned include:

Loose Trussrod – Tightening it just a bit by turning the adjustment nut clockwise;

Loose Tuning Machine or Component – Tightening the nut securing the tuning machine, tightening the wood screw securing the back of the machine, tightening the screw securing the tuning button;

Loose Bridge Pin – Replacing the pin with an oversize pin. These are fitted and installed in the same way as a standard size pin;

Sloppy Saddle Fit – Constructing a new saddle, taking care of fit in the saddle slot;

Loose Neck Bolts – Tightening them a bit;

Loose Brace – A loose brace must be glued down. The basic strategy is to work woodworking glue between the brace and the plate to which it will be attached, using a palette knife, and then to clamp the brace in place until the glue cures. Any loose area of a brace that is within 4˝ (101.6mm) of the soundhole can usually be clamped using a cam clamp and a fashioned caul. Clamping farther away from the soundhole is usually done using a *go bar*, a flexible piece of wood that is cut a bit longer than the distance between the brace and the opposite plate, and then wedged into place (**figure 23-5**).

Clamping Caul – The caul is removed.

There are certainly other potential sources for rattles, but the ones listed are by far the most common ones that could be encountered on a newly constructed guitar.

String Buzzes

String buzzes are the result of some vibrating part of a string coming in contact with something while it vibrates. That contact is possible anywhere along the vibrating length of the string. It is also possible along the part of the string between the nut and the fretting finger, even though this portion of the string is not intended to vibrate. Tracking down a string buzz often takes a little detective work. As is done when tracking down a rattle, the first step in the process is to figure out how to reliably produce the buzz. Once that is done, it is usually quite simple to identify the source of the buzz.

The evaluation description at the beginning of the Troubleshooting section should be followed to elicit the buzz. Careful notes should be made about which string or strings are involved, and for fretted notes, the frets at which the buzzing occurs.

Buzzing on an open string that does not occur when that string is fretted is usually caused by either a poorly cut string slot in the nut, or the string slot cut too deep. If the floor of the string slot in the nut is not angled properly or is not flat, a sitar-like buzz may be heard, due to the nut not providing a positive termination of the vibrating length of the string. The fix here is to reshape the floor of that slot to be sure it is properly angled and flat. If the buzzing is the result of a slot that is too narrow and doesn't allow the string to sit firmly on the slot floor, the fix is to widen the slot appropriately. Note that a slot which is too narrow can often be diagnosed when the string is pulled up out of the slot, because the slot will grab the string and only let it go with some additional pull.

If the buzzing is the result of a nut slot that is cut too deep, the open string is usually buzzing against the first fret while it vibrates. If a slot has been cut too wide, the string may be buzzing against the walls of the slot. The fixes for the latter two issues are to either fill and then re-file that string slot, or to construct a new nut.

Photo 23-27– *The two example instruments, ready to play.*

Paradoxically, buzzing on a fretted string can also be the result of the string slot in the nut being cut too deep. Here, it is the length of string between the nut and the fretting finger that is sympathetically vibrating against (usually) the first fret. This can be checked by damping the strings behind the fretting finger with a piece of cloth between strings and fret tops. If this makes the buzzing go away, then the depth of the string slot in the nut is suspect and should be checked.

Buzzing on a string that is played either open or fretted, the latter possibly at more than one fret, is usually due to an issue with the bridge saddle. If the top of the saddle is not sharp at the point where the string passes over it, or if the string touches any part of the bridge between the saddle and the bridge pin hole slot, buzzing may be heard. It is usually possible to dampen this kind of buzzing by pressing firmly down on the string, just behind where it passes over the saddle. If this action stops the buzz, the saddle top may have to be reworked for that string.

The most common cause of string buzzes that occur while fretting is a low fret at the fretting position, or one or more high frets between where the string is fretted and the bridge. High frets can usually be identified with the use of a short straightedge, which will rock on a single high fret when placed on the fret tops. A single low fret is often difficult to identify, because the differences in height are usually quite subtle. If a high fret is identified, the fret should be examined carefully to see if it has popped up a bit out of its slot. If so, it should be pressed back in place, gluing it down if necessary, following the descriptions in the book on fret installation.

There are two fixes for a string buzz due to fret height issues. The first is to raise the action a bit. Usually the easiest way to do this (or to at least try this) is to increase the amount of relief by adjusting the trussrod. The second way to fix this is to re-level and dress the frets to eliminate the height difference. The general way to make the decision on how to fix this is to try raising the action, and if this fixes the problem at an action that is acceptable, then all is well. If not, re-working the fret tops will be necessary.

Although it may seem appropriate to simply file down the top of the offending fret and then dress it again, due to the subtle height differences involved this approach rarely works. Attempting this usually just makes this fret a bit low, which just moves the problem farther up the fretboard. The appropriate fix here is to re-level the frets in the entire affected area of the fretboard, checking for flatness along the string paths in the same manner as was discussed in the section of the book on fret dressing. Following re-leveling, the affected frets are dressed and polished.

Three Month Checkup

Usually an instrument will have settled enough in three months of being strung up to pitch to warrant another check, and possible adjustment, of relief and action. Note that wood exhibits cold creep and so the instrument will change in shape throughout its life. But these changes generally happen a lot more slowly than the changes that happen in the first few months.

Luthiers should be aware of seasonal changes. There are often noticeable relief and action changes with changes in temperature and humidity. These can be limited by attempting to maintain the instrument in conditions of fairly constant temperature and humidity.

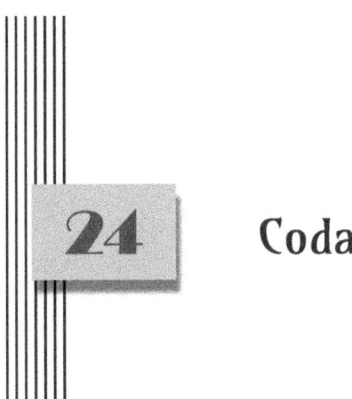

24 Coda

The guitar construction process detailed in this book is an optimal approach to the construction of the acoustic steel string guitar for the lutherie novice. It is based on my observations of lutherie novices over many years and in many contexts. First-time guitar builders come at their projects in different ways, and many of them complete their guitars. What happens after a first guitar has been completed is something that has interested me throughout my lutherie career, and is another area which I have observed in some detail. I'll end this book with a few observations on what first-time luthiers do after their initial guitar construction projects, and the ways in which those that continue lutherie work tend to go about that.

A certain number of novice luthiers complete one guitar and then go on to something else. But to me the more interesting group is those that build one or more additional instruments. The motivations for doing so seem to vary a lot. Some builders simply find the process interesting enough to want to pursue it further. Others, motivated by issues that arose during the construction of their first instruments, want to continue building until they achieve some level of mastery of the process. Still others want to pursue the craft in order to further optimize the construction process or to attempt to improve the performance of the instrument itself.

Probably the most frequently asked (or at least privately considered) question posed by lutherie novices that desire to better master the craft is: How long will it take to attain a level of mastery? Although personal goals vary, most continuing luthiers want to know what it will take to reach a point where they can consistently produce guitars of high quality. It may seem simplistic, but most experienced luthiers I know will answer this question by giving some number of guitars to be completed. Everyone has a different idea of what that number is. In my experience most dedicated luthiers reach a high level of proficiency after having built about 20 instruments.

This is by no means a hard and fast number. One of my New England Luthiers colleagues, Boston, Massachusetts, luthier Burton LeGeyt, was producing exquisite guitars from the get go. His third instrument was fantastic, and he's gone on from there.

That it is pretty much universally accepted by experienced luthiers that some level of mastery requires some number of instruments to be built has resulted in a number of luthiers considering if it may be possible to reduce that number. The first luthier I know to take a serious look at solving this problem, at least as far as the sound of the instrument goes, was Hawaiian classical guitar and ukulele luthier David Hurd. He proposed a process of measuring compliance (flexibility) of the top as a path to reducing the number of instruments a luthier has to build to reliably make instruments of high sound quality. That process is detailed in his still-popular book *Left Brain Lutherie*. Other luthiers have also considered this problem.

Many of those that choose to continue lutherie will spend considerable time and effort in learning more about the craft. There was a time, and it wasn't all that long ago, when doing so would have been a formidable and mostly solitary task. These days there is a wealth of resources available, enough so that students of the craft can pick and choose their sources of additional information.

Informal information sources abound on the Internet. Lutherie-specific forums and discussion groups, while not abundant, are numerous enough to allow those interested to pick and choose among them. General Internet searches will also turn up lots of lutherie-specific information available from various builders' sites.

Another good learning option available to the continuing luthier is a local lutherie organization. These are invariably located in population centers, and unfortunately not all locations can support such a group. I am very fortunate to live in the Boston area, which is the home of New England Luthiers, a long-established group of luthiers that holds regular meetings and maintains an online discussion group. Other areas have similarly active local groups. The value of face-to-face contact with other makers of stringed instruments cannot be overstated.

For those looking for more formal sources of advanced lutherie information, options include regular publications such as *American Lutherie*, the journal of the Guild of American Luthiers. Although it may not always be obvious in the age of voluminous online information, there is immense value is carefully curated sources of information. A carefully edited journal will almost always present a far more information-dense experience than is generally available through more informal sources.

Guitar lutherie and guitar lutherie instruction is mature enough at this point that a number of books aimed at the more advanced luthier are available. As with most formal sources of information, these must be purchased, but the depth of information available in such books makes them a great bargain. Because video production can be done these days in a cost-effective manner, another source of advanced lutherie information is commercial video instruction. This is particularly suited to those operations that are simply easier to demonstrate live. And there are a number of people that are just more comfortable acquiring information in this format than from other media.

My final recommendation for acquiring more advanced lutherie information is hands-on lutherie courses. This is always an expensive option, but the possibility of learning directly and interactively from an established master luthier is probably the most optimal way to obtain as much information as possible in a short amount of time.

Some suggestions for sources of formal advanced lutherie information appear in the Sources of Advanced Guitar Building Information section of the Online Annex of this book, found in Appendix A.

I hope the information I've provided here has been interesting. Continuing luthiers will find that they will modify a number of the construction techniques described in this book as they gain experience, and that they will simply leave some behind for techniques more suitable to their new level of skill. This is as it should be. To those novice luthiers that have decided to continue building stringed musical instruments, please let me welcome you to our craft.

Appendix A: Online Annex

Information that can change quickly, at least in the context of the printing of a book, is kept online so that it may be updated when necessary. Information maintained online includes the plans and templates for the example guitars built in the book; a list of suppliers of lutherie materials, tools and services; and errata that were found in the text of the book following its publication. The URLs of external website resources are also included in the online annex because these are subject to change as well. This page includes the URLs of the home page of the online annex as well as links to the specific types of information maintained in the annex.

The Online Annex

This is the home page of the online annex. All parts of the annex are available from here.

https://LiutaioMottola.com/books/steelAnnex.htm

Errata (Errors in the Text of the Book)

All known errors in the current edition of the book are listed in this section. It is wise to refer to this section as the first step before beginning the book. Instructions are also included here for reporting any errors you find to the author.

https://LiutaioMottola.com/books/steelAnnex.htm#errata

Plans and Templates

The plans and templates for the example instruments described in this book may be downloaded from this section. Note that all plans and templates are available only as PDF files, delivered as email attachments.

https://LiutaioMottola.com/books/steelAnnex.htm#plans

Specific Tools Referenced in the Book

General information and purchasing information for any specific tools that were mentioned in the construction descriptions in this book are included in this section.

https://LiutaioMottola.com/books/steelAnnex.htm#tools

Specific Finishing Materials Referenced

General information and purchasing information for any specific finishing products that were mentioned in the construction descriptions in this book are included in this section.

https://LiutaioMottola.com/books/steelAnnex.htm#finishing

Sources of Lutherie Tools and Supplies

A list of sources, organized by type of supplier. There are general lutherie suppliers which offer a wide variety of tools, wood, finishing supplies and other supplies, as well as specialist suppliers such as lutherie wood dealers. Some specialty suppliers are quite specific, offering only one particular tool or part.

https://LiutaioMottola.com/books/steelAnnex.htm#sources

Sources of Lutherie Services

A number of steps in the guitar construction process can be contracted out. Probably the most common services that a luthier may want to procure are those for custom inlay, custom machining of guitar wood parts, and spray finishing. Listings here are organized by type of service.

https://LiutaioMottola.com/books/steelAnnex.htm#services

Sources of Advanced Guitar Building Information

As mentioned in the final chapter, there are many sources of advanced lutherie information including books, video and online instruction, and hands-on classes and other forms of personal instruction. Listings here are ordered by media type.

https://LiutaioMottola.com/books/steelAnnex.htm#advanced

Appendix B: Simple Router Jig for Planing Thin Plates

Planing larger pieces of wood to the thin thicknesses required for the plates and ribs of the guitar can be done by the wood supplier, or it can be accomplished easily using a thickness sander. That tool is quite expensive and not all luthiers have one. A less expensive method for doing this makes use of a router and a large diameter bottom cleaning bit. The router is supported by a simple, easy to build jig. The jig consists of two parts, a movable sled to which the router is attached, and a base to which the wood to be planed is affixed (**photo B-1**). The jig as described can be used to accurately plane down any piece of wood that is thinner than ¾″ (19.1MM) thick. This is about the simplest jig of this type that can be made.

The largest diameter bottom cleaning bit that will fit the router should be used. The bigger the bit, the cleaner the planing will be.

Construction of the Planing Jig

The jig is made from ¾″ (19.1MM) thick melamine-covered particle board (**photo B-2**), and 1⅛″ (28.6MM) steel angle stock. Note that the steel angle stock is important to keep the router sled part of the jig stiff. The dimensions of the jig are not critical but the jig should be designed to handle either one plate half or two side pieces. This means the base piece should be approximately 12″ (304.8MM) wide by 36″ (914.4MM) long, and the sled should be approximately 8″ (203.2MM) wide by 24″ (609.6MM) long.

The base is made by attaching 1″ (25.4MM) rails made of the same melamine board material along the long edges of the base piece, attached with countersunk wood screws (**photo B-3**). If the base slips around too much on the bench, its bottom surface can be covered with PSA sandpaper of a coarse grit.

The sled is made by drilling a large diameter hole in its center to provide clearance for the bottom cleaning bit, and mounting holes for the router to be screwed to it, using the router baseplate hardware. The router baseplate can be removed and used as a template for locating these holes (**photos B-4** and **B-5**). Then the angle steel stiffeners are cut to length, their sharp edges are removed, and they are drilled for mounting holes. The stiffeners are screwed down along the edges of the sled using wood screws (**photo B-6**).

After the base and sled are built, spacers must be attached to the bottom of the sled to prevent the router bit from contacting the rails of the base (**photo B-7**). The router is bolted to the sled (**photo B-8**) and the bottom cleaning bit is mounted in the router. Two pieces of some ⅛″ (3.2MM) thick material are used as spacers. These are temporarily attached to the inside surfaces of the two rails on the base. The sled is placed on top of

Photo B-1 – *A simple planing jig for planing guitar plates and sides to thickness. The jig uses a router with a bottom cleaning router bit.*

***Photo B-2** – The jig is built out of melamine-covered particleboard.*

***Photo B-6** – The stiffening angle stock pieces are aligned with the edges of the sled piece and screwed down with wood screws.*

***Photo B-3** – Two rails are added at the edges of the base piece.*

***Photo B-7** – Stops must be added to the sled to prevent the bit from contacting the inside surfaces of the base rails.*

***Photo B-4** – The router baseplate is used as a template to mark mounting holes for the router on the sled piece.*

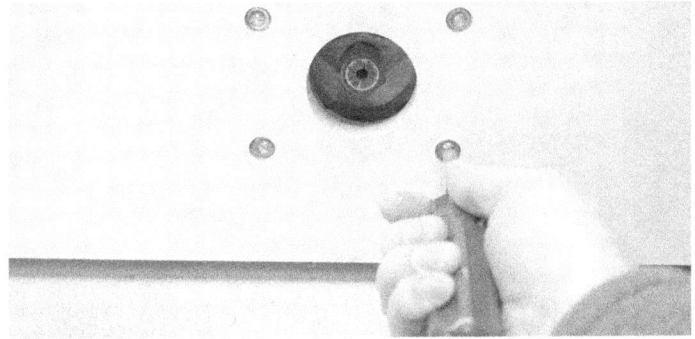

***Photo B-8** – The router is screwed to the sled using the same hardware that was used to attach its baseplate.*

***Photo B-5** – A large diameter hole provides clearance for the bottom cleaning bit. Countersunk mounting holes for the router are drilled.*

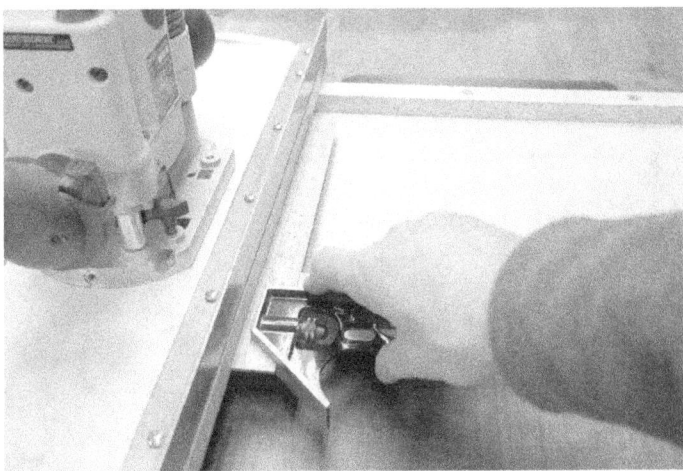

***Photo B-9** – A square is used to orient the sled square to the base.*

Photo B-10 – *The outside edge of the rail is traced on the underside of the sled, to locate the position of the stop.*

Photo B-11 – *The attached stop looks like this.*

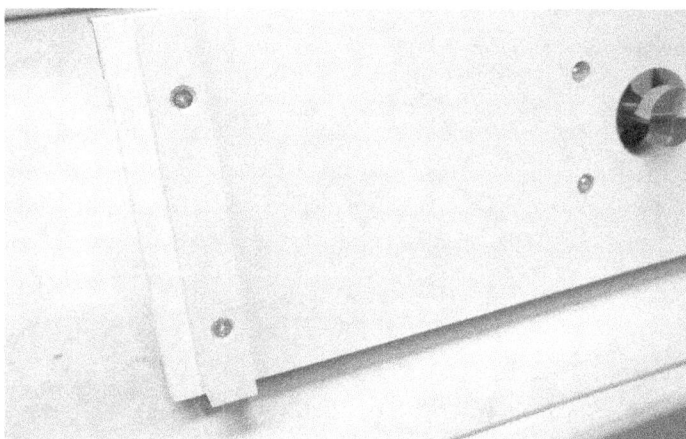

Photo B-12 – *The stop is screwed to the underside of the sled using wood screws.*

Photo B-13 – *After planing, the work must be carefully removed from the base using a thin putty knife to separate the double-sided tape.*

the base and the side of the router bit is pressed against the spacer on one rail, while a square is used to keep the sled perpendicular to the base (**photo B-9**). Then a mark is made on the underside of the opposite end of the sled against the outside of the rail (**photo B-10**). The other end of the sled is similarly marked. Small wood stops are attached at these marks using wood screws (**photos B-11** and **B-12**). The stops prevent the bit from contacting and chewing up the walls of the rails. But note that in use the material to be planed must be positioned on the base at least ⅛″ (3.2mm) from inside surfaces of the rails.

Using the Planing Jig

Material to be planed to thickness that is more than ¾″ (19.1mm) thick is first reduced in thickness via other means. The material to be planed is attached to the base using *small* pieces of double-sided tape. Enough tape to hold the material down flat to the base is used, but not so much that it will be difficult to remove the material after it is planed.

In use, the router is moved in clockwise circular motions so that the bit is never cutting directly into the grain. For the smoothest surface finish, the router should not be pressed down while planing. The weight of the router and sled is all that is needed to keep them in place on the rails. Even though the sled is stiff, pressing down on the router can still flex it enough to slightly gouge the material.

The jig leaves slight circular marks on the surface of the material which are easily removed using a handheld sander and 100-grit sandpaper. After planing and sanding, the material is removed using a thin putty knife to carefully separate the double-sided tape (**photo B-13**).

Appendix C: Guitar Body Vise

There are a few guitar construction operations that are a lot easier to accomplish when the guitar body is rigidly supported in a tail-up position. These include work on the end graft pocket and installing the end pin. This easy-to-build guitar body vise (**photo C-1**) is modeled after one described by Duane Waterman in an early *Guild of American Luthiers Data Sheet*, and currently reprinted in the GAL book *Lutherie Tools*.[1] It is constructed from readily available materials and is based on pipe clamps.

The component parts are shown in **photo C-2**. Two ¾″ (19.1mm) pipe clamps on 14″ (355.6mm) threaded pipe nipples are used for the clamping parts of the vise (**photo C-3**). In use, the sides of the guitar body could possibly contact the pipes. To prevent this, the part of each pipe that is between the clamp ends is covered with a 3″ (76.2mm) long piece of split foam pipe insulation.

The jaws of the vise are made of two pieces of ¼″ (6.4mm) thick Baltic birch plywood covered on one side with ¼″ (6.4mm) thick sheet cork. The jaw pieces are each 20″ (508mm) long and 6″ (152.4mm) high, with the corners rounded over. Cut near each end of each jaw is a 1³⁄₁₆″ (30.2mm) clearance slot, which allows the jaws to sit on the pipe nipples. The clearance slots are cut on 16″ (406.4mm) centers. The jaw pieces are cut out, then the cork sheeting is glued to one surface of each. After the glue dries, the cork is trimmed to the outsides of the jaws and the clearance slots.

The pipe nipples are mounted using pipe flanges (**photo C-4**). These can be mounted on the front surface of the bench. Although it is not obvious from the photos here, on my bench the flanges are mounted on the back side of the front board of the bench, behind holes drilled through the front of the bench. The vise is easily disassembled and removed when not in use, leaving only the pipe flanges permanently attached to the bench. It is also possible to screw the pipe flanges to a baseboard that can be clamped to the bench when the vise will be used, and unclamped and removed when the vise is not needed.

In use, the jaws are made of material thin enough to bend to follow the arching of the guitar body plates. Although the jaws hold the body quite securely, it is possible that pressing down hard on the body could push the guitar body out through the bottom of the vise. It is always a good idea when using the guitar body vise to provide some backup support or padding on the floor, to prevent serious damage to the instrument should this happen.

Photo C-1 *– A simple shop-built vise for holding the guitar body in a tail-upright orientation. The screw mechanism is made of pipe clamps and the jaws are made of cork-lined plywood. The vise can be removed from the bench when not in use.*

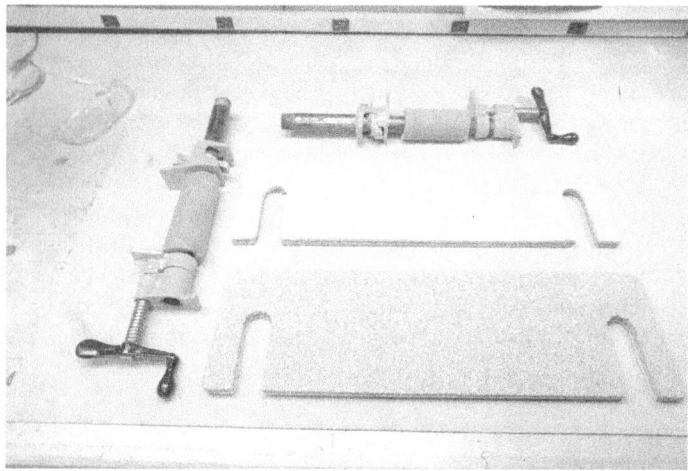

Photo C-2 – *The basic assemblies of the guitar body vise include two pipe-clamp screw mechanisms and two flexible padded jaw pieces.*

Photo C-3 – *The vise is mounted on any vertical surface using two pipe flanges. The vise can be removed from the flanges and stored out of the way when not in use.*

Photo C-4 – *The assembled vise, ready for use.*

---

1. Waterman, Duane. (1984) Guitar Body Vise. *Lutherie Tools: Making Hand and Power Tools For String Instrument Building*, p.50. Guild of American Luthiers,

Appendix D: Guitar Neck Rest

Once the neck is attached to the body, the guitar has to be positioned as a whole and somewhat awkward unit. One of the most useful tools for working on the guitar while it is sitting top-up on the bench is a guitar neck rest. This cradles the underside of the neck shaft and lifts the neck off the bench (**photo D-1**). In so doing it makes the guitar more stable in position. It also lifts the headstock up enough so it does not contact the bench top. A neck rest of the appropriate height presents the fretboard and guitar top at a horizontal or nearly horizontal attitude. This is useful when doing all sorts of later construction operations, including work on the frets (**photo D-2**).

Guitar neck rests are available from lutherie suppliers. In their simplest form they can be nothing more than a block of appropriate dimensions with a concave trough cut into the top. The trough can be cut using rasps, gouges or sanding drums. After it is cut, sheet cork or some other padding material is glued into the trough. This provides a cradle that supports the underside of the neck shaft.

The height of the neck rest is whatever is required to position the neck so the fretboard is more or less horizontal. The simple neck rest pictured here (**photo D-3**) is about 3¼″ (82.6mm) tall from the bottom of the block to the center of the padded trough. This works out well for the body depths of the two example instruments, and would work out well for just about all acoustic guitars.

The block can be made of any material available. The one pictured here is made from an off-cut from a mahogany heel blank, but it can just as well be made from laminated pieces of MDF. I like to glue some cork to the bottom of the block as well, to make it more non-slip when it is sitting directly on the bench top.

Photo D-2 – The guitar neck rest in use, in preparation for doing work on the frets.

Photo D-3 – A simple shop-built guitar neck rest made of a block of wood with a shallow trough cut into the top. The trough and the bottom of the block are padded with sheet cork.

Photo D-1 – A simple shop-built guitar neck rest in use.

Appendix E: Finish Scrapers

Scrapers are generally useful woodworking hand tools. Many of the surface refinement steps demonstrated throughout the book show the use of the card scraper. Preparing the edge of the card scraper involves sharpening a thin side flat and square, drawing out an edge using the scraper burnisher, then using that same tool to turn the edge, so a hook with a sharp scraping edge is formed. This provides a stiff and robust edge which will provide a lot of wood scraping service before needing to be refreshed.

Scraping edges can be formed by simply using the scraper burnisher to turn the edge on the blade of just about any cutting tool (**figure E-1**). Hand tool aficionados are probably familiar with scraper planes, the blades of which are generally sharpened with a single bevel in the conventional manner, then the edge is turned to form a hook. This same technique can be used to form various scraper tools. This is especially useful for making a special-purpose small scraper for scraping off the finish so the bridge can be glued to the guitar top.

Two such scrapers are described here. The first is a simple disposable scraper made out of a single-edge razor blade (**photo E-1**). These are extremely useful for all sorts of applications, but their small size makes them ideal for scraping finish. I first saw these mentioned by Athens, Ohio, luthier and repair guru Dan Erlewine, and have been using them ever since. The edges are already sharp, so no additional sharpening is necessary. The edge must be turned, and the scraper is ready for use. Because the material and the sharpened edge is so thin, the turned edge can bend back straight fairly quickly, so it is not possible to get a lot of use out of one of these. After a razor blade scraper no longer scrapes, the best thing to do is to toss it, get a fresh blade, and make another one.

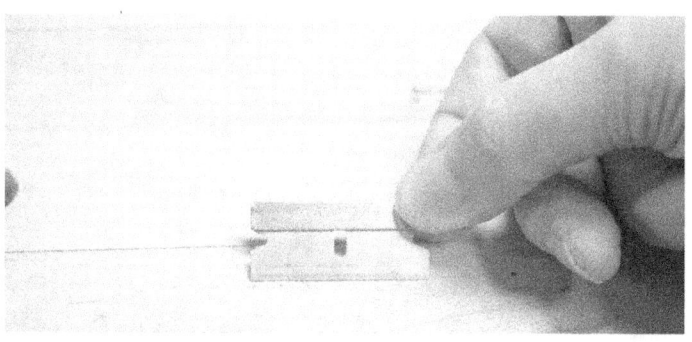

Photo E-1 – *The edge of a standard single-edge razor blade can be turned to make a small disposable scraper.*

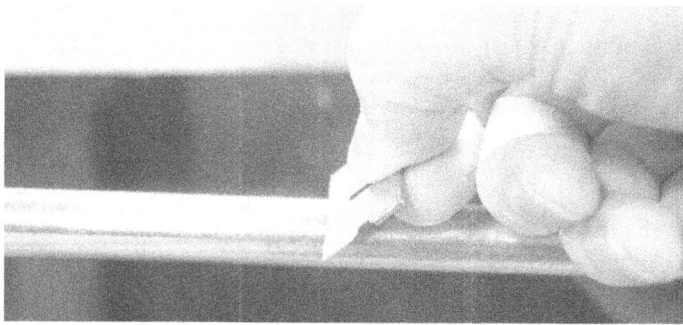

Photo E-3 – *The blade is angled less acutely for the second pass of the edge over the surface of the burnisher.*

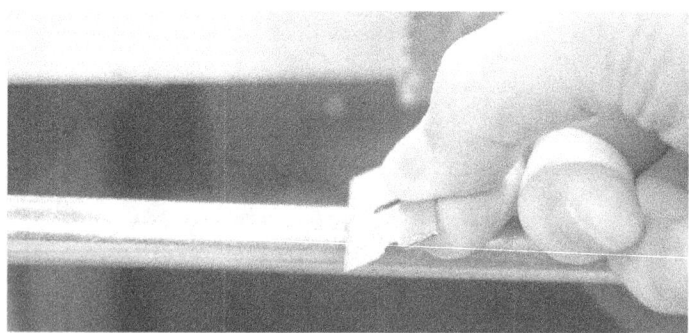

Photo E-2 – *The edge is turned a little at a time. The first pass is with the blade at an acute angle to the surface of the burnisher.*

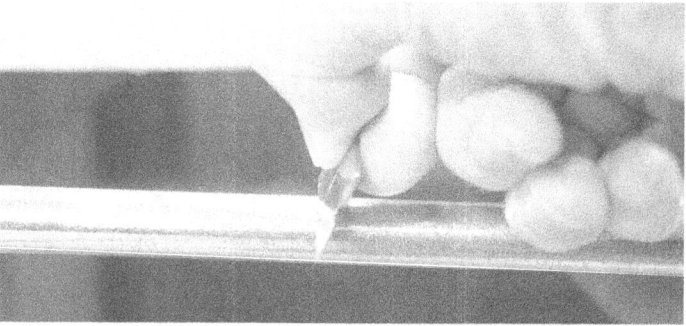

Photo E-4 – *The blade is nearly perpendicular with the surface of the burnisher for the third and final pass over the burnisher surface.*

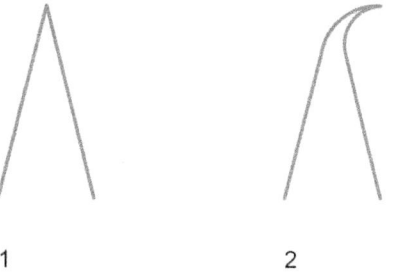

1 2 3 4

Figure E-1 – *A double-bevel edge, such as those found on knife blades and the blades of carving chisels (1) can be turned to form a scraping edge (2). A single-bevel edge like those of plane blades (3) can also be turned to form a scraping edge (4). The latter edges should be turned toward the flat back side of the blade.*

Although the edge can be turned by holding the razor blade in the vise and using the scraper burnisher in the conventional manner, I find it much quicker and easier to hold the blade in my hand and just draw the edge across the surface of the burnisher. In fact I rarely even take the time to find and use the scraper burnisher for this task, preferring instead to simply turn the edge on the metal handle of my bench vise (**photos E-2** through **E-4**).

For scraping the finish off the guitar top in preparation for attaching the bridge, I like to make a small special-purpose scraper out of a small plane blade. A spokeshave blade is ideal because it is small enough for most of this task but it is also big enough to hold comfortably (**photo E-5**). Although replacement spokeshave blades are readily available they are generally of high quality and are quite expensive. The blade shown in the accompanying photos is from a cheap imported spokeshave. This was so inexpensive that I bought it just for the blade, and chucked the rest of the tool.

The blade is sharpened and polished in the conventional manner, just like it would be for use in the spokeshave. Then it is clamped edge-up in the vise and the scraper burnisher is used to turn the edge (**photos E-6** and **E-7**). Note that the edge is turned toward the flat back surface of the blade. Since the scraper will be held in the hands in use, lightly rounding over all of the other edges of the blade will make it much more comfortable to use, and will prevent those edges from cutting into the hands,

The turned edge will hold up for a good long time, particularly if the tool is only used for scraping finish. As is the case with card scrapers and scraper planes, once the hook starts to bend back, the edge can be refreshed by simply turning the hook again. This works one or two times, but eventually the blade will have to be re-sharpened and polished, and then the hook turned again.

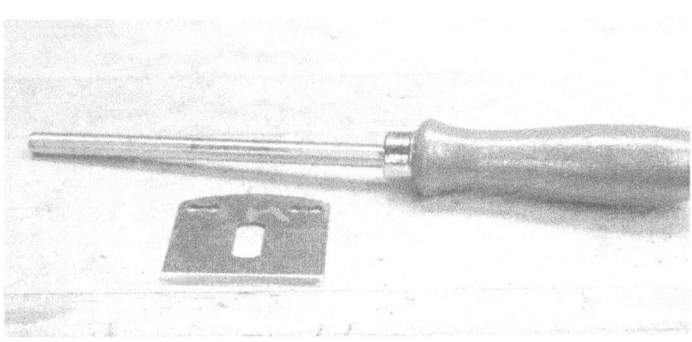

Photo E-5 – The spokeshave blade is sharpened and polished in preparation for turning the edge.

Photo E-6 – The first pass across the edge is with the burnisher held at a fairly acute angle.

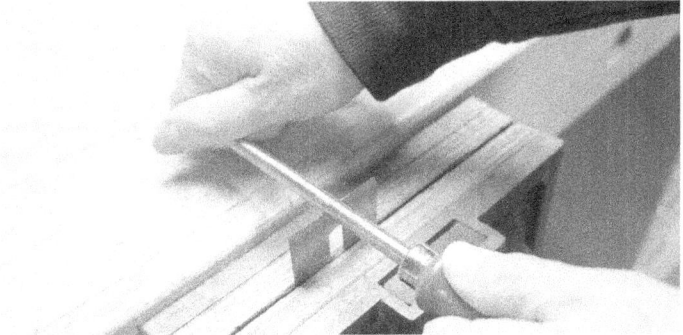

Photo E-7 – With subsequent passes the angle of the burnisher is reduced to near horizontal to the top of the bench.

Glossary of Lutherie Terms

There is a lot of terminology introduced throughout the book. Most often, short definitions are provided at the point in the book where each term is first introduced, but this appendix puts all these terms in one place for easy reference. Some of these terms have been introduced specifically to unambiguously identify things in the descriptions in this book, but most are conventional lutherie terminology. The definitions of the latter are taken directly from my comprehensive lutherie dictionary, *Mottola's Cyclopedic Dictionary of Lutherie Terms*. Readers looking for a deeper dive into lutherie and its terminology may be interested in that book. See its information page at https://www.liutaiomottola.com/books/dictionary.htm.

ad hoc arching *n*. Plate arching of a form that does not follow any simple geometric model. There are many different types of plate arching, but for the purposes of guitar assembly we can generally reduce that number to two; spherical doming, where the arching is patterned after a section of the surface of a sphere, and ad hoc arching, which is everything else.

American Lutherie *n*. The quarterly journal of the Guild of American Luthiers. It features articles on lutherie and other topics of interest to luthiers. See also: Guild of American Luthiers.

assembled neck blank *n*. Although not a term that is used universally in lutherie, this book makes a distinction between rectangular cross section neck blanks and assembled neck blanks. The former is a rectangular solid or laminated block of wood that is larger than the entire headstock/neck shaft/heel assembly in every dimension, while the latter is built up from separate headstock, shaft, and heel parts. The assembled neck blank requires more effort to put together but it makes more efficient use of wood.

back purfling *n*. Purfling on the back plate of a guitar or similar instrument, between the binding and the rest of the back. See also: purfling.

back reinforcing strip *n*. Thin strip of cross grain wood used to reinforce the center seam or other seams of the back of flattop guitars.

back strip *n*. Decorative strip on the centerline of the back plate of a flattop guitar. Syn.: back stripe.

bastard grain *adj*. Describing wood with grain angle that varies across the width of the board when viewing the end grain. The term is sometimes also used to describe any board that cannot be classified as quartersawn or flat sawn. See also: flat sawn, quartersawn.

belly bridge *n*. A style of bridge used in flat top steel string guitars. The tops of the bridge wings of this style of bridge are flat, and they transition to the central portion of the bridge with rounded curves. See also: bridge wing.

bending strap *n*. A flexible metal strap used to provide support against cracking when bending the ribs of the guitar. A bending strap is usually the same length and height as the side being bent. In use it is placed behind the wood to be bent, and the wood and the strap are bent at the same time. The strap prevents the back surface of the bend from being subject to tension, which could crack or split the wood.

binding *n*. Edging on instrument bodies, also found on fingerboards and headstocks. The binding is decorative but also serves to protect the edge and to seal the end grain. Bindings are typically made of wood or plastic, and may be combined with purflings, which decorate and contrast the inside edges of the bindings.

bookmatched *adj*. The plates of most stringed instruments are made of two pieces of wood. These pieces are generally cut as successive slices from the same billet. If the two slices are opened up like a book, each side will be a mirror image of the other, more or less. This orientation of two successive slices of wood is called bookmatched. Bookmatched tops and backs are standard for most musical instruments, even inexpensive modern instruments. But there are a number of examples of historical instruments, some extremely well regarded, that do not have bookmatched plates.

bottom surface (neck blank) *n*. The surface of the neck blank which is opposite the fretboard surface.

breakover angle *n*. The strings pass over the bridge (saddle) of a stringed instrument at an angle. The breakover angle is the angle between the projection of the straight path of the string past the bridge, and the actual path of the after length of the string.

bridge wing *n*. On flattop guitar bridges, the wings are the thin, flat ends of the bridge, the parts that do not contain either the saddle or the string anchor holes.

burn in *n*. The quality of finishes applied in multiple coats which describes how well those coats fuse with one another. A coat of a finish with good burn in will fuse completely with the previously applied coats. Evaporative finishes like shellac and lacquer offer good burn in. Waterborne finishes have good burn in if subsequent coats are applied soon after previous coats. Reactive finishes like varnish don't burn in at all.

camber *n*. The curvature of the playing surface of the fingerboard of some stringed instruments. With the exception of most classical guitars and early instruments, the fingerboards of stringed instruments are shaped so that the playing surface exhibits an arch. This is considered by some to make barring easier as it follows the natural curve of the insides of the fingers. In lutherie the term radius is also used as a synonym for camber. Syn.: radius.

camber radius *n*. The playing surface of the fretboard of most steel string guitars is cambered such that this surface is shaped like a section from the surface of a cylinder of some radius. The camber radius is the radius of that cylinder. A longer radius yields a flatter camber.

catalyzed finish *n*. Any finishing material that requires a catalyst to be added just prior to application. Catalyzed finishes are also called two-part or two-pack finishes. Catalyzed finishes generally cure hard and fast and go on thick so that multiple coats are not necessary. Drawbacks include toxicity and the fact that they are often insoluble once they cure. The latter property means they can be difficult to repair, and letting them cure in the spray gun can mean the end for the gun.

cellulose *n*. The chemical composition of wood contains two basic components, lignin and carbohydrate. The cell structure of wood is composed mostly of carbohydrates, which in turn are composed mostly of cellulose and hemicelluloses. A simplified model of the structure of wood is of cells with cellulose cell walls glued together with lignin. See also: lignin.

chasing *v*. Sequential hammering along a line. Frets are hammered into place by chasing. This slowly embeds the tang of the fret in the fret slot without crimping the fret anywhere.

coalescing finish *n*. Any finishing material in which the liquid form is an emulsion containing solids that coalesce to form a homogeneous mass in the cured finish. All waterborne finishes are coalescing finishes.

compass gramil *n*. Hand tool used to make a circular knife cut. The tool consists of a body which holds the knife blade and a pivot pin. The distance from blade to pin is adjustable as is the depth of cut of the knife blade. In use the pin is placed in a drilled hole at the center of the circle and the tool is rotated around the pivot pin. Each pass is made a bit deeper than the previous one until the desired depth of cut is achieved. In lutherie this tool is used to cut out round sound holes and to cut the walls of soundhole rosette pockets. See also: gramil.

compensation *n*. Change in saddle or nut position from calculated locations to compensate for the sharping affect of fretting strings and the bending stiffness of strings. Instruments which use less elastic strings such as those made of steel generally require more compensation than do instruments with more elastic strings. Bridge saddle compensation is generally found on all fretted instruments with steel strings and on most nylon strung instruments as well. Nut compensation is found on some steel and nylon strung instruments. In general, compensation values are not included in descriptions of the scale length of instruments, but are given as separate values. For all practical purposes compensation values are not precisely calculable, as the inputs to such calculations require the longitudinal stiffness of the core of the string, values for which are not readily available and vary from string set to string set and are affected by action and relief. In addition, same-note pitch variability is quite high for steel string instruments. Instruments with fixed bridges such as flattop guitars generally use some conventional value for compensation that has worked well in the past.

compression trussrod *n*. Also sometimes called single-acting, and, interestingly enough, tension trussrods. These can be tightened to provide more neck back bow only. A strategy for using this style of trussrod to provide limited front bow adjustment is to install the trussrod and then tighten it to slightly back bow the fingerboard. Then the fingerboard is planed flat.

course *n*. A group of strings that are all fretted at the same time. For example a 12 string guitar has six courses of two strings each, and a mandolin has four courses of two strings each. If an instrument has a combination of single strings and multi-string courses, the single strings are also each referred to as a course.

cutoff bar *n*. A brace of a typical fan braced top plate. The cutoff bars run diagonally across the bottom of the plate from a point near the tail end of the center fan brace to a point near the side at the width of the lower bout. An instrument with cutoff bars usually has two, one on each side. Syn.: closing bar. See also: fan bracing.

dished workboard *n*. The plates of modern flattop instruments are not really flat but are instead slightly arched. In a production environment, the plates are domed by being assembled on a dished workboard. Braces and patches are glued onto the plate while it is sitting face down on a dished workboard. The clamps used to glue the braces down also bend the plate into the workboard so it takes on the dish shape. When the glue dries and the plate is removed it retains its dished shape. Turning the plate face up shows the plate domed on the outside surface.

double acting trussrod *n*. Trussrod that can be adjusted to provide more back bow or more front bow. See also: compression trussrod, trussrod.

downcut router bit *n*. Router bit used to excavate shallow pockets and groves with clean upper edges. In operation the groves of the bit spiral down, which does not work well for chip removal but also does not usually tear up the grain on the upper edge of the pocket being excavated, particularly in soft wood. Syn.: spiral down router bit, down spiral router bit. See also: upcut router bit.

drop fill *n, v*. Liquid filler material that is applied using a dropper or by letting a drop fall off the end of a small stick or other applicator. The verb form of the term is the application of such filler.

elastic deformation *n*. The deformation of the shape of a component under load such that when the load is removed the component will return to its original shape. In the context of guitar side bending, cold and dry wood demonstrates elastic deformation. It can be bent, but when bending pressure is released it will return (mostly) to its original shape. See also: plastic deformation.

end graft *n*. See tail graft.

end pin *n*. Pin or button on/in the end of the instrument. For violin family instruments and some archtop guitars, the end pin secures the tail gut, which attaches the tailpiece to the body.

For other instruments the end pin is used as a strap button, to secure the end of a strap.

evaporative finish *n*. Any finish which hardens by the evaporation of its solvent, leaving behind the hard solute. Shellac and lacquer are examples of evaporative finishes.

fall off *n*. Bending down of the fretboard extension (that part of the fretboard that is over the top of the guitar), out of the plane of the part of the fretboard on the neck shaft. Fall off sometimes occurs as a side effect of the neck/body geometry, but many luthiers engineer in some fall off to help prevent buzzing of the vibrating strings against the upper frets.

fan bracing *n*. A bracing pattern that uses a number of radially arranged braces to brace the area of the top below the soundhole. This is the most typical bracing pattern for classical guitars, which generally use five to seven braces, but sometimes more or fewer. The typical bracing pattern uses a transverse brace above the soundhole, another transverse brace below the soundhole, and the fan braces below that. This pattern also often uses two diagonal cutoff bars below the fan braces. See also: cutoff bar, ladder bracing, X bracing.

figure *n*. Any visually interesting or appealing pattern of wood.

fittings *n*. The mechanical and generally non-vibrating parts of the instrument, generally used to support the ends of the strings or provide other utility functionality. Tuning machines or pegs, tail pieces, end pins, pickguards and similar pieces are generally referred to as the fittings.

flat sawn *n*. A board that is sawn so that, when viewed from the end grain, the grain lines run more or less parallel with the width of the board. Wood is flat sawn (as opposed to quartersawn) for two reasons: 1. It is easier to saw; 2. some species look better when sawn this way. Syn.: back sawn, slab sawn. See also: quartersawn.

French polish *n*. A hand-applied shellac finish. French polish is built up in many layers using a hand held cloth pad called a rubber, tampon or muñeca. The shellac is dissolved in alcohol and then padded on. The major steps in the process include sealing, grain filling, bodying, spiriting off, and glazing.

fret crowning file *n*. A small file with a concave surface, used to restore the crown to a fret after fret leveling has flattened it. Fret crowning files are special purpose tools available from lutherie suppliers.

fret dressing file *n*. A triangular profile file used to smooth the fret ends and also the crowns. The sharp edges of fret dressing files are generally ground smooth so they can contact the fretboard surface when used and not scratch it.

fret tang *n*. The part of a fret that, when the fret is installed in the fretboard, goes into the fret slot and ends up below the playing surface of the fretboard. See also: fret, fret slot.

fretboard surface (neck blank) *n*. The surface of the neck blank that will eventually have the fretboard glued to it in the finished neck.

fretboard extension *n*. The part of the fretboard that extends over the body of the guitar.

GAL *abbr*. See Guild of American Luthiers.

garland *n*. The assembled rib, lining and block subassembly of a stringed musical instrument.

gramil *n*. A cutting gauge used to mark out purfling channels and the rabbets for guitar binding. Syn.: purfling cutter. See also: purfling.

Guild of American Luthiers *n*. Founded in 1972 by Tim Olsen, the Guild of American Luthiers is the largest and oldest organization of luthiers worldwide. Based in Tacoma WA, USA, the GAL publishes the quarterly journal *American Lutherie* as well a number of lutherie books and plans, and hosts a lutherie convention. Syn.: GAL.

gut string *n*. Guitar string made from the intestines of animals. Gut strings are used in antique instruments and in some instruments of the violin family.

head plate *n*. The front of the headstock of some instruments is covered with a thin plate of decorative wood called the head plate.

headplate veneer *n*. One or more sheets of veneer are often glued between the head plate and the rest of the guitar headstock. In the finished instrument, the edges of these veneers are visible and form decorative lines.

heel cap *n*. Decorative piece of wood that covers the bottom of the heel of the neck of an acoustic guitar or similar instrument.

kerfed lining *n*. Lining material used primarily in guitars and mandolins. It consists of wood strips that are kerfed (cut almost all the way through) at close regular intervals. The kerfs allow the lining to be bent cold, which speeds assembly time. Syn.: kerfing, kerf lining

ladder bracing *n*. A bracing pattern that makes use of braces that are parallel to each other and perpendicular to the instrument centerline. Ladder bracing was commonly used on the tops of all flattop stringed instruments before the use of fan bracing and X bracing and is still the most common bracing pattern for backs. See also: fan bracing, X bracing.

Latin binomial *n*. Wood species are unambiguously identified by their genus and species combined. Together, these are referred to as a Latin binomial. For example, mahogany is of the genus *Swietenia* and the species *macrophylla*. The Latin binomial for mahogany is the combination of these two words.

layout surface *n*. The surface of a component that will be shaped that is used to draw on. See also: reference surface.

lignin *n.* (LIG-nin) Part of the micro structure of wood. The "glue" which holds the micro structural components of wood together.

lining *n.* Strips or blocks of wood at the junction of the ribs and plates of most stringed instruments. The purpose of the linings is to increase the gluing area at the rib/plate joint. See also: kerfed lining

lutherie *n.* (LOO-ther-ee) The craft of constructing stringed musical instruments. The term is generally used to describe the construction of bowed and plucked instruments.

luthier *n.* (LOO-thee-er) Person that builds or repairs stringed musical instruments. The word is French (pronounced loo-tea-AY) but the common anglicized pronunciation is given. Its original definition is a person (and specifically a male) that makes lutes, but it is currently used in the USA to indicate any person that builds any kind of stringed musical instrument.

mastic *n.* 1. A resin from the mastic tree (*Pistacia lentiscus*) used as a component of violin varnishes. 2. Any thick, hardening mixture of binder and pigment materials, used as a surround for decorative inlay. Mastics were often made of hide glue and ebony dust, or shellac and wood dust or mineral pigment. A common use of mastic was as the background material for shell inlays used to decorate the soundholes of guitars.

medullary ray *n.* Part of the structure of wood. Medullary rays appear as radial structures which run lengthwise through the tree. These structures are more prominent in some species than in others. They are most observable in wood that has been quartersawn, i.e. where the grain lines are vertical to the wide surface of the board. Syn.: medullary. See also: quartersawn.

moustache bridge *n.* A style of guitar bridge that features elongated wings that curl up or down in a decorative fashion, in the style of a 19th century mustache.

neck block *n.* A block of wood inside the body of an instrument near the neck. The neck block is used as the structure that supports the attachment of the neck to the body.

neutral axis *n.* The axis in the cross section of a beam on which there is no longitudinal stress and strain. Consider a simple beam, simply supported at its ends, supporting a weight at its center and deflecting under that weight. The upper surface of the beam is in compression and the lower surface is in tension. The axis through the beam between these surfaces that is neither in tension nor compression is the neutral axis. Syn.: elastic axis.

nut *n.* The termination structure for the vibrating part of the strings of a stringed musical instrument. The nut usually contains a slot for each string. The walls of the slot laterally locate the string, and the floor of the slot locates the string in relation to the top of the fingerboard or frets. Nuts are typically made of a variety of materials for steel string and electric guitars. The nuts of bowed instruments are traditionally made of ebony, and the nuts of early guitars and classical guitars are traditionally made of ivory or bone.

oil varnish *n.* Varnish made from some kind of resin, polymerized or non-polymerized oil, and solvent. Oil varnishes are used primarily in violin family instruments but they are sometimes used for mandolins and guitars. The varnish is relatively slow drying and does not burn in. Applied coats do not melt into each other.

orthographic projection *n.* A 2D drawing representation of a three dimensional object. An orthographic representation includes three 2D drawings, one from each direction. A typical representation will include top, side, and end views.

pattern *v.* Refers to whether or not the pattern for an instrument plate can be cut from a particular board. Plate boards are generally rectangular and often contain defects and irregularities that should not impact their use because these defects will not appear inside the template of the plate of the finished instrument. A board with no defects is easy to pattern – the template for the plate can be positioned anywhere on it. A board with a lot of defects may be difficult to pattern – the template may only fit in one place that provides elimination of all defects. And of course some boards will not pattern – there is no place on it the template can be placed that would eliminate all defects from the finished instrument plate.

peón *n.* (pey-OWN) Small block of wood used as the gluing surface (lining) between the plate of an instrument and the ribs. Peones are typically used only as linings for the top plate, and are found most often in Spanish style guitars. Syn.: glue block, tentellón. See also: lining. Plural: peones.

pickguard *n.* A plate attached to the top of an instrument to protect the top from being scratched up by playing the instrument with a pick. Pickguards are common features of instruments generally played with a pick such as electric guitars and steel string acoustic guitars.

pitch *n.* In lutherie the terms yaw, pitch, and roll, used to describe rotation of an object in space, are most often used to describe adjustments necessary to fit an instrument's neck onto its body. When the instrument is viewed from the side, pitch is up and down rotation of the neck about an axis extending from your eye to the neck/body join. See also: roll, yaw.

plastic deformation *n.* The deformation of the shape of a component under load such that when the load is removed the component will not return to its original shape. In the context of guitar side bending, hot and wet wood demonstrates plastic deformation. It can be bent, and when bending pressure is released it will retain (mostly) its bent shape. See also: elastic deformation.

plate arching *n.* For flattop guitars, plate arching means any arching that has been forced into the plate by the application of braces with arched surfaces.

playing surface *n.* On a fretless instrument, the surface of the fingerboard that the strings contact during playing. On a fretted instrument, this term is also used to denote the surface described by the tops of the frets.

proportional spacing *n.* In the context of the placement of guitar strings on an instrument, proportional spacing means placing the strings next to each other so that the spaces between each adjacent pair of strings is equal to that of all the other adjacent pairs. When so placed, the string centers are located proportionally to the their individual thicknesses.

PSA *abbr.* Pressure Sensitive Adhesive.

purfling *n.* Decorative strips on the plates and possibly the ribs, near the edges. On guitars and similar instruments the purfling strips can be found between the bindings and the rest of the surface of the plate. Guitar purflings are composed of wood or fiber lines and also marquetry strips and shell pieces. Violin family instruments have no bindings and the purflings on these instruments are located just inboard of the edges of the plates. Violin purflings are always composed of simple lines. See also: bindings.

quartered *syn.* quartersawn

quartersawn *adj.* This term refers to a method for cutting a log into boards and also to the resulting grain orientation of the boards. To saw quartersawn lumber, a log is cut axially into quarters. Then for each quarter section, a slice is taken from one of the flat sides, then the quarter is rotated and a slice is taken from the other flat side. This process is repeated until the quarter section is all sawn into boards. When viewed from the end, each board will show grain lines (annular rings) oriented more or less perpendicular to the width of the board. There are other ways logs can be cut to yield boards that show this grain orientation, but for lutherie purposes we refer to the resulting boards as quartersawn or simply quartered, no matter the method used to cut the wood. Note that some wood merchants use a very liberal definition of quartersawn lumber and may consider any board with grain oriented less than 45 degrees from vertical to be quartersawn, but generally lutherie wood dealers consider boards with grain angle of less than 20 degrees to be quartersawn, and are usually even more demanding where instrument top wood is concerned. Quartersawn lumber is valued in lutherie as it is generally more dimensionally stable than flat sawn lumber, and generally easier to bend without distorting or breaking. Syn: quarter sawn, quartered.

radial *adj.* Used to specify the relationship of a surface of a board to the growth rings of the tree from which is was cut. A radial surface is perpendicular to the growth rings and thus to the grain of the board when viewed from the end. The broad surfaces of a quartersawn board are radial surfaces.

radiused *adj.* Cambered. See camber.

rectangular cross-section neck blank *n.* Although not a term that is used universally in lutherie, this book makes a distinction between rectangular neck blanks and assembled neck blanks. The former is a rectangular solid or laminated block of wood that is larger than the entire headstock/neck shaft/heel assembly in every dimension, while the latter is built up from separate headstock, shaft, and heel parts. The rectangular cross section neck blank requires little or no effort to put together, but it is potentially wasteful of wood. However, most of the waste wood after the neck is cut out of the blank is in a single big piece, which can be effectively used for other parts of the guitar.

reference surface *n.* The surface of a component that will be shaped that is used as a reference for the shaping operation and tool. When power tools are used, the reference surface is generally the surface that will be in contact with the table of the power tool during shaping. See also: layout surface.

rib jack *n.* Jacks (the opposite of clamps) used to hold the ribs of an instrument in position inside an outside mold. The jacks are used during the process of gluing on the top or back plate. Once the glue dries, the jacks are removed through the soundhole.

roll *n.* In lutherie the terms yaw, pitch, and roll, used to describe rotation of an object in space, are most often used to describe adjustments necessary to fit an instrument's neck onto its body. When the instrument is viewed from the end, roll is rotation of the neck about an axis extending from your eye through the instrument. See also: pitch, yaw.

rosette *n.* Decoration around or in a soundhole.

rule of 18 *n.* Historical technique used to calculate fret locations. The scale length was divided by 18, the result of which was the distance from nut to first fret. That distance was subtracted from the scale length and that value was divided by 18 to yield the distance from the first fret to the second fret. The process was repeated for all frets. The technique does not yield the same results as the modern twelfth root of 2 method for performing these calculations, but the results may be within the range of human pitch differentiation for stringed musical instruments. See also: twelfth root of 2, compensation.

runout *n.* Lack of parallelism between the grain lines and the long dimension of a board. Split boards generally do not exhibit runout, while most sawn boards have at least some. Severe runout can lead to structural weakness, but woodworkers need to be aware of even small amounts of runout because it affects the direction in which a board can be planed. Runout present in bookmatched pieces makes the two halves look different.

saddle *n.* Hard, protruding component over which the strings or other wire components run. The bridge saddle of guitar family instruments is the termination of the speaking length of the string. The saddle on violin family instruments is a piece of hard material inlaid into the edge of the top at the tail end, over which the tail gut runs.

safe edge *n.* An edge or side of a file or rasp that is smooth and devoid of cutting teeth. The safe edge of a file can be rubbed against a surface without cutting into that surface.

sandpaper pull method *n.* A technique for fitting two flat parts together. The parts are roughly shaped to fit each other, then are held together with a piece of course grit sandpaper in between. The sandpaper is pulled one way and then the other while the pieces are held together. This sands the surface of one of the pieces to the contour of the other. A variation of the technique is used to angle the heel back in a neck reset or neck fitting for a guitar. Here the sandpaper is positioned between the heel and the instrument body and facing the heel. On each stroke the sandpaper is completely pulled out, which causes the heel to be sanded more deeply at the back end than at the top end. This angles the heel back. Syn.: floss sanding.

scallop *n*. A valley carved into a wood component. Some guitar top and back braces feature scalloped ends, and some have scallops cut in the central portion of the brace.

scallop *v*. To form a scallop.

setback *n*. The distance an object's location is offset from its nominal position. Lutherie use of the term generally refers to the position of the bridge saddle or nut of a guitar, or the distance of one of the outer strings to the edge of the fingerboard.

shooting board *n*. A board used as a platform for boards to be jointed using a hand plane. The boards to be jointed are placed on the shooting board with the edges to be jointed overhanging the edge of the shooting board a bit. Then the edge is planed with a plane resting on its side.

side purfling *n*. Purfling on the ribs of a guitar or similar instrument, between binding and the rest of the rib. See also: purfling.

silking *n*. See medullary ray.

single-acting trussrod *n*. See compression trussrod.

solera *n*. (so-LAIR-ah) Workboard fixture used in the construction of Spanish guitars. The fixture includes an outline of the body and generally has provisions for some side supports to aid in the bending of the ribs of the instrument.

spherical doming *n*. Plate arching of a form that results in the surface of the plate shaped like a section of a sphere. There are many different types of plate arching, but for the purposes of guitar assembly we can generally reduce that number to two; spherical doming, where the arching is patterned after a section of the surface of a sphere, and ad hoc arching, which is everything else. Guitars built in a production environment are usually spherically domed.

spirit varnish *n*. Varnish using alcohol as the solvent. Spirit varnishes are generally quick drying. Subsequent coats burn in to previous coats, forming a continuous mass. Spirit varnishes are often used for violins. See also: oil varnish.

spp. *abbr*. This abbreviation for the word "species" is used in the species part of a Latin binomial to indicate two or more species of the same genus. For example, the binomial for ebony is *Diospyros* spp. which indicates that two or more species of the genus *Diospyros* are included. See also: Latin binomial.

springback *n*. The tendency of bent wood to partially return to its unbent shape. Wood sides and bindings are often slightly over-bent on a bending iron and then allowed to relax and cool in a mold. Wood bent in a bending machine is generally left to cool and dry in the machine to help eliminate springback.

stacked heel *n*. Neck heel that is made up of a number of pieces of wood stacked together. Stacked heels make efficient use of wood, as a single board can be cut to length for headstock, neck shaft, and a number of pieces that can be stacked and laminated together for the heel.

stiffness *n*. The property of resisting bending. Rigidity. This property of an object is dependent on the material it is made of and on its shape.

stiffness to weight ratio *n*. The ratio of the stiffness of a material or a structural component to its weight. For the components of the top of the guitar, we generally use materials that have a high stiffness to weight ratio. These materials are both stiff and light in weight. See stiffness.

successive approximation *n*. The process of approaching a final value by making progressively smaller changes. The term is applied to woodworking to describe the usual method by which raw materials are fashioned into finished and often complex shapes. For example, an instrument neck shaft starts out as rectangular stock sawn to the rough dimensions of the finished neck. The vertical and horizontal profiles are then cut, bringing the piece a bit closer to the final shape. Facets cut on the shaft roughly approximate the final curved profile, and secondary facets approximate that profile even more accurately. Final scraping and sanding bring the piece to finished dimensions. Syn.: sequential refinement.

tail block *n*. Structural component of stringed instruments. The tail block is a block of wood located at the tail end of the body. Its function is to serve as a gluing surface for the ends of the ribs and to support the end pin or strap button. Syn.: butt block. See also: end pin.

tail graft *n*. A decorative feature of flattop guitars and other instruments. The tail graft is an inlaid strip of wood at the end seam of the ribs. It often contrasts with the ribs and is often of the same material as the bindings or back strip. There are two basic configurations for the tail graft, tapered or straight. Syn.: butt graft, end graft, tail strip.

tangential *adj*. Used to specify the relationship of a surface of a board to the growth rings of the tree from which is was cut. A tangential surface is tangential (approximately parallel) to the growth rings and thus to the grain of the board when viewed from the end. The broad surfaces of a flat sawn board are tangential surfaces.

top purfling *n*. Purfling on the top plate of a guitar or similar instrument, between the binding and the rest of the top. See also: purfling.

torrefied *adj*. Heat treated. Torrefied wood is used primarily in lutherie for guitar tops and braces. Heat treatment techniques vary, but generally involve heating the wood for some period of time. Some processes control humidity or available oxygen during treatment. Heat treating affects a number of physical properties of the wood. The wood ends up darker in color, stiffer, heavier, and with reduced breaking strength and ability to take up moisture. This latter property makes the wood more dimensionally stable with changes in humidity. There are various "brand names" of heat treatment. The most commonly known is Torrefaction. In lutherie contexts a common generic term for such heat treatment is torrefication.

trussrod *n*. A rod or system of rods used to reinforce the neck of a stringed instrument. There are three general types of trussrods. Non-adjustable trussrods provide stiffening only. Steel rods, bars or channels are often used in this application, as are rods and bars made of carbon fiber composite material. Adjustable trussrods include single-acting and double-acting types. Single-acting rods, also sometimes called compression rods or tension rods, can be adjusted to provide more neck back bow only. Double-acting rods can be adjusted to provide more back bow or more front bow.

twelfth root of two *n*. The number which, when raised to the 12th power, equals 2. Its value is approximately 1.059463. The twelfth root of 2 is used in lutherie to describe the fret spacing relationship of fretted instruments in equal temperament. A simple way to make use of this constant in locating frets is to use a fret position constant derived from it, 17.817. The scale length is divided by this, the result of which is the distance from nut to first fret. That distance is subtracted from the scale length and the resulting value is divided by the fret position constant to yield the distance from the first fret to the second fret. The process is repeated for all frets. While the technique yields mathematically correct results, resulting pitches are not quite accurate. With added compensation the results may be within the range of human pitch differentiation for stringed musical instruments. See also: compensation, rule of 18.

upcut router bit *n*. Router bit which spirals up in operation, which helps to clear chips out of the routed pocket but can fuzz the upper edge of the pocket. Syn.: Spiral-up router bit, up-spiral router bit. See also: downcut router bit.

UV cured finish *n*. Finishing material that cures with exposure to ultraviolet light.

vibrating length *n*. The portion of the string of a musical instrument that vibrates. For an unstopped string, the vibrating length is the portion between nut and bridge; for a stopped string, the vibrating length is the portion between the stopping finger/fret and the bridge. The term is generally used to differentiate the active portion of the string from the "inactive" portions located above the nut and below the bridge, generally referred to as the after length. Syn.: speaking length.

waterslip decals *n*. Graphics transfers made of printed pieces of thin clear vinyl. The pieces are adhered to a backing sheet covered in water soluble glue. In use, the decals are soaked in warm water which softens the glue, then slipped off the backer sheet and transferred to an object to be decorated. These are traditionally used to decorate the headstocks of inexpensive factory-built guitars.

wet inspection *n*. Inspection of the surfaces of worked wood pieces such as instruments by first wetting the surfaces with an evaporating solvent. The solvent gives some impression of what the surface will look like under finish. It also can highlight flaws in the surface which may not be visible when the surface is dry.

witness line *n*. A defect in the application of varnish finishes or other finishes that are applied in layers that remain distinct rather than burning in to form a single continuous layer. When such a finish is leveled using abrasives, it is possible to cut through, that is, to completely abrade the top layer in places, exposing an underlying layer. The visible boundary line between the layers is called a witness line. The fix for witness lines is to apply additional layers of finish and to level so as not to cut through the top layer.

X bracing *n*. A bracing strategy for the top of flattop guitars that features two main braces configured in an X pattern, the center point of which is positioned on the centerline of the plate just above the bridge position. X bracing is used primarily on modern steel string guitars. See also: fan bracing, ladder bracing.

yaw *n*. In lutherie the terms yaw, pitch, and roll, used to describe rotation of an object in space, are most often used to describe adjustments necessary to fit an instrument's neck onto its body. When the instrument is viewed looking at its top, yaw is rotation of the neck from side to side about an axis extending from your eye to the centerline of the instrument at the neck/body join. See also: pitch, roll.

Wood Species Mentioned in this Book

More information about the various wood species mentioned throughout the book is provided here. Note that this data is presented in Latin binomial order. Although common names are more, well, common, they can be quite ambiguous in practice. The only definitive way to identify wood species in by their Latin binomials.

Information here is largely gleaned from various public sources. But the single best source for consistent information about wood is Eric Meier's website called The Wood Database. Eric also offers an excellent book on the subject entitled *Wood! Identifying and Using Hundreds of Woods Worldwide*. I highly recommend the site and the book.

Most of the entries here list common names, where the wood grows, and some general information about what the wood looks like and how it behaves as a material. Specific properties such as density, stiffness, and shrinkage are generally included. These are presented as specific gravity, modulus of elasticity, and shrinkage percentages, respectively. Although these technical terms may not be familiar to all readers, it should be noted that they can still be used to compare the woods presented here to each other. The higher the specific gravity number, the denser the wood is. The higher the modulus of elasticity, the stiffer the wood is. The shrinkage percentages represent how much wood shrinks from green to dry enough to use. Higher shrinkage numbers means the wood is less stable with changes in humidity, so the lower the shrinkage numbers, the more stable the wood is. Also note that there are two shrinkage numbers presented. The closer these numbers are to each other, the more dimensionally stable the wood is.

Acer macrophyllum– Bigleaf maple, broadleaf maple, Oregon maple. Found in the western part of the US and Canada. The wood of the tree is moderately hard, moderately heavy, and moderately dense, and light in color. It is somewhat stringy and does not carve as well as other maples. Specific gravity of dry wood is approximately 0.55. Modulus of elasticity is 10 GPa. Figured wood can display a flamed or quilted pattern. It is commonly used for drop tops for electric guitars and is often used for mandolin backs and sides.

Acer platanoides– Norway maple, European maple. European hardwood used for backs and sides of violin family and similar instruments. Can exhibit a tiger or flame pattern. The wood of the tree is moderately hard, moderately heavy and moderately dense, and light in color. Specific gravity of typical dry wood is 0.65. Modulus of elasticity is 10.6 GPa.

Acer pseudoplatanus– European sycamore, sycamore, European maple. Not a true sycamore but a maple, this European hardwood is used for backs and sides of violin family and similar instruments. Note that this is not the wood generally referred to as sycamore in the USA (*Platanus occidentalis*). Can exhibit a tiger or flame pattern. The wood of the tree is moderately hard, moderately heavy and moderately dense, and light in color. Specific gravity of typical dry wood is 0.61. Modulus of elasticity is 9.92 GPa.

Acer rubrum– Red maple, swamp maple, Eastern soft maple. Found in the eastern part of the US and Canada. The wood of the tree is moderately hard, moderately heavy and moderately dense, and light in color. Specific gravity of typical dry wood is 0.54. Modulus of elasticity is 11.3 GPa. Figured soft maple can display a tiger or flame pattern. It is used for the backs, sides and necks of archtop guitars and mandolins, and for drop tops for solid body electric guitars.

Acer spp.– Any species (or all species) of the *Acer* (maple) genus.

Betula spp.– American birch. Found in the northeastern part of the US. The wood is moderately hard, moderately heavy, and moderately dense, and light in color. The following specs are for *B. alleghaniensis* (yellow birch) but are similar for other species. Specific gravity of typical dry wood is 0.62. Modulus of elasticity is 13.8 GPa. Shrinkage (radial, tangential): 5.8%, 7.4%.

Carya spp.– Hickory, pecan. Found in the eastern to midwestern parts of the US. The sapwood is white, tinged with brown, while the heartwood is pale to reddish brown. The wood is very strong, heavy and dense. It is difficult to dry. Specific gravity of typical dry wood is 0.69. Modulus of elasticity is 11.38 Gpa. Shrinkage (radial, tangential): 5.8%, 9.2%.

Dalbergia latifolia– An Indian rosewood commonly used in lutherie. The wood is hard, heavy, stiff and strong. Colors range from dark brown to lighter shades of brown with black, brown and purple streaking. It is used for guitar backs and sides and also for fingerboards and bridges. The trees are grown for shade in Indian tea plantations and production of the wood is managed by the Indian government. Specific gravity of dry wood is 0.83 and modulus of elasticity is 11.5 GPa. Syn.: East Indian rosewood, EIR, Indian rosewood.

Dalbergia nigra– Brazilian rosewood. This rosewood is hard, dense and red/brown in color. It was the traditional wood for top-of-the-line steel string guitars and classical guitars for some time, but it is now essentially unavailable except at extremely high prices. It grows in Brazil, but it is endangered by loss of habitat as forests have been converted to farmland. It is CITES listed. The dry wood has a typical specific gravity of 0.84 and a modulus of elasticity of 13.9 GPa.

Dalbergia spp.– Any species (or all species) of the *Dalbergia* (rosewood) genus.

Diospyros spp.– Ebony wood. Ebony is from a number of species of the genus *Diospyros*, and there are a number of other black or nearly black woods that are called ebony as well. *Diospyros ebenum* is more generally called Ceylon, Sri Lanka, or Indian ebony. It is hard, dense, brittle and ranges from black to somewhat black in color. World supplies are being decimated and the wood is expensive and sometimes difficult to obtain. It is used in lutherie for fingerboards and headstock veneers, also for the fittings of violin family instruments and archtop guitars. Ebony shrinks a lot when drying and takes a long time to air dry.

Entandrophragma cylindricum– Sapele. The wood is found in various African countries. The wood looks much like mahogany and is a medium brown color, and often shows the same kinds of figure found in mahogany. It is a popular species for guitar necks, and also for backs and sides. It is moderately hard, moderately heavy, and moderately dense. Specific gravity of dry wood is 0.67. Modulus of elasticity is 12 Gpa. Shrinkage (radial, tangential): 4.9%, 7.2%.

Juglans hindsii– Claro walnut, California walnut. Found in the western part of the US. The wood is light brown to chocolate brown (heartwood) with off white colored sapwood. It is a popular domestic species for acoustic guitar backs and sides. It is moderately hard, moderately heavy and moderately dense. Specific gravity of dry wood is 0.64. Modulus of elasticity is 11.6 GPa. Shrinkage (radial, tangential): 4.3%, 6.4%.

Juglans nigra– Black walnut. Black walnut is found throughout the eastern United States. Black walnut wood is heavy, strong, and highly resistant to shock. It is a popular domestic species for acoustic guitar backs and sides. Specific gravity of typical dry wood is 0.66. Modulus of elasticity is 11.6 GPa. Shrinkage (radial, tangential): 5.5%, 7.8%.

Liriodendron tulipifera– North American tree generally called yellow poplar, tulip poplar or just poplar. It is not a true poplar. The wood sees limited use in lutherie but is sometimes used for blocks and for electric guitar bodies that will be painted. It is moderately dense and moderately stiff. It machines well but can be fuzzy when sanded. Specific gravity (dry) 0.46. Modulus of elasticity is 10.9 GPa. Shrinkage (radial, tangential): 4.6%, 8.2%.

Picea abies– The species generally known as German spruce, Norway spruce, or European spruce (also called Swiss, French, Yugoslavian and Italian spruce). A European softwood used for the tops on many instruments. This species was used in many old Spanish classical guitars and, as a local species, is used in many modern European instruments. It is imported into the USA and used by American luthiers as well. It grows throughout Europe. It is light in color with darker latewood bands. Specific gravity of dry wood is 0.41. Modulus of elasticity is 9.7 GPa.

Picea engelmannii– Engelmann spruce. This softwood from the Pacific Northwest is used for the top plates of guitars and other acoustic instruments. It is light in color with darker latewood bands. The dry wood has an average specific gravity of 0.39 and a modulus of elasticity of 9.44 GPa.

Picea rubens– Red or Adirondack spruce. A North American softwood used for tops of many instruments. This species was used in many pre-World-War-II Martin guitars and is preferred by a number of modern flattop guitar builders. It is one of three species commonly referred to as eastern Spruce. It grows primarily in New England and in the Appalachian mountains. Dry wood has a typical specific gravity of 0.43 and a modulus of elasticity of 10.8 GPa. Syn.: Adirondack spruce, red spruce.

Picea sitchensis– Sitka spruce. Softwood from the Pacific Northwest of North America. Used primarily for steel string guitar and mandolin tops. The typical specific gravity of Sitka spruce is 0.40 for dry wood. The modulus of elasticity of Sitka spruce grown in the United States is 11 GPa. Syn.: Sitka spruce, yellow spruce.

Picea spp.– Any species (or all species) of the *Picea* (spruce) genus.

Prunus serotina– Black cherry, cherry, American cherry. Found in eastern North America. Heartwood is a light pinkish brown when freshly cut, darkening to a medium reddish brown with time and upon exposure to light. Sapwood is a pale yellowish color. The wood has no discernible pores, so no pore filling is required when finishing it. The wood is easy to work. It is easy to heat bend. Dry wood has a typical specific gravity of 0.56 and a modulus of elasticity of 10.4 GPa. Shrinkage (radial, tangential): 3.7%, 7.1%.

Quercus alba– White oak. Found in the eastern US. Heartwood and sapwood are white to light brown. Quartersawn wood shows a medullary fleck pattern. The wood is stringy and heavy, and it is easy to heat bend. Dry wood has a typical specific gravity of 0.75 and a modulus of elasticity of 12.3 GPa. Shrinkage (radial, tangential): 5.6%, 10.6%.

Quercus spp.– Any species (or all species) of the *Quercus* (oak) genus.

Robinia pseudoacacia– Black locust. Species native to the USA, it has density and stiffness similar to Brazilian rosewood (*Dalbergia nigra*) and is considered by some to be a viable domestic alternative for guitar backs and sides.

Swietenia macrophylla– Honduras mahogany. A medium dark, medium density tropical hardwood. Honduras (sometimes called true or genuine) mahogany is used in lutherie for guitar and mandolin backs and sides and necks, and also for blocks and linings. The wood is extremely stable due to its low shrinkage (radial: 2.9%, tangential: 4.3%), low shrinkage ratio, and interlocking grain structure. It is very easy to carve. It has pronounced pores, which are generally filled when the wood is finished. The wood is native to northern South America. It has a typical specific gravity of 0.59 in dry wood, and a modulus of elasticity of 10 GPa.

Thuja plicata– Western red cedar. Softwood, not of the cedar genus (C*edrus*), used for guitar tops. It is light in weight, moderately stiff, and soft. Dry wood has a specific gravity of 0.37 and a modulus of elasticity of 7.7 GPa. Syn.: western red cedar, red cedar.

Tilia americana– Basswood. Fine grained hardwood native to the eastern United States. Used for painted electric guitar bodies and blocks for acoustic instruments. Plain white in color. Carves easily. Specific gravity of dry wood is 0.42. Modulus of elasticity is 10.1 GPa. Syn.: basswood, lime, linden.

Luthiers Mentioned in this Book

As you may have noticed, I refer to the work of a lot of different luthiers in this book. Usually it is in the context of illustrating some detail, but it is often just in passing. I do this for a few reasons. One is simply to point out that there are a lot of people around the world that are engaged in guitarmaking. Another reason is to make it clear that I have been and continue to be influenced in ways large and small by so many talented luthiers. But to me the most important reason to present some idea of the number of individuals involved in this work is to show that there are a variety of ways in which lutherie may be done. There is no one way and there certainly is no "right" way to build a guitar. As I pointed out in the introduction, I've made a long study of how the most accomplished luthiers do what they do, and it is clear that there are many different paths to excellence. The luthiers named in this book represent just a sampling of some of this excellence. I highly recommend looking some of these people up on the Internet and checking out their websites. I am confident that any aspiring luthier will gain great inspiration by doing so.

Kevin Aram

André Brunet

James Buckland

Cyndy Burton

John Calkin

Todd Cambio

William Cumpiano

Mark Dalton

Mike Doolin

Sjaak Elmendorp

Dan Erlewine

Harry Fleishman

Gerard Gilet

Bob Gleason

Trevor Gore

John Greven

David Hurd

Jeff Jewitt

Sergei de Jonge

Howard Klepper

Grit Laskin

Burton LeGeyt

C.F. Martin

Graham McDonald

Jim Mouradian

Jonathan Natelson

Louis Panormo

Alberto Paredes

Anamaría Paredes

Andy Powers

Francisco Sanguino

Richard Schneider

Tim Shaw

Charles Tauber

Bob Taylor

Antonio de Torres Jurado

Kevin Waldron

Sylvan Wells

James Westbrook

Kathy and Jimmi Wingert

Index

#5 jack plane 173
#7 jointer plane 173

A

"A" grading system 194
abalone 50, 68–70, 193, 197, 209–211, 213–215
Acer pseudoplatanus 17, 481. See Also European sycamore
Acer rubrum 17, 36, 481. See Also eastern soft maple
Acer saccharum 19, 130
acetone 11, 302, 306
action 31, 54, 316, 384, 386, 417, 420, 440, 452–457, 462, 475
    general action 454, 456
    relative action 454–456
    string action gauge 454–455
alcohol 275, 308, 349, 354, 476, 479
Allen key 31, 33, 237, 253, 257, 340, 414, 452
American cherry 17, 482. See Also Prunus serotina
American Lutherie vii–ix, 1–2, 14, 54, 66, 97, 112, 148, 195, 216, 340, 354, 358–359, 382, 412, 426, 448, 463, 474, 476
application container 360, 362–364
application temperature range 352, 359
aquarium pump 75–77
Kevin Aram 354, 483
arbor press 301
assembly board 24–27, 65–66, 264, 271
automotive compound 382, 459–460
Avery 73, 442, 444
awl 22–23, 26–27, 32, 52–53, 59–61, 66, 94, 126, 197–199, 256, 390–391, 427–428, 455–456

B

back bow 31, 452, 461, 475, 480
back braces 170–171, 186–190, 192, 219, 235, 259, 479
back joint 169
back plate v, 7–8, 114, 129, 150, 157, 162, 169–174, 176, 181–190, 192, 193, 196–198, 217, 219, 222–223, 243, 253, 257–260, 262–263, 265–266, 268–269, 274, 278–280, 282–285, 287–290, 298–300, 333–334, 337, 344, 357, 371, 374, 378, 432, 474, 478
back reinforcement strip 170, 172, 183–186, 189–192, 257–259, 433
back strip 169–170, 176–177, 179–184, 259, 262–264, 270–271, 274, 278–279, 282–284, 287–290, 298, 300, 355–356, 474, 479
back taper 161
backsaw 3, 41, 44, 153, 267, 335
ball peen hammer 312
Baltic birch plywood 219, 469
bandsaw 3, 22–24, 30–31, 47, 76, 91–94, 116, 128, 163–165, 183, 238, 264, 309
basswood 17, 482. See Also Tilia americana
bastard grain 17–19, 474
beeswax 76, 404, 431–432, 447
belly bridge 384, 474
belt sander 72, 97, 124, 145, 152, 157, 161, 439
bench hook 40, 47, 71, 264
bench vise 33, 318–320, 323–324, 334, 371, 373, 473
bending characteristics of wood 132
bending iron 113–114, 129, 131, 133–142, 147–148, 207–208, 270, 273, 293, 299, 309, 344, 479
bending pressure 131, 136–142, 148, 310, 475, 477
Betula spp. 130, 132, 149, 481
binding 71, 128, 142–143, 177, 207, 214, 262, 270–300, 315, 320–321, 331, 337, 340, 343–344, 354, 356, 359, 367, 447–448, 474, 476, 479
    binding strip 142–143, 177, 207, 262, 270–273, 276–280, 282–285, 287–288, 290–294, 296–297, 299–300
bindings 113, 130, 142, 145, 170, 176–177, 261–262, 264, 270–276, 278, 284, 287, 290–291, 293, 295, 297, 299–300, 304, 320–322, 331–332, 339–340, 342, 344, 354, 356, 359, 376, 474, 478–479
    plastic bindings 262
    wood bindings 142, 262
birch 130, 132, 149, 219, 469, 481
black cherry 67, 132, 149, 355, 384, 482
black locust 37, 482
black walnut 17, 132, 355, 482. See Also Juglans nigra
block plane 3, 95–96, 161–162, 182, 269, 330, 335–336
blocks (neck and tail) 6, 17, 114, 149–153, 157–158, 161–162, 168, 389, 482
blowout 89, 94
body contact surface 32, 55–57, 62, 95–96, 108, 111, 149, 303, 316–320, 322, 324–327, 334, 336–337
body mold v, 14, 113–114, 140, 172, 270
body outline 114–117, 122–126, 129, 135–136, 148, 172, 185, 188–189, 192, 221, 223–224, 229, 232, 234–236, 238, 245, 249, 272
    body outline segment tape. See outline segment tape
boiling water 81, 208–209
bookmatched 129–130, 142–143, 169, 173, 193–194, 474, 478
box joint 219, 223–232, 234
    box joint cap 219, 231–232
boxwood 387
brace 171–172, 186–192, 217–219, 221–232, 234–242, 243–250, 252, 254, 257–259, 336, 338, 433, 460–461, 475–476, 479
    brace blank 171–172, 186–189, 219, 221–227, 234–237, 240, 258
    brace end 187–189, 191–192, 228–230, 232, 234–235, 237, 239–241, 243–250, 252, 258–259
        floating brace end 250
        pocket 246–250, 258–259
braces 6, 170–172, 184, 186–192, 193, 217–232, 234–235, 237–242, 243–247, 249–250, 258–259, 316, 379, 475–477, 479–480
bracewood 172, 187–188, 219
bracing pattern 171, 193, 217–219, 237, 476
brackets 250
brad 82–86, 87–91, 388, 400, 402–404, 427, 438

Brazilian rosewood   36, 130–131, 481–482
breakover angle   316–317, 474
bridge   v, 6–7, 9, 35, 37–40, 47, 169, 179, 181, 193, 217, 219, 221–224, 228–231, 233, 237, 241, 262, 315–317, 322, 325–326, 341, 378, 382, 383–412, 415, 427, 429, 437–438, 441, 449–453, 455–458, 460–462, 472–475, 477–480
    bridge height   316–317
    bridge pin   39, 222, 383–392, 395–396, 400, 405–410, 427, 429, 449–452, 458, 460–462
        bridge pin hole   39, 384–385, 387–392, 395–396, 400, 405–408, 410, 449–450, 462
        bridge pin reamer   388
        bridge pin spacing   39
        string slot saw   409–410
    bridge plate   169, 219, 221–224, 228–231, 233, 241, 262, 387–388, 400, 402–403, 405, 407, 449–450, 456
    saddle. See saddle
        saddle slot   387–393, 395, 397, 399–400, 405–407, 410–412, 437, 456, 458, 461
    bridge wing   384, 393–394, 400, 405, 474
bridge blank   387–388, 390
bridge clamps   388, 403–404
André Brunet   165, 483
James Buckland   vii, 1, 38, 199, 483
buffing wheel   425
burn in   350–351, 358, 377–378, 474, 477, 479
Cyndy Burton   353, 483
butt joint   55, 150, 154–156, 213, 215, 290, 298, 300
Buxus sempervirens   387
buzzes   417, 449, 457–458, 460–462

C

calipers   9, 197, 205, 207, 210–211, 454
John Calkin   vii, 97, 195, 483
cam clamp   8–9, 25, 116, 156, 191, 230, 403–406, 461
Todd Cambio   68, 483
CAMI   12, 378–379, 382
candling the plate joint   173
capo   452
card scraper   3, 8–9, 124, 157, 178, 181–182, 196, 204–205, 209–210, 215–216, 265, 271, 273–274, 283, 299–300, 340, 343, 377, 388, 402, 472–473
card stock   14, 51, 53, 58–59, 72, 154–155, 167, 318, 389, 399, 434, 455
Carya spp.   37, 481
catalyzed finish   350–351, 475
cathedral arch   186–187, 192
caul   26–27, 82–86, 87–91, 145, 148, 183–186, 221–222, 230–231, 236–237, 241, 251, 301, 330, 332–333, 336–338, 340, 388, 402–407, 416, 460–461
cellulose   133, 475
cereal box cardboard   98, 213, 413–414, 453
chamfer   208–209, 273–274, 310, 400–403, 408, 410, 422, 439, 457–459
chasing   310–311, 475
cheeks   56
chisel   57, 78, 82, 85–86, 91, 95, 186, 190, 192, 197, 199–201, 222, 228, 233–234, 240, 242, 245–249, 253, 260, 265–268, 270, 283–286, 288–290, 292–294, 299–300, 320, 346–347, 356–357, 359, 377, 388, 402, 407
    micro chisel   199–201, 346
circle cutter   198–199, 202–203, 208–209. See Also compass, compass gramil
circular arc segment   135, 140
CITES   132, 481
clamping pressure   9, 25, 82, 87, 100, 141, 153, 156, 165, 179–180, 192, 229, 232, 253, 337
claro walnut   132, 482
clear label stock   68–69, 73
clear packaging tape   154–155
climb cut   48, 96, 253, 281
clothes iron   78, 81, 299
clothespins   165, 271
CNC   37, 40–41, 43, 68–71, 74
coalescing finish   350, 475
cold bent   207, 209
compass   28, 115–116, 135, 161, 199–200, 212, 214
    compass gramil   198–199, 475
        disposable compass gramil   199–200, 216
compensation   38, 384–386, 412, 475, 478, 480
computer drawing software   68, 70, 73
cone point set screws   255
construction level   176, 180–181
construction lumber   99
contact thermometer   134, 137
coping saw   91–94, 220, 391
corning   275, 378
cotton gardening gloves   137
countersink   388, 403, 407–408
cover plate   202–203
cracking   13, 17, 36, 69, 131, 138, 150, 217–218, 260, 474
credit card   358–359
creep   462
cross-grain scratches   108
cross-grain stiffening   223
William Cumpiano   97, 483
curved shell pieces   204, 207
cut through   379–380, 382, 480
cyanoacrylate glue   11, 63–64, 69, 82, 88, 142, 162, 199–200, 208, 215, 248, 273, 293–294, 302, 305–306, 311, 346, 377, 408, 416, 438, 454, 460
    cyanoacrylate glue solvent   11, 302

D

Dalbergia latifolia   36, 130, 481
Dalbergia nigra   36, 130, 481–482
Mark Dalton   201, 483
damping   460–462
dent steaming   343
dental pick   210–211, 213, 377
Diospyros spp.   36, 71, 386, 479, 481
disc sander   20, 24, 72
dishwashing liquid   378–379
disposable miter fixture   293–294
distorting effects of string tension   223
domestic hardwoods   131
domestic species   37, 130–132, 386–387, 482
doming   7, 171, 474, 479
Mike Doolin   viii, 40, 55, 483

dot marker location gauge 51
double-sided tape 41–44, 48, 57–61, 76–77, 79–80, 91–92, 318, 330, 334–335, 427–428, 468. See Also double-stick tape
double-stick tape 48–49, 79, 95, 164–167, 243, 258, 288–289, 318–319, 391–393, 395, 403–404
drill bit 32, 53–54, 59–63, 76–77, 87–88, 123, 199–201, 203, 256, 397, 400, 406, 431
    brad point 32, 52, 59–61, 93–94, 199–200, 254, 256–257, 391, 428–429
    micro drill bit 76–77
    stop collar 61–62
    twist bit 54, 61–62, 257, 429
drill press 3, 8–9, 18, 20, 22, 29–30, 32, 52–54, 57, 60–61, 93–94, 116–118, 152, 157, 188–189, 200, 203, 207–209, 220, 235, 251, 256, 305, 391, 397, 402–403, 427–428
drilling guide 256–257, 427
drop-fill 215, 345–346, 376–377
drum sander 30, 93, 130, 189, 227, 391, 394. See Also sanding drum
dry brush 367, 369–376
dry-fitted 156, 211, 214
duct tape 199

E

East Indian rosewood 36, 130, 481
eastern soft maple 17, 481. See Also Acer rubrum
ebony 36, 70–71, 76, 82, 131, 314, 388, 477, 479, 481–482
    ebony dust 76, 477
elastic deformation 133, 475, 477
Sjaak Elmendorp vii–viii, 384, 483
end graft 156, 469, 475, 479. See Also tail graft
end nippers 87–88, 302, 307–308, 310–312, 412
    flush cutting 307–308, 312, 412
end pin 149–150, 156, 261, 263, 341, 387, 427–431, 469, 475–476, 479
Engelmann spruce 193–194, 482
engraving scriber 81
Entandrophragma cylindricum 17, 482. See Also sapele
epoxy 11, 20–21, 76, 79–80, 82, 94, 124, 214–215, 308, 314, 344–346, 409
ergonomics 171
Dan Erlewine 472, 483
European spruce 193, 482
European sycamore 17, 481. See Also Acer pseudoplatanus
evaporative finish 350, 474, 476
example guitars 5, 19–21, 23–24, 27, 31, 33, 37, 42–43, 46, 55–56, 114, 120, 139–140, 143, 159, 161, 215, 218, 384, 388, 465
example instruments 7, 13, 18, 22, 31–32, 35, 37, 39–40, 42, 50–51, 55, 65, 71–72, 115, 118, 125, 130–131, 135–136, 143, 145, 148, 150–151, 160, 163, 170–171, 184, 188–189, 194, 197, 217–219, 221, 223, 231, 235–237, 240, 263, 270, 303, 310, 318, 322, 338, 388–389, 399, 404, 434, 441, 452, 455, 465, 471
exterior plywood 114

F

facet 98, 100, 102–103, 105–106, 160, 422, 459

neck shaft
    primary 102, 105
    secondary 103
    tertiary 107
fall off 329, 414, 419–420, 438, 475–476
fan bracing 217–218, 475–476, 480
feeler gauge 9, 34, 54, 58, 61–62, 158–159, 161–162, 164, 200, 240, 328–329, 395, 437–439, 443, 452–454
FEPA 12, 377–378, 382
file 14, 32, 51, 74, 79, 81, 86, 144–145, 220, 273, 302, 308, 310, 312–313, 318, 339–340, 388, 396, 407–410, 413, 417–423, 426, 439–443, 445–448, 449, 451, 453–454, 456, 459, 461–462, 476, 478
fillet 435, 459
finger brace 223–224, 237–241, 250
finishing nail 99
fittings 337, 341, 427, 476, 482
flat sawn 17–19, 131, 474, 476, 478–479
flat washers 115, 157, 255, 257
flattening agents 363
Harry Fleishman 32, 483
flip-matched 18–19
flow-out 359–360, 371, 376, 381
foam brush 351, 358, 360, 363, 377
foam earplugs 353–354, 401
font viii, 4, 75
Forstner bit 30, 115, 117–118, 220
freehand arc 101–102, 106
French polish 351, 476
fret v, 3–4, 31, 35–47, 49–52, 87–88, 91, 97–98, 100–102, 104–105, 109, 267, 301–302, 304–305, 307–314, 321–322, 328–329, 344, 385–386, 413–426, 437–439, 443, 452–456, 461–462, 475–476, 478, 480
    barbs 310–311
    bead 88, 301–302, 310–311, 415, 417, 420–421
    crowning 413, 420–421, 476
        fret crowning file 413, 420–421, 476
    end 36, 310, 312–314, 344, 413, 417–418, 421–424, 426, 476
        fret end bevel 313
        fret end dressing 417, 421–422, 426
    fret dressing file 413, 421, 426, 476
    fretwire 39, 301–302, 307–310, 314. See Also fret, wire
        alloy 302
    installation 44, 301–302, 307–310, 462
    leveling 308, 312, 328, 413, 417–421, 476
    location 38, 41–43, 45, 478
    placement 4, 38
    polishing 421, 423, 426
    slot 35–37, 39–46, 49, 88, 91, 267, 301–302, 304–305, 310–314, 475–476
        fret slot cleaning tool 302, 305
    slotting saw 44–45, 267
    slotting template 43–44
    spacing 37–39, 416, 480
    tang 35, 41, 301, 308–314, 322, 418, 475–476
    tied fret 38
    wire 3, 41, 302, 311–313, 413
fret leveler file 302, 308, 417

fretboard v, 4, 6, 14, 20–28, 31–34, 35–37, 39–54,
57–59, 62–64, 67, 72, 83, 85–86, 87–91, 93–96, 97,
99–102, 104–110, 112, 149–150, 160–161, 201, 204,
207, 214–215, 235, 254–255, 257, 301–314,
315–332, 334, 336–338, 340, 342, 348, 354–357,
359, 363, 365–368, 372–377, 380–382, 385–390,
397–400, 413–426, 436–438, 441–447, 450–454,
457–458, 462, 471, 474, 476
    blank 36–37, 39–41, 43, 45, 47–48
        pre-slotted 37, 40–41, 46
    camber 35–36, 39–40, 54, 301–302, 304–305,
308–310, 418, 420–421, 437, 474–475, 478
    dot markers 36, 40, 46, 49–53
    extension 37, 46, 88, 90–91, 95, 99–100, 149,
201, 204, 207, 215, 235, 257, 303–305,
311–312, 315–331, 334, 336–338, 340, 357, 359,
363, 365–367, 374, 377, 380–382, 413–414, 416,
420, 422, 424, 438, 476
    fretboard radius 39, 302, 304
    marker dots 50, 54, 91, 112, 301–302, 305–306
    playing surface 35–36, 39–40, 43–44, 46, 48–50,
52–53, 91, 99, 108, 112, 301–305, 308, 310,
342, 354, 356–357, 359, 366, 373, 414, 474,
476–477
    position markers 36, 40
    side marker dot 50, 54, 91, 306
fretboard radius sanding block 302, 304
front bow 31, 475, 480
furniture powder 76, 80, 82

G

garland v, 114, 149–150, 155–163, 165–168, 171,
184, 187, 243–247, 249–252, 258–259, 261, 275, 476
German spruce 193, 482
Gibson 17, 156
Gerard Gilet 86, 483
Bob Gleason 358, 483
glue allowance 197, 205, 207, 209, 211, 213
glue blocks. See peones
glue brush 205, 271
glue line 11, 20, 31, 197
glue stick 432–433
glue-proof 25, 27, 65, 121, 124, 177, 198,
204–206, 264, 270, 293–294
gluing surface 23, 25–27, 40, 42, 46–48, 50, 53, 65,
87, 171–172, 219, 223, 226, 271–274, 397, 401,
404, 477, 479
go bar 461
goggles 76
Goldilocks principle 26, 362
Trevor Gore 86, 483
gouge 63, 152, 215, 236, 285–286, 468
grain filler 358, 377, 382
graining 345–346, 348
gramil 198–201, 205, 210, 216, 270, 283–287,
475–476
John Greven 97, 358, 483
growth rings 16–17, 478–479
guide block 256, 427–429
Guild of American Luthiers vii–ix, 1, 354, 463,
469–470, 474, 476
guitar body vise vi, 267–268, 427–428, 469–470

guitar sides 9, 113–115, 124, 126, 128, 129,
132–134, 136–137, 139, 141, 153, 155–156, 262,
271–274, 300, 309, 356. See Also rib
gum eraser 378, 414–415, 423–424

H

hacksaw 61, 302
half pencil 161, 437–439, 443, 456–458
hand drill 32, 57, 83, 87, 123, 199, 254, 257, 400,
406, 428, 432
hand plane 8–9, 21, 23–24, 40, 47, 71, 130, 143,
170, 173, 479
hand saw 22, 69, 75
hand-applied finishes 350, 354, 358
hard maple 19
hardwood 17–18, 32, 36, 93–94, 115, 129, 131,
149, 157, 163, 199, 219, 222, 256, 262, 342, 359,
391, 397, 404, 456, 481–482
headband magnifier 42, 288
headplate v, 28, 37, 67–73, 75–86, 87, 90–91, 261,
329–330, 332, 342, 355–356, 361, 363, 371–373,
380–381, 415, 432, 442–443, 476
    headplate blank 71, 329–330
    headplate veneer 67–68, 71, 476
headstock 6, 17–31, 33, 55–56, 65–66, 67–68,
71–74, 77, 80, 82–83, 86, 87, 91–95, 98–103, 106,
109, 111–112, 304, 310, 316, 342, 348, 352, 354,
357, 359, 361, 371, 373, 376–377, 380–382,
430–431, 445–446, 450, 452–453, 458, 461, 471,
474, 478–479, 481
    angle 21–22, 24, 28, 71
    ears 18–19, 65–66
    headstock side of the nut 21–23, 26–27, 66, 445,
447, 453
    thickness of 27–28, 30, 354, 381
heat bending 129, 132–133
heat lamp 358, 360–361, 370–373, 376
heel 6, 15–19, 22–23, 26–28, 31–34, 55–65, 87–88,
90–91, 94–96, 97–98, 101–103, 105–109, 111–112,
149, 255, 257, 301, 303–304, 310–312, 314,
315–328, 331–337, 339–340, 342, 357, 359, 368,
370–371, 373, 375, 377–379, 381–382, 413–414,
426, 427, 471, 474, 476, 478–479
    block 19, 23, 26–27
    dowel 15, 32
    heel cap 112, 314, 317, 331–333, 335–337, 357,
373–374, 476
herringbone pattern 191, 271
hickory 37, 481
hide glue 10–11, 68, 477
high speed grinder 80
hobby knife 28, 41–44, 199–200, 302, 345–347,
401, 407, 416
    blade 199–200, 302, 346–347
Honduras mahogany 5, 16–17, 130–131, 149, 482. See
Also Swietenia macrophylla
hop-hornbeam 386
humidity 7, 10, 13, 16–17, 19, 36, 131, 149, 171,
194, 217–218, 462, 479–481
David Hurd 463, 483

I

impact resistance 131

inlay 40, 67–76, 78–82, 156, 170, 176, 182, 193, 201, 341–342, 348, 465, 477
insertion tool 59–64
intonation 38, 40–41, 46, 302, 384–386, 397–398, 412, 420, 437, 440, 446–447, 452

J

jeweler's saw 69–70, 75–77, 80–81
Jeff Jewitt 350, 483
jigsaw 115–116, 118, 126, 128, 409
jointer 21, 143, 170, 172–173
jointing 8, 67, 169–170, 172–176, 196
Sergei de Jonge 132, 483
Juglans hindsii 132, 482
Juglans nigra 17, 132, 355, 482. See Also black walnut

K

kerf 41, 44, 46, 75, 163–165, 246–248, 253, 255, 310, 322, 409–410, 476
kerfed lining 149, 162–163, 165, 246–247, 250, 476–477
    tooth 247
kinking 141
Howard Klepper 262, 483
knot 143
kraft paper tape 290, 294, 304

L

label stock 14, 68–69, 73
lacquer fill stick 344
ladder bracing 171, 193, 217–218, 476, 480
laminate trimmer. See router, trim router
laminated shell sheet 69
landing stroke 362, 367
laser cutting machine 74
Grit Laskin 70, 483
ledges 270, 274–276, 278, 283–284, 286, 288, 290, 294–295, 299
left-handed 5, 50, 112, 173, 223, 237, 240, 311, 388–389, 392, 434–435, 439, 444–446, 452, 457
Burton LeGeyt 463, 483
Leonardo Guitar Research Project 131
lever 316
lignin 133, 475, 477
linings 9, 114, 149–151, 161–163, 165, 167–168, 187, 240, 242, 243–248, 250, 253, 258–259, 263, 270, 281–282, 477, 482
Liriodendron tulipifera 17, 130, 149, 482. See Also tulip poplar
locating pins 87, 397, 400, 404, 406–407
lower bout 135–136, 147, 154–155, 157, 196, 275, 281, 295–296, 475
lower bout secondary arc segment 147
lower bout segment 147
lutherie iv, vi–ix, 1–5, 8–14, 16, 18–19, 27, 31, 36–37, 39–41, 43–44, 50, 54, 57, 61, 66, 69–71, 80, 97, 106, 112, 113–114, 129–132, 134, 136, 141–142, 148, 149, 151, 163, 165, 169–173, 177, 187, 190, 194–197, 199, 201–202, 205, 207, 210, 213, 216, 218–219, 222, 239, 246, 258, 261–262, 270–271, 275–276, 283, 301–302, 305, 308, 332, 340, 345, 350, 354, 358–359, 378, 382, 387–388, 401–402, 408–409, 412, 413, 416, 420–421, 426, 427, 434, 440, 442, 448, 454–456, 463–464, 465, 469–471, 474–483
lutherie supplier 9, 11–12, 19, 27, 31, 36–37, 40–41, 43–44, 50, 57, 69, 71, 80, 132, 134, 151, 163, 170, 194, 197, 199, 201, 205, 207, 210, 213, 270–271, 275–276, 283, 301–302, 305, 308, 345, 354, 378, 387–388, 402, 408–409, 413, 427, 434, 440, 442, 455, 465, 471, 476
lutherie wood supplier 9–10, 16, 18, 36–37, 39, 71, 129–130, 132, 141–142, 149, 169, 172, 177, 187, 194, 196, 219, 222, 262, 387
luthier vii–viii, 1, 9, 11, 13, 32, 36, 55–56, 67–71, 82, 91, 95, 97–98, 109–111, 113–115, 127, 129–132, 134–138, 143, 147, 149, 154, 160, 165, 167, 169–170, 172, 183, 195, 197, 200, 205, 207, 209–211, 213, 217–219, 244, 250, 252, 261–262, 267, 270, 272, 281, 288, 304, 308, 311, 315, 320, 337, 342, 349–350, 353–354, 356–359, 363, 365, 367, 369–374, 377–379, 384, 387, 389, 391–393, 396, 414–415, 428, 433, 440, 446, 452, 457–458, 463–464, 465, 472, 477, 483

M

machinist's scriber 81, 412
magnifying headgear 41. See Also headband magnifier
marking gauge 27, 31, 40, 395
marking knife 41–44
marquetry 70, 75, 170, 176–177, 195, 197, 207–210, 262, 478
Martin 6, 17, 37, 194–195, 217, 434, 482–483
C.F. Martin 6, 37, 194–195, 217
masking tape 10, 57–59, 61–62, 72, 87–88, 90, 145, 177, 179–181, 183–185, 205, 224, 227, 230, 353–354, 358–359, 390, 398–399, 402, 406, 414, 416, 423, 425–426, 432, 435–436, 454
mastic 195, 477
Graham McDonald vii, 149, 483
MDF 12, 41, 45, 47–48, 57–58, 61, 83, 87–88, 91–93, 95, 113–115, 119–121, 125, 154, 173–174, 179, 184, 199–200, 221, 230, 250–251, 303, 312, 333–334, 338, 391–393, 404, 471
medium density fiberboard. See MDF
melamine board 12, 24–25, 41, 48, 58–59, 62, 65, 79–80, 113–115, 119–121, 124–125, 127–128, 177–179, 198, 205–206, 211, 264, 271, 317–318, 329–330, 466–467
mensure. See scale length
Marin Mersenne 385
mill file 302, 308, 312–313, 413, 417
mineral spirits 354, 356
miter box 41
miter gauge 30–31, 41, 46, 163
miter joint 290, 296, 346–347
mold v, 14, 113–128, 133, 135–137, 140–142, 144–148, 149, 151–162, 166–168, 172, 182–183, 185, 198, 207–210, 243–245, 248, 251–253, 258–259, 270, 272–273, 315, 478–479
    floor 126–128, 144, 148, 153–158, 160–162, 243, 253, 258
    insert 127–128, 144, 153, 158, 161–162, 166–167, 243, 251, 253, 258
    mold half 116–117, 120, 122

open frame mold   114–115, 118, 120, 123–125, 157, 273
  solid construction mold   115, 125
MOP   50, 69
mother of pearl   50, 68–69, 75. See Also MOP
Jim Mouradian   viii, 1, 483
mustache bridge   384

N

naphtha   275, 308, 403, 414, 426, 448
Jonathan Natelson   97, 483
neck angle   28, 30–31, 55, 158, 315
  neck angle bevel   158
neck assembly   33, 57–59, 62–65, 71–72, 83, 87–88, 91, 129
neck blank   15–23, 27–28, 30, 65, 130, 163, 474, 476, 478
  assembled   15–17, 19–20, 22–23, 30, 474, 478
  rectangular cross-section   18–20, 478
    laminated   11, 15, 17–19
    solid wood   15
  surface
    bottom surface   20–21, 23, 28
    fretboard surface   20–23, 25–28, 32–33, 44, 58, 62, 67, 72, 83, 86, 87–88, 90
    layout surface   20–23, 28
    reference surface   20–23, 26–28, 30, 33
neck block   55–56, 123, 149–152, 155–156, 159–162, 165–167, 184–186, 235–236, 243–244, 247, 250, 252, 254–258, 269, 315, 337–338, 340, 449, 477
neck bolts   255, 321, 328, 331, 337–338, 340, 449, 460–461
neck carving   97–98, 113, 129
neck carving holding fixture   98–100, 102–103
neck end   6–7, 55, 114, 123, 125, 127–128, 135, 142–144, 147–148, 149–150, 154–162, 166–168, 172, 182–186, 188–189, 191, 197–198, 204–206, 211–212, 214–215, 217, 221–222, 231, 235–239, 243–244, 246–247, 249–250, 252–254, 256–259, 265, 267, 274–275, 278, 280–281, 283, 290, 296–300, 315–316, 319, 321, 333, 366, 373, 435
neck end seam   156, 159, 166–167, 258, 316
neck flat segment   148
neck joint   v, 7, 15, 18, 32, 55–56, 66, 315, 320, 340
  bolt-on   32, 55–57, 340
  dovetail   7, 55
neck rest   vi, 354, 358, 365, 369, 416–417, 449, 452, 471
neck shaft   6, 18–19, 23–28, 64–65, 87–88, 94–95, 97–98, 100, 106–107, 110, 307, 310, 357, 378, 381, 416, 424, 471, 474, 476, 478
  facet. See facet
needle file   76, 78–79, 81, 144, 220, 310, 340, 388, 407–410, 413, 440, 442–443, 449, 451, 459
neutral axis   132–133, 477
New England Luthiers   viii–ix, 463
nitrocellulose lacquer   349
Norway spruce   193, 482
notched plastic spreader   21
nut   14, 18–19, 21–23, 26–28, 35, 37–49, 51, 54, 66, 67, 73, 82–86, 87–88, 90–91, 94–95, 101–103, 105–106, 304, 310, 322, 341, 359, 372–373, 375–376, 382, 384–390, 397–400, 411, 414–416, 419–420, 425, 427, 431, 437, 439–448, 449, 451–454, 456–462, 475, 477–480
  (string) slot   440–442, 445, 448, 451, 453, 458–461
  nut blank   387–388, 440, 442
  nut file   440, 444, 446, 448, 451, 453, 456
  nut material   387, 440
  nut razor saw   440
  nut slot   91, 359, 373, 376, 389–390, 399, 416
  nut stop   399–400, 415–416, 419
  slotting template   14, 442, 444–445
nut compensation   475

O

oak   17, 130, 482. See Also Quercus spp.
oblique brace   218, 237, 240–242, 250
off cut   16, 144
oil varnish   349–351, 358–359, 477, 479
oil wiping varnish   351, 354
opaque black filler   80, 82
open end wrench   63–64, 431–432
Ostrya virginiana   386
outline segment tape   144–145, 272

P

paint thinner   275, 308, 354, 361, 414, 426
Louis Panormo   383–384, 433, 483
paper label   242, 432
paper towel   353, 382
paraffin   76, 404, 431–432, 447
Anamaría Paredes   viii, 13, 195, 483
Alberto Paredes   viii, 195, 483
paste wax   25, 404
patterned   172, 474, 479
peones   162, 477
permanent marker   124–126, 242, 318–319, 417
phenolic impregnated paper composite   388
phenolic impregnated wood   36, 70–71, 76, 314
Picea abies   193, 482
Picea engelmannii   194, 482
Picea rubens   194, 482
Picea sitchensis   194, 482
Picea spp.   149, 172, 193, 482
pickguard   427, 433–437, 448, 477
pigment bleeding   354, 358–359
pigmented filler   68, 80
pilot hole   58–64, 428–429, 431–432
pin vise   76–77
pipe flange   469–470
pipe nipple   469
pitch (musical)   385–386, 447, 450–453, 458, 460, 462, 475
pitch (neck orientation)   7, 150, 315–320, 322–327, 330, 337, 477–478, 480
pivot pin   198–204, 208–209, 215–216, 475
planer   9, 23, 40, 45, 130, 188
plastic deformation   133, 475, 477
plastic mallet   118, 199, 301
plastic rod   40, 49–50, 305–306
plastic scraper   358–359
plastic soda straw   83–84, 87

plastic straw 86, 90–91, 155–156, 185–186, 192, 222, 230, 236, 340, 406
plasticization 133
plate arching 7, 170–171, 253, 474, 477, 479
pliers 63–64, 84, 86, 87–88, 91, 141, 147, 201, 205–210, 213, 255, 297, 300, 301–302, 306, 310, 406–407, 451–452
    sheet-metal pliers 141
    side cutting 87–88, 310
point source light 352
"Popsicle stick" brace 235–237, 243–247, 250, 252, 254, 257–258, 336, 338
pore filler 351
power tool vii, 3, 8–9, 20, 93, 130, 169, 197, 274, 470, 478
Andy Powers 218, 483
practice sides 132, 138–140, 142
printer paper 53, 452–453
proportional spacing 441, 451, 478
protractor 21–22, 24, 28, 31, 71–72, 99, 288–289, 333–334
Prunus serotina 17, 67, 132, 149, 355, 482. See Also American cherry
PSA sandpaper 12, 59–61, 80, 117, 121–122, 124, 152, 170, 175–176, 179, 185–186, 216, 266, 302, 304–305, 317–318, 334–335, 396, 466
PTFE plastic 207, 209–210, 213
purfling 71, 170, 176–177, 179, 182, 184, 205, 210, 262–264, 270–272, 274–280, 282–284, 286–300, 331–333, 341, 343, 345–348, 354, 456, 474, 476, 478–479
    purfling bundle 263, 279, 282, 290–291, 293–298, 300, 343, 345–348
purflings 261–264, 270–300, 331–332, 340, 343, 345, 347, 354, 356, 359, 376, 474, 478
    back purflings 262
    side purflings 262, 264, 270–274, 276–278, 280–282, 284–288, 290, 292–293, 295, 297, 299–300, 331–332
    top purflings 262
putty 11, 94, 313–314, 344–346, 348
putty knife 48–49, 264, 330, 468
PVC sheet 318

Q

quartered 17, 37, 129, 478. See Also quartersawn
quartersawn 10, 16–17, 36, 131, 172, 186, 188, 194, 222, 386–387, 474, 476–478, 482
Quercus alba 130, 482
Quercus spp. 17, 482. See Also oak

R

rabbeting bit sets 275
rabbets 270, 275–279, 283, 286–290, 476
raking light 342–343, 352, 354, 357, 360–361, 363, 369, 371, 376–377, 379
random orbital sander 275, 342
rasp 98, 102–103, 106–107, 157, 234, 236, 255, 257, 265, 268–269, 285–286, 297, 299, 321, 439, 478
    cabinet rasp 98
    cheese grater 8, 98
rattles 449, 457–458, 460–461
razor blade scraper 402, 414–416, 435, 472
razor saw 189–190, 227, 244–245, 248, 254, 259, 269, 291–292, 299–300, 309, 332, 334, 338, 412, 440, 443
red spruce 193–194, 482
reference line 27, 32, 87
relaxation of the wood 139–140
relief 31, 452–453, 455–457, 462, 475
respirator 76, 137
rib 14, 114, 147, 149, 157–158, 161–162, 184, 243, 245, 248–249, 253, 258, 263, 265, 267, 273, 300, 371, 377, 380–382, 476–479
    jack 149, 157–159, 161–162, 167–168, 173, 243, 253, 258, 478
rift sawn. See bastard grain
right-handed 5, 7, 20, 50, 112, 143, 175, 206, 209, 212, 218–219, 223, 237, 240, 370, 385, 388–389, 392, 399–400, 434, 439, 444–446, 452, 457
riser block 91–93, 175
Robinia pseudoacacia 37, 482
roll 315–316, 320–321, 477–478, 480
ROS 275
rosette v, 193–205, 207–210, 213, 215–216, 219, 221, 262, 264, 290, 434–436, 475, 478
    rosette channel 197–201, 203, 208–210, 215–216, 219
router
    circle-cutting baseplate 197
    collet adapter 203
    edge guide 33–34, 391–394
    hand-held 33
    jig vi, 71, 466
    plunge 8, 34, 201–202, 391, 393
    router base plate 82, 201–204, 208–209
    router bit 9, 12, 33, 48–49, 55, 58, 82, 95, 116, 118–119, 176–177, 198, 201–204, 215–216, 275–276, 278, 466, 468, 475, 480
        bottom bearing 48–49, 118–119, 253, 260, 275
        bottom-cleaning 57–58
        downcut 201, 203–204, 216, 475, 480
        flush-cutting router bit 48
            pattern bit 47–48, 57–58, 94–95, 119, 127, 253
        micro router bit 198
        rabbeting router bit 275–276
        spiral router bit 33, 475, 480
        top bearing 48–49, 57–58, 94, 118–119
        upcut 201, 475, 480
    router pad 256, 280–281
    table 33
    trim router 8, 58, 95, 118, 275, 278
rubbing out 351, 378, 380
rule of 18 38–39, 478, 480
ruler 14, 31, 41–47, 50, 100–102, 189, 198, 222, 224, 238, 240–242, 247, 250, 254, 287–289, 322, 326, 389, 398–400, 427, 431, 442, 444–445, 451, 454–455
    flexible ruler 9, 98, 287–289, 444–445, 451
    flexible plastic ruler 31
runout 17, 40, 47, 131, 194, 207, 403, 478

runs 354, 356–359, 363, 367, 370–373, 375–377, 386, 393, 414

S

saber saw. See jigsaw
saddle 35, 37–38, 40, 316–317, 322, 383–393, 395–397, 399–400, 405–412, 427, 437–442, 449, 451, 455–462, 474–475, 478–479
    saddle exposure 40, 396, 456
safe edge 86, 421–422, 442, 478
safety glasses 76
sandbag 302, 306–307, 310, 358, 373–374, 376, 416
sanding block 30, 57, 80, 82, 92, 108–109, 111–112, 117–118, 122–124, 183, 185–186, 215–216, 234, 236, 269, 275, 300, 301–302, 304–305, 314, 319–320, 335–336, 341–342, 378–382, 394, 415, 423
sanding board 8, 12–14, 22, 24, 26–27, 30–32, 47, 66, 119, 152, 157–162, 167–168, 197, 227, 230–231, 238, 240, 263–264, 275, 306, 314, 317–320, 322–327, 330, 332, 334–336, 345, 347, 390–392, 395, 399, 409–412, 439–440, 442–443, 448, 457–459
    neck-fitting sanding boards 317–319, 322, 330, 332
sanding drum 8, 18, 22, 29–30, 116, 152, 157, 186, 192, 207, 220, 235, 251, 471
sandpaper 8–9, 12–13, 47, 53, 57, 59–61, 66, 80, 82, 92–94, 107–109, 112, 117, 120–122, 124, 151–152, 157, 170, 175–176, 179, 183, 185–186, 192, 196, 208–209, 215–216, 220–221, 231, 233–234, 236, 238, 245, 251, 266, 269, 274–275, 283–284, 286, 288, 302, 304–307, 314, 317–320, 323–325, 327, 329–330, 334–337, 339–340, 341–342, 345–346, 348, 358–359, 377–382, 396–398, 410–411, 413–415, 423–425, 435, 442, 458–459, 466, 468, 478–479
    sandpaper pull method 323, 330, 478
    silicon carbide 358, 378–379, 382, 413, 423
    wet or dry 358, 378–379, 382, 422
Francisco Sanguino 217, 483
sapele 17, 482. See Also Entandrophragma cylindricum
scale length 37–39, 41–43, 322, 384–386, 388–390, 397–399, 437–438, 475, 478, 480
scale length stick 388–390, 397–399, 437–438
scallop 187, 190–192, 234–235, 479
scarf joint 67, 298
Richard Schneider 283, 483
scissors 28, 41, 43, 48, 51, 56, 58, 72–73, 98, 101, 115, 125, 192, 213–214, 220, 223, 232, 235, 355, 389, 432–435, 444, 446, 455
scorching 137, 142, 157, 275
scraper plane 330, 472–473
scratch awl. See awl
scribing 27, 58, 66, 81, 116, 161–162, 167, 266–268, 401
    scribing tool 161
sealing 114–115, 124–125, 127–128, 354, 356, 358–359, 476
segments of the sides 125, 140
setup (guitar) 449–450, 452, 456
Tim Shaw 115, 483
sheet cork 388, 404, 469, 471
shell inlay 68–70, 81, 341–342, 477

shell material 50, 68–70, 75–76, 80–81, 112, 197, 204, 207, 210, 214, 262, 348
shell particles 78
shellac 124, 345, 349, 351, 474, 476–477
shim 37, 46, 55, 99, 154–155, 167, 275, 456
shipping tape 125
shoeshine sanding 107–108
shooting board 170, 173–176, 479
side bending 113–114, 129, 132, 135–138, 157, 208, 272, 475, 477
silicone sealer 87, 89–90, 360–361
single-edge razor blade 348, 354, 356–359, 377, 402, 413, 472
Sitka spruce 193–195, 482
skew knife 248–249, 320, 345
softwood 129, 193, 196, 216, 482
soldering iron 86, 91, 343–344, 406–407
solera 114, 479
solid linings 162–163
soundhole 6, 35, 39, 45–50, 54, 56, 158–160, 166–168, 190, 193, 195, 197–201, 203, 206, 215–216, 217–223, 227, 229, 231–232, 235–236, 253, 259–260, 262, 290, 320, 327, 353, 363–367, 370–372, 374, 380, 388, 401, 404–406, 414, 416–418, 425, 432–435, 449, 451–452, 461, 475–476, 478
soundhole reinforcement ring 219–223, 229, 231–232, 235–236
special router base 80, 82
spindle sander 8, 22, 29–30, 93, 116–117, 152, 157, 186, 188–189, 207, 235, 251, 391, 394, 439, 443
spirit varnish 349, 351, 479
spokeshave 8, 98, 102–103, 106, 162, 227, 233, 388, 473
spray gun 350, 382, 475
spring back 139, 141, 148
spring clamp 9, 54, 66, 83–85, 87–88, 165, 177–178, 228–230, 271, 333, 397
spruce 149, 170, 172, 183–184, 186, 188, 193–196, 201, 219–220, 231, 251, 253, 255, 344, 382, 482
square (tool) 21–28, 42, 52, 63–64, 66, 85, 145, 154, 159, 174, 188–189, 221, 224, 227, 236, 241–242, 272, 275, 289–290, 292–293, 393–394, 412, 467–468
    combination square 292–293
    drafting square 159–160, 188–189, 221, 236, 241–242, 289–290
    framing square 189
squeegee 178, 294, 296, 362, 367, 375, 436
squeeze bottle 355–356, 382
squeeze-out 21, 26, 66, 81, 84, 86, 90–91, 95, 120, 155, 167, 180–181, 185–186, 192, 207, 211, 222, 230–232, 236–237, 239–241, 252–253, 274, 299–300, 337, 340, 343–346, 348, 403–406, 460
stacked heel 19, 479
stearated sandpaper 377
steel angle stock 466
steel wool 342, 354, 356–358
straightedge 21, 28, 47, 56, 58, 84, 98, 101–102, 105–106, 110, 127, 135, 143, 187–188, 192, 197, 224–225, 227, 234–235, 238, 246–247, 254,

266–267, 275, 288–289, 304, 319, 335, 389, 395, 414, 419–420, 428, 431–432, 437, 462
    flexible straightedge 101–102, 105–106, 288–289
strap button 427, 476, 479
string i, vii, 1, 5–7, 10, 13, 17, 19, 21, 31, 35, 37–40, 47, 54, 55–56, 130, 148, 149, 162–163, 169–171, 193–195, 217–218, 222–223, 237, 261, 302, 313, 315–317, 329, 383–388, 397, 404, 407–410, 412, 419–420, 438–448, 449–462, 463, 470, 474–478, 480–482
    string spacing 35, 39, 47, 388, 441–442, 451
    string tension 6, 10, 13, 31, 171, 193, 217, 223, 237, 316, 385, 449, 452–453, 460
string balls 222
successive approximation 97–98, 479
sugar maple. See Acer saccharum
surfactant 379
sweat 342
swelling allowance 197
Swietenia macrophylla 5, 17, 36, 57, 130–131, 149, 246, 482. See Also Honduras mahogany

T

T-shirt material 345, 354–355, 358, 361, 365, 406
table saw 18, 20, 33, 41, 46, 59, 72, 122, 143, 163, 165, 172, 179, 207
    zero clearance insert 46, 143, 164–165, 176, 207
tabs (mold) 113, 116–117, 121–124, 167
tack rag 354, 356–358, 363
tacking iron 299
tail block 149–152, 154–157, 160, 162, 167–168, 185, 259, 261, 263, 265, 389, 429, 479
tail end 6, 114–115, 124–127, 142–144, 146–148, 149–156, 158, 161–162, 166–168, 172, 182–183, 185, 215, 217–218, 222–224, 229, 235–239, 241, 244, 246, 250, 252, 258–259, 261, 263, 265, 267, 269, 274–275, 277, 279, 281–284, 286–291, 293–300, 315, 356–357, 361, 364, 367–370, 381, 396, 427–428, 435–436, 450, 461, 475, 478–479
tail graft 156, 169, 261–269, 274–275, 277–278, 280–286, 288–290, 293, 296, 299, 332, 355, 427, 475, 479
tail seam 153, 155, 261
tapering of the sides 157
Charles Tauber 132, 483
Bob Taylor. See Taylor Guitars
Taylor Guitars 55, 218, 315
tear-out 40
template
    brace half template 188, 190, 192
    bridge template 388–390, 399
    circle 28
    French curve 101
    fret-slotting. See fret, slotting template
    headstock template 65, 72–74, 91
    heel end 57, 59
    template book 14, 50–51, 56, 65, 150, 219, 223, 388–389, 394, 434, 455
thickness sander 3, 9, 23, 40, 45, 143, 172, 188, 466
threaded insert 28, 32, 56–64, 66, 109, 255, 303, 340, 427
    threaded insert fitting jig 58, 60, 62–63
threaded rod 123, 157
threadlocker fluid 337
three ring rosette pattern 197
Thuja plicata 194, 482
Tilia americana 17, 482. See Also basswood
tonewood 132
toothpick 80, 82, 305, 314, 344–346, 415, 454
top plate v, 6–8, 14, 126, 157, 169, 188, 193–198, 200–202, 204–206, 208–209, 211, 213–216, 217–222, 224, 227–230, 234–239, 241–242, 243–246, 250–251, 253, 257–259, 262, 265, 270, 272, 274, 277–278, 282–289, 291–296, 298–299, 315–316, 319–320, 331, 338, 340, 343, 356, 365, 369, 373, 383, 389, 398–400, 403, 407, 475, 477, 479, 482
torrefied wood 194, 479
Antonio de Torres Jurado 217, 483
transfer pipette 11, 302, 305–306, 311, 346, 358, 376, 416, 454, 460
transition curve 30–31, 91–93, 102, 106
    heel to neck shaft 20, 102, 106
    neck shaft to headstock 91–93
tropical hardwoods 36, 131–132, 387
tropical species 130, 132
trussrod 3, 6, 15–16, 28, 31–34, 57–58, 87, 89–90, 95, 109, 237, 253–255, 257, 278, 280, 296–297, 299, 303, 312, 318, 320–323, 330, 414, 437, 449, 452–453, 456–457, 460–462, 475, 479–480
    adjuster nut 34, 89, 253–254, 257, 318, 322, 456
    compression. See trussrod, single-acting
    double-acting 31, 480
    neutral position 33
    single-acting 31, 475, 479–480
    slot 33–34, 57–58, 87, 89–90, 95, 278, 280
tulip poplar 17, 130, 149, 482. See Also Liriodendron tulipifera
tuning machine 3, 6, 27, 69–72, 91, 93–94, 352–354, 401, 427, 430–432, 449, 451, 453, 459–461, 476
    bushings 430, 432
tweezers 79, 306
twelfth root of two 38–39, 385, 480
twisting 142

U

unbending 141, 147
upper bout 124, 135–136, 139–140, 146–147, 169, 183, 275, 281, 296, 300, 370
upper bout secondary arc segment 147
upper transverse brace 219, 234–237, 247, 338
UV-cured polyester finish 349

V

veneer lines 71, 195, 197–198, 204–207, 209–211, 215, 262
veneer sheets 177, 332
vinyl sealer 345
visual inspection 112, 425
VOC 351
volatile organic compounds 350

W

waist 6, 116, 125–126, 131, 135–136, 142, 145–148, 155, 157, 167, 183, 237, 273, 275, 281,

283–286, 291–293, 296, 298, 342, 369, 373–374, 376, 381
waist segment   145–147
Kevin Waldron   132, 483
waterborne finish   342, 349, 377, 474–475
waterslip decal   68, 480
wax block   77–78, 81
wax paper   10, 12, 154–157, 178–182, 205–207, 213, 269, 302, 305, 330, 332–333, 352–353, 382
wedges   33, 64, 95, 229–230, 280–281, 329–330
Sylvan Wells   15, 483
James Westbrook   1, 483
western red cedar   194, 482
wet inspection   354, 480
wet sanding   377–382, 414
wetting agent   379
white oak   130, 482
white plastic label stock   69, 73
wing nuts   157
Kathy and Jimmi Wingert   70, 483
wipe-on varnish   349
wood
    grain orientation
        bastard grain. See bastard grain
        flatsawn. See flat sawn
        quartersawn. See quartersawn
    mechanical properties
        dimensional stability   17
        easy to carve   17, 172, 482
        shrinkage   36, 131, 481
            longitudinal   17
        stiffness   6, 16, 31, 131, 149, 162, 187, 193–194, 217, 219, 235, 237, 385–386, 475, 479, 481–482
        stiffness to weight ratio   194, 479
        strength   16, 480
    phenolic impregnated. See phenolic impregnated wood
    selection for
        back and sides   129
        fretboard   36
        neck blank   15
    species
        American cherry (Prunus serotina). See American cherry, Prunus serotina, black cherry
        basswood (Tilia americana). See Tilia americana, basswood
        birch (Betula spp.). See Betula spp., birch
        black locust (Robinia pseudoacacia). See Robinia pseudoacacia, black locust
        black walnut (Juglans nigra). See Juglans nigra, black walnut
        boxwood (Buxus sempervirens). See boxwood, Buxus sempervirens
        Brazilian rosewood (Dalbergia nigra). See Dalbergia nigra, Brazilian rosewood
        claro walnut (Juglans hindsii). See Juglans hindsii, claro walnut
        East Indian rosewood (Dalbergia latifolia). See Dalbergia latifolia, East Indian rosewood
        eastern soft maple (Acer rubrum). See Acer rubrum, eastern soft maple
        ebony (Diospyros spp.). See ebony, Diospyros spp.
        Engelmann spruce (Picea engelmannii). See Picea engelmannii, Engelmann spruce
        European sprice (Picea abies). See European spruce, German spruce, Norway spruce, Picea abies
        European sycamore (Acer pseudoplatanus). See European sycamore, Acer pseudoplatanus
        hard maple (Acer saccharum). See hard maple, Acer saccharum
        hickory (Carya spp.). See Carya spp., hickory
        Honduras mahogany (Swietenia macrophylla). See Swietenia macrophylla, Honduras mahogany
        hop-hornbeam (Ostrya virginiana). See hop-hornbeam, Ostrya virginiana
        oak (Quercus spp.). See oak, Quercus spp.
        red spruce (Picea rubens). See red spruce, Picea rubens
        sapele (Entandrophragma cylindricum). See Entandrophragma cylindricum, sapele
        Sitka spruce (Picea sitchensis). See Picea sitchensis, Sitka spruce
        tulip poplar (Liriodendron tulipifera). See tulip poplar, Liriodendron tulipifera
        western red cedar (Thuja plicata). See western red cedar, Thuja plicata
        white oak (Quercus alba). See white oak, Quercus alba
wood glue   20, 75–77, 81, 83, 85–86, 87, 90, 94, 119–121, 178, 205, 214, 314, 344

X

X bracing   217–219, 237, 476, 480

Y

yaw   315–319, 325–327, 337, 477–478, 480

www.ingramcontent.com/pod-product-compliance
Lightning Source LLC
Chambersburg PA
CBHW081343230426
43667CB00017B/2705